ADVANCED
FINANCIAL
ACCOUNTING

THIRD EDITION

CLARENCE BYRD
UNIVERSITY OF OTTAWA

IDA CHEN
CLARENCE BYRD INC.

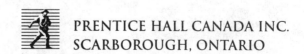

PRENTICE HALL CANADA INC.
SCARBOROUGH, ONTARIO

Canadian Cataloguing in Publication Data

Byrd, Clarence E.
        Advanced financial accounting
3rd ed.
Includes index.
ISBN 0-13-779935-7
1. Accounting. I. Chen, Ida. II. Title.
HF5635.B95 1999 657'.046 C98-931639-4

© 1999, 1996, 1994 Clarence E. Byrd Inc.

ALL RIGHTS RESERVED

No part of this book may be reproduced in any form without permission in writing from the publisher.

Prentice-Hall, Inc., Upper Saddle River, New Jersey
Prentice-Hall International (UK) Limited, London
Prentice-Hall of Australia, Pty. Limited, Sydney
Prentice-Hall Hispanoamericana, S.A., Mexico City
Prentice-Hall of India Private Limited, New Delhi
Prentice-Hall of Japan, Inc., Tokyo
Simon & Schuster Southeast Asia Private Limited, Singapore
Editora Prentice-Hall do Brasil, Ltda., Rio de Janeiro

ISBN 0-13-779935-7

Publisher: Patrick Ferrier
Developmental Editor: Anita Smale
Production Editor: Kelly Dickson
Production Coordinator: Jane Schell
Cover Design: Alex Li
Cover Image: Image Farm Texture and Background Volume 4 and KTP Power Photos Volume 1

1 2 3 4 5   03 02 01 00 99

Printed and bound in Canada.

Visit the Prentice Hall Canada Web site! Send us your comments, browse our catalogues, and more at **www.phcanada.com**. Or reach us through e-mail at **phcinfo_pubcanada@prenhall.com**.

Preface

What Is "Advanced" Financial Accounting?

Most Canadian universities and colleges offer either one or two courses in "advanced" financial accounting. Depending on the organization and the Province in which it operates, all of Canada's professional accounting organizations require their students to complete one or both of such courses. Clearly there is a need for a text which deals with this subject.

Unfortunately, there is no general agreement as to the content that should be included in such a text. This was confirmed by a survey conducted by Prentice Hall Canada, the publisher of this book. While there was general agreement that business combinations and the preparation of consolidated financial statements, as well as the translation of foreign currency transactions and foreign currency financial statements should be included, there was little agreement as to the other subjects that should be included under the general designation of "advanced" financial accounting.

In our view, any distinction between "advanced" and "intermediate" subjects in financial accounting is fairly arbitrary. We are devoting considerable effort to the idea that, subsequent to some type of introductory exposure to basic accounting skills, accounting should be taught on a subject by subject basis. Rather than relegating a subject such as long term investments to an intermediate accounting course because it is on the asset side of the balance sheet, we believe that it should be taught in a comprehensive and integrative manner. This requires recognition that some of the accounting procedures related to this subject cannot be dealt with in the absence of knowledge of consolidation procedures, the income tax law related to the cost and equity methods, and the possibility that such investments involve a business combination transaction.

Until this approach finds its way into university and college courses and professional accounting programs, we have produced this new edition of our version of what constitutes advanced financial accounting in Canada. The first nine Chapters cover the mandatory subjects of long term investments, business combinations, preparation of consolidated financial statements, and the translation of foreign currency transactions and foreign currency financial statements. The remaining Chapters, along with the justification for their inclusion, is as follows:

Chapter 10 This Chapter covers accounting for partnerships. While this subject is given some coverage in introductory courses, it is not generally covered in intermediate texts. It is an important subject in terms of professional practice and, as a consequence, we believe that it should be covered here.

Chapter 11   The subject matter of this Chapter is bankruptcy and reorganization. Here again, these matters are not covered in intermediate texts. In addition, we believe that they are of considerable significance, particularly with the addition of Section 1625, "Comprehensive Revaluation Of Assets And Liabilities", to the *CICA Handbook*.

Chapters 12 And 13   These two Chapters deal with the subjects of segment disclosures and interim reporting. While we do not view this material as being particularly "advanced" in nature, it is not covered in intermediate texts and is of considerable significance. This is particularly true in the case of segment disclosures. This is the only text which currently (September, 1998) provides coverage of the new Section 1701 of the *CICA Handbook* which was issued in September, 1997. This important new material, which was developed in cooperation with the Financial Accounting Standards Board in the U.S. and the International Accounting Standards Committee, introduces a significantly different approach to providing this type of information.

Chapter 14   The subject here is not-for-profit accounting. In 1996 and 1997, the Accounting Standards Board issued seven new *CICA Handbook* Sections dealing with this subject. For the first time, these organizations have a fairly comprehensive set of accounting standards for dealing with the problems that are unique to their needs. This is the only currently available text which provides coverage of these important new materials.

Chapter 15   The subject of this Chapter is financial instruments. It provides coverage of *Handbook* Section 3860 which was issued in September, 1995, as well as content from the still outstanding portions of the 1994 Re-Exposure Draft on this subject. While the material here is almost overwhelming in its scope and importance, it is not dealt with in intermediate texts. As a consequence, we have included the material we have available in this text. We would also note that we considered not including this Chapter. It does not provide a focus on issues that will be comfortable for most students and it is not supported by an appropriate body of problem material. In the end, we concluded that providing this material was superior to having no coverage available in any Canadian accounting text.

Chapters 16 And 17   With the introduction of the new Section 3465 to the *CICA Handbook*, "Income Taxes" in December, 1997, there is no question in our mind that accounting for income taxes is no longer an appropriate inclusion in an intermediate accounting course. To begin, it is not reasonable to discuss the complex temporary differences that are presented in this new Section without having had at least a first course in Canadian income taxation. More importantly, a considerable portion of this new *Handbook* Section deals with accounting for taxes related to both business combinations and foreign currency translation. Simply put, this material is not comprehensible in the context of an intermediate accounting course. As a consequence, we have included two Chapters dealing with this important new material.

There are many other candidates for coverage under the banner of "advanced" financial accounting. It is our personal belief that both accounting for leases and accounting for pensions are subjects of sufficient complexity to warrant coverage here. In addition, subjects such as related party transactions and impaired loans involve very complex issues that would be difficult to deal with at the intermediate level. However, we believe that this book contains a relevant group of materials that can provide the basis for either a one semester or a two semester course in advanced financial accounting.

If you have alternative views on the appropriateness of the subjects we have chosen, we would very much like to hear from you.

Work In Process

This book is not a finished product. In fact, we suspect that it will never be finished in a sense that it will satisfy our belief in the need for current and comprehensive coverage of its subject matter.

With respect to the material in Chapters 1 through 7 on long term investments, business combinations, and the preparation of consolidated financial statements, we have been developing this material for over 20 years. Our coverage of these subjects is the most comprehensive available in Canada and, in addition, it is supported by an extensive selection of problem material.

In a consistent manner, Chapters 8 and 9 provide coverage of both existing accounting standards and proposed changes as they relate to the translation of foreign currency transactions and foreign currency financial statements. In similar fashion, Chapter 10's coverage of partnership accounting is comprehensive, dealing with all of the substantive issues related to this area. As was the case in Chapter 1 through 7, these Chapters are supported by a large selection of problem material.

Beyond Chapter 10, the coverage is less complete. In particular, Chapters 12 (segment disclosures), 13 (interim reporting), 14 (not-for-profit accounting), and 15 (financial instruments) have only limited problem material. In addition, the material in Chapter 15, while comprehensive in its coverage, will be very difficult for students to deal with in its present form.

Chapters 16 and 17 provide guidance on the new material related to accounting for income taxes. However we would have been more comfortable if we could have had the time to provide a larger array of problem material.

While we apologize for these shortfalls, we would point out that, in deciding to proceed with this new edition, we were faced with three alternatives:

- leave out subjects, such as financial instruments or not-for-profit accounting, for which the text or problem material is not fully developed;

- delay publication of a new edition until the 1999-2000 academic year; or

- provide all the material that we currently have in a new edition that is available for the 1998-99 academic year.

We have, of course, chosen the last alternative. As a result of making this choice, we are providing a book which provides at least as much coverage as any other Canadian advanced financial accounting text and, in addition, provides coverage of new and developing areas of financial reporting that is not generally available in any other text.

We believe that students are better off having somewhat limited coverage of the current rules for segment information and not-for-profit accounting, as opposed to having the more comprehensive coverage that is available in other texts of accounting standards that are now totally obsolete. In similar fashion, we believe that providing students with less than perfectly organized coverage of the issues involved in financial instruments is better than having no coverage at all of these issues.

Current economic conditions in the publishing industry do not permit publication of annual editions of a text such as this. However, with the assistance of Prentice Hall, we would hope to have a new edition in two years (the 2000-2001 academic year). Without question, some of the shortcomings of this edition will be corrected. In the meantime, we would suggest that you keep in contact with your Prentice Hall representative. We are constantly developing new problem materials on the subjects covered in this text and it may be possible to make some of them available to you prior to the issuance of a new edition.

Using This Book

Official Pronouncements

This book contains a large number of quotations from the *Handbook* of the Canadian Institute of Chartered Accountants. In the *CICA Handbook*, the paragraphs which represent required disclosure are printed in *italics*. We will observe this convention in the quotations presented in our material.

In previous editions, relevant Abstracts issued by the Emerging Issues Committee (EIC) were integrated into the appropriate Chapters. Some users of this text have advised us that they are not interested in such in-depth coverage of the material under consideration. In response to this view, we have, for the most part, relegated these Abstracts to Chapter Supplements. This leaves users with a clear cut choice of either leaving out this material or integrating the issues covered into their study programs.

With respect to Recommendations of the Accounting Standards Board, the material in this text is current to *CICA Handbook* Revision No. 93 (September, 1997). In addition, the content of the 1996 Re-Exposure Draft, "Foreign Currency Translation" is covered.

Problem And Reference Material

Chapters 2 through 17 all have some assignment problem material. Solutions to assignment problems and cases are only available to instructors through a solutions manual that is made available on adoption of the text.

Chapter 2 through 10 also have self study problems. Unlike the assignment problems, solutions to these problems are provided at the end of the text.

In appropriate locations, there are lists of additional current literature readings that may be of interest to some users of this text.

The text has both a table of contents and a comprehensive index. As the index is electronically generated, it has a high level of accuracy and should be of considerable assistance in locating material that is of interest.

Other Matters

The materials in this text have been developed over the course of many years. During this period they have been used by thousands of Canadian accounting students. Many of these students, as well as their instructors, have contributed to the development process by making suggestions for improvements and by helping us find the errors and omissions that are integral to such a process. We would like to thank all of these people for their assistance in improving these materials as well as for their patience in dealing with any problems found in earlier editions.

Through the efforts of Prentice Hall, a number of people have reviewed the previous edition of this text. They are:

- Betty L. Bracken, Niagara College
- Al Hunter, University Of Lethbridge
- Ross Johnston, University Of Windsor
- Deirdre Taylor, Ryerson Polytechnic University

Suggestions made by Donald Lockwood of the University of British Columbia have been particularly influential. He has noted his impatience with our use of iterative examples (i.e., different versions of the same consolidation problem). We hope he is pleased to see that we have eliminated a significant amount of such material.

We would especially like to acknowledge the work of Lucie Courteau of Laval University. Ms. Corteau was largely responsible for producing the material in Chapter 11 of this text.

In addition, she provided an invaluable sounding board for dealing with new ideas and emerging issues.

We are very much aware that this book would not be possible without the efforts of the staff at Prentice Hall Canada. Anita Smale provided constant assistance with all of our needs in the development of this book. We look forward to working with Ms. Smale on the new edition of *Canadian Tax Principles* which will be available in the Fall of 1998.

Also of great importance to us is our long standing relationship with Prentice Hall Canada's acquisitions editor, Patrick Ferrier. We are notoriously difficult folk to work with. Fortunately, with Mr. Ferrier's assistance we have been able to satisfy our need for editorial independence within the context of publishing books under the banner of one of Canada's largest publishing organizations. Mr. Ferrier must be congratulated on his dancing skills.

Clarence Byrd University Of Ottawa
Ida Chen   Clarence Byrd Inc.

Table of Contents

Chapter 3
Business Combinations

Chapter 3, continued

Chapter 4
Consolidated Balance Sheet
At Acquisition

Chapter 5
Consolidation Subsequent To Acquisition (No Unrealized Intercompany Profits)

Chapter 6
Consolidation Subsequent To Acquisition (Including Unrealized Intercompany Profits)

Chapter 7
Advanced Topics In Consolidations

Chapter 8
Foreign Currency: Basic Concepts And Translation Of Transactions

Chapter 9

Translation Of Foreign Currency Financial Statements

Chapter 9, continued

Chapter 10

Accounting For Partnerships

Chapter 11
Bankruptcy and Reorganization

Chapter 12
Segment Disclosures

Chapter 13

Interim Financial Reporting To Shareholders

Chapter 14

Accounting For Not-For-Profit Organizations

(continued)

Chapter 14, continued

Chapter 15
Financial Instruments

Chapter 15, continued

Chapter 16

Accounting For Income Taxes
Part One:
Basic Concepts And Procedures

Chapter 17

Accounting For Income Taxes
Part Two:
Additional Issues

Chapter 1

Business Combinations and Long Term Investments: Introduction and Overview

Introduction

1-1.   The first seven Chapters of this text deal with a group of related subjects which typically constitute the core material of most advanced financial accounting courses. With their respective individual designations, these related subjects are:

- Long Term Investments
- Business Combinations
- Preparation Of Consolidated Financial Statements

1-2.   When a long term investment is made, the result may or may not be a business combination. Correspondingly, some business combination transactions result in an ongoing long term investment situation. Other such transactions may result in a single legal entity with no continuing intercorporate holding of securities. In those business combinations where there is a continuing long term investment relationship, the preparation of consolidated financial statements will be required.

1-3.   Given this situation, the purpose of this Chapter is to provide a description of each of the individual subject areas and a general explanation of how the subjects relate to each other. While the content of this Chapter is non technical in nature, a familiarity with the individual subjects, as well as with the basic relationships between them is essential to an understanding of the more technical material which follows in Chapters Two through Seven.

Definitions And Classification

Long Term Investments

Long Term Vs. Temporary

1-4. The *CICA Handbook* contains Recommendations for both temporary investments (Section 3010) and long term investments (Section 3050 and 3055). While an investment in a security that matures in less than one year — for example, a Government of Canada

90 day Treasury Bill, is clearly temporary — the classification of other securities is less obvious. Such other securities would include both debt securities with various maturity dates, as well as equity securities which generally have no maturity date.

1-5. In general, the classification of these other securities is dependent on the intent of management. As an example of this, consider a company which acquires 1,000 shares of another publicly traded company. If the investment simply reflects a temporary excess of cash and management intends to dispose of the shares in the next six months, the shares would be classified as a temporary investment. Alternatively, if management has acquired the shares as part of a long term strategy of investing in a particular industry segment, the investment would be accounted for as a long term investment.

Separate Legal Entities

1-6. A corporation can invest in another business entity either by acquiring assets or, alternatively, by acquiring securities. When the asset approach is used, the assets are recorded on the books of the acquiring company and accounted for as per the other assets of the corporation.

1-7. Alternatively, when debt or equity securities are acquired, there is a continuing investment relationship between two separate and distinct legal entities. This is depicted in Figure 1-1.

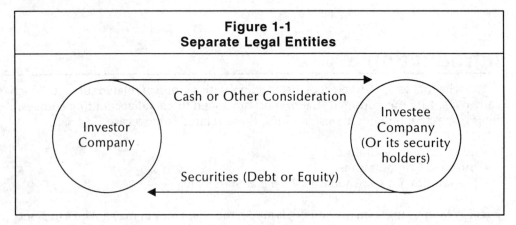

Figure 1-1
Separate Legal Entities

Cash or Other Consideration

Investor Company

Investee Company (Or its security holders)

Securities (Debt or Equity)

1-8. As can be seen in Figure 1-1, the enterprise which has paid the consideration and acquired the securities will be referred to as the investor company. This enterprise can either acquire the other company's securities directly from the other company or, alternatively, the securities can be acquired in secondary markets from other investors. Regardless of the route chosen, the company's whose securities are held will be referred to as the investee company.

1-9. As noted in Figure 1-1, the investor company can acquire either debt or equity securities of the investee company. However, most of our Chapter Two discussion of long term investments will focus on the acquisition and holding of equity securities. This focus reflects the fact that there are few accounting problems associated with long term holdings of debt securities.

1-10. We would also note that long term investments can be made by unincorporated businesses. However, *CICA Handbook* Recommendations are more generally applicable to incorporated businesses and, as a consequence, our references will largely be to long term investments held by corporations.

Classification

1-11. There are a variety of ways in which we could classify long term investments in equity securities. From the point of view of determining the appropriate accounting treatment, the most useful classification system is based on the degree of control which the investor is able to exercise over the affairs of the investee.

1-12.   In actual fact, degree of control is a continuous variable which is not subject to completely defensible divisions. However, we will find it useful for accounting purposes to identify three categories of long term investment that are defined in terms of the degree of control involved. These categories can be described as follows:

- Situations in which the investor company has no influence or control over the investee company.

- Situations in which the investor company has significant influence over the investee company.

- Situations in which the investor company has control over the investee company.

1-13.   In those situations where the investor has no significant degree of control over the investee, there is little that would distinguish a long term investment from any other asset included in the investor's Balance Sheet. As a result of this fact, the holding of the investee's securities will be treated in a manner analogous to the treatment of most other assets. This method is known as the cost method of accounting for long term investments. It will be explained in detail in Chapter 2.

1-14.   Between investment situations involving no control and those involving complete control, there are situations in which the investor is able to exercise a significant amount of influence over the affairs of the investee. When this is the case, the accounting will be modified to reflect this ability to significantly influence the investee. The accounting method that results from these modifications is referred to as the equity method of accounting for long term investments. As it is more complex than the cost method, the equity method will be covered in both Chapter 2 and Chapter 6.

1-15.   The final category of long term investments, those situations in which the investor is able to exercise control over the affairs of the investee, will generally be identified by the investor holding a majority of the outstanding voting shares of the investee. In this situation, the investor is generally in a position to operate the two separate legal entities as a single economic entity. Given the presence of the entity assumption which requires the accountant to focus on the economic entity, it is necessary to prepare financial statements which reflect the presence of this single economic entity. These statements, which ignore the separate legal existence of the investor company and investee company, are referred to as consolidated financial statements. Chapter 4 through 7 will deal with the complex procedures associated with the preparation of such statements.

Business Combinations

Definition

1-16.   The term business combination is used to refer to those situations in which two or more independent business entities (also referred to as economic entities) join together to form a single business entity. This is shown graphically in Figure 1-2 (following page).

1-17.   In examining Figure 1-2, it is important to understand that there is a difference between the legal and the accounting meanings of the term, business combination. In some situations, the economic unification of two businesses will be accompanied by an actual legal amalgamation of their assets. For example, if Company A pays cash to acquire all of the assets of Company B, the combined assets of the two companies will wind up on the books of a single legal entity. A similar result would occur if the assets of both Company A and Company B were transferred to a new corporation established for this purpose. In such situations, the economic and legal entities coincide, and this serves to clearly establish the appropriate accounting entity.

1-18.   Alternatively, the combination may be accomplished through one business entity gaining control over the other through an acquisition of shares. For example, Company A

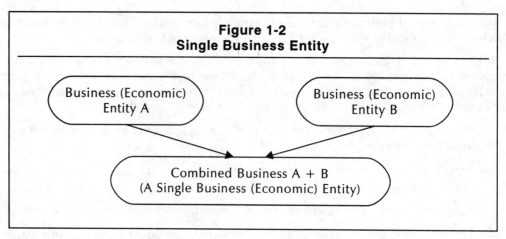

Figure 1-2
Single Business Entity

Business (Economic) Entity A

Business (Economic) Entity B

Combined Business A + B
(A Single Business (Economic) Entity)

might acquire 100 percent of the outstanding voting shares of Company B. In this case the combining enterprises, Company A and Company B, retain their separate identities and, from a legal point of view, no business combination has taken place. In substance, however, this situation is no different from the one described in the preceding paragraph. The assets of both Companies are now under common control and, from an economic point of view, a business combination has occurred. As accountants are primarily interested in economic substance rather than legal form, accounting procedures will focus on the fact that there has been a business combination which has resulted in a single economic entity. The resulting financial statements, which ignore the separate legal existence of the two Companies, are referred to as consolidated financial statements.

Classification

1-19. In international practice, two major alternatives exist for the classification of business combination transactions. In the United States, classification is based largely on the nature of the consideration used to effect the business combination transaction. The accounting treatment is determined by whether cash was used in the transaction or, alternatively, if the combination was effected through an exchange of shares.

1-20. In contrast, Canadian practice concentrates on the economic substance of the transaction. In most business combination transactions, the owners of one of the combining companies will, subsequent to the transaction, have control over the combined operations. This type of business combination is distinguished by the accountant's ability to identify one of the combining companies as the acquirer.

1-21. In the majority of business combinations it will be fairly easy to identify a dominant or acquiring company. When that is the case, the transaction will be classified as a purchase. There are, however, some situations in which companies combine without any one of the predecessor companies being in control. This could happen if the combination involved companies of equal size and value or, alternatively, if more than two enterprises were involved in the combination. When such situations occur, it will not be possible to identify an acquirer.

Accounting Treatment – Identifiable Acquirer

1-22. As was the case with long term investments, classification of the business combination transaction leads logically to the choice of the accounting method that will be used. In those transactions in which one of the combining enterprises can be identified as the acquirer, this enterprise would simply be engaged in the purchase of assets. In fact, the only significant difference between this type of business combination transaction and any other purchase of assets is the fact that the consideration given by the acquiring enterprise must be allocated among a number of identifiable assets, identifiable liabilities, and goodwill. It follows that when an acquiring enterprise can be identified, the business combination transaction should be accounted for in a manner that is consistent with any other acquisition of assets by the acquiring enterprise. This approach is reflected in what is called the purchase method of accounting for business combinations, the use of which is required for those Canadian business combinations in which an acquirer can be identified. The great majority of business combination transactions would fall into this category.

Accounting Treatment - No Identifiable Acquirer

1-23.   In those unusual circumstances in which none of the combining enterprises can be identified as the acquirer, the Canadian position is that there is no new basis of accounting for the net assets of any of the combining enterprises. This interpretation, which also requires retroactive restatement of all prior periods reported, is referred to as the pooling of interests method of accounting for business combinations.

1-24.   A somewhat different approach to this type of combination transaction takes the view that the combined enterprises represent a new enterprise and this provides a new basis of accountability for the net assets of all of the combining enterprises. This interpretation, referred to as the new entity or fair value pooling approach, has not been established as a generally accepted accounting principle in either Canada or the United States. As a result, it will be given no attention in this text.

The Overlap

1-25.   In reading the preceding material it may have occurred to you that certain situations may involve both a business combination transaction and an ongoing long term investment relationship. From the point of view of long term investments, this involves a situation in which the investor and investee entities are treated as a single accounting entity. The same situation, described from the point of view of business combinations, could be described as a business combination in which the companies retain their separate legal identities. This is shown graphically in Figure 1-3 on the following page.

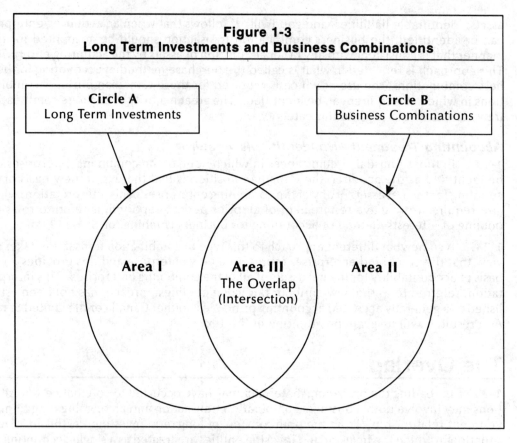

Figure 1-3
Long Term Investments and Business Combinations

Circle A
Long Term Investments

Circle B
Business Combinations

Area I   Area III
The Overlap
(Intersection)   Area II

1-26.   As can be seen in Figure 1-3, if Circle A represents the subject matter of long term investments and Circle B the subject matter of business combinations, there is an overlap or intersection between the two circles. Including this intersection, three separate areas are created. These areas can be described as follows:

Area I   This area represents long term investments that have not resulted in an economic unification of the investor and investee companies. Stated alternatively, these are the long term investment situations where the investor and investee companies have retained both their separate legal status as well as their separate economic status. In practical terms both portfolio investments (i.e., investments where no control is involved) and investments involving significant influence would be found in this area. However, situations where the investor company has acquired control would be excluded.

Area II   This area represents business combinations in which there is no continuing long term investment relationship between the combining companies. Stated alternatively, these are the business combination transactions where the assets and liabilities of the two companies have been combined into a single legal entity. As there is both a legal and an economic amalgamation of the two business entities, the legal and economic entities coincide.

Area III (Overlap)   In Areas I and II, there was no conflict between the legal and economic entities involved. In Area III, this situation changes. Area III involves situations where the two companies have achieved economic unification but, for reasons that will be explained in detail in Chapter 3, have retained their separate legal existence. This means that we are dealing with two separate legal entities that are being operated as a single economic unit. When accountants are confronted with a conflict between the economic entity and the legal entity, the entity assumption requires that attention be directed to the economic entity. This means that when dealing with the situations found in this area, the two separate legal entities will have to be accounted for as a single unified business. As noted previously, this is accomplished through the preparation of consolidated financial statements. The investor and investee companies that are involved in this type of situation are referred to as the parent company and the subsidiary company, respectively.

Canadian Pronouncements

Handbook Recommendations

1-27. Given the broadly based nature of the subjects of long term investments and business combinations, it is necessary to refer to a large number of the Recommendations contained in the *CICA Handbook*. However, the following six Sections are of particular relevance to these subjects.

Section 1580: "Business Combinations"   This Section was added to the *CICA Handbook* in 1973. While there have been minor revisions since that date, the basic content of this Section has remained unchanged since its introduction into the *CICA Handbook*. Included here is guidance on the selection of the appropriate method of accounting for particular business combination transactions as well as the specific rules for the application of the purchase and pooling of interests methods.

Section 1590: "Subsidiaries"   This brief Section was added to the *CICA Handbook* in 1991. It defines a subsidiary as an enterprise controlled by another enterprise and defines control as the continuing power of an enterprise to determine operating, investing and financing policies of the controlled enteprise. The Section also specifies that all subsidiaries must be consolidated.

Section 1600: "Consolidated Financial Statements"   This Section was first added to the *CICA Handbook* in 1975, with a major revision occurring in 1991. It contains detailed rules for both the preparation of consolidated financial statements, as well as the application of the equity method to long term investments.

Section 1625: "Comprehensive Revaluation Of Assets And Liabilities"   This Section was added to the *CICA Handbook* in December, 1992. It deals with recording revised asset and liability amounts in two different situations. The one that is relevant here involves an investor acquiring control over an investee (subsidiary). In these circumstances, there will be differences between the fair values of the subsidiary's assets and liabilities and the carrying values in the subsidiary's records. As the purchase price of the subsidiary will be based on fair values, it is the fair value amounts that must be included in the consolidated financial statements. While this can be done through the consolidation procedures, it can be more convenient to record the fair values of the subsidiary's assets on its books at the time of acquisition. This procedure is called "push down" accounting and it is dealt with in Section 1625.

Section 3050: "Long Term Investments"   This Section was first added to the *CICA Handbook* in 1972 and has been subject to several revisions. As it presently stands, it contains rules with respect to the accounting methods to be used for portfolio investments and significantly influenced companies, procedures for the application of the cost and equity methods of accounting for long term investments, and disclosure requirements applicable to situations in which non consolidated financial statements are presented for subsidiaries. It also requires the write down of long term investments in some circumstances and specifies the use of average values for the cost of long term investments that are being sold.

Section 3055: "Interests In Joint Ventures"   This Section was added to the *CICA Handbook* in 1977 and was subject to a significant revision in 1994. It defines joint ventures, requires the use of proportionate consolidation to account for joint venture arrangements, and provides specific procedural rules which reflect the unique nature of joint venture arrangements.

EIC Abstracts

1-28.   The preceding pronouncements constitute a comprehensive set of guidelines for dealing with the subjects of business combinations, long term investments and the preparation of consolidated financial statements. However, the complexity of these subjects has made them a frequent topic on the agenda of the Emerging Issues Committee (EIC, hereafter). Seventeen of the Abstracts issued to date (December, 1997) by this Committee have direct bearing on the subjects of long term investments, business combinations, and consolidated financial statements. They are as follows:

No. 8	Recognition Of An Equity Accounted Investee's Losses In Excess Of The Investment (October, 1989)
No. 10	Reverse Takeover Accounting (January, 1990)
No. 12	Capitalization Of Interest Costs On Investments In Potential Takeover Targets (January, 1990)
No. 14	Adjustments To The Purchase Equation Subsequent To The Acquisition Date (June, 1990)
No. 20	Reacquisition Of Troubled Franchises By The Franchisor (December, 1990)
No. 29	Dilution Gains And Losses In Oil And Gas Companies Using The Full Cost Method Of Accounting (Jul9, 1991)
No. 38	Accounting By Newly Formed Joint Ventures (July, 1992)
No. 41	Presentation Of Assets And Liabilities Held For Disposal (November, 1992)
No. 42	Costs Incurred On Business Combinations (December, 1992)
No. 48	Tax Effecting Dilution Gains And Losses (October, 1993)
No. 55	Identifiable Assets Acquired In A Business Combination (August, 1994)
No. 56	Exchangeable Debentures (November, 1994)
No. 62	Measurement Of Cost Of A Business Acquisition Effected By Issuing Shares (March, 1995)
No. 64	Goodwill Disclosures (August, 1995)
No. 66	Transfer Of A Business Between Entities Under Common Control (November, 1995)
No. 73	Buy Out Transactions (June, 1996)
No. 76	Fair Value Of Shares Issued As Consideration In A Purchase Business Combination (November, 1996)

1-29.   Most of these Abstracts will be given some attention in Chapters 2 through 7 of this text. In some cases, their content will be incorporated directly into the text. However, in those cases where the subject covered by the Abstract is less important, the coverage will be in a Supplement to the relevant Chapter.

Long Term Investments and Business Combinations in Canadian Practice

1-30.   Both business combinations and long term investments are important areas in Canadian practice. The 1997 edition of *Financial Reporting In Canada* states that, for 1996, 192 of the 200 survey companies indicated that the statements presented were on a consolidated basis. This, of course, indicates the presence of one or more subsidiaries. Also for 1996, 134 of the 200 companies reported the presence of long term investments other than subsidiaries and joint ventures, and 102 of the companies reported the presence of joint ventures.

1-31.   With respect to business combinations, statistics on the number of these 200 companies disclosing business combination transactions occurring during the current year are as follows:

Year	1996	1995
Purchase Transactions	76	66
Pooling Of Interests Transactions	1	2

1-32.   For reasons that will be apparent when we discuss the Recommendations contained in Section 1580 of the *CICA Handbook*, pooling of interests accounting is very rare in Canada. This is in contrast to the U.S. situation where pooling of interests accounting is a commonly used procedure.

Approaching The Subject

1-33.   With the completion of this brief introductory Chapter, Chapters 2 through 7 will provide a systematic and detailed presentation of the concepts and procedures associated with long term investments, business combinations, and the preparation of consolidated financial statements. Chapters 2 and 3 will be largely conceptual in their content, dealing with the pronouncements contained in Sections 1580, 1590, 1625, 3050, and 3055 of the *CICA Handbook*. With these concepts in hand, we will then be in a position to turn our attention to the procedures that are required in the preparation of consolidated financial statements.

1-34.   Chapter 4 will introduce this subject by dealing with the preparation of the consolidated Balance Sheet at the date of acquisition of a subsidiary. This will include material on the conceptual alternatives in consolidation, as well as on the allocation of the investment cost to fair value changes and goodwill.

1-35.   Chapter 5 extends the analysis to cover consolidation in periods subsequent to the acquisition and covers the preparation of the consolidated Income Statement and the consolidated Statements Of Retained Earnings. Material on the preparation of a consolidated Statement Of Cash Flows will be deferred until Chapter 7. Procedures dealt with here include write offs of fair value changes and goodwill, elimination of intercompany assets and liabilities, elimination of intercompany expenses and revenues and the elimination of intercompany dividends.

1-36.   Chapter 6 further expands the coverage of basic consolidation procedures by providing a comprehensive analysis of unrealized intercompany profits. The analysis includes consideration of unrealized profits in opening and closing inventories, unrealized profits on the sale of non depreciable capital assets, and unrealized profits on the sale of depreciable capital assets.

1-37.   Chapters 2 through 6 provide in depth coverage of basic consolidation procedures, including some material on conceptual alternatives in the preparation of consolidated financial statements. In some advanced financial accounting courses, this may be viewed as adequate coverage of this subject, with no consideration being given to more advanced consolidation procedures.

1-38.   There are, however, a large number of more advanced topics that relate to the preparation of consolidated financial statements. While it is unlikely that any instructor would choose to cover all of these advanced topics, there does not appear to be a consensus as to which subjects are the most important. In order to deal with this situation, we have relegated coverage of all of these topics to a separate Chapter 7. In addition, the problem material which accompanies this Chapter is clearly segregated by subject matter. This will allow instructors to choose to cover as many or as few of these topics as they wish.

1-39.   As a final point, we would note that we have dealt with the subject of income taxes related to business combination transactions and consolidated financial statements in a separate Chapter 17. This reflects the fact that Section 3465 of the *CICA Handbook*, "Income Taxes", which was issued in December, 1997, contains a significant number of Recommendations dealing with these issues.

Chapter 2

Long Term Investments

Introduction

Subject Matter

Temporary Investments

2-1.   Canadian companies make investments in other companies for a variety of reasons. The least complicated situations are those in which the enterprise has a temporary excess of funds and uses these funds to acquire the securities of other companies. In such cases, management will have an intent to dispose of the securities as soon as the invested funds are needed for the ongoing operations of the business. Such temporary investments will be classified as current assets and accounted for as per the Recommendations of Section 3010 of the *CICA Handbook*.

Long Term Investments

2-2.   In this volume we are concerned only with long term investments that have been acquired as part of the overall business strategy of the investor company. Such investments vary widely in the degree of control or influence that the investor company is able to exercise. Further, the specific investment arrangement used will be influenced by a wide variety of legal and tax considerations. For example, differing provincial income tax rules and rates may make it desirable to establish a separate corporate entity in each province where the investor company operates. Another example, making use of the fact that corporations have limited legal liability to their creditors, would involve a corporation setting up a separate corporation to undertake a particularly risky business venture.

2-3.   As was pointed out in Chapter 1, long term investment situations are distinguished by the presence of two separate and distinct legal entities. One of these legal entities (the investor) will be holding the securities issued by the other legal entity (the investee). All types of securities are included within this framework and there is no necessity for the investment to be intercorporate for Sections 3050 or 3055 to apply. However, it is clear that the major concern of these Sections of the *CICA Handbook* is with investments in corporate equity securities by corporate investors. Some attention will, however, be given to long term investments in debt securities.

Branch Accounting

2-4.   If an enterprise was interested in starting operations in a different province, an alternative to establishing a new corporate entity to carry out those operations would be the establishment of a branch. This represents a fairly simple way to begin operating in the other province as no new legal entity is required.

2-5. Such a branch may keep a separate set of accounts, recording assets, liabilities, revenues and expenses in much the same fashion as would an incorporated subsidiary. However, unlike the subsidiary, a branch is not a separate legal entity. This means that it will not be required to prepare separate financial statements for external users. The accounting procedures to be used by such a branch are an internal matter and not subject to the constraints created by *CICA Handbook* recommendations. As the focus of this volume is financial reporting under generally accepted accounting principles, no further attention will be given to branch accounting.

Issues To Be Covered

2-6. The material in Sections 1590 (Subsidiaries), 3050 (Long Term Investments), and 3055 (Interests In Joint Ventures) can be grouped into coverage of three broad issues, accompanied by material on a number of more detailed problems. In very general terms, these broad issues can be outlined as follows:

1. **Classification** The *CICA Handbook*'s classification of long term investments is largely in terms of the degree of control involved. The types of long term investments that are identified are as follows:

   - Subsidiaries
   - Significantly Influenced Companies
   - Portfolio Investments
   - Joint Ventures

2. **Accounting Methods** The *Handbook* Recommendations also identify the various methods of accounting to be used for long term investments. They are as follows:

   - Cost Method
   - Equity Method
   - Proportionate Consolidation
   - Full Consolidation

   This Chapter will provide complete coverage of the cost method as well as a general introduction to the equity method and proportionate consolidation. However, both the application of the equity method and the use of proportionate consolidation require an understanding of the procedures that are used in full consolidation. As a consequence, additional coverage of the equity method and proportionate consolidation will be included in later Chapters, after the relevant full consolidation techniques have been presented.

3. **Recommended Methods For Specific Investment Classifications** Given the types of long term investments identified in the preceding item 1 and the accounting methods identified in item 2, the third broad issue that is dealt with in the *CICA Handbook* Recommendations under consideration here is the determination of which methods should be used with each of the investment types that have been defined.

4. **Other Problems** Other problems that are dealt with in Section 3050 are as follows:

   - Non temporary declines in the value of an investment.
   - Gains and losses on sales of investments.
   - Financial statement presentation of long term investments.

Classification Of Long Term Investments

An Overview

2-7.   Long term investments are those investments that management intends to hold for more than one year after the Balance Sheet date. As previously noted, the classification of such long term investments is based largely on the degree of influence that can be exercised by the investor company. In general, the degree of influence is related to the portion of the investor company voting shares which are held by the investor company. This means that we can depict long term investment classifications in terms of the following Figure 2-1:

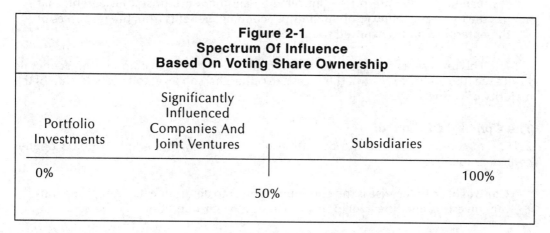

Figure 2-1
Spectrum Of Influence
Based On Voting Share Ownership

2-8.   As shown in the preceding Figure, the long term investment classification involving the highest degree of influence is subsidiaries. In general, this type of long term investment involves situations where the investor company owns more than 50 percent of the outstanding voting shares of the investee company. However, as will be subsequently pointed out, such majority ownership is no longer a required part of the definition of subsidiaries.

2-9.   At the other extreme we find the classification of portfolio investments. These are long term investment situations in which the investor company has little or no influence over the affairs of the investee company and, as can be seen in the display, this situation normally involves proportionately small holdings of investee voting shares.

2-10.   The final two classifications are significantly influenced companies and joint ventures. Both of these classifications involve situations where the investor company has a significant influence over the affairs of the investee company, but the influence falls short of control. Joint ventures are distinguished from other situations where the investor has influence on the basis of the manner in which each joint venture investor relates to the other joint venture investors.

2-11.   This provides you with a somewhat simplified picture of the long term investment classifications that are found in the Recommendations of the *CICA Handbook*. With this in hand, we can now turn to a more detailed consideration of the individual categories.

Subsidiaries

Defined

2-12.   Prior to 1991, the *CICA Handbook* defined a subsidiary as an investee for which the investor held a majority of the outstanding voting shares. In general, this was a reasonable definition because majority ownership generally meant that an investor company would be able to elect a majority of the investee company's board of directors and, thereby, exercise control over the operating, investing, and financing policies of that company. However, there was a problem in that, under this definition, no recognition was given to situations in which the investor company was able to exercise control without having majority ownership. The failure to recognize this possibility resulted in situations where an investor company which did in fact have full control of the investee company would account for its long term investment using methods which were intended for situations involving only significant influence. In other words, the original *Handbook* Recommendation represented an emphasis on legal form, rather than economic substance.

2-13.   Section 1590, issued in 1991, corrects this situation. The definition of a subsidiary found in Paragraph 1590.03 is as follows:

> A *subsidiary* is an enterprise controlled by another enterprise (the parent) that has the right and ability to obtain future economic benefits from the resources of the enterprise and is exposed to the related risks.

2-14.   This represents an improved definition in that it places an emphasis on economic substance (the ability to control the investee) rather than on legal form (ownership of the majority of voting shares).

The Concept Of Control

2-15.   In conjunction with the definition of a subsidiary, Paragraph 1590.03 defines control as follows:

> **Control** of an enterprise is the continuing power to determine its strategic operating, investing and financing policies without the co-operation of others.

2-16.   While this definition appears to be very straightforward, it is subject to varying interpretations. The most restrictive interpretation of this definition would be that control requires ownership of 100 percent of the outstanding shares of the investee. This is based on the fact that, as long as there are any minority shareholders in the investee company, corporate legislation will prevent the investor company from undertaking transactions that are harmful to the interests of that group. For example, if the investor owns 100 percent of the outstanding shares, there is nothing to prevent the investor from selling products to the investee at prices in excess of fair market value. However, if there is a minority interest present in the investee company, this type of transaction could not take place because it would be detrimental to the economic position of the minority shareholders.

2-17.   While this very restrictive interpretation of control has some appeal from a legal point of view, it fails to recognize that control over the great majority of operating and financing decisions can be achieved with less than 100 percent ownership. This suggests the use of a less restrictive interpretation of control in practical situations.

2-18.   A second possible interpretation of control could be based on the fact that corporate legislation generally requires a two-thirds majority vote for passage of special resolutions. Such transactions as changes in the corporate objectives, amalgamations with other companies, and other changes in the corporate charter would require such a super majority. This means that an interpretation of control based on two-thirds ownership of voting shares would have some appeal from a legal point of view. Again, however, this interpretation is too restrictive in that many of the operating and financing decisions could be controlled with less than two-thirds ownership of the investee company's voting shares.

2-19.   A more practical interpretation of control is based on the idea that, in terms of economic substance, the key factor is the ability of the investor company to determine policy for the great majority of operating and financing decisions that are made by the investee company. This ability is generally associated with simple majority ownership of outstanding voting shares. It is this interpretation of control that is contained in the *CICA Handbook* which states:

Paragraph 1590.08   The level of equity interest in one enterprise held by another leads to a presumption regarding control. An enterprise is presumed to control another enterprise when it owns, directly or indirectly, an equity interest that carries the right to elect the majority of the members of the other enterprise's board of directors, and is presumed not to control the other enterprise without such ownership. In a particular situation, these presumptions may be overcome by other factors that clearly demonstrate that control exists or does not exist. The greater the difference in an enterprise's voting interest from the 50% level, the more persuasive these other factors must be in overcoming the applicable presumption.

2-20.   While this statement clearly establishes voting share ownership as the primary measure of control, it leaves open the possibility of other measures being used. Two examples of such other measures are cited:

Paragraph 1590.13(a)   Ownership of less than the majority of voting shares combined with an irrevocable agreement with other owners to exercise voting rights may result in majority voting power and may, therefore, confer control.

Paragraph 1590.13(b)   Control may exist when an enterprise does not own the majority voting interest if it has the continuing ability to elect the majority of the members of the board of directors through ownership of rights, options, warrants, convertible debt, convertible non-voting equity such as preferred shares, or other similar instruments that, if converted or exercised, would give the enterprise the majority voting interest.

2-21.   An investor may find situations where its use of the resources of the investee company are subject to certain restrictions. Examples of this would be debt covenants which restrict the investee company's ability to pay dividends or regulatory restrictions which control the prices that can be charged by the investee company. Such normal business restrictions do not preclude control by the investor and the classification of the investee as a subsidiary. However, in some cases the restrictions may involve a transfer of voting rights and this could result in the investor no longer being able to exercise control.

2-22.   Section 1590 also notes that a brief interruption of power is not a loss of control. An example of this would be the appointment of a receiver to seize a specific group of assets in order to satisfy a creditor claim. Further, the investor company can have control without choosing to exercise it on a day to day basis. In addition, control can be exercised in situations where the investee has obligations that exceed its resources. None of these conditions would prevent the investor's holding from being classified as a subsidiary.

2-23.   However, there are situations in which the restrictions on the investor company's ability to exercise its ownership rights are so severe that control can no longer be considered present. An example of this would be a foreign investee operating in a country which places severe restrictions on the repatriation of earnings. In such cases, the investment would no longer be classified as a subsidiary, despite the presence of majority ownership of voting shares.

2-24.   Another situation where majority ownership of voting shares would not result in a parent/subsidiary relationship arises when there is a demonstrable intent to dispose of the investment in the foreseeable future. Section 1590 notes that when the investor/investee relationship is established for a short term or where it can be terminated other than by a decision of the acquiring enterprise, the investment should be classified as temporary and accounted for by the methods specified in Section 3010 of the *CICA Handbook*.

Indirect Ownership

2-25.   The preceding discussion of control dealt only with situations in which the investor company had direct ownership of the investee company's outstanding voting shares.

However, an investor company can have indirect control of another company, even in situations where the investor company owns none of the shares of that company. Two examples of such indirect control are provided in Figure 2-2.

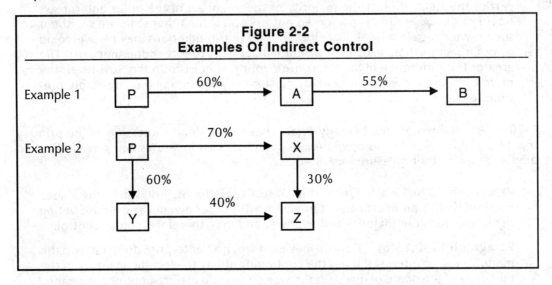

Figure 2-2
Examples Of Indirect Control

2-26.   In Example 1, P owns 60 percent of A. This would give P control over A and make this company a subsidiary. In turn, A owns 55 percent of B, giving A control and making B a subsidiary of A. In addition, P's control of A gives P indirect control over B, making B a subsidiary of P as well as a subsidiary of A.

2-27.   In Example 2, P controls both X and Y. Between them, these two companies own 70 percent of Z, giving them joint control over this company. Because P controls both X and Y, P has indirect control over Z. This means that Z, as well as X and Y are subsidiaries of P.

2-28.   The preceding examples are commonly referred to as multi-level affiliations. Even more complex relationships can develop if companies acquire shares of other companies that are above them in the chain of control. For example, Z might acquire some of the shares of X or P in Example 2. Shareholdings of this type are referred to as reciprocal shareholdings. The procedures to be used in dealing with both multi-level affiliations and reciprocal shareholdings are dealt with in Chapter 7.

2-29.   A final point here relates to measurement based on indirect interests. Returning to Example 1, when we measure P's indirect interest in B, it will be based on the product of the ownership percentages. For example, P's interest in B's earnings is based on 33 percent ([60%][55%]) of those earnings. While such percentages must be used in measurement calculations, they have nothing to do with determining the existence of control. In general, control is based on majority ownership at each stage in the chain of ownership. The fact that an equitable interest, as established by the product of the ownership percentages, is less than 50 percent has nothing to do with whether an indirect interest represents control.

Significantly Influenced Companies

2-30.   The *CICA Handbook* does not provide a specific definition of the category of long term investments known as significantly influenced companies. However, the basic idea is that they are investees in which an investor company is able to exercise a significant degree of influence without actually having control of the investee company. These situations are described as follows:

Paragraph 3050.04   Significant influence differs from control and joint control. An investor may be able to exercise significant influence over the strategic operating, investing and financing policies of an investee even though the investor does not control or jointly control the investee. The ability to exercise significant influence may be indicated by, for example, representation on the board of directors, participation in policy-making processes, material intercompany transactions, interchange of managerial personnel or provision of technical information. If the investor holds less than 20% of the voting interest in the investee, it is presumed that the investor does not have the ability to exercise significant influence, unless such influence is clearly demonstrated. On the other hand, the holding of 20% or more of the voting interest in the investee does not in itself confirm the ability to exercise significant influence. A substantial or majority ownership by another investor would not necessarily preclude an investor from exercising significant influence.

2-31.   At first glance, the preceding would appear to make the determination of significant influence a matter of professional judgment. However, the inclusion of a specific percentage of share ownership will, almost certainly, be used by many accountants as an administratively convenient guideline for the determination of significant influence. In view of the fact that the determination of significant influence is clearly something that must be determined through the application of judgment on a situation by situation basis it seems unfortunate that any particular percentage of share ownership was even mentioned. There is no logical reason to believe that 20 percent will be more effective in the determination of significant influence than any other arbitrarily determined percentage of share ownership. Therefore, it is possible to make a case that the exercise of judgment would have received more encouragement had this 20 percent guideline been omitted.

2-32.   In applying professional judgment, representation on the board of directors is probably the most reliable indicator of the ability of the investor corporation to exercise significant influence. If the investor company is able to elect one or more members to the investee's board, it would generally be clear that influence is present. The ability to get this representation is a function of the percentage of shares owned and the number of positions on the board. It is also dependent on the type of voting that is used by the investee company. For example, assume an investor owns 10 percent of the shares and there are 10 directors on the board. If the investee corporation uses cumulative voting, the investor will be in a position to elect one director. If the investee corporation uses non cumulative voting, a majority group of shareholders can, in fact, elect all of the directors.

Portfolio Investments

2-33.   The *CICA Handbook* presents a definition of portfolio investments as follows:

> **Paragraph 3050.02(b)   Portfolio investments** are long-term investments that are not interests in joint ventures or partnerships of the reporting enterprise, nor investments in companies that are subject to significant influence by the reporting enterprise.

2-34.   The preceding definition is, of course, straightforward and non controversial. The statement is in terms of what a portfolio investment is not. However, it is clear that what is being described is those long term investment situations in which the investor is not in a position to exert influence over or become involved in the affairs of the investee. This would include all long term holdings of debt securities, as well as long term holdings of equity securities where the investor company does not have significant influence. As our earlier discussion should have made clear, distinguishing equity investments in which significant influence is present from those in which it is not, will sometimes involve the exercise of considerable professional judgment.

2-35.   It should also be noted that the 1984 CICA Research Study, *Accounting For Portfolio Investments*, recommends a somewhat different approach to defining portfolio investments. The definition found in this Study is as follows:

Portfolio investments are investments that are intended to fulfill a long term investment strategy of an enterprise and that are generally passive in nature. Portfolio investments include both fixed term and equity investments, but exclude non passive investments such as investments in subsidiaries, joint ventures, partnerships, and companies subject to significant influence by the investor.

2-36.   This definition provides a description of portfolio investments based on their passive nature. We believe that it is preferable to the existing definition in that it defines portfolio investments in terms of what they are, rather than in terms of what they are not.

Joint Ventures

Definition

2-37.   A considerable amount of difficulty has been experienced in establishing a clear cut definition of what constitutes a joint venture. This reflects the fact that it is often difficult to distinguish this type of long term investment from other long term investment situations where the investor has the ability to exercise significant influence. Section 3055 of the *CICA Handbook* defines joint venture arrangements as follows:

> **Paragraph 3055.03(c)**   A **joint venture** is an economic activity resulting from a contractual arrangement whereby two or more venturers jointly control the economic activity.

2-38.   This definition contains a number of terms which require further clarification. This clarification is provided in two additional Section 3055 definitions:

> **Paragraph 3055.03(b)**   **Joint control** of an economic activity is the contractually agreed sharing of the continuing power to determine its strategic operating, investing and financing policies.

> **Paragraph 3055.03(e)**   A **venturer** is a party to a joint venture, has joint control over that joint venture, has the right and ability to obtain future economic benefits from the resources of the joint venture and is exposed to the related risks.

2-39.   With respect to the meaning of control, it can be assumed that the definition of that concept which was provided in Section 1590 (see Paragraph 2-15 of this Chapter) will be equally applicable in this context.

2-40.   From the preceding definitions it can be concluded that the most important distinguishing feature of a joint venture is that its economic activity is subject to joint control by two or more venturers. Such joint control would preclude any one of the venturers from having unilateral control over the venture's economic activity. If the control agreement that is in place allows any one of the investors to exercise such unilateral control, none of the investors will be able to classify their interest as a joint venture. The investor with unilateral control would classify its investment as a subsidiary, while the other investors would classify their interests as either portfolio investments or significantly influenced investees, as appropriate.

2-41.   There may be investors with an economic interest in a joint venture that do not participate under the agreement for joint control. This does not preclude the investors who do participate under the control agreement from classifying their investment as a joint venture. However, investors who do not participate under the agreement would not be able to use this classification and would have to classify their investment as either a portfolio investment or a significantly influenced investee, as appropriate.

2-42.   From the point of view of an individual interest in a joint venture, the venturer must have the right and ability to obtain future economic benefits from the resources of the joint venture and must be exposed to the risks related to the use of these resources. If the interest does not involve such risk and reward sharing, it should be viewed as a loan rather than as an equity interest in a joint venture. Long term loan arrangements are normally classified as portfolio investments.

2-43.   The control agreement may take a variety of different forms. It may involve a contract between the various venturers or, alternatively, the agreement may be incorporated in the articles of incorporation or by-laws of the joint venture. The arrangement will normally be in writing and cover such matters as the activities, duration, policies and procedures of the joint venture, the allocation of ownership, the decision making process, the capital contributions by the venturers and the sharing by the venturers of the output, revenue, expenses or results of the joint venture.

2-44.   The joint venture definitions do not prevent one of the venturers from acting as manager for the enterprise. As long as this manager is acting within policies that have been agreed on under the terms of the contractual agreement for the venture, the enterprise can be viewed as a joint venture arrangement. However, if the manager has the continuing power to determine the strategic operating, investing, and financing policies of the enterprise, without review by the other equity interests, then the manager is in control of the venture and should classify the investment as a subsidiary.

Forms Of Organization

2-45.   Section 3055 provides a discussion of the various forms and structures that can be used to carry out joint venture operations. Three basic forms are identified and they can be described as follows:

1.   **Jointly Controlled Operations**   This form involves the use of the assets and other resources of the individual venturers, rather than the establishment of a corporation, partnership or other enterprise, or a financial structure that is separate from the venturers themselves. Characteristics of this form would include:

    - Each venturer uses its own property, plant and equipment, and carries its own inventories for purposes of the joint venture activities.
    - Assets remain under the individual ownership and control of each venturer.
    - Each venturer incurs its own expenses and liabilities and raises its own financing.
    - The arrangement will provide for the sharing of revenues and of common expenses among the various venturers.

    An example of this form might involve several venturers combining their efforts to manufacture a product. In this situation, different parts of the manufacturing operation might be carried out by each of the venturers using their own assets and other resources. While each venturer would incur their own costs, they would receive a share of the revenues from the product, as per the terms of the joint venture agreement.

2.   **Jointly Controlled Assets**   In this situation, the joint venture involves the joint control and possible joint ownership by the venturers, of one or more assets contributed to or acquired for the use of the joint venture. Each venturer will take a share of the output from the assets and each will be responsible for a share of the expenses incurred. As was the case with jointly controlled operations, this type of joint venture does not involve the establishment of a corporation, partnership, other enterprise, or financial structure that is separate from the venturers themselves.

    Examples of this form of operation could involve the joint control of a rental property or the joint development of a natural resource property.

3.   **Jointly Controlled Enterprise**   This form of joint venture involves establishing a separate corporation or partnership in which each venturer has an investment interest. The separately established entity would operate much like other

investment entities, except for the fact that it would be subject to the joint control of the various venturers. Characteristics of this form would include:

- While each venturer contributes cash or other resources to the joint venture, the venture itself will own the assets, assume the liabilities, receive the revenues, and incur the expenses of the joint venture operations.
- The venture may enter into contracts in its own name and raise financing for the purposes of joint venture activity.
- In most cases, each venturer will share in the income of the jointly controlled enterprise. In a minority of cases, the venturers will share in the output of the enterprise, rather than the income.

Examples of this form would include any situation where two or more venturers transfer relevant assets into a separate corporation or partnership.

Classification Example

2-46. The following example illustrates the investment classification process for joint ventures.

A new company, the Venture Company, is formed and all of the shares are acquired by four investor Companies. These Companies and their proportionate ownership interests are as follows:

- Company A holds 60 percent of the shares.
- Company B holds 20 percent of the shares.
- Company C holds 15 percent of the shares.
- Company D holds 5 percent of the shares.

The four investor Companies sign an agreement which provides that Company A and Company D will not participate in the affairs or operations of the business. The agreement further specifies that in all areas essential to the operation of the business, decisions will be made by and require the consent of both Company B and Company C. The classification of the investment in the Venture Company by each of the investor Companies would be as follows:

Company A   While Company A holds a majority of the voting shares in the Venture Company, the joint venture agreement prevents the Company from exercising the control that we normally associate with majority ownership. Further, it does not appear that Company A will have any real influence on the affairs of Venture Company. As a consequence, Company A would classify Venture Company as a portfolio investment.

Companies B And C   There is a contractual agreement in place under which two or more venturers control the enterprise. Further, under this agreement, B and C have joint control. Given their participation under the agreement and the fact that no single investor has unilateral control, Companies B and C would classify their long term investments in Venture Company as joint venture investments.

Company D   This investor, because of its exclusion from any share of joint control, would classify the investment as a portfolio investment.

Methods Of Accounting For Long Term Investments

General Description

2-47.   As was indicated earlier, the *CICA Handbook* refers to four methods of accounting for long term investments. These are the cost method, the equity method, full consolidation, and proportionate consolidation. Of these methods, the cost method is defined and described completely in Section 3050. In addition, the general requirements for the application of the equity method are provided in Section 3050. However, one of the requirements specified in Section 3050 is that, if the equity method is used, it must produce the same investor net income amount that would have been calculated if the investee had been consolidated. This means that a complete understanding of consolidation procedures is required in order to fully implement the equity method. Similarly, proportionate consolidation is given a general definition in Section 3055 but its application in more complex situations requires an understanding of full consolidation procedures.

2-48.   As a major portion of this text will be required to provide a complete presentation of consolidation procedures, it is clear that the only method that can be dealt with in a comprehensive fashion in this Chapter is the cost method. However, in order to understand the relevant Recommendations on which methods should be used for the various identified classifications of long term investments, a general description of all methods is provided. In addition, this Chapter will also present simple examples of the application of the equity method, full consolidation, and proportionate consolidation. More complex applications of these methods will be presented in Chapter 6, subsequent to our discussion of the more detailed aspects of consolidation.

2-49.   Before leaving this general description, you should note that there is no mention in Section 3050 or Section 3055 of the use of market or lower of cost or market as a general method of accounting for long term investments. While these methods are used in accounting for temporary investments, they are not acceptable for long term investment holdings. The reason for this is that market values reflect the amount that would be received if the investment were liquidated. Such values are relevant in the case of temporary investments because there is an intent to liquidate. However, in the case of investments that management intends to hold for the long term, such values are clearly not appropriate as a basis for valuation.

Cost Method Defined

General Procedures

2-50.   The cost method of accounting for long term investments is a specific application of the general procedures used in accounting for most non current assets. It is based on the historical cost principle and the fact that an equity investor company's only legal claim to income is based on the amount of dividends declared by the investee company. This method is defined as follows:

> **Paragraph 3050.02(c)**   The **cost method** is a basis of accounting for long-term investments whereby the investment is initially recorded at cost; earnings from such investments are recognized only to the extent received or receivable. When the investment is in the form of shares, dividends received in excess of the investor's pro rata share of post acquisition income are recorded as a reduction of the amount of the investment.

2-51.   As stated in the preceding Paragraph, the cost method records the investment at its cost and, in most circumstances, the investor company will continue to carry the asset at this value until it is disposed of. In general, the investor will recognize income only when the investee declares dividends ("extent received or receivable"). No recognition is given to increases or decreases in the Retained Earnings of the investee company, nor is any disclosure provided to indicate that the investee has recorded extraordinary items, results of discontinued operations, or prior period adjustments.

Return Of Capital

2-52.   An exception to the preceding general rules occurs when the dividends declared by the investee represent a return of capital to the investor. This happens when the investee's cumulative dividends since the date of the investor's acquisition of shares exceed the cumulative Net Income of the investee since that date. Stated alternatively, this happens when an investee pays dividends out of Retained Earnings that were present when the investor acquired its shares. A simple example will serve to illustrate this situation:

Example On December 31, 1998, the Fastee Company has the following Shareholders' Equity:

Common Stock - No Par	$3,400,000
Retained Earnings	4,600,000
Total Shareholders' Equity	$8,000,000

On this date, the Fastor Company acquires 10 percent of Fastee's outstanding voting shares at a cost of $800,000. During 1999, Fastee has Net Income of nil and declares dividends of $400,000.

2-53. As Fastee had no Net Income in 1999, the 1999 dividends are being paid out of the December 31, 1998 Retained Earnings balance. From the point of view of Fastee this is not a liquidating dividend. It is an ordinary dividend being paid on the basis of a Retained Earnings balance that is legally available for this purpose. However, from the point of view of Fastor, the $40,000 dividend that they receive from Fastee represents a return of capital. This position is based on the fact that, when they paid $800,000 for their 10 percent share of Fastee, they acquired a 10 percent share of the $4,600,000 Retained Earnings balance that was present in Fastee's December 31, 1998 Balance Sheet. As this balance is being used by Fastee as the basis for their 1999 dividend payment, the $40,000 received by Fastor constitutes a return of part of their original investment and not investment income. The journal entry to record the receipt of the dividend is as follows:

Cash	$40,000	
Investment In Fastee		$40,000

Equity Method Defined

Basic Procedures

2-54. The equity method is defined in the *CICA Handbook* as follows:

Paragraph 3050.02(a) The **equity method** is a basis of accounting for long-term investments whereby the investment is initially recorded at cost and the carrying value adjusted thereafter to include the investor's pro rata share of post acquisition earnings of the investee, computed by the consolidation method. The amount of the adjustment is included in the determination of net income by the investor and the investment account of the investor is also increased or decreased to reflect the investor's share of capital transactions and changes in accounting policies and corrections of errors relating to prior period financial statements applicable to post acquisition periods. Profit distributions received or receivable from an investee reduce the carrying value of the investment.

2-55. Ignoring for the moment special disclosure requirements and the need for consolidation adjustments, we can describe the equity method either in terms of asset value or income amounts. These descriptions are as follows:

Investment (Asset) Value The investment account is initially recorded at cost. In each subsequent accounting period, it is adjusted up or down to reflect the investor company's share of the change in Retained Earnings of the investee company. This adjustment could also be described as a two stage process in which the investment account is increased (decreased) for the investor's share of the investee's Net Income (Net Loss) and reduced for the investor's share of the investee's dividends declared.

Investment Income   Investment Income under the equity method is simply the investor company's share of the reported Net Income of the investee company.

Special Disclosure Requirements

2-56.   When an investee that is to be accounted for by the equity method has recorded discontinued operations, extraordinary items, capital transactions, or prior period adjustments related to accounting changes or errors, the *CICA Handbook* makes the following Recommendation:

> **Paragraph 3050.09**   *In accounting for an investment by the equity method, the investor's proportionate share of the investee's discontinued operations, extraordinary items, changes in accounting policy, corrections of errors relating to prior period financial statements and capital transactions should be disclosed in the investor's financial statements according to their nature.* (April, 1996)

2-57.   This means that if, for example, an investee company has an extraordinary gain, the investor company's share of this gain will be disclosed as an extraordinary gain in the financial statements of the investor company. This provision will be illustrated in an example of the application of the equity method later in this Chapter.

2-58.   A second equity method disclosure Recommendation is as follows:

> **Paragraph 3050.10**   *When the fiscal periods of an investor and an investee, the investment in which is accounted for by the equity method, are not coterminous, events relating to, or transactions of, the investee that have occurred during the intervening period and significantly affect the financial position or results of operations of the investor should be recorded or disclosed, as appropriate.* (August, 1978)

2-59.   This would generally be a problem only when the investor's year end is later than the year end that is reflected in the investee figures used. The appropriate disclosure for the relevant events would follow the pattern required for subsequent events in general (See Section 3820 of the *CICA Handbook)*. This Recommendation will not be illustrated in the examples contained in this Chapter.

2-60.   Disclosure is also required under the equity method of the treatment given to any difference between the cost of the investment and the investor's share of the underlying net book value of the investee's assets as follows:

> **Paragraph 3050.32**   *When investments are accounted for by the equity method, disclosure should be made, in the notes to the financial statements, of the amount of any difference between the cost and the underlying net book value of the investee's assets at the date of purchase, as well as the accounting treatment of the components of such difference.* (January, 1973)

2-61.   This disclosure relates to the need to incorporate various consolidation adjustments into the equity method. As will be explained in the following paragraphs, these consolidation adjustments will be covered in Chapter 6.

Consolidation Adjustments

2-62.   The need to incorporate consolidation adjustments into equity method procedures is clearly established in the following Recommendation:

> **Paragraph 3050.08**   *Investment income as calculated by the equity method should be that amount necessary to increase or decrease the investor's income to*

that which would have been recognized if the results of the investee's operations had been consolidated with those of the investor. (August, 1978)

2-63.   This requirement means that investment income under the equity method must be adjusted for all of the same factors that influence consolidation procedures. While these terms will not mean very much to you at this stage, adjustments would be required for fair value and goodwill write offs, upstream unrealized profits, and downstream unrealized profits. These consolidation adjustments will be covered in Chapters 5 and 6 and, as a consequence, the equity method examples in this Chapter will involve simple situations where such adjustments are not required. We will, of course, have to return to the equity method in Chapter 6 in order to fully illustrate this method of accounting for long term investments.

Consolidation Defined

2-64.   We have previously noted that long term investments sometimes involve situations in which the investor company has complete control over the affairs of the investee company. In such situations, the two companies are being operated as if they were a single business or economic entity and, as a consequence, accounting should focus on the economic resources and operations of the combined companies. Consolidation is an accounting method which accomplishes this goal. It accounts for the investor and investee companies as if they were a single entity, adding together all of the assets, liabilities, expenses and revenues of the two companies. However, these procedures always begin with the single entity accounting records of the two companies. Given this, the procedures required to adjust various asset values and to eliminate the effects of the different intercompany transactions are quite complex. As a consequence, only a very elementary example of the application of consolidated procedures will be presented in this Chapter.

2-65.   We would note, however, that when consolidation procedures are applied, the investment account will always be replaced by the investee's individual assets and liabilities. This means that no investment account will be included in the consolidated financial statements presented by the investor company. As a result, investor companies use a variety of different methods to account for the investment account in their single entity records. Since the investment account will not be disclosed in the consolidated financial statements, the method by which this balance will be accounted for in the single entity records of the investee company is not subject to generally accepted accounting principles.

Proportionate Consolidation Defined

2-66.   Under this modified version of consolidation, only the investor's share of the investee's assets, liabilities, expenses, and revenues are added to those of the investor. This is in contrast to full consolidation where 100 percent of the investee's assets, liabilities, expenses, and revenues are added to those of the investor company, with the minority interest in these items being disclosed as a separate item in the financial statements. When the investor company owns 100 percent of the investee company's shares, there is no difference between full and proportionate consolidation.

2-67.   While a complete application of proportionate consolidation requires the same adjustments as those required by full consolidation, we will provide a simple example to illustrate this procedure in this Chapter. However, as was the case with the equity method, it will be necessary to return to this subject in Chapter 6, after we have given more complete consideration to consolidation procedures.

Application Of The Cost And Equity Methods

Example One

2-68.   The example which follows involves no fair value changes, goodwill, or intercompany transactions. It will serve to fully illustrate the cost method and to introduce the equity method of accounting for long term investments.

Example One   On December 31, 1998, the Stor Company purchases 30 percent of the outstanding voting shares of the Stee Company for $6 million in cash. On this date, the carrying value of the net identifiable assets of the Stee Company total $20 million. All of the Stee Company's identifiable assets and liabilities have fair values that are equal to their carrying values. There are no intercompany transactions other than dividend payments during the three years subsequent to December 31, 1998. Dividends are declared on November 1 of each year and paid on December 1 of the same year. The Stee Company's Net Income and Dividend Declared Snd Paid for this period are as follows:

Year	Net Income	Dividends Declared And Paid
1999	$2,000,000	$1,500,000
2000	500,000	1,500,000
2001	3,500,000	1,700,000

The Net Income of the Stee Company does not include any extraordinary items in any of the years under consideration. In terms of bookkeeping procedures to be used, we will assume that Stor records the Stee dividends when received and, in applying the equity method, adjusts accounts for its share of Stee's Net Income at the end of each year.

Required   Provide the journal entries for the Stor Company related to its investment in the Stee Company for the years 1999 through 2001. They should be prepared under the assumption that the Stor Company accounts for its Investment In Stee using (A) the cost method and (B) the equity method.

Example One Part A Solution - Cost Method Journal Entries

2-69.   The journal entry required to record the initial investment on December 31, 1998 is as follows:

Investment In Stee	$6,000,000	
Cash		$6,000,000

2-70.   The journal entry that would be required for the 1999 receipt of dividends is as follows:

Cash	$450,000	
Investment Income		$450,000

(To record the receipt of 30 percent of the Stee Company's $1,500,000 dividends declared.)

2-71.   The journal entry that would be required for the 2000 receipt of dividends is as follows:

Cash	$450,000	
Investment In Stee		$150,000
Investment Income		300,000

(To record the receipt of 30 percent of the Stee Company's dividends and the resulting decrease in the investment account due to a return of capital.)

Note   At this point the Stee Company has paid dividends of $3,000,000 but has only earned $2,500,000 since the Stor Company acquired the Stee Company shares. This means that there has been a return of capital and the Stor Company will write down its investment account by $150,000 (30 percent of $500,000). The Investment Income totals $750,000 for the two years since acquisition ($450,000 + $300,000) and this is equal to 30 percent of the sum of the Stee Company's income for the two years ($2,000,000 for 1999 plus $500,000 for 2000).

2-72.   The journal entry that would be required for the 2001 receipt of dividends is as follows:

Cash $510,000
     Investment Income $510,000
(To record the receipt of 30 percent of the Stee Company's dividends of $1,700,000.)

Note   This entry leaves the balance in the Investment In Stee account at $5,850,000. It could be argued that since the Stee Company has retained sufficient earnings in 2001 to replace the pre acquisition retained earnings that were disbursed in 2000, the investment account should be restored to its original balance of $6,000,000. This would be accomplished with a debit to the Investment In Stee and a credit to Investment Income. This would bring the total Investment Income for the three years to $1,410,000 ($450,000 + $300,000 + $660,000) which is equal to 30 percent of the $4,700,000 in dividends that have been paid by the Stee Company during the three years since Stor Company acquired its shares. We would note that, while the *CICA Handbook* does not deal with this issue, practitioners appear to leave the investment account at its reduced value in these situations.

Example One Part B Solution - Equity Method Journal Entries

2-73.   The journal entry required to record the initial investment on December 31, 1998 is the same as under the cost method:

Investment In Stee $6,000,000
    Cash $6,000,000

2-74.   Under the procedures that we are using, two entries are required during 1999. The first is to record the receipt of the Stee dividends and the second is to make the year end adjustment to reflect Stor's share of Stee's Net Income.

Cash $450,000
    Investment In Stee $450,000
(To record the receipt of 30 percent of the Stee Company's $1,500,000 of dividends declared as a reduction in Stor's equity interest in Stee.)

Investment In Stee $600,000
    Investment Income $600,000
(To record Stor's 30 percent share of Stee's $2,000,000 Net Income as an increase in Stor's equity interest in Stee and as a revenue)

Note   It is possible to accomplish the same result with a single net entry as follows:

Cash $450,000
Investment In Stee   150,000
    Investment Income $600,000

The difference in these two approaches is a matter of bookkeeping. The two entry approach reflects the way the entries would normally be recorded in practice. However, the single net entry approach is sometimes used as a shortcut in textbook examples.

2-75.   For 2000, two entries would again be required under the equity method:

Cash	$450,000	
Investment In Stee		$450,000

(To record the receipt of 30 percent of the Stee Company's $1,500,000 of dividends declared as a reduction in Stor's equity interest in Stee.)

Investment In Stee	$150,000	
Investment Income		$150,000

(To record Stor's 30 percent share of Stee's $500,000 Net Income as an increase in Stor's equity interest in Stee and as a revenue.)

2-76. For 2001, two entries would again be required under the equity method:

Cash	$510,000	
Investment In Stee		$510,000

(To record the receipt of 30 percent of the Stee Company's $1,700,000 of dividends declared as a reduction in Stor's equity interest in Stee.)

Investment In Stee	$1,050,000	
Investment Income		$1,050,000

(To record Stor's 30 percent share of Stee's $3,500,000 Net Income as an increase in Stor's equity interest in Stee and as a revenue.)

Application Of The Equity Method

Example Two

2-77. It was noted previously that the equity method requires special disclosure when the investee has results of discontinued operations, extraordinary items, capital transactions or prior period adjustments. This provision can be illustrated by extending the preceding example.

Example Two On December 31, 1998, the Stor Company purchased 30 percent of the outstanding shares of the Stee Company. At the time of the acquisition, the identifiable assets and liabilities of the Stee Company had fair values that were equal to their carrying values and the purchase price was equal to the Stor Company's proportionate share of these carrying values. The Stor Company uses the equity method to account for its investment in the Stee Company. We have examined the Stor Company's accounting for 1999, 2000, and 2001 under the equity method. The 2002 condensed Income Statements of the two companies are as follows:

	Stor Company	Stee Company
Sales	$3,500,000	$750,000
Expenses	3,000,000	550,000
Income Before Extraordinary Items	$ 500,000	$200,000
Extraordinary Loss	-0-	(80,000)
Net Income	$ 500,000	$120,000

There are no intercompany transactions between the Stee Company and the Stor Company during 2002.

Required: Prepare the condensed Income Statement of the Stor Company for 2002.

Solution

2-78. The Stor Company's 2002 Income Statement using the equity method of accounting would be as follows:

Sales	$3,500,000
Ordinary Investment Income (30% of $200,000)	60,000
Total Revenues	$3,560,000
Expenses	3,000,000
Income Before Extraordinary Items	$ 560,000
Extraordinary Investment Loss (30% of $80,000)	(24,000)
Net Income	$ 536,000

2-79.   As can be seen in the preceding Income Statement, the investee's extraordinary items would be disclosed as an extraordinary item in the Income Statement of the investor enterprise. This would be true, even if some or all of the items were ordinary transactions from the point of view of the investor company. This is because they remain extraordinary transactions from the point of view of the investee and the related investment income.

Application Of The Equity Method, Proportionate Consolidation And Full Consolidation

Example Three

2-80.   An additional example of accounting methods for long term investments will provide a simple illustration of the application of the equity method, full consolidation, and proportionate consolidation. The example is as follows:

Example Three   On January 1, 1998, Marker Ltd. acquires 25 percent of the outstanding voting shares of Markee Inc. for $250,000. On this date, the Markee Inc. has Common Stock - No Par of $400,000 and Retained Earnings of $600,000. The identifiable assets and liabilities of Markee Inc. have fair values that are equal to their carrying values on this date. Both Companies have a December 31 year end.

During the year ending December 31, 1998, Markee Inc. has Net Income of $80,000 and declares and pays dividends of $30,000. Other than the payment of dividends, there are no intercompany transactions during the year and Markee has no results of discontinued operations, extraordinary items, capital transactions or accounting changes or errors requiring prior period adjustments. Marker Ltd. carries its investment in Markee Inc. using the equity method. Given this, Marker Ltd.'s journal entries to record its share of Markee's 1998 Dividends Declared and Markee's 1998 Net Income would be as follows:

Cash ([25%][$30,000])	$ 7,500	
Investment In Markee		$ 7,500
Investment In Markee ([25%][$80,000])	$20,000	
Investment Income		$20,000

The Balance Sheets of the two Companies as at December 31, 1998 and the Income Statements for the year ending December 31, 1998 would be as follows:

Marker Ltd. And Markee Inc.
Equity Method Balance Sheets
As At December 31, 1998

	Marker Ltd.	Markee Inc.
Cash	$ 175,000	$ 105,000
Accounts Receivable	425,000	220,000
Inventories	937,500	550,000
Investment In Markee (At Equity)	262,500	-0-
Plant And Equipment	2,700,000	725,000
Total Assets	$4,500,000	$1,600,000
Current Liabilities	$ 250,000	$ 125,000
Long Term Liabilities	750,000	425,000
Common Stock - No Par	1,200,000	400,000
Retained Earnings	2,300,000	650,000
Total Equities	$4,500,000	$1,600,000

Marker Ltd. And Markee Inc.
Equity Method Income Statements
For Year Ending December 31, 1998

	Marker Ltd.	Markee Inc.
Sales	$4,200,000	$1,500,000
Investment Income (Equity Method)	20,000	-0-
Total Revenues	$4,220,000	$1,500,000
Cost Of Goods Sold	$2,700,000	$ 975,000
Other Expenses	1,200,000	445,000
Total Expenses	$3,900,000	$1,420,000
Net Income	$ 320,000	$ 80,000

Proportionate Consolidation Solution

2-81.   The preceding financial statements reflect the application of the equity method to this situation. Note that in this simple example the $262,500 equity value of the Investment In Markee is exactly equal to 25 percent of the net assets of Markee ([25%][$1,600,000 - $125,000 -$425,000]). Proportionate consolidation would simply replace this $262,500 with 25 percent of the individual assets and liabilities of Markee Inc. This will result in the following Balance Sheet and Income Statement:

Marker Ltd. And Markee Inc.
Proportionate Consolidation Balance Sheet
As At December 31, 1998

Cash [$175,000 + (25%)($105,000)]	$ 201,250
Accounts Receivable [$425,000 + (25%)($220,000)]	480,000
Inventories [$937,500 + (25%)($550,000)]	1,075,000
Investment In Markee (Replaced By Marker's Share Of Markee's Net Assets)	-0-
Plant And Equipment [$2,700,000 + (25%)($725,000)]	2,881,250
Total Assets	$4,637,500
Current Liabilities [$250,000 + (25%)($125,000)]	$ 281,250
Long Term Liabilities [$750,000 + (25%)($425,000)]	856,250
Common Stock - No Par (Marker's Only)	1,200,000
Retained Earnings (Marker's Only)	2,300,000
Total Equities	$4,637,500

Marker Ltd. And Markee Inc.
Proportionate Consolidation Income Statement
For Year Ending December 31, 1998

Sales [$4,200,000 + (25%)($1,500,000)]	$4,575,000
Cost Of Goods Sold [$2,700,000 + (25%)(75,000)]	$2,943,750
Other Expenses [$1,200,000 + (25%)($445,000)]	1,311,250
Total Expenses	$4,255,000
Net Income	$ 320,000

2-82.   Note that the Net Income under proportionate consolidation is $320,000, the same figure that we arrived at for Marker Ltd. as a single entity using the equity method to account for its investment in Markee Inc. This makes clear that the basic difference between these two methods is one of disclosure. Under the equity method, Marker records $20,000 or 25 percent of Markee's Net Income as a single line item called Investment Income. In contrast, proportionate consolidation incorporates 25 percent of all of Markee's Revenues and Expenses into the Income Statement. While the detail contained in the statements looks very different, the bottom line figure of $320,000 is not changed.

Full Consolidation Solution

2-83.   It is somewhat more difficult to explain the appearance of the statements that result from using full consolidation procedures. Under these procedures, 100 percent of the assets, liabilities, expenses, and revenues of Markee will be added to those of Marker. However, since Marker does not own 100 percent of these amounts, a new equity interest will have to be disclosed in both the Income Statement and the Balance Sheet. In the usual situation in which full consolidation is being applied, the investor's ownership represents control over the investee and this equity interest would be referred to as a Minority Interest or Non Controlling Interest. In this situation, it will have to be referred to as a Majority Interest. In the Consolidated Balance Sheet, this Majority Interest is simply the majority's 75 percent share of the net assets of Markee. Correspondingly, in the Consolidated Income Statement, the Majority Interest is 75 percent of Markee's Net Income. The required financial statements are as follows:

Marker Ltd. And Markee Inc.
Full Consolidation Balance Sheet
As At December 31, 1998

Cash ($175,000 + $105,000)	$ 280,000
Accounts Receivable ($425,000 + $220,000)	645,000
Inventories ($937,500 + $550,000)	1,487,500
Investment In Markee (Replaced By Markee's Net Assets)	-0-
Plant And Equipment ($2,700,000 + $725,000)	3,425,000
Total Assets	**$5,837,500**

Current Liabilities ($250,000 + $125,000)	$ 375,000
Long Term Liabilities ($750,000 + $425,000)	1,175,000
Majority Interest ([75%][$400,000 + $650,000])	787,500
Common Stock - No Par (Marker's Only)	1,200,000
Retained Earnings (Marker's Only)	2,300,000
Total Equities	**$5,837,500**

Marker Ltd. And Markee Inc.
Full Consolidation Income Statement
For Year Ending December 31, 1998

Sales ($4,200,000 + $1,500,000)	$5,700,000
Cost Of Goods Sold ($2,700,000 + $975,000)	$3,675,000
Other Expenses ($1,200,000 + $445,000)	1,645,000
Total Expenses	**$5,320,000**
Total Income	$ 380,000
Majority Interest ([75%][$80,000])	(60,000)
Consolidated Net Income	**$ 320,000**

2-84.   Note that this is the same $320,000 of Net Income that resulted from the application of both the equity method and proportionate consolidation.

Application Of The Equity Method - EIC Abstract No. 8

Example Four

2-85.   A final example will be used to illustrate a further aspect of the general application of the equity method:

Example Four   On January 1, 1998, Duster Ltd. acquires 35 percent of the outstanding voting shares of Dustee Ltd. for $3,500,000 in cash. At the time of this acquisition, the net book value of Dustee Ltd. was $50,000,000. Duster Ltd. was able to acquire these shares at this price because it was anticipated that Dustee Ltd. was going to experience severe losses during the next two years. This anticipation was correct and Duster's 1998 loss from its Investment In Dustee was $4,200,000.

Example Four Solution

2-86.   Under the usual equity method procedures, the journal entry to reflect this result would be as follows:

Investment Loss	$4,200,000	
Investment In Dustee		$4,200,000

2-87.   The problem here is that this entry would create a credit balance of $700,000 in the Investment In Dustee account and this balance would have to be reported as a liability. Since equity investments in corporations are protected by limited liability, the recording of a liability in these circumstances would generally not be appropriate. As a consequence, an investor company would usually stop recording further equity method losses when the related asset balance reaches nil.

2-88.   However, the Emerging Issues Committee was asked if there were any circumstances in which it would be appropriate to continue recording losses after an equity investment balance reached nil. Their response is reflected in EIC Abstract No. 8 in which they indicate that continuing to record such losses would be appropriate if the investor was likely to share in them. In their view, this would be the case if any of the following conditions are present:

- the investor has guaranteed obligations of the investee; or
- the investor is otherwise committed to provide further financial support for the investee; or
- the investee seems assured of imminently returning to profitability.

2-89.   The other issue dealt with in this EIC Abstract was the question of what disclosure should be provided in those cases where the investor does not continue to record equity method losses. In general, they indicated that the information to be disclosed would be a matter of professional judgment but could include:

- disclosure of unrecognized losses for the period and accumulated to date; and
- the investor's accounting policies with respect to the investment, including the policy to be followed should the investee return to profitability.

2-90.   The Committee also indicated that, when losses have not been recorded on an investee that later returns to profitability, the investor should resume recognizing its share of those profits only after its share of the profits equals its share of the losses not recognized.

Application Of The Cost Method - Debt Securities
Example
2-91.   As previously indicated, long term investments in debt securities would be classified as portfolio investments. While procedures for dealing with these securities are given extensive treatment in most intermediate accounting texts, a simple example is useful in the context of our general discussion of long term investments:

On January 1, 1998, Barton Inc. acquires debt securities with a par value of $2,000,000 at a cost of $2,250,000. The bonds mature in 10 years and pay interest annually on December 31 at a coupon rate of 8 percent. It is the intent of management to hold these securities until their maturity.

Solution
2-92.   The acquisition of the bonds would be recorded as follows:

Bonds Receivable - Par Value	$2,000,000	
Bonds Receivable - Premium	250,000	
Cash		$2,250,000

2-93.   As we are dealing with a long term investment in debt securities, it is appropriate to amortize the premium on the bonds. For the sake of simplicity, we will assume straight line amortization of this amount, resulting in an annual write off of $25,000 ($250,000 ÷ 10 years). The following annual entry would be required to record interest received and the premium amortization:

Cash ([8%][$2,000,000]) $160,000
    Bonds Receivable - Premium $ 25,000
    Interest Revenue   135,000

2-94. If the bonds are held, as intended, until their maturity, the premium will have been eliminated through amortization. The following entry would be required to record the receipt of the par value amount:

Cash $2,000,000
    Bonds Receivable - Par Value $2,000,000

2-95. Alternatively, if the bonds are sold prior to maturity, the proceeds of disposition will be compared to the book value of the debt securities including the unamortized premium. The difference will then be recorded as a gain or loss.

Evaluation Of Cost And Equity Methods

2-96. If an individual who was familiar with the accounting procedures used for most of the long term assets of an enterprise were asked to develop an accounting method to be used for long term investments, the individual would probably arrive at a set of procedures that look very much like the cost method. This method uses acquisition cost as its basic measure of value. Income is subsequently recognized only when there is a clear legal basis for such recognition. In the case of long term investments in equity securities, this legal basis would require a dividend declaration. In contrast, the equity method records as income and includes in asset values the investor's claim to the undistributed earnings of the investee. From a legal point of view, the investor has no real claim to these balances and, in many situations, will never realize the amounts that have been recorded.

2-97. The preceding analysis suggests that the cost method is more consistent with general accounting procedures than the equity method in situations where there is less than full control over the investee. Unfortunately there is a problem with this conclusion. Under the cost method, Investment Income is based on the dividend declarations of the investee. This income is the investor's share of the investee's dividends declared, without regard to the GAAP determined earnings of the investee. While economic reality requires that there be a long run relationship between reported income and dividend declarations, the directors of the investee have great discretion in determining short run variations in this relationship. This does not create a problem when the investor company is not in a position to influence the board of directors. However, there are many situations short of full control of the investee, where the investor is able to exercise considerable influence on the actions of the investee's directors. In these cases, the use of the cost method would allow the investor company to have significant influence over its own Investment Income.

2-98. For this reason, the equity method is required in situations where the investor company has influence over the investee. This would generally include all long term investments in significantly influenced investees. In requiring the equity method in these circumstances, a potential problem is also dealt with. This is the possibility that the investor company could influence the terms of intercompany transactions between the investor and investee enterprises. As was noted previously and as will be illustrated in subsequent chapters, the application of the equity method requires the elimination of all intercompany profits, both those of the investor and those of the investee, from the reported Investment Income.

2-99. Even in those situations where the investor is not in a position to influence the investee, there is a problem with the use of the cost method. The 1984 CICA Research

Study, *Accounting For Portfolio Investments*, concluded that the use of market values for these investments would provide the most useful information for decision making purposes. Further, the study group recommended that gains or losses should be recognized as they occur on the basis of market related values. This is in contrast to the current situation in which gains and losses are recorded when there is a long term investment disposition, a transaction over which the investor company has complete discretion as to timing.

Evaluation Of Consolidation

Proportionate Consolidation

2-100.   Prior to the October, 1994 revision of Section 3055, joint ventures were most commonly accounted for by the equity method. The previous version of Section 3055 indicated that, if a substantial portion of the investor's operations were in the form of joint ventures, it was permissible to use proportionate consolidation. However, the use of this method was never required.

2-101.   In general, the use of the equity method for joint ventures was a reasonable approach. The cost method had to be rejected because, by the very definition of a joint venture investment, the investor had to be involved in the management of the investee. The definition of joint venture investments also precluded any investor having the full control over the investee that would justify the use of the full consolidation method. With the elimination of both the cost method and full consolidation for joint ventures, the use of the equity method was an almost inevitable choice.

2-102.   However, there was a problem with the application of the equity method in some joint venture situations. Companies existed which had no real economic activity other than their investment in joint ventures. For such companies, the use of the equity method would result in a one line Balance Sheet (Investment In Joint Ventures) and a one line Income Statement (Investment Income From Joint Ventures). This was clearly an inadequate form of disclosure and, given this problem, the use of proportionate consolidation provided an effective solution.

2-103.   In response to this problem, the Accounting Standards Board concluded that proportionate consolidation was the appropriate method to be used for all joint venture situations. This is stated as follows:

> **Paragraph 3055.17**   *Interests in joint ventures should be recognized in the financial statements of the venturer using the proportionate consolidation method.* (January, 1995)

2-104.   While it is not clear to us that it was necessary to require proportionate consolidation for all joint venture situations, this Recommendation represents an unquestionable improvement in situations where a substantial portion of the investor's operations are in the form of joint ventures.

Full Consolidation

2-105.   There is general agreement that, when an investor company has achieved sufficient control over an investee that resources are freely interchangeable and the two entities can be operated as a single economic unit, the application of full consolidation procedures is appropriate. At one point in time, the *CICA Handbook* listed a limited number of situations where subsidiaries could be excluded from consolidation. However, current *Handbook* Recommendations in this area leave no choice. If control over an investee exists, the investee is a subsidiary and must be consolidated with the financial statements of the parent or investor company.

2-106.   While there is general agreement on the usefulness of consolidated financial statements for measuring the financial position and results of operations for a controlled group of companies, there is criticism of the fact that these are normally the only financial statements presented by the parent company. For a large corporation, these consolidated statements might aggregate financial data for a hundred or more individual companies. Further, these companies could be involved in dozens of different lines of business or in many different geographic locations around the world.

2-107.   To some extent, the segmented information requirements of Section 1701, "Segment Disclosures", alleviate this problem by providing for disclosure of reportable operating segments. However, segmented information fails to take into account the legally defined interests of creditors, tax authorities, and non controlling interest (minority) shareholders. Creditors can only take legal action against individual legal entities. In fact, an individual company can be in bankruptcy without threatening the overall health of the consolidated group. Further, tax returns must be filed by each individual corporation and non controlling interest shareholders must look to the individual corporation in which they hold shares for their expected return on investment.

2-108.   This leads some to argue that consolidated statements should be presented in conjunction with the single entity statements of the companies which comprise the consolidated group. This, in fact, is the approach that is taken in many industrialized countries other than Canada and the United States. As the whole area of consolidated financial statements is currently under comprehensive review in the United States, we may see changes in this situation in the next few years.

Recommended Accounting Methods For Long Term Investments

Portfolio Investments

2-109.   We have now completed our presentation of the classification of long term investments and the description of the methods that are available to account for them. We are now in a position to consider which of the methods described is most appropriate for each of the long term investment classifications that have been defined. The least complex Recommendation in this area pertains to portfolio investments. With respect to these investments, the *CICA Handbook* states the following:

> **Paragraph 3050.18**   *The cost method should be used in accounting for portfolio investments.* (August, 1978)

2-110.   This Recommendation reflects the fact that the investor company is not in a position to exercise significant influence or control over the investee. While it is consistent with other Recommendations for dealing with the valuation of long term assets, there is some question as to its usefulness for decision making purposes.

2-111.   There are no exceptions to this accounting treatment for portfolio investments. However, as noted previously, the cost of the investment can be reduced in situations where there is a return of the investor company's capital. In addition, investments that have experienced a non temporary decline in value must be written down, without regard to the method being used to account for them (see the discussion which begins at Paragraph 2-144). There are no circumstances under which the value of portfolio investments would be increased.

2-112.   As we have noted, all long term investments in debt securities are considered to be portfolio investments. Given this, the *CICA Handbook* notes the following:

> **Paragraph 3050.19**   In the case of fixed term securities, it would be appropriate to amortize any discount or premium arising on purchase over the period to maturity. As a result of the amortization, earnings from the investment would reflect a yield based on purchase costs, not on coupon rates, and the carrying value of the investment would be adjusted systematically, during the period it is held, toward

the amount expected to be realized at maturity or an earlier call date.

2-113.   While this suggests that discount or premium on long term debt should be amortized, it does not specify the method to be used for this amortization. The statement that the "carrying value of the investment would be adjusted systematically" would permit the use of either the straight line or the effective yield approach.

Significantly Influenced Companies

2-114.   As was noted in our evaluation of the equity method, if investors in significantly influenced companies were allowed to use the cost method, it would be possible for them to manipulate investment income via their influence over the investee's dividend policy. Given this possibility, the *CICA Handbook* makes the following Recommendation:

Paragraph 3050.06   *An investor that is able to exercise significant influence over an investee that is neither a subsidiary as defined in "Subsidiaries", Section 1590, nor a joint venture as defined in "Interests In Joint Ventures", Section 3055, should account for the investment by the equity method.* (January, 1995)

2-115.   The equity method would continue to be used until such time as significant influence is no longer present and significantly influenced company is no longer the appropriate classification for the investee. While this is not specifically dealt with in the *Handbook*, in some situations significant influence may evolve into control over the investee. This would normally follow the acquisition of additional voting shares and would result in the investee being classified as a subsidiary. In such situations, the investor company would switch from using the equity method to using consolidation procedures.

2-116.   It is also possible that an investor company will lose its ability to exercise significant influence. If this occurs, the following Recommendation is applicable:

Paragraph 3050.07   *When an investor ceases to be able to exercise significant influence over an investee, the investment should be accounted for by the cost method.* (January, 1992)

2-117.   You should note that there are alternative approaches to the application of this Recommendation. This reflects the fact that, when an investor has applied the equity method to an investment, the investment account will no longer be carried at its original cost. In most cases it will be at a value in excess of original cost, reflecting the investor's share of the investee's Retained Earnings since acquisition. In switching over to the cost method, the accounting change could be applied on either a retroactive or prospective basis.

2-118.   If it were applied retroactively, the investment would have to be restored to its original cost. In most situations, this would require the investment to be written down, resulting in the recognition of a loss. In contrast, prospective treatment would use the equity value at the date of the change as the deemed cost, applying cost method procedures to those accounting periods subsequent to the change. Under this prospective treatment, no loss or gain would be recognized at the time of the accounting change.

2-119.   While not a formal Recommendation, Paragraph 3050.16 notes that cost is deemed to be the carrying value (equity value) at the time of the switch from the equity method to the cost method. This suggests the use of prospective treatment when an investor no longer able to exercise significant influence over an investee. This Paragraph also notes that this might be an appropriate time to consider whether there has been an impairment in the value of the investment that would require a write down under Paragraph 3050.20 (see our Paragraph 2-144).

2-120.   The use of prospective treatment in these situations creates an additional problem in the application of the cost method. As cost is deemed to be the equity value at the time of the change from the equity method to the cost method, the investment account will reflect the Retained Earnings of the investee up to the time of the switch. This is in contrast to the usual cost procedures in which the investment account reflects the investee Retained Earnings only to the date on which the investment was made. This difference has an influence on the measurement of whether or not an investee dividend represents a return of capital to the investor. In this situation, a return of capital occurs when the cumulative amount of dividends exceeds income in the period subsequent to the date of the accounting change.

Joint Ventures

General Requirements

2-121.   As noted in our discussion of the nature of joint ventures, an investor must participate in the management of an investee in order for the investment to be classified as a joint venture. This means that such investors will be in a position to influence the policies of the investee, including decisions related to the declaration of dividends. In view of this, it would not be appropriate to allow joint venture investors to use the cost method.

2-122.   The definition of a joint venture also specifies that none of the participant investors can have unilateral control. As full consolidation is only appropriate in situations where the investor has control over the investee, we can conclude that full consolidation is never appropriate for a joint venture investment.

2-123.   This process of elimination appears to lead directly to the use of the equity method. However, in some situations there is a serious problem with the use of the equity method for joint ventures. There are Canadian companies whose total economic activity consists of investments in a variety of joint venture arrangements. As we noted previously, if such investor companies are allowed to use the equity method, their financial statements would consist of a Balance Sheet in which there is only a single asset (Investment In Joint Ventures) and an Income Statement made up of a single revenue (Investment Income). This would not constitute effective disclosure and, as a consequence, Section 3055 specifies the use of proportionate consolidation. This is indicated as follows:

> **Paragraph 3055.17**   *Interests in joint ventures should be recognized in the financial statements of the venturer using the proportionate consolidation method.* (January, 1995)

2-124.   In making this Recommendation the Accounting Standards Board argues that it is essential that each venturer reflect the substance and underlying economic reality of its interest, without regard to the structures or forms under which the joint venture activities take place. By providing financial statement users with the most appropriate information about the resources, obligations and operations of a venturer that conducts business through one or more joint ventures, the proportionate consolidation method achieves this essential objective.

Forms And Structures

2-125.   The example presented in Paragraph 2-80 was used to provide a simple illustration of the application of proportionate consolidation. This example was based on the form of the joint venture being an investment in a separate enterprise. The application of proportionate consolidation in this type of situation results in the venturer recognizing:

1.   in its balance sheet, its share of the assets and its share of the liabilities of the jointly controlled enterprise;

2.   in its income statement, its share of the revenue and its share of the expenses of the jointly controlled enterprise.

2-126.   While this separate enterprise arrangement is, for most of us, the most familiar type of joint venture arrangement, other forms and structures exist.

2-127.   Joint venture activities may be undertaken without establishing a separate enterprise through arrangements involving jointly controlled operations (see Paragraph 2-45). When this is the case, Paragraph 3055.19 indicates that using the proportionate consolidation method results in the venturer recognizing:

1. in its balance sheet, the assets that it controls and the liabilities that it incurs; and

2. in its income statement, its share of the revenue of the joint venture and its share of the expenses incurred by the joint venture.

2-128.   A further alternative involves carrying on joint venture activities through arrangements involving only jointly controlled assets (see Paragraph 2-45). In this situation, Paragraph 3055.20 indicates that use of the proportionate consolidation method results in the venturer recognizing:

1. in its balance sheet, its share of the jointly controlled assets and its share of any liabilities incurred jointly with the other venturers in relation to the joint venture; and

2. in its income statement, any revenue from the sale or use of its share of the output of the joint venture, and its share of any expenses incurred by the joint venture.

2-129.   Many of the procedures used in proportionate consolidation are the same as those used in the application of full consolidation. This would include the treatment of fair values changes and their related amortization, as well as the elimination of unrealized intercompany profits. These complications mean that we will have to return to the proportionate consolidation method in Chapter 6, after we have completed our discussion of basic consolidation procedures.

2-130.   While recognizing the existence of alternative approaches to organizing joint venture activities, the more complex examples of joint venture procedures that will be presented in Chapter 6 will be based on situations in which the joint venture activities are carried out through a separate enterprise.

Cessation Of Joint Control

2-131.   In situations where a separate enterprise has been established to carry out joint venture activities, proportionate consolidation will be required as long as the joint venture agreement is in effect. However, if joint control ceases to exist, other methods will have to be used.

2-132.   If joint control has been lost because one investor has acquired unilateral control over the enterprise, the enterprise that has gained unilateral control will become subject to the Recommendations of Section 1590, "Subsidiaries". In general, this will result in this investor using full consolidation procedures.

2-133.   An individual investor may cease to participate in joint control for a variety of reasons. This could happen through one of the other investors acquiring unilateral control or, alternatively, through a change in the joint venture agreement such that the particular investor no longer participates in the control mechanism. For investors in this position, the requirements of Section 3050, "Long Term Investments", become applicable. This would result in the application of either the cost method or the equity method, depending on how the investment was classified.

2-134.   A further possibility here is that joint venture operations would be discontinued. In this situation, the provisions of Section 3475, "Discontinued Operations" would be applicable.

Subsidiaries

General Rule

2-135.   When an investor company has control over the operating, investing, and financing activities of an investee company, the two companies can normally be considered a single economic entity. In such circumstances, it is a well established practice for accountants to concentrate on the single economic entity, rather than on the separate investor and investee legal entities. As the definition of a subsidiary is based on control, it is not surprising that consolidation is the required accounting method. Paragraph 1590.16 of the *CICA Handbook* makes the following Recommendation with respect to the accounting treatment of subsidiaries:

> **Paragraph 1590.16**   *An enterprise should consolidate all of its subsidiaries.*
> (January, 1992)

2-136.   This is a very restrictive rule which provides no flexibility with respect to the consolidation of investments that are classified as subsidiaries. This reflects the fact that, under earlier rules which were less rigid, it appeared that investor companies used the available flexibility to enhance their consolidated statements by excluding certain subsidiaries (e.g., subsidiaries with large debt loads).

Non Consolidated Financial Statements

2-137.   In some circumstances, non consolidated financial statements may be prepared for subsidiaries or joint ventures. While such statements do not comply with the Recommendations of Section 1590, "Subsidiaries", or Section 3055, "Interests In Joint Ventures", if they otherwise comply with generally accepted accounting principles, Paragraph 3050.45 of the *CICA Handbook* indicates that they may be prepared in the following circumstances:

(a) a reporting enterprise is itself a wholly-owned subsidiary, and the sole owner has access to all pertinent information concerning the resources and results of operations of the group;

(b) a reporting enterprise that prepares consolidated financial statements also prepares non consolidated financial statements for income tax or other special purposes; or

(c) the owners of the reporting enterprise have access to all pertinent information concerning the resources and results of operation of the group; and the owners, including those not otherwise entitled to vote, unanimously consent to the preparation of non-consolidated financial statements.

2-138.   With respect to these non consolidated statements, the following Recommendations are applicable:

> **Paragraph 3050.39**   *When non-consolidated financial statements are prepared in the situations described in paragraph 3050.45, the following information should be disclosed:*
>
> *(a) the reason that non-consolidated financial statements are issued;*
>
> *(b) the fact that, as the non-consolidated financial statements have not been prepared for general purposes, some users may require further information;*
>
> *(c) a reference to consolidated financial statements, if any exist;*
>
> *(d) the fact that the financial statements are in accordance with generally accepted accounting principles except that they are prepared on a non-consolidated basis;*

(e) the method of accounting for subsidiaries; and

(f) the method of accounting for interests in joint ventures. (January, 1995)

Paragraph 3050.40 *Investments in non-consolidated subsidiaries should be shown separately. (January, 1992)*

Paragraph 3050.41 *Income from investments in non-consolidated subsidiaries should be shown separately. (January, 1992)*

Paragraph 3050.42 *Interests in joint ventures not accounted for using the proportionate consolidation method should be shown separately. (January, 1995)*

Paragraph 3050.43 *Income from interests in joint ventures not accounted for using the proportionate consolidation method should be shown separately. (January, 1995)*

Paragraph 3050.44 *The particulars of any shares or other securities issued by the reporting enterprise and owned by subsidiaries excluded from consolidation should be disclosed in the financial statements of the reporting enterprise. (January, 1992)*

Accounting Methods Summarized

2-139.   The conclusions reached in Sections 1590, 3050, and 3055 on the appropriate accounting methods to be used for each investment classification can be summarized in Figure 2-3 which follows:

Figure 2-3 Accounting Methods Summarized		
Investment Classification	**Degree Of Control**	**Accounting Method**
Portfolio Investments	None	Cost
Significantly Influenced Companies	Significant	Equity
Joint Ventures	Shared	Proportionate Consolidation
Subsidiaries	Complete	Consolidation

2-140.   As is clear from Figure 2-3, the cost method is only used in those cases where the investor is not in a position to exercise significant influence over the affairs of the investee. As was previously explained, this prevents the investor company from manipulating investment income in those situations where it is in a position to control the dividend policy of the investee.

2-141.   Correspondingly, the equity method is required in the cases where the investor can exercise significant influence. This prevents the investor company from manipulating investment income via intercompany transactions using arbitrary transfer prices.

2-142.   In the case of joint ventures, proportionate consolidation is required. This reflects the fact that the investor company will have influence over the investee through its shared control of that enterprise

2-143.   Finally, in those cases where the investor company has control over the investee, the investor and investee companies are accounted for as a single operating unit. This is accomplished through the preparation of consolidated financial statements.

Other Provisions Of Sections 3050 And 3055

Declines In The Value Of Long Term Investments

General Provisions

2-144.   The general *Handbook* provision dealing with the question of when a long term investment should be written down is as follows:

> **Paragraph 3050.20**   *When there has been a loss in value of an investment that is other than a temporary decline, the investment should be written down to recognize the loss.* The write-down would be included in the determination of income and may or may not be an extraordinary item. (See "Extraordinary Items", Section 3480) (January 1973)

2-145.   This provision would apply, regardless of the method that was being used to account for the investment. In those cases where the investment is carried by the cost or equity method, the *CICA Handbook* notes:

> **Paragraph 3050.25**   When either the equity method or the cost method is used, a decline in value that is other than temporary would be recognized by writing down the investment.

2-146.   While you will not fully understand this point until we have covered consolidation procedures, the investment account for subsidiaries is always eliminated from the consolidated financial statements. Given this, the write down of an investment in a subsidiary will take the form of a reduction in the value of specific assets in the consolidated Balance Sheet. The usual choice for this write down would be any Goodwill that was recognized when the subsidiary was acquired.

Debt Securities

2-147.   The implementation of Paragraph 3050.20 to holdings of debt securities does not present any major problems. The only circumstances that would lead an investor to conclude that an investment in debt securities should be written down are:

- The possibility that the securities will be disposed of before they mature at a value that is less than their carrying value; or

- The possibility that the investee may default on some part of the interest or principal prior to the maturity of the securities.

2-148.   Changes in the market value of debt securities are not of significance in those cases where the investor intends to hold the investment to its maturity date, provided such changes do not reflect the possibility that the creditor enterprise will default on its obligations under the debt agreement.

Equity Securities

2-149.   The implementation of Paragraph 3050.20 with respect to securities that do not have either a fixed maturity date or a fixed maturity value will generally be more difficult than was the case with holdings of debt securities. There are some fairly obvious situations which indicate there has been a non temporary loss in value, such as an investee in bankruptcy or one for which there is an agreement to sell at a price which will result in a loss. However, in the majority of situations, the investor will have to examine a number of factors to determine if a write down is appropriate. Paragraph 3050.24 suggests that the following be taken into consideration:

- a prolonged period during which the quoted market value of the investment is less than its carrying value;
- severe losses by the investee in the current year or current and prior years;
- continued losses by the investee for a period of years;
- suspension of trading in the securities;
- liquidity or going concern problems of the investee;
- the current fair value of the investment (an appraisal) is less than its carrying value.

2-150.   This Paragraph goes on to note the following with respect to the use of these factors:

> ...... when a condition, indicating that an impairment in value of an investment may have occurred, has persisted for a period of three or four years, there is a general presumption that there has been a loss in value which is other than a temporary decline. This presumption can only be rebutted by persuasive evidence to the contrary.

Subsequent Increase In Value

2-151.   It is possible that, after a long term investment has been written down, the fortunes of the investee will improve and the investment will increase in value. This, of course, raises the question of whether the investment should be written back up to its original value. The *CICA Handbook* takes the position that, once an investment has been reduced in value, this new value should be viewed as the cost for subsequent accounting purposes. This view is reflected in the following Recommendation:

> **Paragraph 3050.21**   *A write-down of an investment to reflect a loss in value should not be reversed if there is a subsequent increase in value.* (August, 1978)

2-152.   This Recommendation can only be defended on grounds of conservatism. It is difficult to understand why the same kind of evidence which was used to support a write down of the long term investment could not be used to support a reversal of such a write down. However, this approach is consistent with the treatment of capital asset write downs under the Recommendations of Section 3060 (see Paragraph 3060.43).

Gains And Losses On The Sale Of Investments

2-153.   A long term investment may consist of a group of identical securities which have been acquired at different points in time and, as a consequence, at different prices. When part of such a group is disposed of, some assumption must be made as to the flow of costs to be allocated to the sale. The normal alternatives would be specific identification, LIFO (last-in, first-out), FIFO (first-in, first-out), or average cost. The *CICA Handbook* takes the position that average cost best reflects the gain or loss that would be recognized if the entire investment were disposed of. This is reflected in the following Recommendation:

> **Paragraph 3050.27**   *For the purposes of calculating a gain or loss on the sale of an investment, the cost of the investment sold should be calculated on the basis of the average carrying value.* (January, 1973)

2-154.   This Recommendation is consistent with the required income tax treatment of gains and losses on such identical properties (See Section 47 of the *Income Tax Act*).

Transfers Of Non Cash Assets To Joint Ventures

The Problem

2-155.   In making a long term investment in the shares or debt securities of an investee company, the consideration used by the investor company could be cash, shares or debt of the investor company, or non cash assets owned by the investor company. While non cash assets could be used to acquire any type of investment, this does not appear to be a common occurrence in the case of subsidiaries, portfolio investments, or significantly influenced companies. As a consequence, the *CICA Handbook* has not given any attention to this issue in Section 3050.

2-156.   However, contributions of non cash assets to joint ventures are sufficiently common that attention has been given to the problems associated with such contributions, both by the Accounting Standards Board and by the Emerging Issues Committee.

2-157.   Problems arise with non cash investment contributions when the assets contributed are carried, on the venturer's books, at values other than current fair market value. For example, a venturer might contribute land with a carrying value of $500,000 and a current fair market value of $1,000,000. The issues that arise in this type of situation are as follows:

- To what extent, if any, should gains be recognized on the transfer of non cash assets to a joint venture in return for an equity interest in that venture?

- To what extent, if any, should losses be recognized on the transfer of non cash assets to a joint venture in return for an equity interest in that venture?

- How are these conclusions altered when the venturer receives cash or other assets in addition to an equity interest in the joint venture?

- If a gain or loss is to be recognized on the transfer of non cash assets to a joint venture, how is the amount of gain or loss to be determined?

Relevant Pronouncements

2-158.   Prior to the 1994 revision of Section 3055 of the *CICA Handbook*, the basic source of guidance on non monetary contributions to joint ventures was EIC Abstract No. 28. With the revision of Section 3055, this Abstract was no longer relevant and it was withdrawn.

2-159.   While Section 3055 is the major source of guidance in this area, note that two other *Handbook* Sections have some bearing on the issues related to the transfer of non monetary assets to joint ventures. These are Section 3830, "Non Monetary Transactions", and Section 3060, "Capital Assets". The relevance of these Sections to the issue under discussion will be considered in the next two Sections of this Chapter.

Section 3830 - Non Monetary Transactions

2-160.   Consider the following example:

Example   Company A and Company B form a joint venture. Company A's capital contribution consists of a factory with a fair market value of $1,000,000 and a carrying value of $200,000. Company B's capital contribution consists of equipment with a fair market value of $1,000,000 and a carrying value of $350,000. Each venturer receives a 50 percent equity interest in the joint venture.

2-161.   From the point of view of both venturers, they have exchanged ownership of productive assets for an interest in similar productive assets. The assets are not assets that are held for resale and no monetary consideration is involved.

2-162.   Section 3830, "Non Monetary Transactions", is relevant here. It states:

Paragraph 3830.08 *Non-monetary exchanges that do not represent the culmination of the earnings process should be recorded at the carrying value of the asset or service given up in the exchange adjusted by any monetary consideration received or given.* (January, 1990)

2-163.   An example of a transaction that would not represent the culmination of the earnings process is found in Paragraph 3830.09(b) as follows:

Paragraph 3830.09(b)   ... an exchange of productive assets not held for sale in the ordinary course of business for similar productive assets or for an equivalent interest in the same or similar productive assets.

2-164.   A contribution of non cash assets to a joint venture in return for an equity interest in the joint venture, all of the assets of which consist of similar assets, would be a transaction described by Paragraph 3830.09(b). As a result, such a transaction would not involve the culmination of an earnings process and Paragraph 3830.08 would require that the transaction be recorded at the carrying value of the assets transferred. This leads us to the conclusion that no gains should be recorded by a venturer when non cash assets are transferred to a joint venture in return for only an equity interest. Note, however, Paragraph 3830.08 indicates that the carrying value can be adjusted for any monetary consideration received and this provides for the possibility of recognizing some amount of gain on the transfer. Section 3055 reflects this analysis of the applicability of Section 3830 to non cash asset contributions to joint ventures.

Section 3060 - Capital Assets

2-165.   As noted, Section 3830 requires that transfers of non cash assets in return for an interest in similar assets be recorded at the carrying value of the assets transferred. This clearly prohibits a given venturer from recognizing his share of any gain on assets transferred to a joint venture in return for an equity interest in that venture. In turn, it would seem to suggest that losses would be similarly prohibited on such transfers. However, the loss situation is also influenced by the requirements of Section 3060, "Capital Assets". Consider the following example:

Example   Company X and Company Y form a joint venture. Company X's capital contribution consists of a factory with a fair market value of $500,000 and a carrying value of $900,000. Company Y's capital contribution consists of equipment with a fair market value of $500,000 and a carrying value of $350,000. Each venturer receives a 50 percent equity interest in the joint venture.

2-166.   Company X, in dealing with an arm's length party, has agreed to accept an equity interest that is worth $500,000 in return for an asset with a carrying value of $900,000. This is clear and objective evidence that the net recoverable amount of this asset has declined below the net carrying value of the factory. In these circumstances, the *CICA Handbook* Recommends the following:

Paragraph 3060.42 *When the net carrying amount of a capital asset, less related accumulated provision for future removal and site restoration costs and future income taxes, exceeds the net recoverable amount, the excess should be charged to income.* (December, 1990)

2-167.   If we believe that the transfer of an asset to a joint venture in return for an equity interest with a value that is less than the carrying value of the asset, is evidence of a decline in the recoverable amount of the asset, then Paragraph 3060.42 would require recognition of the loss on such assets prior to their transfer. Subsequent to the write down under Paragraph 3060.42, the assets could be transferred at their carrying value as per the provisions of Paragraph 3830.08 for exchanges of non monetary assets. In effect, this requires that losses on investment contributions of non cash assets to joint ventures in exchange for an equity interest must be recognized. Section 3055 reflects this analysis of the applicability of Section 3060 to situations where venturers contribute non monetary assets to joint ventures.

Section 3055 - General Approach

2-168.   When a venturer transfers an asset to a joint venture in return for an equity interest in the venture, he has given up unilateral control of the asset in exchange for participation in joint control of the asset by the various parties to the joint venture agreement. Provided the venturer making the transfer is dealing at arm's length with the other parties to the joint venture agreement, the asset transfer can be viewed as an arm's length transaction. This is important in that it creates a presumption that the transfer was made at the asset's fair market value and this, in turn, provides a basis for recognizing some portion of any gain or loss arising on the transfer.

Section 3055 - Losses On Transfer

2-169.   To illustrate the Recommendations of Section 3055 with respect to losses, assume that a venturer has land with a current fair market value of $400,000 and an original cost of $500,000. The venturer intends to transfer this land to a joint venture in which he will have a 25 percent equity interest.

2-170.   One possibility here would be that, after acquiring his 25 percent interest through an investment of cash, the land is transferred to the joint venture in return for cash equal to its fair value of $400,000. While Section 3055 does not deal explicitly with this situation, the Section's view that such transfers are arm's length transactions would suggest that the entire loss of $100,000 would be taken into income at the time of transfer. As cash is involved, Section 3830 would not be applicable and, as a consequence, there would be no constraint on the venturer's ability to recognize losses or gains. In addition, the transfer would be evidence of a non temporary decline in value, resulting in a need to write down the entire value of the asset under the provisions of Section 3060.

2-171.   The situation becomes more complex if the asset is exchanged for an equity interest in the venture, rather than for cash or other monetary assets. This situation is covered in Section 3055 as follows:

> **Paragraph 3055.26**   *When a venturer transfers assets to a joint venture and receives in exchange an interest in the joint venture, any loss that occurs should be charged to income at the time of the transfer to the extent of the interests of the other non-related venturers. When such a transaction provides evidence of a decline that is other than temporary in the carrying amount of the relevant assets, the venturer should recognize this decline by writing down that portion of the assets retained through its interest in the joint venture.* (January, 1995)

2-172.   Returning to the example from Paragraphs 2-169 and 2-170, the preceding Recommendation would require that at least $75,000 of the total loss of $100,000 ($400,000 - $500,000) be taken into income at the time of transfer. With the venturer in our example having a 25 percent equity interest, the $75,000 would represent the 75 percent interest of the other non related venturers.

2-173.   While at least $75,000 of the loss must be taken into income because of the Recommendation in Paragraph 3055.26, we would expect that, in most situations, the value established by the terms of the transfer to the joint venture would provide a strong indication that there has been a non temporary decline in value. This would mean that Paragraph 3055.26, as reinforced by the Recommendation in Paragraph 3060.42, would require a full write down of the asset to its fair value. Such a write down would mean that the full $100,000 loss would have to be taken into income.

Section 3055 - Gains On Transfer

2-174.   With respect to the recognition of gains, the general Recommendation is as follows:

> **Paragraph 3055.27**   *When a venturer transfers assets to a joint venture and receives in exchange an interest in the joint venture, any gain that occurs should be recognized in the financial statements of the venturer only to the extent of the interests of the other non-related venturers, and accounted for in accordance with paragraphs 3055.28 and 3055.29.* (January, 1995)

2-175.   Note carefully the difference between this Recommendation on gains and the Paragraph 3055.26 Recommendation on losses. The latter Recommendation requires that losses be taken into income, not just recognized in the financial statements. The Paragraph 3055.27 Recommendation on gains refers only to recognition in the financial statements. When we examine Paragraphs 3055.28 and 3055.29, we will find that, in some situations, none of the recognized gain will be taken into income at the time the asset is transferred to the joint venture. This would be accomplished by setting up a Deferred Gain account in the joint venturer's proportionate consolidation Balance Sheet.

2-176.   While it is possible that no gain will be taken into income at the time the asset is transferred to the joint venture, all of the gain that must be recognized as a result of the Recommendation in Paragraph 3055.27 will eventually be included in income. To the extent that this gain is not taken into income at the transfer date, it will be taken into income in some later accounting period. The timing of this income inclusion is governed by the following two Recommendations:

> **Paragraph 3055.28**   *When the contributing venturer receives cash or other assets that do not represent a claim on the assets of the joint venture, only that portion of the gain that relates to the amount of cash received or the fair value of the other assets received should be taken to income at the time of the transfer.* (January, 1995)
>
> **Paragraph 3055.29**   *Any remaining portion of the gain that does not meet the conditions in paragraph 3055.28 should be deferred and amortized to income in a rational and systematic manner over the life of the contributed assets. If the contributed assets are non-depreciable, the deferred gain should be taken to income on a basis appropriate to the expected revenue or service to be obtained from their use by the joint venture. If the contributed assets are disposed of by the joint venture, any unamortized portion of the deferred gain should be taken to income.* (January, 1995)

2-177.   In situations where the contributing venturer receives only an equity interest in the joint venture, Paragraph 3055.27 would require that the other venturers' percentage interest in the gain be recognized at the time the asset is transferred by the contributing venturer. However, Paragraph 3055.28 would prevent any portion of this recognized gain from being included in the contributing venturer's income at the time of transfer. The recognized portion of the gain would have to be included in income in subsequent periods as per the Recommendation in Paragraph 3055.29.

2-178.   If the contributing venturer receives cash or other assets in addition to an equity interest, all or part of the recognized gain can be included in the contributing venturer's income at the time of transfer. Note, however, in applying Paragraph 3055.28, the amount of cash or other assets received must be reduced to the extent that they have been financed by the borrowing of the joint venture. This requirement is reflected in the following Recommendation:

> **Paragraph 3055.30**   *For purposes of paragraph 3055.28, in determining the portion of the gain that should be taken to income, the amount of cash received or*

the fair value of the other assets received should be reduced by the contributing venturer's proportionate interest in cash or other assets derived from, or financed by, borrowings of the joint venture and by any obligation assumed by the contributing venturer that would in substance reverse or negate the original receipt of cash or other assets. (January, 1995)

2-179.   The process of calculating the gain to be recognized under Paragraph 3055.28 is described as follows:

Paragraph 3055.34   Where the contributing venturer concurrently receives in exchange cash or other assets that do not represent in any way an investment in, or a claim on, the assets of the joint venture and where the venturer has no commitments to reinvest such consideration received in the joint venture, the portion of the gain that would be taken to income referred to in paragraph 3055.28 would be the difference between:

(a) the fair value of the consideration received, i.e. the amount of cash received or the fair value of the other assets received less the portion of cash or other assets represented by the contributing venturer's proportionate interest in cash or other assets derived from, or financed by, borrowings of the joint venture and less any obligation assumed by the contributing venturer that in substance would reverse or negate the original receipt of cash or other assets; and

(b) the net carrying value of the assets considered to be partly sold, i.e. that portion of the aggregate carrying value of those assets determined by applying the ratio of the fair value of the consideration received over the fair value of the assets transferred.

2-180.   After we have recognized the portion of the total gain specified in Paragraph 3055.27 and taken all or part of this gain into income under the Recommendation contained in Paragraph 3055.28, we may be left with a Deferred Gain. This Deferred Gain will be taken into income using the Recommendation in Paragraph 3055.29. For depreciable assets, this will be in a rational and systematic manner over their remaining life. For non depreciable assets, the Paragraph requires that the Deferred Gain be taken into income on a basis appropriate to the expected revenues that the asset will produce. Paragraph 3055.29 also Recommends that, if the transferred asset is sold by the joint venture, any portion of the Deferred Gain that has not been taken into income in previous periods, should be taken into income when the sale occurs.

Example One

2-181.   As a first example of the preceding Recommendations, consider the following example from the point of view of Alpha Company:

Example One   Alpha Company and Beta Company, two unrelated corporations, form a joint venture. Alpha contributes a manufacturing plant with an estimated fair value of $1,000 and a net carrying value of $250. Alpha receives cash of $800 and a 40 percent interest in the joint venture. Alpha is not obligated to reinvest the cash or make further contributions. Beta contributes cash of $300 to the joint venture in return for a 60 percent interest in the joint venture. The joint venture borrows $650 from a bank.

2-182.   The Recommendation in Paragraph 3055.27 would require that Alpha give recognition to Beta's 60 percent share of the gain. This would result in the recognition of $450 [(60%)($1,000 - $250)]. The amount of gain to be taken into Alpha's income at the time of transfer would be calculated as follows:

Proceeds Of Disposition [$800 - (40%)($800 - $300)]	$600
Cost Of Assets Considered To Be Sold [($600 ÷ $1,000)($250)]	(150)
Gain To Be Recognized On Transfer	$450

2-183.   Note that in the calculation of the Proceeds Of Disposition, recognition is given to the fact that only $300 of the $800 in cash received by Alpha came from Beta. The remainder came from the proceeds of the bank loan and Alpha is responsible for 40 percent of this $500 amount. This serves to illustrate the application of Paragraph 3055.30.

2-184.   Also note that the gain to be taken into income is the same amount as the total gain to be recognized. This results from the fact that the $600 Proceeds Of Disposition is equal to 60 percent of the total value of the asset transferred, the same percentage as Beta's share of the joint venture. Given this situation, there is no further gain to be taken into income in subsequent periods.

2-185.   The carrying value for Alpha's initial investment in the joint venture, before the application of proportionate consolidation procedures, would be calculated as follows:

Carrying Value Of The Plant	$250
Total Gain Recognized	450
Value Of Capital Contribution	$700
Equity Returned	(800)
Initial Investment	($100)

2-186. Based on the fact that the amount received by Alpha from the joint venture exceeds the value of its contribution as measured under Section 3055, the interest in the joint venture is a liability rather than an asset.

Example Two

2-187.   As a second example of the application of Section 3055 Recommendations, consider the following from the point of view of Alpha Company:

Example Two   Alpha Company and Beta Company form a joint venture. Alpha contributes a manufacturing plant with an estimated fair value of $700 and a carrying value of $300. Alpha receives cash of $100 from the joint venture and a 40 percent interest in the joint venture. Alpha is not obligated to reinvest the cash or make further contributions. Beta contributes cash of $900 to the joint venture in return for a 60 percent interest in the joint venture.

2-188.   The gain to be recognized under the Recommendation in Paragraph 3055.27 would again be Beta's 60 percent share of the total. This amount would be $240 [(60%)($700 - $300)].

2-189.   The portion of the gain to be taken into income at the time of transfer would be calculated as follows:

Proceeds Of Disposition	$100
Cost Of Assets Considered To Be Sold [($100 ÷ $700)($300)]	(43)
Gain To Be Recognized On Transfer	$ 57

2-190.   Notice that, in this case, no bank financing was involved and, as a consequence, the Proceeds Of Disposition is equal to the full amount of the cash received.

2-191.   Alpha's initial investment in the joint venture, before the application of proportionate consolidation procedures, would be as follows:

Carrying Value Of The Plant	$300
Total Gain Recognized [(60%)($700 - $300)]	240
Value Of Capital Contribution	$540
Equity Returned	(100)
Initial Investment	$440

2-192.   In both of the preceding Examples, the joint venturer would have to apply proportionate consolidation procedures in accounting for the joint venture investment. However, we will not illustrate these procedures in this Chapter as these will be covered, subsequent to our coverage of basic consolidation procedures, in Chapters 4 through 6.

Accounting For The Joint Venture - EIC Abstract No. 38

2-193.   Section 3055 provides guidance on the accounting required for non cash investments in joint ventures from the point of view of the investor. It does not, however, deal with the question of how the joint venture should account for the non cash assets that have been contributed to the joint venture. This issue is dealt with in EIC Abstract No. 38 (note that this Abstract was issued prior to the 1994 revision of Section 3055 of the *CICA Handbook*).

2-194.   The Committee concluded that the accounting basis used by the joint venturer for assets transferred as a capital contribution does not determine the basis of accounting to be used by the joint venture. The Abstract goes on to note that existing practice includes the use of several alternative approaches by the joint venture. These are:

- Valuation of the net assets at their fair values (fair values may differ from the values agreed upon in the joint venture agreement).

- Valuation of the net assets at the carrying value of the net assets to the joint venturers.

- Valuation of the net assets at the carrying value of the joint venturers' investment in the joint venture. This would include any gain recorded by a joint venturer on the portion of the assets considered to be sold.

2-195.   The EIC is of the opinion that any of these alternatives is acceptable under Canadian generally accepted accounting principles. They note, however, that the joint venture should disclose the basis of valuation that is adopted.

Additional Disclosure Requirements

Subsidiaries

2-196.   We have previously noted that control will normally be identified by the presence of majority ownership of voting shares. However, Section 1590 recognizes that this is not always the case. Control can exist without majority ownership and lack of control may occur where there is majority ownership. As these situations are not the usual ones, Paragraphs 1590.22 and 1590.23 specify additional disclosure requirements:

Paragraph 1590.22   *When a reporting enterprise does not own, directly or indirectly through subsidiaries, an equity interest carrying the right to elect the majority of the members of the board of directors of a subsidiary, the reporting enterprise should disclose (i) the basis for the determination that a parent-subsidiary relationship exists, (ii) the name of the subsidiary, and (iii) the percentage ownership (if any).* (January, 1992)

Paragraph 1590.23   *When a reporting enterprise owns, directly or indirectly through subsidiaries, an equity interest carrying the right to elect the majority of* *the members of the board of directors of an investee that is not a subsidiary, the reporting enterprise should disclose (i) the basis for the determination that a parent-subsidiary relationship does not exist, (ii) the name of the investee, (iii) the percentage ownership, and (iv) either separate financial statements of the investee, combined financial statements of similar investees or, provided all information significant to the consolidated financial statements is disclosed, condensed financial statements (including notes) of the investee. (January, 1992)*

Portfolio Investments And Significantly Influenced Companies

2-197.   Section 3050 contains several Recommendations with respect to the disclosure of portfolio investments and significantly influenced companies. They are as follows:

Paragraph 3050.29   *The basis of valuation of long-term investments should be disclosed. (January, 1973)*

Paragraph 3050.30   *Investments in companies subject to significant influence, other affiliated companies and other long-term investments should each be shown separately. (January, 1992)*

Paragraph 3050.31   *Income from investments in companies subject to significant influence, other affiliated companies and other long-term investments should each be shown separately. Income calculated by the equity method should be disclosed separately. (January, 1992)*

Paragraph 3050.32   *When investments are accounted for by the equity method, disclosure should be made, in the notes to the financial statements, of the amount of any difference between the cost and the underlying net book value of the investee's assets at the date of purchase, as well as the accounting treatment of the components of such difference. (January, 1973)*

Paragraph 3050.33   *When portfolio investments include marketable securities, the quoted market value of such securities as well as their carrying value should be disclosed. (January, 1973)*

Joint Ventures

General Disclosure

2-198.   In order that investors will be able to better understand the extent to which the venturer's activities are carried out in the form of joint ventures, separate disclosure of the venturer's share of assets, liabilities, revenues, expenses, net income, and cash flows of the joint venture are required. This is reflected in the following Recommendation:

Paragraph 3055.41   *A venturer should disclose the total amounts and the major components of each of the following related to its interests in joint ventures:*

(a) current assets and long-term assets;
(b) current liabilities and long-term liabilities;
(c) revenues, expenses and net income;
(d) cash flows resulting from operating activities;
(e) cash flows resulting from financing activities; and
(f) cash flows resulting from investing activities. (January, 1995)

2-199.   This information would normally be presented on a combined basis for all of the venturer's joint venture activities. In those situations where substantially all of the activities of a venturer are carried out through joint ventures, a statement that this is the case would be sufficient disclosure.

2-200.   Joint venture arrangements involve contingencies and commitments, even to the extent of an individual venturer becoming responsible for other venturers' shares of joint venture obligations. The need for disclosure in this type of situation is reflected in the following Recommendation:

> **Paragraph 3055.42**   *A venturer should disclose its share of any contingencies and commitments of joint ventures and those contingencies that exist when the venturer is contingently liable for the liabilities of the other venturers of the joint ventures.* (January, 1995)

2-201.   Paragraph 3055.44 indicates that it is generally desirable to disclose a listing and description of significant interests in joint ventures, including the names and the proportion of ownership interest held in particular ventures. Other disclosure requirements may arise for joint ventures as the result of the application of other *CICA Handbook* Sections. For example, some of the Recommendations of Section 3840, "Related Party Transactions" would often be applicable to joint ventures.

Long Term Investments In Canadian Practice

Statistics From Financial Reporting In Canada

Long Term Investments Other Than Joint Ventures

2-202.   Of the 200 companies surveyed for the 1997 edition of *Financial Reporting in Canada*, 134 disclosed the presence of long term investments other than joint ventures in their 1996 annual reports. With respect to the valuation of these investments, 59 companies used both cost and equity, 27 used cost only, and 27 used equity only. The remaining 21 companies either did not disclose the basis of valuation or, alternatively, used some method other than cost or equity.

2-203.   Again looking at the 134 companies that disclosed the presence of long term investments other than joint ventures, only 58 segregated investment assets by type of investment, and only 22 provided investment income segregated by type.

Joint Ventures

2-204.   Of the 200 companies surveyed for the 1997 edition of *Financial Reporting In Canada*, the majority (102 companies) indicated in their 1996 annual reports that they participated in one or more joint ventures arrangements. Almost all of these companies accounted for these arrangements using proportionate consolidation.

2-205.   With respect to other types of disclosure, the following additional statistics are included for the 200 companies surveyed for the 1997 edition of *Financial Reporting In Canada:*

- 56 companies provided separate disclosure of the current and non current assets of their joint ventures;
- 53 companies provided separate disclosure of the current and long term liabilities of their joint ventures; and
- 52 companies disclosed the operating, financing, and investing cash flows of their joint venture arrangements.

Examples From Canadian Practice

Long Term Investments Other Than Joint Ventures

2-206.   The following example is from the annual report of ALCAN ALUMINIUM LIMITED for the reporting period ending December 31, 1996. It illustrates extensive disclosure of long term investments in the Balance Sheet, the Income Statement, as well as in the notes to the financial statements.

Balance Sheet Disclosure

(in millions of US$)

December 31	1996	1995	1994
Investments (Notes 3, 8 and 11)	$428	$695	$1,193

Income Statement Disclosure

(in millions of US$)

December 31	1996	1995	1994
Income before other items	$421	$542	$128
Equity loss (Note 8)	(10)	(3)	(29)
Minority interests	(1)	4	(3)
Net income before extraordinary item	$410	$543	$ 96

Notes To Financial Statements

Note 2   Summary Of Significant Accounting Policies (In Part)

Principles of Consolidation

The consolidated financial statements, which are expressed in U.S. dollars, the principal currency of Alcan's business, are prepared in accordance with generally accepted accounting principles (GAAP) in Canada. They include the accounts of companies controlled by Alcan, virtually all of which are majority owned. Joint ventures, irrespective of percentage of ownership, are proportionately consolidated to the extent of Alcan's participation. Consolidated net income also includes Alcan's equity in the net income or loss of companies owned 50% or less where Alcan has significant influence over management, and the investment in these companies is increased or decreased by Alcan's share of their undistributed net income or loss and deferred translation adjustments since acquisition. Investments in companies in which Alcan does not have significant influence over management are carried at cost less amounts written off.

Intercompany balances and transactions, including profits in inventories, are eliminated.

Note 8   Investments

	1996	1995	1994
Companies accounted for under the equity method	$421	$688	$1,185
Other investments - at cost, less amounts written off	7	7	8
	$428	$695	$1,193

The activities of the major equity-accounted companies are diversified aluminum operations in Japan and India. On December 31, 1996, the quoted market value of the Company's investments in Nippon Light Metal Company, Ltd. (NLM) and Indian Aluminium Company, Limited (Indal) exceeds their book value by $632. Their combined results of operations and financial position are included in the summary below. The 1996 information for NLM excludes, from the date of acquisition, the interest in those subsidiaries acquired by the Company from NLM as a result of the restructuring of the Company's holdings in Asia, explained in Note 11.

The information for 1994 also includes the results of operations and financial position for an aluminum rolling operation in Germany and for operations related to the procurement and processing of raw materials in Australia, Brazil and Guinea. Beginning in 1995, these joint ventures are proportionately consolidated and summarized financial information about these is included in Note 7.

	1996	1995	1994
Results of operations for the year ended December 31			
Revenues	$6,483	$7,896	$8,073
Costs and expenses	6,457	7,816	7,892
Income before income taxes	26	80	181
Income taxes	65	84	218
Net income (Loss)	($ 39)	($ 4)	($ 37)
Alcan's share of Net income (Loss)	($ 10)	($ 3)	($ 29)
Dividends received by Alcan	$ 11	$ 9	$ 22
Financial position at December 31			
Current assets	$3,013	$3,842	$4,029
Current liabilities	2,735	3,438	3,699
Working capital	278	404	330
Property, plant and equipment - net	1,916	2,347	4,209
Other assets - net	261	153	261
	2,455	2,904	4,800
Debt not maturing within one year	1,422	1,351	1,713
Net assets	$1,033	$1,553	$3,087
Alcan's equity in net assets	$ 421	$ 688	$1,185

Note 11   Restructuring Of Holdings In Asia

In the third quarter of 1996, the Company sold its equity-accounted investment in Toyo Aluminium K.K. (Toyal) to the Company's Japanese affiliate, Nippon Light Metal Company, Ltd. (NLM), for cash proceeds of $207. The after-tax gain of $128, including deferred translation adjustments, on this sale has been deferred. Approximately one half of the gain is being recognized over the period related to the utilization of the underlying assets by Toyal, while the remainder will be recognized if certain non-depreciable assets are sold by Toyal.

In November 1996, the Company and NLM created a new company, Alcan Nikkei Asia Holdings Ltd. (ANAH), owned 60% by Alcan and 40% by NLM. In exchange for shares in ANAH the Company contributed a portion of its holdings in NLM while NLM contributed its shareholdings in a number of companies located in Malaysia, Thailand and China. The Company's effective ownership of ANAH, including the interests held through NLM, is 78.2% and the minority interest in ANAH's subsidiaries is presented on this basis.

As a result of this transaction, Alcan's effective ownership in NLM falls from 47.4% to 45.6%. The gain on the partial sale of the Company's investment in NLM has been deferred and will be recognized over the period related to the utilization or disposition of the underlying assets by ANAH's subsidiaries.

Included in the Company's balance sheet at the date of acquisition were the following assets and liabilities of ANAH's Asian subsidiaries:

Working capital	$ 49
Property, plant and equipment	99
Other assets - net	9
	157
Long-term debt	4
Minority interest	71
Net assets	$ 82

The Company's share of net income for the month since acquisition is not significant.

Joint Ventures

2-207.   The following example is from the annual report of SHAW INDUSTRIES LTD. for the reporting period ending October 26, 1996. It illustrates the general disclosure of a joint venture arrangement, as well as specific disclosure related to the formation of a new joint venture.

Notes To Financial Statements

Note 1   Significant Accounting Policies (in part)
a)   Principles Of Consolidation
The consolidated financial statements include the accounts of Shaw Industries Ltd., its wholly owned subsidiaries and its joint venture interests (collectively, the "company"). The company accounts for its joint venture interests by the proportionate consolidation method. The Dresser-Shaw joint venture includes an associated company accounted for on an equity basis and certain non-wholly owned subsidiaries accounted for on a consolidated basis giving rise to a non-controlling interest in the net assets and net results.

Note 10   Joint Venture Operations
a)   Formation Of The Dresser-Shaw Joint Venture
Effective February 29, 1996, Dresser Industries, Inc. and the company contributed their respective worldwide pipecoating operations, Bredero Price and Shaw Pipe Protection into an incorporated joint venture owned 50.1% by Dresser Industries and 49.9% by the company. The joint venture is comprised of Dresser-Shaw Company and Bredero-Shaw, Inc. (collectively, the "Dresser-Shaw joint venture"). Joint control of the operations is exercised by a board of directors consisting of three appointees from each of the shareholders.

The formation of the joint venture represents an exchange of productive assets for an equivalent interest in similar productive assets and therefore has been accounted for by the company at the carrying value of the net assets given up with no gain or loss being recognized on the transaction. The book value of the net assets initially contributed to the joint venture by the company was $54,416,000.

For the first three years of the joint venture, Canadian profits are attributed to Shaw Industries, North Sea profits are attributed to Dresser Industries and the balance is shared on the basis of ownership. After the third year, all profits will be shared on the basis of ownership.

The initial term of the joint venture is four years from February 29, 1996, with provision for both early termination after two years and renewal beyond four years. The company has the option to sell, and Dresser Industries has the option to acquire the Shaw Industries interest in the joint venture on February 28, 1998 or February 29, 2000 for an amount determined in accordance with an earnings formula, subject to a minimum price of $US 175 million.

b)   Proportionately Consolidated Financial Information
The company's joint venture operations include the Dresser-Shaw joint venture and Arabian Shaw Pipecoaters (Thailand) Ltd. which was 65% owned by the company from its formation in 1994 until being contributed to the Dresser-Shaw joint venture on February 29, 1996. In December 1996, the remaining 35% interest in Arabian Shaw Pipecoaters was acquired for consideration of $2,449,000 being the company's proportionate share.

The company's share of joint venture assets and liabilities, accounted for on the basis of ownership; of revenue, expenses, and net income (loss), accounted for on the basis of entitlement under the relevant shareholders' agreements; and of cash flow, is summarized below:

(In thousands)	1996	1995
Current assets	$118,234	$ 3,598
Fixed assets, net	46,085	9,127
Other assets	8,707	-
Current liabilities	102,543	17,974
Deferred income taxes	270	-
Non-controlling interest in subsidiaries	2,689	-
Revenue	200,431	10,296
Operating and other expenses	182,127	17,091
Non-controlling interest in loss of subsidiaries	551	-
Net income (loss)	18,855	(6,795)
Cash provided by (used in):		
Operating activities	37,679	4,165
Investing activities	(23,434)	(138)
Financing activities	(17)	-

The company has provided guarantees for certain joint venture bank facilities and performance obligations of $19,064,000 (1995 - $17,515,000). Additional bank and performance guarantees have been provided by the other venture, and by the joint venture itself in the normal course of carrying out pipecoating projects for customers.

During the year, the company received a dividend of $12,899,000 from the Dresser-Shaw joint venture.

Additional Readings

2-208.   The following readings may be of interest to those wishing to pursue the issues that were discussed in this Chapter.

CICA Research Study   *Accounting For Portfolio Investments,* 1984, CICA Research Study Group.

CA Magazine Article   "Portfolio Investment Proposals Redirected", Jonathan M. Kligman, September, 1987.

CA Magazine Article   "Consolidated Effort", Peter Martin, October, 1991.

CA Magazine Article   "The Revolution That Wasn't", Carla Daum, April, 1993. This article contains a discussion of *CICA Handbook* Section 1625, "Comprehensive Revaluation Of Assets And Liabilities".

CA Magazine Article   "Demystifying Dilution", Lynne Clark, May, 1993.

CA Magazine Article   "The Goodwill Game", Tony Brookes, March, 1995.

CA Magazine Article   "Joint Enterprise", Patsy Willett, June/July, 1995.

International Accounting Standard No. 25   *Accounting For Investments,* March, 1986.

Journal Of Accountancy Article   "Consolidation And The Equity Method -Time For An Overhaul", Benjamin S. Neuhasen, February, 1982.

Journal Of Accountancy Article   "Unchartered Territory: Subsidiary Financial Reporting", Terry E. Allison and Paula Bevels Thomas, October, 1989.

Journal Of Accountancy Article   "The Portfolio Accounting Controversy", James T. Parks, November, 1989.

Supplement To Chapter Two
Other Emerging Issues Committee Abstracts

Introduction

2-209.   Some users of this text do not wish to have comprehensive coverage of the issues dealt with by the Emerging Issues Committee (EIC) of the Canadian Institute of Chartered Accountants. While it is clear that some of this Committee's Abstracts are of considerable significance (e.g., EIC 10 which is the only source of guidance for reverse takeovers), other are not of general interest.

2-210.   We have dealt with this situation by integrating only what we believe to be the more important of these Abstracts into the text material. However, we believe that it is important for some users to have more comprehensive coverage of this material. As a consequence, we are providing coverage of less important EIC Abstracts in a Supplement to the relevant text Chapters. This allows individual users to either ignore this material or, alternatively, include the Supplement as part of their course requirements.

EIC No. 20 - Reacquisition Of Troubled Franchises By The Franchisor

2-211.   When a franchisor has reacquired a troubled franchise, a basic issue is whether the amounts paid should be recorded as an asset or, alternatively, charged to income. The EIC concludes that, in most cases, the appropriate answer is to charge the related amount to income. As a consequence, a long term investment or capital asset will normally not result from such a reacquisition and we will not cover EIC Abstract No. 20 in this Chapter.

EIC No. 56 - Exchangeable Debentures

2-212.   This EIC Abstract deals with situations where a company ("the issuer") issues a debenture which requires it, at maturity, to deliver issued and outstanding shares of another entity ("the underlying shares"). The terms of the debenture may specify that the settlement amount is adjustable in the event that the market value of the underlying shares at maturity varies from a specified amount (e.g., their market value at the issue date of the debenture). Such a settlement adjustment mechanism may establish a minimum and/or maximum settlement amount.

2-213.   The issuer may already own sufficient underlying shares to satisfy the maximum repayment obligation under the debenture. The issuer may also have the option to repay the debenture in cash or other assets having a fair value equivalent to the amount determined in accordance with the settlement adjustment mechanism in the debenture agreement.

2-214.   The issues considered by the EIC, along with the conclusions reached by the Committee, are as follows:

Issue One   Should the issuer re-measure the carrying amount of the debenture, based upon the fair value of the underlying shares, at each balance sheet date?

The EIC reached a consensus that the issuer should remeasure the carrying amount of the exchangeable debenture on each Balance Sheet date, using the fair value of the underlying shares. This value can be modified for any settlement adjustment mechanism contained in the debt instrument.

Issue Two   If the issuer remeasures the carrying amount of the debenture at each balance sheet date, should the issuer recognize the resultant gains or losses in net income as they arise?

The EIC reached a consensus that the changes in the carrying value of the debenture which result from the remeasurement process should be included in income as they occur. An exception to this would be situations where hedge accounting is being used.

Issue Three   To the extent that the issuer has an investment in the underlying shares, is hedge accounting appropriate?

The EIC reached a consensus that hedge accounting would be appropriate only if the debenture is designated as a hedge. To be designated as a hedge, gains or losses on the debentures would have to offset losses or gains on the shares. This would only happen if the shares were going to be sold. As a consequence, hedge accounting can only be used if there is an intent to dispose of the underlying shares. In the absence of such intent, gains and losses on the debenture would have to be taken into income, rather than deferred as would be the case if hedge accounting were being used.

Issue Four   If the issuer uses hedge accounting, what additional information should the issuer disclose?

The EIC reached a consensus that if the issuer uses hedge accounting, then the issuer should disclose the fact that the designation of the debenture as a hedge contemplates disposition of the underlying investment, and also the impact of disposition of the underlying investment.

Issue Five   How should the issuer classify and present the debenture, and any gains or losses deferred as a result of hedge accounting, on the balance sheet?

The EIC reached a consensus that the issuer should classify the debenture as debt on the balance sheet. Any gains and losses deferred as a result of hedge accounting should be presented separately from the debt on the balance sheet.

Problems For Self Study

(The solutions for these problems can be found following Chapter 17 of the text.)

SELF STUDY PROBLEM TWO - 1

On July 1, 1995, the Miser Company purchased 25 percent of the outstanding voting shares of the Mercy Company for $4 million in cash. On the acquisition date all of the net identifiable assets of the Mercy Company had fair values that were equal to their carrying values. The carrying value of Mercy Company's net assets was $16 million. Net Income and Dividends Declared of the Mercy Company for the year of acquisition and the three subsequent years are as follows:

Year	Net Income (Net Loss)	Dividends
1995	$ 600,000	$ 600,000
1996	(2,000,000)	400,000
1997	1,500,000	500,000
1998	3,000,000	1,000,000

Net Income accrued uniformly over the year 1995 and one-half of that year's dividends were declared between July 1, and December 31. Both Companies close their books on December 31 of each year. The 1998 Net Income figure of the Mercy Company includes an Extraordinary Loss of $800,000. There were no intercompany transactions, other than dividend payments, during any of the four years.

Required: Provide the Miser Company's journal entries to account for its investment in the Mercy Company for each of the four years assuming:

A. that its 25 percent shareholding does not result in significant influence over the Mercy Company;

B. that its 25 percent shareholding does result in significant influence over the Mercy Company.

SELF STUDY PROBLEM TWO - 2

On January 1, 1995, the Buy Company purchased 25 percent of the outstanding voting shares of the Sell Company for cash of $1,500,000. On this date, the Sell Company had net assets of $6,000,000. This was reflected in the Sell Company's Shareholders' Equity which consisted of No Par Common Stock of $7,000,000 and a deficit or debit balance in Retained Earnings of $1,000,000. On the acquisition date, all of the identifiable assets and liabilities of the Sell Company had fair values that were equal to their carrying values.

Between January 1, 1995 and December 31, 1997, the Sell Company had a total Net Income of $3,000,000 and paid dividends which totalled $2,000,000. During this period, dividend payments were the only intercompany transactions. The Sell Company does not have any investment income in the years under consideration.

For the year ending December 31, 1998, prior to the Buy Company taking into account any amounts for Investment Income from the Sell Company, the two Companies have the following Income Statements:

	Buy	Sell
Sales	$5,000,000	$2,000,000
Cost of Goods Sold	(3,000,000)	(1,800,000)
Other Expenses	(800,000)	(400,000)
Income (Loss) Before Investment Income and Extraordinary Items	$1,200,000	($ 200,000)
Extraordinary Gain (Net of $400,000 in Taxes)	-0-	600,000
Income Before Investment Income	$1,200,000	$ 400,000

On January 1, 1998, the Retained Earnings balance of the Buy Company was $15,000,000. This balance included the investment income calculated by the equity method for Buy's Investment In Sell during the period January 1, 1995 through December 31, 1997. During the year ending December 31, 1998, the Buy Company declares and pays dividends in the amount of $500,000 while the corresponding dividend figure for the Sell Company is $150,000.

Also during 1998, the Sell Company discovers an expense which was overlooked in 1997 for tax and accounting purposes of $50,000 (net of taxes of $20,000). This error is deducted in the Sell Company's Statement of Retained Earnings.

Required:

A. Assume that the Buy Company's 25 percent investment in the shares of the Sell Company gives it significant influence over the Sell Company. Prepare the Buy Company's Income Statement and Statement of Retained Earnings for the year ending December 31, 1998, assuming that the equity method has been used to account for its Investment In Sell.

B. Assume that the Buy Company's 25 percent investment in the shares of the Sell Company does not give it significant influence over the Sell Company. Prepare the Buy Company's Income Statement and Statement of Retained Earnings for the year ending December 31, 1998, assuming that the cost method has been used to account for its Investment In Sell since the acquisition date. (This will require a recalculation of the Buy Company's January 1, 1998 Retained Earnings balance.)

C. Calculate the balance in the Investment In Sell account as at December 31, 1998, under the Part A assumptions.

SELF STUDY PROBLEM TWO - 3

Case One   On December 31, 1998, Condor Ltd. (CL) and Vulture Inc. (VI) form an incorporated joint venture, Scavengers Ltd. (SL). CL contributes a manufacturing plant with a carrying value of $2,200,000 and an estimated fair value of $5,000,000. In return, CL receives $3,500,000 in cash and a 60 percent equity interest in the joint venture. CL is not obligated to reinvest the cash. Also on December 31, 1998, VI invests $1,000,000 in cash for a 40 percent equity interest in SL, and SL borrows $2,800,000 from a bank.

Case Two   On December 31, 1998, Condor Ltd. (CL) and Vulture Inc. (VI) establish a new corporation, Scavengers Ltd. (SL), over which they have joint control. CL contributes a manufacturing plant with a fair value of $2,650,000 and a carrying value of $1,400,000. CL receives cash of $650,000 and a 40 percent interest in SL. CL is not obligated to reinvest the cash. VI contributes $3,000,000 in cash in return for a 60 percent equity interest in SL.

Required: For both of the preceding independent Cases, assume that in CL's single entity financial statements, the Investment In SL will be accounted for by the equity method and that, in determining the gain or loss on the transfer of the manufacturing plant to SL, CL will follow the Recommendations contained in Section 3055 of the *CICA Handbook*. Determine:

A. the maximum gain or loss to be recognized on CL's transfer of the manufacturing plant to SL and the amount of this gain or loss that can be taken into income at the time of transfer; and

B. the value to be recorded in CL's single entity financial statements as the initial Investment In SL.

Assignment Problems And Cases

(The solutions to these problem are only available in
the solutions manual that has been provided to your instructor.)

ASSIGNMENT PROBLEM TWO - 1

On January 1, the Lestor Company purchased 20 percent of the outstanding voting shares of the Rapone Company. The purchase price, all of which was paid in cash, amounted to $5 million. On the acquisition date, the fair value of the Rapone Company's net assets was $25 million. During the three years following the acquisition date the Rapone Company had Net Income and paid dividends as follows:

Year	Net Income (Net Loss)	Dividends
1	$1,500,000	$1,000,000
2	(1,000,000)	1,000,000
3	4,000,000	1,000,000

All dividends were paid in the year in which they were declared. That is, there were no Dividends Payable at the end of any of the three years. There were no intercompany transactions, other than dividend payments, during any of the years under consideration. Both Companies close their books on December 31.

Required:

A. Assume that the Lestor Company's 20 percent shareholding does not result in significant influence over the Rapone Company. Provide the Lestor Company's dated journal entries to account for its investment in the Rapone Company for each of the three years.

B. Assume that the Lestor Company's 20 percent shareholding does result in significant influence over the Rapone Company. Provide the Lestor Company's dated journal entries to account for its investment in the Rapone Company for each of the three years.

C. Calculate the balance in the Investment In Rapone account as at December 31 of the third year for both Part A and Part B of this problem.

ASSIGNMENT PROBLEM TWO - 2

On January 1, 1995, Tribble Company purchased 40 percent of the outstanding voting shares of the Marcus Company for $320,000 in cash. On that date, Marcus had Common Stock - No Par of $500,000, Retained Earnings of $300,000 and all of its identifiable assets and liabilities had fair values that were equal to their carrying values. Between January 1, 1995 and December 31, 1997, Marcus had Net Income and paid dividends as follows:

	1995	1996	1997
Net Income (Loss)	$300,000	($400,000)	$320,000
Dividends	100,000	50,000	70,000

There were no extraordinary items or prior period adjustments for Marcus in the 3 years 1995 through 1997. For the year ending December 31, 1998, the Income Statements of the Tribble and Marcus Companies, before recognition of any investment income, were as follows:

	Tribble	Marcus
Sales	$2,300,000	$850,000
Other Revenues	200,000	-0-
Total Revenues	$2,500,000	$850,000
Cost Of Goods Sold	$1,000,000	$500,000
Other Expenses	500,000	80,000
Total Expenses	$1,500,000	$580,000
Income Before Extraordinary Items	$1,000,000	$270,000
Extraordinary Loss	-0-	20,000
Net Income	$1,000,000	$250,000

Assuming the use of the cost method to account for its Investment in Marcus, Tribble had a Retained Earnings balance of $4,600,000 on January 1, 1998. Tribble declared $150,000 in dividends in that year. Marcus declared and paid dividends of $120,000 in 1998.

During 1998, Marcus initiated a change in accounting policy. The change was accounted for retroactively, resulting in a prior period addition to the Company's Retained Earnings balance in the amount of $700,000.

Required:

A. Assume that the Tribble Company carries its investment in Marcus by the cost method. Prepare the dated journal entries for the Tribble Company related to its investment in the Marcus Company for the years 1995 through 1998, the Income Statement for the Tribble Company for the year ending December 31, 1998, and the Statement of Retained Earnings for the Tribble Company for the year ending December 31, 1998.

B. Assume that, since its acquisition, the Tribble Company has carried its investment in Marcus by the equity method. Prepare the dated journal entries for the Tribble Company related to its investment in the Marcus Company for the years 1995 through 1998, the Income Statement for the Tribble Company for the year ending December 31, 1998, and the Statement Of Retained Earnings for the Tribble Company for the year ending December 31, 1998. (Note that the Retained Earnings balance of the Tribble Company given in the problem is based on the assumption that the cost method has been used since the acquisition.)

ASSIGNMENT PROBLEM TWO - 3

On January 1, 1995, the Bronson Company purchased 18 percent of the outstanding shares of the Somerset Company. The purchase price, all of which was paid in cash, amounted to $1.8 million. On the acquisition date, the fair value of the Somerset Company's net assets was $10 million and all of the assets and liabilities had fair values that were equal to their carrying values. Both Companies have a fiscal year which ends on December 31.

During the four years following the Bronson Company's acquisition of the Somerset Company's shares, the Somerset Company had income and declared and paid dividends as follows:

Year	Net Income (Net Loss)	Dividends
1995	$ 950,000	$350,000
1996	(1,140,000)	140,000
1997	750,000	160,000
1998	840,000	320,000

Other Information:

1. The Somerset Company's 1997 Net Income includes an Extraordinary Loss of $163,000.

2. During 1998, the Company changed its accounting policy with respect to the calculation of Depreciation Expense. The change was accounted for retroactively, resulting in an addition to Retained Earnings of $246,000 to reflect the effects of this change on prior periods.

3. There were no intercompany transactions between Bronson and Somerset, other than dividend payments, during any of the years under consideration.

Required:

A. Assume that the Bronson Company's 18 percent shareholding does not result in significant influence over the Somerset Company. Provide the Bronson Company's dated journal entries to account for its Investment In Somerset for the years 1995 through 1998.

B. Assume that the Bronson Company's 18 percent shareholding does result in significant influence over the Somerset Company. Provide the Bronson Company's dated journal entries to account for its Investment In Somerset for the years 1995 through 1998.

ASSIGNMENT PROBLEM TWO - 4
The Fostor Company purchased 30 percent of the outstanding voting shares of the Festee Company for $1,200,000 in cash on January 1, 1996. On that date, the Festee Company's Shareholders' Equity was made up of Common Stock ($50 par, $2 million issued and outstanding), other Contributed Capital of $500,000 and Retained Earnings of $1.5 million. There were no differences between the carrying values and the fair values of any of its identifiable assets or liabilities. The net income and dividends declared and paid by the Festee Company for the two years subsequent to its acquisition were as follows:

	1996	1997
Net Income (Loss)	($100,000)	$160,000
Dividends	40,000	50,000

The Income Statements for the year ending December 31, 1998, prior to the recognition of any Investment Income, for the Fostor and Festee Companies are as follows:

	Fostor	Festee
Sales	$2,000,000	$550,000
Other Revenues	100,000	-0-
Total Revenue	$2,100,000	$550,000
Cost Of Goods Sold	$1,000,000	$300,000
Other Expenses	200,000	50,000
Total Expenses	$1,200,000	$350,000
Income Before Extraordinary Items	$ 900,000	$200,000
Extraordinary Loss	-0-	30,000
Net Income	$ 900,000	$170,000

During 1998, the Fostor Company declared and paid dividends of $100,000 while Festee Company declared and paid dividends of $70,000. The Festee Company declares and pays its dividends on December 31 of each year.

Required:

A. Assume that the Fostor Company cannot exercise significant influence over the affairs of the Festee Company. Provide the journal entry of the Fostor Company related to its investment in the Festee Company for the year ending December 31, 1998.

B. Assume that the Fostor Company can exercise significant influence over the affairs of the Festee Company. Provide the following:

1. The dated journal entries of the Fostor Company related to its investment in Festee Company for the years ending December 31, 1996, 1997 and 1998.

2. The Income Statement of the Fostor Company, including recognition of any investment income or loss, for the year ending December 31, 1998.

3. The balance in the Investment In Festee Company account as it would appear on the December 31, 1998 Balance Sheet of the Fostor Company.

ASSIGNMENT PROBLEM TWO - 5

On January 1, 1998, Flor Company acquires 650,000 of the outstanding common shares of Flee Company at a cost of $20,800,000. On this date, the Shareholders' Equity of Flee Company was as follows:

Common Stock - No Par (1,000,000 Shares)	$10,000,000
Retained Earnings	22,000,000
Total Shareholders' Equity	$32,000,000

At this time, all of the identifiable assets and liabilities of Flee Company have fair values that are equal to their carrying values. Both Companies have a December 31 year end.

During the year ending December 31, 1998, Flee Company has Net Income of $1,800,000, and declares and pays dividends of $600,000. For 1998, Flee Company does not report any results of discontinued operations, extraordinary items or capital transactions. Other than Flee's Dividends Declared, there are no transactions between the two Companies during the year. Flor Company carries its Investment In Flee Company using the equity method.

The single entity Balance Sheets for the two companies as at December 31, 1998 and the Income Statements for the year ending December 31, 1998, are as follows:

Flor And Flee Companies
Balance Sheets As At December 31, 1998

	Flor Company	Flee Company
Cash	$ 7,400,000	$ 1,300,000
Accounts Receivable	12,600,000	7,700,000
Inventories	27,600,000	12,600,000
Investment In Flee (Note One)	21,580,000	-0-
Plant And Equipment (Net)	15,820,000	20,400,000
Total Assets	$85,000,000	$42,000,000

	Flor Company	Flee Company
Current Liabilities	$17,800,000	$ 1,620,000
Long Term Liabilities	23,400,000	7,180,000
Common Stock - No Par	12,500,000	10,000,000
Retained Earnings	31,300,000	23,200,000
Total Equities	$85,000,000	$42,000,000

Note One   The value of the Investment In Flee under equity method procedures would be calculated as follows:

Initial Cost Of Investment	$20,800,000
Equity In Flee Earnings ([65%][$1,800,000])	1,170,000
Dividends Received ([65%][$600,000])	(390,000)
Investment At Equity - December 31, 1998	$21,580,000

Flor And Flee Companies
Income Statements For The Year Ending December 31, 1998

	Flor Company	Flee Company
Sales	$14,600,000	$7,260,000
Investment Income ([65%][$1,800,000])	1,170,000	-0-
Total Revenues	$15,770,000	$7,260,000
Cost Of Sales	$ 8,240,000	$2,780,000
Depreciation Expense	4,260,000	1,260,000
Other Expenses	1,100,000	1,420,000
Total Expenses	$13,600,000	$5,460,000
Net Income	$ 2,170,000	$1,800,000

Required:

A.   Assume that Flor Company intends to account for its Investment In Flee Company using proportionate consolidation. Prepare the Balance Sheet as at December 31, 1998 and the Income Statement for the year ending December 31, 1998 for the Flor Company.

B.   Assume that Flor Company intends to account for its Investment In Flee Company using full consolidation. Prepare the consolidated Balance Sheet as at December 31, 1998 and the consolidated Income Statement for the year ending December 31, 1998 for the Flor Company and its investee.

ASSIGNMENT PROBLEM TWO - 6

Each of the following independent cases involves three companies which deal with each other at arm's length. They are Acres Ltd. (AL), Barrus Ltd. (BL), and Caron Ltd. (CL). In all cases presented, the three companies are forming a joint venture called Collusive Ventures Ltd. (CVL) and the joint venture agreement gives them the following equity interests in this new enterprise:

Venturer	AL	BL	CL
Equity Interest In CVL	25 Percent	35 Percent	40 Percent

We will be concerned with accounting for the capital contribution being made by AL and, as a consequence, the capital contributions of BL and CL will be the same in all cases. They are as follows:

BL   This venturer contributes cash of $600,000 and other assets with a fair value of $450,000. The carrying value of these assets on BL's books is $220,000.

CL   This venturer contributes cash of $400,000 and other assets with a fair value of $800,000. The carrying value of these assets on CL's books is $1,115,000.

Case One   In return for its 25 percent equity interest in CVL, AL contributes non monetary assets with a fair value of $750,000 and a carrying value of $1,000,000. AL receives no other assets from CVL and CVL does not assume any additional debt at the time of its incorporation.

Case Two   In return for its 25 percent equity interest in CVL, AL contributes non monetary assets with a fair value of $1,100,000 and a carrying value on AL's books of $600,000. In addition to its 25 percent equity interest, AL receives $350,000 in cash. CVL does not assume any additional debt at the time of its incorporation.

Case Three   In return for its 25 percent equity interest in CVL, AL contributes cash of $350,000 and non monetary assets with a fair value of $400,000. The carrying value of these non monetary assets on the books of AL is $250,000. AL receives no other assets from CVL and CVL does not assume any additional debt at the time of its incorporation.

Case Four   In return for its 25 percent equity interest in CVL, AL contributes non monetary assets with a fair value of $1,400,000 and a carrying value on AL's books of $1,100,000. In addition to its 25 percent equity interest, AL receives $650,000 in cash. At the time of incorporation, CVL borrows $1,000,000. The three venturers are responsible for this debt in proportion to their equity interests in CVL.

Case Five   In return for its 25 percent equity interest in CVL, AL contributes non monetary assets with a fair value of $2,500,000 and a carrying value on AL's books of $2,000,000. In addition to its 25 percent equity interest, AL receives $1,750,000 in cash. At the time of incorporation, CVL borrows $1,000,000. The three venturers are responsible for this debt in proportion to their equity interests in CVL.

Required: Following the Recommendations of Section 3055 of the *CICA Handbook*, determine the amount of the gain or loss that would be recognized by AL at the time the Company makes its capital contribution to CVL.

ASSIGNMENT CASE TWO - 1

Carson Investments is a manufacturing company with a variety of investments in Canadian companies. These investments can be described as follows:

Best Parts Inc.   Carson Investments owns 45 percent of the outstanding common shares of Best Parts Inc. Over 90 percent of this company's sales are made to Carson Investments. In addition to the holding of common shares, Carson owns 60 percent of the outstanding 12 percent, cumulative preferred shares of Best Parts Inc.

Research Tech Ltd.   Carson owns 25 percent of the outstanding common shares of Research Tech Ltd., a company established with three other investors to do research on a new manufacturing process. The other investors each have 25 percent of the outstanding common shares. However, two of these investors do not participate in the management of the Company, leaving all operating decisions in the hands of Carson and one other investor.

Entell Ltd. Carson owns 46 percent of the outstanding voting shares of Entell Ltd. Included in the assets of Entell is an investment in 18 percent of the outstanding common shares of Chelsea Distributors Inc. In recent years Chelsea has experienced adverse operating results and there is some question as to whether it will be able to continue as a going concern.

Chelsea Distributors Inc. Carson owns directly 37 percent of the outstanding common shares of Chelsea Distributors Inc. In addition, Chelsea owns 3 percent of the outstanding voting shares of Carson Investments Ltd.

Required: Describe and justify the recommended accounting treatment for each of the intercorporate investments, including those made by Carson Investments' investees.

ASSIGNMENT CASE TWO - 2

Small World Limited owns a chain of retail stores which sell children's books and toys. The President of Small World, Ted Kidd, hopes that his company will eventually achieve vertical integration with many of its suppliers. At the moment, Small World owns 55 percent of the outstanding common shares of Blocks N Things, a toy wholesaler.

Blocks N Things owns 22 percent of the outstanding common shares and 53 percent of the outstanding non cumulative, non participating preferred shares of Craftco Limited, a manufacturer of wooden toys. No other Craftco shareholder or group of related shareholders holds preferred or common shares to the same extent as Blocks N Things.

Craftco currently owns 13 percent of the outstanding common shares of Delta Inc., a major Canadian pulp and paper company. The market value of Delta's shares has decreased substantially since acquisition.

Small World Limited also owns 40 percent of the outstanding common shares of Delta Inc.

Required: Describe and justify the recommended accounting treatment for each of the above intercorporate investments.

(SMA adapted)

Chapter 3

Business Combinations

Introduction

Business Combinations Defined

3-1.   The *CICA Handbook* defines a business combination transaction in the following manner:

> **Paragraph 1580.01**   In this Section, the term "business combination" is used to include any transaction whereby one business unites with or obtains control over the assets of another business. Although the transaction may be achieved through various legal avenues, the result of the combination is the bringing together of separate businesses into one economic entity.

3-2.   Section 1580 continues by providing examples of situations that would be included in this definition:

> **Paragraph 1580.02**   Business combinations include transactions where an incorporated company unites with or obtains control of:
>
> (a) another incorporated company;
>
> (b) a group of assets which constitutes a business entity, including a division of another company; or
>
> (c) an unincorporated business entity.
>
> A business combination would not include transactions involving the purchase of a single asset or a group of assets which does not constitute a business entity.

3-3.   It is clear from the preceding that the key factor in identifying a business combination transaction is the fact that two or more independent economic entities have joined to become a single economic entity. This economic unification may or may not be accompanied by an actual legal unification.

3-4.   In defining those transactions which can be described by the term business combination, three additional points should be made. They are:

   1. While Section 1580 does not specifically cover such situations, the principles de-

scribed would be applicable to combinations of unincorporated business enterprises.

2. The acquisition of an investee which becomes subject to significant influence by the investor will never be viewed as a business combination. This means that, with respect to long term investment situations, only those in which the investor acquires control over the investee are considered to be business combination transactions. In most situations, control will be obtained through the acquisition of a majority of the voting shares of the investee company.

3. If companies that are under common control (i.e., two subsidiaries of the same parent) engage in a transfer of assets or an exchange of shares, it will not be accounted for as a business combination. Rather, the transaction will be given the treatment that is appropriate for other intercompany transactions.

Legal Avenues To Combination

Basic Example

3-5.   Assume that two companies, the Alpha Company and the Beta Company have, for a variety of reasons, decided to come together in a business combination transaction and continue their operations as a single economic entity. The basis for this decision may involve marketing, distribution, industrial relations, finance, taxes or virtually any other aspect of operating a business enterprise. In any case, a decision has been made that the objectives of the firms can be better achieved through some form of combined operations.

3-6.   The date of the combination transaction is December 31, 1998 and, on that date the Balance Sheets of the two companies are as follows:

Alpha And Beta Companies
Balance Sheets As At December 31, 1998

	Alpha Company	Beta Company
Current Assets	$153,000	$ 35,000
Non Current Assets	82,000	85,000
Total Assets	$235,000	$120,000
Liabilities	$ 65,000	$ 42,000
Common Stock:		
(5,000 Shares Issued And Outstanding)	95,000	—
(10,000 Shares Issued And Outstanding)	—	53,000
Retained Earnings	75,000	25,000
Total Equities	$235,000	$120,000

3-7.   In order to simplify the use of this Balance Sheet information in the examples which follow, we will assume that all of the assets and liabilities of the two companies have fair values that are equal to their carrying values. In addition, we will assume that the shares of the two Companies are trading at their book values, $34.00 per share for Alpha [($95,000 + $75,000) ÷ 5,000] and $7.80 per share for Beta [($53,000 + $25,000) ÷ 10,000]. This indicates a total market value for Alpha Company of $170,000 and a corresponding value for Beta Company of $78,000.

Legal Form Vs. Economic Substance

3-8.   Once the decision to combine has been made, the combining Companies are faced with a second decision. This is the question of what legal format will be most advantageous in implementing the combination. Like the initial decision to combine the two Companies, this is an extremely complex decision which would involve consideration of almost every aspect of the operation of the business. While the economic substance of the combination transaction could have some influence on the legal format chosen, it is unlikely that it would be the dominant consideration. However, in the determination of the appropriate accounting method to be used, we will find that the economic substance of the combination transaction will be the primary consideration. Since the legal format will not necessarily reflect this economic substance and, given the fact that economic substance is the primary consideration in determining the accounting procedures to be used, it follows that the legal format chosen will offer little or no guidance to the accountant in choosing the correct method to account for the combination transaction.

3-9.   The fact that the legal format does not provide guidance in the choice of accounting methods for a particular business combination would suggest that we need not be concerned with understanding the possible legal formats. However, this is not the case. In implementing the accounting methods for business combinations, it is necessary to understand the various legal avenues to combination in order to make a correct application of the appropriate procedures. Further, we will find that in some cases the statutory requirements that can be associated with certain legal formats will override the accounting recommendations associated with the economic substance of the particular transaction. This is particularly true in the area of the combined company's shareholders' equity. As a consequence, we will provide descriptions and illustrations of the basic legal avenues that could be used to effect a business combination.

3-10.   Referring to our basic example involving the Alpha and Beta Companies, the alternative legal forms that could be used to combine these two companies can be outlined as follows:

1. Alpha Company could acquire the net assets of Beta Company through a direct purchase from that Company. The consideration paid to Beta could be cash, other assets, or Alpha Company debt or equity securities.

2. A new organization, Sigma Company, could be formed. Sigma Company could then issue shares to both Alpha Company and Beta Company in return for their net assets. The proportion of shares issued would be based on their respective market values, 68.55% ($170,000 ÷ [$170,000 + $78,000]) for Alpha and 31.45% for Beta. As the newly formed Sigma Company would not have any assets to use as consideration in this transaction, Alpha and Beta would receive debt or equity securities of Sigma Company.

3. Alpha could acquire the shares of Beta Company directly from the shareholders of that Company. The consideration paid to the Beta shareholders could be cash, other assets, or Alpha Company debt or equity securities.

4. A new organization, Sigma Company, could be formed. Sigma Company could then issue its debt or equity securities directly to the shareholders of Alpha Company and Beta Company in return for the shares of the two Companies.

3-11.   There are other possibilities here. For example, if Alpha had a subsidiary, Alpha could gain control over Beta by having the subsidiary acquire the Beta Company shares from the Beta shareholders. In addition, from a tax point of view, business combination transactions often involve rollover procedures (e.g., ITA 87 amalgamations). However, an understanding of the four basic approaches listed above is adequate for the purposes of this Chapter.

Acquisition Of Assets By Alpha Company

3-12.   Perhaps the most straightforward way in which the Alpha and Beta Companies could be combined would be to have one of the Companies simply acquire the net identifiable assets of the other. Using our basic example, assume that the Alpha Company gives

Beta Company cash of $78,000 (Beta's net book value) to acquire the assets and liabilities of Beta Company. This approach is depicted in Figure 3-1.

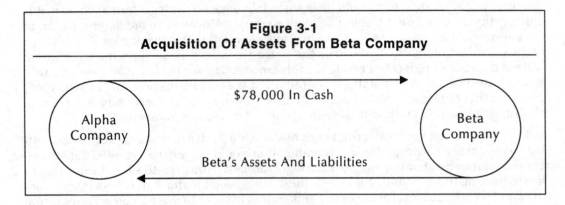

Figure 3-1
Acquisition Of Assets From Beta Company

$78,000 In Cash

Alpha Company

Beta Company

Beta's Assets And Liabilities

3-13.   At this point, it is likely that the Beta Company would go through a windup operation by distributing the cash received from Alpha Company to its shareholders in return for the outstanding Beta Company shares. If this were to happen, the Beta Company shares would be canceled and the Beta Company would cease to exist as a separate legal entity. However, no matter what course of action is taken by Beta Company after the sale of its net assets, the net assets of the combined Companies will be recorded on Alpha Company's books and the accounting for the combined Companies will take place as a continuation of this Company's books. This means that the business combination transaction has been carried out in such a fashion that both Companies' operations have been transferred to a single continuing legal entity. Alpha Company's Balance Sheet subsequent to the business combination transaction would be as follows:

Alpha Company
Balance Sheet As At December 31, 1998
Acquisition Of Beta Assets For Cash

Current Assets ($153,000 - $78,000 + $35,000)	$110,000
Non Current Assets ($82,000 + $85,000)	167,000
Total Assets	$277,000
Liabilities ($65,000 + $42,000)	$107,000
Common Stock (5,000 Shares Issued And Outstanding)	95,000
Retained Earnings	75,000
Total Equities	$277,000

3-14.   It would not be necessary for Alpha to acquire 100 percent of the net assets of Beta in order to have the transaction qualify as a business combination transaction. If Alpha were to acquire, for example, the manufacturing division of Beta, this transaction would be subject to the accounting rules for business combinations. The key point is that Alpha must acquire a group of assets sufficient to be viewed as a separate economic or business entity. As was noted previously, the acquisition of a single asset or group of assets which does not constitute a business entity would be outside the coverage of Section 1580 of the *CICA Handbook*.

3-15.   You should also note that this business combination transaction could have been carried out using Alpha Company shares rather than cash. While the economic outcome would be the same unification of the two Companies, the resulting Alpha Company Balance Sheet would be somewhat different. More specifically, the Current Assets would not have been reduced by the $78,000 outflow of cash and there would be an additional $78,000 in Common Stock outstanding. If the new shares were issued at their December 31, 1998 market value of $34.00 per share, this transaction would have required 2,294 new Alpha shares to be issued ($78,000 ÷ $34.00). This alternative Balance Sheet would be as follows:

Alpha Company
Balance Sheet As At December 31, 1998
Acquisition Of Beta Assets For Shares

Current Assets ($153,000 + $35,000)	$188,000
Non Current Assets ($82,000 + $85,000)	167,000
Total Assets	$355,000
Liabilities ($65,000 + $42,000)	$107,000
Common Stock (7,294 Shares Issued And Outstanding)	173,000
Retained Earnings	75,000
Total Equities	$355,000

Acquisition Of Assets By Sigma Company

3-16.   The acquisition of assets approach could also be implemented through the use of a new corporation. Continuing to use our basic example, assume that a new Company, the Sigma Company, is formed. Based on their respective market values, Sigma issues 17,000 shares to Alpha Company and 7,800 shares to Beta Company in return for the assets and liabilities of the two Companies. This assumes a value of $10 per share for the new Sigma Company shares. You should note, however, that any value could have been used for the Sigma Company shares as long as the number of shares issued to Alpha and Beta was proportionate to the market values of the two companies. For example, a value of $5 could have been used for the Sigma shares, provided 34,000 shares were issued to Alpha and 15,600 shares to Beta. This approach is depicted in Figure 3-2.

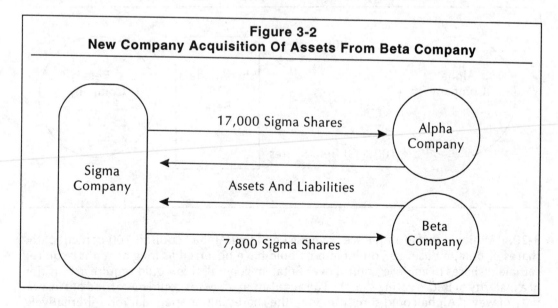

Figure 3-2
New Company Acquisition Of Assets From Beta Company

3-17.   Under this approach, Sigma Company acquires the net assets of both Alpha and Beta Companies. As Sigma is a new company, the only consideration that can be used would be newly issued Sigma shares. Sigma Company's Balance Sheet subsequent to the business combination transaction would be as follows:

Sigma Company
Balance Sheet As At December 31, 1998

Current Assets ($153,000 + $35,000)	$188,000
Non Current Assets ($82,000 + $85,000)	167,000
Total Assets	**$355,000**
Liabilities ($65,000 + $42,000)	$107,000
Common Stock (24,800 Shares Issued And Outstanding)	248,000
Total Equities	**$355,000**

3-18. As was the case when Alpha acquired the net assets of Beta on a direct basis, the result of the business combination is that both Companies' operations have been transferred to a single continuing legal entity. The only difference here is that the continuing legal entity is a new company rather than one of the combining Companies. The resulting Sigma Company Balance Sheet is fundamentally the same as would have resulted from Alpha Company acquiring the net assets of Beta using Alpha shares as consideration. The only difference is that, because Sigma is a new Company, all of the Shareholders' Equity must be allocated to Common Stock, rather than being split between Common Stock and Retained Earnings.

Acquisition Of Shares By Alpha Company

3-19. Another legal route to the combination of Alpha and Beta would be to have one of the two Companies acquire a majority of the outstanding voting shares of the other Company. Continuing to use our basic example, the Alpha Company will give $78,000 in cash to the Beta shareholders in return for 100 percent of the outstanding shares of the Beta Company. This approach is depicted in Figure 3-3.

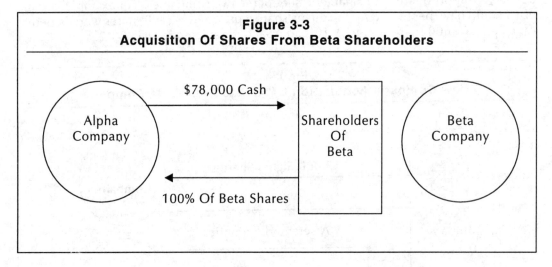

Figure 3-3
Acquisition Of Shares From Beta Shareholders

3-20. While in this example we have assumed that Alpha acquired 100 percent of the shares of Beta, a business combination would have occurred as long as Alpha acquired sufficient shares to achieve control over Beta. In general, this would require acquisition of a majority of Beta's voting shares. The acquisition of shares could be carried out in a variety of ways. Alpha could simply acquire the shares in the open market. Alternatively, they could be acquired from a majority shareholder, through a public tender offer to all shareholders, or through some combination of these methods.

3-21. Regardless of the method used, acquisition of a majority of the outstanding voting shares of Beta Company would mean that Alpha Company was in a position to exercise complete control over the affairs of the Beta Company. As a result of this fact, the two Companies could be viewed as a single economic entity and a business combination could be said to have occurred. This would be the case despite the fact that the two Companies have retained their separate legal identities. In this situation, in order to reflect the economic unification of the two Companies, consolidated financial statements would have to be prepared. While we have not, as yet, provided detailed coverage of consolidation procedures, the basic idea is that the investee's (subsidiary's) assets and liabilities will be added to those of the investor (parent). The resulting consolidated Balance Sheet would be as follows:

Alpha Company And Subsidiary
Consolidated Balance Sheet As At December 31, 1998

Current Assets ($153,000 - $78,000 + $35,000)	$110,000
Non Current Assets ($82,000 + $85,000)	167,000
Total Assets	**$277,000**
Liabilities ($65,000 + $42,000)	$107,000
Common Stock (5,000 Shares Issued And Outstanding)	95,000
Retained Earnings	75,000
Total Equities	**$277,000**

3-22.   There are a number of advantages that can be associated with acquiring shares rather than assets to effect the business combination transaction. First, the acquisition of shares can be a method of going around a company's management if they are hostile to the idea of being acquired. In addition, less financing is needed as only a majority share ownership is required for control over 100 percent of the net assets. Also in the area of financing, if the purchase is timed properly, it may be possible to acquire shares when the stock market is depressed, thereby paying less than the fair values of the identifiable assets of the business. Another advantage would arise should the acquiring company ever wish to dispose of its investment. Shares, particularly if they are publicly traded, are a much more liquid asset than would be the individual assets of an operating company. Finally, this form of business combination provides for the continuation of the acquired company in unaltered legal form. This means it retains its identity for marketing purposes, the tax basis of all of its assets remain unchanged, and there is no interruption of the business relationships that have been built up by the acquired company. As a result of all of these advantages, this form of business combination appears to be the most commonly used when large publicly traded companies are involved.

Acquisition Of Shares By A New Company

3-23.   As was the case with business combinations based on an acquisition of assets, an alternative to having one entity acquire the shares of the other is to establish a new company to acquire the shares of both predecessor companies. As in our earlier example, we will call the new company Sigma Company. We will assume that it issues 17,000 of its shares to the shareholders of Alpha Company in return for all of their outstanding shares. Correspondingly, 7,800 shares will be issued to the shareholders of Beta Company in return for all of their outstanding shares. This business combination transaction is depicted in Figure 3-4 (following page).

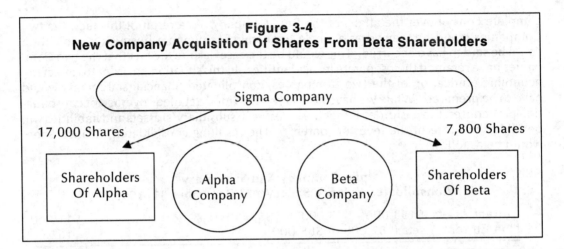

Figure 3-4
New Company Acquisition Of Shares From Beta Shareholders

3-24.   In this case there will be three ongoing legal entities. These would be the parent Sigma Company, as well as Alpha Company and Beta Company, which have now become subsidiaries. Once again we are faced with a situation in which, despite the presence of more than one separate legal entity, the underlying economic fact is that we have a single unified entity. This requires the information for these three Companies to be presented in a single consolidated Balance Sheet as follows:

Sigma Company And Subsidiaries
Consolidated Balance Sheet As At December 31, 1998

Current Assets ($153,000 + $35,000)	$188,000
Non Current Assets ($82,000 + $85,000)	167,000
Total Assets	**$355,000**
Liabilities ($65,000 + $42,000)	$107,000
Common Stock (24,800 Shares Issued And Outstanding)	248,000
Total Equities	**$355,000**

3-25.   You will note that the only differences between this consolidated Balance Sheet and the one that was prepared when Alpha acquired the shares of Beta are:

• Current Assets are $78,000 higher because Alpha used Cash as consideration where Sigma issued Common Stock.

• Shareholders' Equity consists only of Common Stock with no Retained Earnings balance because Sigma is a new Company.

An Important Point
3-26.   The preceding Paragraphs have provided a description of the basic legal routes by which a business combination can be effected. It must be stressed that, while the legal form of the combination will have some influence on the accounting procedures to be used, such form does not provide a clear indication of the economic substance of the transaction. From this fact it follows that the legal form of the combination does not provide guidance as to the appropriate choice of accounting methods to be used. In terms of the requirements of Section 1580 of the *CICA Handbook*, it is possible that a combination using any of the preceding legal formats could be classified as either a purchase transaction or a pooling of interests transaction. As we shall clarify later in this Chapter, the appropriate classification will be based on the question of whether we can identify an acquirer.

Legal Avenues And Tax Considerations

Acquisition Of Assets

3-27.　While it would not be appropriate in a financial reporting text to provide a comprehensive discussion of the tax provisions that are associated with the various legal avenues to combination, these matters are of sufficient importance that a brief description of major tax features is required. Looking first at combinations involving the acquisition of assets, there is a need to distinguish between situations in which cash or other assets was the consideration and those situations in which new shares were issued. If a company acquires the assets of another business through the payment of cash or other assets, the acquired assets will have a completely new tax base, established by the amount of non share consideration given. There would be no carry over of any of the tax values (i.e., adjusted cost base or UCC) that are associated with the business which gave up the assets.

3-28.　The same analysis could apply to situations in which shares are issued to acquire the assets of another business. While the transfer might take place at new tax values, there is also the possibility that different values might be used. As long as the transferor of the assets is a Canadian corporation, the parties to the combination can use the *Income Tax Act* Section 85 rollover provisions. In simplified terms, ITA Section 85 allows assets to be transferred at an elected value that could be anywhere between the fair market value of the assets and their tax values in the hands of the transferor.

3-29.　In general, investors will prefer to acquire assets rather than shares. In most situations, the value of the acquired assets will exceed their carrying values and, if the investor acquires assets, these higher values can be recorded and become the basis for future capital cost allowance (CCA) deductions. In contrast, if the investor acquires shares, the investee company will continue to use the lower carrying values as the basis for CCA, resulting in higher taxable income and taxes payable. In addition, if the investor acquires shares, any problems involving the investee's tax returns for earlier years are acquired along with the shares. When the investor company acquires assets, it simply has a group of assets with a new adjusted cost base and any investee tax problems are left with the selling entity.

3-30.　From the point of view of a person selling an existing business, they will generally have a preference for selling shares. If shares are sold, any resulting income will be capital gains, only three-quarters of which is taxable. In the alternative sale of assets, income will include capital gains but may also include fully taxable recapture of CCA. Further, for the seller to have access to the funds resulting from the sale, it may be necessary to go through a complex windup procedure. If the corporation being sold is a qualified small business corporation, there is an additional advantage to selling shares rather than assets. Gains on the sale of shares of this type of corporation may be eligible for the special $500,000 lifetime capital gains deduction.

Acquisition Of Shares

3-31.　In looking at situations in which the combination is carried out through an acquisition of shares, the type of consideration used also has some influence. If shares are acquired through the payment of cash or other assets, the shares will have a new tax base equal to their fair market value as evidenced by the amount of consideration given. In addition, any excess of consideration over the adjusted cost base of the shares given up will create an immediate capital gain in the hands of the transferor. However, if new shares are issued to acquire the desired shares, Section 85.1 of the *Income Tax Act* can be used. This Section provides that in a share for share exchange, any gain on the shares being transferred can effectively be deferred. Under the provisions of this Section, the old shares are deemed to have been transferred at their adjusted cost base and, in turn, the adjusted cost base of the old shares becomes the adjusted cost base of the new shares that have been received.

3-32.　While the type of consideration used to effect the business combination can make a significant difference to the transferor of the shares, it does not influence the tax status of the assets that have been indirectly acquired through share ownership. As this legal form of combination results in both parties continuing to operate as separate legal entities, the assets remain on the books of the individual companies and their tax bases are not affected in any way by the transaction. As noted previously, in most cases these tax bases will be lower than the fair market values of the assets and, as a result, lower than the tax bases that would normally arise if the assets were acquired directly.

Economic Substance Of Combination Transactions

Combinations Involving An Acquirer

Purchase Transactions Described

3-33.   Accountants generally attempt to concentrate on the economic substance of transactions rather than their form. This fact is particularly important in accounting for business combinations. As previously described, these combination transactions can assume a great variety of legal forms. However, these forms should not be allowed to obscure the fact that, in the great majority of business combinations, one of the combining business entities will have a dominant or controlling interest in the combined business entity. This dominant or controlling company can be viewed as the acquiring company and, given this analysis, the business combination transaction can then be thought of as an acquisition of assets. Under this view, the economic substance of most business combination transactions is simply that one business entity (the acquirer) is purchasing the net assets of another business entity (the acquiree). It would follow that most business combination transactions should be accounted for in a manner that is analogous to the treatment which is accorded to other acquisitions of assets. The "purchase" method of accounting for business combination transactions accomplishes this goal.

General Characteristics Of Purchase Accounting

3-34.   The preceding paragraph stated that the purchase method of accounting for business combination transactions treats the event as an ordinary acquisition of assets. This is made very clear if the general characteristics of the purchase method are examined. They are described in Figure 3-5.

Figure 3-5 Characteristics Of Purchase Method	
Specific Characteristic	**Purchase Method Procedure**
Asset Valuation	The assets and liabilities of the acquiree are recorded at fair values while those of the acquiring enterprise remain at carrying values.
Results Of Operations	The income of the acquired company is added to that of the acquirer only from the date of acquisition.
Shareholders' Equity	The acquiring company's shareholders' equity accounts are not affected by the combination transaction.
Costs Of Combination	All of the direct costs required to implement the business combination transaction become part of the cost of the acquired assets.

3-35.   These general characteristics of the purchase method of accounting for business combinations would constitute an appropriate description of the procedures applicable to the acquisition of any asset by a business enterprise. For example, if an enterprise acquires an inventory of merchandise, the merchandise would be recorded at its fair value, any profit resulting from its resale would be added to the acquirer's income only after it has been acquired and resold, its acquisition would have no effect on the acquiring enterprise's shareholders' equity, and any costs associated with acquiring the merchandise would be added to its cost. In fact, there is only one real difference between the procedures required to record a business combination under the purchase method and the procedures used to record the acquisition of a single asset. When a business entity is acquired, the cost of the purchase must be allocated to a number of different tangible and intangible assets and liabilities. This complex allocation process will be covered later in this Chapter when we provide a more complete presentation of the purchase method.

CICA Handbook Recommendation

3-36. The preceding two paragraphs suggest that whenever it is possible to identify an acquiring company, the combination should be treated as an acquisition of assets and the purchase method of accounting accomplishes this end. This view is reflected in the *CICA Handbook* which states the following:

> **Paragraph 1580.15** *The purchase method should be used to account for all business combinations, except for those rare transactions where an acquirer cannot be identified.* (April, 1974)

Identification Of An Acquirer

3-37. The implementation of the Paragraph 1580.18 Recommendation will require that we determine, in every business combination transaction, whether one of the combining companies can be identified as an acquirer. In those situations where the combination is carried out using cash or other assets as consideration, there is no difficulty with this process.

3-38. Referring to the various cases that we considered in our discussion of legal forms, assume that Alpha Company gives cash to either Beta Company in order to acquire the net assets of that Company, or to the Beta Company shareholders in order to acquire a controlling interest in its voting shares. Where the cash is given to Beta Company to acquire net assets, all of the assets and liabilities of both companies are now on the books of Alpha Company. Since neither Beta Company nor its shareholders have received any of the shares of Alpha Company as part of the combination transaction, they have no continuing participation in the combined company. Clearly Alpha Company is the acquirer. If the cash had gone to the Beta Company shareholders, a similar situation would exist. While in this case Beta Company would continue as a legal entity after the combination transaction, its former shareholders would not participate in its ownership. As was the case when the assets were acquired for cash, we would conclude that Alpha Company is the acquirer.

3-39. The situation becomes more complex when voting shares are used as consideration. This reflects the fact that voting shares allow all shareholders a continuing participation in the control of the combined company. The general rule to be applied in this case is as follows:

> **Paragraph 1580.14** In situations where voting shares are issued or exchanged to effect the combination, the factors relating to control over the resultant combined company must be considered. One of the key factors is the extent of holdings of voting shares in the combined company by the shareholders (as a group) of any of the combining companies. A company whose shareholders (as a group) hold more than 50 percent of the voting shares of the combined company will normally be identified as the acquirer.

3-40. While the preceding guideline sounds fairly simple, its implementation can be somewhat confusing. Consider, for example, the case depicted in Figure 3-6:

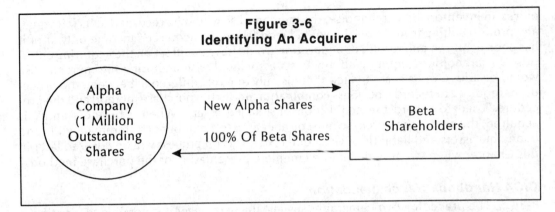

Figure 3-6
Identifying An Acquirer

Alpha Company (1 Million Outstanding Shares)

New Alpha Shares

100% Of Beta Shares

Beta Shareholders

3-41.   In this legal form, the combined entity will be the consolidated enterprise consisting of Alpha Company and its subsidiary Beta Company. The Alpha shareholder group will consist of both the original Alpha shareholders and the new shareholders who were formerly Beta shareholders. In the usual case, fewer than one million shares would have been issued to the Beta shareholders and, as a consequence, the original Alpha shareholders will be in a majority position.

3-42.   This means that, generally, Alpha Company will be identified as the acquirer. However, even when the Alpha shareholders are in the majority, Section 1580 goes on to recognize that other factors may have to be considered:

> **Paragraph 1580.15**   An exception to this general presumption could occur where the shareholders (as a group) of one of the combining companies hold more, but not significantly more, than 50% of the voting shares of the resultant combined company. In such a situation, other factors such as the composition of the board of directors, the holding of major blocks of voting shares, active participation in management, and voting trusts could prevent that combining company from exercising the prerogatives of an acquirer or could give another combining company a dominant position. Where the other combining company is identified as the dominant company, it should be considered to be the acquirer.

3-43.   While the usual combination in this legal form will be as described, with the original parent company shareholders retaining a majority interest, there are other possibilities. If Alpha had issued 2 million shares to the Beta shareholders, they would have assumed the majority position in the combined company, with the result that the subsidiary would be identified as the acquirer. This type of transaction is referred to as a reverse takeover and will be given further attention in this and subsequent Chapters.

3-44.   A further possibility would be that Alpha would issue exactly 1 million shares to the Beta shareholders. In this case, because neither shareholder group has a majority of voting shares, it would be possible to argue that neither of the Companies is the acquirer.

3-45.   The preceding paragraphs illustrate the identification of an acquirer in situations where one of the combining companies issues shares to acquire the shares of the other combining company. You should also consider how this identification process would work when one company acquires the assets of the other company, when a new company is formed to acquire the assets of both companies, and when a new company is formed to acquire the shares of both companies.

Reverse Takeovers - EIC Abstract No. 10

3-46.   Reverse takeovers have become fairly common in recent years. Referring back to Figure 3-6, we noted that if Alpha Company were to issue 2 million new shares to the shareholders of Beta Company in return for their shares, these former Beta Company shareholders would now be the majority shareholders in the combined company. This means that, while Beta Company has been legally acquired and has become a subsidiary, it would be identified as the acquirer for accounting purposes.

3-47.   The most common reason for such transactions is a desire on the part of a company to be listed on a stock exchange. In many of these transactions, the parent company will be a relatively inactive listed company and the subsidiary will be a private company. The consolidated entity which results from the reverse takeover transaction will be under the control of the former shareholders of the private company. However, the shares that are held by these shareholders will now be listed on a public stock exchange. This procedure may be less costly than applying directly for such listing.

3-48.   The concepts involved in such reverse takeovers are no different from those that are applicable in other business combination transactions in which an acquirer can be identified. However, the procedures required to implement these concepts are more difficult to apply in these situations. In view of this, the Emerging Issues Committee issued Abstract No. 10, "Reverse Takeover Accounting". This EIC Abstract provides guidance on the procedures to be used in these situations, including examples to illustrate the application of the suggested procedures. Reflecting the fact that reverse takeovers commonly involve the acquisition of shares, the examples in the Abstract involve preparing a consolidated Balance Sheet for a parent and its subsidiary. Given this need to deal with consolidated financial statements, we will defer presenting a reverse takeover example until we have introduced basic consolidation procedures in the next Chapter.

Combinations With No Acquirer

Pooling Transactions Described

3-49.   In some situations it will not be possible to identify an acquirer. Continuing with the example in Figure 3-6, we noted that, if Alpha Company issues 1 million of its shares to the shareholders of Beta Company in return for their shares, neither shareholder group has a majority of the shares and no acquirer can be readily identified. This means that, while Alpha has legally acquired control over Beta, in terms of economic substance there may be no acquiring company.

3-50.   Note, however, that judgment is required in such circumstances. If the original directors and management of Alpha Company remain in place and the former Beta Company shareholders make no attempt to actively use their management rights, Alpha might still be identified as the acquirer. Perhaps the best statement here would be to indicate that near equality of holdings by the two shareholder groups is a necessary but not sufficient condition to indicate that no acquirer can be identified.

CICA Handbook Recommendation

3-51.   When an acquirer cannot be identified, we are dealing with a voluntary coming together of independent enterprises which have decided to carry on future operations on a combined basis. In our opinion, this voluntary coming together of previously separate enterprises results in the formation of a new and different enterprise. This would suggest that all of the assets of the combining enterprises should be recorded at new values, that the combined company's shareholders' equity should consist entirely of contributed capital and that income for this new enterprise should only be recognized from the date of its formation through the combination transaction. This would be the "new entity" or "fair value pooling" approach to accounting for business combinations.

3-52.   While many authorities believe that fair value pooling is the most appropriate solution to dealing with business combinations where no acquirer can be identified, this view is not acceptable under the requirements of the *CICA Handbook*. In situations where an acquirer cannot be identified, the following Recommendation is applicable:

Paragraph 1580.21   *The pooling of interests method should be used to account for those rare business combinations in which it is not possible to identify one of the parties as the acquirer.* (April, 1974)

General Characteristics Of Pooling Of Interests Accounting

3-53.   The pooling of interests method of accounting is not a very logical or reasonable method of accounting. It views the combination transaction as though it were not a real economic event but rather, a simple coming together of two or more companies with no new basis of accountability for the assets of any of the companies. Given the magnitude of the changes that will be engendered by a transaction which combines two or more existing companies, it is difficult to attach credibility to this economic interpretation which underlies the pooling of interests method.

3-54.   It is probable that the continued existence of the pooling of interests method results from its widespread use in the United States. In that country, the pooling of interests method can be used for virtually any business combination transaction in which shares are used as the consideration. While U.S. accounting bodies have made a number of attempts to limit the usage of this method, to date, none of these attempts have been successful.

3-55.   The underlying reason for this is the fact that, in many situations, pooling of interests accounting can have a very positive influence on reported income subsequent to the combination transaction. Unlike the situation with purchase accounting, the assets of all of the combining companies remain at their old carrying values. The excess of the price paid for the assets over their old carrying values does not have to be recorded as either increases in the value of identifiable assets or as goodwill. As the excess does not have to be recorded, subsequent depreciation and amortization charges will be correspondingly lower, resulting in higher reported net income figures. In individual cases, the differences between purchase accounting results and those reported under pooling of interests can be enormous.

3-56.   The general characteristics of this method, along with those of the purchase method for comparative purposes, are presented in Figure 3-7.

Figure 3-7 Characteristics Of Purchase And Pooling Of Interests Methods		
Specific Characteristic	**Purchase Method Procedure**	**Pooling Of Interests Procedure**
Asset Valuation	The assets and liabilities of the acquiree are recorded at fair values while those of the acquiring enterprise remain at carrying values.	The assets and liabilities of both of the combining companies will be recorded at their carrying values.
Results Of Operations	The income of the acquired company is added to that of the acquirer only from the date of acquisition.	The income of the combining companies will be combined for all prior periods reported.
Shareholders' Equity	The acquiring company's shareholders' equity accounts are not affected by the combination transaction.	The shareholders' equity accounts of the combining companies will be added together on the books of the combined company.
Costs Of Combination	All of the direct costs required to implement the business combination transaction become part of the cost of the acquired assets.	All of the direct costs required to implement the business combination transaction will be treated as an adjustment of the shareholders' equity accounts.

3-57. While some further attention will be given to the pooling of interests procedures in a later section of this Chapter, you should note that the use of this method is fairly rare in Canada. This makes an understanding of these procedures much less important than a full understanding of the procedures associated with the more commonly used purchase method.

Application Of The Purchase Method

Determination Of The Purchase Cost

General Rules

3-58. Having covered the general background on accounting for business combinations, we can now turn to the detailed application of the purchase and pooling of interests methods of accounting for such transactions. Primary attention will be given to the more widely used of the two methods, the purchase method. The first step in this method is the determination of the cost of the purchase.

3-59. Determination of the cost in applying the purchase method involves the same general principles as those used in determining the cost of any asset which has been acquired by the enterprise. This is reflected in the following Recommendation:

> **Paragraph 1580.29** *Where the purchase method is used to account for the combination, the cost of the purchase to the acquiring entity should be determined by the fair value of the consideration given, except as specified in NON-MONETARY TRANSACTIONS, paragraph 3830.08. In those cases where the fair value of the consideration given is not clearly evident, the acquirer's share of the fair value of the net assets acquired should be used as the cost of the purchase to the acquiring entity.* (January, 1990)

3-60. The problems involved in implementing this Recommendation would vary with the nature of the consideration given. The following guidelines would cover most situations:

- If the acquirer pays cash there is no significant problem.

- If the acquirer gives other assets, the fair value of the assets provided may be used as the purchase price. However, if the assets being given are productive assets not held for sale in the ordinary course of business, and they are being exchanged for similar productive assets, Paragraph 1580.29 would require that the exchange take place at the carrying values of the other assets on the books of the acquirer. This is noted through the reference to Paragraph 3830.08 of the *CICA Handbook* Section, "Non Monetary Transactions" that is contained in Paragraph 1580.29. This means that, if the acquiring company gave equipment with a carrying value on its books of $500,000 in return for similar equipment of the acquiree, the newly acquired equipment would be recorded at $500,000, without regard to the current values of either the equipment given up or the equipment acquired.

- If shares with a quoted market price are issued by the acquirer, this market price will normally be used as the primary measure of the purchase price.

- If the acquirer issues shares that do not have a market price or if it is agreed that the market price of the shares issued is not indicative of their fair value, the fair value of the net assets acquired would serve as the purchase price in the application of this method of accounting for business combinations. It is not likely that any goodwill would be recorded if this approach to the determination of the purchase price were used.

3-61. The preceding represents an application of the familiar idea that assets are recorded at the fair value of the consideration given or, if there are significant problems in determining the fair value of that consideration, the fair value of the assets acquired.

Direct Costs Of Combination - General Rules

3-62.   Another familiar idea is that all of the direct costs related to the acquisition of a particular asset should be included as a part of the cost of the acquisition. This general rule would, of course, apply to the assets acquired in a business combination that is accounted for by the purchase method of accounting. This is reflected in the following Recommendation:

> **Paragraph 1580.52** *Expenses directly incurred in effecting a business combination accounted for as a purchase should be included as part of the cost of the purchase.* (April, 1974)

3-63.   This would not apply to the costs of registering and issuing shares if the shares were issued to effect the combination transaction. These costs would be treated as a capital transaction. However, all other direct costs of the acquisition would be treated as a part of the cost to be allocated to the identifiable net assets of the acquiree and to goodwill.

Contingent Consideration

3-64.   It is possible for a business combination agreement to provide for the payment of additional consideration if some specified event or transaction occurs in future accounting periods. The issue that is created by such contingent consideration is whether the consideration should be recorded at the time of the combination transaction or only when the contingency is resolved and the additional amounts are issued or become payable. The following general Recommendation is applicable:

> **Paragraph 1580.33** *Where the amount of contingent consideration can be reasonably estimated at the date of acquisition and the outcome of the contingency can be determined beyond reasonable doubt, it should be recorded at that date as part of the cost of the purchase. Where the amount of contingent consideration or the outcome of the contingency cannot be determined beyond reasonable doubt, details of the contingency should be disclosed in a note to the financial statements; when the contingency is resolved, the consideration should be recorded as an additional cost of the purchase.* (April, 1974)

3-65.   Additional Recommendations provide more detailed guidance for two common forms of contingency payments. Specific statements are made with respect to contingency payments related to earnings performance of the acquiree and contingent payments related to the future market prices of shares issued to effect a combination transaction.

Payments Contingent On Earnings

3-66.   It is not uncommon for an acquiree to make the argument that the enterprise is really worth more than is being offered by the acquirer and that the earnings of some future period will support this contention. A way of dealing with this possibility is for the acquirer to offer to pay additional consideration should the acquiree's belief about the future earnings prove to be correct. This results in a situation where there is contingent consideration based on the acquiree's future earnings.

3-67.   When additional payment is contingent on the future earnings of the acquiree, the following Recommedation is made:

> **Paragraph 1580.35** *In situations where additional consideration becomes payable as the result of maintaining or achieving specified earnings levels in periods*

*subsequent to the acquisition, such consideration should be recorded, when de-
terminable, as an additional cost of the purchase. Details of such contingent consideration should be disclosed. (April, 1974)*

3-68.   The accounting treatment of contingent consideration based on earnings can be
illustrated by the following simple example:

Example   On January 1, 1998, the Mor Company issues 3 million of its no par value
voting shares in return for all of the outstanding voting shares of the Mee Company.
On this date the Mor Company shares have a fair value of $25 per share. In addition,
the Mor Company agrees that if the 1998 earnings per share of the Mee Company is in
excess of $3.50, the Mor Company will pay an additional $10 million in cash to the
former shareholders of the Mee Company. The entry on January 1, 1998 would be as
follows:

Investment In Mee	$75,000,000	
No Par Common Stock		$75,000,000

At the end of 1998, the Mee Company's earnings per share has exceeded the contingency level of $3.50 and the following entry to record the contingency payment
would be required:

Investment In Mee	$10,000,000	
Cash		$10,000,000

3-69.   This additional $10 million would have to be allocated to goodwill (or an adjust-
ment of the allocation of negative goodwill) in the preparation of the consolidated financial statements.

Payments Contingent On Share Prices

3-70.   When shares are used as consideration in a business combination transaction, the
acquirer may make the argument that the shares being offered are worth more than the
acquiree has calculated and that this additional value will be supported by some future
market price for the stock. In this case, the acquirer may agree to pay additional amounts
if the market value of the shares does not reach a certain price at some future point in
time.

3-71.   In situations where additional payments are contingent on future price performance of the acquirer's shares, the following Recommendation is applicable:

Paragraph 1580.38   *Any contingent consideration which will be payable if the
market price of the shares issued to effect the combination does not reach a specified value by a specified future date should not change the amount recorded as the
cost of the purchase. If additional consideration becomes payable, the current fair
value of such consideration should be offset by a simultaneous reduction in the
value placed on the shares issued at the date of acquisition to their lower current
fair value. (April, 1974)*

3-72.   The accounting treatment of contingencies based on share prices can be illustrated by extending the previous example used to illustrate the accounting treatment of
contingencies based on earnings. The revised example is as follows:

Example   On January 1, 1998, the Mor Company issues 3 million of its no par value
voting shares in return for all of the outstanding voting shares of the Mee Company.
On this date the Mor Company shares have a fair value of $25 per share. In this case
we will assume that the Mor Company has agreed to pay an additional $15 million if,
on December 31, 1998, the market price of the Mor Company shares is not equal to at

least $30 per share. In this situation, the Mor Company has, in effect, guaranteed the Mee Company shareholders a value of $30 per share for the Mor Company shares. If the market price does not move from its current $25 per share up to $30 per share, the Mor Company will provide the difference by paying $15 million (3 million shares at $5 per share). In view of this fact, the purchase price should include this contingency payment as follows:

Investment In Mee	$90,000,000	
No Par Common Stock		$90,000,000

If the Mor Company shares reach $30 by the end of 1998, no further entries will be required and the No Par Common Stock will remain at $90,000,000. On the other hand, if they fail to achieve the specified level and the contingency payment must be made, the No Par Common Stock will be reduced by the following entry:

No Par Common Stock	$15,000,000	
Cash		$15,000,000

Note that the payment of contingent consideration does not affect the cost of the purchase of the Mee Company.

Establishment Of The Acquisition Date

3-73. The acquisition date will generally be the date on which the assets are received and the consideration given. However, the key factor is the transfer of control and this may take place on a different date than the actual transfer of the assets or the payment of the consideration. If there is a material lag between the effective date for accounting purposes and the date on which the consideration must be paid, the cost of the purchase and the net income of the acquirer should be reduced to reflect imputed interest for this period.

3-74. Once the effective date of acquisition has been established, the *Handbook* notes that:

> **Paragraph 1580.40** *The cost of the purchase and the amounts assigned to assets acquired and liabilities assumed should be determined as of the date of the acquisition.* (April, 1975)

3-75. The acquisition date is also significant in the determination of the income of the combined companies under the purchase method of accounting. This is noted as follows:

> **Paragraph 1580.41** *The financial statements of an acquiring company for the period in which a business combination occurs should reflect the operations of the acquired company from the date of acquisition.* (April, 1974)

3-76. This is in contrast to the pooling of interests method of accounting in which the income of the combining companies would be added together on a retroactive basis.

General Procedures For The Allocation Of The Purchase Price

3-77. It was previously noted that the purchase method of accounting for business combinations is simply a way of treating these transactions in a manner that is analogous to other asset acquisition transactions. The only real complicating factor is the fact that a single purchase price must be allocated over a large group of identifiable assets, identifiable liabilities, and goodwill. The guidelines for this allocation process are as follows:

> **Paragraph 1580.44** *The cost of purchase should be allocated as follows:*
>
> *(a) the acquiring company's interest in identifiable assets acquired and liabilities*

assumed should be based on their fair values at the date of acquisition;

(b) the excess of the cost of the purchase over the acquiring company's interest in identifiable assets acquired and liabilities assumed should be reflected as goodwill.

The interest of any non-controlling shareholders in the identifiable assets acquired and liabilities assumed should be based on their carrying values in the accounting records of the company acquired. This interest should be included in the amount disclosed as non-controlling interest on the liabilities side of the balance sheet. Where the acquiring company's interest in the identifiable assets acquired and liabilities assumed, based on their fair values, exceeds the cost of the purchase, the amounts assigned to identifiable non-monetary assets should be reduced to the extent that the excess is eliminated. The allocation of the reduction to individual non-monetary assets or groups of non-monetary assets requires a re-examination of values previously assigned; this is a matter of judgment and should be determined having regard to the circumstances of the acquisition. (April, 1975)

3-78.   A thorough understanding of the preceding Paragraph is essential to your ability to deal with both business combinations and the preparation of consolidated financial statements. In virtually all real world business combinations it is possible to identify an acquirer and, as a consequence, the purchase method of accounting will be used. This means that in virtually all business combination problems, including those in which the legal format requires the preparation of consolidated financial statements, the purchase price will have to be allocated to identifiable net assets and goodwill.

3-79.   In procedural terms, this allocation problem can be dealt with in the following two steps:

Step A   Determine the fair values of the acquiree's identifiable assets and liabilities. In practical situations, this is a complex process which will involve considerable effort on the part of both accountants and appraisers. This process is discussed in more detail in the Section titled "Determination Of Fair Values".

Step B   It is unlikely that the purchase price will be equal to the acquirer's share of the sum of the fair values of the identifiable assets and liabilities of the acquiree. As a consequence, it is necessary to compare the purchase price with the investor's share of the fair values of the identifiable net assets that have been acquired. This comparison can have two possible outcomes:

1. If the purchase price is the larger figure, the excess will be allocated to goodwill. This possibility will be discussed in the Section titled "Goodwill".

2. If the purchase price is less than the acquirer's share of the fair values, the deficiency will be deducted from the individual non-monetary assets. This possibility will be discussed in the Section titled "Negative Goodwill".

Determination Of Fair Values

3-80.   We are concerned here with assigning individual values to the identifiable assets and liabilities that are acquired in the business combination transaction. The general approach that is found in the *CICA Handbook* could be characterized as attempting to establish net realizable values for most current assets and replacement costs for non current assets. However, a fairly detailed set of guidelines is provided as follows:

Paragraph 1580.45   General guidelines for arriving at the fair value of individual identifiable assets and liabilities are as follows:

(a) Marketable securities at current net realizable values.

(b) Receivables based on the amounts to be received, less allowances for uncollectibility and collection costs, if necessary.

(c) Inventories:
   (i) Finished goods and merchandise at estimated selling prices less the sum of (a) costs of disposal and (b) a reasonable profit allowance for the selling effort;
   (ii) Work in process at estimated selling prices of finished goods less the sum of (a) costs to complete, (b) costs of disposal and (c) a reasonable profit allowance for the completing and selling effort based on profit for similar finished goods;
   (iii) Raw materials at current replacement costs.

(d) Plant and equipment:
   (i) to be used, at current replacement costs for similar capacity unless the expected future use of the assets indicates a lower value to the acquirer;
   (ii) to be sold or held for later sale rather than used, at current net realizable value; and
   (iii) to be used temporarily, at current net realizable value with depreciation to be recognized in the periods of use.
   Replacement cost may be determined directly if a market for used assets exists; otherwise, an estimate of depreciated replacement cost should be used. The accumulated depreciation of the acquired company should not be carried forward by the acquiring company. Current net realizable value will have to take into account factors such as whether there is a demand for such plant and equipment; whether it will have to be dismantled, thereby incurring dismantling costs; whether such demand is within the particular locality, thereby avoiding heavy transportation costs, etc.

(e) Intangible assets which can be identified and named, including contracts, patents, franchises, customer and supplier lists, and favourable leases, at estimated or appraised values.

(f) Other assets, including land, natural resources and non marketable securities, at estimated or appraised values.

(g) Net pension assets or obligations, for defined benefit pension plans:

   (i) When the plan is to continue in operation, the actuarial present value of accrued pension benefits would be calculated using best estimate assumptions following the Recommendations in Section 3460. Similarly, the value of pension fund assets would be determined according to the established policy of the acquiring company, in accordance with Section 3460.

   (ii) When the plan is to be wound up, the net pension asset or obligation should be valued based on the amount expected to be received or paid on settlement.

(h) Long-term liabilities, accruals, debts, etc., based on the amount required to discharge the obligation.

(i) Other liabilities and commitments, including unfavourable leases (as lessee), contracts and commitments, and plant closing expense incident to the acquisition, based on the amount required to discharge the obligation.

Discounting may be considered to be an aid in valuation where an asset would not be realized or an obligation would not be discharged in the current operating cycle.

Liabilities

3-81.   The preceding offers fairly detailed guidelines for dealing with particular assets and liabilities. In general terms, these guidelines require the use of net realizable value for current and non current assets that are to be sold, and the use of replacement costs for non current assets that will be used. With respect to liabilities, the requirement that they be recorded at the amount required to discharge the obligation has a meaning that will vary with the circumstances:

Short Term Obligations   The amount to be used here will be the face value of the obligations.

Long Term Obligations   In the absence of some special provision for the retirement of the obligation, the present value at current market rates would be used. When marketable obligations are involved, this amount would simply be the current market value of the obligations. When a call provision or other special retirement arrangement is available on marketable debt, this value might be used. However, we feel that it would only be appropriate when it is less than the current market value of the obligations. This view reflects the fact that such provisions are not likely to be exercised when the call price exceeds the current market value. This analysis leads to the conclusion that the fair value of long term debt obligations would be the lesser of their current fair market value and their call price.

Acquiree Goodwill

3-82.   Another problem arises when an acquiree has goodwill that has been recorded on its books. The previously quoted Recommendation from Paragraph 1580.44 of the *CICA Handbook* requires that the non controlling interest be based only on identifiable assets. Since this term refers to all assets except for goodwill, this suggests that the non controlling interest share of any goodwill recorded by the acquiree would not be recorded. However, this is in conflict with Paragraph 1600.15 of the *CICA Handbook* which requires that the non controlling interest be based on all subsidiary assets. We are of the opinion that the Section 1600 Recommendation is more consistent with the general approach used to account for the non controlling interest in preparing consolidated financial statements. Note that business combinations which do not involve the acquisition of shares (parent/subsidiary) legal form cannot have a non controlling interest.

Asset Restrictions

3-83.   The *CICA Handbook* provides the following guideline when there are restrictions on the use of assets:

Paragraph 1580.46   Any assets, including cash, which are subject to particular restrictions would be valued with consideration given to those restrictions.

Tax Considerations - Temporary Differences At The Combination Date

3-84.   In many business combination transactions, the fair values of acquired assets will differ from their tax values on the books of the acquired company. This situation can result from two possible causes:

- In situations where shares have been acquired to effect the business combination, the acquired subsidiary will continue as a separate legal entity and will retain old tax values for its assets, without regard to their fair values at the time of the business combination.

- In situations where assets have been acquired to effect the business combination, the transfer of assets may involve a rollover provision (e.g., ITA 85) under which assets are transferred at elected values without regard to their fair values at the time of the business combination.

3-85. Prior to the 1997 introduction of Section 3465, "Income Taxes", to the *CICA Handbook*, Section 1580 indicated that these alternative tax values should be taken into consideration in the determination of fair values. Consider, for example, an item of equipment for which fair value is determined on the basis of its replacement cost. If its tax value is less than its normal replacement cost, its fair value would have to be reduced to reflect the fact that the tax deductions associated with the acquired asset are less than those associated with a purchase of a new asset at full replacement cost.

3-86. The introduction of Section 3465 has changed this situation as is reflected in the following Recommendation:

Paragraph 1580.47 The values placed by an acquirer on the assets and liabilities of an acquired company are determined based on their fair values, without reference to their values for tax purposes, or tax bases. "Income Taxes", Section 3465, requires that the tax effects of differences between the assigned values of the identifiable assets and liabilities acquired and their tax bases be recorded as future income tax assets and liabilities and included in the allocation of the cost of the purchase.

3-87. This revised Recommendation requires that fair values be determined without regard to tax values and that future income tax assets or liabilities be established at the time of the business combination transaction. Further attention will be given to this issue in Chapter 17 when we give detailed consideration to the tax aspects of business combinations.

Tax Considerations - Acquiree Future Income Tax Assets And Liabilities

3-88. Paragraph 1580.47 requires that future income tax assets and liabilities be established at the time of a business combination transaction on the basis of temporary differences between the tax values and fair values of assets and liabilities acquired. Given this, future income tax assets and liabilities on the books of the acquiree can be ignored in the process of determining fair values. This is reflected in the following Recommendation:

Paragraph 1580.48 Future income tax liabilities and assets reported by the acquired company would not be included in the allocation of the cost of the purchase or in the consolidated financial statements. Instead the amounts of future income tax liabilities and assets to be included in the allocation of the cost of the purchase and in the consolidated financial statements would be determined as described in paragraph 1580.47.

3-89. As noted previously, these issues will be discussed more fully in Chapter 17.

Tax Considerations - Acquiree Loss Carry Forwards

3-90. In some business combinations, the acquiree may have either a recognized or an unrecognized loss carry forward. If the amount involved is significant, care will be taken to insure that any benefits associated with this loss carry forward are legally available to the combined company. This is complicated by the fact that most business combination transactions involve an acquisition of control and this event triggers special tax rules for loss carry overs. While a complete discussion of the tax treatment of loss carry overs when there is an acquisition of control would not be appropriate in a text on financial reporting, several points should be made:

- An acquisition of control creates a deemed year end at that point in time. This will generally shorten the carry over period for time limited loss carry overs.

- Net capital loss carry overs, current allowable capital losses, and allowable business investment losses expire with the deemed year end. While there are elections which will allow for the use of all or part of such amounts, the inability to carry these losses forward means that any unused balances have no future value.

- With respect to non capital losses that are carried forward beyond the acquisition of control, their use is dependent on the combined company carrying on the same business or a line of business similar to that in which the loss occurred, and on having sufficient taxable income in that line of business to fully utilize the losses. Otherwise, the carry forwards cannot be used and will have no value to the combined company.

3-91.   If the loss carry forward and its associated benefit legally survive the combination transaction, a question then arises as to how such benefits should be dealt with in the allocation of the purchase price. With respect to this issue, the *CICA Handbook* Recommends the following:

> **Paragraph 1580.47**   ... In addition, the benefit of any unused tax losses or income tax reductions that meet the recognition criteria set out in INCOME TAXES, Section 3465, would be recognized as future income tax assets and included in the allocation of the cost of the purchase. Similarly, the benefit of any previously unrecognized unused tax losses or income tax reductions of the acquirer that, at the time of the business combination, meets the recognition criteria would also be recognized as future income tax assets and included in the allocation of the cost of the purchase.

3-92.   The preceding should make clear that, in any business combination transaction which involves an acquiree with significant loss carry overs, designing the combination's legal form in such a fashion that the benefit of the loss is legally available to the combined entity is an important consideration. Equally important is the need to structure the combination in a manner that permits the potential benefit of the loss to be realized.

Push Down Accounting

The Concept

3-93.   When the legal form of the business combination transaction is such that one legal entity acquires the assets of the other party, the fair values of the assets and liabilities will be recorded on the books of the legal acquirer. Once these fair values are recorded they become the actual book values in the records of the acquirer and no adjustments are required in subsequent accounting periods.

3-94.   The situation is different when the legal form of the combination transaction involves the acquisition of shares in a subsidiary. As the old book values of assets and liabilities will remain on the single entity records of the subsidiary, any fair value changes arising as part of the combination transaction as well as any subsequent amortization that is required, will only be recorded as working paper entries in the preparation of consolidated financial statements. This results in a sort of dual accounting system in which old book values are retained and dealt with in the legal records of the subsidiary while a significantly different set of values is used in the consolidated financial statements.

3-95.   As a way of avoiding the additional effort required by this dual system of valuation, some use has been made of push down accounting. Under these procedures, the fair values that are determined at the time of the business combination transaction are recorded in the actual books of the subsidiary, not just in the consolidated financial statements. This means that, as was the case when the combination was carried out through an acquisition of assets, no further adjustments will be required in periods subsequent to the combination transaction to reflect the differences between the fair values and book values at acquisition.

3-96.   These push down accounting procedures clearly reduce the effort required in the preparation of consolidated financial statements. However, the fact that the subsidiary replaces its existing book values with different values is not consistent with the general use of historical costs for asset valuation.

3-97.   In those cases where the parent owns 100 percent of the subsidiary's shares, this is not a problem. The only statements that will be issued to the public will be on a consolidated basis and the financial information presented in these statements will be the same whether fair value changes are dealt with through push down accounting or through the more conventional working paper approach. However, when there is a publicly traded minority interest, the subsidiary will have to issue single entity financial statements and, if push down accounting has been used, these statements will no longer reflect the historical costs that are normally required under generally accepted accounting principles.

CICA Handbook Recommendations

3-98. In December, 1992, Section 1625, "Comprehensive Revaluation Of Assets And Liabilities", was added to the *CICA Handbook*. As push down accounting is an application of comprehensive revaluation procedures, this Section is relevant to our discussion of the use of this method. In general, comprehensive revaluation is permitted when the following conditions are satisfied:

> **Paragraph 1625.04** *The following conditions are required to be satisfied for an enterprise's assets and liabilities to be comprehensively revalued:*
>
> (a) *All or virtually all of the equity interests in the enterprise have been acquired, in one or more transactions between non-related parties, by an acquirer who controls the enterprise after the transaction or transactions; or*
>
> (b) *The enterprise has been subject to a financial reorganization, and the same party does not control the enterprise both before and after the reorganization;*
>
> *and in either situation new costs are reasonably determinable.* (January, 1993)

3-99. Paragraph (a) of this Recommendation describes a business combination situation in which the acquirer has purchased shares of the acquiree. This means that the Recommendation permits, but does not require, push down accounting whenever all or virtually all of the equity interests of an enterprise have been acquired. As to the meaning of "virtually all" in this Recommendation, the *CICA Handbook* provides the following guidance:

> **Paragraph 1625.10** An acquirer that holds at least 90% of the equity interests after the acquisition is presumed to have acquired virtually all of the enterprise's equity interests.

3-100. While this suggestion does leave some room for the application of professional judgment, the 90 percent guideline will likely become the dominant criteria for the use of push down accounting. The Section also notes that push down accounting is only appropriate when the acquirer, representing an individual or group's collective interest, controls the enterprise as per the Recommendations of Section 1590.

3-101. Paragraph 1625.13 reinforces the point that, in the absence of an ability to reasonably determine values for individual assets and liabilities, push down accounting is not appropriate. As an example of this, the Paragraph describes a situation where there is a basket purchase and the enterprise does not have, and cannot obtain from the acquirer, details of the purchase price and its allocation among assets and liabilities.

Application

3-102. Section 1625 makes a number of Recommendations with respect to the application of push down accounting, including the specification of appropriate disclosure requirements for this method. In addition, an Appendix to the Section contains examples of the application of push down accounting. However, examples of push down accounting require some understanding of consolidation procedures. As we have not yet presented any material on consolidation procedures, it would be difficult to explain a push down accounting example involving these procedures. As a consequence, we will defer any examples involving the application of push down accounting until we have introduced basic consolidation procedures at acquisition in Chapter 4.

Goodwill

The Concept

3-103.   In Step A (see Paragraph 3-79) we determined the current fair values of the identifiable assets and liabilities of the acquiree on an individual basis. When these assets are put together as a business enterprise, it is unlikely that the sum of these fair values will be equal to the value of the business as an operating economic entity. If the assets were used in an effective and efficient manner, it is possible for the business to be worth considerably more than the sum of its individual asset values. Alternatively, ineffectual management or other factors can depress the value of a business well below the sum of the fair values of its assets. Note that this is not a clear indication that the assets should be liquidated on an individual basis. Fair values are based on the value of an asset to a going concern and, while in some cases they may be equal to liquidation values, this is not likely to be the case for most non current assets.

3-104.   If the business is worth more than the sum of its individual asset values, this will be reflected in the prices paid by an acquirer in a business combination. In this situation, when the acquisition cost exceeds the acquirer's share of the fair values of the acquiree's identifiable net assets, the excess is generally referred to as goodwill. From a conceptual point of view, goodwill is the capitalized expected value of enterprise earning power in excess of a normal rate of return for the particular industry in which it operates. As an example of this concept, consider the following:

> **Example**: Ryerson Ltd. has net identifiable assets with a current fair value of $1 million. Its annual income has been $150,000 for many years and it is anticipated that this level of earnings will continue indefinitely. A normal rate of return in Ryerson's industry is 10 percent as reflected in business values that are typically 10 times reported earnings.

3-105.   Given this information, it is clear that Ryerson has goodwill. Normal earnings on Ryerson's $1 million in net assets would be $100,000, well below the Company's $150,000. Based on these earnings and a valuation benchmark of 10 times earnings, the value of Ryerson as a going concern would be $1.5 million. This would suggest the presence of goodwill as follows:

Value Of Ryerson As A Going Concern	$1,500,000
Fair Value Of Ryerson's Net Identifiable Assets	(1,000,000)
Goodwill	$ 500,000

3-106.   While it is clear that, in this simplified example, Ryerson clearly has goodwill, it is unlikely that it will be recorded in the Company's Balance Sheet. Even in situations where an enterprise has incurred significant costs for the creation of goodwill (e.g., management training or advertising directed at enhancing the image of the enterprise), GAAP does not permit the recognition of internally generated goodwill. This reflects the belief that there is no reliable procedure for the measurement of such amounts. In fact, this belief prevents the recognition of most internally generated intangibles. The only major exception to this is the recognition of certain development costs as assets under the provisions of Section 3450 of the *CICA Handbook*, "Research and Development Costs".

Measurement In Practice

3-107.   While it is not possible under GAAP to recognize internally generated goodwill, we often find goodwill in corporate balance sheets. In fact, in many cases, it can be a very significant item. However, these amounts usually reflect goodwill that has been recognized as the result of a business combination transaction accounted for by the purchase method.

3-108.   In practical terms, the only useful definition of goodwill under GAAP is the excess of the purchase price over the acquirer's proportionate share of the fair values of the acquiree's net identifiable assets at the date of a business combination accounted for by the purchase method. Returning to our example involving Ryerson Ltd., if another enterprise were to purchase either the net assets or the shares of this enterprise, the acquirer would record the goodwill of $500,000 that was calculated in the example.

3-109.   In general, this is the only basis for recording significant amounts of goodwill. One sometimes sees nominal amounts of goodwill added to corporate Balance Sheets without the purchase of another enterprise. However, this is a procedure that is acceptable only if the amount involved is immaterial. In addition, if one or both of the combining companies in a pooling of interests transaction has previously recorded goodwill, this will be carried forward on the books of the combined company. However, such goodwill would have originated in an earlier business combination transaction accounted for by the purchase method.

Accounting Procedures

3-110.   Prior to the inclusion of Section 1580 in the *CICA Handbook*, goodwill was subject to a considerable variety of accounting treatments. This is no longer possible. When it is determined that there is an excess of the purchase price over the acquirer's share of the fair value of the acquiree's net identifiable assets, the *CICA Handbook* requires the following disclosure:

> **Paragraph 1580.61**   *The amount attributed to goodwill should be shown separately on the balance sheet as an intangible asset, to the extent that it has not been amortized or written down. It should not be shown as a deduction from shareholders' equity.* (April, 1974)

3-111.   Once the goodwill balance has been measured and recorded, Section 1580 also specifies the subsequent accounting treatment:

> **Paragraph 1580.58**   *The amount reflected as goodwill at the date of acquisition should be amortized to income by the straight-line method over the estimated life of such goodwill; however, such period should not exceed forty years. The period of amortization should be disclosed.* (April, 1974)

3-112.   The preceding requirement for systematic amortization of goodwill balances would seem to preclude immediate write offs of such balances. However, it is permitted under certain circumstances:

> **Paragraph 1580.62**   *Where there has been a permanent impairment in value of the unamortized portion of goodwill, it should be written down. The write down should be treated as a charge against income.* (April, 1974)

3-113.   Depending on the circumstances which give rise to the impairment in value, the write down may be treated as a charge against Income Before Extraordinary Items And Discontinued Operations, an Extraordinary Item, or a Result Of Discontinued Operations. One would expect that the application of this provision would not be common.

International Accounting Standard No. 22, "Business Combinations"

3-114.   This International Accounting Standard was subject to a major revision in 1993 and is likely to be influential in changing accounting for goodwill in both Canada and the United States. Two of the Recommendations of this revised Standard are of particular significance:

- It requires a review at each Balance Sheet date to determine if the unamortized balance of goodwill is likely to be recovered. If the review indicates that all or part of the balance will not be recoverable, the non recoverable amount should be charged to expense immediately.

- The Standard Recommends that the maximum period of amortization for goodwill should be five years.

3-115.   Given the somewhat ephemeral nature of the factors that contribute to goodwill, these Recommendations would appear to be very appropriate. In general, goodwill reflects an advantageous competitive position, resulting in superior earnings for as long as this position can be maintained. In today's rapidly changing business environment, it is difficult to believe that such an advantageous position could have a life of 40 years. Given this, it is likely that both Canadian and U. S. standards will be altered to reflect the Recommendations of this International Accounting Standard.

3-116.   A further issue identified in this Standard is the fact that corporate takeovers can result in bidding wars that push up the amount paid for goodwill to unreasonable levels. For a good discussion of all of the issues raised by this revision of International Accounting Standard No. 22, we would recommend the *CA Magazine* article, "The Goodwill Game". It was written by Tony Brookes and appeared in the March, 1995 issue.

Negative Goodwill

3-117.   As was previously noted, a business enterprise which is being operated in an ineffective manner may have a total value which is less than the sum of its individual asset values. If such a business is an acquiree in a business combination transaction, the purchase price will be less than the acquirer's share of the fair values of the net identifiable assets of the acquiree. While the *CICA Handbook* does not use the term, this deficiency is often referred to as negative goodwill. Conceptually, it would represent the capitalized expected value of an earnings deficiency with respect to a normal rate of return in the industry in which the enterprise operates. In short, it is simply the reverse of the positive goodwill situation which was discussed in the previous Section.

3-118.   We are of the opinion that negative goodwill should be given a treatment which would be analogous to the treatment which is accorded positive goodwill. This would suggest that it be established as a valuation account related to the total enterprise and deducted from the total asset values of the combined company. If the negative goodwill is perceived to have a limited life, it should be amortized to income over that life.

3-119.   However, this is not the approach that is required under the recommendations of the *CICA Handbook*. The relevant *Handbook* Recommendation was quoted previously and the relevant portion is reproduced here:

> **Paragraph 1580.44**   *Where the acquiring company's interest in the identifiable assets acquired and liabilities assumed, based on their fair values, exceeds the cost of the purchase, the amounts assigned to identifiable non-monetary assets should be reduced to the extent that the excess is eliminated. The allocation of the reduction to individual non-monetary assets or groups of non-monetary assets requires a re-examination of values previously assigned; this is a matter of judgment and should be determined having regard to the circumstances of the acquisition.* (April, 1975)

3-120.   This Recommendation is conceptually unsound in that it fails to recognize that negative goodwill is not associated with any single asset or group of assets. Rather, negative goodwill reflects the fact that the enterprise is not being operated in a manner that produces an adequate rate of return on the assets being used. It makes no more sense to subtract negative goodwill from an individual non monetary asset than it would to add positive goodwill to such an asset.

3-121.   Even if there were a sound conceptual basis for the *Handbook* Recommendation on negative goodwill, the guidelines for its implementation are inadequate. Leaving the allocation of such amounts as completely a matter of judgment would allow such diverse treatments as subtracting the amount either from land or from inventories. In the former case, the negative goodwill might never have any influence on income. In contrast, if the amount is allocated to inventories, the entire amount of the negative goodwill will be added to income within one year.

Treatment Of Shareholders' Equity

3-122. From a conceptual point of view, the shareholders' equity of a combined company resulting from a purchase transaction would simply be the shareholders' equity of the acquiring company. However, under some of the legal forms of combination this may be in violation of relevant corporate legislation. For example, if the net assets of two existing companies are transferred to a newly established corporation, the *Canada Business Corporations Act* would require that all of the shareholders' equity of the new corporation be classified as contributed capital. This is, of course, in conflict with the purchase accounting requirement that the shareholders' equity of the combined company have the same amounts of contributed capital and retained earnings as the acquiring company. When conflicts of this sort arise, the relevant corporate legislation would be the determining factor in the presentation of the combined company's shareholders' equity.

Reporting Operations

3-123. As we have noted previously, the purchase method of accounting for business combinations treats the combination transaction as an acquisition of assets by the acquiring business entity. As the earnings produced by newly acquired assets are only added to income from the date on which they are acquired, it follows that the earnings of an acquiree in a business combination transaction would only be added to those of the acquirer from the effective date of the combination transaction. This means, for example, that if a business combination takes place on the last day of the acquiring company's fiscal year, the reported earnings of the combined company will only include those of the acquirer. If the transaction takes place earlier in the year, a proportionate part of the acquiree's earnings will have to be added to those of the acquirer.

Required Disclosure

3-124. The *CICA Handbook* contains a general Recommendation that is applicable to both purchase and pooling of interests transactions:

> **Paragraph 1580.78** *For each business combination, disclosure should be made, in the financial statements of the combined entity for the period in which the combination took place, of the method of accounting for the combination, the net assets brought into the combination, the consideration given and other pertinent information.* (April, 1974)

3-125. For those business combinations where purchase accounting is used, the following Recommendation is applicable:

> **Paragraph 1580.79** *For a combination accounted for as a purchase, information disclosure should include the following:*
>
> *(a) the name and a brief description of the business acquired and, where shares are acquired, the percentage of voting shares held;*
>
> *(b) the method of accounting for the combination - that is by the purchase method;*
>
> *(c) the date of acquisition and the period for which results of operations of the acquired business are included in the income statement of the acquiring*

company;

(d) *net assets acquired:*
  (i) *total assets, including intangible assets other than goodwill, at the amount assigned thereto;*
  (ii) *total liabilities at the amount assigned thereto;*
  (iii) *amount of non controlling interest in such net assets;*
  (iv) *amount of goodwill arising from the acquisition together with the period of amortization;*

(e) *amount of consideration given, at fair value, by way of the following:*
  (i) *common shares (description and number);*
  (ii) *preferred shares (description and number);*
  (iii) *long term debt (description);*
  (iv) *cash; and*
  (v) *other consideration (description);*

(f) *description and amount of any contingent consideration.* (April, 1975)

3-126. This Paragraph also notes that information relating to a number of relatively minor acquisitions may be combined for disclosure purposes.

Purchase Method Example

Example

3-127. The preceding material has provided a discussion and description of the various procedures that are required in the application of the purchase method of accounting for business combinations. The example which follows will serve to illustrate the application of these procedures.

On December 31, 1998, the Balance Sheets of the Dor and Dee Companies, prior to any business combination transaction, are as follows:

Balance Sheets
As At December 31, 1998

	Dor Company	Dee Company
Cash	$ 1,200,000	$ 600,000
Accounts Receivable	2,400,000	800,000
Inventories	3,800,000	1,200,000
Plant And Equipment (Net)	4,600,000	2,400,000
Total Assets	$12,000,000	$5,000,000
Liabilities	$ 1,500,000	$ 700,000
Common Stock - No Par*	6,000,000	2,500,000
Retained Earnings	4,500,000	1,800,000
Total Equities	$12,000,000	$5,000,000

*On this date, prior to the transactions described in the following paragraphs, each Company has 450,000 common shares outstanding.

On December 31, 1998, the Dor Company issues 204,000 shares of its No Par Common Stock to the Dee Company in return for 100 percent of its net identifiable assets. On this date the shares of the Dor Company are trading at $25 per share. All of the identifiable assets and liabilities of the Dee Company have fair values that are equal to their carrying values except for the Plant And Equipment which has a fair value of $2,700,000 and a remaining useful life of ten years.

Identification Of An Acquirer

3-128. Since the Dor Company issued fewer shares to the Dee Company than it had outstanding prior to the business combination, the shareholders of the Dor Company would be the majority shareholders in the combined company and the Dor Company would be identified as the acquirer.

Determination Of Purchase Price

3-129. With a market value of $25 per share, the 204,000 shares issued to effect the business combination would have a total market value in the amount of $5,100,000. This would be the purchase price of the Dee Company.

Investment Analysis Schedule

3-130. Whenever the purchase method of accounting for business combination transactions is used, it will be necessary to allocate the cost of the purchase to the fair values of identifiable assets and liabilities and to establish a value for either a positive or negative value for goodwill. As a common legal form for such purchase transactions is the acquisition of shares of a subsidiary, this analysis and allocation of the investment cost will continue to be required any time that we are preparing consolidated financial statements. This means that we will be involved with this process throughout the remainder of this text.

3-131. In a simple problem such as the one under consideration, there is little need to have detailed schedules or procedures to carry out this process. The fair values of the Dee Company's net identifiable assets would be calculated as follows:

Carrying Values - Dee's Net Assets ($5,000,000 - $700,000)	$4,300,000
Fair Value Change On Plant ($2,700,000 - $2,400,000)	300,000
Fair Values - Dee's Net Assets	$4,600,000

3-132. Given the purchase price and the fair values, the Goodwill that will be recognized from this business combination can be calculated in the following manner:

Purchase Price	$5,100,000
Fair Values - Dee's Net Assets	(4,600,000)
Goodwill To Be Recognized	$ 500,000

3-133. In subsequent Chapters we will be dealing with more complex examples, in some cases involving a large number of fair value changes. The calculations are further complicated in that, in situations where the parent does not acquire 100 percent of the subsidiary's shares, only the parent's proportionate interest in the fair value changes will be recognized. This means that a more systematic approach to the investment analysis is required.

3-134. Different texts use a variety of approaches to this problem and any of these approaches will provide a correct solution. The investment analysis approach that we find to be effective can be described as follows:

- Subtract the subsidiary's book value (or, in those cases where the acquiring company purchases less than 100 percent of the subsidiary's shares, the investor's proportionate interest in this book value) from the cost of the investment. We will refer to the resulting balance as a differential (other terms used for this balance are "purchase price discrepancy" and "excess of cost over book value"). If it is a positive number, it indicates that the investor is paying more than his proportionate share of the subsidiary's book values and that there is a debit amount to be allocated. A negative number reflects a credit balance to be allocated. Note that, as the differential reflects the total of all fair value changes and goodwill to be recognized, a positive balance does not necessarily indicate the presence of goodwill.

- Once the differential has been established, we will then add or subtract the various fair value changes that have been determined for the subsidiary's identifiable assets. As a positive differential reflects a debit balance to be allocated, we will subtract any fair value changes which require allocation of debits (increase in assets or decreases in liabilities). Correspondingly, we will add any fair value changes that require credits (decreases in assets or increases in liabilities).

- The resulting balance will be allocated to goodwill if it is positive. If the balance is negative, it will be deducted from the identifiable non monetary assets.

3-135. Applying these rules to Dor Company's purchase of Dee Company's net assets results in the following schedule:

Investment Cost	$5,100,000
Book Value - Dee's Net Assets ($5,000,000 - $700,000)	(4,300,000)
Differential	$ 800,000
Fair Value Increase On Plant ($2,700,000 - $2,400,000)	(300,000)
Goodwill	$ 500,000

Journal Entry

3-136. Using the preceding investment analysis, we are now in a position to record the business combination. It would be recorded on the books of the Dor Company as a simple acquisition of net assets. Except for Dee's Plant And Equipment and the Goodwill to be recorded as a result of the business combination, the carrying values from the books of the Dee Company would be used. The entry is as follows:

Cash	$ 600,000	
Accounts Receivable	800,000	
Inventories	1,200,000	
Plant And Equipment	2,700,000	
Goodwill	500,000	
Liabilities		$ 700,000
Common Stock - No Par (Dor)		5,100,000

Combined Balance Sheet

3-137. The resulting Balance Sheet for the combined company as at December 31, 1998 would be as follows:

The Dor Company And Subsidiary
Balance Sheet
As At December 31, 1998

Cash ($1,200,000 + $600,000)	$ 1,800,000
Accounts Receivable ($2,400,000 + $800,000)	3,200,000
Inventories ($3,800,000 + $1,200,000)	5,000,000
Plant And Equipment ($4,600,000 + $2,700,000)	7,300,000
Goodwill	500,000
Total Assets	$17,800,000
Liabilities ($1,500,000 + $700,000)	$ 2,200,000
Common Stock - No Par ($6,000,000 + $5,100,000)	11,100,000
Retained Earnings (Dor's Only)	4,500,000
Total Equities	$17,800,000

Application Of The Pooling Of Interests Method

Valuation Of Assets And Liabilities

3-138.   We will now turn our attention to a fairly detailed look at the application of the pooling of interests method of accounting for business combinations. Given the view that this type of business combination does not give rise to a new basis of accountability for either company's net assets, we will find procedures here to be considerably less complex than they were in the application of purchase accounting.

3-139.   In the application of purchase accounting, the first two steps involved the determination of the purchase price and the allocation of this price to identifiable net assets and goodwill. These steps are not required here. Since there is no new basis of accountability for either company's net assets, these two steps can be ignored in the process of retaining old carrying values. This view is reflected in the *CICA Handbook* as follows:

> **Paragraph 1580.64**   *Where the pooling of interests method is used to account for a business combination, the combined company should reflect assets and liabilities at the values recorded by the combining companies. If adjustments have been made to put the accounting methods used by the combining companies on a common basis, such adjustments should be made retroactively and financial statements of the combined company presented for prior periods should be restated.* (April, 1974)

Expenses Related To The Combination

3-140.   Since under the pooling of interests concept, no acquisition of assets is involved, the costs that are directly related to effecting the combination would not be viewed as a part of the cost of any of the assets. Rather, such costs would be accounted for as a reduction in the capital of the combined company. This is noted as follows:

> **Paragraph 1580.72**   *Expenses directly incurred in effecting a business combination accounted for as a pooling of interests should be reflected as a capital transaction in the financial statements of the resulting combined company for the period in which such expenses are incurred.* (See "Capital Transactions", Section 3610) (April, 1974)

3-141.   While the preceding Recommendation makes it clear the direct costs of implementing the business combination must be deducted from the combined company's shareholders' equity, no guidance is provided on the specific accounts to be charged. Given the fact that contributed capital must be retained in the business and cannot form the basis of dividend payments, it would appear logical to deduct these costs from earned capital (retained earnings).

Reporting Operations

3-142.   The view that is inherent in the pooling of interests concept is that the two companies have, in effect, always been combined. This would call for retroactive treatment for the operating results of the combined company. This is noted in Paragraph 1580.69:

> **Paragraph 1580.69**   *In business combinations accounted for by the pooling of interests method, the results of operations for the period in which the combination occurs and for all prior periods should be reflected on a combined basis.* (April, 1974)

3-143.   In cases where a company's historical reporting extends beyond comparative statements for the current and preceding year — for example a ten year summary of selected financial information — this Recommendation would require all of this information to be restated on a combined basis.

Intercompany Transactions

3-144.   If the legal form of the business combination is such that the combining companies remain legally separate, there will continue to be intercompany transactions subsequent to the combination transactions. Under both the purchase method and the pooling of interests method, the effects of transactions between the combining companies subsequent to the combination would be removed from all accounts. However, for transactions between the two companies which took place prior to the combination, the purchase method would view them as arm's length transactions and would not adjust the combined company's accounts. In contrast, pooling of interests accounting is based on the concept that the two companies have always been combined and, as a consequence, the effects of both pre combination and post combination intercompany transactions would have to be eliminated. This is noted in the following Recommendation:

> **Paragraph 1580.70**   *The effect of intercompany transactions on assets, liabilities, retained earnings, revenue and expenses should be eliminated.* (April, 1974)

Depooling Transactions

3-145.   The retroactive approach would also apply in a depooling or a reversal of a pooling of interests transaction. This is noted as follows:

> **Paragraph 1580.74**   *Where the shares and/or assets of one of the combining companies are returned to its shareholders in substantially the same form as they were contributed to the combined company, the financial statements of the combined company should be restated to reflect the financial position and results of operations of the combining company as if the combination had not taken place.* (April, 1974)

Combinations Subsequent To The Balance Sheet Date

3-146.   If the combination transaction is consummated subsequent to the Balance Sheet date, financial statements will not be retroactively restated. However, disclosure will be required as specified in the following Recommendation:

> **Paragraph 1580.76**   *Where a pooling of interests is consummated subsequent to the fiscal year end of the combining companies but prior to issuance of their financial statements, the combination should be disclosed as a subsequent event in notes to the financial statements of the combining companies. Supplemental information should be provided to disclose the substance of the combination and the effects of the combination on reported financial position and results of operations.* (April, 1974)

Shareholders' Equity

General Rules

3-147.   The shareholders' equity for the combined company that would be consistent with the conceptual view that is inherent in the pooling of interests method of accounting for business combinations would simply be the sum of the shareholders' equities of the combining companies. This fact is reflected in the following Recommendation:

> **Paragraph 1580.67**   *Where the pooling of interests method is used to account for the business combination, the shareholders' equity of the combined company should be the sum of the shareholders' equities of the combining companies.* (April, 1974)

3-148. The preceding explains the obvious fact that, if the assets and liabilities of both of the combining companies are recorded at their respective book values, the shareholders' equity of the resulting combined company will have to equal the sum of the shareholders' equities of the combining companies. It does not, however, provide guidance as to how the total shareholders' equity balance should be allocated among the various possible components of this balance. The answer to this more difficult question will depend on whether the legal entity which survives the business combination has par value or no par value shares outstanding.

Par Value Shares

3-149. For corporations chartered under the *Canada Business Corporations Act* or under most Provincial Acts, the use of par value shares is prohibited. Par value shares, however, can still be used under several Provincial Acts. Therefore, the complications created by such shares in pooling of interests accounting will be covered. When par value shares are used, construction of the combined company's shareholders' equity in a pooling of interests transaction can be described in the following steps:

A. Determine the combined company's total shareholders' equity by summing the total shareholders' equity of the combining companies (quantity A). This total would have to be reduced for any unrealized intercompany profits that were present at the time of combination and for the direct costs of the combination transaction.

B. Determine the par value of the outstanding shares of the legally surviving company subsequent to the combination transaction (quantity B). This amount will be allocated to the par value account on the books of the combined company.

C. Subtract quantity B from quantity A. This balance will be allocated to the combined company's retained earnings and/or contributed surplus. In making this allocation, the procedures are as follows:

1. If the A minus B quantity is greater than the sum of the retained earnings of the combining companies, the excess will be allocated to contributed surplus and the retained earnings of the combined company will be equal to the sum of the retained earnings of the combining companies. Note again, however, that the total Retained Earnings would have to be reduced for unrealized intercompany profits and the direct costs of the business combination transaction.

2. If the A minus B quantity is less than the sum of the retained earnings of the combining companies, there will be no allocation to contributed surplus and the combined company's retained earnings will be limited to the excess of the combined company's total shareholders' equity over the amount allocated to par value. As in item C(1), the allocation to Retained Earnings would be reduced for unrealized intercompany profits and the direct costs of the business combination transaction.

Shares Without Par Value

3-150. Construction of the combined company's shareholders' equity in a pooling of interests transaction involving shares without par value shares can be described in the following steps:

A. The No Par Common Stock account of the combined company will be equal to the sum of the contributed capital accounts of the combining companies.

B. The retained earnings account of the combined company will be equal to the sum of the earned capital accounts of the combining companies. As in the par value case, the allocation to Retained Earnings would be reduced for unrealized intercompany profits and the direct costs of the business combination transaction.

3-151.   The procedures described in the preceding two paragraphs are consistent with the view of the nature of the business combination transaction that is inherent in the pooling of interests method. As with the purchase method, the application of these procedures may produce a shareholders' equity section that is in conflict with the requirements of corporate legislation. In this case, the legislative requirements would prevail with disclosure of the resulting differences.

Required Disclosure

3-152.   As was noted previously, for all business combinations, the combined entity is required to disclose the method of accounting used, the net assets brought into the combination, and the nature of the consideration used. As was the case in purchase accounting, a considerable amount of additional disclosure is required. These requirements are stated in Paragraph 1580.81 as follows:

> **Paragraph 1580.51**   *For a combination accounted for as a pooling of interests, information disclosed should include the following:*
>
> (a) *the name and a brief description of each company brought into the combination;*
>
> (b) *the percentage of each company's voting shares exchanged to effect the combination;*
>
> (c) *the method of accounting for the combination — that is, by the pooling of interests method;*
>
> (d) *date of combination;*
>
> (e) *net assets brought into the combination by each of the combining companies:*
>> (i)   *total assets at book value;*
>> (ii) *total liabilities at book value;*
>> (iii) *amount of non-controlling interest at book value;*
>
> (f) *the description, number and fair value of the combined company's voting shares held by the shareholders of each of the combining companies immediately after the combination; the description and fair value for each type of other consideration received by the shareholders of each of the combining companies;*
>
> (g) *the revenue, discontinued operations, extraordinary items and net income (after adjusting for intercompany transactions) of each of the combining companies and the non-controlling interest in the net income from the commencement of the fiscal period of the combined company to the date the combination is consummated. (April, 1975)*

Pooling Of Interests Method Example

Example

3-153.   The preceding material has provided a discussion and description of the various procedures that are required in the application of the pooling of interests method of accounting for business combinations. The example which follows will serve to illustrate the application of these procedures.

Example   On December 31, 1998, the Balance Sheets of the Bor and Bee Companies are as follows:

Balance Sheets
As At December 31, 1998

	Bor Company	Bee Company
Cash	$1,100,000	$ 900,000
Accounts Receivable	1,800,000	2,100,000
Inventories	2,700,000	3,400,000
Plant And Equipment (Net)	3,400,000	3,600,000
Total Assets	$9,000,000	$10,000,000
Liabilities	$1,800,000	$ 1,200,000
Common Stock - Par $10	4,000,000	4,500,000
Contributed Surplus	500,000	2,000,000
Retained Earnings	2,700,000	2,300,000
Total Equities	$9,000,000	$10,000,000

At this time, the Bor Company issues 400,000 of its Common Stock - Par $10 shares to the shareholders of the Bee Company in return for 100 percent of the outstanding shares of this latter company. At this time, the shares of the Bor Company are trading at $45 per share while the shares of the Bee Company are trading at $40 per share. All of the identifiable assets and liabilities of both Companies have carrying values that are equal to their fair values except for the inventories of the Bor Company which have a fair value of $3,000,000 and the Plant And Equipment of the Bee Company which has a fair value of $2,800,000. The direct costs of implementing the business combination transaction amount to $100,000.

Identification Of An Acquirer

3-154.   Since the Bor Company issued 400,000 of its shares to the shareholders of the Bee Company, both groups of shareholders now have exactly one half of the outstanding shares in the combined company. In the absence of other considerations, pooling of interests accounting would be appropriate.

Investment Analysis

3-155.   Given the fact that pooling of interests accounting can be used for this business combination, the information on the per share market prices and the fair values of the two companies is irrelevant. Therefore, no investment analysis is required. The Bor Company would record its investment in the Bee Company as an asset and the Bee Company will continue to carry on its separate legal existence as a subsidiary of the Bor Company.

Combined Shareholders' Equity

3-156.   The only possible complicating factor is the construction of the combined company's shareholders' equity. The total would be the sum of the shareholders' equities of the combining companies, less the $100,000 costs of combination, an amount of $15,900,000. Of this balance, $8,000,000 would be allocated to the Common Stock - Par $10 account, reflecting the fact that there are now 800,000 shares outstanding. This would leave $7,900,000 to be allocated to the combined Retained Earnings and the combined Contributed Surplus. Of this amount, $4,900,000 would be credited to the combined Retained Earnings (the sum of the combining companies' Retained Earnings, less the $100,000 costs of combination) and the balance of $3,000,000 would go to the combined Contributed Surplus.

Combined Balance Sheet

3-157.   The consolidated Balance Sheet as at December 31, 1998 would largely involve adding the accounts of the two Companies in the following manner:

The Bor Company And Subsidiary
Consolidated Balance Sheet
As At December 31, 1998

Cash ($1,100,000 + $900,000 - $100,000)	$ 1,900,000
Accounts Receivable ($1,800,000 + $2,100,000)	3,900,000
Inventories ($2,700,000 + $3,400,000)	6,100,000
Plant And Equipment ($3,400,000 + $3,600,000)	7,000,000
Total Assets	$18,900,000

Liabilities ($1,800,000 + $1,200,000)	$ 3,000,000
Common Stock - Par $10 (800,000 Shares)	8,000,000
Contributed Surplus (See Explanation In Text)	3,000,000
Retained Earnings (Sum Of Bee And Bor, Less $100,000)	4,900,000
Total Equities	$18,900,000

Additional Readings

3-158.   The following readings may be of interest to those wishing to pursue the issues that were discussed in this Chapter. You may also wish to consult the Additional Readings provided at the end of Chapters 2 and 4.

CA Magazine Article   "Accounting Options For Section 85 Rollovers", James M. Sylph and Eric G. Percival, July, 1981.

CA Magazine Article   "Push Down Accounting: Is The U.S. Lead Worth Following?", James M. Sylph, October, 1985.

CA Magazine Article   "Consolidated Effort", Peter Martin, October, 1991.

CA Magazine Article   "The Goodwill Game", Tony Brookes, March, 1995.

International Accounting Standard No. 22   *Accounting For Business Combinations*, November, 1983 (Revised In 1993).

Journal Of Accountancy Article   "Business Combinations: Some Unresolved Issues", Enrico Petri and Clyde P. Stickney, April, 1982.

Journal Of Accountancy Article   "Push-Down Accounting: Pros and Cons", Michael E. Cunningham, June, 1984.

Journal Of Accountancy Article   "Allocating Purchase Price In An Acquisition: A Practical Guide", Stephen L. Key and Simon S. Strauss, November, 1987.

Journal Of Accountancy Article   "LBO Accounting: Unveiling The Mystery Of Carryover Basis", Jerry Gorman, October, 1988.

Journal Of Accountancy Article   "Consolidations: An Overview Of The FASB Discussion Memorandum", Paul Pacter, April, 1992.

Journal Of Accountancy Article   "Goodwill Accounting: Time For An Overhaul", Michael Davis, June, 1992.

Supplement To Chapter Three - Other Emerging Issues Committee Abstracts

Introduction

3-159.   Given the complexity that can be associated with business combination transactions, it is not surprising that a large number of issues related to this area have turned up on the agenda of the Emerging Issues Committee (EIC). As noted in Chapter 2, some users of this text do not wish to have comprehensive coverage of the issues dealt with by this Committee. While it is clear that some of this Committee's Abstracts are of considerable significance (e.g., EIC 10 which is the only source of guidance for reverse takeovers), other are not of general interest.

3-160.   As was the case in Chapter 2, we have dealt with this situation by integrating only what we believe to be the more important of these Abstracts into the text material of Chapter 3. The remaining Abstracts related to business combination transactions are summarized in this Supplement to the Chapter.

Interest Capitalization - EIC Abstract No. 12

3-161.   A problem related to establishing the purchase cost in a business combination transaction involves situations in which the acquirer establishes control over an extended period of time. An acquirer may either choose to or be forced to establish a controlling interest in a gradual manner over a period of time which may encompass more than a single accounting period. This possibility has resulted in two issues being presented to the Emerging Issues Committee. As described in EIC Abstract No. 12, "Capitalization Of Interest Costs On Investments In Potential Takeover Targets", they are:

- Is it permissible to capitalize interest on financing required to acquire control over a period of time?

- If it is permissible, what is the period during which interest may be capitalized and what criteria should be applied in determining how much interest can be capitalized?

3-162.   The Committee notes that the *CICA Handbook* does not currently provide comprehensive guidance on the capitalization of interest. Further, there is no established tradition of allowing interest to be capitalized as an element of the cost of a takeover. Given these facts, the Committee concludes that it would not be appropriate to capitalize interest costs on investments in takeover targets. In view of the Committee's consensus on this issue, there is no need to address the questions of over what period interest can be capitalized or how much interest can be added to the cost of an acquired company.

Adjustments To Purchase Price - EIC Abstract No. 14

3-163.   While financial reporting considerations require the timely completion of financial statements, there is often considerable uncertainty associated with the values to be assigned to assets and liabilities in a business combination transaction accounted for by the purchase method. This has led the Emerging Issues Committee to issue EIC Abstract No. 14, "Adjustments To The Purchase Equation Subsequent To The Acquisition Date". This Abstract considers the following two issues:

- Is it appropriate to adjust a previously reported purchase price allocation in a business combination accounted for by the purchase method? If so, under what circumstances would it be appropriate?

- If adjustments to the purchase price allocation are considered to be appropriate, should there be a limited defined allocation period during which adjustments can be made? If so, how long should it be?

3-164.   With respect to the first issue, the Committee points out that it is generally inappropriate to make adjustments to the amounts allocated to the assets and liabilities of the acquired company. Such adjustments should only be made in unusual circumstances. If the complexity or timing of the transaction is such that it is impractical to complete the allocation process in a satisfactory manner, it is acceptable to prepare statements based on the best allocation available and, if required, adjust the allocation at a later date. In no case should such adjustments be treated retroactively.

3-165. Subsequent to acquisition, the acquired company may be required to make adjustments to its financial statements for prior period adjustments or the correction of errors. Such adjustments in the records of the acquiree should not result in adjustments to the allocation of the purchase price. However, if, in the allocation process, the acquiring company makes an error as described in Section 1506 of the *CICA Handbook*, the necessary correction should be made retroactively.

3-166. With respect to the second issue, the Committee does not believe that there should be a defined period for the making of adjustments. In most cases, the necessary allocation can be made within the period of acquisition. If this is not the case, the Committee believes that the financial statements of the period should disclose that the amounts assigned to assets and liabilities acquired may be subject to later adjustments. This disclosure should identify the particular assets and liabilities subject to adjustment and, where possible, the nature of the possible adjustments. The Committee also indicates that, only in the most unusual circumstances, can a period of more than one year after the date of acquisition be justified for completing the allocation process.

3-167. In those circumstances where it is necessary to make adjustments of allocation values, the Committee believes that the financial statements of all previously reported periods should be restated on a retroactive basis.

Assets Held For Disposal - EIC Abstract No. 41

3-168. When two companies are combined, it is likely that there will be some duplication of productive assets. Management will normally plan to dispose of such redundant assets and, as a consequence, there is some question as to the accounting procedures to be applied to these assets. The Emerging Issues Committee has dealt with these issues in EIC Abstract No. 41, "Presentation Of Assets And Liabilities Held For Disposal". The specific issues dealt with in this Abstract are:

- May the liabilities that are expected to be assumed by a purchaser or that are expected to be discharged from the proceeds of the sale be offset against the assets held for disposal?

- May assets that were previously classified as non current assets be classified as current assets as a result of adopting the plan of disposal?

3-169. With respect to disclosure of liabilities, the Committee indicates that the expectation that liabilities are to be assumed by a purchaser or to be discharged from the proceeds of the sale does not justify offsetting the liabilities against the assets held for disposal. The liabilities are still obligations of the acquiree and should be so disclosed.

3-170. On the second issue, the Committee reached a consensus that assets that are to be disposed of should generally not be reclassified as current assets. The exception to this would be when the entity has actually sold them prior to the completion of the financial statements and the proceeds of the sale will be realized within a year from the Balance Sheet date, or within the normal operating cycle where that is longer than a year. If this exception applies and certain assets are reclassified as current, any liabilities to be assumed by the purchaser or required to be discharged on disposal of the assets should be classified as current liabilities.

Direct Costs Of Combination - EIC Abstract No. 42

3-171. While capitalization of the direct costs of implementing business combination transactions is a very straightforward concept, it appears that there have been problems in its implementation. Various policies have been followed as to which costs can be capitalized as part of the purchase cost and which costs must be charged to expense as incurred. In particular, there are problems associated with dealing with restructuring and integration costs that are only planned at the time of the combination transaction. As a consequence, the Emerging Issues Committee has issued Abstract No. 42, "Costs Incurred On Business Combinations". This Abstract elaborates on the general principle by noting that direct expenses consist of incremental costs incurred to acquire control of the business. This would include finders fees and other amounts paid to lawyers, accountants, appraisers, and other consultants. Excluded would be all allocations of internal costs, including the costs of maintaining an acquisitions department.

3-172.   With respect to planned restructuring and integration costs, the Committee reached a consensus that they may be included in the purchase price only when:

(a) the costs are directly related to the acquisition and are incremental (i.e., they would not be incurred without the acquisition);

(b) the costs form part of a program defined at the time of the acquisition;

(c) the costs are specified in a reasonable level of detail at the time the purchase price is allocated; and

(d) (i)   the costs relate to the acquired business, or

(ii)   the costs relate to the acquiring entity and are:

- direct substitutes for costs that would otherwise be incurred with respect to the acquired business. Costs would be considered direct substitutes if they are similar in nature and relate to similar functions or similar lines of business, or

- incurred as a result of the intervention of a government regulator or similar body.

3-173.   The discussion in the Abstract emphasizes that only the costs that would not be incurred without the acquisition are eligible for capitalization. The Committee also notes that establishing a restructuring program and setting out the detail of costs to be incurred provides an appropriate basis for recording such amounts as part of the purchase price and the related liability. This is of particular importance in view of the fact that EIC Abstract No. 14 generally discourages adjustments to the initial allocation of the purchase price.

3-174.   With respect to criteria (d) for the recognition of planned restructuring costs as assets, the Committee notes that most of the costs that will be included in the purchase price will relate to the operations of the acquired business. However, this will not always be the case. For example, an acquirer may plan to keep operating only eight of the combined company's ten existing plants. If management decides that it would be best to close one of the acquirer's plants, this can be considered a direct substitute for closing an acquiree's plant. As a consequence, the cost of closing this plant can be considered a direct cost to be capitalized.

3-175.   The Committee also points out that, whenever planned restructuring and integration costs are included in the purchase price in a business combination transaction, the amounts should be disclosed in reasonable detail in the notes to the financial statements.

Identifiable Assets Acquired In A Business Combination - EIC Abstract No. 55

3-176.   This EIC Abstract is concerned largely with situations in which the acquiree has chosen to capitalize research and development expenditures. Provided that these expenditures have a positive fair value, a problem arises when the accounting policies of the acquirer are such that the costs that were capitalized by the acquiree would have been charged to expense by the acquiree. This is, of course, only a problem when the business combination has been classified as a purchase transaction.

3-177.   The specific issues dealt with in EIC No. 55 are as follows:

1.   Should the acquiring entity include the fair value of all identifiable assets in determining the allocation of the cost of the purchase even if, under its own accounting policy, some of those costs would be expensed immediately if incurred directly?

2.   How should the acquiring entity account for such assets on acquisition?

3-178.   With respect to the first issue, the Committee reached a consensus that, on the acquisition of another business, the acquiring entity should, in complying with Section 1580 of the *CICA Handbook*, include the fair value of all identifiable assets in determining the allocation of the cost of the purchase even if, under its own accounting policy, some of those costs would be expensed immediately if incurred directly.

3-179.   On the issue of how to subsequently account for these capitalized costs, the Committee reached a consensus that the acquiring entity should reflect, as assets on its Balance Sheet, the portion of the cost of the purchase which it allocates to acquired identifiable assets and that, in the absence of specifically identifiable changes in circumstances, the carrying amount of such assets would not be immediately written down.

3-180.   The Committee also noted that the accounting treatment described in this Abstract can be applied prospectively.

Goodwill Disclosure - EIC Abstract No. 64

3-181.   This Abstract, issued on August 21, 1995, is applicable to entities that have goodwill recorded in their financial statements. It deals with two issues that arise with respect to such goodwill balances. These are:

1.   Should the entity disclose how it determines whether there is a permanent impairment in value of the unamortized portion of goodwill?

2.   What disclosures should the entity make when it recognizes a write down of the unamortized portion of goodwill?

3-182.   With respect to the first issue, the Committee notes that Section 1505, "Disclosure Of Accounting Policies", requires disclosure of an entity's significant accounting policies. The Committee believes that disclosure of methods for determining whether there has been a permanent impairment of goodwill is a significant policy. This information provides financial statement users with an understanding of the criteria used by the entity to assess whether a write down is necessary and also provides information to assist users in assessing the likelihood of future impairment of goodwill. Based on this analysis, the Committee indicates that an entity should disclose how it determines whether there is a permanent impairment in the unamortized balance of goodwill, even if no impairment exists. They also note that the approach used should be applied consistently from period to period.

3-183.   With respect to the second issue, the Committee reached a consensus that, if an entity recognizes a write down of the unamortized portion of goodwill, it should disclose the following:

- the amount of the write down;
- the reason for the write down, including a description of the events or changes in circumstances that caused the permanent impairment;
- the identity of the business to which the permanent impairment relates; and
- a description of how the amount of the permanent impairment was determined, including whether discounting was used.

3-184.   It is noted that a write down may require a review of the amortization period applicable to any remaining balance of goodwill. The Committee also notes that conclusions reached in this Abstract apply to goodwill that is included in the carrying value of investments accounted for by the equity method.

Transfer Of A Business Between Entities Under Common Control - EIC Abstract No. 66

3-185. This EIC Abstract deals with a situation in which two business entities that are under common control exchange control of another business. For example, a subsidiary of a particular parent company sells the assets of its manufacturing division to another subsidiary of its parenty company. This is a related party transaction and the acquiring company concludes (see Paragraph 3840.26) that, because the transaction represents the culmination of an earnings process, it should be recorded at exchange value. The issue here is how should the acquiring entity account for the transaction?

3-186. The Committee reached a consensus that the acquiring entity should account for the acquired business in the same manner as a business combination accounted for by the purchase method. For purposes of applying these paragraphs, the exchange amount is used to determine the cost of the purchase.

Buy Out Transactions - EIC Abstract No. 73

3-187. The issue dealt with here arises when a group of investors form a company (Company A) for the sole purpose of facilitating the acquisition of control of another company (Company B) through an arm's-length transaction (neither Company A's investors nor Company A are related to Company B's investors or Company B before the acquisition of control). Company A arranges financing and makes an offer for the common shares of Company B but undertakes no other activities and holds no other assets. Company A acquires a controlling interest in Company B but not all or virtually all of its common shares. The issue is how should the acquiring company, Company A, account for the transaction?

3-188. The Committee reached a consensus that Company A should account for the transaction by applying the purchase method of accounting. Company A would allocate the fair value of the consideration paid to the assets and liabilities of Company B based on their fair values at the date of the acquisition and consolidate Company B. The non-controlling interest in Company B reported in the consolidated financial statements would be based on the carrying values recorded in Company B's accounting records.

3-189. While noting that the assets, liabilities and operations of Company A on a consolidated basis are substantially the same as those of Company B, the Committee viewed the transaction as an acquisition of Company B's assets and liabilities by another entity as a result of an arm's-length transaction. The Committee concluded that the users of Company A's consolidated financial statements are better informed about its financial position and results of operations when its assets and liabilities are measured on the basis of their cost to Company A. In support of its position, the Committee noted that, if Company A had acquired significant influence but not control over Company B, it would measure its investment initially at the fair value of the consideration paid and apply the equity method of accounting subsequently, with the result that its earnings would be determined on the same basis as if it had consolidated Company B in accordance with the consensus set out above.

3-190. The Committee also noted that CICA 1625 could be applied in the type of transaction described above only if Company A had acquired all or virtually all of the equity interests in Company B and Company B elected to apply push-down accounting to its financial statements. Otherwise, Company B would not change the basis of measuring its assets and liabilities in its own financial statements.

Fair Value Of Shares Issued As Consideration In A Purchase Business Combination - EIC Abstract No. 76

3-191. This EIC Abstract deals with two issues related to situations in which shares are issued as consideration in a business combination transaction. The issues, along with the conclusions reached by the Committee, are as follows:

Issue One   When should the acquirer use quoted market prices for the class of shares issued in the business combination as the basis for determining the fair value of the shares issued?

Consensus   The Committee reached a consensus that the acquirer should use quoted market prices for the class of shares issued in the business combination as the basis for determining the fair value of the shares issued unless:

(a) the market for the class of shares issued is inactive or illiquid; or
(b) the shares issued to effect the business combination are subject to significant restrictions preventing them from being traded for some time following their issuance.

When quoted market prices cannot be used, fair values will have to be determined directly for the various assets acquired and liabilities assumed.

Issue Two   How should the acquirer determine the fair value of shares issued to effect a purchase business combination when the market for the class of shares is active and liquid and the shares are not subject to significant restrictions preventing them from being traded for some time following their issuance?

Consensus   The Committee reached a consensus that, when the market for the class of shares issued to effect a purchase business combination is active and liquid and the shares issued are not subject to significant restrictions preventing them from being traded for some time following their issuance, the acquirer should determine the fair value of the shares by:

(a) establishing an average of quoted market prices for shares of the same class over a reasonable period before and after the date of acquisition; and
(b) reducing the average quoted market price of the shares for the transaction costs incurred to issue them.

The acquirer would not make other types of adjustment to quoted market prices in determining the fair value of its shares.

Transaction costs that may be incurred to issue shares commonly include fees and commissions paid to underwriters, dealers and agents, levies by regulatory agencies and stock exchanges, and taxes and duties. The acquirer would reduce the average quoted market price of its shares by the costs incurred to issue them. The acquirer may further reduce the average quoted market price by other transaction costs normally incurred when issuing shares for cash but avoided in the business combination.

The Committee noted that, when an acquirer in a business combination offers all sellers a substantially equivalent choice of shares or cash consideration, the cash price per share would establish the fair value of the acquirer's shares issued.

Problems For Self Study

(The solutions for these problems can be found following Chapter 17 of the text.)

SELF STUDY PROBLEM THREE - 1

On December 31, 1998, the Balance Sheets of the Graber and the Grabee Companies are as follows:

	Graber	Grabee
Cash	$ 50,000	$ 70,000
Accounts Receivable	250,000	330,000
Inventories	400,000	300,000
Plant and Equipment (Net)	1,200,000	600,000
Land	800,000	400,000
Goodwill	150,000	50,000
Total Assets	$2,850,000	$1,750,000
Current Liabilities	$ 75,000	$ 50,000
Long Term Liabilities	800,000	400,000
Future Income Tax Liabilities	200,000	100,000
Common Stock - Par $20	800,000	-0-
Common Stock - Par $100	-0-	560,000
Contributed Surplus	400,000	340,000
Retained Earnings	575,000	300,000
Total Equities	$2,850,000	$1,750,000

On December 31, 1998, the Graber Company issues 40,000 of its Par $20 common shares to the Grabee Company in return for 100 percent of its net assets. The December 31, 1998 market price of the Graber Company shares is $35 per share while the Grabee shares are trading at $250 per share on this date. After selling its net assets, the Grabee Company distributes the Graber shares to its shareholders in return for their shares. The Grabee shares are then cancelled and the Company ceases to exist as a separate legal entity. The direct expenses of carrying out this business combination transaction amount to $10,000 and are paid in cash.

Other Information

1. All of the net identifiable assets of the two Companies have fair values that are equal to their carrying values except for the Grabee Company's Goodwill and Deferred Taxes and the following other accounts:

	Fair Values	
	Graber	Grabee
Plant and Equipment (Net)	$1,800,000	$800,000
Land	1,000,000	300,000
Long Term Liabilities	750,000	450,000

2. The Net Income of the Graber Company for the year ending December 31, 1998 was $125,000 while that of the Grabee Company amounted to $200,000.

3. The 1998 Net Income of the Graber Company included a $20,000 gain resulting from the sale of land to the Grabee Company on July 8, 1998.

4. The 1998 Net Income of the Grabee Company included a $50,000 gain on sales of merchandise to the Graber Company. All of this merchandise remained in the December 31, 1998 Inventories of the Graber Company.

As the problem is designed to illustrate the concepts involved in accounting for business combinations, your solutions should be consistent with the concepts associated with these procedures and should ignore any effects that corporate legislation might have on the shareholders' equity of the combined company.

Required:

A. Assume that, because the directors and management of the Graber Company are unchanged after this business combination transaction, the Graber Company is identified as the acquirer. Prepare the combined company's Balance Sheet as at December 31, 1998 and calculate the combined company's Net Income and Basic Earnings Per Share for the year ending December 31, 1998.

B. Assume that neither Company can be identified as the acquirer. Prepare the combined company's Balance Sheet as at December 31, 1998 and the combined company's Net Income and Basic Earnings Per Share for the year ending December 31, 1998.

SELF STUDY PROBLEM THREE - 2

On December 31, 1998, the condensed Balance Sheets of the Ero Company and the Tick Company are as follows:

	Ero	Tick
Monetary Assets	$ 200,000	$1,000,000
Non Monetary Assets	3,800,000	4,000,000
Total Assets	$4,000,000	$5,000,000
Monetary Liabilities	$ 100,000	$ 800,000
Common Stock - Par $10	2,000,000	-0-
Common Stock - No Par	-0-	3,000,000
Contributed Surplus	500,000	-0-
Retained Earnings	1,400,000	1,200,000
Total Equities	$4,000,000	$5,000,000

On December 31, 1998, the Tick Company has 100,000 common shares outstanding. On that same date, the Monetary Assets and Liabilities of both Companies have fair values that are equal to their carrying values. The fair values of Ero's Non Monetary Assets are $400,000 greater than their carrying values while Tick's Non Monetary Assets are $600,000 less than their carrying values. For both Companies, the Non Monetary Assets have an estimated remaining useful life of 4 years. Any goodwill that is recognized in the business combination should be amortized over 20 years. Both Companies use the straight line method for all depreciation and amortization calculations.

The Net Income of the Ero Company for the year ending December 31, 1998 is $400,000 and the Net Income of the Tick Company for the year ending December 31, 1998 is $600,000. If there had been no business combination on December 31, 1998, the 1999 Net Income of Ero would have been $700,000 and that of Tick would have been $800,000. There are no intercompany transactions or dividends declared in 1998 or 1999.

These two Companies can effect a business combination by several different legal avenues. Each of the following cases assumes that one of these available avenues has been chosen and that a business combination takes place on December 31, 1998. The cases are completely independent and in selecting the accounting method to be used, assume that the Company whose shareholders have majority share ownership in the combined business entity is deemed to be the acquiring Company. As the problem is designed to illustrate the concepts involved in the application of purchase and pooling of interests accounting, your solutions should be consistent with the concepts associated with these procedures and should ignore any effects that corporate legislation might have on the shareholders' equity of the combined company.

A. Ero issues 100,000 of its shares to Tick in return for 100 percent of Tick's net assets. The shares of Tick are cancelled and Ero is the sole survivor of the combination. Ero shares are trading at $40 per share on this date.

B. Ero issues 200,000 of its shares to the shareholders of Tick in return for 100 percent of their outstanding shares. Tick continues to exist as a separate legal entity. At the date of combination, the shares of Ero are trading at $25 per share while those of Tick are trading at $50 per share.

C. Ero Company and Tick Company cease to exist as separate legal and economic entities. A new Company, the Erotick Company is formed which issues 300,000 shares without par value. Of these new shares, Tick receives 180,000 in return for 100 percent of its net assets and Ero receives 120,000 shares in return for 100 percent of its net assets. On the date of the combination, Ero shares are trading at $24 per share and Tick shares are trading at $72 per share.

D. A new Company is formed which acquires all of the net assets of Ero and Tick. This new Company, the Erotique Company, is authorized to issue shares without par value. It issues 50,000 shares of its stock to the Ero Company and 50,000 of its shares to the Tick Company. These shares of the Erotique Company trade at $120 per share immediately after the combination.

Required: For each of the preceding cases, prepare the appropriate combined Balance Sheet as at December 31, 1998. In addition, compute Net Income and Basic Earnings Per Share figures for the business entity resulting from the combination for both 1998 and 1999.

Assignment Problems And Cases

(The solutions to these problem are only available in
the solutions manual that has been provided to your instructor.)

ASSIGNMENT PROBLEM THREE - 1

On December 31, 1998, the condensed Balance Sheets of the Hyper Company and the
Tension Company are as follows:

	Hyper	Tension
Monetary Assets	$1,400,000	$ 800,000
Non Monetary Assets	4,600,000	2,200,000
Total Assets	$6,000,000	$3,000,000
Monetary Liabilities	$ 500,000	$ 200,000
Common Stock - Par $20	2,000,000	-0-
Common Stock - Par $75	-0-	750,000
Contributed Surplus	1,000,000	1,250,000
Retained Earnings	2,500,000	800,000
Total Equities	$6,000,000	$3,000,000

(Handwritten annotations: "4,000,000" next to Non Monetary Assets Hyper; "2,000,000" next to Tension; "400,000" next to Monetary Liabilities Hyper; "250,000" next to Tension)

The Monetary Assets of both Companies have fair values that are equal to their carrying
values. The fair value of the Hyper Company's Non Monetary Assets is $4 million and the
fair value of its Monetary Liabilities is $400,000. The fair value of the Tension Company's
Non-monetary Assets is $2 million and the fair value of its Monetary Liabilities is
$250,000.

These two Companies can effect a business combination by several different legal avenues. Each of the following cases assumes that one of these available avenues has been
chosen and that a business combination takes place on December 31, 1998. The cases
are completely independent and in selecting the accounting method to be used, assume
that the Company whose shareholders have majority share ownership in the combined
business entity is deemed to be the acquiring Company. As the problem is designed to illustrate the concepts involved in the application of purchase and pooling of interests accounting, your solutions should be consistent with the concepts associated with these
procedures and should ignore any effects that corporate legislation might have on the
shareholders' equity of the combined company.

A. The Hyper Company issues 70,000 of its shares in return for the net assets of the Tension Company. The shares of Tension are cancelled and Tension ceases to exist as a
separate legal entity. At the date of the combination the shares of the Hyper Company
are trading at $45 per share.

B. The Tension Company issues 10,000 of its shares in return for the net assets of the Hyper Company. The shares of the Hyper Company are cancelled and Hyper ceases to
exist as a separate legal entity. At the date of the combination the shares of the Hyper
Company are trading at $60 per share and Tension Company's shares are trading at
$600 per share.

C. The Tension Company issues 15,000 of its shares in return for the net assets of the Hyper Company. The shares of the Hyper Company are cancelled and the Hyper
Company ceases to exist as a separate legal entity. At the date of the combination the
shares of the Hyper Company are trading at $75 per share and the shares of the Ten-
sion Company are trading at $500 per share.

D. A new Company, the Hypertension Company, is formed. This new Company issues

15,000 no par value shares to the Hyper Company in return for all of its net assets and 10,000 no par value shares to the Tension Company in return for all of its net assets. Both the Hyper Company and the Tension Company distribute the Hypertension Company shares to their shareholders in return for all of their outstanding shares. The Hyper Company and Tension Company shares are cancelled and the two Companies cease to exist as separate legal entities. At the date of the combination the Hyper Company shares are trading at $90 per share and the Tension Company shares are trading at $600 per share.

Required: For each of the preceding cases, prepare the appropriate combined Balance Sheet as at December 31, 1998.

ASSIGNMENT PROBLEM THREE - 2

On December 31, 1998, the condensed Balance Sheets of the Gold Company and the Medal Company are as follows:

	Gold	Medal
Monetary Assets	$ 500,000	$ 300,000
Non Monetary Assets	5,500,000	3,200,000
Total Assets	$6,000,000	$3,500,000
Monetary Liabilities	$ 300,000	$ 100,000
Common Stock - Par $30	3,000,000	-0-
Common Stock - Par $10	-0-	1,000,000
Contributed Surplus	1,200,000	1,000,000
Retained Earnings	1,500,000	1,400,000
Total Equities	$6,000,000	$3,500,000

During 1998, the Net Income of the Gold Company was $1 million while the Net Income of the Medal Company was $200,000. For 1999, if we assume that there is no business combination on December 31, 1998, the corresponding Net Income figures would be $1.5 million and $500,000. No dividends were paid by either Company in 1998 or 1999. No intercompany transactions occurred during 1999.

The Monetary Assets and Liabilities of both Companies have fair values that are equal to their carrying values. The fair values of the Non-monetary Assets are $6 million for Gold and $3 million for Medal. The Non-monetary Assets consist of Plant And Equipment with an estimated useful life of 5 years with no anticipated net salvage value. Any goodwill that is recognized in the business combination transaction should be amortized over 40 years. Both Companies use the straight line method for all depreciation and amortization calculations.

On December 31, 1998, there are several different legal avenues that the two Companies can use to effect a business combination. Four different possibilities are as follows:

A. Medal issues 90,000 of its shares in return for the net assets of Gold. At the date of the combination the shares of Medal are trading at $65 per share. Gold continues to exist as a separate legal entity.

B. Gold issues 80,000 of its shares in return for the net assets of Medal. The shares of Medal are cancelled and Medal ceases to exist as a legal entity. At the date of the combination the shares of Gold are trading at $50 per share.

C. A new Company, the Goldmedal Company, is formed and issues 50,000 no par value common shares to Gold in return for all of its net assets and 30,000 shares to Medal in return for all of its net assets. The Gold Company and the Medal Company distribute the Goldmedal shares to their shareholders and cease to exist as separate legal and economic entities. At the date of the combination the Gold Company shares are trading at $75 and the Medal Company shares are trading at $45 per share.

D. Medal issues 100,000 shares to the shareholders of Gold Company in return for all of their outstanding shares. The shares of Gold are cancelled and Gold ceases to exist as a legal entity. At the date of the combination the shares of Gold are trading at $50 and the shares of Medal are trading at $90.

Required: For each of the preceding independent cases, prepare the combined Balance Sheet as at December 31, 1998. In addition, compute Net Income and Earnings Per Share figures for the business entity resulting from the combination for both the year ending December 31, 1998 and the year ending December 31, 1999. In selecting the accounting method to be used, assume that the Company whose shareholders have majority ownership in the combined business entity is deemed to be the acquiring Company.

ASSIGNMENT PROBLEM THREE - 3

On December 31, 1998, the assets and liabilities of the Davis Company and the Jones Company have fair values and book values as follows:

	The Davis Company		The Jones Company	
	Book Value	Fair Value	Book Value	Fair Value
Cash	$ 450,000	$ 450,000	$ 375,000	$ 375,000
Accounts Receivable	560,000	545,000	420,000	405,000
Inventories	1,200,000	1,150,000	875,000	950,000
Net Plant And Equipment	2,800,000	3,200,000	1,450,000	1,250,000
Goodwill	-0-	-0-	125,000	-0-
Total Assets	$5,010,000	$5,345,000	$3,245,000	$2,980,000
Current Liabilities	$ 325,000	$ 325,000	$ 295,000	$ 295,000
Bonds Payable	1,200,000	1,400,000	870,000	910,000
Future Income Tax Liability	780,000	N/A	430,000	N/A
No Par Common Stock	2,100,000	N/A	1,200,000	N/A
Retained Earnings	605,000	N/A	450,000	N/A
Total Equities	$5,010,000		$3,245,000	

On December 31, 1998, the Davis Company issues 30,000 shares of its No Par Common Stock in return for all of the assets and liabilities of the Jones Company. On this date the Davis Company shares are trading at $65 per share while the Jones Company shares are trading at $32.50 per share.

Other Information:

1. The No Par Common Stock of the Davis Company consists of 42,000 shares issued at an average price of $50 per share. The No Par Common Stock of the Jones Company consists of 60,000 shares issued at an average price of $20 per share.

2. The Jones Company has an unrecognized loss carry forward of $300,000. Both Companies are subject to a combined provincial and federal tax rate of 40 percent. The two Companies feel that there is reasonable assurance that the carry forward benefit will be realized if they are brought together in a business combination transaction.

Required: Prepare the December 31, 1998 Balance Sheet that would be required for the combined company resulting from the business combination transaction.

ASSIGNMENT PROBLEM THREE - 4

As at December 31, 1998, the condensed Balance Sheets of the Monson, Barrister, and Flex Companies, are as follows:

Monson Ltd.

	Values	Fair Values
Current Assets	$ 24,200	$ 25,000
Non Current Assets	186,500	193,200
Total Assets	$210,700	
Liabilities	$ 78,400	$ 75,600
No Par Common Stock (11,000 Shares)	93,500	
Retained Earnings	38,800	
Total Equities	$210,700	

Barrister Ltd.

	Values	Fair Values
Current Assets	$ 35,800	$ 34,500
Non Current Assets	220,600	168,400
Total Assets	$256,400	
Liabilities	$ 56,300	$ 58,200
No Par Common Stock (5,500 Shares)	66,000	
Retained Earnings	134,100	
Total Equities	$256,400	

Flex Ltd.

	Values	Fair Values
Current Assets	$ 46,300	$ 47,300
Non Current Assets	152,200	156,600
Total Assets	$198,500	
Liabilities	$ 62,400	$ 59,800
No Par Common Stock (18,000 Shares)	45,000	
Retained Earnings	91,100	
Total Equities	$198,500	

The three companies intend to combine their activities and are considering a variety of approaches. Four possible approaches are as follows:

Approach One   Flex Ltd. would borrow $303,000. Using the loan proceeds, Flex Ltd. would pay cash of $160,000 to Monson Ltd. and cash of $143,000 to Barrister Ltd., in return for all of the assets and liabilities of the two companies. There will be a wind up of the operations of both Monson Ltd. and Barrister Ltd. The business combination will be accounted for by the purchase method.

Approach Two Barrister Ltd. would borrow $326,000. Using the loan proceeds, Barrister Ltd. would pay cash of $170,000 to the shareholders of Monson Ltd. and cash of $156,000 to the shareholders of Flex Ltd., in return for all of the outstanding shares of these two companies. The business combination will be accounted for by the purchase method.

Approach Three Monson Ltd. will issue 11,000 new common shares to the shareholders of Barrister Ltd. and 11,000 new common shares to the shareholders of Flex Ltd. In return, Monson Ltd. will receive all of the outstanding common shares of these two companies. At this time, the common stock of Monson Ltd. is trading at $12.25 per share. The business combination will be accounted for by the pooling of interests method.

Approach Four Monson Ltd. will issue 11,000 new common shares to Barrister Ltd. and 11,000 new common shares to Flex Ltd. In return, Monson Ltd. will receive all of the assets and liabilities of the two companies. There would be a wind up of the activities of the two companies. At this time, the common stock of Monson Ltd. is trading at $13.50 per share. As neither Barrister Ltd. nor Flex Ltd. are given representation on the Monson Ltd. Board Of Directors, the business combination will be accounted for by the purchase method.

Required: Prepare the December 31, 1998 Balance Sheet for the combined company that would result from each of the four approaches described.

ASSIGNMENT PROBLEM THREE - 5

On December 31, 1998, Public Ltd. acquires all of the oustanding shares of Private Inc. The consideration consists of 100,000 Public Ltd. shares plus $1,200,000 in cash. At the time of issue, the Public Ltd. shares are trading at $10.50. As part of the acquisition contract, Public Ltd. agrees that, if by the end of 1999 their shares are not trading at a price of $12.00 or more, it will pay an additional $150,000 in cash to the former shareholders of Private Inc.

On December 31, 1998, the pre business combination Balance Sheets of the two Companies are as follows:

	Public Ltd.	Private Inc.
Cash	$1,892,000	$ 342,000
Accounts Receivable	767,000	-0-
Inventories	1,606,000	641,000
Land	462,000	107,000
Plant And Equipment - Cost	3,272,000	2,727,000
Accumulated Depreciation	(1,203,000)	(776,000)
Patent	-0-	103,000
Goodwill	372,000	100,000
Total Assets	$7,168,000	$3,244,000
Current Liabilities	$ 458,000	$ -0-
Bonds Payable - Par	1,507,000	800,000
Bond Payable - Premium	48,000	23,000
Public Common Stock - No Par (250,000 Shares)	2,500,000	N/A
Private Common Stock - No Par	N/A	1,200,000
Retained Earnings	2,655,000	1,221,000
Total Equities	$7,168,000	$3,244,000

Other Information:

1. The stock of Public Ltd. is traded on a national stock exchange. As a consequence, they are required to prepare audited financial statements. Private Inc. is a Canadian controlled private corporation and has never needed audited financial statements.

2. As there has been no need for Private Inc. to comply with generally accepted accounting principles (GAAP), the Company records revenues and current expenses on a cash basis. After some investigation, it is determined that on January 1, 1998, Private Inc. had unrecorded Accounts Receivable of $220,000 and unrecorded Accounts Payable of $273,000. The corresponding balances on December 31, 1998 are $326,000 for Accounts Receivable and $473,000 for Accounts Payable.

3. Public Ltd. records Inventories at lower of cost and market. Private Inc.'s Inventories are carried at cost. On December 31, 1998, the net realizable value of Private Inc.'s Inventories was $607,000.

4. On December 31, 1998, the appraised value of Private Inc.'s Land was $93,000.

5. The December 31, 1998 fair value of Private Inc.'s Plant And Equipment is $2,103,000.

6. The Patent on Private Inc.'s books was purchased on January 1, 1993 and is being amortized over what was expected to be its useful life, ten years. However, the process that is covered by the Patent has been replaced by a less costly procedure, and is no longer used by the Company.

7. The Goodwill that is present on Private Inc.'s books arose when the owner of the Company noted that many other companies were showing Goodwill on their books. As a result he made an angry phone call to his accountant, stating that his Company had as much Goodwill as anyone else and demanding the immediate recording of at least $100,000. His accountant, not wishing to offend him, complied by recording the $100,000 in Goodwill and crediting Retained Earnings.

8. Private Inc.'s Bonds Payable were privately placed with a large Insurance Company. At current market rates of interest they have a present value of $790,000. However, they can only be retired by paying the Insurance Company a premium of 10 percent over their par value.

Required: Prepare the December 31, 1998 Balance Sheet for the combined companies Public Ltd. and its subsidiary, Private Inc. Ignore all tax considerations.

ASSIGNMENT CASE THREE - 1

The Haggard Corporation Limited (Haggard, hereafter), a federally chartered Canadian company, has concluded negotiations with the Jones Corporation Limited (Jones, hereafter) for the purchase of all of the latter corporation's assets at fair market value, effective January 1, 1998. An examination at that date by independent experts disclosed that the fair market value of Jones' inventories was $150,000, and of its machinery and equipment was $160,000. The original cost of the machinery and equipment was $140,000 and its undepreciated capital cost at December 31, 1997 was $110,000. It was determined that accounts receivable were fairly valued at book value.

Jones held 1,000 of the common shares of Haggard and the fair market value of these shares was $62,000. This value corresponds with the value of Haggard's common shares in the open market and would be expected to hold for transactions involving a substantially larger number of shares.

The purchase agreement provides that the total purchase price of all assets will be $490,000, payable as follows:

1. Assumption of the current liabilities of Jones at their book value;

2. Settlement of the Jones debenture debt at its current value in a form acceptable to Jones debenture holders;

3. Haggard shares held by Jones and acquired by Haggard as a result of the transaction would be subsequently returned to Jones at fair market value as part of the consideration;

4. Haggard holds 1,000 shares of Jones and these would be returned to Jones. The value to be ascribed to these shares is 1/10 of the difference between the total purchase price of all assets stated above ($490,000) less the current value of its liabilities.

5. The balance of the purchase consideration was to be entirely in Haggard common shares, except for a possible fractional share element which would be paid in cash.

The Jones debenture holders, who are neither shareholders of Haggard nor Jones, have agreed to accept Haggard bonds in an amount equal to the current value of the Jones debentures which are yielding 10 percent. The Haggard bonds carry a 12 percent coupon and trade at par. The face value of each bond is $1,000.

Jones, upon conclusion of the agreement, would be wound up. The Balance Sheets of both corporations, as at the date of implementation of the purchase agreement (January 1, 1998), are as follows:

Balance Sheets
As At January 1, 1998

	Haggard	Jones
Cash	$ 100,000	$ -0-
Accounts Receivable	288,000	112,000
Inventories At Cost	250,000	124,000
Investment In Jones (1,000 Shares)	20,000	-0-
Investment In Haggard (1,000 Shares)	-0-	40,000
Machinery And Equipment - Net	412,000	100,000
Total Assets	$1,070,000	$376,000
Current Liabilities	$ 60,000	$ 35,000
7% Percent Debentures - Due December 31, 2002 (Note One)	-0-	100,000
12% Percent Bonds - Due December 31, 2002 (Note One)	500,000	-0-
Premium On Bonds	20,000	-0-
Common Stock (Note Two)	200,000	100,000
Retained Earnings	290,000	141,000
Total Equities	$1,070,000	$376,000

Note One Interest is paid annually.

Note Two Each company has issued 10,000 shares.

Both corporations have fiscal years that are identical to the calendar year.

The present value of an annuity of $1 for 5 periods at 10 percent is $3.7908. The present value of $1 to be received at the end of 5 periods at 10 percent is $.6209.

Required:

A. Prepare Haggard's pro-forma Balance Sheet as at January 1, 1998.

B. Draft a note to the 1998 financial statements disclosing the purchase of Jones' net assets.

C. Indicate how this purchase would be presented in Haggard's 1998 Statement Of Changes In Financial Position.

D. Assume that Jones had a noncapital loss carry forward for tax purposes of $500,000. Should the form of the purchase of Jones differ? Explain your conclusion.

(CICA Adapted)

ASSIGNMENT CASE THREE - 2

You have just started work as a management accountant with Aristotle Capital Corporation (ACC), a well capitalized, privately held holding company, with a wide variety of investment holdings in Canada. Your first project relates to the proposed acquisition of a significant interest in the common shares of General Chisel Limited (GCL).

GCL has recently gone public, and has shown rapid growth. Its operations include the Canadian manufacture of small hand tools as well as the importation of tools from several Pacific Rim countries. All products are packaged under the GCL label, a registered trademark, and sold to independent retailers and a number of smaller hardware chains.

Comparative draft financial statements for GCL for the years 1997 and 1998 are attached as Exhibit 1 and drafts of several of the notes to the financial statements are shown in Exhibit 2.

You have been asked to prepare a report for the acquisitions committee. Your objectives are to develop a list of potential problem areas and risks which may affect the proposed acquisition decision. Each of the items identified should be briefly analyzed.

Required: Based on the information provided, prepare a report for the acquisitions committee regarding GCL.

(SMA Adapted)

Exhibit 1
General Chisel Limited
Comparative Financial Statements

Draft Consolidated Balance Sheet
As At December 31
('000s)

	1998	1997
Current assets		
Cash	$ 1,075	$ 3,712
Accounts receivable	14,140	10,770
Inventories	22,543	17,125
Other	836	528
Current assets	$38,594	$32,135
Property, plant and equipment	12,834	11,515
Intangible assets	2,178	1,854
Other long-term assets	876	724
Total Assets	$54,482	$46,228

	1998	1997
Current liabilities		
Bank debt	$ 4,705	$ 3,802
Accounts payable	9,013	7,697
Dividends payable	169	169
Current portion of long-term debt	3,355	2,067
Taxes payable	1,768	833
Current Liabilities	$19,010	$14,568
Long-term debt		
Mortgage and notes	$ 8,867	$ 6,466
Convertible debentures (8%)	6,000	6,000
Long Term Liabilities	$14,867	$12,466
Future Income Tax Liabilities	$ 1,568	$ 1,302
Shareholders' equity		
Common shares	$ 6,375	$ 6,270
Retained earnings	12,953	11,881
Cumulative translation loss	(291)	(259)
Shareholders' Equity	$19,037	$17,892
Total Equities	$54,482	$46,228

Draft Consolidated Income Statement
For The Year Ended December 31
('000s)

	1998	1997
Sales	$98,703	$76,021
Cost of goods sold and operating expenses	91,620	70,356
Operating income	$ 7,083	$ 5,665
Expenses:		
Depreciation	$ 1,614	$ 1,377
Amortization	184	102
Interest	1,734	1,619
Foreign currency gain	(33)	(92)
Expenses Other Than Operating	$ 3,499	$ 3,006
Earnings before tax	$ 3,584	$ 2,659
Income tax:		
Current	$ 1,526	$ 707
Future	309	511
Income Tax Expense	$ 1,835	$ 1,218
Net income	$ 1,749	$ 1,441
Earnings per share:		
Basic	$0.13	$0.11
Fully diluted	$0.11	$0.10

Draft Consolidated Statement Of Retained Earnings
For The Year Ended December 31
('000s)

	1998	1997
Opening balance as previously reported	$10,418	$ 9,828
Change in accounting policy (Note 2)	1,463	1,215
Opening balance as restated	$11,881	$11,043
Add: Net income	1,749	1,441
Balance Available For Dividends	$13,630	$12,484
Deduct: Dividends	677	603
Closing balance	$12,953	$11,881

Exhibit 2
General Chisel Limited
Excerpts From The Notes To The
Comparative Financial Statements

1. **Accounting Policies: Foreign Currency Translation**   All foreign operations are considered self-sustaining. Assets, liabilities, revenues and expenses are translated using the current rate method, in accordance with the recommendations of the *CICA Handbook*.

2. **Change in Accounting Policy**   During 1998, the company decided to change its method of revenue recognition for sales to new wholesale customers from the installment sales method to recognition of all revenue at the point of sale. The amounts reported reflect the cumulative effect on income of that change.

4. **Earnings per share**   These amounts are based on the weighted average common shares outstanding. Fully diluted earnings per share reflect the dilutive effect which would have resulted had all convertible securities been converted into common shares as of the beginning of the current year.

7. **Contingencies**   There are several outstanding claims and legal actions involving the company and its subsidiaries. In the opinion of management, the outcome of these matters should not have a material effect on the financial position of the company.

Chapter 4

Consolidated Balance Sheet At Acquisition

Introduction To Consolidations

The Objective Of Consolidation

4-1.   As noted in the previous Chapter, in some business combinations, the combining entities maintain their separate legal existence. This means that each of the companies will maintain a separate, single entity, set of books. However, since there has been a business combination, it is necessary to prepare a combined set of financial statements to present to the investors in the acquiring or parent company. This follows from the view that when two or more companies are being operated as a single economic entity, the accounting records should reflect that fact. Consolidated financial statements are designed to accomplish that goal. The objective in preparing consolidated financial statements is to account for the parent and its subsidiaries as if they were a single economic entity. This form of accounting will, of course, look through the separate legal existence of the various companies in the business combination.

Consolidated Financial Statements And User Needs

4-2.   General purpose financial statements find their way into the hands of a wide variety of users. Investors, creditors, government organizations and consumer interest groups would constitute only a partial list of the individuals and organizations that are interested in the external financial reports of Canadian business organizations. Because consolidated financial statements do not reflect the activities of a real legal entity, users of such statements should have a clear understanding of the limits that this situation places on the usefulness of these statements. As was implied in the preceding paragraph, consolidated financial statements are prepared primarily to meet the needs of the shareholders of the parent or acquiring company. There are other groups that have some interest in one or more of the combining companies. For the most part, however, these groups will not receive a significant benefit from consolidated financial statements.

4-3.   Consolidated financial statements are of primary interest to the group which is in a position to control the consolidated entity, the majority shareholders of the parent company. The legal position of other interested parties is as follows:

Creditors   Since the consolidated entity has no status as a legal entity, it cannot have creditors. The liabilities that are disclosed in the consolidated Balance Sheet are those of the individual legal entities (parent and subsidiary companies) and creditor claims must be satisfied out of the assets of these legal entities. This conclusion may be modified by the presence of intercompany guarantees on debt obligations.

Taxation Authorities   In Canada, there is no legal basis for filing a consolidated tax return. The parent and each of its individual subsidiaries must file separate tax returns and the consolidated financial statements are essentially ignored by the taxation authorities. Since the *CICA Handbook* requires income tax allocation, this means that consolidated income will generally be different than the aggregate taxable income of the combined companies. This situation is given detailed consideration in Chapter 17.

Non Controlling Shareholders   If there are non controlling shareholders in one or more of the subsidiary companies, their primary interest will be in the single entity statements of the subsidiary. They have no real way in which to participate in the operating results of the combined company.

4-4.   The position of other potentially interested groups could be analyzed in a similar manner.

Consolidation Policy

4-5.   Most published consolidated financial statements provide a note regarding consolidation policy (i.e., which investees are included in the consolidated financial statements). Since the objective of consolidation is to treat a group of legally separate companies that are being operated as a single entity as a single accounting entity, consolidation would be conceptually appropriate for investees where the investor has control, has the right and ability to obtain future economic benefits from the resources of the enterprise, and is exposed to related risks. As we noted in Chapter 2, investees that fit this description are called subsidiaries and this means that consolidation is only appropriate for those investees that can be classified as subsidiaries.

4-6.   Despite the fact that companies have no real alternatives with respect to the consolidation of subsidiaries, it remains common to have the basis of consolidation discussed in the Statement Of Accounting Policies. In the survey of the 1996 annual reports of 200 companies that we included in the 1997 edition of *Financial Reporting In Canada*, 190 of these companies discussed their basis of consolidation in their Statement of Accounting Policies.

4-7.   With respect to the content of this disclosure, a fairly typical example from the 1996 annual report of BCE Inc. is as follows:

Note 1   Accounting Policies
Consolidation
The financial statements of entities which are controlled by the Corporation are consolidated, entities which are jointly controlled by the Corporation, referred to as joint ventures, are accounted for using the proportionate consolidation method, associated companies, which the Corporation has the ability to significantly influence, generally representing 20% to 50% ownership, are accounted for using the equity method; investments in other companies are accounted for using the cost method.

Intercompany earnings on the sales of telecommunications equipment from Northern Telecom Limited (Nortel) to the regulated subsidiaries of BCE are deemed to be realized and are not eliminated on consolidation. The sales price on such equipment is recognized for rate-making purposes by the CRTC and other regulators. All other significant intercompany transactions have been eliminated in the consolidated financial statements.

A Note On Terminology

4-8.   When a parent company owns less than 100 percent of the outstanding shares of a subsidiary, disclosure will have to be given to the interests of shareholders other than the parent company. Prior to 1991, subsidiaries were defined in terms of majority ownership and, as a consequence, it was always appropriate to refer to the interests of non controlling shareholders as a minority interest.

4-9.   With the 1991 change in the definition of a subsidiary, it is now possible for a parent's control to be based on less than a majority of the voting shares of that subsidiary. This means that there can be situations in which the non controlling interest is not, in fact, a minority interest. As a reflection of this revision, all of the *CICA Handbook* references to minority interest were changed to non controlling interest. Consistent with these changes in the *CICA Handbook*, we will use the term non controlling interest throughout the remainder of this text. You should note, however, that the term minority interest is just as appropriate in most situations. In fact, minority interest is the term that is usually used in practice to refer to the non controlling interest in subsidiaries.

Conceptual Alternatives In Consolidation

Basis For Alternatives

4-10.   When consolidated financial statements are being prepared with subsidiaries in which the parent company has 100 percent ownership of the outstanding shares, there is no controversy as to the procedures that are to be used. However, the presence of less than 100 percent ownership introduces non controlling shareholders into the consolidation process. As there are a variety of views as to the nature of the relationship between the non controlling shareholders and the consolidated entity, it follows that there are several ways in which this group's interest in the consolidated net income and net assets could be dealt with.

4-11.   The literature on consolidations generally makes reference to three different views of the nature of the non controlling interest and, correspondingly, presents three conceptual alternatives in the preparation of consolidated financial statements. These three approaches are normally referred to as the entity approach, the proprietary approach, and the parent company approach. You should note that what is referred to here as the proprietary conceptual approach is, in fact, the basis for proportionate consolidation procedures. As noted previously, proportionate consolidation is the required method for dealing with joint ventures.

4-12.   For a variety of reasons, we believe that you should have some understanding of these three conceptual alternatives. The reasons for this view include:

- An understanding of these conceptual alternatives will enhance your ability to understand the specific procedures that are required in Canada.

- An understanding of these conceptual alternatives will allow you to evaluate proposed changes that are likely to take place in this area.

- Canadian consolidation requirements do not adopt a consistent conceptual approach. An understanding of the available alternatives will facilitate your understanding of the inconsistencies found in current CICA Recommendations.

4-13.   This Chapter will provide you with a description of the view of the non controlling interest that is inherent in each of the three conceptual alternatives. This will be followed by a description of the consolidation procedures that would be consistent with the view of the non controlling interest that is inherent in each of the alternatives. A simple example will be used to illustrate the alternatives as they apply to the valuation of subsidiary assets. Other procedural alternatives will be illustrated in later Chapters.

4-14.   When the three alternatives have been described, the associated procedures listed, and asset valuation procedures illustrated, there will be an evaluation of the three different concepts. Subsequent to this evaluation will be a summary of the procedures that have been adopted in Section 1600 of the *CICA Handbook*. This additional listing is necessitated by the fact that Section 1600 does not consistently recommend a single conceptual alternative.

4-15. In reviewing the procedures that are listed under each conceptual alternative, do not be disturbed if you do not fully understand what is being described. They are listed at this point only to give you an overall picture of the relevant conceptual alternatives. You may, however, wish to return to these lists periodically as you develop a more complete understanding of specific consolidation procedures. This is particularly true with respect to the Recommendations found in Section 1600. The Section 1600 requirements are of sufficient importance that we will return to this Chapter's summary description of the conceptual alternatives Recommended by Section 1600 at the end of Chapter 6, after we have given detailed attention to specific consolidation procedures.

The Entity Concept

Nature Of The Entity Concept

4-16. This conceptual approach to consolidation is based on the view that the non controlling shareholders are simply another class of residual ownership interest and differ from the controlling shareholders' interest only in the size of their holdings. We have found it helpful to think of the non controlling interest under the entity concept as being analogous to the position of preferred shareholders in a non consolidated situation. That is, the non controlling interest is still clearly part of the residual equity of the business even though its claim may differ somewhat from that of the majority or controlling shareholders.

Associated Procedures

4-17. The following procedures and disclosure would be consistent with the adoption of the entity concept of the nature of the non controlling interest:

Asset Valuation   Both the controlling and the non controlling share of the fair values, as determined at the acquisition date, of the subsidiary's net identifiable assets would be recorded on the consolidated Balance Sheet. The same would be true for any goodwill that is being recognized as part of the business combination transaction.

Non Controlling Interest In The Balance Sheet

- **Disclosure**   The Non Controlling Interest would be a component of total shareholders' equity.

- **Calculation**   The Non Controlling Interest in the consolidated Balance Sheet would consist of its proportionate share of the fair values of the subsidiary's net identifiable assets and goodwill, adjusted for all of the same factors that require adjustments to be made to the majority interest. These factors would include depreciation, depletion, and amortization of fair value changes and goodwill, and the elimination of all of the unrealized intercompany profits of the subsidiary company.

Non Controlling Interest In The Income Statement

- **Disclosure**   Since the non controlling shareholders are viewed as a residual ownership interest, their proportionate share of subsidiary income would not be deducted in the computation of consolidated net income. Rather, their share would be viewed as a distribution of income in the consolidated Statement Of Retained Earnings. Note the similarity of the treatment given to the non controlling shareholders to that given to preferred shareholders in non consolidated situations. The income applicable to both groups would be disclosed as a distribution of income in the Statement Of Retained Earnings, not as a determinant of net income.

- **Calculation** The Non Controlling Interest in the consolidated Income Statement would consist of its proportionate share of the reported income of the subsidiary, adjusted for all of the same factors that require adjustments to be made to the majority interest. These factors would include the current charge for depreciation, depletion, and amortization of fair value changes and goodwill, the elimination of current subsidiary intercompany profits that are still unrealized from the consolidated point of view, and the addition of subsidiary intercompany profits from previous years that have become realized for consolidation purposes during the current year.

Unrealized Intercompany Profits Of The Subsidiary The entity concept's view that the non controlling shareholders occupy a residual ownership position would mean that both the controlling and the non controlling share of unrealized intercompany profits of the subsidiary be treated in a similar fashion. This would require the elimination of all such subsidiary profits with the amounts being charged proportionately to the controlling and non controlling interests. This approach is sometimes referred to as 100 percent pro rata elimination of unrealized intercompany profits of the subsidiary company.

Asset Valuation Illustrated

4-18. The only consolidation procedure that is relevant to this Chapter's subject of the consolidated Balance Sheet at acquisition is asset valuation. A simple example will be used to illustrate asset valuation procedures under the three conceptual alternatives:

Example Acker Inc. acquires 60 percent of Bloom Ltd. Acker has Land with a carrying value of $2,300,000. At the time of acquisition, Bloom has Land with a carrying value of $400,000 and a fair value of $450,000.

4-19. Under the entity approach, the value for Land that would be included in the consolidated Balance Sheet would be calculated as follows:

Acker Inc. - Carrying Value	$2,300,000
Bloom Ltd. - 100 Percent Of Fair Value	450,000
Consolidated Land	$2,750,000

The Proprietary Concept

Nature Of The Proprietary Concept

4-20. This conceptual approach is based on the view that the non controlling shareholders are complete outsiders to the consolidated entity. Their interest in the subsidiary's assets, liabilities, expenses, and revenues would not even be considered in the preparation of consolidated financial statements. Stated another way, the proprietary approach is based on the somewhat legalistic view that, with respect to the subsidiary's assets, liabilities, expenses, and revenues, the consolidated entity includes only the parent company's proportionate share of these balances.

Associated Procedures

4-21. The following procedures and disclosure would be consistent with the adoption of the proprietary concept of the nature of the non controlling interest:

Asset Valuation Only the majority share of fair values, as determined at the acquisition date, of the subsidiary's net identifiable assets and goodwill would be recorded in the consolidated Balance Sheet.

Non Controlling Interest In The Balance Sheet Since the proprietary approach excludes the non controlling stockholders' share of the subsidiary's net identifiable assets from the consolidated balances, no Non Controlling Interest would be included in the consolidated Balance Sheet.

Non Controlling Interest In The Income Statement   As this approach excludes the non controlling share of the subsidiary's expenses and revenues from the consolidated balances, no Non Controlling Interest would be disclosed in the consolidated Income Statement.

Unrealized Intercompany Profits Of The Subsidiary   As the proprietary approach does not include the non controlling share of any of the subsidiary balances in the consolidated account balances, it would only be necessary to eliminate the majority share of the subsidiary's unrealized intercompany profits. This is sometimes referred to as fractional elimination of unrealized intercompany profits of the subsidiary.

Asset Valuation Illustrated

4-22.   The same example that was used to illustrate the entity approach to asset valuation will be used here. It is repeated for your convenience:

Example   Acker Inc. acquires 60 percent of Bloom Ltd. Acker has Land with a carrying value of $2,300,000. At the time of acquisition, Bloom has Land with a carrying value of $400,000 and a fair value of $450,000.

4-23.   Under the proprietary approach, the value for Land that would be included in the consolidated Balance Sheet would be calculated as follows:

Acker Inc. - Carrying Value	$2,300,000
Bloom Ltd. - 60 Percent Of Fair Value ($450,000)	270,000
Consolidated Land	$2,570,000

The Parent Company Concept

Nature Of The Parent Company Concept

4-24.   This conceptual approach is essentially a modification of the proprietary approach. The non controlling shareholders are still considered an outside interest. However, this approach takes the view that the non controlling share of assets, liabilities, expenses, and revenues are a part of the consolidated economic entity. The difference from the entity approach is that the non controlling participation is perceived as being a fixed, creditor like claim. This would lead to the conclusion that the non controlling interest will not be affected by any of the adjustments or eliminations that are applied to the controlling interest in the preparation of consolidated financial statements. In other words, the non controlling shareholders participate in the net assets and results of operations of the consolidated entity, but only to the extent of the book values from the single entity financial statements of the subsidiary.

Associated Procedures

4-25.   The following procedures and disclosure would be consistent with the adoption of the parent company concept of the nature of the non controlling interest:

Asset Valuation   The consolidated net identifiable assets would include 100 percent of the subsidiary's carrying values but only the parent's share of any fair value changes and/or goodwill that was present at the acquisition date.

Non Controlling Interest In The Balance Sheet

• **Disclosure**   As the parent company approach views the Non Controlling Interest as an outside interest analogous to creditors in non consolidated statements, it would follow that the Non Controlling Interest would be grouped with long term liabilities in the consolidated Balance Sheet.

• **Calculation**   The Non Controlling Interest in the consolidated Balance Sheet would be based on the non controlling shareholders' proportionate share of the carrying values of the net identifiable assets of the subsidiary company. As this interest is viewed as a fixed or creditor like claim, no adjustments to the single entity records of the subsidiary would be required in the determination of the Non Controlling Interest that would be disclosed in the consolidated Balance Sheet.

Non Controlling Interest In The Income Statement

- **Disclosure** As this approach views the non controlling shareholders as an outside interest similar to creditors, the Non Controlling Interest would be treated in the same manner as interest charges. That is, it would be deducted in the computation of consolidated Net Income. Note that it would be deducted as a single figure, not from the individual expenses and revenues as in the proprietary approach.

- **Calculation** The Non Controlling Interest in the consolidated Income Statement would be based on the non controlling shareholders' proportionate share of the reported net income of the subsidiary company. As this interest is viewed as a fixed or creditor like claim, no adjustments to the single entity records of the subsidiary would be required in the determination of the Non Controlling Interest in the consolidated Income Statement.

Unrealized Intercompany Profits Of The Subsidiary As the parent company approach views the Non Controlling Interest as an outside claim that is based on the single entity records of the subsidiary, the non controlling interest's share of subsidiary unrealized intercompany profits would not be eliminated. In other words, only the controlling interest's share of the subsidiary's unrealized intercompany profits would be eliminated. This is referred to as fractional elimination.

Asset Valuation Illustrated

4-26.   The same example that was used to illustrate the entity and proprietary approaches to asset valuation will be used here. The example is repeated for your convenience:

Example Acker Inc. acquires 60 percent of Bloom Ltd. Acker has Land with a carrying value of $2,300,000. At the time of acquisition, Bloom has Land with a carrying value of $400,000 and a fair value of $450,000.

4-27.   One way in which the required consolidated Land value could be calculated under the parent company approach is as follows:

Acker Inc. - Carrying Value	$2,300,000
Bloom Ltd.:	
40 Percent Of Carrying Value ($400,000)	160,000
60 Percent Of Fair Value ($450,000)	270,000
Consolidated Land	$2,730,000

4-28.   While the preceding calculation reflects the concept underlying the parent company approach (i.e., assets valued at the minority's share of carrying value and the parent's share of fair value), an alternative calculation is often more convenient to use. This alternative approach starts with 100 percent of the subsidiary's carrying value. This amount is then increased or decreased for the parent company's share of any fair value change. This alternative calculation is as follows:

Acker Inc. - Carrying Value		$2,300,000
Bloom Ltd.:		
Carrying Value	$400,000	
[(60%)($450,000 - $400,000)]	30,000	430,000
Consolidated Land		$2,730,000

Evaluation Of The Conceptual Alternatives

Proprietary Concept

4-29.   The preceding paragraphs have provided you with a general description of the procedures and disclosure that would be required under the three major conceptual alternatives in the preparation of consolidated financial statements. With respect to the proprietary approach, there is little support for this concept as a general solution to the problem of preparing consolidated financial statements. It is not difficult to understand the reason for this. The objective that is being satisfied in the preparation of consolidated financial statements is the portrayal of the financial position and the results of operations of the parent and its various subsidiaries as if they were a single economic entity. This is based on the assumption that all of the net assets of the entire group of affiliated companies is under the common control of the parent company management. It is not some legalistically determined fraction of subsidiary net assets that is under common control, it is 100 percent of such assets. In view of this fact, the proprietary concept's procedures, which only include the parent company's share of the subsidiary's assets, liabilities, expenses, and revenues in the consolidated financial statements, does not seem to be an appropriate solution. An exception to this would be its previously noted application as the proportional consolidation method used in accounting for corporate and unincorporated joint ventures.

Parent Company Concept

4-30.   If the proprietary concept is rejected as a general solution to the problem of preparing consolidated financial statements, one is left with a choice between the parent company concept and the entity concept. Both of these concepts are the same in that they see the non controlling shareholders as having an interest in the net assets and income of the consolidated entity. The difference is their divergent views on the nature of that interest. As a consequence, the choice between the procedures and disclosures inherent in the two methods should be based on an analysis of the nature of the claims of the non controlling shareholders.

4-31.   The parent company concept views the interest of the non controlling shareholders as being a creditor like interest. For this to be a reasonable position, the non controlling shareholders would possess rights similar to those which are associated with other creditor claims. The rights that we normally associate with creditor claims are (1) a contractually specified claim to income, (2) a contractually specified claim to principal and (3) the right to receive this principal sum on a contractually specified future date. It is clear that the relationship of the non controlling shareholders to the consolidated entity does not have any of these characteristics. Given this fact, it is difficult to support the parent company concept as it is based on the view that the non controlling interest is a creditor like claim.

Entity Concept

4-32.   In our opinion, the non controlling shareholders have a claim that is best described as a residual equity position. The shares held by this group do not mature, they do not promise any specified return, nor do they purport to return to the investor any specified principal amount under any circumstances that might be encountered by the firm. These characteristics describe an equity relationship and they describe the position of the non controlling shareholders. This leads us to the conclusion that the entity concept and its associated procedures and disclosures is the most appropriate approach to the preparation of consolidated financial statements.

The Conceptual Approach Of Section 1600

4-33.   The preceding paragraph presents a case for the adoption of the entity concept in the preparation of consolidated financial statements. We believe that Section 1600 of the *CICA Handbook* should have adopted this approach in its entirety. If it was decided that one of the other concepts was a better alternative, we would have hoped that the recommendations would have applied the concept in a consistent manner. Unfortunately, this did not happen. In one area or another of Section 1600, we find examples of all of the previously described conceptual approaches. These inconsistencies are one of the major sources of difficulty in the process of learning to prepare consolidated financial statements. As an initial step towards helping you deal with this difficulty, the following paragraph provides a summary list of the approaches that were adopted with respect to each of the major issues in the preparation of consolidated financial statements. In this and subsequent Chapters, we will provide detailed illustrations of all the procedures described in this list.

4-34.   The following procedures reflect the recommendations of the *CICA Handbook* with respect to the preparation of consolidated financial statements:

Asset Valuation   The recommended approach to asset valuation is the parent company concept. That is, only the majority interest in fair value changes and goodwill are recognized at the time of acquisition or combination. As a consequence, only the majority's share of the depreciation, depletion, and amortization of these values is recorded in subsequent periods.

Non Controlling Interest In The Balance Sheet

- **Disclosure**   Section 1600 is not explicit on this issue. It simply states that the Non Controlling Interest in the consolidated net assets of the subsidiary companies should be shown separately from shareholders' equity. This eliminates the entity approach and the fact that a non controlling interest is present eliminates the proprietary approach. This seems to leave the parent company approach. However, in the absence of a clear statement that the Non Controlling Interest should be disclosed as a part of long term liabilities, it often ends up presented in a somewhat ambiguous fashion between the long term liabilities and the consolidated shareholders' equity.

- **Calculation**   The inconsistencies of Section 1600 become apparent in the calculation of the Non Controlling Interest on the Balance Sheet. In general, this computation follows the parent company approach and bases the Non Controlling Interest on the non controlling shareholders' proportionate share of the carrying values of the subsidiary. However, because the entity approach is used for the elimination of unrealized subsidiary profits, these transactions must be taken into account in determining the appropriate balance. Stated generally, the Non Controlling Interest in the consolidated Balance Sheet would be computed by taking the non controlling shareholders' proportionate interest in the net book value of the subsidiary's assets after they have been adjusted for any unrealized intercompany profits of the subsidiary company.

Non Controlling Interest In The Income Statement

- **Disclosure**   With respect to income before extraordinary items, Section 1600 requires that Non Controlling Interest be given separate disclosure in the consolidated Income Statement. This, of course, reflects an adoption of the parent company approach. For no apparent reason, extraordinary items are dealt with by a different conceptual alternative. Only the parent company's proportionate interest in these items is disclosed and this is an application of the proprietary concept.

- **Calculation**   As was the case with the computation of the Non Controlling Interest for purposes of disclosure in the consolidated Balance Sheet, the computation here is complicated by the presence of inconsistencies in the Recommendations of Section 1600. Generally, the Non Controlling Interest in the consolidated Income Statement is based on the reported income of the subsidiary. Once again, however, adjustments must be made for the adoption of the entity approach in dealing with unrealized subsidiary profits. Stated generally, the Non Controlling Interest in the consolidated Income Statement is calculated by taking the non controlling shareholders' proportionate interest in the reported income of the subsidiary with the elimination of current subsidiary intercompany profits that are still unrealized from the consolidated point of view and the addition of subsidiary intercompany profits from previous years that have become realized for consolidation purposes during the year.

Unrealized Intercompany Profits Of The Subsidiary   As already noted, Section 1600 adopts the entity approach here and requires 100 percent pro rata elimination of unrealized intercompany subsidiary profits.

Conceptual Alternatives In Text Material

Chapter 4

4-35.   Conceptual alternatives are relevant to the material in this Chapter only with respect to the procedures used for asset valuation and disclosure of the Non Controlling Interest in the consolidated Balance Sheet. In our discussion of the three conceptual alternatives, we used a simple example to illustrate the alternative procedures with respect to asset valuation. As a consequence, we will not give further attention to that issue in this Chapter. We will, however, give some further attention to disclosure of the Non Controlling Interest in the consolidated Balance Sheet.

4-36.   This means that, in the remainder of this Chapter, the consolidation procedures that will be developed are based on the parent company approach to asset valuation. That is, the values recorded in the consolidated financial statements for the various assets and liabilities of the subsidiary will include the parent's share of their fair values, plus the non controlling interests share of their book values.

Chapters 5 And 6

4-37.   Chapter 5 will contain a brief example of the income statement disclosure associated with the three conceptual alternatives. Correspondingly, Chapter 6 will use an example to illustrate the alternative approaches to dealing with unrealized intercompany profits. The remainder of these Chapters will focus on the consolidation procedures that are required by the Recommendations of the *CICA Handbook*.

A Procedural Approach To Preparing Consolidated Financial Statements

Use Of Worksheets

4-38.   With the preceding survey of the conceptual alternatives completed, we can now turn our attention to the development of a procedural approach to the preparation of consolidated financial statements. Some current textbooks rely on the use of a worksheet as the basis for the development of consolidation procedures. Under this approach, the various Income Statement and Balance Sheet accounts are listed in the first columns of the work sheet, followed by columns for adjustments, eliminations, Non Controlling Interest, consolidated Balance Sheet, and consolidated Income Statement.

4-39.   While this may be justified by the complex situations encountered in practice, it has very little utility to the student preparing for university or professional examinations. In the context of an examination situation, the mere preparation of the worksheet format would absorb most of the time available for completing a consolidation problem. This would be unfortunate in that preparing the worksheet format is basically a copying process and it would generally not provide even a partial contribution to the total marks allocated to the question.

4-40.   Perhaps of even greater importance is the fact that we have consistently found that students whose only exposure to consolidations is through the use of a worksheet do not usually achieve a level of understanding that extends beyond the procedures that are involved in this type of process. They very quickly learn to fill in the appropriate boxes as required by this mechanical approach. However, if they are asked, for example, to determine or explain consolidated Net Income, they will not be able to provide this information. This means that, unless a consolidation problem is presented in work sheet form, students will generally not be able to solve it. This is further complicated in that there are alternative work sheet formats and the ability to manipulate one does not guarantee an ability to deal with alternative formats.

4-41.   As a consequence of these factors, we have rejected the worksheet approach to the preparation of consolidated financial statements.

Direct Definitional Calculations And Journal Entries

4-42.   If you have a thorough understanding of the consolidation process, the most efficient method of preparing consolidated financial statements is to be in a position to make an independent computation of each of the consolidated account balances. However, it would be very difficult to teach this type of approach directly and, as a reflection of this fact, we will develop a set of procedures using journal entries to adjust the existing account balances. These journal entries will be added to or subtracted from the account balances given in the problem in order to arrive at the correct balances for inclusion in the consolidated financial statements.

4-43.   Two points should be made with respect to these journal entries. First, we view them largely as an interim teaching device. We encourage you to discontinue using them as soon as you feel that you understand the concepts well enough to make direct computations of the balances that are required for inclusion in the consolidated financial statements.

4-44.   However, during the period that you are using these entries, a second point relates to the nature of these entries. They are only working paper entries and are not recorded in the single entity records of either the parent or subsidiary companies (there would some exceptions to this if push down accounting is used). It is particularly important to keep this fact in mind when dealing with consolidation subsequent to acquisition. You must recognize that any entries that were made in preparing the 1997 consolidated financial statements will have to be repeated in preparing the 1998 statements.

General Approach Outlined

4-45.   Anticipating the material which follows, our procedures will use three Steps in the development of consolidation procedures. These will be referred to as Steps A, B, and C, and they can be described as follows:

Step A   This Step will involve the elimination of the investment account against the subsidiary shareholders' equity at the time of acquisition. Also included in this Step will be the establishment of the Non Controlling Interest for the Balance Sheet at acquisition, as well as the allocation of the various fair value changes and goodwill that have been established by the purchase price. The procedures involved in this Step are given complete coverage in this Chapter.

Step B   This Step involves a number of adjustments and eliminations for such things as intercompany assets and liabilities, goodwill amortization, intercompany expenses and revenues, and the elimination of unrealized intercompany profits. As these adjustments and eliminations are only required in periods subsequent to acquisition, they will be dealt with in Chapters 5 and 6.

Step C   This final Step will allocate any remaining balance in the Retained Earnings of the subsidiary between the Non Controlling Interest in the consolidated Balance Sheet and the consolidated Retained Earnings. As was the case with the Step B procedures, the Step C procedures are only required in periods subsequent to acquisition. This means that the Step C procedures will also be dealt with in Chapters 5 and 6.

Consolidated Balance Sheet At Acquisition

Consolidations And Business Combinations

4-46.   While we have made this point several times before, we would like to remind you again that, in all cases where a parent has acquired control over a subsidiary, a business combination transaction has occurred. As with business combinations that use other legal forms, combinations involving the acquisition of the shares of a subsidiary could qualify for either purchase accounting or pooling of interests accounting. However, in the great majority of situations, purchase accounting will be appropriate and, as a consequence, all of the consolidation examples in this and following Chapters will be based on the assumption that an acquirer can be identified and that the purchase method of accounting is being used.

4-47.   You will recall from Chapter Three's discussion of the purchase method that one of its features is that the identifiable assets and liabilities of the acquiree must be recorded at fair values. In the great majority of subsidiary acquisitions, the parent is the acquirer and the subsidiary is the acquiree. As a consequence, the fair values of the identifiable assets and liabilities of the subsidiary must be determined and recorded in the consolidated financial statements. In addition, if the investment cost (purchase price) exceeds the parent's share of these fair values, goodwill must also be recorded in the consolidated financial statements. This feature of the purchase method of accounting will be reflected in the development of procedures to be used in preparing a consolidated Balance Sheet at acquisition.

Examples To Be Used

4-48.   The least complex type of consolidation problem involves the preparation of a consolidated Balance Sheet as at the date of acquisition. The presentation of the procedures required to prepare a consolidated Balance Sheet as at the date of acquisition will use four examples. They can be briefly described as follows:

Example One   This very simple example will have the parent company owning 100 percent of the subsidiary company's shares with the investment cost equal to book value and no fair value changes or goodwill present.

Example Two   This will also involve 100 percent ownership. However, the investment cost will differ from book value. This differential will be allocated to fair value changes and goodwill.

Example Three   We will return to our first assumption of the investment cost being equal to book value with no fair value changes. However, the investor's proportionate share of the subsidiary shares will be less than 100 percent.

Example Four   The final example will involve less than 100 percent ownership of the subsidiary's outstanding shares and will also incorporate fair value changes and a differential between cost and book value.

Example One - 100 Percent Ownership
With No Fair Value Changes

Example

4-49.   In this Example, the parent will own 100 percent of the outstanding shares of the subsidiary. There are no fair value changes on any of the subsidiary's identifiable assets or liabilities and the investment cost will be equal to book value.

On December 31, 1998, the Pert Company purchases 100 percent of the outstanding voting shares of the Sert Company for $5 million in cash. On that date, subsequent to the business combination transaction, the Balance Sheets of the two Companies are as follows:

Balance Sheets
As At December 31, 1998

	Pert	Sert
Cash	$ 800,000	$ 500,000
Accounts Receivable	1,500,000	1,100,000
Inventories	3,400,000	2,500,000
Investment In Sert	5,000,000	-0-
Plant And Equipment (Net)	6,300,000	3,900,000
Total Assets	$17,000,000	$8,000,000
Current Liabilities	$ 800,000	$1,000,000
Long Term Liabilities	2,200,000	2,000,000
No Par Common Stock	8,000,000	2,000,000
Retained Earnings	6,000,000	3,000,000
Total Equities	$17,000,000	$8,000,000

Other Information:

A. All of the net identifiable assets of the Sert Company have fair values that are equal to the carrying values that are presented in the preceding Balance Sheet.

B. During 1998, the Sert Company sold merchandise to the Pert Company for $100,000 and recognized a gross profit on these sales of $40,000. On December 31, 1998, one half of this merchandise remains in the inventories of the Pert Company.

C. On December 31, 1998, the Pert Company owes the Sert Company $25,000 on open account for merchandise purchased during the year.

Required: Prepare a consolidated Balance Sheet for the Pert Company and its subsidiary, the Sert Company, as at December 31, 1998.

Procedures

4-50.   In somewhat simplified terms, preparation of the consolidated Balance Sheet at acquisition involves adding together all of the assets and equities of the parent and subsidiary companies. However, special procedures are required for certain of these balances. Specifically, these procedures relate to the Pert Company's Investment In Sert account and to the Sert Company's shareholders' equity. In addition, in this example it is also necessary to deal with the intercompany receivable and the intercompany profit.

Investment In Sert

4-51.   The Investment In Sert account on the books of the Pert Company reflects the ownership of the net identifiable assets of the Sert Company. Since in preparing consolidated financial statements we are trying to show the two companies as if they were a single economic entity, the net identifiable assets of the Sert Company will be included in the consolidated net identifiable assets. If, in addition, we include the Investment In Sert account, we will be counting these net identifiable assets twice. Therefore, it will always be necessary to eliminate 100 percent of the investment account. This will remain the case under our procedures even as the problems become more complex and begin to deal with preparing consolidated financial statements subsequent to acquisition.

Subsidiary Shareholders' Equity

4-52.   From the point of view of the consolidated entity, the Sert Company has no shares outstanding. That is, no individual or organization outside of the consolidated entity is holding any of the common shares of the Sert Company. This would mean that in the consolidated financial statements, any Contributed Capital of Sert that is present at the time of acquisition should be eliminated. With respect to Retained Earnings, the purchase method of accounting only includes the income of the acquiree from the date of acquisition forward. As a consequence, none of the Retained Earnings of an acquired company that is present at the time of acquisition would be included in the combined or consolidated company's Retained Earnings. This is reflected in the following *CICA Handbook* Recommendation:

> **Paragraph 1600.22**   *The retained earnings or deficit of a subsidiary company at the date(s) of acquisition by the parent should not be included in consolidated retained earnings.* (April, 1975)

4-53.   This would necessitate the elimination of any subsidiary Retained Earnings that are present at the time of acquisition. As a general conclusion, it follows that we will always eliminate 100 percent of the subsidiary shareholders' equity at acquisition. Under the procedures that we are developing, this will remain the case even as the problems become more complex and deal with fractional ownership and consolidation subsequent to the date of acquisition.

Elimination Entry

4-54.   In the preceding paragraphs, we have developed our first two procedures for preparing consolidated financial statements. As these two Procedures are a part of Step A in our general approach to preparing consolidated financial statements, we will designate these procedures as Step A-1 and A-2, respectively.

> **Step A-1 Procedure**   Always eliminate 100 percent of the Investment In Subsidiary account.

> **Step A-2 Procedure**   Always eliminate 100 percent of all the balances in the subsidiary's shareholders' equity that are present on the acquisition date.

4-55.   The journal entry required to carry out these two Steps is as follows:

No Par Common Stock (Sert)	$2,000,000	
Retained Earnings (Sert)	3,000,000	
Investment In Sert		$5,000,000

Intercompany Asset And Liability

4-56.   In preparing consolidated financial statements, the Pert Company and the Sert Company are viewed as constituting a single economic entity. From this point of view, any intercompany asset and liability balances do not exist and must be eliminated. The following *CICA Handbook* Recommendation is applicable:

> **Paragraph 1600.19**   *Intercompany balances should be eliminated upon consolidation.* (April, 1975)

4-57.   This provides the basis for a third procedure in preparing consolidated financial statements. However, we will be required to eliminate intercompany asset and liability balances in years subsequent to acquisition as well as at acquisition. As a consequence, it will become part of Step B in our general approach to consolidations. Given this, we will designate this procedure as Step B-1.

Step B-1 Procedure Always eliminate 100 percent of intercompany assets and liabilities.

4-58. In our example, Pert Company owes Sert Company $25,000 on open account. Given this, the entry that is required to implement Step B-1 is as follows:

Current Liabilities	$25,000	
Accounts Receivable		$25,000

Intercompany Gains And Losses

4-59. In contrast to the intercompany asset and liability balances which are still present at the time of the acquisition, intercompany expense and revenue transactions, as well as any resulting profits, are events which occurred prior to the combination transaction. Further, at the time they occurred, they were not intercompany transactions but, rather, transactions between two independent companies dealing at arm's length. Given this, it is not appropriate to eliminate these amounts or to even think of them as intercompany transactions. This is reflected in the following Recommendation:

Paragraph 1600.24 *Where the carrying value of the assets of the parent company or a subsidiary company include gains or losses arising from intercompany transactions which took place prior to the date of acquisition, such gains or losses should not be eliminated unless the transactions were made in contemplation of acquisition.* (April, 1975)

4-60. Since there is no indication in the problem that the 1998 transactions were in contemplation of the business combination, no entry is required for these events.

Preparing The Consolidated Balance Sheet

4-61. As indicated in our discussion of the procedural approach to be used, the preparation of the consolidated Balance Sheet involves adding together the asset and equity balances from the individual Balance Sheets of the two companies and then adjusting these amounts for the various journal entries that have been made. In this Example One, the resulting consolidated Balance Sheet, with all of the calculations shown parenthetically, is as follows:

Pert Company And Subsidiary
Consolidated Balance Sheet
As At December 31, 1998

Cash ($800,000 + $500,000)	$ 1,300,000
Accounts Receivable ($1,500,000 + $1,100,000 -$25,000)	2,575,000
Inventories ($3,400,000 + $2,500,000)	5,900,000
Investment In Sert ($5,000,000 - $5,000,000)	-0-
Plant And Equipment ($6,300,000 + $3,900,000)	10,200,000
Total Assets	$19,975,000
Current Liabilities ($800,000 + $1,000,000 - $25,000)	$ 1,775,000
Long Term Liabilities ($2,200,000 + $2,000,000)	4,200,000
No Par Common Stock (Pert's Only)	8,000,000
Retained Earnings (Pert's Only)	6,000,000
Total Equities	$19,975,000

Notes On Example One   Two points are relevant with respect to the procedures and disclosure for Example One:

- In the actual presentation of the consolidated Balance Sheet, the Investment In Sert account would simply not be shown. It is included here to call your attention to the fact that the account was there on the Pert Company's books and has been eliminated.

- Both components of the consolidated shareholders' equity are identical to those of the parent company. This will always be the case in the consolidated Balance Sheet as at the date of acquisition, a result that follows from the rules that are generally applicable in the purchase method of accounting for business combinations. This will not be the case in periods subsequent to the acquisition date unless the parent company carries the investment by the equity method.

Example Two - 100 Percent Ownership With Fair Value Changes And Goodwill

Example

4-62.   As was the case in Example One, the parent in this Example Two will own 100 percent of the outstanding shares of the subsidiary. However, in this Example Two we have added fair value changes on the subsidiary assets as well as a goodwill balance. As a consequence we will have to use the procedures developed in Chapter 3 to analyze the investment cost and allocate the appropriate amounts to fair value changes and goodwill. The basic data for Example Two is as follows:

On December 31, 1998, the Pend Company purchases 100 percent of the outstanding voting shares of the Send Company for $3,500,000 in cash. On that date, subsequent to the business combination transaction, the Balance Sheets of the two Companies are as follows:

Balance Sheets
As At December 31, 1998

	Pend	Send
Cash	$ 500,000	$ 300,000
Accounts Receivable	1,200,000	800,000
Inventories	1,800,000	1,200,000
Investment In Send	3,500,000	-0-
Plant And Equipment (Net)	3,000,000	2,700,000
Total Assets	$10,000,000	$5,000,000
Current Liabilities	$ 800,000	$ 500,000
Long Term Liabilities	1,700,000	1,500,000
No Par Common Stock	4,000,000	1,000,000
Retained Earnings	3,500,000	2,000,000
Total Equities	$10,000,000	$5,000,000

Other Information:

A. All of the net identifiable assets of the Send Company have fair values that are equal to their carrying values except for Plant And Equipment which has a fair value that is $300,000 more than its carrying value and the Long Term Liabilities which have fair values that are $100,000 less than their carrying values.

B. Prior to the business combination there were no intercompany transactions between the two companies. On the date of the combination there are no intercompany asset and liability balances.

Required: Prepare a consolidated Balance Sheet for the Pend Company and its subsidiary, the Send Company, as at December 31, 1998.

Procedures

4-63. As described in Example One, Steps A-1 and A-2 are used to eliminate 100 percent of the Investment In Subsidiary account and 100 percent of the subsidiary's shareholders' equity at acquisition. Applying these procedures in this Example results in the following journal entry:

No Par Common Stock (Send)	$1,000,000	
Retained Earnings (Send)	2,000,000	
Differential	500,000	
Investment In Send		$3,500,000

4-64. The application of Steps A-1 and A-2 in this Example results in a journal entry that does not balance, a situation that we have corrected by adding a $500,000 debit that has been temporarily designated Differential. This is a typical result. In most consolidation problems, there will be a difference between the cost of the investment and the investor's share of the book value of the subsidiary that has been acquired. This means that eliminating the investment account against the subsidiary shareholders' equity will result in an imbalance that requires an additional debit or credit. If a debit Differential is required, it reflects an excess of investment cost over the investor's share of subsidiary book value. A credit Differential indicates that the investment cost was less than the investor's share of subsidiary book value. Learning to deal with these differentials is the next step in our development of consolidation procedures.

Treatment Of Differentials

4-65. The first thing to understand about such differentials is that they will not disappear. The preceding $500,000 must be included somewhere in the consolidated Balance Sheet. Further, it must be allocated to one or more specific accounts. It cannot simply be included in the consolidated Balance Sheet with the account title Differential or Excess Of Cost Over Book Value.

4-66. In attempting to allocate such differentials to specific asset and liability accounts, it is essential to understand why they exist. That is, what factors contributed to the Pend Company's decision to pay $500,000 more than the book value of the Send Company's net assets in order to acquire 100 percent of its outstanding shares? From a conceptual point of view, three possible explanations for this situation can be developed. Note that these explanations are not mutually exclusive and, in fact, would usually occur in various combinations. The three possibilities are as follows:

Specific Identifiable Assets Specific identifiable assets and identifiable liabilities of the Send Company may have fair values that are different from their carrying values. For example, the $500,000 excess of cost over book value in the present example could be explained if the Send Company's Plant And Equipment had a fair value of $3,200,000 or $500,000 more than the carrying value of $2,700,000.

Subsidiary Goodwill A second possible explanation of any differences between investment cost and book value relates to how successfully the enterprise is being operated. As was discussed in Chapter Three, if the enterprise is being operated in an unusually successful manner, it is likely that the enterprise as a going concern will have a fair value that is in excess of the sum of the fair values of its identifiable net assets. Such an excess would be allocated to goodwill and could be the explanation of the $500,000 excess in the problem that is under consideration. A similar analysis would apply to situations in which the enterprise is being operated at a less than average level of success, resulting in the need to deal with a negative goodwill balance.

Consolidated Goodwill   A final possibility is that extra value is created in the business combination process. There may be so many advantages associated with bringing a particular subsidiary into a combination with a parent company that the parent is prepared to pay more than the net identifiable assets and goodwill of the subsidiary are worth as a single entity. This excess is sometimes referred to as consolidated goodwill and could be the explanation of the $500,000 excess in the problem under consideration. Note that, unlike the two previous explanations for differentials, the consolidated goodwill argument could not be used to explain a credit differential. It is very difficult to believe that the shareholders of the subsidiary would be willing to sell their shares for less than the value of the enterprise simply because there are so many disadvantages associated with affiliation.

4-67.   We would note that while there is clearly a conceptual distinction between subsidiary goodwill and consolidated goodwill, it is of no practical significance. In the application of the purchase method of accounting for business combination transactions, goodwill is measured as the excess (deficiency) of the investment cost over the investor's share of the investee's fair values. No attempt is made to segregate this total goodwill into a component that was present prior to the business combination transaction and a component that results from the business combination transaction.

4-68.   Based on the preceding analysis of the reasons for the existence of debit or credit differentials, it is clear that the *CICA Handbook* Recommendations for the application of the purchase method of accounting for business combinations requires that such balances be allocated to fair value changes on identifiable assets, fair value changes on identifiable liabilities, and to positive or negative goodwill. This provides the basis for an additional procedure in the preparation of consolidated financial statements. As this procedure is part of Step A in our general approach to preparing consolidated financial statements, it will be designated Step A-3.

Step A-3 Procedure   The total amount of any debit or credit Differential must be allocated to the parent company's share of fair value changes on identifiable assets, fair value changes on identifiable liabilities, and to positive or negative goodwill. Note that we will only recognize the parent company's share of any fair value changes or goodwill. This reflects the fact that the *CICA Handbook* requires the use of the parent company approach for the valuation of subsidiary assets.

Investment Analysis Schedule

4-69.   As was noted in Chapter 3, in more complex problems it is useful to have a systematic approach to the allocation of fair value changes and goodwill. While it is was not really necessary in the relatively simple example that was presented in that Chapter, we introduced such a systematic approach in the form of an investment analysis schedule. The rules that were presented in Chapter 3 for the preparation of such schedules are repeated here for your convenience:

Calculating The Differential   Subtract the subsidiary's book value, or the parent company's proportionate interest therein in cases where the parent company owns less than 100 percent of the subsidiary shares,) from the investment cost. This results in a balance that we will refer to as a Differential. If it is a positive number, it indicates that the investor is paying more than his proportionate share of subsidiary book values and that there is a debit amount to be allocated. A negative number reflects a credit balance to be allocated. Note that, as the Differential reflects the total of all fair value changes and goodwill to be recognized, a positive balance does not clearly indicate the presence of goodwill.

Allocating The Differential   Once the Differential has been established, we will then add or subtract the various fair value changes that have been determined for the subsidiary's identifiable assets. As a positive differential reflects a debit balance to be allocated, we will subtract any fair value changes which require the allocation of debits (increase in assets or decreases in liabilities). Correspondingly, we will add any fair value changes that require credits (decreases in assets or increases in liabilities). In this example, both the $300,000 fair value increase on Plant And Equipment and the $100,000 fair value decrease on Long Term Liabilities involve debits and will be subtracted.

Dealing With Goodwill   The resulting balance will be allocated to goodwill if it is positive. If the balance is negative, it will be deducted from the identifiable non monetary assets as per the Recommendations of Section 1580 of the CICA Handbook. As note in Chapter 3, the particular assets that will be charged with this negative goodwill is a matter of professional judgment.

4-70.   For our Example Two, involving the Pend Company and its subsidiary Send Company, the investment analysis schedule would be prepared as follows:

Investment Cost	$3,500,000
Book Value Of The Send Company ($1,000,000 + $2,000,000)	(3,000,000)
Differential	$ 500,000
Fair Value Changes:	
Increase On Plant And Equipment	(300,000)
Decrease On Long Term Liabilities	(100,000)
Goodwill	$ 100,000

4-71.   This goodwill balance can be verified in order to check the computations in the schedule. Goodwill is defined as the excess of the investment cost over the investor's share of the fair values of the net identifiable assets of the investee. In this example, the investment cost was $3,500,000 while the investor's share of the fair values of the investee's net identifiable assets was $3,400,000. This is calculated by taking the carrying values of $3,000,000, plus the fair value increase of $300,000 on the Plant And Equipment plus the fair value decrease of $100,000 on Long Term Liabilities. Thus, the investment cost, less the investor's 100 percent share of fair values is equal to $100,000 ($3,500,000 - $3,400,000), which verifies the amount of goodwill determined in the investment analysis schedule.

Journal Entry

4-72.   Using the information provided by the preceding investment analysis schedule, we can now complete the journal entry needed for the preparation of the required consolidated Balance Sheet at acquisition. In this entry we will combine Step A-1 (elimination of the investment account), Step A-2 (elimination of the subsidiary shareholders' equity at acquisition), and Step A-3 (allocation of the Differential to fair value changes and goodwill). The entry is as follows:

No Par Common Stock	$1,000,000	
Retained Earnings	2,000,000	
Plant And Equipment (Net)	300,000	
Long Term Liabilities	100,000	
Goodwill	100,000	
Investment In Send		$3,500,000

4-73.   Note that this entry still eliminates 100 percent of both the Investment In Send and the shareholders' equity of the Send Company. In addition, the $500,000 balance which we temporarily designated Differential has been allocated to identifiable assets, identifiable liabilities, and goodwill.

Consolidated Balance Sheet

4-74.   Using the same procedures as in Example One, the Example Two consolidated Balance Sheet can be prepared as follows:

Pend Company And Subsidiary
Consolidated Balance Sheet
As At December 31, 1998

Cash ($500,000 + $300,000)	$ 800,000
Accounts Receivable ($1,200,000 + $800,000)	2,000,000
Inventories ($1,800,000 + $1,200,000)	3,000,000
Investment In Send ($3,500,000 - $3,500,000)	-0-
Plant And Equipment (Net)	
($3,000,000 + $2,700,000 + $300,000)	6,000,000
Goodwill	100,000
Total Assets	**$11,900,000**
Current Liabilities ($800,000 + $500,000)	$ 1,300,000
Long Term Liabilities ($1,700,000 + $1,500,000 -$100,000)	3,100,000
No Par Common Stock (Pend's Only)	4,000,000
Retained Earnings (Pend's Only)	3,500,000
Total Equities	**$11,900,000**

4-75.   The only difference between the procedures used in preparing this consolidated Balance Sheet and those used in preparing the Example One consolidated Balance Sheet is that allocations are made for the fair value changes and goodwill. Note that the consolidated shareholders' equity is still simply the shareholders' equity of the parent company.

Example Three - Fractional Ownership With No Fair Value Changes Or Goodwill

Example

4-76.   This example introduces a situation where the parent company owns less than 100 percent of the subsidiary shares (fractional ownership). As a result of this change, we will have to consider the calculation and disclosure of Non Controlling Interest in the consolidated Balance Sheet. The basic data for this Example is as follows:

On December 31, 1998, the Pack Company purchases 80 percent of the outstanding voting shares of the Sack Company for $3,200,000 in cash. On that date, subsequent to the business combination transaction, the Balance Sheets of the two Companies are as follows:

Balance Sheets
As At December 31, 1998

	Pack	Sack
Cash	$ 600,000	$ 400,000
Accounts Receivable	1,500,000	1,100,000
Inventories	2,100,000	1,400,000
Investment In Sack	3,200,000	-0-
Plant And Equipment (Net)	5,600,000	2,100,000
Total Assets	**$13,000,000**	**$5,000,000**
Current Liabilities	$1,200,000	$ 400,000
Long Term Liabilities	2,800,000	600,000
No Par Common Stock	5,000,000	1,000,000
Retained Earnings	4,000,000	3,000,000
Total Equities	**$13,000,000**	**$5,000,000**

Other Information:

A. All of the identifiable assets and liabilities of the Sack Company have fair values that are equal to the carrying values that are presented in the preceding Balance Sheet.

B. Prior to the business combination there were no intercompany transactions between the two Companies. It follows that on the date of the combination there are no intercompany asset and liability balances.

Required: Prepare a consolidated Balance Sheet for the Pack Company and its subsidiary, the Sack Company, as at December 31, 1998.

Procedures

4-77.   With no fair value changes, no goodwill, and no intercompany balances, Steps B-1 and A-3 are not relevant in this Example. However, Steps A-1 and A-2 are still required, even with the presence of a non controlling interest. You will have no difficulty in understanding the continued need for Step A-1, the requirement that we eliminate 100 percent of the Investment In Subsidiary account. However, with some of the subsidiary's shares held by investors outside the consolidated entity, Step A-2's requirement that we eliminate 100 percent of the subsidiary's shareholders' equity does not seem reasonable. In this Example Three, 20 percent of Sack Company's shares are in the hands of such outsiders and, in the preparation of both the entity and parent company approach consolidated Balance Sheets, the interest of these shareholders in Sack Company's shareholders' equity must be included in the consolidated Balance Sheet.

4-78.   The reason for this seemingly unreasonable requirement is a procedural one. It is true that the non controlling interest's 20 percent share of Sack Company's shareholders' equity will be included in the parent company and entity approach consolidated Balance Sheets. However, this interest will not be disclosed as No Par Common Stock or Retained Earnings. Rather, it will be disclosed as a Non Controlling Interest. Therefore, in our approach to preparing consolidated financial statements, we will continue to eliminate 100 percent of the subsidiary's shareholders' equity at acquisition (Step A-2), but we will add a further procedure. As this new procedure is part of Step A in our general approach to consolidated financial statements, it will be designated Step A-4.

Step A-4 Procedure   The non controlling interest's share of the book value of the subsidiary Shareholders' Equity at acquisition must be allocated to a Non Controlling Interest account in the consolidated Balance Sheet.

4-79.   The fact that we base the Non Controlling Interest on the book value of the subsidiary's net assets means that we are not recognizing the non controlling interest's share of either fair value changes or goodwill. This follows from the fact that the *CICA Handbook* requires the use of the parent company approach to asset valuation.

Investment Analysis Schedule

4-80.   Given that there are no fair value changes or goodwill in this Example, no investment analysis schedule is required.

Journal Entry

4-81.   Based on the preceding analysis, we can complete the journal entry needed to prepare the required consolidated Balance Sheet. In this entry we will use Step A-1 (elimination of the investment account), Step A-2 (elimination of 100 percent of the subsidiary shareholders' equity at acquisition), and the new Step A-4 (allocation of 20 percent of Sack Company's shareholders' equity to the Balance Sheet account Non Controlling Interest).

No Par Common Stock	$1,000,000	
Retained Earnings	3,000,000	
Investment In Sack		$3,200,000
Non Controlling Interest (20% Of $4,000,000)		800,000

Treatment Of The Non Controlling Interest

4-82. The preceding journal entry creates an account titled Non Controlling Interest. Unless the subsidiary has accumulated a deficit sufficiently large to create a negative balance in shareholders' equity, this account will have a credit balance and, as a consequence, it will be allocated to the equity side of the consolidated Balance Sheet. Some further discussion, however, is required with respect to both the computation and disclosure of this balance.

Computation With respect to computation, the Non Controlling Interest in the consolidated Balance Sheet is simply the non controlling shareholders' proportionate share of the carrying values of the net assets of the subsidiary. This is the approach that is required by the *CICA Handbook*:

> **Paragraph 1600.15** *The non-controlling interest in the subsidiary's assets and liabilities should be reflected in terms of carrying values recorded in the accounting records of the subsidiary company.* (April, 1975)

Disclosure With respect to the disclosure of the Non Controlling Interest in the consolidated Balance Sheet, the *CICA Handbook* makes the following somewhat ambiguous Recommendation:

> **Paragraph 1600.69** *Non-controlling interest in consolidated subsidiary companies should be shown separately from shareholders' equity.* (April, 1975)

While this Recommendation would allow the Non Controlling Interest to be shown as part of the long term liabilities, it is most commonly disclosed in practice as a separate item between the long term liabilities and shareholders' equity.

Other Factors You should also understand that, in real world situations, the Non Controlling Interest in the consolidated Balance Sheet is a highly aggregated piece of information. If the parent company has fractional ownership of a large number of subsidiary enterprises, all of the interests of the various non controlling shareholder groups would be included in a single Non Controlling Interest figure. Further, for those subsidiaries with different classes of non voting or preferred shares outstanding, these additional equity interests would also become part of the Non Controlling Interest in the consolidated Balance Sheet. It would be unusual for outstanding subsidiary preferred shares to be disclosed as a separate item in a consolidated Balance Sheet.

Consolidated Balance Sheet

4-83. Using the same procedures as in Examples One and Two, the Example Three consolidated Balance Sheet would be prepared as follows:

Pack Company And Subsidiary
Consolidated Balance Sheet
As At December 31, 1998

Cash ($600,000 + $400,000)	$ 1,000,000
Accounts Receivable ($1,500,000 + $1,100,000)	2,600,000
Inventories ($2,100,000 + $1,400,000)	3,500,000
Investment In Sack ($3,200,000 - $3,200,000)	-0-
Plant And Equipment (Net) ($5,600,000 + $2,100,000)	7,700,000
Total Assets	$14,800,000

Current Liabilities ($1,200,000 + $400,000)		$ 1,600,000
Long Term Liabilities ($2,800,000 + $600,000)		3,400,000
Total Liabilities		$5,000,000
Non Controlling Interest [(20%)($4,000,000)]		800,000
Shareholders' Equity:		
No Par Common Stock (Pack's Only)	$5,000,000	
Retained Earnings (Pack's Only)	4,000,000	9,000,000
Total Equities		$14,800,000

4-84.   Note that we have disclosed the Non Controlling Interest as a separate item between the Total Liabilities and Shareholders' Equity.

Example Four - Fractional Ownership With Fair Value Changes And Goodwill

Example

4-85.   In this final example, we will continue to have fractional ownership. However, we will add fair value changes and goodwill. The basic data for this Example is as follows:

On December 31, 1998, the Peak Company purchases 90 percent of the outstanding voting shares of the Seek Company for $5,220,000 in cash. On that date, subsequent to the business combination transaction, the Balance Sheets of the two Companies are as follows:

Balance Sheets
As At December 31, 1998

	Peak	Seek
Cash	$ 1,000,000	$ 700,000
Accounts Receivable	2,100,000	1,200,000
Inventories	3,440,000	2,500,000
Investment In Seek	5,220,000	-0-
Plant And Equipment (Net)	4,240,000	4,600,000
Total Assets	$16,000,000	$9,000,000
Current Liabilities	$ 1,200,000	$1,000,000
Long Term Liabilities	2,800,000	2,000,000
No Par Common Stock	7,000,000	2,000,000
Retained Earnings	5,000,000	4,000,000
Total Equities	$16,000,000	$9,000,000

Other Information:

A. All of the identifiable assets of the Seek Company have fair values that are equal to their carrying values except for Plant And Equipment which has a fair value that is $600,000 less than its carrying value and Inventories with fair values that are $100,000 more than their carrying values.

B. Prior to the business combination there were no intercompany transactions between the two Companies. It follows that on the date of the combination there are no intercompany asset and liability balances.

Required: Prepare a consolidated Balance Sheet for the Peak Company and its subsidiary, the Seek Company, as at December 31, 1998.

Procedures

4-86. This final Example provides a complete illustration of the procedures that are required in preparing a consolidated Balance Sheet as at the date of acquisition. However, no new procedures are required. As with all of the preceding examples, we will continue to use Step A-1 (eliminate the investment account) and Step A-2 (eliminate 100 percent of the subsidiary's shareholders' equity at acquisition). As in Example Three, we will need Step A-4 to establish a Non Controlling Interest to be included in the consolidated Balance Sheet. In addition, we will need Step A-3 from Example Two to allocate the Differential to fair value changes and goodwill.

Investment Analysis Schedule

4-87. The investment analysis schedule that will be used in this Example is as follows:

	90 Percent	100 Percent*
Investment Cost	$5,220,000	$5,800,000
Book Value Of The Seek Company	(5,400,000)	(6,000,000)
Differential	($ 180,000)	($ 200,000)
Fair Value Changes:		
Decrease On Plant And Equipment	540,000	600,000
Increase On Inventories	(90,000)	(100,000)
Goodwill	$ 270,000	$ 300,000

*The 100 percent figure for the investment cost is the total value for the business that is implied by the price paid for 90 percent of the business ($5,220,000 equals 90 percent of $5,800,000).

4-88. In general terms, this schedule operates exactly as it did in the 100 percent ownership case. However, because we are only going to recognize the parent company's share of fair value changes and goodwill, all of the information has to be calculated on a 90 percent basis.

4-89. You will note that, in our schedule, we have retained the 100 percent figures along with the 90 percent figures. As only the fractional calculations are required in preparing a consolidated Balance Sheet at acquisition, it is not really necessary to calculate both the fractional and 100 percent amounts. However, we would urge you to do so since in most consolidation problems some of the information is given on a fractional basis (investment cost) while other data is given on a 100 percent basis (fair value changes). As a result, one of the most common errors made in solving consolidation problems is to add or subtract a fractional figure to or from a 100 percent figure. This two column analysis will virtually eliminate this type of error, particularly if the final goodwill figure is verified using a definitional calculation. In this Example the investment cost is $5,220,000 and the investor's share of the subsidiary's fair values is $4,950,000 [(90%)($6,000,000 - $600,000 + $100,000)]. This verifies the 90 percent goodwill figure of $270,000 ($5,220,000 -

$4,950,000).

Journal Entry

4-90.   The required journal entry would be as follows:

No Par Common Stock	$2,000,000	
Retained Earnings	4,000,000	
Inventories	90,000	
Goodwill	270,000	
Plant And Equipment (Net)		$ 540,000
Non Controlling Interest (10% of $6,000,000)		600,000
Investment In Seek		5,220,000

4-91.   This journal entry uses Step A-1 (elimination of 100 percent of the investment account) and A-2 (elimination of 100 percent of the subsidiary shareholders' equity at acquisition). In addition, under Step A-3, it uses the figure from the 90 percent column in the investment analysis schedule to allocate the investor's proportionate share of fair value changes and goodwill. Finally, under Step A-4, it establishes a Non Controlling Interest to be included in the consolidated Balance Sheet at acquisition. This Non Controlling interest is based on the $6,000,000 ($2,000,000 + $4,000,000) book value of Seek Company's Shareholders' Equity.

Consolidated Balance Sheet

4-92.   The required consolidated Balance Sheet is as follows:

Peak Company And Subsidiary
Consolidated Balance Sheet
As At December 31, 1998

Cash ($1,000,000 + $700,000)		$ 1,700,000
Accounts Receivable ($2,100,000 + $1,200,000)		3,300,000
Inventories ($3,440,000 + $2,500,000 + $90,000)		6,030,000
Investment In Seek ($5,220,000 - $5,220,000)		-0-
Plant And Equipment (Net)		
($4,240,000 + $4,600,000 - $540,000)		8,300,000
Goodwill		270,000
Total Assets		**$19,600,000**
Current Liabilities ($1,200,000 + $1,000,000)		$ 2,200,000
Long Term Liabilities ($2,800,000 + $2,000,000)		4,800,000
Total Liabilities		**$ 7,000,000**
Non Controlling Interest [(10%)($6,000,000)]		600,000
Shareholders' Equity:		
No Par Common Stock (Peak's Only)	7,000,000	
Retained Earnings (Peak's Only)	5,000,000	12,000,000
Total Equities		**$19,600,000**

Note On Asset Valuation   The consolidated asset and liability balances that are required under the Recommendations of the *CICA Handbook* can be calculated in two different ways. One approach is to take 100 percent of the parent company's book values, the non controlling interest's 10 percent share of subsidiary book values, and the parent company's 90 percent share of subsidiary fair values. Applying this to the Inventories in the preceding example gives $6,030,00 [$3,440,000 + (10%)($2,500,000) + (90%)($2,500,000 + $100,000)]. An alternative approach takes 100 percent of the carrying values of the parent company's individual assets and liabilities, plus 100 percent of the carrying values of the subsidiary's individual assets and liabilities, plus or minus the parent company's 90 percent interest in the fair value changes on the subsidiary's individual assets and liabilities. This would give the same $6,030,000 [$3,440,000 + $2,500,000 + (90%)($2,600,000 - $2,500,000)]. While either of these approaches will produce the required solution, we believe the latter approach is somewhat more efficient in most problem situations. As a consequence, it will be more commonly used throughout the remainder of this text. Given this, we would suggest that you use this approach in solving assignment and self study problems.

Note On Non Controlling Interest   The Non Controlling Interest has been disclosed as a separate item between the Total Liabilities and Shareholders' Equity.

Push Down Accounting

General Concepts

4-93.   Throughout the preceding discussion of the consolidated Balance Sheet at the time of acquisition, no adjustments were made to the subsidiary's accounting records as a result of its being acquired. As was noted in Chapter 3, the acquisition of majority ownership in a subsidiary is a business combination transaction which will normally be accounted for by the purchase method. Further, such an acquisition may also represent the acquisition of all or virtually all of the equity interest in the subsidiary, a situation in which Section 1625 of the *CICA Handbook*, "Comprehensive Revaluation Of Assets and Liabilities", permits the use of push down accounting. Push down accounting represents an alternative to the procedures that we have described throughout this Chapter, in that it allows fair value changes to be recorded on the books of the subsidiary. In those situations where it is applicable, normally situations involving the ownership of 90 percent or more of the outstanding voting shares of the subsidiary, the use of push down accounting will significantly simplify the procedures required in the preparation of consolidated financial statements.

Example

Basic Data

4-94.   As we noted in the preceding Chapter, an understanding of push down accounting requires some familiarity with basic consolidation procedures. Now that we have examined consolidation procedures, at least to the extent they apply at the time of acquisition, we can present an example of the push down accounting procedures. As 90 percent ownership was involved in the preceding Example Four (Paragraph 4-85), we will use the same data to illustrate push down accounting. This will give you an opportunity to compare the procedures that will be used when push down accounting is used, with those applicable in situations where this approach is not used. The Example Four data is repeated here for your convenience:

On December 31, 1998, the Peak Company purchases 90 percent of the outstanding voting shares of the Seek Company for $5,220,000 in cash. On that date, subsequent to the business combination transaction, the Balance Sheets of the two Companies are as follows:

Balance Sheets
As At December 31, 1998

	Peak	Seek
Cash	$ 1,000,000	$ 700,000
Accounts Receivable	2,100,000	1,200,000
Inventories	3,440,000	2,500,000
Investment In Seek	5,220,000	-0-
Plant And Equipment (Net)	4,240,000	4,600,000
Total Assets	$16,000,000	$9,000,000
Current Liabilities	$ 1,200,000	$1,000,000
Long Term Liabilities	2,800,000	2,000,000
No Par Common Stock	7,000,000	2,000,000
Retained Earnings	5,000,000	4,000,000
Total Equities	$16,000,000	$9,000,000

Other Information:

A. All of the identifiable assets of the Seek Company have fair values that are equal to their carrying values except for Plant And Equipment which has a fair value that is $600,000 less than its carrying value and Inventories with fair values that are $100,000 more than their carrying values.

B. Prior to the business combination there were no intercompany transactions between the two Companies. It follows that on the date of the combination there are no intercompany asset and liability balances.

Required: Prepare a push down accounting Balance Sheet for the Seek Company as at December 31, 1998. Using this Balance Sheet as a basis for your procedures, prepare a consolidated Balance Sheet for the Peak Company and its subsidiary, the Seek Company, as at December 31, 1998.

CICA Handbook Recommendations

4-95.   In applying push down accounting to this example, three Recommendations of Section 1625 are relevant. The first is as follows:

Paragraph 1625.23   *When a comprehensive revaluation of an enterprise's assets and liabilities is undertaken as a result of a transaction or transactions as described in 1625.04(a), push-down accounting should be applied. The portion of the assets and liabilities related to non-controlling interests should be reflected at the carrying amounts previously recorded by the acquired enterprise.* (January, 1993)

4-96.   This Recommendation reflects the fact that the parent company approach to asset valuation at the time of acquisition is required in the preparation of consolidated financial statements. By indicating that the non controlling interest must be based on carrying values, it is made clear that asset and liability values can include only the acquiring company's share of fair value changes and goodwill. This means that the 90 percent column in the Example Four investment analysis can also be used here.

4-97.   The second relevant Recommendation on the application of push down accounting is as follows:

Paragraph 1625.29   *When a comprehensive revaluation of an enterprise's assets and liabilities is undertaken as a result of a transaction or transactions as described in 1625.04(a), that portion of retained earnings which has not been included in the consolidated retained earnings of the acquirer or is not related to any continuing non-controlling interests in the enterprise should be reclassified to either share* *capital, contributed surplus, or a separately identified account within sharehold-ers' equity.* (January, 1993)

4-98.   The Paragraph 1625.29 Recommendation requires that, with the exception of two types of items, the Retained Earnings of the subsidiary at acquisition must be reclassi-fied in the application of push down accounting. The two exceptions are:

- Amounts belonging to a non controlling interest.

- Amounts that have been included in the calculation of Retained Earnings of the ac-quirer as the result of an equity interest which existed prior to obtaining control over the subsidiary.

4-99.   The amounts which are reclassified can be allocated to share capital, contributed surplus, or a separately identified account within shareholders' equity. While the Recom-mendation is flexible in this regard, we would be inclined to allocate the acquirer's share of the subsidiary's contributed capital to a separately identified account within share-holders' equity. This would serve to distinguish this balance from the usual types of con-tributed capital balances.

4-100.   The third relevant *Handbook* Recommendation is as follows:

Paragraph 1625.30   *The revaluation adjustment arising from a comprehensive revaluation of an enterprise's assets and liabilities undertaken as a result of a trans-action or transactions as described in 1625.04(a) should be accounted for as a capital transaction,* (see CAPITAL TRANSACTIONS, Section 3610), *and recorded as either share capital, contributed surplus, or a separately identified account within shareholders' equity.* (January, 1993)

4-101.   With respect to the revaluation adjustment arising from altered asset and liabil-ity values, Paragraph 1625.30 also provides for alternative disclosure. Our preference in this case would be to again use a separate account for this amount. An appropriate title would be Capital Arising On Comprehensive Revaluation Of Assets.

Journal Entry - Push Down Accounting

4-102.   The journal entry required to implement push down accounting on the books of the Seek Company as at December 31, 1998 would be as follows:

Retained Earnings ([90%][$4,000,000])	$3,600,000	
Inventories	90,000	
Goodwill	270,000	
Capital Arising On Comprehensive		
Revaluation Of Assets (Differential)	180,000	
Plant And Equipment (Net)		$ 540,000
Contributed Surplus [(90%)($4,000,000)]		3,600,000

4-103.   This entry reclassifies the majority share of Retained Earnings as Contributed Surplus, records Peak's proportionate share of the fair value changes on Inventories and Plant And Equipment on Seek's books, records Peak's share of the Goodwill on Seek's books, and establishes a capital revaluation account for the excess of the cost of the in-vestment over Seek's book value (this is the Differential from the Example Four invest-ment analysis schedule - see Paragraph 4-87)).

Subsidiary Balance Sheet - Push Down Accounting

4-104.   Given the preceding journal entry, the push down accounting Balance Sheet of Seek Company on December 31, 1998 would be prepared as follows:

Seek Company
Push Down Accounting Balance Sheet
As At December 31, 1998

Cash	$ 700,000
Accounts Receivable	1,200,000
Inventories ($2,500,000 + $90,000)	2,590,000
Plant And Equipment (Net) ($4,600,000 - $540,000)	4,060,000
Goodwill	270,000
Total Assets	$8,820,000

Current Liabilities	$1,000,000
Long Term Liabilities	2,000,000
No Par Common Stock	2,000,000
Contributed Surplus	3,600,000
Capital Arising On Comprehensive Revaluation Of Assets	(180,000)
Retained Earnings (Non Controlling Interest)	400,000
Total Equities	$8,820,000

4-105.   Given this push down accounting Balance Sheet, the procedures for preparing the required consolidated Balance Sheet are simplified. The required journal entry would be as follows:

No Par Common Stock (Seek's)	$2,000,000	
Contributed Surplus (Seek's)	3,600,000	
Retained Earnings (Seek's)	400,000	
Capital Arising On Comprehensive		
Revaluation Of Assets		$ 180,000
Investment In Seek		5,220,000
Non Controlling Interest		600,000

4-106.   This entry eliminates all of the subsidiary's Shareholders' Equity balances, eliminates Peak's Investment In Seek, and establishes the Non Controlling Interest at acquisition.   This Non Controlling Interest balance is equal to their $200,000 [(10%)($2,000,000)] share of No Par Common Stock, plus the $400,000 Retained Earnings Balance. In keeping with the Paragraph 1625.23 requirement that the Non Controlling Interest must be based on carrying values, the $600,000 can also be calculated by taking 10 percent of the $6,000,000 in Shareholders' Equity from the pre acquisition Balance Sheet of Seek. Given this entry, the required consolidated Balance Sheet is identical to the parent company approach Balance Sheet presented in Example Four:

Peak Company And Subsidiary
Consolidated Balance Sheet
As At December 31, 1998

Cash ($1,000,000 + $700,000)	$ 1,700,000
Accounts Receivable ($2,100,000 + $1,200,000)	3,300,000
Inventories ($3,440,000 + $2,590,000)	6,030,000
Investment In Seek ($5,220,000 - $5,220,000)	-0-
Plant And Equipment (Net) ($4,240,000 + $4,060,000)	8,300,000
Goodwill	270,000
Total Assets	$19,600,000

Current Liabilities ($1,200,000 + $1,000,000)		$ 2,200,000
Long Term Liabilities ($2,800,000 + $2,000,000)		4,800,000
Total Liabilities		$ 7,000,000
Non Controlling Interest [(10%)($6,000,000)]		600,000
Shareholders' Equity:		
No Par Common Stock (Peak's Only)	7,000,000	
Retained Earnings (Peak's Only)	5,000,000	12,000,000
Total Equities		$19,600,000

Disclosure Requirements

4-107.   Before leaving the subject of push down accounting, we would note that the *CICA Handbook* has several disclosure Recommendations that are applicable when this method is used. These are as follows:

> **Paragraph 1625.34**   *In the period that push-down accounting has been first applied the financial statements should disclose the following:*
>
> (a) *the date push-down accounting was applied, and the date or dates of the purchase transaction or transactions that led to the application of push-down accounting;*
>
> (b) *a description of the situation resulting in the application of push-down accounting; and*
>
> (c) *the amount of the change in each major class of assets, liabilities and shareholders' equity arising from the application of push-down accounting.* (January, 1993)
>
> **Paragraph 1625.35**   *For a period of at least three years following the application of push down accounting the financial statements should disclose:*
>
> (a) *the date push down accounting was applied;*
>
> (b) *the amount of the revaluation adjustment and the shareholders' equity account in which the revaluation adjustment was recorded; and*
>
> (c) *the amount of retained earnings reclassified and the shareholders' equity account to which it was reclassified.* (January, 1993)

Reverse Takeovers

The Concept

4-108.   As noted in Chapter 3, there are business combination transactions in which the acquiring company from a legal point of view is, in fact, the acquiree from an economic point of view. This can only happen when the legal acquirer uses its own shares to obtain either the assets or shares of the legal acquiree. If, for example, an acquirer issues such a large block of shares to the shareholders of an acquiree that, subsequent to the business combination transaction, the acquiree shareholders hold a majority of shares in the acquirer, we have a reverse takeover. To help clarify this situation, we will assume that Alpha Company is combining with Beta Company and the legal form of the combination is an acquisition of 100 percent of the Beta Company shares. This transaction is diagrammed in Figure 4-2.

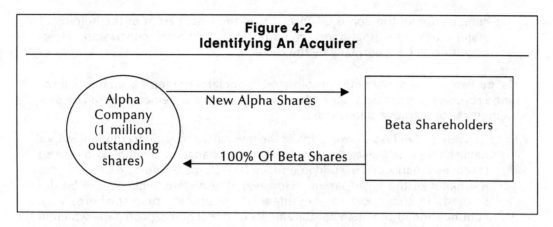

Figure 4-2
Identifying An Acquirer

Alpha Company (1 million outstanding shares) → New Alpha Shares → Beta Shareholders

Beta Shareholders → 100% Of Beta Shares → Alpha Company

4-109.   From a legal point of view, Alpha has acquired control of Beta through ownership of 100 percent of Beta's outstanding voting shares. Stated alternatively, Alpha is the parent company and Beta is its subsidiary. If you were to discuss this situation with a lawyer, there would be no question that Alpha Company is the acquirer from a legal point of view.

4-110.   However, the economic picture is not so clear. If, for example, Alpha has issued 1,500,000 new shares to the former shareholders of Beta, they now hold 60 percent (1,500,000 ÷ 2,500,000) of the outstanding shares of Alpha. As a group, the Beta shareholders own a majority of shares in the combined economic entity and, under the requirements of the *CICA Handbook*, Beta is deemed to be the acquirer. In other words, the economic outcome is the "reverse" of the legal result.

4-111.   Reverse takeovers are surprisingly common in practice and are used to accomplish a variety of objectives. One of the more common, however, is to obtain a listing on a public stock exchange. Referring to the example just presented, assume that Alpha is an inactive but listed public company. It is being used purely as a holding company for a group of relatively liquid investments. In contrast, Beta is a very active private company that would like to be listed on a public stock exchange. Through the reverse takeover procedure that we have just described, the shareholders of Beta have retained control over Beta. However, the shares that they hold to exercise that control are those of Alpha and these shares can be traded on a public stock exchange. The transaction could be further extended by having Alpha divest itself of its investment holdings and change its name to Beta Company. If this happens, Beta has, in effect, acquired a listing on a public stock exchange through a procedure that may be less costly than going through the usual listing procedures.

EIC Abstract No. 10 - Reverse Takeover Accounting

4-112.   We noted in the preceding Chapter that the concepts involved in reverse takeover accounting are no different than those involved in other business combinations where an acquirer can be identified. However, there are sufficient complications in the application of these concepts that the Emerging Issues Committee has issued Abstract No. 10, "Reverse Takeover Accounting". In this Abstract, the Committee reaches a consensus on six specific issues related to reverse takeovers. The issues, as well as the consensus reached, are as follows:

> **Issue One**   In what circumstances is it appropriate to apply reverse takeover accounting principles?
>
> > **Consensus On Issue One**   In general, reverse takeover accounting is appropriate when there has been a business combination transaction in which the shareholders of the legal subsidiary become owners of more than 50 percent of the voting shares of the legal parent. Other factors, such as the ultimate

composition of the Board Of Directors of the legal parent or the holding of major blocks of voting shares, could result in a different conclusion. However, this will not normally be the case.

Issue Two How should the consolidated financial statements prepared following a reverse takeover be described and what financial statements should be presented as comparative statements?

Consensus On Issue Two Unless the reverse takeover is accompanied by a name change for the legal parent (such name changes are common in reverse takeover situations), consolidated financial statements must be issued under the name of the legal parent. However, these statements should be described, in the notes to the financial statements or elsewhere, as a continuation of the financial statements of the acquiring company which in this type of situation is the legal subsidiary.

With respect to comparative figures, the fact that the combined company is a continuation of the business of the legal subsidiary means that statements from previous years will be those of the legal subsidiary. The fact that the capital structure of the consolidated entity, being the capital structure of the legal parent, is different from that appearing in the financial statements of the legal subsidiary in earlier periods due to the reverse takeover accounting should be explained in the notes to the consolidated financial statements.

Issue Three How should the cost of the purchase be determined and allocated in a reverse takeover transaction?

Consensus On Issue Three The general principle here is that the cost of the purchase should be based on the fair value of the consideration given or, where the fair value of the consideration given is not evident, the fair value of the net assets acquired. In a reverse takeover, the consideration is not given by the legal parent. Rather, it is deemed to be given by the legal subsidiary. The actual amount is determined by calculating the number of shares the legal subsidiary would have had to issue in order to provide the percentage of ownership in the combined company to the shareholders of the legal parent that they have retained in the combined company through the reverse takeover transaction. The fair value of these deemed new shares, usually determined by the fair market value of the legal subsidiary shares before the business combination would be used as the cost of the purchase. (There may be circumstances where the fair value of the legal parent's shares or the fair values of the identifiable assets and liabilities acquired would be used.) This process will be clarified in a subsequent example.

With respect to the allocation of this purchase price, the usual rules from Section 1580 would be applied. Note, however, in a reverse takeover it would be allocated to the fair values of the legal parent's assets and liabilities. The legal subsidiary's assets and liabilities would continue to be recorded at their original carrying values.

Issue Four How should the shareholders' equity be determined and presented in the consolidated balance sheet following a reverse takeover transaction?

Consensus On Issue Four Again it is noted that the combined company in a reverse takeover is a continuation of the legal subsidiary. This means that the combined company's Retained Earnings balance subsequent to the business combination transaction should be equal to that of the legal subsidiary. The amount shown as contributed capital should be that of the subsidiary prior to the business combination transaction, plus the fair value of the additional shares deemed to have been issued (the purchase cost). Note, however, the actual number and type of shares would have to reflect the capital structure of the legal parent, including any shares that were actually issued to effect the reverse takeover. In those cases where a reverse takeover is accompanied by a legal amalgamation, legislation may require that the contributed capital of the amalgamated company be equal to the aggregate of the contributed capital of the amalgamating companies prior to the amalgamation transaction. In such cases, any excess of legally required capital over the amounts required by these accounting recommendations should be shown as a separate balance in Shareholders' Equity. Additional note disclosure will usually be appropriate.

Issue Five   How should the earnings per share be determined for a fiscal year during which a reverse takeover occurs and for the years for which comparative statements are presented?

Consensus On Issue Five   For the current year, the number of shares to be used in the denominator of the earnings per share calculation will be the weighted average number of legal parent shares outstanding. For the portion of the year prior to the reverse takeover, this calculation would be based on the number of shares issued by the legal parent to the shareholders of the legal subsidiary. For the portion of the year subsequent to the reverse takeover, this calculation would be based on the actual number of legal parent shares outstanding. The income figure in the numerator would be that of the legal subsidiary, with the earnings of the legal parent added for the portion of the year subsequent to the reverse takeover transaction. In the comparative figure for previous years, the earnings per share calculation would involve dividing the earnings of the legal subsidiary by the number of shares issued in the reverse takeover by the legal parent.

Issue Six   When not all the shareholders of the legal subsidiary exchange their shares for shares in the legal parent, how should the interest of such shareholders be accounted for in the consolidated financial statements?

Consensus On Issue Six   From the point of view of the combined entity, these shareholders are a minority interest in the legal subsidiary. As the legal subsidiary is the acquirer in a reverse takeover transaction, this subsidiary's assets and liabilities would continue to be carried at their pre combination book values. As a consequence, this minority interest in the consolidated Balance Sheet would reflect the minority shareholders' proportionate interest in the book value of the net assets of the legal subsidiary.

Examples

Example With No Non Controlling Interest

4-113.   EIC Abstract No. 10 includes two examples which illustrate the various conclusions reached on reverse takeover accounting issues. The first of these examples involve a situation in which all of the subsidiary shares are acquired and there is no non controlling interest:

Alpha Company - Balance Sheets

	December 31 1997	September 30 1998
Current Assets	$ 400	$ 500
Fixed Assets	1,200	1,300
Total Assets	$1,600	$1,800
Current Liabilities	$ 200	$ 300
Long Term Liabilities	300	200
Deferred Income Taxes	100	100
Redeemable Preferred Shares (100 Shares)	100	100
Common Shares (100 Shares)	300	300
Retained Earnings	600	800
Total Equities	$1,600	$1,800

Beta Company - Balance Sheets

	December 31 1997	September 30 1998
Current Assets	$1,000	$ 700
Fixed Assets	2,000	3,000
Total Assets	$3,000	$3,700
Current Liabilities	$ 500	$ 600
Long Term Liabilities	700	800
Deferred Income Taxes	200	300
Common Shares (60 Shares)	600	600
Retained Earnings	1,000	1,400
Total Equities	$3,000	$3,700

Other Information:

1. For the nine months ended September 30, 1998, Alpha Company had Net Income of $200 while Beta had Net Income of $400. No dividends were declared by either Company during the period. Neither Company had any Extraordinary Items or Results Of Discontinued Operations during this period.

2. At September 30, 1998, the fair value of Alpha's common shares was $12 per share while that of Beta's shares was $40 per share.

3. On September 30, 1998, the fair values of Alpha's identifiable assets and liabilities are the same as their book values except for fixed assets which have a fair value of $1,500.

4. On September 30, 1998, Alpha issues 150 common shares in exchange for all 60 of the outstanding common shares of Beta.

Investment Analysis

4-114.   As the former Beta shareholders now own 60 percent [150 ÷ (100 + 150)] of the outstanding Alpha shares as compared to 40 percent (100 ÷ 250) for the ongoing Alpha shareholders, we are dealing with a reverse takeover. Had this combination been carried out through an issue of Beta shares, Beta would have had to issue 40 additional shares to Alpha in order to give the Alpha shareholders the same 40 percent interest [40 ÷ (60 + 40)] in the combined company. Using the fair value of Beta shares as the basis for determination, this gives a purchase cost of $1,600 [(40 Shares)($40)]. Given this, Goodwill can be calculated as follows:

Purchase Price	$1,600
Alpha's Book Value ($300 + $800)	(1,100)
Differential	$ 500
Fair Value Change On Alpha's Fixed Assets ($1,500 - $1,300)	(200)
Goodwill	$ 300

Consolidated Balance Sheet

4-115.   Based on these calculations, the required consolidated Balance Sheet can be prepared as follows:

Alpha Company And Subsidiary
Consolidated Balance
As At September 30, 1998

Current Assets ($700 + $500)		$1,200
Fixed Assets ($3,000 + $1,300 + $200)		4,500
Goodwill (See Preceding Calculation)		300
Total Assets		$6,000
Current Liabilities ($600 + $300)		$ 900
Long Term Liabilities ($800 + $200)		1,000
Deferred Taxes ($300 + $100)		400
Shareholders' Equity:		
Redeemable Preferred Shares (100)	$ 100	
Common Shares (Note One)	2,200	
Retained Earnings (Beta's)	1,400	3,700
Total Equities		$6,000

Note One   While the number of shares outstanding is Alpha's 250, the $2,200 is made up of Beta's original contributed capital of $600, plus the $1,600 resulting from the deemed issue of 40 additional shares in the reverse takeover.

Consolidated Net Income

4-116.   In calculating consolidated Net Income for the year ending December 31, 1998, Alpha's income for the nine month period ending September 30, 1998 would be excluded. On this basis, assume that the consolidated Net Income for combined entity's first full year ending December 31, 1998 is $800. This would be divided by a weighted average Alpha Company shares outstanding using 150 shares (the number issued to Beta in the reverse takeover transaction) for the first nine months of 1998 and 250 (the actual number outstanding for this period) for the remaining three months. The weighted average would be calculated as follows:

First Nine Months ([150 Shares][3/4])	112.5
Remaining Three Months ([250][1/4])	62.5
Weighted Average Shares Outstanding	175.0

4-117.   Given this weighted average for shares outstanding, the 1998 earnings per share would be calculated as follows:

$$\frac{\text{Consolidated Net Income}}{\text{Weighted Average Shares Outstanding}} = \frac{\$800}{175} = \$4.57$$

If we assume that Beta's Net Income for 1997 was \$600, the corresponding comparative figure for 1997 would be calculated as follows:

$$\frac{\text{Consolidated Net Income}}{\text{Weighted Average Shares Outstanding}} = \frac{\$600}{150} = \$4.00$$

Example With Minority Interest

4-118.   The preceding example assumed that all of the Beta shareholders exchanged their shares for those of Alpha. As noted in Issue Six, this may not always be the case and, when it is not, a minority interest is created. Note, however, that this is not the usual minority or non controlling interest. While it is an interest in the subsidiary, it is not an interest in the acquiree. Rather, it is a minority or non controlling interest in the acquirer. This means that its presence will not influence the cost of the purchase or the amounts to be allocated to fair value changes or goodwill.

Investment Analysis And Consolidated Balance Sheet

4-119.   To illustrate this possibility, we will modify the original example. The example will be altered by assuming that 150 Alpha shares are offered for the full 60 shares of Beta (2.5 Alpha shares for each Beta share). However, in this version of the example only 56 shares of Beta are tendered for exchange, resulting in the issue of only 140 Alpha shares. This means that the former Beta shareholders own 58.3 percent (140 ÷ 240) of the Alpha shares that are outstanding after the reverse takeover. If the combination had been carried out by issuing Beta shares, the issuance of 40 Beta shares would have resulted in the Beta shareholders retaining their 58.3 percent ownership interest (56 ÷ [56 + 40]) in the combined company. This means that the \$1,600 purchase price [(40 Shares)(\$40 Per Share)] would be the same as in the previous example, as would the amount of Goodwill to be recorded in the consolidated Balance Sheet. Given this, the consolidated Balance Sheet would be as follows:

Alpha Company And Subsidiary
Consolidated Balance Sheet
As At December 31, 1998

Current Assets (\$700 + \$500)	\$1,200
Fixed Assets (\$3,000 + \$1,300 + \$200)	4,500
Goodwill	300
Total Assets	\$6,000
Current Liabilities (\$600 + \$300)	\$ 900
Long Term Liabilities (\$800 + \$200)	1,000
Deferred Income Taxes (\$300 + \$100)	400
Total Liabilities	\$2,300
Non Controlling Interest (Note One)	134
Shareholders' Equity:	
Redeemable Preferred Shares (100) \$ 100	
Common Shares (Note Two) 2,160	
Retained Earnings (Note Three) 1,306	3,566
Total Equities	\$6,000

Note One   The \$134 Non Controlling Interest is based on 6.7 percent (4 Shares ÷ 60 Shares) of the carrying value of Beta's net assets (\$600 + \$1,400) prior to the reverse takeover.

Note Two   This note would disclose that there are 240 Alpha shares outstanding. The total amount of $2,160 is made up of the $560 associated with 56 of Beta's pre acquisition shares, plus the $1,600 associated with the 40 shares deemed to be issued in the reverse takeover transaction.

Note Three   The Retained Earnings reflects the majority's 93.3 percent share (56 Shares ÷ 60 Shares) of the $1,400 in Beta Retained Earnings at the time of the reverse takeover.

Summary Of Consolidation Procedures

4-120.   As described in this Chapter, we are developing a set of consolidation procedures involving three steps. This Chapter has focused on Step A and has introduced all of the procedures required to complete this Step. In addition, one procedure from Step B has been introduced. The procedures introduced in this Chapter are as follows:

Step A-1 Procedure   Eliminate 100 percent of the Investment In Subsidiary account.

Step A-2 Procedure   Eliminate 100 percent of all the balances in the subsidiary's shareholders' equity that are present on the acquisition date.

Step A-3 Procedure   Allocate any debit or credit Differential that is present at acquisition to the investor's share of fair value changes on identifiable assets, fair value changes on identifiable liabilities, and positive or negative goodwill.

Step A-4 Procedure   Allocate to a Non Controlling Interest account in the consolidated Balance Sheet, the non controlling interest's share of the book value of the total at acquisition Shareholders' Equity of the subsidiary.

Step B-1 Procedure   Eliminate 100 percent of all intercompany assets and liabilities.

4-121.   The preceding list includes all of the procedures that are required in Step A. These four Procedures will be used in all subsequent consolidation problems. We will also continue to use Step B-1. However, in Chapters 5 and 6, a number of additional procedures will be added to Step B and the Step C procedures will be introduced.

Summary Of Definitional Calculations

4-122.   You may recall from our discussion of the procedural approach to be used in preparing consolidated financial statements, that we encouraged you to work towards preparing the required balances in these statements by using direct definitional calculations. To assist you in this work, we offer the following definitions that have been developed in the course of this Chapter.

Identifiable Assets And Liabilities   The consolidated balance for any identifiable asset or liability is calculated as follows:

- 100 percent of the carrying value of the identifiable asset or liability on the books of the parent company at the balance sheet date; *plus*

- 100 percent of the carrying value of the identifiable asset or liability on the books of the subsidiary company at the balance sheet date; *plus (minus)*

- the parent company's share of the fair value increase (decrease) on the asset or liability (i.e., the parent company's share of the difference between the fair value of the subsidiary's asset or liability at time of acquisition and the carrying value of that asset or liability at the time of acquisition).

Goodwill The Goodwill to be recorded in the consolidated balance sheet is equal to the excess of the cost of the investment over the parent company's share of the fair values of the subsidiary's net identifiable assets as at the time of acquisition.

Non Controlling Interest - Balance Sheet The Non Controlling Interest to be recorded in the consolidated Balance Sheet will be an amount equal to the non controlling interest's ownership percentage of the book value of the subsidiary's common stock equity at the Balance Sheet date.

Contributed Capital The Contributed Capital to be recorded in the consolidated Balance Sheet will be equal to the Contributed Capital from the single entity Balance Sheet of the parent company.

Retained Earnings Consolidated Retained Earnings will be equal to the Retained Earnings balance that is included in the Balance Sheet of the parent company.

4-123.   We would note that these definitions reflect the current Recommendations of the *CICA Handbook*. As you might expect, some of these definitions will have to be modified as new consolidation procedures are developed in subsequent Chapters.

Additional Readings

(See also the Additional Readings listings in Chapters 2 and 3)

CA Magazine Article   "Consolidations Simplified - Part 1", George C. Baxter, Brenda M. Mallouk, And John R. E. Parker, November, 1981.

CA Magazine Article   "Consolidations Simplified - Part 2", George C. Baxter, Brenda M. Mallouk, And John R. E. Parker, January, 1982.

CA Magazine Article   "Consolidated Effort", Peter Martin, October, 1991.

CA Magazine Article   "The Revolution That Wasn't", Carla Daum, April, 1993.

CA Magazine Article   "Demystifying Dilution", Lynne Clark, May, 1993.

International Accounting Standard No. 27   *Consolidated Financial Statements And Accounting For Investments In Subsidiaries*, April, 1989.

Journal Of Accountancy Article   "Minority Interest: Opposing Views", Paul Rosenfield Versus Steven Rubin, March, 1986.

Journal Of Accountancy Article   "Uncharted Territory: Subsidiary Financial Reporting", Terry E. Allison and Paula Bevels Thomas, October, 1989.

Journal Of Accountancy Article   "APB 16: Time To Reconsider", Michael Davis, October, 1991.

Journal Of Accountancy Article   "Consolidations: An Overview Of The FASB Discussion Memorandum", Paul Pacter, April, 1992.

Journal Of Accountancy Article   "Understanding The FASB's New Basis Project", G. Michael Crooch and James A. Largay III, May, 1992.

Journal Of Accountancy Article   "Goodwill Accounting: Time For An Overhaul", Michael Davis, June, 1992.

Walk Through Problem

Note   This is the first example of what we refer to as walk through problems. In these walk through problems you are provided with a fill-in-the-blank solution format to assist you in solving the problem. This solution format begins on the following page and a complete solution to the problem follows the solution format. These problems are designed to be an easy way to get started with solving the type of problem illustrated in the Chapter. Having completed this problem, you should proceed to the Problems For Self Study which you will have to work without the assistance of a solution format. Also note that this same problem will be continued and extended in Chapters 5 and 6. This is to provide you with a basis for comparison as you move into more difficult procedures that are introduced in these subsequent Chapters.

Basic Data   On December 31, 1998, the Puff Company purchased 60 percent of the outstanding voting shares of the Snuff Company for $720,000 in cash. On that date, subsequent to the completion of the business combination, the Balance Sheets of the Puff and Snuff Companies and the fair values of Snuff's identifiable assets and liabilities were as follows:

| | Balance Sheets | | Fair Values |
	Puff	Snuff	Snuff
Cash And Accounts Receivable	$ 350,000	$ 200,000	$200,000
Inventories	950,000	500,000	450,000
Investment In Snuff	720,000	-0-	N/A
Plant And Equipment (Net)	2,400,000	700,000	800,000
Total Assets	$4,420,000	$1,400,000	
Current Liabilities	$ 400,000	$ 100,000	$100,000
Long Term Liabilities	1,000,000	400,000	360,000
No Par Common Stock	1,000,000	800,000	N/A
Retained Earnings	2,020,000	100,000	N/A
Total Equities	$4,420,000	$1,400,000	

Required: Prepare a consolidated Balance Sheet for the Puff Company and its subsidiary, the Snuff Company, as at December 31, 1998. Your answer should comply with the Recommendations of the *CICA Handbook*.

Walk Through Problem Solution Format

Investment Analysis

	60 Percent	100 Percent
Purchase Price	$	$
Book Value	($)($)	
Differential	$	$
Fair Value Change:		
On Inventories	$	$
On Plant And Equipment	($)($)	
On Long Term Liabilities	($)($)	
Goodwill	$	$

Investment Elimination Entry

No Par Common Stock	$	
Retained Earnings	$	
Long Term Liabilities	$	
Plant and Equipment (Net)	$	
Goodwill	$	
Inventories		$
Investment in Snuff		$
Non Controlling Interest		$

Puff Company And Subsidiary
Consolidated Balance Sheet
As At December 31, 1998

Cash And Accounts Receivable $

Inventories $

Investment in Snuff $

Plant And Equipment (Net) $

Goodwill $

Total Assets $

Current Liabilities $

Long Term Liabilities $

Non Controlling Interest $

No Par Common Stock $

Retained Earnings $

Total Equities $

Walk Through Problem Solution

Investment Analysis

	60 Percent	100 Percent
Purchase Price	$720,000	$1,200,000
Book Value	(540,000)	(900,000)
Differential	$180,000	$ 300,000
Inventories	30,000	50,000
Plant And Equipment	(60,000)	(100,000)
Long Term Liabilities	(24,000)	(40,000)
Goodwill	$126,000	$ 210,000

Investment Elimination Entry

No Par Common Stock	$800,000	
Retained Earnings	100,000	
Long Term Liabilities	24,000	
Plant and Equipment (Net)	60,000	
Goodwill	126,000	
Inventories		$ 30,000
Investment in Snuff		720,000
Non Controlling Interest (40% of $900,000)		360,000

Puff Company
Consolidated Balance Sheet
As At December 31, 1998

Cash and Accounts Receivable	$ 550,000
Inventories	1,420,000
Investment in Snuff	-0-
Plant And Equipment (Net)	3,160,000
Goodwill	126,000
Total Assets	$5,256,000
Current Liabilities	$ 500,000
Long Term Liabilities	1,376,000
Non Controlling Interest	360,000
No Par Common Stock	1,000,000
Retained Earnings	2,020,000
Total Equities	$5,256,000

Problems For Self Study

(The solutions for these problems can be found following Chapter 17 of the text.)

SELF STUDY PROBLEM FOUR - 1

On December 31, 1998, the Shark Company pays cash to acquire 70 percent of the outstanding voting shares of the Peril Company. On that date the Balance Sheets of the two Companies are as follows:

	Shark	Peril
Cash	$ 590,000	$ 200,000
Accounts Receivable	2,000,000	300,000
Inventories	2,500,000	500,000
Investment In Peril (At Cost)	910,000	-0-
Plant And Equipment (Net)	4,000,000	1,000,000
Total Assets	$10,000,000	$2,000,000
Liabilities	$ 2,000,000	$ 400,000
Common Stock (No Par)	4,000,000	400,000
Retained Earnings	4,000,000	1,200,000
Total Equities	$10,000,000	$2,000,000

On the acquisition date, the fair values of the Peril Company's assets and liabilities are as follows:

Cash	$ 200,000
Accounts Receivable	250,000
Inventories	550,000
Plant And Equipment (Net)	700,000
Liabilities	(500,000)
Net Fair Values	$1,200,000

Required: Prepare a consolidated Balance Sheet for the Shark Company and its subsidiary the Peril Company as at December 31, 1998. Your solution should comply with the Recommendations of the *CICA Handbook.*

SELF STUDY PROBLEM FOUR - 2

On December 31, 1998, the Potvin Distributing Company purchased 60 percent of the outstanding voting shares of the Shroder Company. On that date, subsequent to the acquisition transaction, the Balance Sheets of the two Companies were as follows:

	Potvin	Shroder
Cash	$ 300,000	$ 100,000
Accounts Receivable	2,000,000	200,000
Inventories	3,000,000	400,000
Investment In Shroder (At Cost)	1,200,000	-0-
Plant And Equipment (At Cost)	6,000,000	1,300,000
Accumulated Depreciation	(2,000,000)	(500,000)
Total Assets	$10,500,000	$1,500,000

	Potvin	Shroder
Accounts Payable	$ 1,500,000	$ 200,000
Long Term Liabilities	2,000,000	300,000
Common Stock (No Par)	3,000,000	1,500,000
Retained Earnings (Deficit)	4,000,000	(500,000)
Total Equities	$10,500,000	$1,500,000

On December 31, 1998, all of the identifiable assets and liabilities of both Companies have carrying values that are equal to their fair values except for the following accounts:

Fair Values	Potvin	Shroder
Inventories	$2,800,000	$450,000
Plant and Equipment	$4,500,000	$550,000
Long Term Liabilities	$1,600,000	$400,000

In addition to the preceding information, Shroder holds a copyright which was developed by its employees, but is not recorded on its books. On December 31, 1998, the copyright held by Shroder has a fair value of $200,000 and a remaining useful life of 5 years.

During 1998, the Shroder Company sold merchandise to the Potvin Company for a total amount of $100,000. On December 31, 1998, all of this merchandise has been resold by the Potvin Company, but Potvin still owes Shroder $10,000 on open account for these merchandise purchases.

Required: Prepare a consolidated Balance Sheet for the Potvin Distributing Company and its subsidiary, the Shroder Company as at December 31, 1998. Your solution should comply with the Recommendations of the *CICA Handbook*.

SELF STUDY PROBLEM FOUR - 3

On December 31, 1998, the Pentogram Company purchased 70 percent of the outstanding voting shares of the Square Company for $875,000 in cash. The Balance Sheets of the Pentogram Company and the Square Company before the business combination transaction on December 31, 1998 were as follows:

	Pentogram	Square
Cash	$1,200,000	$ 50,000
Accounts Receivable	400,000	250,000
Inventories	2,000,000	500,000
Plant And Equipment	4,000,000	1,400,000
Accumulated Depreciation	(1,000,000)	(300,000)
Total Assets	$6,600,000	$1,900,000
Current Liabilities	$ 200,000	$ 150,000
Long Term Liabilities	1,000,000	350,000
No Par Common Stock	2,000,000	1,000,000
Retained Earnings	3,400,000	400,000
Total Equities	$6,600,000	$1,900,000

All of the Square Company's identifiable assets and liabilities have carrying values that are equal to their fair values except for Plant and Equipment which has a fair value of $800,000, Inventories which have a fair value of $600,000 and Long Term Liabilities which have a fair value of $400,000.

Required: Prepare a consolidated Balance Sheet for the Pentogram Company and its subsidiary, the Square Company as at December 31, 1998, subsequent to the business combination. Your solution should comply with all of the requirements of the *CICA Handbook*.

Assignment Problems

(The solutions to these problem are only available in
the solutions manual that has been provided to your instructor.)

ASSIGNMENT PROBLEM FOUR - 1

The Excelsior Company purchased 80 percent of the outstanding voting shares of the Excelsiee Company for $120,000 in cash. On the acquisition date, after the business combination transaction, the Balance Sheets of the two Companies and the fair values of the Excelsiee Company's identifiable assets and liabilities were as follows:

	Book Values Excelsior	Book Values Excelsiee	Fair Values Excelsiee
Cash	$ 100,000	$ 120,000	$ 120,000
Accounts Receivable	1,500,000	500,000	400,000
Inventories	2,300,000	400,000	200,000
Investment in Excelsiee (At Cost)	120,000	-0-	-0-
Plant and Equipment (Net)	3,980,000	1,100,000	1,300,000
Total Assets	$8,000,000	$2,120,000	
Accounts Payable	$1,000,000	$ 400,000	$ 350,000
Mortgage Payable	-0-	120,000	120,000
Long Term Liabilities	2,000,000	1,400,000	1,600,000
Common Stock No Par	2,000,000	150,000	
Retained Earnings	3,000,000	50,000	
Total Equities	$8,000,000	$2,120,000	

Required: Prepare a consolidated Balance Sheet for the Excelsior Company and its subsidiary the Excelsiee Company as at the acquisition date. Your answer should comply with the Recommendations of the *CICA Handbook*.

ASSIGNMENT PROBLEM FOUR - 2

On December 31, 1998, the Balance Sheets of the Pike Company and the Stirling Company were as follows:

	Pike	Stirling
Cash	$ 195,000	$ 118,500
Accounts Receivable (Net)	472,500	253,500
Inventories	883,500	596,700
Plant And Equipment (Net)	4,050,000	2,251,500
Goodwill	142,500	45,000
Total Assets	$5,743,500	$3,265,200
Current Liabilities	$ 13,500	$ 45,000
Long Term Liabilities	1,080,000	1,673,700
Preferred Stock - Par $100	-0-	30,000
Common Stock - No Par	2,550,000	1,500,000
Retained Earnings	2,100,000	16,500
Total Equities	$5,743,500	$3,265,200

On December 31, 1998, the net identifiable assets and goodwill of both Companies had fair values that were equal to their carrying values except for the following fair values:

Fair Values	Pike	Stirling
Accounts Receivable	$470,000	$ 237,000
Inventories	976,300	571,500
Goodwill	-0-	-0-
Long Term Liabilities	800,000	1,050,000

The Pike Company has 50,000 No Par Common Shares outstanding with a current market price of $36 per share. The Stirling Company has 20,000 No Par Common Shares outstanding. The Preferred Shares of the Stirling Company are cumulative, nonparticipating, and have no dividends in arrears. There have been no intercompany transactions prior to December 31, 1998.

Required: Prepare, in accordance with the Recommendations of the *CICA Handbook*, the consolidated Balance Sheet as at December 31, 1998 for both of the following independent cases:

A. Assume that the Pike Company issued 37,500 of its shares to acquire 75 percent of the outstanding shares of Stirling on December 31, 1998. On this same date, Pike purchased one half of the issue of Stirling Preferred Stock for $15,000 in cash.

B. Assume that Pike Company issued 50,000 of its shares on December 31, 1998 to acquire all of the outstanding shares of Stirling and in addition purchased the entire issue of Stirling Preferred Stock for $30,000 in cash on this date. Neither Company can be identified as the acquirer in this transaction.

ASSIGNMENT PROBLEM FOUR - 3

On December 31, 1998, the closed Trial Balances of the Pass Company and the Sass Company were as follows:

	Pass	Sass
Cash and Receivables	$ 100,000	$ 10,000
Inventories	3,300,000	290,000
Plant And Equipment (At Cost)	9,000,000	3,000,000
Accumulated Depreciation	(3,400,000)	(1,200,000)
Total Assets	$9,000,000	$2,100,000
Current Liabilities	$ 300,000	$ 200,000
Long Term Liabilities	3,500,000	800,000
Mortgage Payable	-0-	300,000
Common Stock - No Par	1,000,000	-0-
Common Stock - Par $50	-0-	900,000
Contributed Surplus	-0-	300,000
Retained Earnings (Deficit)	4,200,000	(400,000)
Total Equities	$9,000,000	$2,100,000

The Pass Company has 25,000 shares outstanding on December 31, 1998 which are trading at $50 per share on this date. On December 31, 1998, the net identifiable assets of both Companies had fair values that were equal to their carrying values except for the following fair values:

Fair Values	Pass	Sass
Plant and Equipment (Net)	$7,000,000	$1,500,000
Long Term Liabilities	3,000,000	900,000

Prior to the business combination, in 1998, Pass sold merchandise to Sass for $200,000 and Sass sold Pass merchandise for $100,000. On December 31, 1998, one-half of these intercompany purchases had been resold to parties outside the consolidated entity. These sales provide both Companies with a 20 percent gross margin on sales prices. On December 31, 1998, Sass owed Pass $50,000 on its intercompany merchandise purchases.

Required: Prepare the combined Companies' Balance Sheet as at December 31, 1998 for each of the following independent cases:

A. Assume that Pass has issued 15,000 of its shares to acquire 75 percent of the outstanding shares of Sass on December 31, 1998. Pass can be identified as the acquirer.

B. Assume that Pass has issued 25,000 of its shares on December 31, 1998 to acquire all of the outstanding shares of Sass. Neither Company can be identified as the acquirer.

Your solutions should comply with the Recommendations of the *CICA Handbook*.

ASSIGNMENT PROBLEM FOUR - 4

The Peretti Company and the Blakelock Company are two successful Canadian companies operating on Prince Edward Island. On December 31, 1998, the condensed Balance Sheets and the identifiable fair values of the Peretti Company and the Blakelock Company are as follows:

Peretti Company
December 31, 1998

	Balance Sheet	Fair Values
Current Assets	$2,220,000	$2,340,000
Non Current Assets (Net)	3,600,000	3,900,000
Total Assets	$5,820,000	
Current Liabilities	$ 420,000	$ 420,000
Long Term Liabilities	1,500,000	1,440,000
Common Stock - No Par	1,800,000	
Retained Earnings	2,100,000	
Total Equities	$5,820,000	

Blakelock Company
December 31, 1998

	Balance Sheet	Fair Values
Current Assets	$1,800,000	$1,980,000
Non Current Assets (Net)	3,540,000	2,400,000
Total Assets	$5,340,000	
Current Liabilities	$ 720,000	$ 720,000
Long Term Liabilities	2,400,000	2,520,000
Common Stock - No Par	1,200,000	
Retained Earnings	1,020,000	
Total Equities	$5,340,000	

The Peretti Company has 300,000 common shares outstanding with a market price of $12 per share. The Blakelock Company has 60,000 common shares outstanding with a market price of $23 per share. On December 31, 1998, Peretti owes Blakelock $48,000 for the use of Blakelock's accounting staff during 1998.

Required: Assume that on December 31, 1998, subsequent to the preparation of the preceding single entity Balance Sheets, the Peretti and Blakelock Companies enter into a business combination. The following list describes three independent cases based on differing assumptions with respect to how the combination was effected. In each case, prepare the appropriate Balance Sheet for the combined business entity as at December 31, 1998, subsequent to the business combination.

A. The Peretti Company purchases 60 percent of the outstanding shares of the Blakelock Company for $900,000 in cash. The consolidated Balance Sheet will be prepared using the entity approach to consolidated financial statements.

B. The Peretti Company issues 75,000 of its shares and uses them to acquire 60 percent of the Blakelock Company shares. The consolidated Balance Sheet will be prepared in compliance with the recommendations of the *CICA Handbook*.

C. The Peretti Company issues 300,000 common shares to the shareholders of Blakelock Company in exchange for all of the Blakelock Company's outstanding shares. Blakelock Company continues to exist as a separate legal entity. No acquirer can be identified in this transaction.

ASSIGNMENT PROBLEM FOUR - 5

On December 31, 1998, the Poplin Company acquires 95 percent of the outstanding shares of Silk Company in return for cash of $1,235,000. The remaining 5 percent of the Silk Company shares remain in the hands of the public.

Immediately after this acquisition transaction, the Balance Sheets of the two Companies were as follows:

Poplin And Silk Companies
Balance Sheets
As At December 31, 1998

	Poplin	Silk
Cash	$ 220,000	$ 78,000
Accounts Receivable	1,140,000	125,000
Inventories	2,560,000	972,000
Investment In Silk	1,235,000	N/A
Land	665,000	137,000
Plant And Equipment (Net)	2,750,000	430,000
Total Assets	$8,570,000	$1,742,000
Current Liabilities	$ 560,000	$ 225,000
Long Term Liabilities	1,340,000	517,000
Common Stock - No Par	2,800,000	450,000
Retained Earnings	3,870,000	550,000
Total Equities	$8,570,000	$1,742,000

At the time of this acquisition, all of the identifiable assets and liabilities of Silk Company had fair values that were equal to their carrying values except the Land which had a fair value of $337,000, and the Plant And Equipment which had a fair value of $380,000. Poplin Company will use push down accounting, as described in Section 1625 of the *CICA Handbook* to account for its Investment in Silk.

Required:

A. Prepare the Silk Company's Balance Sheet that is to be used in preparing the December 31, 1998 consolidated Balance Sheet.

B. Prepare the consolidated Balance Sheet for Poplin Company and its subsidiary Silk as at December 31, 1998.

ASSIGNMENT PROBLEM FOUR - 6
The Balance Sheets of the Fortune Company and the Gold Company as at December 31, 1997 and July 1, 1998 prior to any business combination transaction, were as follows:

	Fortune Company		Gold Company	
	1/7/98	31/12/97	1/7/98	31/12/97
Current Assets	$ 420,000	$ 410,000	$ 620,000	$ 604,000
Fixed Assets (Net)	1,320,000	1,400,000	2,920,000	2,996,000
Total Assets	$1,740,000	$1,810,000	$3,540,000	$3,600,000
Current Liabilities	$ 220,000	$ 230,000	$ 350,000	$ 360,000
Long Term Liabilities	430,000	680,000	520,000	930,000
Contributed Capital:				
Redeemable Preferred Shares	200,000	200,000	-0-	-0-
Common Shares	500,000	500,000	1,200,000	1,200,000
Retained Earnings	390,000	200,000	1,470,000	1,110,000
Total Equities	$1,740,000	$1,810,000	$3,540,000	$3,600,000

Other Information:

1. For the six month period ending July 1, 1998, the Fortune Company had Net Income of $190,000 and the Gold Company had Net Income of $360,000. These figures did not contain any Extraordinary Items or Results Of Discontinued Operations. Neither Company declared any dividends during this period.

2. On both Balance Sheet dates, the Fortune Company had 20,000 Redeemable Preferred Shares and 50,000 Common Shares outstanding. On July 1, 1998, the Common Shares were trading at $22 per share.

3. On both Balance Sheet dates, the Gold Company had 40,000 Common Shares outstanding. On July 1, 1998, these shares were trading at $75 per share.

4. On July 1, 1998, all of the fair values of Fortune Company's and Gold Company's identifiable assets and liabilities had book values that were equal to their fair values except for Fixed Assets. Fortune's Fixed Assets had a fair value of $1,900,000, while Gold's Fixed Assets had a fair value of $2,800,000.

Required: For the following two independent cases, use the guidelines provided by the Emerging Issues Committee (EIC) Abstract No. 10 to prepare the July 1, 1998 Consolidated Balance Sheet for Fortune Company and its subsidiary Gold Company. In addition, calculate Consolidated Net Income and Basic Earnings Per Share for the six month period ending July 1, 1998.

A. On July 1, 1998, Fortune Company issues 100,000 additional Common Shares in exchange for all of the outstanding Common Shares of Gold Company.

B. On July 1, 1998, Fortune Company issues 85,000 additional Common Shares in exchange for 36,000 (90 percent) of the outstanding Common Shares of Gold Company.

Chapter 5

Consolidation Subsequent To Acquisition (No Unrealized Intercompany Profits)

Procedures Subsequent To Acquisition

5-1.   Once we move beyond the date on which the parent acquired its controlling interest in the subsidiary shares, the preparation of consolidated financial statements becomes much more complex. We will have to deal with the concept of consolidated Net Income and the preparation of a consolidated Income Statement. Further, both the Statement Of Retained Earnings and the Statement Of Changes In Financial Position will have to be prepared on a consolidated basis. Even the preparation of a consolidated Balance Sheet in the periods subsequent to the date of acquisition will become more complex as we have to write off fair value changes and goodwill, eliminate intercompany assets and liabilities, and allocate the retained earnings of the subsidiary since acquisition.

5-2.   We will begin this Chapter with a simple example of the conceptual alternatives in the presentation of the consolidated Income Statement. While we will find that the *CICA Handbook* requires the use of the parent company approach in preparing a consolidated Income Statement for a parent company and its subsidiaries, this example will also illustrate other alternatives. In addition, you should note that the proprietary approach consolidated Income Statements illustrated do have a practical application. They are identical to the Income Statements that would be prepared when proportionate consolidation is used to account for joint ventures.

Conceptual Alternatives For The Consolidated Income Statement

Example

5-3.   In order to provide an illustration of the various possible approaches to the preparation of the consolidated Income Statement, we will use the following example:

The Pick Company owns 60 percent of the outstanding shares of the Stick Company. The purchase was made at a time when all of the identifiable assets and liabilities of the Stick Company had carrying values that were equal to their fair values. The purchase price was equal to 60 percent of the carrying values of the Stick Company's net identifiable assets. In a subsequent year the condensed Income Statements of the two Companies are as follows:

	Pick	Stick
Sales	$4,000,000	$2,000,000
Cost of Goods Sold	$2,500,000	$1,000,000
Other Expenses	700,000	400,000
Total Expenses	$3,200,000	$1,400,000
Net Income	$ 800,000	$ 600,000

Proprietary Concept Solution

5-4.   Under this conceptual approach, the expenses and revenues that are disclosed in the consolidated Income Statement consist of 100 percent of the parent company's expenses and revenues plus a share of the subsidiary's expenses and revenues that is based on the parent company's ownership interest (60 percent in this example). The resulting Income Statement is as follows:

Sales ($4,000,000 + $1,200,000)	$5,200,000
Cost Of Goods Sold ($2,500,000 + $600,000)	$3,100,000
Other Expenses ($700,000 + $240,000)	940,000
Total Expenses	$4,040,000
Consolidated Net Income	$1,160,000

5-5.   Since the consolidation procedures remove the non controlling interest's share of the individual subsidiary expenses and revenues, there is no necessity to disclose a separate Non Controlling Interest in the consolidated Income Statement. This, of course, is analogous to the procedures that were used in preparing the consolidated Balance Sheet under the proprietary concept. You might also note that the consolidated Net Income of $1,160,000 is equal to the sum of the Pick Company's Net Income of $800,000, plus 60 percent of the Stick Company's Net Income of $600,000.

Parent Company Concept Solution

5-6.   This conceptual approach views the non controlling interest as a part of the consolidated entity and, as a consequence, the consolidated Income Statement includes 100 percent of the expenses and revenues of both the parent and the subsidiary company. With respect to the nature of the non controlling interest's participation in the consolidated entity, the parent company approach views these shareholders as having a creditor like interest. Given this view, the non controlling interest in the income of the consolidated entity would be viewed as a claim analogous to interest charges on creditor interests. This would require that the Non Controlling Interest be deducted in the computation of consolidated Net Income. The resulting consolidated Income Statement would appear as follows:

Sales ($4,000,000 + $2,000,000)	$6,000,000
Cost Of Goods Sold ($2,500,000 + $1,000,000)	$3,500,000
Other Expenses ($700,000 + $400,000)	1,100,000
Total Expenses	$4,600,000
Combined Income	$1,400,000
Non Controlling Interest (40 Percent Of $600,000)	240,000
Consolidated Net Income	$1,160,000

5-7.   There are several aspects of this presentation that you should note. First, in our disclosure we have calculated a separate subtotal for Combined Income. This has been done for illustrative purposes only. Normal disclosure would have the Non Controlling Interest grouped and deducted with the other expenses of the consolidated entity.

5-8.   As a second point, note that the Non Controlling Interest is based on the reported income of the subsidiary. Consistent with the view that the non controlling shareholders have a creditor like interest, there is no recognition of their share of the adjustments required in the application of consolidation procedures (e.g., fair value changes). As a consequence, the Non Controlling Interest in the consolidated Income Statement is simply their 40 percent share of Stick Company's reported Net Income of $600,000.

5-9.   Finally, note that the consolidated Net Income is the same figure that we arrived at using the parent company approach. This will always be the case as both the proprietary and the parent company approach ignore the non controlling interest's share of the various adjustments required in applying consolidation procedures. The difference between these two approaches is one of disclosure, with the parent company approach including the Non Controlling Interest in the consolidated Income Statement while the proprietary approach excludes this amount.

Entity Concept Solution

5-10.   As was the case with the parent company approach, the entity approach views the non controlling interest as being a part of the consolidated entity. This would mean that the consolidated expenses and revenues would again include 100 percent of the reported expenses and revenues of both the parent company and the subsidiary company. The difference is that the entity approach views the non controlling interest as an additional class of owner's equity. Given this, the non controlling interest in the income of the consolidated entity must be treated in a manner analogous to the treatment of dividends on preferred shares. That is, it will be viewed as a distribution of Net Income rather than as a determinant of Net Income. Therefore, instead of being a deduction in the computation of consolidated Net Income, the Non Controlling Interest under the entity concept would be shown as a distribution of income in the consolidated Statement of Retained Earnings. The entity approach consolidated Income Statement would be as follows:

Sales ($4,000,000 + $2,000,000)	$6,000,000
Cost Of Goods Sold ($2,500,000 + $1,000,000)	$3,500,000
Other Expenses ($700,000 + $400,000)	1,100,000
Total Expenses	$4,600,000
Consolidated Net Income	$1,400,000

5-11.   Note that the figure that was designated Combined Income under the parent company approach has become consolidated Net Income. Further, it is equal to the combined Net Incomes of the individual entities ($800,000 for Pick and $600,000 for Stick). In this example, with no fair value changes or goodwill, the Non Controlling Interest would still be $240,000 or 40 percent of the reported income of the subsidiary. As can be seen in the example, however, it would not be disclosed in the consolidated Income Statement. Rather, it would be shown as a deduction in the consolidated Statement Of Retained Earnings in a manner analogous to the disclosure accorded dividends on preferred stock.

CICA Handbook Requirements

5-12.   The position of the *CICA Handbook* on the choice of conceptual approaches to be used in the preparation of the consolidated Income Statement is not internally consistent. With respect to the treatment of the Non Controlling Interest in Income Before Discontinued Operations And Extraordinary Items, the *Handbook* makes the following Recommendation:

> **Paragraph 1600.67**   *The non-controlling interest in the income or loss before discontinued operations and extraordinary items for the period should be disclosed separately in the consolidated income statement.* (January, 1990)

5-13.   This position reflects the parent company approach in that it requires a Non Controlling Interest (thus, rejecting the proprietary approach) that is shown in the consolidated Income Statement (thus, rejecting the entity approach). However, with respect to the treatment of subsidiary results of discontinued operations and extraordinary items, the Recommendation continues as follows:

> **Paragraph 1600.67**   *Where there are discontinued operations or extraordinary items, the parent company's portion of such items should be disclosed.* (January, 1990)

5-14.   This, of course, is a reflection of the proprietary conceptual approach to consolidations. There is no explanation offered for this apparent inconsistency.

General Approach To Problem Solving

The Problem With Consolidation Procedures

5-15.   The preparation of consolidated financial statements, to an extent not approached by any other area of financial accounting, has seen a tremendous amount of attention devoted to the development of detailed and extensive technical procedures. In addition to several alternative work sheet approaches, consolidation problems have been solved using a variety of computerized approaches using spreadsheets and linear programming. Indeed, it seems that anyone that has ever taught this subject has reached the conclusion that they have found a "better way" to deal with such problems.

5-16.   In our opinion, there are two basic drawbacks with relying on any set of consolidation procedures, including those that will be used in this text:

1.   You can develop great facility with any of the available detailed procedural approaches, without acquiring any real understanding of the content of consolidated financial statements. We have often encountered situations where a student, having developed lightning like speed in manipulating a work sheet, will be completely at a loss when asked to do a simple calculation of consolidated Net Income or the Non Controlling Interest to be included in a consolidated Balance Sheet. It appears that focusing on detailed procedures does little to facilitate an understanding of the real content of consolidated financial statements.

2.   An equally serious problem with detailed procedural approaches is that they only work when the data for a consolidation problem is presented in the format for which the procedural approach was developed. For example, if you develop a set of procedures that will work when the investment in the subsidiary is carried in the underlying records of the parent company by the cost

method, these procedures will not work if the investment is carried by the equity method. Similarly, if procedures are developed for problems which require both a consolidated Income Statement and a consolidated Balance Sheet, they will not work when only a consolidated Balance Sheet is required. If detailed procedures are to be relied on, the only solution to this problem is to develop a full blown set of procedures for each possible problem format.

15-17. As we noted in Chapter 4 (see Paragraph 4-42), it is our belief that if you develop a thorough understanding of the consolidation process, the most efficient method of preparing consolidated financial statements is to be in a position to make an independent computation of each of the consolidated account balances. This approach does not rely on detailed work sheet or journal entry procedures and, as a consequence, there is no need to learn alternative sets of consolidation procedures.

15-18. The problem remains, however, of getting you to the stage where you can efficiently make definitional calculations of the various balances that may be required in a consolidation problem. This will require some type of organized procedural approach and, as we indicated in Chapter 4, we will base our procedures on the use of journal entries applied to the balances that are given in the basic problem data. We would remind you that we view these procedures as an interim teaching device. We encourage you to discontinue using them as soon as you feel that you understand the concepts well enough to make direct computations of the balances that are required for inclusion in the consolidated financial statements.

Classification Of Problems

Problem Requirements

5-19. As was indicated in the preceding Section, consolidation problems can be presented in a variety of formats. While there is an almost unlimited number of possibilities in this area, we have found it useful to classify problems in terms of (1) problem requirements and (2) method of carrying the investment.

5-20. With respect to problem requirements, there are two basic types of problems. We have designated these two types as open trial balance problems and closed trial balance problems. The two types of problems can be described as follows:

Open Trial Balance Problems This is the designation that we will use for any problem that requires the preparation of any consolidated statement or the calculation of any consolidated information, other than all or part of a consolidated Balance Sheet. The use of this designation reflects the fact that such problems are often, but not always, presented as an open trial balance (i.e., a trial balance prepared before expenses and revenues have been closed to retained earnings). A typical problem of this variety would require the preparation of a consolidated Income Statement, a consolidated Statement Of Retained Earnings, and a consolidated Balance Sheet. Procedures are required here to deal with both the beginning of the year balance in subsidiary Retained Earnings, as well as items of expense or revenue that occur during the year.

Closed Trial Balance Problems This is the designation that we will use for problems which require only the preparation of all or part of a consolidated Balance Sheet. The use of this designation reflects the fact that such problems are often, but not always, presented as a closed trial balance (i.e., a trial balance prepared after expenses and revenues have been closed to retained earnings.) The procedures developed for this type of problem do not have to deal with either the opening Retained Earnings or expense and revenue items that occur during the year.

Accounting Method

5-21. When consolidated financial statements are prepared, the parent's Investment In Subsidiary account will be eliminated and replaced by the various assets and liabilities of the subsidiary. This means that the parent company can carry this Investment In Subsidiary account by any method they choose. As the account will not be included in the published consolidated financial statements, *CICA Handbook* Recommendations are not applicable.

5-22.   While it is not possible to establish this from published financial statements, it is likely that most companies carry their Investment In Subsidiary accounts at cost. It is a less complicated method and, in addition, cost is generally the tax basis for such assets. However, it is possible that a problem will be presented with the investment carried at equity. This results in a second approach to the classification of problems — problems in which the Investment In Subsidiary is accounted for by the cost method versus problems in which the Investment In Subsidiary is carried by the equity method.

Classifications To Be Covered

5-23.   Given the two types of problem requirements that we have designated and the two methods by which the investment may be carried, we can identify the following general types of problems:

1.   **Open** Trial Balance with the investment at **Cost**
2.   **Closed** Trial Balance with the investment at **Cost**
3.   **Open** Trial Balance with the investment at **Equity**
4.   **Closed** Trial Balance with the investment at **Equity**

5-24.   In previous editions of this book we have developed procedures to deal with each of these possible problem formats. Our experience has been that this does not enhance your understanding of consolidated financial statements, nor does it assist in arriving at the ultimate goal of preparing consolidated financial statements by using direct definitional calculations.

5-25.   In particular, there seemed to be difficulty in understanding the somewhat awkward procedures that are required when the Investment In Subsidiary account is carried by the equity method. It is our impression that few students ever really mastered these procedures. Further, we do not believe that it is a useful expenditure of your time to make the effort that would be required to fully understand these procedures.

5-26.   Given this situation, the comprehensive example that will be used in this Chapter, as well as in Chapter 6, will illustrate only the two types of problems where the Investment In Subsidiary is carried by the cost method. We will not, in either this Chapter or Chapter 6, develop procedures to be used when the investment is carried by the equity method. Note, however, that if you wish to pursue such procedures, a discussion of these requirements can be found in Chapter 7 which deals with advanced topics in consolidations.

The Procedures

5-27.   As was indicated in Chapter 4, we are going to develop a set of procedures which use the basic data of the problem, adjust and eliminate parts of this basic data using journal entries, and use this information to arrive at final figures to be included in the consolidated financial statements. As outlined in that Chapter, there are three basic Steps involved in these procedures and they can be described as follows (this description assumes that the investment in the subsidiary is accounted for by the cost method):

Step A - Investment Elimination   This first Step will eliminate 100 percent of the investment account against the subsidiary shareholders' equity at the time of acquisition. As a part of this Step, entries will also be made to record the investor's share of the acquisition date fair value changes and goodwill of the subsidiary. In addition, a Non Controlling Interest will be established, representing the non controlling shareholders' interest in carrying values of the net identifiable assets of the subsidiary as at the date of acquisition.

This Step was dealt with in a comprehensive fashion in Chapter Four and was codified into a set of four specific procedures to be used. These procedures are repeated here for your convenience:

Step A-1 Procedure   Eliminate 100 percent of the Investment In Subsidiary account.

Step A-2 Procedure   Eliminate 100 percent of all the balances in the subsidiary's shareholders' equity that are present on the acquisition date.

Step A-3 Procedure   Allocate any debit or credit Differential that is present at acquisition to the investor's share of fair value changes on identifiable assets, fair value changes on identifiable liabilities, and positive or negative goodwill.

Step A-4 Procedure   Allocate to a Non Controlling Interest account in the consolidated Balance Sheet, the non controlling interest's share of the book value of the total Shareholders' Equity of the subsidiary at acquisition.

Note that these procedures will have to be implemented, even in periods subsequent to the year of acquisition. This reflects the fact that consolidation entries are only working paper entries and are not entered on the books of the individual legal entities. Unless push down accounting is used, the Step A entries required in the year of acquisition, will have to be repeated in each subsequent year.

Step B - Adjustments And Eliminations   This Step involves making adjustments and eliminations to the various accounts that will be included in the consolidated information. At this stage of the development of our consolidation procedures, we can identify four types of adjustments and eliminations that we must be prepared to deal with. They are as follows:

1. If intercompany asset and liability balances are present, they must be eliminated. This procedure was discussed and illustrated in Chapter Four. It was also stated in terms of a specific procedure as follows:

    Step B-1 Procedure   Eliminate 100 percent of all intercompany assets and liabilities.

2. In Step A, the parent company's share of all of the acquisition date fair value changes on the subsidiary's assets and liabilities was recorded. To the extent that these fair value changes were recorded on assets with an unlimited economic life, the recorded fair value changes can be left in place until such time as the assets are sold. If such assets are sold, there will be a need to adjust any resulting gain or loss recorded on the books of the subsidiary to reflect the realization of the fair value change.

    When the fair value changes are recorded on assets or liabilities with a limited life, the subsidiary will record amortization, depletion, or depreciation on these assets based on their carrying values. As a consequence, there will be a need to adjust these amortization, depletion, or depreciation amounts to reflect the realization of the fair value changes on these assets and liabilities. If such assets are sold prior to the end of their economic life, the resulting gain or loss must be adjusted for the unrealized balance of the fair value change.

    In addition to the preceding adjustments, the consolidation procedures that will be used subsequent to acquisition will require amortization of any goodwill recognized at the time of acquisition.

3. If intercompany expenses and revenues are present, they must be eliminated. Note that, in this Chapter, we are dealing only with intercompany expenses and revenues, no unrealized intercompany profits.

4. If intercompany dividends have been declared, they must be removed from

the revenues and dividends declared account.

Step C - Distribution Of Subsidiary Retained Earnings   Step A left a balance in the retained earnings of the subsidiary. This balance represents the retained earnings of the subsidiary that have been accumulated since the date of acquisition. If the parent owned 100 percent of the subsidiary and there were no Step B adjustments or eliminations, the subsidiary's retained earnings since acquisition balance would simply become a part of consolidated Retained Earnings.

However, these assumptions are usually not applicable. In most situations there will be less than 100 percent ownership and a portion of the subsidiary retained earnings since acquisition will have to be allocated to the Non Controlling Interest in the consolidated Balance Sheet. Further, there will almost always be Step B adjustments and eliminations, some of which will alter the subsidiary's retained earnings since acquisition balance. This is further complicated by the fact that some of these Step B changes will apply only to the controlling interest in subsidiary retained earnings since acquisition, while others will alter both the controlling and the non controlling shares of this balance. (This latter situation does not turn up until Chapter 6 when we introduce unrealized intercompany profits.) As a consequence, it is not possible to allocate the controlling and non controlling shares of the subsidiary's retained earnings since acquisition until we have completed the Step B adjustments and eliminations.

This brings us to Step C. At this point, our one remaining task will be to take the subsidiary retained earnings since acquisition balance, as adjusted by the Step B adjustments and eliminations, and allocate it between the Non Controlling Interest in the consolidated Balance Sheet and consolidated Retained Earnings.

5-28.   Given this general outline of the procedures to be followed, we can now turn our attention to the application of these three Steps to the various relevant versions of a comprehensive problem.

Comprehensive Example - Open Trial Balance With Investment At Cost

Basic Data

5-29.   Our first example involves a problem in which you are asked to prepare more than just a consolidated Balance Sheet. While consolidated Statement Of Cash Flows is required, a consolidated Income Statement and a consolidated Statement of Retained Earnings are required, in addition to a consolidated Balance Sheet. This means that this problem would be classified as an open trial balance problem. As will always be the case in this Chapter, the Investment In Subsidiary will be carried at cost.

On January 1, 1994, the Pleigh Company purchases 80 percent of the outstanding shares of the Sleigh Company for $3,200,000 in cash. On that date the Sleigh Company had No Par Common Stock of $2,000,000 and Retained Earnings of $1,500,000. On December 31, 1998, the adjusted trial balances of the Pleigh Company and its subsidiary, the Sleigh Company are as follows:

	Pleigh	Sleigh
Cash	$ 500,000	$ 300,000
Current Receivables	800,000	400,000
Inventories	2,500,000	1,700,000
Long Term Note Receivable	200,000	-0-
Investment In Sleigh - At Cost	3,200,000	-0-
Land	1,500,000	1,000,000
Plant And Equipment (Net)	4,500,000	1,900,000
Cost Of Goods Sold	2,800,000	1,500,000
Depreciation Expense	200,000	100,000
Other Expenses	364,000	616,000
Interest Expense	240,000	84,000
Dividends Declared	350,000	100,000
Total Debits	$17,154,000	$7,700,000
Current Liabilities	$ 500,000	$ 200,000
Long Term Liabilities	2,000,000	700,000
No Par Common Stock	8,000,000	2,000,000
Retained Earnings (January 1)	2,550,000	2,300,000
Sales	4,000,000	2,500,000
Interest Revenue	24,000	-0-
Dividend Revenue	80,000	-0-
Total Credits	$17,154,000	$7,700,000
1998 Net Income	$ 500,000	$ 200,000
December 31, 1998 Retained Earnings	$ 2,700,000	$2,400,000

Other Information:

A. At the date of Pleigh Company's acquisition of the Sleigh Company's shares, all of the identifiable assets and liabilities of the Sleigh Company had fair values that were equal to their carrying values except Inventories which had fair values that were $100,000 more than their carrying values, Land with a fair value that was $150,000 less than its carrying value and Plant And Equipment which had a fair value that was $250,000 greater than its carrying value. The Plant And Equipment had a remaining useful life on the acquisition date of 20 years while the inventories that were present on the acquisition date were sold during the year ending December 31, 1994. The Land is still on the books of the Sleigh Company on December 31, 1998. Any goodwill is to be amortized over 10 years. Both Companies use the straight line method to calculate depreciation and amortization.

B. Sleigh Company's Sales during 1998 include sales of $300,000 to Pleigh Company. All of this merchandise has been resold by the Pleigh Company.

C. On December 31, 1998, the Pleigh Company is holding Sleigh Company's long term note payable in the amount of $200,000. Interest at 12 percent is payable on July 1 of each year. Pleigh Company has been holding this note since July 1, 1996.

D. Between January 1, 1994 and December 31, 1997, the Sleigh Company earned a total of $2,500,000 and paid dividends of $1,700,000.

Required Prepare a consolidated Income Statement and a consolidated Statement Of Retained Earnings for the year ending December 31, 1998 and a consolidated Balance Sheet as at December 31, 1998 for the Pleigh Company and its subsidiary, the Sleigh Company.

Step A Procedures
Investment Analysis
5-30. As indicated in Chapters 3 and 4, in business combination transactions for which the purchase method of accounting is applicable, it is useful to prepare an analysis of the investment cost. Using the procedures developed in those Chapters, the analysis of the Pleigh Company's investment in the Sleigh Company is as follows:

	80 Percent	100 Percent
Investment Cost	$3,200,000	$4,000,000
Book Value At Acquisition	(2,800,000)	(3,500,000)
Differential	$ 400,000	$ 500,000
Fair Value Changes:		
Inventories	(80,000)	(100,000)
Land	120,000	150,000
Plant And Equipment (Net)	(200,000)	(250,000)
Goodwill	$ 240,000	$ 300,000

5-31. Note that this analysis is based on the values for Sleigh Company's assets at the time of acquisition. This reflects the fact that fair value and goodwill amounts to be recognized are established at this time.

5-32. At acquisition, the total fair value of the net assets of the Sleigh Company is $3,700,000 ($3,500,000 + $250,000 - $150,000 + $100,000). The Goodwill of $240,000 can be verified by comparing the investment cost of $3,200,000 to $2,960,000, the investor's 80 percent share of the fair values of $3,700,000.

Investment Elimination
5-33. Based on the preceding analysis and using the procedures developed in Chapter 4, the journal entry to eliminate the investment account is as follows:

No Par Common Stock	$2,000,000	
Retained Earnings	1,500,000	
Plant And Equipment (Net)	200,000	
Inventories	80,000	
Goodwill	240,000	
Land		$ 120,000
Non Controlling Interest		700,000
Investment In Sleigh		3,200,000

Step B(1) - Intercompany Assets And Liabilities
Procedure
5-34. The first type of adjustment or elimination that is required in Step B involves the elimination of intercompany assets and liabilities. As was noted in Chapter 4, it is not uncommon for intercompany debts to arise between a parent and a subsidiary. When these two legal entities are viewed as a single economic entity, such intercompany debt has no real economic existence and should be eliminated. The appropriate procedure for this was described in Chapter Four and codified as Step B-1.

Comprehensive Example

5-35.   There are two such items in this problem. The most obvious is the $200,000 long term note payable from Sleigh to Pleigh. An additional intercompany balance relates to the fact that the last interest payment on this note was July 1, 1998. This would mean that on December 31, 1998, Sleigh would have recorded interest payable and Pleigh would have recorded interest receivable of $12,000 [(6/12)(12%)($200,000)]. The required elimination entries would be as follows:

Long Term Liabilities	$200,000	
Long Term Note Receivable		$200,000
Current Liabilities	$ 12,000	
Current Receivables		$ 12,000

5-36.   You should note that the purpose of this entry is to avoid the overstatement of the total consolidated assets and equities. The elimination of such intercompany liabilities will never have any influence on either the Non Controlling Interest in the consolidated Balance Sheet or the amount of consolidated Retained Earnings.

Step B(2) - Fair Value And Goodwill Write Offs

General Procedures

5-37.   In Step A we recorded the parent company's share of fair value changes on the subsidiary's identifiable assets and liabilities, as well as that company's share of unrecorded subsidiary goodwill. In making the Step A entry you should have noticed that, despite the fact that we are several years past acquisition, the amounts that were recorded were the same as those that would have been recorded at the time of acquisition. This means that, at this point, we need a further procedure to recognize the extent to which these fair value changes have been realized in the period subsequent to acquisition.

5-38.   Realization of these amounts can take place in one of two ways. In the case of non current assets with limited lives (Plant And Equipment or Goodwill in our example), realization will occur as the asset is used up. On the books of the subsidiary, the carrying values of these assets would be charged to depreciation or amortization expense on the basis of their carrying values. In the consolidated Financial Statements these depreciation or amortization amounts must be adjusted to reflect the depreciation or amortization of the related fair value changes. A similar analysis can be made of liabilities with limited lives.

5-39.   The alternative way in which a fair value change can be realized is through disposal of the asset by the subsidiary. In the case of current assets (Inventories in our example), this will take place in the normal course of business operations in the one year period following acquisition. On the books of the subsidiary, the disposal will result in the carrying value of the current asset being charged to expense. In a manner analogous to the adjustment of depreciation or amortization expense on depreciable assets, the expense to which the current asset was charged must be adjusted for the realization of the fair value change. In the case of Inventories, the adjustment would be to the consolidated cost of goods sold.

5-40.   It is also possible that a non current asset with a limited life might be sold prior to the end of that life. This would usually result in the recognition of a gain or loss by the subsidiary with the amount being calculated on the basis of the carrying value of the asset. In this situation, the unamortized portion of the fair value change would be considered realized and, in preparing consolidated financial statements, would be treated as an adjustment of the gain or loss recognized by the subsidiary.

5-41.   For fair value changes on non current assets with an unlimited life (Land in our example), it may not be necessary to record any adjustment in Step B. If the asset is still owned by the consolidated entity, the fair value change has become a part of its consolidated carrying value. This adjustment would be recorded as part of Step A. As the asset has an unlimited life, there is generally no need to amortize either the asset or the related fair value change in Step B. However, if the asset is sold in the periods subsequent to acquisition, any gain or loss recorded by the subsidiary will have to be adjusted to reflect the fact that all of the fair value change that was recognized in the consolidated financial statements has become realized.

5-42. A further complication in dealing with the adjustments required by realization of fair value changes is caused by the fact that such realization may occur in either the current period or in an earlier period subsequent to the acquisition date. As all of the subsidiary's expenses and revenues that relate to prior periods would now be accumulated in the subsidiary Retained Earnings, adjustments for fair value realizations that relate to prior periods will have to be recorded as adjustments of that balance. In contrast, the adjustments for fair value realizations during the current period can be made to current expenses or revenues.

5-43. All of the preceding can be stated as Step B-2 as follows:

Step B-2 Procedure Give recognition to the post acquisition realization of acquisition date fair value changes on assets and liabilities that have been used up or sold during the post acquisition period. To the extent that this realization occurred in prior periods, this recognition will require an adjustment of the opening Retained Earnings of the subsidiary. Alternatively, if the realization occurred in the current period, the adjustment will be to the subsidiary's current period expenses, revenues, gains, or losses.

5-44. We will now turn our attention to applying this procedure to the fair value changes in our comprehensive example.

Inventories

5-45. With respect to the Inventories, these were charged at their carrying value to the Cost Of Goods Sold of the Sleigh Company during 1994. This means that all of Sleigh Company's $80,000 share of the fair value increase on Inventories was realized during that prior year. As the subsidiary would have recorded Cost Of Goods Sold on the basis of the $1,700,000 carrying value of the Inventories, an $80,000 addition to this expense is required. In addition, as the Inventories are no longer the property of the subsidiary, it is necessary to reverse that $80,000 increase in Inventories that was recorded in Step A. The entry required in 1994 is as follows:

Cost Of Goods Sold	$80,000	
Inventories		$80,000

5-46. Since this entry was not recorded on the books of the Sleigh Company, the Retained Earnings of the Sleigh Company will be $80,000 too high in all subsequent years. This would mean that in these subsequent years, including the current 1998 period, the following adjustment will be required in the preparation of consolidated financial statements:

Retained Earnings - Sleigh	$80,000	
Inventories		$80,000

5-47. While the preceding debit is to the Retained Earnings of Sleigh, you should note that because we are only recognizing the investor's share of the fair value change, this adjustment would only affect the Pleigh Company's share of the Retained Earnings of Sleigh. This would be true of all of the adjustments of depreciation, depletion and amortization of fair value changes and goodwill that are required in the process of preparing consolidated financial statements.

Plant And Equipment

5-48. When a fair value change has been recorded on an asset or liability that is being allocated to income over several accounting periods, this Step B-2 in the consolidation procedures is somewhat more complex. This is due to the fact that adjustments are required for each accounting period in which income is influenced by the presence of the asset. In the problem under consideration, we allocated a fair value change of $200,000 [(80%)($200,000)] to Plant And Equipment which had a useful life of 20 years at the time of the acquisition on January 1, 1994. This will require a $10,000 ($200,000 ÷ 20) adjustment to Depreciation Expense in each year for the 20 years subsequent to the acquisition date. For example, the required entry for 1994 would be as follows:

Depreciation Expense	$10,000	
Plant And Equipment (Net)		$10,000

5-49.   This entry serves to increase Depreciation Expense by $10,000 and to reverse 1/20 of the fair value change that was recorded in Step A. In each subsequent year, the credit to Plant And Equipment (Net) will increase by $10,000. However, the debit to Depreciation Expense will remain at $10,000 and will be accompanied by a debit to Retained Earnings for adjustments to Depreciation Expense for prior periods. Note that in this "open trial balance" version of the problem, any adjustments that are made to Sleigh's Retained Earnings are to the opening balance in this account.

5-50.   Based on this analysis, the entries that would have been required in 1995, 1996, and 1997 are as follows:

1995

Retained Earnings - Sleigh's Opening	$10,000	
Depreciation Expense	10,000	
Plant And Equipment (Net)		$20,000

1996

Retained Earnings - Sleigh's Opening	$20,000	
Depreciation Expense	10,000	
Plant And Equipment (Net)		$30,000

1997

Retained Earnings - Sleigh's Opening	$30,000	
Depreciation Expense	10,000	
Plant And Equipment (Net)		$40,000

5-51.   The entry specifically required in this problem would adjust Sleigh's opening Retained Earnings for the four years 1994 through 1997 and the Depreciation Expense for the current year. This entry would be as follows:

Required Entry

Retained Earnings - Sleigh's Opening	$40,000	
Depreciation Expense	10,000	
Plant And Equipment (Net)		$50,000

5-52.   Here again, the adjustment to the Retained Earnings of the Sleigh Company will only affect the parent company's share of this balance, a reflection of the parent company conceptual approach to the asset valuation problem in the preparation of consolidated financial statements.

Goodwill

5-53.   In Step A we recognized Goodwill in the amount of $240,000. The Other Information (Item A) in the problem indicate that this balance is to be allocated to income over 10 years so that the appropriate charge to consolidated income is $24,000 per year. The debit to Goodwill Amortization Expense will be accompanied by a credit to the Goodwill balance that was established in Step A of these procedures, resulting in the following entry for 1994:

Goodwill Amortization Expense	$24,000	
Goodwill		$24,000

5-54.   In each subsequent year the credit to the asset Goodwill will increase by $24,000 and, as was the case with the entries for the fair value change on Plant And Equipment, the expense debit will remain the same. This reflects the fact that the expense adjustment for previous years must be to Sleigh's opening Retained Earnings balance. Given this, the entries that would have been made in the years 1995 through 1997 are as follows:

1995

Retained Earnings - Sleigh's Opening	$24,000	
Goodwill Amortization Expense	24,000	
Goodwill		$48,000

1996

Retained Earnings - Sleigh's Opening	$48,000	
Goodwill Amortization Expense	24,000	
Goodwill		$72,000

1997

Retained Earnings - Sleigh's Opening	$72,000	
Goodwill Amortization Expense	24,000	
Goodwill		$96,000

5-55.   The entry that would be specifically required in this problem for 1998 would be as follows:

Required Entry

Retained Earnings - Sleigh's Opening	$96,000	
Goodwill Amortization Expense	24,000	
Goodwill		$120,000

5-56.   This entry will leave a net balance in the Goodwill account of $120,000 ($240,000 - $120,000).

Land

5-57.   This problem also involves a fair value change on a piece of land which was owned by the Sleigh Company on the acquisition date. This fair value change was recorded in Step A and, since land is not normally subject to depreciation or depletion, no further entry is required here as long as the Sleigh Company still owns the land. Since the problem indicates that Sleigh is still holding the land on December 31, 1998, no Step B entry is required for the land.

Summary

5-58.   The preceding illustrates the procedures required by the three different types of fair value changes that you will encounter. These are fair value changes on current assets, fair value changes on assets with unlimited lives and fair value changes on long term assets and liabilities with limited lives. You will encounter these types of fair value changes in virtually every consolidation problem, which makes it essential that you understand these procedures. We also remind you that under the parent company approach to asset valuation, these adjustments have no effect on the interest of the non controlling shareholders, either in the consolidated Balance Sheet or in the consolidated Income Statement.

Step B(3) - Intercompany Expenses And Revenues

General Procedure

5-59.   The third type of adjustment or elimination that is required in Step B involves the elimination of intercompany expenses and revenues. The principles that are involved here are identical to those involved in intercompany asset-liability situations. If we view a parent company and its subsidiaries as a single accounting entity, intercompany expenses and revenues reflect transactions which have no real economic existence. Stated as a procedure, the required elimination is as follows:

Step B-3 Procedure   Eliminate 100 percent of all intercompany expenses and revenues.

5-60.   Note that in both Step B-1 which deals with the elimination of intercompany assets and liabilities and with this new Step B-3, we eliminate 100 percent of the relevant items, without regard to the percentage of subsidiary shares which are owned by the parent company.

Intercompany Sales

5-61.   In this problem, Sleigh Company sells merchandise to the Pleigh Company for $300,000. Assume (this information is not part of the basic problem) that Sleigh purchased this merchandise for $180,000 and Pleigh resold it for $350,000. If we simply added together the single entity results for this transaction, the result would be as follows:

Sales ($300,000 + $350,000)	$650,000
Cost Of Goods Sold ($180,000 + $300,000)	(480,000)
Gross Margin	$170,000

5-62.   From the perspective of the two Companies as a single consolidated entity, the correct figures would be a revenue from sales outside the consolidated entity of $350,000 and an expense resulting from purchases outside the consolidated entity of $180,000. To achieve this result we must eliminate both the intercompany expense and intercompany revenue. The required entry is as follows:

Sales	$300,000	
Cost Of Goods Sold		$300,000

5-63.   The effect of this entry is to reduce total expenses and total revenues. It has no influence on gross margin which will remain at $170,000 ($350,000 - $180,000). Further, it will not influence either the non controlling interest's share or the majority shareholder's portion of that income.

5-64.   You should also note that this entry is based on the fact that all of the merchandise that Pleigh has acquired from Sleigh has been resold. If this were not the case, any profit resulting from the sale would be viewed as unrealized and the procedures here would have to be altered. We will deal with this issue when we get to Chapter 6.

Intercompany Interest Expense And Revenue

5-65.   There is a second item in this problem to which this general procedure applies. This is the interest of $24,000 (12 percent of $200,000) on the intercompany note payable. The entry to eliminate this item is as follows:

Interest Revenue	$24,000	
Interest Expense		$24,000

5-66.   As was the case with the intercompany sales entry, the purpose of the preceding entry is to reduce total revenues and expenses. Neither the non controlling nor the consolidated share of Net Income is influenced by this elimination.

Step B(4) - Intercompany Dividends

5-67.   The final Step B elimination in this problem involves the intercompany dividends. The Sleigh Company declared and paid $100,000 in dividends during 1998 and the Pleigh Company recorded the $80,000 of these which it received as a dividend revenue. Obviously, some type of elimination is required.

5-68.   To understand this elimination you must recall that under the requirements of the *CICA Handbook*, consolidated Net Income is defined using the parent company concept. This means that consolidated Net Income does not include the Non Controlling shareholders' share of subsidiary income. As a consequence, in the consolidated Statement Of Retained Earnings, when we show distributions of consolidated Net Income in the form of dividends, the dividends to be disclosed will be those of the parent company only. Since the consolidated Statement Of Retained Earnings discloses only the parent company's dividends, we will have to eliminate 100 percent of the Dividends Declared of the subsidiary. Of this total, the parent company's share will be eliminated from the Dividend Revenues of the parent company while the remainder will be treated as a direct reduction of the Non Controlling Interest in the Balance Sheet. This analysis can be expressed in the form of Step B-4 as follows:

> **Step B-4 Procedure** Eliminate 100 percent of subsidiary dividends declared. The controlling share of this amount will be deducted from the revenues of the parent company and the non controlling share of this amount will be deducted from the Non Controlling Interest in the consolidated Balance Sheet.

5-69. Using this procedure the required entry is as follows:

Dividend Revenue	$80,000	
Non Controlling Interest (Balance Sheet)	20,000	
Dividends Declared		$100,000

5-70. With the $20,000 in dividends to the non controlling shareholders being charged directly to the Non Controlling Interest account on the consolidated Balance Sheet, the only separate disclosure of this $20,000 item will be in the consolidated Statement Of Changes In Financial Position.

5-71. As a final point you should note that there is no need to make any adjustments for dividends paid by the subsidiary in earlier periods. In periods after the dividends are declared, the $80,000 controlling interest share will be included in the Retained Earnings of the parent company and will become a component of consolidated Retained Earnings. This is appropriate in that these resources are still within the consolidated entity.

Summary Of Step B Adjustments And Eliminations

5-72. The preceding paragraphs have demonstrated and explained the four basic adjustments that are required in Step B for this problem. An additional adjustment will be introduced in Chapter Six which deals with unrealized intercompany profits. All of these adjustments are common to the great majority of consolidation problems that you will encounter and are, as a consequence, of considerable significance. We will now turn our attention to the final Step C of our consolidation procedures.

Step C - Distribution Of The Subsidiary Retained Earnings

The Problem

5-73. At this point our one remaining task is to determine the appropriate distribution of the balance that is left in the Retained Earnings account of the Sleigh Company. In the original trial balance, the January 1, 1998 balance in this account was $2,300,000. The remaining balance in this account can be calculated as follows:

Balance - January 1, 1998	$2,300,000
Step A Elimination (Balance At Acquisition)	(1,500,000)
Step B Adjustments:	
Fair Value Change On Inventories	(80,000)
Fair Value Change On Plant And Equipment (Net)	(40,000)
Goodwill Amortization	(96,000)
Balance After Step A And B Procedures	$ 584,000

5-74. As this remaining balance represents Sleigh earnings that have accrued subsequent to the business combination transaction in which Pleigh acquired Sleigh, a portion of this will be included in the Retained Earnings of the consolidated entity. However, we must also allocate an appropriate portion of this amount to the Non Controlling Interest in the consolidated Balance Sheet.

5-75.   As more factors enter into our consolidation problems, the computation involved in this distribution becomes fairly complex. A good deal of this complexity results from the fact that the *CICA Handbook* is not consistent with respect to the conceptual approach that is required in the preparation of consolidated financial statements. However, in this Section the only adjustments that have an effect on this distribution are related to fair value changes and goodwill and, as we have previously noted, these adjustments follow the approach that is used for the valuation of consolidated net assets. This is the parent company approach.

5-76.   It follows that none of the Step B adjustments affect the non controlling interest's share of these Retained Earnings. This means that the non controlling interest's share of the subsidiary's Retained Earnings since acquisition can simply be based on the carrying value of the subsidiary's Retained Earnings. Despite this simplicity, we will introduce an approach to this computation that can be applied without regard to how complex the problem becomes. While this approach and schedule are not really essential at this stage, it will serve us well when we introduce unrealized intercompany profits in Chapter 6.

Retained Earnings Distribution Schedule

5-77.   This schedule begins with the opening Retained Earnings balance of the subsidiary and immediately removes the portion of this balance that was present at the time of acquisition. In more complex situations, the next step would be to adjust the remaining amount for unrealized upstream profits, the only adjustment which has an effect on the non controlling interest in subsidiary Retained Earnings. Since there are no unrealized intercompany profits in this problem, we can proceed immediately to the computation and deduction of the non controlling interest in the Retained Earnings of the subsidiary since acquisition. All other Step B adjustments are then accounted for to arrive at the amount which represents the parent company's share of the adjusted Retained Earnings of the subsidiary since acquisition. This amount, often referred to as an equity pickup, will then be allocated to consolidated Retained Earnings. Stated as a procedure, this allocation can be described as follows:

> **Step C-1 Procedure**   Determine the appropriate allocation of the subsidiary's adjusted Retained Earnings since acquisition. The non controlling interest's share will be based on book value. In contrast, the allocation to consolidated Retained Earnings will be the parent company's share of book values, adjusted for the realization of fair value changes that have occurred since acquisition.

5-78.   Based on this Step, the required schedule can be completed as follows:

Retained Earnings Distribution Schedule

Balance As Per The Trial Balance	$2,300,000
Balance At Acquisition	(1,500,000)
Balance Since Acquisition	$ 800,000
Non Controlling Interest [(20%)($800,000)]	(160,000)
Available To The Controlling Interest	$ 640,000
Step B Adjustments:	
Inventories	(80,000)
Plant And Equipment (4 Years At $10,000)	(40,000)
Goodwill (4 Years At $24,000)	(96,000)
To Consolidated Retained Earnings	$ 424,000

5-79.   Note that the Step B adjustments in this schedule reflect the journal entries that were made in the Step B procedures.

5-80.   With the information from this schedule, we can now make the Step C distribution entry.

Retained Earnings Distribution Entry

5-81.   The final procedure can be stated as follows:

> **Step C-2 Procedure**   Eliminate the subsidiary's adjusted Retained Earnings since acquisition. This amount will be allocated to the Non Controlling Interest in the consolidated Balance Sheet and to consolidated Retained Earnings as determined in Step C-1.

5-82.   The entry required to distribute the Sleigh Company's retained earnings since acquisition is as follows:

Retained Earnings - Sleigh	$584,000	
Non Controlling Interest (Balance Sheet)		$160,000
Consolidated Retained Earnings		424,000

5-83.   This journal entry reduces the Sleigh Company's Retained Earnings balance to zero, distributing the remaining balance to the controlling and non controlling interests in the consolidated entity. With this entry completed we have established the opening balance for consolidated Retained Earnings. It is simply the Pleigh Company's January 1, 1998 balance of $2,550,000 plus the $424,000 allocation resulting from the preceding journal entry, for a total of $2,974,000.

Preparation Of Consolidated Financial Statements

5-84.   With the addition of the Step C distribution entry, we have completed all of the procedures necessary for the preparation of consolidated financial statements. We will now take the individual account balances from the original trial balance, add and subtract the adjustments that have been made in Steps A, B, and C of our procedures, thereby arriving at the figures to be included in the consolidated financial statements. These computations will be disclosed parenthetically, a method of disclosure that we would recommend for use on examinations. We remind you again that, if your grasp of the procedures which we are using is sufficiently solid, the most efficient approach to the preparation of consolidated financial statements is the direct computation of the individual statement items without taking the time to prepare the preceding working paper journal entries.

Consolidated Income Statement

Statement Disclosure

5-85.   The consolidated Income Statement of the Pleigh Company and its subsidiary for 1998 would be prepared as follows:

Pleigh Company And Subsidiary
Consolidated Income Statement
Year Ending December 31, 1998

Sales ($4,000,000 + $2,500,000 - $300,000)	$6,200,000
Interest Revenue ($24,000 - $24,000)	-0-
Dividend Revenue ($80,000 - $80,000)	-0-
Total Revenues	$6,200,000
Cost Of Goods Sold ($2,800,000 + $1,500,000 - $300,000)	$4,000,000
Depreciation Expense ($200,000 + $100,000 + $10,000)	310,000
Interest Expense ($240,000 + $84,000 - $24,000)	300,000
Other Expenses ($364,000 + $616,000)	980,000
Goodwill Amortization Expense	24,000
Total Expenses	$5,614,000
Combined Income	$ 586,000
Non Controlling Interest (20 Percent Of $200,000)	40,000
Consolidated Net Income	$ 546,000

5-86.   We note again that the subtotal for Combined Income is not normal disclosure. It has been included only for computational purposes. Normal disclosure under the required parent company approach would have the Non Controlling Interest included among the other deductions from revenue. Similarly, there would not be disclosure of either Interest Revenue or Dividend Revenue in an actual consolidated Income Statement. We have included these items here to emphasize that procedures were required to remove them.

Definitional Calculation

5-87.   In addition to being able to prepare a consolidated Income Statement in the manner illustrated, it is useful to know how to prepare an independent calculation of the final consolidated Net Income figure. This calculation can be used to verify the consolidated Net Income figure which results from the preparation of a consolidated Income Statement or, in those problems that only require a final consolidated Net Income figure and not a complete statement, this calculation can save you the time that would be required to calculate individual consolidated expenses and revenues. Further, there are some problems which ask for this calculation, without providing you with individual expense and revenue information. When this is the case, it is essential that you know how to make such calculations.

5-88.   There are a variety of ways in which this calculation can be made. However, we have found that the approach which is sometimes referred to as the definitional calculation seems to be the easiest to understand. This calculation is as follows:

Pleigh Company's Net Income	$500,000
Intercompany Dividend Revenues	(80,000)
Pleigh's Net Income Less Dividends	$420,000
Pleigh's Equity In The Net Income Of Sleigh ([80%][$200,000])	160,000
Income Before Adjustments	$580,000
Adjustments:	
Fair Value Depreciation	(10,000)
Goodwill Amortization	(24,000)
Consolidated Net Income	$546,000

Consolidated Statement Of Retained Earnings

Statement Disclosure

5-89.   Using the preceding Net Income data, we can now prepare the consolidated Statement Of Retained Earnings for 1998 of the Pleigh Company and its subsidiary. It would be as follows:

Pleigh Company And Subsidiary
Consolidated Statement Of Retained Earnings
Year Ending December 31, 1998

Balance - January 1, 1998 ($2,550,000 + $424,000)	$2,974,000
1998 Net Income	546,000
1998 Dividends (Parent's Only)	(350,000)
Balance - December 31, 1998	$3,170,000

Definitional Calculation

5-90.   As was the case with consolidated Net Income, you will frequently find it useful to be able to make an independent computation of the end of the year balance in the Retained Earnings account. Here again, this independent computation can be used to verify the figure that was arrived at in the preparation of the consolidated Statement Of Retained Earnings or as a more efficient method of determining this balance when the complete Statement Of Retained Earnings is not required. The definitional approach to the computation of this amount is as follows:

Pleigh's Closing Balance	$2,700,000
Pleigh's Share Of Sleigh's Retained Earnings Since	
Acquisition (80 Percent Of [$2,400,000 - $1,500,000])	720,000
Adjustments:	
Inventories	(80,000)
Plant (5 Years At $10,000)	(50,000)
Goodwill (5 Years At $24,000)	(120,000)
Consolidated Retained Earnings As At December 31, 1998	$3,170,000

5-91.   Note that, in this calculation, the calculation of Pleigh's share of Sleigh's Retained Earnings since acquisition is based on that Company's book figures ($900,000) with no adjustments. This reflects the fact that, to this point, all of our consolidation procedures are based on the parent company approach, with all of the adjustments being charged against the controlling interest's share of Retained Earnings. This will change when we introduce unrealized intercompany profits in Chapter 6. Also note that, because we are dealing with end of the period Retained Earnings, the fair value adjustments are for five years. This is in contrast to our earlier adjustments to the opening Retained Earnings which were for only four years.

5-92.   If you are required to prepare a consolidated Statement of Retained Earnings on an examination, there may be marks allocated to both the opening and closing balances. The procedures we are using calculate the opening balance first. If this is done correctly and you have the appropriate figures for both Net Income and Dividends Declared, then the statement itself will calculate the correct closing balance. However, an error in the opening balance calculation, in Net Income or in Dividends Declared will produce an incorrect closing balance. If this happens and you do not make a separate calculation of the closing balance, you may lose all of the marks allocated to this total. Therefore, we would suggest that you always make an independent verification of the closing balance.

Consolidated Balance Sheet

Non Controlling Interest

5-93.   While it is not the most efficient way to solve this problem, we can use the procedures that we have just developed to calculate the Non Controlling Interest on the Balance Sheet. Using this approach, the calculation would be as follows:

Step A Allocation (Balance At Acquisition)	$700,000
Step B Adjustment For Dividends	(20,000)
Step C Allocation (Retained Earnings Since Acquisition)	160,000
Non Controlling Interest In Income (From Income Statement)	40,000
Non Controlling Interest (Balance Sheet)	$880,000

5-94.   A more conceptual approach would be based on the fact that the December 31,
1998 Sleigh Company's Shareholders' Equity consists of $2,000,000 in No Par Common
Stock and $2,400,000 in Retained Earnings. This means that the subsidiary's net assets
total $4,400,000 and since, in this problem, none of the adjustments or eliminations have
any influence on the Non Controlling Interest, this interest can be calculated by simply
taking the non controlling share of these net assets. That is, 20 percent of $4,400,000 is
the required $880,000.

Statement Disclosure

5-95.   With the Non Controlling Interest established, the consolidated Balance Sheet as
at December 31, 1998 of the Pleigh Company and its subsidiary would be prepared as follows:

Pleigh Company And Subsidiary
Consolidated Balance Sheet
As At December 31, 1998

Cash ($500,000 + $300,000)	$ 800,000
Current Receivables ($800,000 + $400,000 - $12,000)	1,188,000
Inventories ($2,500,000 + $1,700,000 + $80,000 -$80,000)	4,200,000
Long Term Notes Receivable ($200,000 - $200,000)	-0-
Investment In Sleigh ($3,200,000 - $3,200,000)	-0-
Land ($1,500,000 + $1,000,000 - $120,000)	2,380,000
Plant And Equipment (Net)	
($4,500,000 + $1,900,000 + $200,000 - $50,000)	6,550,000
Goodwill ($240,000 - $120,000)	120,000
Total Assets	$15,238,000

Current Liabilities ($500,000 + $200,000 - $12,000)	$ 688,000
Long Term Liabilities ($2,000,000 + $700,000 - $200,000)	2,500,000
Non Controlling Interest (See preceding discussion)	880,000
No Par Common Stock (Pleigh's Balance)	8,000,000
Retained Earnings (See Retained Earnings Statement)	3,170,000
Total Equities	$15,238,000

5-96.   Most of the preceding computations follow directly from the trial balance data
adjusted by the various journal entries that we have made. The exceptions to this are the
Retained Earnings balance and the Non Controlling Interest which were computed in the
preceding sections. Note that the Investment In Sleigh and Long Term Note Receivable
accounts would not be disclosed in actual consolidated financial statements. They have
been included in this presentation simply to show the disposition of all of the balances included in the problem data.

Comprehensive Example - Closed Trial Balance With Investment At Cost

Basic Data

5-97.   In this second version of the comprehensive example, the only requirement is the preparation of a consolidated Balance Sheet. As a consequence, the data is presented in the form of a closed trial balance.

On January 1, 1994, the Pleigh Company purchases 80 percent of the outstanding voting shares of the Sleigh Company for $3,200,000 in cash. On that date the Sleigh Company had No Par Common Stock of $2,000,000 and Retained Earnings of $1,500,000. On December 31, 1998, the adjusted trial balances of the Pleigh Company and its subsidiary, the Sleigh Company are as follows:

	Pleigh	Sleigh
Cash	$ 500,000	$ 300,000
Current Receivables	800,000	400,000
Inventories	2,500,000	1,700,000
Long Term Note Receivable	200,000	-0-
Investment In Sleigh - At Cost	3,200,000	-0-
Land	1,500,000	1,000,000
Plant And Equipment (Net)	4,500,000	1,900,000
Total Debits	$13,200,000	$5,300,000
Current Liabilities	$ 500,000	$ 200,000
Long Term Liabilities	2,000,000	700,000
No Par Common Stock	8,000,000	2,000,000
Retained Earnings	2,700,000	2,400,000
Total Credits	$13,200,000	$5,300,000

Other Information:

A.   At the date of Pleigh Company's acquisition of the Sleigh Company's shares, all of the identifiable assets and liabilities of the Sleigh Company had fair values that were equal to their carrying values except Inventories which had fair values that were $100,000 more than their carrying values, Land with a fair value that was $150,000 less than its carrying value and Plant And Equipment which had a fair value that was $250,000 greater than its carrying value. The Plant And Equipment had a remaining useful life on the acquisition date of 20 years while the inventories that were present on the acquisition date were sold during the year ending December 31, 1994. The Land is still on the books of the Sleigh Company on December 31, 1998. Any goodwill is to be amortized over 10 years. Both Companies use the straight line method to calculate depreciation and amortization.

B.   Sleigh Company's Sales during 1998 include sales of $300,000 to Pleigh Company. All of this merchandise has been resold by the Pleigh Company.

C.   On December 31, 1998, the Pleigh Company is holding Sleigh Company's long term note payable in the amount of $200,000. Interest at 12 percent is payable on July 1 of each year. Pleigh Company has been holding this note since July 1, 1996.

D.   Between January 1, 1994 and December 31, 1997, the Sleigh Company earned a total of $2,500,000 and paid dividends of $1,700,000.

Required: Prepare a consolidated Balance Sheet as at December 31, 1998 for the Pleigh Company and its subsidiary, the Sleigh Company.

Procedural Approach

5-98.   The procedural approach here is similar to that used in our first version of this problem. The basic differences can be described as follows:

- All of the Step B fair value and goodwill write off entries will now be made to Sleigh's closing Retained Earnings account.

- The Step C entry will involve distributing the December 31, 1998 retained earnings, rather than the January 1, 1998 balance.

- As no consolidated Income Statement is being prepared, there is no need to adjust or eliminate any expense or revenue items.

- As all dividends received have been closed to Retained Earnings, there is no need to eliminate intercompany dividends declared.

Step A Procedures

Investment Analysis

5-99.   The analysis of the investment in Sleigh will be identical to the one used in the "open trial balance" version of this problem. It is as follows:

	80 Percent	100 Percent
Investment Cost	$3,200,000	$4,000,000
Book Value	(2,800,000)	(3,500,000)
Differential	$ 400,000	$ 500,000
Fair Value Changes:		
Inventories	(80,000)	(100,000)
Land	120,000	150,000
Plant And Equipment (Net)	(200,000)	(250,000)
Goodwill	$ 240,000	$ 300,000

Investment Elimination

5-100.   As was the case with the investment analysis, the journal entry here will be the same as in the "open trial balance" version of the problem. It is as follows:

No Par Common Stock	$2,000,000	
Retained Earnings	1,500,000	
Plant And Equipment (Net)	200,000	
Inventories	80,000	
Goodwill	240,000	
Land		$ 120,000
Non Controlling Interest		700,000
Investment In Sleigh		3,200,000

Step B(1) - Intercompany Assets And Liabilities

5-101.   The elimination of intercompany asset and liability balances is also the same as in the "open trial balance" version of this problem. The required entries are:

Long Term Liabilities	$200,000	
Long Term Note Receivable		$200,000
Current Liabilities	$ 12,000	
Current Receivables		$ 12,000

Step B(2) - Fair Value And Goodwill Write Offs

General Procedures

5-102. With the investment at cost, recognition will have to be given to realization of fair value changes for the entire period since acquisition. This means that the entries in this version of the problem will have the same effect on the asset and liability accounts as did the entries which were made in the first version of this comprehensive problem. The only difference in the entries is that, since we are working with a closed trial balance, it is no longer possible to adjust expense and revenue accounts. These accounts have been closed into Sleigh's ending Retained Earnings balance and, as a consequence, the portion of the adjustments that were allocated to expenses and revenues in the open trial balance versions of this problem will now go to Retained Earnings.

Inventories

5-103. Since the fair value change on Inventories had no effect on the 1998 expenses or revenues, the entry here will be the same as it was in the open trial balance version of this problem. It is as follows:

Retained Earnings - Sleigh's Closing	$80,000	
Inventories		$80,000

Plant And Equipment

5-104. As was the case in the previous version of this problem, we will credit the Plant And Equipment account for 5 years (January 1, 1994 through December 31, 1998) of additional depreciation expense on the fair value change. However, instead of splitting the debits between Retained Earnings and the current Depreciation Expense, the entire amount will go to Retained Earnings. The entry would be as follows:

Retained Earnings - Sleigh's Closing	$50,000	
Plant And Equipment (Net)		$50,000

Goodwill

5-105. The Goodwill adjustment will follow the same pattern as the fair value depreciation adjustment on the Plant And Equipment. Five years of Goodwill amortization will be charged against the asset account and, in this version of the problem, the total amount will be removed from the retained earnings balance of the subsidiary. The entry is as follows:

Retained Earnings - Sleigh's Closing	$120,000	
Goodwill		$120,000

Land

5-106. As the Land is still on the books of the Sleigh Company, no entry is required to adjust the fair value change on this account.

Step B(3) - Intercompany Expenses And Revenues

5-107. In the "open trial balance" version of this problem, we made an entry here to eliminate intercompany expenses and revenues. We noted that this entry was simply to avoid overstating expenses and revenues. Since all of the expenses and revenues are now closed to retained earnings, no entry is required in this closed trial balance version of the problem.

Step B(4) - Intercompany Dividends

5-108. In the "open trial balance" version of this problem, we made an entry here to eliminate intercompany dividend payments. The entry involved reducing Dividend Revenue or Investment Income and Dividends Declared. Since all of these accounts have been closed to Retained Earnings, no entry is required for intercompany dividends in this closed trial balance version of the problem. The Non Controlling Interest in consolidated net assets in the previous version of this problem was reduced to the extent of dividend payments to non controlling shareholders. This effect will be automatically picked up in Step C when we base the allocation to the Non Controlling Interest on the end of the year Retained Earnings balance of the Sleigh Company. This end of year balance has, of course, had all of the Sleigh Company's 1998 dividends deducted as part of the closing entries.

Step C - Distribution Of The Subsidiary Retained Earnings

Retained Earnings Balance

5-109.   Our one remaining task at this point is to determine the appropriate distribution of the balance that is left in the Retained Earnings account of the Sleigh Company. Note that, in this closed trial balance version of our comprehensive problem, we are concerned with the closing balance of Sleigh's Retained Earnings. The balance that is left in this account can be calculated as follows:

Balance - December 31, 1998	$2,400,000
Step A Elimination (Balance At Acquisition)	(1,500,000)
Balance Since Acquisition	$ 900,000
Step B Adjustments:	
Inventories	(80,000)
Plant And Equipment (5 Years At $10,000)	(50,000)
Goodwill (5 Years At $24,000)	(120,000)
Balance To Be Distributed	$ 650,000

5-110.   Since we are dealing with Sleigh's closing Retained Earnings balance, all of the Step B adjustments are for five years, rather than for four years as was the case in the open trial balance version of this comprehensive problem.

Retained Earnings Distribution Schedule

5-111.   As indicated in the preceding calculation, $650,000 remains in the Retained Earnings account of the Sleigh Company. We will use the same type of schedule that was introduced in the "open trial balance" version of this problem to analyze the distribution of this amount. It is as follows:

Retained Earnings Distribution Schedule

Balance As Per The Trial Balance	$2,400,000
Balance At Acquisition	(1,500,000)
Balance Since Acquisition	$ 900,000
Non Controlling Interest [(20%)($900,000)]	(180,000)
Available To The Controlling Interest	$ 720,000
Step B Adjustments:	
Inventories	(80,000)
Plant And Equipment (5 Years At $10,000)	(50,000)
Goodwill (5 Years At $24,000)	(120,000)
To Consolidated Retained Earnings	$ 470,000

Retained Earnings Distribution Entry

5-112.   Using this schedule, we can now make the required Step C distribution entry. The journal entry required to distribute the Sleigh Company's Retained Earnings since acquisition is as follows:

Retained Earnings - Sleigh	$650,000	
Non Controlling Interest		$180,000
Consolidated Retained Earnings		470,000

5-113. When the $470,000 from the preceding entry is added to the balance of $2,700,000 that is in the Pleigh Company's Retained Earnings account, we have the December 31, 1998 consolidated Retained Earnings figure of $3,170,000.

Consolidated Balance Sheet

Non Controlling Interest

5-114.   Here again, the easiest way to compute the Non Controlling Interest is to take 20 percent of the end of the year net assets of the Sleigh Company. This 20 percent of $4,400,000 gives the required Non Controlling Interest of $880,000. Alternatively, the procedures can be used to arrive at the same result. This calculation would be as follows:

Step A Allocation	$700,000
Step C Allocation	180,000
Non Controlling Interest	$880,000

Statement Disclosure

5-115.   We are now in a position to complete the required consolidated Balance Sheet as at December 31, 1998 of the Pleigh Company and its subsidiary. It would be prepared as follows:

Pleigh Company And Subsidiary
Consolidated Balance Sheet
As At December 31, 1998

Cash ($500,000 + $300,000)	$ 800,000
Current Receivables ($800,000 + $400,000 - $12,000)	1,188,000
Inventories ($2,500,000 + $1,700,000 + $80,000 - $80,000)	4,200,000
Long Term Note Receivable ($200,000 - $200,000)	-0-
Investment In Sleigh ($3,200,000 - $3,200,000)	-0-
Land ($1,500,000 + $1,000,000 - $120,000)	2,380,000
Plant And Equipment (Net)	
($4,500,000 + $1,900,000 + $200,000 - $50,000)	6,550,000
Goodwill ($240,000 - $120,000)	120,000
Total Assets	$15,238,000
Current Liabilities ($500,000 + $200,000 - $12,000)	$ 688,000
Long Term Liabilities ($2,000,000 + $700,000 - $200,000)	2,500,000
Non Controlling Interest (See Preceding Discussion)	880,000
No Par Common Stock (Pleigh's Balance)	8,000,000
Retained Earnings (See Retained Earnings Distribution)	3,170,000
Total Equities	$15,238,000

Application Of The Equity Method

Basic Concepts

5-116.   In Chapter 2, we indicated that the Net Income of an investor using the equity method for an investee had to be equal to the consolidated Net Income that would result from the consolidation of that investee. This requirement is based on the following Recommendation:

Paragraph 3050.08 *Investment income as calculated by the equity method should be that amount necessary to increase or decrease the investor's income to that which would have been recognized if the results of the investee's operations had been consolidated with those of the investor.* (August, 1978)

5-117.   With respect to this Chapter, this means that all of the adjustments for fair value write offs and goodwill amortization that would be required in the consolidation process, are also required in the application of the equity method. There is, however, a major difference in the disclosure of these adjustments. In consolidation, the various adjustments are included in specific consolidated account balances. For example, a goodwill balance is recorded in the consolidated Balance Sheet, and the related amortization is disclosed as Goodwill Amortization Expense in the consolidated Income Statement. In contrast, the equity method deals with all of these adjustments as modifications of the Investment Asset and Investment Income accounts. This means that an investor using the equity method would not record a Goodwill amount in its single entity Balance Sheet, nor would such an investor record a Goodwill Amortization Expense. Rather, the goodwill amortization amount would be calculated and deducted from Investment Income and from the equity pickup which is added to the Investment Asset account. This is why the application of the equity method is sometimes referred to as a "one line consolidation".

Comprehensive Example

Income Statement

5-118.   To illustrate the basic procedures under the equity method, we will use the same comprehensive example that we have been working with throughout this Chapter. The basic data for this problem have been presented several times and will not be repeated here. The only change is that we will assume that Pleigh Company's majority ownership does not give it control over the Sleigh Company and, as a consequence, the investment cannot be consolidated.

5-119.   From our previous experience with the Pleigh Company problem, we know that consolidated Net Income for 1998 amounts to $546,000. Since the Pleigh Company's net income without the inclusion of any revenues from its Investment In Sleigh amounts to $420,000, the only Investment Income that would satisfy the requirement stated in Paragraph 3050.08 is $126,000.

5-120.   Using this Investment Income, the Income Statement of the Pleigh Company with the Investment In Sleigh carried by the equity method would be as follows:

Pleigh Company
Income Statement
Year Ending December 31, 1998

Sales	$4,000,000
Interest Revenue	24,000
Investment Income	126,000
Total Revenues	$4,150,000
Cost Of Goods Sold	$2,800,000
Depreciation Expense	200,000
Interest Expense	240,000
Other Expenses	364,000
Total Expenses	$3,604,000
Net Income	$ 546,000

5-121.   Under this approach, we have determined Investment Income as a "plug" figure which serves as an amount that will result in Pleigh Company's Net Income satisfying the condition that it must be equal to the amount that would result from the application of consolidation procedures. Note, however, that this amount can be calculated directly as follows:

Pleigh's Interest In Sleigh's Income [(80%)($200,000)]	$160,000
Fair Value Adjustments:	
Depreciation	(10,000)
Goodwill	(24,000)
Pleigh's Equity Method Investment Income	$126,000

Balance Sheet

5-122. If Pleigh was not consolidating its investment in Sleigh, and used the equity method in its single entity statements, the Balance Sheet account Investment In Sleigh would have to be increased to reflect Pleigh's equity in this investee. As is the case with Investment Income under the equity method, this Balance Sheet account would be subject to the same types of adjustments that would be required in the preparation of consolidated financial statements. The required balance would be calculated as follows:

Investment In Sleigh At Cost		$3,200,000
Equity Pickup:		
Sleigh's December 31 Retained Earnings	$2,400,000	
Balance At Acquisition	(1,500,000)	
Balance Since Acquisition	$ 900,000	
Pleigh's Share	80%	720,000
Fair Value Adjustments:		
Inventories		(80,000)
Plant And Equipment [(5 Years)($10,000)]		(50,000)
Goodwill [(5 Years)($24,000)]		(120,000)
Investment In Sleigh At Equity		$3,670,000

5-123. If this amount is used on the asset side of Pleigh's single entity Balance Sheet, there will have to be a corresponding $470,000 ($3,670,000 - $3,200,000) adjustment to Retained Earnings on the equity side of the single entity Balance Sheet. This will leave Pleigh with the following single entity Balance Sheet under the equity method:

Pleigh Company
Single Entity Balance Sheet
As At December 31, 1998

Cash	$ 500,000
Current Receivables	800,000
Inventories	2,500,000
Long Term Note Receivable	200,000
Investment In Sleigh (At Equity)	3,670,000
Land	1,500,000
Plant And Equipment (Net)	4,500,000
Total Assets	$13,670,000

Current Liabilities	$ 500,000
Long Term Liabilities	2,000,000
No Par Common Stock	8,000,000
Retained Earnings ($2,700,000 + $470,000)	3,170,000
Total Equities	$13,670,000

5-124.   Note that, when the equity method is used, the resulting Retained Earnings figure in Pleigh's single entity Balance Sheet is equal to the consolidated Retained Earnings figure resulting from the application of consolidation procedures. This result follows from the Paragraph 3050.08 requirement that investment income as calculated by the equity method must be the amount necessary to increase or decrease the investor's income to that which would have been recognized if the results of the investee's operations had been consolidated with those of the investor.

Step By Step Acquisitions

Definition And Accounting Recommendations

5-125.   A step by step acquisition involves a situation in which an investor acquires control of an investee in a sequence of two or more purchases. Several purchases and a considerable period of time might elapse before a particular investee becomes a subsidiary. However, when control is achieved, the accounting procedures are not conceptually different than those used in dealing with a single step acquisition of a subsidiary. This is reflected in the following *CICA Handbook* Recommendation:

> **Paragraph 1600.13**   *Where an investment in a subsidiary is acquired through two or more purchases, the parent company's interest in the subsidiary's identifiable assets and liabilities should be determined as follows:*
>
> (a) *the assignable costs of the subsidiary's identifiable assets and liabilities should be determined as at each date on which an investment was required;*
>
> (b) *the parent company's interest in the subsidiary's identifiable assets and liabilities acquired at each step in the purchase should be based on the assignable costs of all such assets and liabilities at that date.* (April, 1975)

5-126.   The meaning of assignable costs in the preceding Recommendation is fair values adjusted, if applicable, for any excess of such values assigned over the cost of the purchase. This means that this Recommendation calls for the establishment and allocation of fair values at each purchase date. While these are the same procedures that would be used in the case of a single step acquisition, implementation difficulties may arise as a result of the step by step acquisition process.

Implementation Problems

5-127.   As indicated in the previous paragraph, the appropriate solution to accounting for this type of situation would require the determination and allocation of fair value changes and goodwill at each step of the acquisition. However, there are situations in which, at the time of one or more of the early share acquisitions, there is no intent to acquire controlling ownership. If these initial investments are classified as portfolio investments they will be accounted for by the cost method. Since under this method there is no requirement that fair values be determined, this information may not be available when it becomes appropriate to consolidate or apply the equity method. In view of this problem, the following suggestion is made:

> **Paragraph 1600.11**   For practical purposes, assignable costs will normally be determined as at the time the first use of equity accounting becomes appropriate (or as at the time the first use of consolidation becomes appropriate, if equity accounting has not previously been appropriate) and at each further major purchase.

5-128.   For those purchases where fair value data is not available there will still be a differential between investment cost and the investor's proportionate share of book values. This differential, if a debit amount, will have to be allocated to goodwill. If a credit is involved, it will be deducted from identifiable non monetary assets.

5-129.   An additional modification of general procedures is also suggested. This involves situations in which there are a large number of small purchases. It is stated as follows:

> **Paragraph 1600.11**   Where there are numerous small purchases, it is appropriate to group a series of such purchases into one step, in order to treat the series in the same way as a major purchase.

Example - Step-By-Step Acquisition

Basic Data

5-130.   While the concepts involved in step by step acquisitions are identical to those used in single step acquisitions, the procedures involved are sufficiently different to warrant the presentation of a simple illustration of this situation. The basic data for this example is as follows:

> **Example**   On December 31, 1996, the Alpha Company purchases 30 percent of the outstanding shares of the Morgan Company for $2,250,000. On this date the carrying values of the Morgan Company's net identifiable assets amount to $5,000,000. All of the fair values of the individual identifiable assets and liabilities of the Morgan Company have carrying values that are equal to their fair values except for an item of Plant And Equipment. This item has a remaining useful life of six years and a fair value that exceeds its carrying value by $1,000,000. Both Companies use the straight line method to calculate depreciation and amortization.
>
> On December 31, 1997, the Alpha Company purchases an additional 40 percent of the outstanding shares of the Morgan Company for $3,500,000. On this date the carrying values of the Morgan Company's net identifiable assets total $6,000,000. All of the fair values of the identifiable assets and liabilities of the Morgan Company have carrying values that are equal to their fair values except for the item of Plant And Equipment. This is the same item on which there was a fair value change on December 31, 1996. However, the fair value change has increased to a total of $1,500,000 on December 31, 1997. The remaining useful life of this asset is now five years. Goodwill is to be amortized over a period of 10 years from the date at which the individual amounts purchased are recognized.
>
> During the years 1996, 1997, and 1998 there are no intercompany transactions between the Alpha Company and its subsidiary the Morgan Company. Also during this period, the Morgan Company's contributed capital remains unchanged. The Alpha Company carries its investments in the Morgan Company using the cost method. On December 31, 1998, the condensed Balance Sheets of the Alpha Company and its subsidiary the Morgan Company are as follows:

	Alpha	Morgan
Investment In Morgan Company	$5,750,000	$ -0-
Other Identifiable Assets	4,150,000	6,500,000
Total Assets	$9,900,000	$6,500,000
No Par Common Stock	$5,000,000	$2,000,000
Retained Earnings	4,900,000	4,500,000
Total Equities	$9,900,000	$6,500,000

Required: Prepare a consolidated Balance Sheet for the Alpha Company and its subsidiary, the Morgan Company, as at December 31, 1998.

Procedures

5-131.   In a problem such as this, the easiest solution usually involves direct computations of the balances to be included in the consolidated Balance Sheet. While they can be used, our general procedures are somewhat awkward when dealing with a multiple step acquisition. As a consequence, the solution to this problem will be presented in terms of direct computations of all of the required account balances.

Analysis Of Investments

5-132.   Before proceeding to the direct computation of the various accounts for inclusion in the consolidated Balance Sheet, it is useful to analyze the two investment transactions through which the Alpha Company acquired control of the Morgan Company. The analysis of the first transaction is as follows:

	30 Percent	100 Percent
Investment Cost	$2,250,000	$7,500,000
Book Value - Net Assets	(1,500,000)	(5,000,000)
Differential	$ 750,000	$2,500,000
Fair Value Change On Plant	(300,000)	(1,000,000)
Goodwill	$ 450,000	$1,500,000

5-133.   In similar fashion, the analysis of the second investment transaction would appear as below:

	40 Percent	100 Percent
Investment Cost	$3,500,000	$8,750,000
Book Value - Net Assets	(2,400,000)	(6,000,000)
Differential	$1,100,000	$2,750,000
Fair Value Change On Plant	(600,000)	(1,500,000)
Goodwill	$ 500,000	$1,250,000

Consolidated Net Identifiable Assets

5-134.   At the end of Chapter 4 we provided the following definitional calculation for identifiable assets and liabilities:

Identifiable Assets And Liabilities   The consolidated balance for any identifiable asset or liability is calculated as follows:

- 100 percent of the carrying value of the identifiable asset or liability on the books of the parent company; *plus*

- 100 percent of the carrying value of the identifiable asset or liability on the books of the subsidiary company; *plus (minus)*

- the parent company's share of the increase (decrease) in the fair value of the subsidiary's asset (liability) balance.

5-135.   As we are now in a period subsequent to acquisition, a further component must be ad5ded to this definition to recognize that parts of the fair value changes have been realized and must be charged to income. This further component could be stated as follows:

- *minus (plus)* the portion of the fair value increase (decrease) that has become realized since acquisition through usage of the asset, or through its disposal.

5-136.   This definition can be used in dealing with this step-by-step acquisition. The only difference here is that there are two acquisition dates and fair values must be picked up with respect to both of them. The calculation, including accumulated amortization on the fair value changes to December 31, 1998, would be as follows:

December 31, 1998 Book Values:		
Alpha Company's		$ 4,150,000
Morgan Company's		6,500,000
Total Book Values - December 31, 1998		$10,650,000
Fair Value Changes:		
December 31, 1996 Purchase	$300,000	
Depreciation [(2)($300,000 ÷ 6)]	(100,000)	200,000
December 31, 1997 Purchase	$600,000	
Depreciation ($600,000 ÷ 5)	(120,000)	480,000
Consolidated Net Identifiable Assets		$11,330,000

5-137.   Note carefully that fair value changes are only included to the extent that they are purchased. Changes in fair values that occur subsequent to a particular purchase are not retroactively picked up. As an example, in this situation you would not record the first purchase's 30 percent share of the increase in the fair value change on the Plant item from $1,000,000 on December 31, 1996 to $1,500,000 on December 31, 1997. This is, of course, consistent with the general approach under the parent company concept in that only the investor's purchased share of fair value changes and goodwill is recognized.

Goodwill

5-138.   In Chapter 4, a definitional calculation of Goodwill was provided as follows:

Goodwill   The Goodwill to be recorded in the consolidated Balance Sheet is equal to the cost of the parent company's investment in the subsidiary, less the parent company's share of the fair value of the subsidiary's net assets.

5-139.   Now that we have moved into periods subsequent to acquisition, amortization of this balance has to be taken into consideration. This can be accomplished by adding the following sentence to the preceding definition:

This amount is reduced by amortization for the period from acquisition to the current consolidated Balance Sheet date.

5-140.   Using this definition, the amortized balance to be disclosed in the consolidated Goodwill account as at December 31, 1998, can be calculated as follows:

First Purchase	$450,000	
Amortization [(2)($450,000 ÷ 10)]	(90,000)	$360,000
Second Purchase	$500,000	
Amortization ($500,000 ÷ 10)	(50,000)	450,000
Consolidated Goodwill		$810,000

Consolidated Retained Earnings

5-141.   A definitional calculation can be made here of the required balance for the consolidated Retained Earnings as at December 31, 1998. The only difference that is created by the multiple steps in the acquisition is that multiple equity pickups will be recorded. The calculation is as follows:

Alpha Company's Retained Earnings	$4,900,000
Equity Pickups:	
First Purchase [(30%)($4,500,000 - $3,000,000)]	450,000
Second Purchase [(40%)($4,500,000 - $4,000,000)]	200,000
Depreciation Of Fair Value Changes	(220,000)
Goodwill Amortization	(140,000)
Consolidated Retained Earnings	$5,190,000

Consolidated Balance Sheet

5-142. Using the preceding information, the consolidated Balance Sheet would be prepared as follows:

Alpha Company And Subsidiary
Consolidated Balance Sheet
As At December 31, 1998

Net Identifiable Assets	$11,330,000
Goodwill	810,000
Total Assets	$12,140,000
Non Controlling Interest (30 Percent Of $6,500,000)	$ 1,950,000
No Par Common Stock (Alpha Company's Balance)	5,000,000
Retained Earnings	5,190,000
Total Equities	$12,140,000

Summary Of Consolidation Procedures

5-143. In Chapter 4, we began the development of a set of procedures that could be used in the preparation of a consolidated Balance Sheet at the date of the subsidiary's acquisition. As this Chapter 5 begins to deal with the preparation of a complete set of consolidated financial statements for periods subsequent to acquisition, it contains a significant expansion of these procedures. Further, some modifications of the procedures developed in Chapter 4 were required in order to deal with periods subsequent to acquisition and the need to prepare additional types of consolidated statements. At this point, we will provide you with a complete summary of the procedures developed in Chapters 4 and 5, including any required modification of procedures originally developed in Chapter 4. This summary is as follows:

Step A-1 Procedure Eliminate 100 percent of the Investment In Subsidiary account.

Step A-2 Procedure Eliminate 100 percent of all the acquisition date balances in the subsidiary's shareholders' equity (includes both contributed capital and earned capital).

Step A-3 Procedure Allocate any debit or credit Differential that is present at acquisition to the investor's share of fair value changes on identifiable assets, fair value changes on identifiable liabilities, and positive or negative goodwill.

Step A-4 Procedure Allocate to a Non Controlling Interest account in the consolidated Balance Sheet, the non controlling interest's share of the at acquisition book value of the total Shareholders' Equity of the subsidiary (includes both contributed capital and earned capital.

Step B-1 Procedure Eliminate 100 percent of all intercompany assets and liabilities.

Step B-2 Procedure Give recognition to the post acquisition realization of acquisition date fair value changes on assets and liabilities that have been used up or sold during the post acquisition period. To the extent that this realization occurred in prior periods, recognition will require an adjustment of the opening Retained Earnings of the subsidiary. Alternatively, if the realization occurred in the current period, the adjustment will be to the subsidiary's current period expenses, revenues, gains, or losses.

Step B-3 Procedure   Eliminate 100 percent of all intercompany expenses and revenues.

Step B-4 Procedure   Eliminate 100 percent of subsidiary dividends declared. The controlling share of this amount will be deducted from the revenues of the parent company and the non controlling share of this amount will be deducted from the Non Controlling Interest in the Balance Sheet.

Step C-1 Procedure   Determine the appropriate allocation of the subsidiary's adjusted Retained Earnings since acquisition. The Non Controlling Interest's share will be based on book value. In contrast, the allocation to consolidated Retained Earnings will be the parent company's share of book values, adjusted for the realization of fair value changes that have occurred since acquisition.

Step C-2 Procedure   Eliminate the subsidiary's adjusted Retained Earnings since acquisition. This amount will be allocated to the Non Controlling Interest in the consolidated Balance Sheet and to consolidated Retained Earnings as determined in Step C-1.

5-144.   The preceding represents a complete set of consolidation procedures for dealing with problems that do not have unrealized intercompany profits. The development of the procedures for dealing with unrealized intercompany profits will be found in Chapter 6.

5-145.   We would call your attention to the fact that, as stated, the listed procedures apply to open trial balance problems in which the investment is carried at cost. In other types of problems, modifications will be required. For example, in applying Step B-2 in a closed trial balance problem, there will be no adjustments to current expenses, revenues, gains, or losses as these amounts have been closed to the subsidiary's Retained Earnings account. Such required modifications were illustrated in the closed trial balance version of our comprehensive example.

Summary Of Definitional Calculations

5-146.   We continue to encourage you to work towards preparing the required balances in consolidated financial statements by using direct definitional calculations. To assist you in this work, we offer the following definitions that have been developed in the course of Chapters 4 and 5.

Identifiable Assets And Liabilities   The amount to be included in the consolidated Balance Sheet for any identifiable asset or liability is calculated as follows:

- 100 percent of the carrying value of the identifiable asset or liability on the books of the parent company at the Balance Sheet date; *plus*

- 100 percent of the carrying value of the identifiable asset or liability on the books of the subsidiary company at the Balance Sheet date; *plus (minus)*

- the parent company's share of the fair value change on the asset or liability (i.e., the parent company's share of the difference between the fair value of the subsidiary's asset or liability at time of acquisition and the carrying value of that asset or liability at the time of acquisition); *minus (plus)*

- amortization of the parent company's share of the fair value change on the asset or liability for the period since acquisition to the current Balance Sheet date.

Goodwill   The Goodwill to be recorded in the consolidated Balance Sheet is equal to:

- the excess of the cost of the investment over the parent company's share of the fair values of the subsidiary's net assets at the time of acquisition; *minus*

- amortization of that excess over the period since acquisition to the current Balance Sheet date.

Non Controlling Interest - Balance Sheet   The Non Controlling Interest to be recorded in the consolidated Balance Sheet will be an amount equal to the non controlling interest's ownership percentage of the book value of the subsidiary's common stock equity at the Balance Sheet date.

Contributed Capital   The Contributed Capital to be recorded in the consolidated Balance Sheet will be equal to the contributed capital from the single entity Balance Sheet of the parent company.

Retained Earnings   The Retained Earnings amount to be included in the consolidated Balance Sheet is calculated as follows:

- 100 percent of the Retained Earnings of the parent company; *plus (minus)*

- the parent company's share of the subsidiary's Retained Earnings (Deficit) since acquisition; *plus (minus)*

- 100 percent of the adjustments to consolidated expenses, revenues, gains, and losses for realized fair value changes during the period since acquisition to the current Balance Sheet date; *minus*

- 100 percent of goodwill amortization for the period since acquisition to the current Balance Sheet date.

Revenue   The amount of any revenue to be included in the consolidated Income Statement is calculated as follows:

- 100 percent of the amount reported in the parent company's financial statements; *plus*

- 100 percent of the amount reported in the subsidiary's financial statements; *minus*

- 100 percent of any intercompany amounts included in the parent or subsidiary figures; *plus (minus)*

- the parent's share of any fair value changes realized during the period through usage or sale of subsidiary assets (fair value amortization, depreciation, or depletion and amounts realized through sale of subsidiary assets prior to the end of their economic life). It would be unusual for fair value realizations to be related to revenues. However, it could happen. For example, amortization of the a fair value change on a long term receivable would be treated as an adjustment of interest revenue. An additional example could result from the sale of an asset on which a fair value change has been recorded in the consolidated financial statements. If there was a gain (revenue) on the transaction, it would have to be adjusted for the realized fair value change.

Expense   The amount of any expense to be included in the consolidated Income Statement is calculated as follows:

- 100 percent of the amount reported in the parent company's financial statements; *plus*

- 100 percent of the amount reported in the subsidiary's financial statements; *minus*

- 100 percent of any intercompany amounts included in the parent or subsidiary figures; *plus (minus)*

- the parent's share of any fair value changes realized during the period through usage or sale of subsidiary assets (fair value amortization, depreciation, or depletion and amounts realized through sale of subsidiary assets prior to the end of their economic life).

Goodwill Amortization Expense   In general, this is a new expense added by the consolidation procedures. The amount to be included here is the annual amortization of the Goodwill balance recognized at the time of the subsidiary's acquisition.

Non Controlling Interest - Income Statement   The non controlling interest in the consolidated Income Statement is an amount equal to the non controlling interest's ownership percentage of the reported Net Income. Note that, if the subsidiary has extraordinary items or results from discontinued operations, this Non Controlling Interest will be based on the subsidiary's Income Before Extraordinary Items And Discontinued Operations.

Consolidated Net Income   Consolidated Net Income can be calculated as follows:

- 100 percent of the parent company's Net Income, excluding dividends received from the subsidiary; *plus (minus)*

- the parent's share of the subsidiary's reported Net Income (Net Loss); *plus (minus)*

- the parent's share of any fair value changes realized during the period through usage or sale of subsidiary assets (fair value amortization, depreciation, or depletion and amounts realized through sale of subsidiary assets prior to the end of their economic life).

5-147.   These definitions are applicable to problems which do not involve the presence of unrealized intercompany profits. When we introduce unrealized intercompany profits in the next Chapter, these definitions will require significant modification.

Walk Through Problem

Note   This problem is an extension of the Walk Through Problem that was presented at the end of Chapter 4. As was explained in that Chapter, these problems provide you with a fill-in-the-blank solution format to assist you in solving the problem. These problems are designed to be an easy introduction to solving the type of problem illustrated in the Chapter.

Basic Data   On December 31, 1998, the Puff Company purchased 60 percent of the outstanding voting shares of the Snuff Company for $720,000 in cash. On that date, subsequent to the completion of the business combination, the Balance Sheets of the Puff and Snuff Companies and the fair values of Snuff's identifiable assets and liabilities were as follows:

	December 31, 1998 Balance Sheets Puff	Snuff	Fair Values For Snuff
Cash And Accounts			
Receivable	$ 350,000	$ 200,000	$200,000
Inventories	950,000	500,000	450,000
Investment In Snuff	720,000	-0-	N/A
Plant And Equipment (Net)	2,400,000	700,000	800,000
Total Assets	$4,420,000	$1,400,000	
Current Liabilities	$ 400,000	$ 100,000	$100,000
Long Term Liabilities	1,000,000	400,000	360,000
No Par Common Stock	1,000,000	800,000	N/A
Retained Earnings	2,020,000	100,000	N/A
Total Equities	$4,420,000	$1,400,000	

The December 31, 1998 Inventories of Snuff are sold during 1999. The Plant And Equipment of Snuff on December 31, 1998 has an estimated useful life of 10 years while the Long Term Liabilities that were present on that date mature on December 31, 2001. Any goodwill arising from the business combination should be amortized over 30 years. Both Companies use the straight line method of depreciation and amortization. Puff carries its Investment In Snuff by the cost method.

The Income Statements for the year ending December 31, 2000 and the Balance Sheets as at December 31, 2000 of the Puff and Snuff Companies are as follows:

Income Statements
For The Year Ending December 31, 2000

	Puff Company	Snuff Company
Sales	$2,500,000	$1,300,000
Other Revenues	100,000	30,000
Total Revenues	$2,600,000	$1,330,000
Cost Of Goods Sold	$1,200,000	$ 750,000
Depreciation Expense	400,000	250,000
Other Expenses	800,000	180,000
Total Expenses	$2,400,000	$1,180,000
Net Income	$ 200,000	$ 150,000

Balance Sheets
As At December 31, 2000

	Puff Company	Snuff Company
Cash	$ 100,000	$ 70,000
Accounts Receivable	430,000	180,000
Inventories	1,150,000	400,000
Investment In Snuff	720,000	-0-
Plant And Equipment (Net)	2,150,000	850,000
Total Assets	$4,550,000	$1,500,000
Current Liabilities	$ 300,000	$ 40,000
Long Term Liabilities	1,000,000	400,000
No Par Common Stock	1,000,000	800,000
Retained Earnings	2,250,000	260,000
Total Equities	$4,550,000	$1,500,000

Other Information:

1. During 2000, the Puff Company declared and paid $100,000 in dividends while the Snuff Company declared and paid $40,000.

2. Included in the 2000 Sales of the Snuff Company are sales of $200,000 to the Puff Company. The Puff Company has resold all of this merchandise to purchasers outside of the consolidated entity. Puff owes Snuff $100,000 on December 31, 2000 for the merchandise purchases.

3. On December 31, 2000, Snuff still owes Puff for management fees earned during 2000. Fees of $25,000 have been charged by Puff and none of this amount has been paid by Snuff in 2000.

Required: For the Puff Company and its subsidiary the Snuff Company, prepare:

A. A consolidated Income Statement for the year ending December 31, 2000.

B. A consolidated Statement Of Retained Earnings for the year ending December 31, 2000.

C. A consolidated Balance Sheet as at December 31, 2000.

In addition, provide calculations which verify consolidated Net Income for the year ending December 31, 2000, the December 31, 2000 consolidated Retained Earnings, and the December 31, 2000 Non Controlling Interest in net assets.

Walk Through Problem Solution Format

Step A - Investment Analysis

	60 Percent	100 Percent
Purchase Price	$	$
Book Value	($)	($)
Differential	$	$
Fair Value Change On Inventories	$	$
Fair Value Change On Plant And Equipment	($)	($)
Fair Value Change On Long Term Liabilities	($)	($)
Goodwill	$	$

Step A - Investment Elimination Entry

No Par Common Stock	$	
Retained Earnings	$	
Plant And Equipment (Net)	$	
Long Term Liabilities	$	
Goodwill	$	
Investment In Snuff		$
Inventories		$
Non Controlling Interest		$

Step B(1) - Intercompany Assets And Liabilities

Current Liabilities	$	
Accounts Receivable		$
Current Liabilities	$	
Accounts Receivable		$

Step B(2) - Fair Value Adjustment On The Inventories

Inventories	$	
Retained Earnings		$

Step B(2) - Fair Value Adjustment On Plant And Equipment

Retained Earnings - Snuff	$	
Depreciation Expense	$	
Plant and Equipment (Net)		$

Step B(2) - Fair Value Adjustment On Long Term Liabilities

Retained Earnings - Snuff	$	
Other Expenses	$	
Long Term Liabilities		$

Step B(2) - Goodwill Amortization

Retained Earnings - Snuff	$	
Other Expenses	$	
Goodwill		$

Step B(3) - Intercompany Expenses And Revenues

Sales	$	
Cost Of Goods Sold		$
Other Revenues	$	
Other Expenses		$

Step B(4) - Intercompany Dividends

Other Revenues	$	
Non Controlling Interest	$	
Dividends Declared		$

Step C - Retained Earnings Distribution Schedule

Snuff's January 1, 2000 Balance	$	
Snuff's Balance At Acquisition	($	)
Balance Since Acquisition	$	
Non Controlling Interest [(40%)( )]	($	)
Available To The Controlling Interest	$	
Step B Adjustments:		
Fair Value Change On Inventories	$	
Fair Value Change On Plant and Equipment	($	)
Fair Value Change On Long Term Liabilities	($	)
Goodwill Amortization	($	)
To Consolidated Retained Earnings	$	

Step C - Retained Earnings Distribution Entry

Retained Earnings - Snuff	$	
Non Controlling Interest	$	
Consolidated Retained Earnings		$

Puff Company And Subsidiary
Consolidated Income Statement
For The Year Ending December 31, 2000

Sales	$
Other Revenues	$
Total Revenues	$
Cost Of Goods Sold	$
Depreciation Expense	$
Other Expenses	$
Non Controlling Interest	$
Total Expenses	$
Consolidated Net Income	$

Verification Of Consolidated Net Income

Puff Company's Net Income	$	
Intercompany Dividend Revenues	($	)
Puff's Net Income Less Dividends	$	
Puff's Equity In The Net Income Of Snuff	$	
Income Before Adjustments	$	
Step B Adjustments:		
Fair Value Change On Plant and Equipment	($	)
Fair Value Change On Long Term Liabilities	($	)
Goodwill Amortization	($	)
Consolidated Net Income	$	

Puff Company And Subsidiary
Consolidated Statement Of Retained Earnings
For The Year Ending December 31, 2000

Balance - January 1, 2000	$
Consolidated Net Income	$
Available For Distribution	$
Dividends Declared	$
Balance - December 31, 2000	$

Verification Of Consolidated Retained Earnings

Puff's Closing Balance	$	
Puff's Share Of Snuff's Retained Earnings Since Acquisition	$	
Step B Adjustments:		
Fair Value Change On Inventories	$	
Fair Value Change On Plant and Equipment	($	)
Fair Value Change On Long Term Liabilities	($	)
Goodwill Amortization	($	)
Consolidated Retained Earnings As At December 31, 2000	$	

Puff Company And Subsidiary
Consolidated Balance Sheet
As At December 31, 2000

Cash	$
Accounts Receivable	$
Inventories	$
Investment In Snuff	$
Plant And Equipment (Net)	$
Goodwill	$
Total Assets	$
Current Liabilities	$
Long Term Liabilities	$
Non Controlling Interest	$
No Par Common Stock	$
Retained Earnings	$
Total Equities	$

Verification Of The Non Controlling Interest In Consolidated Net Assets

At Acquisition (Step A)	$
Dividends Declared By Snuff (Step B)	($)
Retained Earnings Distribution (Step C)	$
From Consolidated Net Income	$
Non Controlling Interest As At December 31, 2000	$

Walk Through Problem Solution

Step A - Investment Analysis

	60 Percent	100 Percent
Purchase Price	$720,000	$1,200,000
Book Value	(540,000)	(900,000)
Differential	$180,000	$ 300,000
Inventories	30,000	50,000
Plant And Equipment	(60,000)	(100,000)
Long Term Liabilities	(24,000)	(40,000)
Goodwill	$126,000	$ 210,000

Step A - Investment Elimination Entry

No Par Common Stock	$800,000	
Retained Earnings	100,000	
Plant And Equipment	60,000	
Long Term Liabilities	24,000	
Goodwill	126,000	
Investment In Snuff		$720,000
Inventories		30,000
Non Controlling Interest		360,000

Step B(1) - Intercompany Assets And Liabilities

Current Liabilities	$100,000	
Accounts Receivable		$100,000
(Intercompany Merchandise Sales)		

Current Liabilities	$25,000	
Accounts Receivable		$25,000
(Management Fees)		

Step B(2) - Fair Value Adjustment On The Inventories

Inventories	$30,000	
Retained Earnings - Snuff		$30,000

Step B(2) - Fair Value Adjustment On Plant And Equipment

Retained Earnings - Snuff	$6,000	
Depreciation Expense	6,000	
Plant And Equipment (Net)		$12,000
(Annual Adjustment = $60,000/10 = $6,000/Year)		

Step B(2) - Fair Value Adjustment On Long Term Liabilities

Retained Earnings - Snuff	$8,000	
Other Expenses	8,000	
Long Term Liabilities		$16,000
(Annual Adjustment = $24,000/3 = $8,000/Year)		

Step B(2) - Goodwill Amortization

Retained Earnings - Snuff	$4,200	
Other Expenses	4,200	
Goodwill		$8,400
(Annual Adjustment = $126,000/30 = $4,200/Year)		

Step B(3) - Intercompany Expenses And Revenues

Sales	$200,000	
Cost Of Goods Sold		$200,000
(Intercompany Merchandise Sales)		
Other Revenues	$25,000	
Other Expenses		$25,000
(Management Fees)		

Step B(4) - Intercompany Dividends

Other Revenues (60% of $40,000)	$24,000	
Non Controlling Interest (Balance Sheet)	16,000	
Dividends Declared		$40,000

Step C - Retained Earnings Distribution Schedule

Snuff's January 1, 2000 Balance ($260,000 - $150,000 + $40,000)	$150,000
Snuff's Balance At Acquisition	(100,000)
Balance Since Acquisition	$ 50,000
Non Controlling Interest ([40%][$50,000])	(20,000)
Available To The Controlling Interest	$30,000
Step B Adjustments:	
Fair Value Change On Inventory	30,000
Fair Value Change On Plant And Equipment	(6,000)
Fair Value Change On Long Term Liabilities	(8,000)
Goodwill Amortization	(4,200)
To Consolidated Retained Earnings	$41,800

Step C - Retained Earnings Distribution Entry

Retained Earnings - Snuff	$61,800	
Non Controlling Interest		$20,000
Consolidated Retained Earnings		41,800

Puff Company And Subsidiary
Consolidated Income Statement
For The Year Ending December 31, 2000

Sales ($2,500,000 + $1,300,000 - $20 0,000)	$3,600,000
Other Revenues ($100,000 + $30,000 - $25,000 - $24,000)	81,000
Total Revenues	$3,681,000
Cost Of Goods Sold ($1,200,000 + $750,000 - $200,000)	$1,750,000
Depreciation Expense ($400,000 + $250,000 + $6,000)	656,000
Other Expenses ($800,000 + $180,000 + $8,000 + $4,200 - $25,000)	967,200
Non Controlling Interest (40%)($150,000)	60,000
Total Expenses	$3,433,200
Consolidated Net Income	$ 247,800

Verification Of Consolidated Net Income

Puff Company's Net Income	$200,000
Intercompany Dividend Revenues	(24,000)
Puff's Net Income Less Dividends	$176,000
Puff's Equity In The Net Income Of Snuff (60% of $150,000)	90,000
Income Before Adjustments	$266,000
Step B Adjustments:	
Fair Value Change On Plant and Equipment	(6,000)
Fair Value Change On Long Term Liabilities	(8,000)
Goodwill Amortization	(4,200)
Consolidated Net Income	$247,800

Puff Company And Subsidiary
Consolidated Statement Of Retained Earnings
For The Year Ending December 31, 2000

Opening Balance ($2,150,000 + $41,800)	$2,191,800
Consolidated Net Income	247,800
Available For Distribution	$2,439,600
Dividends Declared (Puff's Only)	100,000
Closing Balance	$2,339,600

Verification Of Consolidated Retained Earnings

Puff's Closing Balance	$2,250,000
Puff's Share Of Snuff's Retained Earnings	
Since Acquisition (60% of $160,000)	96,000
Step B Adjustments:	
Inventories	30,000
Plant (2 Years At $6,000)	(12,000)
Long Term Liabilities (2 Years At $8,000)	(16,000)
Goodwill (2 Years At $4,200)	(8,400)
Consolidated Retained Earnings As At December 31, 2000	$2,339,600

Puff Company And Subsidiary
Consolidated Balance Sheet
As At December 31, 2000

Cash ($100,000 + $70,000)	$ 170,000
Accounts Receivable ($430,000 + $180,000 - $100,000 - $25,000)	485,000
Inventories ($1,150,000 + $400,000 - $30,000 + $30,000)	1,550,000
Investment In Snuff ($720,000 - $720,000)	-0-
Plant And Equipment (Net) ($2,150,000 + $850,000 + $60,000 - $12,000)	3,048,000
Goodwill ($126,000 - $8,400)	117,600
Total Assets	$5,370,600

Current Liabilities ($300,000 + $40,000 - $100,000 - $25,000)	$ 215,000
Long Term Liabilities ($1,000,000 + $400,000 - $24,000 + $16,000)	1,392,000
Non Controlling Interest (40%)($1,060,000)	424,000
Common Stock (Puff's Only)	1,000,000
Retained Earnings (See Statement)	2,339,600
Total Equities	$5,370,600

Verification Of The Non Controlling Interest In Consolidated Net Assets

At Acquisition (Step A)	$360,000
Dividends Declared By Snuff (Step B)	(16,000)
Retained Earnings Distribution (Step C)	20,000
From Consolidated Net Income	60,000
Non Controlling Interest As At December 31, 2000	$424,000

Problems For Self Study

(The solutions for these problems can be found following Chapter 17 of the text.)

SELF STUDY PROBLEM FIVE - 1

On December 31, 1993, the Pastel Company purchased 90 percent of the outstanding voting shares of the Shade Company for $5,175,000 in cash. On that date, the Shade Company had No Par Common Stock of $2,000,000 and Retained Earnings of $4,000,000. All of the Shade Company's identifiable assets and liabilities had carrying values that were equal to their fair values except for:

1. Equipment which had fair values that were $1,000,000 less than their carrying values and a remaining useful life of 10 years.

2. Land which had a fair value that was $100,000 greater than its carrying value.

3. Accounts Receivable with fair values that were $50,000 less than their carrying values.

4. Long Term Liabilities which had fair values that were $200,000 less than their carrying values and mature on December 31, 1998.

The Balance Sheets of the Pastel Company and the Shade Company as at December 31, 1998 were as follows:

	Pastel	Shade
Cash and Current Receivables	$ 2,625,000	$ 800,000
Inventories	8,000,000	2,000,000
Equipment (Net)	24,000,000	4,000,000
Buildings (Net)	10,000,000	2,000,000
Investment in Shade (Cost)	5,175,000	-0-
Land	2,000,000	1,200,000
Total Assets	$51,800,000	$10,000,000
Dividends Payable	$ -0-	$ 100,000
Current Liabilities	1,800,000	900,000
Long Term Liabilities	10,000,000	1,000,000
No Par Common Stock	20,000,000	2,000,000
Retained Earnings	20,000,000	6,000,000
Total Equities	$51,800,000	$10,000,000

The Income Statements of the Pastel and Shade Companies for the year ending December 31, 1998 were as follows:

	Pastel	Shade
Sales	$8,000,000	$2,000,000
Gain on Sale of Land	500,000	-0-
Other Revenues	800,000	100,000
Total Revenues	$9,300,000	$2,100,000
Cost of Goods Sold	$3,800,000	$ 800,000
Depreciation Expense	1,400,000	300,000
Other Expenses	2,000,000	400,000
Total Expenses	$7,200,000	$1,500,000
Net Income	$2,100,000	$ 600,000

Other Information:

1. Any goodwill arising from the business combination should be amortized over 30 years.

2. Both Companies use the straight line method to calculate all depreciation and amortization charges and the First-In, First-Out inventory flow assumption.

3. Pastel uses the cost method to carry its Investment In Shade.

4. The Sales account in the Pastel Company's Income Statement includes only sales of merchandise. All other income is accounted for in Other Revenues.

5. During 1998, Pastel charged Shade $100,000 for management fees. None of this amount has been paid during 1998.

6. During 1998, dividends of $200,000 were declared and paid by Pastel and dividends of $100,000 were declared by Shade. On December 31, 1998, the dividends that were declared by the Shade Company during 1998 had not yet been paid.

7. During 1998, Shade sold to Pastel $500,000 worth of merchandise which was totally resold by Pastel in 1998. Pastel owes Shade $75,000 on December 31, 1998 due to these purchases.

8. During 1998, Pastel sold merchandise to Shade for $150,000. All of this merchandise was resold in 1998. Shade has not paid for these purchases as at December 31, 1998.

Required   Prepare, for the Pastel Company and its subsidiary, the Shade Company:

A. The consolidated Income Statement for the year ending December 31, 1998.

B. The consolidated Statement Of Retained Earnings for the year ending December 31, 1998.

C. The consolidated Balance Sheet as at December 31, 1998.

SELF STUDY PROBLEM FIVE - 2

On December 31, 1991, the Prude Company purchased 60 percent of the outstanding voting shares of the Sybarite Company for $750,000 in cash. On that date, the Balance Sheet of the Sybarite Company and the fair values of its identifiable assets and liabilities were as follows:

	Carrying Values	Fair Values
Cash	$ 10,000	$ 10,000
Current Receivables	200,000	150,000
Inventories	1,090,000	640,000
Plant and Equipment	1,000,000	1,050,000
Accumulated Depreciation	(300,000)	-0-
Total Assets	$2,000,000	
Current Liabilities	$ 200,000	$ 200,000
Long Term Liabilities	500,000	600,000
No Par Common Stock	1,000,000	
Retained Earnings	300,000	
Total Equities	$2,000,000	

The difference between the carrying value and fair value of the Plant and Equipment relates to a building with a remaining useful life of 14 years. The Long Term Liabilities all mature on January 1, 1997. Any goodwill arising from the business combination is to be amortized over 20 years.

On December 31, 1998, the Balance Sheets of the Prude Company and its subsidiary, the Sybarite Company are as follows:

	Prude	Sybarite
Cash	$ 50,000	$ 300,000
Current Receivables	300,000	400,000
Inventories	700,000	1,750,000
Investment in Sybarite (Cost)	750,000	-0-
Plant and Equipment	9,000,000	1,000,000
Accumulated Depreciation	(3,000,000)	(650,000)
Total Assets	$7,800,000	$2,800,000
Current Liabilities	$ 300,000	$ 100,000
Long Term Liabilities	1,000,000	300,000
No Par Common Stock	4,000,000	1,000,000
Retained Earnings	2,500,000	1,400,000
Total Equities	$7,800,000	$2,800,000

Other Information:

1. Both Companies use the straight line method for the calculation of all depreciation and amortization.

2. The Prude Company's Sales include sales of $50,000 to the Sybarite Company. Although this merchandise has been sold by Sybarite, it has not paid Prude for any of this merchandise during the year. Prude has levied an interest charge of $5,000 on this unpaid amount which is also outstanding on December 31, 1998.

3. There have been no additions or disposals of Plant and Equipment by Sybarite since December 31, 1991.

4. During 1998, Prude had Net Income of $1,000,000 and declared dividends of $200,000, while Sybarite had Net Income of $600,000 and declared and paid dividends of $100,000.

Required: Prepare a consolidated Balance Sheet as at December 31, 1998 for the Prude Company and its subsidiary, the Sybarite Company.

SELF STUDY PROBLEM FIVE - 3

On December 31, 1996, the Port Company acquired 30 percent of the outstanding voting shares of the Ship Company for $3,000,000. On December 31, 1997, the Port Company acquired an additional 30 percent of the Ship Company's outstanding voting shares for $3,600,000. The Ship Company's Balance Sheets as at December 31, 1996 and December 31, 1997 were as follows:

Ship Company
Balance Sheets
As At December 31

	1996	1997
Net Monetary Assets	$2,000,000	$3,500,000
Plant and Equipment (Net)	5,000,000	4,500,000
Total Assets	$7,000,000	$8,000,000
Common Stock - No Par	$4,000,000	$4,000,000
Retained Earnings	3,000,000	4,000,000
Total Equities	$7,000,000	$8,000,000

On December 31, 1996, the fair value of the Ship Company's Plant and Equipment was $2,000,000 greater than its carrying value and its remaining useful life on that date was 10 years. At the time of the second purchase the fair value of the Ship Company's Plant and Equipment was $3 million greater than its carrying value and there had been no additions to the account during the year. Any goodwill arising from either transaction should be amortized over 20 years. All depreciation and amortization charges are calculated on a straight line basis for both Companies. On December 31, 1998, the Balance Sheets of the two Companies were as follows:

Port and Ship Companies
Balance Sheets
As At December 31, 1998

	Port	Ship
Net Monetary Assets	$ 3,400,000	$4,500,000
Investment in Ship (Cost)	6,600,000	-0-
Plant and Equipment (Net)	10,000,000	4,000,000
Total Assets	$20,000,000	$8,500,000
Common Stock - No Par	$10,000,000	$4,000,000
Retained Earnings	10,000,000	4,500,000
Total Equities	$20,000,000	$8,500,000

Required: Prepare, for the Port Company and its subsidiary the Ship Company, a consolidated Balance Sheet as at December 31, 1998.

SELF STUDY PROBLEM FIVE - 4

On January 1, 1992, the Puberty Company acquired 80 percent of the outstanding voting shares of the Senile Company for $4,000,000 in cash. On that date, the Senile Company had outstanding common shares with a total Par Value of $400,000, Contributed Surplus of $600,000 and Retained Earnings of $2,000,000. At the acquisition date, all identifiable assets and liabilities of the Senile Company had fair values equal to their carrying values except for a building with a remaining useful life of 25 years which had a fair value that was $4,000,000 greater than its carrying value and an issue of 20 year bonds that had a fair value that was $2,000,000 greater than the value at which they were carried on Senile's books. The bonds were issued on January 1, 1988. In addition, on January 1, 1992, Senile had Goodwill of $1,000,000 on its books, which was being amortized over 5 years.

On December 31, 1998, the adjusted trial balances of the Puberty Company and its subsidiary, the Senile Company are as follows:

	Puberty	Senile
Cash and Current Receivables	$ 1,100,000	$ 400,000
Long Term Receivables	1,000,000	200,000
Inventories	4,000,000	1,300,000
Plant and Equipment (Net)	6,000,000	6,000,000
Investment in Senile (Cost)	4,000,000	-0-
Cost of Goods Sold	5,000,000	1,500,000
Other Expenses	3,000,000	800,000
Dividends Declared	400,000	300,000
Total Debits	$24,500,000	$10,500,000
Current Liabilities	$ 300,000	$ 400,000
Notes Payable	200,000	600,000
Long Term Liabilities	2,000,000	2,500,000
Common Stock - Par Value	3,000,000	400,000
Contributed Surplus	1,000,000	600,000
Retained Earnings	8,000,000	3,200,000
Sales	9,000,000	2,500,000
Other Revenues	1,000,000	300,000
Total Credits	$24,500,000	$10,500,000

Other Information:

1. Any goodwill arising from the acquisition of Senile is to be amortized over 40 years. Puberty carries its investment in Senile by the cost method.

2. Both Companies use the straight line method to calculate all amortization and depreciation charges.

3. Puberty's 1998 Sales include $1,000,000 in sales to Senile which were priced to provide Puberty with a gross profit of 30 percent of the sales price. This merchandise has been resold by Senile in 1998.

4. Puberty holds a 12 percent, $500,000 Note which is payable by Senile in 2002. Interest is payable April 1 and October 1 on the principal. Puberty has been holding this Note since July 1, 1998.
5. Puberty's Other Revenues include any Investment Income received, as well as $100,000 in management fees which are payable by Senile in 1999.

Required: Prepare, for the Puberty Company and its subsidiary, the Senile Company:

A. the consolidated Income Statement for the year ending December 31, 1998;

B. the consolidated Statement of Retained Earnings for the year ending December 31, 1998; and

C. the consolidated Balance Sheet as at December 31, 1998.

Assignment Problems

(The solutions to these problem are only available in
the solutions manual that has been provided to your instructor.)

ASSIGNMENT PROBLEM FIVE - 1

On December 31, 1993, the Percy Company purchased 75 percent of the outstanding voting shares of the Stern Company for $3 million in cash. On that date, Stern had Common Stock - No Par of $2 million and Retained Earnings of $1 million. On December 31, 1993 all of the identifiable assets and liabilities of Stern had fair values that were equal to their carrying values with the following exceptions:

1. Inventories with fair values that were $400,000 less than their carrying values.

2. Land with a fair value that was $800,000 greater than its carrying value.

3. Long Term Liabilities, maturing on January 1, 1999, with fair values that were $200,000 less than their carrying values.

Any goodwill arising from this business combination is to be amortized over 30 years. Both Companies use the straight line method to calculate all depreciation and amortization. The land which was on the books of the Stern Company on December 31, 1993 has not been sold as at December 31, 1998. The Percy Company accounts for its investment in Stern Company using the cost method.

Other data for the year ending December 31, 1998 is as follows:

Income Statements
For The Year Ending December 31, 1998

	Percy	Stern
Merchandise Sales	$5,000,000	$2,000,000
Other Revenues	1,000,000	500,000
Total Revenues	$6,000,000	$2,500,000
Cost of Goods Sold	$2,000,000	$1,000,000
Depreciation Expense	400,000	300,000
Other Expenses	600,000	400,000
Total Expenses	$3,000,000	$1,700,000
Net Income	$3,000,000	$ 800,000

Retained Earnings Statements
For The Year Ending December 31, 1998

	Percy	Stern
Opening Balance	$10,000,000	$1,600,000
Net Income	3,000,000	800,000
Balance Available	$13,000,000	$2,400,000
Dividends Declared	1,000,000	400,000
Closing Balance	$12,000,000	$2,000,000

Balance Sheets
as at December 31, 1998

	Percy	Stern
Cash and Current Receivables	$ 1,500,000	$1,200,000
Note Receivable	1,000,000	-0-
Inventories	4,500,000	1,000,000
Investment in Stern (At Cost)	3,000,000	-0-
Plant and Equipment (Net)	9,000,000	3,000,000
Land	2,000,000	800,000
Total Assets	$21,000,000	$6,000,000
Current Liabilities	$ 500,000	$ 200,000
Long Term Liabilities	3,500,000	1,800,000
Common Stock - No Par	5,000,000	2,000,000
Retained Earnings	12,000,000	2,000,000
Total Equities	$21,000,000	$6,000,000

Other Information:

1. During 1998, Stern had sales of $1,500,000 to Percy while Percy had $500,000 in sales to Stern. All of the merchandise which was transferred in these intercompany sales has been resold during 1998 to companies outside of the consolidated entity.

2. The Long Term Liabilities of the Stern Company include a $1 million note that is payable to the Percy Company. During 1998, interest expense on this note was $110,000 and on December 31, 1998, $100,000 of this interest had not been paid by Stern. The note is to be paid on December 31, 2001.

Required: Prepare, for the Percy Company and its subsidiary, the Stern Company, the following:

A. The consolidated Income Statement for the year ending December 31, 1998.

B. The consolidated Statement of Retained Earnings for the year ending December 31, 1998.

C. The consolidated Balance Sheet as at December 31, 1998.

ASSIGNMENT PROBLEM FIVE - 2

On January 1, 1993, the Prospect Company purchases 80 percent of the outstanding voting shares of the Suspect Company for $1,760,000 in cash. On that date, the Shareholders' Equity of the Suspect Company is as follows:

Common Stock - No Par	$1,050,000
Retained Earnings - Unrestricted	560,000
Reserve For Contingencies	140,000
Total	$1,750,000

On the acquisition date, all of the assets and liabilities of the Suspect Company have fair values that are equal to their carrying values except for a patent. The patent is carried on Suspect's books at $500,000. Its fair value on the acquisition date is $700,000 and its remaining useful life on that date is 10 years. Any goodwill that arises on this acquisition date will be amortized over 20 years.

Between January 1, 1993 and December 31, 1998, the Suspect Company earns $980,000 and pays dividends of $280,000. The Company's Reserve For Contingencies is unchanged during this period.

During the year ending December 31, 1998 the Prospect Company has Net Income of $300,000 and Suspect has Net Income of $100,000. Prospect pays no dividends during 1998 while Suspect pays $50,000. On December 31, 1998, the Prospect Company has Retained Earnings of $2,000,000.

Prospect carries the Investment In Suspect at cost and its Net Income includes Investment Income calculated by this method. Both Companies calculate all depreciation and amortization charges using the straight line method and, during 1998, there are no intercompany transactions other than dividend payments.

Required:

A. Compute consolidated Net Income for the year ending December 31, 1998 for the Prospect Company and its subsidiary the Suspect Company.

B. Compute the carrying value of the Patent, the amount of Goodwill, the Non Controlling Interest, and the Retained Earnings balance that would be shown on the consolidated Balance Sheet of the Prospect Company and its subsidiary the Suspect Company, as at December 31, 1998.

ASSIGNMENT PROBLEM FIVE - 3

The Palma Company acquired 84 percent of the outstanding voting shares of the Gratton Company for $4,200,000 in cash on December 31, 1992. On that date, the Balance Sheet of the Gratton Company and the fair values of its identifiable assets and liabilities were as follows:

	Carrying Values	Fair Values
Cash	$ 350,000	$ 350,000
Accounts Receivable	250,000	200,000
Inventories	500,000	600,000
Land	3,000,000	3,800,000
Plant and Equipment (Net)	1,800,000	1,200,000
Total Assets	$5,900,000	$6,150,000
Current Liabilities	$ 250,000	$ 250,000
Long Term Liabilities	950,000	800,000
Common Stock - No Par Value	1,700,000	N/A
Retained Earnings	3,000,000	N/A
Total Equities	$5,900,000	

The difference between the carrying value and fair value of the Plant and Equipment arises from a piece of equipment which has an estimated remaining useful life of 15 years on December 31, 1992. The long term liabilities of Gratton mature on December 31, 2010. Palma carries its investment in Gratton by the cost method.

On December 31, 1998, the adjusted trial balances of the Palma Company and its subsidiary, the Gratton Company are as follows:

	Palma	Gratton
Cash	$ 873,000	$ 470,000
Accounts Receivable	950,000	580,000
Inventories	960,000	800,000
Land	8,500,000	4,750,000
Plant and Equipment (Net)	6,500,000	2,750,000
Investment in Gratton (Cost)	4,200,000	-0-
Goodwill	425,000	-0-
Cost of Goods Sold	4,500,000	3,500,000
Other Expenses	327,000	2,750,000
Dividends Declared	500,000	350,000
Total Debits	$27,735,000	$15,950,000
Current Liabilities	$ 727,000	$ 350,000
Long Term Liabilities	975,000	800,000
Common Stock - No Par Value	9,500,000	1,700,000
Retained Earnings	6,805,800	6,100,000
Sales	9,000,000	6,500,000
Other Revenues	727,200	500,000
Total Credits	$27,735,000	$15,950,000

Other Information:

1. Any goodwill arising from the acquisition of Gratton is to be amortized over 15 years. If negative goodwill results from the acquisition, it is to be applied to the plant and equipment.

2. Both Companies use the straight line method to calculate all amortization and depreciation charges. The fiscal year end of both Companies is December 31.

3. The Plant and Equipment and Land that was owned by Gratton on December 31, 1992 are still on the books of Gratton on December 31, 1998. The December 31, 1992 Accounts Receivable and Inventories were received and sold, respectively, during 1993.

4. Palma's 1998 Sales include $750,000 in sales to Gratton which were priced to provide Palma with a gross profit of 40 percent of the sales price. On December 31, 1998, Gratton has not yet paid for 35 percent of its purchases from Palma. Gratton had sales of $500,000 to Palma in 1997 and $450,000 in 1998. All merchandise obtained through these sales has been resold to the public in the year of purchase.

5. During 1998, Palma repaired equipment for Gratton and charged $2,500 in service fees. As at December 31, 1998, this payable is still outstanding. These fees are included in Palma's Other Revenues, along with any Investment Income received.

Required: For the Palma Company and its subsidiary, the Gratton Company:

A. Prepare the consolidated Income Statement for the year ending December 31, 1998.

B. Prepare the consolidated Statement of Retained Earnings for the year ending December 31, 1998.

C. Prepare the consolidated Balance Sheet as at December 31, 1998.

D. Assume that the Palma Company has carried the Gratton Company using the equity method since its acquisition. Calculate the Investment in Gratton that would be disclosed on the single entity Balance Sheet of the Palma Company as at December 31, 1998 and the Investment Income that would be disclosed on the single entity Income Statement of the Palma Company for the year ending December 31, 1998.

ASSIGNMENT PROBLEM FIVE - 4

On January 1, 1996, the Perry Company purchased 72 percent of the outstanding voting shares of the Styan Company for $3,675,000 in cash. On that date, the Styan Company had No Par Common Stock of $1,680,000 and Retained Earnings of $3,570,000. All of the Styan Company's identifiable assets and liabilities had carrying values that were equal to their fair values except for:

1. Inventories which had fair values of $1,806,000 and book values of $2,037,000.

2. Buildings which had fair values that were $175,000 more than their carrying values and a remaining useful life of 20 years.

3. Land which had a fair value of $1,596,000 and a carrying value of $1,400,000.

4. A Patent with a book value of $154,000 and a nil fair value which was being amortized at $77,000 per year.

5. Long Term Liabilities which had fair values that were $210,000 more than their carrying values and mature on December 31, 2005.

The Balance Sheets of the Perry Company and the Styan Company as at December 31, 1998 were as follows:

	Perry	Styan
Cash	$ 175,000	$ 17,500
Current Receivables	910,000	140,000
Inventories	1,709,750	1,050,000
Equipment (Net)	3,584,000	2,248,750
Buildings (Net)	3,727,500	2,187,500
Investment in Styan (Cost)	3,675,000	-0-
Land	1,706,250	1,400,000
Total Assets	$15,487,500	$7,043,750
Dividends Payable	$ -0-	$ 70,000
Current Liabilities	840,000	350,000
Long Term Liabilities	3,587,500	1,064,000
Preferred Stock	280,000	-0-
No Par Common Stock	9,100,000	1,680,000
Retained Earnings	1,680,000	3,879,750
Total Equities	$15,487,500	$7,043,750

The Income Statements of the Perry and Styan Companies for the year ending December 31, 1998 were as follows:

	Perry	Styan
Sales	$3,800,000	$1,120,000
Other Revenues	62,400	200,000
Total Revenues	$3,862,400	$1,320,000
Cost of Goods Sold	$1,412,000	$ 623,000
Depreciation Expense	525,000	175,000
Other Expenses	1,567,000	235,000
Total Expenses	$3,504,000	$1,033,000
Income Before Extraordinary Items	$ 358,400	$ 287,000
Extraordinary Loss (Net of Taxes of $17,000)	-0-	52,500
Net Income	$ 358,400	$ 234,500

Other Information:

1. Any goodwill arising from the business combination should be amortized over 20 years.

2. Both Companies use the straight line method to calculate all depreciation and amortization charges and the First-In, First-Out inventory flow assumption.

3. Perry uses the cost method to carry its Investment In Styan.

4. The Sales account in both Companies' Income Statements include only sales of merchandise. All other income is accounted for in Other Revenues.

5. The Styan Company has sold no Land since January 1, 1996.

6. During 1998, dividends of $175,000 were declared and paid by Perry and dividends of $70,000 were declared by Styan.

7. During 1998, Perry sold to Styan merchandise worth $217,000 which was resold by Styan for a gross profit of $162,000 outside of the consolidated entity in 1998. Styan owes Perry $84,000 on December 31, 1998 due to these purchases.

8. During October, 1998, Styan charged the Perry Company $70,000 for the services of a team of computer programmers. The wages paid to the programmers with respect to this work was $58,500. Perry still has a balance of $3,500 outstanding with respect to this charge on December 31, 1998.

Required:

A. Prepare the consolidated Income Statement for the year ending December 31, 1998 of the Perry Company and its subsidiary, the Styan Company.

B. Prepare the consolidated Statement Of Retained Earnings for the year ending December 31, 1998 of the Perry Company and its subsidiary, the Styan Company.

C. Prepare the consolidated Balance Sheet as at December 31, 1998 of the Perry Company and its subsidiary, the Styan Company.

D. Assume that the Perry Company, despite its majority ownership, does not have control over Styan and carries its Investment In Styan using the equity method. Calculate and disclose the amount(s) of investment income that would be shown in the Perry Company's Income Statement under this assumption. (An Income Statement is not required.)

ASSIGNMENT PROBLEM FIVE - 5

The book value and fair value of the net identifiable assets of the Slice Company are as follows:

	Book Value	Fair Value
December 31, 1996	$4,265,000	$4,365,000
December 31, 1997	$4,865,000	$5,065,000

On December 31, 1996, the Piece Company acquires 20 percent of the outstanding voting shares of the Slice Company for cash of $904,000. The remaining useful life of the Slice Company assets on which the fair value changes exist is 10 years and no salvage value is anticipated.

On December 31, 1997, the Piece Company acquires an additional 50 percent of the outstanding voting shares of the Slice Company for cash of $2,873,000. The remaining life of the Slice Company assets on which the fair value changes exist is 9 years.

On December 31, 1998, the book values of the net identifiable assets of the Piece Company and the Slice Company are as follows:

	Piece	Slice
Total Net Identifiable Assets	$8,973,000	$5,653,000

On December 31, 1998, the Retained Earnings balance of the Piece Company is $4,235,000.

Other Information:

1. Both Companies amortize all assets and liabilities using the straight line method.

2. Goodwill is to be amortized over a period of 10 years from the date of its recognition.

3. During the period January 1, 1996 through December 31, 1998, neither the Piece Company nor the Slice Company issues or retires any of their shares of common stock.

4. During the period January 1, 1996 through December 31, 1998, the only intercompany transactions were dividends declared and paid to the Piece Company by the Slice Company.

5. The Piece Company carries its Investment In Slice Company using the cost method.

6. There is no Goodwill on the books of either the Piece Company or the Slice Company.

Required: Calculate the amounts that would be shown in the consolidated Balance Sheet of the Piece Company and its subsidiary the Slice Company on December 31, 1998 for the following accounts:

A. Net identifiable assets
B. Goodwill
C. Non Controlling Interest
D. Retained Earnings.

ASSIGNMENT PROBLEM FIVE - 6

On January 1, 1996, the Perle Company acquired 70 percent of the outstanding voting shares of the Thane Company for $1,785,000 in cash. On this date the book value of the Thane Company's Shareholders' Equity was $2,600,000 and all of the Thane Company's identifiable assets and liabilities had fair values that were equal to their carrying values except for the following:

	Carrying Value	Fair Value
Marketable Securities	$ 28,000	$ 35,000
Fleet of Trucks	324,000	365,000
Division F - Building and Equipment (Net)	631,000	453,000
Land	96,000	118,000
Long Term Liabilities - Par $2,000,000	1,983,000	2,010,000

The Marketable Securities were sold on March 17, 1997 for $33,000. The fleet of trucks have an estimated remaining useful life of four years on January 1, 1996 and no anticipated salvage value. The Division F Building and Equipment cost $1,457,500 when purchased on January 1, 1984 and had an estimated useful life of 20 years on that date. When purchased they had an anticipated salvage value of $80,000 and there is no change in the estimates of salvage value or total useful life on January 1, 1996. The parcel of Land is being held in anticipation of expansion in 2002. The Long Term Liabilities are scheduled to mature on December 31, 2001.

The Perle Company amortizes goodwill over a period of 20 years. Both Companies use the straight line method for all depreciation and amortization calculations and the Perle Company carries its investment in Thane Company using the cost method. The Perle Company's investment income consists of $5,000 in interest revenue and its income from the Thane Company. During the period January 1, 1996 until December 31, 1998, neither the Perle Company nor the Thane Company issue or retire shares of common stock.

For the year ending December 31, 1998, the Income Statements for the Perle Company and the Thane Company are as follows:

	Perle	Thane
Sales Revenue	$4,887,000	$1,450,000
Investment Income	29,500	12,000
Total Revenues	$4,916,500	$1,462,000
Cost Of Goods Sold	$2,117,000	$ 829,000
Depreciation Expense	935,000	135,000
Other Expenses	1,284,000	246,000
Total Expenses	$4,336,000	$1,210,000
Income Before Discontinued Operations	$ 580,500	$ 252,000
Loss From Discontinued Operations	-0-	(63,250)
Net Income	$ 580,500	$ 188,750

Other Information:

1. On January 1, 1998, the Retained Earnings balance of the Perle Company was $8,463,000. During 1998, the Perle Company paid dividends totalling $115,000.

2. Between January 1, 1996 and December 31, 1997, Thane earned Net Income of $192,000 and declared dividends totalling $46,000.

3. On January 1, 1998, the Thane Company sold Division F to someone outside the consolidated entity for $430,000, creating a loss from discontinued operations of $63,250. The sale consisted of the Building and Equipment which had the fair value changes on January 1, 1996.

4. To help with the paperwork in closing the division, the Thane Company used the services of several of the Perle Company's accountants and agreed to pay a fee of $5,600 for these services. On December 31, 1998, this fee remains unpaid. This amount is included in the Sales Revenues of the Perle Company and in the Other Expenses of the Thane Company. The salaries paid to the accountants by the Perle Company for the work done on the Thane Company amount to $4,200 and are included in the Other Expenses of the Perle Company.

5. On January 1, 1998, the Perle Company rented a building from the Thane Company for a monthly rent of $2,000. On December 31, 1998, the Perle Company owed three months rent. The rent is included in the Sales Revenues of the Thane Company and in the Other Expenses of the Perle Company.

Required:

A. For the year ending December 31, 1998, prepare the consolidated Income Statement and the consolidated Statement Of Retained Earnings of the Perle Company and its subsidiary the Thane Company.

B. Calculate the Non Controlling Interest that would be shown in the December 31, 1998 consolidated Balance Sheet of the Perle Company and its subsidiary the Thane Company.

ASSIGNMENT PROBLEM FIVE - 7

On January 1, 1997, the Shareholders' Equity of the Trak Company was as follows:

Common Stock - No Par (120,000 Shares Outstanding)	$ 4,680,000
Preferred Stock - Par $250 - Cumulative 10 Percent Dividend	1,250,000
Retained Earnings	6,270,000
Total	$12,200,000

On this date, Nordeek Ltd. acquired 90,000 of the outstanding Trak common shares at a cash price of $105 per share. The legal and accounting fees associated with this acquisition of shares were $25,000.

At the time of this business combination, all of the identifiable assets and liabilities of the Trak Company had fair values that were equal to their carrying values with the following exceptions:

- Trak had developed a patent which had a fair value of $850,000 and a remaining useful life of 10 years at the time of the business combination. The costs of developing this patent had been expensed as incurred and, as a consequence, its carrying value on Trak's books was nil.

- Accounts Receivable were carried on the books of Trak at their face value of $924,000. At the time of the business combination, it is estimated $50,000 of these accounts will be uncollectible. Actual amounts that prove to be uncollectible amount to $62,500, with all other amounts being collected during 1997.

- Inventories have a fair value that is $320,000 in excess of their carrying value on Trak's books. All of these inventories are sold during 1997.

- Plant Assets have a cost of $4,600,000 and accumulated depreciation of $2,400,000. The fair value of these assets is $2,500,000 and they have a remaining useful life of 20 years.

- At the time of the business combination, Trak has bonds outstanding with a carrying value of $2,000,000, a maturity value of $2,000,000, and a maturity date of January 1, 2002. Because of their high coupon rate of interest, these bonds are trading at a value of $2,250,000. A provision in the bond indenture allows the bonds to be called at 105 (a total price of $2,100,000). On December 31, 1998, this call provision is exercised.

It is the policy of the Nordeek Company to amortize any goodwill arising as the result of business combination transactions over a period of 25 years using the straight line method.

Other Information:

1. Both companies have a December 31 year end.

2. It is the policy of Trak Company to write off all of their tangible and intangible assets using the straight line method. The straight line method is also used for the amortization of bond premium or discount.

3. During the year ending December 31, 1997, Trak had Net Income of $463,000, paid preferred stock dividends of $125,000 and common stock dividends of $240,000. There were no arrearages of preferred stock dividends on January 1, 1997.

4. During the year ending December 31, 1998, Trak had Net Income of $372,000, paid preferred stock dividends of $125,000 and common stock dividends of $90,000.

5. During 1998, Nordeek sold merchandise to Trak Company for $325,000. The cost of this merchandise to Nordeek was $175,000 and it was resold in 1998 by Trak for $410,000.

6. During 1998, Trak provided a variety of consulting services to Nordeek for a fee of $92,000. On Trak's books, the cost of providing these services was $64,500.

7. For the year ending December 31, 1998, Nordeek recorded Net Income of $1,563,000 in its single entity statements. On December 31, 1998, the Retained Earnings balance of Nordeek Company is $10,523,000. Nordeek carries its investment in Trak using the cost method.

Required: Calculate the following:

A. Consolidated Net Income for the Nordeek Company and its subsidiary Trak Company for the year ending December 31, 1998.

B. Consolidated Retained Earnings for the Nordeek Company and its subsidiary Trak Company as at December 31, 1998.

C. The Non Controlling Interest that would be shown in the consolidated Income Statement for the year ending December 31, 1998.

D. The Non Controlling Interest that would be shown in the consolidated Balance Sheet as at December 31, 1998.

ASSIGNMENT PROBLEM FIVE - 8

On January 1, 1998, Saytor Ltd. acquires 35 percent of the outstanding common shares of Saytee Inc. at a cost of $3,066,000. On this date, the Shareholders' Equity of Saytee Inc. was as follows:

Common Stock - Par $20	$2,500,000
Contributed Surplus	2,000,000
Retained Earnings	3,700,000
Total Shareholders' Equity	$8,200,000

At this time, all of the identifiable assets and liabilities of Saytee Inc. have fair values that are equal to their carrying values. This means that the $196,000 excess of the purchase price ($3,066,000) over Saytor's 35 share of Saytee's book value ($2,870,000) will be allocated to Goodwill. This Goodwill will be amortized on a straight line basis over 10 years. Both Companies have a December 31 year end.

During the year ending December 31, 1998, Saytee Inc. has Net Income of $462,000 and declares and pays dividends of $250,000. For 1998, Saytee does not report any results of discontinued operations, extraordinary items or capital transactions. Other than Saytee's Dividends Declared, there are no transactions between the two Companies during the year. Saytor Ltd. carries its Investment In Saytee using the equity method.

The Balance Sheets for the two companies as at December 31, 1998 and the Income Statements for the year ending December 31, 1998, are as follows:

Saytor And Saytee Companies
Balance Sheets As At December 31, 1998

	Saytor Ltd.	Saytee Inc.
Cash	$ 420,000	$ 270,000
Accounts Receivable	1,340,000	896,000
Inventories	2,370,000	3,560,000
Investment In Saytee (Note One)	3,120,600	-0-
Plant And Equipment (Net)	3,170,000	5,708,000
Total Assets	$10,420,600	$10,434,000
Current Liabilities	$ 872,000	$ 462,000
Long Term Liabilities	2,100,000	1,560,000
Common Stock - No Par	3,700,000	-0-
Common Stock - Par $20	-0-	2,500,000
Contributed Surplus	-0-	2,000,000
Retained Earnings	3,748,600	3,912,000
Total Equities	$10,420,600	$10,434,000

Note One   The equity value for the Investment In Saytee is calculated as follows:

Cost On January 1, 1998	$3,066,000
Equity Pickup For 1998 ([35%][$462,000 - $250,000])	74,200
Goodwill Amortization ($196,000 ÷ 10)	(19,600)
Investment At Equity	$3,120,600

Saytor And Saytee Companies
Income Statements For The Year Ending December 31, 1998

	Saytor Ltd.	Saytee Inc.
Sales	$12,572,300	$8,623,000
Investment Income (Note Two)	142,100	-0-
Total Revenues	$12,714,400	$8,623,000
Cost Of Sales	$ 7,926,000	$5,824,000
Depreciation Expense	3,116,000	1,326,000
Other Expenses	1,132,000	1,011,000
Total Expenses	$12,174,000	$8,161,000
Net Income	$ 540,400	$ 462,000

Note Two   The equity method Investment Income would be calculated as follows:

Saytor's Share Of Saytee's Reported Income ([35%][$462,000])	$161,700
Goodwill Amortization ($196,000 ÷ 10)	(19,600)
Equity Method Investment Income	$142,100

Saytor Ltd. intends to account for its Investment In Saytee Inc. using proportionate consolidation.

Required: Using proportionate consolidation procedures, prepare the consolidated Balance Sheet as at December 31, 1998 and the consolidated Income Statement for the year ending December 31, 1998 for Saytor Ltd. and its investee, Saytee Inc. Your solution should comply with the Recommendations of Section 3055 of the *CICA Handbook*.

Chapter 6

Consolidation Subsequent To Acquisition (Including Unrealized Intercompany Profits)

Unrealized Intercompany Profits

Basic Concepts

6-1.   From the point of view of the consolidated entity, profits on intercompany transactions are said to be unrealized until verified by an arm's-length transaction with an individual or organization that is outside or independent of the consolidated entity. For example, if a subsidiary sells merchandise to a parent company and recognizes a profit on the transaction, the profit of the subsidiary is said to be unrealized until such time as the parent resells the merchandise outside of the consolidated entity. Correspondingly, if there is an intercompany sale of a capital asset, any gain or loss recognized by the vendor is unrealized until such time as the purchaser either sells the asset or uses it up.

6-2.   To say that these profits are unrealized from the point of view of the consolidated entity is the equivalent of saying that they do not exist from the consolidated point of view. This problem is the major focus of this Chapter. We will be concerned with introducing procedures for the elimination of these unrealized intercompany profits in the preparation of consolidated financial statements. We would also note the possibility of unrealized intercompany losses. Similar procedures will be required when such losses arise. The required procedures will involve adjustments to both expenses and revenues in the consolidated Income Statement, as well as to assets and liabilities in the consolidated Balance Sheet.

6-3.   The problem of unrealized intercompany profits should not be confused with the problem of intercompany expenses and revenues. While they are often related, they should be dealt with as two separate and distinct issues. For example, if there is an intercompany payment of interest on a note that is carried on both companies' books at face value, there is an intercompany expense and revenue but no unrealized intercompany profit or loss. In other situations an unrealized profit may arise at the time of an intercompany expense and revenue. This would be the case, for example, if there was an intercompany sale of merchandise. Note, however, if the purchasing company has resold the merchandise to parties outside the consolidated entity, there will still be an intercompany expense and revenue to be eliminated. However, there will not be an intercompany unrealized profit.

6-4.   A final point here is that a profit that is unrealized in one accounting period may become realized in a subsequent period. If, for example, the ending inventories of a subsidiary contained goods purchased from the parent, any profit recorded by the parent on the sale of these goods is unrealized and must not be included in the consolidated figures. However, the ending inventories that contained the unrealized profit are likely to be sold during the following accounting period. If the goods are sold to a party outside of the consolidated entity, the parent company's profit becomes realized at that point and should be included in the consolidated income figures. The point being made here is that the procedures that will be developed in this Chapter must deal with both the removal of unrealized intercompany profits, and with adding them back when they become realized in some future period or periods.

Classification

6-5.   From a conceptual point of view, all types of unrealized intercompany profits are the same. However, in terms of the procedures to be used in preparing consolidated financial statements, we will find it useful to classify such profits into three groups. These groups are as follows:

1.   Unrealized profits on intercompany sales of assets with unlimited lives. The primary example of this situation would be intercompany sales of land.

2.   Unrealized profits on intercompany sales of assets that are subject to depreciation, depletion, or amortization. This would include plant and equipment, natural resources and intangibles.

3.   Unrealized profits on intercompany sales of current assets. The most common example of this situation would be intercompany sales of merchandise or manufactured items that are being held for resale.

6-6.   In the this Chapter's comprehensive example we will find that the procedures are somewhat different for each of these categories.

Conceptual Alternatives In The Consolidated Income Statement

Downstream Unrealized Profits

6-7.   With respect to downstream profits (those resulting from the parent recording a profit on a sale to a subsidiary), there are no conceptual alternatives. Since the profit is that of the parent company, there is no non controlling interest in it. As a consequence, all such profits will be subject to 100 percent elimination. The elimination will, of course, be charged against consolidated Net Income and consolidated Retained Earnings.

Upstream Unrealized Profits

6-8.   With upstream profits (those resulting from the subsidiary recording a profit on a sale to the parent), there is the possibility of a non controlling interest being present. Such a non controlling interest would have a claim on the profits of the subsidiary and this would raise the possibility of different concepts being applied in the elimination of such profits. A simple example will be used to illustrate these conceptual alternatives. The basic data for this example is as follows:

Example   The Play Company owns 70 percent of the outstanding voting shares of the Stay Company. The purchase was made at a time when all of the identifiable assets and liabilities of the Stay Company had carrying values that were equal to their fair values. The purchase price was equal to 70 percent of the carrying value of the

Stay Company's net identifiable assets. In a subsequent year the Income Statements of the two Companies are as follows:

	Play	Stay
Sales Revenue	$7,500,000	$2,200,000
Gain On Sale Of Land To Play Company	-0-	400,000
Total Revenues	$7,500,000	$2,600,000
Expenses	5,600,000	1,900,000
Net Income	$1,900,000	$ 700,000

Proprietary Concept Solution

6-9.   You will recall that under this conceptual approach, the expenses and revenues that are disclosed in the consolidated Income Statement consist of 100 percent of the parent company's expenses and revenues plus a share of the subsidiary's expenses and revenues that is based on the parent company's ownership interest (70 percent in this example). In addition, because the Gain On Sale Of Land is an unrealized intercompany profit, the parent's share of this item would also be removed. The resulting consolidated Income Statement would appear as follows:

Sales Revenue ($7,500,000 + $2,200,000 - $660,000)	$9,040,000
Gain On Sale Of Land To Play Company ($400,000 - $120,000 - $280,000)	-0-
Total Revenues	$9,040,000
Expenses ($5,600,000 + $1,900,000 - $570,000)	6,930,000
Consolidated Net Income	$2,110,000

6-10.   As was the case when this concept was illustrated in Chapter 5, the removal of the non controlling interest's share of the individual expenses and revenues eliminates the need to disclose a Non Controlling Interest in the consolidated Income Statement. With respect to the treatment of the unrealized intercompany profit, we eliminated the non controlling interest's share as part of the general application of the proprietary concept. The balance or parent company share was removed because it was unrealized. This procedure is sometimes referred to as fractional elimination of the unrealized intercompany profit. The consolidated Net Income of $2,110,000 can be verified by taking Play Company's Net Income of $1,900,000 plus $210,000, 70 percent of Stay Company's realized income of $300,000 ($700,000 - $400,000).

Parent Company Concept Solution

6-11.   This conceptual approach views the non controlling interest as a part of the consolidated entity and, as a consequence, the consolidated Income Statement would include 100 percent of the expenses and revenues of both the parent and the subsidiary company. With respect to the nature of the non controlling interest's participation in the consolidated entity, it is viewed as being a creditor like interest, somewhat akin to an issue of long term debt. Given this view, the Non Controlling Interest in the income of the consolidated entity would be viewed as a claim analogous to interest charges on creditor interests and would be deducted in the computation of consolidated Net Income. The resulting consolidated Income Statement would appear as follows:

Sales Revenue ($7,500,000 + $2,200,000)	$9,700,000
Gain On Sale Of Land To Play Company ($400,000 - $280,000)	120,000
Total Revenues	$9,820,000
Total Expenses ($5,600,000 + $1,900,000)	7,500,000
Combined Income	$2,320,000
Non Controlling Interest (30 Percent Of $700,000)	210,000
Consolidated Net Income	$2,110,000

6-12.   Note that this is the same consolidated Net Income that we arrived at under the proprietary approach, indicating that in some respects, the parent company approach is simply a modified version of the proprietary approach.

6-13.   Also note that the Non Controlling Interest continues to be based on the reported income of the subsidiary. This result, which is inherent in the application of the parent company approach, could only be achieved in this situation by leaving the non controlling interest's share of the unrealized intercompany profit in the consolidated revenues.

Entity Concept Solution

6-14.   You will recall that under the entity approach, the non controlling interest is viewed as a part of the consolidated entity. However, in contrast to the parent company approach, the non controlling interest here is viewed as an additional class of owner's equity. It would follow that the non controlling interest should be dealt with in a manner that is equivalent to the treatment accorded the controlling interest. With respect to unrealized intercompany profits of the subsidiary company, this view would require the elimination of both the non controlling and the controlling interests' shares of such profits with the reduction in income being charged in a proportionate manner to the two respective interests. This approach is normally referred to as 100 percent pro rata elimination of subsidiary unrealized profits. It is illustrated in the following consolidated Income Statement:

Sales Revenue ($7,500,000 + $2,200,000)	$9,700,000
Gain On Sale Of Land To Play Company ($400,000 -$400,000)	-0-
Total Revenues	$9,700,000
Expenses ($5,600,000 + $1,900,000)	7,500,000
Consolidated Net Income	$2,200,000

6-15.   Note that the consolidated Net Income is equal to the sum of the two Companies' Net Incomes ($1,900,000 + $700,000), less the $400,000 unrealized intercompany profit. No Non Controlling Interest is shown in the preceding Income Statement. Rather, it would be shown in the consolidated Statement Of Retained Earnings as a distribution of consolidated Net Income. Note that this treatment is analogous to the treatment that would be given to dividends on preferred shares and that this is consistent with the entity concept view that the non controlling interest is an equity interest. Because we have eliminated 100 percent of the unrealized intercompany profit, the non controlling interest in the consolidated Statement Of Retained Earnings would be $90,000. This is 30 percent of $300,000 (the reported income of the Stay Company of $700,000, less the unrealized intercompany profit of $400,000).

CICA Handbook Requirements

6-16.   The current Canadian requirements for dealing with unrealized intercompany profits in consolidated financial statements can be found in two Paragraphs of the *CICA Handbook*. The first is as follows:

> **Paragraph 1600.30** *Unrealized intercompany gains or losses arising subsequent to the date of an acquisition on assets remaining within the consolidated group should be eliminated. The amount of elimination from assets should not be affected by the existence of a non-controlling interest.* (April, 1975)

6-17.   This calls for 100 percent elimination of all unrealized intercompany profits but does not indicate specifically whose interest should be charged with the elimination. This latter question is clarified as follows:

> **Paragraph 1600.32** *Where there is an unrealized intercompany gain or loss recognized by a subsidiary company in which there is a non-controlling interest, such gain or loss should be eliminated proportionately between the parent and non-controlling interest in that company's income.* (April, 1975)

6-18.   Taken together, these two Paragraphs call for 100 percent, pro rata elimination of unrealized intercompany profits. This, of course, is an adoption of the entity approach for dealing with this issue. It is somewhat difficult to understand this Recommendation as, in dealing with most of the other issues in consolidation, the *CICA Handbook* has taken the view that the parent company approach is the most appropriate conceptual alternative. While we have already noted our disagreement with the parent company view of the nature of the non controlling interest, we would have found its adoption considerably more acceptable had it been applied in a consistent manner. However, this is not the case and this inconsistency in dealing with unrealized intercompany profits is one of the major sources of confusion and difficulty in the preparation of consolidated financial statements.

6-19.   Using the data for the example that was previously presented, the consolidated Income Statement of the Play Company and its subsidiary which would comply with all of the requirements of the *CICA Handbook* would be as follows:

Sales Revenue ($7,500,000 + $2,200,000)	$9,700,000
Gain On The Sale Of Land To	
Play Company ($400,000 - $400,000)	-0-
Total Revenues	$ 9,700,000
Expenses ($5,600,000 + $1,900,000)	7,500,000
Combined Income	$2,200,000
Non Controlling Interest (30 Percent Of $300,000)	90,000
Consolidated Net Income	$2,110,000

6-20.   This is the same consolidated Net Income that was computed under the parent company approach. However, the non controlling share of the unrealized profit has been removed from both Total Revenues and the Non Controlling Interest.

6-21.   We will now turn our attention to a comprehensive example which will illustrate in greater detail the treatment of unrealized intercompany profits. We will use the same basic problem that was used in the comprehensive example in Chapter 5 with unrealized intercompany profits added. Also, as was the case in Chapter 5, we will deal with two versions of this problem, both with the investment in the subsidiary being carried by the cost method on the books of the parent company. A version of this problem with the investment carried by the equity method on the books of the parent company can be found in Chapter 7.

Comprehensive Example - Open Trial Balance With Investment At Cost

Basic Data

6-22.   The basic data for this open trial balance version of our comprehensive problem is as follows:

On January 1, 1994, the Pleigh Company purchases 80 percent of the outstanding voting shares of the Sleigh Company for $3,200,000 in cash. On that date the Sleigh Company had No Par Common Stock of $2,000,000 and Retained Earnings of $1,500,000. On December 31, 1998, the adjusted trial balances of the Pleigh Company and its subsidiary, the Sleigh Company are as follows:

	Pleigh	Sleigh
Cash	$ 500,000	$ 300,000
Current Receivables	800,000	400,000
Inventories	2,500,000	1,700,000
Long Term Note Receivable	200,000	-0-
Investment In Sleigh - At Cost	3,200,000	-0-
Land	1,500,000	1,000,000
Plant And Equipment (Net)	4,500,000	1,900,000
Cost Of Goods Sold	2,800,000	1,500,000
Depreciation Expense	200,000	100,000
Other Expenses	364,000	616,000
Interest Expense	240,000	84,000
Dividends Declared	350,000	100,000
Total Debits	$17,154,000	$7,700,000
Current Liabilities	$ 500,000	$ 200,000
Long Term Liabilities	2,000,000	700,000
No Par Common Stock	8,000,000	2,000,000
Retained Earnings (January 1)	2,550,000	2,300,000
Sales	4,000,000	2,500,000
Interest Revenue	24,000	-0-
Dividend Revenue	80,000	-0-
Total Credits	$17,154,000	$7,700,000
1998 Net Income	$ 500,000	$ 200,000
December 31, 1998 Retained Earnings	$ 2,700,000	$2,400,000

Other Information:

A.   At the date of Pleigh Company's acquisition of the Sleigh Company's shares, all of the identifiable assets and liabilities of the Sleigh Company had fair values that were equal to their carrying values except Inventories which had fair values that were $100,000 more than their carrying values, Land with a fair value that was $150,000 less than its carrying value and Plant And Equipment which had a fair value that was $250,000 greater than its carrying value. The Plant And Equipment had a remaining useful life on the acquisition date of 20 years while the inventories that were present on the acquisition date were sold during the year ending December 31, 1994. The Land is still on the books of the Sleigh Company on December 31, 1998. Goodwill, if any, is to be amortized over 10 years. Both Companies use the straight line method to calculate depreciation and amortization.

B. Sleigh Company's Sales include sales of $300,000 to Pleigh Company. The December 31, 1998 Inventories of the Pleigh Company contain $100,000 of this merchandise purchased from Sleigh Company during 1998. In addition, the January 1, 1998 Inventories of the Pleigh Company contained $70,000 in merchandise purchased from Sleigh Company during 1997. All intercompany sales are priced to provide the selling company a gross margin on sales price of 40 percent.

C. On December 31, 1998, the Pleigh Company is holding Sleigh Company's long term note payable in the amount of $200,000. Interest at 12 percent is payable on July 1 of each year. Pleigh Company has been holding this note since July 1, 1996.

D. During 1996, the Pleigh Company sold Land to the Sleigh Company for $100,000 in cash. The Land had a carrying value on the books of the Pleigh Company of $75,000.

E. During 1997, the Sleigh Company sold Land to the Pleigh Company for $150,000. This Land had a carrying value on the books of the Sleigh Company of $110,000.

F. On December 31, 1996, the Sleigh Company sold Equipment to the Pleigh Company for $600,000. The Equipment had originally cost the Sleigh Company $800,000 and, at the time of the intercompany sale, had accumulated depreciation of $350,000. On this date, it was estimated that the remaining useful life of the Equipment was three years with no net salvage value.

Required: Prepare a consolidated Income Statement and a consolidated Statement Of Retained Earnings for the year ending December 31, 1998 and a consolidated Balance Sheet as at December 31, 1998 for the Pleigh Company and its subsidiary, the Sleigh Company.

Procedural Approach

6-23. The same basic approach that was used in solving the comprehensive problem in Chapter Five will be used here. Some modifications will be generated by the presence of unrealized intercompany profits. These modifications will be mentioned briefly here and described in detail in the solution which follows:

Step A This step will not be changed by the inclusion of unrealized intercompany profits.

Step B The adjustments and eliminations that were introduced in this Step in Chapter Five will remain the same. However, the presence of unrealized intercompany profits will require that additional eliminations be made.

Step C From a conceptual point of view, this Step is unchanged from Chapter Five. However, the fact that the *CICA Handbook* recommends the use of the entity approach for the elimination of unrealized intercompany profits creates significant complications in determining the appropriate distribution of the subsidiary's retained earnings since acquisition.

Step A Procedures

Investment Analysis

6-24. The following investment analysis is unchanged from its presentation in the open trial balance version of this comprehensive problem in Chapter 5:

	80 Percent	100 Percent
Investment Cost	$3,200,000	$4,000,000
Book Value	(2,800,000)	(3,500,000)
Differential	$ 400,000	$ 500,000
Fair Value Changes:		
Inventories	(80,000)	(100,000)
Land	120,000	150,000
Plant And Equipment	(200,000)	(250,000)
Goodwill	$ 240,000	$ 300,000

Investment Elimination

6-25.   The investment elimination entry would also be unchanged. It is as follows:

No Par Common Stock	$2,000,000	
Retained Earnings	1,500,000	
Plant And Equipment (Net)	200,000	
Inventories	80,000	
Goodwill	240,000	
Land		$ 120,000
Non Controlling Interest		700,000
Investment In Sleigh		3,200,000

Step B(1) - Intercompany Assets And Liabilities

6-26.   The entries for the elimination of intercompany assets and liabilities are unchanged from Chapter 5. They are as follows:

Long Term Liabilities	$200,000	
Long Term Note Receivable		$200,000
Current Liabilities	$12,000	
Current Receivables		$12,000

Step B(2) - Fair Value And Goodwill Write Offs

6-27.   The entries required for depreciation, depletion, and amortization of fair value changes and goodwill are unchanged from the Chapter Five version of this comprehensive problem. They are as follows:

Retained Earnings - Sleigh's Opening	$80,000	
Inventories		$80,000
Retained Earnings - Sleigh's Opening	$40,000	
Depreciation Expense	10,000	
Plant And Equipment (Net)		$50,000
Retained Earnings - Sleigh's Opening	$96,000	
Goodwill Amortization Expense	24,000	
Goodwill		$120,000

Step B(3) - Intercompany Expenses And Revenues

6-28.   The entries for the elimination of intercompany expenses and revenues are unchanged from Chapter 5. They are as follows:

Sales	$300,000	
Cost Of Goods Sold		$300,000
Interest Revenue	$ 24,000	
Interest Expense		$ 24,000

6-29.   Note that under our procedures, the entry for eliminating the intercompany expense and revenue related to the sale of merchandise has not been affected by the fact that a part of the goods remain in the inventories of the purchasing company. That is, we continue to eliminate 100 percent of the intercompany amount. While there are other approaches to dealing with intercompany merchandise sales, we believe that it is best to leave the intercompany expense and revenue procedure unchanged by the presence of an intercompany inventory profit. Using this approach, an additional entry will be required to remove the unrealized profit from the ending inventories of the Pleigh Company. This, however, will not alter the fact that we always eliminate 100 percent of intercompany expenses and revenues. This procedure will be discussed more fully in the material which follows.

Step B(4) - Intercompany Dividends

6-30.   The entry to eliminate the effects of intercompany dividends is unchanged from the Chapter 5 example. It is as follows:

Dividend Revenue	$80,000	
Non Controlling Interest	20,000	
Dividends Declared		$100,000

Step B(5) - Unrealized Intercompany Profits

Elimination Of Unrealized Profits

6-31.   The only new material in this problem is the addition of unrealized intercompany profits. Four such items have been added:

- There is a downstream unrealized profit resulting from Pleigh Company's 1996 sale of Land to Sleigh Company.

- There is an upstream unrealized profit resulting from Sleigh Company's 1997 sale of Land to Pleigh Company.

- There are unrealized upstream profits in both the opening and closing inventories of Pleigh, resulting from Sleigh's sales of merchandise to that company in 1997 and 1998. Recognition will also have to be given to the fact that the opening inventory profit that was unrealized at the beginning of 1998 has become realized during 1998.

- There is an upstream unrealized profit resulting from Sleigh Company's 1996 sale of Plant And Equipment to Pleigh Company. Recognition will also have to be given to the fact that a portion of this profit has become realized since the year of the sale.

6-32.   The presence of these unrealized intercompany profits creates the need to introduce the final procedures that are required in the preparation of basic consolidated financial statements. The first of these procedures involves the elimination of any unrealized profits that are present at the end of the current period and can be stated as follows:

Step B-5(a) Procedure   Eliminate 100 percent of all unrealized intercompany profits (losses) that are present at the end of the current period. The amounts will be deducted from (added to) the appropriate assets and, to the extent they were recognized in the current period income of the parent or subsidiary, they will be added to (subtracted from) current period expenses or revenues. If profits recognized by the parent or subsidiary in previous periods are still unrealized at the end of the current period, the adjustment will be to the opening consolidated retained earnings, rather than to the current period expenses or revenues. The elimination of downstream profits (losses) will be charged (credited) exclusively to consolidated Net Income and consolidated Retained Earnings. The elimination of upstream profits (losses) will be charged (credited) proportionately to consolidated figures and to any non controlling interest that is present.

Realization Of Previously Unrealized Profits

6-33.   We have noted previously that profits that are unrealized from a consolidated point in view in one period, may become realized in subsequent periods. If a parent sells merchandise to a subsidiary during 1998 and that merchandise remains in the December 31, 1998 Inventories of the subsidiary, the profit is unrealized and must be eliminated in the preparation of the 1998 consolidated financial statements. However, in most situations, the subsidiary will sell this merchandise during 1999, thereby realizing the profit from the point of view of the consolidated entity. As the profit will not be included in the 1999 single entity income records of the parent company, it must be added back in the preparation of consolidated financial statements. In other words, unrealized intercompany profits and losses must be eliminated in the preparation of the 1998 consolidated financial statements and the amounts recorded in the preparation of the 1999 consolidated financial statements. While Step B-5(a) can be used to eliminate the 1998 profit, we need an additional procedure to record the 1999 realization of this profit. This procedure can be described as follows:

> **Step B-5(b) Procedure**   Recognize the amount of previously unrealized intercompany profits or losses that have become realized during the period, either through the sale of the related asset or through usage of that asset. The amount which was previously unrealized from the consolidated point of view would be included in the opening single entity retained earnings of the parent or subsidiary companies. This means there must be an adjustment to a current period expense or revenue and to the consolidated opening retained earnings. The realization of previously unrealized downstream profits (losses) will be credited (charged) exclusively to consolidated Net Income and consolidated Retained Earnings. The realization of previously unrealized upstream profits (losses) will be credited (charged) proportionately to consolidated figures and to any non controlling interest that is present.

Implementation

6-34.   In the case of intercompany profits on inventories or non depreciable assets, the realization will take place through a sale transaction that occurs in a specific accounting period. This means that Step B-5(a) will be first implemented in the period in which the parent or subsidiary records the unrealized profit and will continue to be applied until the relevant asset is sold. In the period of sale, Step B-5(b) will be used to recognize the realization of the profit in the consolidated financial statements. In other words, for these types of unrealized intercompany profits, Steps B-5(a) and B-5(b) will be applied separately.

6-35.   In contrast, when the unrealized profit is related to the sale of a depreciable asset, the profit becomes realized through usage of the asset. Perhaps the best way to understand this is to think of a depreciable asset as a bundle of economic services. In effect, these services are being sold on a piecemeal basis as the asset is used and depreciated. This means that the intercompany profit will become realized as the asset is being depreciated. Because this realization process is carried out over several accounting periods, we have generally found it easier to net Steps B-5(a) and B-5(b). That is, when dealing with unrealized profits resulting from the intercompany sale of depreciable assets, we will not use separate entries to record the unrealized amount and the amount realized during subsequent periods. Rather, we will use a single net entry which reflects the amount realized during the current period and the remaining unrealized amount at the beginning of the current period.

Presentation Of Material

6-36.   In presenting this material on unrealized intercompany profits, we will often provide you with the entries that were recorded in the single entity records of the parent or subsidiary companies. Such entries are certainly not a required part of the consolidation procedures. However, we believe that the best way to understand this difficult material is to compare the values that are contained in the underlying records of the individual companies with the amounts that are required for consolidation purposes. Once these amounts are carefully established, the appropriate adjustment or elimination becomes a relatively simple bookkeeping problem.

Step B(5) - Downstream Profit On Land

Current Procedures

6-37.   In 1996, Pleigh Company sold Land with a carrying value of $75,000 to Sleigh Company for $100,000. To record this transaction, the following entry was made in Pleigh's single entity records:

Cash	$100,000	
Land		$75,000
Gain On Sale Of Land		25,000

6-38.   At the same time, the Sleigh Company would have recorded the purchase of Land in its single entity records as follows:

Land	$100,000	
Cash		$100,000

6-39.   From the point of view of the consolidated entity, this transaction did not occur. This would mean that the Land should still be in the consolidated statements at the old value of $75,000 and that no Gain On Sale should be included in consolidated income. The Step B-5(a) elimination entry which would have accomplished this result in 1996 would be as follows:

Gain On Sale Of Land	$25,000	
Land		$25,000

6-40.   This restores the Land value to $75,000 and removes the gain from the records of the Pleigh Company. While this entry would have been made in the process of preparing consolidated financial statements in 1996, it was a working paper entry and the unadjusted values would still remain in the records of the two Companies. That is, the Land would still be on the Sleigh Company's books at $100,000 and the $25,000 Gain would be included in the Retained Earnings of the Pleigh Company. Consequently, in every year subsequent to 1996 (including the current year), the following elimination entry would be required:

Retained Earnings - Pleigh	$25,000	
Land		$25,000

6-41.   You should note that since this is a downstream profit, this elimination will have no effect on the Non Controlling Interest in either the consolidated Income Statement or the consolidated Balance Sheet.

Future Events

6-42.   Consolidation procedures would require that this entry be continued until the Land is sold by the Sleigh Company to someone outside of the consolidated entity. In the year in which such a sale takes place, separate entries would be required for Steps B-5(a) and B-5(b). They would be as follows:

Retained Earnings - Pleigh	$25,000	
Land		$25,000
Land	$25,000	
Gain On Sale Of Land		$25,000

6-43.   This Gain would be added to any additional gain recorded on the sale by Sleigh in its single entity records and the total would be disclosed in the consolidated Income Statement. If, for example, Sleigh had sold the Land for $130,000, they would have recorded a gain of $30,000 ($130,000 - $100,000) in their records and this would result in a total gain of $55,000 being shown in the consolidated Income Statement.

6-44.   Subsequent to a sale of the Land, no further entries would be required and the Gain would become a legitimate part of the Retained Earnings of Pleigh and consolidated Retained Earnings.

Step B(5) - Upstream Profit On Land

Current Procedures

6-45.   With respect to the 1997 transaction in which Sleigh sold Land with a carrying value of $110,000 to Pleigh for $150,000, the procedures are basically the same as those required on the downstream sale. In the underlying records of the two Companies, Sleigh would have recorded the sale of Land and Pleigh would have recorded the purchase as follows:

Cash	$150,000	
Land		$110,000
Gain On Sale Of Land		40,000
Land	$150,000	
Cash		$150,000

6-46.   The 1997 Step B-5(a) entry to eliminate this Gain and reduce the Land value to the appropriate $110,000, is as follows:

Gain On Sale Of Land	$40,000	
Land		$40,000

6-47.   In contrast to the previous case, this elimination will be charged on a pro rata basis to the non controlling and controlling interests in income. More specifically, the 1997 Non Controlling Interest in the consolidated Income Statement would have been reduced by $8,000 (20 percent of $40,000) and consolidated Net Income would have been reduced by $32,000 (80 percent of $40,000). This is necessary because the unrealized intercompany profit is an upstream one and relates to the income of the subsidiary.

6-48.   As a final point on this upstream profit, you should note that the fact that the elimination of this profit will be split on a pro rata basis does not alter the fact that 100 percent of the profit must be removed from the consolidated revenues. The consolidated expenses and revenues include 100 percent of the parent and subsidiary expenses and revenues and, under the *CICA Handbook* requirements 100 percent of both upstream and downstream profits must be removed from these figures. When a non controlling interest is involved, the effect of this elimination must be split between that interest and the controlling interest. However, this does not take place in the disclosure of consolidated expenses and revenues. This pro rata split takes place only in the calculation of the Non Controlling Interest and consolidated Net Income.

Future Periods

6-49.   Because the 1997 entry was only recorded in the consolidation working papers, it will be necessary to reduce the Land account and remove the profit from the Retained Earnings of the subsidiary in 1998 and all subsequent years the Land is on the consolidated books. The entry to accomplish this is as follows:

Retained Earnings	$40,000	
Land		$40,000

6-50.   Here again, the effect of this entry will be split between the non controlling and controlling interests in the consolidated entity. The Non Controlling Interest in the consolidated Balance Sheet will be reduced $8,000 while consolidated Retained Earnings will decline by $32,000.

Step B(5) - Upstream Inventory Profits

Determining The Amount

6-51. Most problems you encounter will give you the amount of sales that remain in the inventories of the purchasing company. For example, in this problem we know that the Sleigh Company sold $300,000 in merchandise to the Pleigh Company and that $100,000 of this merchandise is still in the closing inventories of the parent company. However, the amount to be eliminated is not the sales price of the merchandise that is still in the inventories of the purchasing company. Rather, it is the amount of gross profit that was recognized by the selling company when these goods were sold. The amount of this gross profit can be communicated by the problem in a variety of ways. The more common ones are as follows:

- The most straightforward situation is when the amount of the profit is simply stated. For example, this problem could have indicated that the amount of gross profit on the goods that were sold to Pleigh Company and remain in its inventories was $40,000.

- The most common approach is the one used in this comprehensive problem, that is, to provide you with a gross margin percentage based on sales prices. This problem states that intercompany transfers are priced to provide the selling company with a gross margin of 40 percent. We then multiply this 40 percent times the $100,000 in merchandise that is still on hand at the end of 1998 to arrive at the unrealized intercompany profit in the ending inventories of $40,000.

- Some problems will state a gross margin percentage that is based on cost rather than selling prices. For example, our problem could have stated that intercompany transfers are priced to provide the selling company with a gross margin equal to two-thirds of cost. We would then have to solve the following simple equation:

$[(Cost)(166\text{-}2/3\%)]$ = $100,000

Cost = ($100,000 ÷ 166-2/3%)

Cost = $60,000

Subtracting this cost from the sales price of $100,000 would give us the same $40,000 gross profit to be eliminated.

- In unusual cases, nothing will be stated with respect to profit amounts or percentages. In these cases, a gross margin percentage must be extracted from the income statement data. The Sleigh Company had Sales Revenue of $2,500,000 and a Cost Of Goods Sold of $1,500,000. Its gross margin of $1,000,000 is equal to 40 percent of Sales Revenue. Applying this 40 percent to the merchandise in the inventories of the Pleigh Company gives an unrealized profit in the ending inventories of $40,000. The application of the same percentage to the Sleigh Company sales in the opening inventories of the Pleigh Company gives $28,000 (40 percent of $70,000). We would note that this approach relies on the somewhat unreasonable assumption that the gross margin percentage on intercompany sales is the same as the gross margin percentage on all other sales.

6-52. The preceding establishes that the upstream profits to be eliminated from the opening inventories amount to $28,000 and the corresponding figure for the closing inventories is $40,000.

Procedures - Ending Inventory Profits

6-53. In Step B-3 we noted that we would continue to eliminate 100 percent of intercompany sales, even in those case where some of the transferred merchandise remained in the closing inventories of the purchasing company. This point requires some additional explanation.

6-54.   During 1998, Sleigh sold merchandise to Pleigh for $300,000. Based on a 40 percent gross margin, the cost of this merchandise to Sleigh and the real cost of the merchandise to the consolidated entity is $180,000. If Pleigh had resold all of this merchandise, the $300,000 transfer price would have been included in that Company's Cost Of Goods Sold and the elimination of $300,000 of both Sales and Cost Of Goods Sold is an obvious requirement. This leaves the consolidated Cost Of Goods Sold equal to the appropriate $180,000 as recorded in Sleigh's single entity statements.

6-55.   In the actual data of the problem, $100,000 of this merchandise remains in Pleigh's Inventories and only $200,000 has been included in Pleigh's Costs Of Goods Sold. This would suggest that only $200,000 of Pleigh's Cost Of Goods Sold should be eliminated. Further, the $40,000 profit that was recorded on this intercompany transfer would have to be removed from Pleigh's Inventories and, since from the point of view of the consolidated entity this merchandise has not been sold, its original $60,000 cost would have to be removed from Sleigh's Cost Of Goods Sold. This would suggest the use of the following elimination entry:

Sales	$300,000	
Cost Of Goods Sold (Pleigh's)		$200,000
Cost Of Goods Sold (Sleigh's)		60,000
Inventories (Pleigh's)		40,000

6-56.   This approach has logical appeal and will, of course, provide you with a correct solution. However, we have found it preferable to keep separate the individual consolidation procedures and will use an alternative but equivalent approach. This alternative approach uses the basic Cost Of Goods Sold equation which is as follows:

Cost Of Goods Sold = Opening Inventories + Purchases - Closing Inventories

6-57.   Under our alternative procedure, separate entries are made to reflect the need for adjustments to Purchases and to Closing Inventories. Continuing with the data from the comprehensive problem, the full $300,000 of intercompany sales would be included in the Purchases component of the equation and this means we will eliminate 100 percent of this amount. This is consistent with the entry that we made in Step B-3 which is repeated here for your convenience:

Sales	$300,000	
Cost Of Goods Sold		$300,000

6-58.   A second entry will then be used to reflect the fact that the Closing Inventories contained a $40,000 unrealized profit. Removing this from the Closing Inventories figure in the preceding equation requires an increase in Cost Of Goods Sold. The entry to accomplish this and to remove the profit from the Inventories figure in the consolidated Balance Sheet is as follows;

Cost Of Goods Sold	$40,000	
Inventories		$40,000

6-59.   As you can see, the net effect of these two entries is identical to that of the single entry used in the alternative analysis. This latter approach has the advantage of clearly separating Step B-3 from Step B-5 and we have found it to be somewhat easier to understand. As a consequence, this two entry approach will be used in all of the problem solutions that follow.

6-60.   Note that since the increase in the Cost Of Goods Sold is related to the elimination of an unrealized upstream profit, the effect will be shared pro rata by the controlling and the non controlling interests. The Non Controlling Interest in the consolidated Income Statement will be reduced by $8,000, while consolidated Net Income will be reduced by the balancing $32,000.

Procedures - Opening Inventories

6-61.   The profits that were unrealized in the opening inventories were included in the income of the selling company in the previous year and would be included in the opening balance of that company's Retained Earnings for the current year. This would mean that our elimination would have to take these profits out of the opening Retained Earnings of the selling company. In addition, the selling company would have calculated the current year's Cost Of Goods Sold using the overstated opening inventory figure and this would result in a Cost Of Goods Sold figure that would be overstated in a corresponding manner. Consequently, our elimination entry would have to reduce the current year's Cost Of Goods Sold. The resulting increase in income would reflect the fact that any unrealized inventory profits that were present at the beginning of the current year would normally be realized by the end of the year. This means that we need to apply Step B-5(b) using the following journal entry:

Retained Earnings - Sleigh's Opening	$28,000	
Cost Of Goods Sold		$28,000

6-62.   Since we are again dealing with an upstream profit, the effect of the $28,000 reduction in the Cost Of Goods Sold would be split between the non controlling and controlling interests. That is, the Non Controlling Interest in the consolidated Income Statement would be increased by $5,600 (20 percent of $28,000) and consolidated Net Income would go up by $22,400 (80 percent of $28,000).

Step B(5) - Upstream Profit On Depreciable Assets

Basic Concepts

6-63.   Within the context of preparing consolidated financial statements, we have defined realization in terms of transactions with individuals or enterprises that are outside the consolidated entity. That is, an intercompany profit is said to be unrealized until such time as it is verified by a transaction with some entity that is independent of the consolidated group. This idea is very easy to grasp in the case of intercompany profits on the sale of land or inventories. As we have seen, these profits are treated as unrealized until such time as the land or inventories are resold outside of the consolidated entity. The same general principles apply in the case of assets with limited lives of more than one accounting period. In fact, if such assets were resold to an outsider subsequent to an intercompany sale, any unrealized profit that is present at the time of the sale would be considered to be realized at that point in time.

6-64.   However, depreciable assets are normally used in the business rather than sold. Further, any unrealized profits resulting from intercompany sales of these assets will become realized through the use of such assets. As we noted earlier, the best way to visualize this process is to think of a depreciable asset as a bundle of economic services that is being sold on a piecemeal basis as the asset is used over its economic life. While alternative approaches could be justified, the normal procedure is to recognize the realization of the unrealized intercompany profit on depreciable assets using the same allocation pattern that is being used to depreciate the asset. As a consequence, this recognition will take the form of an adjustment of consolidated Depreciation Expense.

6-65.   Consider the intercompany sale in our comprehensive example. In this example, Sleigh sold an item of Plant And Equipment with a carrying value of $450,000 ($800,000 - $350,000) to Pleigh for $600,000. As a result of this transaction, Sleigh recorded a gain of $150,000 and Pleigh recorded the Plant And Equipment at a value of $600,000.

6-66.   Using the straight line method, Pleigh will record depreciation on this asset at a rate of $200,000 per year. From the point of view of the consolidated entity, the correct depreciation base is $450,000 (Sleigh's old carrying value) and this amount would be depreciated over the three year remaining life at a rate of $150,000 per year. The required $50,000 per year reduction of consolidated Depreciation Expense ($200,000 - $150,000) would give recognition to the annual realization of the $150,000 intercompany profit that the Sleigh Company recorded on this sale. Over the three year life of the asset, the $50,000 per year reduction in Depreciation Expense would accommodate the realization of the entire intercompany profit on this transaction.

Presentation

6-67.   As we noted earlier, in dealing with depreciable assets, the fact that realization of the intercompany profit takes place over a number of accounting periods means that it is generally easier to combine Steps B-5(a) and B-5(b) into a single net entry for each year. We will follow that approach in the presentation which follows.

6-68.   We also believe that it is useful to discuss all of the annual entries that would have been made since the time of the intercompany asset sale. As a consequence, the following presentation includes entries for 1996, 1997, 1998, and 1999. We remind you that the 1996, 1997, and 1999 entries are for discussion purposes only and are not required to complete the solution. Only the entry for 1998 is needed to prepare the consolidated financial statements for that year.

Profit On Depreciable Asset - Required Entry For 1996

6-69.   When the intercompany sale took place on December 31, 1996, the Sleigh Company would have made the following entry on its books:

Cash	$600,000	
Plant And Equipment (Net)		$450,000
Gain On Sale		150,000

6-70.   At the same time, the Pleigh Company would have recorded the acquisition of the asset as follows:

Plant And Equipment (Net)	$600,000	
Cash		$600,000

6-71.   As a result of these two entries, the Plant And Equipment is $150,000 too high for inclusion in the consolidated Balance Sheet and the Sleigh Company has recorded a $150,000 Gain On Sale which should not be included in consolidated Net Income. To remedy this situation, the following elimination entry is required:

Gain On Sale	$150,000	
Plant And Equipment (Net)		$150,000

6-72.   This entry leaves Plant And Equipment at the correct figure of $450,000 and eliminates the unrealized intercompany Gain On Sale. You should note that none of the intercompany profit becomes realized during 1996 as there would have been no usage of the asset subsequent to the December 31 transfer date. As a consequence, there is no adjustment of the 1996 Depreciation Expense.

Profit On Depreciable Asset - Required Entry For 1997

6-73.   The entry for 1997 would be more complex in that additional accounts would require adjustment. On the books of the Pleigh Company, the Plant And Equipment is written down to $400,000 ($600,000 - $200,000). As the appropriate figure for consolidation purposes is $300,000 ($450,000 - $150,000), this balance will require adjustment. As previously indicated, the current year's Depreciation Expense will have to be adjusted downward by $50,000 ($200,000 - $150,000). Finally, the entire 1996 unrealized profit of $150,000 has been recorded in the Retained Earnings of the Sleigh Company. Since on January 1, 1997, none of this profit had been realized through reduced depreciation expense, the full $150,000 must be removed from Sleigh's opening Retained Earnings. The entry to accomplish all of the preceding would be as follows:

Retained Earnings - Sleigh's Opening	$150,000	
Depreciation Expense		$ 50,000
Plant And Equipment (Net)		100,000

6-74.   Since we are dealing with an upstream profit, all of the effects of this entry will be reflected in pro rata adjustments of the non controlling and controlling shares of income and net assets. That is, the $150,000 debit to Retained Earnings will reduce the beginning of the year non controlling interest in net assets by $30,000 (20 percent of $150,000) and the opening consolidated Retained Earnings by $120,000 (80 percent of $150,000). The $50,000 reduction in Depreciation Expense will increase the Non Controlling Interest in the 1997 consolidated Income Statement by $10,000 (20 percent of $50,000) and consolidated Net Income by $40,000 (80 percent of $50,000). Note that, at the end of the year, the net adjustment would be $100,000, the original unrealized amount of $150,000, less the $50,000 realization which took place during 1997. If end of the period figures were being calculated, the elimination of this $100,000 would reduce the Non Controlling Interest in the consolidated Balance Sheet by $20,000 [(20%)($100,000)] and consolidated Retained Earnings by $80,000 [(80%)($100,000)].

Profit On Depreciable Asset - Required Entry For 1998

6-75.   For the problem under consideration, the relevant entry is the one for 1998. This entry would be as follows:

Retained Earnings - Sleigh's Opening	$100,000	
Depreciation Expense		$50,000
Plant And Equipment (Net)		50,000

6-76.   On the books of the Pleigh Company, the Plant And Equipment has been written down to a value of $200,000 ($600,000 - $400,000) while the correct figure for consolidation purposes is $150,000 ($450,000 - $300,000). The $50,000 credit to Plant And Equipment provides the adjustment for this difference. As at January 1, 1998, the Retained Earnings balance of the Sleigh Company contains the full $150,000 of intercompany profit that was recognized on the sale of the depreciable asset. Since $50,000 of this was realized through reduced Depreciation Expense in 1997, the remaining unrealized balance on January 1, 1998 is $100,000. It is this amount that the preceding journal entry removes from the Retained Earnings of the Sleigh Company. The credit to Depreciation Expense serves to reduce the 1998 Depreciation Expense from the $200,000 that is on the books of the Pleigh Company to the appropriate $150,000 for consolidation purposes.

6-77.   As was explained in conjunction with the 1997 entry, both the reduction in the Retained Earnings of the Sleigh Company and the increase in current income resulting from the reduced depreciation expense, will be reflected on a pro rata basis in both the controlling and non controlling interests in net assets and income.

Profit On Depreciable Asset - Required Entry For 1999

6-78.   As was the case with the 1996 and 1997 entries, the 1999 entry is not a necessary part of the solution. However, it will be presented in order to provide a complete illustration of the treatment of a profit on the intercompany sale of a depreciable asset. The entry is as follows:

Retained Earnings - Sleigh's Opening	$50,000	
Depreciation Expense		$50,000

6-79.   The debit to the Retained Earnings of the Sleigh Company reflects the fact that of the original unrealized profit of $150,000, $100,000 was realized through reduced depreciation expense in 1997 and 1998, leaving an unrealized balance of $50,000. The $50,000 credit to Depreciation Expense is the usual reduction in this expense from $200,000 to $150,000. Note that the credit to Plant And Equipment is no longer present since the asset would now be fully depreciated. It would have a net book value of zero in the records of the Pleigh Company and this is the appropriate figure for consolidation purposes.

6-80.   As in the entries for the previous two years, the effects of the reduced Retained Earnings and Other Expenses would be allocated on a pro rata basis to the controlling and non controlling interests.

6-81.   One additional point needs to be made in this final year of the asset's life. In 1996, the year of the intercompany sale, we removed the $150,000 Gain On Sale from income in the process of preparing consolidated financial statements. In the subsequent three years, we reversed this elimination by increasing income at a rate of $50,000 per year. As at December 31, 1999, these two effects will have netted out and no further adjustments or eliminations will be required in subsequent years. This conclusion assumes that the asset will be retired at this time.

Step C - Distribution Of The Subsidiary Retained Earnings

The Problem

6-82.   At this point our one remaining task is to determine the appropriate distribution of the balance that is left in the Retained Earnings account of the Sleigh Company. The amount of this balance can be determined as follows:

Sleigh's Opening Balance	$2,300,000
Step A Elimination	(1,500,000)
Balance Since Acquisition	$ 800,000
Step B Adjustments:	
Fair Value on Inventories	(80,000)
Plant (4 Years At $10,000)	(40,000)
Goodwill (4 Years At $24,000)	(96,000)
Unrealized Upstream Profit On Land Sale	(40,000)
Unrealized Upstream Profit In Opening Inventories	(28,000)
Unrealized Upstream Profit On Equipment	(100,000)
Balance After Adjustments	$ 416,000

6-83.   As this schedule indicates, we are left with $416,000 as the January 1, 1998 adjusted balance of the Sleigh Company's Retained Earnings since acquisition. We must now determine the appropriate distribution between the Non Controlling Interest in consolidated net assets and consolidated Retained Earnings. We will find that the presence of unrealized upstream profits will significantly complicate this process.

6-84.   If we were consistently using the entity conceptual approach, all of the Step B adjustments would be reflected proportionately in both the non controlling interest and the controlling interest. The distribution of the remaining balance would be a simple matter of allocating it in proportion to the two respective ownership interests. That is, we could split the remaining $416,000 on a 20 percent, 80 percent basis.

6-85.   Correspondingly, if we were applying the parent company concept in a consistent manner, none of the Step B adjustments would have any influence on the amount of the non controlling interest in net assets. We could calculate the non controlling interest in Retained Earnings since acquisition by multiplying the non controlling percent times the unadjusted Retained Earnings of the subsidiary since acquisition. Then all of the Step B adjustments and eliminations would be charged against the parent company's share of the subsidiary's Retained Earnings since acquisition. In this example, the non controlling interest in Sleigh's Retained Earnings since acquisition would be $160,000 ([20%][$800,000]), and all of the Step B adjustments for the realization of fair value changes and goodwill amortization would be deducted from the controlling interest.

6-86.   Unfortunately, the *CICA Handbook* did not adopt a consistent conceptual approach to the preparation of consolidated financial statements. While most of the Recommendations are based on the parent company concept, there is one important exception. This is the fact that the entity approach is used in the elimination of unrealized intercompany profits. This means that, unlike the adjustments for the realization of fair value changes, the adjustments for unrealized upstream profits will influence the calculation of the non controlling interest. As a consequence, we will need a two stage distribution schedule in which unrealized upstream profits are dealt with separately from the other Step B adjustments related to the realization of fair value changes and goodwill amortization.

Retained Earnings Distribution Schedule

6-87.   As was the case in Chapter 5, this schedule begins with the Retained Earnings balance of the subsidiary and, using Step A procedures, removes the portion of this balance that was present at the time of acquisition. As indicted in the preceding section, the presence of unrealized upstream profits means that we cannot calculate the non controlling interest as a percentage of total retained earnings since acquisition. We must first modify this total for all of the Step B adjustments and eliminations which involve upstream profits that are unrealized at the beginning of the year. Note that we are concerned with the beginning of the year unrealized profits because, in this open trial balance problem, we are distributing the opening Retained Earnings since acquisition balance.

6-88.   After the removal of the non controlling interest from the modified balance, all other Step B adjustments and eliminations are added or subtracted to arrive at the appropriate allocation to consolidated Retained Earnings. This two stage schedule reflects a combination of entity and parent company procedures and would appear as follows:

Balance As Per The Trial Balance	$2,300,000
Balance At Acquisition	(1,500,000)
Balance Since Acquisition	$ 800,000
Unrealized Upstream Profits:	
Land	(40,000)
Opening Inventories	(28,000)
Equipment - Beginning Of The Year	(100,000)
Adjusted Balance Since Acquisition	$ 632,000
Non Controlling Interest [(20%)($632,000)]	(126,400)
Available To The Controlling Interest	$ 505,600
Other Step B Adjustments:	
Fair Value Change On Inventories	(80,000)
Fair Value Change On Plant And Equipment	(40,000)
Goodwill Amortization	(96,000)
To Consolidated Retained Earnings	$ 289,600

Retained Earnings Distribution Entry

6-89.   Using the information from the preceding schedule, the journal entry to distribute Sleigh's Retained Earnings since acquisition is as follows:

Retained Earnings - Sleigh's Opening	$416,000	
Non Controlling Interest		$126,400
Consolidated Retained Earnings		289,600

6-90.   This entry reduces the Sleigh Company's Retained Earnings balance to zero and distributes the total to the controlling and non controlling interests. With this entry completed we have established the opening balance for consolidated Retained Earnings. It is simply the Pleigh Company's January 1, 1998 balance of $2,550,000, less the $25,000 downstream profit on land, plus the $289,600 allocation resulting from the preceding journal entry, for a total of $2,814,600.

Consolidated Income Statement

Non Controlling Interest Computation

6-91.   With the addition of the Step C distribution entry, we have completed all of the procedures necessary for the preparation of consolidated financial statements. As was the case in Chapter 5 we will begin with the consolidated Income Statement.

6-92.   In Chapter 5, the calculation of the Non Controlling Interest in the consolidated Income Statement was simply a matter of multiplying the reported income of the subsidiary by the non controlling ownership percentage. With the introduction of upstream unrealized profits, the calculation becomes more complex. The reason for this is, of course, the fact that the elimination of these profits is being dealt with using entity concept procedures. This means that we must adjust the reported income of the subsidiary for included profits that have not been realized during the year (e.g., closing inventory profits), as well as for previously unrealized profits that have become realized during the year (e.g., opening inventory profits). Only then can we calculate the appropriate Non Controlling Interest for inclusion in the consolidated Income Statement. The required calculation would be as follows:

Sleigh Company's Reported Income	$200,000
Realized Gain On Equipment	50,000
Profits In Opening Inventories	28,000
Profits In Ending Inventories	(40,000)
Adjusted Subsidiary Income	$238,000
Non Controlling Percent	20%
Non Controlling Interest	$ 47,600

6-93.   In presenting this calculation, we stress the fact that upstream unrealized profits are the only adjustments or eliminations that have any influence on the amount of the Non Controlling Interest. This statement is always true and would apply to both the Non Controlling Interest in the consolidated Income Statement and the Non Controlling Interest in the consolidated Balance Sheet.

Statement Disclosure

6-94.   The consolidated Income Statement would be prepared as follows:

Pleigh Company And Subsidiary
Consolidated Income Statement
Year Ending December 31, 1998

Sales ($4,000,000 + $2,500,000 - $300,000)	$6,200,000
Interest Revenue ($24,000 - $24,000)	-0-
Dividend Revenue ($80,000 - $80,000)	-0-
Total Revenues	$6,200,000
Cost Of Goods Sold ($2,800,000 + $1,500,000 - $300,000 + $40,000 - $28,000)	$4,012,000
Interest Expense ($240,000 + $84,000 - $24,000)	300,000
Depreciation Expense ($200,000 + $100,000 + $24,000 - $50,000)	274,000
Other Expenses ($364,000 + $616,000)	980,000
Goodwill Amortization Expense	10,000
Total Expenses	$5,576,000
Combined Income	$ 624,000
Non Controlling Interest (See previous calculation)	47,600
Consolidated Net Income	$ 576,400

6-95. Note again that the subtotal for Combined Income is not normal disclosure. Rather, it has been included for computational purposes. Normal disclosure would have the Non Controlling Interest included among the other deductions from revenue.

Verification Of Consolidated Net Income

6-96. As was explained in Chapter 5, it is often useful to be able to make a schedular calculation of consolidated Net Income. In this version of the comprehensive problem, the schedular calculation of consolidated Net Income is as follows:

Pleigh Company's Net Income	$500,000
Intercompany Dividend Revenues	(80,000)
Pleigh's Net Income Less Dividends	$420,000
Pleigh's Equity In Sleigh's Adjusted Net Income (80% of $238,000)	190,400
Income Before Adjustments	$610,400
Adjustments:	
Fair Value Depreciation	(10,000)
Goodwill Amortization	(24,000)
Consolidated Net Income	$576,400

6-97. Note that Pleigh's interest in the income of the Sleigh Company is not based on the reported income of the Sleigh Company. Rather, it is based on the same $238,000 adjusted subsidiary income figure which was used in the computation of the Non Controlling Interest in consolidated Net Income.

Consolidated Statement Of Retained Earnings

Statement Disclosure

6-98. Using the Net Income data, we can now prepare a consolidated Statement Of Retained Earnings. It would be as follows:

Pleigh Company And Subsidiary
Consolidated Statement Of Retained Earnings
Year Ending December 31, 1998

Balance - January 1, 1998 (See Discussion In Step C)	$2,814,600
1998 Net Income (See Income Statement)	576,400
1998 Dividends Declared (Pleigh's Only)	(350,000)
Balance - December 31, 1998	$3,041,000

Verification Of Consolidated Retained Earnings

6-99. As was the case with consolidated Net Income, you will often find it useful to be able to make an independent computation of the end of the year balance in the consolidated Retained Earnings account. The definitional approach to the computation of this amount is as follows:

Pleigh's Closing Balance	$2,700,000
Pleigh's Share Of Sleigh's Retained Earnings Since Acquisition	
(See following Equity Pickup Calculation)	616,000
Inventories	(80,000)
Plant (5 Years At $10,000)	(50,000)
Goodwill (5 Years At $24,000)	(120,000)
Downstream Profit On Land	(25,000)
December 31, 1998 Consolidated Retained Earnings	$3,041,000

Equity Pickup Calculation

6-100.   In picking up Pleigh's share of the Retained Earnings of the Sleigh Company since acquisition, we must remove the effects of unrealized intercompany profits. The $616,000 equity pickup included in the verification of consolidated Retained Earnings would be calculated as follows:

Sleigh's Closing Retained Earnings		$2,400,000
Balance At Acquisition		(1,500,000)
Balance Since Acquisition		$ 900,000
Unrealized Upstream Profits:		
Land	($40,000)	
Ending Inventories	(40,000)	
Equipment	(50,000)	(130,000)
Adjusted Balance		$ 770,000
Controlling Percent		80%
Equity Pickup		$ 616,000

Consolidated Balance Sheet

Non Controlling Interest

6-101.   There are two basic ways to determine the Non Controlling Interest that is shown on the Balance Sheet. One approach would be to use the Sleigh Company's book values adjusted for upstream unrealized profits. This calculation follows:

December 31, 1998 - No Par Common Stock		$2,000,000
December 31, 1998 - Retained Earnings		2,400,000
Unrealized Upstream Profits:		
Land	($40,000)	
Ending Inventories	(40,000)	
Equipment	(50,000)	(130,000)
Sleigh's Adjusted Book Values		$4,270,000
Non Controlling Percent		20%
Non Controlling Interest		$ 854,000

6-102.   An alternative calculation of the Non Controlling Interest would start with the Step A allocation of $700,000, deduct the $20,000 Step B adjustment for dividends to non controlling shareholders, add the Step C allocation of $126,400 and the Non Controlling Interest of $47,600 from the consolidated Income Statement.

Statement Disclosure

6-103.   The consolidated Balance Sheet at December 31, 1998 of the Pleigh Company and its subsidiary would be prepared as follows:

Pleigh Company And Subsidiary
Consolidated Balance Sheet - As At December 31, 1998

Cash ($500,000 + $300,000)	$ 800,000
Current Receivables ($800,000 + $400,000 - $12,000)	1,188,000
Inventories ($2,500,000 + $1,700,000	
+ $80,000 - $80,000 - $40,000)	4,160,000
Long Term Note Receivable ($200,000 - $200,000)	-0-
Investment In Sleigh ($3,200,000 - $3,200,000)	-0-
Land ($1,500,000 + $1,000,000 - $120,000 - $40,000 - $25,000)	2,315,000
Plant And Equipment ($4,500,000 + $1,900,000	
+ $200,000 - $50,000 - $50,000)	6,500,000
Goodwill ($240,000 - $120,000)	120,000
Total Assets	$15,083,000

Current Liabilities ($500,000 + $200,000 - $12,000)	$ 688,000
Long Term Liabilities ($2,000,000 + $700,000 -$200,000)	2,500,000
Non Controlling Interest (See previous calculation)	854,000
No Par Common Stock (Pleigh's Balance)	8,000,000
Retained Earnings (See previous calculation)	3,041,000
Total Equities	$15,083,000

6-104.   Most of the preceding computations follow directly from the trial balance data adjusted by the various journal entries that we have made. The exceptions to this are the Retained Earnings balance which was computed in the consolidated Statement Of Retained Earnings, and the Non Controlling Interest which was previously calculated.

Comprehensive Example - Closed Trial Balance With Investment At Cost

Basic Data

6-105.   In this version of the problem, Investment In Sleigh will continue to be carried at cost. However, the data will be presented in the form of a closed trial balance and only a consolidated Balance Sheet will be required. The data is as follows:

On January 1, 1994, the Pleigh Company purchases 80 percent of the outstanding voting shares of the Sleigh Company for $3,200,000 in cash. On that date the Sleigh Company had No Par Common Stock in the amount of $2,000,000 and Retained Earnings of $1,500,000. On December 31, 1998, the adjusted trial balances of the Pleigh Company and its subsidiary, the Sleigh Company are as follows:

	Pleigh	Sleigh
Cash	$ 500,000	$ 300,000
Current Receivables	800,000	400,000
Inventories	2,500,000	1,700,000
Long Term Note Receivable	200,000	-0-
Investment In Sleigh - At Cost	3,200,000	-0-
Land	1,500,000	1,000,000
Plant And Equipment (Net)	4,500,000	1,900,000
Total Debits	$13,200,000	$5,300,000
Current Liabilities	$ 500,000	$ 200,000
Long Term Liabilities	2,000,000	700,000
No Par Common Stock	8,000,000	2,000,000
Retained Earnings	2,700,000	2,400,000
Total Credits	$13,200,000	$5,300,000

Other Information:

A. At the date of Pleigh Company's acquisition of the Sleigh Company's shares, all of the identifiable assets and liabilities of the Sleigh Company had fair values that were equal to their carrying values except Inventories which had fair values that were $100,000 more than their carrying values, Land with a fair value that was $150,000 less than its carrying value and Plant And Equipment which had a fair value that was $250,000 greater than its carrying value. The Plant And Equipment had a remaining useful life on the acquisition date of 20 years while the inventories that were present on the acquisition date were sold during the year ending December 31, 1994. The Land is still on the books of the Sleigh Company on December 31, 1998. Goodwill, if any, is to be amortized over 10 years. Both Companies use the straight line method to calculate depreciation and amortization.

B. Sleigh Company's Sales include sales of $300,000 to Pleigh Company. The December 31, 1998 Inventories of the Pleigh Company contain $100,000 of this merchandise purchased from Sleigh Company during 1998. In addition, the January 1, 1998 Inventories of the Pleigh Company contained $70,000 in merchandise purchased from Sleigh Company during 1997. All intercompany sales are priced to provide the selling company a gross margin on sales price of 40 percent.

C. On December 31, 1998, the Pleigh Company is holding Sleigh Company's long term note payable in the amount of $200,000. Interest at 12 percent is payable on July 1 of each year. Pleigh Company has been holding this note since July 1, 1996.

D. During 1996, the Pleigh Company sold Land to the Sleigh Company for $100,000 in cash. The Land had a carrying value on the books of the Pleigh Company of $75,000.

E. During 1997, the Sleigh Company sold Land to the Pleigh Company for $150,000. This Land had a carrying value on the books of the Sleigh Company of $110,000.

F. On December 31, 1996, the Sleigh Company sold Equipment to the Pleigh Company for $600,000. The Equipment had originally cost the Sleigh Company $800,000 and, at the time of the intercompany sale, had accumulated depreciation of $350,000. On this date, it was estimated that the remaining useful life of the Equipment was three years and no salvage value was anticipated.

Required: Prepare a consolidated Balance Sheet as at December 31, 1998 for the Pleigh Company and its subsidiary, the Sleigh Company.

Procedural Approach

6-106.   The procedural approach here is similar to that used in the open trial balance, cost method version of this problem. The basic difference is that all of the Step B adjustments to expenses and revenues will now be made to Sleigh's Retained Earnings account and the Step C entry will involve distributing the December 31, 1998 Retained Earnings, rather than the January 1, 1998 balance.

Step A Procedures

Investment Analysis

6-107.   The analysis of the investment will be identical to the one used in the open trial balance, cost method version of this problem. It is as follows:

	80 Percent	100 Percent
Investment Cost	$3,200,000	$4,000,000
Book Value	(2,800,000)	(3,500,000)
Differential	$ 400,000	$ 500,000
Fair Value Changes:		
Inventories	(80,000)	(100,000)
Land	120,000	150,000
Plant And Equipment	(200,000)	(250,000)
Goodwill	$ 240,000	$ 300,000

Investment Elimination

6-108.   Based on the preceding analysis, the journal entry to eliminate the Investment In Sleigh account is as follows:

No Par Common Stock	$2,000,000	
Retained Earnings	1,500,000	
Plant And Equipment (Net)	200,000	
Inventories	80,000	
Goodwill	240,000	
Land		$ 120,000
Non Controlling Interest		700,000
Investment In Sleigh		3,200,000

Step B(1) - Intercompany Assets And Liabilities

6-109.   The elimination of intercompany asset and liability balances is the same in both open trial balance and closed trial balance versions of this problem. The entries are:

Long Term Liabilities	$200,000	
Long Term Note Receivable		$200,000
Current Liabilities	$ 12,000	
Current Receivables		$ 12,000

Step B(2) - Fair Value And Goodwill Write Offs

6-110.   The entries in this version of the problem will have the same effect on the asset and liability accounts as did the entries in the first version of this problem. The only difference is that since we are working with a closed trial balance it is no longer possible to adjust expense and revenue accounts. As these accounts have been closed into the ending retained earnings balances, adjustments will now go to the Retained Earnings account of the Sleigh Company.

6-111.   Since the fair value change on Inventories had no effect on the 1998 expenses or revenues, the entry here will be the same as it was in the first version of this problem. It is as follows:

Retained Earnings - Sleigh's Closing	$80,000	
Inventories		$80,000

6-112.   As was the case in the first version of this problem, we will credit Plant And Equipment for 5 years (January 1, 1994 through December 31, 1998) of additional depreciation expense on the fair value change. However, instead of splitting the debits between Retained Earnings and the current Depreciation Expense, the entire amount will go to Retained Earnings. The entry is as follows:

Retained Earnings - Sleigh's Closing	$50,000	
Plant And Equipment (Net)		$50,000

6-113.   The goodwill adjustment will follow the same pattern as the fair value depreciation adjustment on the Plant And Equipment. Five years of Goodwill amortization will be charged against the asset account and, in this version of the problem, the total amount will be removed from the retained earnings balance of the subsidiary. The entry is as follows:

Retained Earnings - Sleigh's Closing	$120,000	
Goodwill		$120,000

6-114.   As the Land is still on the books of Sleigh, no entry is required to adjust the fair value change on this account.

Step B(3) - Intercompany Expenses And Revenues

6-115.   In the "open trial balance" versions of this problem, we made an entry here to eliminate intercompany expenses and revenues. We noted that this entry was simply to avoid overstating expenses and revenues. Since all of the expenses and revenues are now closed to retained earnings, no entry is required in this closed trial balance version of the problem.

Step B(4) - Intercompany Dividends

6-116.   In the open trial balance versions of this problem we made an entry here to eliminate dividend payments. The entry involved reducing Pleigh's revenues, Dividends Declared and the Non Controlling Interest in the consolidated Balance Sheet. As Pleigh's revenues and the Dividends Declared accounts have been closed to retained earnings, no entry is required for these adjustments. With respect to the reduction of the Non Controlling Interest in the consolidated Balance Sheet, this effect will be automatically picked up in Step C when we base our allocation to this account on the end of the year Retained Earnings balance of the Sleigh Company. This end of year balance has, of course, had all of the Sleigh Company's 1998 dividends taken out as part of the closing entries.

Step B(5) - Unrealized Intercompany Profits

6-117.   In the open trial balance version of this problem, our adjustments and eliminations for unrealized intercompany profits had to take into consideration such profits in the opening consolidated Retained Earnings balance, the current period's consolidated expenses and revenues, and the closing balances for inclusion in the consolidated Balance Sheet. In this closed trial balance version of the problem, we are only concerned with unrealized intercompany profits to the extent that they have an effect on the accounts to be included in the December 31, 1998 consolidated Balance Sheet. We will find that this will simplify and, in the case of profits in the opening inventories, eliminate the entries that are required in dealing with unrealized intercompany profits.

Downstream And Upstream Profits On Land

6-118.   This problem contains a 1996 intercompany profit of $25,000 on the sale of Land from Pleigh Company to Sleigh and a similar 1997 profit of $40,000 on the sale of Land from Sleigh to Pleigh. The amounts of these profits are unchanged from the beginning of the current accounting period and, as a consequence, the appropriate elimination entries to be used here are the same as those that were required in the open trial balance version of this problem in which the Investment In Sleigh account was carried at cost. The entry for the downstream profit is as follows:

Retained Earnings - Pleigh's Closing	$25,000	
Land		$25,000

6-119.   For the upstream profit, the entry is:

Retained Earnings - Sleigh's Closing	$40,000	
Land		$40,000

Upstream Inventory Profits

6-120.   In this problem there are Sleigh Company profits in the opening Inventories of the Pleigh Company in the amount of $28,000 and a similar balance in the closing Inventories of the Pleigh Company of $40,000.

6-121.   With respect to the $28,000 opening inventory profit, in the open trial balance, investment at cost version of this problem we found it necessary to reduce the opening Retained Earnings of the Sleigh Company and the 1998 consolidated Cost Of Goods Sold. The combined effect of these two adjustments on the December 31, 1998 Retained Earnings of Sleigh would be zero as the reduction in the January 1, 1998 Retained Earnings would be offset by the increase in 1998 income created by the decrease in Cost Of Goods Sold. As a reflection of this situation, no entry is required for opening inventory profits in closed trial balance, investment at cost type problems. An additional way of looking at this situation would be to note that the Inventories that Pleigh was holding at the beginning of 1998 have been sold and the Sleigh Company's unrealized opening inventory profit has now been realized. Therefore, no elimination entry is required.

6-122.   The unrealized profit in the closing Inventories of the Pleigh Company does, however, require an adjustment. The consolidated Inventories must be reduced as was the case in the open trial balance version of the problem. However, the accompanying debit can no longer go to the Cost Of Goods Sold account. Since this account has been closed into the ending Retained Earnings, the adjustment must be to Retained Earnings and would appear as follows:

Retained Earnings - Sleigh's Closing	$40,000	
Inventories		$40,000

Upstream Profit On Equipment

6-123.   On December 31, 1996, there was a profit of $150,000 recognized by the Sleigh Company on the sale of a depreciable asset with a three year life to the Pleigh Company. During 1997, $50,000 of this profit was realized through a reduction in consolidated Depreciation Expense. This left $100,000 to be removed from the January 1, 1998 Retained Earnings of the Sleigh Company in the open trial balance, investment at cost version of this problem. Now that we are dealing with a closed trial balance, we must account for the fact that an additional profit realization of $50,000 occurred during 1998. This means that at the end of 1998, the only adjustment will be for the remaining $50,000 which is still unrealized on this date. The entry would be as follows:

Retained Earnings - Sleigh's Closing	$50,000	
Plant And Equipment (Net)		$50,000

6-124.   Note that, as with the other intercompany profit eliminations, there is no adjustment of the current year's expenses or revenues as they have been closed to Retained

Earnings in this closed trial balance problem.

Step C - Distribution Of The Subsidiary Retained Earnings

Retained Earnings Balance

6-125.   The Retained Earnings account of the Sleigh Company in the trial balance for this problem was $2,400,000. In Step A we removed $1,500,000 of this amount, leaving a balance in the amount of $900,000 which had accrued between the acquisition date of January 1, 1994 and the current date of December 31, 1998. Our one remaining task in this problem is to determine how much of this balance is left after the Step B adjustments and to distribute this balance to the non controlling and controlling interests. The remaining balance can be determined as follows:

Balance Since Acquisition	$ 900,000
Step B Adjustments:	
Fair Value on Inventories	(80,000)
Plant (5 Years At $10,000)	(50,000)
Goodwill (5 Years At $24,000)	(120,000)
Unrealized Upstream Profits On Land Sale	(40,000)
Unrealized Upstream Profits In Closing Inventories	(40,000)
Unrealized Upstream Profits On Equipment	(50,000)
Balance After Adjustments	$ 520,000

Retained Earnings Distribution Schedule

6-126.   The schedule for allocating the balance from the preceding Paragraph would be as follows:

Sleigh's Closing Retained Earnings	$2,400,000
Balance At Acquisition	(1,500,000)
Balance Since Acquisition	$ 900,000
Unrealized Upstream Profits:	
Land	(40,000)
Closing Inventories	(40,000)
Plant	(50,000)
Adjusted Balance Since Acquisition	$ 770,000
Non Controlling Interest ([20%][$770,000])	154,000
Available To The Controlling Interest	$ 616,000
Other Step B Adjustments:	
Inventories	(80,000)
Plant	(50,000)
Goodwill	(120,000)
To Consolidated Retained Earnings	$ 366,000

6-127.   With the information from this schedule, we can now make the required Step C distribution entry.

Retained Earnings Distribution Entry

6-128.   Using the information from the preceding schedule, the journal entry to distribute Sleigh's Retained Earnings since acquisition is as follows:

Retained Earnings - Sleigh	$520,000	
Non Controlling Interest		$154,000
Consolidated Retained Earnings		366,000

6-129.   This entry reduces the Sleigh Company's Retained Earnings balance to zero and distributes the total to the controlling and non controlling interests. When the credit of $154,000 to the Non Controlling Interest is added to the Step A credit to this account of $700,000, we have established the appropriate balance of $854,000 for inclusion in the consolidated Balance Sheet as at December 31, 1998. Further, if we take the Pleigh Company's Retained Earnings balance of $2,700,000 from the trial balance, subtract the downstream profit on the intercompany sale of land of $25,000 and add the allocation from above of $366,000, we arrive at a figure of $3,041,000. This figure is the correct figure for consolidated Retained Earnings to be included in the December 31, 1998 Balance Sheet.

Consolidated Balance Sheet

6-130.   With the addition of the Step C distribution entry, we have completed all of the procedures necessary for the preparation of the consolidated Balance Sheet. In this "closed trial balance" version of the problem there are no significant complicating factors. All of the balances flow directly from the preceding journal entries, resulting in the consolidated Balance Sheet which is presented as follows:

Pleigh Company And Subsidiary
Consolidated Balance Sheet As At December 31, 1998

Cash ($500,000 + $300,000)	$ 800,000
Current Receivables ($800,000 + $400,000 - $12,000)	1,188,000
Inventories ($2,500,000 + $1,700,000 + $80,000 - $80,000 - $40,000)	4,160,000
Long Term Note Receivable ($200,000 - $200,000)	-0-
Investment In Sleigh ($3,200,000 - $3,200,000)	-0-
Land ($1,500,000 + $1,000,000 - $120,000 - $40,000 - $25,000)	2,315,000
Plant And Equipment ($4,500,000 + $1,900,000 + $200,0000 - $50,000 - $50,000)	6,500,000
Goodwill ($240,000 - $120,000)	120,000
Total Assets	$15,083,000
Current Liabilities ($500,000 + $200,000 - $12,000)	$ 688,000
Long Term Liabilities ($2,000,000 + $700,000 -$200,000)	2,500,000
Non Controlling Interest	854,000
No Par Common Stock	8,000,000
Retained Earnings	3,041,000
Total Equities	$15,083,000

Review Of The Conceptual Alternatives Adopted By Section 1600

6-131.   Now that you have an understanding of all of the basic consolidation procedures, including unrealized intercompany profits, the summary of the conceptual alternatives that was originally presented in Chapter 4 will be reviewed. The following procedures reflect the recommendations of the *CICA Handbook* with respect to the preparation of consolidated financial statements:

Asset Valuation   The recommended approach is the parent company concept. That is, only the parent company's interest in fair value changes and goodwill are recognized at the time of acquisition or combination and only the parent company's share of the depreciation, depletion, and amortization of these values is recorded in subsequent periods.

Non Controlling Interest On Balance Sheet - Disclosure   Section 1600 states that the Non Controlling Interest in the consolidated net assets of the subsidiary companies should be shown separately from shareholders' equity. This appears to be the parent company approach. However, in the absence of a clear statement that the Non Controlling Interest should be disclosed as part of the long term liabilities, it often ends up being presented in a somewhat ambiguous fashion between the long term liabilities and the consolidated shareholders' equity.

Non Controlling Interest On Balance Sheet - Calculation   The inconsistencies of Section 1600 become apparent in this calculation. In general, this computation would follow the parent company approach and base the Non Controlling Interest on the non controlling shareholders' proportionate share of the carrying values of the subsidiary. However, because the entity approach is used for the elimination of unrealized subsidiary profits, these transactions must be taken into account in determining the appropriate balance here. Stated generally, the Non Controlling Interest in the consolidated Balance Sheet would be computed by taking the non controlling shareholders' proportionate interest in the net book value of the subsidiary's assets after they have been adjusted for any unrealized intercompany profits of the subsidiary company.

Non Controlling Interest On Income Statement - Disclosure   With respect to income before the results of discontinued operations and extraordinary items, Section 1600 requires that Non Controlling Interest be given separate disclosure in the consolidated Income Statement. This reflects an adoption of the parent company approach. For no apparent reason, the results of discontinued operations and extraordinary items are dealt with by a different conceptual alternative. Only the parent company's proportionate interest in these items is disclosed and this is an application of the proprietary concept.

Non Controlling Interest On Income Statement - Calculation   Again, our computation here is complicated by the presence of inconsistencies in the recommendations of Section 1600. Generally, the Non Controlling Interest in the consolidated Income Statement is based on the reported income of the subsidiary. However, adjustments must be made for the adoption of the entity approach in dealing with unrealized subsidiary profits. Stated generally, the Non Controlling Interest in the consolidated Income Statement would be calculated by taking the non controlling shareholders' proportionate interest in the reported income of the subsidiary with the elimination of current unrealized subsidiary intercompany profits and the addition of subsidiary intercompany profits from previous years that have become realized for consolidation purposes during the year.

Unrealized Intercompany Profits Of The Subsidiary   As we have already noted, Section 1600 adopts the entity approach here and requires 100 percent pro rata elimination of unrealized intercompany subsidiary profits.

Application Of The Equity Method

Basic Concepts

6-132.   In Chapter 5 (see Paragraph 5-116), we indicated that the Net Income of an investor using the equity method for an investee had to be equal to the consolidated Net Income that would result from the consolidation of that investee. This requirement was based on the following Recommendation:

> **Paragraph 3050.08** *Investment income as calculated by the equity method should be that amount necessary to increase or decrease the investor's income to that which would have been recognized if the results of the investee's operations had been consolidated with those of the investor.* (August, 1978)

6-133.   In Chapter 5 this meant that all of the adjustments for fair value write offs and goodwill amortization that would be required in the consolidation process, are also required in the application of the equity method. As you would expect, similar adjustments are required for the unrealized intercompany profits that were introduced in this Chapter. As was noted in Chapter 5, however, there is a major difference in the disclosure of these adjustments when the equity method is applied. In consolidation, the various adjustments are included in specific consolidated account balances. In contrast, the equity method deals with all of these adjustments as modifications of the Investment Asset and Investment Income accounts.

Comprehensive Example

Income Statement

6-134.   As we did in Chapter 5, we will use the comprehensive example that we have been working with throughout this Chapter to illustrate the application of the equity method. The basic data for this problem have been presented several times and will not be repeated here. The only change is that we will assume that Pleigh Company's majority ownership does not give it control over the Sleigh Company and, as a consequence, the investment cannot be consolidated.

6-135.   From our previous experience with the Pleigh Company problem, we know that consolidated Net Income for 1998 amounts to $576,400. Since the Pleigh Company's net income without the inclusion of any revenues from its Investment In Sleigh amounts to $420,000, the only Investment Income that would satisfy the requirement stated in Paragraph 3050.08 is $156,400. This figure can be verified as follows:

Pleigh's Interest In Sleigh's Income:		
Sleigh's Reported Net Income	$200,000	
Opening Inventory Profits	28,000	
Closing Inventory Profits	(40,000)	
Realization Of Equipment Profit	50,000	
Sleight's Adjusted Income	$238,000	
Pleigh's Proportionate Interest	80%	$190,400
Fair Value Adjustments:		
Depreciation		(10,000)
Goodwill		(24,000)
Pleigh's Equity Method Investment Income		$156,400

6-136.   Using this Investment Income, the Income Statement of the Pleigh Company with the Investment In Sleigh carried by the equity method would be as follows:

Pleigh Company
Income Statement
Year Ending December 31, 1998

Sales	$4,000,000
Interest Revenue	24,000
Investment Income	156,400
Total Revenues	$4,180,400
Cost Of Goods Sold	$2,800,000
Depreciation Expense	200,000
Interest Expense	240,000
Other Expenses	364,000
Total Expenses	$3,604,000
Net Income	$ 576,400

Balance Sheet

6-137.   If Pleigh was not consolidating its investment in Sleigh, and used the equity method in its single entity statements, the Balance Sheet account Investment In Sleigh would have to be increased to reflect Pleigh's equity in this investee. As is the case with Investment Income under the equity method, this Balance Sheet account would be subject to the same types of adjustments that would be required in the preparation of consolidated financial statements. The required balance would be calculated as follows:

Investment In Sleigh At Cost		$3,200,000
Equity Pickup:		
Sleigh's December 31 Retained Earnings	$2,400,000	
Balance At Acquisition	(1,500,000)	
Balance Since Acquisition	$ 900,000	
Unrealized Upstream Profits:		
Land	(40,000)	
Closing Inventories	(40,000)	
Equipment	(50,000)	
Adjusted Balance Since Acquisition	$ 770,000	
Pleigh's Share	80%	616,000
Fair Value Adjustments:		
Inventories		(80,000)
Plant And Equipment [(5 Years)($10,000)]		(50,000)
Goodwill [(5 Years)($24,000)]		(120,000)
Downstream Profit On Land		(25,000)
Investment In Sleigh At Equity		$3,541,000

6-138.   If this amount is used on the asset side of Pleigh's single entity Balance Sheet, there will have to be a corresponding $341,000 ($3,541,000 - $3,200,000) adjustment to Retained Earnings on the equity side of the single entity Balance Sheet. This will leave Pleigh with the following single entity Balance Sheet under the equity method:

Pleigh Company
Single Entity Balance Sheet
As At December 31, 1998

Cash	$ 500,000
Current Receivables	800,000
Inventories	2,500,000
Long Term Note Receivable	200,000
Investment In Sleigh (At Equity)	3,541,000
Land	1,500,000
Plant And Equipment (Net)	4,500,000
Total Assets	$13,541,000

Current Liabilities	$ 500,000
Long Term Liabilities	2,000,000
No Par Common Stock	8,000,000
Retained Earnings ($2,700,000 + $341,000)	3,041,000
Total Equities	$13,541,000

6-139.   Note that, when the equity method is used, the resulting Retained Earnings figure in Pleigh's single entity Balance Sheet is equal to the consolidated Retained Earnings figure resulting from the application of consolidation procedures. This result follows from the Paragraph 3050.08 requirement that investment income as calculated by the equity method must be the amount necessary to increase or decrease the investor's income to that which would have been recognized if the results of the investee's operations had been consolidated with those of the investor.

Alternative Disclosure

6-140.   In the example we have just considered, there were no downstream intercompany profits in the 1998 Net Income of the Pleigh Company. If such profits had been present, it would have been acceptable under the requirements of the *CICA Handbook* to simply deduct them from the Investment Income total. In view of the fact that such downstream profits are not included in the reported income of the Sleigh Company, this does not seem to be a particularly desirable form of disclosure. This inappropriateness is recognized in the *CICA Handbook* which provides for alternative disclosure of unrealized downstream profits. The relevant provision is as follows:

> **Paragraph 3050.15**   The elimination of an unrealized intercompany gain or loss has the same effect on net income whether the consolidation or equity method is used. However, in consolidated financial statements, the elimination of a gain or loss may affect sales and cost of sales otherwise to be reported. In the application of the equity method, the gain or loss is eliminated by adjustment of investment income from the investee or by separate provision in the investor's financial statements, as is appropriate in the circumstances.

6-141.   This Paragraph permits the disclosure of unrealized downstream profits as a separate item in the Income Statement of the investor company which is applying the equity method. It would be our view that such disclosure would be preferable to the deduction of such profits from the Investment Income account.

Summary Of Consolidation Procedures

6-142.   In Chapter 4, we began the development of a set of procedures that could be used in the preparation of a consolidated Balance Sheet at the date of the subsidiary's acquisition. In Chapter 5 we made substantial additions to this list involving intercompany expenses and revenues, fair value amortization, and the distribution of subsidiary Retained Earnings since acquisition. In this Chapter, in addition to modifying some of the Chapter 5 procedures to reflect the presence of unrealized intercompany profits, we added new Step B procedures for eliminating and restoring such items. We are now in a position to provide a complete summary of basic consolidation procedures as developed in this text. This summary is as follows:

Step A-1 Procedure   Eliminate 100 percent of the Investment In Subsidiary account.

Step A-2 Procedure   Eliminate 100 percent of all the acquisition date balances in the subsidiary's shareholders' equity (includes both contributed capital and earned capital).

Step A-3 Procedure   Allocate any debit or credit Differential that is present at acquisition to the investor's share of fair value changes on identifiable assets, fair value changes on identifiable liabilities, and positive or negative goodwill.

Step A-4 Procedure   Allocate to a Non Controlling Interest account in the consolidated Balance Sheet, the non controlling interest's share of the at acquisition book value of the total Shareholders' Equity of the subsidiary (includes both contributed capital and earned capital).

Step B-1 Procedure   Eliminate 100 percent of all intercompany assets and liabilities.

Step B-2 Procedure   Give recognition to the post acquisition realization of acquisition date fair value changes on assets and liabilities that have been used up or sold during the post acquisition period. To the extent that this realization occurred in prior periods, recognition will require an adjustment of the opening Retained Earnings of the subsidiary. Alternatively, if the realization occurred in the current period, the adjustment will be to the subsidiary's current period expenses, revenues, gains, or losses.

Step B-3 Procedure   Eliminate 100 percent of all intercompany expenses and revenues.

Step B-4 Procedure   Eliminate 100 percent of subsidiary dividends declared. The controlling share of this amount will be deducted from the revenues of the parent company and the non controlling share of this amount will be deducted from the Non Controlling Interest in the Balance Sheet.

Step B-5(a) Procedure   Eliminate 100 percent of all unrealized intercompany profits *(losses)* that are present at the end of the current period. The amounts will be deducted from *(added to)* the appropriate assets and, to the extent they were recognized in the current period income of the parent or subsidiary, they will be added to *(deducted from)* current period expenses or revenues. If profits recognized by the parent or subsidiary in previous periods are still unrealized at the end of the current period, the adjustment will be to the opening consolidated retained earnings, rather than to the current period expenses or revenues. The elimination of downstream profits *(losses)* will be charged *(credited)* exclusively to consolidated Net Income and consolidated Retained Earnings. The elimination of upstream profits *(losses)* will be charged *(credited)* proportionately to consolidated figures and to any non controlling interest that is present.

Step B-5(b) Procedure   Recognize the amount of previously unrealized intercompany profits or losses that have become realized during the period, either through the sale of the related asset or through usage of that asset. The amount which was previously unrealized from the consolidated point of view would be included in the opening single entity retained earnings of the parent or subsidiary companies. This means there must be an adjustment to a current period expense or revenue and to the consolidated opening retained earnings. The realization of previously unrealized downstream profits *(losses)* will be credited *(charged)* exclusively to consolidated Net Income and consolidated Retained Earnings. The realization of previously unrealized upstream profits *(losses)* will be credited *(charged)* proportionately to consolidated figures and to any non controlling interest that is present.

Step C-1 Procedure   Determine the appropriate allocation of the subsidiary's adjusted Retained Earnings since acquisition. The book value of the subsidiary Retained Earnings since acquisition will first be adjusted for upstream profits that are unrealized as of the date applicable to the Retained Earnings balance (opening Retained Earnings in open trial balance problems). This adjusted balance will be multiplied by the ownership percentage of the non controlling interest, with the product being allocated to the non controlling interest. After the non controlling interest is subtracted, the resulting balance will be adjusted for the fair value and goodwill write offs called for in Step B(2). The balance remaining after these adjustments will be allocated to consolidated Retained Earnings.

Step C-2 Procedure   Eliminate the subsidiary's adjusted Retained Earnings since acquisition. This amount will be allocated to the Non Controlling Interest in the consolidated Balance Sheet and to consolidated Retained Earnings as determined in Step C-1.

6-143.   As we did in Chapter 5, we would remind you that, as stated, the listed procedures apply to open trial balance problems with the investment in the subsidiary carried by the cost method. In dealing with closed trial balance problems, or problems in which the investment is carried by the equity method, these procedures will need to be modified. Such required modifications were illustrated in the closed trial balance version of our comprehensive example.

Summary Of Definitional Calculations

6-144. With this Chapter's coverage of the procedures required to deal with unrealized intercompany profits, we can now provide you with a comprehensive list of the definitions to be used in preparing consolidated financial statements. We continue to encourage you to work towards preparing the required balances in consolidated financial statements by using these direct definitional calculations. The list is as follows:

Identifiable Assets And Liabilities The amount to be included in the consolidated Balance Sheet for any identifiable asset or liability is calculated as follows:

- 100 percent of the carrying value of the identifiable asset (liability) on the books of the parent company at the Balance Sheet date; *plus*

- 100 percent of the carrying value of the identifiable asset (liability) on the books of the subsidiary company at the Balance Sheet date; *plus (minus)*

- the parent company's share of the fair value increase (decrease) on the asset (liability); *minus (plus)*

- amortization of the parent company's share of the fair value increase (decrease) on the asset (liability) for the period since acquisition to the current Balance Sheet date; *minus (plus)*

- upstream and downstream intercompany profits (losses) that are unrealized as of the Balance Sheet date.

Goodwill The Goodwill to be recorded in the consolidated Balance Sheet is equal to:

- the excess of the cost of the investment over the parent company's share of the fair values of the subsidiary's net assets at the time of acquisition; *minus*

- amortization of that excess over the period since acquisition to the current Balance Sheet date.

Non Controlling Interest - Balance Sheet The Non Controlling Interest to be recorded in the consolidated Balance Sheet will be an amount equal to the non controlling interest's ownership percentage multiplied by:

- the book value of the subsidiary's common stock equity at the Balance Sheet date; *minus (plus)*

- upstream intercompany profits (losses) that are unrealized as of the Balance Sheet date.

Contributed Capital The Contributed Capital to be recorded in the consolidated Balance Sheet will be equal to the contributed capital from the single entity Balance Sheet of the parent company.

Retained Earnings The Retained Earnings amount to be included in the consolidated Balance Sheet is calculated as follows:

- 100 percent of the Retained Earnings of the parent company; *plus (minus)*

- the parent company's share of the subsidiary's Retained Earnings (Deficit) since acquisition, adjusted for upstream profits (losses) that are unrealized as of the Balance Sheet date; *plus (minus)*

- 100 percent of the adjustments to consolidated expenses, revenues, gains, and losses for realized fair value changes during the period since acquisition to the current Balance Sheet date; *minus*

- 100 percent of goodwill amortization for the period since acquisition to the current Balance Sheet date; *minus (plus)*

- downstream intercompany profits (losses) that are unrealized as of the Balance Sheet date.

Revenue   The amount of any revenue to be included in the consolidated Income Statement is calculated as follows:

- 100 percent of the amount reported in the parent company's financial statements; *plus*

- 100 percent of the amount reported in the subsidiary's financial statements; *minus*

- 100 percent of any intercompany amounts included in the parent or subsidiary figures; *minus (plus)*

- the recorded amount (parent's share) of any fair value increase (decrease) on an asset (liability) that is realized during the year (e.g., fair value increase on land that is sold during the current year); *minus (plus)*

- 100 percent of any upstream or downstream unrealized profits (losses) that are included in the parent or subsidiary company revenues (e.g., gain on an intercompany sale of land during the current year); *plus (minus)*

- 100 percent of any upstream or downstream unrealized profits (losses) that were unrealized in a previous period but have become realized during the current period (e.g., gain on an intercompany sale of land in a previous year, with the land being resold outside the consolidated entity during the current year).

Expense   The amount of any expense to be included in the consolidated Income Statement is calculated as follows:

- 100 percent of the amount reported in the parent company's financial statements; *plus*

- 100 percent of the amount reported in the subsidiary's financial statements; *minus*

- 100 percent of any intercompany amounts included in the parent or subsidiary figures; *plus (minus)*

- the recorded amount (parent's share) of any fair value increase (decrease) on an asset (liability) that is realized during the year (e.g., depreciation on the parent's share of a fair value increase that was recorded at the time of acquisition); *plus (minus)*

- 100 percent of any upstream or downstream unrealized profits (losses) that are included in the parent or subsidiary company expenses (e.g., unrealized intercompany profits in the closing inventories would be added to the consolidated Cost Of Goods Sold); *minus (plus)*

- 100 percent of any upstream or downstream unrealized profits (losses) that were unrealized in a previous period but have become realized during the current period (e.g., unrealized intercompany profits in the opening inventories would be subtracted from the consolidated Cost Of Goods Sold)).

Goodwill Amortization Expense   In general, this is a new expense added by the consolidation procedures. The amount to be included here is the annual amortization of the Goodwill balance recognized at the time of the subsidiary's acquisition.

Non Controlling Interest - Income Statement   The Non Controlling Interest to be recorded in the consolidated Income Statement will be an amount equal to the non controlling interest's ownership percentage multiplied by:

- the reported Net Income of the subsidiary; *minus (plus)*

- 100 percent of upstream unrealized intercompany profits (losses) that are included in the Net Income of the subsidiary (e.g., upstream unrealized profits in the closing inventories); *plus (minus)*

- 100 percent of upstream profits that were eliminated in a previous period because they were unrealized, but that have become realized during the current period (e.g., upstream unrealized profits in the opening inventories).

Note that, if the subsidiary has extraordinary items or results from discontinued operations, this Non Controlling Interest will be based on the subsidiary's Income Before Extraordinary Items And Discontinued Operations. Also note that, in situations where there are preferred shares with a prior claim on the income of the subsidiary, the Non Controlling Interest to be disclosed in the consolidated Income Statement will include such claims.

Consolidated Net Income   Consolidated Net Income can be calculated as follows:

- 100 percent of the parent company's Net Income, excluding dividends received from the subsidiary; *plus (minus)*

- the parent's share of the sum of:
  - the subsidiary's reported Net Income (Net Loss); *minus (plus)*
  - 100 percent of upstream unrealized intercompany profits (losses) that are included in the Net Income of the subsidiary (e.g., upstream unrealized profits in the closing inventories); *plus (minus)*
  - 100 percent of upstream profits that were eliminated in a previous period because they were unrealized, but that have become realized during the current period (e.g., upstream unrealized profits in the opening inventories).

  minus (plus)

- the recorded amount (parent's share) of any fair value increase (decrease) on an asset (liability) that is realized during the year (e.g., depreciation on a fair value change recorded at the time of acquisition); *minus (plus)*

- 100 percent of downstream profits (losses) that are included in the Net Income of the parent (e.g., downstream unrealized profits in the closing inventories); *plus (minus)*

- 100 percent of downstream profits that were eliminated in a previous period because they were unrealized, but that have become realized during the current period (e.g., downstream unrealized profits in the opening inventories).

6-145.   This comprehensive list of definitions can be used to solve any basic consolidation problem in which the investment in the subsidiary is carried by the cost method. We would encourage to make use of them in solving the self study problems which accompany this Chapter.

Transactions Between A Venturer And A Joint Venture

General Rules

6-146.   As was noted in Chapter 2, the October, 1994 revision of Section 3055 of the *CICA Handbook* requires that interests in joint ventures be accounted for by the proportionate consolidation method. This would suggest that joint venture accounting will require the usual full consolidation adjustments for fair value write offs, goodwill amortization, and upstream and downstream unrealized intercompany profits. However, the fact that joint ventures are defined in a manner which creates a special relationship between its venturers has led the Accounting Standards Board to make a different Recommendation for dealing with profits arising on the intercompany transactions between a joint venture and its venturers.

6-147.   To illustrate the differences, we will use an example in which an investee sells merchandise with a cost of $80,000 to one of its investor companies for $100,000, recording a profit of $20,000 which has not been realized through a subsequent resale by the investor. Consider how this situation would be dealt with if the investee were a subsidiary, a significantly influenced company accounted for by the equity method, and a joint venture accounted for by proportionate consolidation:

Subsidiary   If the investee were a subsidiary, consolidation procedures would require that both the intercompany expense and revenue of $100,000 and the unrealized intercompany profit of $20,000 be eliminated. This conclusion results from the view that the parent and subsidiary are parts of a single accounting entity and, as a consequence, a real sales transaction did not occur.

Significantly Influenced Company - Equity Method   In this case the investor and investee are accounted for as separate entities and, under this view, a real transaction did take place. As a consequence, there would be no elimination of the $100,000 intercompany expense and revenue. However, the presence of significant influence makes this a non arm's length transaction, raising questions about the reliability of any profit figures that are reported. Given this, the *Handbook* Recommendations require the elimination of 100 percent of any unrealized intercompany profits in the application of the equity method. This is accomplished by a reduction in the Investment Income account, rather than through adjustments of specific expenses and revenues.

Joint Ventures - Proportionate Consolidation   As any investor who classifies an investment as a joint venture must participate in its management, venturers clearly have influence over the joint venture. As a consequence, transactions between venturers and the joint venture must be viewed as non arm's length. However, there is a difference from the usual situation where the investor has influence over the investee. In joint ventures, all of the venturers participate under the management agreement and are likely to pay careful attention to transactions that take place between the joint venture and other venturers. In fact, it would be unusual to find a joint venture agreement that does not specify the terms and conditions under which intercompany transactions can take place. Given this, it is usually reasonable to view transactions between a joint venture and its venturers as being arm's length in the sense that they are controlled by the relationship established in the joint venture arrangement or by an informal agreement among the joint venturers. This assumes that the various venturers are, in fact, dealing at arm's length.

However, there is a problem. To the extent that the venturer has an interest in the joint venture, the intercompany transaction is, in effect, a transaction between the venturer and itself as represented by its interest in the joint venture. As a consequence, recognition of the particular venturer's share of the profit or loss does not appear to be appropriate.

The preceding discussion would suggest that, in the application of proportionate consolidation in joint venture situations, only the individual venturer's share of intercompany expenses, revenues, and unrealized profits would be eliminated. As will be discussed in the following Section, this is the position taken by Section 3055 of the *CICA Handbook*.

Section 3055 Recommendations

Downstream Transactions

6-148.   When there is a sale in the normal course of business operations from the venturer to the joint venture, Section 3055 makes the following Recommendation:

Paragraph 3055.36   *When a venturer sells assets to a joint venture in the normal course of operations and a gain or loss occurs, the venturer should recognize the gain or loss in income to the extent of the interests of the other non-related venturers. When such a transaction provides evidence of a reduction in the net realizable value, or a decline in the value, of the relevant assets, the venturer should recognize the full amount of any loss in income.* (January, 1995)

6-149.   To illustrate this provision, consider the following:

Example   On January 1, 1998, a group of joint venturers form Jointly Ltd.(JL) with a total investment of $1,000 in cash. One of the investors, Nordwell Inc. (NI), has received a 30 percent interest in return for $300 in cash. NI is a holding Company formed for this investment transaction and, on this date, the Company has no other assets or liabilities. The Balance Sheets of the two Companies on January 1, 1998 would be as follows:

Balance Sheets
As At January 1, 1998

	Nordwell	Jointly
Cash	Nil	$1,000
Investment In JL	$300	Nil
Total Assets	$300	$1,000
Capital Stock	$300	$1,000

During the year ending December 31, 1998, NI purchases merchandise on credit for $100 and sells it to JL for $160. The merchandise has not been resold at year end. Neither Company had other transactions during the year ending December 31, 1998. The Balance Sheets for the two Companies as at December 31, 1998 and the Income Statements for the year ending December 31, 1998 are as follows:

Balance Sheets
As At December 31, 1998

	Nordwell	Jointly
Cash	$160	$ 840
Inventory	Nil	160
Investment In JL	300	Nil
Total Assets	$460	$1,000

	Nordwell	Jointly
Accounts Payable	$100	Nil
Capital Stock	300	$1,000
Retained Earnings	60	Nil
Total Equities	$460	$1,000

Income Statements
Year Ending December 31, 1998

	Nordwell	Jointly
Sales	$160	Nil
Cost Of Sales	100	Nil
Net Income	$ 60	Nil

6-150.   The first step in the consolidation procedures would be to eliminate the Investment In JL, JL's Capital Stock and, because we are using proportionate consolidation, the 70 percent interest of the other joint venturers in Jointly's assets. The entry would be as follows:

Capital Stock (JL)	$1,000	
Cash [(70%)($840)]		$588
Inventory [(70%)($160)]		112
Investment In JL		300

6-151.   As JL had no Income Statement items, there is no need for an entry to eliminate the interest of the other joint venturers in expenses or revenues. This means that the only other elimination entry is the one required to deal with the downstream sale. As NI can recognize this transaction to the extent of the interests of the other joint venturers, only NI's shares of the Sales, Costs Of Sales, and unrealized profit will have to be eliminated. The required entry is as follows:

Sales [(30%)($160)]	$48	
Inventory [(30%)($160 - $100)]		$18
Cost Of Sales [(30%)($100)]		30

6-152.   Given the preceding eliminations, the proportionate consolidation Balance Sheet and Income Statement can be prepared as follows:

Nordwell Inc.
Proportionate Consolidation Balance Sheet
As At December 31, 1998

Cash ($160 + $840 - $588)	$412
Inventory (Nil + $160 - $112 - $18)	30
Investment In JL ($300 - $300)	Nil
Total Assets	$442

Accounts Payable	$100
Capital Stock	300
Retained Earnings ($60 - $18)	42
Total Equities	$442

Nordwell Inc.
Proportionate Consolidation Income Statement
Year Ending December 31, 1998

Sales ($160 - $48)	$112
Cost Of Sales ($100 - $30)	70
Net Income	$ 42

6-153.   Note that, if full consolidation procedures had been applied, the entire intercompany transaction would have been eliminated and there would have been no content in the consolidated Income Statement for the year ending December 31, 1998.

6-154.   As a final point on downstream transactions, note that the Paragraph 3055.36 Recommendation contemplates the possibility of recognizing 100 percent of the loss when the transaction provides evidence of a reduction in net realizable value. This is consistent with the Paragraph 3055.26 Recommendation on capital contributions to joint ventures, which also permitted full recognition of a loss under these circumstances.

Upstream Transactions

6-155.   When there is a sale from the joint venture to one of the venturers, the following Recommendation applies:

Paragraph 3055.37 *When a venturer purchases assets from a joint venture in the normal course of operations, the venturer should not recognize its share of the profit or loss of the joint venture on the transaction until the assets are sold to a third party. However, when the transaction provides evidence of a reduction in the net realizable value, or a decline in the value of the relevant assets, the venturer should recognize its share of the loss in income immediately. (January, 1995)*

6-156.   In order to illustrate this provision, we will use the same basic example that was presented in Paragraph 6-149, modified to include an upstream rather than a downstream transaction. The example is as follows:

Example   On January 1, 1998, a group of joint venturers form Jointly Ltd.(JL) with a total investment of $1,000 in cash. One of the investors, Nordwell Inc. (NI), has received a 30 percent interest in return for $300 in cash. NI is a holding Company formed for this investment transaction and, on this date, its only other asset or liability is cash of $220. The Balance Sheets of the two Companies on January 1, 1998 would be as follows:

Balance Sheets
As At January 1, 1998

	Nordwell	Jointly
Cash	$220	$1,000
Investment In JL	300	Nil
Total Assets	$520	$1,000
Capital Stock	$520	$1,000

During the year ending December 31, 1998, JL purchases merchandise for $150 and sells it to NI for $220. The merchandise has not been resold at year end. Neither Company had other transactions during the year ending December 31, 1998. The Balance Sheets for the two Companies as at December 31, 1998 and the Income Statements for the year ending December 31, 1998 are as follows:

Balance Sheets - As At December 31, 1998

	Nordwell	Jointly
Cash	Nil	$1,070
Inventory	$220	Nil
Investment In JL	300	Nil
Total Assets	$520	$1,070
Capital Stock	$520	$1,000
Retained Earnings	Nil	70
Total Equities	$520	$1,070

Income Statements - Year Ending December 31, 1998

	Nordwell	Jointly
Sales	Nil	$220
Cost Of Sales	Nil	150
Net Income	Nil	$ 70

6-157.   A first entry is required to eliminate NI's Investment in JL, JL's Capital Stock, and the other venturers' interest in the assets, liabilities, expenses, and revenues of JL:

Capital Stock (JL)	$1,000	
Sales [(70%)($220)]	154	
Cost Of Sales [(70%)($150)]		$105
Cash [(70%)($1,070)]		749
Investment In JL		300

6-158.   If there had been an opening balance in JL's Retained Earnings, the preceding entry would have also eliminated that balance.

6-159.   A second entry is required to eliminate NI's share of the intercompany Sales, Cost Of Sales, and the unrealized profit in the ending Inventory:

Sales [(30%)($220)]	$66	
Inventory [(30%)($70)]		$21
Cost Of Sales [(30%)($150)]		45

6-160.   Using the preceding journal entries, the proportionate consolidation Balance Sheet as at December 31, 1998 and Income Statement for the year ending December 31, 1998, can be prepared as follows:

Nordwell Inc.
Proportionate Consolidation Balance Sheet
As At December 31, 1998

Cash (Nil + $1,070 - $749)	$321
Inventory ($220 + Nil - $21)	199
Investment In JL ($300 - $300)	Nil
Total Assets	$520
Accounts Payable ($220 + Nil - $220)	Nil
Capital Stock	520
Retained Earnings	Nil
Total Equities	$520

Nordwell Inc.
Proportionate Consolidation Income Statement
Year Ending December 31, 1998

Sales ($220 - $154 - $66)	Nil
Cost Of Sales ($150 - $105 - $45)	Nil
Net Income	Nil

6-161.   With respect to the proportionate consolidation Income Statement, we have not included any disclosure of the intercompany transaction. This reflects the fact that, while we can recognize the other venturers' share of the intercompany profit, it is not disclosed in the proportionate consolidation income statement. If full consolidation procedures were being applied, the other venturers' share of Sales, Cost Of Sales, and the intercompany profit would have been disclosed. However, under the rules applicable to intercompany transactions between a parent and a subsidiary, this would have been eliminated, resulting the same Income Statement disclosure.

Upstream And Downstream Transactions Compared

6-162.   With both upstream and downstream intercompany profits, the venturer is allowed to recognize the share of such profits that belongs to the other non affiliated venturers in its consolidated financial statements. However, because proportionate consolidation is being used, the resulting disclosure is somewhat confusing.

6-163.   To see the results with downstream profits, return to the example presented in Paragraph 6-149. You will note that in the proportionate consolidation Balance Sheet (Paragraph 6-152), none of the $60 intercompany profit is included in the Inventory balance. The $30 balance in this account is simply NI's 30 percent share of the $100 original cost of the Inventory. This does not mean, however, that we have not recognized the other venturer's 70 percent share of the profit. This is clear from the proportionate consolidation Income Statement which shows a profit equal to $42 (70 percent of $60). The reason that this $42 does not show up in the Inventory figure is that the Inventory belongs to JL and this means that proportionate consolidation procedures will remove 70 percent of all of JL's accounts. The $42 has been removed here, not because it is intercompany, but because proportionate consolidation procedures remove all values that belong to the other joint venturers.

6-164.   A similar analysis can be made of upstream transactions using the example from Paragraph 6-156. In this case, the Inventory figure in the proportionate consolidation Balance Sheet includes the 70 percent share of the $70 intercompany profit that belongs to the other joint venturers {$199 = [$150 + (70%)($70)]}. The reason that the profit is included in the consolidated Inventory figure in this case is that the Inventory is on the books of NI. This means that it will not be eliminated by proportionate consolidation procedures.

6-165.   However, the $49 profit is not included in the proportionate consolidation Income Statement. This reflects the fact that, in upstream transactions, the Sales and Cost Of Sales figures are from the books of JL. This means that 70 percent of these figures will be eliminated through proportionate consolidation procedures, thereby eliminating in the proportionate consolidation Income Statement the $49 profit that was included in the proportionate consolidation Balance Sheet.

Capital Contributions

6-166.   As noted in Chapter 2, it is not uncommon for a venturer to make a capital contribution in the form of non cash assets. This raises the question of whether or not any difference between the fair market value of the non cash assets contributed, and their carrying value on the books of the joint venturer prior to contribution, should be recognized at the time of contribution. As this issue was discussed at length in Chapter 2, the coverage will not be repeated here.

Comprehensive Example

Basic Data

6-167.   The following comprehensive example will serve to illustrate the application of proportionate consolidation procedures:

On January 1, 1998, Laroo Ltd. (LL) and Rotan Inc. (RI) establish a new corporation which will market products that both Companies produce. LL has no affiliation with RI other than their common ownership of the new corporation. The new corporation will be called Cooperative Enterprises Inc. (CEI).

LL's capital contribution consists of a Building with a carrying value of $1,500,000 and a fair value of $2,000,000. The building is situated on leased land. The lease payments are at current fair market value and the lease is transferred to CEI at the time of its incorporation. At January 1, 1998, the remaining term of the lease is 20 years and this is also the remaining economic life of the building. In return for the building, LL receives 60 percent of CEI's voting shares and $200,000 in cash. LL records a gain of $500,000 on the transfer of the building.

RI's capital contribution consists of $1,200,000 in cash. In return, RI receives 40 percent of CEI's voting shares.

LL and RI sign an agreement which provides for joint control over CEI. All significant operating and financing decisions must be approved by both of the investor Companies.

For the year ending December 31, 1998, the single entity Balance Sheets and Income Statements for LL and CEI are as follows:

	LL	CEI
Cash And Receivables	$ 1,500,000	$ 300,000
Inventories	4,800,000	1,500,000
Investment In CEI (At Cost)	1,800,000	-0-
Land	1,100,000	-0-
Building	3,500,000	2,000,000
Accumulated Depreciation	(1,200,000)	(100,000)
Total Assets	$11,500,000	$3,700,000
Liabilities	$ 2,200,000	$ 200,000
Common Stock - No Par	5,000,000	3,000,000
Retained Earnings	4,300,000	500,000
Total Equities	$11,500,000	$3,700,000
Sales	$4,200,000	$2,800,000
Gain On Sale Of Building	500,000	-0-
Cost Of Goods Sold	(2,500,000)	(1,500,000)
Depreciation Expense	(700,000)	(100,000)
Other Expenses	(400,000)	(700,000)
Net Income	$1,100,000	$ 500,000

Other Information:

1. During the year ending December 31, 1998, CEI sells merchandise to LL for $420,000. This merchandise had cost CEI $350,000 and none of it has been re-

sold by LL.

2. During the year ending December 31, 1998, LL sells merchandise to CEI for $860,000. This merchandise had cost LL $740,000 and one-half of it has been re-sold by CEI.

3. Neither LL nor CEI declare or pay dividends during the year ending December 31, 1998.

Required: Using proportionate consolidation procedures, prepare a consolidated Balance Sheet as at December 31, 1998 and a consolidated Income Statement for the year ending December 31, 1998, for LL and its investee CEI. Your solution should comply with the Recommendations in Section 3055 of the *CICA Handbook*.

Analysis Of Gain

6-168. In transferring the Building to CEI, LL recognized a gain of $500,000 ($2,000,000 - $1,500,000). Under the provisions of Section 3055, this gain can only be recognized to the extent of the interest of the other non affiliated venturer. This provides the following analysis:

Total Gain	$500,000
LL's Share (60 Percent)	(300,000)
Gain To Be Recognized	$200,000

6-169. To the extent that LL received cash or assets other than an equity interest in NVI, this gain can be taken into income at the time of transfer. The calculation of the amount to be taken into income at the time of transfer is as follows:

Cash Received At Transfer	$200,000
Cost Of Asset Considered To Be Sold:	
[($200,000 ÷ $2,000,000)($1,500,000)]	(150,000)
Gain To Be Taken Into Income At Transfer	$ 50,000

6-170. The remaining $150,000 ($200,000 - $50,000) of the gain that can be recognized, will be taken into income over the 20 year life of the Building. This will be at a rate of $7,500 per year.

6-171. As the $300,000 unrecognized gain will have to be removed from the consolidated carrying value of the Building, the consolidated Depreciation Expense will have to be decreased annually by $15,000 ($300,000 ÷ 20 Years).

Investment Elimination

6-172. The journal entry to eliminate the Investment In CEI, CEI's Common Stock - No Par, CEI's Retained Earnings at Acquisition, and RI's share of the individual assets, liabilities, expenses, and revenues of CEI would be as follows:

Common Stock - No Par (CEI's)	$3,000,000	
Retained Earnings At Acquisition	Nil	
Accumulated Depreciation (40%)	40,000	
Liabilities (40%)	80,000	
Sales (40%)	1,120,000	
Cash And Receivables (40%)		$120,000
Inventories (40%)		600,000
Building (40%)		800,000
Cost Of Goods Sold (40%)		600,000
Depreciation Expense (40%)		40,000
Other Expenses (40%)		280,000
Investment In CEI		1,800,000

6-173.   Note that, at this point, we are left with 60 percent of the carrying values of CEI's assets, liabilities, expenses, and revenues. Because we are using proportionate consolidation, there is no account balance to reflect RI's interest in the assets, liabilities, expenses, and revenues of CEI.

Gain Adjustment - Building

6-174.   A second entry is required to deal with the gain recognized by LL on the transfer of the Building. The entry will leave the $50,000 of the gain that can be recognized at transfer in the Gain On Sale Of Building account. The $300,000 of the gain that cannot be recognized will be removed from the Building account, while the $150,000 portion of the gain that will be recognized over the life of the Building will be allocated to a Deferred Gain account. The required entry is as follows:

Gain On Sale Of Building ($500,000 - $50,000) $450,000
      Building (Unrecognized Portion) $300,000
      Deferred Gain   150,000

6-175.   This entry, when combined with the earlier elimination of RI's 40 percent share of the Building, leaves a balance of $900,000 ($2,000,000 - $800,000 - $300,000). As would be expected, this is equal to LL's 60 percent share of the original $1,500,000 carrying value for the Building.

Deferred Gain Amortization

6-176.   As one year has passed since the Building was transferred to CEI, one-twentieth of the Deferred Gain has been realized and can be taken into income. The appropriate entry is as follows:

Deferred Gain $7,500
      Gain On Sale Of Building $7,500

6-177.   As CEI has recorded depreciation on the $2,000,000 fair value of the Building, this must be adjusted to reflect the removal of the $300,000 unrecognized gain from this asset. This will require an annual adjustment of $15,000 ($300,000 ÷ 20 Years) as follows:

Accumulated Depreciation $15,000
      Depreciation Expense $15,000

6-178.   This entry, when combined with the earlier elimination of RI's 40 percent share of the Building, leaves Accumulated Depreciation and Depreciation Expense at $45,000. As was the case with the Building account, this is equal to depreciation at 5 percent on LL's $900,000 share of the original carrying value of the building.

6-179.   There are intercompany expenses and revenues arising from both upstream ($420,000) and downstream ($860,000) sales of merchandise. In the case of joint ventures, intercompany sales and any related intercompany profit can be recognized to the extent of the share of the other non affiliated venturers (Paragraphs 3055.36 and 3055.37). In the case of downstream transactions, this means that we must eliminate the selling venturer's share of the sale and any unrealized profit resulting from the transaction. The remainder of the downstream sale and the related profit will remain in the proportionate consolidation results. When an upstream transaction is involved, all of the sale and unrealized profit must be eliminated. While we can recognize the other non related venturer's share of the profit in the consolidated Balance Sheet (it is included in an asset on the books of the venturer and not subject to proportionate consolidation procedures), the sale and profit belong to the other non related venturer and will be removed by the proportionate consolidation procedures.

6-180.   With respect to the entry to eliminate the intercompany sales, RI's 40 percent share of the upstream sale was eliminated in our first journal entry. This means that we will only need to eliminate $1,112,000 [(60%)($420,000 + $860,000)] of these sales. The required entry is as follows:

Sales	$1,112,000	
Cost Of Goods Sold		$1,112,000

6-181.   As some of the merchandise has not been resold, there are also unrealized inter-company profits to be eliminated. The upstream amount is $70,000 ([100%][$420,000 - $350,000]) and the downstream amount is $60,000 ([50%][$860,000 - $740,000]). As was the case with upstream intercompany sales, we have already eliminated RI's 40 per-cent share of all of CEI's profits and, as a consequence, we only need eliminate $42,000 ([60%][$70,000]) of the unrealized upstream profit of $70,000. With respect to the downstream profit, we will need to eliminate 60 percent of this total, an amount of $36,000 ([60%][$60,000]). The entry to eliminate this total of $78,000 ($42,000 + $36,000) is as follows:

Cost Of Goods Sold	$78,000	
Inventories		$78,000

6-182.   Given these entries, the required consolidated Balance Sheet can be prepared as follows:

LL And Investee CEI
Consolidated Balance Sheet (Proportionate Basis)
As At December 31, 1998

Cash And Receivables ($1,500,000 + $300,000 - $120,000)	$ 1,680,000
Inventories ($4,800,000 + $1,500,000 - $600,000 - $78,000)	5,622,000
Investment In CEI ($1,800,000 - $1,800,000)	-0-
Land (LL's Only)	1,100,000
Building ($3,500,000 + $2,000,000 - $800,000 - $300,000)	4,400,000
Accumulated Depreciation ($1,200,000 + $100,000 -$40,000 - $15,000)	(1,245,000)
Total Assets	**$11,557,000**
Liabilities ($2,200,000 + $200,000 - $80,000)	$2,320,000
Deferred Gain ($150,000 - $7,500)	142,500
Common Stock - No Par (LL's Only)	5,000,000
Retained Earnings (See Note)	4,094,500
Total Equities	**$11,557,000**

Note   The balance in consolidated Retained Earnings can be verified with the fol-lowing calculation:

LL's Balance - December 31, 1998	$4,300,000
Unrecognized Gain On Building Transfer	(300,000)
Deferred Gain On Building Transfer	(150,000)
Gain Realized During 1998	7,500
Depreciation Adjustment	15,000
Downstream Inventory Profit [(60%)($60,000)]	(36,000)
BL's Adjusted Balance	$3,836,500
Equity Pickup [(60%)($500,000 - $70,000)]	258,000
Consolidated Retained Earnings	**$4,094,500**

6-183.   The required consolidated Income Statement would be prepared as follows:

LL And Investee CEI
Consolidated Income Statement (Proportionate Basis)
Year Ending December 31, 1998

Sales ($4,200,000 + $2,800,000 - $1,120,000 -$1,112,000)	$4,768,000
Gain On Sale Of Building ($500,000 - $450,000 +$7,500)	57,500
Cost Of Goods Sold ($2,500,000 + $1,500,000 -$600,000 - $1,112,000 + $78,000)	(2,366,000)
Depreciation Expense ($700,000 + $100,000 - $40,000 -$15,000)	(745,000)
Other Expenses ($400,000 + $700,000 - $280,000)	(820,000)
Consolidated Net Income	$894,500

6-184.   The consolidated Net Income figure can be verified with the following calculation:

LL's 1998 Net Income	$1,100,000
Unrecognized Gain On Building Transfer	(300,000)
Deferred Gain On Building Transfer	(150,000)
Gain Realized During 1998	7,500
Depreciation Adjustment	15,000
Downstream Inventory Profit [(60%)($60,000)]	(36,000)
BL's Adjusted Balance	$ 636,500
Equity Pickup [(60%)($500,000 - $70,000)]	258,000
Consolidated Retained Earnings	$ 894,500

6-185.   Note that the preceding adjustments to BL's Net Income are the same as the adjustments in the verification of consolidated Retained Earnings. This is because it is the first year of operations of NVI.

Walk Through Problem

Note   This problem is an extension of the Walk Through Problem that was presented at the end of Chapters Four and Five. As previously explained, these problems provide you with a fill-in-the-blank solution format to assist you in solving the problem. These problems are designed to be an easy introduction to solving the type of problem illustrated in the Chapter.

Basic Data   On December 31, 1998, the Puff Company purchased 60 percent of the outstanding voting shares of the Snuff Company for $720,000 in cash. On that date, subsequent to the completion of the business combination, the Balance Sheets of the Puff and Snuff Companies and the fair values of Snuff's identifiable assets and liabilities were as follows:

| | December 31, 1998 Balance Sheets | | Fair Values |
	Puff	Snuff	For Snuff
Cash And Accounts Receivable	$ 350,000	$ 200,000	$200,000
Inventories	950,000	500,000	$450,000
Investment In Snuff	720,000	-0-	N/A
Plant And Equipment (Net)	2,400,000	700,000	$800,000
Total Assets	$4,420,000	$1,400,000	
Current Liabilities	$ 400,000	$ 100,000	$100,000
Long Term Liabilities	1,000,000	400,000	$360,000
No Par Common Stock	1,000,000	800,000	N/A
Retained Earnings	2,020,000	100,000	N/A
Total Equities	$4,420,000	$1,400,000	

The December 31, 1998 Inventories of Snuff are sold during 1999. The Plant And Equipment of Snuff on December 31, 1998 has an estimated useful life of 10 years while the Long Term Liabilities that were present on that date mature on December 31, 2001. Any goodwill arising from the business combination should be amortized over 30 years. Both Companies use the straight line method of depreciation and amortization. Puff carries its Investment In Snuff by the cost method.

The Income Statements for the year ending December 31, 2002 and the Balance Sheets as at December 31, 2002 of the Puff and Snuff Companies are as follows:

Income Statements
For The Year Ending December 31, 2002

	Puff Company	Snuff Company
Sales	$3,700,000	$2,000,000
Other Revenues	200,000	50,000
Total Revenues	$3,900,000	$2,050,000
Cost Of Goods Sold	$2,000,000	$1,100,000
Depreciation Expense	600,000	400,000
Other Expenses	900,000	350,000
Total Expenses	$3,500,000	$1,850,000
Net Income	$ 400,000	$ 200,000

Balance Sheets
As At December 31, 2002

	Puff Company	Snuff Company
Cash	$ 80,000	$ 75,000
Accounts Receivable	500,000	325,000
Inventories	1,375,000	750,000
Investment In Snuff	720,000	-0-
Plant And Equipment (Net)	2,325,000	1,100,000
Total Assets	$5,000,000	$2,250,000
Current Liabilities	$ 400,000	$ 220,000
Long Term Liabilities	1,000,000	750,000
No Par Common Stock	1,000,000	800,000
Retained Earnings	2,600,000	480,000
Total Equities	$5,000,000	$2,250,000

Other Information:

1. During 2002, Puff declared and paid $150,000 in dividends while Snuff declared and paid $75,000 in dividends.

2. Included in the 2002 Sales of Snuff are sales of $300,000 to Puff on which Snuff earned a gross profit of $125,000. Of these sales, $60,000 remain in the December 31, 2002 inventories of Puff. The January 1, 2002 inventories of Puff contained merchandise purchased from Snuff for $75,000 on which Snuff had earned a gross profit of $35,000. Puff owes Snuff $45,000 on December 31, 2002 for the merchandise purchases.

3. During 2002, Puff had sales of $175,000 to Snuff. Of these sales, $80,000 are on hand in the December 31, 2002 inventories of Snuff. Of the $250,000 of sales from Puff to Snuff in 2001, $110,000 were not resold in 2001. Puff's intercompany sales are priced to provide a gross margin of 40 percent of sales price.

4. On January 1, 1999, the Snuff Company sold the Puff Company a machine for $250,000. The machine had been purchased by Snuff on January 1, 1998 for $360,000 and had an estimated useful life on that date of six years with no salvage value expected. On December 31, 1998, the date of the business combination, this machine had a fair value that was equal to its carrying value.

5. On January 1, 2002, the Snuff Company sold a piece of land that it had purchased for $15,000 on December 31, 2000 to Puff for $33,000. This price is to be paid on January 1, 2003.

Required: Prepare a consolidated Income Statement and Consolidated Statement Of Retained Earnings for the year ending December 31, 2002 and a Consolidated Balance Sheet as at December 31, 2002 for the Puff Company and its subsidiary, the Snuff Company that complies with the *CICA Handbook*. Provide verifications for the 2002 consolidated Net Income, December 31, 2002 consolidated Retained Earnings and the December 31, 2002 Non Controlling Interest in net assets.

Walk Through Problem Solution Format

Step A - Investment Analysis

	60 Percent	100 Percent
Purchase Price	$	$
Book Value	($)	($)
Differential	$	$
Fair Value Change On Inventories	$	$
Fair Value Change On Plant And Equipment	($)	($)
Fair Value Change On Long Term Liabilities	($)	($)
Goodwill	$	$

Step A - Investment Elimination Entry

No Par Common Stock	$	
Retained Earnings	$	
Plant And Equipment (Net)	$	
Long Term Liabilities	$	
Goodwill	$	
Investment In Snuff		$
Inventories		$
Non Controlling Interest		$

Step B(1) - Intercompany Assets And Liabilities

Current Liabilities	$	
Accounts Receivable		$
Current Liabilities	$	
Accounts Receivable		$

Step B(2) - Fair Value Adjustment On The Inventories

Inventories $

    Retained Earnings $

Step B(2) - Fair Value Adjustment On Plant And Equipment

Retained Earnings - Snuff $

Depreciation Expense $

    Plant and Equipment (Net) $

Step B(2) - Fair Value Adjustment On Long Term Liabilities

Retained Earnings - Snuff $

Other Expenses $

    Long Term Liabilities $

Step B(2) - Goodwill Amortization

Retained Earnings - Snuff $

Other Expenses $

    Goodwill $

Step B(3) - Intercompany Expenses And Revenues

Sales $

    Cost Of Goods Sold $

Step B(4) - Intercompany Dividends

Other Revenues $

Non Controlling Interest $

    Dividends Declared $

Step B(5) - Upstream Intercompany Inventory Profits

Cost Of Goods Sold $

    Inventories $

Retained Earnings - Snuff $

    Cost Of Goods Sold $

Step B(5) - Downstream Intercompany Inventory Profits

Cost Of Goods Sold $

    Inventories $

Retained Earnings - Puff $

    Cost Of Goods Sold $

Step B(5) - Upstream Sale Of Machine

Plant And Equipment $

Depreciation Expense $

    Retained Earnings - Snuff $

Step B(5) - Upstream Sale Of Land

Other Revenues $

    Plant And Equipment (Net) $

Step C - Retained Earnings Distribution Schedule

Snuff's January 1, 2002 Balance	$	
Snuff's Balance At Acquisition	($	)
Balance Since Acquisition	$	
Upstream Profits: Inventories	($	)
Equipment	$	
Adjusted Balance Since Acquisition	$	
Non Controlling Percent	%	
To The Non Controlling Interest	$	
Available To The Majority	$	
Step B Adjustments:		
Fair Value Change On Inventories	$	
Fair Value Change On Plant and Equipment	($	)
Fair Value Change On Long Term Liabilities	($	)
Goodwill Amortization	($	)
To Consolidated Retained Earnings	$	

Step C - Retained Earnings Distribution Entry

Retained Earnings - Snuff	$	
Non Controlling Interest	$	
Consolidated Retained Earnings		$

Puff Company And Subsidiary
Consolidated Income Statement
For The Year Ending December 31, 2002

Sales	$
Other Revenues	$
Total Revenues	$
Cost Of Goods Sold	$
Depreciation Expense	$
Other Expenses	$
Non Controlling Interest	$
Total Expenses	$
Consolidated Net Income	$

Puff Company And Subsidiary
Consolidated Statement Of Retained Earnings
For The Year Ending December 31, 2002

Balance - January 1, 2002	$
Consolidated Net Income	$
Available For Distribution	$
Dividends Declared	
Balance - December 31, 2002	$

Verification Of Consolidated Net Income

Puff Company's Net Income		$
Intercompany Dividend Revenues		($)
Puff's Net Income Less Dividends		$
Snuff Company's Reported Income	$	
Upstream Adjustments:		
Profits In Ending Inventories	($)	
Profits In Opening Inventories	$	
Realized Loss On Equipment	($)	
Upstream Gain on Land Sale	($)	
Adjusted Subsidiary Income	$	
Controlling Percent		%
Controlling Interest		$
Step B Adjustments:		
Fair Value Change On Plant and Equipment		($)
Fair Value Change On Long Term Liabilities		($)
Goodwill Amortization		($)
Downstream Adjustments:		
Profits in Ending Inventories		($)
Profits in Opening Inventories		$
Consolidated Net Income		$

Verification Of Consolidated Retained Earnings

Puff's Closing Balance $

Snuff's Closing Balance $

Balance At Acquisition   ($)

_____

Balance Since Acquisition $

Upstream Adjustments:

    Profits in Ending Inventories   ($)

    Unrealized Loss on Equipment $

    Unrealized Gain on Land Sale   ($)

_____

Realized Balance Since Acquisition $

Controlling Percent   %

_____

Controlling Interest $

Step B Adjustments:

    Inventories $

    Fair Value Change On Plant and Equipment   ($)

    Fair Value Change On Long Term Liabilities   ($)

    Goodwill Amortization   ($)

    Downstream Closing Inventory Profits   ($)

_____

Consolidated Retained Earnings As At December 31, 2002 $

_____
_____

Puff Company And Subsidiary
Consolidated Balance Sheet
As At December 31, 2002

Cash	$
Accounts Receivable	$
Inventories	$
Investment In Snuff	$
Plant And Equipment (Net)	$
Goodwill	$
Total Assets	$
Current Liabilities	$
Long Term Liabilities	$
Non Controlling Interest	$
No Par Common Stock	$
Retained Earnings	$
Total Equities	$

Verification Of The Non Controlling Interest In Consolidated Net Assets

At Acquisition (Step A)	$
Dividends Declared By Snuff (Step B)	($)
Retained Earnings Distribution (Step C)	$
From Consolidated Net Income	$
Non Controlling Interest As At December 31, 2002	$

Walk Through Problem Solution

Step A - Investment Analysis

	60 Percent	100 Percent
Purchase Price	$720,000	$1,200,000
Book Value	(540,000)	(900,000)
Differential	$180,000	$ 300,000
Inventories	30,000	50,000
Plant And Equipment	(60,000)	(100,000)
Long Term Liabilities	(24,000)	(40,000)
Goodwill	$126,000	$ 210,000

Step A - Investment Elimination Entry

No Par Common Stock	$800,000	
Retained Earnings	100,000	
Plant And Equipment	60,000	
Long Term Liabilities	24,000	
Goodwill	126,000	
Investment In Snuff		$720,000
Inventories		30,000
Non Controlling Interest		360,000

Step B(1) - Intercompany Assets And Liabilities

Current Liabilities	$45,000	
Accounts Receivable		$45,000
(Intercompany Merchandise Sales)		

Current Liabilities	$33,000	
Accounts Receivable		$33,000
(Intercompany Land Sale)		

Step B(2) - Fair Value Adjustment On The Inventories

Inventories	$30,000	
Retained Earnings - Snuff		$30,000

Step B(2) - Fair Value Adjustment On Plant And Equipment

Retained Earnings - Snuff	$18,000	
Depreciation Expense	6,000	
Plant And Equipment (Net)		$24,000
(Annual Adjustment = $60,000/10 = $6,000/Year)		

Step B(2) - Fair Value Adjustment On Long Term Liabilities

Retained Earnings - Snuff	$24,000	
Other Expenses	-0-	
Long Term Liabilities		$24,000
(There is no effect on consolidated Net Income since the Long Term Liabilities have matured.)		

Step B(2) - Goodwill Amortization

Retained Earnings - Snuff	$12,600	
Other Expenses	4,200	
Goodwill		$16,800

(Annual Adjustment = $126,000/30 = $4,200/Year)

Step B(3) - Intercompany Expenses And Revenues

Sales ($300,000 + $175,000)	$475,000	
Cost Of Goods Sold		$475,000

Step B(4) - Intercompany Dividends

Other Revenues (60% of $75,000)	$45,000	
Non Controlling Interest (Balance Sheet)	30,000	
Dividends Declared		$75,000

Step B(5) - Upstream Intercompany Inventory Profits

Cost Of Goods Sold	$25,000	
Inventories		$25,000

(Unrealized Intercompany Profits in Closing Inventories =
[($60,000/$300,000)($125,000)])

Retained Earnings - Snuff	$35,000	
Cost Of Goods Sold		$35,000

(Unrealized Profits in Opening Inventories - Given)

Step B(5) - Downstream Inventory Profits

Cost Of Goods Sold	$32,000	
Inventories		$32,000

(Unrealized Profits in Closing Inventories = 40% of $80,000)

Retained Earnings - Puff	$44,000	
Cost Of Goods Sold		$44,000

(Unrealized Profits in Opening Inventories = 40% of $110,000)

Step B(5) - Upstream Sale Of Machine

Plant And Equipment (Net)	$10,000	
Depreciation Expense	10,000	
Retained Earnings - Snuff		$20,000

(Annual Adjustment = [$360,000 - $60,000 - $250,000]/5 years = $10,000/Year)

Step B(5) - Upstream Sale Of Land

Other Revenues ($33,000 - $15,000)	$18,000	
Plant And Equipment (Net)		$18,000

Step C - Retained Earnings Distribution Schedule

Snuff's January 1, 2002 Balance ($480,000 - $200,000 + $75,000)	$355,000
Snuff's Balance At Acquisition	(100,000)
Balance Since Acquisition	$255,000
Opening Upstream Profits:	
Inventories	(35,000)
Equipment	20,000
Adjusted Balance Since Acquisition	$240,000
Non Controlling Percent	40%
To The Non Controlling Interest	$ 96,000

Available To The Controlling Interest	$144,000
Step B Adjustments:	
Fair Value Change On Inventory	30,000
Fair Value Change On Plant And Equipment	(18,000)
Fair Value Change On Long Term Liabilities	(24,000)
Goodwill Amortization	(12,600)
To Consolidated Retained Earnings	$119,400

Step C - Retained Earnings Distribution Entry

Retained Earnings - Snuff	$215,400	
Non Controlling Interest		$ 96,000
Consolidated Retained Earnings		119,400

Puff Company And Subsidiary
Consolidated Income Statement
For The Year Ending December 31, 2002

Sales ($3,700,000 + $2,000,000 - $475,000)	$5,225,000
Other Revenues ($200,000 + $50,000 - $45,000 - $18,000)	187,000
Total Revenues	$5,412,000
Cost Of Goods Sold ($2,000,000 + $1,100,000 - $475,000	
+ $25,000 - $35,000 + $32,000 - $44,000)	$2,603,000
Depreciation Expense ($600,000 + $400,000 + $6,000 + $10,000)	1,016,000
Other Expenses ($900,000 + $350,000 + $4,200)	1,254,200
Non Controlling Interest [(40%)($200,000 -	
$25,000 + $35,000 - $18,000 - $10,000)]	72,800
Total Expenses	$4,946,000
Consolidated Net Income	$ 466,000

Puff Company And Subsidiary
Consolidated Statement Of Retained Earnings
For The Year Ending December 31, 2002

Opening Balance (See Note)	$2,425,400
Consolidated Net Income	466,000
Available For Distribution	$2,891,400
Dividends Declared (Puff's Only)	150,000
Closing Balance	$2,741,400

Note - The opening consolidated Retained Earnings consists of Puff's opening balance of $2,350,000 ($2,600,000 - $400,000 + $150,000) plus the Step C allocation of $119,400 less the opening unrealized downstream inventory profits of $44,000.

Verification Of Consolidated Net Income

Puff Company's Net Income		$400,000
Intercompany Dividend Revenues		(45,000)
Puff's Net Income Less Dividends		$355,000
Snuff Company's Reported Income	$200,000	
Upstream Adjustments:		
Profits In Ending Inventories	(25,000)	
Profits In Opening Inventories	35,000	
Realized Loss On Equipment	(10,000)	
Upstream Gain on Land Sale	(18,000)	
Adjusted Subsidiary Income	$182,000	
Controlling Percent	60%	109,200
Fair Value Depreciation		(6,000)
Liability Amortization		-0-
Goodwill Amortization		(4,200)
Downstream Adjustments:		
Profits in Ending Inventories		(32,000)
Profits in Opening Inventories		44,000
Consolidated Net Income		$466,000

Verification Of Consolidated Retained Earnings

Puff's Closing Balance		$2,600,000
Snuff's Closing Balance	$480,000	
Balance At Acquisition	(100,000)	
Balance Since Acquisition	$380,000	
Upstream Adjustments:		
Profits in Ending Inventories	(25,000)	
Unrealized Loss on Equipment	10,000	
Unrealized Gain on Land Sale	(18,000)	
Realized Balance Since Acquisition	$347,000	
Controlling Percent	60%	208,200
Adjustments:		
Inventories		30,000
Plant (4 Years At $6,000)		(24,000)
Long Term Liabilities (Matured)		(24,000)
Goodwill (4 Years At $4,200)		(16,800)
Downstream Closing Inventory Profits		(32,000)
Consolidated Retained Earnings As At December 31, 2002		$2,741,400

Puff Company And Subsidiary
Consolidated Balance Sheet
As At December 31, 2002

Cash ($80,000 + $75,000)	$ 155,000
Accounts Receivable ($500,000 + $325,000 - $45,000 - $33,000)	747,000
Inventories ($1,375,000 + $750,000 - $30,000 + $30,000 - $25,000 - $32,000)	2,068,000
Investment In Snuff ($720,000 - $720,000)	-0-
Plant And Equipment (Net) ($2,325,000 + $1,100,000 + $60,000 - $24,000 + $10,000 - $18,000)	3,453,000
Goodwill ($126,000 - $16,800)	109,200
Total Assets	$6,532,200
Current Liabilities ($400,000 + $220,000 - $45,000 - $33,000)	$ 542,000
Long Term Liabilities ($1,000,000 + $750,000 - $24,000 + $24,000)	1,750,000
Non Controlling Interest [(40%)($1,280,000 - $25,000 + $10,000 - $18,000)]	498,800
Common Stock (Puff's Only)	1,000,000
Retained Earnings (See Statement)	2,741,400
Total Equities	$6,532,200

Verification Of The Non Controlling Interest In Consolidated Net Assets

At Acquisition (Step A)	$360,000
Dividends Declared By Snuff (Step B)	(30,000)
Retained Earnings Distribution (Step C)	96,000
From Consolidated Net Income	72,800
Non Controlling Interest As At December 31, 2002	$498,800

Problems For Self Study

(The solutions for these problems can be found following Chapter 17 of the text.)

SELF STUDY PROBLEM SIX - 1

Note - This is the same basic problem as *SELF STUDY PROBLEM FIVE - 1*, except that unrealized intercompany profits have been added.

On December 31, 1993, the Pastel Company purchased 90 percent of the outstanding voting shares of the Shade Company for $5,175,000 in cash. On that date, the Shade Company had No Par Common Stock of $2,000,000 and Retained Earnings of $4,000,000. All of the Shade Company's identifiable assets and liabilities had carrying values that were equal to their fair values except for:

1. Equipment which had fair values that were $1,000,000 less than their carrying values and a remaining useful life of 10 years.

2. Land which had a fair value that was $100,000 greater than its carrying value.

3. Accounts Receivable with fair values that were $50,000 less than their carrying values.

4. Long Term Liabilities which had fair values that were $200,000 less than their carrying values and mature on December 31, 1998.

The Balance Sheets of the Pastel Company and the Shade Company as at December 31, 1998 were as follows:

	Pastel	Shade
Cash and Current Receivables	$ 2,625,000	$ 800,000
Inventories	8,000,000	2,000,000
Equipment (Net)	24,000,000	4,000,000
Buildings (Net)	10,000,000	2,000,000
Investment in Shade (Cost)	5,175,000	-0-
Land	2,000,000	1,200,000
Total Assets	$51,800,000	$10,000,000
Dividends Payable	$ -0-	$ 100,000
Current Liabilities	1,800,000	900,000
Long Term Liabilities	10,000,000	1,000,000
No Par Common Stock	20,000,000	2,000,000
Retained Earnings	20,000,000	6,000,000
Total Equities	$51,800,000	$10,000,000

The Income Statements of the Pastel and Shade Companies for the year ending December 31, 1998 were as follows:

	Pastel	Shade
Sales	$8,000,000	$2,000,000
Gain on Sale of Land	500,000	-0-
Other Revenues	800,000	100,000
Total Revenues	$9,300,000	$2,100,000
Cost of Goods Sold	$3,800,000	$ 800,000
Depreciation Expense	1,400,000	300,000
Other Expenses	2,000,000	400,000
Total Expenses	$7,200,000	$1,500,000
Net Income	$2,100,000	$ 600,000

Other Information:

1. Any goodwill arising from the business combination should be amortized over 30 years.

2. Both Companies use the straight line method to calculate all depreciation and amortization charges and the First-In, First-Out inventory flow assumption.

3. Pastel uses the cost method to carry its Investment in Shade.

4. The Sales account in the Pastel Company's Income Statement includes only sales of merchandise. All other income is accounted for in Other Revenues.

5. During 1998, Pastel charged Shade $100,000 for management fees. None of this amount has been paid during 1998.

6. During 1998, dividends of $200,000 were declared and paid by Pastel and dividends of $100,000 were declared by Shade. On December 31, 1997, the dividends that were declared by the Shade Company had not yet been paid.

7. During 1997, Shade sold to Pastel $500,000 worth of merchandise of which 75 percent had been resold by Pastel in 1998. Pastel owes Shade $75,000 on December 31, 1998 due to these purchases. The December 31, 1997 Inventories of Pastel contained $300,000 of merchandise purchased from Shade in 1997. The Shade Company's sales are priced to provide it with a 60 percent gross margin on its sales price.

8. During 1997, Pastel sold $300,000 of merchandise to the Shade Company and earned a total gross profit of $120,000 on these sales. On December 31, 1997, $150,000 of this merchandise is still in the inventories of Shade. During 1998, Pastel sold merchandise which had cost it $60,000 to Shade for $150,000. None of this merchandise was resold in 1998. Shade has not paid for these 1998 purchases as at December 31, 1998.

9. On January 1, 1995, Shade sold a piece of equipment that it had purchased on January 1, 1992 for $180,000 to Pastel for $120,000. On January 1, 1992, the machine had an estimated useful life of 18 years with no net salvage value and there is no change in these estimates at the time of the sale to Pastel.

10. On December 30, 1998, Pastel sold to Shade for cash of $1,500,000, a Building with a net book value of $800,000 and the Land it was situated on which had originally cost $200,000. Shade allocated $1,100,000 of the purchase price to the Building and the

remainder to the Land. The Building has an estimated remaining useful life of 25 years on this date. The gain on this sale is disclosed separately for reporting purposes on Pastel's books.

Required:

A. Prepare the consolidated Income Statement for the year ending December 31, 1998 of the Pastel Company and its subsidiary, the Shade Company.

B. Prepare the consolidated Statement of Retained Earnings for the year ending December 31, 1998, of the Pastel Company and its subsidiary, the Shade Company.

C. Prepare the consolidated Balance Sheet as at December 31, 1998 of the Pastel Company and its subsidiary, the Shade Company.

SELF STUDY PROBLEM SIX - 2

On December 31, 1993, the Plate Company purchased 80 percent of the outstanding shares of the Stone Company for $7,800,000 in cash. On this date, the identifiable assets and liabilities of the Stone Company had carrying values and fair values as follows:

	Carrying Values	Fair Values
Cash	$ 500,000	$ 500,000
Accounts Receivable	1,500,000	1,500,000
Inventories	3,000,000	4,000,000
Land	1,500,000	1,000,000
Plant and Equipment	9,000,000	8,000,000
Accumulated Depreciation	(3,000,000)	-0-
Loss Carry Forward Benefit	-0-	500,000
Total Assets	$12,500,000	

	Carrying Values	Fair Values
Current Liabilities	$ 1,000,000	$ 1,000,000
Long Term Liabilities	4,500,000	6,000,000
Common Stock - No Par	3,000,000	
Unrestricted Retained Earnings	3,000,000	
Reserve for Contingencies	1,000,000	
Total Equities	$12,500,000	

On December 31, 1993, the Plant and Equipment of the Stone Company had a remaining useful life of 20 years. The December 31, 1993 Inventories of Stone were sold in 1994. On December 31, 1993, the Plate Company could claim that the Stone Company's Loss Carry Forward Benefit was reasonably assured of being realized.

Both Companies use the straight line method to calculate depreciation and amortization.

On December 31, 1998, the adjusted trial balances for the Plate Company and the Stone Company are as follows:

	Plate	Stone
Cash	$ 3,000,000	$ 700,000
Accounts Receivable	7,500,000	2,100,000
Inventories	14,300,000	5,600,000
Land	9,000,000	2,500,000
Plant and Equipment	26,400,000	12,000,000
Patents	1,400,000	-0-
Investment in Stone (At Cost)	7,800,000	-0-
Cost of Goods Sold	6,400,000	3,400,000
Other Expenses	3,800,000	1,600,000
Dividends Declared	2,000,000	1,000,000
Total Debits	$81,600,000	$28,900,000
Accumulated Depreciation	$10,600,000	$ 6,500,000
Current Liabilities	8,500,000	1,200,000
Long Term Liabilities	15,000,000	4,500,000
Common Stock - No Par	20,000,000	3,000,000
Unrestricted Retained Earnings	11,000,000	6,200,000
Reserve for Contingencies	-0-	500,000
Total Revenues	16,500,000	7,000,000
Total Credits	$81,600,000	$28,900,000

Other Information:

1. There have been no additions or disposals of Plant and Equipment by the Stone Company between December 31, 1993 and December 31, 1998. The land on the books of the Stone Company on December 31, 1993 has not been sold.

2. Any goodwill arising from the business combination will be amortized over 40 years.

3. All of the Long Term Liabilities of the Stone Company mature on December 31, 2003.

4. On January 1, 1995, the Stone Company purchased a Patent for $1,100,000. On that date, the remaining legal life of the Patent was 11 years. On January 1, 1996 the Patent had a carrying value on the Stone Company's books of $1,000,000. At this time the Patent was sold to the Plate Company for $2,000,000.

5. During 1998, the Plate Company sold Land to the Stone Company for $1,000,000. The carrying value of the Land on the books of the Plate Company was $500,000.

6. During 1998, $2,000,000 of the Stone Company's Sales were made to the Plate Company. A total of $500,000 of this merchandise remains in the December 31, 1998 Inventories of the Plate Company. The December 31, 1997 Inventories of the Plate Company contained merchandise purchased from the Stone Company for $800,000. All intercompany sales are priced to provide the selling Company with a gross profit margin on sales price of 30 percent.

Required:

A. Prepare a consolidated Income Statement for the Plate Company and its subsidiary the Stone Company for the year ending December 31, 1998.

B. Prepare a consolidated Statement of Retained Earnings for the Plate Company and its subsidiary the Stone Company for the year ending December 31, 1998.

C. Prepare a consolidated Balance Sheet for the Plate Company and its subsidiary the Stone Company as at December 31, 1998.

SELF STUDY PROBLEM SIX - 3

On January 1, 1997, the Prime Company acquired 60 percent of the outstanding voting shares of the Sublime Company for $3 million in cash. On this date, the Sublime Company had No Par Common Stock of $3 million and Retained Earnings of $2 million. All of Sublime's identifiable assets and liabilities had fair values that were equal to their carrying values except for the Accounts Receivable which had a total net realizable value that was $100,000 less than its stated value and a piece of equipment with a fair value that was $400,000 less than its carrying value and a remaining useful life of 3 years.

Both Companies use the straight line method to calculate all depreciation and amortization expenses. Any goodwill arising from the business combination is to be amortized over 30 years. Prime carries its investment in Sublime by the cost method.

On December 31, 1998, the Balance Sheets of the Prime Company and its subsidiary, the Sublime Company are as follows:

Balance Sheets
As At December 31, 1998

	Prime	Sublime
Cash and Current Receivables	$ 1,600,000	$ 1,000,000
Inventories	2,400,000	1,500,000
Investment in Sublime (At Cost)	3,000,000	-0-
Long Term Receivables	1,500,000	-0-
Plant and Equipment (Net)	14,000,000	8,500,000
Land	5,000,000	2,000,000
Total Assets	**$27,500,000**	**$13,000,000**
Current Liabilities	$ 4,500,000	$ 2,000,000
Long Term Liabilities	5,000,000	3,000,000
No Par Common Stock	6,000,000	3,000,000
Retained Earnings	12,000,000	5,000,000
Total Equities	**$27,500,000**	**$13,000,000**

Other Information:

1. The Prime Company sold merchandise to the Sublime Company in 1997 of which $300,000 remained in the December 31, 1997 Inventories of Sublime. This merchandise was sold in 1998 and Prime made no further sales of inventories to Sublime in 1998. Prime's sales are priced to provide it with a 40 percent gross margin on cost.

2. Sublime's Sales in 1998 included $500,000 in sales to Prime. Of these sales, $200,000 remain in the December 31, 1998 Inventories of Prime. Prime's January 1, 1998 inventories contained $400,000 of merchandise purchased from Sublime of which $300,000 was purchased in 1997 and sold in 1998. The remaining $100,000 was specialized merchandise purchased in 1996, prior to the business combination and $50,000 of this specialized merchandise remains in Prime's December 31, 1998 Inventories. Sublime's sales are priced to provide it with a 25 percent gross margin on cost.

3. On July 1, 1998, the Sublime Company sold a machine it had built for a cost of $200,000 to the Prime Company for $150,000. The machine had an estimated useful life on July 1, 1998 of 5 years. On December 31, 1998, the Prime Company has a liability outstanding of 80 percent of the purchase price and this will be paid in 1999.

4. The Sublime Company purchased Land for $2 million from Prime on November 1, 1997. The land was originally purchased by Prime for $1 million. The purchase price is to be paid in 5 equal installments of $400,000 on January 1 of each year subsequent

to the sale.

5. During 1998, Prime earned Net Income of $2,000,000 and paid dividends of $400,000 and Sublime earned Net Income of $500,000 and paid dividends of $100,000.

Required: Prepare a consolidated Balance Sheet for the Prime Company and its subsidiary, the Sublime Company as at December 31, 1998.

SELF STUDY PROBLEM SIX - 4

On December 31, 1990, the Rosebud Company purchased 20 percent of the outstanding voting shares of the Ginko Company for $600,000 in cash. On that date, the Ginko Company's Balance Sheet and the fair values of its identifiable assets and liabilities were as follows:

	Carrying Values	Fair Values
Cash And Current Receivables	$ 300,000	$ 300,000
Inventories	1,000,000	800,000
Plant And Equipment (Net)	2,000,000	2,400,000
Total Assets	$3,300,000	
Current Liabilities	$ 200,000	$ 200,000
Long Term Liabilities	600,000	600,000
Common Stock - No Par	1,000,000	
Retained Earnings	1,500,000	
Total Equities	$3,300,000	

On this date, the remaining useful life of the Ginko Company's Plant And Equipment is estimated to be 10 years. The Rosebud Company amortizes all Goodwill over 20 years.

On December 31, 1993, the Rosebud Company purchased an additional 55 percent of the outstanding voting shares of the Ginko Company for $1,705,000 in cash. This increases its total percentage of ownership to 75 percent. On that date, the Ginko Company's Balance Sheet and the fair values of its identifiable assets and liabilities were as follows:

	Carrying Values	Fair Values
Cash And Current Receivables	$ 500,000	$ 500,000
Inventories	1,375,000	1,375,000
Land	425,000	475,000
Plant And Equipment (Net)	1,400,000	1,600,000
Total Assets	$3,700,000	
Current Liabilities	$ 300,000	$ 300,000
Long Term Liabilities	600,000	700,000
Common Stock - No Par	1,000,000	
Retained Earnings	1,800,000	
Total Equities	$3,700,000	

There has been no purchase or sale of Plant And Equipment by the Ginko Company during the years 1991 through 1993. The Long Term Liabilities mature on December 31, 2013. The Rosebud Company accounts for its Investment In Ginko by the cost method.

The Income Statements and Statements of Retained Earnings of the Rosebud and Ginko Companies for the year ending December 31, 1998, and their Balance Sheets as at December 31, 1998 were as follows:

Balance Sheets
As At December 31, 1998

	Rosebud	Ginko
Cash And Current Receivables	$ 500,000	$ 600,000
Inventories	600,000	1,200,000
Investment In Ginko	2,305,000	-0-
Land	795,000	500,000
Plant And Equipment (Net)	2,900,000	2,200,000
Total Assets	$7,100,000	$4,500,000
Current Liabilities	$ 500,000	$ 400,000
Long Term Liabilities	1,000,000	600,000
Common Stock - No Par	2,000,000	1,000,000
Retained Earnings	3,600,000	2,500,000
Total Equities	$7,100,000	$4,500,000

Income Statements
For The Year Ending December 31, 1998

	Rosebud	Ginko
Sales Of Merchandise	$5,000,000	$2,000,000
Other Revenues	200,000	100,000
Total Revenues	$5,200,000	$2,100,000
Cost Of Goods Sold	$2,500,000	$ 800,000
Other Expenses and Losses	1,000,000	900,000
Total Expenses and Losses	$3,500,000	$1,700,000
Net Income	$1,700,000	$ 400,000

Statements Of Retained Earnings
For The Year Ending December 31, 1998

	Rosebud	Ginko
Opening Balance	$2,500,000	$2,200,000
Net Income	1,700,000	400,000
Balance Available	$4,200,000	$2,600,000
Dividends Declared	600,000	100,000
Closing Balance	$3,600,000	$2,500,000

Other Information:

1. There has been no sale of Plant And Equipment or Land by the Ginko Company during the years under consideration except for a piece of equipment which was purchased on January 1, 1994 for $300,000. On that date it had an expected useful life of 6 years. The piece of equipment was sold to Rosebud for $100,000 on January 1, 1996.

2. During 1997, Rosebud had sales of $400,000 to Ginko of which $150,000 were not resold by Ginko until 1998. In 1998, of the $550,000 in total sales from Rosebud to Ginko, $220,000 remained in the December 31, 1998 inventories of Ginko. On December 31, 1998, Ginko still owes Rosebud $175,000 for 1998 merchandise purchases. All of Rosebud's sales to Ginko are priced to provide a gross margin on sales prices of 50 percent.

3. In 1997, Ginko had sales of $160,000 to Rosebud of which all but $20,000 was resold by Rosebud during 1997. During 1998, Rosebud purchased $190,000 of merchandise from Ginko of which $45,000 remained in the December 31, 1998 inventories of Rosebud. All of Ginko's sales to Rosebud are priced to provide a gross margin on sales prices of 60 percent.

4. The Rosebud Company and the Ginko Company account for inventories on a first-in, first-out basis. Both Companies use the straight line method to calculate all depreciation and amortization.

5. On December 15, 1998, the Rosebud Company sold a parcel of Land to the Ginko Company for $75,000, payable in two equal installments on December 15, 1998 and January 15, 1999. The Rosebud Company had purchased this parcel of land for $118,000 in 1992.

Required: Prepare a consolidated Income Statement and Statement of Retained Earnings for the year ending December 31, 1998, and a consolidated Balance Sheet as at December 31, 1998 for the Rosebud Company and its subsidiary the Ginko Company.

SELF STUDY PROBLEM SIX - 5

On January 1, 1995, the Pork Company purchased 80 percent of the outstanding voting shares of the Salt Company for $1 million in cash. At the acquisition date, the carrying value of the net assets of Salt was equal to $1 million and all of its identifiable assets and liabilities had fair values that were equal to their carrying values, except for an issue of 10 percent coupon Bonds Payable which had a fair value which was $100,000 less than its carrying value. The bonds mature on January 1, 2005. Any goodwill arising from this transaction is to be amortized over 30 years. Both Companies use the straight line method to calculate depreciation and amortization.

On January 1, 1997, the Salt Company sold a building to the Pork Company for $4,500,000. When Salt purchased the building on January 1, 1992 for $5,500,000 it had an estimated useful life of 20 years. During 1998, Pork paid $100,000 in dividends and no dividends were paid by Salt.

The condensed Income Statements for the two Companies for the year ending December 31, 1998 are as follows:

	Pork	Salt
Sales	$600,000	$400,000
Cost of Goods Sold	$250,000	$300,000
Other Expenses	300,000	150,000
Total Expenses	$550,000	$450,000
Income (Loss) Before Extraordinary Items	$ 50,000	($ 50,000)
Extraordinary Gain (Loss)	100,000	(200,000)
Net Income (Loss)	$150,000	($250,000)

Required:

A. Prepare a consolidated Income Statement for the Pork Company and its subsidiary the Salt Company for the year ending December 31, 1998.

B. Assume that the Pork Company does not classify the Salt Company as a subsidiary. Prepare an Income Statement for the Pork Company for the year ending December 31, 1998 assuming it uses the equity method to account for its investment in the Salt Company.

SELF STUDY PROBLEM SIX - 6

On January 1, 1996, the Plantor Company purchased 75 percent of the outstanding voting shares of the Plantee Company for $850,000 in cash. This amount was $100,000 greater than the Plantor Company's share of the carrying values of the Plantee Company's net assets. The entire $100,000 is allocated to goodwill and will be charged to income over a 20 year period.

No dividends were paid by either Company in 1998. Plantor Company carries its investment in Plantee Company using the cost method. The Income Statements of the two Companies for the year ending December 31, 1998 are as follows:

Income Statements
For The Year Ending December 31, 1998

	Plantor	Plantee
Sales	$500,000	$200,000
Cost of Goods Sold	$300,000	$100,000
Other Expenses	140,000	76,000
Total Expenses	$440,000	$176,000
Income Before Extraordinary Items	$ 60,000	$ 24,000
Extraordinary Gain	-0-	6,000
Net Income	$ 60,000	$ 30,000

Other Information:

1. During 1998, the Plantor Company sold $100,000 in merchandise to the Plantee Company. Of these sales, $15,000 remains in the December 31, 1998 Inventories of the Plantee Company. All intercompany purchases are priced to provide the selling Company with a normal gross profit.

2. During 1998, the Plantee Company sold $50,000 in merchandise to the Plantor Company. Of these sales, $20,000 remains in the December 31, 1998 Inventories of the Plantor Company. There were no intercompany inventory sales prior to 1998.

3. On January 2, 1996, the Plantee Company sold equipment to the Plantor Company for $100,000. On that date the equipment was carried on the Plantee Company's books at $135,000 and had a remaining useful life of 5 years.

4. Both Companies use the straight line method to calculate all depreciation and amortization.

Required:

A. Prepare a consolidated Income Statement for the Plantor Company and its subsidiary the Plantee Company for the year ending December 31, 1998.

B. Assume that the Plantor Company does not classify the Plantee Company as a subsidiary. Prepare the Plantor Company's Income Statement for the year ending December

31, 1998 assuming it uses the equity method to account for its investment in the Plantee Company.

SELF STUDY PROBLEM SIX - 7

On April 1, 1997 Sentinel Resources Ltd. and the Molar Oil Company jointly purchase Numa Inc. The enterprise will be operated as a joint venture and fits the joint venture definition contained in Section 3055 of the *CICA Handbook*. The main objective of Numa Inc. will be to develop oil fields in northern Alberta. Sentinel Resources contributes $450,000 in cash for 45 percent of Numa Inc.'s outstanding voting shares while Molar Oil purchases the remaining 55 percent for $550,000. Other than the joint venture agreement, there is no affiliation of any sort between the two investor Companies.

On April 1, 1997, after the purchase of Numa Inc., the condensed Balance Sheets of the three Companies and the fair values of the identifiable non current assets are as follows:

	Sentinel	Molar	Numa
Net Current Assets	$1,050,000	$ 950,000	$100,000
Investment in Numa	450,000	550,000	-0-
Other Non Current Assets	5,300,000	7,600,000	840,000
Total Assets	$6,800,000	$9,100,000	$940,000
Common Stock - No Par	$4,000,000	$5,000,000	$940,000
Retained Earnings	2,800,000	4,100,000	-0-
Total Equities	$6,800,000	$9,100,000	$940,000
Non Current Assets - Fair Values	$5,700,000	$9,800,000	$900,000

The fair values of the net current assets are equal to their carrying values. In each of the three Companies, the difference between the fair values and carrying values of the non current assets arises from Land.

For the year ending March 31, 1998, the condensed Income Statements, before the recognition of any investment income, and the dividends declared of the three Companies are as follows:

	Sentinel	Molar	Numa
Revenues	$7,800,000	$9,600,000	$660,000
Expenses and Losses	6,400,000	8,500,000	480,000
Net Income	$1,400,000	$1,100,000	$180,000
Dividends Declared	$ 300,000	$ 500,000	$ 40,000

Also during the year ending March 31, 1998, the following transactions occurred between Numa Inc. and its investor companies:

1. On March 1, 1998, Molar Oil purchased crude oil from Numa Inc. for $390,000. The cost allocated to the oil by Numa Inc. is $314,000. All of this oil is being stored by Molar Oil and it will be sold in April, 1998.

2. On March 31, 1998, Sentinel Resources purchased Equipment from Numa Inc. for

$95,000. The Equipment had been carried on the books of Numa Inc. at a net book value of $175,000. The resulting $80,000 loss is included in the Expenses And Losses of Numa.

Both investor Companies will amortize any goodwill arising from the acquisition of Numa Inc. over 20 years.

Required: Assume that both Sentinel Resources and Molar will account for their investments in Numa Inc. using the Recommendations of Section 3055 of the CICA Handbook.

A. Prepare the condensed proportionate consolidation Balance Sheet of Sentinel Resources as at April 1, 1997, after the acquisition of 45 percent of Numa Inc.

B. Prepare the condensed proportionate consolidation Income Statement of Sentinel Resources for the year ending March 31, 1998.

C. Prepare the condensed proportionate consolidation Income Statement of Molar for the year ending March 31, 1998.

Assignment Problems

(The solutions to these problem are only available in
the solutions manual that has been provided to your instructor.)

ASSIGNMENT PROBLEM SIX - 1

Note - This is the same basic problem as *ASSIGNMENT PROBLEM FIVE - 1*, except that unrealized intercompany profits have been added.

On December 31, 1993, the Percy Company purchased 75 percent of the outstanding voting shares of the Stern Company for $3 million in cash. On that date, Stern had Common Stock - No Par of $2 million and Retained Earnings of $1 million. On December 31, 1993 all of the identifiable assets and liabilities of Stern had fair values that were equal to their carrying values with the following exceptions:

1. Inventories with fair values that were $400,000 less than their carrying values.

2. Land with a fair value that was $800,000 greater than its carrying value.

3. Long Term Liabilities, maturing on January 1, 1999, with fair values that were $200,000 less than their carrying values.

Any goodwill arising from this business combination is to be amortized over 30 years. Both Companies use the straight line method to calculate all depreciation and amortization. The land which was on the books of the Stern Company on December 31, 1993 has not been sold as at December 31, 1998. The Percy Company accounts for its investment in Stern Company using the cost method.

Other data for the year ending December 31, 1998 is as follows:

Income Statements
For The Year Ending December 31, 1998

	Percy	Stern
Merchandise Sales	$5,000,000	$2,000,000
Other Revenues	1,000,000	500,000
Total Revenues	$6,000,000	$2,500,000
Cost of Goods Sold	$2,000,000	$1,000,000
Depreciation Expense	400,000	300,000
Other Expenses	600,000	400,000
Total Expenses	$3,000,000	$1,700,000
Net Income	$3,000,000	$ 800,000

Retained Earnings Statements
For The Year Ending December 31, 1998

	Percy	Stern
Opening Balance	$10,000,000	$1,600,000
Net Income	3,000,000	800,000
Balance Available	$13,000,000	$2,400,000
Dividends Declared	1,000,000	400,000
Closing Balance	$12,000,000	$2,000,000

Balance Sheets
as at December 31, 1998

	Percy	Stern
Cash and Current Receivables	$ 1,500,000	$1,200,000
Note Receivable	1,000,000	-0-
Inventories	4,500,000	1,000,000
Investment in Stern (At Cost)	3,000,000	-0-
Plant and Equipment (Net)	9,000,000	3,000,000
Land	2,000,000	800,000
Total Assets	$21,000,000	$6,000,000
Current Liabilities	$ 500,000	$ 200,000
Long Term Liabilities	3,500,000	1,800,000
Common Stock - No Par	5,000,000	2,000,000
Retained Earnings	12,000,000	2,000,000
Total Equities	$21,000,000	$ 6,000,000

Other Information:

1. The Long Term Liabilities of the Stern Company include a $1 million note that is payable to the Percy Company. During 1998, interest expense on this note was $180,000 and on December 31, 1998, $100,000 of this interest had not been paid by Stern. The note is to be paid on December 31, 2001.

2. Stern had sales of $1,500,000 to Percy during 1998 of which $400,000 remained in the December 31, 1998 inventories of Percy. The 1997 sales of $2,000,000 from Stern to Percy left $800,000 of merchandise in the December 31, 1997 inventories of Percy.

3. Stern's purchases for 1998 included $500,000 of merchandise from Percy. Of these purchases 60 percent remained in the December 31, 1998 inventories of Stern. There had been no purchases from Percy remaining in the December 31, 1997 inventories of Stern. All intercompany sales and purchases are priced to provide the selling company with a gross margin of 50 percent of the sales price.

4. On January 1, 1996, Stern sold a machine with a net book value of $250,000 to Percy for $350,000. At that time, the machine had a remaining useful life of 5 years.

5. On September 1, 1998, Percy sold a parcel of land which was purchased in 1994 for $100,000, to Stern for $350,000. The gain on this sale is included in Other Revenues.

Required: Prepare, for the Percy Company and its subsidiary, the Stern Company, the following:

A. The consolidated Income Statement for the year ending December 31, 1998.

B. The consolidated Statement of Retained Earnings for the year ending December 31, 1998.

C. The consolidated Balance Sheet as at December 31, 1998.

ASSIGNMENT PROBLEM SIX - 2

On January 1, 1993, the Brooks Company purchased 60 percent of the outstanding voting shares of the Bolt Company for $12 million in cash. On that date, the Bolt Company had No Par Common Stock of $14 million and Retained Earnings of $10 million. All of the Bolt Company's identifiable assets and liabilities had carrying values that were equal to their fair values except for:

1. Equipment which had fair values that were $3,000,000 less than their carrying values and a remaining useful life of 9 years with no anticipated salvage value.

2. Long Term Liabilities which had fair values that were $2,000,000 greater than their carrying values and mature on December 31, 2000.

The condensed Income Statements of the Brooks and Bolt Companies for the year ending December 31, 1998 were as follows:

	Brooks	Bolt
Total Revenues	$15,000,000	$ 5,000,000
Cost of Goods Sold	$ 8,000,000	$ 2,000,000
Depreciation Expense	1,000,000	400,000
Other Expenses and Losses	2,000,000	600,000
Total Expenses and Losses	$11,000,000	$ 3,000,000
Net Income	$ 4,000,000	$ 2,000,000

Other Information:

1. Any goodwill arising from the business combination should be amortized over 15 years.

2. Both Companies use the straight line method to calculate all depreciation and amortization charges and the First-In, First-Out inventory flow assumption.

3. Brooks uses the cost method to carry its Investment in Bolt.

4. On January 1, 1995, the Bolt Company sold a patent to the Brooks Company for $3 million. The Bolt Company had purchased the patent on January 1, 1990 for $3 million and had been amortizing it over its remaining legal life of 15 years. On January 1, 1995 the remaining legal life is 10 years.

5. Between January 1, 1993 and January 1, 1998, the Bolt Company had earnings of $16 million and paid dividends of $10 million. On January 1, 1998, the Brooks Company has a Retained Earnings balance of $60 million.

6. On January 1, 1998, Brooks sold to Bolt a machine for $30,000. It had originally cost $75,000 and had been depreciated at a rate of $8,750 annually for 3 years prior to the sale. The remaining useful life of the machine on January 1, 1998 was 5 years with an estimated net salvage value of $5,000.

7. During 1998, dividends of $1,500,000 were declared and paid by Brooks and dividends of $1,000,000 were declared by Bolt.

8. During 1998, 40 percent of the Bolt Company's Total Revenues were sales to the Brooks Company. One-half of this merchandise remains in the December 31, 1998 inventories of Brooks. On January 1, 1998, the inventories of Brooks contained purchases from the Bolt Company totalling $500,000. Bolt's sales are priced to provide it with a 55 percent gross margin on its sales price.

Required:

A. Prepare the consolidated Income Statement for the year ending December 31, 1998 of the Brooks Company and its subsidiary, the Bolt Company.

B. Prepare the consolidated Statement of Retained Earnings for the year ending December 31, 1998, of the Brooks Company and its subsidiary, the Bolt Company.

C. Compute the Non Controlling Interest that would be shown on the consolidated Balance Sheet as at December 31, 1998 of the Brooks Company and its subsidiary, the Bolt Company.

ASSIGNMENT PROBLEM SIX - 3

On January 1, 1993, the Paul Company acquired 75 percent of the outstanding voting shares of the Saul Company for $6,000,000 in cash. On this date the Saul Company had No Par Common Stock of $6,200,000 and Retained Earnings of $2,800,000. At this acquisition date, the Saul Company had Plant And Equipment that had a fair value that was $600,000 less than its carrying value, Long Term Liabilities that had a fair value that was $200,000 more than their carrying values and Inventories with a fair value that was less than their carrying values in the amount of $800,000. All of the other identifiable assets and liabilities of the Saul Company had fair values that were equal to their carrying values on the date of acquisition. The remaining useful life of the Plant And Equipment was 12 years with no anticipated salvage value. The Long Term Liabilities were issued at par of $4,000,000 and mature on January 1, 2003. Goodwill is to be amortized over 10 years.

On January 1, 1996, the Saul Company sells a patent to the Paul Company for $900,000. On this date the carrying value of this patent on the books of the Saul Company was $1,000,000 and the remaining useful life was five years. All depreciation and amortization is accounted for on a straight line basis by both companies.

Between January 1, 1993 and January 1, 1998, the Saul Company had Net Income of $2,200,000 and paid dividends of $800,000. On January 1, 1998, the Retained Earnings of the Paul Company were $30,000,000. During 1998, the Paul Company declared and paid dividends of $200,000 and the Saul Company declared and paid dividends of $100,000. The Paul Company carries its Investment in Saul by the cost method.

The condensed Income Statements of the two Companies for the year ending December 31, 1998 are as follows:

	Paul	Saul
Total Revenues	$5,000,000	$2,000,000
Cost Of Goods Sold	$3,000,000	$1,200,000
Other Expenses	1,500,000	600,000
Total Expenses	$4,500,000	$1,800,000
Net Income	$ 500,000	$ 200,000

During 1998, 40 percent of the Saul Company's Revenues resulted from sales to the Paul Company. Half of this merchandise remains in the ending inventories of the Paul Company and has not yet been paid for. The December 31, 1998 inventory balances for the Paul and Saul Companies are $950,000 and $380,000 respectively.

On January 1, 1998, the inventories of the Paul Company contained purchases from the Saul Company of $500,000. All intercompany merchandise transactions are priced to provide Saul with a gross margin on sales prices of 40 percent.

The Saul Company has not issued any additional Common Stock or Long Term Liabilities since the date of its acquisition by the Paul Company. On December 31, 1998, the Paul Company had $15,000,000 in Long Term Liabilities.

Required:

A. Prepare the consolidated Income Statement for the year ending December 31, 1998 for the Paul Company and its subsidiary, the Saul Company, in compliance with the Recommendations of the *CICA Handbook*.

B. Calculate the amounts, showing all computations, that would be included in the consolidated Balance Sheet as at December 31, 1998 of the Paul Company and its subsidiary, the Saul Company for the following accounts:

1. Retained Earnings
2. Non Controlling Interest
3. Inventories
4. Patent
5. Long Term Liabilities

ASSIGNMENT PROBLEM SIX - 4

On December 31, 1994, the Pumpkin Company purchased 75 percent of the outstanding voting shares of the Squash Company for $4,200,000 in cash. On that date, the Squash Company had No Par Common Stock of $3,900,000 and Retained Earnings of $600,000. All of the Squash Company's identifiable assets and liabilities had carrying values that were equal to their fair values except for:

1. Equipment which had a fair value of $270,000 more that its carrying value and a useful life of 20 years when purchased by Squash on December 31, 1989.

2. Land which had a fair value that was $300,000 greater than its carrying value.

3. Inventories with fair values that were $60,000 more than their carrying values.

4. Long Term Liabilities which had fair values that were $90,000 more than their carrying values and mature on December 31, 2000.

The Balance Sheets of the Pumpkin Company and the Squash Company as at December 31, 1998 were as follows:

	Pumpkin	Squash
Cash and Current Receivables	$ 1,620,000	$ 930,000
Inventories	1,800,000	660,000
Long Term Receivables	840,000	300,000
Plant and Equipment (Net)	4,500,000	2,700,000
Investment in Squash (Cost)	4,200,000	-0-
Land	2,400,000	1,200,000
Total Assets	$15,360,000	$5,790,000
Current Liabilities	$ 480,000	$ 240,000
Long Term Liabilities	660,000	390,000
No Par Common Stock	10,200,000	3,900,000
Retained Earnings	4,020,000	1,260,000
Total Equities	$15,360,000	$5,790,000

The Income Statements of the Pumpkin and Squash Companies for the year ending December 31, 1998 were as follows:

	Pumpkin	Squash
Sales	$5,610,000	$1,770,000
Interest Revenue	84,000	30,000
Other Revenues	90,000	-0-
Total Revenues	$5,784,000	$1,800,000
Cost of Goods Sold	$3,900,000	$1,260,000
Interest Expense	66,000	45,000
Other Expenses	690,000	240,000
Total Expenses	$4,656,000	$1,545,000
Net Income	$1,128,000	$ 255,000

Other Information:

1. Any goodwill arising from the business combination should be amortized over 20 years.

2. Both Companies use the straight line method to calculate all depreciation and amortization charges and the First-In, First-Out inventory flow assumption.

3. Pumpkin uses the cost method to carry its Investment in Squash.

4. During 1998, dividends of $360,000 were declared and paid by Pumpkin and dividends of $120,000 were declared and paid by Squash.

5. The Pumpkin Company manufactures machines with a five year life. Its Sales total in the Income Statement includes only sales of these machines. Intercompany sales of these machines are priced to provide Pumpkin with a 20% gross profit on sales prices in all the years under consideration. On December 31, 1996, Pumpkin sold machines it had manufactured to Squash for $150,000. Squash uses the machines in its production process. On January 1, 1998, Pumpkin sold an additional $300,000 of these machines to the Squash Company. There were no other intercompany sales of these machines in any of the years under consideration.

6. The Squash Company manufactures paper products used in offices. During 1997, Squash sold to Pumpkin $18,000 worth of office supplies of which all but $3,000 were used by Pumpkin in 1997. During 1998, Pumpkin purchased $15,000 worth of merchandise from Squash. During 1998, the Pumpkin Company used $9,000 worth of the paper products purchased from Squash. Squash's intercompany sales are priced to provide it with a 50 percent gross margin on its sales price.

7. On January 1, 1996, Squash sold a piece of equipment to Pumpkin that it had purchased on January 1, 1991. On January 1, 1991, the machine had an estimated useful life of 13 years with no net salvage value and there is no change in this estimate at the time of the sale to Pumpkin. Pumpkin paid 20 percent more than the $300,000 carrying value of the equipment on Squash's books on January 1, 1996.

8. During 1997, Squash sold land that had a carrying value of $240,000 to Pumpkin for a profit of $30,000. One half of the proceeds was paid at that date and the remainder is due on July 1, 1999. The Land that had the fair value increase on December 31, 1994 is still on the books of Squash.

9. On December 31, 1998, Squash had current receivables of $6,000 from Pumpkin and Pumpkin is owed $18,000 by Squash. Intercompany interest which was paid during 1998 on outstanding intercompany payables totalled $1,000 for Squash and $1,400 for Pumpkin.

Required:

A. Prepare the consolidated Income Statement for the year ending December 31, 1998 of the Pumpkin Company and its subsidiary, the Squash Company.

B. Prepare the consolidated Statement of Retained Earnings for the year ending December 31, 1998, of the Pumpkin Company and its subsidiary, the Squash Company.

C. Prepare the consolidated Balance Sheet as at December 31, 1998 of the Pumpkin Company and its subsidiary, the Squash Company.

ASSIGNMENT PROBLEM SIX - 5

On December 31, 1995, the Plain Company acquired 25 percent of the outstanding voting shares of the Steppe Company for $1,250,000. On December 31, 1997, the Plain Company acquired an additional 40 percent of the outstanding voting shares of the Steppe Company for $1,680,000. The fair values of the identifiable assets and liabilities of the Steppe Company were equal to their carrying values except for Current Assets and Long Term Liabilities. The condensed Balance Sheets and the fair values of the Steppe Company on the acquisition dates were as follows:

Balance Sheets
As At December 31

	1997	1995
Current Assets	$ 800,000	$1,200,000
Plant and Equipment (Net)	5,400,000	5,300,000
Total Assets	$6,200,000	$6,500,000
Current Liabilities	$ 300,000	$ 500,000
Long Term Liabilities	2,000,000	2,000,000
Common Stock - No Par	3,000,000	3,000,000
Retained Earnings	900,000	1,000,000
Total Equities	$6,200,000	$6,500,000

Fair Values

	1997	1995
Current Assets	$ 600,000	$ 800,000
Long Term Liabilities	$1,700,000	$1,800,000

The Long Term Liabilities were issued on December 31, 1985 and mature on December 31, 2005. Any goodwill that arises from a business combination is amortized by the Plain Company over 20 years. The Plain Company carries its investment in the Steppe Company by the cost method. Both Companies use the straight line method to calculate all depreciation and amortization.

The condensed Balance Sheets of the Plain Company and the Steppe Company as at December 31, 1998 are as follows:

Balance Sheets
As At December 31, 1998

	Plain	Steppe
Current Assets	$ 2,070,000	$1,400,000
Investment in Steppe	2,930,000	-0-
Plant and Equipment (Net)	9,000,000	6,200,000
Total Assets	**$14,000,000**	**$7,600,000**
Current Liabilities	$ 1,000,000	$ 600,000
Long Term Liabilities	5,000,000	2,000,000
Common Stock - No Par	3,000,000	3,000,000
Retained Earnings	5,000,000	2,000,000
Total Equities	**$14,000,000**	**$7,600,000**

During 1998, the Steppe Company declared and paid $100,000 in dividends and the Plain Company declared $150,000 in dividends which were not paid until January, 1999.

The Steppe Company sold $300,000 of merchandise to the Plain Company during 1998. Of these sales, merchandise which contained a $50,000 gross profit for the Steppe Company remained in the December 31, 1998 inventories of the Plain Company. Merchandise containing a gross profit of $75,000 for the Steppe Company had been included in the December 31, 1997 inventories of the Plain Company. There were no intercompany inventory sales prior to 1997.

Required: Prepare a consolidated Balance Sheet for the Plain Company and its subsidiary, the Steppe Company as at December 31, 1998.

ASSIGNMENT PROBLEM SIX - 6

On January 1, 1998, the Miller Company purchased 75 percent of the outstanding voting shares of the Hughes Company for $950,000 in cash. This amount was $200,000 greater than the Miller Company's share of the carrying values of the Hughes Company's net assets. The entire $200,000 is allocated to goodwill and will be charged to income over 10 years.

No dividends were paid by either Company in 1998. Miller Company carries its investment in Hughes Company using the cost method. Both Companies use the straight line method to calculate all depreciation and amortization. The condensed Income Statements of the two Companies for the year ending December 31, 1998 are as follows:

Income Statements
For The Year Ending December 31, 1998

	Miller	Hughes
Sales	$1,000,000	$500,000
Cost of Goods Sold	$ 600,000	$350,000
Other Expenses	200,000	50,000
Total Expenses	**$ 800,000**	**$400,000**
Net Income	**$ 200,000**	**$100,000**

Other Information

1. During 1998, the Miller Company sold $200,000 in merchandise to the Hughes Company. Of these sales, $100,000 remains in the December 31, 1998 Inventories of the

Hughes Company. The intercompany sales of Miller are priced to provide it with a 40 percent gross profit.

2. During 1998, the Hughes Company had sales of $150,000 to the Miller Company. Of these sales, one-half remains in the December 31, 1998 Inventories of the Miller Company. There were no intercompany inventory sales prior to 1998. The intercompany sales of Hughes are priced to provide it with a 30 percent gross profit.

Required: Prepare the Income Statement for the year ending December 31, 1998 for the Miller Company assuming:

A. the Miller Company prepares consolidated financial statements.

B. the Miller Company does not classify the Hughes Company as a subsidiary and uses the equity method of accounting for its Investment in Hughes.

ASSIGNMENT PROBLEM SIX - 7

On January 1, 1994, the Pompano Company acquires 85 percent of the outstanding voting shares of the Snapper Company in return for a cash payment of $2,125,000. On this date all of the Snapper Company's assets and liabilities had fair values that were equal to their carrying values except for the following:

- Inventories with a carrying value of $672,000 had a fair value of $742,000.

- Plant And Equipment with a net book value of $883,000 had a fair value of $723,000. The estimated remaining useful life of this equipment is 15 years with no anticipated salvage value.

The total carrying value of the Snapper Company's net identifiable assets on January 1, 1994 was $2,370,000. Any goodwill arising from this business combination is to be amortized over 20 years. Both the Pompano Company and the Snapper Company use the straight line method to calculate depreciation and amortization charges.

The Pompano Company carries its investment in the Snapper Company by the cost method and, on this basis, the Income Statements of the Pompano Company and the Snapper Company for the year ending December 31, 1998 are as follows:

	Pompano	Snapper
Sales Revenue	$565,000	$286,000
Investment Income	53,000	-0-
Other Revenue	27,000	36,000
Total Revenues	$645,000	$322,000
Cost Of Goods Sold	$297,000	$134,000
Depreciation Expense	94,000	62,000
Other Expenses	217,000	86,000
Total Expenses	$608,000	$282,000
Income Before Extraordinary Items	$ 37,000	$ 40,000
Extraordinary Gain	-0-	120,000
Net Income	$ 37,000	$160,000

Other Information:

1. On October 1, 1998, the Pompano Company loaned the Snapper Company $45,000 at a rate of 13 percent per annum. Interest is to be paid each year on October 1.

2. During 1998, the Snapper Company declared dividends of $40,000 while the Pompano Company declared dividends of $10,000. All of Snapper's dividends were paid

during the year while only one half of those declared by Pompano were paid.

3. During 1998, the Snapper Company had sales of merchandise in the amount of $78,000 to the Pompano Company of which $32,000 remains in the December 31, 1998 inventories of the Pompano Company. Also during 1998, the Pompano Company sold merchandise to Snapper Company in the amount of $53,000 of which $18,000 remains in the December 31, 1998 inventories of the Snapper Company. There were no intercompany merchandise sales during 1997 and all of the 1998 sales were priced to provide the selling company with a gross profit of 45 percent on sales prices. Both Companies use a First-In, First-Out inventory cost flow assumption.

4. During 1998, the Pompano Company paid the Snapper Company $15,000 for engineering fees.

5. On January 1, 1997, the Snapper Company sold equipment to the Pompano Company for $126,000. This equipment had cost the Snapper Company $200,000 on January 1, 1995 and was being depreciated on Snapper's books over a total expected life of 10 years with no anticipated salvage value.

Required:

A. Prepare the consolidated Income Statement for the Pompano Company and its subsidiary the Snapper Company for the year ending December 31, 1998.

B. Assume that the Pompano Company does not classify the Snapper Company as a subsidiary and uses the equity method to account for its Investment in Snapper. Provide a detailed calculation of the ordinary and extraordinary investment income that would be shown in the Income Statement of the Pompano Company in place of the current figure of $53,000.

ASSIGNMENT PROBLEM SIX - 8

The single entity and consolidated Balance Sheets and Income Statements for the Pomp Company and its subsidiary, the Sircumstance Company for the year ending December 31, 1998, are as follows:

Balance Sheets
As At December 31, 1998

	Pomp	Sircumstance	Consolidated
Cash	$ 20,000	$ 15,000	$ 35,000
Accounts Receivable	400,000	250,000	520,000
Inventories	380,000	335,000	635,000
Investment in Sircumstance	1,500,000	-0-	-0-
Land	800,000	1,200,000	2,100,000
Plant and Equipment (Net)	3,000,000	2,300,000	5,500,000
Goodwill	-0-	-0-	150,000
Total Assets	$6,100,000	$4,100,000	$8,940,000
Current Liabilities	$ 200,000	$ 100,000	$ 190,000
Dividends Payable	50,000	25,000	55,000
Bonds Payable	2,000,000	1,475,000	3,475,000
Non Controlling Interest	-0-	-0-	524,000
Common Stock (No Par)	3,000,000	1,000,000	3,000,000
Retained Earnings	850,000	1,500,000	1,696,000
Total Equities	$6,100,000	$4,100,000	$8,940,000

Income Statements
For The Year Ending December 31, 1998

	Pomp	Sircumstance	Consolidated
Sales	$3,200,000	$2,500,000	$5,400,000
Cost of Goods Sold	(2,000,000)	(1,000,000)	(2,720,000)
Other Expenses	(800,000)	(1,400,000)	(2,310,000)
Investment Income	40,000	-0-	-0-
Non Controlling Interest	-0-	-0-	4,000
Net Income	$ 440,000	$ 100,000	$ 374,000
Dividends Declared	(200,000)	(50,000)	(200,000)
Increase in Retained Earnings	$ 240,000	$ 50,000	$ 174,000

Other Information: Pomp Company acquired its investment in the Common Stock of the Sircumstance Company on January 1, 1994. At that time, all of the identifiable assets and liabilities of the Sircumstance Company had fair values that were equal to their carrying values except for Land which had a fair value that was $125,000 in excess of its carrying value. The Land is still on the books of the Sircumstance Company on December 31, 1998. The Goodwill that was created in this business combination is being amortized over a period of 20 years. Both Companies calculate depreciation and amortization using the straight line method.

The Sircumstance Company regularly sells merchandise to the Pomp Company and, after further processing, the merchandise is resold by the Pomp Company. On January 1, 1996, the Sircumstance Company sold Equipment to the Pomp Company at a loss. At the time, the remaining useful life of this Equipment was five years. Since the Pomp Company acquired its investment in the Sircumstance Company, there has been no change in the number of Sircumstance Company common shares outstanding.

Required: On the basis of the information you can develop from an analysis of the preceding individual and consolidated financial statements, provide answers to the following questions:

A. What percentage of the outstanding common shares of the Sircumstance Company were purchased by the Pomp Company on January 1, 1994?

B. Does the Pomp Company carry its investment in the Common Stock of the Sircumstance Company by the cost method or the equity method? Explain the basis for your conclusion.

C. Assume that $1,500,000 was the cost of the Pomp Company's investment in the Common Stock of the Sircumstance Company. What was the balance in the Retained Earnings account of the Sircumstance Company on January 1, 1994?

D. What is the amount of intercompany inventory sales that the Sircumstance Company made to the Pomp Company during 1998?

E. What is the explanation for the difference between the consolidated Cost of Goods Sold and the combined Cost of Goods Sold of the two affiliated companies?

F. On January 1, 1996, what was the amount of unrealized loss on the intercompany sale of Plant by Sircumstance Company to the Pomp Company?

G. Prepare a schedule of intercompany debts and, if possible, indicate which company is the creditor and which is the debtor.

H. Show how the $4,000 Non Controlling Interest in consolidated Net Income was determined.

I. Show how the Non Controlling Interest of $524,000 in the consolidated Balance

Sheet was determined.

J. Prepare a schedule in which you derive the $1,696,000 balance in consolidated Retained Earnings on December 31, 1998.

K. Prepare a schedule in which you derive the $374,000 in consolidated Net Income for the year ending December 31, 1998.

ASSIGNMENT PROBLEM SIX - 9

On January 1, 1998, the Daunton Company, Etna Company, and Lerner Company establish DEL Ltd. The three Companies sign an agreement which specifies that in all areas essential to the operation of DEL Ltd., decisions must be made by and require the consent of each of the three Companies. Other than this agreement, there is no affiliation of any sort between the three investor Companies. The new Company is organized to do pharmaceutical research, with emphasis on a cure for the common cold. The Daunton Company and the Etna Company each hold 40 percent of DEL Ltd's outstanding voting shares while the Lerner Company holds the remaining 20 percent.

During the year ending December 31, 1998, DEL Ltd. had Net Income of $475,000 and declared dividends of $75,000. On November 1, 1998, the Daunton Company purchased excess laboratory chemicals from DEL Ltd. for $16,000. They had been purchased by DEL Ltd. for $52,000 and had a limited shelf life. On December 31, 1998, the Etna Company purchased a patented process from DEL Ltd. for $183,000. The cost allocated to this process by DEL Ltd. was $100,000.

On December 31, 1998, the Joffry Company, which has no affiliation with the original investors, purchases all of the outstanding voting shares of DEL Ltd. held by the Daunton Company and the Etna Company. On that date the condensed Balance Sheets of the Joffry Company and DEL Ltd. and the fair values of DEL Ltd.'s assets and liabilities are as follows:

	Joffry Book Value	DEL Ltd. Book Value	DEL Ltd. Fair Value
Current Assets	$ 780,000	$ 300,000	$320,000
Noncurrent Assets	1,500,000	700,000	$650,000
Investment In DEL (At Cost)	720,000	-0-	
Total Assets	$3,000,000	$1,000,000	
Liabilities	$ 500,000	$ 200,000	$160,000
Common Stock (No Par)	1,000,000	400,000	
Retained Earnings	1,500,000	400,000	
Total Equities	$3,000,000	$1,000,000	

Required:

A. Provide the journal entries related to the Etna Company's income and dividends from its Investment in DEL Ltd. for the year ending December 31, 1998, prior to the sale of DEL Ltd. Etna Company uses the equity method to account for its investment in DEL Ltd. in its single entity records. Your solution should show the calculation of Investment Income and comply with all of the requirements of the *CICA Handbook*.

B. Assume that the Joffry Company signs an agreement which specifies that in all areas essential to the operation of DEL Ltd., decisions must be made by and require the consent of both the Lerner Company and the Joffry Company. Prepare the Balance Sheet for the Joffry Company as at December 31, 1998 assuming the Joffry Company uses proportionate consolidation to account for its Investment in DEL Ltd.

C. Assume that there is no agreement that provides for participation in the affairs or operations of DEL Ltd. by the Lerner Company. Prepare the consolidated Balance Sheet for the Joffry Company and its subsidiary DEL Ltd. as at December 31, 1998, using the parent company conceptual approach to consolidations.

D. Assume that there is no agreement that provides for participation in the affairs or operations of DEL Ltd. by the Lerner Company. Prepare the consolidated Balance Sheet for the Joffry Company and its subsidiary DEL Ltd. as at December 31, 1998, using the entity conceptual approach to consolidations.

ASSIGNMENT PROBLEM SIX - 10

High Venture Ltd. (HVL, hereafter) is a research and development company with 1,000,000 outstanding voting shares that are held by three sponsoring corporations. When the Company was formed on January 1, 1998, Alpha Company invested $1,500,000 in cash in return for 300,000 of the HVL shares and Beta Company paid $2,000,000 in cash for 400,000 HVL shares. Chi Company provided an office building and the land on which it is situated in return for the remaining 300,000 HVL shares. The land was on Chi's books at a carrying value of $450,000 while the building was carried at a net book value of $650,000 and has a remaining useful life of ten years. At the time of the transfer, the fair value of the land was $500,000 and the fair value of the building was $1,000,000. Chi recognizes a gain of $400,000 on the transfer of this property to HVL.

Other Information:

1. During the year ending December 31, 1998, HVL reports a Net Income of $250,000. Included in this figure is a gain of $30,000 resulting from the December 31, 1998 sale of unused equipment to Alpha Company. HVL does not declare any dividends during this year.

2. For the year ending December 31, 1998 and without including any investment income related to HVL, Alpha reports a Net Income of $350,000, Beta reports a Net Income of $675,000, and Chi reports a Net Income of $852,000. Alpha's Net Income includes a $20,000 gain resulting from the sale of merchandise to HVL. This merchandise is still in the December 31, 1998 inventories of HVL. Beta's 1998 Net Income includes a $60,000 gain on the sale of land to HVL at the end of 1998.

3. The joint venture agreement which governs the activities of HVL gives joint control of the operation to Alpha and Chi and prohibits Beta from exercising any influence over the affairs of HVL. Other than the joint venture agreement, there is no affiliation of any sort between the three investor companies. The joint venture agreement covers the terms of all intercompany transactions.

Required:

A. Indicate the accounting method that should be used by each of the three investor companies for dealing with their investment in HVL.

B. For each of the three investor Companies, calculate 1998 Net Income, including their appropriate share of the earnings of HVL.

Your answer should comply with the Recommendations of Section 3055 of the *CICA Handbook*.

ASSIGNMENT PROBLEM SIX - 11

On January 1, 1998, Barton Ltd. (BL) and Systems Inc. (SI) establish a new corporation which will market products that both Companies produce. BL has no affiliation with SI other than their common ownership of the new corporation. The new corporation will be called New Venture Inc. (NVI).

BL's capital contribution consists of a Building with a carrying value of $400,000 and a fair value of $1,200,000. The building is situated on leased land. The lease payments are at current fair market value and the lease is transferred to NVI at the time of its incorporation. At January 1, 1998, the remaining term of the lease is 10 years and this is also the remaining economic life of the building. In return for the building, BL receives 45 percent of NVI's voting shares and $300,000 in cash. BL records a gain of $800,000 on the transfer of the building.

SI's capital contribution consists of $1,100,000 in cash. In return, SI receives 55 percent of NVI's voting shares.

BL and SI sign an agreement which provides for joint control over NVI. All significant operating and financing decisions must be approved by both of the investor Companies.

For the year ending December 31, 1998, the single entity Balance Sheets and Income Statements for BL and NVI are as follows:

	BL	NVI
Cash And Receivables	$1,600,000	$ 420,000
Inventories	3,420,000	1,160,000
Investment In NVI (At Cost)	900,000	-0-
Land	620,000	-0-
Building	2,120,000	1,200,000
Accumulated Depreciation	(630,000)	(120,000)
Total Assets	$8,030,000	$2,660,000
Liabilities	$ 470,000	$ 120,000
Common Stock - No Par	4,800,000	2,000,000
Retained Earnings	2,760,000	540,000
Total Equities	$8,030,000	$2,660,000
Sales	$3,500,000	$2,300,000
Gain On Sale Of Building	800,000	-0-
Cost Of Goods Sold	(2,200,000)	(1,490,000)
Depreciation Expense	(220,000)	(120,000)
Other Expenses	(340,000)	(150,000)
Net Income	$1,540,000	$ 540,000

Other Information:

1. During the year ending December 31, 1998, NVI sells merchandise to BL for $250,000. This merchandise had cost NVI $200,000 and none of it has been resold by BL.

2. During the year ending December 31, 1998, BL sells merchandise to NVI for $940,000. This merchandise had cost BL $860,000 and one-half of it has been resold by NVI.

3. Neither BL nor NVI declare or pay dividends during the year ending December 31, 1998.

Required: Using proportionate consolidation procedures, prepare a consolidated Balance Sheet as at December 31, 1998 and a consolidated Income Statement for the year ending December 31, 1998, for BL and its investee NVI. Your solution should comply with the Recommendations of Section 3055 of the *CICA Handbook*.

Chapter 7

Advanced Topics In Consolidations

Introduction

7-1.   In the preceding six Chapters, we have provided detailed coverage of business combinations , long term investments, as well as the more basic aspects of preparing consolidated financial statements. With respect to financial statement coverage, we have illustrated the preparation of the consolidated Balance Sheet, the consolidated Income Statement, and the consolidated Statement Of Retained Earnings. We have also given complete coverage of the procedures required in dealing with fair value changes and their amortization, goodwill and its amortization, and unrealized intercompany profits.

7-2.   A thorough understanding of the material in the first six Chapters will allow you to deal with the great majority of consolidation problems that you will encounter in any of Canada's professional accounting programs and, for many individuals, the coverage found in these Chapters is adequate. There are, however, a large number of other issues and procedures that are related to the preparation of consolidated financial statements. We have relegated this additional issues and procedures to this Chapter on Advanced Topics In Consolidations. For individuals who wish to develop their understanding of consolidated financial statements beyond basic issues, this Chapter provides comprehensive coverage of more advanced issues and procedures. Other individuals, who find their needs in this area satisfied by the material in the first six Chapters, can simply ignore this Chapter.

7-3.   The topics that will be included in this Chapter are as follows:

- Consolidation With The Investment Carried By The Equity Method
- Intercompany Bondholdings
- Multi-Level Affiliations
- Reciprocal Shareholdings
- Subsidiary Preferred Stock
- Transactions Involving Subsidiary Shares
- Consolidated Statement Of Cash Flows

7-4.   As compared to previous editions of this text, there are several changes in this list of "advanced" topics and, as a consequence, some comment is appropriate:

Consolidation With Investment At Equity   In previous Chapters, we have always assumed that the parent company carries its investment in the subsidiary using the cost method. When the investment in a subsidiary is carried by the equity method, a completely different set of procedures must be used. In previous editions of this text, we have had extensive coverage of these alternative procedures. In contrast, in this edition we have confined coverage of these procedures to a single example in this Chapter. We have made this change for two reasons:

1. We believe that requiring students to learn a second set of procedures places far too much emphasis on the procedural aspects of consolidation. As a result, less time is spent in understanding the concepts involved in the preparation of these statements.

2. Through the earlier Chapters, we have encouraged the use of direct definitional calculations to prepare consolidated financial statements. When this approach is used, the format of the problem (e.g., investment at cost vs. investment at equity) is irrelevant. Given this, learning a second full set of procedures in order to deal with investment at equity problems is not an efficient use of your time.

Consolidated Statement Of Cash Flows   In previous editions of this text, the consolidated Statement Of Cash Flows was given coverage in both Chapter 5 and Chapter 6. However, we have found that this material could not be successfully covered without spending a significant amount of time reviewing the preparation of a single entity Statement Of Cash Flows. As we do not believe this to be appropriate in an advanced financial accounting course, we have moved this subject to this Chapter on advanced topics.

Taxes In Consolidated Financial Statements   In previous editions of this text, taxes in consolidated financial statements was included in the coverage of this Chapter. However, Section 3465 of the *CICA Handbook* on income taxes, which was issued in December, 1997, provides extended coverage of taxes related to business combination transactions. As a consequence, we have added a separate Chapter on this subject. This material is now contained in Chapter 17 of this text.

Consolidation With Investment At Equity

Basic Data

7-5.   In order to illustrate the consolidation procedures that must be used when the investment in a subsidiary is carried by the equity method, we will use the same basic example that was used in Chapters 5 and 6. This example involved the Pleigh and Sleigh Companies and the basic data is as follows:

On January 1, 1994, the Pleigh Company purchases 80 percent of the outstanding voting shares of the Sleigh Company for $3,200,000 in cash. On that date the Sleigh Company had No Par Common Stock of $2,000,000 and Retained Earnings of $1,500,000. On December 31, 1998, the adjusted trial balances of the Pleigh Company and its subsidiary, the Sleigh Company are as follows:

	Pleigh	Sleigh
Cash	$ 500,000	$ 300,00
Current Receivables	800,000	400,000
Inventories	2,500,000	1,700,000
Long Term Note Receivable	200,000	-0-
Investment In Sleigh - At Equity	3,541,000	-0-
Land	1,500,000	1,000,000
Plant And Equipment (Net)	4,500,000	1,900,000
Cost Of Goods Sold	2,800,000	1,500,000
Depreciation Expense	200,000	100,000
Other Expenses	364,000	616,000
Interest Expense	240,000	84,000
Dividends Declared	350,000	100,000
Total Debits	**$17,495,000**	**$7,700,000**
Current Liabilities	$ 500,000	$ 200,000
Long Term Liabilities	2,000,000	700,000
No Par Common Stock	8,000,000	2,000,000
Retained Earnings (January 1)	2,814,600	2,300,000
Sales	4,000,000	2,500,000
Interest Revenue	24,000	-0-
Investment Income	156,400	-0-
Total Credits	**$17,495,000**	**$7,700,000**

	Pleigh	Sleigh
1998 Net Income	$ 576,400	$ 200,000
December 31, 1998 Retained Earnings	$ 3,041,000	$2,400,000

Other Information:

A. At the date of Pleigh Company's acquisition of the Sleigh Company's shares, all of the identifiable assets and liabilities of the Sleigh Company had fair values that were equal to their carrying values except Inventories which had fair values that were $100,000 more than their carrying values, Land with a fair value that was $150,000 less than its carrying value and Plant And Equipment which had a fair value that was $250,000 greater than its carrying value. The Plant And Equipment had a remaining useful life on the acquisition date of 20 years while the inventories that were present on the acquisition date were sold during the year ending December 31, 1994. The Land is still on the books of the Sleigh Company on December 31, 1998. Goodwill, if any, is to be amortized over 10 years. Both Companies use the straight line method to calculate depreciation and amortization.

B. Sleigh Company's Sales include sales of $300,000 to Pleigh Company. The December 31, 1998 Inventories of the Pleigh Company contain $100,000 of this merchandise purchased from Sleigh Company during 1998. In addition, the January 1, 1998 Inventories of the Pleigh Company contained $70,000 in merchandise purchased from Sleigh Company during 1997. All intercompany sales are priced to provide the selling company a gross margin on sales price of 40 percent.

C. On December 31, 1998, the Pleigh Company is holding Sleigh Company's long term note payable in the amount of $200,000. Interest at 12 percent is payable on July 1 of each year. Pleigh Company has been holding this note since July 1, 1996.

D. During 1996, the Pleigh Company sold Land to the Sleigh Company for $100,000 in cash. The Land had a carrying value on the books of the Pleigh Company of $75,000.

E. During 1997, the Sleigh Company sold Land to the Pleigh Company for $150,000. This Land had a carrying value on the books of the Sleigh Company of $110,000.

F. On December 31, 1996, the Sleigh Company sold Equipment to the Pleigh Company for $600,000. The Equipment had originally cost the Sleigh Company $800,000 and, at the time of the intercompany sale, had accumulated depreciation of $350,000. On this date, it was estimated that the remaining useful life of the Equipment was three years and no salvage value was anticipated.

Required Prepare a consolidated Income Statement and a consolidated Statement Of Retained Earnings for the year ending December 31, 1998 and a consolidated Balance Sheet as at December 31, 1998 for the Pleigh Company and its subsidiary, the Sleigh Company.

Equity Method Data

Differences From Cost Method

7-6. As compared to the cost method version of this problem, the use of the equity method changed three items in the trial balance of the Pleigh Company. These are the Investment In Sleigh, Investment Income, and the Retained Earnings of Pleigh. The following schedules explain these changes.

Investment In Sleigh

7-7. The Investment In Sleigh account was increased to reflect the Pleigh Company's interest in the unremitted earnings of the Sleigh Company since it was acquired. However, this equity pickup has to be adjusted for fair value write offs, goodwill amortization and both upstream and downstream unrealized intercompany profits. The relevant calculation would be as follows:

Investment Cost		$3,200,000
Equity Pickup:		
Retained Earnings - December 31, 1998	$2,400,000	
Retained Earnings At Acquisition	(1,500,000)	
Retained Earnings Since Acquisition	$ 900,000	
Unrealized Upstream Profits:		
Land	(40,000)	
Closing Inventories	(40,000)	
Equipment	(50,000)	
Adjusted Balance Since Acquisition	$ 770,000	
Controlling Interest Share	80%	616,000
Adjustments:		
Inventories		(80,000)
Plant (5 Years At $10,000)		(50,000)
Goodwill (5 Years At $24,000)		(120,000)
Downstream Profit On Land		(25,000)
Investment In Sleigh		$3,541,000

Retained Earnings Of Pleigh

7-8. Note that Pleigh's opening Retained Earnings balance of $2,814,600 is the same figure that we arrived at for consolidated Retained Earnings as at January 1, 1998 in the cost method version of this problem. As was noted in Chapter 5, this is not an accidental result. Rather, it is a result that will always occur in the application of the equity method as it is described in Section 3050 of the *CICA Handbook*. When the equity method is applied, both investor Net Income and investor Retained Earnings must be equal to the consolidated figures that have resulted from preparing consolidated financial statements with the investor included.

7-9.   The opening Retained Earnings balance of $2,814,600 can be verified with the following calculation:

Pleigh's Opening Retained Earnings Balance		
From Cost Method Version Of The Problem		$2,550,000
Equity Pickup:		
Retained Earnings - January 1, 1998	$2,300,000	
Retained Earnings At Acquisition	(1,500,000)	
Retained Earnings Since Acquisition	$ 800,000	
Unrealized Upstream Profits:		
Land	(40,000)	
Opening Inventories	(28,000)	
Equipment	(100,000)	
Adjusted Balance Since Acquisition	$ 632,000	
Controlling Interest Share	80%	505,600
Adjustments:		
Inventories		(80,000)
Plant (4 Years At $10,000)		(40,000)
Goodwill (4 Years At $24,000)		(96,000)
Downstream Profit On Land		(25,000)
Opening Retained Earnings Of Pleigh		$2,814,600

Investment Income

7-10.   The balance in this account can be calculated as follows:

Sleigh's Reported Net Income	$200,000
Opening Inventory Profits	28,000
Closing Inventory Profits	(40,000)
Realization Of Equipment Profit	50,000
Sleigh's Adjusted Net Income	$238,000
Controlling Percent	80%
Controlling Interest	$190,400
Plant Depreciation	(10,000)
Goodwill Amortization	(24,000)
Investment Income	$156,400

Procedural Approach

7-11.   Except for the fact that the investment is carried by the equity method, this problem is identical to the one previously presented in Chapter 6. However, we will find that this change results in considerable alterations in the specific procedures that are required. We will still be using the basic three Step procedure that was developed in the previous Chapters. However, there will be a number of differences in its detailed application. These differences will be explained as we move through these Steps.

Step A Procedures

Investment Analysis

7-12.   The investment analysis schedule is complicated by the fact that the $3,541,000 balance in the Investment In Sleigh account reflects the Retained Earnings of Sleigh from acquisition to January 1, 1998, and the 1998 Investment Income in excess of intercompany dividends of $76,400 [$156,400 - (80%)($100,000)]. Further, both the equity pickup and the Investment Income have been adjusted for fair value write offs, goodwill amortization, and both upstream and downstream unrealized profits. As a consequence, both the analysis of the Investment In Sleigh and the investment elimination entry will have to reflect all of these factors. Since 100 percent of any downstream unrealized profits are being charged against the investor's proportionate share of other financial data, our usual two column fractional and 100 percent investment analysis schedule cannot be used. The following single column analysis will provide the information that is required:

Investment At Equity		$3,541,000
Book Value - January 1, 1998 [(80%)($4,300,000)]		(3,440,000)
Differential		$ 101,000
Fair Value Change:		
On Inventories		-0-
On Land [(80%)($150,000)]		120,000
On Plant [(80%)($250,000) - $40,000]		(160,000)
Investment Income In Excess Of Dividends		(76,400)
Unrealized Upstream Profits:		
Land	$ 40,000	
Opening Inventories	28,000	
Equipment	100,000	
Unrealized Upstream Profits	$168,000	
Controlling Interest Share	80%	134,400
Downstream Profit On Land [(100%)($25,000)]		25,000
Goodwill		$ 144,000

7-13. The unrealized intercompany profits are added in this schedule since they are like fair value decreases on assets and require a credit in the investment elimination entry.

Investment Elimination

7-14. An additional complication in making the investment elimination entry in this situation is that the Non Controlling Interest will be affected by the presence of unrealized upstream profits. More specifically, the entry will eliminate 100 percent of these profits and the credit to the Non Controlling Interest will be based on 20 percent of the $4,300,000 book value less the $168,000 in unrealized upstream profits. The resulting 20 percent of $4,132,000 would be equal to $826,400. The entry is as follows:

No Par Common Stock	$2,000,000	
Retained Earnings	2,300,000	
Plant And Equipment (Net)	160,000	
Goodwill	144,000	
Investment Income	76,400	
Investment In Sleigh		$3,541,000
Non Controlling Interest		826,400
Land ($120,000 + $40,000 + $25,000)		185,000
Inventories		28,000
Plant And Equipment (Net)		100,000

7-15. In this type of situation, the investment elimination entry accomplishes a great deal. It removes all of the shareholders' equity of the subsidiary, eliminates the entire Investment In Sleigh account, establishes the adjusted beginning of the year balances for all of the fair value changes and goodwill, eliminates all of the beginning of the year unrealized intercompany profits, establishes the adjusted Non Controlling Interest as at the beginning of the current year, and reduces the Investment Income account to the amount of intercompany dividends for the period.

Step B(1) - Intercompany Assets And Liabilities

7-16.   The eliminations required by the presence of intercompany assets and liabilities are not affected by the use of the equity method. As a consequence, the entries will be the same as those used in the cost method version of the problem. The entries would be as follows:

Long Term Liabilities	$200,000	
Long Term Note Receivable		$200,000
Current Liabilities	$ 12,000	
Current Receivables		$ 12,000

Step B(2) - Fair Value And Goodwill Write Offs

7-17.   This limination relates to the depreciation, depletion and amortization of fair value changes and goodwill. Because the equity method records these adjustments in investment income and the investment account, in Step A we recorded the fair value change and goodwill balances net of depreciation and amortization for the period from January 1, 1994 to January 1, 1998. However, as this is an "open trial balance" version of the problem, we will have to record any additional write offs for 1998 in order to correctly state the consolidated expenses.

Inventories

7-19.   The Inventories that were present on January 1, 1994 were sold during that year. The related fair value change was fully reflected in the Investment Income and Investment In Sleigh account during that year. No further adjustment would be required at this point.

Plant And Equipment

7-19.   An adjustment for one year's depreciation on the fair value change will be required here. The amount is $10,000 and it would be recorded as follows:

Depreciation Expense	$10,000	
Plant And Equipment (Net)		$10,000

7-20.   This entry would leave the net Plant And Equipment adjustment at the appropriate year end figure of $150,000 (the $160,000 adjustment in Step A, less $10,000 here).

Goodwill

7-21.   As was the case with the Plant And Equipment, an additional adjustment is needed here in order to correctly state the 1998 consolidated expenses. The amount of the adjustment is $24,000 and it would be recorded as follows:

Goodwill Amortization Expense	$24,000	
Goodwill		$24,000

7-22.   This entry would leave the Goodwill at the appropriate year end figure of $120,000 (the $144,000 addition in Step A, less $24,000 here).

Step B(3) - Intercompany Expenses And Revenues

7-23.   The eliminations required by the presence of intercompany expenses and revenues are not affected by the use of the equity method. The entries would be as follows:

Sales	$300,000	
Cost Of Goods Sold		$300,000

Interest Revenue	$ 24,000	
Interest Expense		$ 24,000

Step B(4) - Intercompany Dividends

7-24.   This elimination is required by the presence of intercompany dividends. Under the equity method, the Investment Income that was recorded by the Pleigh Company included both dividends and an appropriate share of the unremitted 1998 earnings of the Sleigh Company. In Step A we eliminated Pleigh's share of the unremitted earnings of Sleigh against the Investment In Sleigh account. This left a balance of $80,000 ($156,400 - $76,400) in the Investment Income account. This $80,000 balance, which reflects the intercompany dividends received from the Sleigh Company, will now be eliminated using an entry similar to that which was required in the previous version of the problem. The entry, which also removes the entire balance in the Dividends Declared account and reduces the Non Controlling Interest in the consolidated Balance Sheet, is as follows:

Investment Income	$80,000	
Non Controlling Interest	20,000	
Dividends Declared		$100,000

Step B(5) - Unrealized Intercompany Profits

7-25.   Our final Step B adjustments and eliminations relate to the treatment of unrealized intercompany profits. When the equity method is being used to carry the investment account in an open trial balance problem, the elimination of the investment balance will require the removal of the intercompany profits that were present as at the beginning of the current year. We saw this procedure demonstrated in our Step A elimination entry. At this stage, we must adjust the current year's expenses and revenues for any changes in the amount of such unrealized intercompany profits that have taken place during the current accounting period.

Unrealized Land Profits

7-26.   You will recall that this problem contains a downstream profit on the sale of land of $25,000 and an upstream profit on a similar sale in the amount of $40,000. These amounts were eliminated from the Land account in Step A. Since there has been no change in the amount of these profits that is unrealized as at the end of 1998, there is no need to make any further entries with respect to these unrealized profits.

Unrealized Opening Inventory Profits

7-27.   In Step A we credited Inventories for $28,000 in Sleigh Company profits that were in the January 1, 1998 Inventories of the Pleigh Company. Under normal circumstances these Inventories would be sold by December 31, 1998 and any profits of the Sleigh Company that were included in the sale would now be considered realized. In view of this, the following entry would be appropriate:

Inventories	$28,000	
Cost Of Goods Sold		$28,000

7-28.   This journal entry serves to reverse the credit to Inventories that was made in Step A and to lower the consolidated Cost Of Goods Sold. This reflects the fact that unrealized profits were present in the beginning inventory that was included in the computation of this figure. The decrease in consolidated Cost Of Goods Sold increases consolidated Net Income by the opening upstream inventory profit which was realized during the current year.

Unrealized Closing Inventory Profits

7-29.   At the end of 1998, $40,000 of the profits of Sleigh Company are still in the ending Inventories of the Pleigh Company. No adjustment was made for this fact in our Step A entry. As a consequence, it is necessary to make the following entry at this point:

Cost Of Goods Sold	$40,000	
Inventories		$40,000

7-30.   This entry serves to reduce the Inventory figure for inclusion in the consolidated Balance Sheet and add a corresponding amount to the consolidated Cost Of Goods Sold. The increase in consolidated Cost Of Goods Sold decreases consolidated Net Income by the closing unrealized upstream profit.

Depreciable Asset Profit

7-31.   On December 31, 1996, the Sleigh Company sold equipment to the Pleigh Company and recognized a profit on the sale of $150,000. Since the asset had a remaining useful life at this time of three years, the profit is being realized through reduced depreciation expense at the rate of $50,000 per year. Since $50,000 would have been realized in 1997, the remaining unrealized balance on January 1, 1998 would have been $100,000. This fact was reflected in Step A when we credited the Plant And Equipment account for $100,000. During the year 1998, an additional $50,000 of the intercompany profit becomes realized so that at the end of 1998, only $50,000 of the profit on the sale of equipment remains unrealized. This fact requires the following entry to be made:

Plant And Equipment (Net)	$50,000	
Depreciation Expense		$50,000

7-32.   This entry serves to reduce the Step A credit to Plant And Equipment to the desired $50,000 and to make an appropriate $50,000 reduction in the amount that will be included in depreciation expense in the consolidated Income Statement.

Step C - Distribution Of The Subsidiary Retained Earnings

7-33.   When the Investment In Sleigh account is carried by the equity method, the Retained Earnings of the subsidiary since the date of acquisition are picked up in Investment Income, the Investment In Sleigh account and the Retained Earnings of the Pleigh Company. This was noted in the Step A investment elimination when we removed the entire balance in Sleigh's Retained Earnings account. With the elimination of the entire Retained Earnings balance against the investment account, no balance remains to be distributed in this step. Therefore, Step C procedures drop out. This would be the case whenever the investment account is carried by the equity method.

Preparation Of Consolidated Financial Statements

7-34.   We have now completed all of the procedures necessary for the preparation of consolidated financial statements. As before, we will take the balances from the original trial balance, add and subtract the adjustments that have been made in our procedures, and arrive at the figures to be included in the consolidated financial statements. As the computations are not altered by the use of the equity method, the schedular verifications of consolidated Net Income and the closing consolidated Retained Earnings will be omitted in this version of the problem.

Consolidated Income Statement

Non Controlling Interest

7-35.   The calculation of the Non Controlling Interest is the same as in the cost method version of the problem. It was as follows:

Sleigh Company's Reported Income	$200,000
Realized Gain On Equipment	50,000
Profits In Opening Inventories	28,000
Profits In Closing Inventories	(40,000)
Adjusted Subsidiary Income	$238,000
Non Controlling Percent	20%
Non Controlling Interest	$ 47,600

Statement Disclosure

7-36.   The consolidated Income Statement for 1998 of the Pleigh Company and its subsidiary would be prepared as follows:

Pleigh Company And Subsidiary
Consolidated Income Statement
Year Ending December 31, 1998

Sales ($4,000,000 + $2,500,000 - $300,000)	$6,200,000
Interest Revenue ($24,000 - $24,000)	-0-
Investment Income ($236,400 - $156,400 - $80,000)	-0-
Total Revenues	$6,200,000
Cost Of Goods Sold ($2,800,000 + $1,500,000 - $300,000 + $40,000 - $28,000)	$4,012,000
Depreciation Expense ($200,000 + $100,000 + $10,000 - $50,000)	260,000
Interest Expense ($240,000 + $84,000 - $24,000)	300,000
Other Expenses ($364,000 + $616,000)	980,000
Goodwill Amortization Expense	24,000
Total Expenses	$5,576,000
Combined Income	$ 724,000
Non Controlling Interest	47,600
Consolidated Net Income	$ 576,400

Consolidated Statement Of Retained Earnings

Statement Disclosure

7-37.   Using the Net Income data, we can now prepare a consolidated Statement Of Retained Earnings. The January 1, 1998 consolidated Retained Earnings is simply the balance from the trial balance of the Pleigh Company. Adjustments, such as those required when the cost method is used, are not needed here. The consolidated Statement of Retained Earnings is as follows:

Pleigh Company And Subsidiary
Consolidated Statement Of Retained Earnings
Year Ending December 31, 1998

Balance - January 1, 1998	$2,814,600
1998 Net Income	576,400
1998 Dividends Declared (Pleigh's Only)	(350,000)
Balance - December 31, 1998	$3,041,000

Consolidated Balance Sheet

Non Controlling Interest

7-38.   In preparing the consolidated Balance Sheet, the only figure that does not flow directly from the journal entries is the Non Controlling Interest. As was the case when the Investment In Sleigh was carried by the cost method, a direct calculation of the Non Controlling Interest can be made by taking 20 percent of the subsidiary's net assets adjusted for end of the year upstream unrealized profits. This would be [(20%)($4,400,000 - $40,000 - $40,000 - $50,000)] and would equal $854,000. Alternatively, we can arrive at this same figure through the various steps in the procedures. Step A allocated $826,400 to the Non Controlling Interest. In Step B this was reduced because of the dividends of $20,000 to the non controlling shareholders. If we take this net amount of $806,400 and add the Non Controlling Interest disclosed in the consolidated Income Statement of $47,600, we get the Non Controlling Interest for the consolidated Balance Sheet of $874,000.

Statement Disclosure

7-39.   Given the preceding analysis, the consolidated Balance Sheet would be prepared as follows:

Pleigh Company And Subsidiary
Consolidated Balance Sheet
As At December 31, 1998

Cash ($500,000 + $300,000)	$ 800,000
Current Receivables ($800,000 + $400,000 - $12,000)	1,188,000
Inventories ($2,500,000 + $1,700,000 - $40,000)	4,160,000
Long Term Note Receivable ($200,000 - $200,000)	-0-
Investment In Sleigh ($3,541,000 - $3,541,000)	-0-
Land ($1,500,000 + $1,000,000 - $185,000)	2,315,000
Plant And Equipment ($4,500,000 + $1,900,000 + $160,000 - $10,000 - $100,000 + $50,000)	6,500,000
Goodwill ($144,000 - $24,000)	120,000
Total Assets	**$15,083,000**
Current Liabilities ($500,000 + $200,000 - $12,000)	$ 688,000
Long Term Liabilities ($2,000,000 + $700,000 -$200,000)	2,500,000
Non Controlling Interest	854,000
No Par Common Stock (Pleigh's Balance)	8,000,000
Retained Earnings (See Retained Earnings Statement)	3,041,000
Total Equities	**$15,083,000**

Intercompany Bondholdings

The Basic Problem

7-40.   We have previously encountered intercompany liabilities. However, in the previous cases the intercompany balance was carried at the same value on the books of both the debtor and creditor company. These situations were further simplified by the fact that this carrying value was the maturity value of the intercompany liability. As a result of these facts, the amount of intercompany interest expense was equal to the amount of intercompany interest revenue and both amounts were equal to the amount of cash that was paid. This meant that when we eliminated the intercompany expense and revenue there was no change in the combined income, the non controlling shareholders' interest in income or consolidated net income. In a similar fashion, the elimination of the intercompany asset and liability served only to reduce the total consolidated assets and liabilities and had no effect on either the Non Controlling Interest in the consolidated Balance Sheet or the Non Controlling Interest in the consolidated Income Statement.

7-41.   Long term marketable debt securities differ from other types of liabilities that we have encountered in our work on consolidations in two ways. First, this type of debt will generally be issued at a premium or discount from the amount that will be payable when it matures. The second difference is that, subsequent to its issuance, it will be traded at various prices which may be above or below its original issue price. These differences introduce complicating factors into the elimination of intercompany assets and liabilities and any related interest expense and interest revenue. These complications can be described as follows:

> **Single Entity Records**   The fact that the bonds may be carried at a value other than their maturity value means that you must have some understanding of the procedures required to amortize bond premium or discount and their effect on the amount of interest expense or interest revenue for the period under consideration. While this situation is not unique to consolidations, it does seem to be a point that causes difficulties for many students.

> **Consolidated Records**   The fact that the bonds trade at prices other than those at which they were issued means that the parent (subsidiary) may purchase the subsidiary (parent) bonds at a price which is different from their carrying value on the books of the issuer. In this situation, the consolidated entity is purchasing the bonds from investors who are outside of the consolidated entity and, if the purchasing price differs from the carrying value of the liability, the consolidated entity will experience a gain or a loss on the retirement of the bonds. In addition, if the bonds are not cancelled, the amount of intercompany interest revenue will not be equal to the amount of intercompany interest expense. This means that the intercompany bondholding will have an influence on the non controlling interest in income and on consolidated Net Income for as long as the bonds continue to pay interest.

7-42.   Intercompany holdings of long term marketable debt securities will be illustrated with a comprehensive three period example. In order to illustrate the income effects in subsequent periods, the example will be followed to the maturity date of the relevant bond issue.

Comprehensive Example

7-43.   The basic data for Plug's acquisition of of 80 percent of Slug's outstanding shares, and for the intercompany purchase of bonds is as follows:

> On December 31, 1992, the Plug Company purchases 80 percent of the outstanding voting shares of the Slug Company for cash in the amount of $3,200,000. On this date the Slug Company's Balance Sheet disclosed No Par Common Stock in the amount of $1,500,000 and Retained Earnings of $2,500,000. All of the identifiable assets and liabilities of the Slug Company had carrying values that were equal to their fair values on that date.

> On December 31, 1993, the Slug Company issues Bonds Payable with a par value of $1,000,000. The bonds have a 10 percent coupon rate, mature on December 31, 1998 and pay interest annually on December 31. They are sold at a price of 105 for total cash proceeds of $1,050,000. The Slug Company accounts for the interest on these bonds by the straight line method.

> On December 31, 1996, the Plug Company purchases the entire $1,000,000 par value of this bond issue. The bonds are purchased in the open market at a price of 96 for a total purchase consideration of $960,000. The Plug Company accounts

for the interest on these bonds by the straight line method.

Except for the intercompany bondholdings and the related Interest Expense and Interest Revenue, there are no intercompany transactions in any of the years under consideration in this example. Further, no dividends were declared or paid by either Company during the years 1996, 1997, or 1998.

Single Entity Information

7-44.   We will eventually deal with the preparation of consolidated financial statements for the years 1996 through 1998. However, in view of the difficulties that most students have with accounting for bond discount or premium amortization, we feel that it is useful to examine the entries that would be made in the single entity records of the two Companies before proceeding to deal with the consolidation aspects of the problem.

7-45.   In the years 1996 through 1998, the Slug Company would make the following annual entry to record Interest Expense:

Interest Expense	$90,000	
Bonds Payable - Premium	10,000	
Cash		$100,000

[To record the coupon interest of 10 percent on $1,000,000 and to amortize premium of $10,000 ($50,000 ÷ 5)]

7-46.   In the years 1997 and 1998, subsequent to the intercompany purchase of the bonds, the Plug Company would make the following entry to record Interest Revenue:

Cash	$100,000	
Bond Investment	20,000	
Interest Revenue		$120,000

[To record the coupon interest of 10 percent on $1,000,000 and to accumulate discount of $20,000 ($40,000 ÷ 2)]

7-47.   For the years under consideration, the end of period balance sheet values for the bonds on the two Companies' books are as follows:

Date	Plug	Slug
December 31, 1996	$ 960,000	$1,020,000
December 31, 1997	980,000	1,010,000
December 31, 1998	1,000,000	1,000,000

1996 Data

7-48.   The December 31, 1996 condensed Balance Sheets and the condensed Income Statements for the year ending December 31, 1996, for the Plug Company and its subsidiary, the Slug Company, are as follows:

Income Statements
For The Year Ending December 31, 1996

	Plug	Slug
Sales Revenue	$3,500,000	$1,200,000
Expenses Other Than Interest	$3,100,000	$ 900,000
Interest Expense	-0-	90,000
Total Expenses	$3,100,000	$ 990,000
Net Income	$ 400,000	$ 210,000

Balance Sheets
As At December 31, 1996

	Plug	Slug
Other Net Assets	$14,500,000	$6,000,000
Investment In Slug's Stock	3,200,000	-0-
Investment In Slug's Bonds	960,000	-0-
Total Assets	$18,660,000	$6,000,000
Bonds Payable - Par	$ -0-	$1,000,000
Bonds Payable - Premium	-0-	20,000
No Par Common Stock	10,000,000	1,500,000
Retained Earnings	8,660,000	3,480,000
Total Equities	$18,660,000	$6,000,000

Required   Prepare a consolidated Balance Sheet as at December 31, 1996 and consolidated Statements Of Income and Retained Earnings for the year ending December 31, 1996.

Step A - Investment Elimination

7-49.   In this example, the investment cost of $3,200,000 was exactly equal to the investor's proportionate share of the subsidiary's book value at the date of acquisition. Further, the problem also states that there are no fair value changes as at the acquisition date. As a consequence, there is no need to do an analysis of the investment account and the relatively simple investment elimination entry is as follows:

No Par Common Stock	$1,500,000	
Retained Earnings	2,500,000	
Non Controlling Interest		$ 800,000
Investment In Slug's Stock		3,200,000

7-50.   The Non Controlling Interest is 20 percent of the at acquisition carrying value of the net identifiable assets of Slug of $4,000,000 ($1,500,000 + $2,500,000).

Step B - Adjustments And Eliminations

7-51.   In the absence of fair value changes or goodwill, there is no need to deal with the problem of write offs of these amounts in subsequent accounting periods. Further, the problem indicates that other than intercompany bondholdings and the related Interest Expense and Interest Revenue, there are no other intercompany transactions or dividends. As a consequence, the only adjustment or elimination to be dealt with here relates to intercompany bondholdings. Before proceeding to the 1996 entry for dealing with these bonds, we will consider the general approach to be used in situations where there are intercompany holdings of long term marketable debt securities.

General Procedures For Intercompany Bondholdings

7-52.   The general procedures for dealing with intercompany holdings of long term marketable debt securities involve three basic steps. These three steps can be generally described in the following manner:

Step One   The first Step in analyzing an intercompany purchase of bonds is to determine the total gain or loss resulting from the purchase. This is accomplished by subtracting the purchase price (asset value) of the bonds from the carrying value on the books of the issuing company (liability value) as at the date of the purchase.

Step Two   If there is a non controlling interest in the subsidiary company, the total gain or loss which was determined in Step One must be allocated to the holding company and the issuing company. While the *CICA Handbook* does not offer recommendations in this area, the general Canadian practice is to allocate on the basis of the relationship between the carrying values on the books of the two companies and the par or maturity value of the bonds. This somewhat arbitrary solution to the problem is called the "par value method".

Step Three   In the real world, bonds would often be cancelled subsequent to an intercompany purchase and no adjustments or eliminations would be required in periods subsequent to their purchase. However, in problem situations the bonds are often left outstanding and this requires that Interest Expense and Interest Revenue be eliminated in these accounting periods. Since the amount of expense and revenue will not usually be equal, this elimination will have a net effect on income. This income effect will, over the remaining life of the bonds, reverse the consolidated gain or loss that was recorded in the year of the intercompany purchase. Therefore, you will have to determine and allocate the annual reversal of the gain or loss that will be reflected in the consolidated Income Statements in the years subsequent to the intercompany transaction.

Step One

7-53.   As previously indicated, the intercompany gain or loss will be determined by subtracting the purchase price of the bonds from their carrying value on the books of the issuer. Using the December 31, 1996 values that were presented in the single entity information, the calculation would be as follows:

December 31, 1996 Liability	$1,020,000
December 31, 1996 Asset	960,000
Gain On Bond Retirement	$ 60,000

7-54.   The logic of the preceding calculation is fairly obvious. The fact that we manage to retire a liability with a book value of $1,020,000 for a cash payment of $960,000 has resulted in a gain of $60,000. Correspondingly, in situations where the asset value used is greater than the liability retired, the preceding calculation will result in a negative number and this will reflect the fact that a loss on the bond retirement has occurred.

Step Two

7-55.   In situations where the parent owns less than 100 percent of the outstanding shares of the subsidiary, the total gain or loss must be allocated between the purchasing company and the issuing company. This is necessary in order to appropriately split the effects of the gain or loss between the Non Controlling Interest in income and consolidated Net Income. In our opinion, all of the possible solutions to this allocation problem are arbitrary in nature. It would be possible to allocate 100 percent of the gain or loss to either the purchasing company or the issuing company. However, as the actions of both of these companies are required in order for the gain or loss to occur, it is impossible to provide a logical defense for choosing one of these methods over the other. As a result, the method that is used most widely is something of a compromise between 100 percent allocation to either the holder or the issuer of the bonds. It is referred to as the par value method as it allocates the gain or loss on the assumption that the bonds were retired by the issuer of the bonds paying an amount equal to par value to the holder of the bonds. The resulting allocation process can be described from the point of view of each of the two companies as follows:

Bondholder   From the point of view of the bondholder, the bonds are an asset. As a consequence, if we assume that the bonds have been retired at par value, this company will have a loss on bonds that are carried at a premium over par value and a gain on bonds that are carried at a discount.

Bond Issuer   From the point of view of the bond issuer, the bonds are a liability. As a consequence, if we assume that the bonds have been retired at par value, this company will experience a gain on bonds that are carried at a premium and a loss on bonds that are carried at a discount.

7-56.   In the illustration that is under consideration, the allocation would be as follows:

Bondholder

Par Value Received	$1,000,000
Book Value Eliminated	960,000
Share Of Total Gain	$ 40,000

Bond Issuer

Book Value Eliminated	$1,020,000
Par Value Given	1,000,000
Share of Total Gain	$ 20,000

Notes On The Step Two Allocation

7-57.   The following points should be made with respect to the preceding allocation of the gain or loss:

A.   The analysis is in terms of the holder and issuer, not the parent and subsidiary. Either company could be the holder or the issuer in a particular situation.

B.   You will note that the Step Two allocations of $40,000 and $20,000 are equal to the total gain of $60,000 that was calculated in Step One. A less obvious fact is that even if there was no total gain or loss resulting from the Step One calculation, an allocation may still be required in Step B when the par value method is being used. For example, if the Plug Company had purchased the bonds for their carrying value on the books of Slug Company of $1,020,000, there would have been no net gain or loss on the retirement. However, if we apply the par value method of allocation we must charge a loss of $20,000 to the Plug Company as holder of the bonds and credit a gain to the Slug Company of $20,000 as the issuer of the liability.

C.   As a final note, we remind you that the *CICA Handbook* is silent as to how this allocation process should be handled. This would appear to permit a variety of procedures in this area.

Step Three

7-58.   The elimination of the intercompany asset and liability for consolidation purposes will, of course, result in subsequent eliminations of intercompany interest expense and revenue (assuming the bonds are not cancelled after the intercompany purchase). The elimination of the intercompany asset and liability results in a gain or loss in those situations in which the premium or discount reflected in the intercompany purchase price is not the same as the premium or discount on the books of the issuer at the time of the intercompany purchase. This difference in premium or discount will also be reflected in the elimination of the intercompany Interest Expense and Interest Revenue. More specifically, there will be a difference in the amount of the expense and revenue that is eliminated in subsequent periods and the effect of this difference will be such that it will just exactly reverse the initial gain or loss on retirement of the bonds. The following calculations pertain to the example that is under consideration (the amounts can be found in the single entity information):

Annual Expense Elimination	$ 90,000
Annual Revenue Elimination	(120,000)
Annual Reduction In Income	($ 30,000)

7-59.   Note that as a result of eliminating the above amounts, the combined income of the consolidated entity will be decreased by $30,000 per year for the two year period 1997 through 1998 and that this will exactly offset the $60,000 gain that was recognized for consolidation purposes in 1996. Apportionment of this $30,000 will be based on the gain allocation that was calculated in 1996. This would be as follows:

Plug's Annual Share Of Gain = $40,000/2 = $20,000
Slug's Annual Share Of Gain = $20,000/2 = $10,000

7-60.   As you would expect, these amounts are equal to the premium and discount amortization in the single entity records of the two companies.

Step B - Bond Elimination Entry

7-61.   With the preceding analysis of the intercompany bondholdings completed, we can now return to Step B of our general consolidation procedures. For 1996, the only entry that is required here is to eliminate the intercompany asset/liability position and to recognize the resulting gain. The entry is as follows:

Bonds Payable - Par	$1,000,000	
Bonds Payable - Premium	20,000	
Gain On Bond Retirement		$ 60,000
Investment In Slug's Bonds		960,000

7-62.   Since the purchase occurred on December 31, 1996, there were no intercompany interest payments and, consequently, no elimination entries for Interest Expense or Interest Revenue.

Step C - Retained Earnings Distribution Schedule

7-63.   The usual Step C schedule would allocate the Retained Earnings of the Slug Company since acquisition:

Book Value - January 1, 1996	$3,270,000
Balance At Acquisition	(2,500,000)
Balance Since Acquisition	$ 770,000
Upstream Gain On Bonds - January 1, 1996	-0-
Modified Balance Since Acquisition	$ 770,000
Non Controlling Interest	20%
Non Controlling Interest In Retained Earnings Since Acquisition	($ 154,000)
To Consolidated Retained Earnings	$ 616,000

7-64.   The January 1, 1996 balance in the Retained Earnings of the Slug Company is the $3,480,000 balance from the December 31, 1996 Balance Sheet, less the $210,000 Net Income from the 1996 Income Statement.

Step C - Allocation Entry

7-65.   The journal entry to implement the allocation determined in the preceding Paragraph is as follows:

Retained Earnings - Slug	$770,000	
Non Controlling Interest		$154,000
Consolidated Retained Earnings		616,000

7-66.   This entry provides the basis for the determination of the January 1, 1996 consolidated Retained Earnings balance of $8,876,000. It is Plug's January 1, 1996 balance of $8,260,000 (December 31, 1996 Balance Sheet amount of $8,660,000, less 1996 Net Income of $400,000) plus the preceding allocation of $616,000.

Non Controlling Interest

7-67.   The only difficult figure to compute for the 1996 consolidated Income Statement is the Non Controlling Interest. It would be based on the reported income of the Slug Company, adjusted for the subsidiary's share of the gain on the intercompany purchase of bonds. This calculation is as follows:

Reported Income Of Slug	$210,000
Slug's Share Of Total Gain	20,000
Adjusted Income	$230,000
Non Controlling Percent	20%
Non Controlling Interest	$ 46,000

1996 Consolidated Income Statement

7-68.   Given the preceding calculation of the Non Controlling Interest, the 1996 consolidated Income Statement can be prepared as follows:

Plug Company And Subsidiary
Consolidated Income Statement
Year Ending December 31, 1996

Sales Revenue ($3,500,000 + $1,200,000)	$4,700,000
Interest Revenue	-0-
Gain On Bond Retirement	60,000
Total Revenues	$4,760,000
Expenses Other Than Interest ($3,100,000 + $900,000)	$4,000,000
Interest Expense	90,000
Total Expenses	$4,090,000
Combined Income	$ 670,000
Non Controlling Interest	46,000
Consolidated Net Income	$ 624,000

1996 Consolidated Statement Of Retained Earnings

7-69.   The consolidated Statement Of Retained Earnings for the year ending December 31, 1996, would be as follows:

Plug Company And Subsidiary
Consolidated Statement Of Retained Earnings
For The Year Ending December 31, 1996

January 1, 1996 Balance (See Step C Allocation Entry)	$8,876,000
Consolidated Net Income	624,000
December 31, 1996 Balance	$9,500,000

December 31, 1996 Consolidated Balance Sheet

7-70.   The consolidated Balance Sheet for the first year of this problem would be prepared as follows:

Plug Company And Subsidiary
Consolidated Balance Sheet
As At December 31, 1996

Other Net Assets ($14,500,000 + $6,000,000)	$20,500,000
Investment In Slug's Stock ($3,200,000 - $3,200,000)	-0-
Investment In Slug's Bonds ($960,000 - $960,000)	-0-
Total Assets	**$20,500,000**

Bonds Payable ($1,000,000 - $1,000,000)	$ -0-
Bonds Payable - Premium ($20,000 - $20,000)	-0-
Non Controlling Interest (See following discussion)	1,000,000
No Par Common Stock (Plug's Only)	10,000,000
Retained Earnings (See Statement of Retained Earnings)	9,500,000
Total Equities	**$20,500,000**

7-71.   The Non Controlling Interest is calculated by taking 20 percent of Slug's net book value ($4,980,000) adjusted for the subsidiary's $20,000 share of the gain on the intercompany bond transaction. That is, [(20%)($4,980,000 + $20,000)] is equal to the Non Controlling Interest of $1,000,000.

1997 Data

7-72.   The December 31, 1997 Balance Sheets and the Income Statements for the year ending December 31, 1997, for the Plug Company and its subsidiary, the Slug Company, are as follows:

Income Statements
For The Year Ending December 31, 1997

	Plug	Slug
Sales Revenue	$4,000,000	$1,500,000
Interest Revenue	120,000	-0-
Total Revenues	**$4,120,000**	**$1,500,000**
Expenses Other Than Interest	$3,700,000	$1,100,000
Interest Expense	-0-	90,000
Total Expenses	**$3,700,000**	**$1,190,000**
Net Income	**$ 420,000**	**$ 310,000**

Balance Sheets
As At December 31, 1997

	Plug	Slug
Other Net Assets	$14,900,000	$6,300,000
Investment In Slug's Stock	3,200,000	-0-
Investment In Slug's Bonds	980,000	-0-
Total Assets	**$19,080,000**	**$6,300,000**
Bonds Payable - Par	$ -0-	$1,000,000
Bonds Payable - Premium	-0-	10,000
No Par Common Stock	10,000,000	1,500,000
Retained Earnings	9,080,000	3,790,000
Total Equities	**$19,080,000**	**$6,300,000**

Required Prepare a consolidated Balance Sheet as at December 31, 1997 and consolidated Statements Of Income and Retained Earnings for the year ending December 31, 1997.

Step A - Investment Elimination

7-73. The following 1997 entry for the elimination of the investment account is identical to the 1998 entry.

No Par Common Stock	$1,500,000	
Retained Earnings	2,500,000	
Non Controlling Interest		$ 800,000
Investment In Slug's Stock		3,200,000

Step B - Adjustments And Eliminations

7-74. The only Step B entry that is required is the entry to deal with the intercompany bondholding and the related Interest Expense and Interest Revenue. This entry would be as follows:

Bonds Payable - Par	$1,000,000	
Bonds Payable - Premium	10,000	
Interest Revenue	120,000	
Interest Expense		$ 90,000
Retained Earnings - Plug		40,000
Retained Earnings - Slug		20,000
Investment In Slug's Bonds		980,000

7-75. The only part of this entry that requires additional explanation is the credits to the Retained Earnings balances of the two Companies. These credits reflect the respective shares of the two Companies in the gain on the intercompany purchase of bonds. These amounts were recognized for consolidation purposes in 1996 but were not entered in the single entity records of either Company. As a consequence, an adjustment is required at this point. Note that the amount of the adjustment is the January 1, 1997 balance of the gain. During 1997, the Interest Expense/Interest Revenue elimination will reverse one half of these amounts, leaving adjustments of $20,000 and $10,000 at the end of 1997.

Step C - Retained Earnings Distribution Schedule

7-76. The usual Step C schedule would be used to allocate the Retained Earnings of the Slug Company since acquisition:

Book Value - January 1, 1997	$3,480,000
Balance At Acquisition	(2,500,000)
Balance Since Acquisition	$ 980,000
Upstream Gain On Bonds - January 1, 1997	20,000
Modified Balance Since Acquisition	$1,000,000
Non Controlling Percent	20%
Non Controlling Interest In Retained Earnings Since Acquisition	($ 200,000)
To Consolidated Retained Earnings	$ 800,000

Step C - Allocation Entry

7-77. The journal entry to implement the allocation determined in the preceding Paragraph is as follows:

Retained Earnings - Slug	$1,000,000	
Non Controlling Interest		$200,000
Consolidated Retained Earnings		800,000

7-78.   This entry provides the basis for the determination of the January 1, 1997 consolidated Retained Earnings balance. As expected, it is equal to the December 31, 1996 balance previously calculated. Alternatively, it can be calculated as follows:

Plug's January 1, 1997 Balance	$8,660,000
Plug's Gain On Bonds As At January 1, 1997	40,000
Preceding Step C Allocation	800,000
Consolidated Retained Earnings Balance - January 1, 1997	$9,500,000

Non Controlling Interest In Income

7-79.   The only difficult figure to compute for the 1997 consolidated Income Statement is the Non Controlling Interest. It would be based on the reported income of the Slug Company, adjusted for the subsidiary's share of the reversal of the gain on the intercompany purchase of bonds. This calculation is as follows:

Reported Income Of Slug	$310,000
Slug's Share Of Gain Reversal	(10,000)
Adjusted Income	$300,000
Non Controlling Percent	20%
Non Controlling Interest	$ 60,000

1997 Consolidated Income Statement

7-80.   Given the preceding calculation of the Non Controlling Interest, the 1997 consolidated Income Statement can be prepared as follows:

Plug Company And Subsidiary
Consolidated Income Statement
For The Year Ending December 31, 1997

Sales Revenue ($4,000,000 + $1,500,000)	$5,500,000
Interest Revenue ($120,000 - $120,000)	-0-
Total Revenues	$5,500,000
Expenses Other Than Interest ($3,700,000 + $1,100,000)	$4,800,000
Interest Expense ($90,000 - $90,000)	-0-
Total Expenses	$4,800,000
Combined Income	$ 700,000
Non Controlling Interest (See Preceding Calculation)	60,000
Consolidated Net Income	$ 640,000

1997 Consolidated Statement Of Retained Earnings

7-81.   The 1997 consolidated Statement Of Retained Earnings would be as follows:

Plug Company And Subsidiary
Consolidated Statement Of Retained Earnings
For The Year Ending December 31, 1997

January 1, 1997 Balance (See Step C Allocation Entry)	$ 9,500,000
Consolidated Net Income (See Income Statement)	640,000
December 31, 1997 Balance	$10,140,000

December 31, 1997 Consolidated Balance Sheet

7-82.   The consolidated Balance Sheet at the end of 1997 would be prepared as follows:

Plug Company And Subsidiary
Consolidated Balance Sheet
As At December 31, 1997

Other Net Assets ($14,900,000 + $6,300,000)	$21,200,000
Investment In Slug's Stock ($3,200,000 - $3,200,000)	-0-
Investment In Slug's Bonds ($980,000 - $980,000)	-0-
Total Assets	**$21,200,000**

Bond Payable ($1,000,000 - $1,000,000)	$ -0-
Bonds Payable - Premium ($10,000 - $10,000)	-0-
Non Controlling Interest (See following discussion)	1,060,000
No Par Common Stock (Plug's Only)	10,000,000
Retained Earnings (See Statement of Retained Earnings)	10,140,000
Total Equities	**$21,200,000**

7-83.   The Non Controlling Interest of $1,060,000 is calculated by taking 20 percent of Slug's net book value adjusted for the subsidiary's remaining $10,000 share of the gain on the intercompany bond transaction ([20%][$1,500,000 + $3,790,000 + $10,000]).

1998 Data

7-84.   The December 31, 1998 Balance Sheets and the 1998 Income Statements for the Plug Company and its subsidiary, the Slug Company, are as follows:

Income Statements
For The Year Ending December 31, 1998

	Plug	Slug
Sales Revenue	$3,000,000	$1,000,000
Interest Revenue	120,000	-0-
Total Revenues	**$3,120,000**	**$1,000,000**
Expenses Other Than Interest	$2,600,000	$ 600,000
Interest Expense	-0-	90,000
Total Expenses	**$2,600,000**	**$ 690,000**
Net Income	**$ 520,000**	**$ 310,000**

Balance Sheets
As At December 31, 1998

	Plug	Slug
Other Net Assets	$15,400,000	$6,600,000
Investment In Slug's Stock	3,200,000	-0-
Investment In Slug's Bonds	1,000,000	-0-
Total Assets	**$19,600,000**	**$6,600,000**
Bonds Payable - Par	$ -0-	$1,000,000
Bonds Payable - Premium	-0-	-0-
No Par Common Stock	10,000,000	1,500,000
Retained Earnings	9,600,000	4,100,000
Total Equities	**$19,600,000**	**$6,600,000**

Required   Prepare a consolidated Balance Sheet as at December 31, 1998 and consolidated Statements Of Income and Retained Earnings for the year ending December 31, 1998.

Step A - Investment Elimination

7-85.   The following 1998 entry for the elimination of the investment account is identical to the entries for 1996 and 1997.

No Par Common Stock	$1,500,000	
Retained Earnings	2,500,000	
Non Controlling Interest		$ 800,000
Investment In Slug's Stock		3,200,000

Step B - Adjustments And Eliminations

7-86.   Here again, the only Step B entry that is required is the one to deal with the intercompany bondholding and related Interest Expense and Interest Revenue. This entry would be as follows:

Bond Payable - Par	$1,000,000	
Interest Revenue	120,000	
Interest Expense		$ 90,000
Retained Earnings - Plug		20,000
Retained Earnings - Slug		10,000
Investment In Slug's Bonds		1,000,000

7-87.   Most of the preceding journal entry is fairly obvious. The one possible difficulty would be with the credits to the opening Retained Earnings balances of the two Companies. These credits reflect the respective shares of the two Companies in the gain on the intercompany purchase of bonds, less one year's reversal of this gain through the elimination of Interest Revenue in excess of Interest Expense. By the end of 1998, the entire amount of the gain will be reversed and this will coincide with the fact that the bonds mature at this time.

Step C - Retained Earnings Distribution Schedule

7-88.   The usual Step C schedule would be used to allocate the Retained Earnings of the Slug Company since the date of acquisition:

Book Value - January 1, 1998	$3,790,000
Balance At Acquisition	(2,500,000)
Balance Since Acquisition	$1,290,000
Upstream Gain On Bonds - January 1, 1998	10,000
Modified Balance Since Acquisition	$1,300,000
Non Controlling Percent	20%
Non Controlling Interest In Retained Earnings Since Acquisition	($ 260,000)
To Consolidated Retained Earnings	$1,040,000

Step C - Allocation Entry

7-89.   The journal entry to implement the allocation determined in the preceding Paragraph is as follows:

Retained Earnings - Slug	$1,300,000	
Non Controlling Interest		$ 260,000
Consolidated Retained Earnings		1,040,000

7-90.   This entry provides the basis for the determination of the January 1, 1998 consolidated Retained Earnings balance. It can be calculated as follows:

Plug's January 1, 1998 Balance	$ 9,080,000
Plug's Gain On Bonds As At January 1, 1998	20,000
Preceding Step C Allocation	1,040,000
Consolidated Retained Earnings Balance - January 1, 1998	$10,140,000

Non Controlling Interest In Income

7-91.   The only difficult figure to compute for the 1998 consolidated Income Statement is the Non Controlling Interest. It would be based on the reported income of the Slug Company, adjusted for the subsidiary's share of the reversal of the gain on the intercompany purchase of bonds. This calculation is as follows:

Reported Income Of Slug	$310,000
Slug's Share Of Gain Reversal	(10,000)
Adjusted Income	$300,000
Non Controlling Percent	20%
Non Controlling Interest	$ 60,000

1998 Consolidated Income Statement

7-92.   Given the preceding calculation of the Non Controlling Interest, the 1998 consolidated Income Statement can be prepared as follows:

Plug Company And Subsidiary
Consolidated Income Statement
For The Year Ending December 31, 1998

Sales Revenue ($3,000,000 + $1,000,000)	$4,000,000
Interest Revenue ($120,000 - $120,000)	-0-
Total Revenues	$4,000,000
Expenses Other Than Interest ($2,600,000 + $600,000)	$3,200,000
Interest Expense ($90,000 - $90,000)	-0-
Total Expenses	$3,200,000
Combined Income	$ 800,000
Non Controlling Interest (See Preceding Calculation)	60,000
Consolidated Net Income	$ 740,000

1998 Consolidated Statement Of Retained Earnings

7-93.   The consolidated Statement Of Retained Earnings for the year ending December 31, 1998 would be as follows:

Plug Company And Subsidiary
Consolidated Statement Of Retained Earnings
For The Year Ending December 31, 1998

January 1, 1998 Balance (See Step C Allocation Entry)	$10,140,000
Consolidated Net Income (See Income Statement)	740,000
December 31, 1998 Balance	$10,880,000

December 31, 1998 Consolidated Balance Sheet

7-94.   The consolidated Balance Sheet at the end of 1998 would be prepared as follows:

Plug Company And Subsidiary
Consolidated Balance Sheet
As At December 31, 1998

Other Net Assets ($15,400,000 + $6,600,000)	$22,000,000
Investment In Slug's Stock ($3,200,000 - $3,200,000)	-0-
Investment In Slug's Bonds ($980,000 - $980,000)	-0-
Total Assets	$22,000,000

Bonds Payable ($1,000,000 - $1,000,000)	$ -0-
Bonds Payable - Premium	-0-
Non Controlling Interest (See following discussion)	1,120,000
No Par Common Stock (Plug's Only)	10,000,000
Retained Earnings (See Statement Of Retained Earnings)	10,880,000
Total Equities	$22,000,000

7-95.   The Non Controlling Interest at this point is simply 20 percent of the net book value of the Slug Company. That is, 20 percent of $5,600,000 is equal to the Non Controlling Interest of $1,120,000.

A Final Note

7-96.   The gain that was included in the computation of consolidated Net Income for 1996 has been reversed by the process of eliminating a larger amount of Interest Revenue than Interest Expense in 1997 and 1998. This means that the accounts now stand as they would have if the intercompany purchase of bonds had never taken place. We can see this by noting that the preceding consolidated Retained Earnings figure can be calculated without reference to the bonds. The calculation is as follows:

Plug Company's Balance		$9,600,000
Slug's Balance	$4,100,000	
Balance At Acquisition	(2,500,000)	
Balance Since Acquisition	$1,600,000	
Controlling Interest	80%	1,280,000
Consolidated Balance		$10,880,000

7-97.   A further confirmation of this point is that the Non Controlling Interest in the Balance Sheet is based on the carrying values of the subsidiary's net assets. In other words, the consolidated balances are at the levels they would be at if the intercompany purchase of bonds had not occurred. You should understand the reason for this before leaving the material on intercompany bondholdings.

Multiple Investment Situations

Introduction

7-98.   It is possible to classify three types of situations in which more than one investment holding is included in a single consolidated entity. In two of these situations, multi-company and multi-level relationships, two or more subsidiaries are engendered by the multiple investments. In the third situation (reciprocal holdings) only one subsidiary is required as the investment moves both upstream and downstream. A brief description, including some indication of the nature of the accounting problems that will be encountered, is provided for each of these situations.

Multi-Company Affiliation

7-99.   The term multi-company affiliation is used to describe situations in which a single parent company has acquired, by direct investment in each investee, two or more subsidiaries. This type of arrangement is shown in Figure 7-1. There are no particular complications in this situation. It is simply a matter of dealing with each subsidiary as though it were the only investee of this type and then summing the resulting financial data.

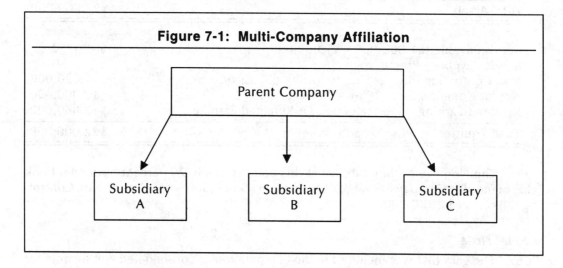

Figure 7-1: Multi-Company Affiliation

Multi-Level Affiliation

7-100.   The distinguishing feature of multi-level affiliations is the presence of indirect ownership. That is, control is achieved, not through the more usual channel of holding the investee's voting shares, but through holding voting shares of a company which in turn owns a controlling interest in an additional investee's shares. This type of arrangment is shown in Figure 7-2. The term multi-level affiliation also encompasses situations in which control is accomplished via a combination of direct and indirect ownership. However, to remain in this category, all of the investment must be in one direction. While multi-level affiliations do not involve any real conceptual differences from those present in single investment situations, the application of these procedures is somewhat more complex. As a consequence, we will provide two examples in this Chapter of multi-level affiliations.

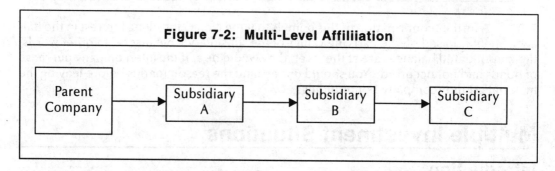

Figure 7-2: Multi-Level Affiliiation

Reciprocal Holdings

7-101.   The distinguishing feature of reciprocal holdings is the presence of both upstream and downstream investment. That is, we find situations in which a parent has invested in a subsidiary and the subsidiary, in turn, has acquired shares of the parent. This latter investment creates the reciprocal holdings situation. This type of situation is shown in Figure 7-3.

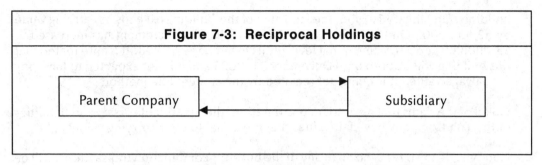

Figure 7-3: Reciprocal Holdings

7-102.   Reciprocal holdings add considerable complexity to problems. The basic reason for this is that in order to determine the parent's share of the retained earnings of the subsidiary since acquisition, you must determine the subsidiary's share of the retained earnings of the parent subsequent to the date of the investment. Since this latter figure involves the former, simultaneous equations are necessary to arrive at a solution to this problem. We will provide three examples in this Chapter which illustrate the procedures required to deal with reciprocal investment relationships.

Multi-Level Affiliations

Approach

7-103.   We will examine two different cases involving multi-level relationships. In order to reduce the amount of facts that you will be required to deal with, the same basic data will be used in both of these illustrations. The investment patterns will be varied in the two cases in order to demonstrate the two types of situations that arise in this area. In the first case, a parent will acquire a subsidiary and this subsidiary will subsequently acquire a second subsidiary. The second case will involve the ultimate parent company acquiring a subsidiary that has already entered into a business combination transaction with another subsidiary.

Basic Data

7-104.   The basic data involves three companies which we will designate the Run Company, the Sun Company, and the Tun Company. Data on the No Par Common Stock, Retained Earnings and Net Income of the three Companies is as follows:

	Run	Sun	Tun
No Par Common Stock	$ 5,000,000	$1,000,000	$3,500,000
Retained Earnings - January 1, 1996	$ 5,000,000	$1,000,000	$ 500,000
1996 Net Income	1,500,000	1,000,000	500,000
Retained Earnings - December 31, 1996	$ 6,500,000	$2,000,000	$1,000,000
1997 Net Income	2,500,000	1,000,000	500,000
Retained Earnings - December 31, 1997	$ 9,000,000	$3,000,000	$1,500,000
1998 Net Income	2,000,000	1,500,000	500,000
Retained Earnings - December 31, 1998	$11,000,000	$4,500,000	$2,000,000

Other Information   Other information on the three Companies is as follows:

A. During the period January 1, 1996 to December 31, 1998, none of the Companies paid or declared dividends or issued additional shares of common stock.

B. On all of the dates that are under consideration, the identifiable assets and liabilities of the Sun Company had fair values that are equal to their carrying values except for a building. On January 1, 1996, the fair value of this building exceeds its carrying value by $2,500,000. On December 31, 1996, this fair value increment has increased to $3,000,000 and it remains at that level until December 31, 1998. It is anticipated that this building will be used until December 31, 2005 and it is not expected to have any net salvage value. It is being depreciated by the straight line method.

C. On all of the dates that are under consideration, the identifiable assets and liabilities of the Tun Company have fair values that are equal to their carrying values.

D. Goodwill, if any is recognized in any of the business combination transactions, will be amortized over 40 years on a straight line basis.

E. All long term investments that arise in either version of this problem are carried by the cost method.

F. During 1998, the Tun Company sells merchandise to the Sun Company for $2,000,000 and to the Run Company for $2,800,000. Of these sales, $500,000 made to the Sun Company and $250,000 made to the Run Company remain in the December 31, 1998 inventories of the purchasing Company. The Tun Company's sales are priced to provide it with a gross margin of 20 percent on sales prices. There have been no intercompany sales prior to 1998.

Case One

Description Of Affiliation

7-105.   In this first situation, assume that on January 1, 1996, the Run Company acquires 80 percent of the outstanding voting shares of the Sun Company for $5,000,000 in cash. One year later, on December 31, 1996, the Sun Company acquires 75 percent of the outstanding voting shares of the Tun Company for $3,375,000 in cash. On that same date, the Run Company purchases 10 percent of the outstanding voting shares of the Tun Company for $450,000 in cash.

> **Required For Case One**   Compute consolidated Net Income for the year ending December 31, 1998 and the Non Controlling Interest that would be shown in the December 31, 1998 consolidated Balance Sheet. In addition, prepare a consolidated Statement Of Retained Earnings for the year ending December 31, 1998.

Investment Analysis - Run In Sun

7-106.   The analysis of the Run Company's investment in the Sun Company is as follows:

	80 Percent	100 Percent
Investment Cost	$5,000,000	$6,250,000
Book Value	(1,600,000)	(2,000,000)
Differential	$3,400,000	$4,250,000
Fair Value Change	(2,000,000)	(2,500,000)
Goodwill	$1,400,000	$1,750,000

7-107.   The fair value change on the Building would be depreciated over 10 years at the rate of $200,000 per year while the Goodwill is to be amortized over 40 years at the rate of $35,000 per year.

Investment Analysis - Run In Sun In Tun

7-108.   On December 31, 1996, the net book value of the assets of the Tun Company amounts to $4,500,000. When, on this date, the Run Company purchases 10 percent of Tun for $450,000 and the Sun Company buys 75 percent of Tun for $3,375,000, the investments are made at a price that is equal to the investor's proportionate share of the book value of the Tun Company. Since the basic data for the problem states that all of the Tun Company's net identifiable assets have fair values that are equal to their carrying values, it will not be necessary to make any adjustments for depreciation, or amortization of fair value changes or goodwill.

Procedures

7-109.   While it would be possible to apply our general consolidation procedures involving the use of journal entries to this problem, it is much more convenient to provide the information required using definitional calculations. This approach will be used here and in the Case Two version of this problem.

Consolidated Net Income

7-110.   Tun Company's Net Income must be adjusted for the $150,000 [(20%)($500,000 + $250,000)] unrealized intercompany inventory profit. The consolidated Net Income for the year ending December 31, 1998 can be calculated as follows:

Run Company's Net Income	$2,000,000
Run Company's Share Of The Net Income Of	
Sun Company [(80%)($1,500,000)]	1,200,000
Run Company's Direct Share Of The Adjusted Net Income	
Of Tun Company [(10%)($500,000 - $150,000)]	35,000
Run Company's Indirect Share Of The Adjusted Net Income	
Of The Tun Company [(80%)(75%)($500,000 -$150,000)]	210,000
Depreciation On Fair Value Change On Building	(200,000)
Goodwill Amortization	(35,000)
Consolidated Net Income	$3,210,000

Consolidated Statement Of Retained Earnings

7-111.   In preparing this consolidated financial statement, we will begin with the following calculation of the opening balance in consolidated Retained Earnings:

Run Company's Opening Balance		$ 9,000,000
Equity Pickup In Sun:		
Sun's Opening Balance	$3,000,000	
Balance At Acquisition	(1,000,000)	
Balance Since Acquisition	$2,000,000	
Run's Proportionate Interest	80%	1,600,000
Equity Pickup In Tun:		
Tun's Opening Balance	$1,500,000	
Balance At Acquisition	(1,000,000)	
Balance Since Acquisition	$ 500,000	
Run's Proportionate Interest -		
{[(80%)(75%)] + 10%}	70%	350,000
Balance Before Fair Value Adjustments		$10,950,000
Fair Value Adjustments:		
Building Depreciation (2 Years At $200,000)		(400,000)
Goodwill Amortization (2 Years At $35,000)		(70,000)
Consolidated Opening Balance		$10,480,000

7-112.   Given this calculation, the consolidated Statement Of Retained Earnings would be prepared as follows:

Run Company And Subsidiaries
Consolidated Statement Of Retained Earnings
For The Year Ending December 31, 1998

Balance - January 1, 1998	$10,480,000
Consolidated Net Income	3,210,000
Balance - December 31, 1998	$13,690,000

7-113.   The closing balance of $13,690,000 can be verified by the following calculation:

Run Company's Closing Balance		$11,000,000
Equity Pickup In Sun:		
Balance Since Acquisition	$3,500,000	
Run's Proportionate Interest	80%	2,800,000
Equity Pickup In Tun:		
Balance Since Acquisition	$1,000,000	
Unrealized Inventory Profits	(150,000)	
Adjusted Balance	$ 850,000	
Run's Proportionate Interest		
{[(80%)(75%)] + 10%}	70%	595,000
Balance Before Fair Value Adjustments		$14,395,000
Fair Value Adjustments:		
Building Depreciation (3 Years At $200,000)		(600,000)
Goodwill Amortization (3 Years At $35,000)		(105,000)
Consolidated Closing Balance		$13,690,000

7-114.   The preceding calculation serves to verify the balance that was computed in the consolidated Statement Of Retained Earnings by adding consolidated Net Income to the opening balance of consolidated Retained Earnings.

Non Controlling Interest

7-115.   The remaining requirement of this Case One is to compute the Non Controlling Interest that would be shown in the consolidated Balance Sheet as at December 31, 1998. This Non Controlling Interest is made up of the interests of two groups of shareholders. These are the non controlling shareholders in the Sun Company and the non controlling shareholders in the Tun Company. Note, however, that there are three components to the non controlling interest. They can be described as follows:

Sun In Sun   The 20 percent non controlling shareholder group in Sun Company have a direct interest in all of the net assets of that Company. This interest will be based on unadjusted carrying values as Sun's assets do not include any unrealized intercompany profits.

Tun In Tun   The 15 percent non controlling shareholder group in Tun Company have a direct interest in all of the net assets of that Company. This interest will be based on the carrying value of the Tun Company's net assets, less the $150,000 unrealized intercompany profit.

Sun In Tun   The non controlling shareholders in Sun Company have an indirect interest in the realized Retained Earnings of the Tun Company that have accrued since it was acquired by the Sun Company. If Sun carried its Investment In Tun by the equity method, this interest would be reflected in the net assets of the Sun Company and would be picked up in the calculation of the direct interest of the non controlling shareholders of Sun. However, as Sun carries its Investment In Tun by the cost method, a separate calculation of this indirect non controlling interest is required. Note that the Tun Retained Earnings will have to be adjusted for the $150,000 unrealized intercompany profit.

7-116.   The relevant calculations are as follows:

Sun Shareholders' Direct Interest In Sun:		
Common Stock [(20%)($1,000,000)]		$ 200,000
Retained Earnings (20%)($4,500,000)		900,000
Sun Shareholders' Indirect Interest In Tun:		
Retained Earnings Balance	$2,000,000	
Balance At Acquisition	(1,000,000)	
Balance Since Acquisition	$1,000,000	
Unrealized Inventory Profits	(150,000)	
Adjusted Balance	$ 850,000	
Proportionate Interest [(20%)(75%)]	15%	127,500
Tun Shareholders' Direct Interest In Tun:		
Common Stock (15%)($3,500,000)		525,000
Realized Retained Earnings (15%)($1,850,000)		277,500
Total Non Controlling Interest		$2,030,000

Case Two

7-117.   In this situation we will assume that on December 31, 1996, the Sun Company acquires 75 percent of the outstanding voting shares of the Tun Company for $3,375,000 in cash. One year later, on December 31, 1997, the Run Company acquires 80 percent of the outstanding voting shares of the Sun Company for $7,500,000 in cash.

Required For Case Two   Compute consolidated Net Income for the year ending December 31, 1998 and the Non Controlling Interest that would be shown in the December 31, 1998 consolidated Balance Sheet. In addition, prepare a consolidated Statement Of Retained Earnings for the year ending December 31, 1998.

Investment Analysis - Sun in Tun

7-118.   On December 31, 1996, the net book value of the assets of the Tun Company amounts to $4,500,000. When on this date, the Sun Company buys 75 percent of Tun for $3,375,000, the investment is made at a price that is equal to the investor's proportionate share of the book value of the Tun Company. Since the basic data for the problem states that all of the Tun Company's net identifiable assets have fair values that are equal to their carrying values, it will not be necessary to make any adjustment for depreciation or amortization of fair value changes or goodwill.

Investment Analysis - Run In Sun

7-119.   The analysis of the Run Company's investment in the Sun Company is as follows:

	80 Percent	100 Percent
Investment Cost	$7,500,000	$9,375,000
Book Value (See Note)	(3,500,000)	(4,375,000)
Differential	$4,000,000	$5,000,000
Fair Value Change	(2,400,000)	(3,000,000)
Goodwill	$1,600,000	$2,000,000

Note On Book Value   At the time the Run Company acquired its interest in the Sun Company, the Sun Company had been holding a controlling interest in the Tun Company for a period of one year. During this period, the Tun Company earned and retained income of $500,000 (the Tun Company's 1997 Net Income). Since the Sun

Company is carrying its investment in Tun by the cost method, Sun's equity in Tun's income since acquisition is not reflected on the books of the Sun Company. However, it should be included as part of the book value that is being purchased by the Run Company. Therefore, the book value for the Sun Company that is included in the investment analysis schedule is computed as follows:

Sun's Common Stock	$1,000,000
Sun's Retained Earnings	3,000,000
Sun's Equity Pickup In Tun's Earnings [(75%)($500,000)]	375,000
Total	$4,375,000

7-120.   With respect to the treatment of the fair value change and Goodwill in subsequent accounting periods, the fair value changes on the building would be amortized over 8 years at a rate of $300,000 per year while the Goodwill would be written off over 40 years at the rate of $40,000 per year.

Procedures

7-121.   Here again, we will not become involved with a complete application of the procedures that were developed in previous Chapters. Rather, we will use direct calculations of the various balances that are required in completing the problem.

Consolidated Net Income

7-122.   The first computation that is required in this Case Two is consolidated Net Income for the year ending December 31, 1998. This figure is calculated as follows:

Run Company's Net Income	$2,000,000
Run Company's Share Of The Net Income Of The Sun Company [(80%)($1,500,000)]	1,200,000
Run Company's Share Of Adjusted Net Income Of The Tun Company [(80%)(75%)($500,000 - $150,000)]	210,000
Depreciation On Fair Value Change On Building	(300,000)
Goodwill Amortization	(40,000)
Consolidated Net Income	$3,070,000

Consolidated Statement Of Retained Earnings

7-123.   Since the Run Company acquired the combined Sun and Tun Companies on December 31, 1997, the consolidated Retained Earnings balance on that date would simply be that of the Run Company or a balance of $9,000,000. Given this fact, the consolidated Statement Of Retained Earnings would be prepared as follows:

Run Company And Subsidiaries
Consolidated Statement Of Retained Earnings
For The Year Ending December 31, 1998

Balance - January 1, 1998	$ 9,000,000
Consolidated Net Income	3,070,000
Balance - December 31, 1998	$12,070,000

7-124.   As usual, we would recommend that you verify the final balance in this consolidated financial statement using a definitional calculation. This calculation would be as follows:

Run Company's Closing Balance		$11,000,000
Equity Pickup In Sun:		
Sun's Closing Balance	$4,500,000	
Balance At Acquisition	(3,000,000)	
Balance Since Acquisition	$1,500,000	
Run's Proportionate Interest	80%	1,200,000
Equity Pickup In Tun:		
Tun's Closing Balance	$2,000,000	
Balance At Acquisition	(1,500,000)	
Balance Since Acquisition	$ 500,000	
Unrealized Inventory Profits	(150,000)	
Tun's Adjusted Balance	$ 350,000	
Run's Proportionate Interest [(80%)(75%)]	60%	210,000
Balance Before Fair Value Adjustments		$12,410,000
Fair Value Adjustments - Building Depreciation (1 Year)		(300,000)
Fair Value Adjustment - Goodwill Amortization (1 Year)		(40,000)
Consolidated Closing Balance		$12,070,000

7-125.   This serves to verify the balance that was computed in the consolidated Statement Of Retained Earnings by adding consolidated Net Income to the opening balance of consolidated Retained Earnings.

Non Controlling Interest

7-126.   The Non Controlling Interest as at December 31, 1998, is again made up of the interest of two groups of non controlling shareholders. These are the non controlling shareholders of the Sun Company and the non controlling shareholders of the Tun Company. Further, the non controlling shareholders of the Sun Company have an interest in the net assets of both the Sun Company and the Tun Company. As the Sun Company is once again carrying its investment in the Tun Company by the cost method, a separate computation will have to be made in order to pick up the Sun Company non controlling shareholders' interest in the Retained Earnings of the Tun Company since its acquisition by the Sun Company. The complete calculation is as follows:

Sun Shareholders' Interest In Sun:		
Common Stock [(20%)($1,000,000)]		$ 200,000
Retained Earnings [(20%)($4,500,000)]		900,000
Sun Shareholders' Interest In Tun:		
Retained Earnings Balance	$2,000,000	
Balance At Acquisition	(1,000,000)	
Balance Since Acquisition	$1,000,000	
Unrealized Intercompany Profit	(150,000)	
Adjusted Balance	$ 850,000	
Sun Shareholders' Proportionate		
Interest [(20%)(75%)]	15%	127,500
Tun Shareholders' Interest In Tun:		
Common Stock [(25%)($3,500,000)]		875,000
Realized Retained Earnings		
[(25%)($2,000,000 - $150,000)]		462,500
Total Non Controlling Interest		$2,565,000

7-127.   This schedule completes the requirements of Case Two and the presentation of the problems associated with preparing consolidated financial statements in multi-level affiliations.

Reciprocal Shareholdings

The Basic Problem

7-128.   We have previously dealt with situations involving multi-level affiliations. You will recall that this involved the indirect ownership of subsidiaries with more than one level of investment existing below the parent company. However, at that time we confined ourselves to those cases in which all of the investment affiliations were downstream from the parent to each lower level of subsidiary relationship. The term reciprocal holdings refers to the generally more complex situations in which one or more subsidiaries has turned upstream and invested either in a subsidiary at a higher level in the ownership hierarchy or in the parent company itself. We will now turn our attention to illustrating the procedures to be used when there are reciprocal investments.

7-129.   The basic problem that arises in situations where, for example, a parent owns the majority of the outstanding voting shares of a subsidiary and the subsidiary owns some portion of the outstanding shares of the parent, relates to the computation of the proportionate equities in the income and Retained Earnings of the two companies. In order to determine the parent's share of the income of the subsidiary one must first determine the income of the subsidiary and, this in turn, will require the determination of the subsidiary's share of the income of the parent. The solution to this obviously circular process requires the application of simultaneous equations.   While this is a basic algebraic technique for solving a group of equations which have a number of variables that is equal to or less than the number of equations, it is not commonly used by accountants and, as a consequence, can generate a certain amount of difficulty in solving problems involving reciprocal holdings. Other than this problem, however, we will find that reciprocal shareholdings do not involve any new concepts or procedures.

Case One

Basic Data

7-130.   The first example will involve a very simple situation.

Company Aye acquires 70 percent of the voting shares of Company Bye on January 1, 1994 and, also on this date, Company Bye acquires 10 percent of the voting shares of Company Aye. As both companies were newly incorporated on this date, there are no fair value changes, Goodwill or Retained Earnings at acquisition to be dealt with in this problem. On December 31, 1998, the Balance Sheets of the two Companies appeared as follows:

	Aye	Bye
Investment In Bye (At Cost)	$ 140,000	$ -0-
Investment In Aye (At Cost)	-0-	50,000
Other Net Assets	1,060,000	450,000
Total Assets	$1,200,000	$500,000
Common Stock - No Par	$ 500,000	$200,000
Retained Earnings	700,000	300,000
Total Equities	$1,200,000	$500,000

There were no additions or deletions to either Company's Common Stock - No Par accounts during the period January 1, 1994 to December 31, 1998. In addition, there were no intercompany transactions during this period.

Required   Prepare a consolidated Balance Sheet for the Aye Company and its subsidiary, the Bye Company, as at December 31, 1998.

Retained Earnings Allocation

7-131.   The only real difficulty in this problem is the allocation of the $1,000,000 in Retained Earnings to the respective shares of the non controlling and controlling interests. This is where the application of simultaneous equations plays a role. The following two equations can be used to express the respective interest of the two Companies in the balances of the Retained Earnings accounts:

Aye = $700,000 + (70 Percent Of Bye)
Bye = $300,000 + (10 Percent Of Aye)

7-132.   Solving these two equations gives the following values:

Aye = $978,494
Bye = $397,849

7-133.   As would be expected, the sum of these two figures is in excess of the amount to be allocated. This reflects the fact that each amount contains a proportionate share of the other balance. This duplication will not, of course, find its way into the completed financial statements.

Non Controlling Interest

7-134.   The Aye balance of $978,494 contains a 10 percent non controlling interest of $97,849 that is included in the Bye interest and must be removed in order to arrive at the appropriate consolidated Retained Earnings figure of $880,645.

7-135.   The Bye balance of $397,849 contains a controlling interest that is reflected in the preceding consolidated Retained Earnings balance. To arrive at the non controlling interest in Retained Earnings since acquisition, this 70 percent controlling interest of $278,494 must be removed. This will leave $119,355 as the non controlling interest in Retained Earnings since acquisition. If we add the $60,000 non controlling interest in the Common Stock of Bye to this amount, we are left with a total Non Controlling Interest to be presented in the consolidated Balance Sheet of $179,355.

Case One Consolidated Balance Sheet

7-136.   The Balance Sheet that is required in this example can be completed as follows:

Aye Company And Subsidiary
Consolidated Balance Sheet
As At December 31, 1998

Other Net Assets		$1,510,000
Non Controlling Interest		$ 179,355
Shareholders' Equity		
Common Stock - No Par	500,000	
Retained Earnings	880,645	
Shares In Aye Held By Subsidiary	(50,000)	1,330,645
Total Equities		$1,510,000

7-137.   Note that the Bye Company's investment in the shares of the Aye Company has been shown as a deduction from the total consolidated Shareholders' Equity. This reflects the Recommendation of Paragraph 1600.71 of the *CICA Handbook*. This Recommendation is as follows:

Paragraph 1600.71   *Where a subsidiary company holds shares of the parent company, the issued share capital of the parent should be set out in full, with the cost of the shares held by the subsidiary shown as a deduction from shareholders' equity. (See "Share Capital," Section 3240) (April, 1975)*

Case Two

Basic Data

7-138.   This example of reciprocal shareholding procedures involves three companies.

On January 1, 1993, the Ex Company buys 70 percent of the voting shares of the Why Company and 80 percent of the voting shares of the Zee Company. Also on this date, Why purchases 10 percent of the voting shares of the Zee Company and Zee purchases 20 percent of the voting shares of the Why Company. As in the previous example, all of the Companies are newly incorporated on this date and, as a result, there are no problems associated with fair value changes, Goodwill, or Retained Earnings at acquisition. On December 31, 1998, the Balance Sheets of the three Companies are as follows:

	Ex	Why	Zee
Investment In Why	$ 350,000	$ -0-	$100,000
Investment In Zee	320,000	40,000	-0-
Other Net Assets	930,000	710,000	400,000
Total Net Assets	$1,600,000	$750,000	$500,000
Common Stock - No Par	$1,000,000	$500,000	$400,000
Retained Earnings	600,000	250,000	100,000
Total Equities	$1,600,000	$750,000	$500,000

There are no additions or deletions to any Company's Common Stock account during the period January 1, 1993 through December 31, 1998. In addition, there were no intercompany transactions during this period. All investment accounts are carried by the cost method.

Required   Prepare a consolidated Balance Sheet for the Ex Company and its subsidiaries, the Why and Zee Companies, as at December 31, 1998.

Retained Earnings Allocation

7-139.   Here again, our basic problem is the allocation of the Retained Earnings balances to the respective controlling and non controlling interests. The equations on which this allocation is to be based are as follows:

$$Ex = \$600,000 + (70 \text{ Percent Of Why}) + (80 \text{ Percent Of Zee})$$
$$Why = \$250,000 + (10 \text{ Percent Of Zee})$$
$$Zee = \$100,000 + (20 \text{ Percent Of Why})$$

7-140.   Solving these three equations gives the following values:

$$Ex = \$908,163$$
$$Why = \$265,306$$
$$Zee = \$153,061$$

7-141.   As in this case, neither subsidiary has any interest in the earnings of the parent company, the consolidated Retained Earnings balance is simply the $908,163 calculated above for the Ex Company. This also means that there will be no deduction in the consolidated shareholders' equity for subsidiary holdings of parent company shares.

Non Controlling Interest

7-142.   The total non controlling interest can be calculated as follows:

Common Stock - Why (10 Percent Of $500,000)	$ 50,000
Common Stock - Zee (10 Percent Of $400,000)	40,000
Retained Earnings - Why (10 Percent Of $265,306)	26,531
Retained Earnings - Zee (10 Percent Of $153,061)	15,306
Total Non Controlling Interest	$131,837

Case Two Consolidated Balance Sheet

7-143.   The Balance Sheet that is required in this example can be completed as follows:

Ex Company And Subsidiaries
Consolidated Balance Sheet
As At December 31, 1998

Other Net Assets	$2,040,000
Non Controlling Interest	$ 131,837
Common Stock - No Par	1,000,000
Retained Earnings	908,163
Total Equities	$2,040,000

Case Three

Basic Data

7-144.   As should be fairly obvious to you, the preceding examples are very elementary. There have been no fair value changes or goodwill, no unrealized intercompany profits and, in general, a lack of the types of complicating factors that are often found in consolidation problems. As such they are consistent with the examples contained in the Case Studies at the end of Section 1600 of the *CICA Handbook*. This final Case is intended to provide a more complex illustration involving both differential allocations and intercompany profits. In putting this example together, we would note that there are alternative procedures that can be used for dealing with these new issues. Further, it is not completely clear from reading Section 1600 which alternatives are to be used.

7-145.   As noted previously, Paragraph 1600.71 of the *CICA Handbook* requires that the cost of the subsidiary's holdings in the parent be deducted from consolidated shareholders' equity. Further, if the subsidiary has acquired the parent company's shares at a price which is different from the proportionate share of the parent's book value, the non controlling interest in this differential must be recognized. This is reflected in the following Recommendation:

Paragraph 1600.52   *A difference arising from the elimination of reciprocal shareholdings among companies in the consolidated group should be allocated to parent and non-controlling interests on the basis of their proportionate shareholdings.* (April, 1975)

7-146.   Taken together, these two Paragraphs would indicate that any difference between the cost of the subsidiary's investment in the parent and its proportionate share of the related book values would not be allocated to assets at the time of acquisition or written off against income in subsequent accounting periods.

7-147.   When we turn to dealing with any differential that might arise on the parent's investment in the subsidiary and to the treatment of upstream and downstream unrealized profits, Section 1600 does not contain any Recommendations specific to reciprocal holdings situations. However, the general rules would appear to be applicable here and will be used in the example which follows.

Example   On December 31, 1995, the single entity Balance Sheets of the Noar and Soar Companies are as follows:

Condensed Balance Sheets
As At December 31, 1995

	Noar	Soar
Net Assets	$8,000,000	$4,000,000
No Par Common Stock	$5,000,000	$3,000,000
Retained Earnings	3,000,000	1,000,000
Total Shareholders' Equity	$8,000,000	$4,000,000

On this date, the Noar Company purchases 85 percent of the outstanding voting shares of the Soar Company for $3,800,000 in cash, while the Soar Company purchases 10 percent of the outstanding voting shares of the Noar Company for $900,000 in cash. On the acquisition date, all of the identifiable assets and liabilities of both Companies have fair values that are equal to their carrying values. Both Companies carry their Long Term Investments at cost and any goodwill which arises on this business combination transaction will be amortized over 20 years.

The condensed Income Statements of the two Companies for the year ending December 31, 1998, are as follows:

Condensed Income Statements
For The Year Ending December 31, 1998

	Noar	Soar
Revenues	$1,250,000	$960,000
Expenses	1,110,000	840,000
Net Income	$ 140,000	$120,000

During 1998, the sales of Soar Company include an amount of $125,000 which represents sales to Noar Company. Of these sales, merchandise which contains a gross profit of $18,000 remains in the December 31, 1998 Inventories of Noar Company. Also during 1998, Soar Company purchases $85,000 in merchandise from the Noar Company. At the end of 1998, $25,000 of this merchandise remains in the ending inventories of the Soar Company. Included in this amount is a gross profit of $12,000. During 1998, the Noar Company declares and pays dividends of $80,000 while the Soar Company declares and pays dividends of $60,000. There were no other transactions between the two Companies in any of the years that are under consideration.

The condensed Balance Sheets of the two Companies as at December 31, 1998 are as follows:

Condensed Balance Sheets
As At December 31, 1998

	Noar	Soar
Investments	$3,800,000	$ 900,000
Other Net Identifiable Assets	4,540,000	3,410,000
Total Assets	$8,340,000	$4,310,000
No Par Common Stock	$5,000,000	$3,000,000
Retained Earnings	3,340,000	1,310,000
Total Shareholders' Equity	$8,340,000	$4,310,000

Required:

A. Prepare a consolidated Balance Sheet as at December 31, 1995.

B. Prepare a consolidated Income Statement and a consolidated Statement Of Retained Earnings for the year ending December 31, 1998, and a consolidated Balance Sheet as at December 31, 1998.

December 31, 1995 Consolidated Balance Sheet

7-148.   Before preparing this Balance Sheet, an analysis of the two investments must be made:

	Noar In Soar	Soar In Noar
Investment Cost	$3,800,000	$900,000
Book Value:		
85 Percent Of $4,000,000	(3,400,000)	
10 Percent Of $8,000,000		(800,000)
Differential	$ 400,000	$100,000

7-149.   The $400,000 differential which arises on Noar's Investment In Soar will be allocated to Goodwill and amortized at the rate of $20,000 per year ($400,000 ÷ 20). The other differential will be, in effect, part of the amount that is deducted from the consolidated shareholders' equity as a reflection of the Soar Company's $900,000 investment in the common stock of Noar Company.   Given these calculations, the required Balance Sheet is as follows:

Noar Company And Subsidiary
Consolidated Balance Sheet
As At December 31, 1995

Net Identifiable Assets - ($8,000,000		
+ $4,000,000 - $3,800,000 - $900,000)		$7,300,000
Goodwill		400,000
Total Assets		$7,700,000
Non Controlling Interest [(15%)($4,000,000)]		$ 600,000
Shareholders' Equity		
Common Stock	5,000,000	
Retained Earnings	3,000,000	
Shares In Noar Held By Subsidiary	(900,000)	7,100,000
Total Equities		$7,700,000

1998 Consolidated Income Statement

7-150.   Before proceeding to the consolidated Income Statement, it will be necessary to solve the following income equations of the two Companies. The Net Income of both Companies must be adjusted for unrealized inventory profits and intercompany dividends received. In addition, the $20,000 amortization of Goodwill reduces the Noar income equation.

Noar   = $140,000 - $12,000 - [(85%)($60,000)] - $20,000 + [(85%)(Soar)]
Soar   = $120,000 - $18,000 - [(10%)($80,000)] + [(10%)(Noar)]

7-151.   Solving these equations gives:

Noar   = $149,617
Soar   = $108,962

7-152. Given these solutions, the required Income Statement is as follows:

Noar Company And Subsidiary
Consolidated Income Statement
For The Year Ending December 31, 1998

Revenues ($1,250,000 + $960,000 - $125,000	
- $85,000 - $8,000 - $51,000)	$1,941,000
Expenses ($1,110,000 + $840,000 - $125,000	
- $85,000 + $12,000 + $18,000 + $20,000)	(1,790,000)
Non Controlling Interest [(15%)($108,962)]	(16,344)
Consolidated Net Income	$ 134,656

1998 Consolidated Statement Of Retained Earnings

7-153. In order to prepare this statement we need to solve the following equations related to the January 1, 1998 Retained Earnings balance:

Noar = $3,280,000 - $3,000,000 - (2 years @ $20,000) + ([85%][Soar])
Soar = $1,250,000 - $1,000,000 + ([10%][Noar])

7-154. Solving for these equations gives:

Noar = $494,536
Soar = $299,454

7-155. The required consolidated Statement Of Retained Earnings is as follows:

Noar Company And Subsidiary
Consolidated Statement Of Retained Earnings
For The Year Ending December 31, 1998

Opening Balance [$3,000,000 + (90%)($494,536)]	$3,445,082
Consolidated Net Income	134,656
Dividends [(90%)($80,000)]	(72,000)
Closing Balance	$3,507,738

December 31, 1998 Consolidated Balance Sheet

7-156. Using the information from the other financial statements, the consolidated Balance Sheet can be prepared as follows:

Noar Company And Subsidiary
Consolidated Balance Sheet
As At December 31, 1998

Net Identifiable Assets ($4,540,000		
+ $3,410,000 - $12,000 - $18,000)		$7,920,000
Goodwill ($400,000 - $60,000)		340,000
Total Assets		$8,260,000
Non Controlling Interest ($600,000 + [15%][$299,454]		
+ $16,344 - [15%][$60,000])		$ 652,262
Shareholders' Equity:		
No Par Common Stock	5,000,000	
Retained Earnings (From Statement)	3,507,738	
Shares In Noar Held By Subsidiary	(900,000)	7,607,738
Total Equities		$8,260,000

7-157. The only item in the preceding Balance Sheet which requires further explanation is the Non Controlling Interest. We have computed this balance by first calculating the January 1, 1998 Non Controlling Interest [$600,000 + (15%)($299,454)], adding the Non Controlling Interest in 1998 income of $16,344 and subtracting $9,000 in dividends paid to non controlling shareholders. There are, of course, more direct ways of calculating both this year end balance and the year end balance in Retained Earnings. We would suggest that you attempt the direct calculations of the end of year balances as a test of your understanding of this subject.

Subsidiary Preferred Stock

Classification Of Preferred Stock

7-158.   Because of their hybrid nature, preferred shares have always presented accountants with some difficulties in terms of determining the appropriate disclosure in the financial statements. While these securities may have some of the characteristics that we associate with debt securities (a specified rate of income, a claim in liquidation that is prior to the common shareholder), they also have attributes that we normally associate with common stock (no maturity date, no legal claim to income if dividends are not declared).

7-159.   The problem is made more difficult by the fact that not all preferred shares have the same characteristics. For example, there are issues of preferred stock that have all of the characteristics of the corporation's common shares except for the fact that they do not have voting rights. It would seem fairly clear that this type of preferred stock should be classified as an equity item in the Balance Sheet. In contrast, there are issues of preferred stock that not only have a fixed rate of dividends but, in addition, have a guaranteed redemption value. This type of preferred stock is clearly more akin to debt than to equity. This view is reflected in the Recommendations contained in Section 3860 of the *CICA Handbook* which was issued in September, 1995. This Section, "Financial Instruments - Disclosure And Presentation", requires that preferred shares involving a "contractual obligation on one party to the financial instrument (the issuer) either to deliver cash or another financial asset to the other party (the holder) or to exchange another financial instrument with the holder under conditions that are potentially unfavourable to the issuer", should be classified as liabilities.

7-160.   Until the introduction of Section 3860 into the *CICA Handbook*, the common Canadian practice was to deal with all preferred shares as though they were a part of total shareholders' equity. It is likely that this situation will continue, except in situations where the terms of the shares require that they be classified as a liability.

7-161.   A further exception to this disclosure exists when a subsidiary has preferred shares outstanding. In consolidated financial statements, the Canadian practice is to disclose the equity of the subsidiary's preferred shareholders in the net assets of the subsidiary company as a part of the non controlling interest. The basis for this practice is found in the following *Handbook* suggestion:

> **Paragraph 1600.68** Non-controlling interest is shown as a separate item on the balance sheet outside of shareholders' equity and may be composed of more than one class of equity interest.

7-162.   You may recall from our previous discussions of the non controlling interest that Paragraph 1600.69 of the *CICA Handbook* requires that the non controlling interest in the Balance Sheet be disclosed separately from shareholders' equity. In our opinion, this is not consistent with the treatment of other preferred stock balances.

Issues Raised By Consolidation

Non Controlling Interest

7-163.   The presence of preferred stock in the capital structure of a subsidiary, even in those cases where there are no intercompany holdings of the shares, complicates the computation of the Non Controlling Interest and consolidated Retained Earnings in the preparation of consolidated financial statements. The degree of complexity that these shares add to the problem of preparing consolidated financial statements is dependent on the nature of the income provision that has been written into the preferred share agreement. If the dividend claim is non cumulative, the claim of the preferred shareholders against the total shareholders' equity of the subsidiary will not extend beyond the capital that they have contributed. However, if the dividend claim is cumulative and the subsidiary has missed paying the specified dividend in one or more previous periods, these preferred dividend arrearages will constitute a claim against the unappropriated Retained Earnings of the subsidiary. Even more complicated is the situation in which the preferred shareholders have a right to participate in the income beyond the rate that is specified in the preferred share agreement. In this situation, the preferred shareholders will have an interest in their proportionate share of all of the Retained Earnings of the subsidiary.

Differentials

7-164. Further problems can be created when there are parent company purchases of preferred shares. If the shares have been purchased at a price that is equal to their claim on the carrying values of the net assets of the subsidiary, there is no problem as an equal amount of assets and equities will be eliminated and this, of course, will have no effect on anything other than total assets and equities. However, if there is a discrepancy between the amount paid for the stock and its claim against the carrying values of the subsidiary's net assets, the elimination of the share balance and the related investment account will leave a differential to be allocated.

7-165. For example, if subsidiary preferred shares with a book value of $1,000,000 were acquired by the parent company at a cost of $1,200,000, the entry to eliminate the resulting intercompany balances would be as follows:

Preferred Shares	$1,000,000	
Differential	200,000	
Investment In Preferred Shares		$1,200,000

7-166. If common shares were involved, the Recommendations of the *CICA Handbook* would require that this differential be allocated to fair value changes and goodwill (see the discussion of these procedures in Chapters 4 and 5). However, preferred shares generally have a fixed claim in liquidation and, as a consequence, cannot be viewed as having a residual interest in the net assets of the corporation. Given this, we do not believe that differentials arising on the elimination of intercompany preferred shareholdings should be treated in the same manner as differentials on common shares.

7-167. While the *CICA Handbook* does not provide specific guidance on this issue, we are of the opinion that, when a parent company acquires subsidiary preferred shares from individual shareholders other than the subsidiary, from the point of view of the consolidated entity the acquisition constitutes a retirement of these shares. This corresponds to the treatment of intercompany holdings of bonds. As was noted earlier in this Chapter, intercompany acquisitions of bonds are treated as retirements, resulting in a gain or loss to be recorded in the consolidated financial statements. Note, however, the retirement of preferred shares would be a capital transaction and, as a consequence, the differential that arises on elimination of the intercompany balances would not be treated as a gain or loss.

7-168. If we view an acquisition by a parent company of outstanding subsidiary preferred shares as a retirement of these shares, any differential arising on the elimination of intercompany balances would be subject to the rules in *CICA Handbook* Section 3240, "Share Capital". Under these rules, a debit differential would normally be charged to Retained Earnings, while a credit differential would be credited to contributed capital. In the example in Paragraph 7-165, the $200,000 debit would be to Retained Earnings.

Examples - Basic Data

7-169. The problems associated with subsidiary preferred stock will be illustrated in three examples. The first Example is a simple one involving a subsidiary with an issue of non cumulative preferred shares. There is a parent company purchase of these shares at a price that is equal to their carrying value on the books of the subsidiary. Example Two is similar to Example One. However, in addition to the parent company purchase of these shares at a price that is equal to their claims against the carrying values of the subsidiary's net assets, we have added a complicating factor in that the preferred shares have a cumulative dividend provision. Example Three is the most complex version of the problem. The parent company purchase of preferred shares remains in the Example. However, the preferred shares will be assumed to have a provision that provides their holders with full participation in the earnings of the subsidiary.

7-170. The same basic data will be used for all of the Examples to be presented. The parent company will be designated the Peel Company while the subsidiary will be the Seal Company. The basic information on the shareholders' equity, income and dividends of the two Companies is as follows:

	Peel	Seal
No Par Common Stock	$1,800,000	$600,000
Preferred Stock - 8 Percent, Par $50	-0-	300,000
Total Contributed Capital	$1,800,000	$900,000
Retained Earnings - January 1, 1996	$1,200,000	$300,000
1996 Net Income	150,000	60,000
1996 Dividends	-0-	-0-
Retained Earnings - December 31, 1996	$1,350,000	$360,000
1997 Net Income	150,000	60,000
1997 Dividends	-0-	-0-
Retained Earnings - December 31, 1997	$1,500,000	$420,000

7-171. The subsidiary has not paid dividends on the preferred shares in 1996 or 1997 and this, in turn, has prevented the payment of dividends on the common shares. As a result, the Net Income of the Peel Company does not contain investment income in either 1996 or 1997. This is due to the assumption that the Peel Company carries its investment in the Seal Company by the cost method. During 1998, the Peel Company earns a Net Income of $120,000 before the recognition of any investment income from its subsidiary and the Seal Company has a Net Income of $150,000.

Example One - The Non Cumulative Case

7-172. In this first Example, assume that the Preferred Stock of the Seal Company is non cumulative and non participating. The data is as follows:

The Peel Company purchases 40 percent of the Seal Company's 8 percent Preferred Stock for $120,000 in cash and 60 percent of the Seal Company's Common Stock for $540,000 [(60%)($600,000 + $300,000)] in cash. Both of these investment transactions take place on January 1, 1996. The purchases are made at book value and, at this time, the net identifiable assets of the Seal Company have fair values that are equal to their carrying values. During 1998, the Peel Company does not pay any dividends while the Seal Company pays Common Stock dividends of $36,000 and Preferred Stock dividends of $24,000. The Balance Sheets of the two Companies on December 31, 1998 are as follows:

	Peel	Seal
Investment In Seal's Preferred Stock	$ 120,000	$ -0-
Investment In Seal's Common Stock	540,000	-0-
Other Net Assets	2,791,200	1,410,000
Total Assets	$3,451,200	$1,410,000
Preferred Stock - 8%, Par $50	$ -0-	$ 300,000
No Par Common Stock	1,800,000	600,000
Retained Earnings	1,651,200	510,000
Total Equities	$3,451,200	$1,410,000

The Retained Earnings balance of the Peel Company consists of the December 31, 1997 balance of $1,500,000, the 1998 Net Income exclusive of investment income of $120,000, dividends received on Preferred Stock of $9,600 (40 Percent Of $24,000), and dividends received on Common Stock of $21,600 (60 Percent Of $36,000).

Required   Calculate the 1998 consolidated Net Income. In addition, prepare a consolidated Statement Of Retained Earnings for the year ending December 31, 1998, and a consolidated Balance Sheet as at December 31, 1998 for the Peel Company and its subsidiary.

Step A - Investment Elimination

7-173.   As both the common and preferred stock investments are made at prices that are equal to book values and no fair value changes are present on the acquisition date, no investment analysis schedule is necessary. Going directly to the investment elimination entry, where the investment in both the common and preferred stock will be eliminated, it is as follows:

Preferred Stock - 8 Percent, Par $50	$300,000	
No Par Common Stock	600,000	
Retained Earnings	300,000	
Investment In Seal's Preferred Stock		$120,000
Investment In Seal's Common Stock		540,000
Non Controlling Interest		540,000

7-174.   As usual, we have eliminated 100 percent of the investment accounts and 100 percent of the subsidiary's shareholders' equity as at the acquisition date. The only difference here is that the credit to the Non Controlling Interest is made up of a common stock interest (40 percent of $900,000, or $360,000) and a Preferred Stock interest (60 percent of $300,000, or $180,000).

Step B - Adjustments And Eliminations

7-175.   The only adjustment or elimination that is required here is the entry to eliminate the intercompany dividends. Other than the fact that two types of dividends are involved, it is the same entry that we have used for intercompany dividend eliminations in the past and is as follows:

Dividend Revenue ($21,600 + $9,600)	$31,200	
Non Controlling Interest ($14,400 + $14,400)	28,800	
Preferred Dividends Declared		$24,000
Common Dividends Declared		36,000

Step C - Retained Earnings Distribution

7-176.   The Retained Earnings of the Seal Company since acquisition to the beginning of 1998 is equal to $120,000 ($420,000 - $300,000) and since there are no adjustments or eliminations to be made against this amount, it will simply be split between non controlling and controlling interests on the basis of their share of the Seal Company's common shares. That is, the non controlling interest will get 40 percent while the controlling interest is allocated 60 percent. The entry is as follows:

Opening Retained Earnings - Seal	$120,000	
Non Controlling Interest		$48,000
Consolidated Retained Earnings		72,000

7-177. This entry reflects the fact that the non participating Preferred Stock has no claim against the Seal Company's Retained Earnings in this Example.

Consolidated Net Income

7-178. The consolidated Net Income for 1998 of the Peel Company and its subsidiary can be calculated as follows:

Peel's Reported Net Income	$151,200
Less: Intercompany Dividends	31,200
Peel's Income Exclusive Of Dividends	$120,000
Equity Pickup:	
Common [(60%)($150,000 - $24,000)]	75,600
Preferred [(40%)($24,000)]	9,600
Consolidated Net Income	$205,200

Note that the common stock interest is based on the earnings of the common stockholders and not Net Income. That is, the preferred dividend claim must be subtracted from Net Income in order to arrive at the interest of the common stockholders. The fact that the preferred shares are non cumulative means that, if the preferred dividends had not been declared, the claim of the preferred shareholders could have been ignored. In that case, the equity pickup would have been $90,000 (60 percent of $150,000).

Consolidated Statement Of Retained Earnings

7-179. As given in the Basic Data for the examples, on January 1, 1998, the Retained Earnings of the Peel Company amount to $1,500,000. If we add the allocation of $72,000 from the Step C distribution entry, we have the opening consolidated Retained Earnings of $1,572,000. Given this, the consolidated Statement Of Retained Earnings for 1998 of the Peel Company and its subsidiary can be prepared as follows:

Peel Company And Subsidiary
Consolidated Statement Of Retained Earnings
For The Year Ending December 31, 1998

Balance - January 1, 1998	$1,572,000
Consolidated Net Income	205,200
Balance - December 31, 1998	$1,777,200

7-180. You may wish to verify the ending balance in consolidated Retained Earnings using a definitional calculation.

Consolidated Balance Sheet

7-181. The consolidated Balance Sheet as at December 31, 1998, for the Peel Company and its subsidiary would be prepared as follows:

Peel Company And Subsidiary
Consolidated Balance Sheet
As At December 31, 1998

Investment In Seal's Preferred Stock ($120,000 -$120,000)	$ -0-
Investment In Seal's Common Stock ($540,000 -$540,000)	-0-
Other Net Assets ($2,791,200 + $1,410,000)	4,201,200
Total Assets	**$4,201,200**

Preferred Stock - 8 Percent, Par $50 ($300,000 -$300,000)	$ -0-
Non Controlling Interest (See Following Calculation)	624,000
No Par Common Stock (Peel's Only)	1,800,000
Retained Earnings (See Statement)	1,777,200
Total Equities	**$4,201,200**

Non Controlling Interest

7-182.   The Non Controlling Interest in the preceding consolidated Balance Sheet can be calculated as follows:

Preferred Stock Interest [(60%)($300,000)]	$180,000
Common Stock Interest:	
Contributed Capital [(40%)($600,000)]	240,000
Retained Earnings [(40%)($510,000)]	204,000
Total Non Controlling Interest	**$624,000**

Example Two - Cumulative Case

7-183.   This example is based on the same basic data that was used in Example One. The major difference here is that we will assume that the subsidiary preferred shares have a cumulative dividend provision. However, we retain the assumption that these shares do not participate in earnings beyond their specified dividend rate. The data is as follows:

The Peel Company purchases 40 percent of the Seal Company's 8 percent Preferred Stock for $120,000 in cash and 60 percent of the Seal Company's Common Stock for $540,000 in cash. Both of these investment transactions take place on January 1, 1996. The purchases are made at book value and, at this time, the net identifiable assets of the Seal Company have fair values that are equal to their carrying values. On this investment date, there are no dividend arrearages on the shares of Preferred Stock.

During 1998, the Seal Company will pay Common Stock dividends of $36,000. However, because we are now dealing with cumulative Preferred Stock, the Seal Company must make up all dividend arrearages before the $36,000 dividend can be paid on the Common Stock. Since the Basic Data for the examples states that the Seal Company paid no preferred dividends in 1996 and 1997, the 1998 dividends on Preferred Stock will have to total $72,000. This is the annual dividend of $24,000 for a period of three years. The Balance Sheets for the two Companies on December 31, 1998 are as follows:

	Peel	Seal
Investment In Seal's Preferred Stock	$ 120,000	$ -0-
Investment In Seal's Common Stock	540,000	-0-
Other Net Assets	2,810,400	1,362,000
Total Assets	**$3,470,400**	**$1,362,000**

	Peel	Seal
Preferred Stock - 8%, Par $50	$ -0-	$ 300,000
No Par Common Stock	1,800,000	600,000
Retained Earnings	1,670,400	462,000
Total Equities	$3,470,400	$1,362,000

The Retained Earnings balance of the Peel Company consists of the December 31, 1997 balance of $1,500,000, plus the Net Income exclusive of investment income of $120,000, plus dividends received on Preferred Stock of $28,800 (40 percent of $72,000), plus dividends received on Common Stock of $21,600 (60 percent of $36,000).

Required   Calculate the 1998 consolidated Net Income. In addition, prepare a consolidated Statement Of Retained Earnings for the year ending December 31, 1998, and a consolidated Balance Sheet as at December 31, 1998 for the Peel Company and its subsidiary.

Step A - Investment Elimination

7-184.   The investment elimination entry in this Example would be identical to that required in Example One. This is as follows:

Preferred Stock - 8 Percent, $50 Par	$300,000	
No Par Common Stock	600,000	
Retained Earnings	300,000	
Investment In Seal's Preferred Stock		$120,000
Investment In Seal's Common Stock		540,000
Non Controlling Interest		540,000

Step B - Adjustments And Eliminations

7-185.   As in Example One, the only adjustment that is required is to eliminate the intercompany dividends. It is as follows:

Dividend Revenue ($21,600 + $28,800)	$50,400	
Non Controlling Interest ($14,400 + $43,200)		57,600
Preferred Dividends Declared		$72,000
Common Dividends Declared		36,000

Step C - Retained Earnings Distribution

7-186.   The Retained Earnings of the Seal Company since acquisition equal $120,000. However, in this Example Two, there are $48,000 (2 years at $24,000) in preferred dividend arrearages that have a prior claim on this balance. As a result of this fact, the preferred claim is $28,800 (60 percent of $48,000) while the non controlling common shareholders have a $28,800 claim which is 40 percent of the balance of $72,000 ($120,000 - $48,000). Correspondingly, the allocation to consolidated Retained Earnings would be $19,200 (40 percent of $48,000) plus $43,200 (60 percent of $72,000) for a total of $62,400. The entry would be as follows:

Opening Retained Earnings - Seal	$120,000	
Non Controlling Interest		$57,600
Consolidated Retained Earnings		62,400

Consolidated Net Income

7-187.   The consolidated Net Income for 1998 of the Peel Company and its subsidiary can be calculated as follows:

Peel's Reported Net Income ($120,000 + $28,800 + $21,600)	$170,400
Intercompany Dividends	(50,400)
Peel's Income Exclusive Of Subsidiary Dividends	$120,000
Equity Pickups:	
Common Stock [(60%)($150,000 - $24,000)]	75,600
Preferred Stock [(40%)($24,000)]	9,600
Consolidated Net Income	$205,200

7-188.   Note that this is the same consolidated Net Income that we arrived at in Example One. This means that the dividend arrearages and their payment during the current year have had no effect on the current year's consolidated Net Income.

Consolidated Statement Of Retained Earnings

7-189.   As given in the Basic Data, on January 1, 1998, the Retained Earnings of the Peel Company equal $1,500,000. If we add the allocation of $62,400 from the Step C distribution entry, we have opening consolidated Retained Earnings of $1,562,400. Given this, the consolidated Statement Of Retained Earnings for 1998 of the Peel Company and its subsidiary would be prepared as follows:

Peel Company And Subsidiary
Consolidated Statement Of Retained Earnings
For The Year Ending December 31, 1998

Balance - January 1, 1998	$1,562,400
Consolidated Net Income	205,200
Balance - December 31, 1998	$1,767,600

Consolidated Balance Sheet

7-190.   The consolidated Balance Sheet as at December 31, 1998 of the Peel Company and its subsidiary is as follows:

Peel Company And Subsidiary
Consolidated Balance Sheet As At December 31, 1998

Investment In Seal's Preferred Stock ($120,000 -$120,000)	$ -0-
Investment In Seal's Common Stock ($540,000 -$540,000)	-0-
Other Net Assets ($2,810,400 + $1,362,000)	4,172,400
Total Assets	$4,172,400

Preferred Stock - 8 Percent, $50 Par ($500,000 + $500,000)	$ -0-
Non Controlling Interest (See Following Calculation)	604,800
No Par Common Stock (Peel's Only)	1,800,000
Retained Earnings (See Statement)	1,767,600
Total Equities	$4,172,400

Non Controlling Interest

7-191.   The Non Controlling Interest in the preceding consolidated Balance Sheet can be calculated as follows:

Preferred Stock Interest (60%)($300,000)	$180,000
Common Stock Interest:	
Contributed Capital [(40%)($600,000)]	240,000
Retained Earnings [(40%)($462,000)]	184,800
Non Controlling Interest	$604,800

Example Three - Participating Case

7-192.   This final Example will continue to use the same basic data that was provided in Examples One and Two. The difference here will be that, in addition to being cumulative, we will assume that the subsidiary's preferred shares are participating. Participation agreements can be based on percentages of par value or on the basis of the number of shares in the various classes under consideration. Since the Seal Company has No Par Common Stock, we will assume that the $600,000 in No Par Common Stock consists of 12,000 shares and that the participation is on a per share basis. In effect, this means that after each of the 6,000 Seal Company preferred shares have received a dividend of $4 (8 percent of $50), the Seal Company common shares must also receive $4 per share before any further preferred dividends can be paid. After each class of shares have received this $4 per share, any additional dividends must be paid in equal per share amounts to both classes of equity interest. The data for this version of the example is as follows:

The Peel Company purchases 60 percent of the Seal Company Common Stock for $480,000 and 40 percent of the Seal Company Preferred Stock for $160,000. Both of these purchases occur on January 1, 1996 and the prices are equal to the book value of the equity investment acquired (See following Investment Analysis). On this investment date, all of the net identifiable assets of the Seal Company have fair values that are equal to their carrying values.

The total dividends paid by the Seal Company during 1998 amount to $234,000. This amount can be analyzed as follows:

	Common	Preferred
1996 Arrearages At $4	$ 48,000	$24,000
1997 Arrearages At $4	48,000	24,000
1998 Regular At $4	48,000	24,000
1998 Extra At $1	12,000	6,000
Total Dividends	$156,000	$78,000

The Balance Sheets of the two Companies as at December 31, 1998 are as follows:

	Peel	Seal
Investment In Seal's Preferred Stock	$ 160,000	$ -0-
Investment In Seal's Common Stock	480,000	-0-
Other Net Assets	2,904,800	1,236,000
Total Assets	$3,544,800	$1,236,000
Preferred Stock - 8%, Par $50	$ -0-	$ 300,000
No Par Common Stock	1,800,000	600,000
Retained Earnings	1,744,800	336,000
Total Equities	$3,544,800	$1,236,000

The Retained Earnings balance of the Peel Company consists of the December 31, 1997 balance of $1,500,000, the 1998 Net Income exclusive of investment income of $120,000, dividends received on Preferred Stock of $31,200 (40 percent of $78,000), and dividends received on Common Stock of $93,600 (60 percent of $156,000).

Required   Calculate the 1998 consolidated Net Income. In addition, prepare a consolidated Statement Of Retained Earnings for the year ending December 31, 1998, and a consolidated Balance Sheet as at December 31, 1998 for the Peel Company and its subsidiary.

Investment Analysis

7-193.   The fact that the subsidiary's preferred shares are participating means that these shareholders have a claim on subsidiary Retained Earnings. More specifically, since there are 6,000 preferred shares outstanding and 12,000 common shares outstanding, the Seal Company Retained Earnings balance must be divided between the two classes of equity on a one-third (6,000 ÷ 18,000) to two thirds (12,000 ÷ 18,000) basis. This means that the January 1, 1996 book value that would be associated with the Seal Company Common Stock would be $600,000 plus two-thirds of $300,000, a total of $800,000. The corresponding figure for the book value of the Seal Company Preferred Stock would be $300,000 plus one-third of $300,000, or a total of $400,000. This means that both of the investments that were made by the Peel Company on this date were made at book value. This can be seen as follows:

Common Stock Cost = $480,000 = [(60%)($800,000)]
Preferred Stock Cost = $160,000 = [(40%)($400,000)]

7-194.   A similar computation will provide the Non Controlling Interest as at the acquisition date. These calculations are as follows:

Common Stock Non Controlling Interest = $320,000 = [(40%)($800,000)]
Preferred Stock Non Controlling Interest = $240,000 = [(60%)($400,000)]

7-195.   This gives a total Non Controlling Interest of $560,000.

Step A - Investment Elimination

7-196.   Based on the preceding analysis, the investment elimination entry would be as follows:

Preferred Stock - 8 Percent, $50 Par	$300,000	
No Par Common Stock	600,000	
Retained Earnings	300,000	
Investment In Seal's Preferred Stock		$160,000
Investment In Seal's Common Stock		480,000
Non Controlling Interest		560,000

Step B - Adjustments And Eliminations

7-197.   Here again, the only adjustment that is required is for the elimination of intercompany dividends. It is as follows:

Dividend Revenue ($93,600 + $31,200)	$124,800	
Non Controlling Interest ($62,400 + $46,800)	109,200	
Preferred Dividends Declared		$ 78,000
Common Dividends Declared		156,000

Step C - Retained Earnings Distribution

7-198.   The Retained Earnings of the Seal Company since acquisition equal $120,000. Of this amount one-third or $40,000 is a part of the preferred stock equity while the balance or $80,000 belongs to the common shareholders. This means the preferred claim will be $24,000 (60 percent of $40,000) while the non controlling common claim will be $32,000 (40 percent of $80,000). In a similar fashion the controlling claim is $16,000 (40 percent of $40,000) on the preferred holding and $48,000 (60 percent of $80,000) on the common holding. Note that no attention need be given to the two years of dividend arrearages that are present at January 1, 1998. This results from the fact that, whenever a preferred dividend arrearage is paid, an equivalent per share amount must be paid to the common shareholders. This establishes the common shareholders' claim to a two-thirds share of all of Seal's Retained Earnings. The journal entry to distribute the interests that we have just calculated is as follows:

Opening Retained Earnings - Seal $120,000
     Non Controlling Interest ($24,000 + $32,000) $56,000
     Consolidated Retained Earnings ($16,000 + $48,000)   64,000

Consolidated Net Income

7-199.   The consolidated Net Income for 1998 of the Peel Company and its subsidiary can be calculated as follows:

Peel's Reported Net Income ($120,000 + $93,600 + $31,200)	$244,800
Intercompany Dividends	(124,800)
Peel's Income Exclusive Of Dividends	$120,000
Equity Pickups:	
Common Stock [(60%)(2/3)($150,000)]	60,000
Preferred Stock [(40%)(1/3)($150,000)]	20,000
Consolidated Net Income	$200,000

7-200.   Note that with participating preferred stock, both equity pickups are based on Net Income rather than having the equity pickup of the common stock being based on this figure less preferred dividends.

Consolidated Statement Of Retained Earnings

7-201.   As given in the Basic Data, on January 1, 1998, the Retained Earnings balance of the Peel Company is $1,500,000. If we add the allocation of $64,000 from the Step C distribution entry, we have the opening consolidated Retained Earnings balance of $1,564,000. Given this, the consolidated Statement Of Retained Earnings for 1998 of the Peel Company and its subsidiary can be prepared as follows:

Peel Company And Subsidiary
Consolidated Statement Of Retained Earnings
For The Year Ending December 31, 1998

Balance - January 1, 1998	$1,564,000
Consolidated Net Income	200,000
Balance - December 31, 1998	$1,764,000

Consolidated Balance Sheet

7-202.   The consolidated Balance Sheet as at December 31, 1998 of the Peel Company and its subsidiary is as follows:

Peel Company And Subsidiary
Consolidated Balance Sheet
As At December 31, 1998

Investment In Seal's Preferred Stock ($160,000 -$160,000)	$ -0-
Investment In Seal's Common Stock ($480,000 -$480,000)	-0-
Other Net Assets ($2,904,800 + $1,236,000)	4,140,800
Total Assets	$4,140,800

Preferred Stock - 8 Percent, $50 Par ($500,000 + $500,000)	$ -0-
Non Controlling Interest (See Following Calculation)	576,800
No Par Common Stock (Peel's Only)	1,800,000
Retained Earnings (See Statement)	1,764,000
Total Equities	$4,140,800

Non Controlling Interest

7-203. The Non Controlling Interest calculation is complicated by the fact that when preferred shares are participating, they have a claim on the Retained Earnings in much the same manner as do the common shareholders. This claim is reflected in the following calculation of the Non Controlling Interest:

Preferred Stock Interest:	
Contributed Capital [(60%)($300,000)]	$180,000
Retained Earnings [(60%)(1/3)($336,000)]	67,200
Common Stock Interest:	
Contributed Capital [(40%)($600,000)]	240,000
Retained Earnings [(40%)(2/3)($336,000)]	89,600
Total Non Controlling Interest	$576,800

7-204. This completes our most complex Example of the consolidation procedures that are required in dealing with subsidiary issues of preferred stock.

Transactions Involving Subsidiary Shares

Types Of Transactions

7-205. Subsequent to the acquisition of a subsidiary that is to be consolidated, certain transactions involving the shareholders' equity of that subsidiary may affect the proportional equity positions of the parent and non controlling interests. Possible shareholders' equity transactions include the following:

- The purchase of additional subsidiary shares from an outside interest by the parent company.
- The purchase of additional subsidiary shares from an outside interest by the subsidiary company.
- The sale of a portion of the subsidiary shares to an outside interest by the parent company.
- The issue by the subsidiary company of additional shares to an outside interest.

7-206. The first two types of transactions do not involve anything that is really new and, therefore, can be dealt with in a brief manner. The latter two items, however, involve new procedures and will be illustrated in detail.

Parent Purchase Of Additional Subsidiary Shares

7-207. The purchase of additional subsidiary shares by the parent from an interest outside of the consolidated entity is really no different from the earlier purchase of shares which made the investee a subsidiary. It follows that the accounting treatment would be the same. This is reflected in the following *CICA Handbook* suggestion:

Paragraph 1600.39 When a parent company acquires additional shares in a subsidiary, that transaction will be accounted for in accordance with the guidelines provided in paragraphs 1600.07-1600.24.

7-208. As discussed in Chapter 4, Paragraphs 1600.07-.24 deal with consolidation at the date of acquisition and require that amounts paid for subsidiary common shares be allocated to the fair values of the subsidiaries identifiable assets and to goodwill.

Subsidiary Purchase Of Its Own Shares

7-209. The acquisition by a subsidiary of some of its own outstanding shares has an economic effect that is similar to the purchase of additional shares by the parent company. The recommended accounting procedures are based on this view of the economic substance of the event. As found in Paragraph 1600.48, they are as follows:

> **Paragraph 1600.48**   When a subsidiary acquires its own shares for cancellation from outside interests, the proportionate interest of the parent company after the transaction is increased. Since the transaction is similar in effect to the situation where the parent company acquires an additional interest in a subsidiary it may be accounted for in the same manner as a step-by-step acquisition.

7-210.   Since step-by-step acquisitions were covered in Chapter 5, the preceding Recommendation will not be illustrated.

Comprehensive Example For Complex Transactions

7-211.   As indicated previously, both the sale of a portion of the subsidiary shares by the parent company and the issuance of additional shares by the subsidiary are sufficiently different and complex to warrant detailed illustration. In order to do this in an adequate manner, a fairly comprehensive consolidation problem is required. We will illustrate both of these types of shareholders' equity transactions using the same basic example. The example, before the addition of any subsidiary shareholders' equity transactions is as follows:

> On January 1, 1996, the Pure Company purchases 70 percent of the outstanding shares of the Sure Company for $2,100,000 in cash. At the time of this acquisition, the Sure Company had No Par Common Stock outstanding in the amount of $1,500,000 and Retained Earnings of $1,000,000. Also on that date, all of the identifiable assets and liabilities of the Sure Company had carrying values that were equal to their fair values except for a patent which had a fair value that was $300,000 greater than its carrying value. The remaining economic life of this patent is six years and it is being amortized by the straight line method. Any goodwill is to be amortized over 20 years. On December 31, 1998, the adjusted but unclosed condensed trial balances of the two Companies are as follows:

	Pure	Sure
Investment In Sure (Cost)	$2,100,000	$ -0-
Other Net Identifiable Assets	6,500,000	3,200,000
Total Expenses	1,300,000	600,000
Total Debits	**$9,900,000**	**$3,800,000**
No Par Common Stock	$4,000,000	$1,500,000
Retained Earnings	4,100,000	1,500,000
Total Revenues	1,800,000	800,000
Total Credits	**$9,900,000**	**$3,800,000**

> **Required**   Prepare a consolidated Balance Sheet as at December 31, 1998 and consolidated Statements Of Income And Retained Earnings for the year ending December 31, 1998.

Procedures

7-212.   The preceding problem is a very simple one of a variety that we have encountered on several previous occasions. As a result, the journal entries will be presented without explanations, only for your convenience in understanding the basic data for the problem.

Step A - Investment Elimination Entry

7-213.   The required investment elimination entry would be as follows:

No Par Common Stock	$1,500,000	
Retained Earnings	1,000,000	
Other Net Assets (Patent) ([70%][$300,000])	210,000	
Goodwill	140,000	
Non Controlling Interest		$ 750,000
Investment In Sure		2,100,000

Step B - Adjustments

7-214.   The only entry that is required here is for the amortization of the fair value change on the patent and Goodwill. The entry is as follows:

Retained Earnings	$84,000	
Total Expenses ($35,000 + $7,000)	42,000	
Other Net Identifiable Assets ([3][$35,000])		$105,000
Goodwill ([3][$7,000])		21,000

Step C - Retained Earnings Distribution

7-215.   The entry to allocate the balance in the Retained Earnings account of the Sure Company would be as follows:

Retained Earnings	$416,000	
Non Controlling Interest		$150,000
Consolidated Retained Earnings		266,000

7-216.   As usual, this entry establishes the opening balance for consolidated Retained Earnings. It would be the Pure Company's balance of $4,100,000 plus the preceding credit of $266,000 for a total of $4,366,000. This figure will be used in the preparation of the consolidated Statement Of Retained Earnings.

Consolidated Income Statement

7-217.   The 1998 consolidated Income Statement would be prepared as follows:

Pure Company And Subsidiary
Consolidated Income Statement
For The Year Ending December 31, 1998

Total Revenues ($1,800,000 + $800,000)	$2,600,000
Total Expenses ($1,300,000 + $600,000 + $42,000)	1,942,000
Combined Income	$ 658,000
Non Controlling Interest (30 Percent Of $200,000)	60,000
Consolidated Net Income	$ 598,000

Consolidated Statement Of Retained Earnings

7-218.   The consolidated Statement Of Retained Earnings for 1998 would be prepared as follows:

Pure Company And Subsidiary
Consolidated Statement Of Retained Earnings
For The Year Ending December 31, 1998

Balance - January 1, 1998 ($4,100,000 + $266,000)	$4,366,000
Consolidated Net Income	598,000
Balance - December 31, 1998	$4,964,000

Consolidated Balance Sheet

7-219.   The consolidated Balance Sheet as at December 31, 1998 for the Pure Company and its subsidiary would be prepared as follows:

Pure Company And Subsidiary
Consolidated Balance Sheet
As At December 31, 1998

Investment In Sure ($2,100,000 - $2,100,000)	$ -0-
Other Net Identifiable Assets ($6,500,000	
+ $3,200,000 + $210,000 - $105,000)	9,805,000
Goodwill ($140,000 - $21,000)	119,000
Total Assets	**$9,924,000**

Non Controlling Interest (30 percent of $3,200,000)	$ 960,000
No Par Common Stock (Pure's Only)	4,000,000
Retained Earnings (See Statement)	4,964,000
Total Equities	**$9,924,000**

Example One - Parent Sells Subsidiary Shares

7-220.   In the first Example based on the preceding data, assume that prior to the preparation of consolidated financial statements on December 31, 1998, the Pure Company sells 10 percent of the shares of the Sure Company (this would be one seventh of its 70 percent holding of Sure Company shares) for $600,000 in cash. In this situation, the following Recommendation is applicable:

Paragraph 1600.45   *When the parent company sells part of its holdings in a subsidiary to interests outside the consolidated group, any difference between the parent's underlying equity in the shares sold and the sale proceeds should enter into the determination of consolidated net income. (April, 1975)*

7-221.   In the present situation, the application of this requirement will result in a gain on the transaction of $248,000. This is the excess of the sale price of $600,000 over the Pure Company's $352,000 underlying equity in the shares sold. This underlying equity can be calculated as follows:

Investment Cost	$2,100,000
Equity Pickup [(70%)($1,700,000 - $1,000,000)]	490,000
Patent Amortization (3 Years At $35,000)	(105,000)
Goodwill Amortization (3 Years At $7,000)	(21,000)
Total Underlying Equity	$2,464,000
Fraction Sold	1/7
Underlying Equity Sold	$ 352,000

7-222.   This calculation will provide the basis for a new set of 1998 consolidated financial statements for the Pure Company and its subsidiary the Sure Company.

Consolidated Income Statement

7-223.   The main difference in this new consolidated Income Statement would be the gain resulting from the Pure Company's sale of Sure shares. The Income Statement for 1998 of the Pure Company and its subsidiary would be as follows:

**Pure Company And Subsidiary
Consolidated Income Statement
For The Year Ending December 31, 1998**

Total Revenues ($1,800,000 + $800,000 + $248,000)	$2,848,000
Total Expenses ($1,300,000 + $600,000 + $42,000)	1,942,000
Combined Income	$ 906,000
Non Controlling Interest (30 Percent Of $200,000)	60,000
Consolidated Net Income	$ 846,000

7-224.   Note that, because the sale of shares took place at the end of the year, the non controlling interest for the year remains at 30 percent for 1998. In the December 31, 1998 consolidated Balance Sheet and in the consolidated Income Statements of future years it will be at 40 percent.

Consolidated Statement Of Retained Earnings

7-225.   The consolidated Statement Of Retained Earnings for the year ending December 31, 1998 of the Pure Company and its subsidiary would be prepared as follows:

**Pure Company And Subsidiary
Consolidated Statement Of Retained Earnings
For The Year Ending December 31, 1998**

Balance - January 1, 1998 (See Paragraph 7-218)	$4,366,000
Consolidated Net Income	846,000
Balance - December 31, 1998	$5,212,000

Consolidated Balance Sheet

7-226.   The consolidated Balance Sheet as at December 31, 1998 of the Pure Company and its subsidiary would be prepared as follows:

**Pure Company And Subsidiary
Consolidated Balance Sheet
As At December 31, 1998**

Investment In Sure ($2,100,000 - $300,000 -$1,800,000)	$ -0-
Other Net Identifiable Assets ($6,500,000 + $3,200,000 + $210,000 - $105,000 + $585,000)	10,390,000
Goodwill ($140,000 - $21,000 - $17,000)	102,000
Total Assets	$10,492,000
Non Controlling Interest (40 Percent Of $3,200,000)	$ 1,280,000
No Par Common Stock (Pure's Only)	4,000,000
Retained Earnings (See Statement)	5,212,000
Total Equities	$10,492,000

7-227.   Several of the figures in the preceding statement require additional explanation. First, the $585,000 increase in the Other Net Assets reflects two things. One is the added $600,000 in cash which resulted from the sale of the Sure Company shares. The remaining fair value change on the Patents for consolidation purposes is $105,000 (70 percent of $300,000, less three years amortization). Since the Pure Company has sold one-seventh of its holding in the Sure Company, one-seventh of the remaining fair value change must be removed from the accounts. This reduces Other Net Assets by $15,000 ([$105,000][1/7]), resulting in a the net increase is $585,000 ($600,000 - $15,000).

7-228.   The Investment in Sure account has been reduced by one-seventh of the cost of the investment and will be carried at $1,800,000 on the single entity records of Pure. The $17,000 reduction in the Goodwill account is one-seventh of the amortized balance of $119,000. Since Pure is disposing of one-seventh of its holding in Sure, a similar proportion of the Goodwill must be removed from the accounts.

7-229.   Other changes in this consolidated Balance Sheet for Example One have been previously explained.

Example Two - Subsidiary Sells Subsidiary Shares

7-230.   Assume that the Sure Company's shareholders' equity has consisted of 100,000 shares with no par value and that the Pure Company's 70 percent holding amounts to 70,000 of these shares. In this version of the example, assume that the Sure Company issues to outside interests, an additional 16,667 of its common shares in return for $1,000,000 in cash. Subsequent to this sale of shares, the Pure Company's 70,000 shares now represent a holding of approximately 60 percent (70,000 ÷ 116,667). In other words, the Pure Company's economic position is the same as it was in the previous Example in which it sold a portion of its holding of Sure Company shares.

7-231.   In this situation, the *CICA Handbook* requires the following:

> **Paragraph 1600.47**   *When a subsidiary company issues shares to interests outside the consolidated group, the effect of the change in the parent's interest as a result of the share issue should enter into the determination of consolidated net income.* (April, 1975)

7-232.   The implementation of this provision will require the determination of the gain or loss resulting from the issue of shares. In this Example Two we encounter the same gain as in Example One. The Pure Company's 60 percent share of the proceeds from the sale is $600,000 [(60%)($1,000,000)] and the underlying equity sold is again $352,000 or one-seventh of Pure's total underlying equity of $2,464,000 (See Example One calculation). This gives a gain of $248,000 to be included in the consolidated Income Statement. With this information in hand, we can now proceed to the preparation of consolidated financial statements for this Example.

Consolidated Income Statement And Statement Of Retained Earnings

7-233.   The consolidated Income Statement and the consolidated Statement Of Retained Earnings for the year ending December 31, 1998, would be the same in this Example as in Example One and will not be repeated here.

Consolidated Balance Sheet

7-234.   The consolidated Balance Sheet would be prepared as follows:

Pure Company And Subsidiary
Consolidated Balance Sheet
As At December 31, 1998

Investment In Sure ($2,100,000 - $2,100,000)	$ -0-
Other Net Identifiable Assets ($6,500,000	
+ $3,200,000 + $210,000 - $105,000 + $985,000)	10,790,000
Goodwill ($140,000 - $21,000 - $17,000)	102,000
Total Assets	**$10,892,000**
Non Controlling Interest (40 percent of $4,200,000)	$ 1,680,000
No Par Common Stock (Pure's Only)	4,000,000
Retained Earnings (See Statement)	5,212,000
Total Equities	**$10,892,000**

7-235.   Most of the figures here are the same as in Example One. The only real difference is the fact that $1,000,000 in cash came into the consolidated entity in this Example, while only $600,000 was received in Example One. This $400,000 difference is reflected in a larger Other Net Identifiable Assets and by an additional $400,000 in the Non Controlling Interest.

Consolidated Statement Of Changes In Financial Position

Differences In Procedures

7-236.   In general, the procedures for preparing a consolidated Statement Of Changes In Financial Position are very similar to those required for an ordinary Statement Of Changes In Financial Position (specific differences are described in the paragraphs which follow).

7-237.   In most circumstances, it is not necessary to prepare a complete set of consolidated financial statements in order to complete a consolidated Statement Of Changes In Financial Position. However, as a minimum, the data for consolidated Net Income, the change in consolidated cash, and the change in other working capital items is needed. In addition, some of the consolidated expenses and revenues will be required in order to provide an appropriate conversion of consolidated Net Income into consolidated Cash From Operations.

7-238.   As indicated in the preceding paragraph, most of the procedures are the same whether a consolidated or a single entity Statement Of Changes In Financial Position is being prepared. These basic procedures for preparing this financial statement are covered in a number of current texts and, as a consequence will not be presented in detail in this volume. There are, however, some procedures that are unique to preparing the consolidated statement. They are as follows:

- Consolidated Net Income is defined in Section 1600 as being after the deduction of the Non Controlling Interest. Since this deduction does not involve an outflow of consolidated cash, it will be treated in a manner similar to depreciation expense. That is, it will be added back to consolidated Net Income in order to arrive at consolidated Cash From Operations.

- In an ordinary Statement Of Changes In Financial Position, the dividends shown will be the same amount as shown in the Statement Of Retained Earnings. This will not be the case here. The consolidated Statement Of Changes In Financial Position would disclose all dividends which involve an outflow of consolidated funds. This would include both the dividends declared by the parent company and the dividends declared by the subsidiary and payable to the non controlling shareholders. You will recall that in the consolidated Statement Of Retained Earnings, we deducted only the dividends declared by the parent company.

- Also unique to the consolidation situation is the possibility that the parent may acquire additional subsidiary shares. Three possible situations can be identified here:

    1.   If the shares are acquired for cash directly from the subsidiary, it is an intercompany transaction that would be eliminated and would not appear in the consolidated Statement Of Changes In Financial Position.

    2.   If the shares are acquired for cash from the non controlling shareholders, the transaction would be disclosed as an outflow of consolidated cash.

    3.   If the parent issues additional shares of its own to acquire subsidiary shares from the non controlling shareholders, it would be disclosed in this Statement Of Changes In Financial Position as a non cash financial resource transaction.

A similar analysis can be made when a part of the subsidiary shares are sold.

Section 1540 On Business Combinations

7-239.   In addition to providing general guidelines for the preparation of the Statement Of Changes In Financial Position, Section 1540 also provides specific guidance in the area of business combinations. With respect to the acquisition and disposal of subsidiaries, the following guidance is provided:

> **Paragraph 1540.22**   On acquisition of an entity which is to be consolidated, the net assets acquired, other than cash and cash equivalents, would be classified as an investing activity and the financing aspect would be disclosed separately. The increase or decrease in the consolidated cash and cash equivalents resulting from the acquisition, and the assigned costs of the other assets and liabilities acquired, including any goodwill arising from the transaction, would also be disclosed to portray the components of the net assets acquired. The disclosure would be made either in the body of the statement of changes in financial position or in a note to the financial statements. Similar disclosure would be provided when an enterprise disposes of an entity which was previously consolidated. However, where the vendor does not allocate the proceeds of disposal to the components of the entity sold, the statement would disclose the gross proceeds of disposal, with the cash resources of the entity sold being shown as a deduction therefrom.

7-240.   An additional suggestion is with respect to business combinations accounted for by the pooling of interests method:

> **Paragraph 1540.23**   When a business combination is accounted for as a pooling of interests (See "Business Combinations," Section 1580), the statement of changes in financial position would be restated for all periods presented to reflect the pooling.

Example - Consolidated Statement Of Changes

Basic Data

7-241.   In order to illustrate the procedures and concepts that were discussed in the preceding paragraphs, an example of a consolidated Statement Of Changes In Financial Position will be presented. The basic data is as follows:

On December 31, 1995, the Pam Company acquired 80 percent of the outstanding shares of the Sam Company for $3,600,000 in cash. On this date, all of the Sam Company's identifiable assets and liabilities had carrying values that were equal to their fair values.   The carrying values of the Sam Company's net identifiable assets amounted to $4,000,000. Goodwill, if any, is to be amortized over 10 years.

On December 31, 1998, the Pam Company acquired 100 percent of the outstanding shares of the Tam Company for cash in the amount of $2,200,000. On that date, the Tam Company had cash of $100,000, net non cash current assets of $400,000, and net identifiable non current assets of $1,500,000. All of the Tam Company's identifiable assets and liabilities had carrying values that were equal to their fair values. Goodwill, if any, is to be amortized over 10 years.

The condensed Balance Sheets of the Pam Company and its subsidiary, the Sam Company, on December 31, 1997 and December 31, 1998 are as follows:

Pam And Sam Company
Balance Sheets
As At December 31, 1997

	Pam	Sam
Cash	$ 400,000	$ 300,000
Net Non Cash Current Assets	5,600,000	1,700,000
Investment In Sam (At Cost)	3,600,000	-0-
Plant And Equipment	12,000,000	8,000,000
Accumulated Depreciation	(5,600,000)	(2,000,000)
Total Assets	$16,000,000	$8,000,000
Long Term Liabilities	$ 3,000,000	$2,000,000
No Par Common Stock	5,000,000	2,000,000
Retained Earnings	8,000,000	4,000,000
Total Equities	$16,000,000	$8,000,000

Pam And Sam Company
Balance Sheets
As At December 31, 1998

	Pam	Sam
Cash	$ 800,000	$ 600,000
Net Non Cash Current Assets	4,800,000	2,200,000
Investment In Sam (Cost)	3,600,000	-0-
Investment In Tam (Cost)	2,200,000	-0-
Plant And Equipment	13,000,000	8,400,000
Accumulated Depreciation	(6,400,000)	(2,200,000)
Total Assets	$18,000,000	$9,000,000
Long Term Liabilities	$ 3,000,000	$2,500,000
No Par Common Stock	6,000,000	2,000,000
Retained Earnings	9,000,000	4,500,000
Total Equities	$18,000,000	$9,000,000

Other Information:

A. During 1998, the Sam Company issued $500,000 in long term liabilities for cash.

B. During 1998, the Sam Company purchased Plant And Equipment for $800,000 in cash. Also during the year it sold Plant And Equipment with a cost of $400,000 and a net book value of $200,000 for cash of $60,000.

C. During 1998, the Pam Company issued $1,000,000 in No Par Common Stock in return for Plant And Equipment.

D. The 1998 Dividends Declared and Net Income for the three Companies are as follows:

	Pam	Sam	Tam
Net Income	$2,000,000	$1,000,000	$ 300,000
Dividends	1,000,000	500,000	100,000

Required: For the year ending December 31, 1998, prepare a consolidated Statement Of Changes In Financial Position for the Pam Company and its subsidiaries, the Sam Company and the Tam Company. Your solution should comply with the requirements of the *CICA Handbook*.

Preliminary Computations

7-242.   Before proceeding directly to the preparation of the consolidated Statement Of Changes In Financial Position, it will be useful to provide computations for consolidated Net Income and the change in the consolidated working capital and cash position. These calculations are contained in the Paragraphs which follow.

7-243.   We will calculate the consolidated Net Income using the definitional approach. You should note that the Tam Company's Net Income does not have a place in this calculation. This reflects the fact that its acquisition date was December 31, 1998 and, under the purchase method of accounting for this business combination, the Tam Company's income would only accrue to the consolidated entity subsequent to the acquisition date. Given this, the calculation of the 1998 consolidated Net Income is as follows:

Pam Company's Net Income	$2,000,000
Intercompany Dividends (Sam To Pam)	(400,000)
Pam's Net Income Exclusive Of Subsidiary Dividends	$1,600,000
Equity Pickup - 80 Percent Of Sam's Net Income	800,000
Income Before Adjustments	$2,400,000
Goodwill Amortization (See Note One)	(40,000)
Consolidated Net Income	$2,360,000

Note One   The Goodwill Amortization is based on the fact that $3,600,000 was paid for 80 percent of the Sam Company when the carrying values of this Company's net assets were $4,000,000. As there were no fair value changes, the entire $400,000 excess ($3,600,000 - $3,200,000) of investment cost over the Pam Company's share of the net identifiable assets of Sam was allocated to Goodwill. This balance is being amortized over a period of 10 years.

7-244.   On December 31, 1998, the consolidated cash was made up of Pam's $800,000, Sam Company's $600,000, plus the newly acquired Tam Company's cash of $100,000. This is a total of $1,500,000. On December 31, 1997, Pam Company had cash of $400,000 while the Sam Company's balance was $300,000. On this earlier date, the Tam Company had not yet been acquired so that its cash does not have a place in the consolidated cash which totals $700,000 on December 31, 1997. The increase in consolidated cash for the year ending December 31, 1998 is equal to $800,000 ($1,500,000 - $700,000).

7-245.   On December 31, 1998, the consolidated Net Non Cash Current Assets were made up of the Pam Company's $4,800,000, Sam Company's $2,200,000, and the newly acquired Tam Company's Net Non Cash Current Assets of $400,000 which totals $7,400,000. On December 31, 1997, the Pam Company had Net Non Cash Current Assets of $5,600,000 while the Sam Company's balance was $1,700,000. On this earlier date, the Tam Company had not yet been acquired so that its balance does not have a place in the December 31, 1997 consolidated Net Non Cash Current Assets of $7,300,000. The increase in consolidated Net Non Cash Current Assets for the year ending December 31, 1998 is $100,000 ($7,400,000 - $7,300,000).

Consolidated Statement Of Changes In Financial Position

7-246.   The consolidated Statement Of Changes In Financial Position for the year ending December 31, 1998 would be prepared as follows:

Pam Company And Subsidiaries
Consolidated Statement Of Changes In Financial Position (Cash Basis)
Year Ending December 31, 1998

Operating Activities

Cash From Operations (Note Two)	$4,240,000	
Dividends Declared		
($1,000,000 + 20% of $500,000)	(1,100,000)	$3,140,000

Financing Activities

Issuance Of Long Term Debt For Cash	$ 500,000	
Issuance Of Common Stock For Plant	1,000,000	1,500,000

Investing Activities

Acquisition Of Subsidiary (Note Three)	($2,100,000)	
Proceeds From The Sale Of Plant	60,000	
Acquisition Of Plant For Cash	(800,000)	
Acquisition Of Plant For Common Stock	(1,000,000)	(3,840,000)
Increase In Cash		$ 800,000

Note Two   In any Statement Of Changes In Financial Position, the most difficult figure to compute is Cash From Operations. It can be calculated by starting at zero, adding operating revenues which generate cash and deducting operating expenses which involve outflows of cash. However, it is usually easier to start with Net Income and to adjust this figure for non cash expense and revenue items. This latter approach is used in the calculation which follows:

Consolidated Net Income	$2,360,000
Depreciation Expense (See following discussion)	1,200,000
Non Controlling Interest [(20%)($1,000,000)]	200,000
Loss On Sale Of Equipment (See following discussion)	140,000
Goodwill Amortization	40,000
Consolidated Working Capital From Operations	$3,940,000
Decrease In Consolidated Net Non Cash Current Assets	300,000
Consolidated Cash From Operations	$4,240,000

The Depreciation Expense is equal to the increase in Pam's Accumulated Depreciation of $800,000 ($6,400,000 -$5,600,000), the increase in Sam's Accumulated Depreciation of $200,000 ($2,200,000 - $2,000,000), plus the accumulated depreciation of $200,000 on the Plant And Equipment which was retired. The Loss On Sale Of Equipment also relates to this transaction. It is the proceeds from the sale of $60,000, subtracted from the net book value of $200,000.

Note that, while there was an overall increase in Net Non Cash Current Assets of $100,000, this was net of the $400,000 increase which resulted from the acquisition of the Tam Company. As this increase did not relate to operations of the consolidated group it would be removed from the adjustment required to arrive at cash from operations, leaving a decrease of $300,000 (an increase of $100,000, less the $400,000 from the Tam Company acquisition).

Note Three   There are a variety of ways in which the acquisition of the Tam Company could be disclosed. However, the basic idea is to disclose the components of the net assets acquired and one way of accomplishing this is as follows:

Cash Paid For Tam Company Shares	$2,200,000
Tam Company's Cash Acquired	(100,000)
Net Outflow Of Cash	$2,100,000
Tam's Net Non Cash Current Assets Acquired	(400,000)
Tam's Identifiable Non Current Assets Acquired	(1,500,000)
Tam's Goodwill Acquired	$ 200,000

Problems For Self Study

(The solutions for these problems can be found following Chapter 17 of the text.)

SELF STUDY PROBLEM SEVEN - 1

On January 1, 1995, the Pip Company purchased 37,500 of the common shares of the Squeak Company for $130 per share. On that date, the Squeak Company had 50,000 outstanding No Par Common Shares recorded at $5 million and Retained Earnings of $1 million. On January 1, 1995, all of Squeak's identifiable assets and liabilities had carrying values that were equal to their fair values except for:

1. A portfolio of long term government bonds with a fair value $80,000 greater than its carrying value.

2. An issue of long term liabilities maturing on January 1, 2003 which had a fair value that was $200,000 greater than its carrying value.

3. A machine with a fair value that was $500,000 less than its carrying value and a remaining useful life of 5 years.

Any goodwill arising from this business combination should be amortized over 30 years.

On December 31, 1998, the adjusted trial balances of the Pip Company and its subsidiary, the Squeak Company are as follows:

	Pip	Squeak
Cash and Receivables	$ 740,000	$ 400,000
Inventories	3,400,000	2,100,000
Long Term Government Bonds	-0-	150,000
Investment in Squeak (Equity)	6,398,000	-0-
Plant and Equipment (Net)	13,500,000	6,400,000
Cost of Goods Sold	7,000,000	1,850,000
Other Expenses	1,062,000	600,000
Dividends Declared	400,000	200,000
Total Debits	**$32,500,000**	**$11,700,000**
Current Liabilities	$ 977,000	$ 350,000
Long Term Liabilities	1,500,000	1,000,000
No Par Common Stock	5,000,000	5,000,000
Retained Earnings	10,511,000	2,300,000
Sales	14,000,000	3,030,000
Investment Income	512,000	20,000
Total Credits	**$32,500,000**	**$11,700,000**

Other Information:

1. There have been no sales of Government Bonds by Squeak Company since January 1, 1995.

2. Pip's Sales include sales of $400,000 to Squeak Company while Pip's Cost of Goods Sold include purchases of $100,000 from Squeak. None of these sales or purchases remain in the closing inventories of either Company. At December 31, 1998, each Company has paid for 50 percent of its 1998 intercompany merchandise purchases.

3. Between January 1, 1995 and December 31, 1997, the Squeak Company earned a total of $1,500,000 and paid dividends of $200,000.

4. Both Companies use the straight line method to calculate depreciation and amortization charges.

Required:

A. Verify the figures given in the problem for the December 31, 1998 Investment in Squeak (At Equity) and for the 1998 Investment Income recorded by the Pip Company.

B. Calculate what the balance of the January 1, 1998 Retained Earnings of the Pip Company would have been assuming the Investment in Squeak had been carried using the cost method since its acquisition.

C. Prepare, for the Pip Company and its subsidiary the Squeak Company:

   1. a consolidated Income Statement for the year ending December 31, 1998;

   2. a consolidated Statement of Retained Earnings for the year ending December 31, 1998;

   3. a consolidated Balance Sheet as at December 31, 1998.

SELF STUDY PROBLEM SEVEN - 2

Note - This is an extension of *SELF STUDY PROBLEM SIX - 3.*

On January 1, 1997, the Prime Company acquired 60 percent of the outstanding voting shares of the Sublime Company for $3 million in cash. On this date, the Sublime Company had No Par Common Stock of $3 million and Retained Earnings of $2 million. All of Sublime's identifiable assets and liabilities had fair values that were equal to their carrying values except for the Accounts Receivable which had a total net realizable value that was $100,000 less than its stated value and a piece of equipment with a fair value that was $400,000 less than its carrying value and a remaining useful life of 3 years.

Both Companies use the straight line method to calculate all depreciation and amortization expenses. Any goodwill arising from the business combination is to be amortized over 30 years. Prime carries its investment in Sublime by the equity method.

On December 31, 2000, the Balance Sheets of the Prime Company and its subsidiary, the Sublime Company are as follows:

Balance Sheets
As At December 31, 2000

	Prime	Sublime
Cash and Current Receivables	$ 2,003,000	$ 1,000,000
Inventories	3,200,000	2,000,000
Investment in Sublime (At Equity)	5,497,000	-0-
Long Term Receivables	800,000	1,500,000
Plant and Equipment (Net)	17,000,000	8,000,000
Land	5,000,000	-0-
Total Assets	$33,500,000	$12,500,000
Current Liabilities	$ 2,503,000	$ 1,200,000
Dividends Payable	-0-	300,000
Long Term Liabilities	8,500,000	2,000,000
No Par Common Stock	6,000,000	3,000,000
Retained Earnings	16,497,000	6,000,000
Total Equities	$33,500,000	$12,500,000

Other Information:

1. During 2000, Prime sold $700,000 of merchandise to Sublime and 60 percent of these sales remain in the December 31, 2000 Inventories of Sublime. Sublime has not paid for any of the purchases from Prime that it has not resold. The December 31, 1999 Inventories of Sublime contained $280,000 of purchases from Prime. Prime's sales are priced to provide it with a 40 percent gross margin on cost.

2. During 2000, Prime bought and paid for $600,000 of merchandise purchased from Sublime of which 75 percent has been resold by December 31, 2000. The December 31, 1999 Inventories of Prime contained no purchases from Sublime. Sublime's sales are priced to provide it with a 25 percent gross margin on cost.

3. On July 1, 1998, the Sublime Company sold a machine it had built for a cost of $200,000 to the Prime Company for $150,000. The machine had an estimated useful life on July 1, 1998 of 5 years.

4. The Sublime Company purchased Land for $2 million from Prime on November 1, 1997. The land was originally purchased by Prime for $1 million. The purchase price is to be paid in 5 equal installments of $400,000 on January 1 of each year subsequent to the sale. On October 1, 2000, Sublime sold the parcel of land to a party outside the consolidated entity for $2.5 million. This sale will not affect the terms of payment set up on the sale of land from Prime to Sublime in 1997.

5. On January 1, 2000, Prime sold a machine with a 3 year life to Sublime for proceeds of $100,000 which included a gain of $60,000.

6. During 2000, Prime earned Net Income of $2,500,000 and paid dividends of $500,000. Sublime earned Net Income of $600,000 in 2000 and has declared dividends of $300,000 which will be payable on January 15, 2001.

Required:

A. Verify the Investment in Sublime account as it is shown on Prime's Balance Sheet as at December 31, 2000.

B. Prepare a consolidated Balance Sheet for the Prime Company and its subsidiary, the Sublime Company as at December 31, 2000.

SELF STUDY PROBLEM SEVEN - 3

On January 1, 1997, the Pelt Company purchases 80 percent of the outstanding voting shares of the Smelt Company for cash of $800,000. The $280,000 excess of the investment cost over the book value of the Smelt Company's net identifiable assets is allocated as follows:

Land	$ 40,000
Equipment	
(Expected useful life of 7 years with no net salvage value)	140,000
Goodwill (To be amortized over 25 years)	100,000
Total	$280,000

Both Companies use the straight line method to calculate all depreciation and amortization and close their books on December 31 of each year. The Pelt Company's Investment in Smelt Company is accounted for by the cost method.

During 1997, the Pelt Company reported earnings of $320,000 and declared dividends of $40,000. During this same period, the Smelt Company earned $120,000 and declared common stock dividends of $20,000. During the year ending December 31, 1998, the Pelt Company reported earnings of $160,000 and again declared dividends of $40,000. Smelt Company had a loss of $60,000 in 1998, but still declared a dividend of $20,000 for this period. On January 1, 1998, the Pelt Company had Retained Earnings of $2,400,000 and the Smelt Company had Retained Earnings of $340,000.

During 1997, the Smelt Company had purchases from the Pelt Company of $160,000. This merchandise had cost the Pelt Company $120,000. On December 31, 1997, 25 percent of these goods were still in Smelt's inventory. The Pelt Company had purchases from the Smelt Company of $240,000, for which the cost to the Smelt Company was $180,000. On December 31, 1997, one-third of these goods remained in the inventories of the Pelt Company. One year later, in 1998, the downstream unrealized gain in Smelt's closing inventory was only $8,000 while the upstream unrealized gain in Pelt's closing inventory had increased by $4,000.

The December 31, 1998 trial balance of the Smelt Company included 6 percent coupon bonds ($400,000 par value) at a carrying value of $416,000. These bonds will mature on December 31, 2002. On January 1, 1998, the Pelt Company purchased 60 percent of the Smelt Company bonds at a price of $224,000.

During both 1997 and 1998, the Pelt Company charged the Smelt Company an annual management fee of $21,000. This fee is included in the Operating Expenses of the Smelt Company and in the Miscellaneous Revenues of the Pelt Company.

Required   Calculate the consolidated Net Income for the year ending December 31, 1998 and the balance in consolidated Retained Earnings as at December 31, 1998 of the Pelt Company and its subsidiary, the Smelt Company.

SELF STUDY PROBLEM SEVEN - 4

On December 31, 1996, the Above Company acquired 70 percent of the outstanding voting shares of the Center Company for cash of $4,000,000. On this date the Center Company had No Par Common Stock of $3,000,000 and Retained Earnings of $2,000,000. All of the Center Company's identifiable assets and liabilities had fair values that were equal to their carrying values except Plant And Equipment which had a fair value that was $300,000 greater than its carrying value and a remaining useful life of 20 years.

On December 31, 1997, the Center Company acquired 60 percent of the outstanding voting shares of the Below Company for cash of $2,000,000. On this date the Below Company had No Par Common Stock of $2,000,000 and Retained Earnings of $1,000,000. All of the Below Company's identifiable assets and liabilities had fair values that were equal to their carrying values except Plant And Equipment which had a fair value that was $500,000 less than its carrying value and had a remaining useful life of 20 years.

Both the Above and Center Companies carry their investments at cost. All Companies use the straight line method for all depreciation and amortization. Any goodwill which might arise in the preceding business combination transactions is to be amortized over 10 years.

On December 31, 1998, the condensed Balance Sheets and the 1998 Net Incomes of the Above, Center and Below Companies were as follows:

Condensed Balance Sheets
As At December 31, 1998

	Above	Center	Below
Net Monetary Assets	$1,500,000	$ 900,000	$ 700,000
Investments	4,000,000	2,000,000	-0-
Nonmonetary Assets	3,500,000	2,500,000	2,500,000
Total Assets	$9,000,000	$5,400,000	$3,200,000
No Par Common Stock	$6,000,000	$3,000,000	$2,000,000
Retained Earnings	3,000,000	2,400,000	1,200,000
Total Shareholders' Equity	$9,000,000	$5,400,000	$3,200,000

Net Income For The Year Ending December 31, 1998

	Above	Center	Below
Net Incomes	$400,000	$250,000	$200,000

Other Information:

1. No dividends were declared or paid by the Above, Center or Below Companies during the year ending December 31, 1998.

2. The December 31, 1998 Inventories of the Center Company contain merchandise purchased from the Below Company on which the Below Company had recorded a gross profit of $20,000.

3. The December 31, 1998 Inventories of the Above Company contain merchandise purchased from the Center Company on which the Center Company had recorded a gross profit of $30,000.

Required   Prepare a consolidated Balance Sheet as at December 31, 1998 and compute consolidated Net Income for the year ending December 31, 1998 for the Above Company and its subsidiaries the Center and Below Companies.

SELF STUDY PROBLEM SEVEN - 5

On December 31, 1997, the condensed Balance Sheets of the Push Company and the Shove Company were as follows:

Condensed Balance Sheet
As At December 31, 1997

	Push	Shove
Net Identifiable Assets	$10,000,000	$4,000,000
No Par Common Stock	$ 5,000,000	$3,000,000
Retained Earnings	5,000,000	1,000,000
Total Shareholders' Equity	$10,000,000	$4,000,000

On this date the Push Company purchases 80 percent of the outstanding voting shares of the Shove Company for $3,400,000 and the Shove Company purchases 10 percent of the outstanding voting shares of the Push Company for $1,100,000. At this time, all of the identifiable assets and liabilities of both Companies have fair values that are equal to their carrying values.

Both Companies carry their Long Term Investments at cost and any Goodwill arising from the business combination transaction will be amortized over 10 years by the straight line method.

During 1998, the condensed Income Statements of the two Companies are as follows:

Condensed Income Statement
For The Year Ending December 31, 1998

	Push	Shove
Revenues	$2,000,000	$800,000
Expenses	1,500,000	600,000
Net Income	$ 500,000	$200,000

During 1998 the only intercompany transactions were sales of merchandise. The Shove Company's sales to Push totalled $100,000 while the Push Company's sales to Shove were in the amount of $300,000. On December 31, 1998, the Inventories of the Push Company contain merchandise purchased from the Shove Company on which a gross profit of $10,000 had been recognized at the time of sale. Also on this date, the Inventories of the Shove Company contain merchandise purchased from the Push Company on which a gross profit of $75,000 had been recognized.

The condensed Balance Sheets of the two Companies as at December 31, 1998 are as follows:

Condensed Balance Sheet
As At December 31, 1998

	Push	Shove
Investments	$ 3,400,000	$1,100,000
Other Net Identifiable Assets	7,100,000	3,100,000
Total Assets	$10,500,000	$4,200,000
No Par Common Stock	$ 5,000,000	$3,000,000
Retained Earnings	5,500,000	1,200,000
Total Shareholders' Equity	$10,500,000	$4,200,000

Required   Prepare a consolidated Balance Sheet as at December 31, 1997, a consolidated Income Statement for the year ending December 31, 1998 and a consolidated Balance Sheet as at December 31, 1998 for the Push Company and its subsidiary, the Shove Company.

SELF STUDY PROBLEM SEVEN - 6

On December 31, 1998, the Pointer and Setter Companies had the following condensed Balance Sheets:

	Pointer	Setter
Net Identifiable Assets	$1,400,000	$960,000
Preferred Stock - Par $100	$ -0-	$300,000
Common Stock - Par $50	900,000	450,000
Contributed Surplus	230,000	90,000
Retained Earnings	270,000	120,000
Total Equities	$1,400,000	$960,000

At this time, all of the identifiable assets of the Setter Company have fair values that are equal to their carrying values. The annual dividend on the Setter Company's Preferred Stock is 9 percent of par value.

Required Listed below are three independent cases involving an acquisition of the Setter Company's common and preferred shares on December 31, 1998. For each case, prepare a consolidated Balance Sheet as at December 31, 1998.

A. Assume that the Preferred Stock is cumulative and nonparticipating, and that dividends are not in arrears. The Pointer Company pays $175,000 for 50 percent of the Preferred Stock of the Setter Company and $610,000 for 90 percent of the Company's Common Stock.

B. Assume that the Preferred Stock is cumulative, nonparticipating, and that dividends are two years in arrears. The Pointer Company pays $140,000 for 40 percent of the Preferred Stock of the Setter Company and $550,000 for 80 percent of the Company's Common Stock.

C. Assume that the Preferred Stock is cumulative, fully participating on a percentage of par basis, and that dividends are not in arrears. The Pointer Company pays $225,000 for 60 percent of the Preferred Stock of the Setter Company and $600,000 for 90 percent of the Company's Common Stock.

SELF STUDY PROBLEM SEVEN - 7

On December 31, 1997, the Pick Company purchased 80 percent of the 100,000 issued and outstanding voting shares of the Shovel Company for $1,900,000 in cash. On this date, all of the identifiable assets and liabilities of the Shovel Company had fair values that were equal to their carrying values except for Equipment which had a fair value that was $250,000 greater than its carrying value. This Equipment had a remaining useful life of 10 years at the time of this business combination. Any Goodwill which results from this business combination will be amortized over 10 years. Both Companies use the straight line method for all depreciation and amortization computations. The Pick Company carries its Investment in Shovel using the cost method.

The condensed Balance Sheets of the two Companies, immediately after the transaction described in the preceding paragraph and the condensed open trial balances of the two Companies on December 31, 1998, were as follows:

Condensed Balance Sheet
As At December 31, 1997

	Pick	Shovel
Investment In Shovel	$1,900,000	$ -0-
Net Other Identifiable Assets	5,100,000	2,000,000
Total Assets	$7,000,000	$2,000,000
No Par Common Stock	$4,000,000	$1,000,000
Retained Earnings	3,000,000	1,000,000
Total Shareholders' Equity	$7,000,000	$2,000,000

Condensed Trial Balance
As At December 31, 1998

	Pick	Shovel
Investment In Shovel	$ 1,900,000	$ -0-
Net Other Identifiable Assets	5,900,000	2,300,000
Total Expenses	3,200,000	700,000
Total Debits	$11,000,000	$3,000,000
No Par Common Stock	$ 4,000,000	$1,000,000
Retained Earnings	3,000,000	1,000,000
Total Revenues	4,000,000	1,000,000
Total Credits	$11,000,000	$3,000,000

There were no intercompany transactions and neither Company declared any dividends during the year ending December 31, 1998.

On December 31, 1998, all of the identifiable assets and liabilities of the Shovel Company have fair values that are equal to their carrying values except for Equipment which has a fair value that is $300,000 greater than its carrying value.

Required   For each of the following independent cases, prepare a consolidated Income Statement for the year ending December 31, 1998 and a consolidated Balance Sheet as at December 31, 1998 for the Pick Company and its subsidiary, the Shovel Company.

Case One   Assume that there are no changes in the shareholders' equity of the Shovel Company during the year ending December 31, 1998 or the percentage of Shovel Company shares that are held by the Pick Company on December 31, 1998.

Case Two   Assume that there are no changes in the shareholders' equity of the Shovel Company during the year ending December 31, 1998 but that on December 31, 1998, the Pick Company purchases an additional 10,000 of the outstanding Shovel Company shares for $280,000.

Case Three   Assume that there are no changes in the shareholders' equity of the Shovel Company during the year ending December 31, 1998 but that on December 31, 1998, the Pick Company sells 20,000 of its Shovel Company shares for $600,000 in cash.

Case Four   Assume that on December 31, 1998, the Shovel Company issues an additional 25,000 of its authorized No Par Common Shares to investors in return for $750,000 in cash. There is no change in the Pick Company's holding of 80,000 of the Shovel Company's outstanding shares.

SELF STUDY PROBLEM SEVEN - 8

On July 1, 1998, the Patco Company paid $720,000 in cash to acquire 80 percent of the outstanding voting shares of the Stand Company. At this date the fair values of all of Stand Company's identifiable assets and liabilities had fair values that were equal to their carrying values except for a group of fixed assets. These fixed assets had a fair value that exceeded their carrying value by $120,000. These assets have a remaining useful life on July 1, 1998 of four years.

The following condensed financial statements for the two Companies have been provided by the chief accountant for Patco:

1998 Balance Sheets

	January 1 Patco	July 1 Stand	December 31 Patco	December 31 Stand
Cash	$ 25,000	$ 10,000	$ 12,000	$ 6,000
Noncash Current Assets	1,000,000	140,000	663,000	84,000
Investment In Stand	-0-	-0-	720,000	-0-
Fixed Assets (Net)	1,500,000	900,000	1,680,000	1,050,000
Goodwill	700,000	60,000	525,000	54,000
Total Assets	$3,225,000	$1,110,000	$3,600,000	$1,194,000
Current Liabilities	$ 450,000	$ 60,000	$ 450,000	$ 75,000
Long Term Liabilities	600,000	300,000	675,000	300,000
Common Stock	1,500,000	225,000	1,500,000	225,000
Retained Earnings	675,000	525,000	975,000	594,000
Total Equities	$3,225,000	$1,110,000	$3,600,000	$1,194,000

1998 Income Statements

	Patco Year Ended December 31	Stand Six Months Ended December 31
Sales	$4,600,000	$600,000
Cost Of Goods Sold	$2,700,000	$375,000
Depreciation Expense	525,000	120,000
Amortization Of Goodwill	175,000	6,000
Other Expenses	900,000	30,000
Total Expenses	$4,300,000	$531,000
Net Income	$ 300,000	$ 69,000

In addition to the preceding single entity financial statements, Patco's accountant also provides the following consolidated Balance Sheet for Patco Company and its subsidiary Stand Company:

Consolidated Balance Sheet
As At December 31, 1998

Cash	$ 18,000
Noncash Current Assets	730,000
Fixed Assets	2,827,650
Goodwill	598,800
Total Assets	**$4,174,450**
Current Liabilities	$ 525,000
Long Term Liabilities	975,000
Non Controlling Interest	163,130
Common Stock	1,500,000
Retained Earnings	1,011,320
Total Equities	**$4,174,450**

Other Information:

1. The Patco Company carries its Investment In Stand by the cost method. Both Companies use the straight line method for all depreciation and amortization calculations.

2. During the period July 1, 1998 through December 31, 1998, Stand sells merchandise to Patco in the total amount of $170,000. One half of this merchandise is in the closing Inventories of Patco. The intercompany sales are priced to provide a markup of 25 percent on its invoice cost.

3. On October 1, 1998, Stand sold equipment to Patco for $98,000. The Equipment had a carrying value on the books of Stand of $112,000 and, at the time of the sale, its remaining useful life was estimated to be 10 years. On July 1, 1998, the carrying value of this equipment was equal to its fair value.

4. On March 1, 1998, Patco purchased a Building for $218,000. The vendor accepted a $75,000, 5 year mortgage from Patco and the remainder of the purchase price was paid in cash.

Required:

A. Verify the calculations used by the Patco Company accountant in establishing the consolidated Balance Sheet values for:

1. Goodwill
2. Non Controlling Interest
3. Retained Earnings

B. Calculate consolidated Net Income for Patco Company and its subsidiary Stand Company for the year ending December 31, 1998.

C. Prepare a consolidated Statement Of Changes In Financial Position for the Patco Company and its subsidiary Stand Company for the year ending December 31, 1998.

Assignment Problems

(The solutions to these problem are only available in
the solutions manual that has been provided to your instructor.)

ASSIGNMENT PROBLEM SEVEN - 1

On January 1, 1990, the Poof Company purchased 40,000 common shares of the Spoof Company for $125 a share. On that date, Spoof had Common Stock - Par $50 outstanding of $2,500,000, Contributed Surplus of $1,000,000 and Retained Earnings of $1,500,000. When acquired, all of the identifiable assets and liabilities of Spoof had fair values that were equal to their carrying values with the following exceptions:

1. Inventories with fair values that were $200,000 greater than their carrying values.

2. Land in Loof County with a fair value that was $150,000 greater than its carrying value.

3. Plant and Equipment with a fair value that was $600,000 less than its carrying value and a remaining useful life of 16 years.

Any goodwill arising from this business combination is to be amortized over 40 years.

On January 1, 1994, Spoof sold a machine originally purchased for $1,100,000 on December 31, 1991, to Poof for $1,400,000. Spoof had been depreciating the asset over its estimated life of 22 years. Both Companies use the straight line method for all depreciation and amortization calculations. On September 1, 1998, Spoof sold its land in Loof County to Poof for a gain of $1,000,000. This was the same parcel of land that had a fair value that was $150,000 greater than its carrying value on January 1, 1990.

Other data for the year ending December 31, 1998 is as follows:

Income Statements
For The Year Ending December 31, 1998

	Poof	Spoof
Sales	$11,600,000	$3,000,000
Gain on Land Sale	-0-	1,000,000
Investment Income	406,000	-0-
Total Revenues	$12,006,000	$4,000,000
Cost of Goods Sold	$ 8,000,000	$1,500,000
Other Expenses	1,000,000	500,000
Total Expenses	$ 9,000,000	$2,000,000
Net Income	$ 3,006,000	$2,000,000

Balance Sheets
As At December 31, 1998

	Poof	Spoof
Cash and Current Receivables	$ 900,000	$ 300,000
Inventories	4,600,000	2,400,000
Investment in Spoof (At Equity)	7,560,000	-0-
Plant and Equipment (Net)	13,000,000	6,800,000
Land	6,000,000	2,500,000
Total Assets	$32,060,000	$12,000,000
Current Liabilities	$ 900,000	$ 400,000
Long Term Liabilities	6,600,000	1,100,000
Common Stock - No Par	10,000,000	-0-
Common Stock - Par $50	-0-	2,500,000
Contributed Surplus	-0-	1,000,000
Retained Earnings	14,560,000	7,000,000
Total Equities	$32,060,000	$12,000,000

	Poof	Spoof
Dividends Declared and Paid	$1,000,000	$ 500,000
Intercompany Inventory Sales	2,000,000	1,000,000
Intercompany Purchases in:		
January 1, 1998 Inventories	200,000	450,000
December 31, 1998 Inventories	600,000	1,200,000

Poof Company's Investment in Spoof is carried by the equity method and complies with the recommendations of the *CICA Handbook*. Intercompany sales of inventory are priced to provide a gross profit margin on sales price of 33-1/3 percent for the Poof Company and 50 percent for the Spoof Company. Inventories of both Companies turn over within one year. Neither Company has a liability outstanding related to the intercompany inventory sales on December 31, 1998.

Required: Using the preceding information, provide the following:

A. A verification of the balance in the Investment in Spoof account of $7,560,000.

B. A verification of the Investment Income of $406,000 which was recorded by the Poof Company in applying the equity method of accounting.

C. A calculation of what the December 31, 1998 balance of the Retained Earnings of the Poof Company would have been if the Investment in Spoof had been carried using the cost method since acquisition.

D. A consolidated Income Statement for the Poof Company and its subsidiary, the Spoof Company for the year ending December 31, 1998.

E. A consolidated Statement of Retained Earnings for the Poof Company and its subsidiary the Spoof Company for the year ending December 31, 1998.

F. A consolidated Balance Sheet for the Poof Company and its subsidiary the Spoof Company as at December 31, 1998.

ASSIGNMENT PROBLEM SEVEN - 2

On January 1, 1994, the Hades Company purchased 70 percent of the Styx Company's outstanding voting shares. On that date, the identifiable assets and liabilities had fair values that were equal to their carrying values except for inventories which had a fair value that was $32,000 greater than their carrying values and long term liabilities which had a fair value that was $220,000 greater than their carrying values. These long term liabilities mature on December 31, 2001. Both Companies use the straight line method to calculate all depreciation and amortization charges. Any goodwill arising from this business combination is to be amortized over 20 years. The Styx Company has issued no common stock subsequent to January 1, 1994. The Hades Company carries its Investment in Styx using the equity method.

As at December 31, 1998, the Balance Sheets of the Hades Company and the Styx Company are as follows:

	Hades	Styx
Cash And Current Receivables	$ 1,285,162	$ 491,000
Inventories	972,431	1,772,000
Investment In Styx (At Equity)	4,685,538	-0-
Plant And Equipment (Net)	5,621,000	5,705,000
Total Assets	$12,564,131	$7,968,000
Current Liabilities	$ 1,473,593	$ 212,000
Long Term Liabilities	982,000	1,031,000
No Par Common Stock	3,714,000	2,023,000
Retained Earnings	6,394,538	4,702,000
Total Equities	$12,564,131	$7,968,000

During the period January 1, 1994 through December 31, 1997, the Styx Company earned income of $882,000 and declared dividends of $317,000.

Other Information:

1. During the year 1998, the Hades Company sold merchandise to the Styx Company for $872,000 and purchased $331,000 worth of merchandise from the Styx Company. The December 31, 1998 Inventories of the Hades Company contained merchandise of $86,000 purchased from the Styx Company, while the December 31, 1998 Inventories of the Styx Company contained merchandise purchased for $148,000 from the Hades Company. The January 1, 1998 Inventories of both Companies contained 80 percent of the amount of intercompany purchases that were present in the December 31, 1998 Inventories. The gross profit on all Hades Company sales is 35 percent of sales prices while that of the Styx Company is 45 percent of sales prices.

2. Furniture And Fixtures purchased on January 1, 1995 by the Hades Company for $480,000 were sold to the Styx Company on January 1, 1997 for $230,100. When acquired by the Hades Company, the Furniture And Fixtures was expected to last until January 1, 2003 with no salvage value anticipated. There is no change in this estimate at the time of the intercompany sale.

3. The Styx Company purchased a building and the land it was situated on for $142,000 on December 31, 1994. At that time the estimated life of the building was 20 years with no net salvage value. On December 31, 1997, the building and land was sold to the Hades Company for $263,200. At both the time of the original purchase and the

time of the subsequent intercompany sale, it was independently decided that the total value of the land and building should be allocated 75 percent to the building and 25 percent to the land. The Hades Company gave cash of $150,000 to the Styx Company for the land and building with the balance of the purchase price being due on June 30, 1999.

4. During 1998, the Hades Company earned $932,000 and paid $150,000 in dividends and the Styx Company earned $215,000 and paid $65,000 in dividends.

5. The consolidated Goodwill arising from this business combination has an amortized value of $119,700 on December 31, 1998.

Required:

A. Calculate the cost of the Investment In Styx that was made on January 1, 1994.

B. Prepare the consolidated Balance Sheet of the Hades Company and its subsidiary the Styx Company as at December 31, 1998.

C. Assume that the Hades Company has carried its Investment In Styx by the cost method since its acquisition. Calculate the Retained Earnings balance in the single entity records of the Hades Company on December 31, 1998.

ASSIGNMENT PROBLEM SEVEN - 3

On January 1, 1994, the Pronto Company purchased 75 percent of the outstanding voting shares of the Swan Company for $4,500,000 in cash. On that date, the Swan Company had No Par Common Stock of $3,000,000 and Retained Earnings of $2,500,000. All of the assets and liabilities of the Swan Company had fair values that were equal to their carrying values except for:

1. Plant and Equipment which had a fair value that was $200,000 greater than its carrying value and a remaining useful life of 15 years.

2. Long Term Liabilities maturing on January 1, 2000 which had fair values that were $100,000 less than their carrying values.

Any Goodwill that arises from the business combination is to be amortized over a period of 40 years. Both Companies use the straight line method to calculate all depreciation and amortization, including bond premium and discount.

The Pronto Company carries its investment in the Swan Company using the equity method. Any unrealized intercompany profits resulting from a sale by Pronto are shown as an adjustment of Investment Income. The condensed Income Statements of the two Companies, after the recognition of all investment income, for the year ending December 31, 1998 are as follows:

	Pronto	Swan
Total Revenues	$6,400,000	$2,800,000
Cost of Goods Sold	$4,000,000	$1,400,000
Other Expenses	1,000,000	600,000
Total Expenses	$5,000,000	$2,000,000
Net Income	$1,400,000	$ 800,000

Other Information:

1. On December 31, 1995, the Swan Company issues 6 percent coupon bonds payable with a par value of $500,000. The bonds are sold at 106 percent and mature on December 31, 2005. On January 1, 1998, the Pronto Company purchases one-half of these bonds on the open market for $230,000 in cash.

2. On January 1, 1996, the Swan Company sells a machine to the Pronto Company for $300,000. The carrying value of this machine on the books of the Swan Company on this date is $400,000 and its remaining useful life is 5 years.

3. During 1998, the Swan Company sells merchandise to the Pronto Company for $250,000. Of this merchandise, $80,000 is still in the inventories of the Pronto Company on December 31, 1998. On December 31, 1997, the inventories of the Pronto Company contained merchandise purchased from the Swan Company for $75,000. All of the Swan Company's sales to the Pronto Company are priced to provide a gross margin on sales prices of 20 percent.

4. On December 1, 1998, the Pronto Company sells merchandise to the Swan Company for $200,000. None of this merchandise has been resold by the Swan Company to individuals outside the consolidated entity by December 31, 1998. This merchandise was priced to provide the Pronto Company with a gross margin on sales prices of 30 percent.

5. During 1998, the Swan Company declares and pays dividends of $120,000 while the Pronto Company declares and pays dividends of $200,000.

6. Both the Pronto Company and the Swan Company are merchandising companies. As a result, Cost of Goods Sold consists entirely of merchandise that has been purchased and resold.

7. The January 1, 1998 Retained Earnings balance of the Pronto Company was $12,000,000 and that of the Swan Company was $5,120,000.

Required:

A. Calculate the amount of Investment Income from the Swan Company that has been included in the 1998 Total Revenues of the Pronto Company.

B. Prepare the consolidated Income Statement for the Pronto Company and its subsidiary, the Swan Company for the year ending December 31, 1998.

C. Calculate the Non Controlling Interest that would be shown on the consolidated Balance Sheet as at December 31, 1998 of the Pronto Company and its subsidiary, the Swan Company.

D. Calculate the balance in the Investment in Swan account that would be shown on the Balance Sheet as at December 31, 1998 of the Pronto Company prior to consolidation of the Swan Company.

ASSIGNMENT PROBLEM SEVEN - 4

On January 1, 1993, the Pastar Company acquired 80 percent of the outstanding voting shares of the Slone Company for $1,800,000 in cash. On that date, the identifiable assets and liabilities of the Slone Company had fair values that were equal to their carrying values and the book values of the Slone Company's net assets totalled $2,250,000. Goodwill, if any arises as a result of the business combination, is to be amortized over 40 years. Subsequent to the business combination there are no intercompany transactions other than dividend payments and the following bond purchases and sales.

On April 1, 1983, the Pastar Company issued 12 percent coupon bonds with a par value of $1,125,000 which were sold at 105 percent. They mature on April 1, 2003 and pay interest annually on April 1. On April 1, 1995, the Slone Company purchased $700,000 par value of the Pastar Company bonds in the open market at an average price of 101.5 percent.

On January 1, 1997, the Slone Company issued at 98 percent, 5 percent coupon bonds with a par value of $3,000,000. They mature on January 1, 2002 and pay interest annually on December 31. On January 1, 1998, the Pastar Company purchased $1,200,000 par value of the Slone Company bonds in the open market at an average price of 102 percent.

The Pastar Company accounts for its investment in the Slone Company by the cost method. Both Companies use the straight line method to amortize bond discount or premium. Neither Company has issued any Common Stock since January 1, 1993.

Selected account balances from the Income and Retained Earnings Statements for the year ending December 31, 1998 and the Balance Sheets as at December 31, 1998 of Pastar and Slone are as follows:

	Pastar	Slone
Interest Revenue	$ 197,000	$ 104,000
Interest Expense	201,000	626,000
Net Income	673,000	89,000
Dividends Declared	85,000	13,000
Investments in Bonds	1,435,000	825,000
No Par Common Stock	5,000,000	1,500,000
Ending Retained Earnings	7,712,000	2,351,000

Required Calculate the balances that would be shown on the consolidated financial statements of the Pastar Company and its subsidiary the Slone Company for the year ending December 31, 1998 for the following accounts:

A. Interest Revenue
B. Interest Expense
C. Non Controlling Interest on the consolidated Income Statement
D. Consolidated Net Income
E. Investments in Bonds
F. Non Controlling Interest on the consolidated Balance Sheet
G. Closing consolidated Retained Earnings

ASSIGNMENT PROBLEM SEVEN - 5
On December 31, 1994, the Plateau Company acquired 60 percent of the outstanding voting shares of the Valley Company for cash in the amount of $3,000,000. On this date the Valley Company had No Par Common Stock of $3,500,000 and Retained Earnings of $1,500,000. All of the Valley Company's identifiable assets and liabilities had fair values that were equal to their carrying values.

On December 31, 1996, the Crest Company acquired 90 percent of the outstanding voting shares of the Plateau Company for cash in the amount of $9,000,000. On this date the Plateau Company had No Par Common Stock of $5,000,000 and Retained Earnings of $3,000,000. Also on this date, all of the Plateau Company's identifiable assets and liabilities had fair values that were equal to their carrying values except Long Term Liabilities which had a fair value that was $500,000 less than their carrying value and a remaining term to maturity of eight years.

On December 31, 1996, all of the identifiable assets and liabilities of the Valley Company had carrying values that were equal to their fair values. Between December 31, 1994 and December 31, 1996, the Valley Company earned $800,000 and declared dividends of $300,000. No dividends were declared or paid by the Crest, Plateau, or Valley Companies during the year ending December 31, 1998.

On December 31, 1998, the condensed Balance Sheets and the 1998 Net Incomes of the Crest, Plateau, and Valley Companies were as follows:

	Crest	Plateau	Valley
Net Current Assets	$ 2,000,000	$ 1,000,000	$ 500,000
Investments	9,000,000	3,000,000	-0-
Noncurrent Assets	16,000,000	8,000,000	6,500,000
Total Assets	$27,000,000	$12,000,000	$7,000,000
Long Term Liabilities	$ 1,000,000	$ 1,000,000	$1,000,000
No Par Common Stock	10,000,000	5,000,000	3,500,000
Retained Earnings	16,000,000	6,000,000	2,500,000
Total Equities	$27,000,000	$12,000,000	$7,000,000
Net Incomes	$ 1,000,000	$ 2,000,000	$ 400,000

Other Information:

1. Both the Crest Company and the Plateau Company carry their investments using the cost method.

2. All Companies use the straight line method for calculating depreciation and amortization.

3. Any goodwill which might arise in either preceding business combination transaction is to be amortized over 10 years.

4. The December 31, 1998 Inventories of the Plateau Company contain merchandise purchased from the Valley Company on which the Valley Company had recognized a gross profit of $30,000. There were no purchases from the Valley Company in the December 31, 1997 Inventories of the Plateau Company.

5. The December 31, 1998 Inventories of the Crest Company contain merchandise purchased from the Plateau Company on which the Plateau Company had recorded a profit of $100,000. The December 31, 1997 Inventories of the Crest Company contain merchandise purchased from the Plateau Company on which the Plateau Company had recorded a profit of $500,000.

6. On December 15, 1998, the Crest Company sold a parcel of land to the Valley Company for $66,000. The land had been purchased by the Crest Company in 1995 for $94,000.

Required   For the Crest Company and its subsidiaries:

A. Compute consolidated Net Income for the year ending December 31, 1998.

B. Prepare a consolidated Statement Of Retained Earnings for the year ending December 31, 1998.

C. Prepare a consolidated Balance Sheet as at December 31, 1998.

ASSIGNMENT PROBLEM SEVEN - 6

On December 31, 1996, the condensed Balance Sheets of the Pine Company and the Maple Company are as follows:

Balance Sheets As At December 31, 1996
(Prior to Share Acquisitions)

	Pine	Maple
Net Assets	$5,000,000	$2,000,000
No Par Common Stock	$1,000,000	$ 400,000
Retained Earnings	4,000,000	1,600,000
Total Shareholders' Equity	$5,000,000	$2,000,000

On this date, the Pine Company purchases 80 percent of the outstanding voting shares of the Maple Company for $1,850,000 in cash and the Maple Company purchases 5 percent of the outstanding voting shares of the Pine Company for $280,000 in cash. On the acquisition date, all of the identifiable assets and liabilities of both Companies have fair values that are equal to their carrying values.

Both Companies carry their Long Term Investments at cost and any Goodwill arising from the business combination transaction will be amortized over 25 years by the straight line method.

The condensed Income Statements of the two Companies for the year ending December, 31, 1998 are as follows:

Income Statements
Year Ending December 31, 1998

	Pine	Maple
Revenues	$1,000,000	$500,000
Expenses	600,000	350,000
Net Income	$ 400,000	$150,000

During 1998, the sales of Maple include $80,000 of merchandise that is purchased by Pine. Of these sales, merchandise which contains a gross profit of $30,000 to Maple remains in the December 31, 1998 inventories of Pine. The Maple Company also purchases merchandise from the Pine Company for $100,000 during 1998 and carries in its December 31, 1998 inventories, merchandise containing a gross profit of $25,000 to the Pine Company.

No dividends were paid by either Company during 1997 or 1998. There were no intercompany sales prior to 1998.

The condensed Balance Sheets of the two Companies as at December 31, 1998 are as follows:

Balance Sheets As At December 31, 1998

	Pine	Maple
Investments	$1,850,000	$ 280,000
Other Net Identifiable Assets	3,750,000	1,920,000
Total Assets	**$5,600,000**	**$2,200,000**
No Par Common Stock	$1,000,000	$ 400,000
Retained Earnings	4,600,000	1,800,000
Total Shareholders' Equity	**$5,600,000**	**$2,200,000**

Required: Prepare a consolidated Balance Sheet as at December 31, 1996, a consolidated Income Statement for the year ending December 31, 1998 and a consolidated Balance Sheet as at December 31, 1998 for the Pine Company and its subsidiary, the Maple Company. Your answer should be in accordance with the requirements of the *CICA Handbook*.

ASSIGNMENT PROBLEM SEVEN - 7

On December 31, 1997, the Perry Company purchased 90 percent of the 200,000 issued and outstanding common shares of the Dalton Company for $1,350,000 in cash. On this date, all of the identifiable assets and liabilities of the Dalton Company had fair values that were equal to their carrying values except for a Building which had a fair value that was $90,000 greater than its carrying value. The Building had a remaining useful life of 10 years with no anticipated salvage value at the time of this business combination. Any Goodwill which results from this business combination will be amortized over 10 years.

The condensed Balance Sheets of the two Companies, immediately after the transaction described in the preceding paragraph, were as follows:

	Perry	Dalton
Investment In Dalton	$1,350,000	$ -0-
Net Other Identifiable Assets	4,500,000	1,710,000
Total Assets	**$5,850,000**	**$1,710,000**
Preferred Stock - Par $100	$ -0-	$ 360,000
No Par Common Stock	3,600,000	900,000
Retained Earnings	2,250,000	450,000
Total Shareholders' Equity	**$5,850,000**	**$1,710,000**

One year later, on December 31, 1998, before any of the share transactions described in the Required of this problem, the condensed open trial balances of the two Companies were as follows:

	Perry	Dalton
Investment In Dalton	$1,350,000	$ -0-
Net Other Identifiable Assets	4,950,000	2,034,000
Preferred Dividends Declared	-0-	36,000
Total Expenses	2,250,000	900,000
Total Debits	**$8,550,000**	**$2,970,000**
Preferred Stock - Par $100	$ -0-	$ 360,000
No Par Common Stock	3,600,000	900,000
Retained Earnings	2,250,000	450,000
Total Revenues	2,700,000	1,260,000
Total Credits	**$8,550,000**	**$2,970,000**

The Perry Company carries its Investment in Dalton using the cost method. The 10 percent Preferred Stock of Dalton is cumulative and nonparticipating. The preferred dividends were paid on December 30, 1998 and there are no dividends in arrears. There were no intercompany transactions and neither Company declared any common stock dividends during the year ending December 31, 1998.

On December 31, 1998, all of the identifiable assets and liabilities of the Dalton Company have fair values that are equal to their carrying values except for the Building which has a fair value that is $112,500 greater than its carrying value. Both Companies use the straight line method to calculate all amortization and depreciation charges.

Required: For each of the following independent cases, prepare a consolidated Income Statement for the year ending December 31, 1998 and a consolidated Balance Sheet as at December 31, 1998 for the Perry Company and its subsidiary, the Dalton Company.

Case One   Assume that there are no changes in the shareholders' equity of the Dalton Company during the year ending December 31, 1998 or the percentage of Dalton Company common shares that are held by the Perry Company on December 31, 1998.

Case Two   Assume that there are no changes in the shareholders' equity of the Dalton Company during the year ending December 31, 1998 but that on December 31, 1998, the Perry Company purchases 80 percent of the outstanding Dalton Company preferred shares - Par $100 for $310,000.

Case Three   Assume that there are no changes in the shareholders' equity of the Dalton Company during the year ending December 31, 1998 but that on December 31, 1998, the Perry Company purchases an additional 10,000 of the outstanding Dalton Company common shares for $101,250.

Case Four   Assume that there are no changes in the shareholders' equity of the Dalton Company during the year ending December 31, 1998 but that on December 31, 1998, the Perry Company sells 18,000 of its Dalton Company shares for $180,000 in cash.

Case Five   Assume that on December 31, 1998, the Dalton Company issues an additional 25,000 of its authorized No Par Common Shares to investors in return for $337,500 in cash. There is no change in the Perry Company's holding of 180,000 of the Dalton Company's outstanding shares.

ASSIGNMENT PROBLEM SEVEN - 8

On January 1, 1998, the Winter Company purchased 180,000 of the 200,000 issued and outstanding voting shares of the Spring Company for $1,150,000 in cash. On this date, the Spring Company had No Par Value Common Stock of $860,000 and Retained Earnings of $425,000. All of the identifiable assets and liabilities of the Spring Company had fair values that were equal to their carrying values except for a fleet of delivery vans which had a fair value that was $53,250 less than its carrying value. These vans had a remaining useful life of 4 years with no net salvage value on this date. Any Goodwill which results from this business combination will be amortized over 20 years. Both Companies use the straight line method for all depreciation and amortization calculations.

The condensed Income Statements for the year ending December 31, 1998 and the condensed Balance Sheets as at December 31, 1998, prior to the new issue of stock by the Spring Company, were as follows:

Income Statements
Year Ending December 31, 1998

	Winter	Spring
Total Revenues	$1,520,000	$432,000
Total Expenses	903,000	271,000
Net Income	$ 617,000	$161,000

Balance Sheets
As At December 31, 1998
(Prior To Spring's Stock Issue)

	Winter	Spring
Investment In Spring	$1,150,000	$ -0-
Net Other Identifiable Assets	5,478,000	1,515,000
Total Assets	$6,628,000	$1,515,000
Liabilities	$ 215,000	$ 69,000
No Par Common Stock	1,800,000	860,000
Retained Earnings	4,613,000	586,000
Total Equities	$6,628,000	$1,515,000

The Winter Company accounts for its investment in the Spring Company by the cost method. There were no intercompany transactions and neither Company declared any dividends during the year ending December 31, 1998.

On December 31, 1998, the Spring Company issues an additional 22,222 of its authorized No Par Common Shares to investors in return for $150,000 in cash. There is no change in the Winter Company's holding of 180,000 of the Spring Company's outstanding shares. On December 31, 1998, all of the identifiable assets and liabilities of the Spring Company have fair values that are equal to their carrying values except for the fleet of vans which has a fair value that is $46,500 less than its carrying value.

Required   Prepare the consolidated Income Statement for the year ending December 31, 1998, and the consolidated Balance Sheet as at December 31, 1998, for the Winter Company and its subsidiary the Spring Company.

ASSIGNMENT PROBLEM SEVEN - 9

Proxy Corporation acquired 80 percent of the common shares of Surrogate Ltd. on January 1, 1994, for $1,158,000 in cash. At January 1, 1994, the shareholders' equity for Surrogate Ltd. consisted of the following:

Common Stock - No Par (100,000 shares outstanding)	$1,000,000
Retained Earnings	10,000
Shareholders' Equity	$1,010,000

The adjusted trial balances as at December 31, 1998, for Proxy and Surrogate are shown in Exhibit One.

Other Information:

1. The January 1, 1994 fair values of Surrogate's identifiable assets and liabilities equalled their book values with the following exceptions:

	Book Value	Fair Value
Land	$ 180,000	$280,000
8 Percent Debentures	1,200,000	950,000

    The 8% debentures mature December 31, 2001. Surrogate's Land consisted solely of the Spiritwood property it purchased in 1987 for $180,000. During 1998, Surrogate sold the Spiritwood property to Proxy for proceeds of $300,000.

    Any goodwill arising from the purchase of Surrogate is to be amortized over 10 years.

2. Proxy's Deferred Development Costs relate to a new product that will go into commercial production in early 1999. Included in these costs is materials supplied by Surrogate on June 1, 1998 at a price of $70,000. This price included a profit of $30,000. The deferred development costs are to be amortized over two years, beginning in 1999.

3. On February 6, 1998, Proxy sold Short Term Investments with a carrying value of $100,000 to Surrogate. The sale price was $50,000, the fair market value of the Investments on that date.

4. Proxy's 1998 Other Expenses/Revenues consisted of the following:

    * A revenue accrual of $100,000 for a lawsuit launched in 1998 against a supplier. Proxy's legal counsel has advised that the lawsuit is very likely to be won by Proxy in 1999.

    * Receipt of $75,000 from the federal government as part of a relief program, enacted in 1998. The payment was compensation for inventory which was destroyed in a flood during 1997.

    * Interest revenue of $7,000.

5. On December 31, 1998, Surrogate issued an additional 25,000 common shares for $400,000 to finance 1999 operations. None of these shares were acquired by Proxy.

Required: In accordance with *CICA Handbook* recommendations, prepare Proxy's Consolidated Balance Sheet as at December 31, 1998, and Consolidated Income Statement for the year ended December 31, 1998. Include detailed schedules and explanations to support your calculations. Ignore income taxes.

Exhibit One
Adjusted Trial Balances
As At December 31, 1998

	Proxy	Surrogate
Cash	$ 20,000	$ 390,000
Accounts Receivable	152,000	96,000
Short Term Investments	127,000	50,000
Inventory	120,000	179,000
Investment In Surrogate	1,158,000	-0-
Plant And Equipment (Net)	4,160,000	2,499,000
Deferred Development Costs	330,000	-0-
Land	300,000	-0-
Current Liabilities	(230,000)	(75,000)
8% Debentures	-0-	(1,200,000)
Common Stock - No Par	(2,500,000)	(1,400,000)
Opening Retained Earnings	(1,081,000)	(220,000)
Sales	(4,516,000)	(1,235,000)
Dividend Revenue	(8,000)	-0-
Cost Of Goods Sold	1,500,000	666,000
Loss On Sale Of Securities	50,000	-0-
Gain On Land Sale	-0-	(120,000)
Interest Expense	-0-	96,000
Depreciation/Amortization	600,000	280,000
Dividend Paid May 31, 1998	-0-	10,000
Other Expenses/Revenues	(182,000)	(16,000)
Total	$ -0-	$ -0-

(SMA Adapted)

ASSIGNMENT PROBLEM SEVEN - 10

The Norwood Company purchased 75 percent of the outstanding voting shares of the Sollip Company on January 1, 1995 for $2,000,000 in cash. On that date, the Sollip Company's identifiable assets and liabilities had fair values that were equal to their carrying values except for Plant and Equipment, which had a fair value that was $40,000 more than carrying value and long term liabilities with a fair value that was $80,000 less than carrying value. The Plant and Equipment had a remaining life of 10 years with no anticipated salvage value and the long term liabilities mature on January 1, 2005. On the acquisition date, Sollip had Retained Earnings of $1,400,000 and Common Stock of $600,000.

The Norwood Company carries its investment in Sollip by the cost method. Any goodwill arising from the business combination is to be amortized over 25 years. Both Companies use the straight line method to calculate depreciation and amortization.

The comparative Balance Sheets and the condensed Statement of Income and Change in Retained Earnings for the year ending December 31, 1998 of the Norwood Company and its subsidiary the Sollip Company are as follows:

Balance Sheets
As At December 31

	Norwood		Sollip	
	1998	1997	1998	1997
Cash	$1,009,988	$ 360,000	$1,200,000	$ 600,000
Accounts Receivable	1,394,000	64,000	780,000	200,000
Inventories	310,000	170,000	480,000	320,000
Investment in Sollip (At Cost)	2,000,000	2,000,000	-0-	-0-
Plant and Equipment	6,240,000	6,000,000	4,000,000	4,000,000
Accumulated Depreciation	(3,045,667)	(2,800,000)	(1,988,000)	(1,600,000)
Land	120,000	120,000	60,000	-0-
Total Assets	$8,028,321	$5,914,000	$4,532,000	$3,520,000
Current Liabilities	$2,468,321	$ 714,000	$1,452,000	$ 760,000
Long Term Liabilities	900,000	800,000	560,000	360,000
Common Stock - No Par	2,020,000	2,000,000	600,000	600,000
Retained Earnings	2,640,000	2,400,000	1,920,000	1,800,000
Total Equities	$8,028,321	$5,914,000	$4,532,000	$3,520,000

Income Statements
Year Ending December 31, 1998

	Norwood	Sollip
Total Revenues	$2,760,000	$2,000,000
Cost of Goods Sold	$1,200,000	$ 790,000
Depreciation Expense	410,667	548,000
Other Expenses and Losses	849,333	342,000
Total Expenses and Losses	$2,460,000	$1,680,000
Net Income	$ 300,000	$ 320,000
Retained Earnings, January 1	2,400,000	1,800,000
Balance Available	$2,700,000	$2,120,000
Dividends	60,000	200,000
Balance, December 31	$2,640,000	$1,920,000

Other Information:

1. On January 1, 1996, the Sollip Company sold furniture to the Norwood Company for $31,000. The furniture had a net book value of $85,000 and an estimated life on this date of four years with no anticipated salvage value.

2. On December 31, 1997, the Norwood Company had in its inventories $35,000 of merchandise that it had purchased from Sollip during 1997. During 1998, Norwood purchased $200,000 of merchandise from Sollip of which $75,000 remain in the December 31, 1998 inventories of Norwood. The Norwood Company sold $120,000 of merchandise to Sollip during 1998 which was resold during the year for $165,000. Intercompany inventory sales are priced to provide the selling company with a 30 percent gross profit on sales price.

3. On December 31, 1998 due to the intercompany inventory sales, the Norwood Com-

pany owed the Sollip Company $60,000 and the Sollip Company owed the Norwood Company $80,000. There were no intercompany accounts payable balances on December 31, 1997.

4. On January 1, 1998, to raise cash, the Norwood Company took out a $100,000 second mortgage on its assets. In addition, it sold office equipment that had cost $195,000 and had accumulated depreciation of $165,000 for $20,000.

5. On December 31, 1998, the Sollip Company sold a machine to the Norwood Company for $55,000. The machine had been purchased on January 1, 1995 for $200,000 and had an expected life at that date of 5 years with no anticipated salvage value. The Sollip Company had taken depreciation for 1998 on the machine before the sale. The only Plant and Equipment acquisition of the Sollip Company was a $200,000 machine to replace the one sold to Norwood.

6. On June 30, 1998, the Norwood Company also purchased other Equipment for a combination of $360,000 in cash and 4,000 No Par common shares. The stock was trading at $5 per share on this date.

7. On April 1, 1998, the Sollip Company issued 20 year, 14 percent bonds for $200,000 and used part of the proceeds to purchase a parcel of land.

Required:

A. Compute consolidated Net Income for the year ending December 31, 1998 for the Norwood Company and its subsidiary, the Sollip Company.

B. Calculate consolidated Retained Earnings as at December 31, 1998 for the Norwood Company and its subsidiary, the Sollip Company.

C. Compute the Non Controlling Interest that would be disclosed on the consolidated Balance Sheet of the Norwood Company and its subsidiary, the Sollip Company as at December 31, 1998.

D. Prepare the consolidated Statement of Changes in Financial Position (Cash Basis) for the year ending December 31, 1998 for the Norwood Company and its subsidiary, the Sollip Company.

Chapter 8

Foreign Currency: Basic Concepts And Translation Of Transactions

A Note On Current Developments

8-1.   Canadian accounting standards for foreign currency translation are found in Section 1650 of the *CICA Handbook*, "Foreign Currency Translation". Subject to some minor revisions in 1992, this *Handbook* Section has been in place since June, 1983, a period of nearly fifteen years. Given the changes that have taken place in the international business environment over this period, there is some need for a review of the provisions contained in Section 1650.

8-2.   Such a review is under way, a fact that was reflected in the September, 1993 issuance of the Exposure Draft, "Foreign Currency Translation" by the Accounting Standards Board. For largely technical reasons, this Exposure Draft was replaced by a May, 1996 Re-Exposure Draft. The major features of both of these Exposure Drafts can be described as follows:

- Entities, except rate regulated enterprises that meet certain criteria, would recognize exchange gains and losses on monetary items in income as they arise, unless the monetary item meets the criteria for classification as a certain type of hedge. This represents a significant change from the existing Section 1650, which requires that exchange gains and losses on long term monetary items be deferred and amortized.

- Deferral of exchange gains and losses would be permitted when a monetary item or a foreign currency derivative instrument meets the criteria for classification as a hedge of an anticipated future foreign currency exposure or an investment in a self sustaining foreign operation.

- Disclosure would be required of both total and unrealized exchange gains and losses recognized in income.

- Exchange gains or losses on an investment in a self sustaining operation are accumulated in a separate component of shareholder's equity. Under the current Section 1650, a portion of this balance is taken into income when there is a partial disposition or other reduction in the investment. In order to make Canadian standards more compatible with those of the U.S., the revised Section 1650 would only take this accumulated balance into income when there is a complete liquidation of the investment in the self sustaining operation.

8-3.   At this point in time (May, 1998), the AcSB has indicated that further work in this area has been suspended. This decision reflects the fact that the material on hedging is included in both the foreign currency Re-Exposure Draft and the Re-Exposure Draft on financial instruments. This makes it difficult to include material on this subject in the foreign currency Section of the *Handbook* until such time as the content of the financial instruments Section is settled.

8-4.   Given this uncertainty, as well as the fact that many of the Recommendations of Section 1650 are not significantly altered by the Re-Exposure Draft, our Chapter on foreign currency translation will continue to reflect the existing Section 1650. However, we will include those parts of the Re-Exposure Draft which either clarify current Section 1650 Recommendations or reach a different conclusion with respect to the appropriate accounting procedures to be used. To avoid confusion, this material will be clearly identified as being from the Re-Exposure Draft.

Introduction

The Nature Of The Problem

8-5.   Most of Canada's major corporations would have some familiarity with the subject that is under consideration here. Their involvement in the subject can arise in one of two general ways:

Foreign Currency Transactions   They may find themselves engaged in foreign currency transactions. That is, they may be buying or selling goods or services with the prices denominated in a foreign currency, borrowing or lending money with the amounts that are payable or receivable denominated in some foreign currency, or acquiring foreign currency assets, liabilities, revenue streams, or forward exchange contracts which serve as a hedge of some other foreign currency transaction or balance. In these situations, foreign currency translation is required in order to convert individual assets, liabilities, expenses or revenues into Canadian dollars so that they can be included as an integral part of the financial statements of the domestic enterprise. The issues and procedures associated with the translation of foreign currency transactions will be given detailed consideration in this Chapter.

Foreign Currency Financial Statements   A second situation which requires domestic enterprises to become involved in the translation of foreign currencies arises when a Canadian investor company has subsidiaries, significantly influenced companies, or joint ventures that carry on their operations in a foreign country. Generally, the financial statements of these investees will be expressed in the currency of the country in which they operate. Thus, in order to either apply consolidation procedures or the equity method of accounting, the statements of these investees will have to first be translated into Canadian dollars. As the conceptual issues associated with the translation of foreign currency financial statements are related to those that arise in the translation of foreign currency transactions, they will be dealt with simultaneously in this Chapter. However, coverage of the detailed procedures associated with the translation of foreign currency financial statements will be deferred to Chapter 9.

Approach To The Subject

8-6.   As described in the preceding section, this subject really consists of two separable areas. These are the translation of foreign currency transactions and the translation of foreign currency financial statements.

8-7.   In translating foreign currency transactions, we are dealing with individual assets, liabilities, expenses, and revenues which have resulted from a domestic enterprise becoming involved in a situation in which one or more of these items are expressed in amounts of some currency other than the Canadian dollar. There is no other legal entity, operating in and subject to the accounting principles of a foreign environment, that will serve to complicate the situation. Further, all foreign currency amounts will ultimately be converted to Canadian dollars, making irrelevant the question of what is the appropriate unit of measure or the appropriate disposition of translation adjustments. As a consequence, the only sources of controversy in this situation involve the appropriate classification of hedge transactions and the question of when exchange gains and losses should be recognized in the results of operations.

8-8.   Situations involving the translation of foreign currency financial statements are more complex. Here, a separate legal entity is operating in a foreign environment and may be subject to alternative generally accepted accounting principles. Further, many of the balances which must be translated into Canadian dollars may not, in fact, ever be converted into Canadian dollars. This latter point raises questions both with respect to what currency should serve as the unit of measure and as to the appropriate disposition of translation adjustments. The situation is clearly more complex and has been the source of most of the difficulties in developing pronouncements in this area.

8-9.   While there are differences between the issues involved in translating foreign currency transactions and those associated with the translation of foreign currency financial statements, many of the basic concepts involved are the same. More specifically, the objectives of translation, accounting principles to be used, choice of the unit of measure (translation methods), and the treatment to be given translation adjustments are conceptual issues which are common to both of these subjects. As a consequence, before we proceed to a more detailed discussion of the subjects of foreign currency transactions in this Chapter and foreign currency financial statements in Chapter 9, general consideration will be given to these conceptual issues. This will avoid repetitive discussions of these issues in both the material on foreign currency transactions and the material on foreign currency financial statements.

Conceptual Issues

The Objectives Of Translation

8-10.   As with many subjects in accounting, if care is taken in establishing the objective to be accomplished, much of the debate over the selection of particular procedures to be used will be eliminated. This is clearly the case with foreign currency translation. The somewhat traditional view in this area was that we were faced with a choice between two mutually exclusive objectives. These two choices were commonly referred to as the domestic company perspective and the foreign company perspective and they could be described as follows:

> **Domestic Company Perspective**   This approach is also referred to as the parent company perspective or the Canadian dollar approach. Under this approach, the basic objective of translation is to provide translated statements that can be incorporated into those of the Canadian parent or investor corporation in a manner that would be consistent with the other information contained in those statements. That is, the focus of reporting is on the financial statements of the Canadian company, including foreign investee information that is translated in a manner that will be compatible with the other Canadian dollar information that is included in these statements. This general approach requires that the financial statements of foreign investees be converted to Canadian GAAP prior to translation, that the translation process use the Canadian dollar as the unit of measure, and that translation adjustments be included in the investee's income as exchange gains or losses.

> **Foreign Company Perspective**   This approach is also referred to as the local

company perspective or the foreign currency approach. Here the objective is to measure the economic resources and performance of the investee in terms of the foreign economic environment in which it operates. The focus of financial reporting in this context is to provide the most useful information with respect to the operations of the foreign investee, without regard to the consistency of this information with the other Canadian dollar information included in the financial statements of the Canadian investor company. This general approach requires that financial statements of the foreign investee be left in the GAAP of the foreign country in which it operates, that the translation process use the foreign currency in which the investee operates as the unit of measure, and account for translation adjustments that arise in the translation process as additions or deductions from the investee's shareholders' equity.

8-11.   Much of the work that was done in the 1970s and early 1980s on development of foreign currency translation pronouncements attempted to adopt one of these broad perspectives to all aspects of the subject. The same Recommendations were applied to both foreign currency transactions and to the translation of all foreign currency financial statements, without regard to the nature of the foreign investee's operations. However, users refused to accept the standards that resulted from this approach and, in response to the reactions of users, standard setters began to recognize that it was not appropriate to apply the same translation rules to all types of situations. Subsequent pronouncements began to think in terms of specific applications within the broadly based domestic or foreign company perspectives. More specifically, instead of attempting to consistently adopt one of these perspectives, they began to discuss this subject on the basis of three issues. These issues can be briefly described as follows:

> **Issue One - Accounting Principles**   Should the translated statements of a foreign investee reflect generally accepted accounting principles which prevail in the foreign country or, alternatively, the generally accepted accounting principles which prevail in Canada?

> **Issue Two - Unit Of Measure (Methods Of Translation)**   Should the translated statements of a foreign investee be translated in a manner that will retain some foreign currency as a unit of measure or, alternatively, should the translation process insure that the Canadian dollar is retained as the basic unit of measure? As we shall see in our discussion of methods of translation, if we wish to retain the the foreign currency as the unit of measure we will translate using the current rate method. Alternatively, use of the Canadian dollar as the unit of measure will require using the temporal method of translation.

> **Issue Three - Treatment Of Translation Adjustments**   Translation adjustment arise when a foreign currenty amount is translated using current exchange rates. As the current rate rate is constantly changing, the resulting Canadian dollar figures will always be changing. The issue here is whether the resulting adjustment should be included be included in income or, alternatively, allocated directly to a separate component of shareholders' equity?

8-12.   Each of these issues will be given detailed consideration in the following material.

Accounting Principles Issue

8-13.   The problem here relates to the idea that generally accepted accounting principles are developed in response to the economic conditions which prevail in the environment where such principles are applied. This is often described as the major justification for the differences between the generally accepted accounting principles which exist in various countries of the world. A simple example of this idea might involve a country in which social customs are such that individuals do not take their debt obligations very seriously and frequently default on smaller amounts. In such a country, it is likely that revenue recognition would be based on cash collections rather than using accrual accounting for revenues as a generally accepted accounting principle.

8-14.　　To the extent that there is validity in the view that generally accepted accounting principles reflect economic conditions in particular environments, it would follow that the performance of an investee operating in a foreign economic environment could best be measured using the generally accepted accounting principles that have been developed in that environment. In such situations, the foreign currency financial statements of the investee will usually be prepared using the generally accepted accounting principles which prevail in the foreign country. If, as the preceding line of reasoning suggests, the application of these foreign principles results in the most meaningful measure of the performance of the investee, it would suggest that these principles should not be altered before or during the translation process.

8-15.　　The problem, however, with retaining foreign generally accepted accounting principles in the translated statements of foreign investees is that, under either the equity method or consolidation, the foreign investee's statements will be incorporated into the Canadian dollar statements of the investor company. This, of course, would mean that the resulting statements would not be based on the consistent application of a single set of generally accepted accounting principles. The implications of this for the auditor's report are obvious and lead to the conclusion that either the foreign investee must keep its basic records in terms of Canadian generally accepted accounting principles or, if for statutory or other reasons the foreign currency records must be based on foreign generally accepted accounting principles, such statements must be modified to reflect Canadian generally accepted accounting principles prior to translation.

Unit Of Measure (Methods Of Translation) Issue

Exchange Rate Terminology

8-16.　　As we have previously noted, choosing a particular translation method determines the unit of measure to be used. If foreign currency amounts are translated using the temporal method, the resulting statements are based on the Canadian dollar as the unit of measure. In contrast, if the current rate method is used, the foreign currency is being used as the unit of measure.

8-17.　　Before proceeding to our discussion of these methods, it is important to understand some of the terminology that will be used. Differences between methods of translation are based on the exchange rates that are applied to the various items in the foreign currency balance sheet. The exchanges rates that are used can be described as follows:

> **Current Exchange Rate**　　This term is used to refer to the exchange rate that prevails at the particular Balance Sheet date. For the purposes of translating a December 31, 1998 Balance Sheet, the December 31, 1998 exchange rate would be used as the current exchange rate. Note that, when comparative statements are presented, there would be a different current exchange rate for each Balance Sheet date.

> **Historic Exchange Rate**　　This term is used to refer to the exchange rate that prevailed at the time a particular Balance Sheet item was acquired (asset) or incurred (liability). If an item of equipment was acquired on January 1, 1997, the historic rate would be the exchange rate that prevailed on that date, without regard to the date of the Balance Sheet in which the item of equipment was included.

8-18.　　In text book examples, we generally assume that there is a single exchange rate at any point in time. In the real world, this is clearly not the case. As anyone who has exchanged currencies for travel outside of Canada is aware, financial institutions have different rates for buying a currency vs. selling the same currency. For example, you might find that, if you were buying U.S. dollars, the exchange rate might be $1.43 Canadian, but if you were selling U.S. dollars, the exchange rate might be $1.37 Canadian.

8-19.　　As illustrated in the preceding paragraph, at a given point in time, there will be at least two rates for a particular currency — the rate for selling the currency and the rate for buying the currency. These rates are sometimes referred to as the bid and ask rates. In addition, these rates will vary between financial institutions, as well as with the size of the transaction (e.g., better rates are generally available on larger transactions). Further, in less developed countries or countries where the government controls currency exchange, there may be a wide variety of rates depending on the type of transaction involved (e.g., a better rate for export proceeds, as opposed to import costs).

8-20.   We will not illustrate this problem of multiple exchange rates in the material which follows. However, you should be aware that our references to a single exchange rate on a particular date are, in fact, a simplification of real world conditions.

Alternative Translation Methods

8-21.   At different points in time, four different translation methods have been used in Canadian practice. They are

- The Current/Non Current Method;
- The Monetary/Non Monetary Method;
- The Temporal Method; and
- The Current Rate Method.

8-22.   Until the 1980s, the current/non current method was the required method in both Canada and United States. However, it is now recognized to be an inappropriate approach to translation and is no longer used. The monetary/non monetary method is also flawed and, at this point in time, there is no support for or usage of this method. Given this situation, we will not give any further consideration to either of these methods.

8-23.   This leaves the temporal method and the current rate method. Both of these methods are in current use in Canada and in the United States. Further, they are both supported by a sound conceptual basis. As noted previously, the choice between these two methods involves deciding which currency should be used as the unit of measure. The temporal method is consistent with using the Canadian dollar as the unit of measure, while the current rate method is consistent with the use of a foreign currency as the unit of measure. Both of these methods will be given more detailed consideration.

Temporal Method

8-24.   The temporal method is currently defined in the *CICA Handbook* as follows:

> **Paragraph 1650.03   Temporal Method**   A method of translation which translates assets, liabilities, revenues and expenses in a manner that retains their bases of measurement in terms of the Canadian dollar (i.e., it uses the Canadian dollar as the unit of measure). In particular:
>
> (i)   monetary items are translated at the rate of exchange in effect at the balance sheet date;
>
> (ii)   non-monetary items are translated at historical exchange rates, unless such items are carried at market, in which case they are translated at the rate of exchange in effect at the balance sheet date;
>
> (iii)   revenue and expense items are translated at the rate of exchange in effect on the dates they occur;
>
> (iv)   depreciation or amortization of assets translated at historical exchange rates are translated at the same exchange rates as the assets to which they relate.

8-25.   As can be seen in this definition, the temporal approach determines the rate to be used in the translation process by reference to the manner in which the foreign currency balance has been measured. More specifically, those assets and liabilities that are expressed in current amounts of foreign currency are translated using the current rate of exchange. This would include all monetary items [item (i) in the definition) , as well as any non monetary items that are carried at current value [the exception is item (ii) in the definition]. The account balances that are expressed in historic amounts of foreign currency are translated at the historic rate of exchange that prevailed when the historic amount of foreign currency was measured [the general rule in item(ii) of the definition]. Under current GAAP, most non monetary items are carried at historical cost and, as a consequence, when the temporal method is applied they are translated at historical rates.

8-26.   The preceding definition suggests that each revenue and expense transaction, other than the depreciation or amortization of items translated at historical rates, should be translated at the exchange rate which prevailed on the transaction date. As many revenue and expense items involve a large number of transactions, particularly when the complete financial statements of a foreign operation are being translated, this may not be a practial solution. This is noted in the *CICA Handbook* as follows:

> **Paragraph 1650.61**   Literal application of the Recommendations in this Section might require a degree of detail in record keeping and computations that would be burdensome as well as unnecessary to produce reasonable approximations of the results. Accordingly, it is acceptable to use averages or other methods of approximation. For example, translation of the numerous revenues, expenses, gains and losses at the exchange rates at the dates such items are recognized is generally impractical, and an appropriately weighted average exchange rate for the period would normally be used to translate such items.

8-27.   In many cases, it will be acceptable to use a simple average based on dividing the sum of the beginning of the period and end of the period exchange rates by two. However, the use of this unweighted calculation is based on two assumptions. First, the revenue or expense item being translated must have been recognized uniformly over the period, and second, the change in the exchange rate must have occurred uniformly over the period. If either of these assumptions is not appropriate, then some type of weighted average must be used.

8-28.   We would also note that, for parcularly large income items, it may not be appropriate to use any type of averaging process. For example, if there was a significant gain on the disposition of a capital asset, the exchange rate which prevailed at the time of the disposition should be used.

Current Rate Method

8-29.   The major alternative to the use of the temporal method of translation is the current rate method. This method is defined in the *CICA Handbook* as follows:

> **Paragraph 1650.03   Current Rate Method**   A method of translation which translates assets, liabilities, revenues and expenses in a manner that retains their bases of measurement in terms of the foreign currency (i.e., it uses the foreign currency as the unit of measure). In particular:
>
> (i)   assets and liabilities are translated at the rate of exchange in effect at the balance sheet date;
>
> (ii)   revenue and expense items (including depreciation and amortization) are translated at the rate of exchange in effect on the dates on which such items are recognized in income during the period.

8-30.   This definition requires little explanation. When the current rate method is used, all assets and liabilities will be translated at the current rate of exchange as of the Balance Sheet date. This differs from the temporal approach in that assets carried at historical amounts of foreign currency will be translated at current, as opposed to historical, exchange rates.

8-31.   As was the case with the temporal method, the suggestion that revenue and expense items be tranlated at the individual exchange rates in effect on the dates at which such items are recognized in income, may not be practical. This means that, in the application of the current rate method, average exchange rates will often be used for expense and revenue items.

Translation Methods And The Unit Of Measure

8-32.   We have indicated several times that the choice of translation methods is, in effect, a choice of the unit of measure to be used in the translation process. A simple example will serve to clarify this point:

> **Example**   On January 1, 1998, a Swiss subsidiary of a Canadian company purchases land in Switzerland for 500,000 Swiss Francs (SF, hereafter). At the time of the purchase SF1 = $.95. On December 31, 1998, when the Canadian parent company closes its books and prepares consolidated financial statements, the exchange rate is SF1 = $.90.

8-33.   If our objective is to use the Canadian dollar as the unit of measure, it would seem logical that if the historical cost of this land is established as $475,000 at the time of its purchase, it should remain at this value in subsequent accounting periods. The temporal method produces this result by translating assets and liabilities carried at historical amounts of foreign currency at historical exchange rates. In our example this means that the land would be included in the consolidated financial statements of the parent company at its original Canadian dollar cost of $475,000 in all subsequent periods.

8-34.   In contrast, if we want to use the Swiss Franc as our unit of measure, we would focus on the SF500,000 cost of the asset in that currency. With historical cost established in terms of Swiss Francs, we would then find the appropriate year end value by multiplying the historical value of SF500,000 by the December 31, 1998 exchange rate of $.90 to arrive at a value of $450,000. Note that when we use another currency as the unit to measure historical costs, the Canadian dollar value of these balances will change over time. That is, the December 31, 1998 value of $450,000 (SF500,000 at $.90) is less than the January 1, 1998 value of $475,000 (SF500,000 at $.95).

8-35.   A final point here is that we are operating within the framework of historical cost based accounting. If current cost accounting were the prevalent norm, the selection of a unit of measure would no longer be a substantive issue. We would require the Swiss subsidiary to establish the current value of the land on December 31, 1998 in terms of Swiss Francs and this value, regardless of the unit of measure selected, would be translated at the December 31, 1998 exchange rate of $.90. However, as we are seeking to establish a translated historical cost, the unit of measure question must be answered.

Choosing A Unit Of Measure

8-36.   Whether we are translating foreign currency transactions or, alternatively, translating the financial statements of a foreign investee that will be consolidated or accounted for by the equity method, the translated balances will be included in the Canadian dollar financial statements of the reporting company. Given this, it would seem obvious that translation should be based on the Canadian dollar as the unit of measure. If we do not choose this alternative, we will wind up with financial statements that reflect more than one unit of measure, a problem similar to that discussed under the accounting principles issue. This would suggest that, in all cases, the temporal method of translation should be required.

8-37.   With respect to foreign currency transactions, the view expressed in the preceding Paragraph has prevailed. That is, Section 1650 requires the use of the temporal method in the translation of all foreign currency transactions.

8-38.   There is, however, a problem with the use of the temporal method in the translation of foreign currency financial statements. Because this method translates some assets and liabilities at current exchange rates and other assets and liabilities at historic exchange rates, the temporal method consistently alters — some would say distorts — economic relationships that were present in the foreign currency financial statements. A simple example will clarify this point:

Example   On January 1, 1998, a Canadian Company establishes a subsidiary in France by investing $1,000,000 at a time when one French Franc (FF, hereafter) was worth $.20. This gives a total equity investment of FF5,000,000. On this same date, the subsidiary borrows an additional FF5,000,000 and invests the entire FF10,000,000 in Land. The resulting foreign currency Balance Sheet at January 1, 1998 would be as follows:

**Balance Sheet
As At January 1, 1998 (FF)**

Land	FF10,000,000
Liabilities	FF 5,000,000
Shareholders' Equity	5,000,000
Total Equities	FF10,000,000

Using either the temporal or the current rate method of translation, the translated Balance Sheet on this date would be as follows:

**Balance Sheet
As At January 1, 1998 ($)**

Land (At $.20)	$2,000,000
Liabilities (At $.20)	$1,000,000
Shareholders' Equity (At $.20)	1,000,000
Total Equities	$2,000,000

During the year ending December 31, 1998, the exchange rate goes to FF1 = $.25. As there is no other economic activity during this year, the December 31, foreign currency Balance Sheet would be unchanged. However, as there has been a change in the exchange rate, the translated Balance Sheet will vary, depending on whether the temporal or current rate method is used. The two alternative Balance Sheets are as follows:

**Balance Sheet
As At December 31, 1998 ($)**

	Temporal	Current Rate
Land (At $.20 And $.25)	$2,000,000	$2,500,000
Liabilities (At $.25)	$1,250,000	$1,250,000
Shareholders' Equity (As A Residual)	750,000	1,250,000
Total Equities	$2,000,000	$2,500,000

8-39.   A significant economic relationship that is often considered by financial statement users is the percentage of debt to total equities. In the untranslated Balance Sheet, this relationship is 50 percent (FF5,000,000 ÷ FF10,000,000). When the current rate method is used, this 50 percent relationship is maintained ($1,250,000 ÷ $2,500,000).

8-40.   In contrast, when the temporal method is used, this relationship is increased to 62.5 percent ($1,250,000 ÷ $2,000,000). The fact that this method retains the historic rate for the translation of the Land and, at the same time, uses the current rate to translate the monetary Liabilities, results in a Balance Sheet that makes the subsidiary appear to be a more heavily leveraged, and thereby riskier, enterprise.

8-41.   With respect to the translation of foreign currency financial statements, there does not appear to be a single answer to the unit of measure question. Section 1650 of the *CICA Handbook* concludes that the choice of unit of measure should be based on the type of foreign operation for which financial statements are being translated. To facilitate this approach, it identifies two basic types of foreign operations as follows:

Integrated Foreign Operation   A foreign operation which is financially or operationally interdependent with the reporting enterprise such that the exposure to exchange rate changes is similar to the exposure which would exist had the transactions and activities of the foreign operation been undertaken by the reporting enterprise.

Self Sustaining Foreign Operation   A foreign operation which is financially and operationally independent of the reporting enterprise such that the exposure to exchange rate changes is limited to the reporting enterprise's net investment in the foreign operation.

8-42.   In the case of integrated foreign operations, the foreign investee is not conducting its activities in the foreign currency and, as a consequence, it is exposed to exchange risk. For this type of investee, Section 1650 concludes that the domestic currency should be used as the unit of measure. This is reflected in the requirement that the temporal method be used to translate the financial statements of integrated foreign operations.

8-43.   In contrast, a self sustaining foreign operation will be using a foreign currency as the basis for its operations. Because it is operating independently of the domestic or reporting entity, it is not exposed to the risks associated with exchanging currencies. In this case, Section 1650 concludes that the currency used by the foreign operation should be the unit of measure. For this type of foreign operation, the current rate method of translation is required.

8-44.   These two translation methods, as applied to the translation of foreign currency financial statements of integrated and self sustaining foreign operations, will be given more detailed attention in Chapter 9.

8-45.   We would also note, that while the terminology used is different, U. S. accounting standards will, in most cases, result in the same choice of translation method for companies operating under the rules applicable to that country.

Translation Adjustments

Nature Of Translation Adjustments

8-46.   In the preceding section we noted that the current rules with respect to the unit of measure (translation method) issue are as follows:

- The domestic currency will be used as the unit of measure for translating foreign currency transactions and the financial statements of integrated foreign operations. This means that the temporal method will be used in these applications.

- The foreign currency will be used as the unit of measure for translating the financial statements of self sustaining foreign operations.

8-47.   The second major source of controversy in the development of foreign currency translation pronouncements has been the treatment of translation adjustments. These adjustments can be defined as follows:

Translation Adjustment   A translation adjustment is the change in the Canadian dollar value of a foreign currency balance that results from translation at the applicable current exchange rate at two different points in time.

8-48.   As an example of these adjustments, assume that during the entire year 1998, we had a liability of 1,000,000 Deutsche Marks (DM, hereafter). If the exchange rate increases from DM1 = $.80 on January 1, 1998, to DM1 = $.85 on December 31, 1998, the translated balances would be as follows:

December 31, 1998 (DM1,000,000 @ $.85)	$850,000
January 1, 1998 (DM1,000,000 @ $.80)	(800,000)
Increase In Canadian Dollar Value	$ 50,000

8-49.   This $50,000 increase in the translated balance from $800,000 to $850,000 can be referred to as a translation adjustment. We would note that some texts refer to these amounts as exchange gains or losses. While this terminology is applicable in some circumstances, there are important cases where translation adjustments are not treated as gains and losses (e.g., in the translation of self sustaining operations). Given this, we will use the general term translation adjustment, recognizing that the treatment given to these amounts will vary with the type of translation problem under consideration.

8-50.   A further point here is to note that translation adjustments will occur whenever an item is translated at current exchange rates. As both the temporal method and the current rate method translate some balances at current rates, both of these methods will produce translation adjustments. There will, of course, be differences in the amounts as the two methods apply current rates to a different group of items.

8-51.   A second general point that should be made here is that the selection of a particular translation method does not determine the appropriate treatment of these translation adjustments. In particular, there seems to be a general misconception that the temporal method requires the inclusion of translation adjustments in income in the period in which they occur. This is not the case. Any of the alternative treatments of translation adjustments would be compatible with any translation method selected. In short, the selection of a translation method determines only the amount of the translation adjustments that will occur, not their existence or their disposition.

Alternative Treatments Of Translation Adjustments

8-52.   Once we have established which translation method we will use, we are then confronted with the decision of the appropriate disposition of the translation adjustments which arise under the chosen method. Referring again to the example just presented, we will be required under both the temporal and the current rate methods to credit the liability for the $50,000 translation adjustment. This immediately raises the question of the appropriate allocation of the required $50,000 debit. The various possibilities that have been considered can be described as follows:

Adjustment Of The Cost Of Assets   It can be argued that the $50,000 increase in the amount required to discharge the liability should be included in the cost of the assets that have been financed with the debt.

Adjustment Of Interest Cost   The argument here is that translation adjustments such as these are a part of the cost of borrowing amounts that must be repaid in a foreign currency and, as a consequence, they should be included as a part of the interest costs on such debt.

Exchange Gain Or Loss   Supporters of this view would argue that, like any other decrease in the net asset position of the enterprise, this translation adjustment should be treated as a loss.

Adjustment Of Shareholders' Equity   The position here is that such translation adjustments reflect a decrease in the net investment position of the owners of the enterprise and that the adjustment is a capital rather than an income item.

8-53.   With respect to the first of these alternatives, adjusting the cost of assets acquired, the consensus seems to be that this is not an appropriate solution to the problem. The cost of any asset is established at its acquisition date and should not be influenced by subsequent changes in the cost of financing the asset. Stated alternatively, the decision to finance assets in a foreign currency is a separate and avoidable transaction that should not be allowed to have an influence on the amounts allocated to particular assets acquired. This particular point will be the subject of a more comprehensive discussion when we illustrate the procedures to be used in accounting for merchandise transactions.

8-54. Similar arguments rule against treating translation adjustments as a part of interest costs. Interest costs should reflect the cost of borrowing under normal conditions. Companies that borrow amounts that must be repaid in foreign currencies are subjecting their enterprises to risks that extend beyond ordinary debt obligations and it would not seem appropriate to bury the costs and returns of such additional risk in ordinary interest expense. If we do conclude that it is appropriate to charge or credit translation adjustments to income, they should be given separate disclosure in order to indicate their real origin. An additional justification for not using interest expense as a general solution to the problem of translation adjustments is the fact that translation adjustments occur on accounts other than liabilities and these other accounts have no logical linkage with interest expense.

8-55. This leaves two possible dispositions of translation adjustments - allocating them to income as gains and losses or, alternatively, treating them as adjustments of shareholders' equity. The choice between these two alternatives will depend on the circumstances which created the account on which the translation adjustment has occurred. Again referring to the example of Deutsche Mark debt, a DM1,000,000 liability could reflect two distinctly different situations. If the liability is the result of direct borrowing by a Canadian company, then it will normally have to be repaid by using Canadian dollars to purchase the Deutsche Marks required to repay the obligation. This means that there will be an actual exchange of currencies, requiring the company to use $750,000 to acquire sufficient Deutsche Marks to replace those originally borrowed. Since the DM1,000,000 which was originally borrowed was only worth $700,000, there is little question that a $50,000 loss has occurred.

8-56. In situations such as the preceding example, where an actual exchange of currencies is anticipated, there is a general consensus that translation adjustments should be accounted for as gains and losses. There is, of course, significant controversy surrounding the allocation of such gains and losses to particular accounting periods and this issue will be given full consideration later in this Chapter. However, this controversy does not affect the conclusion that translation adjustments resulting from situations where actual exchanges of currency are anticipated should be allocated to income. In general, the balances resulting from foreign currency transactions fall into this category and, as we shall see, both the Canadian and U.S. standard setting bodies agree that translation adjustments on balances resulting from foreign currency transactions should be allocated to income as exchange gains and losses.

8-57. In contrast to the preceding, if we assume that the DM1,000,000 liability was that of a Canadian company's subsidiary operating in Germany, a different conclusion may be appropriate. Such a subsidiary may have borrowed the Deutsche Marks to invest in assets which produce income within Germany. As this income will accrue in Deutsche Marks, the subsidiary is likely to be able to service the debt, both interest and principal amounts, using the Deutsche Marks generated by the German assets. While the Canadian parent company is required to translate all of the subsidiary's Deutsche Mark balances in order to prepare consolidated financial statements, it is not appropriate to view the resulting translation adjustments as gains or losses when no actual exchange of currencies is anticipated. In this case, the translation adjustments should be allocated directly to shareholders' equity until such time as the investment in the subsidiary is liquidated and an actual exchange of currencies takes place. As you have likely anticipated, Section 1650 of the *CICA Handbook* recommends this treatment in the case of self sustaining foreign operations.

Allocation Of Exchange Gains And Losses To Income

8-58. In those cases, where translation adjustments are considered to be exchange gains or losses, the question remains as to how the amounts should be allocated to income. The following simple example will illustrate this issue.

Example On January 1, 1993, a Canadian company borrowed DM1,000,000 which will be repaid on January 1, 1998. The exchange rate on January 1, 1993 was DM1 = $.80 and it remains at that level until January 1, 1995. On January 1, 1995, the rate goes to DM1 = $.85 and remains at this level until the debt is repaid on January 1, 1998. This results in an exchange loss of $50,000 [(DM1,000,000)($.85 - $.80)].

This loss could be allocated to income using a variety of approaches. The more commonly suggested alternatives are as follows:

- **No Deferral** Under this approach, the entire $50,000 would be charged to income in 1995, the year in which the exchange rate change took place.

- **Deferral Until Realization** If the cash approach to realization is used, the entire $50,000 loss would be deferred until 1998, the year in which the liability is settled.

- **Allocation Over The Total Life Of The Liability** Under this approach, the loss would be allocated to income over the entire five year life of the liability at the rate of $10,000 per year. This solution would also raise the question of the appropriate treatment for the amounts allocated to 1993 and 1994, the years prior to the actual exchange rate change.

- **Allocation Over The Remaining Life Of The Liability** Under this alternative, the $50,000 would be allocated to 1995, 1996, and 1997 at the rate of $16,667 per year.

8-59. In examining these alternatives, it is our opinion that the first choice involving no deferrals is the appropriate solution to this problem. Section 1000 of the *CICA Handbook* establishes two criteria for recognition:

- an item has an appropriate basis of measurement and a reasonable estimate can be made of the amount involved; and

- for items which involve obtaining or giving up future economic benefits, it is probable that such benefits will be obtained or given up.

8-60. In the case of exchange gains and losses, there is no controversy over the ability to objectively measure the values involved. In the case that is under consideration, no one would suggest that the liability not be written up to $850,000 on January 1, 1995 when the exchange rate changes. This is clear evidence that the values involved in this issue can be measured with a sufficient degree of reliability to be included in the accounts. Further, despite the possibility that future exchange rate changes will alter the amount that will ultimately be paid, the current value of $850,000 represents our best measure of the amount that will probably be given up. These considerations lead clearly to the conclusion that the entire $50,000 loss should be recognized in 1995.

8-61. The only other alternative that has any reasonable conceptual basis is deferral until realization. There are situations, such as the cash or instalment approach to revenue recognition, where recognition is deferred until the relevant amounts are realized in cash. However, these situations inevitably are associated with measurement problems (i.e., we only use the cash basis of revenue recognition where great uncertainty surrounds our ability to collect the amounts that are due). We have already noted that there does not seem to be a measurement problem associated with exchange gains and losses and, as a consequence, it does not seem reasonable to defer their recognition until realization.

8-62.   With respect to the remaining two alternatives involving deferral over the total or remaining life of the liability, there is no cogent argument that would support these approaches. They have been defended largely on the basis of two arguments, each of which can be easily rebutted. These arguments, along with a consideration of their validity, are as follows:

> It has been stated that these deferral patterns are appropriate because such exchange gains and losses are unrealized. If realization is defined in terms of cash flows, the contention that the gain or loss is unrealized is true. However, we have previously noted that this is not an adequate reason for deferring recognition and, even if it were, the deferral would be to the year in which the liability is paid, not over a number of years.

> It has been argued that these deferral patterns are appropriate because the gains and losses are uncertain or likely to reverse in future periods. This contention is also factual. However, it is equally applicable to any estimate made in accounting and should not serve to deter us from recognizing values on the basis of our best estimate. Any exposed foreign currency position can be eliminated or hedged to protect an enterprise against the effects of future currency movements. If we do not do so, we are accepting continuing foreign exchange risk and the results of this acceptance should be measured on an ongoing basis. If there is a reversal of an unfavourable movement, the resulting gain will show the wisdom of the continuing exposure. If, alternatively, the unfavourable movement continues, the increased losses should be recognized on the basis of our best estimates. The magnitude of uncertainty here is no greater than we are accustomed to dealing with in other areas of accounting and does not serve as a justification for these arbitrary deferral patterns.

8-63.   It would seem clear that there is little merit in the arguments favouring deferral of exchange gains or losses over the total or remaining life of the related item. We should also note a further problem associated with these deferral approaches. When, in our example, we must credit the liability for the $50,000 increase in its translated value, if we defer the resulting loss, it must be set up as an asset in the balance sheet. In other words, under this approach, an unfavourable movement in exchange rates which will require us to pay more dollars to extinguish a foreign currency liability is being treated as an asset. This clearly is in conflict with the definition of assets that is found in Section 1000 of the *CICA Handbook*.

8-64.   From the preceding we would conclude that exchange gains and losses on foreign currency transactions should generally be taken into income in the year in which the exchange rate change occurs. This is the approach taken in the U.S., in International Accounting Standard No. 21, and in the accounting standards of most other industrialized countries. While Section 1650 continues to Recommend deferral over the remaining life of the asset or liability, the 1996 Re-Exposure Draft would require immediate recognition in income, thereby bringing Canada in line with most of the rest of the world. Surprisingly, however, there continues to be significant opposition to this change.

Summary of Concept Applications

8-65.   In this Section we have discussed the major conceptual issues that arise in the translation of foreign currency transactions and foreign currency financial statements. In this and the next Chapter, we will be giving consideration to the detailed procedures which flow from the decisions that the Accounting Standards Board has made with respect to these conceptual issues. However, before proceeding to this more technical material, a summary of the conclusions found in the *CICA Handbook* is useful. This summary is in the following table:

Conceptual Issue	Translation Application		
	Foreign Currency Transactions	Integrated Foreign Operations	Self Sustaining Foreign Operations
Accounting Principles To Be Used	Canadian GAAP	Canadian GAAP	Canadian GAAP
Unit Of Measure	Canadian Dollar	Canadian Dollar	Foreign Currency
Method Of Translation	Temporal	Temporal	Current Rate
Treatment Of Translation Adjustments	Exchange Gain Or Loss	Exchange Gain Or Loss	Component of Shareholders' Equity
Allocation Of Exchange Gains (Losses) To Income	Over Remaining Life	Over Remaining Life	Not Applicable

Translation Of Foreign Currency Transactions

Accounting Recommendations Applicable To Foreign Currency Transactions

General Approach

8-66.   We have noted previously that there are several different types of foreign currency transactions. These are merchandise transactions, hedging transactions, and capital transactions. While recognizing that these different types of transactions exist, Section 1650 approaches the foreign currency transaction area by providing a group of overall Recommendations dealing with the issues discussed in the previous section of this Chapter. That is, the Section contains general Recommendations with respect to the objectives of translation, methods of translation, and the treatment of translation adjustments. Reflecting this approach, we will review these general Recommendations before proceeding to illustrations of specific types of foreign currency transactions.

Objectives Of Translation

8-67.   There is little controversy with respect to the objectives to be accomplished in translating foreign currency transactions. This process only involves translating specific foreign currency amounts. As there is no complete set of foreign currency financial statements, there are no foreign currency economic relationships to be maintained in the translation process. Further, since there is no foreign based legal entity involved, questions associated with the use of foreign generally accepted accounting principles do not arise. As a consequence, the domestic company perspective on the objectives of foreign currency translation is clearly applicable to the translation of foreign currency transactions. This is reflected in the *CICA Handbook* as follows:

> **Paragraph 1650.05**   For foreign currency transactions, the objective of translation is to express such transactions in a manner that achieves consistency with the accounting treatment for domestic transactions. Since domestic transactions are automatically measured in Canadian dollars, the Canadian dollar is the appropriate unit of measure for foreign currency transactions. Accordingly, the temporal method should be used to translate foreign currency transactions.

Methods Of Translation (Unit Of Measure)

8-68.   As noted in our summary of the conceptual alternatives adopted by the Accounting Standards Board, foreign currency transactions must be translated using the temporal method. Stated alternatively, they must be translated on a basis that retains the Canadian dollar as the unit of measure. This point is elaborated on in several of the Recommendations contained in Section 1650. The first of these, dealing with the exchange rates to be applied at transaction dates, is as follows:

> **Paragraph 1650.14**   *At the transaction date, each asset, liability, revenue or expense arising from a foreign currency transaction of the reporting enterprise should be translated into Canadian dollars by the use of the exchange rate in effect at that date, except when the transaction is hedged, in which case the rate established by the terms of the hedge should be used.* (July, 1983)

8-69.   Since foreign currency transactions commonly involve balances which are not settled by the Balance Sheet date, Paragraphs 1650.16 and 1650.18 provide Recommendations for translating Balance Sheet accounts. These Paragraphs are as follows:

> **Paragraph 1650.16**   *At each balance sheet date, monetary items denominated in a foreign currency should be adjusted to reflect the exchange rate in effect at the balance sheet date.* (July, 1983)

> **Paragraph 1650.18**   *At each balance sheet date, for non-monetary assets of the reporting enterprise that are carried at market, the Canadian dollar equivalent should be determined by applying the exchange rate in effect at the balance sheet date to the foreign currency market price.* (July, 1983)

8-70.   While not stated explicitly, the preceding two Recommendations imply that any non monetary items carried at historical values will be translated at historical rates.

Translation Adjustments

8-71.   As we have indicated previously, there is general agreement that any translation adjustment which arises on the translation or settlement of a balance resulting from a foreign currency transaction should be treated as a gain or loss. This view is reflected in the *CICA Handbook* as follows:

> **Paragraph 1650.20**   *An exchange gain or loss of the reporting enterprise that arises on translation or settlement of a foreign currency denominated monetary item or a non-monetary item carried at market should be included in the determination of net income for the current period, except for:*
>
> (a) *any portion that has been included in income of previous accounting periods; and*
>
> (b) *any exchange gain or loss related to a foreign currency denominated monetary item with a fixed or ascertainable life extending beyond the end of the following fiscal year.* (July, 1983)

8-72.   The exceptions specified in the preceding Recommendation relate to the question of when such exchange gains and losses should be taken into income. More specifically, the Recommendation implies that exchange gains and losses on long term monetary items should be deferred. This is made explicit as follows:

> **Paragraph 1650.23**   *Exchange gains and losses of the reporting enterprise relating to the translation of foreign currency denominated monetary items that have a fixed or ascertainable life extending beyond the end of the following fiscal year should be deferred and amortized on a systematic and rational basis over the remaining life of the monetary item. Disclosure should be made of the method of amortization used.* (See "Disclosure Of Accounting Policies," Section 1505) (July, 1983)

8-73. This requirement that exchange gains and losses be deferred over the remaining life of the monetary item will, of course, result in balances to be carried forward. With respect to these balances, the *Handbook* Recommends the following:

> **Paragraph 1650.25** *The unamortized balance of the deferred exchange gains and losses of the reporting enterprise should be recorded as a deferred charge or as a deferred credit.* (July, 1983)

8-74. If long term monetary balances are settled prior to their maturity date, Section 1650 would require that any unamortized gain or loss relating to the balance be written off at the time of settlement. Further, if the term of the monetary balance is renegotiated prior to its settlement, any unamortized gain or loss would be written off over the renegotiated term and any subsequent gains or losses would also be amortized over the renegotiated term.

Re-Exposure Draft

8-75. While there are some differences in terminology, with respect to both the objectives of translation and the method of translation to be used, the Re-Exposure Draft Recommendations are substantially identical to those in the existing Section 1650. However, there is a major difference in the Re-Exposure Draft treatment of translation adjustments. While agreeing with Section 1650 that these adjustments are exchange gains or losses to be included in income, the Re-Exposure Draft generally requires that these amounts be taken into income in the period in which they arise. This is reflected in the Re-Exposure Draft as follows:

> **RE-ED Paragraph .011** *An exchange gain or loss of the reporting entity arising from the translation or settlement of a foreign currency denominated monetary item, or a non monetary item carried at fair value determined in a foreign currency, should be recognized in income as it arises, unless it is deferred in accordance with paragraphs .013, .021 to .023, or .066.* (Note: The exceptions referenced to Paragraph .013, .021, .023, and .066, refer to situations involving either rate regulated enterprises or hedging.)

8-76. This Paragraph establishes that, in general, exchange gains and losses related to foreign currency transactions must be included in income in the period in which they occur. As we have noted previously, Canada is out of line with the rest of the world on this issue. Given that situation, the Recommendation contained in the Re-Exposure Draft represents a welcome change in Canadian accounting standards. We would also note that this change puts Canada in line with both U.S. standards and with the Recommendations made by the International Accounting Standards Committee.

EIC Abstracts

8-77. There are a number of EIC Abstracts which deal with foreign currency translation. As some users of this text are not interested in pursuing foreign currency translation to that level of detail, we have included our coverage of EIC Abstracts related to foreign currency translation as a Supplement to Chapter 9.

Merchandise Transactions

Conceptual Alternatives

8-78. When a Canadian company buys (sells) goods or services in a foreign country and the resulting payable (receivable) is denominated in the currency of that foreign country, there are two views as to the disposition of any adjustment that may be required by changes in the dollar value of the payable (receivable) prior to its settlement. These two views are generally referred to as the one transaction perspective and the two transaction perspective and can be described as follows:

> **One Transaction Perspective** Under this view, when a Canadian company pur-

chases or sells merchandise, the transaction is incomplete until the amount of Canadian dollars required to settle the related payable or receivable is determined. This means that any adjustment of the foreign currency receivable or payable that is required between the transaction date and the settlement date would be viewed as part of the cost of the merchandise purchased or the sales price of the merchandise sold.

Two Transaction Perspective   Under this alternative view, the purchase or sale of merchandise is viewed as a separate and distinct transaction from the ultimate settlement of the related receivable or payable balance. This means that the merchandise cost or sales price is firmly established as at the date of the transaction and any subsequent adjustment of the resulting receivable or payable would be viewed as an exchange gain or loss resulting from the decision to carry exposed foreign currency balances.

Example

8-79.   The following simple example will serve to illustrate the difference between the one transaction and two transaction perspectives.

Example   The Emp Company has a fiscal year end of December 31. It purchases merchandise in France for resale in Canada. The merchandise must be paid for in French Francs (FF, hereafter) on February 1 of the year subsequent to its purchase. In Canada, the merchandise is sold for cash of $11 per unit. All of the merchandise purchased in a year is sold on April 1 of the following year. Purchases, which occur on November 1 of each year, are as follows:

Date Of Purchase	Quantity	Unit Price	Total Price
November 1, 1996	10,000	FF 20	FF200,000
November 1, 1997	12,000	16	192,000
November 1, 1998	-0-	14	-0-

Between January 1, 1996 and December 30, 1997, the exchange rate for French Francs is FF1 = $.20. On December 31, 1997, the exchange rate goes to FF1 = $.25. It remains at this level throughout 1998.

1996 Journal Entry

8-80.   The entry to record the first purchase of merchandise on November 1, 1996 would be the same for both perspectives. It would be as follows:

Merchandise (FF200,000 At $.20)	$40,000	
Accounts Payable		$40,000

1997 Journal Entries

8-81.   Since there has been no movement in the exchange rate, the February 1, 1997 entry to record the payment for the merchandise would be the same for both perspectives. It would be as follows:

Accounts Payable (FF200,000 At $.20)	$40,000	
Cash		$40,000

8-82.   The April 1, 1997 entries to record sales and the related Cost Of Goods Sold would also be the same under both perspectives. They would be as follows:

Cash (10,000 Units At $11)	$110,000	
Sales		$110,000
Cost Of Goods Sold (FF200,000 At $.20)	$ 40,000	
Merchandise		$40,000

8-83.   The entry to record the purchase of merchandise on November 1, 1997 would be the same under both perspectives. It would be as follows:

Merchandise (FF192,000 At $.20)	$38,400	
Accounts Payable		$38,400

8-84.   An entry will be required on December 31, 1997 to adjust the Accounts Payable to reflect the change in the exchange rate. Under the one transaction perspective this adjustment would be added to the cost of Merchandise with the following entry:

Merchandise [(FF192,000)($.25 - $.20)]	$9,600	
Accounts Payable		$9,600

8-85.   Alternatively, under the two transaction perspective the adjustment would be treated as an exchange loss to be included in the computation of the current year's income. The entry under this perspective would be as follows:

Exchange Loss	$9,600	
Accounts Payable		$9,600

1998 Journal Entries

8-86.   The entry to record the payment of the Accounts Payable would be the same under both perspectives and it would be as follows:

Accounts Payable (FF192,000 At $.25)	$48,000	
Cash		$48,000

8-87.   The entry to record Sales on this date would be the same under both perspectives. It would be as follows:

Cash (12,000 Units At $11)	$132,000	
Sales		$132,000

8-88.   The Cost Of Goods Sold entry would vary between the two perspectives. Under the one transaction perspective, the exchange adjustment has been added to the cost of the merchandise and the Cost Of Goods Sold entry would be as follows:

Cost Of Goods Sold (FF192,000 At $.25)	$48,000	
Merchandise		$48,000

8-89.   Alternatively, under the two transaction perspective the adjustment was charged to income in 1997 and will not affect the amount shown as Cost Of Goods Sold:

Cost Of Goods Sold (FF192,000 At $.20)	$38,400	
Merchandise		$38,400

Summary Of Results

8-90.   The results of the preceding journal entries can be summarized in the following condensed Income Statements:

One Transaction Perspective Results

	1997	1998	Cumulative
Sales	$110,000	$132,000	$242,000
Cost Of Goods Sold	40,000	48,000	88,000
Net Income	$ 70,000	$ 84,000	$154,000

Two Transaction Perspective Results

	1997	1998	Cumulative
Sales	$110,000	$132,000	$242,000
Cost Of Goods Sold	40,000	38,400	78,400
Operating Income	$ 70,000	$ 93,600	$163,600
Exchange Loss	9,600	-0-	9,600
Net Income	$ 60,400	$ 93,600	$154,000

8-91.   You will note that the cumulative income for the two years is $154,000 regardless of the perspective that is adopted. However, the choice between the two perspectives does affect both the timing and the disclosure of the exchange adjustment.

Evaluation Of Perspectives

8-92.   At this point in time there appears to be general agreement that the two transaction perspective is the more appropriate interpretation of the economic factors involved in foreign currency merchandise transactions. It would seem clear that in the preceding situation, the Emp Company could have avoided having an exposed payable position by paying the liability at the transaction date, by purchasing sufficient foreign currency at the transaction date to pay the liability at the settlement date, or by entering into a forward exchange contract to hedge the exposed position. The fact that it chose not to do this and that an exchange loss resulted is really a separate decision and it should not be allowed to affect the translated value of the merchandise that was acquired. This view is reflected in the *CICA Handbook* as follows:

> **Paragraph 1650.13**   In the opinion of the Committee, once foreign currency purchases and sales, or inventories, fixed assets and other non-monetary items obtained through foreign currency transactions, have been translated and recorded, any subsequent changes in the exchange rate will not affect those recorded amounts.

Capital Transactions

Basic Example

8-93.   When a Canadian company borrows (lends) funds and the resulting liability (asset) is denominated in some foreign currency, the company is certain to experience exchange gains or losses over the life of the liability (asset). As we have indicated previously, there are alternative approaches to allocating such gains or losses to income. Under the proposed Recommendations of the September, 1996 CICA Re-Exposure Draft, the Recommendations of the International Accounting Standards Committee, and FASB Statement No. 52, such gains and losses would be taken into income in the period in which the exchange rate change occurs. Alternatively, under Section 1650 of the *CICA Handbook*, a portion of these amounts would be deferred, with the resulting balances being allocated over the remaining life of the asset or liability. The following example will illustrate these two alternatives and the procedures required in dealing with exchange gains and losses.

> **Example - Capital Transactions**   On December 31, 1993, a Canadian company with a December 31 year end borrows 1,000,000 Foreign Currency units (FC, hereafter). In order to concentrate on the two alternative approaches to dealing with exchange gains and losses, we will assume that this liability does not require the payment of interest. The liability will mature on December 31, 1998, five years after it was issued. Exchange rates at December 31 for the years 1993 through 1998 are as follows:

December 31, 1993	FC1 = $2.00
December 31, 1994	FC1 = $2.50
December 31, 1995	FC1 = $2.50
December 31, 1996	FC1 = $1.80
December 31, 1997	FC1 = $1.80
December 31, 1998	FC1 = $2.25

Solution With No Deferral (CICA Re-Exposure Draft)

8-94.   The first solution to this example uses the general approach recommended in the 1996 CICA Re-Exposure Draft.

8-95.   The entry on December 31, 1993 records the liability that has been assumed. It would be as follows:

Cash (FC1,000,000 At $2.00)	$2,000,000	
Long Term Liability		$2,000,000

8-96.   By December 31, 1994, the exchange rate has moved to FC1 = $2.50. The resulting exchange loss would be taken into income with the following entry:

Exchange Loss [(FC1,000,000)($2.50 - $2.00)]	$500,000	
Long Term Liability		$500,000

8-97.   As the exchange rate did not change during 1995, there is no need for any entry on December 31, 1995.

8-98.   By December 31, 1996, the exchange rate has moved to FC1 = $1.80. The resulting exchange gain would be taken into income with the following entry:

Long Term Liability [(FC1,000,000)($2.50 - $1.80)]	$700,000	
Exchange Gain		$700,000

8-99.   As the exchange rate remained at $1.80 during 1997, no entry is required on December 31, 1997.

8-100.   **December 31, 1998 Journal Entries**   The first entry on December 31, 1998 would be to recognize the exchange loss resulting from the increase in the exchange rate to $2.25. It would be as follows:

Exchange Loss (FC1,000,000)($2.25 - $1.80)	$450,000	
Long Term Liability		$450,000

8-101.   A final entry would be required to record the payment of the liability. This would be as follows:

Long Term Liability (FC1,000,000 At $2.25)	$2,250,000	
Cash		$2,250,000

8-102.   This completes the accounting for the liability under the procedures that are recommended under the 1996 CICA Re-Exposure Draft. The main feature that you should note is that exchange gains and losses were only recognized in the accounting periods in which there was a change in the exchange rate for the foreign currency units.

Solution With Deferral Over Remaining Life Of The Liability (Section 1650)

8-103.   This second solution to the example uses the approach that is recommended in Section 1650 of the *CICA Handbook*.

8-104.   The entry on December 31, 1993 records the liability that has been assumed. It would be as follows:

Cash (FC1,000,000 At $2.00)	$2,000,000	
Long Term Liability		$2,000,000

8-105.   As the exchange rate has gone to FC1 = \$2.50 on December 31, 1994, the liability must be adjusted upward. The resulting debit would be divided with one-fifth going to an exchange loss and the remaining four-fifths (the remaining portion of the life of the liability) being established as an asset balance. The journal entry is as follows:

Exchange Loss	\$100,000	
Deferred Exchange Loss	400,000	
Long Term Liability (\$2,500,000 - \$2,000,000)		\$500,000

8-106.   Despite the fact that there has been no movement in the exchange rate during 1995, an exchange loss would be recorded as the deferred charge that was established in 1994 is amortized. The December 31, 1995 entry would be as follows:

Exchange Loss (\$400,000 ÷ 4)	\$100,000	
Deferred Exchange Loss		\$100,000

8-107.   While it would be possible to track and amortize the exchange gain or loss on the maturity value of the liability for each year, a much simpler procedure calculates a net gain or loss for the year using the net value of the liability at the beginning of the year (maturity value, plus or minus any deferred credit or charge). Using this approach, the exchange gain for 1996 can be calculated as follows:

Ending Liability [(FC1,000,000)(\$1.80)]	\$1,800,000
Beginning Net Liability (\$2,500,000 - \$300,000)	(2,200,000)
1996 Gain	(\$ 400,000)
Portion To Be Allocated To 1996	1/3
1996 Gain	\$133,333
1996 Deferred Gain [(1/3)(\$400,000)]	\$266,667

8-108.   Note that the gain on the reduction in the translated maturity value of the liability would be \$233,000 [(\$2,500,000 - \$1,800,000) ÷ 3)]. When this is offset by the \$100,000 amortization of the 1994 exchange loss, we have the same net that is produced by the preceding calculation. This demonstrates that this net calculation produces the same results as the more complex procedures required to track and amortize individual gains and losses for each year.

8-109.   The December 31, 1996 journal entry will eliminate the Deferred Exchange Loss balance and set up a new Deferred Exchange Gain balance. It is as follows:

Long Term Liability (\$2,500,000 - \$1,800,000)	\$700,000	
Deferred Exchange Loss		\$300,000
Exchange Gain		133,333
Deferred Exchange Gain		266,667

8-110.   The entry that would be required on December 31, 1997 would amortize an additional one-half of the Deferred Exchange Gain that was recognized in 1996. It would be as follows:

Deferred Exchange Gain (\$266,667 ÷ 2)	\$133,333	
Exchange Gain		\$133,333

8-111.   On December 31, 1998, the exchange rate has increased to \$2.25. Using the net approach, the 1998 exchange loss would be calculated as follows:

Ending Liability [(FC1,000,000)(\$2.25)]	\$2,250,000
Beginning Net Liability (\$1,800,000 + \$133,334)	(1,933,334)
1998 Loss	\$ 316,667

8-112.   As the liability matures at the end of 1998, none of this amount is deferred to subsequent years. Given this, the required journal entry would be as follows:

Exchange Loss	$316,666	
Deferred Exchange Gain	133,334	
Long Term Liability		$450,000

8-113.   A final entry would be required on December 31, 1998 to record the payment of the liability. It would be as follows:

Long Term Liability (FC1,000,000 At $2.25)	$2,250,000	
Cash		$2,250,000

8-114.   This completes the accounting for the example under the recommendations that are contained in Section 1650 of the *CICA Handbook*. As will become obvious in the following comparison, the results are significantly different than those produced by the application of the CICA Re-Exposure Draft Recommendations.

Comparison Of Results

8-115.   We have presented the accounting that would be required in dealing with the foreign currency debt using both the current Section 1650 Recommendations and those that have been proposed under the 1996 Re-Exposure Draft. The income results for the two approaches during the five years that are under consideration are as follows:

Year	December 31 Rate	Exchange Gain (Loss)	
		Re-Exposure Draft	Section 1650
1994	$2.50	($500,000)	($100,000)
1995	$2.50	-0-	(100,000)
1996	$1.80	700,000	133,333
1997	$1.80	-0-	133,333
1998	$2.25	(450,000)	(316,666)
Total Loss		($250,000)	($250,000)

8-116.   You will notice that while the total loss for the five year period is the same under the two approaches, there are very significant differences in the amounts that are recorded in each of the years. It seems clear to us that the Re-Exposure Draft approach produces results that better reflect economic events that are taking place during this five year period.

Hedging Transactions

What Is A Hedge?

8-117.   The unabridged edition of the *Random House Dictionary Of The English Language* defines the verb "to hedge" as follows:

> To protect against a complete loss (of a bet, investment, financial position, etc.) by placing a smaller bet or bets on another contestant or other contestants, by investing in another thing or area in order to compensate for a possible loss, etc.; to mitigate a possible loss by diversifying (one's bets, investments, etc.).

8-118.   Hedging occurs in many areas of business. Various types of hedging arrangements are available for commodities, equity securities, and interest rates, as well as for foreign currency situations. In this Chapter we will focus only on hedges involving foreign currencies.

What Do We Hedge?

8-119.   As noted in the preceding Paragraph, hedging transactions occur in a variety of business and investment situations. It is clear, however, that some of the most important and widely used hedging practices occur in the area of foreign currency transactions. While it is possible to categorize these foreign currency transaction hedges in a variety of ways, the two most common types of situations can be described as follows:

Hedge Of An Anticipated Foreign Currency Exposure Under the current Section 1650, only an anticipated purchase or sale of goods or services in a foreign currency could be identified as a hedged position. The 1996 Re-Exposure Draft broadens the concept of a hedged position to cover any anticipated foreign currency exposure. In addition to a purchase or sale of goods or services in a foreign currency, the Re-Exposure Draft would permit such exposures as an anticipated foreign currency revenue stream to be treated as a hedged position. The purpose of any hedge that might be used here would be to establish the cost of the anticipated foreign currency exposure at the then current exchange rate for Canadian dollars. If the hedge is successful, the Canadian dollar value of the anticipated exposure will not be affected by subsequent changes in the exchange rate between the Canadian dollar and the foreign currency.

Hedge Of Monetary Assets And Liabilities Foreign currency transactions often result in a Canadian company carrying monetary assets or liabilities that are denominated in a foreign currency. The purpose of any hedge that might be used here is to counteract the possibility of incurring an exchange gain or loss on the monetary asset or liability at the settlement date or some earlier financial statement preparation date.

8-120. In addition to hedges involving foreign currency transactions, we will give some attention in this Chapter to hedges of investments in self sustaining foreign operations.

How Do We Hedge?

8-121. Regardless of the foreign currency transaction involved, there are a number of ways that a hedged position can be accomplished. A simple example will serve to make this point clear.

Example On February 1, 1998, a Canadian company purchases merchandise in Germany for 500,000 Deutsche Marks (DM, hereafter). The merchandise must be paid for in Deutsche Marks on May 1, 1998. On February 1, 1998, the exchange rate is DM1 = $.80, resulting in a Canadian dollar liability of $400,000. The company wishes to insure that exchange rate movements during the period February 1, 1998 to May 1, 1998 do not result in exchange gains or losses on this liability. This could be accomplished in one of several ways:

Purchase Of Deutsche Marks The company could simply, on February 1, 1998, purchase DM500,000 in currency and hold this amount until it was needed to extinguish the liability. This simple solution would not be commonly used because the foreign currency does not provide any rate of return over the period in which it is held.

Purchase Of Monetary Assets It will generally be more appropriate for the Canadian company to hedge its position through the purchase of a monetary asset denominated in Deutsche Marks. For example, if they were to make short term investments in debt securities which were receivable in Deutsche Marks, this would hedge the DM500,000 liability and, at the same time, provide some rate of return on the assets held.

Purchase Of Non Monetary Assets It would be possible for the company to hedge its DM500,000 liability by purchasing a non monetary asset denominated in Deutsche Marks. Such assets as German land, inventories, or equipment could serve in this role. However, the acquisition and disposition of such assets would generally be less convenient than the other alternatives and, in addition, the fact that such assets do not have a fixed Deutsche Mark value could make them ineffective as a hedge. As a consequence, this would not be a common solution to the hedging problem.

Entering A Forward Or Futures Exchange Contract   Perhaps the most convenient solution to the problem of hedging the DM500,000 liability would be to simply enter a forward or futures exchange contract to receive DM500,000 on May 1, 1998.   Under this approach the hedging goal is accomplished, no investment of funds is required, and the only cost is the premium required on the contract (see the next Section for an explanation of contract premiums and discounts).

Acquiring A Future Income Stream   A final possibility, in certain circumstances, would be for the company to acquire a foreign currency income stream. The Canadian company might have licensed another German enterprise to produce one of its products and anticipates that the Deutsche Mark royalties on this arrangement will be sufficient to pay the DM500,000 liability.

8-122.   In this Section we will present and discuss the general principles involved in the two types of foreign currency situations which may require hedges and illustrate such hedges as currency, monetary assets, and non monetary assets. Consideration will also be given to situations involving a hedge of a net investment in a self-sustaining foreign operation. Because of the complexity of such contracts and the possibility that they may be used for purposes other than hedging, forward exchange contracts will be dealt with in a separate Section of this Chapter.

Hedge Accounting

8-123.   In order to understand the importance of being able to identify a particular item as a hedging instrument, it is necessary to understand the concept of "hedge accounting". This term has crept into the literature without any very clear cut definition of its meaning. However, in general terms, hedge accounting refers to the fact that, if a particular financial instrument can be identified as a hedge, any gains or losses can either be deferred or used to offset losses and gains on the instrument being hedged.

8-124.   For example, assume a Canadian company acquires 2,000,000 Swiss Francs (SF, hereafter) at a point in time when SF1 = $.95. If the rate changes to SF1 = $.90, the Canadian dollar value of this currency will be reduced from $1,900,000 to $1,800,000. If this balance is not being used as a hedge, a $100,000 foreign exchange loss would have to be included in the company's income.

8-125.   Alternatively, if the SF2,000,000 was serving as a hedge of a SF2,000,000 liability, hedge accounting would permit the loss on the currency to be offset by the gain on the liability. In fact, this would happen through normal accounting procedures, whether or not the term hedge accounting was used.

8-126.   A more important and controversial application of hedge accounting would arise if the SF2,000,000 were designated as a hedge of an anticipated purchase in Swiss Francs. In this case there would be no gain on the anticipated purchase that could be used to offset the loss on the currency position. However, hedge accounting would allow the deferral of the loss on the foreign currency until the anticipated transaction takes place. In situations such as this, the question of identifying a hedging position is a significant issue. If the currency cannot be identified as a hedge, exchange gains and losses resulting from changes in its value will have to be taken into income. Alternatively, if the SF2,000,000 qualifies for hedge accounting, such gains and losses can be deferred.

Identifying Hedges

8-127.   When an existing monetary asset or liability is covered by an offsetting currency balance, monetary item, or forward contract, identification of the hedging relationship presents no real difficulty. As implied in the preceding section, the difficulty arises when a financial instrument is used to hedge an anticipated foreign currency transaction.

8-128. The problem here is that management may be tempted to identify a particular financial instrument as a hedge, simply to avoid including losses on that instrument in income. One solution would be to require that such anticipated transactions be supported by some type of contract. That would mean, for example, that to claim that there is an anticipated purchase of merchandise in a foreign currency, the transaction would have to be supported by a firm purchase commitment.

8-129. While such a legalistic approach would solve the problem of spurious claims about anticipated transactions, the Accounting Standards Board concluded that it would be too restrictive to deal with the types of foreign exchange risk that confront Canadian business. As a consequence, they Recommend only that management take the responsibility for identifying items that are being used as hedges. This is reflected in the following *CICA Handbook* Recommendation:

> **Paragraph 1650.50** *If a foreign exchange contract, asset, liability or future revenue stream is to be regarded as a hedge of a specific foreign currency exposure:*
>
> *(a) it should be identified as a hedge of the item(s) to which it relates; and*
>
> *(b) there should be reasonable assurance that it is and will continue to be effective as a hedge. (July, 1983)*

8-130. In essence, the identification of hedging relationships has been left as a matter of management judgment. If management is willing to designate an item as a hedge and indicates that it is likely to be effective in that role, hedge accounting is permitted.

8-131. The 1996 Re-Exposure Draft provides separate Recommendations for the identification of a hedge, depending on whether the hedge is of an exposed monetary position or, alternatively, an anticipated foreign currency exposure. However, while these Recommendations are somewhat more detailed than those found in the current Section 1650, the general approach is the same. The Re-Exposure Draft Recommendations make it somewhat more explicit that the enterprise must identify both the hedging instrument and the position that is being hedged. However, this idea is implicit in the current Section 1650 Recommendation. A further difference is that the Re-Exposure Draft Recommendations require that there be a high degree of correlation between changes in the exchange rate applicable to the hedging instrument and changes in the exchange rate applicable to the hedged position. This is accompanied by a requirement that the hedging instrument be of a size such that its gains and losses will counterbalance the corresponding losses and gains on the hedged position. In our opinion, these small changes do not alter the basic approach to the identification of hedges.

Accounting For A Hedge Of An Anticipated Foreign Currency Exposure

8-132. Under the current Section 1650, this type of hedging is limited to hedges of anticipated purchases or sales of goods or services denominated in a foreign currency. The purpose of this type of hedge is to establish the Canadian dollar price of the goods or services to be purchased or sold. In view of this intent, the *CICA Handbook* states the following:

> **Paragraph 1650.52** *When a purchase or sale of goods or services in a foreign currency is hedged before the transaction, the Canadian dollar price of such goods or services is established by the terms of the hedge. (July, 1983)*

8-133. A simple example will serve to illustrates this type of hedge:

> **Example** Assume that on June 1, 1998, a Canadian enterprise agrees to purchase goods in France on September 1, 1998 at a price of 800,000 French Francs (FF, hereafter) and that, on this commitment date, the rate of exchange is FF1 = $0.25. On September 1, 1998, the exchange rate is FF1 = $0.22.

8-134. If no hedge was established on the commitment date, the merchandise would be recorded at whatever exchange rate prevailed on September 1, 1998. The cost of the merchandise would be $176,000 (FF800,000 @ $0.22). This would not be the case if the commitment were hedged.

8-135.　　To illustrate this possibility, assume that at the time of the commitment, the Canadian company purchases FF800,000 in currency at FF1 = $0.25, holds this currency until the September 1, 1998 purchase date, and uses the currency to pay for the merchandise. In this case, the merchandise would be recorded at $200,000 (FF800,000 @ $0.25) and there would be no exchange gain or loss on the currency holding or any other aspect of the transaction. The same analysis would apply if the commitment had been hedged by holding a French Franc denominated monetary investment, the only difference being the additional income on the investment. In the unusual situation where the hedge consisted of a non monetary investment, it is not entirely clear what value the Paragraph 1650.52 Recommendation would apply to the merchandise. We would presume that it would continue to be $200,000, not the ultimate French Franc proceeds of the investment translated at some appropriate rate of exchange.

8-136.　　Section 1650 also notes that when a hedge of a commitment to purchase or sell goods or services is terminated or ceases to be effective prior to the date of the related purchase or sale, any exchange gain or loss deferred on the hedge up to that date will continue to be deferred and included as part of the Canadian dollar price of the goods purchased or sold when the transaction takes place. Continuing our previous example, assume that the Canadian company had constructed its hedge using a currency holding and that it decides to sell these French Francs on August 1, 1998. If on this date the exchange rate is FF1 = $0.23, the loss of $16,000 [($0.25 - $0.23)(FF800,000)] would be deferred and included as part of the Canadian dollar price of the goods purchased on September 1, 1998. This would result in a merchandise cost of $192,000 ($176,000 + $16,000).

8-137.　　With respect to the general rules applicable to accounting for a hedge of an anticipated foreign currency transaction, the approach Recommended in the 1996 Re-Exposure Draft is the same as in the current Section 1650. However, the Re-Exposure Draft does contain some differences:

1. The Re-Exposure Draft allows hedge accounting for anticipated transactions other than purchases or sales of goods or services. An example would be the hedge of an anticipated future revenue stream.

2. The Re-Exposure Draft notes that the requirement that the anticipated foreign currency exposure be highly probable would be clearly fulfilled by a contractual commitment (e.g., a written commitment to purchase goods in a foreign currency). In addition, it provides guidance on factors to be considered in determining whether it is highly probable that an anticipated transaction will occur. These include:

   (a) the existence of similar transactions in the past;
   (b) the financial and operational ability of the entity to carry out the anticipated transaction;
   (c) substantial current commitments of resources by the entity to the business activity of which the anticipated transaction is a part;
   (d) the length of time to the anticipated transaction date;
   (e) the extent of loss or disruption to the entity if it does not undertake the anticipated transaction;
   (f) the likelihood that other transactions, subject to different currency risk, might take place to achieve the same business purpose; and
   (g) the likelihood that another party will be willing and able to undertake the anticipated transaction with the entity.

3. The Re-Exposure Draft contains a provision which deals with situations in which options are used as hedging instruments. This Recommendation is as follows:

Re-ED Paragraph .023 *When an anticipated foreign currency transaction and an option are accounted for as a hedging relationship, any asset, liability, equity instrument, revenue, expense, gain or loss arising from the anticipated foreign currency transaction should be translated at the current rate. Any exchange gain or loss arising from the translation of any asset or liability resulting from the anticipated foreign currency transaction should be recognized in income as it arises unless management intends to exercise the option. When management intends to exercise the option, any asset, liability, equity instrument, revenue, expense, gain or loss arising from the anticipated foreign currency transaction should be translated at the strike price of the option. Any cost associated with the option should be recognized as an expense over the term of the option.*

The problem here is that options will only be exercised by management if they are favourable. Therefore, this new rule was required to distinguish between situations where the option will be exercised and situations in which the option will be allowed to expire. In those cases where the option is not going to be exercised, the Paragraph .023 Recommendation will produce results that are different than those produced under the existing Section 1650.

Accounting For A Hedge Of Monetary Assets Or Liabilities

8-138.   As we have stated earlier, the intent of a hedge of a monetary asset or liability is to counteract the possibility of incurring an exchange gain or loss at the settlement date. As a reflection of this view, Paragraph 1650.54 makes the following Recommendation:

Paragraph 1650.54   *If a foreign currency denominated monetary item is covered by:*

(a) *a hedge that is itself a foreign currency denominated monetary item, any exchange gain or loss on the hedge should be offset against the corresponding exchange loss or gain on the hedged item;*

(b) *a hedge that is a non-monetary item, any exchange loss or gain on the foreign currency denominated monetary item should be deferred until the settlement date of that monetary item. (July, 1983)*

8-139.   Once again, a simple example will serve to illustrate these requirements:

Example   Assume that on November 1, 1998, a Canadian company purchases merchandise in Switzerland for 1,000,000 Swiss Francs (SF, hereafter). At this time the exchange rate is SF1 = $0.90 and, as a consequence, both the merchandise and the resulting payable would be recorded at $900,000. The merchandise is paid for on February 1, 1999 when the exchange rate is SF1 = $0.95.

8-140.   If, in this situation, no hedge of the exposed Swiss Franc liability was provided, it would require $950,000 to pay the SF1,000,000 on February 1, 1999 and an exchange loss of $50,000 would have to be recorded on this settlement date. Alternatively, if the Canadian company hedged its Swiss Franc liability by either holding currency or some monetary investment denominated in Swiss Francs, there could be no net gain or loss recorded. While from a detailed technical point of view there would be a loss on the payable, it would be exactly offset by a gain on the monetary asset holding. The previously cited Paragraph 1650.54 Recommends that these amounts be offset against each other.

8-141.   While we would not expect such a transaction to be normal, a hedge could have been created using a non monetary asset such as an investment in Swiss Franc denominated equity securities. Assume that this is the case and that equity securities costing SF1,000,000 on November 1, 1998 are sold on February 1, 1999 for SF1,200,000. When the Canadian company closes its books on December 31, 1998, the relevant exchange rate is SF1 = $0.92. This would mean that, on this closing date, the Accounts Payable would have to be written up to $920,000 and an exchange loss of $20,000 would have to be recorded. Further, there would be no offsetting gain on the non monetary investment as it would be translated at the historical rate of $0.90. In this situation, Paragraph 1650.54 requires the deferral of the $20,000 loss until February 1, 1998. On this settlement date, the SF1,000,000 of the SF1,200,000 proceeds from the sale of the non monetary investments would be applied to the liability, net of the deferred loss, while the remaining SF200,000 would be converted into $190,000 (SF200,000 @ $0.95) and this would be recorded as a gain. The cost of the merchandise would remain at $900,000 and there would be no loss on the Accounts Payable.

8-142.   As was the case with a hedge of a commitment to purchase or sell goods or services, a hedge of a monetary asset or liability may be terminated or cease to be effective. In this situation, Section 1650 offers no specific guidelines. However, Paragraph 1650.53 does note that if a payable or loan is hedged by a future revenue stream, the amount included in the determination of net income of future periods would be the foreign currency amount translated at the exchange rate in effect when the revenue stream is identified as a hedge. The difference arising due to cash received being translated at the current rate would be deferred and offset against the deferred amount relating to the payable or loan. This Paragraph also points out that any costs relating to the hedge would be recognized in income over the period for which the hedge is in effect.

8-143.   The Re-Exposure Draft Recommendation in this area is as follows:

Re-ED Paragraph .020   *When a foreign exchange instrument and a monetary asset or liability denominated in a foreign currency are accounted for as a hedging relationship, any exchange gain or loss on the foreign exchange instrument should be recognized in income as it arises. Any cost associated with the foreign exchange instrument should be recognized as an expense over the term of the instrument.*

8-144.   While this Recommendation is completely consistent with the current Section 1650 Recommendation in this area, it does serve to clarify one point with respect to hedges involving forward exchange contracts. This involves the fact that the exchange rate agreed to in a forward exchange contract will always be different than the current exchange rate on the date at which the contract is entered. The Re-Exposure Draft Recommendation makes it clear that this difference, referred to as the premium or discount on the contract, should be allocated as an expense over the term of the hedge. A simple example will serve to make this point clear:

Example   A forward exchange contract to acquire 1 million French Francs (FF) on May 1, 1999 at $.25 is entered into on November 1, 1998. At that time, the current rate for FF is 1FF = $.24. On December 31, the date on which the enterprise closes its books, the current exchange rate is 1FF = $27.

The exchange gain on the contract will be $30,000 [(FF1,000,000)($.27 - $.24)] and this will be credited to income in full for the year ending December 31, 1998. If the forward exchange contract is being used to hedge a FF1 million liability, there will be an offsetting loss on that liability.

The cost of the forward exchange contract is $10,000 [(FF1,000,000)($.25 - $.24)]. This amount will be charged to expense over the six month term of the contract, with only one-third (2/6 months) of the total being charged to the year ending December 31, 1998.

Discontinuance Of Hedge Accounting

8-145.   The existing Section 1650 does not deal with the discontinuance of hedge accounting. In contrast, the Re-Exposure Draft begins by indicating clearly the circumstances that would lead to a discontinuance of hedge accounting:

Re-ED Paragraph .042   *Hedge accounting should be discontinued when:*

(a) all or part of the anticipated foreign currency transaction is no longer highly

probable; or

(b) *the foreign currency denominated monetary asset, liability or foreign exchange instrument is settled, matured or otherwise nullified; or*

(c) *management decides to discontinue the hedging relationship.*

8-146.   If one of the conditions specified in Paragraph Re-ED.042 leads to a discontinuance of hedge accounting, the Re-Exposure Draft provides the following Recommendations with respect to the appropriate accounting treatment:

Re-ED Paragraph .043   *When hedge accounting is discontinued, any exchange gains and losses that have been deferred should be recognized in income as follows:*

(a) *when all of the anticipated foreign currency transaction is no longer highly probable, all of the deferred exchange gains and losses on the monetary item or foreign exchange instrument should be included in income immediately;*

(b) *when a portion of the anticipated foreign currency transaction is no longer highly probable, that proportion of the deferred exchange gains and losses on the monetary item or foreign exchange instrument should be included in income immediately;*

(c) *when the monetary item or foreign exchange instrument is settled, matured, or otherwise nullified, or management decides to discontinue the hedging relationship, any exchange gains and losses that have been deferred should continue to be deferred and recognized in income in the same period as the anticipated foreign currency transaction is recognized.*

8-147.   As there is no equivalent Recommendation on the discontinuance of hedging in the existing Section 1650, compliance with these Re-Exposure Recommendations would be considered an application of GAAP.

Accounting For A Hedge Of A Net Investment In A Self-Sustaining Foreign Operation

8-148.   Some Canadian companies may undertake a transaction which serves as a hedge of a net investment in a self-sustaining foreign operation. (See the material on the translation of foreign currency financial statements in Chapter Nine for coverage of foreign operations.) An investment in a German subsidiary, for example, might be hedged by borrowing in Deutsche Marks and designating the resulting liability as a hedge of the net investment in the foreign operation. Under the current Section 1650, gains or losses on foreign currency liabilities are charged to income either immediately or over some specified future period. However, when it is clear that the liability serves as a hedge of a net investment in a foreign operation, Section 1650 of the *CICA Handbook* would offset the translation adjustments on the liability against the corresponding adjustments arising on the translation of the financial statements of the foreign operation. The resulting net adjustment would be included in the separate component of shareholders' equity.

8-149.   The Re-Exposure Draft gives more attention to this subject, first by indicating the circumstances under which an investment in a self sustaining foreign operation can be considered to be hedged:

Re-ED Paragraph .065   *A monetary liability denominated in a foreign currency or a foreign exchange instrument and an investment in a self sustaining foreign operation should be accounted for as a hedging relationship when:*

(a) *the hedging relationship is specifically designated as a hedging relationship; and*

(b) it is highly probable that exchange gains and losses which arise on the compo-nents of the hedging relationship will fully or partially counterbalance.

8-150.   A second Recommendation deals with the procedures to be used in dealing with a hedge of a self sustaining foreign operation:

> **Re-ED Paragraph .066**   *When a monetary liability or a foreign exchange instru-ment and a net investment in a self sustaining foreign operation are accounted for as a hedging relationship, any exchange gain or loss on the monetary liability or the foreign exchange instrument should be included in the separate component of eq-uity established in accordance with paragraph .054 only to the extent that the ex-change gain or loss counterbalances the exchange loss or gain on the net investment in the self sustaining foreign operation.*

8-151.   While they are presented in a more detailed and explicit manner, the Re-Exposure Draft Recommendations are consistent with the Recommendations found in the existing Section 1650.

Forward Exchange Contracts

Nature Of Forward Exchange Contracts

8-152.   A forward exchange contract is an agreement to exchange, on a particular future date, a specified quantity of particular currencies at exchange rates established at the time of entering into the contract. In order to fully understand the nature of such con-tracts and the accounting procedures that are used to deal with them, it is necessary to comprehend a number of definitions that are used in connection with such arrange-ments. These definitions are as follows:

- **Forward Contract Commitment Date**   The date of entering into a forward ex-change contract.

- **Spot Rate**   The exchange rates for immediate delivery of currencies exchanged. In the real world there will generally be two such rates at any given point in time. These are the rates applicable to buying the currency and the rate applicable to selling the currency.

- **Forward Rate**   The exchange rate for future delivery of currencies to be exchanged.

- **Premium Or Discount**   The amount of the forward contract multiplied by the differ-ence between the forward rate and the spot rate at the forward contract commitment date.

8-153.   To illustrate these definitions and to serve as a basis for examples of accounting for forward exchange contracts, a simple example will be used. This example is as fol-lows:

> **Example**   On October 1, 1998, a Canadian company enters a forward exchange contract to receive 1,000,000 Deutsche Marks (DM, hereafter) on March 1, 1999 at a rate of DM1 = $.84. The spot rate on October 1, 1998 is DM1 = $.80. On December 31, 1998, when the company closes its books and prepares financial statements, the spot rate is DM1 = $.88 and on March 1, 1999 it is DM1 = $.94.

8-154.   Note that the Canadian company does not purchase the right to receive the Deutsche Marks, it simply enters a non cancelable executory contract agreeing to ex-change Canadian dollars for Deutsche Marks at a future point in time. While some writers would record a receivable and payable on the forward contract commitment date for the full amount of the contract ($800,000 or DM1,000,000 at the spot rate), it would seem clear that this is not in keeping with generally accepted accounting principles. The nor-mal treatment of unperformed or executory contracts is to provide only note disclosure. The one important exception to this is in the area of leases and this exception is specifi-cally justified and provided for in Section 3065 of the *CICA Handbook*. No such exception is provided for forward exchange contracts and none would seem advisable. There is no intention here to actually receive the Deutsche Marks and pay out the Canadian dollars.

8-155. The only cost associated with entering the forward exchange contract described in the example is the premium of $40,000 [(DM1,000,000)($.84 - $.80)]. The amount of such premiums is influenced primarily by two factors. The first of these is expectations with respect to the future movement of the relevant exchange rate. It would appear in this case that the Deutsche Mark is expected to go up relative to the Canadian dollar. If expectations were weaker or there was some belief that the Deutsche Mark would decline, the premium would be smaller or could even become a discount.

8-156. Interest rates are also influential here. Forward exchange contracts are a way of taking a position in a foreign currency without a significant investment of funds. For example, if an enterprise had a liability of £1,000,000, a forward exchange contract to take delivery of £1,000,000 represents an approach to hedging the liability. As such, it is an alternative to simply holding the £1,000,000 in currency. In view of this alternative, the premium on any forward exchange contract cannot exceed the cost of interest on borrowing an equivalent amount of the foreign currency.

8-157. The accounting treatment of this premium or discount will depend on how the forward exchange contract is being used and will be illustrated in the following material.

Forward Contract As A Hedge Of An Anticipated Foreign Currency Commitment

8-158. The preceding forward contract could be used as a hedge of a commitment to purchase goods or services. For example, assume that the Canadian company anticipates that it will purchase and pay for DM1,000,000 in merchandise on March 1, 1999. In this case, the effect of having the forward exchange contract as a hedge is to establish the Canadian dollar price of the merchandise to be purchased. This value is established at $840,000 by the contracted forward rate of $.84. This means that the premium on the contract becomes part of the cost of the merchandise and, given that the Deutsche Marks received under the contract are used to purchase the merchandise on March 1, 1999, there will be no gain or loss on the contract to be taken into income. The following journal entries would be used on the relevant dates.

8-159. **October 1, 1998 Journal Entry** Because of the executory nature of the forward exchange contract, no entry would be required.

8-160. **December 31, 1998 Journal Entry** It would be possible to record the forward exchange contract as an asset with a value of $80,000 [(DM1,000,000)($.84 - $.80)] with the corresponding gain deferred to be included in the cost of the merchandise. However, if it is still the intent of the company to use the Deutsche Marks received under the contract to purchase merchandise, we believe that it would be more appropriate to make no entry at this date.

8-161. **March 1, 1999 Journal Entry** On this date, the company would use $840,000 in cash to purchase the DM1,000,000 in currency. If these Deutsche Marks were used to purchase the merchandise as planned, the entry would be as follows:

Merchandise	$840,000	
Cash		$840,000

8-162. If, for some reason, the merchandise was not purchased, the Deutsche Marks could be sold at the March 1, 1999 spot rate of DM1 = $.94 and this would result in a gain as follows:

Cash ($940,000 - $840,000)	$100,000	
Gain		$100,000

Forward Contract As A Hedge Of A Monetary Asset Or Liability

8-163. The forward exchange contract described in the basic example could also be used to hedge a liability denominated in Deutsche Marks. For example, if the Canadian company were to purchase DM1,000,000 in German merchandise on October 1, 1998, with the resulting payable due on March 1, 1999, the forward exchange contract in the example would serve as a hedge of this monetary liability. In this situation the merchandise would be recorded using the spot rate on October 1, 1998. The $40,000 premium on the contract would become a hedging expense to be recognized over the period in which the forward contract serves as a hedge. The following journal entries would be used at the relevant dates.

8-164.   October 1, 1998 Journal Entry   The only entry required on this date would be to record the purchase of merchandise at the spot rate:

Merchandise (DM1,000,000 At $.80)	$800,000	
Accounts Payable		$800,000

8-165.   December 31, 1998 Journal Entry   As noted previously, the premium on forward exchange contracts must be recognized as an expense over the life of the hedging arrangement. Since the life of the contract is five months and three months have passed as of December 31, 1998, an entry is required to recognize 3/5 of the premium as an expense:

Hedge Expense [(3/5)(DM1,000,000)($.84 - $.80)]	$24,000	
Premium Liability		$24,000

8-166.   Also on this date, it is necessary to adjust the payable to reflect the new spot rate of DM1 = $.88. This entry by itself would result in an exchange loss. However, the forward exchange contract will be used to offset this loss and, as a consequence, this contract should be recognized as an asset at a value which reflects its intended use. These considerations could be recorded with two journal entries as follows:

Exchange Loss [(DM1,000,000)($.88 - $.80)]	$80,000	
Accounts Payable		$80,000

Forward Exchange Contract [(DM1,000,000)($.88 - $.80)]	$80,000	
Exchange Gain		$80,000

8-167.   While the preceding two entries are an accurate solution to the problem, it is clear that the loss and gain will always be equal in a fully hedged situation such as this. As a reflection of this situation, we have previously noted that the *CICA Handbook* suggests that the corresponding gain and loss should be offset for financial statement presentation. Given this suggestion, the more appropriate net entry would be as follows:

Forward Exchange Contract ([DM1,000,000][$.88 - $.80])	$80,000	
Accounts Payable		$80,000

8-168.   March 1, 1999 Journal Entry   Prior to recording the settlement of the payable on this date, it is useful to illustrate the accrual of the hedge expense for the remaining two months of the contract as well as recognize the increased values of the foreign currency liability and related forward exchange contract. These two entries would be as follows:

Hedge Expense [(2/5)(DM1,000,000)($.84 - $.80)]	$16,000	
Premium Liability		$16,000

Forward Exchange Contract [(DM1,000,000)($.94 - $.88)]	$60,000	
Accounts Payable		$60,000

8-169.   With these adjustments in place, the entry to record the settlement of the liability and the forward exchange contract would be as follows:

Accounts Payable	$940,000	
Premium Liability	40,000	
Forward Exchange Contract		$140,000
Cash		840,000

8-170.   It would, of course, be possible to expand this entry significantly by providing separate entries for the exchange of currencies under the forward exchange contract. However, the preceding entry is a better representation of the manner in which the Canadian dollar cash flows will actually take place.

Speculative Forward Exchange Contracts

8-171.   We would expect that the majority of forward exchange contracts entered into by Canadian enterprises serve as hedges of either foreign currency monetary assets or liabilities or, alternatively, anticipations of future foreign currency exposures. Without question, however, there are situations in which contracts are entered for purely speculative reasons. In such a situation, hedge accounting cannot be used. As was discussed in Paragraphs 8-123 through 8-126, when hedge accounting cannot be used, gains and losses on financial instruments cannot be deferred and must be taken into income as they occur. With respect to the measurement of the gain or loss, the amount would be determined by multiplying the foreign currency amount of the forward contract by the difference between the contracted forward rate and the forward rate available for the remaining maturity of the contract. No separate recognition would be given to the discount or premium.

8-172.   We will again use our basic Deutsche Mark example to illustrate the procedures that would be required in this situation. Given the assumption that the forward contract is not serving as a hedge of any other foreign currency transaction or commitment, the journal entries that would be required in this case are found in the Paragraphs which follow.

8-173.   **October 1, 1998 Journal Entry**   No entry would be required at this date.

8-174.   **December 31, 1998 Journal Entry**   Since the Canadian company is closing its books on this date, an entry would be required to recognize a gain on the contract. To determine the amount of the gain we could use the December 31 spot rate. However, our contract gives us delivery two months after this date and it is probably more appropriate to use the two month forward rate to place a value on the contract. Taking this approach, we will assume that the two month forward rate for Deutsche Marks on December 31, 1998 is DM1 = $.90. Given this additional information, the journal entry would be as follows:

Forward Exchange Contract		
([DM1,000,000][$.90 - $.84])	$60,000	
Exchange Gain		$60,000

8-175.   **March 1, 1999 Journal Entry**   When the forward exchange contract is settled on March 1, 1999, the cash inflow would be based on DM1,000,000 times the difference between the current spot rate of $.94 and the contract rate of $.84. Recognition of this inflow of $100,000 and the recognition of the December 31, 1998 to March 1, 1999 gain would be recorded in the following journal entry:

Cash	$100,000	
Forward Exchange Contract		$60,000
Exchange Gain		40,000

8-176.   This entry reflects the fact that the forward exchange contract would be settled on a net basis, with the only cash flow based on the difference between the contract rate of $.84 and $.94 spot rate at the settlement date.

Additional Readings

CICA Re-Exposure Draft - Section 1650 Revision - "Foreign Currency Translation", May, 1996.

CA Magazine Article - "Managing Foreign Exchange Risks", Robert Ferchat, January, 1981.

CA Magazine Article - "Managing Foreign Exchange Risk Successfully", John M. Simke, July, 1983.

CA Magazine Article - "Foreign Currency Translation At Alcan", Paul Dunne and Glenn Rioux, October, 1983.

CA Magazine Article - "Trading On The Future", Paul T. Farrelly, December, 1988.

CA Magazine Article - "Currency Conundrum", Cally Hunt, November, 1993.

CA Magazine Article - "Hedging: A User's Manual", Sylvie Léger and Jacques Fortin, April, 1994.

CA Magazine Article - "Spotlight On Foreign Exchange", Karen Horcher, April, 1994.

Journal Of Accountancy Article - "Forward Contracts - Free Market Financial Tools", Thomas A. Piteo, August, 1982.

Journal Of Accountancy Article - "Currency Translation And The Funds Statement: A New Approach", Frank R. Rayburn and Michael Crooch, October, 1983.

Journal Of Accountancy Article - "Accounting For Foreign Operations", Paul Rosenfield, August, 1987.

Problems For Self Study

(The solutions for these problems can be found following Chapter 17 of the text.)

SELF STUDY PROBLEM EIGHT - 1

The Ambivalent Company is a Mexican subsidiary of a Canadian parent company and its accounts are included in the Canadian dollar consolidated financial statements of the parent company. On December 31, 1998, the following selected amount balances were included in the foreign currency Balance Sheet of the Ambivalent Company (all amounts are expressed in Mexican Pesos which are designated P hereafter):

	Debits	Credits
Cash	P 500,000	
Long Term Receivables	1,500,000	
Inventories	2,000,000	
Plant and Equipment	5,000,000	
Accounts Payable		P 700,000
Long Term Liabilities		1,200,000
Accumulated Depreciation on Plant and Equipment		2,500,000

The Long Term Receivables and Plant And Equipment were acquired several years ago when P1 = $.10. The Long Term Liabilities were also issued at this time. The Inventories were acquired for P2,100,000 when P1 = $.20. However, they are carried at their net realizable value as measured at December 31, 1998. The exchange rate on December 31, 1998 is P1 = $.25.

Required   Translate the above account balances using the following approaches:

    A. Temporal approach
    B. Current Rate approach

SELF STUDY PROBLEM EIGHT - 2

On December 31, 1995, the Jordanian government loans the Canadian Company, Petroteach, 5 million Jordan Dinars (D, hereafter) interest-free. This money is to be used to establish a training center for skilled workers in the oil industry. The loan matures on December 31, 1999. The relevant exchange rates for the next four years are as follows:

December 31, 1995	D1 = $1.80
December 31, 1996	D1 = $2.10
December 31, 1997	D1 = $2.00
December 31, 1998	D1 = $2.00
December 31, 1999	D1 = $1.70

The Petroteach Company closes its books on December 31 of each year and accounts for foreign currency transactions using the recommendations contained in Section 1650 of the *CICA Handbook*.

Required:

A. Prepare the journal entries that would be required to account for the loan on December 31 of each year to maturity.

B. Prepare a schedule which shows the income effects of the loan for the periods under consideration.

SELF STUDY PROBLEM EIGHT - 3

On December 1, 1998, the Canadian Switzcan Company enters into a forward exchange contract to purchase 2,000,000 Swiss Francs (SF, hereafter) on March 31, 1999 at a rate of SF1 = $1.00. The spot rates of exchange on dates relevant to this contract are as follows:

December 1, 1998	SF1 = $ .96
December 31, 1998	SF1 = $ .98
March 31, 1999	SF1 = $1.03

The 3 month forward rate on December 31, 1998 is SF1 = $1.05. The Switzcan Company closes its books on December 31 and accounts for forward exchange contracts using the recommendations of Section 1650 of the *CICA Handbook*.

Required   In the following independent cases, provide the journal entries that would be required on December 1, 1998, December 31, 1998 and March 31, 1999 to account for the forward exchange contract described above and any other transactions that are included in the individual cases.

A. On December 1, 1998, Switzcan Company makes a commitment to its Swiss supplier to purchase merchandise on March 31, 1999. The cost of the merchandise is SF2,000,000, it will be delivered on March 31, 1999, and the invoice is payable on the delivery date.

B. On December 1, 1998, Switzcan purchases merchandise from its Swiss supplier at a cost of SF2,000,000. The invoice must be paid on March 31, 1999.

C. On December 1, 1998, Switzcan decides to speculate in foreign currency via a forward exchange contract.

SELF STUDY PROBLEM EIGHT - 4

On November 1, 1997, the Riskless Company, a Canadian based trading company, sells merchandise to a German distributor for 5 million Deutsche Marks (DM, hereafter). The invoice is to be paid in Deutsche Marks by the German distributor on February 1, 1998. Also on November 1, 1997, the Riskless Company makes a commitment to purchase equipment from a German manufacturer for DM20 million. The equipment is to be delivered on March 1, 1998 and the entire purchase price must be paid on that date in Deutsche Marks.

In view of the preceding transactions, on November 1, 1997 the Riskless Company enters into two forward exchange contracts for hedging purposes. The first contract allows the Company to deliver DM5 million on February 1, 1998 at an exchange rate of DM1 = $.69. The second contract permits Riskless to buy DM20 million on March 1, 1998 at an exchange rate of DM1 = $.75. In implementing these transactions, the financial vice-president of Riskless becomes very impressed with the profit potential inherent in forward exchange contracts. As a consequence, he enters into an additional contract on November 1, 1997. This final contract, which is purely for speculative purposes, calls for Riskless to deliver DM10 million on June 1, 1998 at an exchange rate of DM1 = $.80.

Date	Spot Rate For Deutsche Marks
November 1, 1997	$.70
December 31, 1997	$.73
February 1, 1998	$.74
March 1, 1998	$.76
June 1, 1998	$.82

In addition to the preceding spot rates, on December 31, 1997, the 5 month forward rate for delivering Deutsche Marks is DM1 = $.81. The Riskless Company closes its books on December 31.

Required For each of the following dates, provide the journal entries that would be required to account for the preceding foreign currency transactions:

A. November 1, 1997
B. December 31, 1997
C. February 1, 1998
D. March 1, 1998
E. June 1, 1998

Assignment Problems

(The solutions to these problem are only available in
the solutions manual that has been provided to your instructor.)

ASSIGNMENT PROBLEM EIGHT - 1

The Alpine Company is a Swiss subsidiary of a Canadian Company and its accounts are included in the Canadian dollar consolidated financial statements of the parent Company. At the year end, the following selected account balances were included in the foreign currency Balance Sheet of the Alpine Company (all amounts are expressed in Swiss Francs which are designated SF hereafter):

	Debits	Credits
Cash	SF 800,000	
Long Term Receivables	1,000,000	
Inventories	2,400,000	
Plant And Equipment	8,000,000	
Accounts Payable		SF 600,000
Long Term Liabilities		3,000,000
Accumulated Depreciation on Plant and Equipment		1,700,000

The Long Term Receivables and Plant And Equipment were acquired several years ago when SF1 = $.80. The Long Term Liabilities were also issued at this time. The Inventories were acquired for SF 3,100,000 when SF1 = $.90. However, they are carried at their net realizable value as measured at the year end. The exchange rate at the year end is SF1 = $.95.

Required Translate the account balances under the following general methods of translation:

A. Temporal method
B. Current Rate method

ASSIGNMENT PROBLEM EIGHT - 2

On December 31, 1997, the Maple Leaf Company, a Canadian company, buys $4,000,000 worth of Deutsche Marks (DM, hereafter) at a rate of DM1 = $.80. The resulting DM5,000,000 is used to establish a new German subsidiary company, the Rhine Company, on this same date. Also on this date, the Rhine Company borrows, at an annual rate of 10 percent, an additional DM5,000,000 in Germany. The debt must be repaid after ten years. The Rhine Company then invests the entire cash balance of DM10,000,000 in a tract of land. The land is immediately leased for a period of ten years with the lessee agreeing to pay the Rhine Company DM1,000,000 at the end of each year.

During the subsequent year, the only activities of the Rhine Company are the collection of the lease payment and the payment of the interest on the Long Term Debt. To simplify the problem, all other expenses and revenues of the Company have been ignored.

The Rhine Company's Income Statement for the year ending December 31, 1998 and its Balance Sheet as at December 31, 1998 in Deutsche Marks are as follows:

Income Statement
Year Ending December 31, 1998
(in Deutsche Marks)

Lease Revenue	1,000,000
Interest Expense	500,000
Net Income	500,000

Balance Sheet
As At December 31, 1998
(in Deutsche Marks)

Cash	500,000
Land	10,000,000
Total Assets	10,500,000
Long Term Debt	5,000,000
Contributed Capital	5,000,000
Retained Earnings	500,000
Total Equities	10,500,000

The exchange rate increased to DM1 = $1.00 on January 1, 1998 and remained unchanged at that level until January 1, 1999.

Required: Prepare the Rhine Company's translated Income Statement for the year ending December 31, 1998 and the Company's translated Balance Sheet as at December 31, 1998 in Canadian dollars using the alternative methods described in the following three Cases.

Case One Assume that the temporal method is used for the translation of all assets and liabilities and that exchange adjustments are included in income in the year in which the exchange rate change occurs.

Case Two Assume that the temporal method is used for the translation of all assets and liabilities and that exchange adjustments are treated as an adjustment of the shareholders' equity of the Rhine Company.

Case Three Assume that the current rate method is used for the translation of all assets and liabilities and that exchange adjustments are treated as an adjustment of the shareholders' equity of the Rhine Company.

ASSIGNMENT PROBLEM EIGHT - 3

The Svedberg Company begins operations on January 1, 1994. Its only business is the importation of educational chemistry sets from Sweden. The chemistry sets are paid for in Swedish Krona (Kr, hereafter). Purchases during the first five years of operation are as follows:

Year	Quantity	Unit Price	Total Price
1994	5,000	Kr 500	Kr 2,500,000
1995	10,000	525	5,250,000
1996	12,000	540	6,480,000
1997	2,000	550	1,100,000
1998	-0-	530	-0-

The Svedberg Company sells the sets in Canada for $200 per set. All of the sets are paid for and sold in the year following purchase. Inventories are accounted for under the first-in, first-out inventory flow assumption. The Svedberg Company closes its books on December 31 of each of year.

Exchange rate data for the period under consideration was as follows:

January 1, 1994 to December 30, 1995	Kr1 = $.22
December 31, 1995 to December 30, 1996	Kr1 = $.25
December 31, 1996 to December 31, 1998	Kr1 = $.24

Required: Prepare the condensed Income Statements for years 1995 through 1998 of the Svedberg Company using:

A. The one-transaction approach to recording foreign currency transactions.

B. The two-transaction approach to recording foreign currency transactions.

ASSIGNMENT PROBLEM EIGHT - 4

On December 31, 1994, the Ferber Company, a Canadian company, borrows 3,000,000 Malaysia ringgitt (R, hereafter) from the Malaysian government to finance the construction of a factory. This liability does not require the payment of interest. It will mature in four years on December 31, 1998. The Ferber Company has a December 31 year end and exchange rates at Balance Sheet dates are as follows:

December 31, 1994	R1 = $0.40
December 31, 1995	R1 = $0.50
December 31, 1996	R1 = $0.30
December 31, 1997	R1 = $0.30
December 31, 1998	R1 = $0.42

Required:

A. Prepare the journal entries that would be required to account for the loan on December 31 of each year to maturity assuming the Ferber Company accounts for foreign currency transactions using the recommendations contained in the 1996 CICA Re-Exposure Draft, "Foreign Currency Translation".

B. Prepare the journal entries that would be required to account for the loan on December 31 of each year to maturity assuming the Ferber Company accounts for foreign currency transactions using the recommendations contained in Section 1650 of the *CICA Handbook*.

C. Prepare a schedule which compares the income effects of the loan for the periods under consideration under both assumptions.

ASSIGNMENT PROBLEM EIGHT - 5

On December 1, 1997, the Hedgor Company, a Canadian based trading company, buys merchandise from a French distributor for 2,000,000 French Francs (F, hereafter). The invoice is to be paid in French Francs by the Hedgor Company on April 1, 1998. Also on December 1, 1997, the Hedgor Company receives a commitment from an Italian customer to purchase merchandise for 5,000,000 Italian Lira (L, hereafter). This merchandise is to be delivered on April 1, 1998 and the entire purchase price must be paid on this date. The Hedgor Company, contrary to its normal sales policies, agrees to accept payment in Italian Lira.

In view of the preceding transactions, on December 1, 1997, the Hedgor Company enters into two forward exchange contracts for hedging purposes. The first contract allows the Company to buy F2,000,000 on April 1, 1998 at an exchange rate of F1 = $0.19. The second contract permits Hedgor to deliver L5,000,000 on April 1, 1998 at an exchange rate of L1 = $.0010.

Relevant data on exchange rates is as follows:

Date	Spot Rate For	
	French Francs	Italian Lira
December 1, 1997	$0.20	$.0009
December 31, 1997	$0.17	$.0011
April 1, 1998	$0.16	$.0012

In addition to the preceding spot rates, on December 31, 1997, the 3 month forward rate for receiving French Francs is $0.18 while the 3 month forward rate for delivering Italian Lira is $.0013. The Hedgor Company closes its books on December 31 of each year.

Required: For each of the following dates, provide the journal entries that would be required to account for the foreign currency transactions described in the preceding.

A. December 1, 1997
B. December 31, 1997
C. April 1, 1998

ASSIGNMENT PROBLEM EIGHT - 6

Over the past ten years, Hartford Ltd. has had Deutsche Mark (DM) denominated revenues from sales to customers in Germany of between DM1,500,000 and DM2,500,000 annually. The are no Deutsche Mark expenditures associated with these revenues.

In order to avoid the foreign exchange risk associated with these revenues, Hartford Ltd. decides to borrow its current debt requirements in Deutsche Marks.

On January 1, 1996, Hartford Ltd. borrows DM6,000,000 at an interest rate of 10 percent per annum. The debt is to be repaid on December 31, 1998. The Company designates the long term debt as a hedge of Deutsche Mark revenues expected to be received in the next three years. The estimated and actual revenues received for the three years 1996 through 1998 were as follows:

	Estimated	Actual
Year Ending December 31, 1996	DM2,200,000	DM2,600,000
Year Ending December 31, 1997	2,300,000	2,000,000
Year Ending December 31, 1998	1,500,000	1,800,000
Total	DM6,000,000	DM6,400,000

Relevant exchange rates are as follows:

January 1, 1996	DM1 = $0.70
Average For 1996	DM1 = $0.75
December 31, 1996	DM1 = $0.80
Average For 1997	DM1 = $0.82
December 31, 1997	DM1 = $0.84
Average For 1998	DM1 = $0.80
December 31, 1998	DM1 = $0.76

The revenues were received uniformly over the year, making it appropriate to translate them using average exchange rates.

Required: Prepare the Canadian dollar journal entries required to record:

A. the issuance of the Deutsche Mark debt,
B. the receipt of the Deutsche Mark revenues,
C. the year end changes in the value of the debt resulting from changes in the exchange rate for the Deutsche Mark,
D. the retirement of the debt on December 31, 1998.

Do not make the journal entries required to record the interest payments on the debt.

ASSIGNMENT CASE EIGHT - 1

International Manufacturing Company (IMC) is a large, Canadian-based corporation with worldwide operations. IMC has issued debt instruments in Swiss francs, German marks and US dollars to take advantage of low interest rates. All these financing arrangements were completed on a fixed interest rate basis.

The Canadian dollar has weakened considerably in the past few years, and as a result IMC has accrued substantial foreign exchange losses. The annual amortization of these losses has seriously impaired IMC's ability to report increased earnings during the last few years, in spite of its successful operations.

IMC's investment banker has recommended the following alternatives to management:

1. That IMC consider using the currency swap market to minimize losses on its debt. IMC would enter into an agreement with a third party whereby IMC agreed to pay the obligation of the third party's debt in Canadian dollars in exchange for the third party agreeing to pay the obligation of IMC's foreign debt. Pursuing this option would entail an additional cost if the investment banker were required to guarantee the payment of the foreign debt.

2. That IMC consider buying back the Swiss franc, German mark and US dollar bonds on the bond market and refinancing them now. Interest rates for all currencies are much higher at present than at the time that these bonds were issued.

Management has approached you, the controller, and has asked you to prepare a report that discusses the accounting and financial reporting implications of each of the investment banker's recommendations. Management is considering a third option as well: using the existing debt to hedge IMC's new operations in foreign countries. Management also wants to know the accounting and financial reporting implications of this option.

Required: Prepare the report.

(CICA Adapted)

Chapter 9

Translation Of Foreign Currency Financial Statements

A Note On Current Developments

As was noted in Chapter 8, a Re-Exposure Draft to revise Section 1650 of the *CICA Handbook* was issued in May,1996. Also as noted in that Chapter, the Accounting Standards Board has suspended work on this project, pending the completion of their efforts in the area of financial instruments. Given the situation, this Chapter will continue to largely reflect the existing Section 1650. However, we will include those parts of the Re-Exposure Draft which either clarify current Section 1650 Recommendations or reach a different conclusion with respect to the appropriate accounting procedures to be used.

Accounting Recommendations

Objectives Of Translation

9-1. In Chapter 8 we noted that, in broad general terms, the objectives of foreign currency translation could be based either on the domestic company perspective or, alternatively, on the foreign company perspective. We also noted that each of these perspectives provided solutions to three basic issues:

- the accounting principles to be used;

- the method of translation to be used (unit of measure to be used); and

- the treatment of translation adjustments.

9-2. The point was also made that, in the development of U.S. and Canadian standards in this area, it has not proved practical to adopt a single perspective to be applied to all types of foreign currency translation problems. Rather, different solutions to the three issues listed in the preceding paragraph will be used, depending on the particular problem that is being addressed. While we provided an indication of the solutions to these issues that are applicable to the translation of foreign currency financial statements, we deferred a detailed consideration of the relevant accounting pronouncements to this Chapter.

Integrated And Self Sustaining Foreign Operations

9-3.   To begin, the *CICA Handbook* makes the following general statement on the objectives of the translation process:

> **Paragraph 1650.06**   For **Foreign Operations**, the ultimate objective of translation is to express financial statements of the foreign operation in Canadian dollars in a manner which best reflects the reporting enterprise's exposure to exchange rate changes as determined by the economic facts and circumstances.

9-4.   This general statement opens the door to the possibility that different objectives will be appropriate in different circumstances. More specifically, Section 1650 distinguishes between integrated foreign operations and self-sustaining foreign operations. These types of foreign operations are given the following general definitions in Paragraph 1650.03:

(a) **Integrated Foreign Operation**   A foreign operation which is financially or operationally interdependent with the reporting enterprise such that the exposure to exchange rate changes is similar to the exposure which would exist had the transactions and activities of the foreign operation been undertaken by the reporting enterprise.

(b) **Self-Sustaining Foreign Operation**   A foreign operation which is financially and operationally independent of the reporting enterprise such that the exposure to exchange rate changes is limited to the reporting enterprise's net investment in the foreign operation.

9-5.   In making this distinction, Paragraph 1650.10 notes that professional judgment is required in evaluating the economic factors which determine the exposure of a reporting enterprise to exchange rate changes. Matters which would be taken into consideration include whether:

(a) there are any factors which would indicate that the cash flows of the reporting enterprise are insulated from or are directly affected by the day-to-day activities of the foreign operation;

(b) sales prices for the foreign operation's products or services are determined more by local competition and local government regulations or more by world-wide competition and international prices and whether such sales prices are primarily responsive on a short-term basis to changes in exchange rates or are immune to such changes;

(c) the sales market for the foreign operation's products and services is primarily outside the reporting enterprise's country or within it;

(d) labour, materials and other costs of the foreign operation's products or services are primarily local costs or whether the foreign operation depends on products and services obtained primarily from the country of the reporting enterprise;

(e) the day-to-day activities of the foreign operation are financed primarily from its own operations and local borrowings or primarily by the reporting enterprise or borrowings from the country of the reporting enterprise;

(f) there is very little interrelationship between the day-to-day activities of the foreign operation and those of the reporting enterprise or whether intercompany transactions with the reporting enterprise form a dominant part of the foreign operation's activities.

9-6.   It is this distinction between integrated foreign operations and self sustaining foreign operations that provides the basis used in Section 1650 for establishing the relevant objectives of translation in the area of translating foreign currency financial statements.

Accounting Principles To Be Used

9-7.   Without regard to the type of foreign operation for which financial statements are being translated, the use of Canadian GAAP is required. This is noted in the *CICA Handbook* as follows:

Paragraph 1650.04   Conformity with accounting principles generally accepted in Canada is implicit in and basic to all Recommendations issued by the Accounting Standards Committee. Financial statements of foreign operations would be adjusted, if necessary, to conform with accounting principles generally accepted in Canada when incorporating them in the financial statements of the reporting enterprise.

9-8.   As noted in the preceding quotation, if the foreign currency records of an investee are based on generally accepted principles that are not consistent with Canadian Recommendations, they must be adjusted to a Canadian basis prior to being translated into Canadian dollars.

9-9.   The 1996 Re-Exposure Draft on foreign currency translation reaches the same conclusion with respect to the accounting principles to be used.

Method Of Translation (Unit Of Measure)

Basis For Decision

9-10.   With respect to the method of translation to be used, Paragraphs 1650.07 and 1650.08 of the *CICA Handbook* explain the basis for its conclusions as follows:

For **Integrated Foreign Operations**, the reporting enterprise's exposure to exchange rate changes is similar to the exposure which would exist had the transactions and activities of the foreign operation been undertaken by the reporting enterprise. Therefore, the financial statements of the foreign operation should be expressed in a manner which is consistent with the measurement of domestic transactions and operations. The translation method which best achieves this objective is the temporal method because it uses the Canadian dollar as the unit of measure.

For **Self-Sustaining Foreign Operations**, the reporting enterprise's exposure to exchange rate changes is limited to its net investment in the foreign operation. Therefore, measuring such operations as if they had carried out their activities in Canadian dollars is considered to be less relevant than measuring the overall effect of changes in the exchange rate on the net investment in such operations. The financial statements of the foreign operation should be expressed in Canadian dollars in a manner which does not change financial results and relationships of the foreign operation. The translation method which best achieves this objective is the current rate method because it uses the currency of the foreign operation as the unit of measure.

Integrated Foreign Operations

9-11.   With respect to the method of translation or unit of measure issue, Section 1650 has adopted the domestic company perspective for integrated foreign operations and the foreign company perspective for self-sustaining foreign operations. This general position is reinforced with specific Recommendations on the translation process. The *CICA Handbook* requires the following translation procedures for integrated foreign operations:

Paragraph 1650.29   *Financial statements of an integrated foreign operation should be translated as follows:*

(a) *Monetary items should be translated into the reporting currency at the rate of exchange in effect at the balance sheet date.*

(b) *Non-monetary items should be translated at historical exchange rates, unless such items are carried at market, in which case they should be translated at the rate of exchange in effect at the balance sheet date.*

(c) *Revenue and expense items should be translated in a manner that produces substantially the same reporting currency amounts that would have resulted had the underlying transactions been translated on the dates they occurred.*

(d) *Depreciation or amortization of assets translated at historical exchange rates should be translated at the same exchange rates as the assets to which they relate.* (July, 1983)

9-12.   While the term is not used in the Recommendation, the preceding rules describe the temporal method of translation.

9-13.   The 1996 Re-Exposure Draft reaches the same conclusions with respect to the method of translation to be used for integrated foreign operations.

Self Sustaining Foreign Operations

9-14.   When a foreign operation has been classified as self sustaining, the *CICA Handbook* requires the following:

Paragraph 1650.33   *Financial statements of a self-sustaining foreign operation should be translated as follows:*

(a) *Assets and liabilities should be translated into the reporting currency at the rate of exchange in effect at the balance sheet date.*

(b) *Revenue and expense items (including depreciation and amortization) should be translated into the reporting currency at the rate of exchange in effect on the dates on which such items are recognized in income during the period.*

Where the economic environment of the foreign operation is highly inflationary relative to that of the reporting enterprise, financial statements should be translated in the manner indicated in paragraph 1650.29. (July, 1983)

9-15.   The preceding requires that, in general, the current rate method be used for translating the financial statements of self-sustaining foreign operations.

9-16.   An exception to this occurs when the self sustaining operation is in a highly inflationary economy. The problem here is that the current rate method of translation uses the foreign currency as the unit of measure. If that currency is rapidly losing value because of a high rate of inflation, it may not be an appropriate unit of measure. As an illustration of this problem, consider the following example:

Example   A self sustaining operation acquires Land for 500,000 Foreign Currency Units (FCU, hereafter) at a time when 1FCU = $1.00. During the following year, the local economy experiences a 1000 percent inflation. As would be expected, the exchange rate falls to 1FCU = $0.10.

9-17.   When the land was acquired, its translated value would have been $500,000 [(FCU500,000)($1.00)]. If we continue to use the current rate method of translation, after one year, the translated value would have fallen to $50,000 [(FCU500,000)($0.10)]. This approach would have introduced a degree of instability into the translated figures that was found unacceptable by the Accounting Standards Board. As a consequence, they require the use of the temporal method for self sustaining operations when they operate in an economic environment that is highly inflationary ("translated in the manner indicated in Paragraph 1650.29"). Stated alternatively, when a foreign currency is subject to high rates of inflation, it is not an appropriate unit of measure and, as a consequence, the Canadian dollar should be used as the unit of measure.

9-18.   The 1996 Re-Exposure Draft reaches the same conclusions with respect to the methods of translation to be used for self sustaining foreign operations, including those that operate in highly inflationary economies.

Translation Adjustments (Exchange Gains And Losses) And Their Allocation To Income

Integrated Foreign Operations

9-19.   With respect to integrated foreign operations, the *Handbook* Recommends the following:

> **Paragraph 1650.31** *Exchange gains and losses arising on the translation of financial statements of an integrated foreign operation should be accounted for in accordance with the Recommendations in paragraphs 1650.20, 1650.23 and 1650.25. (July, 1983)*

9-20.   Without repeating the Recommendations here, we would remind you that Paragraphs 1650.20, 1650.23, and 1650.25 require that, in dealing with foreign currency denominated monetary items with a fixed or ascertainable life extending beyond the end of the following fiscal year, exchange gains and losses that arise must be allocated over the remaining life of the item, with the unamortized deferred balance being shown in the Balance Sheet as a deferred charge or deferred credit.

9-21.   In effect, the Recommendation in Paragraph 1650.31 requires that translation adjustments must be treated as gains and losses to be taken into income either immediately, or deferred and amortized over the remaining life of the asset or liability to which they relate. That is, they will be given the same treatment as translation adjustments resulting from the translation of foreign currency transactions. This is, of course, consistent with the fact that, in the case of integrated foreign operations, there will be an actual exchange of currencies, thereby resulting in real economic benefits and costs.

9-22.   The Recommendations contained in the 1996 Re-Exposure Draft are generally consistent with the Section 1650 Recommendations just presented. There is, however, one important exception. This involves the deferral and amortization of gains and losses on long term foreign currency denominated monetary items. As noted, the deferral and amortization approach is normally required by the current Section 1650. In contrast, the Re-Exposure Draft rejects this approach and requires that, in general, exchange gains and losses be included in income in the year in which they arise. This conclusion is reflected in the combined effect of the following Recommendations:

> **RE-ED Paragraph .052** *Exchange gains and losses arising on the translation of financial statements of an integrated foreign operation should be accounted for in accordance with the Recommendation in paragraph .011.*

> **RE-ED Paragraph .011** *An exchange gain or loss of the reporting entity arising from the translation or settlement of a foreign currency denominated monetary item, or a non monetary item carried at fair value determined in a foreign currency, should be recognized in income as it arises, unless it is deferred in accordance with paragraphs .013, .021 to .023, or .066.* [Note: The exceptions referenced to Paragraph .013, .021, .023, and .066, refer to situations involving either rate regulated enterprises or hedging.]

9-23.   Paragraph RE-ED .011 is applicable to foreign currency transactions and requires that exchange gains and losses be generally included in income in the period in which they arise, without regard to the life of the foreign currency balance to which they relate. Paragraph RE-ED .052 makes this Recommendation applicable to the translation of the foreign currency financial statements of integrated operations, as well as to the translation of the foreign currency transactions. As noted in Chapter 8, this change will make Canadian accounting standards more compatible with those of other countries. In our opinion it will also eliminate a very illogical procedure that is required by current Canadian GAAP.

Self-Sustaining Foreign Operations

9-24. The *CICA Handbook* requires the following treatment of translation adjustments arising on the translation of the financial statements of a self-sustaining foreign operation:

> **Paragraph 1650.36** *Exchange gains and losses arising from the translation of the financial statements of a self-sustaining foreign operation should be deferred and included in a separate component of shareholders' equity, except when the economic environment of the foreign operation is highly inflationary relative to that of the reporting enterprise, in which case such exchange gains and losses would be treated in accordance with the Recommendations in paragraphs 1650.20, 1650.23 and 1650.25. (July, 1983)*

9-25. This Recommendation requires that, in general, translation adjustments which arise in the translation of the foreign currency financial statements of a self sustaining operation be allocated to a separate section of shareholders' equity. While Paragraph 1650.36 still uses the term exchange gain or loss, in effect it requires that translation adjustments not be treated as exchange gains or losses. Adjustments arising from the translation of foreign currency items at current rates are not to be included in current income. Further, they will never be included in income unless the investor company disposes of all or part of its investment in the self sustaining operation, the operation ceases to be a self sustaining operation, or the economy in which it operates becomes highly inflationary. In other words, under normal circumstances, the amounts allocated to this separate component of shareholders' equity will remain there indefinitely.

9-26. As was the case in selecting the translation method to be used for self sustaining foreign operations, a different treatment of translation adjustments is required when the economic environment of the foreign operation is highly inflationary. As was discussed in Chapter 8, the Recommendations in Paragraph 1650.20, 1650.23, and 1650.25 require that translation adjustments be included in income as exchange gains and losses either currently or, when long term monetary items are involved, over the life of the item.

9-27. In general, the 1996 Re-Exposure Draft conclusions on the translation of the financial statements of self sustaining foreign operations are the same as those found in the current Section 1650. As you would expect, however, when the operation is located in a highly inflationary environment, all exchange gains and losses are taken into income immediately, with no use of the deferral and amortization approach.

Cumulative Translation Adjustment Account

9-28. As noted in the preceding Section, translation of the financial statements of a self sustaining foreign operation will usually result in translation adjustments being allocated to a separate shareholders' equity account. This separate component of shareholders' equity is disclosed under a number of different titles in published financial statements. The survey results included in the 1997 edition of *Financial Reporting In Canada* indicate that the most common titles are Cumulative Translation Adjustment and Foreign Currency Translation Adjustment.

9-29. In many cases, this separate component of shareholder's equity will contain a substantial balance. Further, it may be made up of a number of different components (e.g., individual components arising from the translation of different foreign currencies). When this is the case, the *CICA Handbook* requires the following disclosure:

> **Paragraph 1650.39** *Disclosure should be made of the significant elements which give rise to changes in the exchange gains and losses accumulated in the separate component of shareholders' equity during the period. (July, 1983)*

9-30. There is no corresponding Recommendation in the 1996 Re-Exposure Draft.

9-31. As noted in Paragraph 9-25, amounts allocated to this separate component of shareholders' equity will remain there indefinitely. However, where there is a sale of part or all of the reporting enterprise's interest in the foreign operation or a reduction in the shareholders' equity of the foreign operation as the result of a capital transaction, the *CICA Handbook* currently requires the following:

> **Paragraph 1650.38** *An appropriate portion of the exchange gains and losses accumulated in the separate component of shareholders' equity should be included in the determination of net income when there is a reduction in the net investment.* (July, 1983)

9-32. This Recommendation is not consistent with U. S. accounting standards in that it permits a portion of the separate component of shareholders' equity to be taken into income when there is a partial liquidation or other reduction in the domestic company's investment in the self sustaining operation. In contrast, U. S. standards only permit this balance to be taken into income when there is a complete liquidation of the investment position. In order to make Canadian standards more compatible with those of the U. S., the 1996 Re-Exposure Draft makes the following Recommendation:

> **RE-ED Paragraph .063** *Upon sale or upon complete or substantially complete liquidation of an investment in a self sustaining foreign operation, the amount attributable to that operation and that has been accumulated in the separate component of equity should be removed and reported as part of the gain or loss on sale or liquidation of the investment in the period during which the sale or liquidation occurs.*

Hedge Of A Self Sustaining Foreign Operation

9-33. This issue was discussed in Chapter 8 (Paragraphs 8-148 through 8-151). You will recall that, when it is clear that the liability serves as a hedge of a net investment in a foreign operation, Section 1650 of the *CICA Handbook* would offset the translation adjustments on the liability against the corresponding adjustments arising on the translation of the financial statements of the foreign operation. The resulting net adjustment would be included in the separate component of shareholders' equity.

9-34. While they are presented in a more detailed and explicit manner, the Re-Exposure Draft Recommendations are consistent with the Recommendations found in the existing Section 1650.

Example

Basic Data

9-35. In this Section we will demonstrate the procedures to be used for both integrated foreign operations and self-sustaining foreign operations. In addition, when considering the procedures to be used for integrated foreign operations, we will look at the procedures required under the current Section 1650, as well as the procedures required under the Recommendations of the May, 1996 Re-Exposure Draft. In illustrating these situations, a single basic example will be used. This example is as follows:

> On December 31, 1995, the Port Company acquires 100 percent of the outstanding voting shares of the Ship Company for 42.2 million Canadian dollars ($, hereafter). Port Company is a Canadian corporation and Ship Company is a trading company located in Switzerland. On the acquisition date, Ship Company had Common Stock of 20 million Swiss Francs (SF, hereafter) and Retained Earnings of SF32 million. The December 31, 1997 and December 31, 1998 Balance Sheets for the two Companies as well as their Income Statements for the year ending December 31, 1998 are as follows:

Balance Sheets
As At December 31, 1997

	Port ($)	Ship (SF)
Cash	2,000,000	2,000,000
Accounts Receivable	7,600,000	8,000,000
Inventories	30,000,000	40,000,000
Investment In Ship (At Cost)	42,200,000	-0-
Plant And Equipment (Net)	132,000,000	60,000,000
Total Assets	213,800,000	110,000,000
Current Liabilities	43,800,000	6,000,000
Long Term Liabilities	30,000,000	40,000,000
No Par Common Stock	60,000,000	20,000,000
Retained Earnings	80,000,000	44,000,000
Total Equities	213,800,000	110,000,000

Balance Sheets
As At December 31, 1998

	Port ($)	Ship (SF)
Cash	6,800,000	2,000,000
Accounts Receivable	18,800,000	14,000,000
Inventories	56,000,000	54,000,000
Investment In Ship	42,200,000	-0-
Plant And Equipment (Net)	120,000,000	50,000,000
Total Assets	243,800,000	120,000,000
Current Liabilities	49,800,000	4,000,000
Long Term Liabilities	30,000,000	40,000,000
No Par Common Stock	60,000,000	20,000,000
Retained Earnings	104,000,000	56,000,000
Total Equities	243,800,000	120,000,000

Income Statements
For Year Ending December 31, 1998

	Port ($)	Ship (SF)
Sales	390,000,000	150,000,000
Cost Of Goods Sold	340,000,000	120,000,000
Depreciation Expense	12,000,000	10,000,000
Other Expenses	14,000,000	8,000,000
Total Expenses	366,000,000	138,000,000
Net Income	24,000,000	12,000,000

Other Information:

A. On December 31, 1995, the carrying values of all identifiable assets and liabilities of the Ship Company are equal to their fair values.

B. Port Company carries its Investment In Ship at cost. Goodwill is to be amortized over 30 years.

C. Neither the Port Company nor the Ship Company declare or pay dividends during 1998.

D. Ship Company has had no additions to its Plant And Equipment account since December 31, 1995.

E. The Ship Company's Long Term Liabilities were issued at par on December 31, 1993 and mature on December 31, 2003.

F. Exchange rates for the Swiss Franc are as follows:

December 31, 1993	SF1 = $0.60
December 31, 1994	SF1 = $0.70
December 31, 1995	SF1 = $0.80
December 31, 1996	SF1 = $0.75
December 31, 1997	SF1 = $0.90
December 31, 1998	SF1 = $1.00
Average For 1998	SF1 = $0.95

G. The December 31, 1997 Inventories of the Ship Company are acquired when SF1 = $.88 and the December 31, 1998 Inventories are acquired when SF1 = $.99. Both Companies account for their inventories using a FIFO assumption.

H. The 1998 Sales of Ship Company contain SF40 million that are made to Port Company. These goods are resold by Port Company during 1998. As at December 31, 1998, the Port Company owes the Ship Company $1,000,000 and the Ship Company owes the Port Company SF2,000,000. These loans do not bear interest and they are to be repaid in 1999. There are no intercompany loans outstanding as at December 31, 1997.

I. Sales, Purchases, Other Expenses and intercompany sales and purchases take place evenly throughout the year, making the use of average exchange rates appropriate. Both Companies use the straight line method for computing all depreciation and amortization charges.

Integrated Foreign Operations - Current Section 1650

Translated Balance Sheets

9-36. If we assume that the Ship Company is an integrated foreign operation as defined in Section 1650 of the *CICA Handbook*, the translated comparative Balance Sheets as at December 31, 1997 and December 31, 1998 would be as follows:

December 31, 1997 Balance Sheet

	Untranslated	Rate	Translated
Cash	SF 2,000,000	$0.90	$ 1,800,000
Accounts Receivable	8,000,000	$0.90	7,200,000
Inventories	40,000,000	$0.88	35,200,000
Plant And Equipment (Net)	60,000,000	$0.80	48,000,000
Deferred Exchange Loss (Note One)	-0-	N/A	3,642,857
Total Assets	SF110,000,000		$95,842,857
Current Liabilities	SF 6,000,000	$0.90	$ 5,400,000
Long Term Liabilities	40,000,000	$0.90	36,000,000
No Par Common Stock	20,000,000	$0.80	16,000,000
Retained Earnings	44,000,000	N/A	38,442,857
Total Equities	SF110,000,000		$95,842,857

December 31, 1998 Balance Sheet

	Untranslated	Rate	Translated
Cash	SF 2,000,000	$1.00	$ 2,000,000
Accounts Receivable	14,000,000	$1.00	14,000,000
Inventories	54,000,000	$0.99	53,460,000
Plant And Equipment (Net)	50,000,000	$0.80	40,000,000
Deferred Exchange Loss (Note One)	-0-	N/A	6,369,047
Total Assets	SF120,000,000		$115,829,047
Current Liabilities	SF 4,000,000	$1.00	$ 4,000,000
Long Term Liabilities	40,000,000	$1.00	40,000,000
No Par Common Stock	20,000,000	$0.80	16,000,000
Retained Earnings	56,000,000	N/A	55,829,047
Total Equities	SF120,000,000		$115,829,047

Note One   The figures in the preceding Balance Sheets, except for the Deferred Exchange Loss, are derived in an obvious manner. The Ship Company's SF40 million in Long Term Liabilities were issued on December 31, 1993 when SF1 = $.60. However, since we are translating for purposes of preparing consolidated financial statements, this date and exchange rate are not relevant. From the point of view of the consolidated entity these bonds have been outstanding only since December 31, 1995. Therefore, the appropriate rate to use in computing the total exchange gain or loss would be SF1 = $.80 which means that the Long Term Liability would be recorded at $32,000,000 [($0.80)(SF40,000,000)] on December 31, 1995. During 1996 there was an exchange gain of $2,000,000 [(SF40,000,000)($.80 - $.75)] or ($32,000,000 - $30,000,000). Of this amount one-eighth or $250,000 would have been recognized in 1996 and the balance of $1,750,000 would have been shown as a deferred credit in the December 31, 1996 Balance Sheet. The calculations for 1997 and 1998 are as follows:

December 31, 1997 Liability At $.90	$36,000,000
January 1, 1997 Liability ($30,000,000 + $1,750,000)	(31,750,000)
1997 Loss	$ 4,250,000
Charged To 1997 Income (1/7)	(607,143)
December 31, 1997 Deferred Loss (Debit Balance)	$ 3,642,857

December 31, 1998 Liability At $1.00	$40,000,000
January 1, 1998 Liability ($36,000,000 - $3,642,857)	(32,357,143)
1998 Loss	$ 7,642,857
Charged To 1998 Income (1/6)	(1,273,810)
December 31, 1998 Deferred Loss (Debit Balance)	$ 6,369,047

9-37.   We could arrive at these current and deferred losses by amortizing the individual losses or gains which occur in each year. However, the approach illustrated in the preceding calculations will produce the desired information in a much more efficient manner.

Translated Income Statement

9-38.   The 1998 translated Income Statement is as follows:

	Untranslated	Rate	Translated
Sales	SF150,000,000	$0.95	$142,500,000
Opening Inventory	SF 40,000,000	$0.88	$ 35,200,000
Purchases	134,000,000	$0.95	127,300,000
Closing Inventory	(54,000,000)	$0.99	(53,460,000)
Depreciation Expense	10,000,000	$0.80	8,000,000
Other Expenses	8,000,000	$0.95	7,600,000
Exchange Loss (Note Two)	-0-	N/A	473,810
Total Expenses	SF138,000,000		$125,113,810
Net Income	SF 12,000,000		$ 17,386,190

Note Two In addition to the previously calculated loss on the long term monetary liability, there is also an exchange gain on the current monetary items. This gain and the overall net exchange loss for 1998 would be calculated as follows:

Opening Current Net Monetary Assets [(SF4,000,000)($0.90)]	$ 3,600,000
Sales [(SF150,000,000)($.95)]	142,500,000
Purchases [(SF134,000,000)($0.95)]	(127,300,000)
Other Expenses (SF8,000,000 @ $0.95)	(7,600,000)
Computed Closing Current Net Monetary Assets	$ 11,200,000
Actual Closing Current Net Monetary Assets (SF12,000,000 @ $1.00)	(12,000,000)
Exchange Gain On Current Net Monetary Items	($ 800,000)
Exchange Loss On Long Term Liabilities (See Previous Calculations)	1,273,810
Exchange Loss To Be Charged To 1998 Income	($ 473,810)

Integrated Foreign Operations - Re-Exposure Draft

Translated Balance Sheets

9-39.   As previously noted, the Re-Exposure Draft would require that all exchange gains and losses arising on the translation of the financial statements of an integrated foreign operation be included in income as they arise. This means that, in contrast to the financial statements that we have just presented, there would be no deferred exchange gains or losses. Based on the Re-Exposure Draft Recommedations, the Balance Sheets as at December 31, 1997 and December 31, 1998 would be as follows:

December 31, 1997 Balance Sheet

	Untranslated	Rate	Translated
Cash	SF 2,000,000	$0.90	$ 1,800,000
Accounts Receivable	8,000,000	$0.90	7,200,000
Inventories	40,000,000	$0.88	35,200,000
Plant And Equipment (Net)	60,000,000	$0.80	48,000,000
Total Assets	SF110,000,000		$92,200,000
Current Liabilities	SF 6,000,000	$0.90	$ 5,400,000
Long Term Liabilities	40,000,000	$0.90	36,000,000
No Par Common Stock	20,000,000	$0.80	16,000,000
Retained Earnings	44,000,000	N/A	34,800,000
Total Equities	SF110,000,000		$92,200,000

December 31, 1998 Balance Sheet

	Untranslated	Rate	Translated
Cash	SF 2,000,000	$1.00	$ 2,000,000
Accounts Receivable	14,000,000	$1.00	14,000,000
Inventories	54,000,000	$0.99	53,460,000
Plant And Equipment (Net)	50,000,000	$0.80	40,000,000
Total Assets	SF120,000,000		$109,460,000
Current Liabilities	SF 4,000,000	$1.00	$ 4,000,000
Long Term Liabilities	40,000,000	$1.00	40,000,000
No Par Common Stock	20,000,000	$0.80	16,000,000
Retained Earnings	56,000,000	N/A	49,460,000
Total Equities	SF120,000,000		$109,460,000

Translated Income Statement

9-40. As no exchange gains or losses are deferred under the Re-Exposure Draft Recommendations, the resulting gain or loss to be included in income is different than the amount calculated under the current Section 1650 Recommendations. Using this new exchange loss, the 1998 translated Income Statement would be as follows:

	Untranslated	Rate	Translated
Sales	SF150,000,000	$0.95	$142,500,000
Opening Inventory	SF 40,000,000	$0.88	$ 35,200,000
Purchases	134,000,000	$0.95	127,300,000
Closing Inventory	(54,000,000)	$0.99	(53,460,000)
Depreciation Expense	10,000,000	$0.80	8,000,000
Other Expenses	8,000,000	$0.95	7,600,000
Exchange Loss (Note Three)	-0-	N/A	3,200,000
Total Expenses	SF138,000,000		$127,840,000
Net Income	SF 12,000,000		$ 14,660,000

Note Three As there is no deferral of the gains and losses on the long term liabilities under the Re-Exposure Draft Recommendations, the exchange gain or loss calculation is based on all of the monetary items, current and long term. Using this approach, the calculation is as follows:

Opening Net Monetary Liabilities [(SF36,000,000)($0.90)]	($ 32,400,000)
Sales [(SF150,000,000)($0.95)]	142,500,000
Purchases [(SF134,000,000)($0.95)]	(127,300,000)
Other Expenses [(SF8,000,000)($0.95)]	(7,600,000)
Computed Closing Net Monetary Liabilities	($ 24,800,000)
Actual Closing Net Monetary Liabilities [(SF28,000,000)($1.00)]	28,000,000
Exchange Loss	$ 3,200,000

Self-Sustaining Foreign Operation

Translated Financial Statements

9-41. If we assume that the Ship Company is a self-sustaining foreign operation as defined in Section 1650 of the *CICA Handbook*, the Balance Sheets as at December 31, 1997 and December 31, 1998 and the Income Statement for the year ending December 31,

1998, are as follows:

December 31, 1997 Balance Sheet

	Untranslated	Rate	Translated
Cash	SF 2,000,000	$0.90	$ 1,800,000
Accounts Receivable	8,000,000	$0.90	7,200,000
Inventories	40,000,000	$0.90	36,000,000
Plant And Equipment (Net)	60,000,000	$0.90	54,000,000
Total Assets	SF110,000,000		$99,000,000
Current Liabilities	SF 6,000,000	$0.90	$ 5,400,000
Long Term Liabilities	40,000,000	$0.90	36,000,000
No Par Common Stock	20,000,000	$0.80	16,000,000
Cumulative Translation Adjustment	N/A	N/A	3,157,143
Retained Earnings	44,000,000	N/A	38,442,857
Total Equities	SF110,000,000		$99,000,000

December 31, 1998 Balance Sheet

	Untranslated	Rate	Translated
Cash	SF 2,000,000	$1.00	$ 2,000,000
Accounts Receivable	14,000,000	$1.00	14,000,000
Inventories	54,000,000	$1.00	54,000,000
Plant And Equipment (Net)	50,000,000	$1.00	50,000,000
Total Assets	SF120,000,000		$120,000,000
Current Liabilities	SF 4,000,000	$1.00	$ 4,000,000
Long Term Liabilities	40,000,000	$1.00	40,000,000
No Par Common Stock	20,000,000	$0.80	16,000,000
Cumulative Translation Adjustment	N/A	N/A	10,157,143
Retained Earnings	56,000,000	N/A	49,842,857
Total Equities	SF120,000,000		$120,000,000

1998 Income Statement

	Untranslated	Rate	Translated
Sales	SF150,000,000	$.95	$142,500,000
Cost Of Goods Sold	SF120,000,000	$.95	$114,000,000
Depreciation Expense	10,000,000	$.95	9,500,000
Other Expenses	8,000,000	$.95	7,600,000
Total Expenses	SF138,000,000		$131,100,000
Net Income	SF 12,000,000		$ 11,400,000

Cumulative Translation Adjustment

9-42.   Given the information in the problem, it is not possible to calculate the balance that should be included in the Cumulative Translation Adjustment account as at December 31, 1997. We do know that this account, when combined with translated Retained

Earnings, must total $41,600,000 (the amount required to balance assets and equities). However, given the information provided, there is no way of determining the appropriate split between the two accounts. This is a problem that would be encountered by any Canadian enterprise which made the transition to the current rate approach from any other alternative translation method. In this situation, the *CICA Handbook* provides the following guidance:

> **Paragraph 1650.73** The difference arising on translating the assets and liabilities of self-sustaining foreign operations at the current rate as of the commencement of the year for which these Recommendations are first applied would be reported as the opening balance of the exchange gains and losses included in a separate component of shareholders' equity.

9-43. While the meaning of this guidance is not entirely clear, it is our opinion that the intent of the preceding Paragraph 1650.73 is that the opening balance of the Cumulative Translation Adjustment account should be based on the difference between net assets calculated by the current rate method and the equivalent total net assets calculated by the method that was previously in use. Assuming the use of the temporal method prior to December 31, 1997, the shareholders' equity would be the $54,442,857 ($16,000,000 + $38,442,857) calculated using the current Section 1650 Recommendations in the integrated foreign operation example. The December 31, 1997 Cumulative Translation Adjustment would be calculated as follows:

Current Rate Method Shareholders' Equity	
($16,000,000 + $3,157,143 + $38,442,857)	$57,600,000
Temporal Method Shareholders' Equity	(54,442,857)
Opening Cumulative Translation Adjustment	$ 3,157,143

9-44. Once we have established the opening balance, the calculation of the change for the year follows the procedures used to calculate the current exchange gain or loss for integrated foreign operations (see Paragraph 9-40). There is, however, an importance difference. As the temporal method is used for integrated foreign operations, only monetary items and non monetary items carried at current values are translated at current rates. This means that only these items are taken into account in the calculation of the exchange gain or loss for the year. This is reflected in the fact that the schedule in Paragraph 9-40 is based on changes in net monetary items (there are no non monetary items carried at current values in this example).

9-45. In contrast, the statements of self sustaining foreign operations are translated using the current rate method. This means that there will be translation adjustments on all of the assets and liabilities. As you would expect, the calculation of the change in the Cumulative Translation Adjustment account is based on changes in all net assets. The required schedule is as follows:

Opening Net Assets [(SF64,000,000)($.90)]	$ 57,600,000
Sales [(SF150,000,000)($.95)]	142,500,000
Cost Of Goods Sold [(SF120,000,000)($.95)]	(114,000,000)
Depreciation Expense [(SF10,000,000)($.95)]	(9,500,000)
Other Expenses [(SF8,000,000)($.95)]	(7,600,000)
Computed Closing Net Assets	$69,000,000
Actual Closing Net Assets [(SF76,000,000)($1.00)]	(76,000,000)
1998 Increase In The Cumulative Translation Adjustment Balance	($ 7,000,000)

9-46.   In this example, all of the changes in net assets occur uniformly over the year and, as a consequence, average exchange rates can be used. Given this, the computed closing balance could be calculated by translating the change in the net assets of SF12,000,000 (SF76,000,000 - SF64,000,000) by the average rate of $.95. When this $11,400,000 [($0.95)(SF12,000,000)] is added to the translated opening balance of $57,600,000, it gives the Computed Closing Balance of $69,000,000. You should note, however, that this only works when all of the changes in net assets occur uniformly over the year. If one or more of the changes does not satisfy this criteria, for example, a dividend declared at the year end, it will have to be translated at an exchange rate other than the simple average for the year. When this is the case, the more detailed schedular calculation is required.

Consolidated Financial Statements

Investment Analysis

9-47.   We are now in a position to prepare consolidated financial statements for the Port Company and its subsidiary, the Ship Company. These consolidated statements will be based on translation in compliance with the Recommendations of Section 1650 of the *CICA Handbook* for self-sustaining foreign operations.

9-48.   The first step in the process of preparing consolidated financial statements would be to analyze the investment account. This can be done as follows:

Investment Cost	$42,200,000
Translated Book Value At Acquisition [(SF52,000,000)($0.80)]	(41,600,000)
Excess Of Cost Over Book Value	$ 600,000

9-49.   Since there are no fair value changes present on the acquisition date, the entire $600,000 would be allocated to goodwill to be amortized over a period of 30 years at a rate of $20,000 per year.

Consolidated Balance Sheet - December 31, 1997

9-50.   The consolidated Balance Sheet, as at December 31, 1997, would be prepared as follows:

Port Company And Subsidiary
Consolidated Balance Sheet
As At December 31, 1997

Cash ($2,000,000 + $1,800,000)	$ 3,800,000
Accounts And Other Receivables ($7,600,000 + $7,200,000)	14,800,000
Inventories ($30,000,000 + $36,000,000)	66,000,000
Investment in Ship ($42,200,000 - $42,200,000)	-0-
Plant And Equipment ($132,000,000 + $54,000,000)	186,000,000
Goodwill [$600,000 - (2)($20,000)]	560,000
Total Assets	$271,160,000

Current Liabilities ($43,800,000 + $5,400,000)	$ 49,200,000
Long Term Liabilities ($30,000,000 + $36,000,000)	66,000,000
Common Stock - No Par (Port's Only)	60,000,000
Cumulative Translation Adjustment	3,157,143
Retained Earnings (See Verification)	92,802,857
Total Equities	$271,160,000

9-51.   The December 31, 1997 consolidated Retained Earnings balance can be verified with the following calculation:

Port Company's Balance		$80,000,000
Ship Company's Translated Balance	$38,442,857	
Ship's Balance At Acquisition		
[($0.80)(SF32,000,000)]	(25,600,000)	12,842,857
Balance Before Adjustments		$92,842,857
Less Goodwill Amortization [(2)($20,000)]		(40,000)
Balance - December 31, 1997		$92,802,857

Consolidated Balance Sheet - December 31, 1998

9-52.   The consolidated Balance Sheet, as at December 31, 1998, would be prepared as follows:

Port Company And Subsidiary
Consolidated Balance Sheet
As At December 31, 1998

Cash ($6,800,000 + $2,000,000)	$ 8,800,000
Accounts And Other Receivables ($18,800,000	
+ $14,000,000 - $1,000,000 - $2,000,000)	29,800,000
Inventories ($56,000,000 + $54,000,000)	110,000,000
Investment in Ship ($42,200,000 - $42,200,000)	-0-
Plant And Equipment ($120,000,000 + $50,000,000)	170,000,000
Goodwill [$600,000 - (3)($20,000)]	540,000
Total Assets	$319,140,000

Current Liabilities ($49,800,000 + $4,000,000	
- $1,000,000 - $2,000,000)	$ 50,800,000
Long Term Liabilities ($30,000,000 + $40,000,000)	70,000,000
Common Stock - No Par (Port Company's)	60,000,000
Cumulative Translation Adjustment	10,157,143
Retained Earnings (See Verification)	128,182,857
Total Equities	$319,140,000

9-53.   The December 31, 1998 consolidated Retained Earnings balance can be verified with the following calculation:

Port Company's Balance		$104,000,000
Ship Company's Translated Balance	$49,842,857	
Ship's Balance At Acquisition		
[($0.80)(SF32,000,000)]	(25,600,000)	24,242,857
Balance Before Adjustments		$128,242,857
Less Goodwill Amortization [(3)($20,000)]		(60,000)
Balance - December 31, 1998		$128,182,857

Consolidated Income Statement

9-54.   The consolidated Income Statement for the year ending December 31, 1998 would be prepared as follows:

Port Company And Subsidiary
Consolidated Income Statement
Year Ending December 31, 1998

Sales ($390,000,000 + $142,500,000 - [($0.95)(SF40,000,000)]	$494,500,000
Cost Of Goods Sold ($340,000,000 + $114,000,000 - [($0.95)(SF40,000,000)]	$416,000,000
Depreciation Expense ($12,000,000 + $9,500,000)	21,500,000
Other Expenses ($14,000,000 + $7,600,000)	21,600,000
Goodwill Amortization Expense	20,000
Total Expenses	$459,120,000
Net Income	$ 35,380,000

Other Issues

EIC Abstracts

9-55.   There are a number of foreign currency translation issues that have been dealt with by the Emerging Issues Committee (EIC). As many users of this text prefer not to deal with this more detailed material, the content of the relevant EIC Abstracts has not been integrated into the main body of Chapters 8 and 9. However, for users wishing to explore these issues, the Abstracts that are directly relevant to foreign currency translation have been included as a Supplement to this Chapter.

Transactions And Operations Of Foreign Operations Which Are Denominated In Another Currency

9-56.   If a foreign operation of a Canadian company has its own foreign currency transactions or foreign currency operations, it will be necessary to translate these amounts and statements into the currency of the Canadian company's foreign operation using the Recommendations of Section 1650. This could involve using either the temporal or the current rate method, depending on whether the nature of the items and, in the case of a foreign operation with a foreign operation of its own, the classification of this second tier investment. Once this has been accomplished, the Canadian company's foreign operation can be translated into Canadian dollars using either the temporal or current rate method as is appropriate.

Changes In Circumstances Relating To Foreign Operations

9-57.   When a foreign operation is either reclassified from integrated to self sustaining or from self sustaining to integrated, Section 1650 makes the following Recommendation (Paragraph .077 of the CICA Re-Exposure Draft contains an identical Recommendation):

> **Paragraph 1650.43**   *When there are significant changes in the economic facts and circumstances which require the translation method applied to a particular foreign operation to be changed, the change in method should be accounted for prospectively. Disclosure should be made of the reasons for the change in the translation method.* (July, 1983)

9-58.   This means that if the change is from self sustaining to integrated, any previously deferred exchange gains and losses will continue to be deferred and the translated amounts for non monetary items at the end of the period prior to the reclassification will become the historical cost base in the application of the temporal method. Correspondingly, if the change is from integrated to self sustaining, the exchange gain or loss attributable to the current rate translation of non monetary items as of the date of the change would become the balance in the separate component of shareholders' equity.

Investments Accounted For By The Equity Method

9-59.   When an investee is accounted for by the equity method, the investment income that is recorded by the investor company is based on the reported income of the investee (subject to the usual consolidation adjustments). In the case of a foreign investee, the statements will have to be translated prior to the application of the equity method. In such situations, the *CICA Handbook* notes the following:

> **Paragraph 1650.45**   The financial statements of a foreign investee accounted for by the equity method (See "Long-Term Investments," Section 3050) first would be translated into Canadian dollars in accordance with the appropriate Recommendations in this Section; then the equity method would be applied.

9-60.   As the equity method could be applicable to either an integrated or a self sustaining foreign operation, either the temporal or the current rate method may be applicable.

Translation After A Business Combination

9-61.   The acquisition of a foreign investee will normally be classified as a business combination transaction. If the combination is to be treated as a purchase, the rate used to translate non monetary assets and liabilities at subsequent Balance Sheet dates will depend on whether the foreign operation is integrated, in which case the historical rate which prevailed at the date of the business combination will be used, or self-sustaining, in which case the current rate will be used. Note that, regardless of when the foreign operation acquired the assets that are being translated, the historical rate will be the rate which prevailed when the investor acquired the assets (i.e., the business combination date).

9-62.   In general, the same type of analysis would apply where the business combination transaction is classified as a pooling of interests. The only difference would be that when the use of historical rates is required, the rates should be based on the rate which prevailed on the date the asset was acquired or the liability assumed by the investee company. However, as a practical expedient, the use of the rates on the date of the combination would be considered acceptable.

Intercompany Balances

Integrated Foreign Operations

9-63.   It is not uncommon for intercompany asset and liability balances to arise between a domestic investor company and its foreign investees. In such cases, translation of the foreign currency balance will usually result in translation adjustments and this, of course, raises the question of what is the appropriate treatment of these balances. With respect to balances related to integrated foreign operations, the *CICA Handbook* suggests the following:

> **Paragraph 1650.57**   With respect to integrated foreign operations, exchange gains and losses relating to intercompany balances recorded by the reporting enterprise or the foreign operation will be treated in the same manner as those relating to other foreign currency receivables or payables in accordance with the Recommendations in paragraphs 1650.20, 1650.23 and 1650.25 (i.e, the amounts will be treated as exchange gains or losses to be taken into income immediately or deferred and amortized).

9-64.   The 1996 Re-Exposure Draft provides further guidance in this area, noting exchange gains or losses on intercompany balances between an integrated foreign operation and the reporting entity will be eliminated when the financial statements of the foreign operation are consolidated with those of the reporting entity.

Self Sustaining Foreign Operations

9-65.   The situation is more complex when a self sustaining foreign operation is involved. In this case, the *CICA Handbook* distinguishes between ordinary intercompany balances (e.g., those arising on intercompany sales of merchandise), as opposed to intercompany balances that form part of the net investment (e.g., a holding of the foreign investee's redeemable preferred shares). Based on this distinction, the following guidance is provided:

> **Paragraph 1650.58**   With respect to self-sustaining foreign operations, exchange gains and losses on intercompany account balances that are not included as part of the net investment would be treated in the same manner as those relating to normal foreign currency trade balances in accordance with the appropriate Recommendations of this Section (i.e., taken into income currently or deferred and amortized). Exchange gains and losses on intercompany account balances that form part of the net investment would be deferred and included in the separate component of shareholders' equity in accordance with paragraph 1650.36 (Paragraph 1650.36 requires allocation to a separate shareholders' equity section).

9-66.   The 1996 Re-Exposure Draft guidance is generally consistent with the current Section 1650. However, additional guidance is provided as follows:

> **Paragraph RE-ED .086**   Exchange gains and losses on the reporting entity's intercompany balances with a self sustaining foreign operation are not eliminated when the financial statements of the foreign operation are consolidated with those of the reporting entity. The exchange gain or loss arising from the translation of the financial statements of the self sustaining foreign operation into the measurement currency of the reporting entity is included in the separate component of equity established in accordance with paragraph .054. The exchange gain or loss on the reporting entity's intercompany balances remains in the income statement of the reporting entity on consolidation.

Elimination Of Intercompany Profits

9-67.   The issue here is related to the elimination of intercompany profits resulting from transactions between a reporting entity and a foreign investee. Specifically, it must be decided whether to make the elimination using the exchange rate which prevailed at the date of the transaction or, alternatively, use the rate which prevails at the balance sheet date. For integrated foreign operations the answer is clearly the use of the transaction date rate. Somewhat surprisingly, the Accounting Standards Board concludes that this is also the most appropriate rate for self sustaining operations. Note that this will require that the transaction date rate also be used for any subsequent realization of unrealized profits that have been previously eliminated. The 1996 Re-Exposure Draft also Recommends this approach.

Differences In Financial Statement Dates

9-68.   It can often happen that a foreign investee will date its financial statements at a different point in time than those of the domestic investor. When this happens, Paragraph 1650.60 provides the following guidance:

> **Paragraph 1650.60**   When the date of the financial statements of the foreign operation differs from that of the reporting enterprise, those assets and liabilities which are translated at the current rate would normally be translated at the rate in effect at the balance sheet date of the foreign operation, not at the rate in effect at the balance sheet date of the reporting enterprise. When there is a major change in exchange rates between the balance sheet dates of the foreign operation and the reporting enterprise, the effect of the change would be disclosed.

9-69.   The 1996 Re-Exposure Draft contains an identical Recommendation in Paragraph RE-ED .098.

Non Controlling Interest

9-70.   In preparing consolidated financial statements, one or more foreign subsidiaries may have a non controlling interest. In this situation, the *CICA Handbook* indicates the following:

> **Paragraph 1650.62**   The non-controlling interest reported in an enterprise's consolidated financial statements would be based on the financial statements of the foreign operation in which there is a non-controlling interest after they have been translated according to the Recommendations in this Section. In particular, the non-controlling interest reported would include the non-controlling interest's proportionate share of exchange gains and losses.

9-71.   Paragraph RE-ED .088 of the 1996 Re-Exposure Draft contains identical guidance in this situation.

Preference Shares

9-72.   With respect to the treatment of preference shares in translation, the *CICA Handbook* states the following:

> **Paragraph 1650.63**   Preference shares of a foreign operation held by the reporting enterprise would be translated in the same manner as common shares (i.e., at historical rates) unless redemption is either required or imminent, in which case the current rate would be used. Preference shares held by non-controlling shareholders in an integrated foreign operation would also be translated at historical rates unless redemption is either required or imminent, in which case the current rate would be used. Preference shares held by non-controlling shareholders in a self-sustaining foreign operation would be translated at the current rate. (Where the economic environment of a self-sustaining foreign operation is highly inflationary, the preference shares of the foreign operation would be translated in the same manner as preference shares of integrated foreign operations.)

9-73.   The 1996 Re-Exposure Draft refers to Section 3860 of the *CICA Handbook*, "Financial Instruments - Disclosure And Presentation". In simple terms, this Section requires redeemable preferred shares to be classified as debt. With respect to preferred shares of integrated foreign operations, they would be translated at current or historic rates, depending on whether they are classified as debt or equity financial instruments.

9-74.   This classification would not influence the rate to be used for preferred shares issued by self sustaining foreign operations as both debt and equity instruments outstanding would be translated using the current rate. However, the Re-Exposure Draft notes that preference shares of self sustaining operations that are held by the reporting entity would be included as part of the net investment balance. This means that they would be translated at historic rates.

Application Of Lower Of Cost And Market

9-75.   The exchange rate used to translate assets of an integrated foreign operation is dependent on the basis of their valuation in the foreign currency financial statements. If they are valued at cost, historical rates will be applicable while if they are valued at market or some other measure of current value, current exchange rates will be used.

9-76.   This would be relevant in the application of lower of cost and market to the problem of inventory valuation. As a result, the translation process may result in the need to write down translated values even when there has been no write down in the foreign currency statements. For example, assume that a German subsidiary has inventories purchased for 1,000,000 Deutsche Marks (DM, hereafter) when the exchange rate was DM1 = $.85. At the Balance Sheet date, these inventories have a market value of DM1,100,000. There is clearly no need to write down the Deutsche Mark value as the market exceeds the cost. However, if we assume that the Balance Sheet date exchange rate has fallen to DM1 = $.75, the translated market value would be $825,000. As this would be lower than the translated cost of $850,000, the market figure would be used.

9-77. It is also possible for the opposite situation to occur. That is, it may be necessary in the translated financial statements to reverse a write down which has occurred in the foreign currency statements. In addition, Section 1650 notes that once an asset has been written down to market in the translated financial statements, that dollar amount would continue to be the carrying amount in the translated financial statements until the asset is sold or a further write down is required.

Deferred Income Taxes

Section 3470

9-78. When a foreign investee has been classified as an integrated foreign operation, there is some question as to whether deferred taxes should be treated as a monetary or a non monetary item. However, in view of the fact that Section 3470 of the *CICA Handbook* adopts the deferred charge approach to interperiod tax allocation, it seems that the required solution is to treat deferred taxes as non monetary. This is reflected in Paragraph 1650.68 as follows:

> **Paragraph 1650.68** The exchange rate adopted to translate deferred income taxes of an integrated foreign operation will depend on the method of calculation of deferred taxes adopted in the financial statements of the foreign operation. When separate computations are made for the tax effect of originating and reversing timing differences, historical rates in effect at the time deferred taxes were set up (i.e., the average exchange rate for the fiscal period) will be applied. When a single computation is made for the net effect of both originating and reversing differences:
>
> (a) the average exchange rate for the fiscal period will be applied with respect to any increase in deferred taxes;
>
> (b) the composite exchange rate at the beginning of the year will be applied with respect to any decrease in deferred taxes.

9-79. For self-sustaining foreign operations the deferred tax balances, along with all other assets and liabilities, would be translated at current exchange rates.

9-80. The guidance found in the 1996 Re-Exposure Draft, "Foreign Currency Translation", takes the same approach to deferred income taxes as the current Section 1650.

Section 3465

9-81. In December, 1997, Section 3465, "Income Taxes", was added to the *CICA Handbook*. This new Section rejects the deferral approach to tax allocation in favour of the future tax asset/liability approach. As the resulting tax allocation balances will be monetary assets and liabilities, they will be translated at current exchange rates. This would be the case for balances on the books of either integrated or self sustaining foreign operations.

Statement Of Changes In Financial Position

9-82. There are a number of problems which arise in the translation of the Statement Of Changes In Financial Position of a self-sustaining foreign operation. Paragraph 1650.69 of the *CICA Handbook* offers guidance on the following points:

(a) Cash from operations would be translated at the exchange rate at which the respective items are translated for income statement purposes.

(b) Other items would be translated at exchange rates in effect when the related transactions took place.

(c) The effect of subsequent exchange rate changes on the cash flows during the period and on cash and cash equivalents at the commencement of the period would be disclosed, so that cash and cash equivalents at the end of the period are translated at the exchange rate in effect on that date.

9-83.   The guidance found in the 1996 Re-Exposure Draft retains the preceding suggestions. In addition, one further item is added in Paragraph RE-ED .097:

(d) the effect of exchange rate changes on cash and cash equivalents held at the commencement of the period are disclosed as a separate part of the reconciliation of the change in cash and cash equivalents, so that cash and cash equivalents at the end of the period are translated at the exchange rate in effect on that date.

Disclosure And Financial Statement Presentation

Current Section 1650

9-84.   The disclosure requirements of Section 1650 of the *CICA Handbook* are not extensive. We have already noted the only specific recommendations found in this Section. These are Paragraph 1650.39's requirement for disclosure of significant elements which give rise to changes in the exchange gains and losses accumulated in the separate component of shareholders' equity, and Paragraph 1650.43's requirement that disclosure be made of the reasons for any change in translation methods used for foreign operations. One other disclosure guideline is included in the *CICA Handbook*:

Paragraph 1650.44   It is desirable to disclose the amount of exchange gain or loss included in income.

9-85.   It is somewhat surprising that in an area as complex as foreign currency translation, more disclosure requirements were not included in the Recommendations of the Accounting Standards Board.

Re-Exposure Draft

9-86.   The disclosure requirements of Section 1650 could be significantly expanded by the Recommendations contained in the 1996 Re-Exposure Draft. With respect to exchange gains and losses to be included in income, the Re-Exposure Draft contains the following Recommendation:

RE-ED Paragraph .101   *An entity should disclose the net amount of exchange gains and losses included in each of:*

(a) income or loss before discontinued operations and extraordinary items;
(b) the results of discontinued operations; and
(c) extraordinary items.

9-87.   As the Re-Exposure Draft no longer Recommends the deferral and amortization of gains and losses on long term monetary items, additional disclosure is required with respect to amounts of such gains and losses that are unrealized:

RE-ED Paragraph .103   *An entity should disclose the net amount of unrealized exchange gains and losses on long term monetary assets and liabilities, unless the necessary financial information is not reasonably determinable.*

9-88.　Disclosure of deferred amounts of exchange gains and losses is covered as follows:

> **RE-ED Paragraph .106**　*An entity should disclose the net amount of exchange gains and losses that have been deferred in accordance with the Recommendations in paragraph .013 and the basis on which they will be recognized in income.*

9-89.　RE-ED Paragraph .013 allows the deferral of certain exchange gains and losses of regulated enterprises.

9-90.　A further Re-Exposure Draft Recommendation covers the Balance Sheet disclosure of amounts of exchange gains and losses that have been deferred:

> **RE-ED Paragraph .094**　*The balance of any deferred exchange gains and losses of the reporting entity should be reported in the balance sheet as a deferred charge or as a deferred credit.*

9-91.　With respect to the currencies used for measurement and display, the Re-Exposure Draft contains the following Recommendation:

> **RE-ED Paragraph .110**　*An entity should disclose:*
>
> *(a)　the measurement currency of the reporting entity if the measurement currency of the reporting entity is not the Canadian dollar;*
> *(b)　the measurement currency and the display currency of the reporting entity if they are not the same currency.*

9-92.　A final disclosure Recommendation covers the exchange gains and losses of self sustaining operations. It is as follows:

> **RE-ED Paragraph .112**　*An entity should disclose:*
>
> *(a)　the nature of the exchange gains and losses accumulated in the separate component of equity established in accordance with paragraph .054;　and*
> *(b)　the items that gave rise to changes in that separate component of equity during the period.*

Current Canadian Practices

Statistics From Financial Reporting In Canada

9-93.　Section 1650 leaves few alternatives in its application. Integrated operations and foreign currency transactions must be translated using the temporal method and self sustaining operations must be translated using the current rate method. Given this lack of alternatives in the translation of foreign currency statements and transactions, the 1997 edition of *Financial Reporting In Canada* does not present a significant amount of data in this area.

9-94.　Of the 200 public companies included in the survey, 19 companies present their 1996 statements in U. S. dollars. Reasons for this include the fact that the enterprise does most of its business in that country, and/or the fact that the securities of the enterprise are traded on U. S. stock exchanges.

9-95.　Paragraph 1650.23 requires that exchange gains and losses on long term monetary items be deferred and amortized. The 1996 data indicates that 87 of the 200 survey companies disclosed deferred exchange gains or losses. However, for the majority of these companies, the only disclosure was a reference in the statement on accounting policies. On the 87 companies disclosing deferred exchange gains or losses, 29 indicated the method of amortization, while 52 indicated only that they were being amortized over their service lives.

9-96.　With respect to self sustaining foreign operations, Section 1650 requires that exchange gains and losses be deferred and included in a separate section of Shareholders'

Equity. A total of 99 companies disclosed such a section, of which 32 referred to it as a "cumulative translation adjustment" and 28 designated the balance a "foreign currency translation adjustment". A wide variety of other terminology was used. Paragraph 1650.39 requires that disclosure be made of significant elements which gave rise to changes in this Shareholders' Equity balance. Such disclosure was made by 24 companies.

9-97.   Paragraph 1650.44 notes that it is desirable to disclose the amount of exchange gain or loss that is included in income. This disclosure was provided by only 17 of the survey companies.

Examples From Practice

9-98.   Disclosure related to foreign currency translation is found either in the statement of accounting policies or, alternatively, in a note to the financial statements. Our first example is from the 1996 annual report of Quebecor Inc. and illustrates both of these forms of disclosure:

Summary Of Significant Accounting Policies (In Part)

Foreign currency translation

Net assets of self-sustaining foreign operations are translated using the current rate method. Adjustments arising from this translation are deferred and recorded as a separate item under shareholders' equity and are included in income only when a reduction in the investment in these foreign operations is realized. Gains or losses on foreign currency balances and transactions that are designated as hedges of a net investment in self-sustaining foreign operations are offset against exchange losses or gains included in the separate item under shareholders' equity.

As of the moment they are identified as a hedge for long-term monetary liabilities, exchange gains or losses realized on a foreign currency future revenue stream are offset against the corresponding losses or gains on the hedged items.

Other foreign currency transactions entered into by the Company are translated using the temporal method. Translation gains and losses are included in income except for unrealized gains and losses arising from the translation of long-term monetary assets and liabilities which are deferred and amortized on the straight-line basis over the remaining life of the related items.

Notes To Financial Statements

Note 10   Translation Adjustment (Referenced From The Balance Sheet)

(dollar amounts are expressed in thousands)	1996	1995
Balance at beginning	$31,435	$44,432
Effect of exchange rate variation on translation of net assets of self-sustaining foreign operations	(3,865)	(9,263)
Effect of exchange rate variation on translation of items designated as hedges of net investments in self-sustaining foreign operations, net of income taxes of $ 3 ($ 951 in 1995)	7	1,569
Portion included in income as a result of reductions in net investments in self-sustaining foreign operations	(431)	(5,303)
Balance at end	$27,146	$31,435

Note 13 Financial Expenses (Referenced From The Income Statement)

	1996	1995	1994
Interest on long-term debt	$160,452	$125,841	$57,433
Interest on bank indebtedness	4,787	8,709	3,808
Investment income	(9,356)	(24,417)	(5,934)
Amortization of deferred exchange losses	2,319	2,336	2,958
Other	2,544	3,292	(2,457)
	160,746	115,761	55,808
Interest capitalized to the cost of fixed assets	(6,308)	(6,918)	(2,348)
	$154,438	$108,843	$53,460

9-99.   While translation procedures are not necessarily involved, another increasingly common form of disclosure in this area involves a reconciliation of income reported under Canadian GAAP with that reported under U. S. GAAP. An example of this is found in the 1996 annual report of Jannock Limited:

Notes To Financial Statements

Note 12   The Effect of Applying U.S. Generally Accepted Accounting Principles

These consolidated financial statements have been prepared in Canadian dollars, in accordance with generally accepted accounting principles in Canada (Cdn. GAAP) which conform in all material respects with those in the United States (U.S. GAAP) except as follows:

(a) Income Taxes

The Corporation adopted, for U.S. GAAP reporting purposes, Financial Accounting Standard No. 109, "Accounting for Income Taxes" effective January 1, 1993 and the cumulative effect was charged to earnings in 1993. This Standard requires the use of the asset and liability method of accounting for income taxes, whereas the deferral method of accounting for income taxes is used under Cdn. GAAP. The cumulative effect as at December 31, 1996 amounted to a $3.1 million decrease in retained earnings.

(b) Post-Retirement Benefits Other than Pensions

The Corporation presents the adoption, for U.S. GAAP reporting purposes, of Financial Accounting Standard No. 106, "Employers' Accounting for Post-Retirement Benefits Other than Pensions" effective January 1, 1995. This requires the projected future cost of providing post-retirement benefits, such as health care costs and life insurance, to be recognized as an expense as employees render services instead of when paid. The effect for 1996 of adopting this accounting method would be a charge to earnings of $1.0 million ($0.6 million after tax). The cumulative effect of adopting this accounting method as at December 31, 1995 would have amounted to $13.9 million ($8.3 million after tax) and would have been charged to earnings in that year.

Statement Of Earnings Effect

The following table reconciles net earnings for the years as reported in the accompanying consolidated statements of earnings to net earnings that would have been reported had the financial statements been prepared in accordance with U.S. GAAP.

(millions of Canadian dollars)	1996	1995
Net earnings for the year under Cdn. GAAP	50.7	19.7
U.S. GAAP		
Taxes (a)	-	-
Post retirement benefits (b)	(0.6)	(8.3)
Net earnings for the year under U.S. GAAP	50.1	11.4
Earnings per share under U.S. GAAP	1.63	0.33
Earnings per share under Cdn. GAAP	1.65	0.61

Balance Sheets Effect

The following table presents the balance sheet amounts in accordance with U.S. GAAP that are different from the amounts reported under Cdn. GAAP.

(millions of Canadian dollars)	1996	1995
Accounts payable and accrued liabilities	197.2	155.2
Deferred income taxes	1.1	4.1
Retained earnings	162.3	128.8

(c) Cash Flow

The definition of cash and equivalents under U.S. GAAP does not include short-term investments with an initial term of greater than 90 days, or current bank loans and overdrafts. Also, under U.S. GAAP $1.1 million of debt assumed on acquisitions in 1996 (1995 - $1.2 million) would be treated as a non-cash investing and financing activity. These would have the following effect on the consolidated statements of changes in financial position:

(millions of Canadian dollars)	1996	1995
Financing activities		
Decrease in short-term investments	-	-
Decrease in bank indebtedness	(17.5)	(6.3)
Decrease in issue of long-term debt	(1.1)	(1.2)
	(18.6)	(7.5)
Investing activities		
Decrease in debt assumed on acquisition	1.1	1.2
	(17.5)	(6.3)

Had the consolidated statement of changes in financial position been prepared in accordance with U.S. GAAP, cash used for financing activities in 1996 would have been $58.8 million (1995 - cash provided of $27.9 million) and cash used for investing activities would have been $51.2 million (1995 - $80.2 million). Cash and equivalents under U.S. GAAP at December 31, 1996 would be $10.7 million (1995 - $7.8 million).

(d) Joint Ventures

As permitted by the Securities and Exchange Commission, the effects of applying proportionate consolidation for joint ventures are not presented. Information related to joint ventures is set out in Note 4.

(e) Stock Based Compensation

Stock-based compensation is measured using the intrinsic value-based method of accounting under which compensation cost is the excess, if any, of the quoted market price of the stock at grant date or other measurement date over the amount an employee must pay to acquire the stock.

Supplement To Chapter Nine - Other Emerging Issues Committee Abstracts

EIC Abstract No. 3 - Mid Term Hedging

9-100.   Abstract No. 3, "Mid Term Hedging Of A Long Term Foreign Currency Denominated Monetary Item" deals with situations where an enterprise has a long term foreign currency denominated asset or liability that has been outstanding for at least one period and, in accordance with *CICA Handbook* Recommendations, gains and losses are being deferred and amortized on a rational and systematic basis. If the enterprise enters into another foreign currency transaction which fully hedges the original transaction to its maturity date, there will be no further net gains or losses to be recognized on the long term monetary item. However, the question remains as to whether the enterprise should continue to defer and amortize any gain or loss accumulated to the date on which the monetary item was hedged.

9-101.   The consensus reached by the Committee is that the enterprise should continue to defer and amortize any accumulated translation gains or losses over the period that the long term monetary item is outstanding. While the presence of the hedge will eliminate future gains or losses, it has no effect on gains or losses that have occurred prior to its establishment. As a result, the treatment of the accumulated gains or losses should not be altered by the introduction of a hedging instrument.

EIC Abstract No. 11 - Changes In Reporting Currency

9-102.   There are circumstances under which an enterprise will change its reporting currency (currency of display), most commonly from using the domestic currency as the unit of measure (temporal method) to using the foreign currency as the unit of measure (current rate method). When this happens, there is a need to restate the comparative figures for earlier years into statements which use the foreign currency as the unit of display. In considering this problem, the Emerging Issues Committee notes that there are two approaches to this restatement process:

- The enterprise can retroactively restate the prior years' figures as if the foreign currency had always been the currency of display and measurement.

- The prior years' figures can be recast in the foreign currency while retaining the domestic currency as the currency of measurement in the prior years. This is accomplished through a "translation of convenience" whereby amounts appearing for prior years are restated from the domestic to the foreign currency using the exchange rate prevailing at the end of the last period for which the domestic currency was the currency of measurement and display.

9-103.   The term "translation of convenience" is, to our knowledge, a new term that has been introduced in this EIC Abstract. While the Abstract does not contain any examples to illustrate this procedure, it would appear to be the type of procedure suggested in the *CICA Handbook*'s discussion of transitional problems (Paragraphs 1650.70 through 1650.73). This procedure is illustrated in our example of the procedures to be used in the translation of self sustaining foreign operations.

9-104.   The two specific issues dealt with in EIC Abstract No. 11, "Changes In The Reporting Currency", along with the consensus reached by the Committee, are as follows:

Issue One   Which method should be used to present the comparative figures if the entity changes both the currency of display and the currency of measurement in the current period?

Consensus On Issue One   The Committee notes that when a change is necessitated by events or transactions that are clearly different from those previously occurring, it is not considered to be an accounting change (see *CICA Handbook* Paragraph 1506.04, "Accounting Changes"). Given this, they conclude that there should not be a retroactive restatement of previous years' statements. Rather, the comparative figures should be developed using the previously described translation of convenience approach. This would apply, for example, when the change in reporting currency resulted from a change in a subsidiary's operations which required a change in its classification from integrated to self sustaining.

Alternatively, where the change in the currency of measurement is made for reasons other than a change in circumstances, comparative statements should be prepared on a retroactive basis. This would apply, for example, if the enterprise had been erroneously using the temporal approach and was required by its auditors to switch to the current rate method.

Issue Two   Should a different method be used if in the current period there has only been a change in the currency of display, but not in the currency of measurement?

Consensus On Issue Two   On this issue, the Committee concluded that comparative figures should be developed using the translation of convenience approach. When there has been no change in the currency of measurement of the operations of the entity or the subsidiary, retroactive restatement would be inappropriate since it results in a re-measurement of income and the net investment in the foreign operation. The Committee could not differentiate this situation from the first issue in that previously issued financial statements should not be re-measured for a change in circumstances occurring in the current period.

9-105.   The Committee also notes in the Abstract that whenever a change in reporting currency is made, there should be full disclosure of the nature of the change and its effect on the financial statements.

EIC Abstract No. 16 - Long Term Debt Facilities

9-106.   Companies that borrow funds in foreign currencies may have a long term "debt facility" arranged with a financial institution. These financial arrangements or "debt facilities" may have some of the following characteristics:

- The actual borrowings are evidenced by short term obligations which are rolled over. Specific types of debt include bankers' acceptances, short term promissory notes, or commercial paper. The borrower may be allowed to select the particular form of the debt.

- The facility may extend over a period of years, during which the borrower has a guaranteed right to roll over the short term obligations.

- The facility may contain a variety of interest rate options.

- The facility may contain fixed repayment terms, with either serial reductions in the balance outstanding or with a balloon payment at maturity. Alternatively, it may specify declining targets for the the maximum amount which may be outstanding with a separate formula for yearly payments.

- The facility may permit the borrower to switch from one currency to another.

- The facility may be revolving with a maximum limit on the amount borrowed at any one time allowing the borrower to temporarily reduce the amount outstanding while retaining the right to borrow up to the maximum in the future.

9-107.   These arrangements raise several issues with respect to the deferral and amortization of gains or losses on long term monetary items. The issues considered by the Emerging Issues Committee in Abstract No. 16, "Short Term Foreign Currency Obligations

Under Long Term Debt Facilities", along with their consensus on each issue, are as follows:

Issue One   Can foreign exchange gains and losses be deferred and amortized on short term obligations issued under a debt facility arrangement?

Consensus On Issue One   The Committee concluded that short term obligations have a fixed or ascertainable life extending beyond the end of the following fiscal year, provided they are issued under a debt facility that is a committed one. A committed debt facility is one in which the lender cannot unilaterally cancel the facility prior to its scheduled maturity unless the borrower has violated its terms. This means that foreign exchange gains or losses on short term obligations issued under a committed long term debt facility would qualify for deferral and amortization.

Issue Two   As noted, the debt facility may permit the borrower to elect to change the currency in which funds are borrowed. When such a change occurs, does it result in a settlement of the debt for purposes of determining whether it is appropriate to continue the deferral of any unamortized foreign exchange gains and losses?

Consensus On Issue Two   The Committee concluded a change in the borrowing currency should be viewed as settlement of the debt existing in the old borrowing currency, combined with an issue of debt in the new borrowing currency. The basis for this view is that such changes in the borrowing currency may constitute a significant change in the borrowing company's exposure to risk. It follows from this conclusion that any deferred gains and losses resulting from debt that was issued in the old borrowing currency must be included in the income of the period in which the change in the borrowing currency takes place.

Issue Three   In some situations a company may repay a portion of the foreign currency borrowings while retaining, under the terms of the debt facility, the right to fully draw on the facility in the future. The issue is whether there has been a settlement of the debt in the amount of the reduction in the borrowings.

Consensus On Issue Three   The Committee concluded that repayment of a portion of the outstanding borrowings, regardless of the terms of the debt facility, constitute a partial settlement of the debt obligation. Given this, a proportionate amount of any deferred exchange gain or loss relating to the overall obligation must be included in income in the period in which the repayment occurs.

EIC Abstract No. 17 - Debt With Contractual Terms

9-108.   There are situations in which the period over which a debt balance is being amortized extends beyond the debt maturity. For example, a debt obligation might call for repayment at the rate of 5 percent per year (amortization over 20 years) while maturing after 10 years. While repayment of such debt at maturity would require a large balloon payment in the year of maturity, it is usually the intention of the borrower to refinance the unamortized balance at the end of the contractual term of the debt. The issue that arises in such situations is whether foreign exchange gains and losses on the debt should be amortized over the contractual term of the debt or, alternatively, over the intended repayment period.

9-109.   The Emerging Issues Committee concluded in Abstract No. 17, "Deferral And Amortization Of Foreign Exchange Gains And Losses On Debt With Contractual Terms That Differ From The Intended Repayment Period" that the amortization should be limited to the contractual term of the debt. Their defence of this position is with reference to Paragraph 1650.22 of the *CICA Handbook* which states that where the remaining life of a debt obligation is only ascertainable within prescribed limits, the exchange gain or loss should be amortized over the minimum period to settlement. In the situation described here, this would be the contractual term of the debt, without regard to intentions for re-payment.

EIC Abstract No. 26 - Reductions In Net Investment In Self Sustaining Operations

9-110.   When a foreign operation is classified as self sustaining, exchange gains and losses arising from the translation of its statements are deferred and included in a separate component of Shareholders' Equity. When the foreign operation incurs a significant loss or it becomes necessary to write down its assets, there is a question as to the appropriate treatment of these deferred exchange gains and losses. Specifically, this Abstract deals with the issue of whether some portion of the exchange gains and losses accumulated in the separate component of Shareholders' Equity should be included in the determination of Net Income when the foreign operation records a write down of its assets or incurs a significant loss.

9-111.   In the Abstract, the Emerging Issues Committee concludes that an asset write down or significant loss in the financial statements of a foreign operation should not cause a portion of deferred exchange gains and losses to be included in the determination of Net Income. They note that Section 1650 requires the inclusion of these deferred exchange gains and losses in income only when there is a reduction in the net investment in the self sustaining operation (Paragraph 1650.38). While a write down or a significant loss may occur together with a sale of part or all of the interest in the foreign operation, it is the sale, rather than the write down or loss, that results in a reduction in the net investment.

Problems For Self Study

(The solutions for these problems can be found following Chapter 17 of the text.)

SELF STUDY PROBLEM NINE - 1

Investco Ltd. is a Canadian real estate and property developer which decided to hold a parcel of land in downtown Munich, West Germany, for speculative purposes. The land, costing DM12,000,000 (deutsche marks) was financed by a five-year bond (DM9,000,000), which is repayable in deutsche marks, and an initial equity injection by Investco of DM3,000,000. These transactions took place on January 1, 1998, at which time a German subsidiary company was created to hold the investment.

Investco plans to sell the land at the end of five years and use the deutsche mark proceeds to pay off the bond. In the interim, rent is being collected from another company which is using the land as a parking lot. Rental revenue is collected and interest and other expenses are paid at the end of each month. The 1998 year end draft financial statements of the German subsidiary company are as follows:

Income Statement
For The Year Ended December 31, 1998

Rental Revenue	DM	1,000,000
Interest Expense		(990,000)
Other Expenses		(10,000)
Net Income	DM	- 0 -

Balance Sheet
As At December 31, 1998

Cash	DM	- 0 -
Land		12,000,000
Total Assets	DM	12,000,000
Bond (Due December 31, 2002)	DM	9,000,000
Common Stock		3,000,000
Total Equities	DM	12,000,000

Assume the exchange rates were as follows:

January 1, 1998	1 DM = $.75
December 31, 1998	1 DM = $.85
Average, 1998	1 DM = $.80

Required:

A. Prepare the translated 1998 income statements and balance sheets at December 31, 1998, following Canadian generally accepted accounting principles and assuming:

   i) the German subsidiary is an integrated foreign operation as defined in Section 1650 of the *CICA Handbook*; and

   ii) the German subsidiary is a self-sustaining foreign operation as defined in Section 1650.

B. Which translation method better reflects Investco's economic exposure to exchange rate movements? Explain.

C. Which translation method would Investco be required to use? Explain.

D. Assume that, instead of incorporating a West German subsidiary, Investco carries the investment (land, debt, etc.) directly on its own books. Some accountants would argue that it is inappropriate to reflect any portion of an unrealized exchange gain or loss on the bond in the 1998 income statement because the land serves as an effective hedge. Explain the reasoning behind this position. Would this approach be acceptable? Explain.

(SMA Adapted)

SELF STUDY PROBLEM NINE - 2

Sentex Limited of Montreal, Quebec, has an 80% owned subsidiary, Cellular Company Inc., which operates in Erewhon, a small country located in Central America. Cellular was formed on January 1, 1998 by Sentex and Erewhon Development Inc. which is located in Erewhon. Advantages to Sentex of locating in Erewhon are: easy access to raw materials, low operating costs, government incentives, and the fact that the plastics market of Erewhon is not well developed. All management, including the Chief Operating Officer, Mr. V. Globe, has been appointed by Sentex. Top management of Cellular is paid directly by Sentex.

Cellular makes plastic coatings from petrochemical feedstock purchased form Mexico. The process is automated but still uses significant amounts of native Erewhonese labour. The government of Erewhon has determined that this type of development is good for the country, and has underwritten 22,000 cuzos (local currency of Erewhon) of staff training expenses in 1998 by reducing the taxes payable by Cellular. This employment assistance is not expected to continue in the future.

Approximately 75% of total sales by Cellular is made to Sentex which uses the plastic coatings in its Montreal operations. These coatings are generally of a heavy grade and require special set-up by Cellular. The Sentex orders are handled directly by Mr. Globe and his assistant, Mr. A Oppong, and the price is set on the basis of variable costs of manufacture, plus freight and a 30% markup, less applicable export tax incentives. The export tax incentive received by Cellular has been about 1,000 cuzos per order. Plastic coatings are also sold to both commercial and wholesale outlets in Erewhon, with commercial users constituting 20% of the total sales revenue of Cellular.

Cellular has agreed with the Erewhon government not to pay any dividends out of profits for two years. After that, it is anticipated that the majority of profits will be remitted by Cellular to Sentex and its other major stockholder, Erewhon Development Inc. The opening balance sheet of Cellular Company Inc. at January 1, 1998, was as follows:

Cellular Company Inc.
Balance Sheet As At January 1, 1998 (in cuzos)

Cash	30,000
Fixed Assets	350,000
Total Assets	380,000
Long-term Debt	180,000
Common Stock	200,000
Total Equities	380,000

All debt financing was provided by Sentex. The debt was incurred on January 1, 1998 in cuzos, and is secured by the assets of Cellular.

Cellular Company Inc.
Income Statement For the Year Ended December 31, 1998
(in cuzos)

Sales		600,000
Cost Of Goods Sold		400,000
Gross Margin		200,000
Selling And Administrative Expenses	70,000	
Interest	20,000	90,000
Net Income Before Taxes		110,000
Local Taxes	33,000	
Less Allowance For:		
Export Incentive	6,500	
Training Costs	22,000	4,500
Net Income After Taxes		105,500

Cellular Company Inc.
Balance Sheet As At December 31, 1998
(in cuzos)

Cash	25,000
Notes Receivable	100,000
Accounts Receivable	65,000
Inventories (at cost)	90,000
Current Assets	280,000
Fixed Assets (at cost less accumulated depreciation of 120,000)	230,000
Land (for future development)	10,000
Total Assets	520,000
Accounts Payable	30,000
Taxes Payable	4,500
Current Liabilities	34,500
Long-term Liabilities, 10% Bonds Payable Due January 1, 2005	180,000
Total Liabilities	214,500
Common Stock	200,000
Retained Earnings	105,500
Total Equities	520,000

Other Information:

1. Raw material and labour costs were incurred uniformly throughout the year.

2. Sales were made uniformly throughout the year.

3. The fixed assets were acquired on January 1, 1998, and are depreciated using the sum-of-the-years'-digits method over four years.

4. The note receivable is a 90-day non-interest-bearing note received from a customer in exchange for merchandise sold in October.

5. Land was purchased on December 31, 1998, for 10,000 cuzos.

6. The following exchange rates were in effect for the 1998 year:

Rate at January 1, 1998	1 cuzo = $2.00 Canadian
Average rate for the year 1998	1 cuzo = $1.82 Canadian
Rate at December 31, 1998	1 cuzo = $1.65 Canadian

7. Cost of sales and inventory include depreciation of 98,000 cuzos and 22,000 cuzos respectively. The calculation of Cost of Goods Sold in cuzos is as follows:

Material Purchases	300,000
Labour	70,000
Total Purchases	370,000
Depreciation	120,000
Total Goods Available	490,000
Closing Inventory	(90,000)
Cost Of Goods Sold	400,000

Required   Sentex is in the process of preparing consolidated financial statements for the year ended December 31, 1998.

A. Which method of translation should Sentex use, according to Canadian generally accepted accounting principles? Justify your selection, using the information from the question.

B. Calculate the translation gain/loss on the accounts of Cellular Company Inc.

C. Prepare the translated Balance Sheet as at December 31, 1998 and the translated Income Statement for the year ending December 31, 1998 for Cellular Company Inc.

(SMA Adapted)

SELF STUDY PROBLEM NINE - 3
The comparative Balance Sheets and the 1998 Income Statement of the Brazal Company, in New Cozos (NC, hereafter) are as follows:

Brazal Company
Comparative Balance Sheets
As At December 31

	1998	1997
Cash And Current Receivables	NC11,000,000	NC 6,500,000
Long-Term Receivable	5,000,000	5,000,000
Inventories	8,000,000	9,500,000
Plant And Equipment	23,000,000	17,000,000
Accumulated Depreciation	(5,000,000)	(4,000,000)
Land	6,000,000	3,000,000
Total Assets	NC48,000,000	NC37,000,000
Current Liabilities	NC 3,000,000	NC 5,000,000
Long-Term Liabilities	10,000,000	-0-
No Par Common Stock	20,000,000	18,000,000
Retained Earnings	15,000,000	14,000,000
Total Equities	NC48,000,000	NC37,000,000

Brazal Company
Income Statement
For The Year Ending December 31, 1998

Sales	NC50,000,000
Interest Revenue	1,000,000
Total Revenues	NC51,000,000
Cost of Goods Sold	NC30,000,000
Taxes	10,000,000
Depreciation Expense	2,000,000
Other Expenses	5,000,000
Total Expenses	NC47,000,000
Income Before Extraordinary Items	NC 4,000,000
Extraordinary Loss	2,000,000
Net Income	NC 2,000,000

Other Information:

1. The Brazal Company was formed as the wholly owned subsidiary of a Canadian public company. On the date of incorporation, January 1, 1991, No Par Common Stock was issued for NC18 million and the proceeds were used to purchase Plant And Equipment for NC17 million on the same day. There were no further purchases or disposals of Plant And Equipment from January 1, 1991 to December 31, 1997. The Brazal Company uses the straight line method to calculate depreciation expense.

2. The Long-Term Receivable resulted from a sales transaction on January 1, 1997 and is receivable on December 31, 2001. Interest at a rate of 20 percent per year is paid on the principal and is recorded in Interest Revenue.

3. The December 31, 1997 Inventories were acquired on October 1, 1997. The Inventories in the December 31, 1998 Balance Sheet were acquired on October 1, 1998.

4. On January 1, 1998, Plant And Equipment with an original cost of NC4 million and a Net Book Value of NC3 million was expropriated by the local government for cash of NC1 million. The loss arising from this transaction is considered extraordinary.

5. On January 1, 1998, Long-Term Liabilities with a maturity date of December 31, 2007 and an interest rate of 12 percent were issued for total proceeds of NC10 million. These funds were used to purchase NC10 million in equipment on April 1, 1998. The equipment has an estimated useful life of 10 years.

6. The Land on the books on December 31, 1997 was acquired on January 1, 1997. The 1998 purchase of Land for NC3 million occurred on July 1, 1998.

7. Sales, Interest Revenue, Purchases and Other Expenses occurred evenly throughout the year. This would make the use of average indexes appropriate.

8. Taxes accrued evenly throughout the year and were paid in two equal installments of NC5 million on July 1, 1998 and NC5 million on December 31, 1998.

9. The foreign exchange rate data for the New Cozo and the Canadian dollar is as follows:

January 1, 1991	NC1 = $.100
January 1, 1997	NC1 = $.060
October 1, 1997	NC1 = $.045
December 31, 1997	NC1 = $.040
Average for 1997	NC1 = $.050
April 1, 1998	NC1 = $.038
July 1, 1998	NC1 = $.035
October 1, 1998	NC1 = $.032
December 31, 1998	NC1 = $.030
Average for 1998	NC1 = $.035

10. Dividends of NC1 million were declared and paid on October 1, 1998.

11. The new issue of NC2 million in No Par Common Stock occurred on April 1, 1998.

12. The inventory is accounted for on the First-In, First-Out cost flow assumption.

Required:

A. Assume that, under the definitions contained in Section 1650 of the *CICA Handbook*, the Brazal Company is classified as an integrated foreign operation. Prepare in Canadian dollars a Balance Sheet as at December 31, 1997, a Balance Sheet as at December 31, 1998, and a Statement of Income and Change in Retained Earnings for the year ending December 31, 1998.

B. Assume that, under the definitions contained in Section 1650 of the *CICA Handbook*, the Brazal Company is classified as a self sustaining foreign operation. Assume that prior to the year ending December 31, 1998 the Brazal Company was classified and accounted for as an integrated foreign operation. Prepare in Canadian dollars a Balance Sheet as at December 31, 1997, a Balance Sheet as at December 31, 1998, and a Statement of Income and Change in Retained Earnings for the year ending December 31, 1998.

Assignment Problems

(The solutions to these problem are only available in
the solutions manual that has been provided to your instructor.)

ASSIGNMENT PROBLEM NINE - 1

The Traders Company, a merchandising company based in Canada, is faced with the following spot and forward exchange rates for the Deutsche Mark (DM, hereafter) on September 1, 1997:

Spot Rate	DM1 = $.812
Three Month	DM1 = $.822
Six Month	DM1 = $.832
One Year	DM1 = $.851

On this date, the Company decides to enter several contracts to exchange Canadian Dollars for Deutsche Marks. The contracts and the Company's explanation for why they were entered are as follows:

1. On September 1, 1997, the Company purchases merchandise in Germany for DM25 million. The German company requires payment in Deutsche Marks on March 1, 1998 and, as a consequence, the Company enters a contract to receive DM25 million on that date.

2. On September 1, 1997, the Company makes a commitment to purchase merchandise in Germany on December 1, 1997. The cost of the merchandise is DM50 million and the amount must be paid in Deutsche Marks on March 1, 1998. Given this situation, the Traders Company enters a contract to receive DM50 million on March 1, 1998. The merchandise is purchased on December 1, 1997.

3. On September 1, 1997, the Traders Company makes a commitment to purchase merchandise in Germany on March 1, 1998. The cost of the merchandise is DM40 million and the amount must be paid in Deutsche Marks on the delivery of the merchandise. Given this situation, the Traders Company enters a contract to receive DM40 million on March 1, 1998. The merchandise is purchased on March 1, 1998.

4. Because the Company's management feels that forward rates are not optimistic enough with respect to the Deutsche Mark, the Company decides to enter an additional contract on September 1, 1997 to receive DM80 million on September 1, 1998.

The Traders Company purchased 100 percent of the outstanding voting shares of the Kuhn Company, a German Company on December 31, 1996. On that date all of the identifiable assets and liabilities of the Kuhn Company had fair values that were equal to their carrying values. On January 1, 1993 the Kuhn Company had purchased a piece of land in return for a 12 year Note Payable for DM35,000,000.

The Traders Company closes its books on December 31 of each year. Additional exchange rate data is as follows:

January 1, 1993	DM1 = $.700
December 31, 1996	DM1 = $.818
September 30, 1997	DM1 = $.812
December 1, 1997	DM1 = $.826
December 31, 1997	DM1 = $.842
March 1, 1998	DM1 = $.818
September 1, 1998	DM1 = $.782
December 31, 1998	DM1 = $.769

The eight month forward rate on December 31, 1997 is DM1 = $.866.

Required:

A. For each of the four forward exchange contracts entered into by the Traders Company on September 1, 1997, provide the dated journal entries that would be required during the period September 1, 1997 through September 1, 1998. This would include any adjusting entries that would be required when the Company closes its books on December 31, 1997. Your answer should comply with the recommendations of the *CICA Handbook*.

B. The Traders Company prepares consolidated financial statements which include the Kuhn Company. Calculate the exchange gain or loss related to the Note Payable for the 1998 consolidated Net Income and the balances that would be shown on the December 31, 1998 consolidated Balance Sheet for the Land, Note Payable and any related accounts arising from the translation process, assuming the Traders Company classifies the Kuhn Company as:

   1. an integrated foreign operation

   2. a self-sustaining foreign operation

ASSIGNMENT PROBLEM NINE - 2

Telemark Inc., a manufacturer of cross-country ski equipment, has incorporated a wholly owned Finnish operating subsidiary, Suomi Inc. All of the subsidiary's capital results from the issuance of a 25 year, 11 percent mortgage for 3,500,000 Finnish markkas (M, hereafter) on April 1, 1997. Suomi Inc. uses the total proceeds to finance the purchase of an office building on that date. The first interest payment of M385,000 and the first principal repayment of M140,000 are payable on April 1, 1998.

The total cost of the real estate has been allocated 80 percent to the building and 20 percent to the land. The building has an estimated useful life of 25 years and no net salvage value. Both Telemark Inc. and Suomi Inc. use the straight line method to calculate depreciation expense.

The exchange rate for the Finnish markka had the following values:

April 1, 1997	M1 = $0.29
March 31, 1998	M1 = $0.25

The exchange rate changed uniformly over the year ending March 31, 1998.

Required:

A. Suomi Inc. can be classified as an integrated foreign operation or a self-sustaining foreign operation by Telemark Inc. For both cases, calculate the effect of the building purchase and related mortgage on the consolidated financial statements of Telemark Inc. for the year ending March 31, 1998. Specifically, translate the Balance Sheet and

Income Statement accounts of Suomi Inc. affected by the building purchase, mortgage and any translation adjustments.

B. What is the principal determinant of whether a foreign operation is classified as integrated or self-sustaining? Provide one example of the factors that should be considered in the analysis. Using your calculations in Part A, briefly discuss which method would provide more favorable results for the shareholders of Telemark Inc. in the current year and in the future.

(SMA Adapted)

ASSIGNMENT PROBLEM NINE - 3

The French Company, Bonnuit Inc., is a wholly owned subsidiary of the Canadian Company, Goodnite Inc. Goodnite Inc. acquired its investment in the shares of Bonnuit Inc. on January 1, 1985. The Statement Of Income And Change In Retained Earnings for Bonnuit Inc. in French Francs (F, hereafter) for the year ending December 31, 1998 is as follows:

Bonnuit Company
Statement of Income and Change in Retained Earnings
Year Ending December 31, 1998

Sales Revenue	F4,500,000
Cost Of Goods Sold	F1,500,000
Depreciation Expense	225,000
Interest Expense	150,000
Selling And Administrative Expense	375,000
Taxes (At 30 Percent)	675,000
Total Expenses	F2,925,000
Income Before Extraordinary Items	F1,575,000
Extraordinary Loss On Expropriation Of Land (Net Of F45,000 In Taxes)	255,000
Net Income	F1,320,000
Dividends Declared	120,000
Increase In Retained Earnings	F1,200,000

Other Information:

1. The Sales Revenue arises from sales of mattresses and bedding. Sales occur evenly throughout the year.

2. The inventory on hand on January 1, 1998 was purchased on September 30, 1997 for F450,000. Purchases during 1998 of F1,800,000 occurred evenly over the first three quarters. The inventory on hand on December 31, 1998 was purchased on September 30, 1998. Inventory is accounted for on a first-in, first-out inventory flow assumption.

3. The Depreciation Expense pertains to a building which was purchased on January 1, 1988.

4. The Interest Expense relates to the 10 percent, 20 year bonds which were issued for F1,500,000 on January 1, 1998.

5. The Selling And Administrative Expenses occurred evenly over the year.

6. Income Taxes on ordinary income accrued evenly over the year.

7. The Extraordinary Loss arises from the expropriation of a parcel of land which was purchased on January 1, 1988 for F750,000. This land was expropriated by the local government on December 31, 1998 for proceeds of F450,000.

8. The dividends of Bonnuit Inc. were declared on September 30, 1998 and paid on December 31, 1998.

9. The net monetary assets of Bonnuit Inc. on January 1, 1998, before the issuance of the F1,500,000 in bonds (see Part 4), totalled F2,250,000.

10. The relationship between the French Franc and the Canadian dollar on relevant dates was as follows:

January 1, 1988	F1 = $.20
September 30, 1997	F1 = $.24
January 1, 1998	F1 = $.25
March 31, 1998	F1 = $.27
June 30, 1998	F1 = $.29
September 30, 1998	F1 = $.31
December 31, 1998	F1 = $.33
Average For 1998	F1 = $.29

Changes in the exchange rate occurred uniformly over the year 1998.

Required: Translate the Statement Of Income And Change In Retained Earnings of the Bonnuit Company for use in the preparation of the 1998 consolidated financial statements of the Goodnite Company assuming:

A. the Bonnuit Company is an integrated foreign operation.
B. the Bonnuit Company is a self sustaining foreign operation.

ASSIGNMENT PROBLEM NINE - 4

Royce Ltd. is a British Company with all of its facilities located in Manchester, England. The Company was founded on December 31, 1993. However, on December 31, 1994, all of its outstanding shares were acquired by Beaver Inc., a publicly traded Canadian Company. You have been assigned the task of translating Royce's financial statements from U.K. Pounds (£) into Canadian dollars for inclusion in the consolidated financial statements of Beaver Inc.

Royce Ltd.'s Balance Sheets as at December 31, 1997 and December 31, 1998, as well as its Statement Of Income And Change In Retained Earnings for the year ending December 31, 1998, are as follows:

Royce Ltd.
Balance Sheets
As At December 31

	1998	1997
Cash	£ 212,000	£ 187,000
Accounts Receivable	350,000	327,000
Inventories	1,856,000	1,528,000
Plant And Equipment (Net)	4,900,000	5,320,000
Land	600,000	800,000
Total Assets	£7,918,000	£8,162,000

	1998	1997
Current Liabilities	£ 87,000	£ 143,000
Long Term Liabilities	700,000	1,000,000
Common Stock - No Par	5,600,000	5,600,000
Retained Earnings	1,531,000	1,419,000
Total Equities	£7,918,000	£8,162,000

Royce Ltd.
Statement Of Income And Change In Retained Earnings
Year Ending December 31, 1998

Sales	£6,611,000
Gain On Sale Of Land	125,000
Total Revenues	£6,736,000
Cost Of Goods Sold	£4,672,000
Depreciation Expense	420,000
Selling And Administrative Expenses	1,230,000
Interest Expense	84,000
Loss On Debt Retirement	50,000
Total Expenses	£6,456,000
Net Income	£ 280,000
Less: Dividends On Common Shares	168,000
Increase In Retained Earnings	£ 112,000

Other Information:

1. All £5,600,000 of Royce's Common Stock - No Par was issued when the Company was founded on December 31, 1993. With respect to the proceeds, £800,000 was used to acquire the Land which is shown in the December 31, 1997 Balance Sheet. Of the remaining proceeds, £4,400,000 was used to acquire Plant And Equipment with an estimated useful life of 20 years. This Plant And Equipment is being depreciated on a straight line basis.

2. One quarter of the Land which was acquired when Royce was founded was sold on July 1, 1998. The proceeds of disposition were £325,000, resulting in a reported gain on the sale of £125,000.

3. Royce still owns all of the Plant And Equipment that was acquired when the Company was founded. In addition, a further £2,000,000 of Plant And Equipment was acquired on January 1, 1997. This more recently acquired Plant And Equipment was estimated to have a useful life of 10 years at the time of its acquisition and is being depreciated by the straight line method over this period.

4. The acquisition of Plant And Equipment described in Item 3 was financed with £1,000,000 of internally generated funds along with £1,000,000 of debt financing. The stated rate of interest on the debt is 12 percent per annum, with payments required on July 1 and January 1 of each year. The debt was issued on January 1, 1997 at its maturity value and is scheduled to mature on December 31, 2006. However, on January 1, 1998, 30 percent of this debt was retired through a payment of £350,000 in cash, resulting in a loss of £50,000.

5. The December 31, 1997 Inventories were acquired on October 1, 1997 and the December 31, 1998 Inventories were acquired on July 1, 1998. The 1998 Sales and Purchases occurred uniformly over the year. The cost of Inventories is determined on a FIFO basis.

6. Because of the nature of Royce's business, a majority of the 1998 Selling And Administrative Expenses were incurred in the second half of the year. Specifically, it is estimated that two-thirds of these expenses were in the second half of 1998 with only one-third being incurred in the first half of the year.

7. The 1998 dividends were declared on October 1, 1998 and paid on December 31, 1998.

8. Selected spot rates for the U.K. Pound are as follows:

December 31, 1993	£1 = $2.20
December 31, 1994	£1 = $2.18
January 1, 1997	£1 = $2.15
October 1, 1997	£1 = $2.11
December 31, 1997	£1 = $2.08
July 1, 1998	£1 = $2.04
October 1, 1998	£1 = $2.02
December 31, 1998	£1 = $2.00

    During 1998, the exchange rate moved uniformly downward throughout the year.

Required: To assist in the preparation of Beaver Inc.'s consolidated financial statements, prepare Royce Ltd.'s translated Balance Sheets as at December 31, 1997 and December 31, 1998, as well as its translated Statement Of Income And Changes In Retained Earnings for the year ending December 31, 1998 assuming:

A. Beaver Inc. has classified Royce Ltd. as an integrated foreign operation.

B. Beaver Inc. has classified Royce Ltd. as a self sustaining foreign operation. To assist in the preparation of these statements, you have been provided with the information that the correct December 31, 1997 balance in the Cumulative Translation Adjustment account is a credit of $772,000.

ASSIGNMENT PROBLEM NINE - 5

On December 31, 1996, the Olaf Company, a Danish retail operation, was acquired by a Canadian company. On this acquisition date, the carrying values of all of the identifiable assets and liabilities of the Olaf Company equalled their fair values and the Canadian parent purchased 100 percent of the voting shares of Olaf at their book value. On December 31, 1996, the Olaf Company had the following account balances in Kroner (Kr, hereafter):

Retained Earnings	Kr 192,000
No Par Common Stock	Kr1,200,000
Land	Kr 600,000
Equipment	Kr 510,000
Accumulated Depreciation - Equipment	Kr 70,000
Building	Kr2,100,000
Accumulated Depreciation - Building	Kr 320,000

The adjusted Trial Balance of the Olaf Company for the year ending December 31, 1998 is as follows:

Cash	Kr 150,000
Accounts Receivable	255,000
Inventory	510,000
Building	2,100,000
Equipment	690,000
Land	600,000
Cost of Goods Sold	2,400,000
Depreciation Expense	240,000
Other Expenses	960,000
Dividends Declared	600,000
Total Debits	**Kr8,505,000**

Accounts Payable	Kr 450,000
Long Term Note Payable	900,000
No Par Common Stock	1,200,000
Retained Earnings	600,000
Sales	4,500,000
Accumulated Depreciation	840,000
Allowance For Doubtful Accounts	15,000
Total Credits	**Kr8,505,000**

Other Information:

1. Sales and inventory Purchases occurred uniformly over the year. The Other Expenses include Kr 6,000 of bad debts which were credited to the Allowance for Doubtful Accounts on December 31, 1998. Also on December 31, 1998, Kr 9,000 in bad debts were written off against the Allowance for Doubtful Accounts. The remainder of the Other Expenses occurred uniformly over the year.

2. The exchange rate for the Danish Krone and the Canadian dollar is as follows:

December 31, 1996	Kr1 = $0.1000
December 31, 1997	Kr1 = $0.1600
Average for the 1997 fourth quarter	Kr1 = $0.1525
December 31, 1998	Kr1 = $0.2000
Average for 1998	Kr1 = $0.1800
Average for the 1998 fourth quarter	Kr1 = $0.1950

3. The Olaf Company had current monetary assets of Kr230,000 and current monetary liabilities of Kr890,000 as at December 31, 1997.

4. Year end Inventories are purchased uniformly over the last quarter of each year. On December 31, 1997 the Inventories totalled Kr750,000 and on December 31, 1998 they totalled Kr510,000.

5. On January 1, 1998, equipment was purchased for Kr180,000. It has an estimated useful life of six years with no anticipated net salvage value. The Olaf Company uses the straight line method to calculate depreciation expense.

6. The December 31, 1998 Accumulated Depreciation balance is allocated Kr240,000 to the Equipment and Kr600,000 to the Building.

7. The Long Term Note Payable was issued on January 1, 1997 and is due on January 1, 2003.

8. The dividends were declared on January 1, 1998.

Required: The Olaf Company is classified as an integrated foreign operation by its Canadian parent. Its financial statements are translated to be included in the consolidated financial statements of the Canadian parent. Prepare the following in accordance with the recommendations of the *CICA Handbook*:

A. The translated Income Statement of the Olaf Company for the year ending December 31, 1998.

B. The translated Balance Sheet of the Olaf Company as at December 31, 1998.

C. An independent calculation of the foreign exchange gain or loss.

ASSIGNMENT PROBLEM NINE - 6

The Statement of Income and Change in Retained Earnings and the comparative Balance Sheets for the year ending March 31, 1998, of the Bayreuth Company, a German company, in Deutsche Marks (DM, hereafter) are as follows:

Bayreuth Company
Statement Of Income And Change In Retained Earnings
For The Year Ending March 31, 1998
(In Deutsche Marks)

Sales	67,263,750
Total Revenues	67,263,750
Cost of Goods Sold	45,000,000
Depreciation Expense	2,700,000
Other Expenses	13,725,500
Taxes	1,650,000
Total Expenses	63,075,500
Net Income	4,188,250
Dividends On Common Stock	1,500,000
Increase in Retained Earnings	2,688,250

Bayreuth Company
Balance Sheets As At March 31
(In Deutsche Marks)

	1998	1997
Cash And Current Receivables	4,938,250	2,900,000
Inventories	3,450,000	3,750,000
Plant And Equipment	27,000,000	27,000,000
Accumulated Depreciation	(7,200,000)	(4,500,000)
Land	7,500,000	4,500,000
Total Assets	35,688,250	33,650,000
Current Liabilities	1,150,000	1,800,000
Long Term Liabilities	9,000,000	9,000,000
No Par Common Stock	22,500,000	22,500,000
Retained Earnings	3,038,250	350,000
Total Equities	35,688,250	33,650,000

Other Information:

1. On April 1, 1995, the date of incorporation of the Bayreuth Company, No Par Common Stock was issued for DM22.5 million. The proceeds were used to purchase Plant And Equipment for DM18,000,000 and Land for DM4,500,000 on the same day. The Plant and Equipment had an estimated service life of ten years with no anticipated salvage value. The Bayreuth Company uses the straight line method to calculate depreciation expense.

2. On April 1, 1996, additional Plant and Equipment was purchased with the proceeds from a DM9 million issue of bonds maturing on April 1, 2006. These additions also have a ten year estimated service life with no anticipated salvage value.

3. The March 31, 1997 Inventories were acquired on January 1, 1997. The Inventories in the March 31, 1998 Balance Sheet were acquired on January 1, 1998. The Bayreuth Company uses the first-in, first-out inventory flow assumption.

4. Sales, Purchases and Other Expenses occurred evenly throughout the year. The taxes were paid quarterly in equal installments.

5. On October 1, 1997, Land was purchased for cash of DM3 million and the dividends on common stock were declared and paid.

6. The exchange rate movements occurred evenly throughout the year. The average exchange rate for the year ending March 31, 1998 was DM1 = $.84. Other foreign exchange rate data for the Deutsche Mark and the Canadian dollar was as follows:

April 1, 1995	DM1 = $.75
April 1, 1996	DM1 = $.78
January 1, 1997	DM1 = $.78
March 31, 1997	DM1 = $.82
July 1, 1997	DM1 = $.85
October 1, 1997	DM1 = $.84
January 1, 1998	DM1 = $.83
March 31, 1998	DM1 = $.85

Required: Prepare in Canadian dollars, a Statement of Income and Change in Retained Earnings for the year ending March 31, 1998 and comparative Balance Sheets as at March 31, 1997 and March 31, 1998 assuming that under the definitions contained in Section 1650 of the *CICA Handbook*, the Bayreuth Company is classified:

A. As an integrated foreign operation.

B. As a self sustaining foreign operation. Assume that prior to the year ending March 31, 1997 the Bayreuth Company was classified and accounted for as an integrated foreign operation.

ASSIGNMENT PROBLEM NINE - 7

Part A   During 1998, XYZ Ltd. purchased all of the 100,000 outstanding Class B shares of Sub Limited. Each share carries one vote. The previous owner, Mr. Bill, retained all 80,000 outstanding Class A shares of Sub Limited, each also carrying one vote. In order to avoid sudden changes, Mr. Bill stipulated in the sale agreement that he was to retain the right to refuse the appointment of management for Sub Limited and to approve any significant transactions of Sub Limited.

Required: Should XYZ Ltd. consolidate the operations of Sub Limited in its 1998 financial statements, which are to be issued in accordance with generally accepted accounting principles? Provide support for your recommendation.

Part B On its year-end date, Donna Ltd. purchased 80% of the outstanding common shares of Gunn Ltd. Before the purchase, Gunn Ltd. had a deferred loss on foreign currency exchange of $10.5 million on its balance sheet.

Required: What amount should be reported in Donna Ltd.'s consolidated financial statements, issued in accordance with generally accepted accounting principles, for Gunn Ltd.'s deferred loss on foreign currency exchange? Provide support for your recommendation.

Part C CE Ltd. purchased 100% of the outstanding common shares of May Ltd. by issuing shares of CE Ltd. to the shareholders of May Ltd. The former shareholders of May Ltd. now own 65% of the outstanding common shares of CE Ltd. Before the purchase date, May Ltd. had a deferred loss on foreign currency exchange of $10.5 million in its balance sheet.

Required: What amount should be reported in CE Ltd.'s consolidated financial statements, issued in accordance with generally accepted accounting principles, for May Ltd.'s deferred loss on foreign currency exchange? Provide support for your recommendation.

(CICA adapted)

ASSIGNMENT PROBLEM NINE - 8

Canco is a Canadian corporation that specializes in the selling of men's and women's pants. In an attempt to diversify its product line, it acquired 80 percent of the outstanding voting shares of the Forco Company on December 31, 1997 for $10 million in cash. Forco is a French based Company that is famous for the extensive line of sweaters that it sells. Because of the extensive use of common distribution channels that will be possible after this business combination, Forco is classified as an integrated foreign operation.

The comparative Balance Sheets of the two Companies as at December 31, 1997 and December 31, 1998 and the Income Statements of the two Companies for the year ending December 31, 1998 are as follows:

Balance Sheets
As At December 31, 1997

	Canco	Forco
Cash	$ 1,000,000	F 8,000,000
Accounts Receivable	1,000,000	10,000,000
Inventories	3,000,000	7,000,000
Investment In Forco (Cost)	10,000,000	-0-
Plant And Equipment (Net)	5,000,000	6,000,000
Land	-0-	2,000,000
Total Assets	$20,000,000	F33,000,000
Current Liabilities	1,000,000	F 3,000,000
Long Term Liabilities	5,000,000	5,000,000
No Par Common Stock	5,000,000	15,000,000
Retained Earnings	9,000,000	10,000,000
Total Equities	$20,000,000	F33,000,000

Balance Sheets
As At December 31, 1998

	Canco	Forco
Cash	$ 2,000,000	F10,000,000
Accounts Receivable	3,100,000	11,200,000
Inventories	4,000,000	9,000,000
Investment In Forco (Cost)	10,000,000	-0-
Plant And Equipment (Net)	4,400,000	4,300,000
Land	-0-	3,000,000
Total Assets	$23,500,000	F37,500,000
Current Liabilities	$ 1,500,000	F 3,500,000
Long Term Liabilities	5,000,000	5,000,000
No Par Common Stock	5,000,000	15,000,000
Retained Earnings	12,000,000	14,000,000
Total Equities	$23,500,000	F37,500,000

Canco And Forco Companies
Income Statements
For The Year Ending December 31, 1998

	Canco	Forco
Sales	$35,000,000	F40,000,000
Cost Of Goods Sold	$28,000,000	F32,000,000
Depreciation Expense	1,000,000	500,000
Selling And Administrative Expenses	1,600,000	1,500,000
Other Expenses and Losses	600,000	1,000,000
Tax Provision	800,000	1,000,000
Total Expenses	$32,000,000	F36,000,000
Net Income	$ 3,000,000	F 4,000,000

Other Information:

1. Selected exchange rates between the French Franc and the Canadian Dollar are as follows:

January 1, 1992	F1 = $.210
March 1, 1992	F1 = $.220
July 1, 1997	F1 = $.230
December 31, 1997	F1 = $.240
Average For 1997	F1 = $.230
May 1, 1998	F1 = $.250
July 1, 1998	F1 = $.255
September 1, 1998	F1 = $.260
December 31, 1998	F1 = $.270
Average For 1998	F1 = $.255

   The exchange rate changed uniformly throughout the period under consideration.

2. At the time Canco acquired its interest in Forco, all of the identifiable assets and liabilities of Forco had carrying values that were equal to their fair values except for

Equipment which had a fair value that was F1,500,000 greater than its carrying value. The remaining useful life of this Equipment on December 31, 1997 was twelve years. Forco's Plant And Equipment was acquired on March 1, 1992. Both Companies use straight line calculations for all depreciation and amortization charges.

3. Any goodwill arising from the acquisition of Forco by Canco is to be amortized over 30 years.

4. Selling And Administration Expenses occurred uniformly over the second half of 1998. Sales, Purchases, Other Expenses, and Taxes took place evenly throughout the year.

5. The December 31, 1997 Inventories of Forco were purchased on July 1, 1997. The December 31, 1998 Inventories of Forco were purchased on September 1, 1998.

6. The Long Term Liabilities of the Forco Company were issued on January 1, 1992 and mature on January 1, 2002. Forco's No Par Common Stock was also issued on January 1, 1992.

7. Neither of the two companies declared or paid dividends during 1998.

8. Forco's Land consists of two parcels. One was acquired on July 1, 1997 for F2,000,000 and the second was purchased for F1,000,000 on September 1, 1998.

9. On May 1, 1998 Canco purchases Equipment from Forco at a price of $250,000. The Equipment has a carrying value of F1,200,000 on the books of Forco and a remaining useful life at the time of the sale of four years. This is not the Equipment on which there was a fair value change at the time Canco acquired Forco.

10. On May 1, 1998, Forco sold F5,000,000 in merchandise to Canco. Of this sale, Canco had F2,000,000 remaining in the December 31, 1998 Inventories. Sales are priced to provide a gross profit of 20 percent on the sales price. Both Companies account for Inventories on a First In, First Out basis.

Required: Prepare translated Balance Sheets as at December 31, 1997 and December 31, 1998, and a translated 1998 Income Statement for the Forco Company. Using these translated financial statements, prepare consolidated Balance Sheets as at December 31, 1997 and December 31, 1998, and a consolidated Income Statement for the year ending December 31, 1998, for the Canco Company and its subsidiary the Forco Company. Ignore the effect of intercompany transactions on the consolidated Tax Provision.

Chapter 10

Accounting For Partnerships

Introduction

Partnerships Defined

10-1.   In the case of the corporate form of organization, a separate legal entity is involved and this separate legal entity can be established under either the Canada Business Corporations Act or one of the provincial corporations acts. In contrast, partnerships do not constitute an entity which is legally separate from the owners of the business. Further, there is no national legislation in Canada that is analogous to the Uniform Partnership Act which prevails throughout the United States. As a consequence, we can discuss the legal aspects of partnerships in Canada only within the context of provincial legislation. Fortunately, this does not present significant problems as differences between legislation in the various provinces do not have significant impact on accounting procedures. In addition, a large part of the legislation is designed to cover situations where some aspects of the partner's rights and obligations have not been covered in the partnership agreement. As a consequence, the contents of the partnership agreement become the dominant consideration in the accounting area.

10-2.   In simple terms a partnership is an agreement between two or more entities to undertake some business enterprise. A somewhat more formal definition is found in the Ontario Partnerships Act as follows:

> Partnership is the relation that subsists between persons carrying on a business in common with a view to profit, but the relation between the members of a company or association that is incorporated by or under the authority of any special or general Act in force in Ontario or elsewhere, or registered as a corporation under any such Act, is not a partnership within the meaning of this act.

10-3.   This more specific definition excludes the possibility of having a partnership with corporate entities as partners and, in effect, restricts the legal meaning of the term to partnerships between individuals. This involves more in the way of legal form than it does substance as, clearly, corporations do form "partnerships" to undertake particular business ventures. However, as a result of this type of definition, in Canada we tend to refer to these corporate "partnerships" as joint ventures.

10-4.   Most of the businesses which fall within the legal definition of partnerships are relatively small. In terms of the nature of their business activities, the majority would be involved in either merchandising activities or professional activities such as accounting, the provision of legal services, or medicine. In fact, provincial legislation frequently prevents certain professionals from incorporating, thereby encouraging the use of the partnership form of organization.

10-5. As is implied in the preceding definition, all that is required to establish a partnership is an agreement between the parties that are involved. This agreement could be as simple as a "handshake deal" based purely on oral discussions. However, if significant amounts of assets are involved, this type of arrangement is likely to be very unsatisfactory. Even between good friends with the best of intentions, disputes will invariably arise and can seriously disrupt the business activities of the enterprise. As a consequence, partnership agreements should be established in writing, preferably with professional advice, and be designed to cover as many of the possible areas of activity as feasible. A normal agreement would deal with at least the following:

The names of the partners, the starting date and duration of the agreement, and the amount and type of assets to be contributed by the partners.

The manner in which profits and losses are to be shared, including any provisions for salaries, interest on drawings, interest on loans from the partnership, and interest on loans to the partnership.

The nature of the activities that the enterprise will undertake.

The authority and responsibilities to be vested in each partner.

The amount of insurance on the lives of the partners to be paid to the surviving partners as beneficiaries.

The procedures to be used in liquidation, including provisions for dealing with the arbitration of disputes.

Characteristics Of Partnerships

10-6. As with other forms of business organizations, the partnership form has certain characteristics with which it can be associated. These characteristics are frequently presented as lists of advantages and disadvantages. However, in actual fact, the situation is somewhat more complex than that and, as a reflection of that fact, our discussion will be somewhat broader in nature. The basic characteristics of the partnership form of business organization are described in the Paragraphs which follow:

Limited Life We have previously noted that a partnership does not generally exist as a legal entity separate from the participating partners. As a consequence, the life of a partnership is terminated by the death or retirement of any of the partners. Further, from a strict legal point of view, even the admission of a partner creates a new partnership and terminates the legal life of the previous organization. The continuing and invariable need to create new legal entities is expensive, can be the source of protracted disputes, and may lead to serious disruptions of the normal business activities of the organization. It would seem clear that, relative to the corporate form of organization, this characteristic must be viewed as a disadvantage of partnerships.

Unlimited Liability Also related to the absence of a separate legal existence for the partnership, is the unlimited liability that confronts the participating partners. What this means is that if the partnership encounters serious financial difficulties, creditors can look not only to the assets of the business for satisfaction but, in addition, can lay claim to the personal assets of the partners. Here again, this characteristic is generally cited as a disadvantage relative to the corporate form of organization as it significantly extends the liability of any potential partner, and, thereby, may reduce their interest in investing. There is a possible way of avoiding the problem of unlimited liability and this is by establishing a certain number of limited partners. This simply means that any partner that is so designated has his liability limited to some specified amount, generally the amount that has been invested. However, legislation on limited partnerships requires that every such organization have at least one general partner with unlimited liability.

Ease Of Formation   This issue is somewhat less clear cut. In general, it is probably fair to say that a partnership is somewhat easier to form than a corporation. Two people can simply make an informal agreement to undertake some business activity and a partnership is formed. In contrast, the process of incorporation involves complying with a number of legislative requirements and will generally involve legal expenses of at least $500 to $1,000. However, small corporations are constructed along a fairly simple format, with the rights and obligations of the owners clearly established by the relevant enabling legislation. In contrast, partnerships often tend to evolve along more individualized patterns. In this type of situation, the construction of an appropriate and comprehensive partnership agreement may, in fact, be more complex than would be incorporation.

Mutual Agency   This simply means that each partner has the authority to act for the partnership and to enter into contracts which are binding with respect to all of the partners. Depending on the particular provincial legislation, this may be limited in cases where the partner has acted beyond the normal scope of business operations and without specific authority resulting from the partnership agreement. When this characteristic is viewed in the context of the unlimited liability to which most partners are exposed, it would seem clear that it can be an undesirable feature of the partnership form of business organization. A bad decision on the part of one partner can have seriously adverse effects on the other participants in the partnership.

Co-ownership Of Property And Profits   The individual partners have no claim to any of the specific assets of the business but, rather, acquire an interest in all of the assets. The property becomes jointly owned by all partners and each partner has an ownership interest in the profits of the partnership. The major difficulty with this arrangement is that when partners are admitted or retired, the amount of the new or retiring partner's interest must be established and this may prove to be a difficult and time consuming process.

Taxation   Here again, the lack of a separate legal identity for enterprises organized as partnerships is influential. As a result of this lack of identity, the Income Tax Act contains no definition of what constitutes a partnership. However, the Act requires that partnership income be calculated on the assumption that the partnership is a separate person resident in Canada and that its fiscal period is its taxation year. Each partner's share of the income from the partnership from any business or property and its capital gains (or losses) is treated as his income or gain from such a source whether distributed to the person or not. In considering taxation, there are a number of complex factors that must be weighed. The taxation issue goes beyond our interest in a book on financial reporting. However, it is an important consideration and, when it is a relevant issue, it is essential to obtain appropriate professional advice.

Regulation Subsequent To Formation   This issue is relatively clear cut. Partnerships have the advantage of being less subject to regulation and supervision by all levels of government than would enterprises which are organized as corporations. This would be particularly true if the corporation were publicly traded and had to comply with the extensive reporting requirements to which such organizations are subjected.

10-7.   A quick review of the preceding list of characteristics makes the position of the partnership form of organization clear. From a legal point of view, partnerships are very little different from proprietorships. The choice between these two forms will hinge largely on the capital needs of the enterprise. The choice between partnership and corporate forms, however, is more complex. While this is not the case for enterprises which involve professional groups that are prohibited from incorporating, for small businesses the choice may be difficult. Limited life and unlimited liability may not be particularly influential here, and the ease of formation and lack of regulation may push the owners in the direction of the partnership form. As we have noted previously, the tax issue could be extremely important and in actual fact, tax considerations may be the primary consideration in making the choice.

10-8.   As we begin to consider larger enterprises, the issue generally becomes easier to resolve. If the capital requirements of an enterprise are such that a large investor group must be involved, the problems associated with limited life, unlimited liability, and mutual agency become virtually insurmountable. In this type of situation, the corporate form of organization becomes the only reasonable alternative.

Partnerships And The Accounting Entity

10-9.   One of the fundamental assumptions or postulates of financial reporting is that accountants should concentrate on providing financial reports for definable business or economic entities. However, much of the accountant's activity takes place in an environment in which various types of legal entities are defined. Since these legal definitions will invariably have some influence on the information needs of financial statement users, the accountant's position is one which involves a potential conflict.

10-10.   In many cases this conflict does not arise. For a simple corporation with no subsidiaries, the legal and economic entities will generally coincide and, as a result, the financial statements prepared to represent the economic entity will be the same as those that would be prepared to meet any of the requirements of the legal entity. (Tax returns would be an exception to this statement.) However, this reflects a difference in accounting principles rather than a difference between the legal and economic entities. This is not always the case. We have already encountered what is perhaps the most important example of conflicts between legal and economic entities in previous Chapters. This is the situation where a parent company has one or more subsidiaries which can be considered a part of the same economic entity as the parent or investor company. In that case, the accountant deals with the conflict by preparing consolidated financial statements which concentrate on the economic entity rather than the separate legal entities that are represented by the parent and subsidiary company. A second important conflict arises here.

10-11.   From a legal point of view, the real entities involved in a partnership are the partners themselves. As we have noted, the law does not make a distinction between the status of a partner's personal dwelling and a building in which there is a joint interest with other partners. While the individual partners may wish to have personal financial statements prepared, in judging the performance or position of the partnership as a business entity, it is important to have financial statements which segregate the assets, liabilities, expenses, and revenues of the partners from those of the partnership. In order to accomplish this goal the accountant must look through the legal form of the organization and prepare statements which reflect the economic substance of the business. This is why we find that, in practice, most accountants are accustomed to viewing partnerships as separate entities with a continuity of life, accounting policies, and asset valuations. It should be noted, however, that the principles and procedures to be used in segregating this accounting entity from its conflicting legal environment, are not nearly as developed and well established as those used in the similar process of preparing consolidated financial statements.

Partnership Owners' Equity Accounts

10-12.   In accounting for a proprietorship, a single owner's equity account is generally adequate as there are no legal or equity apportionment issues which require the segregation of any part of this balance. In contrast, accounting for the owners' equity of a corporation requires, as a minimum, a strict segregation of contributed and earned capital in order to meet the usual legal requirement that dividends can only be paid from earned capital. The situation with partnership owners' equity is less clear cut.

10-13.   From the point of view of general legislation on partnerships, there is no reason to segregate any portion of the owners' equity balance. However, the need to account for the individual equity balances of each partner and information requirements related to implementing the partnership agreement with respect to profit sharing, drawings, and loans, will generally lead to some partitioning of the owners' equity balance. While this may vary from partnership to partnership, the usual pattern will involve three separate types of accounts for each partner. These will normally be:

Capital Accounts   This is the basic account to which each partner's original investment will be credited. In subsequent years, it will be increased by additional investment as well as the partner's share of any net income of the partnership. It will be reduced by any withdrawals by the partner of partnership assets as well as the partner's share of any net losses of the enterprise.

Drawings   In most situations each partner will have a drawing account. This account will generally be used to account for two types of transactions. First, when a partner withdraws any amounts of salary to which he is entitled, it will be debited to this account. In addition, withdrawals that are made by the partner in anticipation of his annual share of profits would also be debited to this account. This account should not be used for withdrawals of partnership assets that could be viewed as permanent reductions in invested capital, nor should the account be used for loans. At the end of the accounting period, this account will generally be closed to the partner's capital account.

Loans   If it is permitted under the partnership agreement, partners may sometimes borrow funds from the enterprise and, in some situations, a partner may loan funds to the organization. In maintaining equitable relationships between the partners, it is important that this type of transaction be carefully segregated from either drawings against salaries or profits, or increases and decreases in invested capital. To facilitate this segregation, it is the usual practice to set up separate loan receivable and payable accounts for each partner where balances exist. These accounts would not be closed at the end of the period but, rather, would be carried until such time as the balance is paid.

10-14.   The preceding describes a typical set of owners' equity accounts for a partnership. There are, of course, many possible variations, the most common of these being a failure to segregate Drawings accounts from Loans accounts. In addition, if the partnership agreement places any specific restrictions on any or all of the capital balances of the partners, additional accounts may be required to reflect these restrictions.

Partnership Formation

10-15.   The obvious starting point for any discussion of accounting for partnerships would be to consider the transactions required at the inception of the business. If the partnership is not formed from any predecessor organizations, it is simply a matter of recording the assets that have been contributed by the partners. For example, if X and Y form a partnership by each investing $100,000 in cash, the journal entry would be as follows:

Cash	$200,000	
X, Capital		$100,000
Y, Capital		100,000

10-16.   The procedures are only slightly more complex when the assets are other than cash or when the partnership assumes one or more liabilities of a partner. The basic point here is that the assets and liabilities should be recorded at their fair values as at the time the partnership is organized. As an example, assume the same situation as presented in Paragraph 10-15 except that X, instead of investing $100,000 in cash, gives the new enterprise a building with a fair value of $150,000 and the enterprise assumes X's mortgage on the building in the amount of $50,000. The required entry would be as follows:

Cash	$100,000	
Building	150,000	
Mortgage Payable		$ 50,000
X, Capital		100,000
Y, Capital		100,000

10-17. In some situations, partners may be credited with capital balances that are not equal or proportionate to the fair values of the identifiable net assets they are contributing. This would generally reflect the fact that one or more partners is bringing some factor other than identifiable net assets into the business. This could involve special skills, a favorable reputation in the industry, or simply personal assets at a level that enhance the fund raising capacity of the partnership. To illustrate, we can return to the example in Paragraph 10-15. Assume, however, that X is granted an interest equal to that of Y in both capital and income, but that X only contributes $80,000 in cash while Y continues to contribute $100,000. The most reasonable interpretation of this situation is that X has contributed, in addition to the $80,000 in cash, goodwill in the amount of $20,000. Under this interpretation, the appropriate entry would be:

Cash	$180,000	
Goodwill	20,000	
X, Capital		$100,000
Y, Capital		100,000

10-18. An alternative interpretation that is frequently used in practice would involve the assumption that Y is granting a bonus to X of $10,000. Under this assumption, no Goodwill would be recorded and both capital accounts would be recorded at $90,000. This effectively assumes that Y has paid $100,000 for a one half interest in a business that is worth $180,000. We are of the opinion that this is not a reasonable interpretation of the economic substance of the transaction.

10-19. It is not uncommon for a partnership to be formed with one or more of the partners contributing an existing proprietorship. This type of transaction is somewhat more complex in that it would be necessary to determine the fair values of all of the identifiable assets and liabilities as well as any existing goodwill for each predecessor enterprise. The guidelines contained in Section 1580 of the *CICA Handbook* for implementing these procedures in business combinations accounted for by the purchase method would generally be applicable in this type of partnership formation situation. Despite these additional complications, the principles involved are no different than in those cases where the partners contribute only identifiable assets. All of the contributed identifiable assets and liabilities and any existing goodwill would be recorded as the new partnership's assets and, at the same time, the partners' capital accounts would be credited for the amounts contributed. If there was a disparity between the net assets contributed and the amount allocated to the various partners' capital accounts, it can be dealt with by recognition of additional goodwill being contributed by one or more partners or on the basis of bonus payments to one or more partners. As we indicated in Paragraph 10-18, we believe that the former interpretation is the more reasonable of the two alternatives.

Partnership Income

General Principles

10-20. The design of an appropriate and equitable system for the allocation of partnership income is one of the more important components of any properly designed partnership agreement. If the agreement fails to specify a plan for sharing the income of the enterprise, most provincial legislation calls for income to be shared equally. As in many cases such equal sharing would not be considered an equitable arrangement, most partnership agreements devote considerable attention to the problem of income allocation.

10-21. The partnership income allocation problem is made complex by the fact that partners may contribute a variety of different services to the enterprise. In most cases, all partners will contribute some portion of the partnership capital, either in cash or in the form of some other types of assets. In addition, it would be normal for some or all of the partners to work in the enterprise on an ongoing basis. Beyond this, one or more of the partners may possess very substantial personal financial resources which may enhance the ability of the enterprise to obtain a better credit rating, resulting in either more financing or financing at a more favorable rate. Such partners must also be rewarded for the fact that they may lose considerably more in the event the partnership experiences financial adversity or bankruptcy. All of this means that, in order to provide a completely equitable income sharing arrangement, the partnership agreement should give consideration to amounts of capital contributed, the worth of services provided to the partnership by working partners, and any differential amounts of risk related to the amount of personal assets owned by the various partners.

10-22. In actual practice, consideration is not always given to all of these matters. While many variations are possible, four types of income sharing arrangements seem to be the most common. They are as follows:

Fixed Ratios The simplest type of arrangement would involve simply sharing on the basis of some agreed upon ratio, other than that established by relative capital contributions. The ratio will generally be the same for both profits and losses but may, in particular circumstances, differ depending on whether or not the business is successful.

Capital Contributions Under this approach, capital balances would be used as a basis for determining each partner's share of partnership profits or losses. When this approach is used, the partnership agreement must make clear which capital balance is to be used in establishing profit sharing ratios. It could be the balance originally invested, the beginning of the year balance, or the end of the year balance. However, the most reasonable approach would seem to be to use the average balance for the year. It would also be necessary to specify the effects of loans and/or drawings on the determination of the relevant capital balance.

Salaries With Ratios For Any Remainder Here salaries are established for the partners that work in the enterprise and any income or loss balance that remains is allocated on the basis of either fixed or capital contribution ratios. Here again, if fixed ratios are used, they will usually apply to both profits and losses.

Salaries And Interest With Ratios For Any Remainder In this type of plan, all factors are considered. Partners are given credit for services rendered in the form of salaries, for capital contributed in the form of interest, and for any other risk considerations in the ratios established for distributing any remaining balance of profit or loss.

10-23. We think that the last approach described will provide the most useful information. There are, of course, difficulties associated with establishing reasonable salary levels in non-arms length situations, and some question as to whether capital contributed at risk should be viewed as earning "interest". However, this type of arrangement allows all of the comonents of the partner's relationship with the business to be given consideration. In addition, it gives a better indication of the performance of the enterprise itself. If, for example, the business is earning less than the fair value of the services rendered by the partners, then a failure to charge enterprise income with salaries will obscure the fact that from an economic point of view the business is losing money.

10-24.   Profit sharing is the most likely source of disputes among the partners. As a consequence, it is important that the partnership agreement not only provide a method for sharing partnership income but that, in addition, the means of determining that income be established as well. The amount of detail required will vary from agreement to agreement. However, at a minimum, the accounting period and the source from which accounting procedures will be adopted should be included as a part of the agreement.

Allocation Procedures

Example

10-25.   In order to illustrate the various types of profit sharing arrangements described in Paragraph 10-22, a simple example will be used.

Two partners, S and T, are involved and the data for the current calendar year is as follows:

	Partner S	Partner T
Original Investment	$40,000	$60,000
Capital Balance, January 1	55,000	65,000
Additional Investment, April 1	5,000	-0-
Drawings, June 30	4,000	6,000
Additional Investment, October 1	-0-	3,000

For the current year ending December 31, the S and T Partnership earned a Net Income of $15,000, before consideration of any salaries to the partners or interest on their capital contributions.

Fixed Ratios

10-26.   This type of arrangement is sufficiently simple that it requires little discussion. If, for example, the agreement called for profits to be shared equally, S and T would be credited with $7,500 each. This amount, along with the balances in the Drawings accounts would be closed to the end of the period Capital accounts, leaving S with a balance of $63,500 and T with a balance of $69,500. This type of profit sharing arrangement would, in most circumstances, be very easy to administer. However, it can be criticized for failing to give weight to the varying capital and service contributions that the two partners may be making to the enterprise.

Capital Contributions

10-27.   As we have previously noted, when profit sharing is to be based on the relative capital contributions of the partners, there are various ways in which this approach can be applied. If it were based on original contributions, the income to be allocated to each partner could be calculated as follows:

S's Share = ([$15,000][$40,000 ÷ $100,000]) = $6,000

T's Share = ([$15,000][$60,000 ÷ $100,000]) = $9,000

10-28.   Alternatively, if unweighted end of the year capital balances, without the inclusion of the year's income were used ($56,000 + $62,000, see Paragraph 10-29), the relative income shares of the two partners would be calculated as follows:

S's Share = ([$15,000][$56,000 ÷ $118,000]) = $7,119

T's Share = ([$15,000][$62,000 ÷ $118,000]) = $7,881

10-29.   Probably the most equitable way of using capital contributions as a basis for profit sharing is to use the weighted average capital balance for the year. In using this approach, the partnership agreement should specify what amounts are to be included in the weighted average capital calculation. In our example, we will assume that drawings are treated as reductions of capital when they occur but that income for the year is not included in the calculation. On this basis, the weighted average capital balances for the two partners would be calculated as follows:

Weighted Average Capitals
For The Year Ending December 31

For Partner S:	Weighted Amount	Weight	Amount
January 1, Balance	$55,000	1.00	$55,000
Added Investment	5,000	.75	3,750
Drawings	(4,000)	.50	(2,000)
Totals	$56,000		$56,750
For Partner T:			
January 1, Balance	$65,000	1.00	$65,000
Added Investment	3,000	.25	750
Drawings	(6,000)	.50	(3,000)
Totals	$62,000		$62,750

10-30.   Given the preceding calculations, the partners' respective shares of income could be calculated as follows:

S's Share = ([$15,000][$56,750 ÷ $119,500]) = $7,123

T's Share = ([$15,000][$62,750 ÷ $119,500]) = $7,877

Salaries With Ratios For Any Remainder

10-31.   As we move to this somewhat more complex type of profit sharing arrangement, we will assume that both S and T work in the partnership and it is their belief that the fair value of their services would be $5,000 for S and $3,000 for T. The partnership agreement then specifies that any profit or loss after the deduction of these salaries should be split on the basis of 40 percent to S and 60 percent to T. On this basis the profit for the year would be split as follows:

S's Share = ([.40][$15,000 - $5,000 - $3,000]) = $2,800

T's Share = ([.60][$15,000 - $5,000 - $3,000]) = $4,200

10-32.   This means that the total distributions to the two partners would be as follows:

	Partner S	Partner T	Totals
Salaries	$5,000	$3,000	$ 8,000
Profit Shares	2,800	4,200	7,000
Total	$7,800	$7,200	$15,000

10-33.   In this type of arrangement, it is important for the partnership agreement to specify exactly what happens in the event income is less than the salaries. In this case, if income before the consideration of salaries had only been $5,000, the deduction of salaries would have created a $3,000 loss. Normally, this loss would be split using the same 40 percent, 60 percent ratio and this would have resulted in a reduction in the capital accounts of the two partners. However, there is nothing to prevent the two partners from putting a clause into the partnership agreement which provides for salaries to be accrued only when partnership income is sufficient to provide for them.

Salaries And Interest With Ratios For Any Remainder

10-34.   In this final case, we will assume that the partnership agreement calls for salaries of $5,000 for S and $3,000 for T, interest at 10 percent on the beginning of the year capital balances, and for the remaining profit or loss to be allocated on the basis of 40 percent to S and 60 percent to T. The balance to be distributed on the basis of these ratios can be calculated as follows:

Income Before Salaries Or Interest	$15,000
Salaries ($5,000 + $3,000)	(8,000)
Balance Before Interest	$ 7,000
Interest [(.10)($55,000 + $65,000)]	(12,000)
Balance To Be Distributed	($ 5,000)

10-35.   On the basis of the 40:60 sharing plan in the partnership agreement, this loss would be distributed $2,000 to S and $3,000 to T and this would result in the following total distribution to the two partners:

	Partner S	Partner T	Totals
Salaries	$5,000	$3,000	$ 8,000
Interest	5,500	6,500	12,000
Loss	(2,000)	(3,000)	(5,000)
Total	$8,500	$6,500	$15,000

10-36.   As was the case when only salaries and fixed ratio sharing was involved, it is important for the partnership agreement to provide a clear indication of what happens when salaries and, in this case, interest on capital balances exceeds income. The normal procedure would be to give priority to salaries, followed by interest on capital contributions, with any remaining profit or loss distributed in agreed upon ratios. Again, however, there is nothing to prevent the partnership agreement from specifying some alternative type of arrangement.

Disclosure

10-37.   In partnership accounting the meaning of the term Net Income is not entirely clear. If the partnership agreement calls for the payment of salaries to the partners, and these amounts are fairly representative of the fair value of the services rendered by the partners, it would seem appropriate to deduct these amounts as operating expenses before arriving at a Net Income figure. However, if the partnership agreement calls for some form of interest on invested capital, our conventional approach to the calculation of Net Income does not provide for deductions of amounts allocated to the ownership interest of the enterprise. If, however, loans by the partners to the partnership were involved, interest on such liability amounts might be included in the determination of Net Income.

10-38.   Probably as a reflection of the fact that transactions between partners and the partnership are less than fully arms length in nature, the conventional procedure is to disclose Net Income before any distributions to the partners. For example, if we assume that the $15,000 income figure from Paragraph 10-25 was based on Revenues of $40,000 and Expenses of $25,000, and that distributions were as calculated in Paragraph 10-35, the partnership Income Statement could be as follows:

S And T Partnership
Income Statement

Revenues	$40,000
Expenses	25,000
Net Income	$15,000

10-39.   The actual distribution of this income would then be disclosed in a Statement Of Partners' Capital as follows:

S And T Partnership
Statement Of Partners' Capital

	Partner S	Partner T	Totals
Balance, January 1	$55,000	$65,000	$120,000
Additional Investment	5,000	3,000	8,000
Balance Before Income and Drawings	$60,000	$68,000	$128,000
Net Income	8,500	6,500	15,000
Drawings	(4,000)	(6,000)	(10,000)
Balance, December 31	$64,500	$68,500	$133,000

Changes In The Partnership Group

The Conceptual Problem

General Problem

10-40.   Under most provincial legislation in Canada, any change in the participating group of partners involves a dissolution of the existing partnership agreement and necessitates the preparation of a new one. In the absence of a specific alternative provision in the partnership agreement, this would include all of the following types of events:

The admission of a new partner.

The retirement or death of one of the existing partners.

The transfer of an existing partnership interest to a new owner.
(Note that this differs from U.S. law which would not view this as a termination of the partnership agreement.)

10-41.   Since the partnership agreement forms the only legal basis for the existence of a partnership, a legal perspective would view the preceding events as involving the formation of a new business enterprise.

10-42.   Under present generally accepted accounting principles, all of the assets and liabilities transferred to a new business should be recorded at their fair values as at the date the business is formed. This would also include the recording of any goodwill that might be contributed by the investors or their predecessor business organizations. We observed this principle in the examples illustrating the formation of a completely new partnership (Paragraphs 10-15 through 10-19) and there is no question as to its applicability in that type of situation. However, we are now faced with a more difficult question. Should the fact that each ownership change involves the formation of a new legal agreement lead us to the application of the asset and liability revaluation procedures that are generally required in the formation of a new business entity? The alternative would, of course, be to assume a continuity of existence similar to that of a corporation. Under this assumption, a change in the ownership interest has no real effect on the continuity of the accounting records and does not provide a basis for any revaluation of asset or liability balances.

10-43.   While the legal answer is clear, it is not necessarily satisfactory. As we have noted previously, the primary concern of accountants is with economic substance rather than with legal form. Therefore, the real question to be answered is does a change in ownership interest of a partnership involve the creation of a new economic entity or, alternatively, do such changes involve only a change in legal form as represented by the new partnership agreement. In the Paragraphs which follow, this issue is considered in the context of the various types of transactions which can result in changes in the partnership group.

Exchange Of Ownership Interest

10-44.   In some situations an exchange of interests takes place outside of the partnership entity. More specifically, there are situations in which an existing partner sells his interest to a new partner, with the consideration being exchanged directly between the individuals. In this type of situation no new assets enter the partnership books, the partnership is generally not directly involved in the negotiations related to the transaction, and the new partner will normally assume exactly the same rights and obligations that were associated with the previous partner. In fact, it is not uncommon for the partnership agreement to provide for the implementation of such transfers without a legal dissolution of the partnership. Given these facts, it would be our view that treating this type of ownership change as the formation of a new business entity would rarely be an appropriate approach. It follows from this position that continuity of the partnership accounting records should be maintained and that no changes would be made in the carrying values of any of the assets or liabilities of the partnership.

Admission And Retirement Of Partners

10-45.   The situation is less clear cut when a partnership admits a new partner or an existing partner leaves through death or retirement. It is our opinion that a single solution to the problem does not exist and, in the absence of clear cut guidelines for determining whether a new economic entity has been created, some amount of judgment will have to be applied. For example, in a large public accounting firm with hundreds of partners, the admission and retirement of partners are events which occur with great frequency. Further, these admissions and retirements will generally not have any real influence on the continuity of the business activities in which the firm is engaged. In these circumstances, it would be extremely unreasonable to view the admission or retirement of a partner as the creation of a new economic entity and, as a consequence, no break in the continuity of the accounting records should occur.

10-46.   Alternatively, assume that we are dealing with a partnership involving only two partners operating a retail store at the same location for a period of twenty years. Continuing the example, assume that a new partner is brought in, contributing cash in an amount equal to the fair value of the existing partnership net assets, and that the three partners intend to use this cash to open a new operation in a different line of business. A similar example could involve a situation where two partners have worked together for many years and one decides to leave, taking with him half of the assets and clients of the partnership. In both of these situations, a case can be made for the idea that a new business entity has been created and that this new entity is acquiring a group of identifiable assets, goodwill, and liabilities that should be recorded at new values measured as at the date of the admission of the new partner or the retirement of the old.

10-47.   Unfortunately, many situations are not as clear cut as those described in the preceding two Paragraphs. Further complicating the problem at the present time is the fact that there are no existing guidelines for the determination of whether the admission or retirement of a partner constitutes the formation of a new economic entity. As a consequence, we find alternative treatments being applied in practice. When it is assumed that the admission or retirement of a partner does not involve the formation of a new business entity, the respective equity interests are allocated on the basis that the newly admitted or retiring partner is either paying a bonus to or receiving a bonus from the other partners in the organization. This approach will be illustrated in the Sections dealing with both admissions and retirements of partners.

10-48.   In contrast, when it is assumed that the admission or retirement of a partner does involve the formation of a new business entity, identifiable assets will be revalued to their fair values and goodwill, if applicable, will be recorded. There is also a compromise solution that is sometimes encountered. There appears to be a continuing reluctance on the part of some accountants to record goodwill in partnership admission and retirement transactions. This leads to procedures under which fair values are recorded for identifiable assets and liabilities, but any goodwill being acquired by the new business is ignored.

It would be our position that this compromise position is not appropriate. If the circumstances of the admission or retirement are such that the resulting partnership can be viewed as a new economic entity, then generally accepted accounting principles would require the recording of any goodwill acquired by this new entity. As a consequence, the examples in the Sections on the admissions and retirements of partners will illustrate only the complete procedures that we associate with the formation of a new entity.

Exchange Of Ownership Interests

10-49.   The following is an example of an exchange in ownership interest.

Example   The Balance Sheet of the STU Partnership on December 31 of the current year is as follows:

STU Partnership
Balance Sheet As At December 31

Total Net Assets	$1,500,000
Partner S, Capital	$ 500,000
Partner T, Capital	500,000
Partner U, Capital	500,000
Total	$1,500,000

The partnership agreement calls for all profits and losses to be shared on an equal basis. On this date, Partner U sells his interest to a new partner V for $600,000, who pays this amount of cash directly to Partner U.

10-50.   You will recall our argument that, in this type of situation, there would rarely be justification for the revaluation of partnership assets. Given this view, the appropriate entry on the partnership books to record the transaction would be as follows:

Partner U, Capital	$500,000	
Partner V, Capital		$500,000

10-51.   This would leave the December 31 Balance Sheet unchanged except for the new name which attaches to one of the capital accounts.

10-52.   You should also note that the entry and the resulting Balance Sheet would not be affected by the amount paid by Partner V for Partner U's proportionate interest. As we have previously noted, it would be very rare for this type of transaction to result in the creation of a new economic entity. As a result, any business valuation information that is implicit in the transfer price of the partnership interest will generally not be used as a basis for any revaluation of assets or recognition of goodwill.

Admission Of New Partners

10-53.   In view of the fact that additions to the partnership's assets are involved and because alternative assumptions as to the nature of the transaction have greater applicability in the case of partnership admissions, accounting for them requires greater elaboration than was the case with an exchange of partnership interests. To facilitate your understanding of the problems involved, a single basic example will be used to illustrate four cases of a partner admission.

Case 1:	Consideration Exceeds Book Value - New Entity Assumption
Case 2:	Consideration Exceeds Book Value - Continuity Assumption
Case 3:	Consideration Below Book Value - New Entity Assumption
Case 4:	Consideration Below Book Value - Continuity Assumption

Example   The Balance Sheet of the AB Partnership as at December 31 of the current year is as follows:

AB Partnership
Balance Sheet As At December 31

Total Net Assets	$500,000

Partner A, Capital	$250,000
Partner B, Capital	250,000
Total	$500,000

The partnership agreement calls for Partners A and B to share all profits and losses equally. In all of the examples which follow, they are admitting Partner C with a one third interest in assets, income and losses. This means that the three partners will each have equal shares after the admission of Partner C. On December 31, before the admission of Partner C, the fair values of the net assets of the AB Partnership are equal to $600,000.

Case One - Consideration Exceeds Book Value - New Entity

10-54.   As a first example, assume that Partner C pays cash of $325,000 to the partnership in return for a one third interest in assets, income, and losses, and that the admission of this partner can be viewed as the creation of a new economic entity. The admission price implies a total value for the new partnership of $975,000 and a value for the combined interest of Partners A and B of $650,000. Since the total fair values of the net assets of the partnership only amount to $600,000, this would imply the existence of Goodwill in the amount of $50,000. As in this Case we are going to assume that the admission of Partner C creates a new business entity, the following entry will be required to recognize these value changes:

Net Assets	$100,000	
Goodwill	50,000	
Partner A, Capital		$75,000
Partner B, Capital		75,000

10-55.   After this adjustment, the entry to record the admission of Partner C would be as follows:

Cash (Net Assets)	$325,000	
Partner C, Capital		$325,000

10-56.   The resulting Balance Sheet for the new partnership would be as follows:

ABC Partnership
Balance Sheet
As At December 31

Net Identifiable Assets	$925,000
Goodwill	50,000
Total	$975,000

Partner A, Capital	$325,000
Partner B, Capital	325,000
Partner C, Capital	325,000
Total	$975,000

Case Two - Consideration Exceeds Book Value - Continuity

10-57.   In this Case we will assume that Partner C makes the same $325,000 investment which we considered in Case One. However, the circumstances are such that the admission does not break the continuity of the existing business entity and, as a consequence, we would not view C's admission to the Partnership as a basis for revaluing assets. Given this interpretation, we must then assume that C is paying a bonus of $25,000 to each of the existing partners. The total assets will amount to $825,000 and C's one third interest will be valued at $275,000. The entry to record C's admission to the partnership would be as follows:

Cash	$325,000	
Partner A, Capital		$ 25,000
Partner B, Capital		25,000
Partner C, Capital		275,000

10-58.   The resulting Balance Sheet would appear as follows;

ABC Partnership
Balance Sheet
As At December 31

Total Net Assets	$825,000
Partner A, Capital	$275,000
Partner B, Capital	275,000
Partner C, Capital	275,000
Total	$825,000

Case Three - Consideration Below Book Value - New Entity

10-59.   In this Case we will assume that C is admitted to a one third interest in the Partnership in return for cash of $200,000 and that the admission can be interpreted as the formation of a new business entity. If we continue to assume that the fair values of the AB Partnership's net assets are $600,000, this means that the investment cost is below both the book value and the fair values of the interests of either Partner A or Partner B. This could mean one of two things. First, this lower value could imply that the existing partnership has negative goodwill. However, this interpretation is not widely used in present practice. Rather, a second interpretation, that Partner C is bringing goodwill into the business, is used. If there is a reasonable basis for this interpretation, then we believe that the assumption that a new business entity is being formed would still require the recording of the identifiable assets at their fair values. While this would often not be done in practice, the solution which follows adjusts these assets to their fair values. The adjusting entry would be as follows:

Net Assets	$100,000	
Partner A, Capital		$50,000
Partner B, Capital		50,000

10-60.   With this adjustment completed, the entry to admit Partner C and to recognize the goodwill that he is bringing into the business would be as follows:

Cash	$200,000	
Goodwill	100,000	
Partner C, Capital		$300,000

10-61.   Note that, if we had not recorded the fair value changes on the Partnership's Net Assets, Partner C would have only been credited with $50,000 in Goodwill and the capital accounts of the three partners would be at $250,000. However, based on the preceding entries, the Balance Sheet of the ABC Partnership would be prepared as follows:

ABC Partnership
Balance Sheet
As At December 31

Net Identifiable Assets	$800,000
Goodwill	100,000
Total	$900,000

Partner A, Capital	$300,000
Partner B, Capital	300,000
Partner C, Capital	300,000
Total	$900,000

Case Four - Consideration Below Book Value - Continuity

10-62.   In this Case, we will assume that C is admitted to the Partnership in return for a cash payment of $220,000 and that the admission does not constitute the formation of a new business entity. Since the admission of C does not constitute a basis for the revaluation of assets, then we must assume that the existing partners are each granting C a bonus of $10,000. The total assets will amount to $720,000 ($500,000 + $220,000) and C's one third interest will amount to $240,000. The entry to record C's admission to the partnership would be as follows:

Cash	$220,000	
Partner A, Capital	10,000	
Partner B, Capital	10,000	
Partner C, Capital		$240,000

10-63.   The resulting Balance Sheet for the ABC Partnership would be as follows:

ABC Partnership
Balance Sheet
As At December 31

Total Net Assets	$720,000

Partner A, Capital	$240,000
Partner B, Capital	240,000
Partner C, Capital	240,000
Total	$720,000

Retirement Of Existing Partners

Example

10-64.   As was the case in our consideration of the admission of new partners, we will use a single basic example for four different Cases illustrating the retirement of partners. The example is as follows:

The Balance Sheet of the XYZ Partnership as at December 31 of the current year is as follows:

XYZ Partnership
Balance Sheet As At December 31

Total Net Assets	$600,000
Partner X, Capital	$200,000
Partner Y, Capital	200,000
Partner Z, Capital	200,000
Total	$600,000

The partnership agreement calls for Partners X, Y, and Z to share all profits and losses equally. On December 31, it has been determined that the fair values of the identifiable Net Assets of the XYZ Partnership total $690,000. In the Cases which follow, Partner Z is being retired through a payment of partnership cash.

Case One - Consideration Exceeds Book Value - New Entity

10-65.   In this first Case, we will assume that Partner Z is retired in return for a payment of $250,000 in partnership cash and the circumstances are such that the remaining partnership can be viewed as a new business entity. The $250,000 payment to Partner Z for his one third interest implies a total value for the business of $750,000. This is $150,000 in excess of the book values of these assets and, given the fact that it has been determined that the identifiable assets have a total fair value of $690,000, this $150,000 excess would be allocated $90,000 to the identifiable assets and $60,000 to Goodwill. The entry to accomplish this allocation is as follows:

Net Assets	$90,000	
Goodwill	60,000	
Partner X, Capital		$50,000
Partner Y, Capital		50,000
Partner Z, Capital		50,000

10-66.   Given the preceding adjustment, the entry to retire Partner Z would be as follows:

Partner Z, Capital	$250,000	
Cash (Net Assets)		$250,000

10-67.   The resulting Balance Sheet, after the retirement of Partner Z would be as follows:

XY Partnership
Balance Sheet As At December 31

Net Identifiable Assets	$440,000
Goodwill	60,000
Total	$500,000
Partner X, Capital	$250,000
Partner Y, Capital	250,000
Total	$500,000

Case Two - Consideration Exceeds Book Value - Continuity

10-68.   In this Case we will again assume that Partner Z is retired in return for partnership cash in the amount of $250,000. However, in this case the interpretation will be that this retirement did not result in a new business entity and a need to revalue assets. This means that we will have to assume that Partner X and Partner Y are each paying a bonus of

$25,000 to Partner Z. The retirement entry which would reflect that assumption is as follows:

Partner X, Capital	$25,000	
Partner Y, Capital	25,000	
Partner Z, Capital	200,000	
Cash		$250,000

10-69.   The resulting Balance Sheet for the XY Partnership would be as follows:

XY Partnership
Balance Sheet
As At December 31

Total Net Assets	$350,000
Partner X, Capital	$175,000
Partner Y, Capital	175,000
Total	$350,000

Case Three - Consideration Below Book Value - New Entity

10-70.   We will assume in this situation that Partner Z is retired in return for a payment of $180,000 and that the retirement can be viewed as resulting in the formation of a new business entity. The price paid to Partner Z for his one third interest implies a total value for the enterprise of $540,000, a value that is $60,000 less than the $600,000 carrying value of the Net Assets and $150,000 less than their fair value of $690,000. This means that either the Partnership has negative goodwill in the amount of $150,000 ($690,000 - $540,000) or that there are factors in Partner Z's personal situation that make him willing to sacrifice a part of his equity in order to retire from the business.

10-71.   If Partner Z has actually made a sacrifice in order to facilitate his retirement, the amount of this sacrifice could be measured by the $20,000 difference between the capital balance of $200,000 and the retirement price of $180,000, and it would be appropriate to credit this amount to the capital accounts of Partners X and Y. This would result in a solution identical to that which would be used if we assume partnership continuity and use the bonus method to retire Z. This solution is illustrated in Case Four.

10-72.   Alternatively, if we assume that the deficiency relates to negative goodwill, present generally accepted accounting principles require such amounts to be charged to specific non monetary assets. This means that we cannot adjust the Net Assets to their current fair values of $690,000. Rather, we will have to write them down to the $540,000 balance implied in the purchase price. The entry for this adjustment would be as follows:

Partner X, Capital	$20,000	
Partner Y, Capital	20,000	
Partner Z, Capital	20,000	
Net Assets		$60,000

10-73.   After the preceding adjustment, the entry that would be required to retire Partner Z would be as follows:

Partner Z, Capital	$180,000	
Cash		$180,000

10-74.   The resulting Balance Sheet for the XY Partnership would be as follows:

XY Partnership
Balance Sheet
As At December 31

Total Net Assets	$360,000
Partner X, Capital	$180,000
Partner Y, Capital	180,000
Total	$360,000

Case Four - Consideration Below Book Value - Continuity

10-75.   We again assume in this Case that Partner Z is retired in return for a payment of $180,000, but that the transaction did not result in the formation of a new business entity. Since there is no basis for the revaluation of any of the Partnership assets, we will have to assume that Z is paying a bonus of $10,000 each to Partners X and Y. The journal entry to retire Partner Z under this assumption would be as follows:

Partner Z, Capital	$200,000	
Partner X, Capital		$ 10,000
Partner Y, Capital		10,000
Cash		180,000

10-76.   The resulting Balance Sheet for the XY Partnership would be as follows:

XY Partnership
Balance Sheet
As At December 31

Total Net Assets	$420,000
Partner X, Capital	$210,000
Partner Y, Capital	210,000
Total	$420,000

Partnership Liquidation

General Procedures

10-77.   In the context of partnership accounting, the term liquidation refers to situations in which the partners agree to terminate their operation of the enterprise, convert the assets to cash, pay off any outstanding liabilities, and distribute the remaining cash to the partners. In some cases, the business may be sold as a unit in a single transaction while, in other cases, the liquidation process may involve individual asset sales over a considerable period of time.

10-78.   Whether sold as a unit or disposed of on a piece by piece basis, the liquidation of the partnership assets will invariably involve gains and losses. While the partnership agreement might have a special provision dealing with gains and losses arising at the time of liquidation, such gains and losses would normally be allocated to the partners on the basis of their usual profit sharing ratios. These gains and losses will then be added or subtracted to the capital accounts of the partners and these capital account balances will serve as the basis for distributing any partnership cash that is left subsequent to the payment of partnership liabilities.

10-79.   If the partnership experiences losses in the liquidation process, one or more partners may end up with a debit or negative balance in their capital account. If this happens, such partners are responsible for eliminating this balance by making additional capital contributions from their personal assets. If, in this process, the concerned partners become personally insolvent and cannot provide the assets necessary to eliminate their debit capital balances, then any remaining debit balance in their accounts will become additional partnership losses to be shared by the remaining partners.

10-80.   If the partnership experiences particularly severe losses in the process of liquidation, it may find itself in a situation in which its liabilities exceed its assets. In this case the partnership is said to be insolvent (for more information on insolvency, see Reorganization, Receivership and Bankruptcy in this Volume) and one or more of the capital accounts will have debit balances. In fact, all of the capital accounts may have such balances. The only statement that can be made with certainty when the partnership is insolvent is that the sum of the debit capital balances exceeds the sum of any credit balances which may exist. As is the case when debit balances develop in the capital accounts of a solvent partnership, the partners in this position must eliminate this debit balance by making additional capital contributions from their personal assets. If they become personally insolvent in the process of making these contributions, any remaining debits must be allocated to other partners, with the process continuing until all of the partners are insolvent or contributions from the partners' personal assets have been sufficient to satisfy all creditor claims.

10-81.   In the Sections which follow, a number of Cases will be presented to illustrate the preceding general procedures. The Cases will cover situations in which there is a single distribution of cash to the partners as well as the somewhat more complex situations in which the cash distributions take the form of a number of installment payments over some period of time.

Single Step Liquidations

Example

10-82.   The following basic example will be used to illustrate three different Cases of single step liquidations:

The Balance Sheet of the JKL Partnership as at December 31 of the current year is as follows:

JKL Partnership
Balance Sheet
As At December 31

Total Assets	$680,000
Liabilities	$250,000
Partner J, Capital	180,000
Partner K, Capital	130,000
Partner L, Capital	120,000
Total	$680,000

The partnership agreement calls for all profits and losses, including any which arise in the process of liquidation, to be shared equally between the three partners.

Case One -
All Capital Balances Sufficient To Absorb Liquidation Loss Shares

10-83.   In this first, relatively simple case we will assume that the assets are sold for $590,000 in cash, resulting in a liquidation loss of $90,000. This would be allocated to the capital balances of the partners as follows:

	Partner J	Partner K	Partner L
Balance Before Liquidation	$180,000	$130,000	$120,000
Share Of Liquidation Loss	(30,000)	(30,000)	(30,000)
Adjusted Balance	$150,000	$100,000	$ 90,000

10-84.   The adjusted balance would be the amount of cash to be distributed to each partner. This means that of the total of $590,000, the creditors would receive $250,000 and the partners would receive $340,000 as per the schedule in the preceding Paragraph.

Case Two -
Some Capital Balances Not Sufficient To Absorb Liquidation Loss Shares

10-85.   In this somewhat more complex case, we will assume that the assets are sold for only $260,000 in cash, resulting in a liquidation loss in the amount of $420,000. This loss would be allocated to the capital balances of the partners as follows:

	Partner J	Partner K	Partner L
Balance Before Liquidation	$180,000	$130,000	$120,000
Share Of Liquidation Loss	(140,000)	(140,000)	(140,000)
Adjusted Balance	$ 40,000	($ 10,000)	($ 20,000)

10-86.   At this point there are a number of possibilities. If Partners K and L are solvent, they will be called on to contribute additional investment funds in the amount of $10,000 and $20,000 respectively. This would give total cash of $290,000 which would be distributed on the basis of $250,000 to the creditors and $40,000 to Partner A.

10-87.   However, things may not go quite so smoothly. Assume, for example, that Partner L has become personally insolvent and is unable to contribute additional funds. Because Partner L has not been able to absorb his full share of the liquidation loss, the additional $20,000 will have to be allocated equally to Partners J and K. This will leave Partner J with a balance of $30,000 and Partner K with a deficit of $20,000. Assuming Partner K to be solvent, he would then have to contribute an additional $20,000 to the partnership, providing a total amount to be distributed of $280,000. This would be distributed on the basis of $250,000 to the creditors and $30,000 to Partner J.

Case Three - Partnership Insolvent

10-88.   In this final example of a single step liquidation, we will assume that the assets are sold for only $230,000, resulting in a loss of $450,000. Further, as the cash balance of $230,000 is smaller than the liabilities of the partnership, the enterprise is now said to be insolvent. As we have noted previously, this means that one or more of the partners will now have debit balances in their capital accounts. This is made evident in the following allocation schedule:

	Partner J	Partner K	Partner L
Balance Before Liquidaton	$180,000	$130,000	$120,000
Liquidation Loss	(150,000)	(150,000)	(150,000)
Adjusted Balance	$ 30,000	($ 20,000)	($ 30,000)

10-89.   If both Partner K and Partner L are solvent, this situation presents no real problem.   These partners will contribute to the Partnership an additional $20,000 and $30,000, respectively.   This will provide a total cash balance of $280,000, of which $250,000 will go to the creditors and $30,000 will be paid to Partner J.

10-90.   Alternatively, if all three of the partners are insolvent, Partner J will not receive his $30,000 adjusted balance and a plan for distributing the $230,000 to the creditors will have to be established

10-91.   However, a more likely scenario lies between these two extremes. This is that some partners will be solvent while others will be insolvent. To illustrate this possibility, assume that Partner L is insolvent, while Partners J and K remain personally solvent. Partner L's debit balance of $30,000 will be split evenly between Partners J and K, leaving a $15,000 credit for Partner J and a $35,000 debit for Partner K. Partner K will then have to contribute an additional $35,000, giving a total cash balance for the Partnership of $265,000. Of this amount, $250,000 will be distributed to the creditors with the remaining $15,000 going to Partner J.

Installment Liquidations

General Principles

10-92.   In situations where the liquidation of the partnership assets takes place over a considerable period of time, it would be possible to delay any cash distributions to the partners until the entire liquidation process is complete. However, in most cases the partners will prefer to have partial distributions made as the liquidation progresses. If it is decided that such installment distributions are to be made, then it becomes necessary to calculate the amount of each installment that will be distributed to each partner. Two factors complicate this calculation. First, until the liquidation is complete, the partnership does not know what the total amount of the gain or loss on liquidation will be. A second factor relates to the possibility that one or more partners may become insolvent and may not be able to make any payments that might be required to eliminate debit balances in their capital accounts.

10-93.   The two problems are generally dealt with by making the following two assumptions at the time of each installment distribution:

1.   Assume that there will be a total loss on any remaining assets and, as a consequence, no further distributions of cash to the partners as a result of additional sales of assets.

2.   Assume that any partner with a capital deficiency will not be able to eliminate it through additional capital contributions to the partnership. This means that there will be no additional funds from this source available for distribution to the partners.

10-94.   In making distributions based on these assumptions, it is likely that a point will be reached where the partners' remaining capital balances are in the same ratios as their profit sharing percentages. At this point, any further distributions can simply be based on the applicable profit sharing percentages.

Example

10-95.   A simple example will be used to illustrate the general principles that have been described.

On December 31 of the current year, the EFG Partnership has the following Balance Sheet:

EFG Partnership
Balance Sheet
As At December 31

Total Assets	$900,000

Liabilities	$300,000
Partner E, Capital	300,000
Partner F, Capital	180,000
Partner G, Capital	120,000
Total	$900,000

The partnership agreement calls for the partners to share all profits and losses equally. Cash from the sale of assets becomes available in four installments during the year. The amounts of the installments are as follows:

First Installment	$330,000
Second Installment	150,000
Third Installment	120,000
Fourth Installment	60,000
Total	$660,000

At this point all of the partnership assets have been sold and there will be no further distributions to the partners.

10-96.   The total assets were $900,000 when the liquidation began and with proceeds of $660,000, this means that the partners will experience a $240,000 loss. If this were a single step liquidation, the amounts to be paid to the partners could be calculated as follows:

	Partner E	Partner F	Partner G
Balance Before Liquidation	$300,000	$180,000	$120,000
Share Of Liquidation Loss	(80,000)	(80,000)	(80,000)
Adjusted Balance	$220,000	$100,000	$ 40,000

10-97.   The preceding calculation provides the goal for our installment distributions. The installments must be allocated in such a fashion that the total amounts distributed to each partner will be equal to the amounts calculated in the preceding Paragraph.

10-98.   With respect to the first installment of $330,000, the first $300,000 will have to be paid to the partnership creditors. This leaves only $30,000 for the partners and, if we assume that they will receive no further distributions, their total loss would be $570,000. The loss would be allocated as follows:

	Partner E	Partner F	Partner G
Balance Before Liquidation	$300,000	$180,000	$120,000
Share Of Liquidation Loss	(190,000)	(190,000)	(190,000)
Adjusted Balance	$110,000	($ 10,000)	($ 70,000)

10-99.   As both Partner F and Partner G have negative balances, all of the $30,000 remaining cash would be paid to Partner E, leaving a balance in that partner's capital account of $270,000.

10-100.   The sum of the first and second installments is $480,000. If this second installment were, in fact, the last payment to the partners, the total loss on the $900,000 in assets would be $420,000. Assuming that Partner G is not able to make up the capital deficiency which arises at this stage, the second installment would be distributed on the basis of the following schedule:

	Partner E	Partner F	Partner G
Balance After First Installment	$270,000	$180,000	$120,000
Share Of Liquidation Loss	(140,000)	(140,000)	(140,000)
Preliminary Balance	$130,000	$ 40,000	($ 20,000)
Distribution Of The Capital Deficiency Of Partner G	(10,000)	(10,000)	20,000
Adjusted Balance	$120,000	$ 30,000	$ -0-

10-101.   Thus, the second installment of $150,000 would be distributed $120,000 to Partner E and $30,000 to Partner F. This would leave the capital balances of both Partner E and Partner F at $150,000. However, these balances remain larger than that of Partner G and, as a consequence, it is not yet possible to distribute future installments on the basis of profit sharing ratios.

10-102.   The third installment brings the total proceeds to $600,000. If this were viewed as the last installment, the total loss on the $900,000 in assets would be $300,000 and this would be distributed as per the following schedule:

	Partner E	Partner F	Partner G
Balance After Second Installment	$150,000	$150,000	$120,000
Share Of Liquidation Loss	(100,000)	(100,000)	(100,000)
Adjusted Balance	$ 50,000	$ 50,000	$ 20,000

10-103.   Based on the preceding schedule, the third installment would be distributed $50,000 each to Partners E and F, and $20,000 to Partner G. Also of importance is the fact that at this point the remaining balance in each of the Partner's capital accounts is $100,000. Since these balances are equal and the profit and loss allocation is based on equal shares, we are now in a position where the Partners' shares of total capital are equal to their income shares. As noted in Paragraph 10-94, when this stage is reached subsequent distributions of cash can be made on the basis of profit and loss sharing ratios. This means that the fourth installment of $60,000 will simply be distributed $20,000 to each partner.

10-104.   We have now completed the allocation of all four installments. We noted in Paragraph 10-96 that, if the liquidation had taken place in a single step, Partner E would have received $220,000, Partner F, $100,000, and Partner G, $40,000. Since our goal was to achieve an identical result through the various installments, it is useful to verify that this has, in fact, happened. The following schedule provides this verification:

	Partner E	Partner F	Partner G
First Installment	$ 30,000	$ -0-	$ -0-
Second Installment	120,000	30,000	-0-
Third Installment	50,000	50,000	20,000
Fourth Installment	20,000	20,000	20,000
Total Distribution	$220,000	$100,000	$40,000

10-105.   This serves to verify that we have distributed the cash that became available in the installment liquidation steps in a manner that complied with the partnership agreement.

Installment Liquidation Distribution Schedules

10-106.   The preceding section illustrated the calculations required to deal with a known schedule of cash distributions as they became available over a period of time. A somewhat different approach to this problem can be involved in administering liquidations. Rather than calculating the allocation of cash distributions as they occur, a schedule of distributions could be required in advance of any specified amounts becoming available. To illustrate the approach to be used in solving this type of problem, the following simple example will be used.

On December 31 of the current year, the PQR Partnership has the following Balance Sheet:

PQR Partnership
Balance Sheet As At December 31

Total Net Assets	$2,400,000
Partner P, Capital	$1,400,000
Partner Q, Capital	650,000
Partner R, Capital	350,000
Total	$2,400,000

The partnership agreement calls for all profits and losses, including any which arise in the process of liquidation, to be shared on the basis of 50 percent for P, 30 percent for Q, and 20 percent for R.

10-107.   If the respective capital balances were in proportion to the profit sharing ratios, the solution to this problem would be very simple. Distributions would simply be made on the basis of the profit sharing percentages. However, in the preceding example, Partner P's capital balance is more than his 50 percent share of profits while the other partner's capital balances are below their share of profits. This makes it necessary to calculate the loss absorbing capacity of each partner's capital account. These calculations are as follows:

Partner P ($1,400,000 ÷ 50%) = $ 2,800,000

Partner Q ($ 650,000 ÷ 30%) = $ 2,166,667

Partner R ($ 350,000 ÷ 20%) = $ 1,750,000

10-108.   As Partner P is in a position to absorb his share of a $2,800,000 loss, all cash distributions would go to Partner P until this loss absorbing capacity is reduced to the next highest amount, the $2,166,667 capacity of Partner Q. This would mean that the first $316,667 ([$2,800,000 - $2,166,667][50%]) would go to Partner P, reducing his capital account to $1,083,333. At this point new loss absorbing capacities could be calculated as follows:

Partner P ($1,083,333 ÷ 50%) = $2,166,667

Partner Q ($ 650,000 ÷ 30%) = $2,166,667

Partner R ($ 350,000 ÷ 20%) = $1,750,000

10-109.   In order to equalize the loss absorbing capacities of all three partners, Partners P and Q will have to receive the next $333,333 in distributions ([$2,166,667 - $1,750,000][80%]) on the basis of a 50:30 ratio. This means that Partner P will receive $208,333 ([50/80][$333,333]) of this amount while Partner Q will receive $125,000 ([30/80][$333,333]). Subsequent distributions of partnership assets can simply be based on the normal profit sharing ratios of each of the three partners. This is a reflection of the fact that, subsequent to the second distribution, the loss absorbing capacities of the three Partners are now equal:

Partner P ($875,000 ÷ 50%) = $1,750,000

Partner Q ($525,000 ÷ 30%) = $1,750,000

Partner R ($350,000 ÷ 20%) = $1,750,000

10-110.   It also means that the capital balances of the three partners are in proportion to their profit and loss sharing ratios. This can be seen in the following schedule:

	Partner P	Partner Q	Partner R	Total
Original Balance	$1,400,000	$650,000	$350,000	$2,400,000
First Distribution	(316,667)	-0-	-0-	(316,667)
Second Distribution	(208,333)	(125,000)	-0-	(333,333)
Remaining Balance	$ 875,000	$525,000	$350,000	$1,750,000

10-111.   A quick verifying calculation will demonstrate that the capital balances of the three partners are now in the ratio 50:30:20, the same basis on which they share profits and losses.

Incorporation Of A Partnership

10-112.   Under some circumstances, successful partnerships may give consideration to the advantages to be gained from incorporating. These advantages could include an improved tax situation, the ability to raise additional funds more efficiently, or the desire to remove personal assets from the risks associated with participating in a partnership.

10-113.   In such situations, the accounting complications are not particularly significant. The fundamental decision that must be made is to decide whether or not the change in legal form constitutes the creation of a new business entity. While there is room for the application of judgment in this situation, we are of the opinion that the incorporation of a partnership generally creates a new business entity. This will mean that there is a need to adjust all of the assets and liabilities that are being transferred to the corporation at their current fair values. It would also be appropriate to record any partnership goodwill that has been acquired by the newly formed corporation. However, because of valuation problems associated with this intangible asset, this will generally not occur in most practical situations.

10-114.   The accounting records for the corporation could be simply a continuation of the old records of the partnership. In most cases, however, a new set of books will be opened. The appropriate entries will simply involve recording the newly acquired assets at the current fair values and setting up a liability to the partners for the value of the net assets transferred. This liability will then be discharged by the issuance of shares of capital stock.

Problems For Self Study

(The solutions for these problems can be found following Chapter 17 of the text.)

SELF STUDY PROBLEM TEN - 1

The partnership of George Brown and Terry Green was formed on February 28 of the current year. At that date the following assets, recorded at their fair values, were contributed:

	George Brown	Terry Green
Cash	$35,000	$ 25,000
Merchandise		45,000
Building		100,000
Furniture And Equipment	15,000	

The building is subject to a mortgage loan of $30,000 which is to be assumed by the partnership. The partnership agreement provides that George and Terry share profits or losses equally.

Required:

A. What are the capital balances of the partners on February 28 of the current year?

B. If the partnership agreement states that the initial capital balances of the partners should be equal, and no recognition should be given to any intangible assets contributed, what are the partners' capital balances on February 28 of the current year?

C. Given the facts stated in requirement B, except that any contributed goodwill should be recognized in the accounts, what are the partners' capital balances on February 28 of the current year? How much goodwill should be recognized?

SELF STUDY PROBLEM TEN - 2

The condensed Balance Sheet of the Portly, Brawn and Large partnership just prior to liquidation is as follows:

Total Assets	$1,032,000
Accounts Payable	$ 72,000
Portly, Loan	48,000
Portly, Capital	112,000
Brawn, Capital	320,000
Large, Capital	480,000
Total Equities	$1,032,000

Portly, Brawn, And Large share profits and losses in the ratio of 1: 4 : 5, respectively.

Required: Construct a systematic plan showing how cash should be distributed to the various equities as it becomes available during the liquidation process.

SELF STUDY PROBLEM TEN - 3

Several years ago, Tom, Dick, and Harry Jones formed a partnership to carry on their professional activities. The partnership agreement calls for profits and losses to be shared according to the following percentages:

Brother	Percent
Tom	20
Dick	30
Harry	50

At the end of the Partnership's current fiscal year, the condensed Balance Sheet of the Partnership was as follows:

Total Identifiable Assets	$164,000
Liabilities	$ 45,000
Tom Jones, Capital	26,000
Dick Jones, Capital	41,000
Harry Jones, Capital	52,000
Total Equities	$164,000

The brothers estimate that the current fair values of the identifiable assets total $189,000.

Required: The brothers are considering a number of alternatives for expanding, contracting, or liquidating their partnership. Provide the information which is indicated for each of the four independent alternatives that are described in the following paragraphs:

A. Tom Jones is prepared to sell his interest in the Jones Brothers Partnership to his sister Shirley. He would give up his interest in return for $31,500 in cash to be paid directly to him. Provide the journal entry(ies) on the books of the Partnership to record this change in ownership interest.

B. The brothers are prepared to admit their sister Shirley into the Partnership with a 20 percent interest in profits and losses. She will be required to contribute $40,000 in cash to the Partnership in return for this interest. The partners believe that the admission of Shirley would be of sufficient importance to account for the transaction on a new entity basis. Provide the journal entry(ies) on the books of the Partnership to record the admission of Shirley Jones to the Partnership.

C. Dick Jones may wish to retire from the Partnership. If this retirement takes place, the brothers have agreed that Dick should receive a cash payment of $54,000 for his 30 percent interest in the Partnership. The partners do not believe that this retirement is a sufficient change in the business to warrant any revaluation of the Partnership assets. Provide the journal entry(ies) that would be required on the books of the Partnership to record the retirement of Dick Jones.

D. As all three of the brothers have developed separate business interests in recent years, they may decide to liquidate the Partnership. It is their belief that the identifiable assets of the partnership could be sold for their fair values which total $189,000. If the liquidation was carried out and the anticipated amount of cash received for the assets, provide the journal entry(ies) to record the transaction and the distribution of the resulting cash balance.

SELF STUDY PROBLEM TEN - 4

Jones, Smith, and Doe are partners in a retailing business which has been operating for a number of years. Their profit sharing and capital balances on December 31 of the current year are as follows:

Partner	Profit Sharing	Capital Balance
Jones	30 Percent	$ 327,000
Smith	45 Percent	482,000
Doe	25 Percent	191,000

Required: The following Cases represent three different and completely independent transactions. In each Case, we will assume that the transaction took place on December 31 of the current year. You are to provide any journal entries that would be required to record the transaction that has been described.

Case 1   Breem is admitted to the partnership with a one third interest in profits and capital. In return for this interest he makes a cash payment of $540,000 to the partnership. It is determined that the price paid by Breem reflects the fact that the Partnership has unrecorded Goodwill. This Goodwill is to be recorded as part of the admission transaction.

Case 2   Doe gives up his share of the partnership in return for a cash payment of $171,000. The remaining partners decide not to revalue assets to reflect the price that was paid to Doe in this transaction.

Case 3   It is decided that the partnership is to be liquidated. Because of the size of the business, the assets will be liquidated in several groups. After the sale of the first group of Partnership assets, some of the proceeds are used to pay off the creditors of the Partnership. After the payments to the creditors have been made, $100,000 in cash remains and this is distributed to the Partners as per the partnership agreement.

Assignment Problems

(The solutions to these problem are only available in
the solutions manual that has been provided to your instructor.)

ASSIGNMENT PROBLEM TEN - 1

Jim Bond and Bob Ray organized the Bond And Ray Partnership on January 1 of the current year. The following entries were made in their capital accounts during the current year:

	Debit	Credit	Balance
Bond Capital:			
January 1		$20,000	$20,000
April 1		5,000	25,000
October 1		5,000	30,000
Ray Capital:			
January 1		40,000	40,000
March 1	$10,000		30,000
September 1	10,000		20,000
November 1		10,000	30,000

Partnership net income, computed without regard to salaries or interest, is $20,000 for the current year.

Required: Indicate the distribution of net income between the partners under the following independent profit-sharing conditions:

A. Interest at 4 percent is allowed on average capital investments, and the remainder is divided equally.

B. A salary of $9,000 is to be credited to Ray; 4 percent interest is allowed each partner on his ending capital balance; residual profits or losses are divided 60 percent to Bond and 40 percent to Ray.

C. Salaries are allowed Bond and Ray in amounts of $8,300 and $9,500, respectively, and residual profits or residual losses are divided in the ratio of average capital balances.

D. A bonus of 20 percent of partnership net income is credited to Bond, a salary of $5,000 is allowed to Ray, and residual profits or residual losses are shared equally. (The bonus and salary are regarded as "expenses" for purposes of calculating the amount of the bonus.)

ASSIGNMENT PROBLEM TEN - 2

Journalize the admission of Brown to the partnership of Black and Blue in each of the following independent cases. The capital balances of Black and Blue are $20,000 and $20,000 and they share profits and losses equally.

A. Brown is admitted to a one third interest in capital, profits, and losses with a contribution of $20,000.

B. Brown is admitted to a one fourth interest in capital, profits, and losses with a contribution of $24,000. Total capital of the new partnership is to be $64,000.

C. Brown is admitted to a one fifth interest in capital, profits, and losses upon contributing $6,000. Total capital of the new partnership is to be $50,000.

D. Brown is admitted to a one fifth interest in capital, profits, and losses by the purchase of one fifth of the interests of Black and Blue, paying $2,000 directly to Black and $2,000 directly to Blue. Total capital of the new partnership is to be $40,000.

E. Brown is admitted to a one fifth interest in capital, profits, and losses by the purchase of one fifth of the interests of Black and Blue, paying $9,000 directly to Black and $8,000 directly to Blue. Total capital of the new partnership is to be $55,000.

F. Brown is admitted to a one third interest in capital, profits, and losses upon contributing $14,000, after which each partner is to have an equal capital equity in the new partnership.

G. Brown is admitted to a one fifth interest in capital, profits, and losses upon contributing $14,000. Total capital of the new partnership is to be $70,000.

ASSIGNMENT PROBLEM TEN - 3

Allison, Brook, And Carey are partners. Douglas is to be admitted to the partnership at the end of the current fiscal year. On this date, the profit sharing ratios and capital balances of the original partners are as follows:

Partner	Profit Sharing	Capital Balance
Allison	60%	$194,000
Brook	30%	$130,000
Carey	10%	$ 76,000

Required:

A. Assume that Douglas is admitted to the partnership by investing $80,000 for a 20 percent interest in capital and profits. What alternative methods could be used to record the admission of Douglas to the partnership? Provide the journal entries for each method.

B. Assume that Douglas purchases a 20 percent interest in the partnership ratably from the existing partners by paying $84,000 cash directly to the partners. What alternative methods could be used to record the admission of Douglas to the partnership? Provide the journal entries for each method.

ASSIGNMENT PROBLEM TEN - 4

At the year end of the current fiscal year, the Balance Sheet of the Norton, Simon, Carly, and Jones Partnership is as follows:

Monetary Assets	$ 573,000
Nonmonetary Assets	1,114,000
Total Assets	$1,687,000
Current Liabilities	$ 71,500
Long Term Liabilities	26,500
Norton, Capital	173,000
Simon, Capital	337,000
Carly, Capital	692,000
Jones, Capital	387,000
Total Equities	$1,687,000

The Partnership agreement calls for profit and loss sharing on the following basis:

Norton	10 Percent
Simon	20 Percent
Carly	40 Percent
Jones	30 Percent

Because of irreconcilable differences between the partners, it has been decided that the Partnership will be liquidated as soon as possible. However, the partners are agreed that the assets should be disposed of in an orderly fashion, even if it requires some delay in their ultimate disposition. The cash proceeds of all sales will be distributed as they become available.

Required: Prepare a schedule for the distribution of the cash which will result from the sale of Partnership assets.

ASSIGNMENT PROBLEM TEN - 5

A number of years ago, John, Joseph, Judas, and Jerry Goody formed a partnership to carry on their professional activities. The partnership agreement calls for profits and losses to be shared according to the following percentages:

Brother	Percent
John	18
Joseph	23
Judas	32
Jerry	27

At the end of the Partnership's current fiscal year, the condensed Balance Sheet of the Partnership was as follows:

Total Identifiable Assets	$978,000
Liabilities	$114,000
John Goody, Capital	162,000
Joseph Goody, Capital	193,000
Judas Goody, Capital	268,000
Jerry Goody, Capital	241,000
Total Equities	$978,000

The brothers estimate that the current fair values of the identifiable assets total $1,200,000.

Required: The brothers are considering a number of alternatives for expanding, contracting, or liquidating their partnership. Provide the information which is indicated for each of the five independent alternatives that are described in the following paragraphs:

A. John Goody is prepared to sell his interest in the Goody Brothers Partnership to his sister Jill. He would give up his interest in return for $197,000 in cash to be paid directly to him by Jill. Provide the journal entry on the books of the Partnership to record this change in ownership interest.

B. Because of poor health, Judas Goody wishes to retire from the partnership and move to Rangoon. If the retirement takes place, the other Brothers are prepared to pay Judas $197,000 for his 32 percent interest in the Partnership. The partners do not believe that this retirement is a sufficient change in the business to warrant any revaluation of the Partnership assets. Provide the journal entry that would be required on the books of the Partnership to record the retirement of Judas Goody.

C. All of the brothers have developed separate business interests in recent years and, as a consequence, they are considering the liquidation of the partnership. It is their belief that the identifiable assets of the Partnership could be sold for their fair values which total $1,200,000. However, to realize this value the assets will have to be sold over an extended period of time. The brothers anticipate that the first sale of assets would bring in cash of $423,000. Provide the journal entry to record the distribution of this $423,000.

D. The brothers are planning to admit their sister Jill into the partnership with a 20 percent interest in profits and losses. She will be required to contribute $312,000 in cash to the Partnership in return for this interest. The partners believe that admission of Jill would be of sufficient importance to account for the transaction on a new entity basis. Provide the journal entry on the books of the Partnership to record the admission of Jill Goody to the Partnership.

E. In order to increase his interest in the partnership, Jerry Goody acquires two percentage points of the interests of each of his brothers. This total of six percentage points will bring his interest to 33 percent and, in order to acquire this additional interest, he pays an additional $96,000 into the partnership. The partners agree that this transaction is not important enough to justify any new basis of accounting for the Partnership's assets. Provide the journal entry to record the change in ownership interests.

ASSIGNMENT PROBLEM TEN - 6

A number of years ago, Ellen, Eileen, Edna, and Edwina Lee formed a partnership to carry on their professional activities. The partnership agreement calls for profits and losses to be shared according to the following percentages:

Sister	Percent
Ellen	13
Eileen	8
Edna	42
Edwina	37

At the end of the Partnership's current fiscal year, the Balance Sheet of the Partnership was as follows:

The Lee Sisters Partnership
Balance Sheet

Total Identifiable Assets	$4,118,000
Liabilities	$ 226,000
Ellen Lee, Capital	511,000
Ellen Lee, Drawing	(52,000)
Eileen Lee, Capital	342,000
Edna Lee, Capital	1,576,000
Edna Lee, Drawing	(108,000)
Edwina Lee, Capital	1,623,000
Total Equities	$4,118,000

The sisters estimate that the current fair values of the identifiable assets total $4,876,000.

Required: The sisters are considering a number of alternatives for expanding, contracting, or liquidating their partnership. Provide the information which is indicated for each of the five independent alternatives that are described in the following paragraphs:

A. Because of personal differences with the other sisters, Edna Lee would like to retire from the Partnership and move to another city. The other sisters have agreed to pay Edna $1,845,000 of Partnership funds and eliminate her $108,000 drawing in return for her 42 percent interest. They also feel that Edna's departure will improve the operations of the business and therefore it is an appropriate occasion to revalue the Partnership's identifiable assets. Provide the journal entry(ies) that would be required on the books of the Partnership to record the retirement of Edna Lee.

B. The youngest sister of the partners, Elvira Lee, would like to enter the partnership. Eileen Lee is prepared to give up her 8 percent interest if Elvira will pay her $423,000 in cash. Provide the journal entry(ies) on the books of the Partnership to record this change in ownership interest.

C. In order to increase her 8 percent interest in the Partnership, Eileen Lee acquires four percentage points of the interests of each of the other sisters. This brings her total interest in the Partnership to 20 percent and reduces the interests of the other sisters correspondingly. To acquire this additional interest, Eileen pays $642,000 in cash to the Partnership. The partners do not believe that this transaction is of sufficient importance to revalue the partnership assets. Provide the journal entry(ies) to record this transaction on the books of the Partnership.

D. It is the intention of the sisters to liquidate the partnership. In order to get satisfactory prices for the various partnership assets, they have decided to sell them in an orderly fashion over the next twelve months. They anticipate that the first sale of assets should bring in $1,250,000 in cash. Indicate the amounts that would be distributed to the partnership creditors and the four sisters if the first sale does bring in this estimated amount.

E. John Chong is to be admitted to the partnership with a 20 percent interest in profits and losses. He will be required to pay cash of $1,263,000 to the Partnership. The partners believe that this admission is of such significance that the transaction should be accounted for using the new entity approach. Provide the journal entry(ies) required to record this transaction on the books of the Partnership.

ASSIGNMENT PROBLEM TEN - 7

Two years ago, Tammy, Jessica and Donna formed a partnership, FHR Enterprises, to carry on various fundraising and publicity activities. The partnership agreement calls for profits and losses to be shared according to the following ratios:

Partner	Ratio
Tammy	3/6
Jessica	2/6
Donna	1/6

At the end of FHR Enterprises' current fiscal year, its Balance Sheet was as follows:

Current Monetary Assets	$527,000
Furniture and Fixtures (Net)	130,000
Total Identifiable Assets	$657,000

Liabilities		$225,000
Tammy, Capital	$216,000	
Jessica, Capital	144,000	
Donna, Capital	72,000	432,000
Total Equities		$657,000

An independent appraisal estimates the current fair values of the furniture and fixtures total $118,000.

Required: Provide the information which is indicated for each of the independent alternatives that are described in the following paragraphs:

A. Donna retires from the Partnership to pursue a new career as an author. She receives a cash payment of $90,000 for her interest in FHR Enterprises. Tammy and Jessica plan to continue in partnership and maintain the original income sharing ratio. Provide the journal entry(ies) that would be required on the books of the Partnership to record the retirement of Donna assuming:

   i. Tammy and Jessica do not believe that this retirement is a sufficient change in the business to warrant any revaluation of the Partnership assets.

   ii. Tammy and Jessica believe that this retirement is a sufficient change that the remaining partnership can be viewed as a new business entity.

B. FHR Enterprises admits Ollie into the Partnership. Ollie is given a 25 percent interest in capital, and profits and losses. Tammy, Jessica and Donna will share the remaining 75 percent of the partnership earnings in the same original ratio existing prior to the admission of Ollie.

   i. FHR Enterprises agrees to admit Ollie into the Partnership for an investment of $120,000 in cash. Before Ollie is admitted, Tammy withdraws $15,000 cash from the partnership. The original partners do not believe that this admission is a sufficient change in the business to warrant any revaluation of the Partnership assets. Provide the journal entry(ies) on the books of the Partnership to record the cash withdrawal and the admission of Ollie to the Partnership.

   ii. FHR Enterprises admits Ollie into the Partnership for an investment of $150,000 in cash. The original partners believe that this admission is a sufficient change that the remaining partnership can be viewed as a new business entity. Provide the journal entry(ies) on the books of the Partnership to record the admission of Ollie to the Partnership.

ASSIGNMENT PROBLEM TEN - 8

Joe Green and his brother Pete have operated as partners in a small greenhouse business for thirty years. They are nearing retirement age and Pete would like to sell his share of the business and move to Florida. Joe's son, Tom, has worked in the greenhouse operation since he was a child and has gradually taken on more responsibility so that he is now acting as manager. He has $20,000 in savings and can borrow $30,000 more to invest in the partnership with his father. Tom would continue as manager and Joe would gradually reduce his involvement, acting as a consultant when required. Tom wants to build a new packing house and implement a hydroponic growing system, but requires more capital to do so.

The Green Partnership currently has a demand loan from the bank with an interest rate of 7 percent. Tom's brother, Robert, a successful doctor, is willing to invest $80,000, but is not sure whether he wants to be a partner in the business.

The partnership Balance Sheet as at December 31, 1998 is as follows:

Green Partnership
Condensed Balance Sheet
December 31, 1998

Cash	$ 10,000
Supplies	5,000
Equipment (Net)	30,000
Land And Buildings (Net)	60,000
Total Assets	$105,000

Accounts Payable	$ 5,000
Bank Loan	15,000
Joe, Capital	42,500
Pete, Capital	42,500
Total Equities	$105,000

An independent appraiser has estimated the following fair values at December 31, 1998:

Supplies	$ 4,000
Equipment	$ 46,000
Land and Buildings	$100,000

Required: The following parts are independent cases.

A. Assume that Pete and Joe dissolve their partnership and that Joe, Tom and Robert form a partnership on January 1, 1999.

1. Prepare the new partnership Balance Sheet. Show all calculations and state your assumptions.

2. What items should be specified in the new partnership agreement?

3. Discuss how the income or loss for 1999 could be allocated to the new partners.

4. How would the Balance Sheet and income allocation change if Robert contributes financially, but is not admitted as a partner?

B. Assume that Pete gives up his share of the partnership for a cash payment of $60,000 on January 1, 1999. Joe decides not to revalue the assets to reflect the price that Pete was paid. Provide the journal entry to record Pete's retirement.

C. Assume that Pete gives up his share of the partnership for a cash payment of $70,000 on January 1, 1999. Joe decides to revalue the assets as he views the resulting enterprise as a new business entity. On that same date, Tom invests $50,000 for a 50 percent share in the partnership and Robert decides to lend the Green partnership $80,000 in the form of a Note Payable. Joe and Tom decide that Tom is bringing goodwill into the partnership.

1. Provide the journal entries to record the preceding transactions and prepare the Balance Sheet of the new partnership as at January 1, 1999.

2. On January 2, 1999, Joe contributes an additional $25,000 in capital to the partnership. Later that day, the partners are informed that their greenhouse is situated on a site that has been contaminated by radioactive waste. They decide to liquidate the partnership immediately and receive a total of $22,000 for the Supplies, Equipment, Land and Buildings of the partnership. Calculate the amount of cash that would be distributed to each partner on the liquidation of the partnership.

D. Assume that Pete gives up his share of the partnership on January 1, 1999 and on that date, both Tom and Robert purchase a one-third share in the partnership. During the year, Joe has drawings of $28,000 and Tom has drawings of $45,000. These withdrawals are equal to the salaries for Joe and Tom, respectively, as stated in the partnership agreement. The agreement also allows each partner a 10 percent interest on his ending capital balance, without inclusion of the year's income or any withdrawals. Any residual profits or losses are shared equally.

The income of the Green Partnership for the year ending December 31, 1999, computed without regard to salaries to the partners or interest on the capital contributions of the partners, was equal to $200,000. The ending capital balances, calculated before consideration of withdrawals or income of the year are equal to $70,000 for Joe, $50,000 for Tom and $80,000 for Robert. Calculate the income share for each partner for the year.

(SMA Adapted)

ASSIGNMENT CASE TEN - 1

You have been shortlisted for a position as financial consultant for a major Canadian consulting firm. As part of the recruitment procedure, you are asked to demonstrate your basic knowledge of partnerships. Specifically, you are presented with the following four independent partnership scenarios and are asked to write a brief note on each, identifying the relevant issues, concerns and implications of the related circumstances.

The situations are briefly summarized as follows:

1. Partnership A has run into financial difficulty. In discussing the problem, Bert and Ernie, two of the partners, conclude that unless additional financing can be found, the business should be sold or wound up. Oscar, the third partner, joins them and announces that their troubles are over as he has just signed an agreement with Sue making her a full partner in exchange for an investment of $200,000. Neither Bert nor Ernie has ever met Sue.

2. Heather and Bernie have just formed Partnership B. Heather has considerable experience and has made a substantial investment in the business. Bernie, on the other hand, has less experience and has made a smaller investment. Bernie will be working full time in the partnership, while Heather, in the short run, will keep her job outside the partnership and assist Bernie only when needed.

3. Partnership C has run into financial difficulty, and one of the partners has just left town, leaving the other partners to pay off all the debts of the business.

4. Moe and Larry are the sole partners in Partnership D. The partnership has been profitable and has expanded rapidly. Moe is in favor of incorporating the business at this time but Larry would like more information before making a decision.

Required: Prepare the required note for each situation.

(SMA adapted)

ASSIGNMENT CASE TEN - 2

Sally Hart, architect, has operated a sole proprietorship in Guelph since 1991. The practice has become quite successful, in no small part due to Sally's aggressive marketing and excellent reputation in the community.

However, it is now August 1998 and Sally has decided to form a partnership with a recent graduate, Mary Seoul. The new partnership is to take effect immediately after her existing fiscal year, August 31, 1998.

Sally has come to you for assistance in the financial accounting aspects of the new partnership. Specifically, she is interested in how the assets being brought into the partnership will be valued on the opening balance sheet.

According to the new partnership agreement, Sally will be contributing all assets and liabilities used in her existing practice to the new partnership. This includes the capital assets, working capital and long term debt. The working capital consists of accounts receivable, supplies and trade accounts payble. There is an extensive amount of "work-in-progress" (WIP) on Sally's accounts that will also be transferred. In the past, Sally has not recorded WIP on her books of account. The capital assets consist of the single office building used in the practice, desks, chairs and drafting tables.

As Mary has no capital assets and no clients, it was agreed her contribution would be in the form of cash.

The agreement stipulates that they will each own 50% of the new partnership as well as sharing equally in all billings made and expenses incurred, effective September 1, 1998.

Sally has informed you that, due to deflation, the property used as an office has a fair market value below its original cost. Its value is also below the existing mortgage. The mortgage is secured by the property as well as a personal guarantee from Sally.

Finally, Sally informed you that she is being sued by a disgruntled client. The lawsuit implicates Sally as the cause of structural damage in a home she designed in 1993. Sally is concerned since the amount of the lawsuit is in excess of her insurance coverage. While the outcome of the lawsuit is not known at this time, it is expected to be resolved within 12 months.

Required: Advise Sally on how each of the assets and liabilities transferred should be valued on the opening balance sheet of the new partnership. The bank, holding the mortgage, requires the financial statements to be prepared in accordance with generally accepted accounting principles.

(OICA Adapted)

ASSIGNMENT CASE TEN - 3

Length, Width and Hite (LWH) is a firm of architects, with one office in a large Canadian city. The firm has been in operation for over 20 years and, as of September 1, 1998, had 18 partners and a staff of 60. LWH owns a building in which it occupies three floors and it rents out the other three. The firm also has ownership interests of 10% to 50% in several properties. The ownership usually arose because the builders had difficulty paying architects' fees to LWH, and the firm accepted equity interests. Most of these properties have mortgages.

The firm's year end is December 31. Your employer, CA & Co., chartered accountants, has performed compilation engagements, for income tax purposes, for LWH for many years. The last compilation engagement was conducted at December 31, 1997 and you were in charge of the assignment.

On September 2, 1998, the managing partner of LWH, Mr. Lee, informed you that LWH has decided to wind up the practice as of November 30, 1998. Apparently, the partners had several disagreements, so they decided to dissolve the partnership. Mr. Lee and 5 other partners of LWH intend to form a new partnership, Vector and Company (VC), and the others will each choose between forming a new partnership or proceeding on their own. The staff will be divided among the new practices. The clients will choose the partner with whom they wish to remain associated.

Mr. Lee has asked CA & Co. to accept two special engagements:

1. The partners of LWH want to wind up the firm "equitably," and want assurance that each partner receives a "fair share" of the equity. Mr. Lee wants CA & Co. to identify the financial information to be used for the winding up of LWH and to explain why this information is necessary. Furthermore, he would like CA & Co. to indicate how it would substantiate the financial information.

   As part of the dissolution agreement, the partners of LWH agreed to have a report prepared describing the financial information other than financial statements that will be useful to the partners in their new practices. CA & Co. has been asked to prepare this report.

2. Mr. Lee requires CA & Co.'s assistance in selecting significant accounting policies for VC.

The engagement partner, Jim Spinney, has asked you to prepare a memo discussing the nature of the special engagements and work to be performed. The memo should address the issues raised and provide the information required by Mr. Lee. Relevant tax considerations should be identified in the memo.

You have made several inquiries, and have learned the following.

1. At November 30, 1998, LWH will have receivables outstanding and a material amount of work in progress. LWH currently has:

   a. Ownership of its building, which has a mortgage with a 12% interest rate, due in 2001.

   b. Several interests in properties, as stated previously.

   c. A copyright on a design for grocery stores, for which it is entitled to royalties over the next 12 to 15 years.

   d. Leases on computer equipment that expire over the period 2000 through 2003. The lease payments exceed current market rates. LWH is required to make monthly payments to the lessor.

   e. Office equipment and architectural materials and equipment.

   f. Artwork, a library, and miscellaneous assets. Most of the costs were expensed several years ago.

   g. Various pension obligations to a few non-partners who hold or have held administrative positions.

2. The building, property interests, copyright, artwork, library, and miscellaneous assets will be transferred to VC. Some computer leases, some equipment, and some pension obligations will not be transferred to VC but will accompany the non-VC partners. The non-VC partners will be occupying separate premises.

3. All vehicles and some equipment are leased from a company owned by the spouses of the three most senior partners of LWH. The leases extend to 2003 and were set at fair market value at the time that they were signed. However, the lease payments are now well above fair market value. All three partners are becoming partners of VC. The vehicles and equipment are to be assigned to VC, under the proposed terms of the

wind-up of LWH.

4. VC will be using a different bank from the one that LWH uses. However, both banks use the same lending formula for maximum loans: 70% of current receivables and 40% of work in progress. LWH's bank has agreed to give the partnership three months after November 30, 1998, to pay the loan that will be outstanding on LWH's wind-up date. Both banks require personal guarantees from each partner. VC's new bank requires the financial statements of VC to be reviewed. Mr. Lee has asked CA & Co. to perform a review of VC as at December 31, 1998, its first fiscal year end.

5. LWH partners who have retired in the past are paid 20% of their equity per year for five years from the date of their retirement.

6. Partners receive interest at the prime rate on their outstanding loans to the LWH partnership. Only some partners have lent funds to LWH.

7. LWH charges each client at a standard cost per hour. This charge to work in progress includes labour, overhead, and a profit element. Generally, the labour cost for non-partners is about 40% of the standard costing rate. Most receivables are invoiced at 80% to 120% of the standard cost shown in the client work in progress account.

Required   Prepare the memo to Jim Spinney.

(CICA Adapted)

Chapter 11

Bankruptcy and Reorganization

Introduction

11-1.   In layman's language, a person (individual or corporation) is said to be insolvent if the amount of his debts exceeds the value of his assets. The definition given by the Bankruptcy and Insolvency Act is much more precise: A corporation is considered insolvent under the Act if it has debts totaling more than $1,000 and it is unable to pay them when they become due, has stopped making payments required on its debts, or has debts which exceed the fair value of its assets.

11-2.   An insolvent corporation, even under the definition given by the Act, is not automatically bankrupt though. Many alternatives exist that can be used in an attempt to remedy a firm's financial difficulties and to avoid bankruptcy. Once all attempts at agreement with the creditors and reorganization have failed, legal bankruptcy procedures may be initiated either by the insolvent firm itself or by one of its creditors. We will first examine bankruptcy as well as the different options offered to the distressed firm and to its creditors before comparing the advantages and drawbacks of each one.

Bankruptcy

Objective

11-3.   The objective of bankruptcy procedures is to distribute the bankrupt firm's assets as fairly as possible between its creditors. The assets are handed over to an independent trustee who is responsible for their safekeeping and who must sell them and distribute the proceeds to the creditors. The order of distribution is determined by the Act and is based on the type of claim held by each class of creditors.

Bankruptcy Procedures

11-4.   For a firm to be declared bankrupt, one of its creditors or itself must petition the provincial court of law and show that an act of bankruptcy such as one of the following has been committed:

- The firm has voluntarily transferred all its assets to a trustee for distribution to its creditors, or

- It has performed actions to defeat creditors such as transferring assets to related parties, giving special treatment to some creditors, etc., or

- It has performed actions indicating insolvency such as default on payment, release of financial statements showing insolvency, default to a reorganization proposal previously accepted by the court.

11-5.   When granting an order of bankruptcy, the court appoints a trustee who takes possession of the bankrupt's assets. The trustee is usually a professional accountant or a lawyer specialized in insolvency. He must make an inventory of the assets and collect proofs of claim from all creditors. Each creditor must provide him with a proof of the existence and the amount of the claim (invoice, loan contract, etc.). The trustee must then call a creditors' meeting where he will present the bankrupt's Statement of Affairs. This statement lists the bankrupt's assets at their net realizable value as well as a plan for their distribution to creditors. The assets transferred to the trustee include all assets that were in the possession of the bankrupt at the time of the petition as well as any income generated by these assets during the liquidation.

11-6.   At the meeting, creditors approve the appointment of the trustee and choose five inspectors who will represent their interests during the liquidation of assets. The creditors may also give the trustee the mandate to continue operations of the bankrupt firm in order to sell it as a going concern and obtain a better price than if assets were sold separately. In this case, the trustee may hire managers to continue operations until the firm becomes attractive to potential investors. The trustee is responsible for all actions taken by the firm during this time and may be held liable for violations to the Environmental Protection Act, for example.

11-7.   When all assets have been disposed of, the trustee distributes the proceeds to creditors, each according to the priority established by the Act. Since the firm is insolvent, the proceeds are not sufficient to cover all claims and some of the creditors will receive only a portion of the amount of their claim, and sometimes nothing at all. Once everything is distributed, the trustee asks the court to release him from his duties.

11-8.   If the bankrupt is a physical person, he or she is then discharged and none of the creditors has any more claim against him or her. A corporation can only be discharged if all its creditors have been paid in full. In almost all cases the corporation ceases to exist and its owners and administrators may create another firm to continue the same activities or to start new ones.

11-9.   During the course of the proceedings, the trustee and the creditors can challenge any of the bankrupt's transactions performed in the 12 months preceding the petition into bankruptcy if they can prove that they were done with the intent to defeat creditors. All related party transactions are subject to such a challenge, as well as all transfers of assets for which the firm has not received fair compensation.

Priority of Creditors

General Approach

11-10.   The order in which creditors are paid in a bankruptcy is determined very precisely by the Act. It depends on the type of claim held by each of them, but it also reflects the Legislator's concerns about social equity and about encouragement of investment. For instance, the Act gives special treatment to the claims of suppliers and employees of the bankrupt firm. It also upholds most clauses of the finance contracts between debtors and creditors.

Payroll Deductions

11-11.   Until the amendment to the Bankruptcy Act, in 1991, all Governments and Crown Corporations were preferred creditors. The current Act has eliminated these privileges. Only the sums owed by the bankrupt firm for payroll deductions (income tax withheld, Employment Insurance premiums, and Canada Pension Plan contributions) are given special consideration. These items are now protected by being excluded from the bankruptcy altogether and, as a consequence, they are paid before any payment is made to secured creditors. The different laws regulating these deductions provide for the creation of statutory trusts in which the employer keeps the amounts deducted or collected until it is paid back to the governments. The sums presumed to be in these trusts do not belong to the employer, which explains why they are excluded from the assets in the bankruptcy.

Secured Creditors

11-12. The claim of a secured creditor is guaranteed by a specific asset belonging to the debtor. The ownership of this asset (the collateral) remains in the hands of the debtor, but he agrees that the creditor may seize and sell it if the debtor does not abide by the terms of the contract. Before seizing the asset, the creditor must notify the court of his intention to take the collateral into receivership. Examples of secured claims are mortgage loans, secured bank loans, and loans secured by equipment. In bankruptcy, the trustee must award secured creditors the proceeds from the sale of their collateral up to the amount of their claim.

Preferred Creditors

11-13. The Act gives priority of payment to certain groups of unsecured creditors. This priority is based on the personality of the creditors rather than the nature of their claim. The preferred creditors are, in order of their priority, the bankruptcy trustee, the bankrupt firm's employees, municipalities for unpaid property taxes, and the bankrupt's landlord. This order is important since the trustee must be paid in full before anything is paid to employees. The same applies to each group of creditors of this class. The trustee comes first because, in many cases, there is little left after the secured creditors have been paid. If the trustee was very uncertain about his fees being paid, it would be nearly impossible to find anyone willing to act as trustee. The preference treatment for the firm's employees comes from the Legislator's concern for social equity. There is a limit on this type of preferred claim, however: the lesser of six months' salary or $2,000. Landlords' preferred claim is limited to three months' rent.

Unsecured Creditors Without Priority

11-14. This class includes the creditors who do not belong to the first two groups. They all have the same priority. If the proceeds from the sale of assets are not sufficient to cover the total of their claims, the remaining funds are pro rated according to the amount of their claims.

11-15. The Act gives special treatment to some creditors who would normally be considered unsecured. The bankrupt firm's suppliers can repossess the goods for which the debtor has not paid and which have been delivered in the 30 days preceding the petition into bankruptcy, before any distribution to a creditor whose claim is secured by inventory. Certain conditions must hold for the effective cancellation of the sale:

- The bankrupt must still be in possession of the goods

- The goods must be identifiable as those delivered at a specific date by a specific supplier

- They must be in the same state as when delivered

- They must not have been sold or promised for sale in good faith to a third party.

11-16. Certain provincial laws allow the landlord to seize the tenant's assets located in the rented premises in case of default. Bankruptcy procedures suspend this right and the landlord is considered as unsecured, although he has preferred status for three months of rent in arrears. He cannot consider his claim as secured by the bankrupt firm's assets once the bankruptcy petition is before the court.

Deferred Creditors

11-17.   Claims by the owners and directors of the bankrupt firm, as well as by parties related to them, are honoured only after all unsecured claims have been completely satisfied. Neither shareholders who have lent money to their distressed firm nor the managers whose salary is unpaid can be considered as unsecured creditors. The same applies for dividends declared but not paid. Moreover, none of the sums invested as share capital are considered as debt so shareholders have no claim in a bankruptcy.

Types of Claims

Lending Arrangements

11-18.   The various federal and provincial corporations acts, the Bank Act and Quebec's Civil Code of Procedures provide for a variety of forms for financing contracts. The form of a contract usually determines the treatment of the claim in bankruptcy proceedings. We present here the most common forms of lending agreements. The laws leave much latitude to parties as to the clauses to be included, however. Each contract is unique and must be examined carefully to determine the effect bankruptcy procedures might have on it.

Secured Bank Loan

11-19.   Section 178 of the Bank Act allows firms to give their inventory as collateral for loans obtained from a chartered bank or another financial institution regulated by the Act. The collateral includes the inventory (raw materials, goods in process, and finished goods) held by the firm at the time the contract is signed as well as a "floating charge" on all new inventory acquired or manufactured and on receivables created by the sale of inventory. In case of default, the financial institution may notify the court of its intent to seize the collateral and to put it into receivership. The floating charge then crystallizes on the firm's current inventory and receivables and these are considered as the loan securities. This gives the financial institution additional security in the case where a distressed firm runs its inventory down in an effort to deal with liquidity problems. If the inventory is insufficient to cover the claim, receivables are also available as securities.

11-20.   Unpaid suppliers of merchandise in the inventory can first repossess the goods delivered in the previous 30 days, subject to the conditions outlined above. In case of bankruptcy the financial institution is a secured creditor and receives the proceeds from the liquidation of inventory and receivables up to the amount of its claim.

Other Secured Loans and Conditional Sales

11-21.   Loan agreements may also be secured by fixed assets of the borrowing firm. The firm retains legal ownership of the assets but the lender has the right to seize and sell them in case of default. When the assets given as securities consist of land and buildings, the loan is called a mortgage and it is registered in the municipal record about the property. The term chattel mortgage is used for loans secured by other types of collateral.

11-22.   When the borrower defaults on the payments, the creditor may seize the collateral by a petition in receivership and liquidate it to recover the balance of the loan. In case of bankruptcy he is entitled to the proceeds of the liquidation of his collateral up to the amount of his claim.

11-23.   In a conditional sale, ownership of the asset sold remains in the hands of the seller until the buyer has paid his debt in full. The buyer is allowed to use the asset, subject to the right of the seller to repossess it if there is breach of contract. Because the ownership of the asset is still in the hands of the creditor, no legal procedure is necessary for repossession.

Transfer of Receivables

11-24.   Firms in need of funds may assign their receivables to a financial institution or to a firm specializing in factoring. The borrower-assignor's customers are notified that their payments must from then on be made to the lender-assignee. In case of insolvency, the assignee retains his right to the receivables and is considered a secured creditor in bankruptcy.

Bonds

11-25. Bonds are securities issued by a firm that needs debt financing. They may be resold by the holder without the approval of the issuing firm and may be secured by specific assets of the firm or by a floating charge which may apply to all current and future assets. Some bonds are secured only by the reputation of the firm, in which case they are called debentures. The bondholders' interests are protected by a trust agreement in which the firm commits to abide by certain conditions and to report regularly to a trustee representing bondholders.

11-26. When the issuing firm defaults on one of the trust agreement clauses, the bond trustee may seize the security to reimburse bondholders. If there is default of payment, the trustee must petition for receivership before seizing the asset. If the bonds are secured by a floating charge, it crystalizes on the firm's current assets at the date of petition. In the event of bankruptcy, bondholders are considered as secured creditors, unless they hold debentures.

Responsibility Of Officers And Directors

11-27. We have seen that at the end of the bankruptcy, the corporation is usually dissolved and that its owners may create another one. Owners and directors of a bankrupt firm may be held personally responsible for some of the bankrupt firm's actions, however.

11-28. Under various laws governing income tax, governmental pension plans, and unemployment insurance, officers and directors of a corporation may be held personally responsible for the payment of payroll deductions made on the salary of its employees. Other laws also hold them responsible for the payment of salaries to employees as well as GST and sales taxes collected from customers. If the firm's assets are not sufficient to cover those debts officers and directors may have to pay them out of their own assets. They are also liable for a jail term of up to three years if they participate in fraudulent acts relating to the bankruptcy.

11-29. Moreover, the Environmental Protection Act states that officers and directors may be held responsible for damage caused to the environment by their firm, bankrupt or not. They may be prosecuted for having allowed the damages to happen, that is, for having taken no action to stop damages they knew were happening.

Receivership

11-30. Receivership is a legal procedure by which a secured creditor takes possession of assets identified as collateral on his claim after breach of the loan contract by the debtor. If the breach is a default on payment, the creditor must file a notice of intent with the court at least ten days before seizing the asset. A copy of this notice must be sent to all other creditors of the debtor. At the end of the waiting period the creditor appoints a receiver, usually an insolvency expert, who seizes the assets and keeps them for the creditor. His mandate is to find a buyer for the assets so that the creditor may be repaid the amount of his claim. All proceeds in excess of this amount have to be returned to the debtor.

11-31. The ten-day advance notice was added to the Bankruptcy and Insolvency Act in 1991. It improves the chances for the other creditors of the distressed firm to assert their rights in a timely fashion. For example, unpaid suppliers may take back the goods delivered to the firm in the previous 30 days, before a financial institution places them in receivership under section 178 of the Bank Act. If the secured creditor has reasons to believe that the debtor will take advantage of the delay to defeat his claim (by selling or otherwise transferring the collateral), he may ask the court to appoint an interim receiver to safeguard the assets until the issue of the receiving order.

11-32.   Even when appointed by a secured creditor, the receiver must report to the court and to the other creditors about his administration of the assets entrusted to him. He must release a statement of receipts and disbursements as well as a report on the distribution of proceeds. Receivership does not automatically lead to bankruptcy. If the assets seized are essential to the firm's operations, however, bankruptcy almost inevitably follows.

11-33.   An alternative to receivership is a more "friendly" supervision. The creditor who sees one of his debtors in financial distress may suggest the appointment of an independent consultant to help the firm straighten out its situation. This way it is often possible to avoid insolvency and the legal procedures it entails.

Reorganization

General Procedures

11-34.   A firm experiencing financial difficulties has the possibility to change its financing structure in an attempt to reduce pressure on its liquidity. Such a reorganization may be accomplished by informal agreement with the creditors affected by it, under the Companies' Creditors Arrangement Act, or under the Bankruptcy and Insolvency Act.

Informal Agreement

11-35.   If the firm can reach an agreement with its creditors about a restructuring plan, it may be able to straighten out its situation without resorting to legal procedures. Such a plan usually includes a combination of the following clauses:

- Extension of debt maturity dates.
- Refinancing of certain debts.
- Decrease of interest rate on certain debts.
- Reduction of the amount of some claims.
- Assignment of property to a creditor as settlement of his claim.
- Share issue to a creditor as settlement of his claim.

11-36.   In return, some of the creditors may request a seat on the board of directors and the right to intervene in the management of the firm.

11-37.   This solution is the least costly for the creditors as well as the firm but it is feasible only when difficulties are minor and all creditors agree that the firm has a good chance to pull out. It requires unanimity of creditors whose claim is to be affected by the reorganization. Moreover, since there is no legal mechanism to enforce the agreement, any of the creditors may change his mind and demand the payment in full of his original claim, jeopardizing the success of the deal.

Creditors Arrangements

11-38.   The distressed firm may petition the court for reorganization under the Companies' Creditors Arrangement Act. It must fulfill three conditions:

- be insolvent or bankrupt;
- operate in Canada; and
- have bonds payable outstanding.

11-39.   The third condition is not as stringent as it looks since the courts have accepted that the issue be minimal (e.g., $100) and be made the day before the petition.

11-40.   Upon receiving the petition, the court may suspend all legal procedures already initiated against the debtor by secured or unsecured creditors. It may also order a stay against all new actions for up to three months. Once the court grants the request and establishes a date for the creditors' meeting, the firm has 30 days to prepare a proposal on which the creditors will vote at the meeting. In the meantime, the firm can continue its operation without any supervision by the court or the creditors.

11-41.   The proposal must provide for creditors to be classified into categories with common interests. Each class of creditors votes on the proposed reorganization. It is accepted if in each class it obtains a majority of votes and the approval of creditors with 75% of the total of claims in the class. It is thus of utmost importance to define classes in a way that maximizes the chances of approval in each. Once it is accepted with this double majority in all classes, the proposal is sanctioned by the court and all creditors are bound by it, even those who voted against it.

Proposal Under The Bankruptcy And Insolvency Act

11-42.   The Bankruptcy and Insolvency Act also provides for reorganization of the distressed firm. To take advantage of this provision, the debtor must file a notice of intent to make a proposal to its creditors. This notice of intent may be filed with the court by any firm who is insolvent or bankrupt, even if legal actions have already been taken against it by its creditors. Filing the notice of intent automatically stops all creditors' recourse against the debtor for a period of 30 days which can be extended by the court for up to five months.

11-43.   Upon receiving the notice of intent, the tribunal appoints a trustee whose duty it is to supervise the firm's financial affairs and to prepare a cash flow statement demonstrating that the creditors' position will not be eroded during the waiting period. This statement must be filed within 10 days of the trustee's appointment.

11-44.   The firm has 30 days to prepare a proposal to be submitted to its creditors. Here again classes of creditors must be defined, based on the nature of claims. The proposal must be approved by a majority of votes and by creditors with 2/3 of the total claims in each class. If one class of secured creditors rejects the proposal while it is accepted in all other classes, it is possible for the reorganization to proceed by excluding the creditors in the dissenting class (and the assets securing their claims) from the plan. The proposal must provide creditors with more than they would obtain in bankruptcy, if it is to have any chance of being accepted. One of the trustee's duties consists of leading negotiations between creditors and the debtor to ensure the success of the reorganization.

11-45.   If the proposal is rejected, the firm is automatically bankrupt, if it was not already. If, on the other hand, it is accepted it must be sanctioned by the court. From then on it replaces all contracts the firm had with its creditors. None of them may demand more than what is provided for in the proposal. As long as the debtor abides by the terms of the proposal, no legal action may be taken against him by creditors existing at the time it was accepted. Debts incurred after that date are not affected by the agreement and default on them may cause legal actions to be taken by the new creditors. If the firm defaults on the proposal, it is automatically bankrupt.

Choosing The Best Solution

Choice For The Debtor

11-46.   A firm that finds itself in financial distress has a choice between many alternatives to attempt a recovery. The feasibility of each depends in a large part on the severity of the difficulties.

Do Nothing

11-47.   The firm can decide to let things go and hope problems will sort themselves out.

A serious analysis of the causes of the difficulties may show that the problem is temporary or that it has its source at a specific point in the organization and may be solved quite easily. In such a case, minor changes may be sufficient to bring the firm back to profitability. In most situations, however, to do nothing will only make things worse and the firm takes the risk that one or more of its creditors will take drastic measures to get paid.

Reorganization

11-48. The second alternative is for the firm to face up to the situation and to propose an agreement to its creditors. This proposal may be made informally to the main creditors, under the Companies' Creditors Arrangement Act, or under the Bankruptcy and Insolvency Act. The informal agreement is simplest but it does not protect the firm from a bankruptcy or receivership petition by a dissident creditor. This protection is guaranteed when the proposal is made under either of the Acts. The first allows the court to order a stay of procedures and the firm can continue to operate without any supervision. It provides for no inspector or trustee and imposes no priority amongst the creditors. Jurisprudence seems to suggest that Governments and Crown Corporations are not bound by proposals made under this Act, however.

11-49. When the firm files a notice of intent under the Bankruptcy and Insolvency Act the tribunal appoints a trustee whose duty it is to defend the creditors' interests. The firm keeps control of its assets, though. Moreover, the stay of all actions by creditors is automatic and not left to the discretion of the court as it is under the Companies' Creditors Arrangement Act. A rejection of a proposal under the Bankruptcy Act automatically leads to bankruptcy, which is not the case with the other type of arrangement.

Liquidation

11-50. If the firm is still solvent, its owners may decide to liquidate it. An orderly liquidation usually generates larger proceeds than a forced liquidation since there is more time to find an interested buyer who would be ready to pay close to the market value of assets. In bankruptcy or receivership, the trustee or the receiver are not allowed to give any guarantee on the quality of an asset they are liquidating. They could be held personally responsible for any claims from buyers on such a guarantee. This fact explains, at least in part, the low proceeds typical of a bankruptcy liquidation.

Bankruptcy

11-51. Bankruptcy is the last resort. If the managers come to the conclusion that nothing can save the firm, they can petition the tribunal for bankruptcy. Its assets are then assigned to a trustee who liquidates them and the firm is wound up.

Choice For The Creditor

Request For Payment

11-52. The first recourse for the creditor of a firm in default of payment is to demand payment and not to lend it any more funds. Suppliers may request payment on delivery of any goods they sell to the firm. The payment delay should be long enough to allow the firm to find alternative financing. It is also possible at this stage to propose an informal agreement which would allow the creditor to more closely monitor the operations of the debtor. The creditor must take into account the fact that he may be held responsible, under the Environmental Protection Act, of pollution caused by the firm while he is taking an active role in management.

Receivership

11-53. If his claim is secured by one or several of the firm's assets, the creditor may seize them in case of default. He must file a notice of intent with the court ten days before taking control of the assets. Meanwhile, the firm may file a notice of intent to present a proposal under the Bankruptcy and Insolvency Act. The latter notice automatically stops the receivership procedure. For the secured creditor, receivership ensures that his own interests will be put forward, whereas in bankruptcy the trustee defends the interests of all creditors.

Bankruptcy

11-54.   For the unsecured creditor, receivership initiated by one or several secured creditors means that the assets will be sold by someone who has no incentive to seek a price higher than the amount of his claim since he must give any surplus back to the debtor. The trustee, on the other hand, will try to get the highest price possible for each asset since he acts for all creditors. Moreover a petition into receivership by a creditor whose claim is secured by assets which are essential to operations will inevitably lead to bankruptcy.

Reorganization

11-55.   A creditor may have to vote on a proposal submitted by a debtor. It is important for him to consider the long term as well as short term advantages of the proposal over bankruptcy. It may be worthwhile for the creditor to accept a reduction of his claim, an extension of its maturity, or a change in the interest rate if the amount he will receive is likely to be higher than what he would receive in the case of bankruptcy. Receiving common shares in repayment of a claim may also be advantageous for the creditor if the probability that the distressed firm will recover is high. The share price is likely to increase and the creditor will be able to sell them to recover his claim. The main advantages of reorganization is that the firm will continue its operations and this may avoid the loss of a customer for the creditor.

Accounting Aspects Of Insolvency

Statement Of Affairs

General Approach

11-56.   One of the first tasks the trustee must perform in a bankruptcy is to make an inventory of assets and a list of creditors with the amount of their claim. Since the going concern assumption clearly does not hold, valuation of assets must represent the value of future benefits they will generate: their net realizable value. The trustee must also prepare a distribution plan for the proceeds of liquidation based on the payment priority of each creditor.

11-57.   The Statement Of Affairs presents both the list of assets and the distribution plan. It is usually disclosed at the first creditors' meeting, as part of bankruptcy procedures. It can also be prepared in anticipation by a creditor who wants to decide whether or not to file a petition into bankruptcy against a firm. As it is always prepared for a limited number of users and for limited use, the Statement Of Affairs does not have a set format. The format depends on its expected use and on the objectives of its expected readers. The only requirement is that information be clear and easy to understand.

11-58.   Since the Statement Of Affairs is often used by creditors who want to know how much of their claim they can expect to receive, a format showing the state of the claim of each class of creditors may be quite useful. It is not the only one possible, though. The format presented in the following material, suggested by Chabot (1991), contains a section for each class of creditors. For each class, the net realizable value of assets available to pay the claims and the total claims are presented. The difference between the two is a realization surplus or deficiency. Surpluses are added to assets available to other classes of creditors, deficiencies on secured claims become unsecured claims.

11-59   The most frequent use of the Statement Of Affairs is in the case of a bankrupt firm. One of the difficulties for the trustee is to ensure that all assets and liabilities are included since the accounting records of a distressed firm are seldom up-to-date. It is the trustee's responsibility to do everything in his power to reach creditors. Among other things, he must publish a notice of bankruptcy in local newspapers in areas where the firm was doing most of its business.

Example

11-60. The following example will serve to illustrate the preparation of a Statement Of Affairs:

You are a consultant in an accounting firm and Mr. Worreed, owner of the Worreed Corp., asks you for advice on one of his customers, Risk Unlimited. It seems that Risk is experiencing difficulty in meeting its obligations and Mr. Worreed would like to know if he should file a petition into bankruptcy. As a supplier of bulk raw material to Risk, Worreed has an unsecured claim of $50,000 and would like to file its petition before any secured creditor files for receivership.

Mr. Worreed gives you some information he has obtained from Risk including a trial balance as at the end of September 1998 and detailed information about some of the items of the trial balance.

Risk Unlimited
Trial Balance
As At September 30, 1998

	Debits	Credits
Accounts Receivable	$ 135,000	
Inventory	350,000	
Prepaid Expenses	20,000	
Long-Term Investments	80,000	
Fixed Assets (Net)	540,000	
Bank Loan		$ 120,000
Accounts Payable		350,000
Payroll Deductions Payable		25,000
Dividends Payable		10,000
Mortgage Payable		560,000
Capital Stock		60,000
Retained Earnings		Nil
Totals	$1,125,000	$1,125,000

Additional Information:

1. The accounts receivable include accounts with credit balances for a total of $10,000. These accounts would be considered as unsecured claims in bankruptcy.

2. If they are sold as they are, the net realizable value of finished goods would amount to 80% of their cost. The percentage would be 10% and 40% of cost for raw materials and goods in process, respectively. The cost of individual components of inventory are as follows:

Raw Materials	$ 30,000
Goods In Process	145,000
Finished Goods	175,000
Total Cost	$350,000

It is possible, however, to complete the goods in progress by investing an additional $30,000 and using the $30,000 of existing raw materials. The new finished goods could then be sold for 80% of their cost.

3. The market value of long-term investments are equal to their book value.

4. Fixed assets have a market value of $560,000. The real estate agent's commission is estimated at $5,000.

5. The bank loan is secured by inventory under Section 178 of the Bank Act so accounts receivables also serve as securities on the loan if inventory is not sufficient to cover the claim. Some of these accounts date back more than 120 days and there is little chance of collecting them. They total $45,000. The percentage of doubtful accounts in the rest of the receivables is estimated at 10%.

6. The mortgage is secured by all of Risk's fixed assets.

7. No liability has been recognized for wages payable. If the firm went bankrupt, these wages would amount to $25,000 for the 50 employees.

8. Bankruptcy trustee fees would amount to approximately $45,000.

9. Prepaid expenses would have no value in a bankruptcy.

10. Interest payable on the bank loan and the mortgage are estimated at $2,000 and $2,500, respectively.

Required: Prepare a Statement of Affairs for Risky Unlimited in order to help Mr. Worreed make a decision.

Solution To Example

11-61. The first step in the preparation of the required Statement Of Affairs is to estimate the net realizable value of each of Risk's assets. With respect to Accounts Receivable, the relevant amount is calculated as follows:

Accounts Receivable

Book Value	$135,000
Creditor Accounts (Debts)	10,000
Book Value Of Receivables	$145,000
120 Day Accounts (Uncollectible)	(45,000)
Balance	$100,000
Collectible Percentage	90%
Net Realizable Value	$ 90,000

11-62. With respect to the net realizable value of the Inventory, this value will depend on whether they are sold as they are or, alternatively, completed and sold as finished goods for a higher price. The decision depends on the amount that has to be invested to complete the production process. The values resulting from these two approaches can be calculated as follows:

Inventory - Sold As Is

Raw Material ([$30,000][10%])	$ 3,000
Goods In Process ([$145,000][40%])	58,000
Finished Goods ([$175,000][80%])	140,000
Net Realizable Value	$201,000

Inventory - If Completed

Cost Of Raw Material	$ 30,000
Cost Of Goods In Process	145,000
Additional Costs	30,000
Cost Of New Finished Goods	$205,000
Cost Of Finished Goods At September 30	175,000
Total Finished Goods	$380,000
Recovery Percentage	80%
Realizable Value	$304,000
Investment Necessary For Completion	(30,000)
Net Realizable Value	$274,000

11-63.   As completion of production would bring higher net sales proceeds, this value will be used in preparing the Statement Of Affairs.

11-64.   As indicated in the additional information, the Prepaid Expenses would have a net realizable value of zero. Also in the additional information is the fact that the net realizable value of the Long Term Investments would be equal to their book value of $80,000. The net realizable value of the Fixed Assets would be calculated as follows:

Fixed Assets

Market Value	$560,000
Real Estate Commission	(5,000)
Net Realizable Value	$555,000

11-65.   The Statement Of Affairs is designed to present the position of each class of creditors. Based on the preceding information, it would be prepared as follows:

Risk Unlimited
Statement of Affairs
As At September 30, 1998

Position Of Secured Mortgage Holder

Net Realizable Value Of Fixed Assets	$555,000
Amount Of Mortgage Claim ($560,000 + $2,500)	(562,500)
Realization Deficiency (Unsecured Claim)	($ 7,500)

Secured Position Of Bank

Net Realizable Value Of Inventory (Note 1)	$274,000
Bank Loan Balance ($120,000 + $2,000)	(122,000)
Realization Surplus (To Pay Unsecured Claims)	$152,000

Position Of Unsecured Creditors

Realization Surplus On Inventory		$152,000
Accounts Receivable		90,000
Long Term Investment At Net Realizable Value		80,000
Total Available Assets		$322,000
Payroll Deductions Payable (Excluded From Bankruptcy)		(25,000)
Assets Available Under Bankruptcy Proceedings		$297,000
Preferred Creditors:		
Bankruptcy Trustee	($ 45,000)	
Wages Payable	(25,000)	(70,000)
Available To Other Creditors		$227,000
Unsecured Creditors Without Priority:		
Accounts Payable	($350,000)	
Due To Customers	(10,000)	
Mortgage Deficiency	(7,500)	(367,500)
Deficit (Note 2)		($140,500)

Note 1   Inventory is a security on the bank loan but unpaid suppliers may repossess goods they have delivered in the last 30 days if they are still identifiable and in the same state as when delivered. Only raw materials can satisfy these condition if it is possible to determine which materials were delivered when and by which supplier. This identification is impossible in the case of bulk materials, for example. An unpaid supplier repossessing goods under the Bankruptcy and Insolvency Act would have precedence over the bank.

Note 2   The assets are not sufficient for full payment of ordinary creditors. As all have the same priority, each would receive his share of the $227,000 balance. Payments would be on the basis of $0.617687 ($227,000 ÷ $367,500) for each dollar of claim, resulting in the following distribution of the $227,000 balance:

Suppliers [($350,000)(0.617687)]	$216,190
Due To Customers [($10,000)(0.617687)]	6,177
Mortgage Deficiency [($7,500)(0.617687)]	4,633
Total Distribution	$227,000

Shareholders of the firm are deferred creditors so the dividends owed to them could not be paid unless all other creditors are paid in full.

11-66.   Given the preceding calculations, the distribution plan for the assets would be as follows:

Mortgage Holder ($555,000 + $4,633)	$559,633
Bank	122,000
Payroll Deductions	25,000
Trustee	45,000
Wages Payable	25,000
Suppliers	216,190
Due To Customers	6,177
Dividend Payable	Nil
Total	$999,000

11-67.   Worreed is a supplier and the fact that it sold bulk goods to Risk makes it unlikely it will be able to repossess any of these goods. In a bankruptcy it would be classified as an ordinary creditor and would receive only $30,884 [($50,000)(.617687)] of its claim. If it does not file a petition into bankruptcy for Risk, it is likely that secured creditors will petition for receivership. If they are successful, they will have control over the sale of most of the assets and Risk will have to go into bankruptcy anyway since secured creditors will have taken assets which are essential for the continuation of operations. It is also unlikely that inventory would be completed since the proceeds from liquidation of unfinished goods would be sufficient to cover the bank's claim. As a result, the proceeds would be $73,000 less. If Risk goes into bankruptcy, the trustee will act in the best interest of all creditors and Worreed is likely to get a larger fraction of its claim. Whether its creditors petition for bankruptcy or receivership, Risk may make a reorganization proposal. This may be the best solution for all concerned if there is a possibility of saving the firm.

Bankruptcy Accounting

General Procedures

11-68.   If Risk Unlimited is forced into bankruptcy, a trustee will be appointed. The trustee must report regularly on his administration of the bankrupt firm to inspectors who represent the creditors. For this he must keep accounting records for the bankrupt firm. The assets are recorded at their net realizable value and the liabilities at their original amount.

Example Continued

11-69.   To illustrate accounting procedures for the bankrupt firm, we will continue with the example presented in Paragraph 11-60. If we assume that Risk Unlimited goes into bankruptcy as of September 30, 1998, the first journal entry into the trustee's accounting records would be as follows:

Accounts Receivable	$ 90,000	
Inventory	274,000	
Long-Term Investment	80,000	
Fixed Assets (Net)	555,000	
Estate Deficit	140,500	
Mortgage Payable		$562,500
Bank Loan		122,000
Wages Payable		25,000
Payroll Deductions Payable		25,000
Provision For Trustee's Fees		45,000
Accounts Payable		350,000
Due To Customers		10,000

11-70.   All asset sales and payments to creditors are recorded in the bankruptcy books. If it is decided to continue the bankrupt firm's operations, these books are used for recording all transactions. The transactions to liquidate the corporation's assets and to make a partial payment of the trustee's fees would be recorded as follows:

Cash	$555,000	
Fixed Assets (Net)		$555,000
(Sale of fixed assets)		
Mortgage Payable	$555,000	
Cash		$555,000
(Partial payment of mortgage)		

| Inventory | $ 30,000 | |
| Cash | | $ 30,000 |

(Completion of goods in process)

Cash	$310,000	
Inventory ($274,000 + $30,000)		$304,000
Estate Deficit		6,000

(Sale of inventories for $310,000, $6,000 in excess of estimated value)

| Cash | $ 90,000 | |
| Accounts Receivable | | $ 90,000 |

(Collection of accounts receivable)

| Cash | $ 80,000 | |
| Long-term Investments | | $ 80,000 |

(Sale of long term investment)

| Provision For Trustee's Fees | $ 20,000 | |
| Cash | | $ 20,000 |

(Partial payment of trustee's fees)

11-71. The trustee is a preferred creditor and cash is set aside to pay his fees, but he is paid in full only at the end of the bankruptcy proceedings.

11-72. The entry to record the distribution to priority creditors would be as follows:

Bank Loan	$122,000	
Wages Payable	25,000	
Payroll Deductions Payable	25,000	
Cash		$172,000

(Distribution to priority creditors)

11-73. It was originally estimated that there would be $227,000 left for the ordinary creditors (see Statement Of Affairs). However, an extra $6,000 was realized on the inventories which brings the available amount to $233,000. This means that the remaining claims can be settled at $.63401 ($233,000 ÷ $367,500) per dollar, rather than the original estimate of $.617867 per dollar. The entry to record this payment would be as follows:

Mortgage Payable [($7,500)(.63401)]	$ 4,755	
Accounts Payable [($350,000)(.63401)]	221,905	
Due To Customers [($10,000)(.63401)]	6,340	
Cash		$233,000

(Distribution to unsecured creditors)

Statement of Realization and Liquidation

11-74. The trustee uses the Statement of Realization and Liquidation to report on his administration of the bankrupt's affairs. This statement must show receipts and disbursements of funds and allow the reader to verify that the trustee is performing his duty with due care. The following is an example of a Statement of Realization and Liquidation for the first month of Risk Unlimited's bankruptcy and the Balance Sheet of Risk Unlimited at the end of the month.

Risk Unlimited, In Bankruptcy
Statement of Realization and Liquidation
For The Month Of October 1998

	Fair Value 10/01/98	Realization Proceeds	Loss (Gain)	Estate Deficit
Estate Deficit, October 1, 1998				$140,500
Assets Realized:				
Accounts Receivable	$ 90,000	$ 90,000	Nil	
Inventory (Note 1)	274,000	280,000	($6,000)	
Long Term Investments	80,000	80,000	Nil	
Plant And Equipment	555,000	555,000	Nil	
Total Assets Realized	$999,000	$1,005,000	($6,000)	(6,000)
Liabilities Liquidated:				
Secured ($555,000 + $122,000)		$677,000		
Preferred ($25,000 + $25,000)		50,000		
Unsecured		233,000		
Total Liabilities Liquidated		$960,000		
Estate Administration Expenses Paid		20,000		
Total Liabilities Liquidated And Expenses		$980,000		
Estate Deficit, October 31, 1998				$134,500

Risk Unlimited, In Bankruptcy
Balance Sheet
As At October 31, 1998

Assets

Cash And Total Assets	$ 25,000

Liabilities and Deficit

Accounts Payable ($350,000 - $221,905)	$128,095
Provision For Trustee's Fee ($45,000 - $20,000)	25,000
Due To Customers ($10,000 - $6,340)	3,660
Mortgage Payable ($562,500 - $555,000 - $4,755)	2,745
Total Liabilities	$159,500
Deficit	(134,500)
Total Liabilities and Deficit	$ 25,000

Note 1   The realization proceeds for the Inventory reflects the $310,000 proceeds from their sale, less the $30,000 additional costs that were required to complete the goods in process.

Reorganization

General Procedures

11-75.   When the creditors of a distressed firm agree to a reorganization plan, the adjustments established by the plan must be recorded in its books. The debts converted into equity must be eliminated and the amount must be decreased for debts that the creditors agreed to reduce. These modifications generate a reorganization adjustment.

11-76.   The *CICA Handbook* recommends revaluation of all assets and liabilities in certain circumstances:

Paragraph 1625.04   *The following conditions are required to be satisfied for an enterprise's assets and liabilities to be comprehensively revalued:*

(a) *All or virtually all of the equity interests in the enterprise have been acquired, in one or more transactions between non-related parties, by an acquirer who controls the enterprise after the transaction or transactions; or*

(b) *The enterprise has been subject to a financial reorganization, and the same party does not control the enterprise both before and after the reorganization;*

and in either situation new costs are reasonably determinable. (January, 1993)

Paragraph 1625.05   *Identifiable assets and liabilities should be comprehensively revalued when the conditions of paragraph 1625.04 are satisfied as a result of a financial reorganization.* (January, 1993)

11-77.   Paragraph 1625.04(a) above refers to "push down" accounting in business combinations and is not of interest here. What is of interest is the recommendation that all assets and liabilities be revalued when control of the firm changes hands in the reorganization, if the *"new costs are reasonably determinable"*. If control of the firm is not held by the same person(s) before and after the reorganization, it is considered to be a "fresh start" for the firm and its assets and liabilities should be valued as if it had been sold.

11-78.   Consistent with this "fresh start" principle, all losses which existed before the reorganization should be recorded by writing off assets having already lost value. Uncollectible receivables, obsolete inventory and overvalued investments should thus be written down and the loss included in the period preceding reorganization.

11-79.   Assets and liabilities remaining in the balance sheet must then be revalued and this valuation problem is not simple. The *Handbook* provides the following guidance:

Paragraph 1625.39   *The new costs of identifiable assets and liabilities of an enterprise comprehensively revalued as a result of a financial reorganization, should reflect the values established in the negotiation of claims among non-equity and equity interests and should not exceed the fair value of the enterprise as a whole, if known.* (January, 1993)

11-80.   The *Handbook* recommends the use of "the values established in the negotiations" leading to acceptance of the reorganization plan by creditors. The firm's tax benefits, deferred taxes and benefits from losses carried forward, must also be revalued. Deferred taxes are eliminated from the balance sheet and taken into account in the valuation of assets and liabilities to which they are attached. Benefits from losses carried forward are recorded as assets only if the firm has virtual certainty that they will materialize. If the total net value of identifiable assets and liabilities determined by revaluation exceeds the fair value of the firm as a whole, the difference must be treated as negative goodwill and be allocated by reducing the value of identifiable non-monetary assets, as is done in business combinations. The adjustment generated by this revaluation is considered a capital transaction and must be recorded as such:

Paragraph 1625.30   *The revaluation adjustment arising from a comprehensive revaluation of an enterprise's assets and liabilities undertaken as a result of a transaction or transactions as described in 1625.04(a) should be accounted for as a capital transaction, (see "Capital Transactions", Section 3610), and recorded as either share capital, contributed surplus, or a separately identified account within shareholders' equity.* (January, 1993)

Paragraph 1625.45 *Expenses directly incurred in effecting a financial reorganization should be accounted for as a capital transaction (see "Capital Transactions", Section 3610). (January, 1993)*

11-81. Since the firm's assets and liabilities are revalued as if they had been sold, retained earnings before reorganization — which usually are negative — are eliminated and reclassified in share capital, contributed surplus, or a separate account within shareholders' equity. The firm can start a new life without an accumulated deficit.

Paragraph 1625.43 *When a comprehensive revaluation of an enterprise's assets and liabilities is undertaken as a result of a financial reorganization, retained earnings that arose prior to the reorganization should be reclassified to share capital, contributed surplus, or a separately identified account within shareholders' equity. (January, 1993)*

11-82. In the years following reorganization, financial statements should not contain comparative numbers for fiscal years before the revaluation. The firm is considered having made a "fresh start" and a comparison with its "previous life" would be misleading. The notes should give detailed information about the reorganization, however. Disclosure should include the date and nature of the restructuring, amounts of revaluation for important classes of assets and liabilities, and the treatment of accumulated deficit. This information must be disclosed for at least three years following the reorganization.

Paragraph 1625.50 *When an enterprise's assets and liabilities have been comprehensively revalued as a result of a financial reorganization, the financial statements for the period in which the financial reorganization took place should disclose the following:*

(a) the date of the financial reorganization;

(b) a description of the financial reorganization; and

(c) the amount of the change in each major class of assets, liabilities and shareholders' equity resulting from the financial reorganization. (January, 1993)

Paragraph 1625.51 *When an enterprise's assets and liabilities have been comprehensively revalued as a result of a financial reorganization, the financial statements should disclose the measurement bases of the affected assets and liabilities for as long as the revalued amounts are significant. (January, 1993)*

Paragraph 1625.52 *For a period of at least three years following the financial reorganization, the financial statements should disclose:*

(a) the date of the financial reorganization;

(b) the amount of the revaluation adjustment and the shareholders' equity account in which the revaluation adjustment was recorded; and

(c) the amount of retained earnings reclassified and the shareholders' equity account to which it was reclassified. (January, 1993)

Example Continued

11-83. Returning to our basic example from Paragraph 11-60, let us suppose that Risk Unlimited has avoided bankruptcy and that, as of September 30, 1998, its creditors have accepted a reorganization plan. The trial balance is as presented earlier:

Risk Unlimited
Trial Balance
As At September 30, 1998

	Debits	Credits
Accounts Receivable	$ 135,000	
Inventory	350,000	
Prepaid Expenses	20,000	
Long-Term Investments	80,000	
Fixed Assets (Net)	540,000	
Bank Loan		$ 120,000
Accounts Payable		350,000
Payroll Deductions Payable		25,000
Dividends Payable		10,000
Mortgage Payable		560,000
Capital Stock		60,000
Retained Earnings		Nil
Totals	$1,125,000	$1,125,000

11-84.   The following adjustments have been made before the reorganization:

- Accounts of more than 120 days ($45,000) have been written off and accounts with credit balances ($10,000) have been reclassified as accounts payable.

- The value of inventories has been decreased by 20% of their cost.

- Salaries payable ($25,000) and interest payable ($4,500) have been recorded.

11-85.   The reorganization plan contains the following five clauses:

1.   Suppliers agree to decrease their claims by a total of $50,000.

2.   The bank agrees to eliminate accrued interest of $2,000 and to receive 36,000 new common shares of Risk in payment of the balance of its claim.

3.   The mortgage holder accepts Risk's long term investment worth $80,000 and 60,000 new shares valued at $200,000 as partial payment of this claim. He also renounces the accrued interest of $2,500.

4.   Risk's shareholders relinquish the unpaid dividend and keep the 4,000 common shares they hold.

5.   Fixed assets are revalued at their market value of $560,000.

Solution

11-86.   Control has clearly changed hands, since the original shareholders now have 4,000 shares while the bank and the mortgage holder have 36,000 and 60,000 respectively.

11-87.   Losses realized before the reorganization must be recorded first, before the adjustments required by the restructuring plan itself. Losses affect the period ending September 30, 1998 and adjustments are reflected in retained earnings before these are eliminated. This elimination reduces share capital in this example, but could also reduce contributed surplus or be debited to a special account within shareholders' equity. The Schedule of Reorganization Adjustments is as follows:

Risk Unlimited
Schedule Of Reorganization Adjustments
As At September 30, 1998

	Prior To Reorganization		Reorganization	Balance After
	Balance	Write Downs	Adjustments	Reorganization
Accounts Receivable	$ 135,000	($ 45,000)		
		10,000		$100,000
Inventories	350,000	(70,000)		280,000
Prepaid Expenses	20,000			20,000
Long Term Investments	80,000		($ 80,000)	Nil
Fixed Assets (Net)	540,000		20,000	560,000
Totals	$1,125,000	($105,000)	($ 60,000)	$960,000
Bank Loan	$120,000		($120,000)	
Accounts Payable	350,000	$10,000	(50,000)	$310,000
Accrued Interest		4,500	(4,500)	Nil
Accrued Salaries		25,000		25,000
Liability For				
Payroll Deductions	25,000			25,000
Dividend Payable	10,000		(10,000)	Nil
Mortgage Payable	560,000		(80,000)	
			(200,000)	280,000
Share Capital (Note 1)	60,000		260,000	320,000
Retained Earnings (Note 2)	Nil	(144,500)	144,500	Nil
Totals	$1,125,000	($105,000)	($ 60,000)	$960,000

Note 1   The $260,000 adjustment to Share Capital is calculated as follows:

Additions To Share Capital:		
Fixed Asset Revaluation	$ 20,000	
Bank Loan Conversion	120,000	
Accounts Payable Reduction	50,000	
Bank Loan And Mortgage Interest Elimination	4,500	
Cancellation Of Dividend Payable	10,000	
Partial Conversion Of Mortgage	200,000	$404,500
Reduction In Share Capital:		
Deficit Elimination		(144,500)
Total Adjustment		$260,000

Note 2   The $144,500 adjustment to Retained Earnings is generated by write downs prior to Reorganization as follows:

Loss On Accounts Receivable	($ 45,000)
Loss On Inventory	(70,000)
Accrued Interest	(4,500)
Accrued Salaries	(25,000)
Adjustment To Retained Earnings	($144,500)

Going Concern Assumption

Going Concern Postulate

11-88.   The going concern postulate, also referred to as the continuity assumption, states the view that most economic entities are organized for indefinite periods of operation. This is an observable phenomena with respect to the operations of most business organizations, and one of the most important implications of this postulate relates to valuation procedures. If we assume that the entity is a going concern, liquidation values are not a relevant solution to the problem of asset valuation. In the case of a bankruptcy, the going concern assumption is no longer valid.

11-89.   The going concern assumption is adopted in Section 1000, "Financial Statement Concepts". This is reflected in Paragraph 1000.58 as follows:

> **Paragraph 1000.58**   Financial statements are prepared on the assumption that the entity is a going concern, meaning it will continue in operation for the foreseeable future and will be able to realize assets and discharge liabilities in the normal course of operations. Different bases of measurement may be appropriate when the entity is not expected to continue in operation for the foreseeable future.

11-90.   With respect to this assumption, the 1991 CICA Research Study, *The Going Concern Assumption: Accounting And Auditing Implications*, by J. E. Boritz deals with the going concern assumption in a very comprehensive manner. This Research Study is summarized in the Supplement at the end of this Chapter.

Reorganizations In Canadian Practice

Statistics From Financial Reporting In Canada

11-91.   In the two years 1995 and 1996, none of the 200 companies surveyed in the 1997 *Financial Reporting in Canada* was subject to a financial reorganization that required comprehensive revaluation of assets and liabilities. However, the nature of the disclosure requirements is such that disclosure continues for several years after the reorganization. As a consequence, the following example contains the footnotes in the annual reports in the two years subsequent to the reorganization.

Example From Canadian Practice

11-92.   The following notes are from the annual reports of DYLEX LIMITED for the reporting periods ending February 3, 1996 and February 1, 1997. They illustrate disclosure of a reorganization that took place in a previous fiscal year.

Notes To Financial Statements - 1995 Annual Report (Year Ending 03/02/96)

> **Note 2   Reorganization Of The Corporation**
> On January 11, 1995 the Corporation, Dylex Fashion Inc., Dylex Purchasing Limited, Canadian Clothiers Stores Limited, Dylex Fashion Rack Limited, Tip Top Retailers Inc., Bi-Way Stores Corporation, Bi-Way Stores Inc., Bi-Way Retail Limited, Fairweather Stores Inc., Steel Fashions Inc., Thriftys Riding & Sports Shop Inc. and on February 20, 1995, Dylex, Inc., (collectively the "CCAA Companies") sought and received the protection of the Ontario Court of Justice (General Division) (the "Court") from their creditors under the Companies' Creditors Arrangement Act ("CCAA"). The following subsidiaries of the Corporation did not seek protection from their creditors: Harry Rosen Inc., Braemar Apparel Inc., Club Monaco Inc., The Wet Seal, Inc. and San Remo Knitting Mills Inc.
>
> On May 4, 1995, under CCAA, the Corporation received approval of a Plan of Ar-

rangement (the "Plan") by the Court after approval of the Plan by the Landlord Class, the Unsecured Creditors, the Subordinated Debenture holders, the Banks and the Shareholders (all terms as defined in the Plan). The Corporation received a Certificate of Arrangement on May 31, 1995 (the "Plan Implementation Date") and implemented the Plan at that time. The period covered by the Plan was from the Plan Implementation Date to January 31, 1996 (the "Plan Period").

The Plan involved a significant capital reorganization of the Corporation (the "Reorganization"). The Reorganization resulted in cash payments to the creditors and the issuance by the Corporation of New Common Shares, Rights and Warrants as follows:

a) Each Class "A" and each Common shareholder received, as applicable, one New Common Share and one Right for every 52.72319 Class "A" or Common Shares held and one Warrant for every 158.62149 Class "A" or Common Shares held on the Plan Implementation Date.

b) Each Class "C" shareholder received, as applicable, one New Common Share and one Right for every 5.86838 Class "C" Shares held and one Warrant for every 0.51495 Class "C" Shares held on the Plan Implementation Date.

c) Each Subordinated Debenture holder received in full satisfaction of its Proven Claim, including accrued interest of $5.5 million, one New Common Share and one Right for each $9.10222 of Proven Claim and one Warrant for each $27.75641 of Proven Claim.

d) On the Plan Implementation Date all Proven Claims of Landlords and Unsecured Creditors against the CCAA Companies over $2,000 were satisfied by the payment of 60% of their Proven Claim in scheduled cash payments and the balance by the issuance of one New Common Share and one Right for each $13.29535 of Proven Claim and one Warrant for each $218.66663 of Proven Claim.

e) On the Plan Implementation Date the Corporation issued Rights to subscribe for and purchase up to 16 million New Common Shares to Landlords, Subordinated Debenture holders, Unsecured Creditors and Shareholders at a price of $2.50 per New Common Share. Rights on up to 16 million New Common Shares which were not exercised were exercised by the Underwriter. The net proceeds from the Rights Offering of approximately $37 million were used as additional working capital and to reduce the Corporation's term debts.

f) On the Plan Implementation Date the Corporation issued to Landlords, Subordinated Debenture holders, Unsecured Creditors and Shareholders transferable Warrants to subscribe for and purchase 9.45 million New Common Shares of the Corporation. One Warrant entitles the holder thereof to purchase one New Common share at a price of $5.00 for each New Common Share until 5:00 p.m. on May 31, 1998. In addition the Plan extinguished of a portion of the unsecured debt and all of the Subordinated Debentures and the existing Common, Class "A" and Class "C" Shares were converted into New Common Shares.

As part of the Reorganization the Corporation negotiated a Canadian $50 million senior revolving loan bearing interest at a floating rate per annum equal to the index rate plus 1% secured by a first charge on inventory and a second charge on other assets. The proceeds of the loan were used to repay the existing operating lines and for working capital requirements of the Corporation.

The Corporation's Consolidated Statement of Financial Position as at January 28, 1995 was presented on a fresh start basis after giving effect to the Reorganization. Applying fresh start accounting, the Corporation's deficit was set at zero. Costs related to the Reorganization were recorded in the Consolidated Statement of Deficit. After giving effect to the Reorganization and the Rights Offering, the shareholders' equity was stated at $96,266,000 as at January 28, 1995.

The effect of recording the adjustments to reflect the implementation of the Plan is summarized in the table below. This table shows the transition of the Consolidated Statement of Financial Position from the historical cost basis to the fresh start basis of accounting by setting out separately the impact of the Reorganization as at January 28, 1995.

(thousands of dollars)	January 28, 1995 before Reorganization adjustments	Reorganization adjustments	January 28, 1995 after Reorganization adjustments
Current assets	$274,946	$ 37,000 (1)	$311,946
Current liabilities	(299,033)	39,128 (2) (3)	(259,905)
Working capital (deficiency)	(24,087)	76,128	52,041
Other assets	158,171	(7,386)(4)	150,785
Assets employed	$134,084	$ 68,742	$202,826
Financed by:			
Other liabilities	$127,452	($ 20,892)(3)	$106,560
Convertible subordinate debentures	117,992	(117,992)(5)	-
Shareholders' equity			
Share capital	150,798	(54,532)(6)	96,266
Excess of appraised value of fixed assets over cost	1,278	(1,278)(7)	-
Cumulative exchange translation adjustments	7,653	(7,653)(7)	-
Deficit	(271,089)	269,544 (6)	-
	-	1,545 (7)	-
Capital employed	$134,084	$ 68,742	$202,836

Notes To The Table:

1) The net proceeds from the Rights Offering of approximately $37 million were used as additional working capital and to reduce the Corporation's term debts.

2) Settlement of 40% of Landlord and Unsecured Creditors' Proven Claim ($60,020,000).

3) Term debt and capital lease obligations, due February 5, 1996, were rescheduled for repayment in 1995 and were reclassified as current liabilities ($20,892,000).

4) Revaluation of certain other assets to reflect fair market values as determined as part of the Reorganization.

5) Settlement of convertible subordinated debentures.

6) The reduction in share capital consists of the reclassification of the deficit ($269,544,000); offset by the settlement of Landlord and Unsecured Creditors' Proven Claims through issue of New Common Shares ($60,020,000); the full settlement of the convertible subordinate debentures ($117,992,000); and the completion of the Rights Offering under the Plan (approximately $37,000,000 net of expenses).

7) The net reduction in deficit of $1,545,000 includes the elimination of the excess

of appraised value of fixed assets over cost ($1,278,000) and cumulative exchange translation adjustments ($7,653,000); offset by the net write-down of certain other assets ($7,386,000).

Notes To Financial Statements - 1996 Annual Report (Year Ending 03/02/97)

Note 2 Reorganization Of The Corporation

(a) CCAA Proceedings And Financial Reorganization (The "Reorganization")

On January 11, 1995 the Company and certain of its subsidiary companies (Dylex Inc. - February 20, 1995) sought and received the protection of the Ontario Court of Justice (General Division) from the Company's creditors under the Companies' Creditors Arrangement Act ("CCAA"). On May 4, 1995, under CCAA, the Company received approval of a Plan of Arrangement (the "Plan") by the Court after approval of the Plan by the creditors of the Company. The Company received a Certificate of Arrangement on May 31, 1995 and implemented the Plan at that time.

The Company's consolidated statement of financial position as at January 28, 1995 was presented on a fresh-start basis after giving effect to the Reorganization. Applying fresh-start accounting, the Company's deficit was set at zero. Costs related to the Reorganization were recorded in the consolidated statement of deficit. After giving effect to the Reorganization and the rights offering, the shareholders' equity was stated at $96,266,000 as at January 28, 1995.

The Plan involved a significant capital reorganization of the Company and a comprehensive revaluation of the Company's assets and liabilities as at January 28, 1995. The revaluation adjustment of $215 million and the $270 million deficit were classified as share capital.

The Reorganization resulted in cash payments to the creditors and the issuance by the Company of new common shares, rights and warrants.

(b) Restatement Of Reorganization Adjustments

During the process of negotiating the Plan, the various equity and non-equity interests determined the Company's aggregate value based on the values of the Company's individual autonomous operating entities as companies rather than on the individual identifiable assets composing such operating entities. These entities included both subsidiaries owned by the Company as well as distinct operating divisions of the Company. As a consequence of this methodology in determining new costs for the purposes of the comprehensive revaluation of its identifiable assets and liabilities, the aggregate net asset value of $96,266,000 of the Company for financial reporting purposes included goodwill attributable to specific operating entities of $16,744,000. The aggregate value of $96,266,000 did not exceed the fair value of the Company as a whole.

A reconsideration of generally accepted accounting principles applicable to comprehensive revaluations has concluded that no recognition should be given to fair values other than those applicable to identifiable assets included in the Company's consolidated statements of financial position.

Accordingly, the consolidated financial statements for fiscal 1997 and 1996 have been restated to eliminate the initial recognition of goodwill in the amount of $16,744,000 and to eliminate the subsequent impact on reported earnings of the amortization of such goodwill. The effect of this restatement is to reduce the Company's shareholders' equity by $16,744,000 as at January 28, 1995 and subsequent reporting periods and to increase net earnings for the 53 weeks ended February 3, 1996 by $546,000.

Supplement - CICA Research Report - The "Going Concern" Assumption

11A-1. The March, 1991 CICA Research Report, *The "Going Concern" Assumption: Accounting And Auditing Implications* by J. E. Boritz contains an extensive list of very practical recommendations for new standards in both accounting and auditing with respect to the going concern assumption. The following summary is on a chapter by chapter basis.

Chapter One - Introduction

Objective
11A-2. Stated simply, the objective of this Research Report is to address the accounting and auditing implications of the going concern assumption and to discuss technique which can support the exercise of professional judgment in this area. Financial institutions are covered by this Report, but non profit organizations are not.

The Concept
11A-3. The "going concern" concept assumes that an entity will continue in operation for the foreseeable future and will be able to realize assets and discharge obligations in the normal course of operations. The use of this assumption must be warranted by the circumstances and, if this is not appropriate, a different basis of measurement must be adopted.

Growing Importance
11A-4. Four factors have brought the "going concern" issue to prominence. They can be described as follows:

Business Failures   Data points out that business failures are of great economic significance in Canada.

Frequency And Timeliness Of Disclosure   Numerous studies have shown that "going concern" disclosures are not provided often enough or soon enough to warn readers about the potential invalidity of the "going concern" assumption and the related impact on the entity's financial statements.

Accounting And Auditing Standards   The *CICA Handbook* provides virtually no guidelines as to what constitutes appropriate disclosure of "going concern" uncertainties.

Macdonald Commission   The June, 1988 *Report Of The Commission To Study The Public's Expectations Of Audits* (the Macdonald Commission), indicated a need to warn the public about the risk of business failure and to consider the auditor's responsibility in connection with "going concern" issues.

Recommendations
11A-5. In connection with the issues raised in this Chapter, the Research Report make two recommendations:

Accounting Recommendation 1.1   The Accounting Standards Committee should initiate a standards setting project to address the financial reporting implications of the "going concern" assumption in the *CICA Handbook*.

Auditing Recommendation 1.2   The Auditing Standards Committee should initiate a standards setting project to modify the *CICA Handbook* to require auditors to examine the support for management's assertion that the "going concern" assumption is valid.

Chapter Two - The Risk Of Business Failure And The "Going Concern" Assumption

Terminology

11A-6.   This Chapter develops terminology that will be used in many of the Study's subsequent recommendations. The term *foreseeable future* is used to cover a period of one year from the date of the current financial statements. Also of use is the association of risk terminology with probabilities of failure. The terms developed are as follows:

> If the likelihood of the occurrence of events confirming the inappropriateness of the "going concern" assumption were estimated to fall between 20 percent and 50 percent, there would be *significant* doubt about the validity of the "going concern" assumption.

> If the likelihood of the occurrence of events confirming the inappropriateness of the "going concern" assumption is estimated to fall at or above 50 percent but below 70 percent, this would represent *substantial* doubt about the validity of the "going concern" assumption.

> If the likelihood of the occurrence of events confirming the inappropriateness of the "going concern" assumption were estimated to fall at 70 percent or more, this would represent a *very substantial* degree of doubt about the validity of the "going concern" assumption.

> If the likelihood of the occurrence of events confirming the inappropriateness of the "going concern" assumption were estimated to fall at 95 percent or more, representing *virtual certainty* about the invalidity of the "going concern" assumption, then the assumption should not be used.

11A-7.   The Chapter concludes that the "going concern" assumption becomes questionable or invalid upon the actual or anticipated occurrence in the foreseeable future of the earliest of the following events:

- The entity becomes unable to meet its obligations without initiating actions outside the ordinary course of operations.

- Management launches actions outside the ordinary course of operations designed to rescue an entity from financial distress or insolvency.

- Management loses control over the assets and operations of an entity to a lender or other creditors through the appointment of a receiver or a less formal involvement by a consultant or monitor.

- Management loses control over their assets and operations to a trustee in bankruptcy.

11A-8.   These ideas are incorporated into the following recommendation.

Accounting Recommendation 2.1   If an entity is unable to meet its obligations, or if it is likely that it will become unable to meet its obligations in the next fiscal period, without initiating actions outside the ordinary course of operations to rescue itself from financial distress or insolvency, then the appropriateness of the "going concern" assumption used in preparing the financial statements should be questioned:

- if management has initiated actions outside the ordinary course of operations to rescue an entity from financial distress or insolvency, or is likely to initiate such actions in the next fiscal period, then this would cast *substantial* doubt upon its ability to continue as a "going concern";

- if management has lost control, or is likely to lose control in the next fiscal period, over the assets and operations of an entity to a lender or other creditors through a formal appointment of a receiver or a less formal involvement by a consultant or monitor, then this arrangement would cast *very substantial* doubt upon its ability to continue as a "going concern";

- if management has lost control, or is likely to lose control in the next fiscal period, over the assets and operations of an entity to a trustee in bankruptcy, then it is no longer a "going concern" and the "going concern" assumption would be considered invalid.

Chapter Three - Accounting Standards And Reporting Practices Regarding "Going Concern" Uncertainties

Accounting Standards

11A-9. The review contained in this Chapter makes it clear that, when compared with many other countries, Canadian standards related to the "going concern" assumption have a number of gaps. These include:

- No discussion of alternative measurement bases where there is doubt about the validity of the "going concern" assumption.

- No specific timing for going concern disclosure.

- No explicit distinction between substantial and significant degrees of doubt.

- No definition of the length of foreseeable future.

- Limited guidance on disclosure criteria to be used.

Canadian Reporting Practices

11A-10. The Study evaluates the reporting practices of Canadian companies in terms of timeliness, completeness, and understandability. While it is not possible to reach a firm conclusion with respect to timeliness, the evidence suggests that disclosures are not provided on a timely basis, even in the most extreme financial distress circumstances.

11A-11. With respect to completeness, the evidence again suggests a negative conclusion. It appears that current "going concern" disclosures do not provide key information that users require. There are also questions with respect to understandability. Standard tests of complexity rate the material very difficult to read, requiring a post-graduate level of university education.

Chapter Four - Recommendations For Changes in Accounting Standards

Timing Of Disclosures

11A-12. Based on the analysis in the preceding Chapters, this Chapter contains a number of accounting recommendations with respect to the "going concern" assumption. The first three of these recommendations relate to the timing of "going concern" disclosures:

Accounting Recommendation 4.1 In preparing the financial statements of an entity, management should consider whether an entity is able to realize its assets and discharge its liabilities in the ordinary course of operations for the foreseeable future without initiating actions to rescue itself from financial distress or insolvency:

- if the entity is unable to meet its obligations or there are indications that the entity will become unable to meet its obligations during the next fiscal period without initiating actions outside the ordinary course of operations, then the validity of the "going concern" assumption should be questioned. In addition, consideration should be given to disclosure of the matters giving rise to the doubt about the validity of the assumption and to disclosure of changes in the accounting measurement bases used for assets and liabilities, which may be required to inform readers of financial statements about this uncertainty and its impact on the recorded values;

- when the doubt about the validity of the "going concern" assumption is *significant*, management should consider the desirability of disclosing the existence of that doubt, taking into consideration the needs of users of financial statements and its plans for dealing with the circumstances giving rise to such doubt at the reporting date;

- when the doubt about the validity of the "going concern" assumption is *substantial*, management should disclose the existence of that doubt, the matters giving rise to the doubt, its plans for dealing with the circumstances giving rise to such doubt at the reporting date, and the potential impact on the recorded values in the financial statements.

Accounting Recommendation 4.2   If management has lost control, or is likely to lose control during the next fiscal period, over the assets and operations of an entity to a lender or other creditors through a formal appointment of a receiver or a less formal involvement by a consultant or monitor, then this arrangement would generally cast *very substantial* doubt upon the entity's ability to continue as a "going concern" and the validity of the "going concern" assumption. If the "going concern" assumption is used in preparing the financial statements, then the doubts surrounding its use and the impact on recorded values in the financial statements should be communicated to readers of financial statements.

Accounting Recommendation 4.3   If management has lost control over the assets and operations of an entity, or is likely to lose control during the next fiscal period, to a trustee in bankruptcy (or equivalent), then the entity is no longer a "going concern". The "going concern" assumption is invalid and it would be inappropriate to use generally accepted accounting principles applicable to a "going concern" in preparing financial statements. If financial statements are prepared, then an appropriate disclosed basis of accounting should be used.

Location Of Disclosures

11A-13.   Recommendation 4.4 deals with the location of "going concern" disclosures:

Accounting Recommendation 4.4   When there are "going concern" matters which require disclosure then, irrespective of any other disclosure provided in the annual report, there should be appropriate disclosure of such "going concern" matters in the notes to the financial statements. The information should be the first note, or should be prominently placed in the first note, and should be cross referenced to the body of the financial statements and other relevant notes.

Content Of Disclosures

11A-14.   Finally, recommendations 4.5 through 4.9 provide guidance on the content of "going concern" disclosures.

Accounting Recommendation 4.5   If there is little or no doubt about the validity of the "going concern" assumption then, to avoid confusing readers of financial statements, no reference should be made in the note describing significant accounting policies. In the absence of disclosure to the contrary, financial statement readers are entitled to assume that the "going concern" assumption used in preparing the financial statements is appropriate.

Accounting Recommendation 4.6 If there is *significant* doubt about the validity of the "going concern" assumption and it is concluded that, to prevent the financial statements from being misleading, this doubt requires disclosure, then the note disclosing such doubt should contain the following information:

- a statement that the financial statements were prepared using generally accepted accounting principles applicable to a "going concern", which assumes that the entity will continue in operation for the *foreseeable* future and will be able to realize its assets and discharge its liabilities in the normal course of operations.

- an explicit reference to the potential inappropriateness of the use of generally accepted accounting principles applicable to a "going concern" because there is *significant* doubt about the validity of the "going concern" assumption.

- identification of the adverse conditions and events which raise *significant* doubt about the validity of the "going concern" assumption.

- management's plans for dealing with these adverse conditions and events including:

- management's evaluation of the significance of these issues and any mitigating factors;

  - management's plans for addressing these issues;
  - the possible effects of these issues if they are not resolved; and
  - the anticipated timing of resolution of uncertainties surrounding the issues.

- a statement that the financial statements do not reflect adjustments that would be necessary if the "going concern" assumption were not appropriate together with the reason for not reflecting such adjustments (for example, management believes that the described actions already taken, or planned to be taken, will mitigate the adverse conditions and events which raise *significant* doubt about the validity of the "going concern" assumption).

- a statement that if the "going concern" assumption were not appropriate, then adjustments would be necessary in the carrying values of assets and liabilities, the reported revenues and expenses, and the balance sheet classifications used.

Accounting Recommendation 4.7 If there is *substantial* doubt about the validity of the "going concern" assumption, then the note disclosing such doubt should contain the same disclosures outlined in Recommendation 4.6 but the term "significant doubt" should be replaced with the term "substantial doubt".

Accounting Recommendation 4.8 If there is *very substantial* doubt about the validity of the "going concern" assumption, then the financial statements should follow the accounting principles established for contingencies and, in addition to the disclosures outlined in Recommendation 4.7, should include information about:

- the assets and liabilities most significantly affected, including changes in carrying values that would be required to reflect their approximate market values;

- anticipated changes in reported revenues and expenses related to the above; and

- anticipated reclassifications of assets and liabilities from long term to current.

Accounting Recommendation 4.9 If there is almost *total disbelief* in the validity of the "going concern" assumption, then disclosure in the note to the financial statements should:

- state that generally accepted accounting principles for a "going concern" are not applicable to the entity because the "going concern" assumption is not valid.

- describe the basis used for preparing the financial statements and , if it is a modification of generally accepted accounting principles for a "going concern", include information about:

  - the assets and liabilities most significantly affected, including changes in carrying values that would be required to reflect their approximate market values;
  - anticipated changes in reported revenues and expenses related to the above; and
  - anticipated reclassifications of assets and liabilities from long term to current.

Chapter Five - Auditing Standards And Practices Regarding "Going Concern" Uncertainties

Auditing Standards

11A-15.   A review of standards in various jurisdictions makes it clear that Canadian standards differ significantly from both U.S. and international standards. These differences include:

- The Canadian auditor is assigned a passive rather than an active role.

- The Canadian criteria for assessing adequacy of disclosure is very narrow, requiring only that the auditor consider whether the information draws the reader's attention to the possibility that the entity may be in difficulty.

- Auditors can give an unqualified opinion if the "going concern" assumption is not appropriate but there is adequate disclosure. This is in conflict with a prohibition against substituting note disclosure for proper accounting.

- Canadian standards do not define the time period considered to be foreseeable.

- There are no mandatory requirements in the Canadian standards.

Auditing Practices

11A-16.   Canadian auditing practices in this area seem highly variable. For the most part, they offer a completely subjective evaluation based on a general awareness of the clients, the industry, and the economy.

11A-17.   The Study also considers the claim that "going concern" disclosures represent a "self fulfilling prophecy". The idea here is that such disclosures create sufficient doubt about the firm's financial viability that even healthy firms could be forced into bankruptcy. The author indicates that the evidence does not support this contention. He also finds little evidence to support the claim that "going concern" disclosures will result in a client changing auditors.

11A-18.   The author concludes that auditors should assume an active role in examining the management's assertions with respect to the "going concern" assumption. Guidance is also needed about the procedures that an auditor should follow during the planning, evidence gathering and evaluation phases of the audit, including a clear definition of the point at which the "going concern" assumption becomes questionable, the length of the foreseeable future, and the point at which the "going concern" assumption is clearly invalid. In addition, attention needs to be given to reporting considerations related to different degrees of doubt about the validity of the "going concern" assumption.

Chapter Six -
Recommendations For Changes In Auditing Standards

Nature And Extent Of Examination

11A-19.   This Chapter provides a number of recommendations with respect to auditing considerations related to the "going concern" assumption.   Recommendations 6.1 through 6.4 deal with the nature and extent of examination:

> **Auditing Recommendation 6.1**   In planning, gathering evidential matter and completing the audit, the auditor should perform procedures designed to provide reasonable assurance that, if there are matters which cast doubt upon the validity of the "going concern" assumption, such matters would be identified.

> **Auditing Recommendation 6.2**   The auditor should evaluate the results of procedures performed in planning, gathering evidential matter and completing the audit to determine whether, when considered in the aggregate, they cast doubt upon the validity of the "going concern" assumption.

> **Auditing Recommendation 6.3**   If other than insignificant doubts are raised about the validity of the "going concern" assumption, the auditor should obtain additional information about management's plans to address the matters that gave rise to those doubts; for example, plans to dispose of assets, borrow money, restructure debt, reduce or delay expenditures, or to increase ownership equity. The auditor should also assess the likelihood that such plans can be effectively implemented.

> **Auditing Recommendation 6.4**   After considering all the information obtained, the auditor should determine whether there is *significant* or *substantial* doubt about the validity of the "going concern" assumption and, if there is, the auditor should consider the adequacy of the financial statement disclosure in connection with these matters.

Reporting Responsibilities

11A-20.   Recommendations 6.5 through 6.8 deal with the auditor's reporting responsibilities:

> **Auditing Recommendation 6.5**   If there is *significant* doubt about the validity of the "going concern" assumption, then the auditor should consider whether the matters that give rise to such doubt need to be disclosed to readers of financial statements to prevent them from being misled and, if so, whether they are adequately disclosed. If disclosure is adequate, then no modification to the auditor's standard report is required. If disclosure is inadequate, the auditor should request that management provide adequate disclosure. If such action is not taken, then the auditor should render a qualified ("except for...") or adverse opinion for inadequate disclosure, in accordance with the *CICA Handbook* Section 5510, "Reservations In The Auditor's Report".

> **Auditing Recommendation 6.6**   If there is *substantial* doubt about the validity of the "going concern" assumption then, even if disclosure is adequate, the auditor should note, in a paragraph following the opinion paragraph, that "substantial doubt exists about the validity of the "going concern" assumption used in preparing the financial statements" (normally using this wording for clarity and uniformity of reporting) and refer the reader to the note disclosure.

Auditing Recommendation 6.7   If there is substantial doubt about the validity of the "going concern"assumption and disclosure is inadequate, the auditor should normally give an adverse opinion due to the pervasive effects of using the assumption.

Auditing Recommendation 6.8   If there is almost *total disbelief* in the validity of the "going concern" assumption, but the assumption is nevertheless used in preparing the financial statements, then even though there may be adequate disclosure of the "going concern" uncertainties, the auditor should normally give an adverse opinion due to the inappropriate use of generally accepted accounting principles applicable to a "going concern" and the pervasive effects of using that assumption.

Chapter Seven - Techniques For Predicting Financial Distress And Bankruptcy

11A-21.   This is a fairly technical Chapter, devoted to describing the various techniques that can be used to identify and measure the extent to which an entity is subject to the risk of business failure. The techniques considered include ratio analysis, statistical models, questionnaires and checklists, graphical aids, rule based expert systems, and group assessment of risk. It is noted, however, that the auditor's main objective is not to draw a firm conclusion about the future existence of the entity. Rather, his/her goal is to establish whether events that have already occurred - or that may occur in the near future - bring into question the validity of the "going concern" assumption. To support this professional judgment process, the Report makes the following recommendations:

Other Recommendation 7.1   The CICA should encourage and assist practitioners in becoming informed about the techniques available to support the professional judgment process regarding the "going concern" assumption.

Other Recommendation 7.2   The CICA should encourage Consumer And Corporate Affairs Canada to make available - on electronically accessible media - more detailed, more accurate, and more complete financial data about bankrupt and other financially distressed entities than it currently does.

Other Recommendation 7.3   To permit effective financial distress prediction models to be developed and revised on an ongoing basis, the CICA should study the feasibility of developing and maintaining a current database covering both bankruptcy and non bankruptcy types of business failures (perhaps on a joint basis with the Canadian Insolvency Association, the Provincial Institutes, and financial institutions).

Additional Readings

Bennett, Frank, *Bennett on Bankruptcy*, CCH Canadian Ltd., 1993.

CA Magazine Article - "What's Really Wrong With Our Bankruptcy Act?", Peter Farkus, June, 1991.

CA Magazine Article - "Timing is Everything", Peter P. Farkas and Sheryl E. Seigel, December, 1993.

CA Magazine Article - "Air Wars", Peter P. Farkas, April, 1994.

CA Magazine Article - "Striking A New Balance", Jonathan E. Fleisher, September, 1991.

CA Magazine Article - "Tracking The Phantom", Lawrence S. Gold and David Pettai, September, 1993.

CA Magazine Article - "Trustees' Roles Redefined", Steven G. Colick, December, 1993.

CA Magazine Article - "Criminal Rates", Barbara L. Grossman, August, 1994.

CA Magazine Article - "Trustees' Roles Redefined", Steven G. Golick, December, 1994.

CA Magazine Article - "It's Not Just The Economy", Brahm Rosen, August, 1995.

CA Magazine Article - "Against A Rainy Day", Ralph H. Kroman, October, 1996.

CA Magazine Article - "Debt Busters", John Lorinc, December, 1996.

CA Magazine Article - "In Succession", Steven G. Golick and Shelley W. Obal, April, 1997.

Canadian Banker, "Bankers And The New Bankruptcy Act", Bernard Wilson, November-December, 1991.

National Creditor/Debtor Review, "Effect Of Bankruptcy On Commercial Leases", J.D. Stringer, October, 1992.

National Creditor/Debtor Review, "Effects Of Bankruptcy On Directors' And Officers' Liability", David H. Jenkins and Rosemary Scott, October, 1993.

National Insolvency Review, "Environmental Risks: Avoiding Lending Hazard", James W. Harbell and David M. Wex, May, 1993.

National Insolvency Review 8, "Environmental Liability In An Insolvency: Bankruptcy And Insolvency Preparing For Troubled Times", Rebecca E. Keeler, 1991.

Windsor Review of Legal and Social Issues, "Throwing The Net Wider: Can Parent Companies And Lenders Be Held Liable For Contaminated Land?", Dianne Saxe, May, 1991.

Assignment Problems

(The solutions to these problem are only available in
the solutions manual that has been provided to your instructor.)

ASSIGNMENT PROBLEM ELEVEN - 1

John Wong, CA, is the controller of GB Distributors Inc. (GB), a wholesale company in the business of buying goods in large quantities at low prices and selling to retailers across the country. GB's head office and main warehouse are in Toronto. Two years ago, at great expense, GB opened a warehouse in Saskatoon to better serve its western customers.

John is concerned about certain accounting issues with respect to the upcoming fiscal year end of July 31, 1998. GB is having cash flow problems. Its operating line of credit is at its maximum (determined by 65% of inventory and accounts receivable). This is despite the fact that its inventory virtually doubled in the past year. Accounts receivable collections are running at approximately 120 days. Condensed Income Statements for the last three years are included in Exhibit I.

However, the prospects for fiscal 1999 are good. The effects of the recession may finally be over and retailers can begin supplying their stores with the goods that are in GB's inventory right now. As a result, cash flow will improve significantly.

Further, management decided at its quarterly meeting, on March 31, 1998, to abandon the warehouse in Saskatoon, effective July 31, 1998. Rising operating costs, poor sales and more efficient distribution methods from the main warehouse forced management to make this decision. The losses from the Saskatoon warehouse are included in the Income Statements in Exhibit I.

With all the above improvements and the closure of the warehouse, John is convinced the company has turned a corner. However, to realize this improvement, GB must convince the bank to continue financing the company. The bank is so concerned with GB's growing debt, it has withheld further financing, pending the release of the audited financial statements for the year ended July 31, 1998.

The president of GB has asked John for a memo discussing the accounting and disclosure issues relating to the potential going concern problem and the closure of the warehouse.

Required: Assume the role of John Wong and prepare the memo for the president.

(OICA Adapted)

Exhibit I
GB Distributors Inc.
Statement Of Operations
For The Year Ended July 31
(in thousands)

	1997	1996	1995
Sales	$3,500	$4,200	$4,000
Cost Of Goods Sold	2,800	2,940	2,500
Gross Margin	$ 700	$1,260	$1,500
Other Expenses	1,600	1,550	1,500
Net Loss	$ 900	$ 290	$ Nil

ASSIGNMENT PROBLEM ELEVEN - 2

Butcher's Choice Inc., a manufacturer of butcher's equipment, has just gone into bankruptcy. You have been appointed as trustee in the bankruptcy and you must prepare for the first creditors' meeting. You have gathered the following information:

Butcher's Choice Inc.
Trial Balance
As At December 1, 1998

	Debits	Credits
Cash	$ 66,000	
Notes Receivable	114,000	
Accounts Receivable	438,000	
Inventory	291,000	
Short-term Investments (At Cost)	60,000	
Fixed Assets (At Cost)	1,040,000	
Accumulated Depreciation		$ 170,000
Notes Payable		210,000
Accounts Payable		960,000
Share Capital		300,000
Retained Earnings		369,000
Totals	$2,009,000	$2,009,000

Additional Information:

1. You have found unrecorded debts of $20,100 for corporate taxes payable and $7,200 for unpaid salaries.

2. The short-term investments have a fair value of $65,000 and have been given as collateral on a note payable of $60,000.

3. Accounts receivable amounting to $180,000 serve as collateral on the rest of the notes payable. You estimate that 95% of notes receivable, 80% of accounts receivable given as collateral, and 75% of other accounts receivable, are collectible.

4. The composition of inventory is as follows:

Raw Materials	$ 90,000
Goods in Process	51,000
Finished Goods	150,000
Inventory	$291,000

    If they are sold as is, the net realizable value for raw materials will be only 20% of their cost and it is estimated at 50% for goods in process and 85% for finished goods. It is also possible to finish the production by incurring additional costs of $70,000.

5. Fixed assets have a market value of $340,000 but their sale will require payment of $10,000 in commissions. Butcher's Choice also owns a patent worth $10,000 which is not recorded in its books.

6. You estimate your fees for this engagement at $15,000.

Required: Prepare the Statement of Affairs for Butcher's Choice Inc. and determine the amount each class of creditors is likely to receive.

ASSIGNMENT PROBLEM ELEVEN - 3

Mr. Smart owns Smart and Logical Inc., a small firm that develops and sells specialized software. He is worried about one of his most important customers, Manufacture Corporation. In the last few years Smart and Logical has sold several programs to Manufacture. However, its $80,000 account has now been outstanding for three months and all of Mr. Smart's efforts to collect it have been unsuccessful.

He has managed to gather some detailed information on Manufacture and has asked you to estimate his chances of recovering his claim. He has given you the following trial balance for Manufacture and the information he has obtained.

Manufacture Corp.
Trial Balance As At October 31, 1998

	Debits	Credits
Cash (Overdraft)		$ 50,000
Accounts Receivable	$180,000	
Inventory	220,000	
Prepaid Expenses	40,000	
Fixed Assets (Net)	360,000	
Goodwill	50,000	
Accounts Payable		180,000
Bank Loan		100,000
Deferred Taxes		20,000
Corporate Tax Payable		10,000
Mortgages Payable		400,000
Share Capital		60,000
Retained Earnings		30,000
Totals	$850,000	$850,000

Additional Information:

1. Manufacture's accounts receivable include $20,000 of 90-day overdue accounts of which only 20% will be collectible. It is estimated that 75% of the other accounts are collectible.

2. The composition of inventory is as follows:

Raw Materials	$ 70,000
Goods in Process	70,000
Finished Goods	80,000
Total Inventory	$220,000

    Raw materials can be sold for 75% of their book value, goods in process for 10%, and finished goods for 80%. If $50,000 of additional costs were invested, all raw material and goods in process could be used to complete the manufacturing process.

3. Prepaid expenses cannot be transferred and, as a consequence, have no market value.

4. Fixed assets include land and building with a fair value of $300,000 and equipment worth $130,000.

5. The bank loan is guaranteed by inventory and accounts receivable under Section 178 of the Bank Act. Accrued interest on the loan of $3,500 has not been recorded.

6. Mortgages payable include a chattel mortgage of $150,000 on the equipment held by a financing firm and a mortgage on land and building held by the bank. The balance is

$250,000 and the interest rate is 12%. Manufacture has made no payment on this loan in the last three months.

7. Mr. Smart has also learned that Manufacture owes close to $20,000 in unpaid salary to its employees.

Required: Write a report briefly explaining the various procedures available to the parties involved as well as the consequences of each procedure on Smart and Logical's claim. Include a Statement of Affairs for Manufacture Corp. in your solution.

ASSIGNMENT PROBLEM ELEVEN - 4

On August 9, 1998 Navalin Inc., one of the most important engineering firms in Canada, closed down because of financial difficulties. A consortium of eight banks, to whom the corporation owed $135 million, had seized Navalin's engineering contracts as well as most of its assets. The consortium had sold them to another engineering firm, SNC Group Inc.

On December 3, 1998, the trustee in the bankruptcy of Navalin released his report at the creditors' first meeting. The report contained the following information on the fair value of Navalin's assets and liabilities:

Assets Of Navalin Inc.

Art Collection (1,300 Pieces Of Contemporary Canadian Art)	$ 12,000,000
Three Real Estate Properties (Includes Condominium In Monaco)	800,000
Vacant Lot Next To The Kemtec Refinery	90,000,000
Amount Receivable On Sale Of Contracts To SNC	35,000,000
Total Assets	**$137,800,000**

Liabilities Of Navalin Inc.

Consortium Of Banks	$111,000,000
Marathon Realty Co.	33,000,000
Régie des installations olympiques	13,000,000
Assurance-vie Desjardins	3,700,000
Corporate Tax Payable	10,000,000
GST Payable	802,000
Other Creditors	36,200,000
Total Liabilities	**$207,702,000**

Additional Information:

1. The vacant lot had been polluted by a refinery operated by Kemtec Petrochemical Corp., a subsidiary of Navalin which was also included in the bankruptcy. It was expected that the government would probably demand its decontamination sooner or later. Decontamination costs were estimated at $80 million.

2. The consortium included eight Canadian and foreign banks that had given Navalin a line of credit of $135 million. The firm had given all its contracts in progress and most of its assets as security on this loan. The proceeds from the sale of these assets in August 1998 amounted to $59 million, of which $35 million had not yet been received.

3. Navalin Inc. owed Marathon $33 million of unpaid rent for space leased in several buildings in Montréal.

4. La Régie des installations olympiques (RIO), a Québec Crown Corporation managing

Montréal's Olympic Stadium, was claiming $13 million in damages from Navalin for breach of contract. The engineering firm was to carry out repairs to the Stadium roof and RIO had already paid for the work.

5. The bankruptcy trustee estimates that his fee will be about $500,000.

Required:

A. What is the order and amounts in which payments would be made to Navalin's creditors, assuming that there are enough assets to satisfy all claims.

B. Prepare a Statement of Affairs for Navalin showing the amount each class of creditors would receive. Evaluate the loss for each class.

C. From the information given, reconstruct the sequence of legal procedures that led to Navalin's bankruptcy.

ASSIGNMENT PROBLEM ELEVEN - 5

M Aluminum Products (MAP) is a manufacturer of doors, windows, greenhouses and sunrooms. Its common shares had been owned in equal percentages by Mr. and Mrs. Mansfield since MAP's federal incorporation. In the year ended December 31, 1997, sales of MAP according to the audited financial statements had been over $6 million. However, as a result of Mr. Mansfield's illness, and due to uncollected receivables, profits were negligible and the cash and liquid assets position had deteriorated.

In August 1998, following a request by one of its secured creditors that MAP be put into receivership, MAP made a reorganization proposal in which Mr. Eric Cooper agreed to buy the common shares of MAP for $90,000. A tax ruling confirmed that for tax purposes no acquisition of control has occurred, since Mr. Cooper is Mrs. Mansfield's brother. The proposal, if accepted by creditors, will be effective September 1, 1998. Following are its principal clauses:

1. Suppliers will be paid $0.60 on the dollar and MAP will make payments to them of $936,000 on September 1, 1998.

2. The mortgage payable liability will be restructured on September 1, 1998 to lower the interest rate to 7% and lengthen the period for repayment of principal from 15 to 20 years. As at August 31, 1998, the interest rate of 10% was equal to current market rates. MAP will issue common shares to the mortgage holders in payment of $400,000 of the mortgage debt.

3. On December 1, 1998, preferred shareholders will receive $0.30 per dollar of investment for their shares.

4. The non-capital loss carry-forward for income tax purposes is $3,180,000. Before the company got into difficulties, a normal annual taxable income for MAP was $950,000.

5. The bank will receive common shares in exchange for its loan and will have two seats on MAP's board of directors.

6. During the negotiations with creditors and Mr. Cooper, the following estimation of MAP's assets were made as of September 1, 1998.

Receivables	$ 200,000
Inventory	500,000
Land	1,400,000
Building	750,000
Equipment	950,000
Total	$3,800,000

As at August 31, 1998, the condensed balance sheet of MAP showed the following:

Assets

Receivables (Note 1)	$1,175,000
Inventory (Note 2	530,000
Land	800,000
Building, Net (Note 3)	895,000
Equipment, Net (Note 3)	1,240,000
Goodwill, Net (Note 4)	610,000
Franchise (Note 5)	470,000
Total	$5,720,000

Liabilities and Shareholders' Equity

Accounts Payable	$1,560,000
Wages Payable	200,000
Payroll Deduction Payable	100,000
Bank Loan (Note 6)	800,000
Mortgage Payable (Note 7)	1,320,000
Preferred Shares	1,200,000
Common Shares	1,000,000
Deficit	(460,000)
Total	$5,720,000

Notes:

1. Only $200,000 of the accounts receivable are expected to be recovered.

2. If inventory was liquidated as is, its net realizable value would be $400,000.

3. The building and the equipment are shown at cost to MAP less accumulated depreciation. The land, building, and equipment could be liquidated at their fair value as established in the proposal but commissions of $50,000 would have to be incurred.

4. Goodwill is shown at cost to MAP less accumulated depreciation. It was acquired more than 10 years ago when MAP acquired one of its competitors.

5. MAP has local rights to manufacture and distribute some types of aluminum products. The cost of these franchise rights is being amortized over 10 years, their estimated useful life. MAP cannot sell these rights.

6. The bank loan is secured by inventory under Section 178 of the Bank Act.

7. The mortgage is secured by land, building, and equipment.

8. Trustee's fees would amount to $200,000 if MAP was put into bankruptcy.

Required:

A. The president of Stanley Inc., one of MAP's suppliers with a $300,000 claim, has asked you if he should vote for MAP's reorganization proposal at the first creditors' meeting. Prepare a brief report outlining the consequences for Stanley Inc. of voting for and against the proposal and giving your recommendation.

B. If the proposal is accepted and approved by the court, present MAP's balance sheet after the reorganization.

(CICA Adapted)

ASSIGNMENT CASE ELEVEN - 1

Canadian Computer Systems Limited (CCS) is a public company engaged in the development of computer software and the manufacturing of computer hardware. CCS is listed on a Canadian stock exchange and has a 40 percent non controlling interest in Sandra Investments Limited (SIL), a US public company that was delisted by an American stock exchange because of financial difficulties. In addition, CCS has three wholly owned subsidiaries.

CCS is audited by Roth & Minch, a large public accounting firm. You, CA, are the audit manager responsible for the engagement.

CCS has a September 30 fiscal year end. It is now mid December, 1998 and the year end audit is nearing completion. CCS's draft financial statements are included in Exhibit I. While reviewing the audit working papers (see Exhibit II), you identify several issues that raise doubts about CCS's ability to realize its assets and discharge its liabilities in the normal course of business.

After you have reviewed the situation with the engagement partner, he asks you to prepare a memo for his use in discussing the going concern problem with the president of CCS. Your memo should include all factors necessary to assess CCS's ability to continue operations. You are also to comment on the accounting and disclosure implications.

Required: Prepare the memo requested by the partner.

(CICA Adapted)

Exhibit I
Canadian Computer Systems Limited
Extracts From Consolidated Balance Sheet
As At September 30
(in thousands of dollars)

	1998	1997
Current Assets:		
Cash	$ 190	$ 170
Accounts Receivable	2,540	1,600
Inventories (Lower Of Cost Or Market)	610	420
	$ 3,340	$ 2,190
Fixed Assets (Net Of Accumulated Depreciation)	33,930	34,970
Fixed Assets Held For Resale	1,850	1,840
Other Assets	410	420
Total Assets	$39,530	$39,420

	1998	1997
Current Liabilities:		
Demand Loans	$ 1,150	$ 3,080
Accrued Interest Payable	11,510	10,480
Accounts Payable	2,500	2,100
Mortgages Payable (Due Currently		
Because Of Loan Defaults)	21,600	21,600
Long Term Debt Due Within One Year	290	1,780
Debt Obligation Of Sandra Investments Ltd.	50,000	55,420
Total Current Liabilities	$ 87,050	$ 94,460
Long Term Debt	26,830	21,330
Other Liabilities	250	330
Total Liabilities	$114,130	$116,120
Share Capital:		
9 Percent Cumulative, Convertible,		
Preferred Shares (261 Shares)	$ 10	$ 10
Class B Preferred Shares (1,000,000 Shares)	250	250
Common Shares (10,243,019 Shares)	100,170	100,010
Total Share Capital	$100,430	$100,270
Deficit	(175,030)	(176,970)
Total Shareholders' Equity	($ 74,600)	($ 76,700)
Total Equities	$ 39,530	$ 39,420

Canadian Computer Systems Limited
Extracts From Consolidated Statement Of Operations And Deficit
For The Years Ended September 30
(in thousands of dollars)

	1998	1997
Sales:		
Hardware	$ 12,430	$ 19,960
Software	3,070	3,890
Total Sales	$ 15,500	$ 23,850
Other Income	1,120	-0-
Total Revenues	$ 16,620	$ 23,850
Expenses:		
Operating	$ 10,240	$ 15,050
Interest	4,590	4,690
General and Administrative	2,970	4,140
Depreciation	2,400	3,630
Provision For Impairment Of Fixed Assets	-0-	2,220
Total Expenses	$ 20,200	$ 29,730
Loss Before Undernoted Items	($ 3,580)	($ 5,880)
Loss From Sandra Investments Limited	(2,830)	(55,420)
Gain (Loss) From Discontinued Operations	8,350	(4,040)
Net Income (Loss)	$ 1,940	($ 65,340)
Deficit, Beginning Of Year	(176,970)	(111,630)
Deficit, End Of Year	($175,030)	($176,970)

Exhibit II
Extracts From Audit Working Papers

1. Cash receipts are collected by one of CCS's banks. This bank then releases funds to CCS based on operating budgets prepared by management. Demand loans bearing interest at 1 percent over the bank's prime rate are used to finance ongoing operations. The demand loans are secured by a general assignment of accounts receivable and a floating charge debenture on all assets.

2. CCS accounts for its interest in SIL on the equity basis. As a result of SIL's recurring losses in prior years, the investment account was written off in 1996. In 1997, CCS recorded in its accounts, the amount of SIL's bank loan and accrued interest, as this amount was guaranteed by CCS. During 1998, CCS made debt payments of $5.42 million and interest payments of $1.8 million on behalf of SIL. In December 1998, SIL issued preferred shares in the amount of US$40 million, used the proceeds to pay down the loan, and was relisted on the stock exchange. Interest expense on the debt obligation in 1998 totalled $2.83 million and has been included in the income statement under "Loss from Sandra Investments Limited."

3. Current liabilities include mortgages payable of $21.6 million due currently. They have been reclassified from long term debt because of CCS's failure to comply with operating covenants and restrictions. The prior year's financial statements have been restated for comparative purposes.

4. Long-term debt is repayable over varying periods of time. However, the banks reserve the right to declare the loans due and payable upon demand. The loan agreements require CCS to obtain advance approval in writing from the bank if it wishes to exceed certain limits on borrowing and capital expenditures. The agreements also prohibit the sale of certain fixed assets, payment of dividends, and transfer of funds among related companies without prior written approval. One loan of $15 million was in default at September 30, 1998.

5. During the year, CCS issued common shares to the directors and officers to satisfy amounts owing to them totalling $160,000. New equity issues are being considered for this year.

6. On November 15, 1998, a claim related to a breach of contract was filed against one of the company's subsidiaries in the amount of $3.7 million plus interest and costs of the action. Management believes that this claim is without merit. However, if any amounts do have to be paid as a result of this action, management believes that the amounts would be covered by liability insurance.

7. In 1998, operating expenses include $1 million in development costs relating to a computer software program. Sales of this software are expected to commence in 1999.

ASSIGNMENT CASE ELEVEN - 2

Metal Caissons Limited (MCL) was incorporated on December 15, 1996, to build metal caissons, which are large containers used for transporting military equipment. John Ladd (president) and Paul Finch (vice-president) each own 50% of MCL's shares. Until September 30, 1997, MCL's first fiscal year end, they applied their energy to planning and organizing the business. John and Paul developed the product, sought government assistance, designed the plant, and negotiated a sales contract.

In October 1997, MCL signed a $7.5 million contract with the Canadian Department of National Defence (DND). The contract stipulates that MCL must deliver one caisson to DND on the first business day of each month over a period of five years, commencing on April 1, 1998. Any delay in delivery entails a $2,000 penalty per day, per caisson delivered late, up to a maximum of $50,000 per caisson. DND has the right to cancel its contract with MCL at any time if the company is unable to meet its commitments. The caissons must be manufactured according to DND's detailed plans and specifications. Any caisson not meeting the specifications will be rejected, thereby causing a delay in delivery.

During November 1997, MCL obtained two government grants. Details of the grant agreements are as follows:

1. A $1 million grant for the construction of a manufacturing plant. The plant must be located in a designated area of the country and must be constructed primarily of Canadian-made components, failing which MCL must repay the grant in full.

2. A $500,000 grant for job creation. As a condition of the grant, MCL must employ at least 85% of its total work force in the plant for a period of three years. If employment at the plant falls below this minimum level, MCL will have to repay the grant in full.

On December 1, 1997, MCL borrowed $1 million from the bank for construction of the plant in northern Quebec, one of the designated areas. Construction was scheduled to start immediately and to be completed by the end of February 1998. Unfortunately, construction was delayed, and the manufacturing section of the plant was not fully operational until the beginning of May. As a result, the April, May and June caissons were delivered 25, 18 and 12 days late respectively. The inexperienced employees had to work quickly but met the delivery deadlines for the July and August caissons. The administrative section of the plant (supervisors' office, etc., representing 5% of the total area) is still under construction.

As a condition of the bank loan and the DND contract, the company must issue audited financial statements commencing with the year ending September 30, 1998.

It is now mid-September, 1998. Linda Presner, a partner with Presner & Wolf, Chartered Accountants, and you, the CA in charge of the audit, have just met with MCL's senior management to discuss the audit. During the meeting, you obtained the internal financial statements of MCL as at August 31, 1998, as well as a comparative balance sheet for the period ended September 30, 1997 (Exhibit I), and other information on MCL (Exhibit II). After the meeting, Linda asks you to prepare a memo for her dealing with the accounting, auditing, tax, and any other significant issues connected with this engagement.

Required: Prepare the memo requested by the partner.

(CICA Adapted)

Exhibit I
Metal Caissons Limited
Extracts From Internal Balance Sheet
(In Thousands Of Dollars, Unaudited)
As At

	August 31 1998	September 30 1997
Current Assets		
Cash	$ 8	$ 2
Accounts Receivable	635	Nil
Government Grants Receivable	1,500	Nil
Inventories (Note 1)	245	Nil
Total Current Assets	$2,388	$ 2
Fixed Assets (Note 1)	$2,234	Nil
Accumulated Depreciation	(80)	Nil
Net Fixed Assets	$2,154	Nil
Capitalized Expenditures - Net Of Amortization (Note 1)	$ 109	$120
Total Assets	$4,651	$122
Current Liabilities		
Accounts Payable And Other Accrued	$2,369	$ Nil
Advances From Shareholders	120	120
Total Current Liabilities	$2,489	$120
Long Term Liabilities	$1,000	Nil
Shareholders' Equity		
Capital Stock	$ 2	$ 2
Retained Earnings	1,160	Nil
Total Shareholders' Equity	$1,162	$ 2
Total Equities	$4,651	$122

Metal Caissons Limited
Extracts From Internal Statements Of Income And Retained Earnings
(In Thousands Of Dollars, Unaudited)
Eleven Months Ending August 31, 1998

Revenues	$2,125
Cost Of Sales	375
Gross Margin	$1,750
Administrative Expenses	590
Net Income And Retained Earnings	$1,160

Exhibit I (Continued)
Metal Caissons Limited
Extracts From Notes To Internal Financial Statements
For The Eleven Months Ended August 31, 1998

1. Accounting policies

    Inventories   Inventories are valued at the lower of cost and replacement value. Cost is determined on a first-in, first-out basis.

    Fixed Assets   Fixed assets are recorded at cost. Depreciation is calculated on a straight-line basis over the following periods:

Plant	50 Years
Production Equipment	15 Years
Office Equipment	20 Years
Computer Equipment	10 years

    Capitalized Expenditures   Capitalized expenditures consist of costs incurred during the start-up of the company. Amortization is calculated on a straight-line basis over a 10-year period.

    Capitalized Interest   The company is capitalizing 100% of the interest on the long-term debt until construction of the plant is complete. This interest is included in the cost of the plant.

2. Capital stock

    Authorized

    *   An unlimited number of class A voting shares.
    *   An unlimited number of class B and class C non-voting shares, with a $10 non-cumulative dividend, redeemable at the amount paid up.

    Issued

    *   2,000 class A shares.

Exhibit II
Information Gathered By CA

The bank loan bears interest at 15% and is secured by a mortgage on the plant. The loan is repayable over 10 years, with monthly payments of interest and principal of $16,135.

The shareholders have not withdrawn any cash from the company. For fiscal 1997, John Ladd believes his expertise and the time he spent is worth $30,000, and Paul Finch believes his efforts are worth $20,000. In addition, for fiscal 1998, each would like to receive $60,000. They are not sure whether they should receive these amounts as salary or dividends.

The head office of MCL, located in Montréal, is strictly an administrative unit. Twenty-four people, including the president and the vice-president work at head office. A bookkeeper who joined MCL in February 1998 supervises the preparation of the various financial and administrative reports. The plant employs 90 people.

Most of the parts used to make the caissons are purchased from a supplier in Germany. As at September 15, 1998, parts with a value of $300,000 are in storage in Germany and are to be delivered at the beginning of November 1998.

The production manager, a close friend of the shareholders, was hired in January 1998. He receives an annual salary of $50,000 plus a $3,000 bonus per caisson delivered, if MCL meets delivery and specification requirements. According to his employment contract, he can acquire a 10% interest in MCL if he manages to meet all delivery deadlines for the first three fiscal years.

As at September 30, 1997, capitalized expenditures included the following items:

Incorporation costs	$ 1,000
Office equipment	9,000
Travel expenses (in Canada and abroad)	19,000
Travel expenses related to search for plant site	16,000
Costs of calls for tenders	12,000
Product development costs	22,000
Grant negotiation costs	13,000
Costs related to contract negotiations with DND	10,000
Miscellaneous administrative costs	11,000
Miscellaneous legal fees	7,000
Total	$120,000

Travel expenses include several trips by John Ladd and his wife to Germany during which John studied the technology in use there.

The legal fees of $7,000 capitalized as at September 30, 1997, include $2,000 in fees related to a $2.5 million lawsuit filed by Deutsch Production (a German company) against MCL for patent infringements. As at September 15, 1998, John Ladd is unable to determine the outcome of the suit. In addition, $3,000 was incurred to negotiate the purchase of the land.

In fiscal 1998, $12,000 in legal fees has been incurred and expensed.

MCL had no income or expenses in its 1997 fiscal year, so it did not prepare an income tax return for that year.

DND did not take any action following the delays in delivery.

Chapter 12

Segment Disclosures

Note On Current Developments

12-1.   Section 1700 of the *CICA Handbook*, "Segmented Information", had remained largely unchanged since its last major revision in June, 1979. During this period, several factors had created the need for changes to this Section:

- Changes in the *CICA Handbook* have been made to require the consolidation of virtually all subsidiaries, leading to less availability of disaggregated information.

- In several Provinces, changes in the securities commissions' requirements for the Management Discussion And Analysis included in annual reports have explicitly called for more segmented information.

- Several other countries have issued new standards in this area in the last several years. In many cases, Canadian requirements vary from both old and new standards in other countries.

- A number of problems with the existing disclosure requirements have been identified in the literature.

12-2.   With respect to this last point, the 1992 CICA Research Study, *Financial Reporting For Segments*, identified two significant problems. One is the fact that many companies provide no segmentation because they claim that they are in one industry ("dominant industry" disclosure). Most analysts believe that many of these companies could provide useful segment information. The second problem is with companies that provide segment information, but have chosen industry segments that are so broad that they do not adequately meet the analysts' needs. This is sometimes referred to as the "broad industry problem". In both of these problem areas, the companies are providing information that is in full compliance with the requirements of Section 1700 of the *CICA Handbook*. As this compliance does not appear to meet the needs of analysts in the area of segmented reporting, changes were required in the *CICA Handbook*.

12-3.   The process of change began with the publication of the previously mentioned CICA Research Study in 1992. This Research Study documented the problems related to the reporting of segmented information and made a number of important Recommendations for improvements. We have included a summary of this important Research Study as an Appendix to this Chapter.

12-4.   Subsequent to the publication of this Research Study, the CICA's Accounting

Standards Board began work on a joint project with the U.S. based Financial Accounting Standards Board. In the United States, this work resulted in the publication in June, 1997 of Statement Of Financial Accounting Standards No. 131, "Disclosures About Segments Of An Enterprise And Related Information". Shortly thereafter, in September, 1997, the CICA issued a new Section 1701, "Segment Disclosures". This new Section replaces Section 1700, "Segmented Information". The reason for the change in the Section number is that the new Section 1701 does not become effective until fiscal years beginning on or after January 1, 1998. As a result, there will be a period of time where companies can use either the old or the new Recommendations. To avoid confusion between the two sets of Recommendations, the new Recommendations were designated Section 1701, while the older Section 1700 was relegated to the *CICA Handbook* Section for Superseded Recommendations.

12-5.   Despite differing titles, Section 1701 and Statement Of Financial Accounting Standards No. 131 are substantially identical. This is in keeping with the CICA's oft cited goal of harmonizing U. S. and Canadian accounting standards. The only real difference between the two Standards is in their scope. The U. S. Standard limits its scope to publicly traded business enterprises. The Canadian Standard expands its coverage to include not only public enterprises, but deposit taking institutions and life insurance enterprises.

12-6.   The content of this Chapter is largely based on the new Section 1701 of the *CICA Handbook*. However, for comparative purposes, some references will be made to the content of the earlier Section 1700.

Introduction To Section 1701

The Basic Issue

12-7.   The financial statements of an enterprise are usually prepared on a consolidated or total enterprise basis, aggregating the financial data of the various activities of the enterprise. While investors and creditors recognize the importance of this aggregate data to the process of reporting the overall performance of the enterprise, they have indicated that disaggregated data is also of use to them. They point out that evaluation of the risk and return of a particular enterprise is a central element in making investment and lending decisions. For a diversified enterprise, such an evaluation is not possible without some information on the segments of the business. Various alternatives for such disaggregation include product lines, operating divisions of the enterprise, geographic regions, and major customers.

12-8.   While the preceding Paragraph provides a general explanation of the desirability of segmented information, there are arguments which suggest that such information should not be required. These arguments include:

- Such information is too interpretive to be classified as accounting information and, thus, does not belong in the financial statements.

- Such information may not be subject to the same degree of verifiability as consolidated information.

- Such information is costly to compile.

- Such information may provide information that is useful to a firm's competitors.

12-9.   It is the last of these arguments that engenders the greatest resistance to increased amounts of segment disclosure. Many enterprises have expressed a strong belief that they can be harmed by providing such information.

12-10.   While there is some validity in all of the preceding arguments, standard setters in the U.S., Canada, and much of the rest of the industrialized world, have concluded that the merits of segmented information outweigh the disadvantages that can be associated with requiring its presentation.

Purpose And Scope

12-11.   Section 1701 requires that public enterprises and some other enterprises disclose certain information about operating segments and also about their products and services, the geographic areas in which they operate, and their major customers. The *CICA Handbook* also requires the disclosure of certain information about operating segments in interim financial reports.

12-12.   The scope of Section 1701 is described as follows:

> **Paragraph 1701.08**   *This Section should be applied by public enterprises, cooperative business enterprises, deposit-taking institutions and life insurance enterprises. Public enterprises are those enterprises that have issued debt or equity securities that are traded in a public market (a domestic or foreign stock exchange or an over-the-counter market, including local or regional markets), that are required to file financial statements with a securities commission, or that provide financial statements for the purposes of issuing any class of securities in a public market.* (January, 1998)

12-13.   As noted previously, the scope of Section 1701 is more extensive than that of the corresponding Statement Of Financial Accounting Standards No. 131 in the U.S., in that it covers deposit taking institutions and life insurance enterprises, in addition to public enterprises.

12-14.   While only the entities referred to in Paragraph 1701.08 are required to provide segment disclosures, other types of enterprises are encouraged to provide some or all of the disclosure required by Section 1701.

Objectives Of Segmented Information

12-15.   As described in Section 1701, the objective of requiring disclosures about segments of an enterprise and related information is to provide:

> **Paragraph 1701.02**   ... information about the different types of business activities in which an enterprise engages and the different economic environments in which it operates to help users of financial statements:
>
> (a) better understand the enterprise's performance;
>
> (b) better assess its prospects for future net cash flows; and
>
> (c) make more informed judgments about the enterprise as a whole.
>
> That objective is consistent with the objectives of general purpose financial reporting.

12-16.   From this description, it is clear that segmented information is directed towards providing information that will be useful in making interperiod comparisons for an individual enterprise. This more detailed disclosure of economic trends should be of significant assistance in projecting the amount, timing and uncertainty associated with prospective future cash flows, as well as understanding the enterprise's performance and making more informed judgments about the enterprise as a whole.

12-17.   It must be noted, however, that segmented information cannot be used to make meaningful comparisons between similar segments of two or more companies. As will become clear as we look at the more detailed Recommendations of Section 1701, the parameters of reportable operating segments will depend on the manner in which management organizes the enterprise for purposes of making operating decisions and assessing performance. Given this approach, the Section does not provide definitions of the items to be disclosed (e.g., segment profit or loss). Under these circumstances, most of the segment disclosures provided will be of little use in making comparisons of what appear to be similar segments in different companies.

12-18.   To alleviate this problem, Section 1701 requires some disclosure of the revenues that the enterprise derives from each of its products or services. This provides a limited basis for comparability between enterprises.

Management Approach

12-19.   The objective described in the preceding Section might be met by providing statements that are disaggregated in several different ways. This could include by products and services, by geography, by legal entity, or by type of customer. The now superseded Section 1700 focused on industry segments which were defined as follows:

> **Paragraph 1700.10(a)**   Industry segment is a distinguishable component of an enterprise engaged in providing a product or service, or a group of related products or services, primarily to customers outside the enterprise.

12-20.   This approach often required an enterprise to create something approaching a completely new accounting system to provide the data required by this product line approach. This reflects the fact that many enterprises are not organized along product lines for decision making or performance assessment purposes. As a reflection of this problem, the new Section 1701 rejects this approach.

12-21.   Section 1701 takes what is referred to as the management approach to segment disclosures. Under this approach, the reportable operating segments are based on the way in which management organizes the segments within the enterprise for making operating decisions and assessing performance. This means that the segments are evident from the structure of the enterprise's internal organizations, and financial statement preparers will be able to provide the required information in a cost effective and timely manner.

Reportable Operating Segments

Operating Segment Defined

12-22.   A 1993 position paper issued by the Association For Investment Management And Research, in its discussion of segment information, stated the following:

> ... priority should be given to the production and dissemination of financial data that reflects and reports sensibly the operations of specific enterprises. If we could obtain reports showing the details of how an individual business firm is organized and managed, we would assume more responsibility for making meaningful comparisons of those data to the unlike data of other firms that conduct their business differently.

12-23.   This statement is indicative of the type of support that exisits for the management approach to segment disclosure. As noted in the previous Section, the basic type of segment information required under the now superseded Section 1700 was based on products or services provided. In contrast, under the management approach required by the new Section 1701, the focus of segment disclosures will be reportable operating segments. The new Section provides the following definition of an operating segment:

> **Paragraph 1701.10**   An operating segment is a component of an enterprise:
>
> (a) that engages in business activities from which it may earn revenues and incur expenses (including revenues and expenses relating to transactions with other components of the same enterprise),
>
> (b) whose operating results are regularly reviewed by the enterprise's chief operating decision maker to make decisions about resources to be allocated to the segment and assess its performance, and
>
> (c) to which discrete financial information is available.

An operating segment may engage in business activities for which it has yet to earn revenues, for example, startup operations may be operating segments before earning revenues.

12-24.   With respect to this definition, Section 1701 makes a number of additional points:

- It is noted that not every part of an enterprise is an operating segment or part of an operating segment. Corporate headquarters and functional departments that do not earn revenues (e.g., accounting) would fall into this category. It is specifically noted that an enterprise's employee future benefit plans should not be considered to be operating segments.

- As the term is used in Paragraph 1701.10, "chief operating decision maker" identifies a function that may be described by a variety of titles. The basic idea is that this individual or group of individuals is responsible for allocating resources and assessing the performance of the operating segments of the enterprise.

- In many cases, the three characteristics described in Paragraph 1701.08 will clearly identify a a single set of operating segments. There are, however, situations in which the chief operating decision maker will use more than one set of segment information. In such cases, other factors may be useful in identifying a single set of components which constitute the operating segments of an enterprise. Such factors might include the nature of the business activities of each component, the existence of managers responsible for them, and the types of information presented to the board of directors.

- In most situations, an operating segment will have a segment manager. Such segment managers are usually accountable to and maintain regular contact with the chief operating decision maker in order to discuss operating activities, financial results, forecasts, or plans for the segment. The chief operating decision maker may also be a segment manager for one or more segments. In addition, a single individual may be a segment manager for more than one segment. In those cases where the characteristics used to identify an operating segment are applicable to more than one set of components of an organization, the set for which segment managers are held responsible should provide the basis for segment disclosures.

- In a matrix form of organization, operating segment characteristics may apply to overlapping sets of components for which managers are held responsible. An example of this would be an organization in which one group of managers is held responsible for certain product or service lines, while a different group is responsible for particular geographic areas. Financial information would be available for both sets of components and the chief operating decision maker would review both sets of information. Section 1701 notes that, in this type of situation, components based on products and services would form the basis for operating segment disclosure.

Reportable Operating Segments Identified
General

12-25.   In the preceding section we discussed the definition of an operating segment under the management approach to segment disclosure. While this definition allows us to identify the operating segments of an organization, it is unlikely that it will be appropriate to provide disclosure for all of the operating segments identified. This means that the next issue to be considered is which of these operating segments should be considered reportable. Section 1701's general statement on identifying reportable operating segments is as follows:

Paragraph 1701.16   *An enterprise should disclose separately information about each operating segment that:*

(a) *has been identified in accordance with paragraphs 1701.10 - .15 or that results from aggregating two or more of those segments in accordance with paragraph 1701.18, and*

(b) *exceeds the quantitative thresholds in paragraph 1701.19.*

Paragraphs 1701.22 - .25 specify other situations in which separate information about an operating segment should be disclosed. (January, 1998)

12-26. Under this Recommendation, an operating segment or group of aggregated operating segments, is considered to be reportable if it meets a specific quantitative threshold. This means that the process of identifying reportable operating segments begins with consideration of which operating segments can be aggregated. When the aggregation process is completed, the individual and aggregated operating segments will then be evaluated on the basis of the quantitative threshold in order to establish whether they should be considered reportable. The aggregation process and the quantitative threshold will be considered in the sections which follow.

Aggregation Of Operating Segments

12-27. As the goal of segment disclosure is to provide information on components of an enterprise that have similar economic characteristics, it would seem appropriate to aggregate those operating segments that have similar economic characteristics. Section 1701 notes that operating segments may be aggregated if:

1. aggregation is consistent with the objective and basic principles of Section 1701;

2. the segments have similar economic characteristics; and

3. if the segments are similar in each of the following areas:

   - the nature of the products and services;
   - the nature of the production processes;
   - the type or class of customer for their products and services;
   - the methods used to distribute their products or provide their services; and
   - if applicable, the nature of the regulatory environment (for example, banking, insurance, or public utilities).

Quantitative Threshold

12-28. Once operating segments have been identified and aggregated as appropriate, they will generally be considered reportable if they meet the following quantitative threshold:

Paragraph 1701.19 *An enterprise should disclose separately information about an operating segment that meets any of the following quantitative thresholds:*

(a) *Its reported revenue, including both sales to external customers and intersegment sales or transfers, is 10 percent or more of the combined revenue, internal and external, of all reported operating segments.*

(b) *The absolute amount of its reported profit or loss is 10 percent or more of the greater, in absolute amount, of:*

   (i) *the combined reported profit of all operating segments that did not report a loss, or*

   (ii) *the combined reported loss of all operating segments that did report a loss.*

(c) *Its assets are 10 percent or more of the combined assets of all operating segments.* (January, 1998)

12-29. A simple example will serve to illustrate the application of the preceding Recommendation:

Example   A company has identified eight operating segments with reported profits or losses as follows:

Segment	Profit (Loss)	Segment	Profit (Loss)
A	$ 63,000	E	($239,000)
B	210,000	F	(64,000)
C	50,000	G	(45,000)
D	277,000	H	(302,000)
Total	$600,000	Total	($650,000)

12-30.   Since the total reported loss of all industry segments that incurred a loss is greater than the total reported profit of all industry segments that earned a profit, a segment would be reportable under Paragraph 1701.19 if its reported profit or loss exceeded $65,000 or 10 percent of $650,000. This would mean that segments B, D, E, and H would be defined as reportable segments under Paragraph 1701.19(b). While segments A, C, F, and G do not qualify as reportable under Paragraph 1701.19(b), they may qualify under either 1701.19(a) or 1701.19(c).

Dominant Industry Disclosure

12-31.   One the major problems identified by the CICA Research Study, *Financial Reporting For Segments*, was that many enterprises failed to provide segment disclosures based on the claim that substantially all of its operations were in one industry segment. This approach was, in fact, condoned by a specific Recommendation in the now superseded Section 1700.

12-32.   The new Section 1701 contains no similar provision. While it is still possible that a particular enterprise could go through the analysis that we have described and still conclude that they have only one operating segment, this practice is not encouraged by a specific Recommendation that provides for this approach. The dominant industry approach is further discouraged by a Recommendation that requires a minimum allocation to operating segments. This Recommendation is as follows:

> **Paragraph 1701.22**   *If the total of external revenue reported by operating segments constitutes less than 75 percent of an enterprise's total revenue, additional operating segments should be identified as reportable segments (even if they do not meet the criteria in paragraph 1701.19) until at least 75 percent of the enterprise's total revenue is included in reportable segments.* (January, 1998)

Non Reportable Operating Segments

12-33.   Even when the minimum segmentation Recommendation of Paragraph 1701.22 is applied, it is likely that there will be other operating activities or segments that will not be given separate disclosure. With respect to these activities and segments, Section 1701 contains the following Recommendation:

> **Paragraph 1701.23**   *Information about other business activities and operating segments that are not reportable should be combined and disclosed in an "all other" category separate from other reconciling items in the reconciliations required by paragraph 1701.35. The sources of the revenue included in the "all other" category should be described.* (January, 1998)

Changes In Reportable Operating Segments

12-34.   It is probable that, from time to time, there will be changes in the group of operating segments that are identified as being reportable. When a reportable operating segment loses that status, the following Recommendation is relevant:

> **Paragraph 1701.24**   *If management judges an operating segment identified as a reportable segment in the immediately preceding period to be of continuing sig-*

nificance, information about that segment should continue to be disclosed separately in the current period even if it no longer meets the criteria for separate disclosure in paragraph 1701.19. (January, 1998)

12-35.   In the alternative situation, where a previously non reportable component of the enterprise is identified as a reportable operating segment during the current period, this Recommendation is applicable:

Paragraph 1701.25   *If an operating segment is identified as a reportable segment in the current period due to the quantitative thresholds, prior period segment data presented for comparative purposes should be restated to reflect the newly reportable segment as a separate segment even if that segment did not satisfy the criteria for separate disclosure in paragraph 1701.19 in the prior period unless it is impracticable to do so. (January, 1998)*

Reportable Operating Segment Disclosures

Types Of Disclosure

12-36.   Section 1701 requires disclosure in three separate categories. These categories are described as follows:

- General information.

- Information about reported segment profit or loss, including certain revenues and expenses included in reported segment profit or loss, segment assets, and the basis of measurement for segmented information.

- Reconciliations of the various types of segment information with the corresponding enterprise amounts.

12-37.   There are also disclosure provisions with respect to previously disclosed information for prior periods. These components of required disclosure are discussed in the subsections which follow.

General Information

12-38.   The required disclosure here relates to the process by which the enterprise determined its reportable segments, as well as the types of products and services from which the reportable segments derive their revenues. The Recommendation is as follows:

Paragraph 1701.29   *An enterprise should disclose the following general information:*

(a) Factors used to identify the enterprise's reportable segments, including the basis of organization (for example, whether management has chosen to organize the enterprise around differences in products and services, geographic areas, regulatory environments, or a combination of factors and whether operating segments have been aggregated).

(b) Types of products and services from which each reportable segment derives its revenues. (January, 1998)

12-39.   The Appendix to Section 1701 of the *CICA Handbook* contains an example of the type of disclosure that would be appropriate under part (a) of this Recommendation. This example is as follows:

Appendix Example   Diversified Company's reportable segments are strategic business units that offer different products and services. They are managed separately because each business requires different technology and marketing strategies. Most of the businesses were acquired as a unit, and the management at the time of the acquisition was retained.

12-40.   The Section 1701 Appendix example also includes the following as an illustration of the disclosure that would be appropriate under part (b) of Paragraph 1701.29:

> **Appendix Example** Diversified Company has five reportable segments: auto parts, motor vessels, software, electronics, and finance. The auto parts segment produces replacement parts for sale to auto parts retailers. The motor vessels segment produces small motor vessels to serve the offshore oil industry and similar businesses. The software segment produces application software for sale to computer manufacturers and retailers. The electronics segment produces integrated circuits and related products for sale to computer manufacturers. The finance segment is responsible for portions of the company's financial operations including financing customer purchases of products from other segments and real estate lending operations.

Information About Profit Or Loss And Assets

12-41.   Section 1701 specifies a fairly extensive list of items to be disclosed for each reportable operating segment:

> **Paragraph 1701.30** *An enterprise should disclose a measure of profit or loss and total assets for each reportable segment. An enterprise also should disclose the following about each reportable segment if the specified amounts are included in the measure of segment profit or loss reviewed by the chief operating decision maker:*
>
> *(a) Revenues from external customers.*
> *(b) Revenues from transactions with other operating segments of the same enterprise.*
> *(c) Interest revenue.*
> *(d) Interest expense.*
> *(e) Amortization of capital assets and goodwill.*
> *(f) Revenues, expenses, gains or losses resulting from items that do not have all of the characteristics of extraordinary items but result from transactions or events that are not expected to occur frequently over several years, or do not typify normal business activities of the entity.*
> *(g) Equity in the net income of investees subject to significant influence.*
> *(h) Income tax expense or benefit.*
> *(i) Extraordinary items.*
> *(j) Significant non cash items other than amortization of capital assets and goodwill.*
>
> *An enterprise should disclose interest revenue separately from interest expense for each reportable segment unless a majority of the segment's revenues are from interest and the chief operating decision maker relies primarily on net interest revenue to assess the performance of the segment and make decisions about resources to be allocated to the segment. In that situation, an enterprise may disclose that segment's interest revenue net of its interest expense and disclose that it has done so. (January, 1998)*
>
> **Paragraph 1701.31** *An enterprise should disclose the following about each reportable segment if the specified amounts are included in the determination of segment assets reviewed by the chief operating decision maker:*
>
> *(a) The amount of investment in investees subject to significant influence.*
> *(b) Total expenditures for additions to capital assets and goodwill. (January, 1998)*

12-42.   The Diversifed Company example that is presented in the Appendix to Section 1701 is extended to illustrate the following disclosure format that could be used to comply with Paragraphs 1701.30 and 1701.31:

	Auto Parts	Motor Vessels	Software	Elec- tronics	Finance	All Other	Totals
Revenues from external customers	$3,000	$5,000	$9,500	$12,000	$5,000	$1,000[a]	$35,500
Intersegment revenues	-	-	3,000	1,500	-	-	4,500
Interest revenue	450	800	1,000	1,500	-	-	3,750
Interest expense	350	600	700	1,100	-	-	2,750
Net interest revenue[b]	-	-	-	-	1,000	-	1,000
Amortization of capital assets and goodwill	200	100	50	1,500	1,100	-	2,950
Segment profit	200	70	900	2,300	500	100	4,070
Other significant noncash items: Cost in excess of billing on long term contracts	-	200	-	-	-	-	200
Segment assets	2,000	5,000	3,000	12,000	57,000	2,000	81,000
Expenditures for segment capital assets	300	700	500	800	600	-	2,900

[a]Revenues from segments below the quantitative thresholds are attributable to four operating segments of Diversified Company. Those segments include a small real estate business, an electronics equipment rental business, a software consulting practice, and a warehouse leasing oepation. None of those segments has ever met any of the quantitative thresholds for determining reportable segments.

[b]The finance segment derives a majority of its revenue from interest. In addition, management primarily relies on net interest revenue, not the gross revenue and expense amount, in managing that segment. therefore, as permitted by paragraph 1701.30, only the net amount is disclosed.

Diversified Company does not allocate income taxes or unusual items to segments. In addition, not all segments have significant noncash items other that amortization of capital assets and goodwill.

12-43.   There are, of course, a number of issues associated with the measurement of the items listed in the preceding Recommendations and illustrated in the Appendix example. These will be discussed in the next section which deals with accounting policies and measurement in segment disclosures.

Reconciliations

12-44.   For a variety of reasons (e.g., different accounting policies for segment disclosures), the sum of the operating segment data for a particular financial statement item is not likely to be equal to the amount actually reported in the aggregate financial statements. Given this, Section 1701 makes the following Recommendation with respect to reconciling these alternative amounts:

Paragraph 1701.35   *An enterprise should disclose reconciliations of all of the following:*

(a) *The total of the reportable segments' revenues to the enterprise's total revenues.*

(b) *The total of the reportable segments' measures of profit or loss to the enterprise's income before income taxes, discontinued operations and extraordinary items. However, if an enterprise allocates items such as income taxes and extraordinary items to segments, the enterprise may choose to reconcile the total of the segments' measures of profit or loss to the enterprise's income after those items.*

(c) *The total of the reportable segments' assets to the enterprise's total assets.*

(d) *The total of the reportable segments' amounts for every other significant item of information disclosed to the corresponding total amount for the enterprise (for example, an enterprise may choose to disclose liabilities for its reportable segments, in which case the enterprise would reconcile the total of reportable segments' liabilities for each segment to the enterprise's total liabilities if the* segment liabilities are significant).

All significant reconciling items should be separately identified and described (for example, the amount of each significant adjustment to reconcile accounting methods used in determining segment profit or loss to the enterprise's total amount would be separately identified and described). (January, 1998)

6-45.   The Section 1701 Appendix example is extended to illustrate the reconciliation disclosures required under Paragraph 1701.35:

Appendix Example

Revenues

Total revenues for reportable segments	$34,500
Other revenues	1,000
Elimination of intersegment revenues	(4,500)
Total enterprise revenues	$31,000

Profit Or Loss

Total profit of loss for reportable segments	$3,970
Other profit or loss	100
Elimination of intersegment profits	(500)
Unallocated amounts:	
Litigation settlement received	500
Other corporate expenses	(750)
Adjustment to pension expense in consolidation	(250)
Income before income taxes and extraordinary items	$3,070

Assets

Total assets for reportable segments	$79,000
Other assets	2,000
Elimination of receivable from corporation headquarters	(1,000)
Goodwill not allocated to segments	4,000
Other unallocated amounts	1,000
Enterprise total	$85,000

Other Significant Items

	Segment Totals	Adjustments	Enterprise Totals
Interest revenue	$3,750	$ 75	$3,825
Interest expense	2,750	(50)	2,700
Net interest revenue (finance segment only)	1,000	-	1,000
Expenditures for capital assets	2,900	1,000	3,900
Amortization of capital assets and goodwill	2,950	-	2,950
Cost in excess of billings on long term contracts	200	-	200

The reconciling item to adjust expenditures for capital assets is the amount incurred for the corporate headquarters building, which is not included in segment information. None of the other adjustments are significant.

Restatement Of Segment Disclosures

12-46.   As we have noted previously, it is likely enterprises will experience year-to-year changes in their group of reportable operating segments. When this happens, Section

1701 favours the retroactive approach as indicated in the following Recommendation:

> **Paragraph 1701.36** *If an enterprise changes the structure of its internal organization in a manner that causes the composition of its reportable segments to change, the corresponding information for earlier periods should be restated unless it is impracticable to do so. Accordingly, an enterprise should restate those individual items of disclosure that it can practically restate but need not restate those individual items, if any, that it cannot practically restate. Following a change in the composition of its reportable segments, an enterprise should disclose whether it has restated the corresponding items of segment information for earlier periods.* (January, 1998)

12-47.   If a retroactive approach is not applied in such situations, the following Recommendation is applicable:

> **Paragraph 1701.37** *If an enterprise has changed the structure of its internal organization in a manner that causes the composition of its reportable segments to change, and if segment information for earlier periods is not restated to reflect the change, the enterprise should disclose in the year in which the change occurs segment information for the current period under both the old basis and the new basis of segmentation unless it is impraticable to do so.* (January, 1998)

Accounting Principles And Measurement

Approach Under Superseded Section 1700

12-48.   The now superseded Section 1700 was based on providing information about industry segments. As this disclosure was based on products sold or services provided, the resulting disclosure did not reflect the manner in which the particular enterprise was organized.

12-49.   Given this situation, the superseded Section 1700 specified that the accounting principles underlying the segmented information should be the same as those followed in the preparation of the general purpose financial statements of the enteprise. In addition, it provided definitions of segment revenue, segment expense, segment operating profit and segment identifiable assets. These definitions were as follows:

> **Segment revenue** is revenue, directly attributable to a segment, derived from sales to customers outside the enterprise and from intersegment sales or transfers of products and services.

> **Segment expense** is an expense that is directly attributable to a segment or the relevant portion of an expense that can be allocated on a reasonable basis to the segments for whose benefit the expense was incurred. The following are excluded from segment expense because they either do not relate to segments or cannot always be allocated to segments: general corporate expenses; losses from investments accounted for on an equity basis; interest expense when the segment's operations are not primarily of a financial nature; income taxes; extraordinary charges; and non-controlling interest.

> **Segment identifiable assets** are all tangible and intangible assets attributable to a segment, including the portion of those used jointly by two or more segments that can be allocated on a reasonable basis. Advances or loans to, or investments in, another segment are not included in identifiable assets of a segment unless its operations are primarily of a financial nature and such items are similar to those arising from transactions with customers outside the enterprise. In computing the amount of a segment's identifiable assets, allowances such as allowance for doubtful accounts and accumulated depreciation would be taken into account.

Measurement Under Section 1701

12-50.   Under the new Section 1701's management approach to segment disclosure, the basic Recommendation on measurement is as follows:

> **Paragraph 1701.32** *The amount of each segment item disclosed should be the measure reported to the chief operating decision maker for purposes of making decisions about allocating resources to the segment and assessing its performance. Adjustments and eliminations made in preparing an enterprise's general purpose financial statements and allocations of revenues, expenses, and gains or losses should be included in determining reported segment profit or loss only if they are included in the measure of the segments' profit or loss that is used by the chief operating decision maker. Similarly, only those assets that are included in the measure of the segment's assets that is used by the chief operating decision maker should be disclosed for that segment. If amounts are allocated to reported segment profit or loss or assets, those amounts should be allocated on a reasonable basis.* (January, 1998)

12-51.   Under this approach, there is no specification of the accounting principles to be used. Further, no definitions of items such as segment revenue, segment expense, or segment profit or loss are required. While the absence of such definitions is consistent with the management approach to segment disclosures, the absence of these definitions is of concern to some. This was the case with James J. Leisenring, a member of the FASB who dissented from the adoption of Statement Of Financial Accounting Standards No. 131 (this Statement is largely identical to Section 1701). A part of his dissent is as follows:

> By not defining segment profit or loss, this Statement allows any measure of performance to be displayed as segment profit or loss as long as that measure is reviewed by the chief operating decision maker. Items of revenue and expense directly attributable to a given segment need not be included in the reported operating results of that segment, and no allocation of items not directly attributable to a given segment is required. As a consequence, an item that results directly from one segment's activities can be excluded from that segment's profit or loss. Mr. Leisenring believes that, minimally, this Statement should require that amounts directly incurred by or directly attributable to a segment be included in that segment's profit or loss and that assets identified with a particular segment be consistent with the measurement of that segment's profit or loss.

> ... Mr. Leisenring supports the management approach for defining reportable segments and supports requiring disclosure of selected segment information in condensed financial statements of interim periods issued to shareholders. Mr. Leisenring believes, however, that the definitions of revenues, operating profit or loss, and identifiable assets should be retained in this Statement and applied to segments identified by the management approach.

12-52.   While both Canadian and U. S. standard setters rejected Mr. Leisenring's view, there is clearly cause for concern with the wide range of approaches that can be used in preparing segment information. To at least partially alleviate that concern, Section 1701 includes a Recommendation requiring fairly extensive disclosure of the manner in which segment profit or loss and segment assets have been determined:

> **Paragraph 1701.34** *An enterprise should disclose an explanation of the measurements of segment profit or loss and segment assets for each reportable segment. At a minimum, an enterprise should disclose the following:*
>
> *(a) The basis of accounting for any transactions between reportable segments.*
> *(b) The nature of any differences between the measurements of the reportable segments' profits or losses and the enterprise's income before income taxes, discontinued operations and extraordinary items (if not apparent from the reconciliations described in paragraph 1701.35). Those differences could include accounting policies and policies for allocation of centrally incurred costs that are necessary for an understanding of the segment information dis-*

closed.

(c) *The nature of any differences between the measurements of the reportable segments' assets and the enterprise's total assets (if not apparent from the reconciliations described in paragraph 1701.35). Those differences could include accounting policies and policies for allocation of jointly used assets that are necessary for an understanding of the segment information disclosed.*

(d) *The nature of any changes from prior periods in the measurement methods used to determine reported segment profit or loss and the effect, if any, of those changes on the measure of segment profit or loss.*

(e) *The nature and effect of any asymmetrical allocations to segments* (for example, an enterprise might allocate amortization expense to a segment without allocating the related capital assets to that segment). (January, 1998)

12-53.   The Section 1701 Appendix example includes the type of disclosure that would be appropriate under Paragraph 1701.34:

> **Appendix Example**   The accounting policies of the segments are the same as those described in the summary of significant accounting policies except that pension expense for each segment is recognized and measured on the basis of cash payments to the pension plan. Diversified Company evaluates performance based on profit or loss from operations before income taxes not including non recurring gains and losses and foreign exchange gains and losses.

12-54.   As was noted in an earlier section, the chief operating decision maker may use more than one measure of a segment's profit or loss, as well as more than one measure of segment assets. Section 1701 suggests that, in this situation, the measures used for segment disclosure should be those that management believes are determined in accordance with the measurement principles most consistent with those used in measuring the corresponding total amounts in the enterprise's financial statements.

Enterprise Wide Disclosures

General

12-55.   As we have indicated previously in this Chapter, the primary focus of segment disclosures under Section 1701 is on reportable operating segments, with such segments identified on the basis of the organization of the business activities of the enterprise. Unless the enterprise's business activities are organized on the basis of products and services, or geographic regions, we may encounter situations in which:

- an operating segment may report revenues from a range of different products or services;

- different operating segments may report revenues from essentially the same products or services;

- assets may be reported in one geographic area with related revenue being included in different geographic areas; or

- more than one operating segment may carry on activities in the same geographic area.

12-56.   Such results are, of course, consistent with the management approach to segment disclosures. However, users of financial statements are clearly interested in having more detailed information about products and services provided by the enterprise, geographic areas in which the enterprise operates, and major customers. As a consequence, Paragraph 1701.39 through 1701.43 include Recommendations requiring the disclosure of such information. Note, however, that this disclosure need be provided only if it is not provided as part of the reportable operating segment information required elsewhere in Section 1701.

Information About Products And Services

12-57.   In order to provide some basis for comparison with enterprises providing similar products and services, Section 1701 includes the following Recommendation:

> **Paragraph 1701.39**   *An enterprise should disclose the revenues from external customers for each product and service or each group of similar products and services unless it is impracticable to do so. The amounts of revenues disclosed should be based on the financial information used to produce the enterprise's general purpose financial statements. If providing the information is impracticable, that fact should be disclosed.* (January, 1998)

12-58.   Diversified Company in the Section 1701 Appendix example has operating segments that are based on different products and services (see Paragraph 12-40). As a consequence, no additional disclosure is required under Paragraph 1701.39.

Information About Geographic Areas

12-59.   As was the case with lines of products and services, Section 1701 requires additional information about geographic areas:

> **Paragraph 1701.40**   *An enterprise should disclose the following geographic information unless it is impracticable to do so:*
>
> *(a) Revenues from external customers:*
>   *(i)   attributed to the enterprise's country of domicile, and*
>   *(ii) attributed to all foreign countries in total from which the enterprise derives revenues.*
>
> *If revenues from external customers attributed to an individual foreign country are material, those revenues should be disclosed separately. An enterprise should disclose the basis for attributing revenues from external customers to individual countries.*
>
> *(b) Capital assets and goodwill:*
>   *(i)   located in the enterprise's country of domicile, and*
>   *(ii) located in all foreign countries in total in which the enterprise holds assets.*
>
> *If assets in an individual foreign country are material, those assets should be disclosed separately.*
>
> *The amounts disclosed should be based on the financial information used to produce the general purpose financial statements. If providing the geographic information is impracticable, that fact should be disclosed.* (January, 1998)

12-60.   As Diversified Company in the Section 1701 Appendix example did not have operating segments based on geographic areas, Paragraph 1701.40 is applicable. The illustration of geographic information included in the Appendix is as follows:

Appendix Example
Geographic Information

	Revenues	Capital Assets and Goodwill
Canada	$19,000	$11,000
United States	4,200	-
Taiwan	3,400	6,500
Japan	2,900	3,500
Other foreign countries	1,500	3,000
Total	$31,000	$24,000

Revenues are attributed to countries based on location of customer.

Information About Major Customers

12-61.   A final type of enterprise wide disclosure required by Section 1701 is information about major customers:

> **Paragraph 1701.42**   *An enterprise should disclose information about the extent of its reliance on its major customers. If revenues from transactions with a single external customer amount to 10 percent or more of an enterprise's revenues, the enterprise should disclose that fact, the total amount of revenues from each such customer, and the identity of the segment or segments reporting the revenues.* (January, 1998)

12-62.   In applying this provision, Section 1701 notes that a group of enterprises under common control should be considered to be a single customer. In contrast, the federal government, a provincial government, a local government, or a foreign government would each be considered to be a single customer.

12-63.   In general, enterprises are reluctant to disclose information about particular customers as such information may be useful to competitors. As a consequence, Section 1701 does not require disclosure of the identity of major customers, or the amount of revenues that each segment receives from such customers.

12-64.   The Section 1701 Appendix example includes the following illustration of disclosure about major customers:

Appendix Example
Major Customer Disclosure

Revenues from one customer of Diversified Company's software and electronics segments represent approximately $5,000 of the Company's total revenues.

Segment Disclosure In Canadian Practice

Basis For Statistics And Examples

12-65.   The statistics and examples which follow are largely from the 1997 edition of *Financial Reporting In Canada*. This survey of Canadian accounting practices gathered data from 1995 and 1996 annual reports and, as a consequence, it does not contain information related to Section 1701. The statistics and examples that are reproduced from this source are based on the now superseded Section 1700. This information will be revised when the 1998 edition of *Financial Reporting In Canada* becomes available.

Statistics From Financial Reporting In Canada

12-69.   The 1997 edition of *Financial Reporting In Canada* states that for 1996, 141 of the 200 surveyed companies provided industry and/or geographic segment information, 21 disclosed that their operations had a dominant industry segment, and the remaining 38 did not provide information on industry or geographic segments. With respect to the form of segmentation, 37 companies reported information on the basis of industry segments only, 22 companies reported on the basis of geographic segments only, 23 companies provided disclosure of geographic segments with an indication that there was a dominant industry, and 59 companies disclosed both industry and geographic segments.

12-70.   For the 96 companies disclosing information about industry segments, 32 provided information about two segments, 34 provided information about three segments, and 30 provided information about four or more segments.

12-71.   For the companies disclosing information about industry segments, the number of companies reporting various types of information was as follows:

Type Of Information	1996
General description of segment products and services	96
Segment revenue	96
Segment operating profit or loss	94
Segment depreciation, depletion, or amortization	93
Segment identifiable assets	92
Segment capital expenditures	88

12-72.   For the 104 companies that provided information about geographic segments, 46 reported two segments, 32 reported three segments, and 26 reported four or more segments.

12-73.   For the companies reporting geographic segments, the number of companies reporting various types of information were as follows:

Types of information	1996
Location of segment	104
Segment revenue	103
Segment operating profit or loss	97
Identifiable assets	96
Basis of accounting for intercompany sales	22

12-74.   The great majority of companies providing segmented information did so on a comparative basis.

Examples From Practice

Example One - Schneider Corporation

12-75.   The following example is from the annual report of SCHNEIDER CORPORATION for the reporting period ending October 26, 1996. This Company provides segmented information on an industry basis only.

Note 10   Segmented Financial Information:
Information is presented according to the following industry segments:

Consumer Foods:
Comprises processed meats sold under the Schneiders, Lifestyle, Fleetwood, Fiorentina, Cappola, Johnsonville, Prince and Charcuterie Roy brands and grocery products (including cheese in 1995 and 1994) sold under the Schneiders, Mother Jackson's Open Kitchens and Charcuterie Roy brands as well as products sold under private label brands.

Agribusiness:
Comprises the fresh pork and poultry business sectors.

	1996	1995	1994
Sales to customers:			
Consumer Foods	$522,015	$542,166	$495,941
Agribusiness	304,085	285,355	271,710
	$826,100	$827,521	$767,651
Earnings (loss) from operations:			
Consumer Foods	$ 15,667	$24,051	$20,263
Agribusiness	(4,463)	(1,564)	5,728
Corporate/unallocated	(6,314)	(5,058)	(4,423)
Unusual item	(12,000)	-	-
	$(7,110)	$17,429	$21,568
Depreciation and amortization:			
Consumer Foods	$ 9,291	$ 9,717	$ 8,547
Agribusiness	3,830	3,471	3,404
Corporate/unallocated	1,543	1,404	1,286
	$ 14,664	$14,592	$13,237
Capital expenditures:			
Consumer Foods	$ 9,201	$ 7,106	$ 7,853
Agribusiness	13,628	7,933	3,460
Corporate/unallocated	11	419	1,201
	$ 22,840	$ 15,458	$ 12,514
Total assets:			
Consumer Foods	$ 90,786	$ 96,682	$101,460
Agribusiness	86,570	72,539	73,219
Corporate/unallocated	75,815	77,611	69,871
	$253,171	$246,832	$244,550

All of the Corporation's operations, employees and assets are located in Canada. Sales to customers in foreign countries amounted to $103,069,000 in 1996 (1995 - $94,074,000, 1994 - $79,832,000).

Example Two - Slater Steel Inc.

12-76.   The following example is from the annual report of SLATER STEEL INC. for the reporting period ending December 31, 1996. It is an extensive example involving a Company which provides both industry and geographic segmented information.

Note 15 Segmented Financial Information:

a) Industry Segments

	Year Ended December 31							
	Steel Mills		Steel Service Centre		Other		Consolidated	
	1996	1995	1996	1995	1996	1995	1996	1995
Total Sales	$430,309	456,274	82,094	76,850	32,345	36,793	544,743	569,917
Inter-segment sales	558	592	41	99	8	39	607	730
Net sales to customers	$429,746	455,682	82,053	76,751	32,337	36,754	544,136	569,187
Segment earnings	$35,380	54,899	3,941	3,947	966	797	40,287	59,643
General corporate expense							(1,842)	(2,837)
Interest							(3,139)	(4,734)
Earnings before income taxes							35,306	52,072
Income tax provision							(11,639)	(18,093)
Net earnings							$23,667	33,979
Identifiable assets	$308,278	283,804	41,780	35,839	16,022	18,270	366,080	337,913
Corporate assets							9,907	9,229
Total assets							$375,987	347,142
Capital expenditures	$43,034	31,554	1,550	461	154	212	44,738	32,227
Depreciation, amortization	$12,262	12,125	873	1,093	606	654	13,741	13,872

b) Geographic Segments

	Year Ended December 31					
	Canada		U.S.		Consolidated	
	1996	1995	1996	1995	1996	1995
Total assets	$355,351	350,289	189,392	219,628	544,743	569,917
Inter-segment sales	553	704	54	26	607	730
Net sales to customers	$354,798	349,585	189,338	219,602	544,136	569,187
Segment earnings	$25,718	29,138	14,569	30,505	40,287	59,643
General corporate expense					(1,842)	(2,837)
Interest					(3,139)	(4,734)
Earnings before income taxes					35,306	52,072
Income tax provision					(11,639)	(18,093)
Net income					$23,667	33,979
Identifiable assets	$221,731	200,192	144,349	137,721	366,080	337,913
Corporate assets					9,907	9,229
Total assets					$375,987	347,142
Capital expenditures	$34,114	19,303	10,624	12,924	44,738	32,227
Depreciation and amortization	$7,186	7,198	6,555	6,674	13,741	13,872
Export sales	$187,621	184,030	2,802	1,904	190,423	185,934

The steel mills segment consists of the manufacture and sale of stainless, carbon and low alloy steels, special bar quality steel shapes, mold, tool and die steels and custom steel forgings. The steel service centre segment consists of sales and distribution of steel products. The other segment consists of the manufacture and sale of electrical transmission hardware and transportation services. Inter-segment sales are accounted for at cost plus a reasonable mark-up for administrative costs.

Additional Readings

FASB Statement Of Financial Accounting Standards No. 131, *Disclosure About Segments Of An Enterprise And Related Information*, June, 1997.

CA Magazine Article - "A Segmented Picture", John M. Boersema and Susan J. Van Weelden, April, 1992.

CA Magazine Article - "Through Management's Eyes", Cally Hunt, May, 1996.

CA Magazine Article - "Accounting Standards: The Management Approach", Peter Martin, November, 1997.

FASB Statement Of Financial Accounting Standards No. 131 *Disclosures About Segments Of An Enterprise And Related Information*, June, 1997.

Accounting Horizons Article "Segment Statements & Informativeness Measures: Managing Capital Vs. Managing Resources", Yuji Ijiri, September, 1995

Accounting Horizons Article "Reporting Financial Information by Segment: A Comment Of The American Accounting ASsociation On The IASC Draft Statement Of Principles", Stephen B. Salter, Edward P. Swanson, Ann-Kristin Achletner, Erik de Lembre, and Bhagwan S. KLhanna, March, 1996.

Assignment Problems

(The solutions to these problem are only available in
the solutions manual that has been provided to your instructor.)

ASSIGNMENT PROBLEM TWELVE - 1

In each of the following independent cases, information on the various operating segments of a particular enterprise is provided. Operating segments have been identified using the guidance provided by Section 1701 of the *CICA Handbook*.

Case A   Quantitative information with respect to identified operating segments for the Allen Company is as follows:

Segment	Profit (Loss)	Assets	Revenues External	Intersegment
1	$125,000	$273,000	$206,000	Nil
2	91,000	342,000	172,000	$ 4,000
3	56,000	147,000	112,000	46,000
4	(104,000)	406,000	73,000	Nil
5	(26,000)	204,000	104,000	116,000
6	(427,000)	526,000	346,000	26,000
7	485,000	407,000	382,000	56,000
8	236,000	268,000	246,000	24,000
Totals	$436,000	$2,573,000	$1,641,000	$272,000

The total revenue reported by the enterprise is equal to the $1,641,000 total shown for the eight identified operating segments.

Case B   Quantitative information with respect to identified operating segments for the Bakin Company is as follows:

Segment	Profit (Loss)	Assets	Revenues External	Intersegment
1	$126,000	$ 310,000	$ 323,000	$250,000
2	82,000	170,000	120,000	Nil
3	94,000	165,000	115,000	Nil
4	573,000	895,000	562,000	375,000
5	55,000	155,000	96,000	Nil
6	23,000	105,000	84,000	Nil
Totals	$953,000	$1,800,000	$1,300,000	$625,000

The total revenue reported by the enterprise is equal to the $1,300,000 total shown for the six identified operating segments.

Case C   Quantitative information with respect to identified operating segments for the Cello Company is as follows:

Segment	Profit (Loss)	Assets	Revenues External	Revenues Intersegment
1	($172,000)	$ 273,000	$ 319,000	$ 26,000
2	46,000	252,000	119,000	Nil
3	32,000	173,000	191,000	34,000
4	(478,000)	561,000	362,000	171,000
5	72,000	219,000	123,000	4,000
6	(342,000)	402,000	247,000	Nil
7	132,000	148,000	429,000	Nil
8	(104,000)	289,000	113,000	Nil
9	28,000	83,000	47,000	8,000
Totals	($786,000)	$2,400,000	$1,950,000	$243,000

The total revenue reported by the enterprise is equal to the $1,950,000 total shown for the nine identified operating segments.

Required: Using the quantitative information provided, indicate which of the operating segments listed in each Case should be considered reportable operating segments. Briefly explain your conclusions.

ASSIGNMENT PROBLEM TWELVE - 2
Company Background

Integrated Inc.'s major business involves the manufacture, wholesale distribution, and retail sales of two unique groups of products. The first group of products is designed to help with home organization. These are marketed under the brand name Home Assistant (HA). The second group of products is directed towards assisting with the management of commercial offices. These are marketed under the brand name Office Assistant (OA).

Retail sales are handled exclusively through the Company's own outlets, with each outlet handling both the Home Assistant line and the Office Assistant line. While the head office of the Company is in Canada, it operates wholly owned subsidiaries in Mexico, France, and Japan.

All of the Company's manufacturing operations are in Mexico. While there are some external sales of manufactured product in Mexico, the majority of the production is shipped to the Company's operations in Canada, France, and Japan. There is no wholesale or retail activity in Mexico. In Canada, France, and Japan, the Company has wholesale and retail operations for both Home Assistant products and Office Assistant products.

When goods are moved from manufacturing to wholesale operations, or from wholesale operations to retail operations, they are transferred at prices which are the same as those used for sales to enterprises outside Integrated's consolidated group.

After trying alternative approaches, management of the Company has concluded that control of enterprise activities should be based on business functions, as opposed to geographic areas or product lines. As a consequence, the chief operating decision maker receives reports on the basis of manufacturing activities, wholesale activities, and retail operations.

At the retail level, interest is charged on overdue receivables. Interest expense is not allocated to operating segments.

Parent And Subsidiary Data

Separate records are kept for Integrated Inc. and each of its subsidiaries. The following information is taken from these records and reflects activities for the current year. This information is used to prepare the reports required by the chief operating decision maker.

Canadian Operations

| | Wholesale Operations | | Retail Operations | |
	HA Products	OA Products	HA Products	OA Products
Profit (Loss)*	$ 47,000	$ 38,000	($ 64,000)	$ 28,000
Total Capital Assets	250,000	164,000	273,000	184,000
External Revenue	32,000	14,000	672,000	239,000
Intersegment Revenues	294,000	156,000	Nil	Nil
Amortization Expense	22,000	13,400	14,600	9,800
Income Tax Expense (Benefit)	23,400	19,500	(31,200)	13,200
Capital Expenditures	16,200	8,600	34,000	26,000
Interest Revenue	Nil	Nil	3,500	4,200

Because of an expropriation of Land by a local government unit, the retail operations of Canadian OA products experienced an Extraordinary Gain (Net Of Tax) of $5,400.

Mexican Subsidiary

| | Manufacturing Operations | |
	HA Products	OA Products
Profit (Loss)*	$ 233,000	$ 32,000
Total Capital Assets	1,456,000	824,600
External Revenue	123,200	78,300
Intersegment Revenues	326,400	142,600
Amortization Expense	123,200	75,400
Income Tax Expense (Benefit)	106,500	11,300
Capital Expenditures	223,400	87,500
Interest Revenue	Nil	Nil

French Subsidiary

| | Wholesale Operations | | Retail Operations | |
	HA Products	OA Products	HA Products	OA Products
Profit (Loss)*	$ 23,000	$ 19,000	$ 32,000	$ 14,000
Total Capital Assets	126,000	87,000	134,000	98,000
External Revenue	Nil	7,200	356,000	114,000
Intersegment Revenues	142,000	72,000	Nil	Nil
Amortization Expense	14,000	6,200	7,800	5,500
Income Tax Expense (Benefit)	14,100	11,300	18,400	8,100
Capital Expenditures	7,500	4,500	16,000	Nil
Interest Revenue	Nil	Nil	3,200	4,100

Japanese Subsidiary

	Wholesale Operations		Retail Operations	
	HA Products	OA Products	HA Products	OA Products
Profit (Loss)*	$ 12,000	$ 8,500	$ 22,000	$ 24,000
Total Capital Assets	63,100	41,200	82,400	73,500
External Revenue	21,200	7,300	192,000	94,000
Intersegment Revenues	74,500	41,400	Nil	Nil
Amortization Expense	12,100	4,300	3,900	2,600
Income Tax Expense (Benefit)	4,300	2,900	7,400	8,200
Capital Expenditures	3,500	2,300	8,400	Nil
Interest Revenue	Nil	Nil	1,200	1,600

*Segment profit or loss is determined on the basis of total external and intersegment revenues for the segment, reduced by expenses other than taxes that can be directly allocated to the segment.

Consolidated Information

The following information will be included in the consolidated financial statements of Integrated Inc. and its subsidiaries:

Total Revenues*	$2,347,000
Income Before Taxes And Extraordinary Items	536,700
Total Capital Assets	4,723,200
Amortization Expense	346,400
Income Tax Expense	231,800
Capital Expenditures	482,300

*No single customer accounts for more than 10 percent of this total.

Required: Provide all of the disclosure that would be required by Section 1701 of the *CICA Handbook* for the current year's annual report of Integrated Inc.

Chapter 13

Interim Financial Reporting To Shareholders

Note On Current Developments

13-1.   In April, 1991 the CICA published a Research Report titled *Interim Financial Reporting*. While this Report is likely to lead to a substantial revision of Section 1750 of the *CICA Handbook*, "Interim Financial Reporting To Shareholders", current Canadian practice is based on the existing Section 1750. However, the Research Report contains many important Recommendations for improvements to information provided to users of interim financial reports. We believe this Report is useful in understanding interim reporting and have provided a summary of the Research Report in the Supplement to this Chapter.

Introduction

The Issues

13-2.   We are concerned here with the application of accounting principles and reporting practices to interim financial information. Such financial information would include both interim financial statements and summarized interim financial data. While the term could apply to any time period, the interim period that is most commonly referred to is three months or one quarter of the annual accounting period that we normally deal with.

13-3.   There are several basic issues involved in this subject matter and, in addition, a number of other general subject areas are influenced by the decisions that are made in dealing with quarterly financial information. These issues can be outlined as follows:

Objectives And Elements   Section 1000 of the *CICA Handbook*, "Financial Statement Concepts" describes the objectives and elements of financial statements. However, there is still the question of whether the objectives of interim financial reports should be the same as those that apply to annual financial reports. A similar question arises with respect to the characteristics of the elements that will be included in the interim financial statements.

Measurement Of Interim Earnings   There are two basic views as to the appropriate solution to the problem of measuring interim earnings. They are referred to as the integral view and the discrete view and they can be described in the following manner:

1. **Integral Approach**   Under the integral approach, the year is considered to be the primary reporting period. Each interim period is viewed as an integral part of the year, and as such it should bear a part of the annual expenses that are related to revenue generation activity for that period. Estimated annual expenses are allocated or assigned to parts of a year in proportion to sales volume or a similar activity basis.

2. **Discrete Approach**   Under the discrete approach, a year and its parts are viewed as discrete periods for which financial results are reported. Accounting is considered to be the recording of transactions or events as they occur, and the basis for recognizing an expense does not change with the period of time covered by an earnings report.

The application of these views is, of course, more or less difficult depending on the particular area that is being dealt with. The most severe problems arise in the areas of accounting changes, accounting for taxes and the quarterly application of LIFO inventory valuation procedures.

Disclosure   The issue here is whether the same types of disclosure that are used in the annual financial reports are necessary and/or appropriate in the preparation of interim financial reports. More specifically, the question is whether to trade off a certain amount of information loss in return for the savings in cost and time that can be achieved by reporting summarized financial data. In addition, if it is decided that the use of summarized information is appropriate, the nature of the summarized information to be reported will have to be determined.

Applicability   The question here is whether certain types of companies should be exempted from any interim reporting standards that are developed. There are several possible reasons for establishing exemptions of this sort. The most obvious reason for exemption would be the fact that the securities of the company that is under consideration are not publicly traded. Size could also provide a basis for exemption. An additional problem would be whether interim disclosure requirements should apply only to quarterly reports or, alternatively, be extended to cover any period of less than one year.

Objectives And Elements In Interim Reporting

13-4.   There are a number of possible uses that can be made of interim reports. The most frequently cited of these would be as follows:

- As a basis for estimating annual earnings.

- As a basis for making forward projections for any relevant future period, including annual periods.

- To assist in identifying turning points in the company's earnings or liquidity patterns.

- As a basis for evaluating management performance.

- To supplement the annual report in a continuing process of conveying information on the financial progress of the enterprise.

13-5.   Some of these potential uses are identical to those for which we prepare annual reports. This leads some accountants to the view that the objectives of interim reports should be the same as those of annual reports. They note that while the shortness of the interim period may call for different measurement methods or require a different type of disclosure, these are not differences in objectives but rather, different means of achieving the same objectives. Opponents of this view would argue that the collective differences between interim and annual financial reports are so significant that such differences must flow from different objectives. This latter view does not necessarily mean that annual statement objectives are wholly inapplicable to interim reports, but that some modification of the proposed objectives is desirable to recognize that uses, qualitative criteria, and measurements may be different for interim periods.

13-6.   With respect to elements of financial statements, the issue is whether assets, liabilities, and other elements of financial statements reported at interim dates and those reported in annual reports have different characteristics. For example, advertising expenditures would generally not be treated as an asset at the end of an annual accounting period.   However, if a large advertising expenditure was consistently made in the third quarter of each year to promote a heavily seasonal sales volume in the fourth quarter, the integral measurement approach would treat this expenditure as an asset in the third quarter Balance Sheet.

Example: Measurement Of Interim Earnings

Basic Data

13-7.   As pointed out earlier, there are two basic views as to the solution to the problem of measuring interim earnings. Under the integral view, estimated annual expenses are allocated or assigned to parts of a year in proportion to sales volume or some similar activity basis. In contrast, with the discrete view, expenses are charged to the income of the interim period in which they are incurred, regardless of the level of activity in that particular period. At this point we will consider a simple example to illustrate the mechanics of the two approaches and to provide a basis for discussing the merits of the alternative views on which the procedures are based.

> **Example**   The Confused Company estimates that sales during the current calendar year will total 1 million units at $5 per unit. The Company provides interim reports for each quarter of the calendar year and its sales follow an extremely seasonal pattern. In past years the pattern has been 20 percent of sales in the first quarter, 20 percent in the second quarter, 50 percent in the July through September quarter and 10 percent in the last quarter. With respect to variable costs, the budget calls for $2.00 per unit in variable manufacturing costs and $.50 per unit in variable selling expenses. Fixed manufacturing costs are estimated at $1 million and fixed selling and administrative costs are anticipated to total $500,000. Both types of fixed costs are incurred in equal quarterly amounts. The total budget for the Confused Company would appear as follows:

Estimated Sales (1,000,000 At $5.00)		$5,000,000
Variable Costs:		
Manufacturing (1,000,000 At $2.00)	$2,000,000	
Selling (1,000,000 At $.50)	500,000	$2,500,000
Fixed Costs:		
Manufacturing	$1,000,000	
Selling And Administrative	500,000	1,500,000
Total Estimated Costs		$4,000,000
Budgeted Profit		$1,000,000

During the year, all of the revenues and costs occurred exactly as anticipated and units produced were equal to units sold. The resulting dollar figures for quarterly sales are as follows:

Quarter	Sales
First	$1,000,000
Second	1,000,000
Third	2,500,000
Fourth	500,000
Total	$5,000,000

Discrete Approach Solution

13-8.   Interim results of the Confused Company, using the discrete approach are as follows:

Quarter	First	Second	Third	Fourth
Sales (At $5)	$1,000,000	$1,000,000	$2,500,000	$500,000
Variable Cost (At $2.50)	(500,000)	(500,000)	(1,250,000)	(250,000)
Contribution	$ 500,000	$ 500,000	$1,250,000	$250,000
Fixed Costs ($1,500,000/4)	(375,000)	(375,00)	(375,000)	(375,000)
Net Income (Loss)	$ 125,000	$ 125,000	$ 875,000	($ 25,000)

13-9.   The discrete approach solution produces the budgeted total income figure of $1,000,000. However, by allocating fixed costs to income as they are incurred on a quarterly basis, it has produced interim income figures that are more variable than the sales pattern would suggest (i.e., the percentage changes in income are less than the percentage changes in sales). Further, the interim earnings figures would not provide a basis for predicting annual income if you knew the seasonal pattern of sales. That is, if first quarter sales were normally 20 percent of the annual total, you could not use the above information to predict annual results because the first quarter income of $125,000 is not 20 percent of the annual total.   You might also question whether the Company really experienced a loss in the fourth quarter.

Integral Approach Solution

13-10.   Interim results using the integral approach are as follows:

Quarter	First	Second	Third	Fourth
Sales (At $5)	$1,000,000	$1,000,000	$2,500,000	$500,000
Variable Cost (At $2.50)	(500,000)	(500,000)	(1,250,000)	(250,000)
Contribution	$ 500,000	$ 500,000	$1,250,000	$250,000
Fixed Costs (At $1.50)	(300,000)	(300,000)	(750,000)	(150,000)
Net Income	$ 200,000	$ 200,000	$ 500,000	$100,000
Deferred Fixed Costs	$ 75,000	$ 150,000	($ 225,000)	$ -0-

13-11.   The integral approach solution also produces the budgeted total income figure of $1,000,000. The Deferred Fixed Costs are calculated by subtracting the cumulative allocated fixed costs from the cumulative actual fixed costs. By allocating fixed costs in proportion to sales, we produce interim income figures that are both proportional to sales and useful for predicting annual results. As an example of this latter point, if we knew that 20 percent of the Company's business occurred in the first quarter, we could use the interim income of $200,000 to predict the annual total of $1,000,000. This would appear to suggest that the integral approach is a better solution to this problem. However, there are problems with this approach.

Problems With The Integral Approach Solution

13-12.   The preceding Paragraph presented the results that would be produced by the applying the integral approach. This solution was based on the assumption that all revenues and costs for the year were exactly as they were budgeted. Two types of problems can cause difficulty and sometimes produce absurd results in the application of the integral approach. These problems are differences between actual and budgeted costs and/or the volume of sales being more or less than was anticipated. We will illustrate the effects of each of these types of problems separately.

Cost Variances

13-13.   To illustrate this type of problem we will assume that all of the Confused Company's costs were exactly as budgeted except that in the fourth quarter the fixed costs incurred were zero. Keeping in mind that there was a deferred credit in fixed costs at the end of the third quarter, the fourth quarter integral approach Income Statement would be as follows:

Sales	$500,000
Variable Costs	(250,000)
Contribution Margin	$250,000
Fixed Costs (Credit)	225,000
Net Income	$475,000

13-14.   This result, which presents a Net Income that is equal to 95 percent of sales, is clearly not reasonable. However, it can easily happen under the integral approach when costs are incorrectly estimated. It is even possible to find examples where income exceeds total revenue in the last quarter of the fiscal year.

Volume Variances

13-15.   To illustrate this type of problem, assume that first quarter costs are exactly as estimated. However, the sales volume is only 100,000 units at $5 for a total of $500,000. If we ignore the effect of this result on the predictions for the year, the first quarter integral approach Income Statement would be as follows:

Sales	$500,000
Variable Costs	(250,000)
Contribution Margin	$250,000
Fixed Costs (At $1.50)	(150,000)
Net Income	$100,000

13-16.   If the first quarter sales volume is a non recurring shortfall, the preceding result is reasonable. However, if it turns out that the sales of 100,000 units is the usual 20 percent of the annual total, then total sales for the year will only be 500,000 units and the fixed costs will have to be allocated on a different basis. In other words, if the $1,500,000 in fixed costs is to be spread over only 500,000 units rather than the anticipated 1,000,000, the per unit charge under the integral approach will be $3.00 instead of the old basis of $1.50. This would result in the following Income Statement for the first quarter:

Sales	$500,000
Variable Costs	(250,000)
Contribution Margin	$250,000
Fixed Costs (At $3.00)	(300,000)
Net Income (Loss)	($ 50,000)

13-17. This, of course, is a significantly different result than was the case when the estimate of total sales was not adjusted on the basis of the first quarter results. It is indicative of the difficulties that misestimating volume can generate in the application of the integral approach to the computation of interim income.

A Compromise Solution

13-18. The preceding solutions have presented the discrete and integral approaches in their unmodified form. In practice, the more usual approach would be to use the integral approach for manufacturing costs and the discrete approach for other types of costs. This avoids the problem of treating deferred selling and administrative costs as assets and/or liabilities. Applying this combination approach to the interim results for the Confused Company produces the following results:

Quarter	First	Second	Third	Fourth
Sales (At $5)	$1,000,000	$1,000,000	$2,500,000	$500,000
Variable Cost (At $2.50)	(500,000)	(500,000)	(1,250,000)	(250,000)
Contribution	$ 500,000	$ 500,000	$1,250,000	$250,000
Fixed Costs:				
Manufacturing (At $1.00)	(200,000)	(200,000)	(500,000)	(100,000)
Selling	(125,000)	(125,000)	(125,000)	(125,000)
Net Income	$ 175,000	$ 175,000	$ 625,000	$ 5,000

Section 1750 Requirements

Applicability Of Interim Reporting Requirements

13-19. The basic issue here is determining for which enterprises interim disclosure standards should be applicable. The various alternatives are:

- All enterprises that make interim financial reports available to parties external to the enterprise.
- All public enterprises.
- Public enterprises above a specified size as measured by revenue, net income, and/or assets.
- Companies for which the volume of publicly traded equity securities is above a specified level.
- A separate (and significantly lesser) disclosure standard for monthly reports if quarterly reports are issued in accordance with established standards.

13-20. The Recommended solution for Canadian companies is as follows:

Paragraph 1750.01 ... The Recommendations in this Section apply to those interim financial reports which are sent by companies to their shareholders on a regular periodic basis.

13-21. In effect, this Recommendation indicates that the Section 1750 Recommendations are applicable only in those cases where the enterprise regularly issues interim statements. This appears to be a reasonable conclusion given that not all enterprises have a legal reason to issue such statements.

Measurement Approach

13-22.   Section 1750 of the *CICA Handbook* fails to take an unambiguous stand on the measurement approach that should be used in the preparation of interim financial reports. The Recommendation on this issue is as follows:

> **Paragraph 1750.14** *The preparation of financial data should be based on accounting principles and practices consistent with those used in the preparation of annual financial statements. Where necessary, appropriate estimates and assumptions should be made to match costs and revenues. Where, due either to the nature of the item or the short period involved, an estimate may be subject to substantial adjustment at the year end, disclosure of this fact should be made.* (November, 1971)

13-23.   While this statement begins by describing the procedures that would be used under the discrete approach (i.e., principles and practices consistent with those used in the preparation of annual financial statements) it goes on to refer to procedures that would be used under the integral approach (i.e., estimates and assumptions should be made to match costs and revenues).

13-24.   It would appear that this Recommendation would allow the use of any measurement approach that the reporting entity feels is "appropriate". This is a very weak Recommendation in that it permits a wide variety of practices to be used. This, in turn results in a lack of comparability between the interim reports of different corporations.

Disclosure In Interim Statements

Basic Issues

13-25.   The issue here is, of course, what disclosure standards should apply to interim financial statements. The possible solutions to this issue are as follows:

- Disclosure essentially the same as for annual financial statements.

- Addition to or deletion from annual disclosure requirements if specified criteria are met. This raises an additional issue in the determination of the criteria that should be used in deciding to add or delete an item from the disclosure that will be required.

- Presentation of selected financial statement items and a summarization of other items in financial statements such that, when viewed together with the latest annual financial statement and subsequent interim statements, the requirements for a fair presentation are met.

13-26.   In addition to the relationship between annual and interim disclosure requirements, other issues related to disclosure include:

- What, if any, segmented information should be included in interim financial statements?

- If financial information is presented on a regular quarterly basis, for which periods should comparable information be presented? The choices here would include the current interim period and comparable period of the prior year, current and prior year-to-date except for the first period, or current and prior year 12 months-to-date.

- How might report users be informed about the effect of seasonality on interim period income? The choices here would include reliance on management discussion and analysis, the use of 12 months-to-date data, use of the integral view of interim measurement and the provision of a sufficient number of periods of unadjusted data so that users could calculate or observe the seasonal effects for themselves.

Basis Of Presentation

13-27.   Section 1750 has several requirements in this area. The first of these Recommendations notes that:

> **Paragraph 1750.04**   *Interim financial data should be presented on a consolidated basis by companies which present their annual financial statements on a consolidated basis. (November, 1971)*

13-28.   With respect to time periods, minimum disclosure would provide data for the current fiscal year to date with all information being presented on a comparative and consistent basis for the corresponding period in the preceding year. These Recommendations are found in the following two Paragraphs:

> **Paragraph 1750.10**   *Interim financial reports should present financial information for at least the current fiscal year to date. (November, 1971)*

> **Paragraph 1750.12**   *All financial summaries included should be presented on a comparative and consistent basis showing the figures for the corresponding period in the preceding year. The figures for the corresponding period in the preceding year should be restated where appropriate. (See "General Standards Of Financial Statement Presentation", Section 1500 and "Accounting Changes", Section 1506.) (November, 1971)*

13-29.   Section 1750 requires separate disclosure for Results Of Discontinued Operations and Extraordinary Items in interim statements. The Section also notes that they should not be prorated over the year as follows:

> **Paragraph 1750.07**   *Discontinued operations and extraordinary items should be shown separately and included in the determination of net income for the interim period in which they occur. (See "Discontinued Operations", Section 3475 and "Extraordinary Items", Section 3480.) (January, 1990)*

Minimum Disclosure Requirements

13-30.   Section 1750's minimum disclosure requirements are as follows:

> **Paragraph 1750.06**   *Interim financial reports should include at least the following:*
>
> *(a) A summary disclosing separately*
> | | |
> |---|---|
> | (i) | revenue; |
> | (ii) | investment income; |
> | (iii) | amount charged for depreciation, depletion and amortization; |
> | (iv) | interest expense; |
> | (v) | income tax expense; |
> | (vi) | income or loss before discontinued operations and extraordinary items; |
> | (vii) | discontinued operations and related income taxes; |
> | (viii) | income or loss before extraordinary items; |
> | (ix) | extraordinary items and related income taxes; and |
> | (x) | net income or loss for the period. |
>
> *(b) Basic and fully diluted earnings per share figures, calculated and presented in accordance with "Earnings Per Share", Section 3500.*
>
> *(c) Information as to significant changes in financial position. This information can often be provided by a statement of changes in financial position together with other information for any changes which are not disclosed in that statement. In some cases this information can be provided in an alternative form, such as a statement of changes in net assets.*

(d) *Information concerning:*
  (i) *Changes in accounting principles or in the methods used in their application (see "Accounting Changes", Section 1506);*
  (ii) *Discontinued operations (see "Discontinued Operations", Section 3475);*
  (iii) *Extraordinary items, if the descriptive titles of the items do not disclose their nature (see "Extraordinary Items", Section 3480);*
  (iv) *Subsequent events (see "Subsequent Events", Section 3820);*
  (v) *Other matters, not previously reported to shareholders as part of the annual financial statements, such as changes in contingencies or commitments, or issue or expiry of convertible securities, rights, warrants or options.* (January, 1990)

Specific Application Problems

Introduction

13-31.   There are a number of specific areas in which the application of interim reporting concepts is particularly difficult. These areas include interim tax provisions, temporary reductions in LIFO inventories, interim period depreciation, and treatment of interim period accounting changes. Section 1750 provides a discussion of some of these issues, but only a limited number of conclusions are reached. A brief examination of some of these more complex issues follows.

Income Taxes

13-32.   There is, of course, no such thing as an interim tax return and this means that the effective rate of taxation for a particular company must be based on annual data. While the estimation of this effective rate might be difficult in terms of implementation, the concepts involved here are no different than with many other types of annual costs. There are, however, problems that do relate specifically to taxes in interim financial statements and are covered in the following *CICA Handbook* Paragraphs.

- **Two Rate System**   When two different effective tax rates apply — for example in situations where the first $200,000 of earnings are eligible for the small business deduction and the earnings in excess of $200,000 are taxed at a higher rate — Section 1750 provides the following guidance:

   Paragraph 1750.17   The two-rate system of corporate income tax raises the question of how to allocate income subject to the low rate of tax to interim periods. The calculation of income taxes under the two-rate system of corporate income tax may be based on either of two methods. One method involves allocating the income subject to the low rate of tax evenly over the interim periods. The other method would involve estimating the income for the year, calculating the income taxes thereon and applying the effective rate so developed to the interim income.

- **Interim Earnings Fluctuations**   With respect to this problem, the Section states the following:

   Paragraph 1750.18   Where the pattern of earnings fluctuates from one interim period to another, such as in a seasonal business where there may be a profit in one interim period and a loss in another, profitable periods should normally show income tax provisions and unprofitable periods should show income tax recoveries provided such recoveries are more likely than not to be realized.

- **Loss Carry Forwards From Prior Years**   Prior to the inclusion of Section 3465, "Income Taxes", into the *CICA Handbook*, this issue was dealt with in Paragraph 1750.19 of Section 1750. As this issue is now covered in Section 3465, Paragraph 1750.19 has been removed.

- **Loss Carry Overs In The Current Year**   This situation is dealt with in two Paragraphs in Section 1750:

    Paragraph 1750.20   Where the loss in the interim period is less than or equal to the income for the prior annual period, recognition of the tax recovery due to loss carryback provisions to the extent of the entire loss for the interim period is appropriate.

    Paragraph 1750.21   Where the loss in the interim period is in excess of the income for the prior annual period, it is appropriate to recognize the tax recovery due to loss carryback provisions.

- **Tax Allocation**   Prior to the introduction of Section 3465 into the *CICA Handbook*, this issue was dealt with in Paragraph 1750.22 of Section 1750. As this issue is now covered in Section 3465, Paragraph 1750.22 has been removed.

Inventory Valuation

13-33.   The problems here are generally described as follows:

Paragraph 1750.23   It is preferable that the determination of interim inventory be on the same basis as annual inventory. Procedures would have to be applied to give the best possible estimate of the figure which would be produced if all the normal inventory procedures had been carried out. In developing an inventory figure for interim financial reports, consideration should be given to declines which may have occurred in market or replacement value of stock on hand, obsolescence, shrinkages due to theft and unreported wastage and the existence of quantities in excess of probable requirements. Temporary encroachments of base quantities of inventories maintained on a LIFO or based stock method should be taken into account. In industries where the retail inventory or gross profit methods are appropriate, these methods could be used.

13-34.   With respect to temporary adjustments of LIFO inventories that we would expect to replace by year end, a credit adjustment will be required in the interim Balance Sheets. This could be disclosed as an adjustment of the inventory account, a deferred credit or an adjustment of the accounts payable.

Depreciation

13-35.   On this issue, Section 1750 notes the following:

Paragraph 1750.24   The basis used for calculating depreciation for interim periods should be consistent with that used for the year. Calculation of the depreciation charge for the interim period is comparatively simple where the annual depreciation charge is based on month-end or quarter-end balances. However, if the annual depreciation charge is based on year-end balances and the annual charge prorated evenly for interim periods, an estimate of additions or deductions in depreciable assets for the entire fiscal year would be required.

13-36.   Similar problems exist with respect to other expenses such as bonuses or volume discounts that are determined on an annual basis.

Annually Determined Costs And Revenues

13-37.   When certain types of costs are determined on an annual basis (e.g., bonuses to management), Section 1750 provides the following guidance:

Paragraph 1750.25   Some costs or revenues based on levels of income or sales are only determined once each year. Examples are management bonuses, volume discounts (on both purchases and sales), and sales commissions or rent based on income or sales. However, effective rates could be calculated at which each cost or revenue would be accrued during the year and the rates could be used in determining the interim portion of these costs and revenues.

Current Canadian Practices

Examples

13-38.   Our basic source on current Canadian accounting practices has been the CICA's *Financial Reporting In Canada*. This source is devoted to a survey of accounting practices as reflected in the annual reports of major Canadian companies and, as a consequence, it does not provide any information related to interim reports. This makes it impossible to comment on either the number of interim reports that are provided or the accounting practices that are found in those reports that are available.

13-39.   As a substitute for more detailed statistical information, the following briefly summarizes the financial reporting information that appeared in the interim reports of five publicly traded Canadian companies:

Biovail   Interim Report for the third quarter which ended September 30, 1997. This report contained:

- a consolidated Balance Sheet with comparative figures as at December 31, 1996

- a consolidated Statement of Income with comparative figures for the three months ending September 30, 1997

- a consolidated Statement of Income with comparative figures for the nine months ending September 30, 1997

- a consolidated Statement of Changes in Financial Position with comparative figures for the nine months ending September 30, 1997

WIC Western International Communications Ltd.   Interim Report for the first quarter which ended November 30, 1997. This report contained:

- a consolidated Statement of Earnings with comparative figures for the three months ending November 30, 1997

- a consolidated Statement of Changes in Financial Position with comparative figures for the three months ending November 30, 1997

- no consolidated Balance Sheet

Unican   Interim Report for the second quarter which ended December 31, 1997. This report contained:

- a Statement of Income with comparative figures for the three months ending December 31, 1997 and the six months ending December 31, 1997

- a Balance Sheet with comparative figures as at December 31, 1996

- a Statement of Changes in Financial Position with comparative figures for the six months ending December 31, 1997

Cognos International   Interim Report for the third quarter which ended November 30, 1997. This report contained two sets of financial statements. The first set was labelled U.S. GAAP and the second set was labelled Canadian GAAP. Both of these sets of statements contained:

- a consolidated Statement of Income with comparative figures for the three months ending November 30, 1997 and the nine months ending November 30, 1997

- a consolidated Balance Sheet with comparative figures as at February 28, 1997

- a consolidated Statement of Cash Flows for nine months with comparative figures for the nine months ending November 30, 1997

Viceroy Resource Corporation   Interim Report for the third quarter which ended September 30, 1997. This report contained:

- a consolidated Balance Sheet with comparative figures as at December 31, 1996

- a consolidated Statement of Earnings with comparative figures for the three months ending September 30, 1997 and the nine months ending September 30, 1997

- a consolidated Statement of Changes in Financial Position with comparative figures for the nine months ending September 30, 1997

13-40.   The reports varied in size, style and content. They were all unaudited. None of the interim reports contained additional information with respect to the accounting principles used in calculating the amounts presented. In view of the wide variety of possibilities permitted by the *CICA Handbook* in this area, this would have to be viewed as a serious deficiency in these statements.

CICA Research Report

13-41.   Also available with respect to current Canadian practices is a survey of 150 Canadian companies, the results of which are described in Chapter 5 of the CICA Research Report, *Interim Financial Reporting*. Major findings reported in this Chapter are:

- Current practices exceed the requirements of both legislation and Section 1750 of the *CICA Handbook*.

- All of the survey companies presented an Income Statement, 93 percent presented a Statement Of Changes In Financial Position, and 80 percent presented a Balance sheet. Notes to the financial statements were presented by 58 percent of the companies.

- Nearly 80 percent of the survey companies presented interim financial statements with the same level of detail as was contained in their annual financial statements.

- Over 90 percent of the survey companies presented interim financial information on a consolidated basis. Only one of the companies that presented consolidated annual information presented non consolidated interim financial statements.

Supplement
CICA Research Report Interim Financial
Reporting: A Continuous Process

13A-1. This Research Report was published by the CICA in April, 1991. A chapter by chapter summary follows.

Basis For The Report

13A-2. The CICA initiated this Research Report in 1989 in order to review Section 1750 of the *CICA Handbook*. The research for the Report indicated that the accounting standards for this subject were out of step with current practices which now, in most aspects, exceed CICA Recommendations. As a result, the Study Group challenges Canadian standard setters to seriously consider the material in this Report as a basis for amending the current *CICA Handbook* Recommendations.

Chapter 1 - Introduction

13A-3. The Report concludes that there is an urgent need for significant revisions to the present standards, which have remained essentially unchanged for over twenty years. This need is clearly evidenced by the concerns of financial statement users and their advisers, by ongoing regulatory initiatives, and by the demand for timely information for decision making purposes. There is also a further need for ongoing consideration of the effect on interim reporting when standards for annual reporting are established or amended.

13A-4. In view of this situation, the Report identifies and analyzes accounting and financial reporting issues and makes recommendations for amending the present standards on interim reporting. Along with proposed changes to Section 1750, two additional recommendations are made:

> **Recommendation 1 - Revise Interim Reporting Standards** In light of the wide ranging nature of the recommendations included in this research report, the CICA's Accounting Standards Committee should give priority to revising the interim reporting standards in *CICA Handbook* Section 1750.

> **Recommendation 2 - Ongoing Consideration Of Interim Reporting** Ongoing consideration should be given to the effect on interim reporting when establishing or amending standards for annual financial reporting.

Chapter 2 - A Framework For Interim Reporting

13A-5. The Report establishes that the primary users of interim reports are investors, creditors, and their advisers. It also establishes that the main purpose of preparing an interim report is to communicate to users credible, relevant information which will facilitate interpretation of an entity's activities for purposes of economic decision making and assessment of management's stewardship and performance. The Report also delineates the qualitative characteristics of interim information such as understandability, comparability, relevance, reliability, and timeliness. Trade offs between these qualitative characteristics are also considered.

13A-6. The Report concludes that, despite the different trade offs to be made for interim periods, the underlying objectives of interim reporting are essentially the same as those of annual reporting. In summary, the three primary objectives of interim reporting are:

- To communicate, in a readily understandable way, timely, reliable and relevant information about an entity's operating, financing, and investing activities to diverse user groups who rely on it as a principal source and who may have limited authority, ability, or resources to obtain such information.

- To provide a focus for making economic decisions by presenting information about an entity to assist users in predicting, comparing, and evaluating potential earnings and cash flows in terms of amount, timing and related uncertainty.

- To report on management's stewardship and financial performance by presenting information about an entity that is useful in assessing management's ability to utilize resources effectively in achieving the primary goals of the entity.

13A-7.   The proposed framework for interim reporting encompasses accounting standards for interim financial statements. Accounting and reporting issues on applicability, presentation and disclosure, measurement and recognition, and other matters are discussed in Chapters 4 to 7. However, to set the stage for dealing with these issues, Chapter 3 describes the environment within which interim reporting takes place.

Chapter 3 - The Interim Reporting Environment
Legal Requirements
13A-8.   While considerable documentation is required to establish this point, Canadian public companies are legally required to present interim financial statements. Such requirements flow from the Canada Business Corporations Act, various provincial securities commissions, and, for companies that are publicly traded in the U.S., that country's Securities And Exchange Commission.

Accounting And Reporting Standards
13A-9.   The three standard setting bodies that have issued specific standards on interim reports are the CICA (Section 1750 of the *CICA Handbook*), the Accounting Principles Board in the U.S. (APB Opinion No. 28), and the New Zealand Society Of Accountants (SSAP-24).

Current Practices
13A-10.   The background research for this Report included a survey of the interim reports of 150 companies. The typical content was as follows:

- Time Period (most commonly cumulative data to end of quarter)
- Report To Shareholders (date of issuance specified and averaged 41 days after statement date)
- Financial/Operating Summary
- Highlights
- Financial Statements (94% marked unaudited)
- Balance Sheet (80% of companies)
- Income/Earnings Report (100% of companies)
- Statement Of Changes (93% of companies)
- Notes To Financial Statements (58% of companies)
- Segmented Information (30% of companies)
- Other Data

Chapter 4 - Applicability Issues
Applicability Of Standards
13A-11.   The first issue dealt with in this Chapter is the question of who should be required to comply with any interim reporting standards that are developed. In general, provincial legislation requires interim reports from all public companies. Focusing on this fact, the Report makes the following Recommendation:

> **Recommendation 3 - Application Of Standards**   Interim reporting standards should apply to all entities that are legally required to issue external interim finan-

cial statements or interim reports. Other entities, including non profit organizations, that voluntarily issue such statements or reports are strongly encouraged to comply with the standards.

Frequency Of Reporting

13A-12. After reviewing various provincial legal requirements, the Report makes the following Recommendation in this area:

Recommendation 4 - Frequency Of Reporting Interim reports should be prepared on a quarterly basis. To be timely, quarterly reports should be issued within 45 days after the end of each of the first three quarters and, for the fourth quarter, within 90 days after the fiscal year-end. A separate fourth quarter report would normally be prepared unless annual, audited financial statements are issued within 90 days after the fiscal year end.

Periods Presented

13A-13. The majority of Canadian companies currently report on the basis of the current fiscal year to date, cumulative to the end of the current quarter. While there is some support for a running 12 months to date approach, the Research Report reinforces current practice:

Recommendation 5 - Periods Presented Interim reports should present information for the most recent fiscal quarter and for the cumulative fiscal year-to-date. Comparative information should be provided for the corresponding periods of the preceding fiscal year.

Chapter 5 - Presentation And Disclosure Issues

Financial Statement Content

13A-14. The survey of Canadian companies revealed that the majority presented a full set of financial statements, including a level of detail consistent with their annual statements. While this exceeds the current Recommendations of Section 1750, the Research Report concludes that the approach used in practice is the appropriate one:

Recommendation 6 - Content Of Interim Financial Statements Interim reports should include the same financial statements as provided in an entity's annual report. Normally this would include a balance sheet, income statement, and statement of changes in financial position in the same level of detail as the annual financial statements, but the notes to financial statements may be presented in condensed or summarized form. Furthermore, interim financial statements should be presented on a consolidated basis by entities which present their annual financial statements on a consolidated basis.

Note Disclosure

13A-15. In current practice, there is considerable variation in note disclosure, ranging from detail comparable to annual reports to others with a much less formal approach. The Research Report concludes that notes to interim financial statements should facilitate user understanding and assessment of the past, present and future activities of the entity. They should also convey information on significant events in the period and major changes that have occurred since the fiscal year end. To encourage this, the Report makes the following four recommendations:

Recommendation 7 - Basis Of Accounting Notes to interim financial statements should disclose:

- that management has prepared the interim financial statements in accordance with generally accepted accounting principles which normally requires the use of the historical cost basis of accounting and approximations and estimates based on professional judgments; and

- that the interim financial statements contain all adjustments that management believes are necessary for a fair presentation of the entity's financial position, results of operations, and changes in financial position.

Recommendation 8 - Accounting Policies   Notes to interim financial statements should disclose that the interim financial statements should be read in conjunction with the entity's most recent annual financial statements and:

- that the significant accounting policies used for preparing the interim financial statements are consistent with those used in preparing the entity's annual financial statements; and (where applicable)

- that certain significant accounting policies, as disclosed, vary from those used in preparing the annual financial statements.

Recommendation 9 - Additional Disclosures   Notes to interim financial statements should cover discontinued operations, extraordinary items, changes in accounting policies, prior period adjustments, earnings-per-share data, changes in capital structure, contingencies and commitments since the previous fiscal year end, subsequent events, and any other matters of significance.

Recommendation 10 - Fourth Quarter Disclosures   In the absence of a separate fourth quarter report, the results of operations for that quarter should be disclosed as unaudited information supplementary to the annual financial statements. Such disclosure would encompass any fourth quarter discontinued operations, extraordinary items and significant but infrequently occurring items, as well as the aggregate effect of any fiscal year end adjustments which are material to the results of the fourth quarter.

Segmented Information

13A-16.   While only about 30 percent of the survey companies provided any form of segmented information in their interim reports (85 percent had such information in their annual reports), there appears to be a strong demand by certain user groups for providing such information. This demand, along with a recognition that it may be impracticable to provide all of the annual requirements in interim reports, is reflected in the following recommendation:

Recommendation 11 - Segmented Information   Segmented information, by industry and geographic area, should be disclosed in notes to interim financial statements in the same level of detail as the most recent annual financial statements. None-the-less, when such detailed disclosure is not practicable, the notes to the interim financial statements should, as a minimum, disclose the following information:

- segment revenue derived from external sales;
- segment revenue derived from inter segment sales or transfers;
- segment operating profit/loss;
- significant unusual items included in determining segment operating profit/loss;
- the carrying amount of identifiable segment assets when there has been a major change since the most recent fiscal year end (e.g., discontinued operations);
- segment capital expenditures for the period.

Seasonality

13A-17.   A major difficulty in the interpretation of interim results is the fact that they often reflect the effects of seasonality. Very few of the survey companies provided any assistance to users in dealing with this problem. The Research Report views this as a serious omission and makes the following recommendation:

Recommendation 12   Entities whose business is seasonal should describe, in a note to the interim financial statements or in management's review of operations, the seasonal nature of their activities and consider providing supplementary information for twelve month periods ended at the interim date for the current and preceding years.

Chapter 6 - Measurement And Recognition Issues

Discrete Versus Integral

13A-18.   There are two divergent approaches to the preparation of interim financial statements. These are the discrete and the integral methods which can be briefly described as follows:

Discrete   This approach recognizes revenues and expenses for the period in question, thus treating that period in isolation. Under this view, the accruals, deferrals and estimations at the end of each interim period are determined by following the same principles and judgments which apply to annual periods.

Integral   This approach appears to modify the discrete approach so that the results for the interim period may better relate to the results of operations for the annual period. It requires that expenses be allocated to interim periods based on estimates of annual revenues and expenses.

13A-19.   Current practice is a compromise, generally favouring the discrete approach while providing for the use in some circumstances of allocations based on annual estimates. The Research Report recommendations reflect the view that interim financial statements should be based on accounting principles and practices consistent with those used in the preparation of annual reports. These recommendations are as follows:

Recommendation 13 - Revenue   Interim period revenue should be measured and recognized on a basis consistent with that used in preparing annual financial statements.   Revenue would normally be recognized when performance is achieved and there is reasonable assurance regarding measurement and collectibility.

Recommendation 14 - Expenses   Interim period expenses should be measured and recognized on a basis consistent with that used in preparing annual financial statements.   Expenses that are directly associated with revenue or allocated to products sold or services rendered would normally be recognized in the same interim period as the revenue. All other costs and expenses would be recognized in interim periods as incurred, or allocated among interim periods based on an estimate of the time expired, benefit received, or activity associated with the period.

Recommendation 15 - Inventories   Interim period inventories should be recognized on the same basis used in preparing annual financial statements (e.g., lower of cost and market). If the interim period method of cost determination (e.g., retail inventory or gross profit method) varies from that used at the fiscal year end, it should be disclosed in the notes to the interim financial statements. Any significant adjustments that later result from the reconciliation of the recorded inventory amounts and the annual physical inventory should also be disclosed.

Recommendation 16 - Amortization   Interim period amortization of capital assets should be recognized on the same basis used in preparing annual financial statements. The calculation of amortization would normally be based on month end or quarter end capital asset balances. If a different method of application is used, it should be disclosed in a note to the interim financial statements. Any significant adjustments between the recorded amounts and the annual amortization should also be disclosed.

Recommendation 17 - Income Taxes   Interim period income taxes should be recognized on the same basis used in preparing the most recent annual financial statements:

- the components of the variation from the basic income tax rate should be disclosed in the notes to the interim financial statements when they vary significantly from those reported in the annual financial statements;

- the related tax effect for discontinued operations and extraordinary items should be shown separately in the income statement with the discontinued operations and extraordinary items;

- interim period loss carry forwards should be recognized only if they are virtually certain of realization or there is reasonable assurance that timing differences will be reversed;

- the current and deferred portions of income tax should be estimated at the end of each quarter and disclosed separately in the interim financial statements.

Recommendation 18 - Foreign Currency Gains And Losses   Interim period foreign currency exchange gains and losses should be measured and recognized at the end of each quarter in accordance with *CICA Handbook* Section 1650, "Foreign Currency Translation".

Recommendation 19 - Discontinued Operations And Extraordinary Items
Discontinued operations and extraordinary items should be shown separately in the interim period income statement and should be included in the determination of net income for the interim period in which they occur, net of applicable income taxes.   Significant, but infrequently occurring items that do not typify normal business activities of the entity should be shown separately in the interim period income statement before "income before discontinued operations and extraordinary items".

Chapter 7 - Other Matters

Accounting Changes, Prior Period Adjustments, Earnings Per Share
13A-20.   In keeping with the idea that interim reports should reflect the same approach that is used in annual reports, the Research Report makes the following recommendations with respect to accounting changes, prior period adjustments, and earnings per share:

Recommendation 20 - Changes In Accounting Policies And Estimates   Interim period changes in accounting policies should be applied retroactively —
with restatement of all comparative prior periods to give effect to the new accounting policies — and disclosed in a note to the interim financial statements. Interim period changes in accounting estimates should be applied prospectively.

Recommendation 21 - Prior Period Adjustments   Prior period adjustments in an interim period should be applied retroactively — with restatement of all comparative prior periods — and disclosed in a note to the interim financial statements (**BYRD/CHEN NOTE**   Section 3600, which permitted prior period adjustments has been removed from the *CICA Handbook*).

Recommendation 22 - Earnings Per Share   Basic and fully diluted earnings per share figures, calculated in accordance with *CICA Handbook* Section 3500, "Earnings Per Share", for the current fiscal quarter and cumulative fiscal year-to-date, should be disclosed in interim financial statements, either on the face of the income statement or in a note cross referenced to the income statement. The number of shares outstanding at the end of the current fiscal quarter should also be disclosed.

Management Review

13A-21.   While it is not specifically required by current *CICA Handbook* Recommendations, most survey companies provide some type of management discussion and analysis. The Research Report would make this a formal requirement:

> **Recommendation 23 - Management's Review Of Operations**   Interim reports should present management's review and analysis of significant matters regarding performance and future prospects. Such commentary should be on a segment basis (where appropriate), review the operations for the current fiscal quarter and cumulative fiscal year-to-date, and discuss net earnings and earning per share.

Auditor Involvement With Interim Financial Statements

13A-22.   There is a wide divergence of views with respect to the need for auditor involvement with interim financial statements. As this issue goes beyond the terms of reference for this Research Report, no position is taken on this issue. However, consistent disclosure is recommended:

> **Recommendation 24 - Auditor Involvement With Interim Financial Statements**   Interim financial statements which have not been audited by an independent public accountant should be clearly marked "unaudited".

Additional Reading

CA Magazine - "Quarters To Spare?", Jacques Fortin, Louise Martel, and Richard Trudeau, October, 1997.

Assignment Problems

(The solutions to these problem are only available in
the solutions manual that has been provided to your instructor.)

ASSIGNMENT PROBLEM THIRTEEN - 1

The Interval Company anticipates that its total annual sales will amount to 3,000,000 units at a price of $10 per unit. The Company provides interim reports for each quarter of the calendar year and its sales follow a seasonal pattern. Over the past 8 years the pattern has been 20 percent of sales in the first quarter, 10 percent in the second quarter, 50 percent in the third quarter and 20 percent in the last quarter of the year. With respect to variable costs, the annual budget calls for $4 per unit in variable manufacturing costs and $1.50 per unit in variable selling and administrative expenses. The annual fixed manufacturing costs are estimated at $6,000,000 and the annual fixed selling and administrative costs are anticipated to be $4,500,000.

The budget presented in the preceding paragraph, can be summarized as follows:

Total Estimated Sales		$30,000,000
Variable Costs:		
Manufacturing	$12,000,000	
Selling And Administrative	4,500,000	$16,500,000
Fixed Costs:		
Manufacturing	$6,000,000	
Selling And Administrative	4,500,000	10,500,000
Total Estimated Costs		$27,000,000
Budgeted Annual Profit		$ 3,000,000

The actual sales for the year did not equal the budgeted sales. The actual sales figures for the four quarters are as follows:

Quarter	Units Sold	Price Per Unit	Sales
First	550,000	$ 10	$ 5,500,000
Second	200,000	10	2,000,000
Third	1,200,000	10	12,000,000
Fourth	500,000	10	5,000,000
Total	2,450,000		$24,500,000

The actual costs that were incurred in each of the four quarters were as follows:

	Variable Costs		Fixed Costs	
Quarter	Manufacturing	Selling	Manu.	Selling
First	$ 2,200,000	$ 825,000	$1,500,000	$1,125,000
Second	800,000	300,000	1,500,000	1,125,000
Third	5,000,000	1,900,000	1,500,000	1,200,000
Fourth	2,300,000	900,000	1,700,000	1,400,000
Total	$10,300,000	$3,925,000	$6,200,000	$4,850,000

The number of units produced was equal to the number of units sold in each of the four quarters and there were no inventories on hand at the beginning of the year.

Required:

A. Prepare Income Statements for the Interval Company for each of the four quarters using the discrete approach to the measurement of interim earnings.

B. Prepare Income Statements for the Interval Company for each of the four quarters using the integral approach to the measurement of interim earnings. All of the variances of the fixed costs from the budgeted figures should be charged to income in the results of the fourth quarter.

ASSIGNMENT PROBLEM THIRTEEN - 2

The Pert Company estimates that its total sales for the year will be 600,000 units at a price of $40 per unit. The Company provides interim reports for each quarter of the calendar year and its sales follow an extremely seasonal pattern. The pattern in past years has been 10 percent of sales in the first quarter, 40 percent in the second quarter, 30 percent in the July to September quarter and 20 percent in the last quarter of the year. With respect to variable costs, the annual budget calls for $15 per unit in variable manufacturing costs and $10 per unit in variable selling and administrative expenses. The annual fixed manufacturing costs are estimated at $2,400,000 and the annual fixed selling and administrative costs are anticipated to be $1,800,000.

This budget, presented in narrative form in the preceding paragraph, can be summarized in the table which follows:

Total Sales		$24,000,000
Variable Costs:		
Manufacturing	$9,000,000	
Selling And Administrative	6,000,000	$15,000,000
Fixed Costs:		
Manufacturing	$2,400,000	
Selling And Administrative	1,800,000	4,200,000
Total Estimated Costs		$19,200,000
Budgeted Annual Profit		$ 4,800,000

The actual sales for the year were somewhat different than anticipated. The actual sales for the four quarters of the year were as follows:

Quarter	Units Sold	Price Per Unit	Sales
First	50,000	$ 40	$ 2,000,000
Second	200,000	40	8,000,000
Third	150,000	40	6,000,000
Fourth	100,000	40	4,000,000
Total	500,000	$ 40	$20,000,000

The actual costs that were incurred in each of the four quarters were as follows:

| | Variable Costs | | Fixed Costs | |
	Manufacturing	Selling	Manu.	Selling
First Quarter	$ 750,000	$ 500,000	$ 600,000	$ 450,000
Second Quarter	3,200,000	1,900,000	600,000	450,000
Third Quarter	2,100,000	1,700,000	650,000	475,000
Fourth Quarter	1,500,000	1,000,000	700,000	500,000
Total	$7,550,000	$5,100,000	$2,550,000	$1,875,000

The number of units produced equals the number of units sold in each of the four quarters and there were no inventories on hand at the beginning of the year.

Required:

A. Prepare Income Statements for each of the four quarters of the year using the integral approach to the measurement of interim earnings. All of the variances of the fixed costs from the budgeted figures should be charged to income in the results of the fourth quarter.

B. Prepare Income Statements for each of the four quarters of the year using the discrete approach to the measurement of interim earnings.

ASSIGNMENT PROBLEM THIRTEEN - 3

In today's rapidly changing financial markets, financial statement users are demanding more information, released more promptly than in the past. Accordingly, the CICA is conducting a research project to review the *CICA Handbook* section, "Interim Financial Reporting To Shareholders", and to recommend revisions to this section. You have agreed to join the study group. At the first meeting, two study group members are engaged in a lively discussion. One is a CA and controller of an international public company, while the other is a senior financial analyst in a securities firm.

Financial Analyst: My review of the *CICA Handbook* leads me to conclude that the objectives of interim reporting should be the same as those of annual reporting.

Controller: I disagree. Interim reports are aimed at different users, serve different purposes, and must be published more quickly than annual reports. It follows that the underlying objectives should also differ.

Financial Analyst: Regardless of the content of interim reports, the interim operating results should be measured on the same basis as the annual results because the interim period is an integral part of the annual period.

Controller: I agree that there is a measurement problem for interim reporting, but I don't see a simple solution. For example, I find it difficult to make interim estimates for various expenses given the cyclical nature of our business. After all, the interim period is only a portion of the annual period.

Required: Prepare a memo for the study group discussing the main issues raised in the preceding conversation.

(CICA Adapted)

Chapter 14

Accounting For Not-For-Profit Organizations

Introduction

14-1.   Until 1989, not-for-profit organizations were not subject to the Recommendations of the *CICA Handbook* and, as a consequence, they were in a position to use virtually any accounting principles that they wished. Not surprisingly, this led to a situation in which different not-for-profit organizations used a wide variety of procedures, resulting in financial statements which made meaningful interpretation by users extremely difficult.

14-2.   This began to change in 1989. While recognizing that its Recommendations were not applicable in all areas of not-for-profit accounting, the *CICA Handbook* became generally applicable to these organizations. This change was accompanied by the addition of Section 4230, "Non Profit Organizations - Specific Items", to the *Handbook*. This small Section provided limited guidance on such matters as pledges, donated materials and services, and restricted amounts.

14-3.   Since 1989, the CICA's Accounting Standards Board and its Not-For-Profits Task Force has worked on developing accounting standards to deal with certain areas where these organizations have unique problems. This process reached fruition with the issuance of six new *CICA Handbook* Sections in 1996 and one additional Section in 1997. These Sections are:

Section 4400   Financial Statement Presentation By Not-For-Profit Organizations

Section 4410   Contributions - Revenue Recognition

Section 4420   Contributions Receivable

Section 4430   Capital Assets Held By Not-For-Profit Organizations

Section 4440   Collections Held By Not-For-Profit Organizations

Section 4450   Reporting Controlled And Related Entities By Not-For-Profit Organizations

Section 4460   Disclosure Of Related Party Transactions By Not-For-Profit Organizations

14-4.   These new Sections were issued during 1996 and early 1997 and are effective for fiscal periods beginning after April 1, 1997.

14-5.   The new Recommendations are likely to lead to improved financial reporting by not-for-profit organizations. While some not-for-profit organizations may choose not to comply with some or all of these Recommendations, the need to have credibility with the users of their financial statements, particularly those who contribute resources, will certainly encourage full or partial compliance.

Not-For-Profit Organizations Defined

14-6.   The definition of not-for-profit organizations does not include government entities. Recommendations applicable to federal, provincial, territorial, and local governments and to other government entities, such as funds, agencies, and corporations are found in the separate Handbook issued by the Public Sector Accounting And Auditing Standards Board (PSAAB).

14-7.   All seven of the *CICA Handbook* Sections repeat the same definition of not-for-profit organizations. This definition is as follows:

> **Paragraph 4400.02(a)   Not-for-profit organizations** are entities, normally without transferable ownership interests, organized and operated exclusively for social, educational, professional, religious, health, charitable or any other not-for-profit purpose. A not-for-profit organization's members, contributors and other resource providers do not, in such capacity, receive any financial return directly from the organization.

14-8.   The preceding definition makes it clear that there are three characteristics associated with being a not-for-profit organization. These are:

- Not-for-profit organizations normally do not have a transferable ownership interest.

- Not-for-profit organizations are operated exclusively for social, educational, professional, religious, health, charitable, or other not-for-profit purpose.

- The resource providers, be they members or contributors, do not stand to benefit because of their status as resource providers.

14-9.   In many cases, the application of this definition is very straightforward. For organizations that have no activity other than raising funds and using these funds in achieving not-for-profit goals, there is little question as to their status as a not-for-profit organization. This would apply to such organizations as the Canadian Cancer Society or the United Way.

14-10.   However, the classification of other organizations may be less clear cut. For example, while golf and country clubs are not usually organized to make a profit, members are usually required to make a contribution. In order to use the facilities, you are normally required to be a member. This means that the members/contributors benefit because of their status as resource providers. Similar problems exist with condominium corporations and various types of agricultural co-ops.

14-11.   There are other problems related to organizations such as hospitals and universities, where a government organization is often the principal contributor. If such organizations are considered to be government agencies, then they are subject to the Recommendations of the Public Sector Accounting And Auditing Standards Board. Alternatively, if they are considered to be not-for-profit organizations, the *CICA Handbook* Recommendations will be applicable.

GAAP For Not-For-Profit Organizations

General Approach

14-12.   One of the major issues considered in the 1980 CICA Research Study, *Financial Reporting For Non-Profit Organizations*, was the question of whether these organizations should be subject to the profit oriented Recommendations of the *CICA Handbook*. One view was that profit and not-for-profit organizations were sufficiently similar that the existing *Handbook* rules could be applied without modification. At the opposite extreme, it was possible to argue that the differences between these two types of organizations were so great that it would be appropriate to establish a completely separate set of generally accepted accounting principles for not-for-profit organizations.

14-13.   After giving the matter considerable attention, the Committee preparing the Research Study decided on a compromise, They concluded that not-for-profit organizations were sufficiently different that some specialized Recommendations were essential. For example, profit oriented enterprises do not usually have to deal with contributions and pledges. In areas such as this, specialized Recommendations were needed. However, in many areas of accounting, not-for-profit organizations were little different than those with a profit making orientation. In these areas, the usual *CICA Handbook* Recommendations would be applicable. An example of this type of situation would be Section 1505 which requires disclosure of accounting policies. Clearly the type of disclosure called for in this Section would be equally applicable to both types of organizations.

14-14.   We previously noted that, in 1989, most of the Recommendations in the *CICA Handbook* became applicable to not-for-profit organizations. In addition, Section 4230 was added to the *CICA Handbook* in that year. These events reflect the adoption of the compromise approach suggested by the 1980 CICA Research Study. The new *Handbook* Sections that were issued in 1996 also reflect this approach.

14-15.   It is interesting to note that a 1980 CICA Research Study on accounting for government organizations reached a very different conclusion. Their recommendation was that a separate body of accounting standards be established for government organizations. This recommendation was implemented with the establishment of the Public Sector Accounting And Auditing Standards Board (PSAAB). The Recommendations of this Board are now found in a separate PSAAB *Handbook*.

14-16.   To assist with user understanding of not-for-profit GAAP, *CICA Handbook* Sections 4400 through 4460 have an introduction which describes the current approach. Included in this introduction is an Appendix which sets out the applicability of the various *CICA Handbook* Sections to not-for-profit organizations. The table from this Appendix is reproduced here for your convenience:

CICA Handbook Section	Generally Applicable	Applicable If Relevant Transactions	Limited Or No Applicability
1000, Financial Statement Concepts	X		
1500, General Standards Of Financial Statements Presentation	X		
1501, International Accounting Standards			X
1505, Disclosure Of Accounting Policies	X		
1506, Accounting Changes	X		
1508, Measurement Uncertainty	X		

CICA Handbook Section	Generally Applicable	Applicable If Relevant Transactions	Limited Or No Applicability
1510, Current Assets And Current Liabilities	X		
1520, Income Statement			X
1540, Statement Of Changes In Financial Position			X
1580, Business Combinations			X*
1590, Subsidiaries			X*
1600, Consolidated Financial Statements		X	
1625, Comprehensive Revaluation Of Assets And Liabilities			X
1650, Foreign Currency Translation		X	
1701, Segment Disclosures			X
1750, Interim Financial Reporting			X
1800, Unincorporated Businesses			X
3000, Cash		X	
3010, Temporary Investments		X	
3020, Accounts And Notes Receivable		X	
3025, Impaired Loans		X	
3030, Inventories		X	
3040, Prepaid Expenses		X	
3050, Long-Term Investments		X	
3055, Interests In Joint Ventures			X*
3060, Capital Assets			X
3065, Leases		X	
3070, Deferred Charges		X	
3210, Long-Term Debt		X	
3240, Share Capital			X
3250, Surplus			X
3260, Reserves			X
3280, Contractual Obligations	X		
3290, Contingencies	X		
3400, Revenue		X	
3450, Research And Development Costs		X	
3460, Pension Costs And Obligations		X	
*Contains guidance that may be relevant.			

CICA Handbook Section	Generally Applicable	Applicable If Relevant Transactions	Limited Or No Applicability
3465, Income Taxes			X
3475, Discontinued Operations		X	
3480, Extraordinary Items		X	
3500, Earnings Per Share			X
3610, Capital Transactions			X
3800, Accounting For Government Assistance			X
3805, Investment Tax Credits			X
3820, Subsequent Events	X		
3830, Non-Monetary Transactions		X	
3840, Related Party Transactions			X
3841, Economic Dependence			X
3850, Interest Capitalized - Disclosure Considerations		X	
3860, Financial Instruments - Disclosure And Presentation		X	
4000, Prospectuses			X
4100, Pension Plans			X
4210, Life Insurance Enterprises			X
4250, Future-Oriented Financial Information		X	
*Contains guidance that may be relevant.			

Overview Of Handbook Sections For Not-For-Profit Organizations

14-17.   The material that is presented in the seven *Handbook* Sections presents a number of new ideas. Some aspects of these new ideas are confusing and, in addition, they are interrelated in a manner that cuts across the boundaries of the individual Sections. Before proceeding to a more detailed consideration of these Sections, we would like to give you a broad overview of their content and the manner in which we intend to present the material.

14-18.   Section 4400 establishes that not-for-profit organizations can use fund accounting in any format that they wish. However, there is a constraint. Unless it is used in the form that the Section describes as the "restricted fund method" the organization will be limited in its approach to revenue (contribution) recognition. This does not become clear until you read Section 4410 which deals with revenue recognition.

14-19.   Section 4410 indicates that not-for-profit contributions must be recognized using either the "restricted fund method" or the "deferral method". The restricted fund method allows restricted contributions to be recognized when they are received, as opposed to being deferred until there is compliance with the restrictions, either through making expenditures or through the passage of time (restrictions may require certain types of expenditures or they may require that the funds be used in specified periods of time). This restricted fund method, which provides for earlier recognition of restricted revenues, can only be used in the context of fund accounting. Further, it is only available when the approach to fund accounting is based on classifying funds in terms of their restrictions.

14-20. The combined Recommendations of Sections 4400 and 4410 result in a situation in which a Canadian not-for-profit organization can use its choice of three different approaches to preparing its financial statements. These approaches can be described as follows:

Aggregated (Non Fund) Accounting If the organization chooses not to use fund accounting, it will present its financial statements on an aggregate basis. If this approach is used, the deferral method of revenue recognition must be adopted.

Fund Accounting - Restricted Fund Basis If the organization uses fund accounting and classifies its funds in terms of externally imposed restrictions, it can use the restricted fund method of revenue recognition for contributions received.

Fund Accounting - Other Basis If the organization uses fund accounting and classifies its funds on any basis other than externally imposed restrictions (e.g., restrictions on use of funds imposed by donors), it must use the deferral approach to revenue recognition for its contributions.

14-21. The preceding results of the combined reading of Sections 4400 and 4410 provides the basis for accounting for not-for-profit organizations in Canada. The other material in the seven Sections can be described as follows:

Section 4400 In addition to providing for the use of fund accounting, Section 4400 contains Recommendations on the form and content of the four financial statements that will be presented by not-for-profit organizations.

Section 4410 This Section provides detailed guidance on the restricted fund and deferral methods of revenue recognition. Guidance is also provided for not-for-profit revenues other than contributions (e.g., investment income).

Section 4420 This brief Section should have been incorporated into Section 4410. Its only content is a Recommendation with respect to the measurement of contributions receivable. Guidance is also provided on pledges and bequests.

Section 4430 This important Section deals with capital assets held by not-for-profit organizations. In the past, most of the organizations have not recognized their capital assets in their Balance Sheets, charging purchased items to expense in the period acquired and, in many cases, not giving any recognition to contributed capital assets. Section 4430 will change this situation by requiring that both purchased and contributed assets be recorded in the Statement Of Financial Position of the organization. It also deals with related issues such as the amortization of capital assets after they have been recorded in the accounts.

Section 4440 This brief Section deals with collections (e.g., the Henry Moore works held by the Art Gallery Of Ontario). It serves to make this type of capital asset exempt from the Recommendations of Section 4430.

Section 4450 This Section deals with the reporting that is required for the controlled, significantly influenced, or other related entities in the financial statements of not-for-profit organizations.

Section 4460 This Section deals with the disclosure standards for related party transactions in the financial statements of not-for-profit organizations. Measurement issues are not dealt with in this Section.

14-22.   In our approach to this material, we will begin by dealing with two of the general issues associated with not-for-profit organizations. These issues are financial statement concepts for not-for-profit organizations and the reporting entity for not-for-profit organizations. This will be followed by a more detailed discussion of both fund accounting and revenue recognition as it applies to not-for-profit organizations. With our coverage of fund accounting and revenue recognition completed, we are in a position to consider the financial statement presentation Recommendations of Section 4400. After reviewing these Recommendations, we will introduce a basic example to illustrate fund accounting and revenue recognition for an organization that does not have capital assets.

14-23.   Following the example will be a discussion of the capital assets provisions of Sections 4430 and 4440. The basic example will be extended to illustrate these provisions.

14-24.   This Chapter will then consider Section 4450 and its Recommendations for dealing with the controlled, significantly influenced and other entities related to the not-for-profit reporting entity. It will conclude by covering the Section 4460 Recommendations on disclosure of related party transactions by not-for-profit organizations.

Financial Statement Concepts For Not-For-Profit Organizations

14-25.   Section 1000 of the *CICA Handbook* presents and discusses such basic financial statement concepts as the objectives of financial reporting, the qualitative characteristics that make financial information useful, the elements of financial statements, and certain measurement and recognition issues. When this Section was first issued in 1988, it dealt with these issues only in the context of profit oriented enterprises. However, in March, 1991, this Section was revised and expanded so that its coverage would include both profit oriented and not-for-profit organizations. This reflects the view of the Accounting Standards Board that not-for-profit organizations are sufficiently similar to profit oriented enterprises that an alternative set of financial statement concepts is not required.

14-26.   Section 1000 specifies the normal set of financial statements for both profit oriented and not-for-profit organizations. This material is reiterated in Section 4400 as follows:

> **Paragraph 4400.05**   Financial statements for a not-for-profit organization normally include:
>
> (a) a statement of financial position;
> (b) a statement of operations;
> (c) a statement of changes in net assets; and
> (d) a statement of cash flows.

14-27.   Section 4400 notes that other titles may be used for these statements. In addition, it may be desirable to combine statements. For example, many organizations will combine the Statement Of Operations with the Statement Of Changes In Net Assets.

The Reporting Entity For Not-For-Profit Organizations

14-28.   In the past, it was not uncommon for not-for-profit organizations to prepare financial reports on the basis of their legally defined parameters. This meant that related entities that were controlled by the reporting entity were included in financial statements only to the extent that an investment was reported by either the cost or equity methods. In situations where the controlled entity was a not-for-profit organization, this could result in a complete absence of disclosure. This results from the fact that not-for-profit organizations do not normally have a transferable ownership. In this situation, the controlling organization may not even have an investment to disclose.

14-29.   The appropriate reporting entity for many, if not most, not-for-profit organizations would include all of the related entities that it controls. Reporting on this basis would require the preparation of consolidated financial statements for the reporting not-for-profit organization and all of the related entities over which it can exercise control. This treatment would be analogous to the treatment that is required for a profit oriented entity and its subsidiaries.

14-30.   The *Handbook* does not go so far as to require consolidation of all controlled entities. However, it does encourage consolidation of these entities and, if consolidation is not used, a significant amount of additional disclosure is required. This will clearly lead to improved disclosure in this area.

14-31.   The Recommendations related to controlled and other related entities are found in Section 4450 of the *CICA Handbook*. These Recommendations will be given detailed consideration in a later Section of this Chapter.

Fund Accounting

Basic Concepts

14-32.   Fund accounting is widely used by both government organizations and not-for-profit organizations. It involves dividing the reporting entity into a number of pieces which are referred to as funds. As defined by the National Council On Governmental Accounting (a U.S. organization), a fund is defined as follows:

> A fund is defined as a fiscal and accounting entity with a self balancing set of accounts recording cash and other financial resources, together with all related liabilities and residual equities or balances, and changes therein, which are segregated for the purpose of carrying on specific activities or attaining certain objectives in accordance with special regulations, restrictions, or limitations.

14-33.   Some of the typical funds that would be used by a not-for-profit organization would be as follows:

- **Current (Or Operating) Fund - Unrestricted**   Unrestricted contributions such as donations, bequests, grants and other income are reported in this fund, together with the day-to-day operating costs.

- **Current Fund - Restricted**   Current restricted funds are expendable funds restricted by the contributors for special purpose expenditures of a current nature.

- **Endowment (Donor Designated) Fund**   This fund contains assets donated to an organization with the stipulation by the donor that only the income earned can be used, either for the general purposes of the organization or for special purposes. The asset is, therefore, restricted and non-expendable. Gains and losses realized on endowment investments may be transferable to other funds, depending on the terms of the original gift.

- **Board Designated Fund**   The difference between this fund and a donor designated endowment fund is that, in the latter case, the board does not have access to the principal. Resources set aside by action of the board of directors can be used if the board wishes to reverse its previous action.

- **Plant Fund**   This grouping normally comprises long term assets such as land, building, furniture and equipment.

- **Custodial Funds**   These are funds held in trust for other organizations.

14-34.   Once the appropriate group of funds have been established, the *CICA Handbook* defines fund accounting as follows:

Paragraph 4400.02(c) **Fund accounting** comprises the collective accounting procedures resulting in a self-balancing set of accounts for each fund established by legal, contractual or voluntary actions of an organization. Elements of a fund can include assets, liabilities, net assets, revenues and expenses (and gains and losses, where appropriate). Fund accounting involves an accounting segregation, although not necessarily a physical segregation, of resources.

Example

14-35.   A very simple example can be used to illustrate these ideas:

Example   Community Sports Ltd. is established on December 31 of the current year to encourage hiking in the summer and skiing in the winter. On this date it receives unrestricted contributions of $500,000. Its Board allocates this contributions as follows:

General Administration	$100,000
Hiking Promotion	250,000
Skiing Promotion	150,000
Total	$500,000

There are no other transactions before the December 31 year end.

14-36.   If fund accounting is not used, the Statement of Operations for the current year and the Statement of Financial Position as at the year end would be as follows:

Community Sports Ltd.
Statement of Operations For The Current Year

Revenues	$500,000
Expenses	Nil
Excess Of Revenues Over Expenses	$500,000

Community Sports Ltd.
Statement of Financial Position As At December 31

Cash	$500,000
Total Assets	$500,000
Unrestricted Net Assets	$500,000

14-37.   If the organization decides to use fund accounting, it would probably have separate funds for hiking and skiing, as well as an operating fund. In applying fund accounting, Community Sports could either put together three separate sets of financial statements or, alternatively, present all of the funds in a multi column format. The latter approach is illustrated as follows:

Community Sports Ltd.
Statement Of Operations For The Current Year

	Operating Fund	Hiking Fund	Skiing Fund	Total
Revenues	$100,000	$250,000	$150,000	$500,000
Expenses	Nil	Nil	Nil	Nil
Excess Of Revenues Over Expenses	$100,000	$250,000	$150,000	$500,000

Community Sports Ltd.
Statement of Financial Position As At December 31

	Operating Fund	Hiking Fund	Skiing Fund	Total
Cash	$100,000	$250,000	$150,000	$500,000
Total Assets	$100,000	$250,000	$150,000	$500,000
Unrestricted Net Assets	$100,000	$250,000	$150,000	$500,000

14-38.   While this example is far too simple to be generally useful, it does serve to illustrate the basic difference between fund accounting and the more familiar aggregated approach to financial reporting. As this is sufficient coverage of fund accounting for many users of this text, we have included a more comprehensive example of fund accounting as a Supplement to this Chapter.

The Need For Fund Accounting

14-39.   While fund accounting has been widely used in both government and not-for-profit organization accounting, there are those who question its usefulness. The two basic problems with fund accounting can be described as follows:

Fund Definition   Individual organizations can define the funds that they will use in a totally arbitrary fashion. This means that similar organizations can be made to appear very different through the use of a different group of funds. Further, the use of arbitrarily defined funds can be used to obscure the overall performance of the organization.

Interfund Transfers   Until Section 4400 was added to the *CICA Handbook*, there were no rules governing the reporting of interfund transfers. Such transfers could be made at the discretion of the organization and could be reported in a manner that suggested more activity than the organization was actually experiencing.

14-40.   These problems lead some authorities to suggest the elimination of fund accounting. However, this form of accounting has a long tradition of use. Further, this approach has many supporters in the not-for-profit accounting community. These supporters point out that a unique feature of not-for-profit organizations is the fact many of the resources that they receive are subject to various types of restrictions on their use. They argue that fund accounting is a very effective way of disclosing and keeping track of these restrictions. This is probably the primary argument that influenced the Accounting Standards Board in their decision to allow continued use of fund accounting in the not-for-profit area.

CICA Recommendations

Section 4400 Content

14-41.   While recognizing that fund accounting has potential difficulties, Section 4400 of the *CICA Handbook* allows the use of the approach in preparing the financial statements of not-for-profit organizations. The Board has, however, made a number of Recommendations that will deal with some of the problems.

14-42.   To deal with the potentially arbitrary nature of fund definitions, Section 4400 makes the following Recommendation:

Paragraph 4400.06   *An organization that uses fund accounting in its financial statements should provide a brief description of the purpose of each fund reported.* (April, 1997)

14-43.   This will require not-for-profit organizations to provide some rationale for the particular array of funds they are using. It is also noted that each fund reported should be presented on a consistent basis from year to year. If there are changes, they will have to be reported as changes in accounting policies.

14-44.   With respect to the form of presentation, the Section notes that fund accounting statements can be presented either individually, or in a multi column format. It is even acceptable to use different formats for different statements of the same organization. The only constraint is that the format or formats used satisfies the Recommendations made in the Section.

14-45.   With respect to the problem of reporting interfund transfers, Section 4400 Recommends the following:

> **Paragraph 4400.12**   *Interfund transfers should be presented in the statement of changes in net assets.* (April, 1997)

> **Paragraph 4400.13**   *The amount and purpose of interfund transfers during the reporting period should be disclosed.* (April, 1997)

> **Paragraph 4400.14**   *The amounts, terms and conditions of interfund loans outstanding at the reporting date should be disclosed.* (April, 1997)

14-46.   These Recommendations will prevent interfund transfers from being treated as revenues in the Statement Of Operations. In addition, it should discourage the use of interfund transfers to give a false impression of activity, in that it requires a statement as to the purpose of these transactions.

14-47.   If the organization uses a multi column approach to disclosure, interfund loans and advances would be presented in the individual funds, but eliminated from the totals column of the statement. If a single column format is used, the only disclosure of these amounts would be in the notes to the financial statements.

Section 4410 Content

14-48.   Other than requiring an explanation of the purpose of each fund used, Section 4400 does not place restrictions on the manner in which fund accounting is applied. However, Recommendations contained in Section 4410, "Contributions - Revenue Recognition", have the effect of creating two distinct applications of fund accounting. As we have noted, Section 4410 requires that revenue from contributions be recognized using either the "deferral method" or the "restricted fund" method. These two methods are defined in both Section 4400 and 4410 as follows:

> **Paragraph 4400.02(d)**   The **restricted fund** method of accounting for contributions is a specialized type of fund accounting which involves the reporting of details of financial statement elements by fund in such a way that the organization reports total general funds, one or more restricted funds, and an endowment fund, if applicable. Reporting of financial statement elements segregated on a basis other than that of use restrictions (e.g., by program or geographic location) does not constitute the restricted fund method.

> **Paragraph 4400.02(e)**   Under the **deferral method** of accounting for contributions, restricted contributions related to expenses of future periods are deferred and recognized as revenue in the period in which the related expenses are incurred. Endowment contributions are reported as direct increases in net assets. All other contributions are reported as revenue of the current period. Organizations that use fund accounting in their financial statements without following the restricted fund method would account for contributions under the deferral method.

14-49.   While it is not stated in the definition provided, the restricted fund method allows restricted contributions to be recognized when they are received, rather than deferring them until the period in which the related expenses are incurred. It is clear from the preceding definition that this method can only be used if the not-for-profit organization has the following grouping of funds (some of these terms will be further explained in the next Section which discusses Section 4410 in detail):

- A general or operating fund.
- One or more restricted funds.
- One or more endowment funds, if applicable.

14-50.   As the restricted fund method allows earlier recognition of revenues from contributions, it is likely that this requirement will encourage not-for-profit organizations to classify their funds in terms of externally imposed restrictions. This would seem appropriate in that the primary argument for the continued use of fund accounting is that it is an effective way of disclosing and keeping track of restrictions on the use of contributions.

14-51.   This is a fairly subtle solution to the problem of fund classification. Organizations are permitted to use any array of funds that they choose. However, if the selection used is not based on restrictions on contributions, they will have to use the deferral method of revenue recognition for contributions. This has the effect of creating two forms of fund accounting:

1.   Fund accounting with funds classified to disclose restrictions.

2.   Fund accounting with funds classified on any other basis (the normal alternative would be to disclose programs).

14-52.   These new Recommendation are likely to produce more consistent and meaningful applications of fund accounting in Canadian practice.

Revenue Recognition - Handbook Section 4410

The Matching Principle Revised

14-53.   You are all familiar with the application of the matching principle in profit oriented accounting. The major goal of a profit oriented enterprise is to generate revenues and, hopefully profits. Revenues are recognized when they are earned and the resulting consideration can be reasonably measured. While this usually occurs when goods are sold, there are variations on this such as the percentage of completion method of recognizing revenue.

14-54.   The situation with contributions received by not-for-profit organizations is different. The goal of these organizations is to deliver services. This means that, instead of starting with recognizing revenues, not-for-profit organizations focus on the cost of delivering services. When these costs are determined, the appropriate revenues are matched against the costs of providing services. In other words, the matching process is reversed, as compared to the situation with a profit oriented enterprise.

14-55.   Because of this reversal, the usual Section 3400 revenue recognition procedures are not applicable to contributions received by not-for-profit organizations. Given this situation, revenue recognition is one of the areas where not-for-profit organizations need their own accounting standards.

Revenues Of Not-For-Profit Organizations

14-56.   Because of the diversity of not-for-profit organizations, different organizations receive different types of revenues. Not all of these require special attention in Section 4410. For example, a not-for-profit hospital may operate a tuck shop to sell various consumer products that its clients and their visitors require. This type of operation is analogous to other similar activities found in profit oriented operations (e.g., a hotel will have a similar operation). Revenues of this type would be subject to the usual revenue recognition rules that apply to profit oriented enterprises.

14-57. Many not-for-profit organizations will also have investment income. While some of these revenues may be equivalent to the investment income received by profit oriented enterprises, there is the possibility that contributors of the income earning assets have attached restrictions to the income produced. Because of this possibility, Section 4410 provides Recommendations for dealing with the investment income of not-for-profit organizations.

14-58. However, the real difference with not-for-profit organizations is the fact that they receive contributions. Section 4410 defines the various types of contributions received by not-for-profit organizations as follows:

> **Paragraph 4410.02(b)** A **contribution** is a non-reciprocal transfer to a not-for-profit organization of cash or other assets or a non-reciprocal settlement or cancellation of its liabilities. Government funding provided to a not-for-profit organization is considered to be a contribution.

There are three types of contributions identified for purposes of this Section:

> (i) A **restricted contribution** is a contribution subject to externally imposed stipulations that specify the purpose for which the contributed asset is to be used. A contribution restricted for the purchase of a capital asset or a contribution of the capital asset itself is a type of restricted contribution.
>
> (ii) An **endowment contribution** is a type of restricted contribution subject to externally imposed stipulations specifying that the resources contributed be maintained permanently, although the constituent assets may change from time to time.
>
> (iii) An **unrestricted contribution** is a contribution that is neither a restricted contribution nor an endowment contribution.

14-59. As further elaboration of the preceding definitions, Section 4410 defines restrictions as follows:

> **Paragraph 4410.02(c)** **Restrictions** are stipulations imposed that specify how resources must be used. External restrictions are imposed from outside the organization, usually by the contributor of the resources. Internal restrictions are imposed in a formal manner by the organization itself, usually by resolution of the board of directors. Restrictions on contributions may only be externally imposed. Net assets or fund balances may be internally or externally restricted. Internally restricted net assets or fund balances are often referred to as reserves or appropriations.

14-60. The important point to note here is that, for purposes of applying the revenue recognition rules of Section 4410, only externally imposed restrictions qualify for defining restricted contributions. While the concept of external restrictions can be fairly complex in practice, the basic idea is that a contribution is restricted if the contributor has some type of recourse if the funds are not used in the manner specified. The degree of formality that is associated with the restriction may vary from situation to situation.

General Rules
Restricted Fund Vs. Deferral Method
14-61. The basic Recommendation for contributions received by a not-for-profit organization is as follows:

> **Paragraph 4410.10** *An organization should recognize contributions in accordance with either:*

(a) the deferral method ; or

(b) the restricted fund method. (April, 1997)

14-62.   In general terms, the deferral method requires that restricted contributions be deferred and only recognized as revenue as the restrictions are fulfilled. In contrast, the restricted fund method allows restricted contributions to be recorded as revenues in the appropriate restricted fund as they are received. As discussed previously, the restricted fund method can only be used by not-for-profit organizations that use fund accounting with the funds classified to disclose restrictions.

14-63.   Section 4410 provides fairly detailed guidance for the application of these rules. These rules will be considered after briefly presenting the other general revenue recognition rules of this Section, as well as the guidance provided by Section 4420 on contributions receivable.

Contributed Materials And Services

14-64.   Many not-for-profit organizations receive contributions of materials and/or services. These services may present severe valuation problems and, in addition, they may be such that the organization would not have acquired them if they had not been contributed. Given this, Section 4410 makes the following Recommendation:

Paragraph 4410.16   *An organization may choose to recognize contributions of materials and services, but should do so only when a fair value can be reasonably estimated and when the materials and services are used in the normal course of the organization's operations and would otherwise have been purchased. (April, 1997)*

Measurement Of Contributions

14-65.   With respect to the measurement of contributions, Section 4410 makes the following Recommendation:

Paragraph 4410.19   *Contributions should be measured at fair value at the date of contribution if fair value can be reasonably estimated. (April, 1997)*

Disclosure Of Contributions

14-66.   Section 4410 requires the following general disclosure related to contributions:

Paragraph 4410.21   *An organization should disclose:*

(a) the policy followed in accounting for endowment contributions; and
(b) the policies followed in accounting for restricted contributions. (April, 1997)

Paragraph 4410.22   *An organization should disclose its contributions by major source. (April, 1997)*

Paragraph 4410.23   *An organization should disclose the policy followed in accounting for contributed materials and services. (April, 1997)*

Paragraph 4410.24   *An organization should disclose the nature and amount of contributed materials and services recognized in the financial statements. (April, 1997)*

Contributions Receivable

14-67.   A separate, very short, Section 4420 was added to the *CICA Handbook* to deal with the contributions receivable of not-for-profit organizations. The basic Recommendation of this Section is as follows:

Paragraph 4420.03   *A contribution receivable should be recognized as an asset when it meets the following criteria:*

(a) the amount to be received can be reasonably estimated; and
(b) ultimate collection is reasonably assured. (April, 1997)

14-68.   The Section points out that these rules are equally applicable to both pledges and bequests. In addition, the Section makes the following Recommendation with respect to the disclosure of contributions receivable:

> **Paragraph 4420.08**   *When a not-for-profit organization has recognized outstanding pledges and bequests in its financial statements, the following should be disclosed:*
>
> *(a) the amount recognized as assets at the reporting date; and*
> *(b) the amount recognized as revenue in the period.* (April, 1997)

Endowment Contributions

General Nature

14-69.   As previously noted, endowment contributions are distinguished by the fact that they must be retained in the organization and will never be available to meet the expenses associated with the organization's service delivery activities. Income from the investment of endowment funds may or may not be restricted.

Deferral Method

14-70.   As endowment contributions will never be generally available to the organization, they should not be treated as normal revenues of the organization. The appropriate treatment under the deferral method is specified in Section 4410 as follows:

> **Paragraph 4410.29**   *Endowment contributions should be recognized as direct increases in net assets in the current period.* (April, 1997)

14-71.   In the Balance Sheet they will be disclosed as part of the net asset balance and designated as permanently invested in the organization.

Restricted Fund Method

14-72.   To use the restricted fund method, the organization must have a separate endowment fund. Given this, the appropriate treatment of these contributions is as follows:

> **Paragraph 4410.60**   *Endowment contributions should be recognized as revenue of the endowment fund in the current period.* (April, 1997)

14-73.   The only revenues of the endowment fund would be these contributions plus any investment income subject to externally imposed restrictions that require it to be added to the fund. Internal allocations to this fund would not be included in revenues.

Unrestricted Contributions

Deferral Method

14-74.   The Recommendation here would be as follows:

> **Paragraph 4410.47**   *Unrestricted contributions should be recognized as revenue in the current period.* (April, 1997)

Restricted Fund Method

14-75.   The corresponding Recommendation here would be as follows:

> **Paragraph 4410.68**   *Unrestricted contributions should be recognized as revenue of the general fund in the current period.* (April, 1997)

Net Investment Income

Deferral Method

14-76.   When a not-for-profit organization using the deferral method has net investment income, the following Recommendation is applicable:

Paragraph 4410.49 *An organization should recognize:*

(a) net investment income that is not externally restricted in the statement of operations;

(b) externally restricted net investment income that must be added to the principal amount of resources held for endowment as direct increases, or decreases, in net assets; and

(c) other externally restricted net investment income in the statement of operations, in the appropriate deferred contributions balance or in net assets, depending on the nature of restrictions, on the same basis as described in paragraphs 4410.31 to .48. (April, 1997) [Note: Paragraphs 4410.31 through .48 are presented in our Paragraph 14-78].

Restricted Fund Method

14-77.   When a not-for-profit organization using the restricted fund method has net investment income, Section 4410 Recommends the following:

Paragraph 4410.70 *An organization should recognize:*

(a) net investment income that is not externally restricted in the statement of operations in the general fund.

(b) externally restricted net investment income that must be added to the principal amount of resources held for endowment in the statement of operations in the endowment fund; and

(c) other externally restricted net investment income in the statement of operations in the appropriate restricted fund or, if there is no appropriate restricted fund, in the general fund on the same basis as that described in paragraph 4410.65. (April, 1997) [Note: Paragraph 4410.65 will be presented in our Paragraph 14-80].

Restricted Contributions

Deferral Method

14-78.   Under this method, restricted contributions must be deferred, a process that engenders some complexity. More specifically, the amount and timing of the deferral will be dependent on the type of restriction that is placed on the contribution. As a consequence, several Recommendations are needed to deal with the various possibilities. These Recommendations are as follows:

**Restricted Contributions For
Expenses Of Future Periods**

Paragraph 4410.31 *Restricted contributions for expenses of one or more future periods should be deferred and recognized as revenue in the same period or periods as the related expenses are recognized.* (April, 1997)

**Restricted Contributions For The
Purchase Of Capital Assets**

Paragraph 4410.33 *Restricted contributions for the purchase of capital assets that will be amortized should be deferred and recognized as revenue on the same basis as the amortization expense related to the acquired capital assets.* (April, 1997)

Paragraph 4410.34 *Restricted contributions for the purchase of capital assets that will not be amortized should be recognized as direct increases in net assets.* (April, 1997)

Restricted Contributions For
The Repayment Of Debt

Paragraph 4410.38 *Restricted contributions for the repayment of debt that was incurred to fund expenses of one or more future periods should be deferred and recognized as revenue in the same period or periods as the related expenses are recognized.* (April, 1997)

Paragraph 4410.39 *Restricted contributions for the repayment of debt that was incurred to fund the purchase of a capital asset that will not be amortized should be recognized as direct increases in net assets.* (April, 1997)

Paragraph 4410.40 *Restricted contributions for the repayment of debt that was incurred for purposes other than those described in paragraph 4410.38 or .39 should be recognized as revenue in the current period.* (April, 1997)

Restricted Contributions For
Expenses Of The Current Period

Paragraph 4410.45 *Restricted contributions for expenses of the current period should be recognized as revenue in the current period.* (April, 1997)

Restricted Fund Method

14-79.   As organizations using this method will be recognizing restricted contributions as they are received, the situation here is less complex. To the extent that restricted contributions will be reported in restricted funds, the following Recommendation is applicable:

Paragraph 4410.62 *Restricted contributions for which a corresponding restricted fund is presented should be recognized as revenue of that fund in the current period.* (April, 1997)

14-80.   As the not-for-profit organization may not have established an individual restricted fund for each type of restricted contribution that it receives, a further Recommendation is required for restricted contributions that will be reported in the general fund:

Paragraph 4410.65 *Restricted contributions for which no corresponding restricted fund is presented should be recognized in the general fund in accordance with the deferral method (see paragraph 4410.31, .33, .34, .38, .39, .40 or .45).* (April, 1997)

Presentation And Disclosure

Deferral Method

14-81.   Section 4410 makes the following Recommendations with respect to the disclosure of deferred contributions:

Paragraph 4410.52 *Deferred contributions balances should be presented in the statement of financial position outside net assets.* (April, 1997)

Paragraph 4410.53 *An organization should disclose the nature and amount of changes in deferred contributions balances for the period.* (April, 1997)

14-82.   One additional Recommendation for the disclosure of net investment income by organizations using the deferral method:

Paragraph 4410.55 *An organization should disclose the following related to net investment income earned on resources held for endowment:*

(a) the amounts recognized in the statement of operations in the period;
(b) the amounts deferred in the period;
(c) the amounts recognized as direct increases or decreases in net assets in the pe-

riod; and

(d) the total earned in the period. (April, 1997)

Restricted Fund Method

14-83.   For organizations using the restricted fund method, the following Recommendations are applicable to deferred contributions:

> **Paragraph 4410.73**   *When restricted contributions are recognized in the general fund in accordance with paragraph 4410.65, any deferred contributions balances should be presented in the statement of financial position outside net assets.* (April, 1997)

> **Paragraph 4410.74**   *When restricted contributions are recognized in the general fund in accordance with paragraph 4410.65, the nature and amount of changes in deferred contributions balances for the period should be disclosed.* (April, 1997)

14-84.   One additional disclosure Recommendation deals with the net investment income of organizations using the restricted fund method:

> **Paragraph 4410.76**   *An organization should disclose the following related to net investment income earned on resources held for endowment:*
>
> *(a) the amounts recognized in the general fund in the period;*
> *(b) the amounts recognized in each restricted fund in the period;*
> *(c) the amounts recognized in the endowment fund in the period;*
> *(d) any amounts deferred in the period; and*
> *(e) the total earned in the period. (April, 1997)*

Financial Statement Presentation Handbook Section 4400

General

14-85.   The general Recommendations of Section 4400 with respect to fund accounting were discussed earlier in this Chapter. There is, however, one other general Recommendation that is of some importance. It is as follows:

> **Paragraph 4400.04**   *A clear and concise description of a not-for-profit organization's purpose, its intended community of service, its status under income tax legislation and its legal form should be included as an integral part of its financial statements.* (April, 1997)

14-86.   The remaining Recommendations of Section 4400 relate to specific financial statements and will be considered in the context of those statements.

Statement Of Financial Position

General Recommendations

14-87.   Without regard to whether or not fund accounting is used, a not-for-profit organization must provide all fund totals for each item presented in the Statement Of Financial Position. This is reflected in the following Recommendation:

> **Paragraph 4400.18**   *For each financial statement item, the statement of financial position should present a total that includes all funds reported.* (April, 1997)

14-88.   The preparation of this Statement will be based on the general *CICA Handbook* rules, including Section 1510 which provides Recommendation on segregating current assets and current liabilities. However, certain additional disclosure items are unique to not-for-profit organizations. Disclosure of these items is required as follows:

Paragraph 4400.19 *The statement of financial position should present the following:*

(a) net assets invested in capital assets;

(b) net assets subject to restrictions requiring that they be maintained permanently as endowments;

(c) other restricted net assets;

(d) unrestricted net assets; and

(e) total net assets. (April, 1997)

14-89. The total net asset figure, a figure analogous to owners' equity for a profit oriented enterprise, may also be referred to as "Fund Balances" or "Accumulated Surplus (Deficit)".

14-90. With respect to the "net assets invested in capital assets" balance, the amount disclosed will be reduced by related debt. (BYRD/CHEN Note: This conclusion does not appear in any Recommendation. However, it is implicit in the use of the term net, and reinforced by the example in the Appendix to Section 4400.) When the deferral method is used, the balance will be further reduced by any amount of deferred restricted contributions received for the purchase of capital assets.

Disclosure Of External Restrictions

14-91. External restrictions are of significance because they limit the organization's financial flexibility. Given this, Section 4400 has additional disclosure Recommendations for these amounts. For organizations using the deferral method, the Recommendation is as follows:

Paragraph 4400.26 *The following should be disclosed:*

(a) the amounts of deferred contributions attributable to each major category of external restrictions with a description of the restrictions; and

(b) the amount of net assets subject to external restrictions requiring that they be maintained permanently as endowments. (April, 1997)

14-92. The corresponding Recommendation for organizations using the restricted fund method is as follows:

Paragraph 4400.28 *The following should be disclosed:*

(a) the amount of net assets (fund balances) subject to external restrictions requiring that they be maintained permanently as endowments;

(b) the amounts of net assets (fund balances) attributable to each major category of other external restrictions with a description of the restrictions; and

(c) the amounts of deferred contributions attributable to each major category of external restrictions with a description of the restrictions. (April, 1997)

Statement Of Operations

General Recommendations

14-93. The objective of this statement is to communicate information about changes in the organization's economic resources and obligations for the period. The information it contains can be used to evaluate the organization's performance during the period, including its continued ability to provide services. The statement can also be used to evaluate management.

14-94. Section 4400 does not contains specific Recommendations as to classification of expenses, recognizing that different organizations may classify by object (e.g., wage, rent, advertising), while others may classify by function or program (e.g., feeding the poor, providing shelter for the poor). To the extent that the organization has such any of the items listed in Section 1520 of the *CICA Handbook*, the individual disclosure requirements of that Section would be applicable here.

14-95. Not-for-profit organizations have a tradition of reporting certain revenue items net of the related expenses. An example of this would be the net proceeds of particular fund raising events. In an effort to limit this type of disclosure, Section 4400 provides the following Recommendation:

> **Paragraph 4400.37** *Revenues and expenses should be disclosed at their gross amounts.* (April, 1997)

14-96. This disclosure could either be in the Statement Of Operations or, alternatively, in notes to the financial statements. To the extent that the items relate to the organization's main, ongoing service delivery activities, disclosure in the Statement Of Operations is preferred.

Deferral Method

14-97. For those organizations using the deferral method, the following Recommendation is applicable:

> **Paragraph 4400.33** *The statement of operations should present*
>
> (a) *for each financial statement item, a total that includes all funds reported; and*
> (b) *total excess or deficiency of revenues and gains over expenses and losses for the period.* (April, 1997)

14-98. The first part of the Recommendation applies when some form of fund accounting is being used in conjunction with the deferral method. It ensures that information will be provided for the organization as a whole. The remainder of the Recommendation calls for the presentation of a not-for-profit organization's equivalent to a "bottom line".

Restricted Fund Method

14-99. Section 4400 contains the following Recommendation that is specific to those organizations using the restricted fund method:

> **Paragraph 4400.35** *The statement of operations should present the following for the period:*
>
> (a) *the total for each financial statement item recognized in the general fund;*
> (b) *the total for each financial statement item recognized in the restricted funds, other than the endowment fund;*
> (c) *the total for each financial statement item recognized in the endowment fund; and*
> (d) *excess or deficiency of revenues and gains over expenses and losses for each of the general fund, restricted funds other than the endowment fund and the endowment fund.* (April, 1997)

14-100. As was the case with the Recommendation for organizations using the deferral method, this Recommendation insures that information is available for the total organization and that a "bottom line" is presented for the specified fund balances.

Statement Of Changes In Net Assets

14-101. This Statement is the not-for-profit equivalent of the Statement Of Changes In Shareholders' Equity for a profit oriented corporation. For a not-for-profit organization it will disclose information about changes in the portions of net assets attributable to endowments, to capital assets, and to other external and internal restrictions. It provides information with respect to the organization's overall accumulation or depletion of assets. For those not-for-profit organizations that use fund accounting, this Statement may also be referred to as a Statement Of Changes In Fund Balances.

14-102.   Disclosure items that are peculiar to not-for-profit organizations are specified in the following Recommendation:

Paragraph 4400.41   *The statement of changes in net assets should present changes in the following for the period:*

(a) net assets invested in capital assets;

(b) net assets subject to restrictions requiring that they be maintained permanently as endowments;

(c) other restricted net assets;

(d) unrestricted net assets; and

(e) total net assets. (April, 1997)

Statement Of Cash Flows

14-103.   The general rules presented in Section 1540 (Statement Of Changes In Financial Position) of the *CICA Handbook* are, for the most part, applicable here. In addition, Section 4400 adds two Recommendations that are specific to the Statements Of Cash Flows of not-for-profit organizations. They are as follows:

Paragraph 4400.44   *The statement of cash flows should report the total changes in cash and cash equivalents resulting from the activities of the organization during the period. The components of cash and cash equivalents should be disclosed.* (April, 1997)

Paragraph 4400.45   *The statement of cash flows should distinguish at least the following:*

(a) cash from operations: the components of cash from operations should be disclosed or the excess of revenues over expenses should be reconciled to cash flows from operations; and

(b) the components of cash flows resulting from financing and investing activities, not included in (a) above. (April, 1997)

14-104.   Section 4400 notes that cash receipts from operations would include unrestricted contributions, restricted contributions that are to be used for operations, and other revenues arising from the organization's ordinary activities, such as fees for services, proceeds on the sale of goods and unrestricted investment income. Cash disbursements for operations would comprise expenditures made by the organization in carrying out its service delivery activities.

14-105.   Components of cash flows from financing activities would include cash contributed that is restricted for the purpose of acquiring capital assets and cash contributed for endowment. Cash receipts and disbursements related to the assumption and repayment of debt would also be presented as components of cash flows from financing activities. Components of cash flows from investing activities would include the acquisition of capital assets, the purchase of investments, and the proceeds on disposal of major categories of assets, such as capital assets and investments.

14-106.   Section 4400 notes that non cash financing and investing transactions (e.g., contributions of capital assets) should be reported as a cash inflow combined with a cash outflow. We would note that, while this is consistent with the existing Section 1540, an outstanding Exposure Draft for a revised Section 1540 would exclude this type of transaction from the Statement Of Changes In Financial Position.

14-107.   The Section also indicates that, in situations where a Statement Of Changes In Financial Position would not provide additional useful information, no such Statement need be prepared. This might apply, for example, to an organization with relatively simple operations and few or no significant financing and investing activities.

Example 1 (No Capital Assets)

Basic Data

14-108. At this point we would like to present an example which illustrates the three accounting approaches that can be used by a not-for-profit organization (i.e., aggregate accounting, restricted fund accounting, and other fund accounting). This example will illustrate a number of the Recommendations for revenue recognition and financial statement presentation. It will not, however, include capital asset considerations. A second version of this example will be presented after we have discussed Sections 4430 (Capital Assets) and 4440 (Collections). This second example will be a continuation of this example with the addition of purchased and contributed capital assets. We will use the data of this example in three different cases in order to illustrate the alternatives that are available in not-for-profit accounting.

14-109. The basic data for this example is as follows:

Organization And Purpose On January 1, 1998, the Local Care Society (LCS) is organized as a not-for-profit organization. Its purpose is to serve the needs of its local community in two areas:

- The provision of meals for elderly individuals who are unable to leave their homes (meals activity).

- The provision of winter clothing for children who are living in poverty (clothing activity).

The organization will have a December 31 year end.

Endowment Contributions Initial funding is provided by a wealthy individual who makes an endowment contribution of $50,000. These funds are invested in debt securities. There are no restrictions on the income that is produced by these investments. During the year ending December 31, 1998, such income amounted to $4,000.

Unrestricted Contributions The organization solicits and receives unrestricted contributions which are then allocated to both meals activity and clothing activity by the organization's Board Of Directors. During the year ending December 31, 1998, $400,000 in contributions were received. At year end, an additional $35,000 in contributions were receivable. The Board believes that this is a reasonable estimate of the amount that will actually be collected. This total was allocated $285,000 to meals activity and $150,000 to clothing activity.

Restricted Contributions The organization accepts additional contributions that are restricted to use in the clothing activity. These funds are segregated and a separate report is made to contributors on their usage. During the year ending December 31, 1998, restricted contributions of $125,000 were received. No contributions are receivable at year end.

Expenses During the year ending December 31, 1998, the organization incurred the following expenses:

	Meals Activity	Clothing Activity
Wages And Salaries	$ 20,000	$ 25,000
Cost Of Materials Provided	180,000	190,000
Transportation Costs	30,000	5,000
Other Expenses	15,000	20,000
Total	$245,000	$240,000

It is estimated that 40 percent of the expenses related to clothing activity have been made from the restricted contributions.

On December 31, 1998, there were outstanding Accounts Payable related to the meals activity expenses of $30,000.

Case One - No Fund Accounting

14-110.   In this Case we will assume that LCS is not using fund accounting. This means that they will have to use the deferral method of revenue recognition. Based on this approach, the required financial statements are as follows:

LCS Organization
Statement Of Operations And Fund Balances
Year Ending December 31, 1998

Revenues:	
Unrestricted Contributions	$435,000
Amortization Of Deferred Contributions*	96,000
Investment Income	4,000
Total Revenues	**$535,000**
Expenses:	
Wages And Salaries	$ 45,000
Cost Of Materials Provided	370,000
Transportation Costs	35,000
Other Expenses	35,000
Total Expenses	**$485,000**
Excess Of Revenues Over Expenses	$ 50,000
Opening Unrestricted Net Assets	Nil
Closing Unrestricted Net Assets	**$ 50,000**

*Contributions restricted to clothing activity can be recognized to the extent of expenses incurred. For LCS, this amount would be $96,000 [(40%)($240,000)].

LCS Organization
Statement Of Cash Flows
Year Ending December 31, 1998

Cash Flows From Operating Activities:	
Unrestricted Contributions	$400,000
Restricted Contributions	125,000
Investment Income	4,000
Expenses	(455,000)
Total	**$74,000**
Cash Flows From Financing And Investing:	
Endowment Contributions	50,000
Investment Of Endowment Contributions	(50,000)
Increase In Cash	$ 74,000
Opening Cash Balance	Nil
Closing Cash Balance	**$ 74,000**

LCS Organization
Statement Of Financial Position
As At December 31, 1998

Cash (See Statement Of Cash Flows)	$ 74,000
Investments	50,000
Contributions Receivable	35,000
Total	**$159,000**

Accounts Payable	$ 30,000
Deferred Contributions*	29,000
Net Assets:	
Restricted For Endowment Purposes	50,000
Unrestricted	50,000
Total	**$159,000**

*Unamortized deferred contributions amount are calculated as follows:

Total Restricted Contributions	$125,000
Expenses Incurred [(40%)($240,000)]	(96,000)
Unamortized Balance	**$ 29,000**

Case Two - Restricted Fund Accounting

14-111.   In this Case we will assume that LCS establishes separate funds for endowment contributions, restricted clothing activity contributions, and a general fund. Given this, the organization will be able to use the restricted fund basis of revenue recognition. The required financial statements are as follows:

LCS Organization
Statement Of Operations And Fund Balances
Year Ending December 31, 1998

	General Fund	Restricted Fund	Endowment Fund
Revenues:			
Unrestricted Contributions	$435,000		
Restricted Contributions		$125,000	
Investment Income	4,000		
Endowment Contributions			$50,000
Total Revenues	**$439,000**	**$125,000**	**$50,000**
Expenses:*			
Wages And Salaries	$ 35,000	$ 10,000	
Cost Of Materials Provided	294,000	76,000	
Transportation Costs	33,000	2,000	
Other Expenses	27,000	8,000	
Total Expenses	**$389,000**	**$ 96,000**	
Excess Of Revenues Over Expenses	**$ 50,000**	**$ 29,000**	**$50,000**
Opening Net Assets	Nil	Nil	Nil
Closing Net Assets	**$50,000**	**$ 29,000**	**$ 50,000**

*All of the meals activity expenses, plus 60 percent of the clothing activity expenses have been allocated to the general fund. The restricted fund has been allocated 40 percent of the clothing activity expenses.

LCS Organization
Statement Of Cash Flows
Year Ending December 31, 1998

	General Fund	Restricted Fund	Endowment Fund
Cash Flows From Operating Activities:			
Unrestricted Contributions	$400,000		
Restricted Contributions		$125,000	
Investment Income	4,000		
Expenses	(359,000)	(96,000)	
Total From Operations	$ 45,000	$ 29,000	Nil
Cash Flows From Financing And Investing:			
Endowment Contributions			$50,000
Investments Acquired	Nil	Nil	(50,000)
Increase In Cash	$ 45,000	$ 29,000	Nil
Opening Cash Balance	Nil	Nil	Nil
Closing Cash Balance	$ 45,000	$ 29,000	Nil

14-112.   Note that when the restricted fund method is used, there is no requirement for showing the totals for all funds in the Statement Of Operations or the Statement Of Cash Flows.

LCS Organization
Statement Of Financial Position
As At December 31, 1998

	General Fund	Restricted Fund	Endowment Fund	Total
Cash	$ 45,000	$ 29,000		$ 74,000
Investments			$ 50,000	50,000
Contributions Receivable	35,000			35,000
Total	$ 80,000	$ 29,000	$ 50,000	$159,000
Accounts Payable	$ 30,000			$ 30,000
Fund Balances:				
Restricted For Clothing*		$ 29,000		29,000
Restricted For Endowment			$ 50,000	50,000
Unrestricted	50,000			50,000
Total	$ 80,000	$ 29,000	$ 50,000	$159,000

*This balance can be calculated as follows:

Total Restricted Contributions	$125,000
Expenses Incurred [(40%)($240,000)]	(96,000)
Restricted Fund Balance	$ 29,000

Case Three - Fund Accounting On Other Basis

14-113. This final version of our Case will also assume that LCS uses fund accounting. However, it will not qualify for the restricted fund method of revenue recognition as it classifies its funds by programs rather than by restrictions. They will use a general fund, a meals activity fund, and a clothing activity fund. Endowment funds will be accounted for through the general fund. The required financial statements are as follows:

LCS Organization
Statement Of Operations And Fund Balances
Year Ending December 31, 1998

	General Fund	Meals Activity Fund	Clothing Activity Fund	Total
Revenues:				
Unrestricted Contributions		$285,000	$150,000	$435,000
Restricted Contributions			96,000	96,000
Investment Income	$4,000			4,000
Total Revenues	$4,000	$285,000	$246,000	$535,000
Expenses:				
Wages And Salaries		$ 20,000	$ 25,000	$ 45,000
Cost Of Materials Provided		180,000	190,000	370,000
Transportation Costs		30,000	5,000	35,000
Other Expenses	Nil	15,000	20,000	35,000
Total Expenses	Nil	$245,000	$240,000	$485,000
Excess Of Revenues Over Expenses	$4,000	$ 40,000	$ 6,000	$ 50,000
Opening Unrestricted Net Assets	Nil	Nil	Nil	Nil
Closing Fund Balances	$4,000	$ 40,000	$ 6,000	$ 50,000

LCS Organization
Statement Of Cash Flows
Year Ending December 31, 1998

	General Fund	Meals Activity Fund	Clothing Activity Fund	Total
Cash Flows From Operations:				
Unrestricted Contributions*		$250,000	$150,000	$400,000
Restricted Contributions			125,000	125,000
Investment Income	$ 4,000			4,000
Expenses		(215,000)	(240,000)	(455,000)
Total From Operations	$ 4,000	$ 35,000	$ 35,000	$ 74,000
Financing And Investing:				
Endowment Contributions	50,000			50,000
Investments Acquired	(50,000)	Nil	Nil	(50,000)
Increase In Cash	$ 4,000	$ 35,000	$ 35,000	$ 74,000
Opening Cash Balance	Nil	Nil	Nil	Nil
Closing Cash Balance	$ 4,000	$ 35,000	$ 35,000	$ 74,000

*All of the receivables and payables have been allocated to the meals activity fund.

LCS Organization
Statement Of Financial Position
As At December 31, 1998

	General Fund	Meals Activity Fund	Clothing Activity Fund	Total
Cash	$ 4,000	$35,000	$35,000	$ 74,000
Investments	50,000			50,000
Contributions Receivable*		35,000		35,000
Total	$54,000	$70,000	$35,000	$159,000
Accounts Payable*		$30,000		$ 30,000
Deferred Contributions			$29,000	29,000
Fund Balances:				
Restricted For Endowment	$50,000			50,000
Unrestricted	4,000	40,000	6,000	50,000
Total	$54,000	$70,000	$35,000	$159,000

*All of the receivables and payables have been allocated to the meals activity fund.

Capital Assets Of Not-For-Profit Organizations Handbook Sections 4430 And 4440

Background To The Problem

14-114.   For both government and not-for-profit organizations, the traditional practice has been not to record assets in the financial statements. In general, such assets were charged to expense when acquired, leaving no balance to be subject to amortization in future periods.

14-115.   While there is still support for this type of approach, the great majority of authorities in this area view such practices as inappropriate. As a reflection of this fact, Section 4430 has been added to the *CICA Handbook*. The basic purpose of this Section is to require not-for-profit organizations to deal with their capital assets in basically the same manner as is specified in Section 3060 for profit oriented enterprises. In fact, much of Section 4430 duplicates the content of Section 3060.

14-116.   As a measure of the controversy surrounding this issue, you should note that the Accounting Standards Board felt obliged to make exceptions to these rules for the capital assets of not-for-profit organizations. These exceptions are dealt with in the next Section.

Exceptions To Capital Assets Rule

Small Organizations

14-117.   The first exception relates to smaller organizations. In order to implement this exception, Section 4430 contains the following statement:

> **Paragraph 4430.03**   Organizations may limit the application of this Section to the Recommendation in paragraph 4430.40 if the average of annual revenues recognized in the statement of operations for the current and preceding period of the organization and any entities it controls is less than $500,000. When an organization reports some of its revenues net of related expenses, gross revenues would be used for purposes of this calculation.

14-118. The additional disclosures that must be provided in these situations is as follows:

> **Paragraph 4430.40** *Organizations meeting the criterion in paragraph 4430.03 and not following the other Recommendations of this Section should disclose the following:*
>
> *(a) the policy followed in accounting for capital assets;*
>
> *(b) information about major categories of capital assets not recorded in the statement of financial position, including a description of the assets; and*
>
> *(c) if capital assets are expensed when acquired, the amount expensed in the current period. (April, 1997)*

Collections

14-119. Collections are defined in Section 4440 as follows:

> **Paragraph 4440.03(b)** **Collections** are works of art, historical treasures or similar assets that are:
>
> (i) held for public exhibition, education or research;
>
> (ii) protected, cared for and preserved; and
>
> (iii) subject to an organizational policy that requires any proceeds from their sale to be used to acquire other items to be added to the collection or for the direct care of the existing collection.

14-120. A typical example of a collection would be a group of paintings held by a not-for-profit art gallery. Such assets often present significant valuation problems. Perhaps, more importantly, they generally do not depreciate in value. If they do experience a change in value, it is more likely to be in an upward direction. Further, they are not a resource that can be used by the organization for any other purpose.

14-121. Given these considerations, it is not surprising that the Accounting Standards Board decided not to apply the requirements of Section 4430 to these assets. This is accomplished in a less than straightforward manner. Section 4430 does not simply say that these assets are exempt from its Recommendations. Rather, it provides the following definition of Capital Assets:

> **Paragraph 4430.05(b)** **Capital assets**, comprising tangible properties, such as land, buildings and equipment, and intangible properties, are identifiable assets that meet all of the following criteria:
>
> (i) are held for use in the provision of services, for administrative purposes, for production of goods or for the maintenance, repair, development or construction of other capital assets;
>
> (ii) have been acquired, constructed or developed with the intention of being used on a continuing basis;
>
> (iii) are not intended for sale in the ordinary course of operations; and
>
> (iv) are not held as part of a collection.

14-122. By excluding collections from the definition of capital assets, the Accounting Standards Board has, in effect, exempted these assets from the Recommendations of Section 4430.

Recognition And Measurement

Cost

14-123. The basic Recommendation here is as follows:

Paragraph 4430.06 *A capital asset should be recorded on the statement of financial position at cost. For a contributed capital asset, cost is considered to be fair value at the date of contribution. In unusual circumstances when fair value cannot be reasonably determined, the capital asset should be recorded at nominal value.* (April, 1997)

14-124.   This Recommendation requires that the capital assets of not-for-profit organizations be recorded at cost and, in addition, it specifies that the cost of a contributed capital asset is its fair value at the time of contribution. Fair value, as defined in Paragraph 4430.05, is the amount of the consideration that would be agreed upon in an arm's length transaction between knowledgeable, willing parties who are under no compulsion to act. Use of nominal values is acceptable when fair value cannot be reasonably determined.

14-125.   The Section makes a number of additional points with respect to capital assets:

- The cost should include all costs necessary to put the asset into use.

- If an asset is acquired by a not-for-profit organization at a cost that is substantially below fair value, it should be recorded at fair value, with the difference reported as a contribution.

- The cost of a basket purchase should be allocated on the basis of the relative fair values of the assets acquired.

- The cost of self constructed or self developed assets should include direct costs of construction or development, along with any overhead costs directly attributable to the construction or development activity. In the case of self developed intangibles, future benefits may be so uncertain that recording the costs of development as an asset cannot be justified.

- A betterment should be capitalized. These are defined as service enhancements which increase capacity, lower operating costs, extend the useful life, or improve the quality of output of the asset.

14-126.   Other than the possibility of recording a contribution as part of an asset acquisition transaction, all of these suggestions are consistent with the treatment given to the capital assets of profit oriented enterprises.

Amortization

14-127.   With respect to amortization, Section 4430 contains the following Recommendation:

Paragraph 4430.16 *The cost, less any residual value, of a capital asset with a limited life should be amortized over its useful life in a rational and systematic manner appropriate to its nature and use by the organization. Amortization should be recognized as an expense in the organization's statement of operations.* (April, 1997)

14-128.   This Recommendation serves to put the capital assets of not-for-profit organizations on virtually the same footing as those of profit oriented enterprises. The discussion in Section 4430 of this Recommendation is similar to that contained in Section 3060 on this subject, providing for the use of different amortization methods and encouraging the estimation of residual value in determining the amount to be written off. There is a small difference from Section 3060 in that the amortization Recommendation in that Section calls for the write off of the greater of cost less salage value over the life of the asset, and cost less residual value over the useful life of the asset.

14-129.   The Section points out that, along with land, works of art and historical treasures may have virtually unlimited lives. This would suggest that amortization would not be appropriate in these circumstances. We would remind you that, if the work of art is part of a collection, Section 4430's Recommendations are not applicable.

14-130. When fund accounting is used, the fund to which amortization will be charged is a matter of judgment. The common answers would be to charge these amounts to either the capital asset fund or the general fund.

14-131. As is the case with Section 3060, Section 4430 requires a periodic review of amortization:

> **Paragraph 4430.23** *The amortization method and the estimate of the useful life of a capital asset should be reviewed on a regular basis.* (April, 1997)

14-132. Events that might indicate a need for revision would include the following:

- a change in the extent the capital asset is used;
- a change in the manner in which the capital asset is used;
- removal of the capital asset from service for an extended period of time;
- physical damage;
- significant technological developments; and
- a change in the law or environment affecting the period of time over which the capital asset can be used.

Future Removal And Site Restoration Costs

14-133. Section 4430 contains a Recommendation that is identical to Section 3060's in this area:

> **Paragraph 4430.25** *When reasonably determinable, provisions for future removal and site restoration costs, net of expected recoveries, should be recognized as expenses in a rational and systematic manner.* (April, 1997)

14-134. Given the nature of not-for-profit organizations, we would expect that the application of this Recommendation to this type of enterprise would be relatively rare.

Write Downs

14-135. Again following the pattern established in Section 3060, Section 4430 makes the following Recommendation in this area:

> **Paragraph 4430.28** *When a capital asset no longer has any long-term service potential to the organization, the excess of its net carrying amount over any residual value should be recognized as an expense in the statement of operations. A write down should not be reversed.* (April, 1997)

Disposals

14-136. The difference between the net proceeds of a disposal and the net carrying value of an asset is normally recorded in the Statement Of Operations. If there are unamortized deferred contributions related to the capital asset disposed of, they would be recognized as revenue in the period of disposal, provided that all related restrictions have been complied with.

Presentation And Disclosure

14-137. For all capital assets of not-for-profit organizations, the following disclosure is required:

> **Paragraph 4430.31** *For each major category of capital assets there should be disclosure of:*
>
> *(a) cost;*
> *(b) accumulated amortization, including the amount of any write downs; and*
> *(c) the amortization method used, including the amortization period or rate.*
> (April, 1997)

> **Paragraph 4430.32** *The net carrying amounts of major categories of capital assets not being amortized should be disclosed.* (April, 1997)

Paragraph 4430.33 *The amount of amortization of capital assets recognized as an expense for the period should be disclosed.* (April, 1997)

Paragraph 4430.34 *The amount of any write downs of capital assets should be disclosed in the financial statements for the period in which the write downs are made.* (April, 1997)

14-138. Further Recommendations are made with respect to contributed capital assets:

Paragraph 4430.37 *The nature and amount of contributed capital assets received in the period and recognized in the financial statements should be disclosed.* (April, 1997)

Paragraph 4430.38 *Information should be disclosed about contributed capital assets recognized at nominal value.* (April, 1997)

Example 2 (Includes Capital Assets)

Basic Data

14-139.   This is an extension of the example that was presented in Paragraph 14-109. It involves the same Local Care Society (LCS) and extends their activities into the year ending December 31, 1999. It is made more complex by the addition of capital assets and their amortization. The basic data for LCS for the year ending December 31, 1999 is as follows:

Endowment Contributions   There are no additional endowment contributions during the year ending December 31, 1999. The endowment investments have income of $3,000 during this period.

Unrestricted Contributions   During the year ending December 31, 1999, $600,000 in unrestricted contributions were received. At year end, there is an additional $40,000 in contributions that are receivable. The Board believes that this is a reasonable estimate of the amount that will actually be collected. This total was allocated $360,000 to meals activity, $180,000 to clothing activity, and $100,000 for the acquisition of a building to be used in the organizations operations.

Capital Assets   On July 1, 1999, the organization acquires a building for a total cost of $100,000. Of this total, $20,000 represents the fair value of the land on which the building is situated and the remaining $80,000 reflects the fair value of the building. The estimated useful life of the building is 10 years and no significant residual value is anticipated. The organization uses straight line amortization, charging only one-half year's amortization in the year in which an asset is acquired.

Restricted Contributions   The organization continues to accept additional contributions that are restricted to use in the clothing activity. During the year ending December 31, 1999, restricted contributions of $175,000 were received. No contributions are receivable at year end.

Expenses   During the year ending December 31, 1999, the organization incurred the following expenses:

	Meals Activity	Clothing Activity
Wages And Salaries	$ 25,000	$ 20,000
Cost Of Materials Provided	210,000	230,000
Transportation Costs	35,000	15,000
Other Expenses	15,000	25,000
Total	$285,000	$290,000

It is estimated that 50 percent of the expenses related to clothing activity have been made from restricted funds. On December 31, 1999, there were outstanding Accounts Payable related to the meals activities expenses of $25,000.

Case One - No Fund Accounting

14-140   In this Case we will assume that LCS is not using fund accounting. This means that they will have to use the deferral method of revenue recognition. Based on this approach, the required financial statements are as follows:

LCS Organization
Statement Of Operations And Fund Balances
Year Ending December 31, 1999

Revenues:	
Unrestricted Contributions	$640,000
Amortization Of Deferred Contributions*	145,000
Investment Income	3,000
Total Revenues	$788,000
Expenses:	
Wages And Salaries	$ 45,000
Cost Of Materials Provided	440,000
Transportation Costs	50,000
Amortization Expense [($80,000/10)(1/2)]	4,000
Other Expenses	40,000
Total Expenses	$579,000
Excess Of Revenues Over Expenses	$209,000
Invested In Capital Assets (Net)	(96,000)
Opening Unrestricted Net Assets	50,000
Closing Unrestricted Net Assets	$163,000

*Contributions restricted to clothing activity can be recognized to the extent of expenses incurred. For LCS, this amount would be $145,000 [(50%)($290,000)].

LCS Organization
Statement Of Cash Flows
Year Ending December 31, 1999

Cash Flows From Operating Activities:	
Unrestricted Contributions ($600,000 + $35,000)	$635,000
Restricted Contributions	175,000
Investment Income	3,000
Expenses ($285,000 + $290,000 + $30,000 - $25,000)	(580,000)
Total	$233,000
Cash Flows From Financing And Investing:	
Purchase Of Building	(100,000)
Increase In Cash	$133,000
Opening Cash Balance	74,000
Closing Cash Balance	$207,000

14-141.   The Unrestricted Contributions have been increased by the $35,000 of contributions receivable from the preceding year. The Expenses have been increased by the $30,000 Accounts Payable from the preceding year.

LCS Organization
Statement Of Financial Position
As At December 31, 1999

Cash (See Statement Of Cash Flows)		$207,000
Investments		50,000
Contributions Receivable		40,000
Capital Assets:		
Land		20,000
Building	$80,000	
Accumulated Amortization	(4,000)	76,000
Total		$393,000

Accounts Payable	$ 25,000
Deferred Contributions*	59,000
Net Assets:	
Restricted For Endowment Purposes	50,000
Invested In Capital Assets	96,000
Unrestricted	163,000
Total	$393,000

*Unamortized deferred contributions amount are calculated as follows:

Balance - December 31, 1998	$ 29,000
Additions	175,000
Expenses Incurred [(50%)($290,000)]	(145,000)
Balance - December 31, 1999	$ 59,000

Case Two - Restricted Fund Accounting

14-142.   In this Case we will assume that LCS establishes a separate fund for endowment contributions, restricted clothing activity contributions, and a separate general fund. Capital assets will be accounted for in the general fund. Given this classification of funds, the organization will be able to use the restricted fund basis of revenue recognition. The required financial statements are as follows:

LCS Organization
Statement Of Operations And Fund Balances
Year Ending December 31, 1999

	General Fund	Restricted Fund	Endowment Fund
Revenues:			
Unrestricted Contributions	$640,000		
Restricted Contributions		$175,000	
Investment Income	3,000		
Total Revenues	$643,000	$175,000	Nil
Expenses:*			
Wages And Salaries	$ 35,000	$ 10,000	
Cost Of Materials Provided	325,000	115,000	
Transportation Costs	42,500	7,500	
Amortization Expense	4,000	-0-	
Other Expenses	27,500	12,500	
Total Expenses	$434,000	$145,000	Nil
Excess Of Revenues Over Expenses	$209,000	$ 30,000	Nil
Invested In Capital Assets (Net)	(96,000)		
Opening Net Assets	50,000	29,000	$50,000
Closing Net Assets	$163,000	$ 59,000	$50,000

*All of the meals activity expenses, plus 50 percent of the clothing activity expenses have been allocated to the general fund. The restricted fund has been allocated 50 percent of the clothing activity expenses.

LCS Organization
Statement Of Cash Flows
Year Ending December 31, 1999

	General Fund	Restricted Fund	Endowment Fund
Cash Flows From Operating Activities:			
Unrestricted Contributions	$635,000		
Restricted Contributions		$175,000	
Investment Income	3,000		
Expenses	(435,000)	(145,000)	
Total From Operations	$203,000	$ 30,000	Nil
Cash Flows From Financing And Investing:			
Capital Assets Acquired	(100,000)		
Increase In Cash	$103,000	$ 30,000	Nil
Opening Cash Balance	45,000	29,000	Nil
Closing Cash Balance	$148,000	$ 59,000	Nil

14-143.   Note that when the restricted fund method is used, there is no requirement for showing the totals for all funds in the Statement Of Operations or the Statement Of Cash Flows.

LCS Organization
Statement Of Financial Position
As At December 31, 1999

	General Fund	Restricted Fund	Endowment Fund	Total
Cash	$148,000	$ 59,000		$207,000
Investments			$ 50,000	50,000
Contributions Receivable	40,000			40,000
Capital Assets:				
Land	20,000			20,000
Building	80,000			80,000
Acc. Depreciation	(4,000)			(4,000)
Total	$284,000	$59,000	$50,000	$393,000
Accounts Payable	$ 25,000			$ 25,000
Fund Balances:				
Restricted For Clothing*		$ 59,000		59,000
Restricted For Endowment			$ 50,000	50,000
Invested In Capital Assets	96,000			96,000
Unrestricted	163,000			163,000
Total	$284,000	$ 59,000	$ 50,000	$393,000

*While the account title is different, the calculation of this balance was shown in Case One under the title Deferred Contributions.

Case Three - Fund Accounting On Other Basis

14-144.   This final version of our Case will also assume that LCS uses fund accounting. However, it will not qualify for the restricted fund method of revenue recognition as it classifies its funds by programs rather than by restrictions. They will use a general fund, a meals activity fund, and a clothing activity fund. Endowment funds will be accounted for through the general fund. The required financial statements are as follows:

LCS Organization
Statement Of Operations And Fund Balances
Year Ending December 31, 1999

	General Fund	Meals Activity Fund	Clothing Activity Fund	Total
Revenues:				
Unrestricted Contributions	$100,000	$360,000	$180,000	$640,000
Restricted Contributions*			145,000	145,000
Investment Income	3,000			3,000
Total Revenues	$103,000	$360,000	$325,000	$788,000
Expenses:				
Wages And Salaries		$ 25,000	$ 20,000	$ 45,000
Cost Of Materials Provided		210,000	230,000	440,000
Transportation Costs		35,000	15,000	50,000
Amortization Expense	$ 4,000			4,000
Other Expenses		15,000	25,000	40,000
Total Expenses	$ 4,000	$285,000	$290,000	$579,000
Excess Of Revenues				
Over Expenses	$ 99,000	$ 75,000	$ 35,000	$209,000
Invested In Capital Assets	(96,000)			(96,000)
Opening Unrestricted				
Net Assets	4,000	40,000	6,000	50,000
Closing Fund Balances	$ 7,000	$115,000	$ 41,000	$163,000

*Contributions restricted to clothing activity can be recognized to the extent of expenses incurred. For LCS, this amount would be $145,000 [(50%)($290,000)].

LCS Organization
Statement Of Cash Flows
Year Ending December 31, 1999

	General Fund	Meals Activity Fund	Clothing Activity Fund	Total
Cash From Operations:				
Unrestricted Contributions*	$100,000	$355,000	$180,000	$635,000
Restricted Contributions			175,000	175,000
Investment Income	3,000			3,000
Expenses*		(290,000)	(290,000)	(580,000)
Total From Operations	$103,000	$ 65,000	$ 65,000	$233,000
Financing And Investing:				
Capital Assets Acquired	(100,000)			(100,000)
Increase In Cash	$ 3,000	$ 65,000	$ 65,000	$133,000
Opening Cash Balance	4,000	35,000	35,000	74,000
Closing Cash Balance	$ 7,000	$100,000	$100,000	$207,000

*All of the receivables and payables have been allocated to the meals activity fund. The Unrestricted Contributions of $355,000 have been adjusted for the contributions receivable ($360,000 + $35,000 - $40,000). The expenses of $290,000 allocated to the meals activity fund have been adjusted for the Accounts Payable ($285,000 + $30,000 - $25,000).

LCS Organization
Statement Of Financial Position
As At December 31, 1999

	General Fund	Meals Activity Fund	Clothing Activity Fund	Total
Cash	$ 7,000	$100,000	$100,000	$207,000
Investments	50,000			50,000
Contributions Receivable*		40,000		40,000
Capital Assets				
Land	20,000			20,000
Building	80,000			80,000
Accumulated Depreciation	(4,000)			(4,000)
Total	$153,000	$140,000	$100,000	$393,000
Accounts Payable*		$ 25,000		$ 25,000
Deferred Contributions			$59,000	59,000
Fund Balances:				
Restricted For Endowment	$ 50,000			50,000
Invested In Capital Assets	96,000			100,000
Unrestricted	7,000	115,000	41,000	159,000
Total	$153,000	$140,000	$100,000	$393,000

*All of the receivables and payables have been allocated to the meals activity fund.

Reporting Controlled And Related Entities Handbook Section 4450

Background

14-145.   In our earlier discussion of the reporting entity, we noted that the *CICA Handbook* does not require the consolidation of all of the entities that might be controlled by a not-for-profit organization. However, when control exists, there are disclosure requirements that apply when consolidation is not used.

14-146.   Section 4450 deals with these issues. It specifies the disclosure that is required when consolidation is not used for a controlled entity. It also deals with the presentation and disclosure that is required when a not-for-profit organization participates in joint venture arrangements, or has significant influence over another organization.

Related Entities

14-147.   Section 4450 begins by defining possible relationships betweeen a not-for-profit organization and other related entities. These definitions are found in Paragraph 4450.02 as follows:

Control of an entity is the continuing power to determine its strategic operating, investing and financing policies without the co-operation of others.

Joint control of an economic activity is the contractually agreed sharing of the continuing power to determine its strategic operating, investing and financing policies.

A **joint venture** is an economic activity resulting from a contractual arrangement whereby two or more venturers jointly control the economic activity.

Significant influence over an entity is the ability to affect the strategic operating, investing and financing policies of the entity.

An **economic interest** in another not-for-profit organization exists if:

(i) the other organization holds resources that must be used to produce revenue or provide services for the reporting organization; or

(ii) the reporting organization is responsible for the liabilities of the other organization.

14-148.   The definitions related to control, joint control, and significant influence are the same as those used by profit oriented enterprises and, as such, require no further explanation. However, the concept of "economic interest" is unique to the not-for-profit accounting area and, as a consequence, warrants further discussion.

14-149.   While the preceding definition lays out the general rules for determining economic interest, Paragraph 4450.10 provides further guidance by listing possible indicators of such an interest:

(a) The other organization solicits funds in the name of and with the expressed or implied approval of the reporting organization, and substantially all of the funds solicited are intended by the contributor or are otherwise required to be transferred to the reporting organization or used at its discretion or direction;

(b) The reporting organization transfers significant resources to the other organization, whose resources are held for the benefit of the reporting organization;

(c) The other organization is required to perform significant functions on behalf of the reporting organization that are integral to the reporting organization's achieving its objectives; or

(d) The reporting organization guarantees significant liabilities of the other organization.

14-150.   Section 4450 provides further guidance in this area as follows:

Paragraph 4450.11   Economic interests can exist in varying degrees of significance. At one extreme, the reporting organization would not be able to function in its current form without the organization in which it has an economic interest. In such cases, the existence of the economic interest may be a strong indicator that control exists. At the other extreme, economic interests are much more limited and exist without control or significant influence.

Paragraph 4450.12   In determining if an economic interest In another organization exists, the reporting organization would consider whether the other organization is required to transfer resources to or perform significant functions for the reporting organization. For example, externally imposed restrictions on the other organization's resources could create an economic interest. However, a funding relationship where the other organization is not obliged to provide resources to the reporting organization may not be considered to be an economic interest. Similarly, a situation where another organization holds fund raising events from time to time for the benefit of the reporting organization may not result in an economic interest.

14-151.   With these definitions in mind, we can now deal with Section 4450's specific Recommendations concerning entities that are related to a not-for-profit organization.

Controlled Not-For-Profit Organizations

Basic Recommendation

14-152.   The basic Recommendation here sets out three possibilities for dealing with controlled not-for-profit organizations. These are as follows:

> **Paragraph 4450.14**   *An organization should report each controlled not-for-profit organization in one of the following ways:*
>
> *(a) by consolidating the controlled organization in its financial statements;*
>
> *(b) by providing the disclosure set out in paragraph 4450.22; or*
>
> *(c) if the controlled organization is one of a large number of individually immaterial organizations, by providing the disclosure set out in paragraph 4450.26.* (April, 1997)

14-153.   The first and probably best choice on this list is consolidation. If the controlling organization rejects this alternative, it must provide the following disclosure for the not-for-profit organization that is controlled:

> **Paragraph 4450.22**   *For each controlled not-for-profit organization or group of similar controlled organizations not consolidated in the reporting organization's financial statements, the following should be disclosed, unless the group of controlled organizations is comprised of a large number of individually immaterial organizations (see paragraph 4450.26):*
>
> *(a) total assets, liabilities and net assets at the reporting date;*
>
> *(b) revenues (including gains), expenses (including losses) and cash flows from operating, financing and investing activities reported in the period;*
>
> *(c) details of any restrictions, by major category, on the resources of the controlled organizations; and*
>
> *(d) significant differences in accounting policies from those followed by the reporting organization.* (April, 1997)

14-154.   Note that there is no mention of using the equity method here. As the controlled entity is a not-for-profit organization, it is unlikely to have equity interests outstanding. In the absence of a measurable equity interest, the equity method cannot be used.

14-155.   A final possibility for dealing with controlled not-for-profit organizations is as follows:

> **Paragraph 4450.26**   *An organization may exclude a group of controlled organizations from both consolidation and the disclosure set out in paragraph 4450.22, provided that*
>
> *(a) the group of organizations is comprised of a large number of organizations that are individually immaterial; and*
>
> *(b) the reporting organization discloses the reasons why the controlled organizations have been neither consolidated nor included in the disclosure set out in paragraph 4450.22.* (April, 1997)

14-156.   This, in effect, allows a not-for-profit organization to provide no disclosure of a group of controlled entities. Judgment would be required in applying this provision. However, it would be applicable in situations where the number of controlled entities is so large that the de facto exercise of control is not practically feasible.

Consolidated Financial Statements

14-157.   The preparation of consolidated financial statements is covered in Section

1600 of the *CICA Handbook*. Most of the procedures listed there will be fully applicable to preparing these statements in the context of not-for-profit organizations. However, the fact that not-for-profit organizations usually do not have a transferable ownership interest may necessitate some modification of these procedures.

Other Considerations

14-158.   The Section notes that control may or may not be accompanied by an economic interest. If such an interest is present, its nature and extent must be disclosed.

14-159.   As an additional point, there is no requirement for consistency in the application of Paragraph 4450.14. A single not-for-profit organization might choose to consolidate some controlled entities, while choosing to only provide additional disclosure for other similar controlled entities.

Controlled Profit Oriented Enterprises

14-160.   Section 4450 provides several Recommendations for dealing with this type of situation:

Paragraph 4450.30   *An organization should report each controlled profit oriented enterprise in either of the following ways:*

(a) *by consolidating the controlled enterprise in its financial statements; or*

(b) *by accounting for its investment in the controlled enterprise using the equity method and providing the disclosure set out in paragraph 4450.32. (April, 1997)*

Paragraph 4450.31   *For a controlled profit oriented enterprise, regardless of whether it is consolidated or accounted for using the equity method, the following should be disclosed:*

(a) *the policy followed in reporting the controlled enterprise; and*

(b) *a description of the relationship with the controlled enterprise. (April, 1997)*

Paragraph 4450.32   *For each controlled profit oriented enterprise or group of similar controlled enterprises accounted for using the equity method, the following should be disclosed:*

(a) *total assets, liabilities and shareholders' equity at the reporting date; and*

(b) *revenues (including gains), expenses (including losses), net income and cash flows from operating, financing and investing activities reported in the period. (April, 1997)*

14-161.   Note that in this case, involving controlled profit oriented enterprises, the equity method is required if consolidation is not used.

Joint Ventures

14-162.   The presentation and disclosure Recommendations for joint ventures are as follows:

Paragraph 4450.36   *An organization should report each interest in a joint venture in either of the following ways:*

(a) *by accounting for its interest using the proportionate consolidation method in accordance with "Interests In Joint Ventures", Section 3055; or*

(b) *by accounting for its interest using the equity method and disclosing the information set out in paragraph 4450.38. (April, 1997)*

Paragraph 4450.37   *For an interest in a joint venture, regardless of whether it is* *reported using the proportionate consolidation or the equity method, the following should be disclosed:*

(a) the policy followed in reporting the interest; and

(b) a description of the relationship with the joint venture. (April, 1997)

Paragraph 4450.38 *For each interest in a joint venture, or group of similar interests, accounted for using the equity method, the following should be disclosed:*

(a) the reporting organization's share of the joint venture's total assets, liabilities and net assets, or shareholders' equity, at the reporting date;

(b) the reporting organization's share of the joint venture's revenues (including gains), expenses (including losses), and cash flows from operating, financing and investing activities reported in the period; and

(c) significant differences in accounting policies from those followed by the reporting organization. (April, 1997)

Significantly Influenced Not-For-Profit Organizations

14-163.   The required presentation and disclosure for this type of related entity is as follows:

Paragraph 4450.40 *When the reporting organization has significant influence in another not-for-profit organization, the following should be disclosed:*

(a) a description of the relationship with the significantly influenced organization;

(b) a clear and concise description of the significantly influenced organization's purpose, its intended community of service, its status under income tax legislation and its legal form; and

(c) the nature and extent of any economic interest that the reporting organization has in the significantly influenced organization. (April, 1997)

14-164.   The fact that the equity method is not required here once again reflects the fact that most not-for-profit organizations do not have a transferable ownership interest.

Significantly Influenced Profit Oriented Enterprises

14-165.   Not surprisingly, the Section 4450 Recommendation here requires the use of the equity method:

Paragraph 4450.43 *When the reporting organization has significant influence over a profit oriented enterprise, the investment should be accounted for using the equity method in accordance with "Long Term Investments", Section 3050. (April, 1997)*

Disclosure Of Economic Interest

14-166.   When a not-for-profit organization has an economic interest in a related entity, the following disclosure is required:

Paragraph 4450.45 *When an organization has an economic interest in another not-for-profit organization over which it does not have control or significant influence, the nature and extent of this interest should be disclosed. (April, 1997)*

Information At Different Dates

14-167.   When the financial statements of the not-for-profit organization and the related entity are not based on the same period, the following disclosure is required:

Paragraph 4450.47 *When the fiscal periods of the reporting organization and the other entity do not substantially coincide, the financial information required to be disclosed in accordance with paragraph 4450.22, .32 or .38 should be as at the other entity's most recent reporting date and the following should be disclosed:*

(a) the reporting period covered by the financial information; and

(b) the details of any events or transactions in the intervening period that are significant to the reporting organization's financial position or results of operations. (April, 1997)

Disclosure Of Related Party Transactions By Not-For-Profit Organizations Handbook Section 4460

Purpose

14-168.   This Section is concerned with the disclosure of related party transactions in the financial statements of not-for-profit organizations. It is analogous to Section 3840 which deals with the related party transactions of profit oriented enterprises. As is the case with Section 3840, this Section does not apply to management compensation arrangements, expense allowances, or other payments to individuals in the normal course of operations.

Definitions

14-169.   Section 4460 contains definitions for not-for-profit organizations, control, joint control, significant influence, and economic interest, that are identical to those found in Section 4450, "Reporting Controlled And Related Entities By Not-For-Profit Organizations". It also contains the same definition of fair value as is found in Section 4430, "Capital Assets Held By Not-For-Profit Organizations". These definitions will not be repeated here. New definitions in this Section are as follows:

> **Related parties** exist when one party has the ability to exercise, directly or indirectly, control, joint control or significant influence over the other. Two or more parties are related when they are subject to common control, joint control or common significant influence. Two not-for-profit organizations are related parties if one has an economic interest in the other. Related parties also include management and immediate family members.

> A **related party transaction** is a transfer of economic resources or obligations between related parties, or the provision of services by one party to a related party, regardless of whether any consideration is exchanged. The parties to the transaction are related prior to the transaction. When the relationship arises as a result of the transaction, the transaction is not one between related parties.

Identification Of Related Parties

14-170.   The Section provides guidance with respect to the identification of related parties. It is expressed in terms of commonly encountered related parties:

Paragraph 4460.04   The most commonly encountered related parties of a reporting organization include the following:

(a) an entity that directly, or indirectly through one or more intermediaries, controls, or is controlled by, or is under common control with, the reporting organization;

(b) an individual who directly, or indirectly through one or more intermediaries, controls the reporting organization;

(c) an entity that, directly or indirectly, is significantly influenced by the reporting organization or has significant influence over the reporting organization or is under common significant influence with the reporting organization;

(d) the other organization when one organization has an economic interest in the other;

(e) management: any person(s) having authority and responsibility for planning, directing and controlling the activities of the reporting organization. (Management would include the directors, officers and other persons fulfilling a senior management function.)

(f) an individual that has either significant influence or joint control over the reporting organization;

(g) members of the immediate family of individuals described in paragraphs (b), (e) and (f). (Immediate family comprises an individual's spouse and those dependent on either the individual or the individual's spouse.);

(h) the other party, when a management contract or other management authority exists and the reporting organization is either the managing or managed party; and

(i) any party that is subject to joint control by the reporting organization (In this instance a party subject to joint control is related to each of the venturers that share that joint control. However, the venturers themselves are not related to one another solely by virtue of sharing of joint control.).

Disclosure
General Recommendation
14-171.   Section 4460 makes the following Recommendation with respect to the disclosure of related party transactions:

> **Paragraph 4460.07** *An organization should disclose the following information about its transactions with related parties:*
>
> *(a) a description of the relationship between the transacting parties;*
>
> *(b) a description of the transaction(s), including those for which no amount has been recorded;*
>
> *(c) the recorded amount of the transactions classified by financial statement category;*
>
> *(d) the measurement basis used for recognizing the transaction in the financial statements;*
>
> *(e) amounts due to or from related parties and the terms and conditions relating thereto;*
>
> *(f) contractual obligations with related parties, separate from other contractual obligations;*
>
> *(g) contingencies involving related parties, separate from other contingencies.* (April, 1997)

Description Of The Relationship
14-172.   The Section encourages the use of accurate terminology when complying with Paragraph 4460.07(a). Terms such as controlled organization, significantly influenced organization, or organization under common control, are preferable to more general descriptions such as affiliate or associate. Disclosure here should include a description of

the manner in which control or influence is exercised.

Description Of Transactions

14-173.   A description of all transactions, including information about the nature of any items exchanged, is required by Paragraph 4460.07(b). As noted in that Paragraph, this would include transactions, for example an exchange of management services, for which no amounts are recorded in the accounting records.

Amounts And Measurement

14-174.   As with Section 3840 for profit oriented enterprises, Section 4460 requires not-for-profit organizations to disclose the aggregate amount of related party transactions, along with the measurement basis used in recording them. This is particularly important here because, unlike Section 3840, Section 4460 does not include Recommendations with respect to how such related party transactions should be measured.

Other Disclosure Considerations

14-175.   Section 4460 makes the following additional points with respect to the disclosure of the related party transactions of not-for-profit organizations:

- When there are amounts due to and from related parties, disclosure includes the relationship between the parties, as well as the nature of the transactions which created the balances.

- When transactions occur between two organizations which will be consolidated, the transactions will be completely eliminated from the financial statements. This means that no disclosure of such transactions will be required. However, when the equity method is used to account for a related party, any profit or loss on the transaction will be eliminated but the other components of the transaction will remain in the records of the related organizations. Therefore, disclosure will be required in this type of situation.

- In disclosing a not-for-profit organization's contractual obligations and contingencies, Section 3280, "Contractual Obligation", and Section 3290, "Contingencies", would be applicable. Separate disclosure is required for the contractual obligations and contingencies of related parties.

Additional Readings

CICA Research Study - *Financial Reporting For Non-Profit Organizations*, 1980.

CA Magazine Article - "Bringing Nonprofit Organizations Into The *CICA Handbook*", Peter D. Walker, June, 1988.

CA Magazine Article - "New Concepts For Nonprofits", Philip Cowperthwaite, February, 1991.

CA Magazine Article - "Costs and the Collective Good", Thomas H. Beechy and Brenda J. Zimmerman, November, 1992.

CA Magazine Article - "Not-For-Profits: The Sequel", Kerry Danyluk, March, 1994.

CA Magazine Article - "Finding The Right Fit", John C. Macintosh, March, 1995.

CA Magazine Article - "Not-For-Profits: The Conclusion", Kerry Danyluk, March, 1996.

CA Magazine Article - "Putting Not-For-Profit Standards Into Practice", Kerry Danyluk and Kiana Hillier, May, 1997.

CA Magazine Article - "Tracking Contributions", Kerry Danyluk, May, 1998.

FASB Statement Of Financial Accounting Standards No. 116 *Accounting For Contributions received And Contributions Made*, June, 1993.

FASB Statement Of Financial Accounting Standards No. 117 *Financial Statement Of Not-For-Profit Organizations*, June, 1993.

FASB Statement Of Financial Accounting Standards No. 124 *Accounting For Certain Investments Held By Not-For-Profit Organizations*, November, 1995.

Journal Of Accountancy Article *"Understanding And Implementing FASB 124"*, March, 1996.

Supplement To Chapter Fourteen
Example of Fund Accounting
With Encumbrances

Basic Data

14-176. It would be easy to construct a very elaborate example of fund accounting. If we established a complete array of funds for a large nonbusiness organization and, in addition, established a complete set of procedures for recording entries in the various funds, we would have an example that could run for as much as 100 pages. We do not believe that this is needed as it would force you through a process of learning an elaborate system that will not be completely applicable to any existing organization. As an alternative, a relatively simple example will be presented. This example will involve accounting for the general fund of a municipality over a single accounting period and will illustrate most of the basic procedures involved in accounting for this type of fund.

14-177. We will be dealing with the municipality of Hartbourne for the year ending December 31, 1998. The beginning Balance Sheet for the municipality as at January 1, 1998 is as follows:

Municipality Of Hartbourne
Balance Sheet For The General Fund
As At January 1, 1998

Assets

Cash		$125,000
Delinquent Taxes Receivable	$220,000	
Less: Estimated Uncollectible Taxes	10,000	210,000
Inventories Of Supplies		250,000
Total		$585,000

Liabilities, Reserves, And Fund Balance

Current Liabilities	$150,000
Reserve For Inventory Of Supplies	250,000
Fund Balance	185,000
Total	$585,000

Other Information:

1. The annual budget calls for estimated total revenues of $12,000,000, made up of $8,000,000 in property taxes and $4,000,000 in grants from other levels of government. Appropriations total $11,600,000.

2. Uncollectible taxes are estimated to be 0.2 percent of total taxes receivable. In addition, the Municipality borrows $5,000,000 in anticipation of tax collections. This amount is repaid as the taxes are collected.

3. Revenue collections consist of $4,000,000 in grants, $165,000 in opening Delinquent Taxes Receivable, $7,750,000 of current Taxes Receivable and $40,000 on the disposal of property sold to recover Delinquent Taxes Receivable of $55,000.

4. Commitments for expenditures equal $7,000,000.

5. Supplies purchased during the year totalled $950,000.

6. Actual expenditures for the year totalled $11,525,000 of which $3,400,000 was

for goods and services, $925,000 was for Inventory Of Supplies used and paid for, $6,950,000 was used to discharge commitments for expenditures and $250,000 was for payments on long term debt.

14-178.   With respect to the opening Balance Sheet, most of the accounts are readily recognizable to the user of profit oriented accounting. Cash, Taxes Receivable, Supplies, and Current Liabilities are very familiar. The Reserve For Inventory Of Supplies is analogous to a retained earnings reserve in that it is designed to indicate that this amount of the Fund Balance is not available for use in next year's appropriations. The Fund Balance could also be titled accumulated surplus or deficit and represents exactly that. It is analogous to owners' equity in profit oriented accounting, except that for a government general fund there would be no contributed capital.

Journal Entries Required

Recording The Budget Estimates

14-179.   The first step in accounting for the general fund would be to establish the 1998 budget. As most municipal revenues are derived from property taxes, assessment values would have to be established for each class of property in the city. Appropriate rates would be applied to arrive at an estimate of total taxes for the period. As indicated in the Other Information, assume that this process results in a total of $8,000,000 in estimated taxes receivable. In addition, the municipality expects to receive a total of $4,000,000 in grants from the federal and provincial levels of government. Based on these expectations, the municipality budgets total expenditures of $11,600,000, leaving a contingency balance of $400,000. This information would be recorded as follows:

Estimated Revenues	$12,000,000	
Appropriations		$11,600,000
Fund Balance		400,000

Recording Taxes And Grants Receivable

14-180.   Entries could then be made to record the receivables related to both estimated taxes and estimated grants from other levels of government. In making these entries it would be the usual practice to make an allowance for uncollectible taxes. Using the estimated uncollectible rate of 0.2 percent, the entry would be as follows:

Taxes Receivable	$8,000,000	
Grants Receivable	4,000,000	
Estimated Uncollectible Taxes		$ 16,000
Revenues		11,984,000

Borrowing In Anticipation Of Taxes

14-181.   It is fairly common for municipalities to borrow in anticipation of tax receipts. If we assume that Hartbourne borrows $5,000,000 on this basis, the entry would be as follows:

Cash	$5,000,000	
Notes Payable		$5,000,000

Collection Of Taxes And Grants

14-182.   During 1998, entries would be made to collect taxes and grants that are receivable. The Other Information indicates that the municipality collects all of the expected grants, $165,000 of the delinquent taxes that were receivable at the beginning of the year, and $7,750,000 of the current year's accrued taxes. This would require the following journal entry:

Cash	$11,915,000	
Delinquent Taxes Receivable		$ 165,000
Taxes Receivable		7,750,000
Grants Receivable		4,000,000

Other Tax Related Entries

14-183.   Several other entries would be required related to Taxes Receivable over the year. These entries would be as follows:

Notes Payable	$5,000,000	
Cash		$5,000,000

(To pay the $5,000,000 in tax anticipation notes.)

Tax Liens Receivable	$55,000	
Delinquent Taxes Receivable		$55,000

(To convert the remaining January 1 Delinquent Taxes Receivable to liens on the related properties.)

Delinquent Taxes Receivable	$250,000	
Taxes Receivable		$250,000

(To transfer the remaining 1998 Taxes Receivable to the Delinquent Taxes Receivable account.)

Recoveries Of Delinquent Taxes

14-184.   In most situations, some additional actions would take place to recover the remaining $55,000 in delinquent taxes receivable. As recorded in the preceding Paragraph, this would usually involve placing a lien on the taxable property and ultimately selling the property to recover the required amounts. Any excess of the sale proceeds over taxes and penalties due would be returned to the taxpayer and any deficiency would then be written off as uncollectible. The Other Information indicated that the property on which the tax liens were recorded in Paragraph 14-183 is sold for $40,000. The journal entry would be as follows:

Cash	$40,000	
Estimated Uncollectible Taxes	15,000	
Tax Liens Receivable		$55,000

Encumbrances

14-185.   An additional peculiarity of government accounting is the recording of commitments to make expenditures. This reflects the importance of the budget and control process in government accounting. The entry serves to indicate that commitments have been made which use up some part of the appropriations budget. By doing so, the municipality is forced to limit its commitments to the amounts appropriated in the budget and will be able to identify potential excess expenditures. In this case, recording the $7,000,000 in Encumbrances indicated in the Other Information requires the following journal entry:

Encumbrances	$7,000,000	
Reserve For Encumbrances		$7,000,000

Recording Expenditures

14-186.   Government organizations accrue expenditures which reflect the cost of goods and services acquired during the period. In some cases, such as Inventory Of Supplies in our example, an attempt is made to segregate the costs of assets acquired from those used up during the period and, thereby, provide a more conventional measure of expense. However, in other cases, all goods and services acquired are charged to the current year's operating report. In this example we have assumed that Hartbourne acquired goods and services during the year totalling $11,300,000. Of this amount, $950,000 was for supplies, $3,400,000 for goods and services and $6,950,000 for the discharge of expenditure commitments. The appropriate entry would be as follows:

Expenditures	$10,350,000	
Inventory Of Supplies	950,000	
Current Liabilities		$11,300,000

Removing Encumbrances

14-187.   Once an expenditure has been made under a commitment, there is no longer any need to retain the related Encumbrance and Reserve For Encumbrances balances. The Other Information indicated that the Expenditures in Paragraph 14-186 included payment on $6,950,000 of the encumbrances recorded in Paragraph 14-185. This would require the following entry:

Reserve For Encumbrances	$6,950,000	
Encumbrances		$6,950,000

Other Expenditure Related Entries

14-188.   Several additional expenditure related entries would be required. They are as follows:

Current Liabilities	$11,275,000	
Cash		$11,275,000

(To record payments of Current Liabilities. Of the purchases of Supplies, $25,000 was on account.)

Fund Balance	$25,000	
Reserve For Inventory Of Supplies		$25,000

(To increase Reserve For Inventory Of Supplies to the new required balance of $275,000.)

Expenditures	$925,000	
Inventory Of Supplies		$925,000

(To record supplies used during 1998.)

Transfers To And From Other Funds

14-189.   In more realistic situations, there would be a large number of transfers between the general fund and other funds established by the governmental organization. In this example we assume only one such transfer, a $250,000 transfer to the debt service fund for payments on the long term debt of the municipality. The required entry for the general fund would be as follows:

Expenditures	$250,000	
Cash		$250,000

14-190.   This entry assumes that this amount was not included in encumbrances recorded in Paragraph 14-185. In addition, you should note that a corresponding entry will be required in the debt fund accounts.

Financial Statements

14-191.   Three statements would normally be prepared for the general fund. These would be a Statement Of Revenues And Expenditures, an Analysis Of Changes In The Fund Balance Account, and a Balance Sheet. These Statements are as follows:

Municipality Of Hartbourne
Statement Of Revenues And Expenditures For The General Fund
Year Ending December 31, 1998

	Budget	Actual
Revenues	$12,000,000	$11,984,000
Expenditures And Encumbrances	11,600,000	11,575,000
Excess Of Revenues Over Expenditures And Encumbrances	$ 400,000	$ 409,000

14-192.   The Expenditures And Encumbrances consists of the actual expenditures of $11,525,000 plus the $50,000 excess of encumbrances over the expenditures to discharge the encumbrances. Note that the final figure in this Statement is not labeled as income. It simply discloses the fact that revenues exceeded expenditures and encumbrances for the period.

Municipality Of Hartbourne
Analysis Of Changes In The Fund Balance Account
Year Ending December 31, 1998

Opening Balance in The Fund	$185,000
Excess of Revenues Over Expenditures And Encumbrances For The Year	409,000
Increase in Reserve For Inventory Of Supplies	(25,000)
Closing Balance In The Fund	$569,000

Municipality Of Hartbourne
Balance Sheet For The General Fund
As At December 31, 1998

Assets

Cash		$ 555,000
Delinquent Taxes Receivable	$250,000	
Less: Estimated Uncollectible Taxes	11,000	239,000
Inventories Of Supplies		275,000
Total		$1,069,000

Liabilities, Reserves, And Fund Balance

Current Liabilities	$ 175,000
Reserve For Inventory Of Supplies	275,000
Reserve For Encumbrances	50,000
Fund Balance	569,000
Total	$1,069,000

Closing Entries

14-193.   The following entries would be required subsequent to the preparation of financial statements for the year:

Revenues	$11,984,000	
Fund Balance	16,000	
Estimated Revenues		$12,000,000
Appropriations	$11,600,000	
Expenditures		$11,525,000
Encumbrances		50,000
Fund Balance		25,000

14-194.   This completes our example. While the amount of detail has been greatly condensed, the basic procedures involved in accounting for funds have been illustrated. In this example involving the general fund of a government organization, we have also illustrated some of the idiosyncrasies associated with this type of nonbusiness entity. Such things as recording budget data and encumbrances are somewhat foreign to the accounting procedures used by business organizations. You should also note that we have shown only general ledger entries and, clearly, a substantial amount of subsidiary ledger data would have to be maintained by the government organization. However, such government subsidiary ledgers would be maintained in exactly the same manner as those of business organizations and, as a consequence, there would seem to be little point in dealing with them here.

Assignment Problems

(The solutions to these problem are only available in
the solutions manual that has been provided to your instructor.)

ASSIGNMENT PROBLEM FOURTEEN - 1

The Bookkeepers' Rehabilitation Fund is a registered Canadian charity, organized to provide rehabilitation for those Chartered Bookkeepers (CB's, hereafter) that have found so much stress in their daily work that they have been driven to various acts of depravity. The fund maintains several residences where such individuals are provided with a comprehensive program of physical and mental therapy. The program is carefully designed to restore them to their former status as esteemed professionals. The work of the fund is supported by a combination of user fees, support from various community organizations, and an annual fund raising dinner.

The accounting system of this organization is based on three funds. These are an Operating Fund, a Capital Fund, and a Capital Asset Fund. The Operating Fund uses an encumbrance system and budgetary accounts to monitor expenditures and control revenues. Revenues and expenditures are accrued in this fund and, at the end of each year, outstanding encumbrances are charged to operations. While the Capital Fund accrues expenditures, this policy is not followed for revenues.

The Capital Asset Fund is designed to include assets purchased from both the Capital Fund and the Operating Fund. However, in the accounts of this Fund, no distinction is made with respect to the source of financing for particular assets.

On January 1 of the current year, the Balance Sheets of the three Funds are as follows:

Operating Fund

Assets

Cash	$290,000
Temporary Investments	605,000
Interest Receivable	28,000
Fees Receivable	47,000
Total	$970,000

Equities

Accounts Payable	$205,000
Wages Payable	155,000
Estimated Commitments	315,000
Unrestricted Balance	295,000
Total	$970,000

Capital Asset Fund

Assets

Furniture and Fixtures	$4,150,000
Buildings	3,110,000
Accumulated Depreciation	(2,585,000)
Total	$4,675,000

Equities

Fund Balance	$4,675,000
Total	$4,675,000

Capital Fund

Assets

Cash	$ 28,000
Term Deposits	895,000
Total	$923,000

Equities

Fund Balance	$923,000
Total	$923,000

For the current year ending on December 31, the Board Of Directors of the Fund approved the following budget for the Operating Fund:

Estimated Revenues

Fees For Services	$ 3,150,000
Community Organization Grants	10,925,000
Fund Raising Dinner (Net Amount)	2,375,000
Total Estimated Revenues	$16,450,000

Estimated Expenditures

Salaries And Wages	$11,360,000
Materials And Supplies	1,975,000
Miscellaneous Administrative	2,620,000
Budgeted Surplus	495,000
Total Estimated Expenditures And Surplus	$16,450,000

Other Information:

1. During the year, the Fund billed user fees totalling $3,395,000. Collections for the year were $3,102,000 while, at the end of the year, $172,000 in billed fees were judged to be uncollectable.

2. During the year, community organizations pledged total contributions of $11,215,000. At the end of the current year, $275,000 of this amount had not been received.

3. The annual fund raising dinner is scheduled for December 1. A separate Dinner Fund is established to account for this event and, on November 1, $875,000 was advanced from the Operating Fund to set up this special Fund. The event was a success, generating total revenues of $3,425,000 and incurring total costs of $1,015,000. All revenues had been collected at the event but there were $130,000 in costs which had not been paid. The Dinner Fund repaid the original $875,000 advanced from the Operating Fund and, in addition, disbursed $2,395,000 as a loan to the Operating Fund.

4. During the year, salaries and wages of $11,422,000 were paid. At the end of the current year, accrued salaries and wages amounted to $217,000.

5. During the year, Operating Fund purchase orders for goods and services totalled $4,133,000. During this same period, invoices were received for $4,427,000. Of these invoices, a total of $345,000 was related to purchase orders issued in the preceding year and reflected in the Operating Fund Balance Sheet as Estimated

Commitments of $315,000. The remaining $4,082,000 was for costs that had been originally estimated at $3,926,000.

6. Operating Fund Accounts Payable of $4,425,000 were paid during the year.

7. The Temporary Investments in the Operating Fund were sold during the year for $617,000. Also during the year, the Operating Fund collected interest of $63,000, including the $28,000 accrual in the January 1 Balance Sheet.

8. Under a special grants program, the Federal Government has agreed to provide $5,000,000 towards the acquisition of an existing building. The building is to be converted into a large new residence to accommodate the increasing numbers of CBs requiring the help of the Fund. The first $2,000,000 of this grant was received during the current year. The Bookkeepers' Rehabilitation Fund incurred costs of $205,000 in anticipation of acquiring the new building. A total of $15,000 of these costs were unpaid at year end. Of the remaining cash, $1,750,000 was invested in term deposits. Both the principal and interest of all term deposits were rolled over every thirty days, with the total balance rising to $2,765,000 on December 31 of the current year.

9. Depreciation Expense on the capital assets amounts to $890,000 for the year.

Required: Provide journal entries to record all of the preceding information. In addition, provide a Statement Of Operations and a Balance Sheet for each of the funds, including the temporary Dinner Fund.

ASSIGNMENT PROBLEM FOURTEEN - 2

The United Agency is a registered Canadian charity, organized to raise funds for a number of social service agencies in the City Of Barren. The Fund itself raises money through user fees, a variety of government grants, and through an annual fund raising drive. In addition to contributing to other social service agencies, the United Agency owns and maintains a number of mission operations which provide food and lodging at minimal rates to those in need. While recognizing that a high proportion of such amounts will not be collectable, users who cannot currently pay for the mission services are billed for all food and lodging received.

The accounting system of this Agency is based on three funds. These are an Operating Fund, a Capital Fund, and a Capital Asset Fund. The Operating Fund uses an encumbrance system and budgetary accounts to monitor expenditures and control revenues. Revenues and expenditures are accrued in this fund and, at the end of each year, outstanding encumbrances are charged to operations. While the Capital Fund accrues expenditures, this policy is not followed for revenues.

The Capital Asset Fund is designed to include assets purchased from both the Capital Fund and the Operating Fund. However, in the accounts of this Fund, no distinction is made with respect to the sources of financing for particular assets.

On January 1, 1998, the Balance Sheets of the three Funds are as follows:

Operating Fund

Cash	$100,900
Temporary Investments	332,200
Interest Receivable	24,100
Fees Receivable	24,100
Total Assets	**$481,300**

Accounts Payable	$107,400
Wages Payable	83,500
Estimated Commitments	147,200
Unrestricted Balance	43,200
Total Equities	**$481,300**

Capital Asset Fund

Furniture/Fixtures	$2,094,700
Buildings	1,482,300
Accumulated Depreciation	(1,226,300)
Total Assets	**$2,350,700**

Fund Balance	$2,350,700
Total Equities	**$2,350,700**

Capital Fund

Cash	$ 15,300
Term Deposits	447,300
Total Assets	**$462,600**

Fund Balance	$462,600
Total Equities	**$462,600**

For the year ending December 31, 1998, the Board Of Directors of the Fund approved the following budget for the Operating Fund:

Estimated Revenues

Fees For Services	$1,572,400
Community Organization Grants	5,456,200
Fund Raising Drive (Net Amount)	1,167,200
Total Estimated Revenues	**$8,195,800**

Estimated Expenditures

Salaries And Wages	$5,672,300
Materials And Supplies	978,400
Miscellaneous Administrative	1,356,800
Budgeted Surplus	188,300
Total Estimated Expenditures And Surplus	**$8,195,800**

Other Information:

1. During the year, community organizations pledged total contributions of $5,726,000. At the end of 1998, $346,000 of this amount had not been received.

2. During 1998, the Agency's missions billed user fees totalling $1,624,200. Collections for the year were $1,314,000 while, at the end of the year, $271,400 in billed fees were judged to be uncollectible.

3. During 1998, salaries and wages of $5,458,000 were paid. At the end of 1998, accrued salaries and wages amounted to $183,000.

4. The annual fund raising drive was held in December, 1998. A separate Annual Drive Fund is established to account for this activity and, on November 1, 1998, $445,000 was advanced from the Operating Fund to set up this special Fund. The event was a success, generating total revenues of $1,987,000 and incurring total costs of $516,000. All revenues had been collected from the drive but, at December 31, 1998, there were $63,500 in costs which had not been paid. The Annual Drive Fund repaid the original $445,000 advanced from the Operating Fund and, in addition, disbursed $1,378,000 as a loan to the Operating Fund.

5. During 1998, Operating Fund purchase orders for goods and services totalled $2,093,000. During this same period, invoices were received for $2,216,000. Of these invoices, a total of $152,000 was related to purchase orders issued in 1997 and reflected in the Operating Fund Balance Sheet as Estimated Commitments of $147,200. The remaining $2,064,000 was for costs that had been originally estimated at $1,994,000.

6. The Temporary Investments in the Operating Fund were sold during 1998 for $342,200. Also during 1998, the Operating Fund collected interest of $47,500, including the $24,100 accrual in the January 1, 1998 Balance Sheet.

7. Operating Fund Accounts Payable of $2,203,000 were paid during the year.

8. Under a special grants program, the Federal Government has agreed to provide $2,200,000 towards the acquisition of an existing building. The building is to be converted into a new mission to accommodate the increasing numbers of individuals coming to these facilities. The first $960,000 of this grant was received during 1998. The United Agency incurred costs of $103,000 in anticipation of acquiring the new building. A total of $12,000 of these costs were unpaid at year end. Of the remaining cash, $793,000 was invested in term deposits. Both the principal and interest of all term deposits were rolled over every thirty days, with the total balance rising to $1,310,000 on December 31, 1998.

9. For the year ending December 31, 1998, Depreciation Expense on the capital assets amounts to $437,000.

Required: Provide journal entries to record all of the preceding information. In addition, provide a Statement Of Operations and a Balance Sheet for each of the funds, including the temporary Annual Drive Fund.

ASSIGNMENT PROBLEM FOURTEEN - 3

On January 1, 1997, the Winter Sports Society (WSS) is organized as a not-for-profit organization. Its purpose is to serve the needs of its local community in two areas:

- Encouraging children to learn ice skating outside of the arena environment.

- The provision of cross country ski equipment to needy senior citizens.

The organization will have a December 31 year end.

Initial funding is provided by a wealthy individual who makes an endowment contribution of $87,000. These funds are invested in debt securities. There are no restrictions on the income that is produced by these investments. During the year ending December 31, 1997, such income amounted to $4,370.

The organization solicits and receives unrestricted contributions. Such contributions are allocated to both skating promotion and ski equipment provision by the organization's Board Of Directors. During the year ending December 31, 1997, $726,000 in contributions were received. At year end, an additional $56,000 in contributions were receivable. The Board believes that this is a reasonable estimate of the amount that will actually be collected. This total was allocated $410,000 to skating activity and $372,000 to skiing activity. All of the receivables are allocated to skating activity.

The organization accepts additional contributions that are restricted to use in the provision of ski equipment to needy senior citizens. These funds are segregated and a separate report is made to contributors on their usage. During the year ending December 31, 1997, restricted contributions of $242,000 were received. No restricted contributions are receivable at year end. All of these restricted contributions are deposited in a separate bank account.

The organization operates out of fully furnished office space that is rented for $2,000 per month. The use of the space is split equally between skating and skiing activities of the organization.

During the year ending December 31, 1997, the organization incurred the following expenses:

	Skating Activity	Skiing Activity
Wages And Salaries	$ 173,000	$ 71,000
Cost Of Materials Provided	32,000	274,000
Transportation Costs	41,000	33,000
Rent	12,000	12,000
Other Expenses	27,000	31,000
Total	$285,000	$421,000

A total of 50 percent ($210,500) of the expenses related to skiing activity have been paid for out of the restricted contributions bank account.

On December 31, 1997, there were outstanding Accounts Payable related to the skating activity expenses of $30,000.

Required: Prepare a Statement Of Operations And Funds Balances, a Statement Of Financial Position, and a Statement Of Cash Flows under each of the following assumptions:

A. WSS does not use fund accounting.

B. WSS uses fund accounting with funds established for endowment contributions and restricted skiing contributions, in addition to a general fund.

C. WSS uses fund accounting with funds established for skating activities and skiing activities in addition to a general fund. Endowment contributions are dealt with through the general fund.

Your solution should comply with the Recommendations of Sections 4400 and 4410 of the *CICA Handbook*.

ASSIGNMENT PROBLEM FOURTEEN - 4

This is an extension of Assignment Problem 14-3. It involves the same Winter Sports Society (WSS) and extends their activities into the year ending December 31, 1998. It is made more complex by the addition of capital assets and their amortization.

There are no additional endowment contributions during the year ending December 31, 1998. The endowment fund investments have income of $4,820 during this period.

During the year ending December 31, 1998, $842,300 in unrestricted contributions were received. At year end, there is an additional $53,250 in contributions that are receivable. The Board believes that this is a reasonable estimate of the amount that will actually be collected. This total was allocated $510,050 to skating activity, $243,500 to skiing activity, and $142,000 for the acquisition of a building to be used in the organization's operations. All of the receivables are allocated to the skating activity.

On July 1, 1998, the organization acquires a building for a total cost of $142,000. Of this total, $37,000 represents the fair value of the land on which the building is situated and the remaining $105,000 reflects the fair value of the building. The estimated useful life of the building is 20 years and no significant residual value is anticipated. The organization uses straight line amortization, charging only one-half year's amortization in the year in which an asset is acquired.

The organization continues to accept additional contributions that are restricted to use in the skiing activity. As in the past, these funds are placed in a separate bank account. During the year ending December 31, 1998, restricted contributions of $317,600 were received. No contributions are receivable at year end.

During the year ending December 31, 1998, the organization incurred the following expenses:

	Skating Activity	Skiing Activity
Wages And Salaries	$345,600	$ 32,400
Cost Of Materials Provided	48,200	362,300
Transportation Costs	19,400	21,600
Rent	6,000	6,000
Other Expenses	23,300	45,900
Total	$442,500	$468,200

The records show that 56 percent of the expenses related to skiing activity were made from restricted funds.

On December 31, 1998, there were outstanding Accounts Payable related to the skating activities expenses of $32,430.

Required: Prepare a Statement Of Operations And Funds Balances, a Statement Of Financial Position, and a Statement Of Cash Flows under each of the following assumptions:

A. WSS does not use fund accounting.

B. WSS uses fund accounting with funds established for endowment contributions and restricted skiing contributions, in addition to a general fund.

C. WSS uses fund accounting with funds established for skating activities and skiing activities in addition to a general fund. Endowment contributions are dealt with through the general fund.

Your solution should comply with the Recommendations of Sections 4400 to 4460 of the *CICA Handbook*.

ASSIGNMENT CASE FOURTEEN - 1

On August 15, 1995, the European Exchange Club (EEC) was formed in an effort to create a united social group out of several separate regional clubs in the vicinity of the city of Decker, located in central Canada. The purpose of the group is to combine resources to meet the recreational, cultural, and social needs of their collective members. EEC was formed through the collaboration of the following clubs and their memberships:

	Members
The Canadian Russian Society	12,300
The Italian Clubs of Canada	10,800
Portuguese Cultural Foundation	4,100
Association Of Greeks Of The World	2,700
The German Groups	1,100
Other	1,700
Total	32,700

It is now December 1999. EEC's executives have spent the past few years planning and preparing for its operation. The club's community centre is expected to be fully completed next year. The facilities of the club will include the following:

- a multi-purpose building to house banquets, meetings and arts activities
- hiking trails
- indoor/outdoor tennis facilities
- bicycle trails
- baseball diamonds
- an indoor/outdoor pool
- a soccer field

The multi-purpose building is 75 percent complete, and EEC's executives have stated that it is "approximately within budget." Estimated building costs were outlined in a 1995 feasibility study, as follows:

Construction Cost	$2,300,000
Site Preparation Costs	400,000
Furniture And Fixtures	550,000
Consulting Fees	120,000
Miscellaneous	80,000
Total	$3,450,000

The four acres of land on which the facility is built were provided by the provincial government by way of a five-year lease at $1 a year. The adjacent land of 60 acres was contributed to the club by The Italian Clubs of Canada. Previously, this land had been leased to a farmer for $54,000 a year. The 64 acres will be used for the following projects, which will incur the additional costs listed below:

Hiking Trails	$ 595,000
Baseball Diamonds	30,000
Soccer Field	22,000
Bicycle Trails	95,000
Indoor/Outdoor Pool	700,000
Indoor/Outdoor Tennis Facilities	300,000
Total	$1,742,000

In addition to these development costs, the club faces annual operating costs of approximately $740,000, outlined in Exhibit I. John Mendez-Smith, the newly elected president of the club, has approached your firm, Young and Kerr Chartered Accountants, to prepare a report that provides recommendations on accounting, finance, and internal control issues. He has also asked you to identify the merits of an audit and potential problems that may exist. Mr. Mendez-Smith had been informed by another CA firm that audit opinions for non-profit organizations are normally qualified and have little or no usefulness. You took the notes appearing in Exhibit II at a meeting with the club's president and executive committee.

Required: Prepare the report.

(CICA Adapted)

Exhibit I
European Exchange Club
Yearly Budget

Operating Revenues	
Membership Fees	$ 91,000
Social Rentals	185,000
Meeting Rentals	50,000
Sport Rentals	23,000
Concessions	61,000
Fundraising Events	225,000
Total Operating Revenues	$635,000
Operating Costs	
Salaries	$363,000
Administrative Costs	39,000
Maintenance	126,000
Utilities	112,000
Educational Scholarships	100,000
Total Operating Costs	$740,000

Exhibit II
Notes Taken From Your Meeting With
Mr. Mendez-Smith And The Executive Committee

1. Under the lease agreement with the Province, EEC is responsible for maintenance and all costs of improvements. The lease agreement provides for 20 renewal terms of five years' duration each. Renewal is based on the condition that EEC makes the club's services available to all present and future EEC member-clubs and their membership.

2. EEC has requested an operating grant from the provincial government. Its proposal requests the Province to provide EEC with annual funds to cover 50% of "approved" operating costs incurred to provide services to all club members.

   The City of Decker wishes to construct an arena and a swimming pool and has opposed the proposed operating grant. The City has asked to be the first in line for available provincial funds. The Province has informed EEC that if funds are granted, EEC will have to supply audited financial statements of the organization for all future fiscal year ends.

   The committee members suspect that they will have to compromise on their proposal and are having problems determining the minimum annual funds required by the club from the Province.

3. The Russian and Italian clubs have been arguing with other clubs over the equalization payments required from each club. Currently, each club makes payments to EEC based upon their proportionate membership. Payments for each calendar year are made on February 1 of the following year.

   The Russian group performs the administrative functions of EEC and has charged, and will continue to charge, the club only 50% of the market value of these services.

4. The accounting function is a major concern of the member-club representatives. In particular, they have raised the following issues:

   a) Several fund raising events are organized by individual member clubs.

   b) Any donations to EEC are received through the member clubs.

   c) No accounting has been made of services donated to EEC by the members of the individual clubs.

   d) EEC has approached a bank to assist in future phases of the club's development. The bank has informed EEC that it is interested in asset values and EEC's ability to repay the loans.

Chapter 15

Financial Instruments

What's The Problem?

Background

15-1.   Deregulation of financial institutions in the United States, volatility in foreign exchange and interest rates, changes in relevant tax laws, and the increased international mobility of capital have resulted in the development of a large number of new and increasingly complex financial instruments. Bunny Bonds, Junk Bonds, Flip-Flop Notes, Zero Coupon Bonds, Securitized Receivables, Collateralized Mortgage Obligations, Options, Interest Rate Swaps, Futures Contracts, and Forward Rate Agreements represent only a small sample of the diverse array of financial instruments that are in use today. These instruments have clouded the once relatively distinct lines between financial and non financial activities. Further, these instruments have been developed at a rate which has significantly exceeded the accounting profession's ability to develop appropriate accounting recommendations. As a consequence, some financial instruments have been favoured because of their accounting implications.

FASB Financial Instruments Project

15-2.   In the United States, the Financial Accounting Standards Board responded in 1986 by initiating a major project on financial instruments and off balance sheet financing. This project is divided into three main components which can be described as follows:

Disclosure   This first phase of the project is concerned with disclosures for all financial instruments, including both on and off the balance sheet items. It deals with the disclosure of credit risks, cash flows, interest rates and market values for each class of financial instruments.

Recognition And Measurement   In this phase of the project, the FASB will address issues such as removing an asset or liability from the balance sheet, distinguishing between a sale and a financing transaction, accounting for transfers of risk, and measuring transactions at cost and market values.

Distinguishing Between Debt And Equity   This phase is concerned with the classification and accounting for securities which have characteristics of both debt and equity.

15-3.   As of May, 1998, the FASB has issued the following pronouncements as a result of this project.

- Statement Of Financial Accounting Standards No. 105, *Disclosure Of Information About Financial Instruments With Off Balance Sheet Risk And Financial Instruments With Concentrations Of Credit Risk.*
- Statement Of Financial Accounting Standards No. 107, *Disclosures About Fair Value Of Financial Instruments.*
- Statement Of Financial Accounting Standards No. 119, *Disclosure About Derivative Financial Instruments And Fair Value Of Financial Instruments.*
- Statement Of Financial Accounting Standards No. 125, *Accounting for Transfers And Servicing Of Financial Assets and Extinguishments Of Liabilities.*

15-4.   In addition, they have issued an Exposure Draft on *Accounting For Derivative And Similar Financial Instruments And For Hedging Activities.*

CICA Response

15-5.   While the problems associated with financial instruments are probably less severe in Canada than they are in the United States, the CICA has felt a need to respond. This process began with the September, 1991 issuance of an Exposure Draft, *Financial Instruments.* This CICA Exposure Draft was prepared in a somewhat careless and hasty fashion and was subjected to heavy and well deserved criticism.   After reviewing the responses to this initial Exposure Draft, a Re-Exposure Draft was issued in April, 1994. This Re-Exposure Draft is a joint effort with the International Accounting Standards Committee and was intended to provide the basis for a new *CICA Handbook* Section.

15-6.   After the issuance of the Re-Exposure Draft, it became clear that it would be some time before the Accounting Standards Board would be able to reach appropriate conclusions on many of the measurement and recognition issues associated with financial instruments.   However, there was a feeling that improved reporting in this important area was such a crucial issue that some action on the part of the Board was essential.   As a consequence, in September, 1995, the Board released Section 3860, "Financial Instruments - Disclosure And Presentation", which implements a portion of the Recommendations contained in the April, 1994 Re-Exposure Draft.

Presentation Of The Materials

15-7.   We are left then, with a somewhat unusual situation.   The April, 1994 Re-Exposure Draft is still outstanding.   However, to the extent that its content deals with disclosure and presentation, it has been replaced by Section 3860 of the *CICA Handbook.* The Re-Exposure Draft content which deals with measurement and recognition issues remains outstanding and will be incorporated, either in its current or in a modified form, into *Handbook* Recommendations in the future.

15-8.   Given the circumstances, the remaining material in this Chapter will deal with the Re-Exposure Draft only to the extent that it is still relevant.   That is, with respect to those issues that are covered by the Recommendations of Section 3860 (disclosure and presentation), we will ignore the content of the Re-Exposure Draft. However, we will discuss the Recommendations of the Re-Exposure Draft in those areas that are not dealt with in Section 3860 (measurement and recognition).   This approach has the advantage of providing you with a single document which provides integrated coverage of both current and proposed *Handbook* Recommendations on financial instruments.

15-9.   A further point here relates to Section 3860's Recommendations with respect to the classification of redeemable preferred shares.   Such shares are widely used by private corporations as part of tax planning strategies, in particular those involving estate freezes. As the Section 3860 Recommendation that such shares be reclassified as debt generated major changes in the financial statements of issuing corporations, there was widespread criticism of these provisions. In response to these criticisms, the Accounting Standards Board has deferred the effective date of these provisions for private companies until the year 2000. It remains to be seen whether they will, in fact, be implemented at that point in time.

Purpose And Scope

CICA Handbook Section 3860

15-10.   The continuing process of innovation in domestic and international financial markets has created a need for sound general principles of accounting for financial instruments. Given this situation, the purpose of Section 3860 is to enhance financial statement users' understanding of the significance of recognized and unrecognized financial instruments to an entity's financial position, performance and cash flows.

15-11.   The presentation Recommendations in this Section deal with classification of financial instruments between liabilities and equity, the classification of related interest, dividends, losses, and gains, and the offsetting of assets and liabilities.

15-12.   The disclosure Recommendations of this Section deal with information about factors that affect the amount, timing and certainty of an entity's future cash flows relating to financial instruments. The Section also encourages disclosure about the nature and extent of an entity's use of financial instruments, the business purposes that they serve, the risks associated with them, and management's policies for controlling those risks.

15-13.   Section 3860 should be applied to presentation and disclosure issues associated with all types of financial instruments, except for the following:

(a) interests in subsidiaries, which are accounted for in accordance with "Subsidiaries", Section 1590;

b) interests in entities subject to significant influence, which are accounted for in accordance with "Long Term Investments", Section 3050;

(c) interests in joint ventures, which are accounted for in accordance with "Interests In Joint Ventures", Section 3055; and

(d) employers' obligations under employee stock option and stock purchase plans.

15-14.   It is also noted that other *Handbook* Sections may contain additional requirements that are more extensive or explicit for particular financial instruments. Examples of such Sections would be Section 3065, "Leases", and 4100, "Pension Plans".

15-15.   The purpose and scope section of the Re-Exposure Draft has essentially the same content as Section 3860, except for the fact that its coverage extends to measurement and recognition issues that are not within the scope of Section 3860.

What Is A Financial Instrument?

Basic Definitions

15-16.   The list of definitions contained in Section 3860 includes all of the definitions listed in the Re-Exposure Draft. As a consequence, the Re-Exposure Draft definitions are no longer relevant.

15-17.   Section 3860's definition of a financial instrument is as follows:

Paragraph 3860.05(a)   A **financial instrument** is any contract that gives rise to both a financial asset of one party and a financial liability or equity instrument of another party.

15-18.   Note that the definition of a financial instrument requires a reciprocal arrangement between two parties. To be a financial instrument, the contract must involve a financial asset for one party and either a financial liability or an equity instrument of a different party. There is, however, no requirement that the financial asset, financial liability, or equity item be recognized on the books of the reporting party. For example, a forward exchange contract is a financial instrument, despite the fact that it may not be recorded in the financial statements of the parties to the contract.

15-19.   Paragraph 3860.05 also defines specific types of financial instruments and the basic methods that will be used for their valuation:

Paragraph 3860.05(b)   A **financial asset** is any asset that is:

(i)   cash;
(ii) a contractual right to receive cash or another financial asset from another party;
(iii) a contractual right to exchange financial instruments with another party under conditions that are potentially favourable; or
(iv) an equity instrument of another entity.

Paragraph 3860.05(c)   A **financial liability** is any liability that is a contractual obligation:

(i)   to deliver cash or another financial asset to another party; or
(ii) to exchange financial instruments with another party under conditions that are potentially unfavourable.

Paragraph 3860.05(d)   An **equity instrument** is any contract that evidences a residual interest in the assets of an entity after deducting all of its liabilities.

Paragraph 3860.05(e)   **Monetary financial assets and financial liabilities** (also referred to as monetary financial instruments) are financial assets and financial liabilities to be received or paid in fixed or determinable amounts of money.

Paragraph 3860.05(f)   **Fair value** is the amount of the consideration that would be agreed upon in an arm's length transaction between knowledgeable, willing parties who are under no compulsion to act.

Paragraph 3860.05(g)   **Market value** is the amount obtainable from the sale, or payable on the acquisition, of a financial instrument in an active market.

Applying The Definitions

15-20.   The key to distinguishing between financial instruments and other types of arrangements is the question of whether the rights and obligations which arise under the contract are financial assets and financial liabilities. This, in turn, means that the contract must involve either exchanges of cash or exchanges of other financial assets, financial liabilities, or equity instruments.

15-21.   Physical assets such as inventories, plant and equipment, assets used under operating leases, and intangibles such as patents, trademarks, and goodwill, are not financial assets. The same view can be taken of prepayments which, in general, involve the right to receive services rather than cash or financial assets. With respect to liabilities included in the Balance Sheet, most items are financial in nature. However, those liabilities, warranty obligations for example, that involve obligations to deliver services would not be considered financial liabilities.

15-22.   Leasing arrangements may or may not involve financial assets and liabilities. If the lease is such that it can be classified as a capital lease by the lessee and as a direct financing or sales type lease by the lessor, the resulting Balance Sheet items involve an obligation to pay or the right to receive the relevant lease payments. These balances would be viewed as financial assets and financial liabilities. Operating leases, however, involve only the physical services of the asset and do not result in financial assets or liabilities.

15-23.   With respect to tax allocation balances, until recently Section 3470 required that such balances be viewed as deferred charges. This changed with the introduction of Section 3465. The Balance Sheet items that result from tax allocation procedures are now treated as future income tax assets and future income tax liabilities. However, these rights and obligations are imposed by statutory authority and are not contracts between parties. As a consequence, Section 3860 indicates that current or future income tax assets and liabilities are not financial instruments.

15-24.   Based on the preceding distinctions, a particular type of contract may or may not be a financial instrument, depending on the nature of the items involved. For example, an option to acquire equity securities is a financial instrument as the asset to be acquired is financial in nature. Alternatively, an option contract to acquire real estate would not be a financial instrument because real estate is not a financial asset. For this reason, various types of commodity contracts would not be considered financial assets or liabilities. Note, however, commodity linked arrangements, where the holder has an option to receive the commodity or some alternative financial asset, would be viewed as financial assets or liabilities.

15-25.   While many financial assets and liabilities are monetary in nature, you should not view the two concepts as being synonymous. While all monetary items can be viewed as financial assets and liabilities, not all financial assets and liabilities are monetary. For example, investments in equity securities are financial assets, but are not monetary in nature.

15-26.   Financial instruments may involve only primary assets and liabilities such as cash, receivables, payables, and equity securities. However, secondary or derivative arrangements are also used. These secondary instruments involve transferring all or part of the risk that is inherent in an underlying primary asset or liability, with the value of the instrument reflecting changes in the value of the underlying primary asset or liability. Examples of such instruments would include future and forward contracts, options, and interest rate swaps. Note that these derivative financial instruments do not involve a transfer of the underlying primary item at the inception of the contract and do not necessarily involve such a transfer at any point in time.

15-27.   While many financial instruments involve only a single financial asset or liability, compound instruments, which involve a combination of assets and liabilities, also exist. An example of this would be a bond which also contains an option to convert to common or preferred stock.

Additional Points Related To The Definitions

15-28.   Section 3860 and other sources make a number of additional points that help explain the basic definitions. These are as follows:

Contract   The terms contract and contractual refer to an agreement between two or more parties that has clear and unavoidable economic consequences that the parties have little, if any, discretion to avoid, usually because the agreement is enforceable at law. A variety of legal forms may be involved and there is no requirement that they be in writing.

Party   Section 3860's definitions use the word party. This term would include individuals, partnerships, incorporated bodies and government agencies.

Primary And Derivative   Financial instruments include both primary instruments (e.g., cash or receivables) and derivative instruments (e.g., options or futures).

Derivative Instruments   These instruments give an entity a contractual right to exchange financial assets (liabilities) with another entity under conditions that are potentially favourable (unfavourable). Some instruments involve both a right and an obligation to make the exchange (e.g., a forward exchange contract). Examples of derivative instruments include put and call options, forward contracts, interest rate and currency swaps, interest rate caps, collars and floors, loan commitments, note issuance facilities, and letters of credit. As the terms of exchange are fixed at the inception of the contract, such instruments may become favourable or unfavourable as prices in financial markets change relative to the fixed terms in the instrument.

Physical Assets And Prepayments   Physical assets such as inventories, property, plant and equipment, leased assets and intangibles are not financial assets. While they provide an opportunity to generate an inflow of cash of other assets, they do not involve a present right to receive financial assets. With respect to prepayments, deferred revenues, and most warranty obligations, they involve the right to receive or the obligation to deliver goods and services. As such, they are not financial instruments.

Recognition   The fact that a financial instrument gives rise to a financial asset, financial liability, or equity instrument does not necessarily lead to the conclusion that these items should be recognized.

Simple And Compound   Financial instruments may be either simple (e.g., cash or receivables) or compound (e.g., bonds that are convertible into stock).

Contractual Rights To Non Financial Assets   Contractual rights to receive goods (e.g., commodity options) or services (e.g., an operating lease for a physical asset) are not financial instruments as defined in this Section.

Commodity Linked Instruments   An instrument that gives the holder the right to receive cash, but which contains an option to receive a commodity instead, is a financial instrument.

Contingent Obligations   Contingent obligations, for example, a financial guarantee of another entity's debt, are financial instruments. However, their recognition is contingent on the usual criteria for the recognition of contingent assets and liabilities.

Obligations To Deliver Equity Instruments   Examples of such obligations would be options and warrants. These obligations are equity instruments, not liabilities, reflecting the fact that there can be no loss on an issue of shares.

Fair Value   In general, the fair value of a financial instrument is best measured using quoted market prices. When such values are not available, other techniques must be used. These include reference to the current market value of another instrument that is substantially the same, discounted cash flow analysis, and option pricing models.

Cash   Cash is a financial asset because it represents the medium of exchange and is therefore the basis on which all transactions are measured and reported in financial statements.

Contractual Rights To Receive Cash   Common examples of financial assets and liabilities which are contractual rights to receive or deliver cash include trade accounts receivable and payable, notes receivable and payable, loans receivable and payable, and bonds receivable and payable.

Other Contractual Rights   Financial instruments also include rights to receive or obligations to give up financial assets other than cash. An example would be a note that is payable in government bonds.

Taxes   Income tax assets or liabilities, both current and deferred amounts, are not financial instruments. They result from statutory requirements and do not represent contracts between entities.

Terminology Used In Practice

15-29.   Section 3860 of the *CICA Handbook* provides a sound conceptual definition of financial instruments. It does not, however, give any real indication of the plethora of arrangements that the financial community has developed in this area. With respect to descriptions of these arrangements, one of the better sources that we have seen is a book published by Coopers & Lybrand titled *Guide To Financial Instruments*.

15-30.   This publication divides financial instruments into three categories; financing instruments, asset based securities, and hedging instruments. In each category, it provides a fairly comprehensive list of available instruments, a description of each, and a brief discussion of the accounting issues related to the particular instrument. Given the large number of instruments and the fact that new types are constantly being developed, it would not be appropriate to include this complete list in a general publication such as this. However, some examples of each category of instruments will help you understand developments in this area. Representative examples are as follows:

Financing Instruments

Bunny Bonds   A bond in which investors reinvest the interest income into additional bonds with the same terms and conditions as the original bonds. Accordingly, the amount of the bonds multiplies "like a bunny".

Dutch Auction Notes   A note issued with a coupon that is periodically reset at a dutch auction. In a dutch auction, investors bid for the notes, which are sold at the lowest yield necessary to sell the entire issue. Investors willing to accept a lower yield than the breakpoint receive the breakpoint yield. Investors requiring a higher yield are excluded from the offering.

Flip-Flop Notes   A note that allows investors to convert to and from another type of security. For example, a floating rate long term bond may grant investors an option to convert into short term or intermediate term fixed rate notes and then back to the long term bond, if desired.

Indexed Debt   Debt with contingent interest payments in addition to a guaranteed minimum interest payment. The contingent payments may be linked to the price of specific commodities (e.g., oil, gold, silver) or indexes (e.g., S&P 500). In some cases, the investor's right to receive the contingent payment may be detachable from the debt instrument.

Asset Backed Securities

Securitized Receivables   Receivables converted into a form that can be sold to investors. For example, a retail company may pool its credit card receivables, or a finance company its car loans. Then, a special purpose vehicle is set up to purchase the receivables using the proceeds of an offering of securities collateralized by the receivables. The issuer uses the underlying cash flows of the receivables to fund debt service on the securities.

Repurchase Agreement   An agreement in which the seller agrees to repurchase securities, usually government securities, at an agreed upon price at a stated time. A repurchase agreement is similar to a secured borrowing and lending of funds equal to the sales price of the related collateral.

Hedging Instruments

Futures Contract   An exchange traded legal contract to buy or sell a standard quantity and quality of a commodity, financial instrument or index at a specified future date and price.

Caps, Floors, And Collars   A cap is the right to receive the excess of a reference interest rate over a given rate. A cap is analogous to a put option on debt securities. Correspondingly, a floor is the right to receive the excess of a given rate, known as the strike price of the floor, over a reference interest rate. A floor is analogous to a call option on debt securities. A collar is a strategy that combines a cap and a floor. The buyer of a collar buys a cap and writes a floor. The writer of a collar writes a cap and buys a floor.

Interest Rate Swap   A contract between two parties to exchange interest payments on a specified principal amount (referred to as the notional principal) for a specified period. In the most common instance, a swap involves the exchange of streams of variable and fixed rate interest payments.

15-31.   While there are many additional types of instruments in use in today's financial markets, the preceding descriptions should provide you with some feeling for the types of arrangements that are being developed.

Recognition - Financial Assets And Liabilities (Not Covered By Section 3860)

Initial Recognition

Basic Recommendation

15-32.   Recognition is the process of recording an item in the financial statements of an entity. General recognition criteria are provided in Section 1000 of the *CICA Handbook*, "Financial Statement Concepts" and specific guidance on revenue recognition is found in Section 3400, "Revenue". In both of these Sections, recognition requires that two criteria be satisfied. One is that the item must have a reasonable basis of measurement. The second criteria involves the occurrence of some event which transfers risks and rewards from one entity to another. The Re-Exposure Draft makes similar requirements in the case of financial assets and liabilities:

> **RE-ED Paragraph .020**   *A financial asset or financial liability should be recognized on an entity's balance sheet when:*
>
> *(a) substantially all of the risks and rewards associated with the asset or liability have been transferred to the entity; and*
>
> *(b) the cost or fair value of the asset to the entity or the amount of the obligation assumed can be measured reliably.*

15-33.   In examining the question of whether the entity has assumed the risks and rewards associated with a financial asset or financial liability, the Re-Exposure Draft indicates that all types of risk should be considered. These types of risk can be described as follows:

(a) **Price Risk**   There are three types of price risk: currency risk, interest rate risk, and market risk. Market rate risk relates to both changes in general market prices and to changes that are caused by factors specific to the individual security or its issuer. Price risk embodies the potential for gain or for loss.

(b) **Credit Risk**   Credit risk is the risk that one party to a financial instrument will fail to discharge an obligation and cause the other party to incur a financial loss.

(c) **Liquidity Risk**   Liquidity risk is the risk that an entity will encounter difficulty in raising funds to meet commitments associated with financial instruments (also referred to as funding risk). Liquidity risk may result from an inability to sell a financial asset quickly at close to its fair value.

Additional Points From Re-Exposure Draft

15-34.   In applying this Recommendation on initial recognition, the Re-Exposure Draft makes the following additional points:

Risks And Rewards   Assumption of risks and rewards is the key indicator as to whether there will be a probable flow of benefits to an asset holder or a probable outflow from the entity with the obligation.

Executory Contracts   Financial assets and financial liabilities arising from financial instruments under which obligations are partially or completely unperformed (executory contracts) should be recognized when they satisfy the criteria specified in Paragraph .020.

Rewards   Rewards associated with financial assets include entitlements to receive interest and principal payments, to pledge the related instrument as collateral for obligations, to dispose of the instrument for consideration, and to use the instrument to settle an obligation.

Transfers Of Risks And Rewards   In assessing whether there has been a transfer of the risks and rewards associated with a financial asset or liability, the entity must first identify the types of risk associated with the asset or liability. For example, a fixed rate loan receivable involves credit risk and interest rate risk, each of which may cause the fair value of the loan to fluctuate.

Measurement Reliability   In most circumstances, entities are able to determine the cost or fair value of financial assets and liabilities without significant doubt as to the reliability of the measurement. If cash consideration is involved, the amount is readily measurable. When non monetary consideration is involved, market value estimates will have to be used.

Recognition   In unusual circumstances, an item may appear to be a financial asset or liability and yet not be recognized because it cannot satisfy the measurement reliability criteria. As an example, consider a situation where an entity gives a loan guarantee and receives, in return, a pledge of non-marketable financial assets. The financial liability will have to be recognized, even though lack of measurement reliability may prevent the recognition of the financial asset.

Discontinuing Recognition Of A Financial Asset Or A Liability

Basic Recommendation

15-35.   The Re-Exposure Draft also deals with the question of when a financial asset or liability should be removed from the Balance Sheet:

RE-ED Paragraph .028   *A recognized financial asset or financial liability should be removed from an entity's balance sheet when:*

(a) *substantially all of the risks and rewards associated with the asset or liability have been transferred to others and the fair value of any risks and rewards retained can be measured reliably; or*

(b) *the underlying right or obligation has been exercised, discharged or canceled, or has expired.*

15-36.   In many situations, the application of this Recommendation is very clear. For example, when a liability is paid, an option expires, or a receivable is collected, there is no question as to the need to remove the previously recognized item from the Balance Sheet. However, in other situations, measuring the transfer of risks and rewards may require the exercise of considerable judgment.

15-37.   In recent years, companies have made increasing use of various techniques to manage the risks associated with financial assets and financial liabilities. These techniques include hedging, risk diversification, risk pooling, guarantees, and various types of insurance. These techniques can serve to significantly reduce or even eliminate certain types of risk associated with financial balances. However, in most situations, some level or type of risk remains, leading to the conclusion that derecognition of the financial balance is not appropriate.

15-38. Consider, for example, an enterprise with a DM1,000,000 receivable balance. The price risk associated with movements in the German currency could be removed by entering a forward contract to make delivery of DM1,000,000 when the receivable is collected. However, the credit risk remains unchanged and, as a consequence, the DM1,000,000 receivable should continue to be included in the Balance Sheet of the enterprise.

15-39. The Re-Exposure Draft makes a number of additional points with respect to this general Recommendation on discontinuing recognition:

Readily Identifiable Situations Many situations that require an entity to discontinue recognition of a financial asset or financial liability are readily identifiable. For example, the collection of an account receivable.

Measurement Of Remaining Risks An entity removes a transferred financial asset or financial liability from its balance sheet only when substantially all of the associated risks and rewards have been transferred and the fair value of any retained risks and rewards can be measured reliably. If there is not an adequate base for measuring any residual risks or rewards, there is no proper basis for determining whether they are insubstantial. Consequently, there is no basis for determining the amount to be retained in the Balance Sheet.

Separate Measurement In determining whether substantially all of the risks and rewards have been transferred, the entity should measure the fair value of the aggregate risks separately from the fair value of the aggregate rewards. Substantially all of the risks and rewards are considered to be transferred only when the fair value of the risks and the fair value of the rewards are each insubstantial. If the net value of the risks and rewards is insubstantial, the asset or liability would continue to be recognized.

Measurement Of Substantially All While recognizing that it is not possible to quantify such matters precisely, the Re-Exposure Draft suggests that substantially all of the risks and rewards have not been transferred unless the fair value of the risks retained and the fair value of the rewards retained are each less than 5 percent of the fair value of the asset or liability.

Substitute Assets In a transaction such as factoring or securitization of accounts receivable, the entity may remove the accounts receivable and replace them with a liability to make good credit losses on the accounts receivable. The replacement liability would be treated like any other financial liability.

Assets Retained When assets have been factored or securitized but do not meet the criteria for removal from the balance sheet, the transaction will be treated as a financing with disclosure of a new liability. This new liability will be accounted for separately on an effective yield basis.

Risk Management Entities commonly use various risk management techniques such as hedging, risk diversification, risk pooling, guarantees and various types of insurance to reduce exposure to financial risks. The Re-Exposure Draft indicates that the entity should continue to recognize a financial asset or financial liability if it remains exposed to risks and rewards assumed at the inception of the financial instrument, even in situations where the risk is mitigated by risk management techniques.

Inability To Determine Fair Value   An inability to measure the fair value of the asset or liability on an ongoing basis is not a basis for discontinuing recognition.

Transfer Of Receivables

15-40.   It is a common practice for enterprises to use outstanding accounts receivable as a basis for raising funds. Arrangements such as factoring and securitization of receivables allow an enterprise to transfer its receivables to a third party who then becomes responsible for collecting the outstanding balances. In return, the transferor receives some portion of the receivable balances transferred as an immediate cash payment.

15-41.   In some of these arrangements, the transferee assumes all of the risks associated with collecting the outstanding receivables and has no recourse to the transferor in the event of defaults. In such non recourse arrangements, all of the risks associated with the receivables balance have been transferred and it is appropriate to remove them from the Balance Sheet.

15-42.   More commonly, the transfer is in a form that leaves the transferee with recourse to the transferor in the event that some of the receivables prove to be uncollectible. While the *CICA Handbook* does not contain a Recommendation on this issue, current practice would allow the receivable to be removed from the transferor's Balance Sheet when recourse is reasonable in relation to expected credit losses. The original 1991 Exposure Draft suggested a much more restrictive approach. Under the Recommendations of this first Exposure Draft, receivables could only be removed from the transferor's Balance Sheet in situations where they have been transferred on a completely non recourse basis. This, of course, meant that the possible recourse had to be reflected in a financial liability.

15-43.   Most respondents to the 1991 Exposure Draft felt that this approach was too restrictive and, as a consequence, the Re-Exposure Draft takes a more judgmental approach. If it can be determined that 95 percent of the risks and 95 percent of the rewards associated with the receivable has been transferred, the financial asset can be removed from the Balance Sheet, eliminating the requirement that a liability for recourse be included on the equity side of the Balance Sheet.

15-44.   The Re-Exposure Draft makes a number of additional points with respect to the transfer of receivables:

Transfer Of Accounts Receivable: Credit Risk   An entity may transfer accounts receivable through transactions such as factoring or securitization. If the transfer is with recourse to the transferor for uncollectible amounts, the transferor has retained some amount of credit risk. If the fair value of the obligation to bear credit losses can be measured reliably and is not substantial relative to the fair value of the accounts receivable, then the transferor treats the transaction as a sale and removes the accounts receivable from its balance sheet.

Transfer Of Accounts Receivable: Interest Rate Risk   In some cases the amount eventually remitted to the transferor will be dependent on future interest rates. If this is the case, the transferor has retained interest rate risk. Such exposures are inherently difficult to measure and this may prevent the removal of the accounts receivable from the balance sheet.

Form Of Recourse   Recourse to the transferor with respect to credit losses can be provided in various forms. These include put options for cash, substitution of good receivables for defaulted receivables, holdback reserves, subordinated interests in a pool of receivables and amounts held in spread accounts available to absorb credit losses. All of these forms should be treated the same way for accounting purposes.

Fair Value   In assessing the fair value of a recourse obligation, consideration should be given both to the statistical loss experience and the degree of concentration of risk within a pool of transferred receivables. Concentrations of risk relate to such factors as a large single obligor, a large number of obligors from a single industry, or obligors concentrated in a single geographic area.

Puts And Calls The existence of a fixed price option held by the transferor results in retention of the potential to benefit from increases in the value of the receivables transferred. Similarly, a fixed price put option held by the transferee results in retention by the transferor of risks associated with the assets transferred and, depending on its terms, exercise of the option may result in a reversal of the transfer.

Participating Interest If the transferor has retained a participating interest in future cash flows from transferred receivables that constitutes more than 5 percent of the fair value of the receivables, it is presumed that substantially all of the receivables have not been transferred.

Defeasance

15-45. An enterprise with outstanding liabilities might choose to contract with a third party to assume the interest and principal obligations under those liabilities in return for a current payment of cash. This would be desirable, for example, in situations where interest rates have significantly increased in the period since the liabilities were issued. In such a situation, the third party would be willing to assume the obligation for a payment that is less than the carrying value of the liabilities. If the debtor can eliminate the liabilities from its Balance Sheet, a gain equal to the difference between the cash paid to the third party and the carrying value of the liabilities could then be recorded.

15-46. If a formal arrangement is established in which the creditor agrees to discharge the debtor enterprise in return for a guarantee of payment from the third party, there is general agreement that removal of the liabilities from the Balance Sheet of the debtor enterprise is appropriate.

15-47. A more difficult problem arises when an arrangement is made with a third party to assume debt obligations, but without the formal agreement of the creditor interest. This type of arrangement is referred to as "in substance" defeasance and, under current Canadian practice, it would generally be acceptable to remove the relevant liabilities from the Balance Sheet of the debtor enterprise. Both the Exposure Draft and the Re-Exposure Draft would eliminate this practice, allowing the debt to be removed only in true defeasance situations, where the creditor has formally agreed to accept payments from the third party and discharge the debtor enterprise from its obligations. This is reflected in the following comments taken from the Re-Exposure Draft:

Defeasance Defeasance is a procedure where a debtor's obligation is discharged by depositing cash or other assets with a third party that agrees to assume the debtor's obligations. The creditor agrees to look only to the third party for payment. It is appropriate for the debtor to remove the liability from its balance sheet.

In Substance Defeasance This is the same as defeasance except that the creditor is not party to the agreement. In this case, the debtor has not transferred the risks and rewards associated with the obligation as the creditor still looks to the debtor for settlement. As a consequence, the debt should remain on the balance sheet, along with recognition of the assets placed in trust.

Classification Between Liabilities And Equity (Covered By Section 3860)

The Financial Reporting Issue

15-48. Canadian practice has traditionally disclosed preferred shares as a component of shareholders' equity in the corporation's Statement Of Financial Position. However, as some of these securities take on more and more of the characteristics of debt, it has become clear that such disclosure is not always appropriate.

15-49.   This issue has important implications both in the Balance Sheet and the Income Statement. Looking at the equity side of the Balance Sheet, the classification of some types of preferred shares as liabilities could result in significant changes in such important indicators of financial health as the debt to equity ratio. Perhaps even more importantly, in the Income Statement, the treatment of preferred shares as debt would mean that the dividends on these shares would be treated like interest. That is, rather than being viewed as a distribution of Net Income, these amounts would be deducted in the determination of Net Income. This could result in a significant reduction in the Net Income of the enterprise. However, earnings per share would not be changed as it is based on the earnings of the common shareholders.

15-50.   We would also note that the problem is made more difficult by the fact that there are various legal and tax constraints associated with the difference between classification as a liability and classification as shareholders' equity.

Section 3860 Recommendation

15-51.   Section 3860 contains the following Recommendation with respect to the classification of liabilities and equity:

> **Paragraph 3860.18**   *The issuer of a financial instrument should classify the instrument, or its component parts, as a liability or as equity in accordance with the substance of the contractual arrangement on initial recognition and the definitions of a financial liability and an equity instrument.* (January, 1996)

15-52.   While we presented these definitions previously, the relevant definitions of financial liabilities and equity instruments are repeated here for your convenience:

> **Paragraph 3860.05(c)**   A **financial liability** is any liability that is a contractual obligation:
>
> (i)   to deliver cash or another financial asset to another party; or
>
> (ii) to exchange financial instruments with another party under conditions that are potentially unfavourable.

> **Paragraph 3860.05(d)**   An **equity instrument** is any contract that evidences a residual interest in the assets of an entity after deducting all of its liabilities.

15-53.   In the application of Paragraph 3860.18, the key consideration in these definitions is the existence of a contractual obligation on one party to the financial instrument (the issuer) to either deliver cash or another financial asset to the other party (the holder) or to exchange another financial instrument with the holder under conditions that are potentially unfavourable to the issuer. When this condition is present, the financial instrument clearly meets the definition of a financial liability.

15-54.   With respect to securities commonly referred to as preferred shares, if such securities provide for mandatory redemption by the issuer for a fixed or determinable amount at a fixed or determinable future, or if they give the holder the right to require the issuer to redeem the share at or after a particular date for a fixed or determinable amount, the securities meet the definition of a financial liability and should be classified as such.

15-55.   The *Handbook* notes that even when there is no explicit redemption provision, there may be terms or conditions in the securities that may indirectly have the same result. Examples of this would be:

• A contractually accelerating dividend provision such that, within the foreseeable future, the issuer will be economically compelled to redeem the securities.

- Redemption may be required by some future event that is likely to occur (e.g., an increase in the prime rate to some specified level).

15-56.   Preferred shares that have either an explicit provision or terms and conditions that will lead to their being redeemed on potentially unfavourable terms should be classified as liabilities and disclosed as such on the Balance Sheet of the enterprise. Correspondingly, the dividends on such shares should be treated like interest in the Income Statement. That is, they should be deducted in the determination of the Net Income of the enterprise. The classification should take place at the time the securities are first issued.

Classification - Interest, Dividends, Gains, Losses

15-57.   The distinction between liability instruments and equity instruments has important implications for income determination. If a financial instrument is classified as a liability, payments made to the holders of the instrument are considered to be interest payments which reduce reported Net Income. In contrast, payments to the holders of equity financial instruments are viewed as dividends which are disclosed as distributions of Net Income and reported in the Statement Of Changes In Net Assets.

15-58.   There are also important differences when financial instruments are redeemed or otherwise retired. If an instrument is classified as a liability, any difference between the carrying value and the amounts required to eliminate the balance will be treated as a gain or loss to be included in the determination of Net Income. In contrast, the elimination of an equity item is viewed as a capital transaction and, as a consequence, differences between carrying value and the amount of assets given up to retire or redeem the equity balance will not be included in Net Income.

15-59.   The classification of these items will, of course, depend on the classification of the Balance Sheet item to which they relate. This view is reflected in the following Recommendation:

> **Paragraph 3860.31**   *Interest, dividends, losses and gains relating to a financial instrument, or a component part, classified as a financial liability should be reported in the income statement as expense or income. Distributions to holders of a financial instrument classified as an equity instrument should be reported by the issuer directly in equity.* (January, 1996)

15-60.   The Paragraph 3860.31 Recommendation means that dividends declared on preferred shares that are classified as financial liabilities will be measured and disclosed in the same manner as interest payments on bonds. This would include accrual of such dividends prior to their declaration date.

15-61.   In addition to this alternative treatment of dividends on preferred shares classified as liabilities, any gains or losses on the redemption, cancellation, or reissue of such shares will have to be taken into income, rather than treated as a capital transaction.

15-62.   Dividends that are being treated as interest expense can be grouped together with and disclosed as a component of interest expense. However, there may be tax or other reasons for separate disclosure of such dividends.

The Tax Issue

15-63.   Redeemable preferred shares are widely used in tax planning. For example, in an estate freeze it is a normal procedure for the freezor (i.e., the wealthy individual wishing to freeze the value of his or her estate) to exchange common or growth shares in an operating corporation for non growth preferred shares. In order to clearly establish the value for these shares, they are often redeemable at the option of the holder. At the time of the freeze, common or growth shares with a nominal value will be issued to the freezor's beneficiaries (e.g., spouse or children). A rollover provision such as that found in Section 86 of the *Income Tax Act* is normally used to implement this plan.

15-64.   The types of preferred shares used in these situations will almost invariably require the issuing corporation to transfer cash to the holder. This means that under the Recommendations of Section 3860, these shares must be classified as liabilities. This has created considerable furor in the tax community and the reasons are not difficult to understand.

15-65.   The reclassification of these preferred shares as liabilities will, in many tax planning situations, create an equity side to the Balance Sheet that is almost entirely debt. In that, in most of these arrangements, the holder of such preferred shares is unlikely to demand redemption of the securities, particularly if it would cause any financial hardship to the issuing corporation. Despite the fact that no change in economic substance is involved, the tax community has expressed their significant concern that bankers and other creditors will be influenced by this reclassification to downgrade the credit rating of the enterprise. This could lead to increased difficulty in obtaining financing for companies which use such preferred shares.

15-66.   The lobbying of the tax community in this area has been sufficient that the Accounting Standards Board has deferred application of these provisions to non public companies until fiscal years beginning on or after January 1, 2000. However, it is unlikely that that there will be a permanent change of mind on the part of the Board on this issue. Redeemable preferred shares involve a non cancelable obligation to transfer cash and, as such, are clearly liabilities of the issuing enterprise. In our opinion, the issue will have to be resolved by educating creditors as to the real nature of the changes that have taken place in this area.

EIC Abstracts Dealing With Liability/Equity Classification

15-67.   The Recommendations with respect to the classification of liabilities and equity have a significant impact on the information presented in financial reports. Given this, it is not surprising that a number of issues in this area have come to the attention of the Emerging Issues Committee. As a result, several EIC Abstracts have been issued dealing with this classification problem. One of these, EIC Abstract No. 13, was issued prior to the inclusion of Section 3860 in the *CICA Handbook*. Several others have been issued since this Section was introduced. As was the case in earlier Chapters, the content of these EIC Abstracts has been relegated to a Supplement included at the end of this Chapter.

Recognition Of Separate Components Of Compound Financial Instruments

Basic Recommendation

15-68.   The most common example of the types of compound financial instruments under consideration here would be convertible securities. These involve either debt securities or preferred shares that are convertible, at the discretion of the holder, into a specified number of common shares. Stated alternatively, the basic security (debt or preferred shares) is accompanied by an option to acquire common shares.

15-69.   Prior to the introduction of Section 3860, when an enterprise issued such convertible securities, no recognition was given to the value associated with the option to acquire common shares. All of the consideration received by the enterprise was allocated either to the basic debt issue or the basic preferred stock issue. This procedure systematically understated the cost of carrying the debt or preferred shares and the value that has been contributed to the common stock equity of the enterprise.

15-70.   Section 3860 changes this situation dramatically as a result of the following Recommendation:

Paragraph 3860.24 *The issuer of a financial instrument that contains both a liability and an equity element should classify the instrument's component parts separately in accordance with paragraph 3860.18. (January, 1996)*

15-71.   As noted previously, *Handbook* paragraph 3860.18 requires the classification of financial instruments in accordance with the substance of the contractual arrangement and the definitions of a financial liability and an equity instrument. This would clearly require that proceeds received from the issuance of convertible securities be divided between a financial liability and an equity instruments.

15-72.   A practical problem here is how to split the total proceeds of the convertible issue into the respective debt and equity components. Section 3860 does not deal with measurement issues and, as a consequence, it does not prescribe the use of any particular approach to this problem. However, Paragraph 3860.29 describes two approaches that might be used:

(a) assigning to the less easily measurable component (often an equity instrument) the residual amount after deducting from the instrument as a whole the amount separately determined for the component that is more easily measurable; and

(b) measuring the liability and equity components separately and, to the extent necessary, adjusting these amounts on a pro rata basis so that the sum of the components equals the amount of the instrument as a whole.

Separate Recognition Illustrated

15-73.   A simple example will serve to illustrate the application of these two approaches:

Example   An entity issues 2,000 convertible bonds at the start of Year 1. The bonds have a three year term, and are issued at par with a face value of $1,000 per bond, giving total proceeds of $2,000,000. Interest is payable annually at a coupon rate of 6 percent. Each bond is convertible at any time up to maturity into 250 common shares.

When the bonds are issued, the prevailing market interest rate for similar debt without conversion options is 9 percent. At the issue date, the market price of one common share is $3. The dividends expected over the three year term of the bonds amount to $0.14 per share at the end of each year. The risk free annual interest rate for a three year term is 5 percent.

15-74.   Using the first valuation approach, we would first determine the value of the bond component of the compound instrument on the basis of a simple present value calculation using the 9 percent market rate for non convertible debt:

PV Principal - $2,000,000 After Three Years	$1,544,367
PV Interest - $120,000 Per Year For Three Years	303,755
Value Of Liability Component	$1,848,122

15-75.   Given the total issue price of $2,000,000, the value of the equity instrument would be calculated as follows:

Total Proceeds	$2,000,000
Market Value - Liability Component	(1,848,122)
Value Of Equity Component	$ 151,878

15-76.   The alternative valuation approach recognizes that it would also be possible to arrive at a separate determination of the fair value of the equity instrument. While this can be done using a variety of option pricing models, both the Re-Exposure Draft and Section 3860 refer to the Black-Scholes model. If this model is applied, a value of $144,683 is arrived at for the equity instrument.

15-77.   When this equity instrument value is combined with the present value of the debt instrument, the total value for the issues is as follows:

Value Of Debt Instrument	$1,848,122
Value Of Equity Instrument	144,683
Total Combined Value	$1,992,805

15-78.   This combined value is $7,195 less than the $2,000,000 proceeds from the convertible issue. If this difference is pro rated to the two instruments on the basis of their independently determined value, the result is an allocation of $1,854,794 to the financial liability and $145,206 to the equity instrument.

Additional Points

15-79.   Several additional points should be made with respect to these compound financial instruments:

Likelihood Of Conversion   Section 3860 notes that classification of the equity and liability components of convertible bonds should not be altered to reflect a change in the likelihood that the conversion option will be exercised. The value of the equity position is established at the time the convertible bonds are issued and, as with other components of Shareholders' Equity, it should not be altered to reflect changes in its value.

Carrying Value: Issuer   As the issuer cannot usually transfer its obligation or terminate it prior to maturity or conversion, it will carry the liability component on a cost basis. Interest costs will be based on the effective yield method.

Carrying Value: Holder   If the holder carries the components of the compound instrument at fair value, it may be unnecessary for it to account separately for the components. If the components are carried at cost, the components will be accounted for separately. The liability component may have to be reduced if there is an increase in credit risk. Correspondingly, the conversion right is subject to impairment as the time value inherent in the carrying amount decreases over time.

Conversion: Issuer   On conversion, the issuer will reclassify the liability component to equity as part of the carrying value of the newly issued common shares. No gain or loss will be recognized on the transaction.

Conversion: Holder   The holder will have a new investment in common shares that will be recorded at the aggregate carrying amount of the debt and conversion option components. No gain or loss will be recognized on the conversion.

Offsetting Of A Financial Asset And A Financial Liability

Basic Recommendation

15-80.   The basic Recommendation in this area is as follows:

Paragraph 3860.34   *A financial asset and a financial liability should be offset and the net amount reported in the balance sheet when an entity:*

(a) has a legally enforceable right to set off the recognized amounts; and
(b) intends either to settle on a net basis, or to realize the asset and settle the liability simultaneously. (January, 1996)

General Rules

15-81.   In general, GAAP does not permit the offsetting of assets and liabilities for the purpose of Balance Sheet disclosure. However, when this procedure reflects the entity's expected future cash flows, Section 3860 requires offsetting.

15-82.   This would generally be the case only when a debtor has the legal right to eliminate all or a portion of an obligation due to a creditor by applying against that obligation an amount due to the debtor. This is referred to as the right to offset the recognized amounts.

15-83.   In addition to having the right of set off, the conditions for offsetting require that the entity actually intends to use that right to settle the liability. If the entity intends to realize the asset and settle the liability separately, offsetting is not permitted. Intent may be influenced by an entity's normal business practice, the requirements of the financial markets in which it operates or other circumstances that may limit its ability to settle net or to settle simultaneously.

15-84.   While it is not a common situation, a debtor may have a legal right to apply an amount due from a third party against the amount due to a a creditor. Provided there is an agreement among the three parties that clearly establishes the debtor's right of offset, Paragraph 3860.34 would be applicable.

15-85.   Section 3860 distinguishes between offsetting a recognized financial asset and a recognized financial liability and the removal of a previously recognized item from the Balance Sheet. The basic difference is that with the removal of a previously recognized item, there may be a gain or loss to be recognized. This could not happen with offsetting.

15-86.   Paragraph 3860.41 notes that offsetting is not appropriate in the following circumstances:

(a) several different financial instruments are used to emulate the features of a single financial instrument (i.e., a "synthetic instrument");

(b) financial assets and financial liabilities arise from financial instruments having the same primary risk exposure (for example, assets and liabilities within a portfolio of forward contracts or other derivative instruments) but involve different counterparties;

(c) financial or other assets are pledged as collateral for non-recourse financial liabilities;

(d) financial assets are set aside in trust by a debtor for the purpose of discharging an obligation without those assets having been accepted by the creditor in settlement of the obligation (for example, a sinking fund arrangement); or

(e) obligations incurred as a result of events giving rise to losses are expected to be recovered from a third party by virtue of a claim made under an insurance policy.

15-87.   Section 3860 notes the existence of "master netting arrangements". These arise when an entity undertakes a large number of financial instrument transactions with a single counterparty. Such agreements provide for a single net settlement of all financial instruments covered by the agreement, usually only in the event of default on, or termination of, any one contract. They are used by financial institutions to provide protection against loss in the event of bankruptcy or events that result in a counterparty being unable to meet its obligations. Since these arrangements normally only come into effect in unusual circumstances, there is no intent to settle on a net basis as part of the normal business operations. As a result, these master netting arrangements do not provide a basis for offsetting.

Measurement Of Financial Assets And Liabilities On Initial Recognition (Not Covered By Section 3860)

Basic Recommendation

15-88.   The basic Recommendation of the Re-Exposure Draft in this area is as follows:

> **RE-ED Paragraph .071**   *When a financial asset or a financial liability is recognized initially, it should be measured at the fair value of the consideration given or received for it.*

Additional Points

15-89.   The Re-Exposure Draft makes a number of additional points with respect to the application of this basic Recommendation:

Terminology   Assets are generally recognized initially at the fair value of the consideration given and liabilities are recognized initially at the fair value of the consideration received. These amounts are normally referred to as the historical cost of the asset or proceeds of the liability.

Transaction Costs   The historical cost of assets should reflect all related transaction costs.

Fair Value Of Liabilities   The fair value of a liability is the present value of the expected future payments discounted at the interest rate currently applied in financial markets to instruments having similar terms, conditions, risk, and collateral.

Estimates   The historical cost of a financial asset is determined on the basis of the entity's best estimate of the amount and timing of future payments.

Non Cash Transactions   The fair value of an exchange transaction not involving cash may be determined by reference to the fair value of either the consideration given up or the assets acquired, whichever is more clearly evident.

All Items Considered   Several items may be involved in the acquisition of a financial asset. For example, if an entity gives a low interest loan to an employee, the loan should be valued at market rates and recognition should be given to the benefit that has been provided to the employee.

Assets Acquired Through Options   When a financial asset is acquired or disposed of through the exercise of an option, the fair value of the consideration received or given is considered to be the exercise price received or paid adjusted for the carrying amount of the option exercised.

Measurement Of Financial Assets And Liabilities Subsequent To Initial Recognition (Not Covered By Section 3860)

General Rules

15-90.   The Recommendations note that there are two distinctly different bases for measuring financial assets and financial liabilities subsequent to initial recognition. The two alternatives are the use of cost and the use of fair values. It is also noted that the basis used for measuring assets and liabilities has implications for income recognition, particularly with respect to gains or losses resulting from changes in fair values.

15-91.   The Recommendations of this Re-Exposure Draft will apply different bases of measurement to different classifications of financial instruments. Classification will be based on management's primary intent in entering into the transaction. For measurement purposes, financial instruments are classified as held for:

- the period to maturity (which may be a relatively short period) or for the long term;

- hedging (when they are held to mitigate an exposure to financial risk, regardless of the expected holding period); or

- purposes other than hedging when there is no intent to hold to maturity or for the long term.

Financial Assets And Financial Liabilities Held For The Long Term Or To Maturity

Measurement Of A Financial Asset Or Financial Liability

15-92.   **Basic Recommendation**   The basic Recommendation in this area is as follows:

RE-ED Paragraph .082   *Subsequent to initial recognition, a financial asset or a financial liability held for the long term or to maturity should be measured and reported in the balance sheet at the amount initially recognized except as provided otherwise by paragraphs .089, .097, .098, .112, .113, and .127.*

15-93.   If the intent is to hold the asset to maturity or for a very long time, the amount that will be received on the asset or paid on the liability will not be influenced by fluctuations in the fair value of the asset. As a consequence, fair values are of little relevance and the cost method of valuation should be used.

15-94.   The maturity of financial assets and liabilities can be long, short, or non existent. However, the accounting treatment of the instrument will be based on the intent of management. This means that the appropriate accounting treatment cannot be determined by whether the item is classified as current or non current in the Balance Sheet.

15-95.   **Intent Of Management**   An intent to hold a financial asset or financial liability for the long term or to maturity must be supported by a demonstrated capacity to carry out that intent. An intention to hold a financial asset or financial liability for the long term or to maturity may be evident from one or more specific purposes associated with the acquisition of the asset or assumption of the liability. Examples of this included in the Re-Exposure Draft are as follows:

- An entity may assume a financial liability or acquire a financial asset for the long term or to maturity in furthering its business plans. For example, an entity may utilize financial instruments to establish and maintain a long term business relationship with a customer, supplier or partner.

- A financial asset or financial liability may arise as a direct result of the normal business operations of the entity. Trade receivables (payables) would be an example of this.

- An entity may fund a financial asset held for the long term or to maturity with a financial liability having payment obligations matching the cash receipts from the asset. For example, financial institutions commonly fund loans with matching deposit liabilities.

- An entity's intention to hold a financial asset primarily to yield a return in the form of a stream of interest, dividends, or similar periodic cash flows or through appreciation in fair value over an extended period of time usually indicates an intention to hold for the long term.

- A financial instrument, particularly a derivative instrument, may be acquired with a view to altering an entity's net cash flows or risk exposures resulting from another instrument. In addition, two or more separate financial instruments, collectively described as a "synthetic instrument", may be used to emulate the characteristics of another type of instrument.

15-96.   When assets are held in a portfolio that may be maintained for a long time, classification of every individual asset or liability for measurement purposes reflects management's intentions with respect to that particular item only.   The classification is independent of the purpose of the overall portfolio.

15-97.   Generally speaking, the primary purpose of derivative financial instruments is to transfer risk. Their characteristics are such that they facilitate hedging and short term speculation and, as a consequence, are commonly carried at fair value. There may, however, be exceptions to this. For example an entity may hold an option for an extended period and exercise it immediately before its expiry in order to acquire the underlying financial asset.

15-98.   **Cost Method Application**   The Recommendation for the application of the cost method to this type of financial instrument is as follows:

> **RE-ED Paragraph .089**   *A financial asset or financial liability held for the long term or to maturity and to be settled through scheduled payments of fixed or determinable amounts should be measured on the amortized cost basis reflecting its effective yield determined on initial recognition. At each balance sheet date, an entity should report such an asset or liability at the amount of the scheduled future payments discounted at the rate of interest inherent in the amount at which the asset or liability was initially recognized, except as provided otherwise by paragraphs .097, .098, and .127.*

15-99.   In simple cases, the application of this Recommendation creates no problems. The asset or liability is valued at the present value of expected future cash flows, discounted at the rate which prevailed at the time of initial recognition. If the instrument is issued at a premium or discount, this process will require amortization of these amounts using the effective yield approach.

15-100.   There are, however, a number of possible complications involving more complex financial assets and liabilities. The Recommendations make the following points with respect to these situations:

Floating Rate Debt   The Recommendations indicate that, in the case of a financial instrument bearing a floating interest rate, the interest rate inherent on initial recognition is the rate as determined from time to time according to the instrument rather than the actual percentage rate in effect at the date of initial recognition.

Changes In Estimates   In situations where the amount of interest is based on a floating rate or the principal amount of the instrument is to be calculated by reference to the fair value of another financial asset, periodic re-estimation of determinable cash flows is required. Changes in the amount of the estimates will change the effective yield. Any changes in the present value of future cash flows are recognized over the remaining term of the asset or liability. In the case of a floating rate asset or liability recognized initially at an amount equal to the principal repayable on maturity, re-estimation has no effect on the carrying amount of the asset or liability. Where the principal amount varies in relation to an index, an increase or decrease in the principal is recognized over the remaining term to maturity through an increase or decrease in the effective yield in a manner similar to amortization of a discount or premium arising on initial recognition.

Commodity Linked Instruments   In this case, Paragraphs .082 and .089 apply only to the financial asset of the holder and the financial liability of the issuer. In some cases the option component may involve an option to receive a cash amount determinable by reference to a commodity price and a fixed quantity of the commodity in lieu of a fixed cash amount. This type of option makes the principal amount of the financial instrument determinable rather than fixed and, accordingly, affects the measurement of the financial asset or financial liability.

Derivatives   Some derivatives, such as interest rate swaps, are settled through scheduled payments of fixed or determinable amounts, but involve a future exchange of amounts between parties rather than a payment by one party only. Such instruments do not incorporate an effective yield and, as a consequence, they will be carried as per the provisions of Paragraph .082 (i.e., original cost).

Impairment In The Carrying Amount Of A Financial Asset With Payments That Are Fixed Or Determinable

15-101.   The two basic Recommendations for assets that are to be settled by scheduled payments of fixed or determinable amounts are as follows:

RE-ED Paragraph .097   *When an entity obtains evidence that a financial asset carried on the cost basis and to be settled by scheduled payments of fixed or determinable amounts may be impaired, the asset's carrying amount should be reviewed. Impairment exists when the holder of the financial asset no longer has reasonable assurance of collection of all amounts when due in accordance with the terms of the underlying financial instrument. In these circumstances, the asset's carrying amount should be reduced to the entity's current estimate of amount and timing of future payments that will be received, discounted at the rate of interest inherent in the financial asset when initially recognized. The amount of the reduction should be charged to income in the period in which it is recognized.*

RE-ED Paragraph .098   *When the carrying amount of a financial asset to be settled by scheduled payments of fixed or determinable amounts has been written down to estimated recoverable amount and the estimated recoverable amount subsequently increases, the write down should be reversed to the extent of the increase. The amount of the reversal should be credited to income in the period in which it is recognized.*

15-102.   The Re-Exposure Draft makes a number of additional points with respect to these Recommendations:

Section 3025   While impaired loans are to be accounted for in accordance with *Handbook* Section 3025, "Impaired Loans", the Recommendations of this Section are consistent with the Recommendations of that Section.

Interest Rate Risk   The fair value of a financial asset may decline as the result of increasing interest rates. This is not a basis for recording an impairment in carrying value. Only a decline in fair value due to expected credit losses reflects an impairment in the carrying amount of a monetary asset.

Indicators Of Credit Deterioration   The Recommendations list a number of factors which may indicate an impairment in value:

- a current default in making interest or principal payments when due;

- a default in other conditions under the financial instrument, such as a breach of a covenant in a bond indenture;

- an adverse change in the credit rating of a financial instrument by a recognized credit rating organization;

- a decline in the market value of a traded financial instrument unrelated to a change in prevailing market interest rates;

- a decline in the current financial position of the debtor, particularly its liquidity, as evidenced by indicators such as severe losses in the current or recent years, a serious deficiency in working capital or cash flow, or an excess of liabilities over assets;

- a decline in the ability of the debtor to generate future cash flow available to service its obligations, as indicated in forecasts of its expected financial results or management discussions of financial condition and prospects; or

- a decline in the fair value of collateral given by the debtor.

Future Events　No consideration is given to future events in determining whether an asset is impaired.

Best Estimates　When an asset carried on the cost basis is impaired, the same basis of measurement continues to be applied to the asset. The difference is that the expected cash flows will be smaller or paid at a later date. Cash flows will be based on the entity's best estimates, a process which is a matter of judgment. A variety of techniques can be used but they must take into consideration the intent of the entity. For example, if the entity intends to seize any assets that were used as collateral, the cash flows from the sale of these assets would replace the principal payments from the debtor.

Portfolio Considerations　If the assets are carried as part of a portfolio and the entity does not have sufficient information to write down individual assets, the estimates can be based on the aggregate expected cash flows from the portfolio.

No Reasonable Estimates　Sometimes it is not practicable to make a reasonable estimate of future cash flows. In these circumstances, the carrying amount of an impaired asset may be determined by reference to either:

(a) the fair value of any security underlying the asset, net of expected costs of realization and any amounts legally required to be paid to the issuer of the financial instrument; or
(b) an observable market price for the asset.

Restructured Loans　Restructuring is a formal arrangement that either reduces or delays contractual cash flows. For accounting purposes, the restructured asset is viewed as a continuation of an existing asset and measured on the same basis as an impaired asset that has not been restructured.

Accounting Subsequent To Impairment　Subsequent to the recognition of impairment, the entity will apply the interest rate inherent in the initial recognition of the asset to the estimated future cash flows to determine the carrying value of the asset. For this purpose, an interest rate that is determinable under the terms of the underlying financial instrument becomes fixed at the rate prevailing when the asset is recognized as being impaired.

Reversals Of Write Downs　If new information is obtained with respect to the debtor's ability to satisfy its obligations, the resulting change in estimated cash flows could increase the value of the asset. If this happens, it is permissible to reverse any previous write downs. However, the asset cannot be written up to a value that is greater than the original carrying value.

Impairment In The Carrying Amount Of A Financial Asset With Payments That Are Not Fixed Or Determinable

15-103.　The two basic Recommendations for assets that are not to be settled by scheduled payments of fixed or determinable amounts are as follows:

RE-ED Paragraph .112　*When a financial asset that is not to be settled by scheduled payments of fixed or determinable amounts is carried on the cost basis and its fair value has declined below its carrying amount, the carrying amount should be reviewed. In the absence of persuasive evidence that the carrying amount of such an asset will be recoverable within the intended holding period, its carrying amount should be reduced to the estimated recoverable amount. The amount of the reduction should be charged to income in the period in which it is recognized.*

When an entity carries the asset at an amount exceeding its fair value, the entity should disclose:

(a) *its reasons for doing so and the nature of the evidence that provides a basis for management's belief that the carrying amount will be recovered; and*

(b) *the carrying amount and the fair value of the asset (or, in the case of a group of assets each of which is carried at an amount in excess of its fair value, the aggregate of the carrying amounts and the aggregate of the fair values of all such assets).*

RE-ED Paragraph .113 *When the carrying amount of a financial asset that is not to be settled by scheduled payments of fixed or determinable amounts has been written down to estimated recoverable amount and the estimated recoverable amount subsequently increases, the write down should be reversed to the extent of the increase. The amount of the reversal should be credited to income in the period in which it is recognized.*

15-104. A financial asset that is not to be settled by scheduled payments of fixed or determinable amounts will be referred to in the remainder of this section as a non monetary financial asset.

15-105. The Recommendations make several additional points with respect to these non monetary financial assets:

Valuation It will not generally be possible to assess impairment of a non monetary financial asset on the basis of the present value of expected future cash flows. Impairment of this type of asset results from exposure to market risk and is presumed to have occurred when the fair value of such an asset has declined below its carrying amount. Such a decline in value should be recognized unless there is clear and persuasive evidence that the circumstances that led to the decline in value will be reversed in the foreseeable future.

Factors To Consider Assessing whether a decline in the fair value of a non monetary financial asset will reverse, an entity will take into account the ability of the issuer of the underlying financial instrument to generate cash flow in the future, including:

(a) changes in the political or legal environment affecting the issuer's business, such as enactment of new environmental protection, tax or trade laws;

(b) changes in the level of demand for the goods or services sold by the issuer resulting from factors such as changing consumer tastes or product obsolescence;

(c) structural changes in the industry or industries in which the issuer operates, such as changes in production technology or the number of competitors; and

(d) changes in the issuer's financial condition evidenced by changes in factors such as its liquidity, credit rating, profitability, cash flows, debt/equity ratio and level of dividend payments.

Use Of Market Prices The existence of active markets for particular non monetary financial assets provides a basis for determining whether fair value has declined. Using these values should include a review of past volatility of the market price and changes in the market price of the asset relative to changes in the market price of other similar assets.

Evidence Of Decline When the fair value of a non monetary financial asset has declined below its carrying amount but a write down has not been recognized because management believes that the carrying amount can be recovered, the situation will have to be monitored to ensure that the evidence remains persuasive. Examples of circumstances that call into question management's beliefs would include:

(a) the market value of the asset remaining below its carrying amount for a period of two years;
(b) suspension of trading in the asset;
(c) severe losses by the investee in the current year;
(d) continued losses by the investee for a period of two years;
(e) liquidity or going concern problems of the investee;
(f) appraisal of the fair value of the asset at less than its carrying amount.

If the decline has not reversed within two years, any evidence that the carrying amount will be recoverable is presumed not to be persuasive.

Write Down Vs. Fair Value   A write down to reflect impairment is based on the holder's best estimate of the amount it will recover from the asset. This amount may be more or less than the current fair value at that time. As a consequence, such write downs are not the same as the mark-to-market adjustment that might be used on a similar asset carried at fair value.

Portfolio Considerations   Financial assets are assessed individually, not on a portfolio basis, in determining whether a reduction in carrying value is required.

Hedged Assets   The existence of a hedge does not influence whether the carrying amount of a financial asset is impaired. However, income on the hedge may offset any loss on the asset.

Assets Carried At Amounts In Excess Of Fair Value   When an asset is exposed to market risk and the holder continues to carry it at an amount in excess of fair value, additional disclosures should separately identify the asset, its carrying amount and its fair value, and explain the circumstances.

Reversals Of Write Offs   It is permissible to reverse a write down for impairment on the basis of new information. Such reversals do not result in increasing the carrying amount of a financial asset above its historical cost.

Restructuring Of A Financial Liability

15-106.   The following Recommendation is applicable when there is a restructuring of a financial liability:

> **RE-ED Paragraph .127**   *When the amounts of scheduled payments in respect of a financial liability carried on the cost basis have been reduced by agreement with the holder of the instrument, the carrying amount of the liability should be reduced to the amount of the revised future payments, discounted at the rate of interest inherent in the financial liability when initially recognized. The amount of the reduction should be credited to income in the period in which it is recognized.*

15-107.   Under GAAP, a debtor does not normally recognize a change in the fair value of its liabilities resulting from a decline in its creditworthiness. However, a restructuring involves a formal reduction in the debtor's contractual obligations and this should be recognized.

15-108.   Recognition of the change in contractual obligations resulting from a restructuring will normally result in a gain for the debtor. The amount will generally be given separate recognition in the financial statements.

15-109.   The revised carrying value after the restructuring is the present value of the new contractual obligations, discounted at the rate inherent in the liability when it was initially recognized.

15-110.   The Section also notes that, in certain limited circumstances, assets and liabilities may be comprehensively revalued under the provisions of Section 1625, "Comprehensive Revaluation Of Assets And Liabilities".

Gain And Loss Recognition

15-111.   The following Recommendation deals with gains and losses on financial assets or financial liabilities held for the long term:

> **RE-ED Paragraph .130**   *Except as provided otherwise by paragraphs .097, .098, .112, .113, .127, and .158, a gain or loss on a financial asset or liability intended to be held for the long term or to maturity should be recognized in income only when it is realized and the asset or liability is removed from the balance sheet.*

15-112.   This Recommendation is consistent with the general application of the cost method in accounting and needs little explanation. It would apply equally in situations where there is a partial disposition or settlement. In these situations, the carrying amount of the asset or liability would be allocated between the portion disposed of or settled and the remaining portion on the basis of relative fair values at the date of the partial disposition or settlement.

15-113.   Some compound and derivative financial instruments provide the holder with a right to acquire another financial asset other than cash or to issue a financial liability through a transaction that extinguishes the right. While the financial asset or liability representing the right would be removed from the balance sheet when it is exercised, no gain or loss would be recorded. The old carrying value of the asset or liability would become a component of the cost of the new asset or liability.

Financial Assets And Financial Liabilities Held For Hedging Purposes

Background

15-114.   In the economic sense, hedging concerns the reduction or elimination of the effects of market risk, interest rate risk or currency risk, some or all of which may be present in a financial instrument. It involves entering into some type of transaction with a view to reducing the entity's exposure to losses due to these types of price risk. In most hedging situations, an additional consequence of the transaction is to reduce the potential for profit associated with a financial instrument.

15-115.   A wide variety of hedging instruments are available in today's financial markets. They include forward contracts, futures contracts, interest rate and currency swaps, caps, collars, floors, as well as various types of option arrangements. For the most part, hedging instruments are derivative in nature and designed to transfer one element of the risks inherent in a particular primary instrument.

15-116.   Accounting procedures for these instruments are complicated by the fact that they are often used for speculative purposes as well as hedging. For example, assume that on January 1, 1998 an enterprise with a December 31 year end enters a forward exchange contract to take delivery of DM1,000,000 on July 1, 1999. If the contract rate is DM1 = $0.90 (equal to the spot rate on that date), and the spot rate on December 31, 1998 is DM1 = $0.80, the question of whether or not this contract is serving as a hedge becomes very significant. If the contract was entered for purely speculative purposes, the forward exchange contract would be classified as an operating instrument subject to fair value accounting procedures. This would mean that a loss of $100,000 [DM1,000,000)][($0.90 - $0.80)] would have to be recorded and taken into 1998 Net Income. Alternatively, if the enterprise has a DM1,000,000 payable that is due on July 1, 1999, the contract is serving as a hedge and hedge accounting becomes appropriate. Under hedge accounting procedures, gains and losses on a hedging instrument are recognized on the same basis as the corresponding loss or gain on the hedged position. This means that the $100,000 loss on the forward contract would be exactly offset by a corresponding gain on the DM1,000,000 payable, resulting in no inclusion in the 1998 Net Income of the enterprise. This somewhat oversimplified example serves to make clear the importance of distinguishing between those financial instruments that are being used as a hedge and those that would be classified as operating transactions.

Identification Of A Hedge

15-117.   The Re-Exposure Draft's basic Recommendation on this issue is as follows:

RE-ED Paragraph .134   *A financial instrument should be accounted for as a hedge when:*

(a) *the position to be hedged is specifically identified and exposes the entity to risk of loss from price changes;*

(b) *the instrument is specifically designated as a hedge; and*

(c) *it is highly probable that changes in the fair value of the instrument designated as a hedge and opposite changes in the fair value of the position being hedged will have a high degree of correlation so that the hedging instrument will be effective as a hedge (i.e., it eliminates or reduces substantially the risk of loss from the position being hedged.)*

15-118.   The Re-Exposure Draft makes a number of additional points with respect to this basic Recommendation:

Purpose Of Hedging   Hedging involves entering into a transaction in the expectation that it will reduce an entity's exposure to loss from price risk, normally with the additional consequence of reducing the potential for profit. Most of the following discussion is directed at hedges of exposed positions related to financial assets or liabilities. The Section does not preclude the possibility of applying hedge accounting to a financial asset or liability that hedges an exposed position arising from a non financial asset or liability.

Increased Risk Exposure   In some situations, an entity may acquire a financial instrument that increases its exposure to price risk. For example, an entity may acquire an interest rate swap that gives it a floating receipt in exchange for a fixed payment and offsets the effect of any fluctuation in the amount of interest payments on a floating rate financial liability. Such transactions do not qualify as hedging transactions but may be carried on the cost basis if they are to be held for the long term.

Applicability Of Hedge Accounting   A financial instrument can be identified as a hedge when an entity has a specifically identified position that is exposed to the risk of loss as a result of adverse price changes in financial markets and the effect of holding the instrument is to mitigate that risk of loss. The hedge will often be imperfect in practice, it may apply to financial liabilities as well as to financial assets, and it may apply to unrecognized as well as recognized financial assets and liabilities.

Derivative Instruments   The more commonly used hedging instruments are derivative instruments that are designed to transfer one element of the risks inherent in a particular primary instrument. As these instruments can be used for other purposes, it is necessary to designate when they are being used as a hedge.

Management Intent   The substance of a hedging agreement is determined partly by management intent. Designation as a hedge subsequent to its initial recognition by an entity is possible. However, retroactive treatment is not acceptable. That is, there can be no adjustment to defer any previously recognized income or expense associated with the hedging instrument.

Entity Wide Exposure   To determine whether the entity has an existing or expected price exposure that can be hedged effectively, management must consider whether the specific exposed position is already offset, in whole or in part, by other financial assets, financial liabilities, or anticipated future transactions, even though not accounted for as hedges.

Limitations   For large entities that operate on a decentralized basis, determining entity wide exposure to risk may not be practicable. In these situations, management of price risks may be assigned to individual business units or groups of business units. In such circumstances, it is appropriate for purposes of identifying a financial instrument as a hedging instrument that the assessment of an entity's price risk exposure be made at the highest level of management at which information is available and decisions about risk are made.

Imperfect Hedges   A hedging instrument may offset only part of a specific risk or may provide coverage for only part of the life of the specific risk. For example, if interest rate risk is hedged for 50 percent of the amount of a liability for only 50 percent of its life, the liability is considered 50 percent exposed for one-half of its life and 100 percent exposed for the remainder. If the hedge is larger or longer than the position being hedged, only a portion of the instrument can be accounted for using hedge accounting.

Monetary Assets Held To Maturity   Such assets are not exposed to interest rate risk that is eligible to be hedged by another instrument.

Unrecognized Or Anticipated Exposures   An entity may have a position that is eligible to be hedged when the entity anticipates undertaking a transaction that results in an exposure to financial price risk. Exposure may also result from unrecognized financial assets or financial liabilities.

Anticipated Transactions   Hedge accounting for anticipated transactions is only appropriate when it is highly probable that the transaction will take place. In evaluating if it is highly probable that an anticipated transaction will occur, an entity considers when the transaction is expected to occur and other factors such as the following:

(a) the frequency of similar transactions in the past;

(b) the financial and operational ability of the entity to carry out the anticipated transaction;

(c) substantial current commitments of resources by the entity to the business activity of which the anticipated transaction is a part;

(d) the extent of loss or disruption to the entity if it does not undertake the anticipated transaction;

(e) the likelihood that other, substantially different transactions might take place to achieve the same business purpose; and

(f) the likelihood that another party will be willing and able to undertake the anticipated transaction with the entity.

Non Financial Business Risks   Hedge accounting is not appropriate when a financial instrument has been acquired to mitigate the effects of financial risks associated with future purchases or sales of other financial instruments that are possible but not highly probable, or to mitigate the possible effects of other, non financial business risks.

Effectiveness Of Hedge   For a financial instrument to be effective as a hedge, there must be a high degree of probability that there will be a correlation between changes in the fair value of the hedging instrument and opposite changes in the fair value of the position being hedged. This means that the economic relationship between the prices of the two items must be clear.

Derivatives As Hedges   If a derivative is used as a hedge, an entity will normally take into consideration only its intrinsic value in determining correlation with the hedged item. (Intrinsic value is the excess of the fair value of the underlying financial instrument over the contractual exercise price contained in the derivative.)

This means that options cannot be used as hedges when they are "out of the money".

Income Recognition Of A Gain Or Loss On A Hedging Instrument

15-119.   The basic Recommendation here is as follows:

RE-ED Paragraph .151   *A gain or loss from a change in the fair value of a financial instrument accounted for as a hedge should be recognized in income when the corresponding loss or gain from a change in the fair value of the hedged position is recognized in income.*

15-120.   The Re-Exposure Draft makes a number of additional points with respect to this basic Recommendation:

Normal Situation   In the normal situation, the hedge and the hedged position will both be carried at fair value. In this situation, changes in value on both the hedging instrument and the hedged position will be recorded as they occur. This means that no special procedures are required to implement the Recommendation in Paragraph .151.

Hedged Position At Cost   In some situations, the hedged position may be carried at cost. If the hedging instrument is carried at fair value, changes in its value will have to be deferred and included in income when the corresponding changes on the hedged position are included.

Imperfect Hedges   If a hedge is imperfect, the gain (loss) on the hedging instrument will not be equal to the loss (gain) on the hedged position. This difference should be taken into income immediately.

Anticipated Future Transactions   When a hedge has been established for an anticipated future transaction, gains or losses on the hedging instrument will occur before the future transaction takes place. In this situation, the gains or losses on the hedging instrument should be carried forward and matched against the corresponding losses or gain on the hedged future position.

Time Value Of Derivative Instruments   When a derivative instrument is used as a hedge, changes in its time value are not correlated to the hedged item. As a consequence, they should be recognized in income over the term of the hedge, regardless of when the changes in the intrinsic value of the derivative instrument are recognized in income. However, if the derivative instrument is carried at fair value, all of the changes in value will be recognized as they occur and it is not necessary to separate the two amounts.

Discontinuance Of Hedge Accounting

15-121.   The basic Recommendation here is as follows:

RE-ED Paragraph .158   *If a financial instrument classified as a hedge ceases to satisfy all of the conditions in paragraph .134, hedge accounting should be discontinued. At the date of discontinuance of hedge accounting, the hedging instrument should be reclassified in accordance with paragraph .166. To the extent that changes in the fair value of the hedging instrument prior to discontinuance of hedge accounting have been correlated with opposite changes in the fair value of the hedged position and have not been recognized in income, such changes should be recognized in income when the corresponding changes in fair value of the hedged position are recognized.*

15-122.   The use of hedge accounting is conditional on meeting the three criteria specified in Paragraph .134. If all of these conditions are not satisfied, then hedge accounting is no longer appropriate. More specifically, hedge accounting should be discontinued if:

1. the position being hedged no longer exists or no longer exposes the entity to the risk of loss from price changes;

2. the hedging instrument may be reclassified because of a change in management's intentions; or

3. the hedging instrument is no longer effective with respect to its price correlation with the item being hedged.

15-123.   Subsequent to discontinuance, the entity will cease to match income on the hedging instrument with income on the hedged item. There will, however, be no restatement of previously reported income figures.

15-124.   If the hedging instrument is carried at fair value, all of the gains and losses prior to discontinuance will have been recognized. However, some portion of these gains and losses may have been deferred for later inclusion in income (e.g., if they relate to an anticipated future transaction). If there is no basis for continuing to defer such amounts, they should be included in income immediately.

15-125.   When the hedged position is made up of instruments carried at cost, there may be a difference between the unrecognized gain or loss on the hedging instrument and the unrecognized gain or loss on the hedged position. Two possibilities arise here:

1. If the gain or loss on the hedged position is equal to or greater than the corresponding loss or gain on the hedging instrument, the loss or gain on the hedging instrument is carried forward and recognized in income when the hedged position is disposed of, settled, or revalued.

2. If the loss or gain on the hedging instrument exceeds the gain or loss on the hedged position, only the loss or gain on the hedging instrument that corresponds to the gain or loss on the hedged position can be carried forward. If the hedging instrument is being carried at cost, the remaining loss or gain will be recognized when the hedging instrument is disposed of or settled.

Other Financial Assets And Liabilities

15-126.   The two basic Recommendations here are as follows:

RE-ED Paragraph .163   *Subsequent to initial recognition and measurement, a financial asset or financial liability that is not intended to be held for the long term or to maturity and is not classified as a hedging instrument should be remeasured at each balance sheet date and reported at its fair value.*

RE-ED Paragraph .164   *A gain or loss from a change in the fair value of a financial asset or financial liability that is not intended to be held for the long term or to maturity and is not classified as a hedging instrument should be recognized in income as it arises.*

15-127.   This residual category of financial instruments is made up of those financial instruments that are not being held for the long term or until maturity and that are not being used as hedging instruments. Examples of such instruments would include:

• Financial instruments that are being used for speculative purposes.

• Financial instruments that are being used by a portfolio manager to enhance the overall yield on the assets in the portfolio.

• Financial instruments that management hopes to hold to maturity but does not have the demonstrated capacity to do so.

Reclassification (Not Covered By Section 3860)

15-128.   The basic Recommendation here is as follows:

> **RE-ED Paragraph .166**   *When a substantive event occurs that causes management of an entity to change its intention with respect to a financial asset or financial liability after initial classification, the asset or liability should be reclassified and the measurement basis changed in accordance with management's revised intention. Except as provided otherwise by paragraph .158, any gain or loss resulting from a change in the measurement basis should be recognized in income in the period of the reclassification and disclosed separately.*

15-129.   Based on consideration of management's intent, an entity may find it appropriate to reclassify a financial instrument. Such a reclassification will often result in a change in the basis of measurement.

15-130.   If the change is from fair value to cost, the new cost is based on the fair value as at the date of reclassification. Except for certain instruments designated as hedges of anticipated transactions, changes in fair value prior to reclassification will have already been included in income and no restatement of these amounts will be made.

15-131.   If the change is from cost to fair value, the difference arising will be included in income of the current period. Again, the exception to this would be with respect to a financial instrument that has been designated as a hedge of an anticipated transaction.

15-132.   Discontinuance of hedging is a form of reclassification. The treatment of this type of reclassification has been previously dealt with in Paragraphs .160 and .162.

Interest Income And Interest Expense (Not Covered By Section 3860)

Basic Recommendations

15-133.   The first Recommendation here is as follows:

> **RE-ED Paragraph .170**   *Interest income or interest expense arising from a financial asset or a financial liability should be recognized and measured on a basis that reflects the effective yield on the instrument.*

15-134.   This Recommendation requires the use of the effective yield approach to measuring income on financial instruments. In the case of financial instruments carried at cost this involves present value calculations using the yield inherent in the initial recognition of the instrument. This yield is the rate which equates the present value of the cash receipts on the instruments with the amount recognized at its acquisition.   These calculations are illustrated in several examples in the Appendix. In this Chapter, we have included these examples in the Section which follows.

15-135.   If the financial instrument is carried at fair value, the total return on the asset comprises the amount of any change in fair value, together with interest, dividends or other receipts.   Correspondingly, the cost of a liability comprises the amount of any change in fair value together with interest or other payments. The periodic remeasurement of the asset or liability incorporates an implicit amortization of any discount or premium existing from time to time.

15-136.   A second Recommendation in this area relates to the various types of fees that may arise in connection with the origination, restructuring, or settlement of a financial instrument:

> **RE-ED Paragraph .171**   *When fees charged or credited in connection with a financial instrument are in substance an integral part of the effective yield on the re-*

sulting financial asset or financial liability, the fees should be accounted for on a basis that reflects the effective yield in accordance with paragraph .170.

15-137. While exceptions are discussed in the Re-Exposure Draft, this Recommendation requires that fees associated with the issuance of specific financial instruments be included in the determination of the yield inherent in the initial recognition of the financial instrument.

Re-Exposure Draft Material On Effective Rate Method

15-138. Paragraphs A.19 through A.25 of the Re-Exposure Draft Appendix contain material on the application of the effective rate method and serve to illustrate the Recommendations of the preceding Section on interest income and interest expense. This material is reviewed here, in conjunction with the Recommendations from the main body of the Re-Exposure Draft.

15-139. The Appendix notes that discounting requires prediction of the amount and timing of future cash flows. As a consequence, this approach is generally only appropriate in situations where the financial asset or financial liability can be settled by scheduled payments of fixed or determinable amounts (monetary assets and monetary liabilities). This approach is not generally appropriate for equity instruments.

Example One - Fixed Payments

15-140. This first example is a simple one in which the interest payments are fixed and there is no default on any of the amounts. The information is as follows:

An entity borrows cash from another party for a 5 year term on a promissory note that provides for payments of interest annually in arrears at the rate of 8 percent on the stated principal amount of $1,000,000. Repayment of principal is to occur on maturity. The note is issued at a discount for net proceeds of $985,000. It is assumed there are no fees or transaction costs.

The effective yield on the note is 8.38 percent, the discount rate that equates the present value of the future payments on account of principal and interest to the initially recognized carrying amount of $985,000. The first year's interest expense of $82,538 is equal to this rate applied to the initially recognized carrying amount. The carrying amount of the note is increased by the accrual of the interest and reduced by the actual payment of $80,000. This process continues until the maturity of the note. The annual interest expense increases each year to reflect the small increase in the carrying amount of the liability as the initial discount is amortized. The accounting is summarized in Table A.

Table A - Debt With Fixed Payment				
	Contractual Payments (Receipts)	PV Of Payments on Inception Of The Note	Carrying Amount	Interest Expense
Beginning - Year 1	($ 985,000)		$985,000	
End Of Year 1	80,000	$ 73,815	987,538	$ 82,538
End Of Year 2	80,000	68,108	990,288	82,750
End Of Year 3	80,000	62,842	993,269	82,981
End Of Year 4	80,000	57,983	996,499	83,230
End Of Year 5	1,080,000	722,252	-0-	83,501
Total	$ 415,000	$985,000	N/A	$415,000
Effective Yield		8.38%		

Table B - Debt With Floating Interest Rate				
	Contractual Payments (Receipts)	PV Of Payments At Beginning Of Year 3	Carrying Amount	Interest Expense
Beginning - Year 1	($ 985,000)		$985,000	
End Of Year 1	80,000		987,538	$ 82,538
End Of Year 2	80,000		990,288	82,750
Beginning - Year 3			990,288	
End Of Year 3	90,000	$ 82,277	993,239	92,951
End Of Year 4	90,000	75,217	996,468	93,229
End Of Year 5	1,090,000	832,794	-0-	93,532
Total	$ 445,000	$990,288	N/A	$445,000
Effective Yield		9.39%		

Example Two - Determinable Interest Payments

15-141.   The calculations become more complex when the rate is determinable but not fixed. An example of this would be an interest rate that floats in relation to some other rate, for example the prime rate. When the rate changes under such provisions, a new effective rate is created and this rate must be used in future calculations. A fairly simple example of this type of situation is as follows:

An entity borrows cash from another party for a 5 year term on a promissory note that provides for payments of interest annually in arrears on the stated principal amount of $1,000,000 at a rate equal to a specific bank's prime rate plus 1 percent. Repayment of principal is to occur on maturity. Due to fees and transaction costs, the entity receives a net amount of $985,000 on inception of the note. The interest rate on the principal is 8 percent in Year 1 and Year 2 under the interest formula in the note. At the beginning of Year 3, the rate under the formula rises to 9 percent.

The effective yield on the note is 8.38% for Years 1 and 2, as in Example One. At the beginning of Year 3, assuming the new rate will persist for the remaining term to maturity, a new effective yield is determined equal to the rate that equates the present value of the remaining cash flows to the carrying amount of $990,288. The new rate is 9.39 percent and will be used for determining the interest expense until the rate in the interest formula changes again, as summarized in Table B.

Example Three - Determinable Principal

15-142.   A third example involves a note in which the interest rate is fixed. However, the principal amount is tied to the market price of oil. As was the case when there was a change in the interest rate on a floating rate note, any change in the expected principal amount will change the effective yield for the remaining life of the note. The example is as follows:

The principal amount of a note to be paid in cash is the market value of 50,000 barrels of oil at the maturity date of the note. The stated interest rate is 8 percent applied to a $1,000,000 notional principal amount. At the beginning of Year 3, the carrying amount of the note is $990,288 and it is estimated that $1,033,000 will be payable on account of principal when the note matures at the end of Year 5 (i.e., it is estimated that the price of oil on the maturity date will be $20.66 per barrel). The analysis of this situation for Years 3, 4, and 5 is found in Table C (on following page).

Table C - Debt With Floating Principal Amount				
	Contractual Payments (Receipts)	PV Of Payments At Beginning Of Year 3	Carrying Amount	Interest Expense
Beginning - Year 3			$ 990,288	
End Of Year 3	$ 80,000	$ 73,135	1,003,268	$ 92,980
End Of Year 4	80,000	66,860	1,017,468	94,200
End Of Year 5	1,113,000	850,293	-0-	95,532
Total	$1,273,000	$990,288	N/A	$282,712
Effective Yield		9.39%		

Example Four - Impaired Notes

15-143.   The effective yield is also changed when the expected payments on a note are changed. This would happen when a financial asset is impaired because payments are expected to be less or later than specified in the debt contract. An example of this situation is as follows:

The holder of the note described in Example One monitors the creditworthiness of the issuer and, early in Year 3, determines that the issuer will not be able to make the contractually required payments of interest and principal. The holder originally advanced the loan and, as a result, its carrying amount is the same as the issuer's prior to the impairment. Following analysis of the available evidence, management of the note holder makes its best estimate of the expected future cash flows from the note and determines that, as at the beginning of Year 3, the present value of the expected future cash flows is $625,643. The expected future cash flows are discounted at the effective yield rate inherent in the note on initial recognition, determined to be 9.39 percent as at the beginning of Year 3. The $364,645 difference between the holder's carrying amount of the note at the beginning of Year 3 ($990,288 as shown in Table B) and the recoverable amount ($625,643) represents the charge against the holder's net income in Year 3 for the loss on impairment. Interest income on the impaired asset is determined for Year 3 and subsequent years by applying the effective yield to the written down balance as at the beginning of the year. The holder accounts for the note on the basis set out in Table D.

Table D - Debt With Impaired Cash Flows					
		Best Estimate Of Payments Expected To Be Received			
	Contractual Payments	Actual Amount	PV Beginning Of Year 3	Carrying Amount	Interest Income
Opening Year 3 After Recording Impairment				$625,643	
End Of Year 3	$ 90,000	$ -0-	$ -0-	684,391	$ 58,748
End Of Year 4	90,000	50,000	41,784	698,655	64,264
End Of Year 5	1,090,000	50,000	38,198	714,259	65,604
End Of Year 6	-0-	50,000	34,919	731,328	67,069
End Of Year 7	-0-	800,000	510,742	-0-	68,672
Total	$1,270,000	$950,000	$625,643	N/A	$324,357
Effective Yield		9.39%			

Disclosure (Covered By Section 3860)

General Requirements

Objectives

15-144.   The disclosures required by this Section are intended to provide information that will enhance users' understanding of the significance of recognized and unrecognized financial instruments to an entity's financial position, performance and cash flows and to assist in assessing the amounts, timing and certainty of future cash flows associated with those instruments.

15-145.   Beyond providing quantitative information on financial instrument balances and transactions, entities are encouraged to provide a discussion of the extent to which financial instruments are used, the associated risks and the business purposes associated with financial instruments, including policies on matters such as hedging of risk exposures, avoidance of undue concentrations of risk and requirements for collateral to mitigate credit risks.

Types Of Risk

15-146.   An important part of financial instrument disclosure involves providing information to assist users in assessing the extent of risk associated with both recognized and unrecognized financial instruments. To assist in organizing the presentation of this information, Paragraph 3860.44 classifies the relevant types of risk as follows:

(a) **Price risk**   There are three types of price risk: currency risk, interest rate risk and market risk. Currency risk is the risk that the value of a financial instrument will fluctuate due to changes in foreign exchange rates. Interest rate risk is the risk that the value of a financial instrument will fluctuate due to changes in market interest rates. Market risk is the risk that the value of a financial instrument will fluctuate as a result of changes in market prices whether those changes are caused by factors specific to the individual security or its issuer or factors affecting all securities traded in the market.

(b) **Credit risk**   Credit risk is the risk that one party to a financial instrument will fail to discharge an obligation and cause the other party to incur a financial loss.

(c) **Liquidity risk**   Liquidity risk, also referred to as funding risk, is the risk that an entity will encounter difficulty in raising funds to meet commitments associated with financial instruments. Liquidity risk may result from an inability to sell a financial asset quickly at close to its fair value.

(d) **Cash flow risk**   Cash flow risk is the risk that future cash flows associated with a monetary financial instrument will fluctuate in amount. In the case of a floating rate debt instrument, for example, such fluctuations result in a change in the effective interest rate of the financial instrument, usually without a corresponding change in its fair value.

Format

15-147.   Section 3860 does not prescribe the format of the required disclosures or its location within the financial statements. In the case of recognized financial instruments, balances will be included in the financial statements. There is no requirement that such information be repeated in the notes to the financial statements. In dealing with unrecognized financial instruments, the required disclosures can only be presented in notes or other supplementary types of information.

15-148.   With respect to the level of detail for the required disclosures, it will be necessary to strike a balance between providing excessive detail that is of little value to users and obscuring significant information by using too much aggregation. Such decisions will require the exercise of professional judgment.

15-149.   For disclosure purposes, management will be required to group financial instruments into appropriate classes. Characteristics that will be used in this process would include:

• Whether the instruments are recognized or unrecognized.

• The measurement basis used (cost vs. fair value).

15-150.   When disclosure of a particular instrument or group of instruments is included in both the notes and the financial statements, users should be able to reconcile the information contained in the two locations.

Accounting Policies

15-151.   As there are alternative accounting polices for dealing with financial instruments, Section 1505, "Disclosure Of Accounting Policies", would be applicable. The disclosure required by Section 1505 for financial instruments could include:

(a) the criteria applied in determining when to recognize a financial asset or financial liability on the balance sheet and when to cease to recognize it;

(b) the basis of measurement applied to financial assets and financial liabilities both on initial recognition and subsequently; and

(c) the basis on which income and expense arising from financial assets and financial liabilities is recognized and measured.

15-152.   Section 3860 lists the following as transactions where it may be necessary to disclose accounting policies:

(a) transfers of financial assets when there is a continuing interest in, or involvement with, the assets by the transferor, such as securitizations of financial assets, repurchase agreements and reverse repurchase agreements;

(b) transfers of financial assets to a trust for the purpose of satisfying liabilities when they mature without the obligation of the transferor being discharged at the time of the transfer, such as an in-substance defeasance trust;

(c) acquisition or issuance of separate financial instruments as part of a series of transactions designed to synthesize the effect of acquiring or issuing a single instrument;

(d) acquisition or issuance of financial instruments as hedges of risk exposures; and

(e) acquisition or issuance of monetary financial instruments bearing a stated interest rate that differs from the prevailing market rate at the date of issue.

15-153.   With respect to disclosure of accounting policies for measuring financial instruments, Section 3860 points out that it is not adequate to simply indicate the use of cost or fair value. Additional information is necessary to allow users to understand how the method has been applied. For example, when cost is used, the entity might be required to disclose how it accounts for:

• Costs of acquisition or issuance;

• Premiums and discounts on monetary financial assets and financial liabilities;

• Changes in the estimated amount of determinable future cash flows associated with a monetary financial instrument such as a bond indexed to a commodity price;

• Changes in circumstances that result in significant uncertainty about the timely collection of all contractual amounts due from monetary financial assets;

- Declines in the fair value of financial assets below their carrying amount; and

- Restructured financial liabilities.

15-154.   For instruments carried at fair value, disclosure should include the methods used in determining these amounts (quoted market prices, appraisals, etc.).

15-155.   Accounting policy disclosure would include the basis for reporting in the income statement realized and unrealized gains and losses, interest, and other items of income and expense associated with financial instruments. When income and expense items are netted in the Income Statement and the corresponding Balance Sheet items are not netted, the reason for such presentation should be disclosed.

Terms And Conditions

15-156.   The basic Recommendation in this area is as follows:

Paragraph 3860.52   *For each class of financial asset, financial liability and equity instrument, both recognized and unrecognized, an entity should disclose information about the extent and nature of the financial instruments, including significant terms and conditions that may affect the amount, timing and certainty of future cash flows.* (January, 1996)

15-157.   The Section makes a number of additional points with respect to general disclosure:

Paragraph 3860.54   ... terms and conditions that may warrant disclosure include:

(a)   the principal, stated, face or other similar amount which, for some derivative instruments, such as interest rate swaps, may be the amount (referred to as the notional amount) on which future payments are based;

(b)   the date of maturity, expiry or execution;

(c)   early settlement options held by either party to the instrument, including the period in which, or date at which, the options may be exercised and the exercise price or range of prices;

(d)   options held by either party to the instrument to convert the instrument into, or exchange it for, another financial instrument or some other asset or liability, including the period in which, or date at which the options may be exercised and the conversion or exchange ratio(s);

(e)   the amount and timing of scheduled future cash receipts or payments of the principal amount of the instrument, including instalment repayments and any sinking fund or similar requirements;

(f)   stated rate or amount of interest, dividend or other periodic return on principal and the timing of the payments;

(g)   collateral held, in the case of a financial asset, or pledged, in the case of a financial liability;

(h)   in the case of an instrument for which cash flows are denominated in a currency other than the entity's reporting currency, the currency in which receipts or payments are required;

(i)   in the case of an instrument that provides for an exchange, information described in items (a) to (h) for the instrument to be acquired in the exchange; and

(j)   any condition of the instrument or an associated covenant that, if contravened, would significantly alter any of the other terms (for example, a maximum debt-to-equity ratio in a bond covenant that, if contravened, would make the full principal amount of the bond due and payable immediately).

Individual Vs. Group Disclosure   If no single instrument is individually significant to the future cash flows of the entity, the essential characteristics of the instruments should be described by reference to appropriate groupings of like instruments.

Other Specific Requirements   Other *Handbook* Sections may have specific disclosure requirements for financial instruments (e.g., Section 3050, "Long Term Investments").

Legal Form   When the Balance Sheet presentation of a financial instruments differs from the instrument's legal form (e.g., preferred stock presented as debt), it is desirable for an entity to explain in the notes to the financial statements the nature of the instrument.

Relationships Between Instruments   Disclosure should be made in a manner that indicates the nature and extent of the associated financial risk exposures and any relationships between instruments that alter the entity's overall risk exposure. Examples of this would include the relationship between a hedging instrument and the related hedged position, or the relationship between the components of a synthetic instrument.

Disclosures Concerning Interest Rate Risk

Basic Recommendation

15-158.   The basic Recommendation in this area is as follows:

Paragraph 3860.57   *For each class of financial asset and financial liability, both recognized and unrecognized, an entity should disclose information about its exposure to interest rate risk, including:*

(a) contractual repricing or maturity dates, whichever dates are earlier; and

(b) effective interest rates, when applicable. (January, 1996)

15-159.   This disclosure would include which of the entity's financial assets are exposed to:

(a) **Interest Rate Price Risk**   An example of this would be monetary financial assets or financial liabilities with a fixed interest rate.

(b) **Interest Rate Cash Flow Risk**   An example of this would be a monetary financial asset or financial liability with a floating interest rate that is reset as market rates change.

(c) **Not Exposed To Interest Rate Risk**   An example of this would be some investments in equity securities.

15-160.   In transactions such as securitization, an entity may retain exposure to interest rate risk on financial assets, even when those assets are removed from the Balance Sheet. Correspondingly, it may be exposed to interest rate risk as the result of a transaction where no financial asset or financial liability is recognized. An example of this latter situation would be a commitment to issue funds at a specified rate of interest. Despite the fact that the relevant financial assets or liabilities are not included in the Balance Sheet, disclosure of the nature and extent of the entity's exposure should be provided.

Repricing Or Maturity Dates

15-161.   Changes in interest rates have a direct impact on the cash flows associated with particular financial assets or financial liabilities. Information about contractual repricing or maturity dates provides users with information as to how long interest rates are fixed. This gives a basis for evaluating interest rate price risk and, thereby, the potential for gain or loss. In the case of instruments that are repriced prior to maturity, the repricing date is clearly more relevant than the maturity date.

15-162.   While the basic Recommendation refers to contractually determined repricing or maturity dates, expected repricing or maturity dates may differ from those specified in the legal arrangement. An example of this would be mortgage loans where the creditor can choose to repay prior to maturity. When management is able to predict with reasonable reliability the expected dates on which the loans will be repaid, disclosure of this information can be useful.

Effective Interest Rate

15-163.   The effective interest rate on a monetary financial instrument is the rate that, when used to discount the future cash flows from the instrument, will equate its value to the carrying amount of the instrument. The future cash flows would extend to the next repricing or maturity date. The rate is a historical one for fixed rate instruments carried at amortized cost and a current market rate for floating rate instruments or instruments carried at fair value.

15-164.   This requirement for disclosure of the effective interest rate applies to bonds, notes, and other similar monetary financial instruments that create a return to the holder and a cost to the issuer which reflects the time value of money. It does not apply to financial instruments that do not provide a determinable interest rate. This would include non monetary financial instruments and most derivative instruments.

Disclosure Format

15-165.   Section 3860 provides a description of several possible formats for providing the required information on interest rate risk:

(a) The carrying amounts of financial instruments exposed to interest rate price risk may be presented in tabular form, grouped by those that are contracted to mature or reprice (i) within one year of the balance sheet date, (ii) more than one year and less than five years from the balance sheet date, and (iii) five years or more from the balance sheet date.

(b) When the performance of an entity is significantly affected by the level of its exposure to interest rate price risk or changes in that exposure, more detailed information is desirable. An entity such as a bank may disclose, for example, separate groupings of the carrying amounts of financial instruments contracted to mature or reprice (i) within one month of the balance sheet date, (ii) more than one and less than three months from the balance sheet date, (and (iii) more than three and less than twelve months from the balance sheet date.

(c) Similarly, an entity may indicate its exposure to interest rate cash flow risk through a table indicating the aggregate carrying amount of groups of floating rate financial assets and financial liabilities maturing within various future time periods.

(d) Interest rate information may be disclosed for individual financial instruments or weighted average rates or a range of rates may be presented for each class of financial instrument. An entity groups instruments denominated in different currencies or having substantially different credit risks into separate classes when these factors result in instruments having substantially different effective interest rates.

Interest Rate Sensitivity

15-166.   Information about interest rate sensitivity may also be useful. This would involve indicating the effect of a hypothetical change in the prevailing level of market interest rates on the fair value of financial instruments and future earnings and cash flows from these instruments.

15-167.   In the case of floating rate instruments, this would involve indicating possible changes in interest income or interest expense. In the case of fixed rate instruments, the reporting would involve disclosing potential gains or losses.

15-168.   Sensitivity disclosure should include information about the basis on which the information is prepared, including any significant assumptions that have been made. The disclosure may or may not be limited to the direct effects of interest rate change on the instruments that are on hand on the Balance Sheet date.

Disclosures Concerning Credit Risk

Basic Recommendation

15-169.   The basic Recommendation in this area is as follows:

> **Paragraph 3860.67**   *For each class of financial asset, both recognized and unrecognized, an entity should disclose information about its exposure to credit risk, including:*
>
> (a) *the amount that best represents its maximum credit risk exposure at the balance sheet date, without taking account of the fair value of any collateral, in the event other parties fail to perform their obligations under financial instruments; and*
>
> (b) *significant concentrations of credit risk.* (January, 1996)

15-170.   This disclosure Recommendation is designed to assist users in assessing the extent to which failures by counterparties to discharge obligations could reduce the amount of future cash inflows from financial assets on hand at the Balance Sheet date. While such failures will give rise to a financial loss to be included in the entity's Income Statement, the Recommendation does not require an entity to disclose an assessment of the probability of losses arising in the future.

15-171.   Note that this disclosure requirement is for amounts exposed to credit risk, without regard to potential recoveries from collateral. Reasons for this approach are as follows:

(a) to ensure that the users of financial statements have a consistent measure of the amount exposed to that risk for all financial assets, whether the assets are recognized or not; and

(b) to take into account the possibility that the exposure to loss may differ from the carrying amount of a recognized financial asset or the fair value of an unrecognized financial asset that is otherwise disclosed in the financial statements.

15-172.   Section 3860 makes several additional points with respect to the disclosure of credit risk:

Recognized Financial Assets   In the case of recognized financial assets exposed to credit risk, the carrying value of the assets in the Balance Sheet, net of an appropriate provision for loss, usually represents the amount of exposure to credit risk. In situations such as this, no additional disclosure, beyond that provided in the Balance Sheet, is required.

Unrecognized Financial Assets   With unrecognized financial assets, the maximum credit risk exposure may be equal to the principal, stated, face or other similar contractual value for the asset. This value would be disclosed in accordance with Paragraph 3860.52 and no further disclosure is required. Similarly, when the maximum credit risk of an unrecognized financial asset is equal to its fair value, this amount would be disclosed in accordance with Paragraph 3860.78 and no further disclosure is required. However, if the maximum possible loss on an unrecognized financial asset differs from the amounts disclosed in accordance with Paragraph 3860.52 or 3860.78, additional disclosure is required.

Set Off Rights   When an entity has a legally enforceable right to set off a financial asset against a financial liability, the net amount will be reported in the Balance Sheet, provided there is an intent to settle on a net basis. Disclosure under Paragraph 3860.67 should include the existence of the legal right of set off. Further, if the financial liability against which a right of set off exists is due to be settled before the financial asset, the entity is exposed to credit risk on the full carrying amount of the asset if the counterparty defaults after the liability has been settled.

Master Netting Arrangements   An entity may have entered into a master netting arrangement that mitigates exposure to credit loss but does not meet the criteria for offsetting. It is desirable for the entity to disclose the terms of the master netting arrangement. Additional disclosure should indicate that:

- the credit risk associated with financial assets subject to a master netting arrangement is eliminated only to the extent that financial liabilities due to the same counterparty will be settled after the assets are realized; and

- the extent to which an entity's overall exposure to credit risk is reduced through a master netting arrangement may change substantially within a short period following the balance sheet date because the exposure is affected by each transaction subject to the arrangement.

Guarantees   If an entity guarantees an obligation of another party, disclosure is required under Paragraph 3860.67. This would include situations such as securitization transactions in which an entity remains exposed by recourse provisions even after the relevant assets have been removed from its Balance Sheet.

Concentrations Of Credit Risk   These must be disclosed separately when they are not inherent in the business of an entity and not apparent from other disclosures. This disclosure should include a description of the shared characteristic that identifies each concentration and the amount of the maximum possible exposure to loss associated with all recognized and unrecognized financial assets sharing that characteristic.

Concentrations of credit risk may arise from exposures to a single debtor or to a group of debtors having similar characteristics. Such concentrations might also arise if a large portion of an entity's debtors are in a single industry or single geographic area. Section 1700, "Segmented Information" may provide useful guidance in identifying the types of credit risk concentrations that may arise and determining the appropriate degree of disaggregation in general purpose financial statements.

Disclosures Concerning Fair Value

15-173.   The basic Recommendation in this area is as follows:

Paragraph 3860.78   *For each class of financial asset and financial liability, both recognized and unrecognized, an entity should disclose information about fair value. When it is not practicable within constraints of timeliness or cost to determine the fair value of a financial asset or financial liability with sufficient reliability, that fact should be disclosed together with information about the principal characteristics of the underlying financial instrument that are pertinent to its fair value.* (January, 1996)

15-174.   Fair value information is crucial to many types of business decisions. It is a value that reflects the judgment of the financial markets as to the present value of the expected future cash flows associated with an instrument. These values provide a neutral basis for assessing management's stewardship by indicating the effects of its decisions to buy, sell, or hold financial assets and, incur, maintain, or discharge financial liabilities. Fair values are essential for making comparisons of financial instruments as they are not influenced by the purpose for which the instrument is being used, or by when or by whom the instrument was issued or acquired.

15-175.   Additional points made by Section 3860 with respect to the disclosure of fair value information are as follows:

Location Of Disclosure   When an entity does not carry a financial asset or financial liability in its Balance Sheet at fair value, the information will have to be provided through note or other supplementary disclosures.

Methods   As fair value can be determined by a variety of methods, disclosure should be made of the methods used.

Going Concern Assumption   In the determination of fair values, the entity should assume that it is a going concern and that the amount that would be paid or received would not be based on a forced transaction or involuntary liquidation. However, the fair value of a financial asset that is to be sold in the immediate future would be influenced by the depth of the market for the asset.

Instruments Traded In Active Markets   For financial instruments traded in active markets, the quoted market price, adjusted for potential transactions costs, would be the best evidence of fair value. When there are separate bid and ask prices, the following would apply:

- For assets held or liabilities to be issued, use the bid price.

- For assets to be acquired or liabilities held, use the ask price.

Instruments Without Usable Market Prices   In situations where market prices do not exist or where the volumes of trading are too small to provide reliable values, estimation techniques will be used to determine fair values. These would include references to other similar instruments, discounted cash flow analysis, and option pricing models.

Transaction Costs   Fair values should include all costs that would be incurred to exchange or settle the underlying financial instrument. These would include taxes and duties, fees and commissions paid to agents, advisers, brokers or dealers, and levies by regulatory agencies or securities exchanges.

Range Of Values   When an instrument is not traded in an active and efficient market, it may be more appropriate to disclose a range in which the fair value is reasonably believed to lie, rather than a single figure.

Inability To Determine Fair Values   When disclosure of fair value information is omitted because it is not possible to arrive at a sufficiently reliable figure, disclosure should be provided to assist users of financial statements in making their own judgments. If there is a reasonable basis for doing so, management may give its opinion as to the relationship between the fair value and carrying value of such instruments.

Other Issues   For those financial instruments that are carried on the Balance Sheet at other than fair values, the disclosure of fair values should be in a form that permits comparison with the carrying values. With respecting to offsetting fair value disclosure, this should happen only to the extent that the related carrying amounts are offset. Fair values for unrecognized financial instruments should be presented separately from the fair values for recognized items.

Financial Assets Carried At An Amount In Excess Of Fair Value

15-176.   The basic Recommendation here is as follows:

Paragraph 3860.89   *When an entity carries one or more financial assets at an amount in excess of their fair value, the entity should disclose:*

(a) *the carrying amount and the fair value of either the individual assets, or appropriate groupings of those individual assets; and*

(b) *the reasons for not reducing the carrying amount, including the nature of the evidence that provides the basis for management's belief that the carrying amount will be recovered.* (January, 1996)

15-177.   The decision to not write down a financial asset when its carrying value is in excess of its fair value involves an exercise of management judgment. The disclosure that is required here provides users with an understanding of this judgment process and with a basis for assessing the possibility that circumstances may eventually lead to a reduction in the asset's carrying value.

15-178.   The entity's approach to dealing with declines in the value of financial assets should be disclosed as per the Recommendation of Section 1505, "Disclosure Of Accounting Policies". This should include an indication of the evidence specific to the asset that leads management to the conclusion that the asset's carrying amount will be recovered.

Disclosures Concerning Hedges Of Anticipated Future Transactions

15-179.   The Recommendation here is as follows:

Paragraph 3860.92   *When an entity has accounted for a financial instrument as a hedge of risks associated with anticipated future transactions, it should disclose:*

(a) *a description of the anticipated transactions, including the period of time until they are expected to occur;*

(b) *a description of the hedging instruments; and*

(c) *the amount of any deferred or unrecognized gain or loss and the expected timing of recognition as income or expense.* (January, 1996)

15-180.   The information required in this Recommendation permits the users of an entity's financial statements to understand the nature and effect of a hedge of an anticipated future transaction. This information may be provided on an aggregate basis when a hedged position comprises several anticipated transactions or has been hedged by several financial instruments.

15-181.   The Paragraph 3860.92(c) Recommendation should be applied without regard to whether the gains or losses have been recognized in the financial statements. This Recommendation is complicated by the fact that the accounting for the hedging instrument may take a variety of forms:

- If the hedging instrument is carried at fair value, any gain or loss will be unrealized, but recorded in the entity's Balance Sheet.

- If the hedging instrument is carried at cost, any gain or loss will be unrecognized.

- If the hedging instrument has been sold or settled, the gain or loss will be realized.

15-182.   In all of these cases, the gain or loss will be deferred until such time as the hedged transaction is completed.

Other Disclosures

15-183.   Paragraph 3860.95 provides examples of other information that may be desirable to disclose:

Paragraph 3860.95   ...

(a) the total amount of the change in the fair value of financial assets and financial liabilities that has been recognized as income or expense for the period;

(b) the total amount of deferred or unrecognized gain or loss on hedging instruments other than those relating to hedges of anticipated future transactions; and

(c) the average aggregate carrying amount during the year of recognized financial assets and financial liabilities, the average aggregate principal, stated, notional or other similar amount during the year of unrecognized financial assets and financial liabilities and the average aggregate fair value during the year of all financial assets and financial liabilities, particularly when the amounts on hand at the balance sheet date are unrepresentative of amounts on hand during the year.

Disclosures Concerning Impaired Financial Assets (Not Covered By Section 3860)

15-184.   The two basic Recommendations in this area are as follows:

RE-ED Paragraph .221   *When monetary financial assets have been written down in accordance with paragraph .097, an entity should disclose separately:*

(a) *for each class of such assets, the amount at which the impaired assets in the class would have been carried in the absence of any impairment and the accumulated reduction in their carrying amount due to impairment;*

(b) *the net charge or credit to income in respect of impairment; and*

(c) *any amount included in interest income in respect of the impaired assets.*

RE-ED Paragraph .222   *For the period in which non monetary financial assets are written down in accordance with paragraph .112 or a write down is subsequently reversed in accordance with paragraph .113, an entity should disclose separately:*

(a) *for each class of such assets, the carrying amount of the written down assets in the class, net of any related valuation allowance; and*

(b) *the net charge or credit to income in respect of impairment.*

15-185.   Note that these two Recommendations segregate the disclosure required for monetary and non monetary financial assets that are impaired. Disclosures for monetary assets are required for each period during which impairment persists, while disclosures for non monetary assets are made only for the period in which the asset is written down or reversed.

15-186.   An entity applies the presentation and disclosure requirements in "Impaired Loans", Section 3025, to financial assets dealt with in that Section. That Section may also provide guidance for disclosures concerning other types of impaired monetary assets.

Derivatives And Synthetic Instruments

Introduction

15-187.   The April, 1994 Re-Exposure Draft "Financial Instruments" contains an extensive Appendix dealing with a number of issues. Much of this material was incorporated into appropriate sections of the preceding text. However, there is some additional material which describes derivative and synthetic instruments and, in some cases, the appropriate accounting procedures. This material will be dealt with in this separate section.

Option Contracts

General Characteristics

15-188.   Options provide the holder with the right to acquire or dispose of an asset at a specified price for a specified period of time. In this Section we are concerned only with those options where the underlying asset is a financial asset. It is also noted that, when an entity issues options to acquire its own shares, there is no financial liability as defined in this Section.

15-189.   A put option is an option to sell a specified asset while a call option is an option to purchase a specified asset. From the point of view of the holder of the option, these derivative instruments are always considered to be financial assets. This is because the holder is not required to exercise the option and will only do so if it is favourable to them. Correspondingly, an option is always a financial liability to the writer of the option as they will be required to purchase or deliver the specified asset at the discretion of the holder.

15-190.   As an example, consider an option to buy $1,000,000 face value in government bonds for their current fair value of $1,000,000. The holder of this option will only exercise the option if the current fair value of the bonds exceeds $1,000,000. This will result in a gain to the holder and a loss to the writer of the options who is required to deliver the bonds.

15-191.   At any point in time the value of an option is equal to the sum of its intrinsic value (fair value of the underlying asset, less the option price) and its time value (the value associated with having a leveraged position in the underlying asset). When the intrinsic value is positive, the option is said to be "in-the-money". For example, with the option described in the preceding paragraph, it would be in-the-money at any point in time when the fair value of the bonds exceeds $1,000,000. When an option is "out-of-the-money", any value associated with the option relates to its time value.

Options As Hedges

15-192.   In most situations, only the intrinsic value of an option will be correlated with changes in the value of a hedged item. For this reason, an option can normally qualify as a hedging instrument only when it is in-the-money.

15-193.   When a position carried at fair value is hedged by an option held, the option is carried on the same basis as the hedged position and the entire amount of the change in fair value of the option is recognized in income each period. This provides for the appropriate matching of gains and losses.

15-194.   When a position carried on the cost basis is hedged by an option, the option may be carried on the cost basis or at fair value. If the option is carried at fair value, the portion of the change in its fair value that represents a change in intrinsic value is deferred for subsequent matching in income with the change in the fair value of the hedged position. The remainder of the change in fair value of the option, constituting the change in its time value, is recognized in income as it arises. If the option is carried on the cost basis, its time value is amortized into income over the term of the contract and any change in its intrinsic value is not recognized until the corresponding change in fair value of the hedged position is recognized in income.

15-195. When an option is used as the hedge of an anticipated transaction, the instrument can be carried at either fair value or cost. Any change in the intrinsic value of the option is deferred to the extent it is recognized and the change in the time value is amortized to income.

Options Carried At Cost

15-196. If an option is acquired with an intent to hold for the long term or until maturity, it may be carried at cost. However, the holder will have to give periodic recognition to impairment. In addition, recognition will have to be given to the fact that the time value of the option declines as it approaches maturity.

Option Writer's Perspective

15-197. The writer of an option is normally unable to transfer or terminate the resulting obligation and, as a consequence, is exposed to the risk of an unfavourable exchange until the exercise or expiry of the contract. If the holder can exercise the option prior to maturity (an "American option"), the writer cannot determine whether the holder will hold for the long term or to maturity and, as a consequence, must carry the option at fair value. If the option can only be exercised at maturity (a "European option"), the cost method can be used by the writer.

Exercise Of Options

15-198. When an option is exercised, the parties to it will discontinue recognition of any assets or liabilities associated with the financial instrument. The Recommendations of the Exposure Draft require that the carrying amount of an asset acquired or liability assumed on exercise of an option equals the exercise price paid or received, adjusted for the carrying value of the option. This means that no gain or loss arises from the exercise of the option, regardless of the basis on which it is carried.

Accounting For Options

15-199. The following example illustrates the application of this Section to an option contract. The information is as follows:

> The option gives the holder the right to purchase government bonds on the maturity of the option in six months time for $1,000,000, the fair value of the bonds on the inception of the option. The holder pays a premium of $25,000. At the holder's year end, three months after acquisition of the option, the fair value of the bonds has increased substantially and, as a result, the fair value of the option is $42,800. The option contract is exercised subsequently on maturity, when the fair value of the bonds is $1,040,000. In this example, transaction costs are ignored. The journal entries are those recorded by the holder of the call option.

15-200. The journal entry for initial recognition of the option contract as an asset is:

Option Contract	$25,000	
Cash		$25,000

15-201. **Cost Basis Of Measurement Subsequent To Acquisition** While it would be unusual, the option may be carried at cost. If this is the case, no entry is required prior to exercise unless a write down is required because the carrying amount of the contract exceeds the amount recoverable under the contract. This is not the case here and, as a consequence, the only additional entry would be the one required at exercise:

Government Bonds	$1,025,000	
Cash		$1,000,000
Option Contract		25,000

15-202. **Fair Value Basis Of Measurement Subsequent To Acquisition** At the holder's year end, the increase in the $17,800 ($42,800 - $25,000) fair value of the option contract would be recognized with the following entry:

| Option Contract | $17,800 | |
| Gain | | $17,800 |

15-203.   Between the holder's year end and the exercise date, there is a $2,800 ($42,800 - $40,000) loss on the option. The entry for this loss is incorporated into the entry to recognize the exercise of the option as follows:

Government Bonds	$1,040,000	
Loss	2,800	
Cash		$1,000,000
Option Contract		42,800

Forward Contracts

General Characteristics

15-204.   A forward contract involves an agreement to exchange specified assets on specified terms at some future date. Unlike options, neither party to the contract has any discretion with respect to its implementation. The exchange that is described in the contract must be carried out.

15-205.   In many cases, the fair values of the right and the obligation of each party to make the future exchange of the underlying financial instruments on the agreed terms will be of equal value. In this type of situation, the contract will require no other exchange of assets (i.e., neither party to the contract pays any fee).

15-206.   An example of a forward contract would be an agreement in which one party promises to deliver $1,000,000 cash in exchange for $1,000,000 face amount of fixed rate government bonds six months later. During this six month period, both parties have a contractual right (a financial asset) and a contractual obligation (a financial liability). If the fair value of the bonds exceeds $1,000,000, the potential purchaser has a financial asset and the other party has a financial liability. If the fair value of the bonds falls below $1,000,000, the situation reverses.

15-207.   With respect to measurement, the appropriate choice depends on management intent. The principal differences between the effects of applying the measurement Recommendation to option contracts and to forward contracts are as follows:

(a) A party to an option contract has either a right to make an exchange (an asset) or an obligation to make an exchange (a liability), but not both. A party to a forward contract has both a right and an obligation, but only one of these has any intrinsic value at a particular time. Accordingly, an entity carrying a forward contract on the fair value basis may present an asset at one reporting date and a liability at another reporting date in respect of the same contract.

(b) Since both parties to a forward contract are obliged to make a future exchange, forward contracts do not share the characteristics of option contracts that limit the extent to which option contracts may be designated as hedging instruments.

15-208.   Like options, the rights and obligations under a forward contract have time value. In some cases these values are equal and offsetting, while in other cases the time value associated with the right is different from the time value associated with the obligation. If a forward contract is designated as a hedge, time value should be separately identified and recognized in income over the life of the contract.

Accounting For Forward Contracts

15-209.   The following example illustrates the application of the Recommendations of this Section to accounting for forward contracts from the point of view of the purchaser:

The entity agrees to purchase $1,000,000 face value of government bonds in six months for $1,000,000 in cash. The bonds have a fixed rate and their fair value at the inception of the contract is $1,000,000. At the entity's year end, the fair value of the bonds has increased and, as a consequence, the fair value of the contract has increased to $50,000. At the maturity of the forward contract, the bonds have a fair value of $1,040,000. In this example, transaction costs are ignored.

15-210.   On inception, the forward contract has no value because the right and the obligation to make the future exchange have equal value and, accordingly, it is not necessary to record any journal entry in practice.

15-211.   **Cost Basis Of Measurement Subsequent To Initial Recognition**   While it would be unusual, there are circumstances in which a forward contract will be carried at cost. If that is the case, no entry would be required at the entity's year end. However, if the fair value of the bonds has fallen below $1,000,000, note disclosure would be appropriate. There would also be the possibility of making a provision under Section 3290, "Contingencies".

15-212.   At maturity, the following journal entry would be made:

Government Bonds	$1,000,000	
Cash		$1,000,000

15-213.   Note that no recognition is given to the $40,000 excess of fair value over $1,000,000 contract price.

15-214.   **Fair Value Basis Of Measurement Subsequent to Initial Recognition**   Again, no entry would be required at the inception of the contract. However, at the entity's year end, the increase in the fair value of the forward contract asset is recorded as follows:

Forward Contract	$50,000	
Gain		$50,000

15-215.   There is a $10,000 ($50,000 - $40,000) loss on the forward contract between the entity's year end and the maturity date of the contract. The entry for this loss is incorporated into the entry for the purchase of the bonds as follows:

Government Bonds	$1,040,000	
Loss	10,000	
Cash		$1,000,000
Forward Contract		50,000

Futures Contracts

General Characteristics

15-216.   A futures contract has the same fundamental characteristics as a forward contract. The differences are as follows:

- Futures contracts are standardized and traded on an exchange. These features facilitate the opening and closing of positions without the need to deliver or take delivery of the underlying instrument. In some cases, futures based on a share price index for example, delivery is not feasible.

- Futures contracts require a margin deposit at their inception. This will be adjusted based on changes in the fair value of the contract. The changes in this margin account must be recognized, regardless of whether the contract is carried at cost or fair value.

Accounting For Futures Contracts

15-217.   The following example illustrates the application of this Section to a futures contract:

An entity sells a share price index futures contract at $132,250, paying a margin deposit of $25,000 at the inception of the contract (in this example, the entity is required to maintain this amount on deposit while the contract is outstanding). The following day, the entity is required to pay a margin call of $1,560 as the futures contract price has increased to $133,810. Three days later, on the entity's first period end following the acquisition of the futures position, the contract price has fallen to $131,720 and the margin call is returned. The futures contract is closed out after 30 days by the entity purchasing one share price index futures contract at $131,550. The original margin deposit is returned.

15-218.   At the inception of the contract, the only entry is the one required to record the margin deposit:

Deposits (Asset)	$25,000	
Cash		$25,000

15-219.   **Cost Basis Of Measurement Subsequent To Acquisition**   While it would be unusual for a futures contract to be carried at cost, there may be circumstances where it happens. If this is the case, the only entries required prior to maturity will be for the margin calls. In this case, margin must be paid on the day after the acquisition and the entry would be as follows:

Deposits (Asset)	$1,560	
Cash		$1,560

15-220.   The return of the margin would be recorded by reversing this entry:

Cash	$1,560	
Deposits (Asset)		$1,560

15-221.   When the futures position is closed out, the following journal entry is required:

Cash	$25,700	
Deposits (Asset)		$25,000
Gain		700

15-222.   **Fair Value Basis Of Measurement Subsequent To Initial Recognition**   In this case, the entry to record the additional margin deposit would be accompanied by an entry to record the loss on the fair value of the contract:

Deposits (Asset)	$1,560	
Cash		$1,560
Loss	$1,560	
Contract (Asset or Liability)		$1,560

15-223.   At the end of the period, the entry to record the return of the margin would be accompanied by an entry to record the $2,090 ($133,810 - $131,720) gain on the futures contract:

Cash	$1,560	
Deposits (Asset)		$1,560
Contract	$2,090	
Gain		$2,090

15-224.   Note that the entry to record the gain reverses the previously recorded liability and creates a net asset of $530 ($2,090 - $1,560). This $530 amount would also be included in the Income Statement as the net gain for the period.

15-225.   When the futures position is closed out, the following entries are required to show the $170 ($131,720 - $131,550) gain on the futures contract since the beginning of the new period and the elimination of the futures contract asset:

Contract	$170	
Gain		$170

Cash	$25,700	
Deposits (Asset)		$25,000
Contract		700

Interest Rate Swaps

General Characteristics

15-226.   Interest rate swaps are essentially a series of forward contracts to exchange, for example, variable interest payments based on a specified floating interest rate for fixed cash payments, both calculated with reference to an agreed notional principal amount. As with forwards and futures, swaps can be either an asset or a liability.

Accounting For Interest Rate Swaps

15-227.   The following example illustrates the application of the Section to an interest rate swap contract:

An entity assumes a fixed term, floating rate debt that it wishes to convert to a net fixed rate to avoid the uncertainty of floating rates on future cash flows. The debt has a principal amount of $100,000 and interest based on a floating bank rate, payable semi-annually in arrears on September 30 and March 31 of each year. On the same date that it assumes the debt, the entity enters into a swap contract to receive floating rate amounts in return for fixed rate payments for a three year term on a notional principal of $100,000. Under the contract, the entity will make a fixed semi-annual payment at an annual rate of 10 percent of the notional principal in exchange for semi-annual receipts in arrears, calculated on the same basis as the interest on the debt. The contract is entered into on April 1 and the entity's fiscal year end is December 31. The following Table E shows the floating rates applicable to the swap contract for the first two years and the amounts of the swap receipts and payments.

Table E Swap Contract - Applicable Floating Rates			
	Floating Interest Rate	Floating Rate Receipt	Fixed Rate Payment
End Of First 6 Month Swap Period (September 30)	10.5%	$5,250	$5,000
End Of Second 6 Month Swap Period (March 31)	9.8%	4,900	5,000
End Of Third 6 Month Swap Period (September 30)	9.0%	4,500	5,000
End Of Fourth 6 Month Swap Period (March 31)	9.5%	4,750	5,000

15-228.   **Cost Basis Of Measurement Subsequent To Initial Recognition**   On a cost basis, the payments and receipts under the swap contract are recognized as they accrue but changes in the fair value of the right and the obligation to make future exchanges of swap payments are not recognized. At the inception of the swap contract, the right and the obligation to make future exchanges are of equal value when the swap contract is based on market interest rates. The notional principal of $100,000 is not recognized because it does not represent the fair value of the rights and obligations under the swap contract. The September 30 journal entry to record interest on the debt obligation at 10.5 percent at the end of the first six month swap period is:

| Interest Expense | $5,250 | |
| Cash | | $5,250 |

15-229.   The net swap receipt is $250 [(10.5% - 10.0%)][($100,000)][(6/12)] for this six month period. It will normally be treated as an adjustment of interest expense as in the following entry:

| Cash | $250 | |
| Interest Expense | | $250 |

15-230.   In practice, the entity would not know the March 31 floating rate at its December 31 year end. However, we will assume that it estimates it to be 9.8 percent and makes the following entries to accrue interest expense and the expected swap payment:

| Interest Expense [(9.8%)][($100,000)][(3/12)] | $2,450 | |
| Interest Payable | | $2,450 |

| Interest Expense [(10.0% - 9.8%)][($100,000)][(3/12)] | $50 | |
| Swap Amount Payable | | $50 |

15-231.   At the March 31 end of the second six month swap period, an entry is required to record the $4,900 [(9.8%)][($100,000)][(6/12)] payment of interest on the floating rate debt:

Interest Expense	$2,450	
Interest Payable	2,450	
Cash		$4,900

15-232.   As the December 31 estimate of the March 31 rate was correct, the full accrual is at the actual rate of 9.8 percent.

15-233.   Also at the March 31 end of the second swap period, an entry is needed to record the $100 [(10.0% - 9.8%)][($100,000)][(6/12)] swap payment:

Swap Amount Payable	$50	
Interest Expense	50	
Cash		$100

15-234.   **Fair Value Basis Of Measurement Subsequent To Initial Recognition** Again, under the assumption that the right to receive and the obligation to make future payments have equal value at the inception of the contract, no entry is required. However, journal entries will be required subsequently for each receipt or payment, as well as for changes in the fair value of the contract.

15-235.   During the first six month swap period, the floating rate was 10.5 percent, making the swap contract favourable. In order to illustrate the required procedures, we will assume that the fair value of the swap contract at the end of the first six month swap period is $1,800. Based on this, the required entries on September 30 are as follows:

| Interest Expense | $5,250 | |
| Cash | | $5,250 |

| Swap Contract | $1,800 | |
| Gain | | $1,800 |

| Cash | $250 | |
| Swap Contract | | $250 |

15-236.   This treatment leaves the Swap Contract as an asset with a net value of $1,550 ($1,800 - $250). Note that the $250 receipt under the swap agreement is treated as a reduction in the fair value of the swap contract, rather than as an income item as it was when the swap agreement was carried on the cost basis.

15-237.   At the entity's December 31 year end, the contract has become unfavourable and constitutes a financial liability. We will assume that this liability has a fair value of $600 on this date. Based on this, the required entries at December 31 are as follows:

Interest Expense	$2,450	
Interest Payable		$2,450
Loss	$2,150	
Swap Contract		$2,150

15-238.   The $2,150 credit to the Swap Contract eliminates the $1,550 debit left from the September 30 entry and establishes the new liability of $600.

15-239.   At the end of the second six month swap period on March 31, we will assume that the fair value of the swap liability has increased to $615. Based on this, the journal entries at that date are as follows:

Interest Expense	$2,450	
Interest Payable	2,450	
Cash		$4,900
Loss	$15	
Swap Contract		$15
Swap Contract	$100	
Cash		$100

15-240.   Once again, note that the $100 payment under the swap agreement is treated as an adjustment of the fair value of the swap agreement, leaving the Balance Sheet value of the Swap Contract as a $515 liability.

Synthetic Instruments

15-241.   The Re-Exposure Draft takes the position that synthetic financial instruments are groupings of separate financial instruments acquired and held to emulate the characteristics of another instrument. For example, a floating rate long term debt combined with an interest rate swap that involves receiving floating payments and making fixed payments, synthesizes a fixed rate long term debt. Based on this view, the Section takes the position that no special Recommendations are needed for these instruments. This means that each financial asset and financial liability that is considered a component of a synthetic instrument is accounted for separately according to the various requirements of the Section.

Changes In Current Practice

15-242.   Section 3860 and the proposals contained in the Re-Exposure Draft on financial instruments have had and will continue to have a very large impact on current accounting practices. The major differences to be expected can be described as follows:

Recognition

- **Convertible Securities**   Section 3860 would require the recognition of amounts contributed for the equity portion of convertible securities.

- **Factoring Of Accounts Receivable**   Under the Re-Exposure Draft, financing arrangements involving accounts receivable could only be recorded as a sale in situations where the transferee has no recourse to the transferor. Current practice allows the sales treatment when recourse is reasonable with respect to expected credit losses.

- **Defeasance**   Again, no *Handbook* provision deals with this area. The Re-Exposure

Draft would eliminate the current practice of removing assets or liabilities from the Balance Sheet in situations involving "in substance" defeasance.

Presentation

- **Redeemable Preferred Shares**   Section 3860 would require that these securities be accounted for as liabilities. This would mean that consideration received for such securities would be allocated to liabilities rather than shareholders' equity. In addition, the dividends paid on these securities would be recorded as an expense rather than as a distribution of income. Note that for non public companies, the effective date of this change has been deferred until the year 2000.

- **Offsetting**   Under Section 3860, the reporting of related financial assets and financial liabilities on a net basis would only be permitted in situations where a formal legal right of offset has been established with all parties to the arrangement and where there is an intent to settle on a net basis.

Measurement - Financial Assets And Liabilities Held For The Long Term Or To Maturity

- **Write Down Reversals**   The Re-Exposure Draft makes provision for reversing the write down of financial assets and financial liabilities that are held for the long term or to maturity.

- **Troubled Debt Restructurings**   Explicit Recommendations are provided for recording gains or losses resulting from modifications to loan terms that arise in troubled debt restructurings.

Hedging Activities

- **Overall Risk**   In the determination of whether or not an item is a hedge, consideration must be given to its overall influence on the risk position of the enterprise.

- **Anticipated Commitments**   At present, hedge accounting can be used for any instrument that is designated as a hedge of a future commitment to purchase goods and services. Under the Re-Exposure Draft, a financial instrument could be designated as a hedge of a broader range of anticipated transactions (see also the Re-Exposure Draft "Foreign Currency Translation").

Disclosure

- Section 3860 contains comprehensive disclosure Recommendations with respect to financial instruments. For the most part, these Recommendations fill a void in current *CICA Handbook* content and are likely to have a significant impact on Canadian reporting practices.

Financial Instruments In Canadian Practice

Statistics From Financial Reporting In Canada

General Disclosure

15-243.   Of the 200 companies surveyed in the 1997 edition of *Financial Reporting In Canada*, 147 provided some type of disclosure of financial instruments in their 1996 annual reports. This is a significant increase from the 1995 annual reports in which only 103 companies had specific content dealing with financial instruments.

15-244.   The most common single type of disclosure was in a note to the financial statements. However, in the 1996 annual reports, 79 companies provided more than one type of disclosure.

Other Disclosure

15-245.   Other statistics on financial instruments disclosure by the 200 companies surveyed in the 1997 edition of *Financial Reporting In Canada* are as follows:

Preferred Shares As Debt   In 1996, 19 companies disclosed preferred shares as debt, up from only two companies in 1995.

Segregation Of Convertible Proceeds   In 1996, 17 companies disclosed that they had split convertible proceeds between its debt and equity components, up from only three companies in 1995.

Offsetting Assets And Liabilities   The number of companies providing disclosure of offsetting increased from two in 1995 to six in 1996.

Extent And Nature Of Financial Instruments   The number of companies providing this type of disclosure increased from 96 in 1995 to 141 in 1996.

Terms And Conditions   In 1996, 116 companies provided disclosure of the terms and conditions applicable to their financial instruments, up from 81 companies in 1995.

Fair Value Information   The number of companies providing information on the fair value of their financial instruments increased from 40 in 1995 to 116 in 1996.

15-246.   These statistics make it clear that the 1996 introduction of Section 3860 into the *CICA Handbook*, as well as the discussion engendered by the Re-Exposure Draft have had a dramatic impact on the disclosure of financial instruments.

Example From Practice

15-247.   The following example is from the annual report of GULF CANADA RESOURCES LIMITED for the reporting period ending December 31, 1996. It illustrates extensive disclosure of financial instruments, including derivatives and risk management.

Summary Of Significant Accounting Policies (In Part)
Derivative Instruments
The Company enters into various contracts to manage its exposure to changes in commodity prices and exchange rates (Note 15). Gains and losses on the contracts which are used to hedge such exposures on future transactions are recognized in the financial statements when the related transactions occur, and are included in the measurement of such transactions. Changes in the market values of contracts that are not hedges, or that arise subsequent to when they cease to be effective hedges, are recognized as gains and losses in the earnings of each period.

The Company also enters into interest rate swap agreements to manage interest rate risk. The initial cost of the contract is amortized over its life, while changes in market value are recognized as they occur.

Note 15   Financial Instruments
(a) Risk management
   The Company is exposed to fluctuations in oil and gas prices, exchange rates and interest rates and has entered into contracts to hedge or manage its exposure. Maximum exposure to credit losses on these instruments approximates their fair value as disclosed below.

   The Company is exposed to credit risk on the oil and gas price and exchange rate instruments to the extent of non performance by counterparties. For the oil and gas price instruments, credit risk is controlled through credit controls, limits and monitoring procedures. Gulf provides margin deposits as collateral for the transactions. The Company deals with multiple brokers and never has a material deposit with one broker. All exchange rate contracts are with financial institutions with credit ratings of at least A-high, and non performance is not expected.

i) *Oil and gas prices*

The Company is exposed to price risks on future oil and gas production. To reduce this risk, at December 31, 1996, the Company sold on a forward basis approximately 28,000 barrels per day of 1997 liquids production at an average minimum floor price of approximately US$19.00 per barrel and an average maximum ceiling price of US$22.25.

The Company also forward sold approximately 148 million cubic feet per day of 1997 gas production at an average plant gate price of approximately C$1.73 per thousand cubic feet (assuming a foreign exchange rate of US$0.75 to C$1.00). This price was achieved through the use of a combination of physical sales and financial forward sales and options. In addition, Gulf has fixed the basis differential through gas aggregator sales, direct physical sales and the use of financial transactions between Henry Hub, Louisiana (the pricing location used by the New York Mercantile Exchange) and Alberta on approximately 113 million cubic feet per day at an average level of approximately US$0.78 discount per million British Thermal Units (BTU). The Company also forward sold approximately 19 million cubic feet per day of 1998 gas production at a price at Henry Hub of US$2.15 per million BTU.

ii) *Exchange rates*

As a large portion of Gulf's sales are based on U.S. dollar pricing, the Company sells U.S. dollars forward to reduce its foreign exchange risk. At December 31, 1996, the Company had entered into the following U.S. dollar forward sale contracts and options:

Settlement year	Total contract amounts	Contract rate range	Average rate
1997	US$135	US$0.706-0.769	US$0.723
1998	125	0.704-0.778	0.725
1999	175	0.762-0.780	0.768
2000	180	0.763-0.780	0.768
2001	210	0.758-0.782	0.753

At December 31, 1995, Gulf had foreign exchange contracts to sell US$115 million, US$105 million, and US$85 million in 1996, 1997 and 1998, respectively at exchange rates between US$0.702 and US$0.738 with an average rate of approximately US$0.717.

In relation to Gulf's offer to acquire Clyde Petroleum plc for a price denominated in Pounds Sterling, the Company has hedged the full value of the anticipated transaction with Sterling - U.S. dollar options at an exchange rate of US$1.66 per £1. The total value of the Clyde offer at December 31, 1996, was £432 million. (See Note 19)

iii) *Interest rates - Refer to Note 12(a).*

(b) *Commodity trading*

The Company engages in a limited amount of commodity trading. All transactions undertaken are exchange traded options and futures. At December 31, 1996, the Company had a small number of open crude oil and natural gas positions with various settlement dates to June, 1997. The value of these contracts and the net gain during the year from this activity were both immaterial.

(c) *Sale of accounts receivable*

In November, 1994, Gulf entered into an agreement giving it the right, on a continuing basis, to sell certain accounts receivable to a third party to a maximum amount of $75 million. The amount sold at December 31, 1996 was $68 million (1995 - $51 million). The agreement calls for purchase discounts, based on Canadian Bankers Acceptance rates, to be paid on an ongoing basis. The average effective rate for 1996 was approximately 5.3 per cent (1995 - 7.7 percent). The corporation has potential exposure to credit loss. However, the exposure is immaterial.

(d) *Oil indexed financial instrument*

A special purpose entity has $200 million 11 per cent public debentures issued and outstanding which mature on October 31, 2000, and assets consisting of a $200 million 5 per cent fixed plus variable rate oil indexed debenture maturing on October 31, 2000 and an interest rate swap agreement for the same amount and term of the debentures which converts the variable rate on the debenture into a 6 per cent fixed rate. These are not included in Gulf's statement of financial position because Gulf does not have the right and ability to obtain future economic benefits from the resources of the entity and is not exposed to the related risks, nor does Gulf have the continuing power to determine the strategic operating, investing, and financing policies of the entity without the cooperation of others.

Gulf has an interest rate conversion agreement whereby Gulf pays to the special purpose entity the fixed rate of 6 per cent and is eligible to receive a variable rate ranging from nil to 16.8 per cent, depending on the average quarterly West Texas Intermediate oil price. The Company's exposure to loss is 6 per cent of $200 million ($12 million) per year until October 31, 2000. In 1993 and 1992, the Company recorded provisions totaling $67 million to recognize the present value of the Company's exposure. The unamortized balance of the provision at December 31, 1996 is $42 million (1995 - $50 million).

Carrying amounts and estimated fair values of Gulf's financial instruments are:

| | Asset (liability) | | | |
| | December 31, 1996 | | December 31, 1995 | |
	Carrying Amount	Fair Value	Carrying Amount	Fair Value
Equity investments	$ 27	$ 34	$ 24	$ 28
Long-term debt (Note 12)				
Committed bank facilities	0	0	(249)	(251)
8.35% notes	(342)	(356)	0	0
9% debentures	(172)	(180)	(171)	(176)
9.25% debentures	(409)	(433)	(409)	(421)
9.625% debentures	(274)	(296)	(273)	(285)
Oil indexed rate conversion agreement	(42)	(41)	(50)	(47)
Other long-term obligation	(29)	(37)	(30)	(33)
Foreign exchange contracts	25	32	0	6
Commodity price contracts	0	(15)	0	(5)

The following methods and assumptions were used in estimating the fair values of financial instruments:

Cash and short-term investments, accounts receivable and accounts payable: Terms are such that their carrying amounts approximate fair values.

Equity investments: Fair value of market traded securities is based on quoted market prices. Other investments are relatively insignificant and their carrying amounts are assumed to approximate fair values.

Oil indexed rate conversion agreement: Fair value is estimated using discounted cash flow analysis based on the applicable current incremental borrowing rate. Income on the variable rate portion of interest is estimated based on a forecast of the average quarterly price of West Texas Intermediate crude oil.

Committed bank facilities and other long-term obligation: Fair values are estimated using discounted cash flow analysis based on current incremental borrowing rates for similar borrowing arrangements.

Notes and debentures: Fair values are based on the quoted market price.

Commodity price and foreign exchange contracts: Fair values are estimated based on quoted market prices of comparable contracts. The differences between the fair values and carrying amounts are equal to the cumulative unrecognized gains or losses on these contracts. Commodity price contracts include those that may be settled by the delivery of product.

Additional Readings

15-248.   Not surprisingly, there has been considerable discussion of financial instruments issues in both *CA Magazine* and *The Journal Of Accountancy*. The following list is fairly comprehensive with respect to this material.

CICA Re-Exposure Draft, *Financial Instruments*, April, 1994.

CICA Research Study, *The Financial Statement Presentation Of Corporate Financing Activities*, October, 1989.

CICA Handbook Section 3860, "Financial Instruments - Disclosure And Presentation", September, 1995.

CA Magazine Article - "When Risk's Not An Option", Paul T. Farrelly, January, 1990.

CA Magazine Article - "Hedge Hopping", Peter Bennett and Craig Vaughan, January, 1990.

CA Magazine Article - "See Spot Hedge", Paul T. Farrelly, April, 1992.

CA Magazine Article - "Tuning Our Instruments", Jeannot Blanchet And Raymond E. Perry, April, 1992.

CA Magazine Article - "ESOPs Change The Rules", Richard M. Wise, Line Racette, and Perry Phillips, September, 1992.

CA Magazine Article - "Financial Instruments Re-Exposed", Peter J. Martin, June/July, 1994.

CA Magazine Article - "Studies And Standards Alert - Financial Instruments", J. Alex Milburn, September, 1994.

CA Magazine Article - "Paying The Boss - And How", Thomas W. Scott and Peter Tiessen, November, 1995.

CA Magazine Article - "Instrumental Section", Peter J. Martin, January/February, 1996.

CA Magazine Article - "Uncertain Balance", Gerard Berube, September, 1997.

CA Magazine Article - "Speaking Of Financial Matters...", Ian Davidson, November, 1997.

CA Magazine Article - "High Concept, Low Blow", Irving L. Rosen, December, 1997.

FASB Statement Of Financial Accounting Standards No. 105   *Disclosure Of Information About Financial Instruments With Off balance Sheet Risk And Financial Instruments With Concentrations Of Credit Risk*, March, 1990.

FASB Statement Of Financial Accounting Standards No. 107   *Disclosures About Fair Value Of Financial Instruments*, December, 1991.

FASB Statement Of Financial Accounting Standards No. 119   *Disclosure About Derivative Financial Instruments And Fair Value Of Financial Instruments*, October, 1994.

FASB Statement Of Financial Accounting Standards No. 125   *Accounting For Transfers And Servicing Of Financial Assets And Extinguishments Of Liabilities*, June, 1996.

FASB Statement Of Financial Accounting Standards No. 126   *Exemption From Certain Required Disclosures About Financial Instruments For Certain Non Public Entities*, December, 1996.

Journal Of Accountancy Article - "An Accountant's Option Primer: Puts And Calls Demystified", William P. Hauworth II and Lailani Moody, January, 1987.

Journal Of Accountancy Article - "An Overview Of The FASB's Financial Instruments Project", Clifford C. Woods III and Halsey G. Bullen", November, 1989.

Journal Of Accountancy Article - "The Challenges Of Hedge Accounting", John E. Stewart, November, 1989.

Journal Of Accountancy Article - "The Fundamental Financial Instrument Approach", Halsey G. Bullen, Robert C. Wilkins, and Clifford C. Woods III, November, 1989.

Journal Of Accountancy Article "Implications Of FASB Statement No. 105", Ronald E. Carlson and Kate Mooney, March, 1991.

Journal Of Accountancy Article - "A Return To The Past: Disclosing Market Values Of Financial Instruments", Dan W. Swenson and Thomal E. Buttross, January, 1993.

Journal Of Accountancy Article - "The Question Of Derivatives", Roger H. D. Molvar and James F. Green, March, 1995.

Journal Of Accountancy Article - "FASB 123: Putting Together The Pieces", James R. Mountain, January, 1996. This article discusses the new American rules for accounting for employee stock options.

Supplement To Chapter Fifteen: Emerging Issues Committee Abstracts

EIC Abstract No. 13 - Preferred Shares Whose Redemption Is Outside Of The Control Of The Issuer

15-249.   EIC Abstract No. 13 was issued in April, 1990, prior to the issuance of the Recommendations related to preferred shares in the Section 3860. To some extent, the Section 3860 eliminates the need for the material in this Abstract. However, the Accounting Standards Board appears to believe that some of the discussion contained in this Abstract is still relevant. This is evidenced by the fact that it was not altered or withdrawn at the time Section 3860 was issued.

Shares With Fixed Premiums

15-250.   The Committee first deals with shares where there is a fixed redemption premium. That is, the shares are redeemable at a specific value that is in excess of the stated value of the shares on the books of the company. The shares must be redeemed at this value and, in addition, they must be redeemed on a specified date. Most such redemption provisions will also require that all accrued and unpaid dividends must be paid at redemption. In this context, accrued and unpaid means all of the dividends promised by the shares. This creates a requirement that all cumulative arrearages must be made up at the time of redemption. However, it would not mean that dividends that have been passed under a non cumulative provision would have to be paid.

15-251.   Two issues related to this type of situation are dealt with in this Abstract. The issues, and the corresponding EIC conclusions, are as follows:

Issue One   Should any undeclared dividends be accrued or is disclosure sufficient? How should the undeclared dividends be treated for purposes of calculating Earnings Per Share?

Consensus On Issue One   On this Issue, the Committee concluded that accrued and unpaid dividends should be accrued as a liability, rather than merely disclosed. They note that the dividends are different than regular cumulative dividends in that there is a specific future date on which they must be paid. The Committee also notes that these dividends have all the characteristics of a liability as set out in Section 1000 of the *CICA Handbook*:

- they embody a duty or responsibility to others that entails settlement by future transfer or use of assets, provision of services or other yielding of economic benefits at a specified or determinable date, on occurrence of a specified event, or on demand;

- the duty or responsibility obligates the entity leaving it little or no discretion to avoid it;

- the transaction or event obligating the entity has already occurred.

With respect to Earnings Per Share calculations, the Committee concludes that all accrued and unpaid dividends should reduce Income Available To The Common Shareholders in the period in which the liability for the dividends is accrued.

Issue Two   Should any redemption premium be accrued over the period to the redemption date? How should the premium be treated for purposes of calculating Earnings Per Share?

Consensus On Issue Two   The Consensus of the Committee is that the redemption premium should be accrued as a liability over the period to redemption. As the shares must be redeemed, there is a fixed and determinable date when the amounts will have to be paid. This means that the premium has all of the characteristics of a liability. Further, the premium complies with the general recognition criteria set out in Section 1000 of the *CICA Handbook*:

- the item has an appropriate basis of measurement and a reasonable estimate can be made of the amount involved; and

- for items involving obtaining or giving up future economic benefits, it is probable that such benefits will be obtained or given up.

The Committee also considered the situation where the premium is payable with consideration other than cash. For example, the premium is sometimes payable in shares having a market value that is equivalent to the specified amount of cash. The Committee indicates that this alternative type of consideration should not change the accounting procedures to be used.

Recognition of the redemption premium could be on a straight line basis over the period to redemption. However, the Committee believes that the use of the effective interest rate method is preferable. This would require determination of the effective dividend rate on the preferred, including the payment of the redemption premium at maturity. This rate would be applied to the carrying value of the preferred shares, including the amount of redemption premium accrued to date, to arrive at the dividend for the period. The difference between this amount and the stated dividend would be the amount of redemption premium to be accrued for the period.

With respect to disclosure of the redemption premium in the Balance Sheet, the accrued amounts can be added to the carrying value of the preferred shares. If legal considerations prevent this treatment, the credits could be recorded in a separate shareholders' equity account.

On the second part of Issue Two, the Committee reached a Consensus that the premium should reduce income available to common shareholders in the calculation of Earnings Per Share. The premium should be viewed as a form of return to the preferred shareholders and, as such, should be given the same treatment as cumulative dividends on senior shares.

Contingent Redemption Premiums

15-252. The second part of Abstract No. 13 deals with situations where the redemption premium is contingent on future events such as movements in the market price of the enterprise's common shares. For example, the premium might be defined as the excess of the common share price over $10 in five years time. There could be similar ties to commodity prices or foreign currencies. An example here would be a redemption price expressed in terms of ounces of gold. The shareholder could have the option of receiving the gold or the equivalent cash value.

15-253. In this Abstract No. 13, the Emerging Issues Committee deals with two issues related to preferred shares with contingent redemption premiums. The issues, and the corresponding EIC conclusions, are as follows:

Issue One   Should the entity accrue the redemption premium when the amount is not readily determinable?

Consensus On Issue One   The Committee concluded that, until the amount involved can be reasonably estimated, the entity should not begin to accrue the redemption premium. This conclusion is consistent with the recognition criteria set out in both Section 1000 and Section 3290 (Contingencies) of the *CICA Handbook*. Consistent with the disclosure requirements for contingencies that are specified in Section 3290, the Abstract suggests that the following supplementary disclosure should be made:

- the amount of the premium indicated at period end based on the formula to determine the amount payable at the redemption date; and

- the effect the change in the indicated premium during the period would have on Earnings Per Share.

In those situations where the preferred shares must be redeemed through the issuance of a fixed number of common shares, we are still dealing with a contingent premium in that the value of the premium is dependent on the future share price. However, the Committee believes that this type of contingent premium creates a convertible share. As a consequence, there would be no recognition of the premium, either in the Balance Sheet or in Earnings Per Share calculations. Accordingly, the common shares issued on redemption of the preferred shares would be recorded at the carrying amount (issue price) of the preferred shares redeemed.

Issue Two   What accounting treatment should be given to the redemption premium in the period of redemption?

Consensus On Issue Two   The Committee concludes that contingent redemption premiums should be accounted for as capital transactions. That is, in the period in which the shares are redeemed, the premium that must be paid will be charged directly to Retained Earnings, without going through the Income Statement. The effect the change in the indicated premium, from the amount in the prior period to the actual premium on redemption, would have on earnings per share should be disclosed. Some companies may wish to also include the actual amount of the premium in the calculation of earnings per share in the period of redemption.

Retractable Preferred Shares

15-254.   The Committee also discussed preferred shares that are redeemable at some future date at the option of the holder. Such shares are commonly referred to as retractable preferred shares. The Committee reached a consensus that, given the fact that these shares are payable on demand, they have all of the characteristics of a liability as set out in Section 1000 of the *CICA Handbook*.

15-255.   The Committee notes that this guidance should be applied in all transactions where the redemption of the shares is or will be outside of the control of the issuer. In these arrangements, the premium can usually be viewed as a form of return to the holders, in a substance very similar to dividends. Therefore, the accounting should follow the same general principles.

Tax Planning

15-256   As part of a tax planning strategy, preferred shares may be issued to related parties in exchange for currently outstanding common shares or on the transfer of assets. Frequently, there is a redemption premium in that the fair market value of the common shares or assets exchanged will often exceed the recorded amount for the preferred shares. These tax planning arrangements with related parties are not necessarily financings as contemplated by this Abstract. While it is necessary to assess the substance of each particular arrangement, the consensuses in this Abstract normally would not be applicable to such tax planning arrangements. Therefore, in these circumstances, any excess of the redemption value of the preferred shares over their recorded value would not be viewed as a form of return to the shareholders. Accordingly, it would not be necessary to record the excess, if any, when the shares are issued, or to accrue it over the period to the redemption date.

EIC Abstract No. 39 - Accounting For The Issuance Of Derivative Instruments

The Issues

15-257. An entity may issue financial instruments which give the purchaser the option to receive an amount determined by reference to an external measure such as a stock exchange index. If the purchaser exercises the option, the issuer will be obligated to pay an amount calculated in accordance with a formula defined in the terms of the instrument. Such instruments are referred to as derivative instruments in that they incorporate the effect of movements in an external measure. They may also include the effects of other variables such as a foreign exchange rate.

15-258. The proceeds from the sale of the derivative instruments compensate the issuing entity for the risk that it will have to make payments in accordance with the formula. The entity may undertake a hedging or other strategy to reduce its exposure to loss from changes in the external measure. In accordance with the entity's accounting policy, the instruments and the components of any hedging position are marked to market on an on going basis (i.e., remeasured and reported at fair value).

15-259. This situation raised two issues which were dealt with in this Abstract from the Emerging Issues Committee:

Issue One   How should fair value be determined when the instruments are marked to market?

Issue Two   Is it appropriate to recognize any portion of the proceeds received in income when the instruments are issued?

15-260. Note that these issues and the related discussion in the Abstract are only relevant when the instrument under consideration is marked to market.

Consensus On First Issue

15-261. In general, fair value is the amount for which an asset could be exchanged or a liability settled, between knowledgeable, willing parties in an arm's length transaction. The fair value of the derivative instruments previously described comprises their intrinsic value (the current settlement value based on the formula and the current market price of the external measure) and their time value (a function of factors such as the volatility of the external measure, the length of the exercise period, interest rates, and the relationship of the current level of the external measure to the strike price). Where the derivative instruments or the components of a hedge are listed on a stock exchange, the quoted market price is generally the best evidence of fair value. However, when there is infrequent activity in a market, the market is not well established, or small volumes are traded relative to the number of trading units of an instrument to be valued, quoted market prices may not be indicative of fair value. Where the instruments or the components of a hedge are not traded on an exchange, or the quoted market price is not indicative of fair value, fair value may be estimated by use of a valuation technique or by reference to similar publicly traded instruments.

15-262. On the first issue, the Committee reached a consensus that, in addition to the factors outlined above, the fair value of the derivative instruments should provide for any remaining risks and any remaining servicing costs associated with the instruments. The entity's remaining exposure to risks and costs will vary from one situation to another, and the identification and assessment of risks and costs and the determination of appropriate provisions will require consideration of the particular circumstances. Provisions for risks and costs may be incorporated into the valuation model (e.g., by using a volatility measure which gives a more conservative value), or they may be provided for separately.

15-263. In particular, provision should be made for the risk, if any, that value determined by the valuation technique does not reflect the fair value of the instrument. In well established financial markets, the estimated value may be determined by reference to similar trades. However, in less established markets, valuation models will often yield less precise estimates of the amount at which an asset could be exchanged or a liability settled. Provision for the risk of error in the estimate of value may be incorporated into the valuation model or may be provided for separately.

15-264.   In valuing instruments in any hedging position, consideration should also be given to the risk that a counterparty to a financial instrument will fail to discharge an obligation when it is due and will cause the entity to incur a financial loss, and the risk that the entity will not be able to quickly acquire or sell an instrument at an amount close to its fair value due to a lack of liquidity in the market.

Consensus On Second Issue

15-265.   As the derivative instruments are marked to market they will be reported as a liability at their fair value which represents the estimated cost to settle the obligation currently. The proceeds received on issuing the derivative instruments may differ from the estimated cost to settle the obligation. This difference may arise because the instruments have been issued in a retail market, because the markets are illiquid, because the valuation techniques are subjective (valuation models and input variables may differ), or because of arbitrage opportunities.

15-266.   On the second issue, the Committee reached a consensus that any excess of the proceeds received on issuing the derivative instruments over the estimated cost to settle the obligation may be recognized in income when the transaction is initiated only if adequate provision has been made for risks and servicing costs in accordance with the first issue. If the estimated cost to settle the obligation including provision for risks and servicing costs exceeds the proceeds received, the excess should be charged to income when the transaction is initiated.

EIC Abstract No. 69 - Recognition And Measurement Of Financial Instruments Presented As Liabilities Or Equity Under CICA 3860

15-267.   The provisions of Section 3860 with respect to the classification of liabilities and equity have engendered significant change in the manner in which some items are reported. These changes have raised several issues with respect to the recognition and measurement of financial instruments whose classification has been changed by Section 3860. The issue, along with the related EIC Consensus, is as follows:

Issue   When a financial instrument is presented on the issuer's balance sheet differently than under practices commonly followed prior to the adoption of CICA 3860, how should the issuer recognize and measure the instrument or its components?

Consensus   The Committee reached a consensus that the issuer of a financial instrument should determine the instrument's balance sheet presentation under CICA 3860 and then recognize and measure it, or its components, in accordance with its balance sheet presentation. The issuer would apply the same accounting treatments to all financial instruments or components thereof in the same balance sheet class.

The Committee noted that the presentation of a financial instrument or component depends upon the contractual arrangement and the definitions in CICA 3860.05. CICA 3860.06 describes a contract as "an agreement between two or more parties that has clear economic consequences that the parties have little, if any, discretion to avoid, usually because the agreement is enforceable at law."

Recognizing and measuring a financial instrument or component on a basis inconsistent with its presentation would require the issuer to hold one view of the substance of the instrument for recognition and measurement purposes and a different view of its substance for presentation purposes. The Committee considered such an approach inconsistent with basic financial statement concepts.

The Committee noted also that its consensus on this issue will have a number of implications in practice. The following are examples.

(a) **Redeemable preferred shares issued at a premium or discount** A redeemable preferred share that is a liability according to the definition in CICA 3860.05 may be issued for proceeds more or less than the stated redemption amount. The issuer would account for such a premium or discount in the same manner as it accounts for an issue premium or discount on a bond or debenture.

(b) **"High/low" preferred shares issued in a tax planning arrangement** In tax planning arrangements, companies commonly reacquire their own common shares in exchange for preferred shares mandatorily redeemable for cash or other financial assets on demand by the holder. The carrying amount of the common shares reacquired is substantially lower than the redemption amount of the preferred shares, which equals the fair value of the common shares at the date of the transaction. The preferred shares (commonly known as "high/low" shares) constitute liabilities under the definition in CICA 3860.05 and, accordingly, would be presented as such on the issuer's balance sheet in accordance with CICA 3860.18.

As in the case of a demand note, the issuer would measure its liability on issuance of "high/low" shares at the current settlement amount, notwithstanding an intention by the holder of the shares not to demand payment for some period of time or an inability of the issuer to redeem the shares if so requested. The difference between the "high/low" share liability assumed and the carrying amount of the common shares reacquired constitutes a direct charge to equity.

(c) **Debt securities convertible at the holder's option into common shares of the issuer** Financial instruments such as bonds and debentures convertible at the holder's option into common shares of the issuer take the form of a debt security but include both liability and equity components as described in CICA 3860.25-.26. The issuer of such financial instruments presents the components separately in accordance with CICA 3860.24.

In most circumstances, the initial carrying amount of the liability component of a convertible debt security will be less than the amount due to the holder on maturity as a result of the allocation of the proceeds received on issuance between the two components (see CICA 3860.29-.30). An issue discount on the liability component would be accounted for in the same manner as an issue discount on a non-convertible debt security.

On initial recognition of the convertible debt security, the carrying amount ascribed to the holder's right of conversion is presented separately as equity on the issuer's balance sheet. This amount would not be reflected in net income of subsequent periods, regardless of whether the convertible debt security is settled through the issuance of common shares or the payment of cash. The holder's right of conversion is substantially similar to a freestanding share purchase warrant and would be accounted for in the same manner.

The settlement of the convertible debt security on maturity according to its original terms, through the payment of cash or the issuance of common shares at the holder's option, would not give rise to any gain or loss (see also EIC-58). Any gain or loss on extinguishment of the convertible debt security in other circumstances would be determined and accounted for in the same manner as on extinguishment of a non-convertible debt security.

(d) **Preferred shares mandatorily redeemable in a foreign currency** A preferred share mandatorily redeemable for cash in a foreign currency is a monetary liability that would be translated in accordance with CICA 1650 at the current exchange rate.

15-268.   The conclusions of EIC Abstract No. 69 should be applied in all financial statements prepared in accordance with Section 3860 of the *CICA Handbook*.

EIC Abstract No. 70 - Presentation Of A Financial Instrument When A Future Event Or Circumstance May Affect The Issuer's Obligations

15-269.   There are some financial instruments that impose a contractual obligation on the issuer to deliver cash or other financial assets only upon the occurrence or non occurrence of some future event. For example, a share may become redeemable by the holder only if its market price has fallen below a certain level. Two issues are raised by this type of situation. These issues, along with the conclusions reached by the EIC, are as follows:

Issue One   On initial recognition, should the issuer present the financial instrument as a liability or as equity?

Consensus On Issue One   The Committee reached a consensus that the issuer should present the financial instrument as a liability on initial recognition if, at that date, it is probable the instrument will be settled in accordance with its terms by delivery of cash or other financial assets to the holder. Otherwise, the instrument should be presented as equity. The issuer would determine the probability of settling the instrument by delivery of cash or other financial assets on the basis of its best estimate of the likelihood that the triggering event or circumstance will occur or not occur.

Issue Two   Subsequent to the initial recognition of the financial instrument, how should the issuer account for any change in the likelihood of the triggering event or circumstance occurring?

Consensus On Issue Two   The Committee reached a consensus that the issuer should remove a liability or equity instrument from its balance sheet when, contrary to its initial assessment, the triggering event or circumstance has subsequently occurred or failed to occur. The issuer's rights and obligations under the instrument have been altered by the occurrence or non occurrence of the triggering event or circumstance.

The occurrence or non occurrence of a triggering event or circumstance may not result in the maturity, expiry, settlement, discharge or cancellation of the financial instrument. In such circumstances, the issuer would recognize a different liability or equity instrument reflecting its revised contractual rights and obligations.

The issuer would not remove a financial instrument from its balance sheet only on the basis of a change in its assessment of the likelihood of a triggering event or circumstance occurring or failing to occur in the future. CICA 3860.19 precludes the issuer from changing the presentation of the financial instrument.

The Committee noted that, when the issuer makes a significant change in its assessment of the likelihood of the triggering event or circumstance occurring or failing to occur in the future, it would disclose that fact and the reasons for the change in its assessment.

15-270.   The conclusions of EIC Abstract No. 70 should be applied in all financial statements prepared in accordance with Section 3860 of the *CICA Handbook*.

EIC Abstract No. 71 - Financial Instruments That May Be Settled At The Issuer's Option In Cash Or Its Own Equity Instruments

Issues Considered

15-271.   This Abstract deals with situations where debt is issued with regular interest payments over the term to maturity. However, at maturity, the issuer has an unrestricted right to settle the principal amount either in cash or, alternatively, in an equivalent value of its own common shares or other equity instruments. The conclusions reached in this Abstract would not be altered by additional features on the debt, including convertibility at the holder's option.

15-272.   The issues discussed and the consensuses reached in this Abstract are as follows:

Issue One   How should the issuer present the security in its financial statements in accordance with CICA 3860?

Consensus On Issue One   The Committee reached a consensus that the principal element of the security is equity and the obligation to make cash payments on account of interest is a liability, each of which should be presented on the issuer's balance sheet in accordance with its nature as required by CICA 3860.24.

In respect of the principal element of the security, the issuer has no contractual obligation to deliver cash or another financial asset to the holder or to make an exchange of financial instruments on terms that are potentially unfavourable. Settlement of the security in cash on maturity would represent a distribution of equity based on a decision by the issuer at that time.

On issuance of the security, the issuer would recognize the obligation to make interest payments in accordance with its substance, i.e., a stream of contractually required future payments. The issuer may determine the amounts to be recorded for the liability and equity elements on one of the bases discussed in CICA 3860.29 to .30.

The Committee noted that some financial instruments similar to the instrument addressed by this Abstract do not provide the issuer with an unrestricted choice in the manner of settling the principal element on maturity. For example, an issuer may be unable to settle the principal element by issuing its own common shares unless the share price exceeds a stated minimum. When circumstances beyond the control of both the issuer and the holder could cause the issuer to lose its option to settle the principal element in its own shares, presentation of the financial instrument as a liability or equity would be determined in accordance with the consensus in EIC-70.

Issue Two   Having presented the liability and equity elements of the security separately on initial recognition in accordance with the consensus on the first issue in this Abstract, how should the issuer account for the elements over the term to maturity of the instrument?

Consensus On Issue Two   The Committee reached a consensus that the carrying amount of the principal element in equity should be increased over the term to maturity through periodic charges to retained earnings or deficit. The amount of the charge each period would be determined on a systematic and rational basis. On maturity, the carrying amount of the principal element would equal the amount of cash payable by the issuer if it chose not to issue its own common shares or other of its own equity instruments to settle the security.

The Committee noted that the liability element should be accounted for in accordance with the consensus in EIC-69, consistent with its nature as a monetary item.

Issue Three   What effect does the security have on the calculation of the issuer's earnings per share?

Consensus On Issue Three   The Committee reached a consensus that the issuer should determine its basic earnings per share by adjusting its reported net income or loss by the increase for the period in the carrying amount of the principal element of the security, less the associated tax recovery. The increase in the carrying amount of the principal element would be treated in the same manner as the prescribed dividend on a cumulative senior share, as discussed in CICA 3500.

The Committee reached a consensus that the issuer should disclose a supplementary fully diluted earnings per share amount when the effect of settling the security by issuing its own common shares would be dilutive. The supplementary amount would be in addition to any fully diluted earnings per share amount required to be disclosed by CICA 3500 because fully diluted earnings per share amounts calculated under CICA 3500 do not normally include the effect of potential conversions at the issuer's option. In calculating the supplementary amount, the issuer would add back to the numerator both the interest on the liability element, less the associated tax recovery, and the increase for the period in the carrying amount of the principal element of the security, less the associated tax recovery. The denominator would include the number of common shares that would be issued in settling the principal element of the security based on the market price of the shares at the balance sheet date. The disclosure of the supplementary fully diluted earnings per share amount would include information permitting users of the financial statements to understand its nature and significance.

15-273.   The conclusions of EIC Abstract No. 71 should be applied in all financial statements prepared in accordance with Section 3860 of the *CICA Handbook*.

Illustrative Example

15-274.   The Abstract contains the following example which serves to illustrate the conclusions reached by the Committee:

15-275.   The following example is illustrative only and does not form part of the consensuses in this Abstract. The purpose of the example is to assist in applying the consensuses by illustrating one of the possible accounting approaches an issuer may adopt. The example assumes a simple factual situation and does not deal with all requirements that may apply in practice.

An entity issues a security with the following terms and conditions:

- 5 year term to maturity.
- principal amount of $1,000.
- interest payments in cash due annually in arrears.
- annual interest calculated at 8% of the principal.
- principal amount may be settled by the issuer in cash or in its own common shares having an aggregate market value at the settlement date equal to the principal amount, subject to a limit on the maximum number of common shares required to be issued.

15-276.   The security is issued at a price of $980. The entity's marginal borrowing rate for a simple five year term instrument with the same security is 8%. The issuer's marginal income tax rate is 40%, and the interest is fully deductible for tax purposes when paid. The $20 discount is not deductible for income tax purposes.

15-277.   On initial recognition of the security, the carrying amount of the liability element may be determined in accordance with the guidance in CICA 3860.30 and CICA 3860.A24 by discounting the interest payments at 8%. The carrying amount of the equity element would be the residual after deducting from the proceeds on issuance the value assigned to the liability element.

	Actual amount	Present value
Year 1	$ 80.00	$ 74.07
Year 2	80.00	68.59
Year 3	80.00	63.51
Year 4	80.00	58.80
Year 5	80.00	54.45
Totals	$400.00	$319.42

15-278.   The allocated values of the liability and equity elements of the security on issuance are, therefore, as follows:

Present value of the interest cash flows (liability element)	$319.42
Remainder of proceeds on issuance (equity element)	660.58
Total	$980.00

15-279.   These values would be recognized as the initial carrying amounts of the liability and equity elements presented separately on the balance sheet. The carrying amounts would be adjusted periodically for the accretion of the liability due to the time value of money and the amortization of the equity element from its initial carrying amount up to the stated principal amount (note that this requires a rate of 8.647 percent, reflecting the fact that the issue sold at a discount). The benefit arising from the tax deductibility of the interest payment would also be recognized. The annual entries are illustrated in the following table.

	Liability Element	Equity Element	Total	Tax Savings
On Issuance	$319.42	$660.58	$980.00	
Year 1 Accretion	25.55		25.55	$ 10.22
		57.12	57.12	21.78
Year 1 Payment	(80.00)		(80.00)	
End of Year 1	264.97	717.70	982.67	32.00
Year 2 Accretion	21.20		21.20	8.48
		62.05	62.05	23.52
Year 2 payment	(80.00)		(80.00)	
End of Year 2	206.17	779.75	985.92	64.00
Year 3 Accretion	16.49		16.49	6.60
		67.42	67.42	25.40
Year 3 Payment	(80.00)		(80.00)	
End of Year 3	142.66	847.17	989.83	96.00
Year 4 Accretion	11.41		11.41	4.57
		73.25	73.25	27.43
Year 4 Payment	(80.00		(80.00)	
End of Year 4	74.07	920.42	994.49	128.00
Year 5 Accretion	5.93		5.93	2.37
		79.58	79.58	29.63
Year 5 Payment	(80.00)		(80.00)	
Settlement		(1,000.00)	(1,000.00)	
Following Settlement	$ 0.00	$ 0.00	$ 0.00	$160.00

15-280.   The entity would record the following journal entries upon issuance of the security and at the end of the first year.

On issuance of the security:

Cash	$980.00	
Liability (interest)		$319.42
Equity (principal)		660.58

End of Year 1:

Interest expense	$ 25.55	
Liability (interest)		$ 25.55
Retained earnings	$ 57.12	
Equity (principal)		$ 57.12

Tax liability	$32.00	
Retained earnings		$21.78
Tax expense		10.22
Liability (interest)	$80.00	
Cash		$80.00

15-281.   The entity would make corresponding entries in years 2 and 5 based on the amounts in the preceding table. The settlement of the security would be recorded by a debit of $1,000 to the "Equity (principal)" account and a credit of $1,000 to cash or to common shares, depending on the manner in which the issuer chooses to settle.

15-282.   For purposes of illustrating the effect of the security on the calculation of the entity's earnings per share, the following additional information is assumed.

• Reported net income for year 1, after recording the preceding journal entries, is $596.00.

• The entity has 1,000 common shares issued and outstanding throughout year 1. Their current market price at year end is $5. Based on this market price, the entity would be required to issue an additional 200 common shares to settle the security discussed in this example.

• The entity has one class of common shares and no preferred shares.

• The entity's only potentially dilutive factor is an option granted to an employee to buy 50 shares at a price of $2.50 per share. The entity assumes it would earn a pre-tax return of 10% on the proceeds received upon exercise of the option.

15-283.   Basic earning per share are calculated in accordance with the consensus on the third issue by reducing reported net income by the amount of the increase in the carrying amount of the equity element of the security, as follows:

$$\frac{\$596.00 - \$35.34}{1,000 \text{ Shares}} = \$0.56 \text{ per Common Share}$$

The $35.34 is a charge against retained earnings to accrete the carrying amount of the principal element of the security ($57.12) less the associated tax recovery credited to retained earnings ($21.78)

15-284.   Fully diluted earnings per share are calculated in accordance with CICA 3500 by assuming exercise of the outstanding stock option as follows:

$$\frac{\$596.00 - \$35.34 + \$7.50}{1,000 \text{ Shares} + 50 \text{ Shares}} = \$0.54 \text{ per Common Share}$$

The $7.50 is the proceeds of issuing the option (50 shares at $2.50 per share = $125), multiplied by the after tax earnings rate of six percent.

15-285.   The supplementary fully diluted earnings per share amount required by the consensus on the third issue is determined on the basis that the security will be settled by the issuance of common shares as follows:

$$\frac{\$596.00 - \$35.34 + \$7.50 + \$15.33}{1,000 \text{ Shares} + 50 \text{ Shares} + 200 \text{ Shares}} = \$0.50 \text{ per Common Share}$$

The $15.33 is the interest expense arising from the security that is charged against income ($25.55), less the associated tax recovery ($10.22).

Basis Of Application

15-286.   The Committee reached a consensus that entities should apply the accounting treatments described in this Abstract in all financial statements prepared in accordance with CICA 3860 for periods ending after June 28, 1996. Consistent with CICA 3860, the accounting treatments described in this Abstract should be applied retroactively.

EIC Abstract No. 74 - Presentation Of Preferred Shares Requiring The Issuer To Make Repurchases

15-287.   This Abstract deals with a very specific type of preferred shares. They contain a provision which requires the issuer to use its best efforts to repurchase for cancellation each year a specified number of the shares in the class at a price not exceeding their stated value plus accrued but unpaid dividends. The repurchase requirement is suspended when dividend payments on the shares are in arrears. It is not a cumulative requirement, in that if the issuer fails to repurchase all or part of the required shares in a particular year, the short fall is not added to the amount that must be repurchased in subsequent years.

15-288.   The issue, along with the consensus arrived at by the Committee, is as follows:

Issue   How should the issuer present the preferred shares on its balance sheet on issuance in accordance with CICA 3860?

Consensus   The Committee reached a consensus that, on issuance, the issuer should present the preferred shares in accordance with CICA 3860 as equity instruments. Under the terms and conditions described above, the issuer of the preferred shares is not contractually obliged to make any repurchases because it is not obliged to pay dividends on the shares.

The Committee noted that preferred shares with repurchase requirements may contain a variety of different terms and conditions, requiring careful analysis. Some terms and conditions would result in the issuer assuming a contractual obligation to make future payments, even though the form and timing of the payments may be uncertain. For example, various terms of a class of preferred shares may impose an unavoidable obligation on the issuer to repurchase all of the shares over time or else to continue paying dividends on them. Such an obligation results in the preferred share containing a liability element that would be presented as such on the issuer's balance sheet.

The Committee noted also that CICA 3240 and CICA 3860 contain requirements to disclose information about preferred shares, including significant terms and conditions that may affect the amount, timing and certainty of future cash flows. Disclosure of the terms of preferred shares requiring repurchases would include information to assist a financial statement user in understanding the balance sheet presentation of the shares as equity or liabilities.

15-288.   The Committee reached a consensus that entities should apply the accounting treatment described in this Abstract in all financial statements prepared in accordance with CICA 3860 for periods ending after August 16, 1996. Consistent with CICA 3860, the accounting treatment described in this Abstract should be applied retroactively.

Assignment Problems

(The solutions to these problem are only available in
the solutions manual that has been provided to your instructor.)

ASSIGNMENT PROBLEM FIFTEEN - 1

On January 1, 1998, Armour Ltd. issues bonds with a maturity value of $5,000,000 and a stated interest rate of 8 percent. The bonds pay interest on a semi annual basis (June 30 and December 31 of each year) and mature on December 31, 2002. Each $1,000 maturity value bond is convertible into 20 shares of the Company's common stock at any time prior to their December 31, 2002 maturity. At the time the bonds are issued, the Company's common stock is trading at $40 per share.

The bond issue sells for $5,207,915, a price which provides investors with an effective semi annual yield of 3.5 percent. If the bonds did not have a conversion feature, it is estimated that the effective semi annual yield would have to be 4.5 percent. Based on this effective yield, the bonds would have sold for $4,802,182.

Because of a significant increase in the dividend rate on the common stock, all of the bonds are converted on January 1, 1999. At this time, the common stock of Armour Ltd. is trading at $55 per share.

Required: Provide the journal entries to record the issuance of the bonds on January 1, 1998, the required interest payments on June 30 and December 31, 1998, and the conversion on January 1, 1999. Your answer should comply with the Recommendations of Section 3860 of the *CICA Handbook*.

ASSIGNMENT PROBLEM FIFTEEN - 2

On July 1, 1998, Chelsea Products Ltd. issues bonds with a maturity value of $2,500,000 and a stated interest rate of 11 percent. The bonds mature on June 30, 2001 and pay interest on a semi annual basis (December 31 and June 30 of each year). Each $1,000 maturity value bond is convertible into 10 shares of the Company's common stock at any time prior to their June 30, 2001 maturity. The Company's common shares are privately held and do not have a quoted market value.

The bond issue sells for $2,696,580, a price which provides the purchasers with an effective semi annual yield of 4.0 percent. At this time it is estimated that, if the bonds did not have a conversion feature, the effective semi annual yield would have been 5.0 percent.

On January 1, 1999, because of a significant increase in the dividend rate on the Company's common shares, all of the bonds are converted. The common shares are still privately held and no market value information is available.

Required: Provide the journal entries to record the issuance of the bonds on July 1, 1998, the required interest payment on December 31, 1998, and conversion of the bonds on January 1, 1999. Your answer should comply with the Recomendations of Section 3860 of the *CICA Handbook*.

Chapter 16

Accounting For Income Taxes Part One: Basic Concepts And Procedures

Introduction

Basic Issues

16-1.   This Chapter and the one which follows deal with one of the most complex and controversial areas in financial reporting — the concepts and procedures involved in accounting for income taxes. In general terms, this subject matter can be divided into two broad areas:

Interperiod Tax Allocation   As will be discussed in this Chapter, there are significant differences between the assets, liabilities, expenses and revenues that will be included in an enterprise's financial statements, and the corresponding figures that will be included in its tax records. Given this situation, Canadian accounting standards require recognition of some parts of taxes payable in periods other than those in which they fall due under the rules established by Revenue Canada. This process is referred to as interperiod tax allocation. Under Section 3465, this process results in the recognition of future income tax assets and future income tax liabilities. It is this area of accounting for income taxes that has generated the most controversy.

Intrastatement Allocation   Once the amount of income taxes to be included in the financial statements has been determined, the question of how it should be disclosed within the statements remains. This is the subject matter of intrastatement allocation, dealing with such issues as whether a portion of the current income tax expense should be included with the extraordinary items, as a part of the results of discontinued operations, or as a capital transaction. No significant controversy is associated with these procedures.

16-2.   Coverage of both of these areas will be found in this Chapter. As will be noted in the next Section, this coverage has been made somewhat more difficult by the fact that, until the year 2000, we will be operating under a dual system in which companies can use their choice of two different sets of rules for dealing with interperiod tax allocation.

Recent Developments

16-3.   For many years, interperiod tax allocation procedures were based on the Recommendations of Section 3470 of the *CICA Handbook*. These Recommendations required interperiod allocation to be based on timing differences between the accounting income reported in the financial statements of the enterprise, and the corresponding figures that were reported in its tax return. Timing differences were defined in terms of revenues and expenses that would have the same total over the life of the enterprise, but that were being charged or credited to income in different periods for tax and accounting purposes (e.g., A capital asset with a cost of $100,000 will result in both tax and accounting deductions of this amount. However, the amounts deducted in particular time periods for depreciation expense will usually be different from the amounts deducted in that period for CCA.). The resulting Balance Sheet amounts were referred to as Deferred Income Taxes and, as they reflected a deferred charge to income, they were not adjusted for changing tax rates. This approach was referred to as the deferred charge approach to interperiod tax allocation.

16-4.   Until the late 1980s, this approach was consistent with the procedures used for dealing with income taxes under the accounting standards of most of Canada's trading partners. However, this deferred charge approach has been gradually discredited, with most other countries opting for the alternative asset/liability approach to interperiod tax allocation. This latter approach was adopted in 1992 in the U. S. when the FASB issued Statement Of Financial Accounting Standards No. 109, *Accounting For Income Taxes*. This left Canada with accounting standards on accounting for taxes that were not only out of line with those of its major trading partner, but also with most of the rest of the world.

16-5.   This was not a situation that could be allowed to continue. Such a major difference between Canadian and international GAAP can only survive when there is a sound conceptual reason for the Canadian position. This is clearly not the case with the deferred charge approach to interperiod tax allocation and, as a consequence, the Accounting Standards Board issued an Exposure Draft for a revised Section 3470 of the *CICA Handbook* in the March, 1996 issue of *CA Magazine*. The proposals of this Exposure Draft, most importantly the adoption of the asset/liability approach for dealing with temporary differences, were incorporated into a new Section 3465 which was added to the *CICA Handbook* in December, 1997.

16-6.   Section 3465 establishes standards for the recognition, measurement, presentation and disclosure of income and refundable taxes in an enterprise's financial statements. Exceptions to some of the Recommendations are made for certain rate regulated enterprises. In addition, special considerations related to the accounting for investment tax credits are dealt with in "Investment Tax Credits", Section 3805. While the Section consistently refers to "enterprises", it is clear that its primary applicability is to corporations.

16-7.   As an indication of just how controversial the Section 3465 Recommendations are, the effective date of this Section is not until fiscal years beginning on or after January 1, 2000. While earlier application of Section 3465 is encouraged, enterprises will be able to use either Section 3465 or 3470 during the period December 1997 through December 31, 1999.

Approach To The Subject

16-8.   In this Chapter we will focus on basic concepts and procedures involved in the implementation of interperiod and intraperiod tax allocation. It will provide you with a thorough understanding of these subjects, including their applicability to loss carry overs and refundable taxes. With this coverage completed, Chapter 17 will turn to the issues associated with income taxes in the context of business combinations and the preparation of consolidated financial statements. Unlike the predecessor Section 3470, Section 3465 provides fairly detailed guidance in this area. As the material requires a good understanding of both accounting and tax concepts, it is very complex and may not be of interest to all users of this text. As a consequence, it has been relegated to a separate Chapter.

16-9. We will begin our coverage in the next Section of this Chapter with a discussion of alternative approaches to dealing with differences between accounting and tax information. The basic alternatives are the taxes payable approach, the deferred charge approach (used in Section 3470), and the asset/liability approach (required by Section 3465). A simple example will be used to illustrate these alternatives and their relative merits will be evaluated. Following this somewhat theoretical material, the remainder of this Chapter will focus on the Recommendations contained in Section 3465. While the Recommendations of Section 3470 can still be used until the year 2000, we believe the deferred charge approach represents material that will quickly fall into total disuse. As a consequence, we do not believe that you should spend valuable time learning the intricacies of a historical relic.

Differences Between Accounting/Tax Information: Alternative Approaches

GAAP Vs. Tax

16-10. All publicly traded corporations must prepare financial statements in accordance with the generally accepted accounting principles (GAAP) that are presented in the *CICA Handbook*. In addition, other corporations that have a need for audited financial statements must also comply with these principles. This means that the great majority of larger Canadian corporations will produce GAAP based financial statements.

16-11. With respect to the objective of these financial statements, the *CICA Handbook* notes the following:

> **Paragraph 1000.15** The objective of financial statements is to communicate information that is useful to investors, members, contributors, creditors and other users ("users") in making their resource allocation decisions and/or assessing management stewardship. Consequently, financial statements provide information about:
>
> (a) an entity's economic resources, obligations and equity/net assets;
>
> (b) changes in an entity's economic resources, obligations and equity/net assets; and
>
> (c) the economic performance of the entity.

16-12. These same corporations will also have to prepare a corporate income tax return and, in the preparation of this tax return, they will be required to prepare a T2S(1) schedule which calculates Net Income For Tax Purposes. This Net Income For Tax Purposes figure provides the basis for Taxable Income. In preparing these tax figures, the corporation's objective is very different from that cited in Paragraph 1000.15 of the *CICA Handbook*. Stated simply, the objective that is usually served in determining Net Income For Tax Purposes and Taxable Income is to minimize the payment of federal and provincial income taxes.

16-13. Given these alternative objectives, it is not surprising that there are significant differences between Accounting Net Income and Taxable Income. Some of the more common of these differences can be described as follows:

- Accounting Depreciation Expense is typically less than the amount deducted for CCA in the determination of Net Income For Tax Purposes. In terms of the frequency of occurrence, as well as amounts involved, this is easily the most important of the differences between accounting income before taxes and Net Income For Tax Purposes.

- Accounting gains and losses on the disposal of capital assets are determined by deducting the net book value of individual assets from the resulting proceeds of disposition. For tax purposes, such disposals may result in capital gains, recapture of CCA, or terminal losses, with the amounts determined by deducting the lesser of the proceeds of disposition and the capital cost of the individual assets from the UCC of the asset's class.

- Some accounting expenses cannot be deducted or may be only partially deducted for tax purposes. Examples of this would include certain automobile costs, the costs of club dues and recreational facilities, and the cost of business meals and entertainment.

- Dividends from other taxable Canadian corporations are included in accounting revenues but are deducted in the determination of Taxable Income.

- Some accounting expenses which are determined on an accrual basis must be deducted for tax purposes on a cash basis. Examples of this would be warranty costs and pension costs.

- The benefits associated with tax loss carry forwards may be recognized for accounting purposes, prior to their realization for tax purposes.

16-14. There are, of course, many other differences between Accounting Net Income and Taxable Income. However, these are among the most common and, as a consequence, they will be used in the examples presented in the remainder of this Chapter.

Alternative Approaches Described
Classification Of GAAP Vs. Tax Differences

16-15. As was noted in Paragraph 16-9, there are three alternative approaches to dealing with differences between tax and accounting figures. These alternatives are as shown in Figure 16-1.

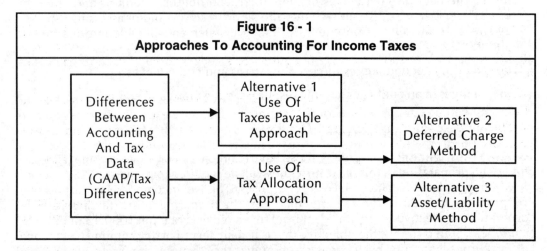

Figure 16 - 1
Approaches To Accounting For Income Taxes

Differences Between Accounting And Tax Data (GAAP/Tax Differences)

Alternative 1
Use Of Taxes Payable Approach

Use Of Tax Allocation Approach

Alternative 2
Deferred Charge Method

Alternative 3
Asset/Liability Method

16-16. Figure 16-1 begins by indicating a situation where differences exist between accounting and tax data. While we have not outlined this problem in Figure 16-1, one of the first difficulties that we will encounter in this Chapter is the fact that there are different approaches to the classification of these differences.

16-17. Under the now superseded Section 3470, classification of GAAP/tax differences were based on income differences. Interperiod tax allocation was used when there were "timing differences" between accounting income and taxable income. Timing differences were defined as situations in which a given cost or revenue is being allocated to accounting income on a different basis than it is being allocated to taxable income. It is expected that over the life of the enterprise, the total amount of the expense (deduction) or revenue (inclusion) will be the same for both tax and accounting records. However, differences arise as a result of alternative methods being used for the allocation of the relevant total to the income of particular accounting or tax years. The classic example of a timing difference situation would be the expenses (deductions) related to the cost of a capital asset. Over the life of the asset, the total depreciation expense subtracted in the determination of accounting Net Income will be equal to the total CCA deducted in calculating Net Income For Tax Purposes. However, because depreciation expense and CCA are often based on different allocation patterns, the two amounts are not likely to be equal in any given year.

16-18.   Under the new Section 3465, the focus of GAAP/tax differences shifts to the Balance Sheet. Whenever there is a difference between the tax basis of an asset or liability, and its carrying amount in the Balance Sheet, it is referred to as a "temporary difference". Consider the capital asset situation referred to in the preceding paragraph. At the Balance Sheet date, a temporary difference would exist if there was a difference between the carrying value of the asset in the accounting records (cost, less accumulated depreciation) and the undepreciated capital cost balance (cost, less accumulated CCA).

16-19.   In many situations, the two concepts are obviously related. Considering again the capital asset situation, the temporary difference at any Balance Sheet date would simply be the sum of all previous timing differences recorded in periods prior to the Balance Sheet date. However, despite the existence of such relationships, the two concepts are different. Section 3470's timing differences are related to income figures, while Section 3465's temporary differences are related to Balance Sheet items. In practical terms, the two approaches can produce different results (e.g., fair value changes recorded in a business combination transaction create a temporary difference, but do not produce timing differences). However, a more complete discussion of the determination of temporary differences will be deferred until a later point in this Chapter.

Alternative 1: Taxes Payable Method

16-20.   Whether GAAP/tax differences are classified as timing differences under Section 3470 or as temporary differences under Section 3465, the next issue becomes whether or not to use interperiod allocation procedures. When tax allocation is not used, all differences between GAAP and tax figures are simply ignored. This approach is referred to as the taxes payable method.

16-21.   Under this taxes payable approach, the Tax Expense or Tax Benefit to be included in the current period's Income Statement is simply the amount of taxes that are payable for the current taxation year. This statement assumes the accounting and taxation years are the same. If this is not the case, the taxes payable amount will have to be pro rated to fit the accounting year. However, the Income Statement item will still be based exclusively on the amount of taxes that are legally required to be paid.

16-22.   With the Tax Expense or Tax Benefit based on tax return figures, the only tax related item that will be disclosed in the Balance Sheet will be the actual amount of taxes that are payable or receivable as a result of filing the current year's tax return. There will be no deferred tax debits or credits, and no future income tax assets or future income tax liabilities.

Alternative 2: Deferred Charge Approach

16-23.   When the deferred charge approach is used, the Tax Expense or Tax Benefit to be disclosed in the current period's Income Statement includes the amount of taxes that are currently payable. However, in order to be consistent with the other revenues and expenses included in the accounting income figure, this amount is increased (when accounting income is larger than taxable income because of timing differences) or decreased (when accounting income is less than taxable income because of timing differences) by an amount equal to the current tax rate multiplied by the current period's timing differences. This amount would be referred to as the deferred portion of the current Tax Expense (Benefit).

16-24. In the Balance Sheet, the deferrals would be accumulated in an account normally referred to as Deferred Income Taxes. A credit balance would reflect a cumulative excess of accounting income over taxable income, while a debit balance would reflect a cumulative excess of taxable income over accounting income. The normal balance would be a credit, reflecting the efforts of the enterprise to minimize taxes.

16-25. As these Balance Sheet items arise as the result of deferring a charge or credit to income, they are viewed as "deferred charges", not as assets and liabilities. As a result, they are not adjusted for changes in the applicable tax rates. This means that deferred income tax balances often reflect a wide variety of tax rates. While our focus in this material is on the Recommendations of Section 3465 which uses the asset/liability approach, we would note that the fact that deferred income tax balances were not adjusted for tax rate changes added considerable complexity to the deferred charge approach.

Alternative 3: Asset/Liability Method

16-26. Under this third alternative, at each Balance Sheet date the enterprise determines the amount of temporary differences between the tax basis of its assets and liabilities, and their respective carrying values in the accounting records. If the tax basis of its assets is less than their carrying value (or the tax basis of its liabilities exceeds their carrying value), a Future Income Tax Liability is recorded. Similarly, if the tax basis of its assets is more than their carrying value (or the tax basis of its liabilities is less than their carrying value), a Future Income Tax Asset results. The amounts to be recorded would be the amount of the temporary difference, multiplied by the tax rate which is expected to be applicable when the asset is realized or the liability settled. In most cases, the tax rate used would be the current rate. However, if different rates have been enacted for the relevant future periods, these future rates would be used.

16-27. As the Balance Sheet items which arise under this method are viewed as assets and liabilities, rather than as deferred charges or credits to income, it follows that they should be adjusted as tax rates change. The guiding valuation principle is that, at each Balance Sheet date, the amount reported as Future Income Tax Assets or Future Income Tax Liabilities should reflect the tax rates that will be applicable when they are realized or settled. This means that they must be adjusted whenever current rates change or applicable future rates are expected to change.

16-28. Unlike the deferred charge method where the Balance Sheet items arise from procedures applied in the Income Statement, under the asset/liability method, the Income Statement inclusion follows from the procedures that have been applied in the Balance Sheet. As was the case with the deferred charge method, the Tax Expense (Benefit) begins with the amount of taxes that are currently payable (receivable). We will then add to (subtract from) this amount the difference between the Future Income Tax Liability (Asset) at the end of the period and the Future Income Tax Liability (Asset) at the beginning of the period. This adjustment will reflect both the change in the temporary differences that took place during the year, as well as any changes in tax rates that have been applied to the balance at the beginning of the year.

Basic Example Data

16-29. We will use a very simple example to illustrate the alternative approaches to tax allocation that we have described. The data for this example is as follows:

Interpro Inc. is established on January 1, 1998 through the investment of $100,000 by its shareholders. The entire $100,000 is used to acquire a capital asset with an estimated useful life of two years. It will be written off on a straight line basis over that period. For income tax purposes, the entire cost of the asset can be deducted in the year of acquisition. The Company will have a December 31 year end for both accounting and tax purposes.

During the year ending December 31, 1998, the asset produces revenues of $110,000. There are no other revenues and the only expense is for depreciation of the asset. The results for the year ending December 31, 1999 are identical to those for 1998. No dividends are paid in either year.

The Company is subject to tax rates of 45 percent in 1998 and 50 percent in 1999. At the end of 1998, the Company knew that its 1999 tax rate would be 50 percent.

Income Statements for the two years 1998 and 1999, and Balance Sheets for the years ending December 31, 1998 and December 31, 1999, before tax factors are taken into consideration, are as follows:

	Year 1998	Year 1999
Revenues	$110,000	$110,000
Depreciation Expense	(50,000)	(50,000)
Pre Tax Income	$60,000	$60,000

	December 31 1998	December 31 1999
Cash	$110,000	$220,000
Capital Asset (Net)	50,000	Nil
Total Assets	$160,000	$220,000
Common Stock	$100,000	$100,000
Retained Earnings (Pre Tax)	60,000	120,000
Total Equities	$160,000	$220,000

Taxes Payable Method

Basic Example

16-30.   If the taxes payable method is used, the Tax Expense will be based on the current taxes payable. For 1998 the amount would be $4,500 [($110,000 - $100,000)(45%)]. For 1999 the figure would be $55,000 [($110,000 - Nil)(50%)]. If we assume that these amounts are paid in cash prior to the year end, the resulting financial statements under this method would be as follows:

	Year 1998	Year 1999
Revenues	$110,000	$110,000
Depreciation Expense	(50,000)	(50,000)
Tax Expense	(4,500)	(55,000)
Net Income	$ 55,500	$ 5,000

	December 31 1998	December 31 1999
Cash	$105,500	$160,500
Capital Asset (Net)	50,000	Nil
Total Assets	$155,500	$160,500
Common Stock	$100,000	$100,000
Retained Earnings	55,500	60,500
Total Equities	$155,500	$160,500

Evaluation

16-31.   Despite the fact that this method has not been widely used, there are a number of arguments which can be made in its favour. As was presented in Paragraph 3470.09 of the *CICA Handbook*, they include the following:

(a) since it is taxable income and not accounting income that attracts taxation, the taxes actually payable for the period represent the appropriate cost to be allocated to that period;

(b) it is unnecessary to provide for income taxes for which there is no legal liability at the end of the financial period;

(c) while timing differences in one period may give rise to the reverse situation in some future period, the date of the reversal may be indefinitely postponed, and accordingly there is no necessity to provide for an amount which may never become payable;

(d) even where the taxes may become payable in some future period, it is usually difficult to estimate the future tax effects with any degree of accuracy.

16-32.   Despite the appeal of these arguments, this approach has always been rejected in favour of some form of tax allocation. Under Section 3470 and its focus on timing differences related to accounting vs. taxable income, the major argument against the taxes payable method was that it was not consistent with the matching principle. That is, under the taxes payable method the Tax Expense is not based on the revenues and other expenses that are included in accounting Net Income. This can clearly be seen in our example. In 1998, the Tax Expense is only $4,500, despite Pre Tax Income of $60,000. In a similar fashion, the 1999 Tax Expense is $55,000 on a Pre Tax Income of the same amount.

16-33.   Under Section 3465, the argument against the taxes payable method shifts to Balance Sheet items. The concern here is that the capital asset that is recorded at a net book value of $50,000 in the December 31, 1998 Balance Sheet has a tax basis of nil. This means that if the carrying value is realized there will be a tax obligation which is not reflected in that Balance Sheet.

16-34.   Other arguments against the taxes payable method include:

the fact that, because the taxes payable calculation involves many discretionary items (e.g., amount of CCA deducted), use of this figure in financial statements could be subject to manipulation;

and the fact that, because taxes payable are not based on the accounting figures included in the Income Statement, the resulting after tax income figures will be more volatile.

16-35.   While the taxes payable method continues to have many supporters, it would appear that tax allocation procedures will continue to carry the day for the foreseeable future.

Deferred Charge Method

Basic Example

16-36.   Under the deferred charge method as described in the now superseded Section 3470, deferred tax balances must be recorded for any timing differences between accounting income and taxable income. In our example, the timing differences and the related deferred tax amounts are based on the difference between Depreciation Expense and CCA. For the two years 1998 and 1999, these timing differences and deferred income tax amounts would be as follows:

	1998	1999
CCA	$100,000	Nil
Depreciation Expense	(50,000)	($50,000)
Timing Differences	$ 50,000	($50,000)
Tax Rate	45%	N/A
Deferred Tax Credit (Debit)	$ 22,500	($22,500)

16-37.   Despite the fact that, at the end of 1998, the new tax rate for 1999 was known, the deferred charge method does not adjust the $22,500 Deferred Income Tax credit to the new rate of 50 percent. This creates a problem in 1999 in that, with the reversal of the 1998 timing difference, the Deferred Income Tax credit balance must be drawn down to zero. This can only be accomplished by using the rate at which it was accumulated, without regard to the current tax rate.

16-38.   Based on the preceding analysis, the financial statements under the deferred charge method would be as follows:

	Year 1998	Year 1999
Revenues	$110,000	$110,000
Depreciation Expense	(50,000)	(50,000)
Pre Tax Income	$ 60,000	$ 60,000
Tax Expense:		
Current	(4,500)	(55,000)
Deferred	(22,500)	22,500
Net Income	$ 33,000	$ 27,500

	December 31 1998	December 31 1999
Cash	$105,500	$160,500
Capital Asset (Net)	50,000	Nil
Total Assets	$155,500	$160,500
Deferred Income Taxes	$ 22,500	Nil
Common Stock	100,000	$100,000
Retained Earnings	33,000	60,500
Total Equities	$155,500	$160,500

Evaluation

16-39.   On the positive side, it can be argued that the deferred charge method is more consistent with the matching principle. Note that the 1998 Tax Expense which totals $27,000 is exactly equal to the 1998 tax rate of 45 percent multiplied by the Pre Tax Income of $60,000. This relationship breaks down in 1999 in that the Expense of $32,500 is not equal to 50 percent of the 1999 Pre Tax Income. This type of problem is inherent in the deferred charge method's failure to adjust the deferred tax balances to reflect current tax rates.

16-40.   The major problem with the deferred charge method is that it results in the recording of deferred charge tax balances in the Balance Sheet. This designation has been used to describe a variety of Balance Sheet accounts, usually after some procedure has been justified in the name of the matching principle. Despite the fact that the term is frequently used, and the fact that there is a *CICA Handbook* Section titled "Deferred Charges", this term does not have a meaningful definition. The elements that should be included in financial statements are defined in Section 1000 of the *CICA Handbook*. This Section indicates that the elements that should be included in the Balance Sheet are assets, liabilities, and owners' equity. If an item does not fall into the definitions which apply to these items, it would not appear to have a place in the Balance Sheet. Given the situation with respect to deferred charges, it is not surprising that the deferral approach has been rejected by standard setters throughout the world.

Asset/ Liability Method

Basic Example

16-41.　This approach recognizes future income tax assets and liabilities on the basis of temporary differences on assets and liabilities in the Balance Sheet. Such temporary differences are based on differences between the tax basis and the carrying values of assets and liabilities included in the Balance Sheet. In our basic example, the temporary differences on the capital asset, as well as the related Future Income Tax Liability, would be calculated as follows:

	December 31 1998	December 31 1999
Carrying Value Of Capital Assets	$50,000	Nil
Tax Basis	Nil	Nil
Temporary Difference	$50,000	Nil
Tax Rate*	50%	50%
Future Income Tax Liability	$25,000	Nil

*As the 1999 rate is known at the end of 1998, the Future Income Tax Liability would be adjusted to reflect that rate in the December 31, 1998 Balance Sheet.

16-42.　The Tax Expense for the two years would include the amount of taxes currently payable (as per the taxes payable method), adjusted for changes in the future income tax liability. Given this, the resulting financial statements for the two years are as follows:

	Year 1998	Year 1999
Revenues	$110,000	$110,000
Depreciation Expense	(50,000)	(50,000)
Pre Tax Income	$ 60,000	$ 60,000
Tax Expense:		
Current	(4,500)	(55,000)
Future	(25,000)	25,000
Net Income	$ 30,500	$ 30,000

	December 31 1998	December 31 1999
Cash	$105,500	$160,500
Capital Asset (Net)	50,000	Nil
Total Assets	$155,500	$160,500
Future Income Tax Liability	$ 25,000	Nil
Common Stock	100,000	$100,000
Retained Earnings	30,500	60,500
Total Equities	$155,500	$160,500

16-43. While this method produces results that are similar to those produced under the deferred charge method, it does shift $2,500 of income out of 1998 and into 1999. This reflects the fact that this method adjusts the Balance Sheet liability for changes in tax rates. Also note that disclosure under this method uses the terms future tax expense and future income tax liability, as opposed to deferred tax expense and deferred income tax credits.

Evaluation

16-44. There is, of course, widespread support for this asset/liability method of tax allocation. This is evidenced by the fact that standard setting bodies throughout the world have, for the most part, adopted this approach. The basic arguments which support this approach are found in the *CICA Handbook* as follows:

Paragraph 3465.02 A fundamental principle in the preparation of financial statements is that an asset will be realized for at least its carrying amount in the form of future economic benefits. In some cases, realization of the carrying amount from sale or use of the asset will give rise to an increase or reduction in income taxes payable in the period of realization or later. For example, an asset with a carrying amount of $1,000 may have a tax basis of $600, such that realization of the carrying amount of $1,000 will give rise to income of $400 that is subject to tax, and an increase in income taxes otherwise payable.

Paragraph 3465.03 Similarly, a fundamental principle in the preparation of financial statements is that a liability will be settled for its carrying amount through the future transfer or use of assets, provision of services or other yielding of economic benefits. In some cases, settlement of the liability for the carrying amount will give rise to a decrease or an increase in income taxes payable in the year of settlement or later. For example, an accrued pension liability of $1,000 might be deductible for tax purposes only when an amount is actually paid. Payment of the accrued amount will give rise to a deduction of $1,000 in computing income that is subject to tax, and a reduction in income taxes otherwise payable.

Paragraph 3465.04 The resultant future tax outflows or inflows from the realization of assets and settlement of liabilities at their carrying amounts meet the conceptual definitions of assets and liabilities. Therefore, a future income tax asset or future income tax liability would be recognized for the tax effects that will arise if an asset is realized or a liability is settled for its carrying amount.

16-45. Without elaborating on this point, we are not comfortable with this reasoning. As the normal result of applying these procedures will be large future income tax liabilities, the question of whether these balances really are liabilities is relevant. Liabilities are defined in the *CICA Handbook* as follows:

Paragraph 1000.32 Liabilities are obligations of an entity arising from past transactions or events, the settlement of which may result in the transfer or use of assets, provision of services or other yielding of economic benefits in the future.

Paragraph 1000.33 Liabilities have three essential characteristics:

(a) they embody a duty or responsibility to others that entails settlement by future transfer or use of assets, provision of services or other yielding of economic benefits, at a specified or determinable date, on occurrence of a specified event, or on demand;

(b) the duty or responsibility obligates the entity leaving it little or no discretion to avoid it; and

(c) the transaction or event obligating the entity has already occurred.

Paragraph 1000.34 Liabilities do not have to be legally enforceable provided that they otherwise meet the definition of liabilities; they can be based on equitable or constructive obligations. An equitable obligation is a duty based on ethical or moral considerations. A constructive obligation is one that can be inferred from the facts in a particular situation as opposed to a contractually based obligation.

16-46. We are of the opinion that the future income tax liabilities that will be recorded under the application of Section 3465 are not consistent with this definition. We would note that, in most cases there is no probable outflow of resources. Further, as it is the earning of taxable income that creates taxes payable, the transaction or event which might cause a future income tax liability to exist has not, in fact, taken place.

16-47. Our view is that the taxes payable approach is the conceptually sound solution to this problem. While this view is shared by a fairly large number of analysts, it is clear that tax allocation on the basis of the asset/liability approach has won the hearts and minds of standard setters.

Other Ideas

Partial Allocation - A Compromise Position

16-48. To this point we have been discussing comprehensive tax allocation. That is, the use of allocation procedures for all timing or temporary differences which arise during the period. There is also a compromise solution involving what is commonly referred to as partial allocation. Under this approach, tax allocation procedures would be applied to some, but not all, timing or temporary differences.

16-49. Several different criterion have been suggested for the implementation of this partial allocation approach. They include; the likelihood that the timing difference will be reversed, the type of transaction which gives rise to the timing or temporary difference, and the one which was adopted in the United Kingdom, the time period in which reversal of the timing difference will occur. While there would be variations in which timing or temporary differences were subject to allocation procedures under these various criteria, all of the proposed criteria would eliminate tax allocation procedures for differences between depreciation and CCA.

16-50. This elimination of tax allocation procedures for differences between depreciation and CCA would serve to significantly reduce the amount of deferred taxes included in published Income Statements and Balance Sheets. However, there does not seem to be much conceptual support for this alternative, particularly in view of the fact that allocation procedures are now going to be based on temporary differences rather than timing differences. In addition, after the long battles required to implement new standards in both Canada and the United States, it is difficult to imagine that standard setters will be eager to revisit this issue in the near future.

Net Of Tax Approach

16-51. While most of the discussion of tax allocation procedures is in terms of the Balance Sheet items being either deferred charges or assets and liabilities, a less well known approach to dealing with these balances is sometimes referred to as the net of tax approach. Proponents of this approach argue that tax allocation balances should be treated as adjustments of the assets or liabilities to which the timing differences relate. For example, when the tax allocation balances relate to the fact that more capital cost allowance than depreciation expense was taken on certain of our limited life assets, proponents of the net of tax view would argue that the resulting tax allocation balances should be subtracted from these assets.

16-52. The most obvious practical problem with this net of tax view is that not all temporary differences relate to specific assets and liabilities and this would prevent the net of tax approach from being a general solution to the problem. More importantly, it is not our present practice to value assets and liabilities on a net of tax basis. Until such time as net of tax valuation becomes a general practice in accounting, the use of this approach to tax allocation would not be a consistent or acceptable solution to the problem.

Future Income Tax Assets And Liabilities

Introduction

16-53.   A fundamental difference between the new Section 3465 and the now superseded Section 3470 is the switch from tax allocation based on timing differences to tax allocation based on temporary differences. Timing differences focused on the Income Statement and were defined in terms of amounts that would be charged or credited to Accounting Income on a different timing basis than they would be charged or credited to Taxable Income, but would total the same amount over the life of the enterprise. As we have noted several times, the classic example of such an item is the annual difference between Depreciation Expense and CCA. Over the life of the enterprise, the total amount deducted for both accounting and tax purposes would be equal to the cost of the asset, less any proceeds resulting from its disposition. However, when these amounts are included in the determination of Accounting Income could be very different from when they are included in the determination of Taxable Income.

16-54.   In keeping with the asset/liability approach to interperiod tax allocation, Section 3465 shifts the focus of these procedures to the Balance Sheet. Instead of applying tax allocation procedures to timing differences, the procedures are applied to temporary differences. These differences are defined as follows:

> **Paragraph 3465.09(c) Temporary differences** are differences between the tax basis of an asset or liability and its carrying amount in the balance sheet. Temporary differences may be either:
>
> (i) **Deductible temporary differences**, which are temporary differences that will result in deductible amounts in determining taxable income of future periods when the carrying amount of the asset or liability is recovered or settled; or
>
> (ii) **Taxable temporary differences**, which are temporary differences that will result in taxable amounts in determining taxable income of future periods when the carrying amount of the asset or liability is recovered or settled.

16-55.   While these terms are not included in Section 3465's list of definitions, it is essential to understand what is meant by the tax basis of assets and liabilities. As informally described elsewhere in Section 3465, these items can be defined as follows:

> **Tax Basis Of Assets**   The tax basis of an asset is the amount that, under the rules established by taxation authorities, could be deducted in the determination of taxable income if the asset were recovered for its carrying amount.

> **Tax Basis Of Liabilities**   The tax basis of a liability is its carrying value, less any amount that will be deductible for income tax purposes with respect of that liability in future periods. If the liability is for the future delivery of goods or services, its tax basis is its carrying value, less any amounts that will not be taxed in future periods.

16-56.   In terms of the Balance Sheet, deductible temporary differences fall into two categories:

> **Deductible Temporary Differences On Assets**   These differences would arise when the tax basis of the asset (deductible amount) exceeds its carrying value (e.g., a long term investment that has been written down to recognize a non temporary decline in value).

> **Deductible Temporary Differences On Liabilities**   These differences would arise when the tax basis of a liability (carrying value, less deductible amount) is less than its carrying value (e.g., estimated warranty liabilities).

16-57.   Again in terms of Balance Sheet items, taxable temporary differences would arise as follows:

Taxable Temporary Differences On Assets   These differences would arise when the tax basis of the asset (deductible amount) is less than its carrying value (e.g., a depreciable asset with a UCC that is less than its net book value).

Taxable Temporary Differences On Liabilities   While this possibility is not listed in Section 3465 (see Paragraph 3465.14), the tax basis of a liability could exceed its carrying value, resulting in a taxable temporary difference. This would occur, for example, when long term bonds are sold at a premium over their face value. As premium amortization is not recognized for tax purposes, the tax basis would remain at the original issue price while the carrying value declines.

16-58.   Summarizing these rules from a different perspective, temporary differences on assets are taxable when the tax basis of the asset is less than its carrying value, and deductible when the tax basis of the asset exceeds its carrying value. With respect to liabilities, temporary differences are deductible when the tax basis of the liability is less than its carrying value, and taxable when the tax basis of the liability is greater than its carrying value.

16-59.   Future income tax assets and liabilities generally result from the presence of deductible and taxable temporary differences. As a consequence, Section 3465 defines such assets and liabilities in terms of temporary differences:

Paragraph 3465.09(d)   Future income tax assets are the amounts of income tax benefits arising in respect of:

(i)   deductible temporary differences;
(ii) the carryforward of unused tax losses; and
(iii) the carryforward of unused income tax reductions, except for investment tax credits.

Paragraph 3465.09(e)   Future income tax liabilities are the amounts of income taxes arising from taxable temporary differences.

16-60.   As is clear from the preceding, the determination of future income tax assets and liabilities is a fairly complex process, requiring a full understanding of the tax basis of assets and liabilities, as well as the meaning of deductible temporary differences and taxable temporary differences. This is further complicated by the fact that these concepts are similar to, but not identical to, the concepts used in calculating deferred tax balances based on timing differences. Given this complexity, the remainder of this section will provide a full discussion of the concepts involved in determining future income tax assets and future income tax liabilities.

Tax Basis Of Assets And Liabilities

Assets

16-61.   As noted previously, the tax basis of an asset is the amount that could be deducted in the determination of taxable income if the asset were recovered for an amount equal to its carrying value. Applying this concept to the usual types of items found on the asset side of the Balance Sheet:

Cash And Cash Equivalents   These assets would invariably have a tax basis equal to their carrying value.

Temporary Investments   The tax basis of Temporary Investments would be their cost. This could be different than their carrying value if the investments were carried at a value other than cost in the accounting records.

Accounts Receivable   In the accounting records, Accounts Receivable are carried at their face value, less an allowance for bad debts. As any tax reserve for bad debts is normally equal to the accounting estimate for bad debts, the tax basis of Accounts Receivable will normally be equal to their carrying value. An exception could occur if accounting revenues were on an accrual basis, with a reserve for unpaid amounts deducted for tax purposes [(ITA 20(1)(n)]. In this situation, the tax basis would be less than the carrying value by the amount of the reserve.

Inventories   In general, inventory valuation methods and inventory cost determination methods are the same for both accounting and tax purposes. This means that the tax basis of inventories would usually be equal to their carrying value. An exception would occur if the enterprise used the LIFO cost determination method for accounting purposes. This method cannot be used for tax purposes and, as a consequence, its use would result in a tax basis that is different than the carrying value for Inventories.

Prepayments   The tax basis of prepayments would normally be equal to their carrying value.

Long Term Investments In Debt Securities   The tax basis of long term investments in debt securities would be their cost, without amortization of any premium over or discount from maturity value. If such premium or discount is amortized in the accounting records, the tax basis of these investments would be different than their carrying value.

Long Term Investment In Equity Securities   The tax basis of long term investments in equity securities is their cost. If such investments are carried in the accounting records at cost, the tax basis will equal the carrying value. If such investments are carried by the equity method, the situation becomes more complex. As the equity method cannot be used for tax purposes, a temporary difference will arise. This type of difference will be discussed in Chapter 17.

Land   Both the tax basis and the carrying value of land will normally be its original cost.

Depreciable Tangible Assets   The tax basis of depreciable assets will generally be their UCC. Their carrying value will be their net book value (cost less accumulated Depreciation Expense), a value that will normally exceed the tax basis of the assets.

Different conclusions may be applicable to certain types of depreciable tangible assets where there are special tax rules. For example, the cost of a passenger vehicle in excess of a specified amount ($26,000 for 1998) cannot be deducted for tax purposes. Going with this restriction is the fact that, if the vehicle is sold for its carrying value, there are no tax consequences. In effect, for tax purposes, the carrying value can be deducted if the vehicle is disposed of for its carrying value. This means that the tax basis of the vehicle is its carrying value.

Intangible Capital Assets   When a company incurs costs in order to develop an intangible asset internally, such costs are usually charged to expense for both tax and accounting purposes. This means that both the carrying value of any resulting asset, as well as its tax basis will be nil. An exception to this may be certain types of development costs which can be capitalized under Section 3450 of the *CICA Handbook*, "Research and Development Costs". This will result in an accounting asset with a positive carrying value. However, such development costs will usually be deducted for tax purposes, resulting in a tax basis for the asset of nil.

With respect to purchased intangible capital assets, if they have a limited life, their cost will be allocated to either Class 14 or Class 44 (patents). The initial carrying value and tax basis for such assets will be equal to their cost. However, as the pattern of Depreciation Expense may be different than the pattern of CCA deductions, the tax basis (UCC) of the assets may be different than their carrying value in future periods.

For tax purposes, purchased intangible assets without a specified life (goodwill)

will have 75 percent of their cost allocated to the cumulative eligible capital balance. As only 75 percent of the proceeds from the disposition of such assets will be considered for tax purposes, the tax basis of such assets includes the non taxable 25 percent of the carrying value that could be received without tax consequences. This means that, at the time of acquisition, the tax basis and the carrying value of such assets would be equal. However, because of differing amortization patterns, these amounts would diverge as the asset is amortized. The tax basis of intangible capital assets, at any point in time, would be 4/3 of the balance in the cumulative eligible capital account.

16-62.   While there are other difficulties in the determination of the tax basis of assets, the preceding analysis deals with those that will be most commonly encountered.

Liabilities

16-63.   As we have previously noted, the tax basis of a liability is defined as its carrying value, less any amount that will be deductible for income tax purposes with respect of that liability in future periods. In similar fashion, if the liability is for the future delivery of goods or services, its tax basis is its carrying value, less any amounts that will not be taxed in future periods. While not mentioned in Section 3465, the definition should also include situations where an amount is added to the carrying value because it will be taxable when the liability is settled in a future period (e.g., settlement of bonds that were originally issued at a premium). The different applications of this concept can be described as follows:

> **Liabilities For Assets Acquired Or Deductible Expenses Incurred**   The majority of accounting liabilities result either from the acquisition of assets or from the incurrence of costs that have been both deducted for tax purposes and charged to expense for accounting purposes.   In either case the settlement of the liability would not generate an item to be included in the determination of accounting income. Examples of this would be liabilities for salaries and liabilities related to the purchase of inventories or capital assets. When such liabilities have also created either tax assets or tax deductions, their settlement would have no tax consequences. This means that their tax basis would be equal to their carrying value and no temporary difference would arise. The previous examples related to salaries and inventories would fall into this classification.

> **Liabilities For Non Deductible Expenses**   Certain liabilities reflect items that can be charged to expense for accounting purposes, but that can never be deducted for tax purposes. Examples of this would be liabilities for non deductible fines and penalties, and liabilities for club dues or recreational facilities. As with liabilities incurred for deductible expenses, no amount can be deducted for tax purposes when such liabilities are settled. Their tax basis would be equal to their carrying value and no temporary difference would arise.

> **Liabilities For Expenses To Be Deducted Or Taxed In Future Periods**   Certain liabilities reflect items that can be charged to expense prior to their deduction for tax purposes. Examples of this would be liabilities for estimated warranty costs and accrued but unfunded pension costs. In both of these cases, the relevant amount can only be deducted for tax purposes when the costs are actually incurred. As the payment of such liabilities will result in a deductible expense for tax purposes, the tax basis of such liabilities is nil (carrying value, less the amount that can be deducted on the payment of the carrying amount). There would be a temporary difference in this situation.

> A less common problem can arise when there is a taxable amount related to the liability. As noted in Paragraph 16-57, tax authorities do not recognize premium amortization on long term bonds, resulting in a situation in where the original premium on the sale of the issue will be a taxable item when the bonds are retired. In

this case, the tax basis of the liability exceeds its carrying value and there is a temporary difference.

Liabilities To Deliver Goods Or Services   As unearned revenues are involved, the settlement of this type of liability will result in an accounting revenue. In most cases, the enterprise will have deducted a reserve for tax purposes for the unearned revenue [ITA 20(1)(m)] and the settlement of the liability would also result in a tax inclusion equal to the accounting revenue. This means that the tax basis of the liability is equal to its carrying value. If, however, no reserve has been deducted, the settlement will not result in a revenue and the tax basis of the liability is nil (carrying value, less the amount that will not be taxed when the goods or services are delivered).

16-64.   As was the case with assets, there are other difficulties in the determination of the tax basis of liabilities. However, the preceding analysis deals with those that will be most commonly encountered.

Temporary Differences

Introduction

16-65.   As noted in Paragraph 16-54, temporary differences are defined as any difference between the tax basis of an asset or liability, and its carrying value in the GAAP based Balance Sheet. Once the tax basis of an asset or liability is established, the calculation of the associated temporary difference presents no real problems. The determination of the tax basis of assets and liabilities was given detailed treatment in the previous section.

16-66.   While further discussion of the determination of temporary differences is not required here, your understanding of this subject will be enhanced by reviewing examples of temporary differences. To this end, we are providing a fairly long selection of examples of the types of temporary differences that you are likely to encounter. While we will come back to this subject in the next section of this Chapter, we would remind you that taxable temporary differences form the basis for future income tax liabilities, while deductible temporary differences indicate the presence of future income tax assets.

Taxable Temporary Differences (Basis For Future Income Tax Liabilities)

16-67.   The following are examples of taxable temporary differences. The amounts indicated will be multiplied by the relevant tax rate, with the product recorded as a future income tax liability.

Accounts Receivable   The enterprise has recorded Accounts Receivable on the delivery of goods in the amount of $75,000. As the amounts are not collectible until the following year, a reserve for unpaid amounts has been deducted for tax purposes under ITA 20(1)(n), leaving the tax basis of the Accounts Receivable as nil. As the carrying value of the asset is greater than its tax basis, there is a taxable temporary difference of $75,000.

Prepaid Pension Costs   The enterprise has made advance funding payments to its registered pension plan, thereby creating an accounting asset with a value of $1,000,000. As these payments have already been deducted for tax purposes, the tax basis of this asset is nil. As the carrying value of the asset is greater than its tax basis, there is a $1,000,000 taxable temporary difference.

Long Term Investments At Equity   The enterprise acquired a long term investment at a cost $1,350,000. As they have significant influence over the investee, the investment is accounted for using the equity method. While the current carrying value of the investment has been increased to $1,560,000, the tax basis remains at $1,350,000. As the carrying value of the investment exceeds its tax basis, there is a taxable temporary difference of $210,000 ($1,560,000 - $1,350,000).

Land Land with a cost of $400,000 is sold for $700,000, resulting in an accounting gain of $300,000. Of the total sale price, $350,000 is still receivable at the end of the year. A capital gains reserve of $150,000 [($350,000 ÷ $700,000)($700,000 - $400,000)] is deducted for tax purposes. With respect to the receivable, its carrying value is $350,000. As the $150,000 reserve will have to be added back to taxable income when the $350,000 receivable is collected, the tax basis of the receivable is $200,000 ($350,000 - $150,000). As the carrying value of the receivable is greater than its tax basis, there is a $150,000 taxable temporary difference.

Depreciable Capital Assets The enterprise has depreciable capital assets with a net book value of $1,250,000. The tax basis of these assets is $675,000, the total UCC for the various CCA classes to which these assets have been allocated. As the carrying value of the assets is greater than their tax basis, there is a taxable temporary difference of $575,000 ($1,250,000 - $675,000).

Depreciable Capital Assets With Investment Tax Credits A depreciable asset is acquired at the beginning of the year for $500,000. It qualifies for a 20 percent investment tax credit and, under the provisions of Section 3805 of the *CICA Handbook*, "Investment Tax Credits", the credit is deducted from the cost of the asset, leaving a balance of $400,000. This balance will be amortized on a straight line basis over ten years, resulting in an annual deduction for depreciation expense of $40,000. For tax purposes, it is a Class 10 asset, with CCA calculated at a rate of 30 percent on the declining balance. It is subject to the first year one-half rules. For tax purposes, the $100,000 investment tax credit is not deducted from the Class 10 UCC until the year following the asset's acquisition. Accounting and tax values at the end of years one and two are as follows:

	Accounting Value	Tax Value
Acquisition	$500,000	$500,000
Investment Tax Credit	(100,000)	N/A
Amortization Base	$400,000	$500,000
Amortization At 10% Of Cost	(40,000)	N/A
Amortization At [(1/2)(30%)]	N/A	(75,000)
Ending Balance Year One	$360,000	$425,000
Investment Tax Credit	N/A	(100,000)
Amortization Base	$360,000	$325,000
Amortization At 10% Of Cost	(40,000)	N/A
Amortization At 30% Of Balance	N/A	(97,500)
Ending Balance Year Two	$320,000	$227,500

At the end of year one, the tax basis of the asset would be $325,000, the amortization base, less the $100,000 investment tax credit (this amount would not be deductible if the asset were settled for its carrying value). This means that the carrying value exceeds the tax basis and there is a $35,000 ($360,000 - $325,000) taxable temporary difference.

At the end of year two, the carrying value is again higher than the tax basis, resulting in a $92,500 ($320,000 - $227,500) taxable temporary difference.

Development Costs The enterprise has incurred development costs of $420,000 which, because they meet the conditions specified in Section 3450 for capitalization, have been recorded as an asset. These costs have been deducted for tax purposes which means that the tax basis of this asset is nil. As the carrying value of the asset is greater than its tax basis, there is a taxable temporary difference of $420,000.

Deductible Temporary Differences (Basis For Future Income Tax Assets)

16-68. The following are examples of deductible temporary differences. The amounts indicated will be multiplied by the relevant tax rate, with the product recorded as a future income tax asset.

Temporary Investments Temporary Investments of equity securities are carried at the lower of cost or market. The enterprise currently holds such securities with a cost of $125,000 and a market value of $115,000. As the carrying value of the asset is less than its tax basis, there is a deductible temporary difference of $10,000 ($125,000 - $115,000).

Inventories In the accounting records, Inventories are carried at cost as determined on a LIFO basis. Their carrying value is $550,000. Cost as determined on a FIFO basis is $575,000 and this is the tax basis of the Inventories. As the carrying value of the asset is less than its tax basis, there is a deductible temporary difference of $25,000 ($575,000 - $550,000).

Portfolio Investments The enterprise has long term portfolio investments with a cost of $325,000. Because these investments have experienced a non temporary decline in value, they have been written down to their net realizable value of $215,000. The tax basis of these investments continues to be their original cost of $325,000. As the carrying value of these investments is less than their tax basis, there is a deductible temporary difference of $110,000 ($325,000 - $215,000).

Goodwill (Eligible Capital Expenditures) In a business combination transaction involving a cash acquisition of assets, the enterprise has paid $620,000 for the goodwill of the acquiree. In the accounting records, it will be amortized on a straight line basis over 10 years at the rate of $62,000 per year. For tax purposes, 75 percent of this amount or $465,000 has been added to the cumulative eligible capital account (CEC). This balance will be amortized at a rate of seven percent per year, applied to the amortized balance.

At any point in time, if the asset was disposed of for its carrying value, 25 percent of this amount would not be taxable (on a disposition of an eligible capital expenditure, only 75 percent of the proceeds are subtracted from the CEC balance). This means that, at acquisition, the tax basis of the goodwill would be equal to the $620,000 carrying value (the CEC balance of $465,000, plus $155,000 which is 25 percent of the $620,000 carrying value).

As the amortization rates applied to the accounting and tax values are different, accounting and tax values will diverge in subsequent periods. For example, after one year, the accounting carrying value would be $558,000 ($620,000 - $62,000). In contrast, the CEC balance would be $432,450 ($465,000, less 7 percent or $32,550). The tax basis of the asset would be $571,950 [$432,450 + (25%)($558,000)]. As the carrying value of the asset is less than its tax basis, there would be a deductible temporary difference of $13,950 ($571,950 - $558,000).

Product Warranty Costs The enterprise has recorded a warranty expense and an estimated liability for warranty cost of $25,000. This amount will be deductible for tax purposes when actual warranty costs are incurred. This means that the tax basis of this liability is nil (carrying value of $25,000, less the $25,000 that will be deductible when the warranty liability is settled by delivering warranty services). As the carrying value of these liabilities is greater than their tax basis, there is a deductible temporary difference of $25,000.

Long Term Bonds Several years ago, the enterprise issued long term bonds with a maturity value of $3,000,000. They were sold for $2,900,000 and, in the accounting records, the $100,000 discount is being amortized over the life of the bonds. The current carrying value of the liability is $2,962,000. However, as discount amortization is not recognized for tax purposes, the tax basis of the bonds is

$2,900,000 (the carrying value of $2,962,000, less the $62,000 that could be deducted if the liability were settled at its carrying value). As the carrying value of these liabilities exceeds their tax basis, there is a deductible temporary difference of $62,000.

Future Site Restoration Costs   In accordance with the provisions of Section 3060 of the *CICA Handbook*, "Capital Assets", the enterprise has recorded a $900,000 liability for future site restoration costs. As these amounts will only be deductible for tax purposes when the expenses are incurred, the tax basis of the liability is nil ($900,000 carrying value, less the $900,000 that will be deductible when the liability is settled). As the carrying value of the liability is greater than its tax basis, there is a deductible temporary difference of $900,000.

Pension Liabilities   The enterprise has accrued a liability for unfunded pension costs of $860,000. For tax purposes, these amounts will be deducted when funding payments are made. This means that the tax basis of this liability is nil ($860,000 carrying value, less the $860,000 that will be deductible when the liability is settled). As the carrying value of the liability is greater than its tax basis, there is a deductible temporary difference of $860,000.

Temporary Differences Vs. Timing Differences

16-69.   As we have noted, the Recommendations of Section 3465 are based on temporary differences that are measured in terms of Balance Sheet accounts. In contrast, the now superseded Section 3470 made its Recommendations on the basis of timing differences which were measured in terms of Income Statement effects. In the great majority of tax allocation calculations, this conceptual change will have no influence on the numbers that will be produced.

16-70.   For example, assume that on January 1, 1998, a company that is subject to a combined federal/provincial tax rate of 40 percent acquires Class 8 assets with a cost of $200,000, and an estimated service life of 20 years. As of this point in time, both the carrying value and the tax basis of these assets is $200,000. Using the straight line method of amortization, the carrying value of the assets on December 31, 1998 would be $190,000 [($200,000 - (5%)($200,000)]. On this same date, the tax basis of the assets would be $180,000 [$200,000 - (20%)(1/2)($200,000)]. Using the alternative terminologies of Sections 3465 and 3470, this situation would be described as follows:

Beginning Of The Year   Using Section 3465 terminology we would state that, at the beginning of 1998, there are no temporary differences and no future income tax assets or liabilities related to these assets. Alternatively, under Section 3470's terminology, we would state that there are no accumulated timing differences and no deferred tax debits or credits related to these assets.

During The Year   Under the Section 3465 approach, there would be a change in temporary differences of $10,000 [nil at the beginning of the year, increasing to ($190,000 - $180,000) at the end of the year]. This amount would be multiplied by the tax rate of 40 percent, with the resulting $4,000 recorded as a Future Tax Expense for the year. Under Section 3470, there would be a timing difference of $10,000 (depreciation expense of $10,000 vs. CCA of $20,000). This amount would be multiplied by the tax rate of 40 percent, with the resulting $4,000 recorded as a Deferred Tax Expense for the year.

End Of The Year   Under Section 3465, we would state that there was a taxable temporary difference at the end of the year of $10,000 ($190,000 - $180,000). This difference would be reflected in a future income tax liability of $4,000 [(40%)($10,000)]. Under Section 3470, we would state that, at the end of the year, there are accumulated timing differences of $10,000. These timing differences would be reflected in a deferred income tax credit of $4,000.

16-71.   As the preceding example makes clear, this two approaches result in the same amount being shown in both the Income Statement and the Balance Sheet. The only difference is in the terminology used to describe the balances. It would appear that this would be the case for most of the items that can be described as temporary differences.

16-72.   There are, however, some differences between the items that would be designated timing differences and those that would be referred to as temporary differences. As the temporary difference concept is more broadly based than the timing difference concept, these differences usually involve items that were considered to be permanent differences under Section 3470.

16-73.   The most important of these items would arise in business combination transactions. When such a transaction is implemented through an acquisition of shares, the subsidiary's assets will be recorded in the consolidated financial statements at their fair values. The tax basis of these assets will be unchanged by the acquisition of shares and, as a consequence, there will generally be differences between the new carrying values for the assets and their tax basis which they have retained from the subsidiary's records. Under Section 3470, such differences were considered to be permanent differences and no deferred tax amounts were required. Under Section 3465, these differences would be considered to be temporary differences and future income tax assets or liabilities would be recorded. The procedures required in this type of situation will be given comprehensive coverage in the following Chapter 17.

16-74.   Other differences between timing differences and temporary differences arise when investment tax credits are accounted for using a deferred charge approach, and when the non monetary assets of an integrated foreign operation are translated using historical rates of exchange.

Converting Temporary Differences To Future Income Tax Assets And Liabilities

16-75.   The definition of future income tax assets and future income tax liabilities was presented in Paragraph 16-63. With respect to liabilities there are no problems. It would appear that all future income tax liabilities can be related to particular assets and liabilities that are presented in the accounting Balance Sheet. This means that once you have determined all of your taxable temporary differences, future income tax liabilities are simply those amounts multiplied by the relevant tax rate. While this issue will be discussed further at a later point in this Chapter, the relevant rate would normally be the rate in effect at the Balance Sheet date.

16-76.   The situation is more complex with respect to the recording of future income tax assets. For those future income tax assets which relate to assets or liabilities in the accounting Balance Sheet, there will be deductible temporary differences. In cases such as this, the future income tax assets will simply be the amount of the deductible temporary difference, multiplied by the relevant tax rate. Here again, the relevant rate will normally be the rate in effect as at the end of the year.

16-77.   As noted in the definition of future income tax assets, there are other future income tax assets which do not relate to assets and liabilities found in the accounting Balance Sheet. The most obvious of these future income tax assets involves unused tax loss carry forwards. If an enterprise has a $1,000,000 non capital loss in the current period and, if this loss cannot be carried back to any of the three preceding taxation years, it becomes a loss carry forward. If we assume that the enterprise has a combined federal/provincial tax rate of 40 percent, there is a potential tax benefit of $400,000. While there is no accounting asset related to this potential benefit, it will be recorded as a future income tax asset if it is more likely than not that it can be realized in the applicable future period.

16-78.   The other type of future income tax asset referred to in the definition of these items relates to the carry forward of unused income tax reductions other than investment tax credits. Section 3465 contains the following examples of such items:

Paragraph 3465.15   ...

(a) a certain percentage of expenditures for mineral property exploration and development may be allowed as an additional deduction for income tax purposes ("earned depletion"). There may be no related asset for financial statement purposes. The difference between the tax basis of the earned depletion base and the carrying amount of nil is a deductible temporary difference which gives rise to a future income tax asset;

(b) research costs are recognized as an expense in the financial statements in the period in which they are incurred but might not be deducted in determining taxable income. The difference between the tax basis of the research costs, being the amount the taxation authorities will permit as a deduction in the future, and the carrying amount of nil is a deductible temporary difference which gives rise to a future income tax asset;

(c) for financial statement purposes, an enterprise might recognize profits on a long-term contract using the percentage of completion method but use the completed contract method when determining taxable income. Income is therefore being deferred for tax purposes, with no corresponding amount being deferred for accounting purposes. The income deferred for tax purposes represents a taxable temporary difference.

16-79.   While no Balance Sheet item would be present for these items, future income tax assets would still be recorded.

Purpose And Scope Of Section 3465

16-80.   The purpose of Section 3465 is to establish standards for the recognition, measurement, presentation, and disclosure of income and refundable taxes in the general purpose financial statements of Canadian enterprises. It is based on the principle that comprehensive tax allocation procedures should be applied in order to record future income tax assets and liabilities related to deductible and taxable temporary differences. It is not applicable to the special considerations related to accounting for investment tax credits. These considerations are covered in Section 3805 of the *CICA Handbook*.

16-81.   For purposes of this Section, income taxes are defined as follows:

Paragraph 3465.09(a)   Income taxes include:

(i)   all domestic and foreign taxes that are based on taxable income;
(ii)   taxes, such as mining taxes, that are based on a measure of revenue less certain specified expenses;
(iii) alternative minimum income taxes, including taxes based on measures other than income and that may be used to reduce income taxes of another period; and
(iv)   taxes, such as withholding taxes, that are based on amounts paid to the enterprise.

16-82.   The position of rate regulated enterprises is different in that, in many cases, future income tax payments will be included in the rates that are charged to customers. In such cases, the future taxes are claims on the resources of the particular enterprise and should not be recorded as liabilities of the enterprise. Given this, Section 3465 includes the following exception to its general scope provision:

Paragraph 3465.102   *A rate regulated enterprise need not recognize future income taxes in accordance with the Recommendations of this Section to the extent that future income taxes are expected to be included in the approved rate charged to customers in the future and are expected to be recovered from future customers. If future income taxes are not recognized in accordance with the Recommenda-*

tions of this Section, the rate regulated enterprise should disclose the following, in addition to the information to be disclosed in accordance with paragraphs 3465.91 and 3465.92:

(a) the reason why future income tax liabilities and future income tax assets have not been recognized; and

(b) the amount of future income tax liabilities, future income tax assets and future income tax expense that have not been recognized. (January, 2000)

16-83. Note that this exception only applies to the extent that future income taxes are expected to be recovered from rates charged to future customers. Otherwise, the provisions of the Section apply and the recording of future income tax assets and liabilities is required. Rate regulated enterprises are defined in the Section as follows:

Paragraph 3465.09(k). A **rate regulated enterprise** is an enterprise which meets all of the following criteria:

(i) the rates for regulated services or products provided to customers are established by or are subject to approval by a regulator or a governing body empowered by statute or contract to establish rates to be charged for services or products;

(ii) the regulated rates are designed to recover the cost of providing the services or products; and

(iii) it is reasonable to assume that rates set at levels that will recover the cost can be charged to and collected from customers in view of the demand for the services or products and the level of direct and indirect competition. This criterion requires consideration of expected changes in levels of demand or competition during the recovery period for amounts recorded as recoverable under the rate formula.

Current Income Tax Assets And Liabilities

16-84. The cost or benefit of current income taxes is defined in Section 3465 as follows:

Paragraph 3465.09(g) The **cost (benefit) of current income taxes** is the amount of income taxes payable (recoverable) in respect of the period.

16-85. The reference here is to taxes that must be paid or that can be recovered as a result of information that is included in the tax return of the enterprise for the current year. Most commonly, this would be the taxes payable as a result of the inclusions and deductions reported for the current taxation year. However, if the current tax return reports a loss, this can be carried back to the three previous years in order to claim a refund of taxes paid in those years. Such a carry back will result in taxes that are currently receivable.

16-86. This means that, at the end of any taxation year, there will be either taxes that are currently payable or taxes that are currently receivable. The current amount payable will reflect taxes that must be paid because of taxable activities during the current or preceding taxation years. Any current amount receivable will reflect taxes paid in previous years that are being recovered because of a loss carry back.

16-87. With respect to these current income tax assets and liabilities, the following Recommendations are applicable:

Paragraph 3465.19 Current income taxes, to the extent unpaid or recoverable, should be recognized as a liability or asset and should not be included in future income tax liabilities or future income tax assets. (January, 2000)

Paragraph 3465.20 The benefit relating to a tax loss arising in the current period that will be carried back to recover income taxes of a previous period should be *recognized as a current asset and not included in future income tax liabilities or future income tax assets.* (January, 2000)

16-88. The use of the term current in the context of the phrase "current income taxes" should not be confused with the use of this term in the classification of assets and liabilities. "Current income taxes", to the extent that they have not been paid or received will be classified as current assets and liabilities. However, current assets and liabilities could also include "future income taxes", provided the amounts would be received or settled within one year of the Balance Sheet date.

Basic Tax Allocation Procedures

Introduction

16-89. At the heart of Section 3465 is the requirement that future income tax assets and liabilities must be recognized for all temporary differences. This reflects an adoption of comprehensive tax allocation procedures, implemented with the asset/liability approach.

16-90. In this section we will present the specific Section 3465 Recommendations which support this approach. We will also discuss possible analytical approaches to implementing these Recommendations. In addition, an example will be presented to illustrate the application of the suggested analytical approach.

16-91. Our concern here will be with basic tax allocation Recommendations. There are a number of more technical issues associated with these Recommendations which, if presented on a simultaneous basis, would tend to obscure the general approach that is being adopted by Section 3465. These more technical issues will be dealt with elsewhere in this Chapter and in Chapter 17.

Basic Tax Allocation Recommendations

Balance Sheet Amounts

16-92. The fundamental Recommendations of Section 3465 require the recognition of future income tax assets and future income tax liabilities at each Balance Sheet date. These Recommendation are as follows:

> **Paragraph 3465.22** *At each balance sheet date, except as provided in paragraphs 3465.33, 3465.35 and 3465.37, a future income tax liability should be recognized for all taxable temporary differences other than those arising from any portion of goodwill which is not deductible for tax purposes.* (January, 2000)

> **Paragraph 3465.24** *At each balance sheet date, except as provided in paragraphs 3465.33, 3465.35 and 3465.37, a future income tax asset should be recognized for all deductible temporary differences, unused tax losses and income tax reductions. The amount recognized should be limited to the amount that is more likely than not to be realized.* (January, 2000)

> **Note** The complications referred to in Paragraph 3465.33, 3465.35, and 3465.37, as well as the treatment of temporary differences related to goodwill, will be dealt with in Chapter 17. Future income tax assets related to unused tax losses will also be considered in more detail at a later point in this Chapter.

Measurement

16-93. With respect to the measurement of the future income tax assets and liabilities, Section 3465 makes the following Recommendation:

> **Paragraph 3465.56** *Income tax liabilities and income tax assets should be measured using the income tax rates and income tax laws that, at the balance sheet date,*

are expected to apply when the liability is settled or the asset is realized, which would normally be those enacted at the balance sheet date. (January, 2000)

16-94.   In some situations, there may be announced changes in the tax rates which are expected to apply when future income tax assets are realized or future income tax liabilities are settled. It would be appropriate to use a substantially enacted future tax rate or future tax law only when there is persuasive evidence that:

- the government is able and committed to enacting the proposed change in the foreseeable future; and

- where the change relates to the current year, the enterprise expects to be assessed based on the announced tax rates or tax laws.

16-95.   The rates used should reflect the expected values of any special tax incentives that are available to the enterprise. This would include such provisions as the small business deduction, the manufacturing and processing profits deduction, and the resource allowance deduction.

16-96.   When different rates apply to different levels of income (e.g., the small business deduction is only available on the first $200,000 of active business income), the tax rate that is expected to apply to taxable income in the period in which temporary differences are expected to reverse should be used. When allocations of incentives must be made to individual companies (e.g, the associated companies rules for the small business deduction), the tax rates should reflect these allocations.

Discounting

16-97.   As future amounts are involved, it would seem that discounting would be an appropriate procedure to be used in the measurement of future income tax assets and liabilities. However, because of the many problems associated with the application of present value concepts, Section 3465 rejects this possibility:

> **Paragraph 3465.57**   *Future income tax liabilities and future income tax assets should not be discounted.* (January, 2000)

16-98.   This conclusion is consistent with Statement Of Financial Accounting Standards No. 109 in the United States.

Income Statement Amounts

16-99.   With respect to amounts to be included in the Income Statement, the following two Recommendations are applicable:

> **Paragraph 3465.63**   *The cost (benefit) of current and future income taxes should be recognized as income tax expense included in the determination of net income or loss for the period before discontinued operations and extraordinary items, ...* (January, 2000)

> **Paragraph 3465.64**   *Changes in future income tax balances recognized in accordance with paragraph 3465.56 as a result of changes in tax laws or rates should be included in future income tax expense reported in income before discontinued operations and extraordinary items.* (January, 2000)

16-100.   Paragraph 3465.63 makes it clear that the current Income Tax Expense or Income Tax Benefit should include both current and future income taxes. The amount of future income taxes to be included would be equal to the change in the net future income tax liability (asset). The change in this net balance would, in turn, be dependent on changes in taxable (deductible) temporary differences during the period. However, Paragraph 3465.64 indicates that this amount would also include changes in the net future income tax liability (asset) related to changes in tax laws or rates.

16-101.   To make these points clear, consider the following simple example:

Example An enterprise has net taxable temporary differences on December 31, 1998 of $1,000,000. At that point in time, the enterprise is subject to a combined statutory tax rate of 40 percent. At December 31, 1999, the net taxable temporary differences total $1,200,000 and the tax rate has increased to 45 percent. The enterprise has a December 31 year end.

16-102. The amount that will added to the 1999 Income Tax Expense for future income taxes would be calculated as follows:

Ending Future Income Tax Liability [(45%)($1,200,000)]	$540,000
Beginning Future Income Tax Liability [(40%)($1,000,000)]	(400,000)
Addition To Future Income Tax Expense	$140,000

16-103. This addition is made up of two components. Of the total of $140,000, $90,000 [(45%)($1,200,000 - $1,000,000)] relates to the increase in taxable temporary differences. The remaining $50,000 results from the 5 percent increase in the tax rate applied to the beginning future tax liability of $1,000,000.

Basic Tax Allocation Disclosure

Income Statement

16-104. **Segregation Of Tax Expense** Section 3465 requires fairly detailed disclosure of amounts related to its basic tax allocation Recommendations. With respect to the general disclosure of Income Tax Expense, the Recommendation is as follows:

Paragraph 3465.85 *Income tax expense included in the determination of net income or loss before discontinued operations and extraordinary items should be presented on the face of the income statement.* (January, 2000)

16-105. This Recommendation is reinforced by a similar requirement in Section 1520, "Income Statement".

16-106. **Current Vs. Future Amounts** In most situations, the Income Tax Expense figure will include both taxes that are currently payable, and amounts that will be payable at some future date. When this is the case, the following Recommendation is applicable:

Paragraph 3465.91 *The following should be disclosed separately:*

(a) *current income tax expense or benefit included in the determination of income or loss before discontinued operations and extraordinary items;*

(b) *future income tax expense or benefit included in the determination of income or loss before discontinued operations and extraordinary items;*

(c) ...

16-107. There are several ways in which the disclosure called for in Paragraph 3465.91 could be implemented. Alternatives are as follows:

• The current and future portions of Income Tax Expense could be segregated in the Income Statement.

• A single total for Income Tax Expense could be shown in the Income Statement, accompanied by note disclosure of the current and future portions.

• A single total for Income Tax Expense could be shown in the Income Statement, accompanied by disclosure of the future portion as an adjustment to cash from operations in the Statement Of Cash Flows.

16-108. **Limited Applicability** Paragraph .92 of Section 3465 contains several additional Recommendations related to Income Tax Expense that are only applicable to public enterprises, life insurance enterprises, deposit taking institutions, or co-operative businesses. For this purpose, the Section defines a public enterprise as follows:

Paragraph 3465.09(j)   A **public enterprise** is an enterprise that:

(i) has issued debt or equity securities that are traded in a public market (a domestic or foreign stock exchange or an over-the-counter market, including local or regional markets);

(ii) is required to file financial statements with a securities commission; or

(iii) provides financial statements for the purpose of issuing any class of securities in a public market.

16-109.   **Nature And Effect Of Temporary Differences**   The first of the Recommendations that are applicable only to public enterprises, life insurance enterprises, deposit taking institutions, or co-operative businesses requires disclosure of:

Paragraph 3465.92(a)   *the nature and tax effect of the temporary differences, unused tax losses and income tax reductions that give rise to future income tax assets and future income tax liabilities. Significant offsetting items included in future income tax assets and liabilities balances should be disclosed;* (January, 2000)

16-110.   What is called for here is a description of the items that are creating the future income tax component of Income Tax Expense. This would include such things as differences between depreciation expense and CCA, other major types of temporary differences, as well as information about unused loss carry forwards.

16-111.   **Components Of Income Tax Expense**   A second Recommendation applicable only to public enterprises, life insurance enterprises, deposit taking institutions, or co-operative businesses requires disclosure of:

Paragraph 3465.92(b)   *the major components of income tax expense included in the determination of income or loss for the period before discontinued operations and extraordinary items;* (January, 2000)

16-112.   This requirement would suggest that the current component of Income Tax Expense should be segregated between taxes that are payable on current taxable income, and taxes that are currently recoverable because of loss carry backs from a subsequent year. The future component of Income Tax Expense would also be segregated. Possible disclosure here would include:

- future tax amounts related to changes in temporary differences during the period;
- future tax amounts related to changes in tax rates;
- future tax amounts resulting from the recognition of previously unrecognized loss carry forwards; and
- future tax amounts resulting from the write down of future tax assets.

16-113.   **Reconciliation With Statutory Rate**   A final Recommendation applicable only to public enterprises, life insurance enterprises, deposit taking institutions, or co-operative businesses requires disclosure of:

Paragraph 3465.92(c)   *a reconciliation of the income tax rate or expense, related to income or loss for the period before discontinued operations and extraordinary items, to the statutory income tax rate or dollar amount, including the nature and amount using percentages or dollar amounts of each significant reconciling item. Significant offsetting items included in the income tax expense should be disclosed even when there is no variation from the statutory income tax rate.* (January, 2000)

16-114.   In addition to temporary differences to which tax allocation procedures are applied, there are many other differences between Accounting Income and Taxable Income. Examples of such differences would include non taxable intercompany dividend revenues, and non deductible amounts related to automobile costs. Under the now superseded Section 3470, such differences were referred to as permanent differences. While Section 3465 has not retained this terminology, such "permanent" differences continue to be present. As no tax allocation procedures are used for permanent differences, their presence can mean that the reported Income Tax Expense does not reflect the statutory rate of taxation. A simple example will make this point clear:

> **Example** A corporation has Accounting Income Before Taxes for the current year of $500,000. As the Accounting Income figure includes $200,000 in dividends from other taxable Canadian corporations, Taxable Income for the year is equal to $300,000. The corporation is subject to a statutory tax rate of 45 percent, resulting in current taxes payable of $135,000.
>
> As the non taxable dividends do not involve a temporary difference, tax allocation procedures would not be applied and the corporation's condensed Income Statement would be as follows:

Accounting Income Before Taxes	$500,000
Income Tax Expense - Current Amount	(135,000)
Accounting Net Income	$365,000

16-115. As this example illustrates, differences such as non taxable dividends can result in an Income Tax Expense which could easily mislead investors and other users as to the statutory tax rate applicable to the enterprise. In such situations, Paragraph 3465.92(c) requires a reconciliation between the actual Income Tax Expense, as compared to the Expense that would result from the application of the statutory income tax rate. The reconciliation that would be required in our simple example would be as follows:

Taxes At Statutory Rate of 45 Percent [(45%)($500,000)]	$225,000
Tax Savings From Non Taxable Dividends [(45%)($200,000)]	(90,000)
Income Tax Expense Reported	$135,000

16-116. In practice, such reconciliations can be very complex, particularly for enterprises involved with mining or other natural resources. We have seen such income tax reconciliation notes occupy a full page of an annual report.

Balance Sheet

16-117. **Segregation And Classification** In the Balance Sheet, Section 3465 requires that income tax assets and liabilities be segregated from other assets and liabilities:

> **Paragraph 3465.86** *Income tax liabilities and income tax assets should be presented separately from other liabilities and assets. Current income tax liabilities and current income tax assets should be presented separately from future income tax liabilities and future income tax assets. (January, 2000)*

16-118. Most enterprises segregate current assets from non current assets, and current liabilities from non current liabilities. The following Recommendations are applicable to such enterprises:

> **Paragraph 3465.87** *When an enterprise segregates assets and liabilities between current and non-current assets and liabilities, the current and non-current portions of future income tax liabilities and future income tax assets should also be segregated. The classification between current and non-current should be based on the classification of the liabilities and assets to which the future income tax liabilities and future income tax assets relate. A future income tax liability or future income tax asset that is not related to a liability or asset recognized for accounting purposes, should be classified according to the expected reversal date of the temporary difference. Future income tax assets related to unused tax losses and income tax reductions should be classified according to the date on which the benefit is expected to be realized. (January, 2000)*

16-119.   Note that, in general, the classification of income tax assets and liabilities between current and non current is based on the classification of the asset or liability to which the tax item relates. For example, income tax liabilities resulting from non current depreciable assets having a net book value in excess of their UCC would be classified as non current. Income tax assets and liabilities that do not relate to particular Balance Sheet items would be classified as current or non current on the basis of when the temporary difference is expected to reverse. The same approach applies to income tax assets related to tax loss carry forwards. The assets would be classified on the basis of when the benefit of the carry forward is expected to be realized. We would expect that, in most cases, income tax assets and liabilities that do not relate to specific Balance Sheet items will be classified as non current, reflecting the uncertainty associated with the timing of the reversal of the related temporary difference or the realization of the future benefit.

16-120.   **Offsetting**   Section 3465 also deals with the problem of offsetting future income tax liabilities against future income tax assets. As was the case with Section 3470, there is a prohibition against offsetting current amounts against non current amounts, provided the enterprise uses such classifications in its Balance Sheet.

16-121.   A new feature in Section 3465 is the recognition that it is not appropriate to offset future income tax liabilities in one tax jurisdiction against future income tax assets in a different tax jurisdiction. For example, It would not be appropriate to offset a future income tax liability that, when settled, will result in taxes payable in Canada, against a future income tax asset that, when realized, will result in tax deductions in a foreign country.

16-122.   Also noted in Section 3465 is the fact that the future income tax liabilities of one taxable entity cannot be eliminated by applying the future income tax assets of a different taxable entity. As there is no statutory provision for filing a consolidated tax return in Canada, the parent and each subsidiary company in a consolidated group are separate taxable entities. In such situations, some companies may have net income tax liabilities, while others may have net income tax assets. Clearly, the income tax assets of one taxable entity cannot be used to eliminate the income tax liabilities of a different taxable entity.

16-123.   In general, Section 3465 Recommends offsetting current income tax assets against current income tax liabilities, and offsetting non current income tax assets against non current income tax liabilities. However, this is only permitted if the assets and liabilities relate to the same taxable entity and to the same tax jurisdiction. The relevant Recommendation is as follows:

> **Paragraph 3465.88**   *Current income tax liabilities and current income tax assets should be offset if they relate to the same taxable entity and the same taxation authority. Future income tax liabilities and future income tax assets should be offset if they relate to the same taxable entity and the same taxation authority. However, when an enterprise classifies assets and liabilities as current and non-current, the current portion of future income tax balances should not offset any future income tax balances classified as non-current.* (January, 2000)

16-124.   In implementing this Recommendation, Section 3465 recognizes the possibility that tax planning strategies can be used to utilize inter entity income tax assets and liabilities (e.g., transfers of profitable assets from an entity with future income tax liabilities to an entity with future income tax assets resulting from loss carry forwards). In this type of situation, offsetting is permitted:

> **Paragraph 3465.89**   *When enterprises in a group are taxed separately by the same taxation authority, a future income tax asset recognized by one enterprise in the group should not be offset against a future income tax liability of another enterprise in the group unless tax planning strategies could be implemented to satisfy the requirements of paragraph 3465.88 when the future income tax liability becomes payable.* (January, 2000)

Solving Tax Allocation Problems

Example

16-125.   As the accounting for tax problems becomes more complex, you are required to deal with both temporary differences, as well as other differences between Accounting Income and Taxable Income. In such cases, it is essential that you have some type of analytical format for dealing with the large amount of information that may be involved.

16-126.   For many years, two alternative formats have been used to assist in preparing financial statements involving income taxes. The first involves a three column schedule in which the bottom line in each column provides the amounts required for the tax journal entry. An alternative approach uses a sequential calculation to move from Financial Statement Income to what is designated Accounting Income, and finally to Taxable Income. The former approach appears to be more widely used and, as a consequence, it will be used in this Chapter and the related problem material.

16-127.   The replacement of Section 3470 with Section 3465 has shifted the focus of tax allocation from timing differences in the Income Statement, to temporary differences in the Balance Sheet. As a reflection of this, the major example of tax allocation presented in the Appendix to Section 3465 (Example 2) based its analysis on Balance Sheet changes. We found this approach to be somewhat awkward and difficult to understand. Further, at this point we have found that the traditional three column approach provided the same results in a manner that was much easier to implement. Given this, we will continue to work with this format. We recognize, however, that as we have further experience with the Recommendations of Section 3465, some other analytical format may evolve.

16-128.   In order to illustrate the three column format in the context of a basic tax allocation problem, we will use the following example:

Example   On December 31, 1997, the Maxin Company had taxable temporary differences of $210,000. As the statutory combined tax rate on this date is 40 percent, the Company's Balance Sheet contains a Future Income Tax Liability of $84,000 [(40%)($210,000)]. The Company's year end is December 31.

During 1998, the Company has Accounting Income Before Taxes of $200,000. In computing this figure, the Company's accountant included $25,000 in Dividend Revenue from taxable Canadian corporations and deducted $10,000 for membership dues in the Inland Golf And Country Club. In addition, the Depreciation Expense deducted in the computation of 1998 accounting income was $50,000 while the maximum capital cost allowance of $75,000 is claimed for tax purposes. For 1998, the Company's statutory combined tax rate is 42 percent. This increase in the tax rate was not anticipated at the end of 1997.

Problem Solving Format

16-129.   Our problem solving format begins by setting up three columns and entering Accounting Income Before Taxes in the first two of these columns as follows:

	Accounting Income	Taxable Income	Temporary Differences
Income Before Taxes	$200,000	$200,000	

16-130.   Before considering the mechanical aspects of this schedule, it is worthwhile to consider what will be contained in each of the three columns. The first column provides the basis for calculating the Income Tax Expense or Income Tax Benefit that will be included in the Company's Income Statement. As we are using comprehensive tax allocation procedures, it will not be adjusted for temporary differences between the current period's Accounting Income and the current year's Taxable Income. However, it will be adjusted for all other differences between the current period's Accounting Income and current year's Taxable Income. This would include such items as non taxable dividends received and non deductible membership dues.

16-131.   When this column total is multipled by the current tax rate, it will give the current Tax Expense or Tax Benefit for the period, as well as the Future Tax Expense or Future Tax Benefit for the period, to the extent that this future item relates to changes in temporary differences that occurred during the current period. A new feature in this analytical format relates to the fact that Section 3465 requires the total balance of future income tax assets and liabilities to be adjusted for changes in tax rates. Since this adjustment must be included in the current period's Future Tax Expense or Future Tax Benefit, the required adjustment will have to be added to the total of this Accounting Income column in order to arrive at the appropriate figure for inclusion in the Income Statement.

16-132.   The Taxable Income column will be used to convert Accounting Income Before Taxes to Taxable Income and will be adjusted for both temporary and other differences between Accounting Income Before Taxes and Taxable Income. The final figure in this column will provide the basis for the calculation of taxes payable using the current tax rate. It will not be altered by adjustments of future income tax assets and liabilities for changes in tax rates. For those of you familiar with corporate tax returns, this column contains the equivalent of the T2S(1) schedule.

16-133.   The Temporary Differences column will then be used to accumulate the current period's temporary differences between accounting and taxable income. Recognizing that taxable temporary differences are more common than deductible differences, taxable differences are added to this column and deductible differences are subtracted. As was the case with the Accounting Income column, adjustments related to the effect of changing tax rates on future income tax assets and liabilities will have to be added to or subtracted from this column. The final figure in this column will become the basis for calculating additions to future income tax liabilities (if positive) or future income tax assets (if negative).

16-134.   Given the preceding anlaysis of the individual columns, rules for dealing with entries that will be made are as follows:

- Temporary differences between current period Accounting Income Before Taxes and current period Taxable Income are added or deducted from both the Taxable Income column and the Temporary Differences column, with the opposite arithmetic signs being applied.

- Other differences (formerly known as permanent differences) between the current period Accounting Income Before Taxes and current period Taxable Income are added or deducted from both the Accounting Income column and the Taxable Income column, with the same arithmetic signs being applied.

- Tax rate adjustments to the opening balance of future income tax assets and/or future income tax liabilities will be added or deducted from both the Accounting Income column and the Temporary Differences column, with the same arithmetic sign being applied. This adjustment is done after the current period totals have been multiplied by the current period tax rate.

16-135.   The completed schedule would appear as follows:

	Accounting Income	Taxable Income	Temporary Differences
Income Before Taxes	$200,000	$200,000	
Membership Fees	10,000	10,000	
Dividend Revenue	(25,000)	(25,000)	
Depreciation		50,000	($50,000)
Capital Cost Allowance		(75,000)	75,000
Balances	$185,000	$160,000	$25,000
Tax Rate	42%	42%	42%
Current Tax Balances	$ 77,700	$ 67,200	$10,500
Effect Of Change In Tax Rate [(42% - 40%)($210,000)]	4,200	N/A	4,200
Total Tax Balances	$ 81,900	$67,200	$14,700

16-136.   As was previously indicated, the bottom line of the preceding schedule provides the required information for preparing the 1998 journal entry to record the Maxin Company's tax balances. Note that the first column, which provides the required debit, will always be equal to the sum of the remaining two columns in which positive balances will be reflected in credit entries. The appropriate journal entry is as follows:

Tax Expense	$81,900	
Taxes Payable		$67,200
Future Income Tax Liability		14,700

16-137.   The Income Statement for 1998, including disclosure of the split between current and future Tax Expense, would be as follows:

Income Before Taxes		$200,000
Tax Expense:		
Current	$67,200	
Future	14,700	81,900
Net Income		$118,100

16-138.   As the reported tax expense does not reflect the current tax rate of 42 percent, additional disclosure is required under Paragraph 3465.92(c) to reconcile these amounts. Appropriate disclosure would be as follows:

Taxes At Statutory Rate [(42%)($200,000]	$84,000
Tax Savings From Non Taxable Dividends [(42%)($25,000)]	(10,500)
Tax Cost Of Non Deductible Dues [(42%)($10,000)]	4,200
Adjustment of Future Income Tax Liability [(42% - 40%)($210,000)]	4,200
Income Tax Expense Reported	$81,900

Intrastatement Allocation

Basic Concept

16-139.   Terms such as "extraordinary items", "results of discontinued operations", "capital transaction", "correction of an accounting error", and "adjustment resulting from a change in accounting policy", are accounting terms which have no meaning in the context of calculating Taxable Income. However, under GAAP, special disclosure requirements require segregated presentation of these various types of changes in equity. For example, adjustments related to changes in accounting policy are charged directly to Retained Earnings, rather than being disclosed as an inclusion or deduction in the Income Statement.

16-140.   In contrast, Taxable Income and the resulting Taxes Payable are single figures that do not segregate the components which make up the totals. The idea that we are concerned with here is that, for financial reporting purposes, taxes which relate to items subject to special disclosure requirements under GAAP should be segregated and given disclosure consistent with the item to which they relate. The basic Recommendation which requires such segregation is as follows:

> **Paragraph 3465.63**   *The cost (benefit) of current and future income taxes should be recognized as income tax expense included in the determination of net income or loss for the period before discontinued operations and extraordinary items, except that:*
>
> (a)   *any portion of the cost (benefit) of current and future income taxes related to discontinued operations or extraordinary items of the current period should be included in the income statement with the results of discontinued operations or extraordinary items, respectively;*
>
> (b)   *any portion of the cost (benefit) of current and future income taxes relating to capital transactions in the current period, or relating to items that are credited or charged directly to equity in the current period, should be charged or credited directly to equity;*
>
> (c)   *any portion of the cost (benefit) of current and future income taxes arising at the time of changes in shareholder status should be treated as a capital transaction (see "Capital Transactions", Section 3610);*
>
> (d)   *any portion of the cost of future income taxes arising at the time an enterprise renounces the deductibility of expenditures to an investor should be treated as a cost of issuing the security to the investor;*
>
> (e)   *any portion of the cost (benefit) of future income taxes arising at the time of acquisition of an asset, other than an asset acquired in a business combination, should be recognized in accordance with paragraph 3465.43* [This issue will be discussed in Chapter 17];
>
> (f)   *any portion of the cost (benefit) of current and future income taxes recognized at the time of a business combination accounted for as a purchase should be included in the allocation of the cost of the purchase (see paragraphs 3465.17 and 3465.46)* [This issue will be discussed in Chapter 17];
>
> (g)   *any other portion of the cost (benefit) of future income taxes related to a business combination, investment in a significantly influenced investee, interest in a joint venture or comprehensive revaluation of assets and liabilities should be recognized in accordance with paragraphs 3465.48, 3465.51, 3465.52, 3465.53 and 3465.54* [This issue will be discussed in Chapter 17];
>
> (h)   *any refundable taxes should be recognized in accordance with paragraphs 3465.71, 3465.72, 3465.73 and 3465.79* [This issue will be discussed in Chapter 17].
>
> (i)   *any portion of the cost (benefit) of current and future income taxes relating to the correction of an error or a change in accounting policy should be recognized in a manner consistent with the underlying item (see "Accounting Changes", Section 1506).* (January, 2000)

16-141.   While the preceding Recommendation requires that taxes be allocated to the accounting item to which they relate (e.g., taxes related to an extraordinary item should be included with the extraordinary item), it does not require that the amount of such taxes be separately disclosed. However, for most of the items listed, separate disclosure of the amount of the tax is required as follows:

Paragraph 3465.91   *The following should be disclosed separately:*

(a) *current income tax expense or benefit included in the determination of income or loss before discontinued operations and extraordinary items;*

(b) *future income tax expense or benefit included in the determination of income or loss before discontinued operations and extraordinary items;*

(c) *income tax expense or benefit related to discontinued operations;*

(d) *income tax expense or benefit related to extraordinary items recognized during the period;*

(e) *the portion of the cost of current and future income taxes related to capital transactions or other items that are charged or credited to equity; and*

(f) *the amount and expiry date of unused tax losses and income tax reductions, and the amount of deductible temporary differences, for which no future income tax asset has been recognized.* (January, 2000)

Example

16-142.   A simple example will illustrate the concept described in the preceding Section:

Example   During the current year, Intra Inc. has income before taxes and extraordinary items of $1,000,000, as well as an extraordinary gain of $250,000 before taxes. There are no differences between these Accounting Income figures and the amounts that will be included in Taxable Income. The Company is subject to a tax rate of 35 percent.

16-143.   In this case, Taxable Income will be $1,250,000 and Taxes Payable will be $437,500 [(35%)($1,250,000)]. For financial reporting purposes, this single figure must be segregated into two components. These would be the $350,000 in Taxes Payable that relate to the $1,000,000 in income before taxes and extraordinary items, and the $87,500 that relates to the Extraordinary Gain. This information would be presented in a condensed Income Statement as follows:

Income Before Taxes And Extraordinary Item		$1,000,000
Income Tax Expense (All Current)		(350,000)
Income Before Extraordinary Item		$650,000
Extraordinary Gain	$250,000	
Related Taxes (All Current)	(87,500)	162,500
Net Income		$812,500

16-144.   Similar treatment would be given to the other types of items listed in Paragraph 3465.63.

A More Complex Example

16-145.   A somewhat more complex example will serve to illustrate situations which involve both interperiod and intrastatement income tax allocation:

Example   At the end of 1997, The Hatch Company has net taxable temporary differences of $900,000. As the tax rate in effect at that point in time was 35 percent, these differences were reflected in a future income tax liability of $315,000. At the beginning of 1998, the government changed the tax rate to 40 percent. This change was not anticipated at the end of 1997.

The 1998 Income Before Taxes And Extraordinary Items for the Hatch Company is $500,000. The computation of this figure included $25,000 in dividends received from taxable Canadian corporations. The capital cost allowance deducted in the calculation of taxable income was $300,000 while the Depreciation Expense charged in the calculation of accounting income was $200,000.

During 1998, the Company experienced an Extraordinary Gain amounting to $37,500 before taxes. This gain qualified as a capital gain for tax purposes.

In addition, there was a change in accounting policy which was applied retroactively. This change involved a change in the amortization method applied to depreciable assets. It increased the accumulated amortization by $75,000, and this amount was deducted from the opening balance of retained earnings. This change did not alter the tax basis of the depreciable assets.

The Company had a December 31, 1997 Retained Earnings balance of $2,000,000. No dividends were declared or paid in 1998.

16-146. The analysis of the Hatch Company's tax balances for 1998 would be as follows:

	Accounting Income	Taxable Income	Temporary Differences
Income Before Taxes	$500,000	$500,000	
Dividend Revenue	(25,000)	(25,000)	
Depreciation		200,000	($200,000)
Capital Cost Allowance		(300,000)	300,000
Ordinary Balance	$475,000	$375,000	$100,000
Tax Rate	40%	40%	40%
Tax Balances Before Rate Change	$190,000	$150,000	$ 40,000
Rate Change [($900,000)(40% - 35%)]	45,000	N/A	45,000
Tax Balances - Ordinary Income	$235,000	$150,000	$ 85,000
Extraordinary Gain	$ 37,500	$37,500	
Non Taxable One-Quarter	(9,375)	(9,375)	
Extraordinary Balance	$ 28,125	$ 28,125	Nil
Tax Rate	40%	40%	
Tax Balances - Extraordinary Item	$ 11,250	$ 11,250	Nil
Prior Period Adjustment	($ 75,000)	($ 75,000)	
Non Deductible Increase In Accumulated Amortization		75,000	($ 75,000)
Prior Period Balance	($ 75,000)	Nil	($ 75,000)
Tax Rate	40%		40%
Tax Balances - Prior Period Adjustment	($ 30,000)	Nil	($ 30,000)

16-147. Based on the preceding schedule, the journal entry to record taxes would be as follows:

Income Tax Expense - Ordinary	$235,000	
Income Tax Expense - Extraordinary	11,250	
Income Tax Benefit - Prior Period Adjustment		$ 30,000
Future Income Tax Liability ($85,000 - $30,000)		55,000
Taxes Payable ($150,000 + $11,250)		161,250

16-148.   Based on this entry, Hatch Company's Income Statement would be as follows:

Income Before Taxes And Extraordinary Items		$500,000
Income Tax Expense (Note One):		
Current [(40%)][($375,000)]	($150,000)	
Future	(85,000)	(235,000)
Income Before Extraordinary Items		$265,000
Extraordinary Gain	$ 37,500	
Applicable Taxes (All Current - Note Two)	(11,250)	26,250
Net Income		$291,250

Note One   The required reconciliation (Paragraph 3465.92) between the actual Income Tax Expense and the expense at the statutory rate would be as follows:

Taxes At Statutory Rate Of 40 Percent [(40%)($500,000)]	$200,000
Tax Savings From Non Taxable Dividends [(40%)($25,000)]	(10,000)
Change In Future Income Tax Liability Resulting From	
Rate Change [(40% - 35%)($900,000)]	45,000
Income Tax Expense Reported	$235,000

Note Two   All of the taxes on the Extraordinary Gain are currently payable. The reason that the effective tax rate is 30 percent rather than the statutory rate of 40 percent is that it is a capital gain and only 75 percent of the amount is taxed.

16-149.   The Hatch Company's Statement of Retained Earnings would be as follows:

Opening Balance - As Previously Reported		$2,000,000
Prior Period Adjustment	($75,000)	
Applicable Taxes (All Future)	30,000	(45,000)
Opening Balance - As Restated		$1,955,000
Net Income		291,250
Closing Balance		$2,246,250

Treatment Of Losses

The Nature Of The Problem

What The Law Allows

16-150.   The rules for loss carry overs as specified in the *Income Tax Act* are as follows:

Non Capital (Operating) Losses   Current period non capital losses can be carried back to be applied against Taxable Income in the three preceding taxation years and carried forward to be applied against Taxable Income in the seven subsequent taxation years. To the extent that such losses relate to farm operations, the carry forward period is extended to ten years. If the farm loss carry overs are restricted by Section 31 of the *Income Tax Act*, they can only be deducted to the extent that there is farm income in the current period.

Net Capital Losses   Current period net allowable capital losses can be carried back to be applied against Taxable Income in the preceding three years and carried forward to be applied against Taxable Income in any subsequent year. However, net capital losses can only be deducted to the extent that there are taxable capital gains in the current period.

16-151.   Loss carry backs are applied to the taxable income of previous years in order to claim a refund of taxes paid during those years. The refund will be at the rates which prevailed during the relevant preceding years. With respect to the carry forwards, these are applied against the taxable income of future periods to reduce the amount of taxes payable in those years. As you would expect, the benefits will be realized at the rates in effect in the relevant future years.

Accounting Problems With Loss Carry Backs

16-152.   With respect to loss carry backs, the accounting problem is not significant. The preceding years' taxable incomes and taxes paid are known quantities and, as a result, there is generally no uncertainty associated with either the amount of the current period loss that can be carried back or the amount of tax refund that will result from this carry back. Since we are certain of realizing (receiving in cash or reducing a tax liability) the loss carry back benefit, it is clear that the benefit should be included in income in the year the loss occurs. This means that an Income Tax Benefit will be included in income, thereby reducing the amount of the Net Loss for the period.

Accounting Problems With Loss Carry Forwards

16-153.   With respect to the benefits associated with loss carry forwards, we are confronted with a significantly more difficult issue. This relates to the fact that the benefit is not certain but, rather, is dependent on the enterprise's ability to generate sufficient income within the loss carry forward period to make use of the benefit. In the case of net capital loss carry forwards, there is an additional restriction in that the income generated must be in the form of taxable capital gains.

16-154.   If sufficient Taxable Income is not generated, the loss carry forward on non capital losses can expire and the potential benefit will be lost. While net capital loss carry forwards do not expire, the inability of the enterprise to generate taxable capital gains may create a situation where the benefit will not be used in the foreseeable future.

16-155.   This uncertainty raises the question of when a benefit related to a loss carry forward should be recognized. Two possible answers to this question include:

1.   The carry forward benefit can be recognized in the period in which the loss which engendered it occurred. This assumes that the enterprise will generate sufficient Taxable Income of the appropriate type to be able to make use of the potential loss carry forward benefit. As the loss is related to items included and deducted in the current period, this solution would be consistent with the matching principal.

2.   Recognition of the carry forward benefit can be deferred until sufficient income is generated to allow the enterprise to actually experience a reduction in future taxes payable. This solution assumes that there is sufficient uncertainty with respect to the realization of the loss carry forward benefit to warrant the deferral of its recognition.

16-156.   There is also the possibility of recognizing part, but not all, of the benefit in the period of loss or, alternatively, recognizing the benefit in a period subsequent to the loss but prior to its application against future taxes payable. This latter alternative would be appropriate when the earnings outlook of the enterprise improves in a period that is after the loss, but before the benefit is actually realized.

16-157.   These issues make the dealing with loss carry forward benefits a fairly complex area of financial reporting. Subsequent to reviewing the specific Recommendations of Section 3465, we will present a number of different examples to illustrate some of these complexities.

Section 3465 Recommendations

Loss Carry Backs

16-158.   As was noted in the previous section, there is no uncertainty with respect to the benefit associated with a loss carry back. As a consequence, this benefit will be treated as a receivable, a view that is reflected in the following Section 3465 Recommendation:

> **Paragraph 3465.20**   *The benefit relating to a tax loss arising in the current period that will be carried back to recover income taxes of a previous period should be recognized as a current asset and not included in future income tax liabilities or future income tax assets.* (January, 2000)

16-159.   When this receivable is recorded, a corresponding amount will be included in the loss period's Income Statement as part of the current component of Income Tax Expense or Income Tax Benefit.

Loss Carry Forwards

16-160.   As noted previously, the situation here is more complex. The basic Recommendation is as follows:

> **Paragraph 3465.24**   *At each balance sheet date, except as provided in paragraphs 3465.33, 3465.35 and 3465.37, a future income tax asset should be recognized for all deductible temporary differences, unused tax losses and income tax reductions. The amount recognized should be limited to the amount that is more likely than not to be realized.* (January, 2000)

16-161.   For this purpose, "more likely than not" is defined as follows:

> **Paragraph 3465.09(i)**   An event is **more likely than not** when the probability that it will occur is greater than 50%.

16-162.   To begin, you should note that Section 3465 makes it much easier to recognize a loss carry forward benefit than it was under the Recommendations of Section 3470. Under the now superseded Section 3470, loss carry forward benefits could generally be recognized as an asset only if there was "virtual certainty" that they would be realized in future periods. The definition of "virtual certainty" included a requirement that there must be assurance beyond a reasonable doubt that the loss carry forward benefit would be realized. In practical terms, it was unusual for an enterprise to be able to make this claim.

16-163.   Under Section 3465, the enterprise is only required to claim that there is a probability greater than 50 percent that the loss carry forward benefit will be realized. As this is a less stringent test than virtual certainty, recognition of future income tax assets in the period of a loss is likely to become more common.

16-164.   Section 3465 provides considerable guidance with respect to assessing whether it is more likely than not that a loss carry forward benefit will be realized. The relevant paragraphs are as follows:

> **Paragraph 3465.25**   Future realization of the tax benefit of an existing deductible temporary difference, unused tax loss or unused income tax reduction ultimately depends on the existence of sufficient taxable income of an appropriate nature, relating to the same taxable entity and the same taxation authority, within the carryback / carryforward periods available under the tax law. The following sources of taxable income may be available under the tax law to realize a tax benefit for deductible temporary differences, unused tax losses or income tax reductions:
>
> (a) future reversals of existing taxable temporary differences;
>
> (b) future taxable income before the effects of reversing temporary differences, unused tax losses and income tax reductions;

(c) taxable income in prior year(s) if carryback is permitted under the tax law; and

(d) tax-planning strategies that would, if necessary, be implemented to realize a future income tax asset.

Paragraph 3465.26   An enterprise would consider tax-planning strategies in determining the extent to which it is more likely than not that a future income tax asset will be realized. Tax planning strategies are actions that:

(a) are prudent and feasible;

(b) an enterprise ordinarily might not take, but would take to prevent a tax loss or income tax reduction from expiring unused; and

(c) would result in realization of future income tax assets.

The carrying amount of any future income tax asset recognized as a result of a tax planning strategy would reflect the cost of implementing that strategy.

Paragraph 3465.27   Forming a conclusion that it is appropriate to recognize a future income tax asset is difficult when there is unfavourable evidence such as cumulative losses in recent years. Other examples of unfavourable evidence include:

(a) a history of tax losses or income tax reductions expiring unused;

(b) losses expected in early future years (by a currently profitable enterprise);

(c) unsettled circumstances that, if unfavourably resolved, would adversely affect future operations and profit levels on a continuing basis in future years; and

(d) a carryback or carryforward period that is so brief that it would limit realization of tax benefits, particularly if the enterprise operates in a traditionally cyclical business.

Paragraph 3465.28   Examples of favourable evidence that might support a conclusion that recognition of a future income tax asset is appropriate despite the existence of unfavourable evidence include:

(a) existing sufficient taxable temporary differences relating to the same taxable entity and the same taxation authority which would result in taxable amounts against which the unused tax losses or income tax reductions can be utilized;

(b) existing contracts or firm sales backlog that will produce more than enough taxable income to realize the future income tax asset based on existing sales prices and cost structures;

(c) an excess of fair value over the tax basis of the enterprise's net assets in an amount sufficient to realize the future income tax asset; or

(d) a strong earnings history exclusive of the loss that created the future deductible amount (unused tax loss carryforward or deductible temporary difference) together with evidence indicating that the loss (for example, an extraordinary item) is an aberration rather than a continuing condition.

Paragraph 3465.29   An enterprise must use judgment in considering the relative impact of unfavourable and favourable evidence on the recognition of a future income tax asset. The weight given to the potential effect of unfavourable and favourable evidence would be commensurate with the extent to which it can be verified objectively. The more unfavourable evidence that exists, the more favourable evidence is necessary and the more difficult it is to support a conclusion that recognition of some portion or all of the future income tax asset is appropriate.

16-165.   If the conclusion on whether it is more likely than not that a loss carry forward benefit will be realized is that some portion, but not all of the benefit should be set up as an asset, Section 3465 makes the following suggestion:

> **Paragraph 3465.30**   An enterprise could recognize a future income tax asset for all deductible temporary differences, unused tax losses and income tax reductions, reduced by a valuation allowance to the extent that it is more likely than not that some portion or all of the assets will not be realized. The valuation allowance would be sufficient to reduce the future income tax asset to the amount that is more likely than not to be realized. This would result in the same net asset as that determined in accordance with paragraph 3465.24 and after applying the considerations described in paragraphs 3465.25-.29 in determining the amount of the valuation allowance.

16-166.   This suggests that the full benefit that is available be set up as an asset, with any amount that cannot be currently recognized included in a valuation allowance that will be deducted from the asset.

Reassessment Of Future Income Tax Assets

16-167.   A new feature of Section 3465 is a Recommendation for the annual reassessment of future income tax assets. It may be necessary to write down assets that have been set up to recognize loss carry forward benefits, or, alternatively, set up assets for loss carry forward benefits that have not been previously recognized. This Recommendation is as follows:

> **Paragraph 3465.31**   *At each balance sheet date:*
>
> (a) *to the extent that it is no longer more likely than not that a recognized future income tax asset will be realized, the carrying amount of the asset should be reduced; or*
>
> (b) *to the extent that it is more likely than not that an unrecognized future income tax asset will be realized, a future income tax asset should be recognized.* (January, 2000)

Disclosure

16-168.   When an enterprise is not able to recognize the benefit of a tax loss carry forward, the amount of the unused tax loss must be disclosed along with its expiry date, if applicable. This Recommendation is in Paragraph 3465.91(f) which was reproduced in our Paragraph 16-141.

Loss Carry Over Examples

Basic Example

16-169.   In this Section we will present several cases designed to illustrate the various Recommendations of Section 3465 with respect to loss carry overs. All of these cases will be based on the following example:

> **Example**   Carrier Ltd. has a December 31 year end. During the year ending December 31, 1998, it experiences an Accounting Loss Before Taxes of $1,000,000. The Company has no temporary differences at either the beginning or the end of 1998 and, for the year, its Taxable Loss is equal to its $1,000,000 Accounting Loss Before Taxes. The statutory combined tax rate in effect for 1998 is 45 percent.

Case One - Loss Carry Back

16-170.   In this case we will assume that in the year ending December 31, 1997, Carrier Ltd. had Accounting Income and Taxable Income in excess of $1,000,000, all of which was taxed at a rate of 50 percent. Given this, the entire 1998 loss of $1,000,000 can be carried back to 1997 and a refund claimed. The relevant journal entry would be as follows:

Current Taxes Receivable [(50%)($1,000,000)]	$500,000	
Income Tax Benefit		$500,000

16-171.   Based on this entry, the condensed Income Statement for Carrier Ltd. for the year ending December 31, 1998 would be as follows:

Loss Before Income Taxes	($1,000,000)
Income Tax Benefit (All Current)	500,000
Net Loss	($ 500,000)

16-172.   Additional disclosure would be required to explain why the Income Tax Benefit does not reflect the statutory rate of 45 percent. This is due to the fact that the tax rate applicable to the tax refund is 50 percent.

Case Two - Loss Carry Forward Benefit More Likely Than Not To Be Realized

16-173.   In this case we will assume that Carrier Ltd. has had no Taxable Income in the three years prior to 1998. However, in 1998, they are able to claim that it is more likely than not that the benefit of the 1998 loss carry forward will be realized. The required journal entry for 1998 would be as follows:

Future Income Tax Asset [(45%)($1,000,000)]	$450,000	
Income Tax Benefit		$450,000

16-174.   Based on this entry, the condensed Income Statement for Carrier Ltd for the year ending December 31, 1998 would be as follows:

Loss Before Income Taxes	($1,000,000)
Income Tax Benefit (All Future)	450,000
Net Loss	($ 550,000)

16-175.   In 1999, the Company's Accounting Income Before Taxes and Taxable Income are equal to $1,500,000. The tax rate in effect for 1999 is 50 percent. The Company was not aware of the 1999 tax rate increase at the end of 1998. Given this, the journal entry for the year ending December 31, 1999 would be as follows:

Income Tax Expense	$700,000	
Future Income Tax Asset (Balance)		$450,000
Current Taxes Payable [(50%)($1,500,000 - $1,000,000)]		250,000

16-176.   Based on this entry, the condensed Income Statement for Carrier Ltd. for the year ending December 31, 1999 would be as follows:

Income Before Income Taxes		$1,500,000
Income Tax Expense:		
Current	($250,000)	
Future	(450,000)	(700,000)
Net Income		$ 800,000

16-177.   Additional disclosure would be required to explain why the Income Tax Expense does not reflect the current rate of 50 percent.

Case Three -
Part Of The Loss Carry Forward Benefit More Likely Than Not To Be Realized

16-178.   In this case we will again assume that Carrier Ltd. has had no Taxable Income in the three years prior to 1998. In 1998, they are able to claim that they are more likely than not to realize the benefit associated with $600,000 of the $1,000,000 loss carry forward. The required journal entry for 1998 would be as follows:

Future Income Tax Asset [(45%)($1,000,000)]	$450,000	
Income Tax Benefit [(45%)($600,000)]		$270,000
Future Income Tax Asset - Allowance For		
Non Realization Of Loss Carry Forward Benefit		
[(45%)($1,000,000 - $600,000)]		180,000

16-179.   Based on this entry, the condensed Income Statement for Carrier Ltd. for the year ending December 31, 1998 would be as follows:

Loss Before Income Taxes	($1,000,000)
Income Tax Benefit (All Future)	270,000
Net Loss	($ 730,000)

16-180.   In the December 31, 1998 Balance Sheet, the Allowance would be deducted from the Future Income Tax Asset, leaving a net balance of $270,000 [(45%)(600,000)].

16-181.   Additional disclosure would be required in this year to indicate that there is a loss carry forward of $400,000 for which the benefit has not been recognized and that it expires in the year ending December 31, 2005. In addition, the Income Tax Benefit would have to be reconciled with the statutory rate of 45 percent.

16-182.   In 1999, the Company's Accounting Income and Taxable Income are equal to $1,500,000. The tax rate in effect for 1999 remains at 45 percent. For the year ending December 31, 1999, the required journal entry would be as follows:

Income Tax Expense	$495,000	
Future Income Tax Asset (Net Of Allowance))		$270,000
Current Taxes Payable [(45%)($1,500,000 - $1,000,000)]		225,000

16-183.   Based on this entry, the condensed Income Statement for Carrier Ltd. for the year ending December 31, 1999 would be as follows:

Income Before Income Taxes		$1,500,000
Income Tax Expense:		
Current	($225,000)	
Future	(270,000)	(495,000)
Net Income		$1,005,000

16-184.   Additional disclosure would be required to explain why the Income Tax Expense does not reflect the current rate of 45 percent.

Case Four -
Loss Carry Forward Benefit Recognized And Subsequently Written Off

16-185.   In this case we will assume that Carrier Ltd. has had no Taxable Income in the three years prior to 1998. However, as in Case Two, in 1998 they are able to claim that it is more likely than not that the benefit of the 1998 loss carry forward will be realized. The required journal entry for 1998 would be as follows:

Future Income Tax Asset [(45%)($1,000,000)]	$450,000	
Income Tax Benefit		$450,000

16-186.   Based on this entry, the condensed Income Statement for Carrier Ltd. for the year ending December 31, 1998 would be as follows:

Loss Before Income Taxes	($1,000,000)
Income Tax Benefit (All Future)	450,000
Net Loss	($ 550,000)

16-187.   In 1999, the Company has Accounting Income Before Taxes and Taxable Income of $100,000, leading management to conclude that it is no longer more likely than not that the benefit of the remaining $900,000 loss carry forward will be realized. The tax rate in 1999 remains unchanged at 45 percent. The journal entry for the year ending December 31, 1999 would be as follows:

Income Tax Expense		
[(45%)($100,000) + ($450,000 - $45,000)]	$450,000	
Future Income Tax Asset (Balance)		$450,000

16-188.   Based on this journal entry, the condensed Income Statement for Carrier Ltd. for the year ending December 31, 1999 would be as follows:

Income Before Taxes	$100,000
Income Tax Expense (All Future)	(450,000)
Net Loss	($350,000)

16-189.   Additional disclosure would be required to indicate that the benefit associated with an unused loss carry forward of $900,000 has not been recognized, and that this carry forward will expire in the year ending December 31, 2005. The Income Tax Expense would also have to be reconciled with the rate in effect of 45 percent.

Case Five - Loss Carry Forward Benefit
Recognized After Year Of Loss But Before Realization

16-190.   In this case we will assume that Carrier Ltd. has had no Taxable Income in the three years prior to 1998. In 1998, they are unable to claim that any of the benefit associated with the $1,000,000 loss carry forward is more likely than not to be realized. In the year ending December 31, 1999, they have Accounting Income Before Taxes and Taxable Income equal to $200,000. This improved performance allows management to claim that it is now more likely than not that the benefit associated with the remaining $800,000 loss carry forward will be realized.   The tax rate in effect for 1999 remains at 45 percent.

16-191.   There would be no tax related journal entry in the year ending December 31, 1998. The condensed Income Statement for Carrier Ltd. for that year would be as follows:

Loss Before Income Taxes	($1,000,000)
Income Tax Benefit	Nil
Net Loss	($1,000,000)

16-192.   Additional disclosure would be required in this year to indicate that there is a loss carry forward of $1,000,000 for which the benefit has not been recognized and that it expires in the year ending December 31, 2005. In addition, the Income Tax Benefit would have to be reconciled with the rate in effect of 45 percent.

16-193.   The required journal entry for the year ending December 31, 1999 would be as follows:

Future Income Tax Asset		
[(45%)($1,000,000 - $200,000)]	$360,000	
Income Tax Benefit		$360,000

16-194.   The condensed Income Statement for Carrier Ltd. for the year ending December 31, 1999 would be as follows:

Income Before Income Taxes	$200,000
Income Tax Benefit (All Future)	360,000
Net Income	$560,000

16-195.   Additional disclosure would be required to reconcile the Income Tax Benefit with the rate in effect of 45 percent.

Transitional Rules

16-196.   As was noted previously, the Recommendations contained in Section 3465 are sufficiently controversial that its effective date is deferred for a significant period of time. (The Section was added to the *CICA Handbook* in December, 1997.) This is reflected in the following Recommendation:

Paragraph 3465.105   *The Recommendations of this Section should be applied for fiscal years beginning on or after January 1, 2000. Earlier adoption is encouraged.* (January, 2000)

16-197.   Section 3465 requires that retroactive treatment be given to the first application of its Recommendations. However, it permits this retroactive application to be made with or without restatement of prior periods:

Paragraph 3465.106   *These Recommendations should be applied retroactively. Restatement of financial statements for prior periods is encouraged, but not required. Any goodwill that arose on a business combination that took place prior to the beginning of the first period for which financial statements are restated should be adjusted only for the effects of future income tax assets not previously recognized, which should be treated as required by paragraph 3465.48 of this Section.* (January, 2000)

16-198.   If restatement is undertaken, the Section provides the following guidance:

Paragraph 3465.108   When financial statements of prior periods have been restated,

(a) future income tax assets and liabilities at the end of each restated period would be measured using the appropriate income tax rates and tax laws at those dates (see paragraph 3465.56); and

(b) the carrying values for assets initially recognized in those periods, and assets (including goodwill) and liabilities, arising from business combinations in those periods, would be adjusted to reflect the application of all Recommendations of this Section in each year restated.

16-199.   A further Recommendation permits financial statements of prior periods to be restated, whether or not the statements are presented in comparative form:

Paragraph 3465.107   *In the period of adoption of the Recommendations of this Section, financial statements of prior periods may be restated, whether or not those statements are presented in comparative form with financial statements of the current period.* (January, 2000)

16-200.   The special transitional rules that are applicable to business combination transactions will be discussed in Chapter 17.

Income Taxes In Canadian Practice

Statistics From Financial Reporting In Canada

16-201. The 1997 edition of *Financial Reporting In Canada* surveyed annual reports for the two years 1995 and 1996. As Section 3465 was not issued until 1997, Section 3470 was applicable to these reports.

16-202. Surprisingly few of the 200 companies surveyed disclosed their method of tax allocation. For 1996, 26 companies indicated the use of the deferred charge method, four indicated the used of the asset/liability method, and two indicated use of both methods.

16-203. Most of the survey companies did disclose the amount by which the current tax provision had been increased or decreased by tax deferrals. For 1996, 76 companies included this disclosure in a note, 49 indicated that it was evident from the statement of changes in financial position, and 38 included this amount as a separate item in the Income Statement.

16-204. In the 1996 Balance Sheets, 133 companies disclosed only deferred income tax credits, 17 disclosed only deferred income tax debits, and 11 companies disclosed both debits and credits. With respect to disclosure of credits, they were usually shown either as a part of non current liabilities (71 companies) or as a separate category (64 companies).

16-205. In 1996, 178 of the 200 survey companies provided a reconciliation of the actual tax expense or benefit with the company's basic tax rate. This was provided both in dollar form (92 companies) and in percentage form (65 companies).

16-206. A total of 75 companies provided some disclosure of unrecognized loss carry forward benefits for 1996. In a majority of cases, both the amount of the loss and its expiry date were provided.

Examples From Practice

Example One

16-207. Our first example is from the annual report of BFC CONSTRUCTION CORPORATION for the reporting period ending December 31, 1996. It illustrates detailed disclosure of the deferred portion of current tax expense, along with an extensive reconciliation of the effective tax rate with the statutory rate. Note that the 1995 effective rate was 293 percent, clearly indicating the need for this reconciliation.

Notes to financial statements

Note 1   Summary Of Significant Accounting Policies (Cdn. $000) (in part)

Income Taxes
The Corporation follows the deferral method of income tax allocation. Deferred income taxes result from timing differences between financial statement and income tax reporting principally relating to the recognition of construction revenue and accelerated depreciation. The portion of deferred income taxes which relates to amounts included in current assets and liabilities is shown as current asset or current liability.

Note 8   Income Taxes (Cdn. $000)
The Canadian and foreign components of the income before income tax and minority interest are as follows:

	1996	1995	1994
Canadian	16,712	(1,015)	1,595
Foreign	523	1,176	6,279
	17,235	161	7,874

Canadian income includes income earned by certain foreign joint ventures which are not taxable in the foreign jurisdictions but are taxable in Canada.

The current and deferred components of the income tax expense are as follows:

	1996	1995	1994
Current:			
Canadian - Federal	1,372	(699)	2,654
- Provincial	509	(404)	708
Foreign	177	911	2
	2,058	(192)	3,364
Deferred:			
Canadian - Federal	3,794	675	(236)
- Provincial	1,968	345	(302)
Foreign	-	(357)	357
	5,762	663	(181)
Income tax expense	7,820	471	3,183

The following is a reconciliation between the Canadian federal statutory and provincial income tax rates and the consolidated effective income tax rate:

	1996	1995	1994
Combined Canadian federal statutory and provincial income tax rates	39.1%	39.1%	38.8%
Expense not included for income tax purposes	8.9	829.9	10.4
Operating losses for which no tax recoveries are currently available	1.8	197.1	-
Tax-exempt portion of capital gain	(0.4)	(74.4)	(1.0)
Rate differentials	4.7	(12.6)	2.4
Taxes based on capital	2.3	196.9	2.8
Utilization of loss carry-forwards not previously recognized for financial statement purposes	(1.7)	(18.9)	(17.9)
Utilization of Canadian development expenses net of acquisition costs	(5.0)	(762.2)	(27.9)
Prior years' tax reassessments	(4.3)	(101.9)	32.8
Consolidated effective income tax rate	45.4%	293.0%	40.4%

Deferred income tax expense results from timing differences in the recognition of revenue and expenses for tax and financial statement purposes. The source of these differences and the income tax effect of each is as follows:

	1996	1995	1994
Depreciation:			
Differences between tax and book depreciation	(4,267)	(1,237)	(660)
Long-term contracts including joint ventures:			
Use of percentage of completion for financial statement purposes and use of billings less costs excluding contractual holdbacks for income tax purposes	4,887	3,257	3,606
Amounts charged to expense for financial statement purposes but not deductible until paid	(76)	(185)	540
Reserve for equipment overhauls:			
Charged to expense for financial statement purposes but not deductible until paid	35	22	639
Loss carry-forwards:			
(Increase) decrease in losses for income tax purposes which were previously recognized for financial statement purposes	6,016	(1,747)	(3,048)
Benefits recognized for financial statement purposes but not for income tax purposes	(606)	-	(1,429)
Tax losses for which no benefit has been recognized	-	301	-
Canadian development expenses	456	660	1,081
Other:			
Expenses accrued or deferred for financial statement purposes, deducted for income tax purposes as paid	(683)	(408)	(910)
Deferred income tax expense (recovery)	5,762	663	(181)

At December 31, 1996 losses for which no potential tax benefit has been reflected in the consolidated financial statements amounted to approximately $807 (1995 - $824). As a result of timing differences in claiming deductions for income tax purposes and recognizing construction revenue, losses for income tax purposes exceed these amounts. At December 31, 1996 losses for income tax purposes amounted to approximately $30,768 (1995 - $42,544), which may be carried forward and applied against future years' taxable income when earned. These losses expire from 1997 to 2003. The Corporation also has available for carry forward $8,506 of unclaimed Canadian development expense that was renounced to it in 1993. The related unamortized acquisition costs carried forward amounts to $1,424. The future tax savings resulting from claiming Canadian development expenses less the amortization of the acquisition costs will be reflected as a reduction of the tax provision when utilized.

Example Two

16-208.   Our second example is from the annual report of METHANEX CORPORATION for the reporting period ending December 31, 1996. It illustrates disclosure of current and deferred taxes, as well as a reassessment proposal from Revenue Canada.

Notes to financial statements

Note 1 Summary of Significant Accounting Policies (in part)

(j) Income taxes:

Deferred income taxes are provided on differences in timing between the treatment for income tax and accounting purposes of various items of income and expenditure.

The Company does not accrue for taxes that will be incurred upon distributions from its subsidiaries unless it is established that it is probable that the earnings will be repatriated.

Note 9 Income and other taxes:

(a) Income tax expense differs from the amounts which would be obtained by applying the Canadian statutory income tax rate to the respective year's earnings before taxes. These differences are as follows:

	1996	1995
Canadian statutory tax rate	45.0%	45.0%
Computed "expected" taxes	(2,177)	$ 114,506
Increase (decrease) in tax resulting from:		
Lower taxes in foreign jurisdictions	(24,657)	(45,335)
Losses not tax-effected	18,448	-
Manufacturing and processing deduction	-	(2,755)
Benefits of losses and other tax		
deductions not previously recognized	(3,697)	(11,457)
Non-deductible costs	15,617	8,723
Other	(520)	(963)
Total income and other taxes	$ 3,014	$ 62,719

Income and other taxes are represented by:		
Cash income tax	$ (2,036)	$ 35,407
Deferred income tax	4,188	26,952
Large corporations tax	862	360
	$ 3,014	$ 62,719

(b) As at December 31, 1996, the Company had available amounts deductible for income tax purposes of $340 million in New Zealand in excess of accounting values. The tax benefits of these excess deductions, which are subject to final determination by taxation authorities, have not been recognized for accounting purposes. When utilized, the benefit of these amounts will be recognized in earnings.

In 1994, the Company purchased property, plant and equipment in Canada which had a cost for accounting purposes in excess of the basis for income tax purposes. This difference is being recognized in the Corporation's income tax provision on a straight-line basis as the assets are depreciated. The unamortized difference at December 31, 1996 is $100 million.

(c) The Company has received a proposal from Revenue Canada to reassess the Company's 1991 Canadian income tax return. The potential reassessment may reduce the amount of tax depreciation available at December 31, 1991 and thereby increase cumulative income taxes and interest to December 31, 1996 in an amount aggregating $90 million.

The Company has responded to Revenue Canada's proposal. It is not determinable whether Revenue Canada's proposal will lead to a reassessment. If a reassessment is issued, the Company will file a notice of objection to appeal the reassessment. Based on advice received from legal counsel, management believes its position should be sustained.

Additional Readings

CICA Research Study - "Accounting For Corporate Income Taxes: Conceptual Considerations And Empirical Analysis", Thomas H. Beechy, May, 1983.

New CICA Handbook Section - Section 3465, "Income Taxes", December, 1997.

CA Magazine Article - "Let's Stop Taking Comprehensive Tax Allocation For Granted", Christina S. R. Drummond and Seymour L. Wigle, October, 1981.

CA Magazine Article - "Comprehensive Tax Allocation: Let's Stop Taking Some Misconceptions For Granted", J. Alex Milburn, April, 1982.

CA Magazine Article - "That Unidentified Growing Object Is Now A Liability", Darroch A. Robertson, March, 1987.

CA Magazine Article - "Timing is Everything", Darroch Robertson, April, 1988.

CA Magazine Article - "Deferred But Not Forgotten", Darroch A. Robertson, January, 1993.

CA Magazine Article - "Here We Go Again", Patsy Willett, September, 1993.

CA Magazine Article - "Tax Talk", Darroch Robertson, April, 1996.

FASB Statement Of Financial Accounting Standards No. 96 - *Accounting For Income Taxes*, December, 1987.

FASB Statement Of Financial Accounting Standards No. 109 - *Accounting For Income Taxes*, February, 1992.

Journal Of Accountancy Article - "No More Deferred Taxes", Paul Rosenfield and William C. Dent, February, 1983.

Journal Of Accountancy Article - "Accounting For Income Taxes: Predicting Timing Difference Reversals", Barry P. Robbins and Steven O. Swyers, September, 1984.

Journal Of Accountancy Article - "Deferred Taxes: The Discounting Controversy", James O. Stepp, November, 1985.

Journal Of Accountancy Article - "FASB Proposed Rules For Deferred Taxes", William R. Read and Robert A. J. Bartsch, August, 1991.

Journal Of Accountancy Article - "Deferred Taxes Under FASB 109", William J. Read and Robert A. J. Bartsch, December, 1992.

Journal Of Accountancy Article - "Evaluating Tax Assets", Thomas R. Petree, George J. Grupoy, Randall J. Vitroy, March, 1995.

Assignment Problems

(The solutions to these problem are only available in
the solutions manual that has been provided to your instructor.)

ASSIGNMENT PROBLEM SIXTEEN - 1

BLM Inc. begins operations on January 1, 1997. Its Balance Sheet on that date, as well as
the comparative figures for December 31, 1997 and December 31, 1998 are as follows:

	January 1 1997	December 31 1997	December 31 1998
Cash And Receivables	$ 50,000	$ 76,000	$ 104,000
Inventory	220,000	290,000	380,000
Deferred Development Costs	Nil	20,000	32,000
Investments	35,000	35,000	35,000
Land	25,000	25,000	25,000
Depreciable Capital Assets (Net)	295,000	279,000	265,000
Total Assets	$625,000	$725,000	$841,000
Accounts Payable	$ 20,000	$ 36,000	$ 48,000
Provision For Warranties	Nil	6,000	12,000
Fines Payable	Nil	Nil	45,000
Accrued Post Retirement Benefits	Nil	Nil	8,000
Long Term Debt	255,000	255,000	255,000
Common Stock	350,000	350,000	350,000
Retained Earnings	Nil	78,000	123,000
Total Equities	$625,000	$725,000	$841,000

These statements have been prepared without any consideration of current or future income tax obligations. This includes the need to recognize and pay for current income tax liabilities.

Other Information:

1. As the Company does not pay any dividends in either 1997 or 1998, Income Before Taxes for the year ending December 31, 1997 is $78,000. The corresponding figure for the year ending December 31, 1998 is $45,000 ($123,000 - $78,000).

2. For the taxation year ending December 31, 1997, the Company's combined federal/provincial tax rate is 40 percent. For the taxation year ending December 31, 1998, the combined rate is 45 percent. This rate increase was not anticipated at the end of 1997.

3. As at January 1, 1997, the tax basis of all of the Company's assets and liabilities is equal to their carrying values.

4. The Company has an accounting policy of deferring certain types of development costs. These deferred costs totaled $20,000 for 1997. During 1998, additional development costs of $15,000 were deferred, while previously incurred costs of $3,000 were written off. For tax purposes, all development costs are written off as incurred.

5. During the two year period ending December 31, 1998, the Company does not acquire additional capital assets and does not dispose of any of the capital assets held on January 1, 1997. On January 1, 1997, the UCC of the depreciable capital assets was equal to their carrying value of $295,000.

During 1997, the Company deducted accounting depreciation of $16,000. For tax purposes, they deducted CCA of $28,000, leaving an ending UCC of $267,000.

During 1998, the Company deducted accounting depreciation of $14,000. For tax purposes, they deducted CCA of $25,000, leaving an ending UCC of $242,000.

6. The Company accrues a liability for warranty obligations in the year in which product is sold. These amounts are not deductible until the warranty services are actually provided and paid for by the Company.

7. During 1998, the Company was fined $45,000 for the violation of certain environmental regulations. These fines are not deductible for tax purposes.

8. During 1998, the Company entered into an agreement to provide certain post retirement benefits to its employees. For accounting purposes, a liability for these costs is accrued on the basis of actuarial estimates. For tax purposes, these amounts cannot be deducted until they are actually paid. For 1998, $8,000 of such benefits were accrued in the accounting records.

9. The Company has determined that it is more likely than not that taxable income will be available against which any resulting deductible temporary difference can be utilized.

Required: For each of the two years ending December 31, 1997 and December 31, 1998, determine BLM's total Tax Expense (Benefit) and Net Income. In addition, prepare the Balance Sheets for the Company at these year ends, including all relevant tax considerations. The Company will prepare its financial statements in compliance with Section 3465 of the *CICA Handbook*.

ASSIGNMENT PROBLEM SIXTEEN - 2

The partial Income Statement of the Compliance Company, a Canadian public company, for the year ending December 31, 1998 is as follows:

Sales	$1,500,000
Other Revenue	150,000
Total Revenue	$1,650,000
Cost Of Goods Sold	$ 800,000
Other Expenses	300,000
Total Expenses Excluding Taxes	$1,100,000
Income Before Taxes And Extraordinary Items	$ 550,000

The Compliance Company's tax rate is 40 percent. The Other Revenue consists of dividends received from taxable Canadian corporations. Cost Of Goods Sold includes straight line depreciation of $500,000.

Other Information:

1. The balance in the Compliance Company's Retained Earnings at January 1, 1998 was $6 million. During 1998, the Compliance Company declared and paid dividends of $200,000.

2. The Compliance Company claimed $750,000 in Capital Cost Allowance for 1998.

3. During 1998, the Compliance Company discovered an expense of $100,000 which related to 1997 that had not been deducted for accounting or tax purposes. This expense is fully deductible for tax purposes at the Company's regular rate.

4. On April 1, 1998, the municipal government expropriated a warehouse owned by the Compliance Company. The building had been purchased for $420,000 of which $120,000 was allocated to the land. The Company received a total of $760,000 of which $520,000 was allocated to the land. The net book value of the building at the time of the expropriation was $240,000. This gain qualifies as an extraordinary item under Section 3480 of the *CICA Handbook*. The building was not the last one in the class and the sale did not create a negative balance in the class. It was not replaced during the current year.

Required: Prepare the journal entry related to taxes for the Compliance Company for the year ending December 31, 1998. In addition, prepare the Income Statement and Statement Of Retained Earnings for the Compliance Company for the year ending December 31, 1998. Your solution should comply with the recommendations of Section 3465 of the *CICA Handbook* and include any required notes.

ASSIGNMENT PROBLEM SIXTEEN - 3

The following information relates to the Evasive Company, a Canadian public company, for the year ending December 31, 1998:

1. On January 1, 1998, the Evasive Company had total taxable temporary differences, all related to the difference between the carrying value and the tax basis of the Company's depreciable assets, of $8,000,000. The related Future Income Tax Liability was $3,600,000, reflecting the Company's December 31, 1997 tax rate of 45 percent.

2. The Company's 1998 accounting income before taxes was $850,000. As of January 1, 1998, the Company's effective tax rate unexpectedly increased to 55 percent. The Evasive Company has a January 1, 1998 balance in its Retained Earnings account of $35,000,000. Dividends totalling $250,000 were declared and paid during 1998.

3. Depreciation Expense for 1998 under generally accepted accounting principles was $700,000. The Company takes maximum Capital Cost Allowance for tax purposes and in 1998 this amounted to $950,000.

4. The 1998 accounting income contains dividends received from other taxable Canadian corporations in the amount of $100,000. The 1998 accounting income was reduced by $35,000 by a provision for the termination of redundant employees. This amount will not be paid until 1999.

5. The Company has a long term investment which has been carried at its original cost of $3,000,000. During 1998, it is decided that this long term investment has experienced a loss in value that is other than a temporary decline. As a result, it is written down to its current market value of $2,000,000. For tax purposes, the loss will qualify as a capital loss when the investment is sold. As the Company has no taxable capital gains in the current year and no taxable capital gains during the previous three years, this loss must be carried forward. Management believes that it is more likely than not that the Company will have adequate taxable capital gains to use this carry forward in future years.

6. During 1998, the Evasive Company discovered an error that overstated a 1997 expense by $105,000 for both accounting and tax records. The resulting increase in income is subject to taxation at the Company's regular rate.

Required: Provide the journal entry to record the Evasive Company's 1998 taxes with separate debits and/or credits for each component of the total Tax Expense. In addition, prepare the condensed Income Statement and Statement Of Retained Earnings of the Evasive Company for the year ending December 31, 1998, including any required notes to the financial statements. Indicate the tax related balances that would be shown on the December 31, 1998 Balance Sheet. Your solution should comply with the Recommendations of Section 3465 of the *CICA Handbook*.

ASSIGNMENT PROBLEM SIXTEEN - 4

At the beginning of 1998 the True Blue Company has a Future Income Tax Liability in its accounts of $2,240,000, all relating to an excess of Capital Cost Allowance claimed over Depreciation Expense recorded. The Company's tax rate in all previous years was 40 percent and both taxable and accounting income were equal to zero in 1995, 1996 and 1997. The Company uses a December 31 year end. These facts provide the starting point for each of the following six independent cases.

Case One   Assume that during 1998 the True Blue Company has a Loss Before Taxes of $2,200,000, records Depreciation Expense of $1,800,000, claims Capital Cost Allowance of $800,000, and can claim that it is more likely than not that it will able to realize the full amount of any loss carry forward benefit. During 1998, the Company's tax rate remains unchanged at 40 percent.

Case Two   Assume that during 1998 the True Blue Company has a Loss Before Taxes of $2,200,000, records Depreciation Expense of $1,800,000, claims Capital Cost Allowance of $800,000, and can claim that it is more likely than not that it will be able to realize the full amount of any loss carry forward benefit. On January 1, 1998, the Company's tax rate increases to 45 percent.

Case Three   Assume that during 1998 the True Blue Company has a Loss Before Taxes of $2,200,000, records Depreciation Expense of $1,800,000, and claims Capital Cost Allowance of $800,000. Management believes that it is more likely than not that they will only be able to realize the benefit associated with $500,000 of any loss carry forward. On January 1, 1998, the Company's tax rate declines to 35 percent.

Case Four   Assume that during 1998 the True Blue Company has a Loss Before Taxes of $2,200,000, records Depreciation Expense of $1,800,000, claims no Capital Cost Allowance, and cannot claim that it is more likely than not that they will be able to realize any part of the benefit of a loss carry forward arising in the year. During 1998, the Company's tax rate remains unchanged at 40 percent.

Case Five   Assume that during 1998 the True Blue Company has a Loss Before Taxes of $2,000,000, but that in 1999 it has Income Before Taxes of $2,400,000. Depreciation Expense is $200,000 per year for both 1998 and 1999. No Capital Cost Allowance is taken in 1998 and $400,000 in Capital Cost Allowance is claimed in 1999. At the end of 1998 the Company can claim that it is more likely than not that it will be able to realize the full amount of any loss carry forward benefit. During 1998 and 1999, the Company's tax rate remains unchanged at 40 percent.

Case Six   Assume that during 1998 the True Blue Company has a Loss Before Taxes of $2,000,000, but that in 1999 it has Income Before Taxes of $2,400,000. Depreciation Expense is $200,000 per year for both 1998 and 1999. No Capital Cost Allowance is taken in 1998 and $400,000 in Capital Cost Allowance is claimed in 1999. At the end of 1998 the Company cannot claim that it is more likely than not that it will able to realize any of the loss carry forward benefit. During 1998, the Company's tax rate remains unchanged at 40 percent. On January 1, 1999, the Company's tax rate increases to 45 percent.

Required: On the assumption that the Company has elected to use the provisions of Section 3465 of the *CICA Handbook*, provide the journal entries required to record taxes and a condensed Income Statement for each year that is under consideration in each of the preceding cases. Your answer should include all required note disclosure.

ASSIGNMENT PROBLEM SIXTEEN - 5

The following data relate to the Assessed Company, a public Canadian company, for the taxation years 1997 through 2000:

Taxation Year	Ordinary Income (Loss) Before Taxes	Depreciation	Capital Cost Allowance
1997	$ 200,000	$ 50,000	$150,000
1998	(2,800,000)	50,000	-0-
1999	350,000	40,000	-0-
2000	3,000,000	150,000	300,000

Other Information:

1. The tax rate for the Assessed Company is 30 percent for all years prior to 1999 and 60 percent for 1999 and 2000. At the end of 1998, the company is not able to claim that any unused tax loss is more likely than not to be realized. However, at the end of 1999, a change in the Company's competitive position allows them to claim that any remaining unused loss is more likely than not to be realized.

2. There was no taxable income or loss in 1995 or 1996. The Assessed Company will not amend any previous year's capital cost allowance. The Assessed Company's December 31, 1996 Balance Sheet contained temporary differences of $300,000, all of which were related to an excess of capital cost allowance taken over depreciation. This was reflected in a December 31, 1996 Future Income Tax Liability of $90,000.

3. In 1997, the Assessed Company pays bribes totalling $100,000 to officials in the country of Graftland. These bribes are not deductible for tax purposes.

4. In both 1998 and 2000, the Assessed Company's income contains dividends from taxable Canadian corporations of $30,000, a total of $60,000 for the two years.

5. There are no Extraordinary Items in 1997, 1998, or in 2000. In 1999, the Assessed Company incurs an Extraordinary Loss of $200,000 from the expropriation of a parcel of land. This loss is a capital loss for tax purposes and it can be deducted in 1999 as the Company's 1999 ordinary income contains a $200,000 capital gain from the sale of a long term investment.

Required: For each of the years under consideration prepare journal entries to record income taxes for the year. Using this information, prepare a condensed Income Statement for each of the four years. Your solution should comply with Section 3465 of the *CICA Handbook* and include any required notes.

ASSIGNMENT PROBLEM SIXTEEN - 6

The following data relate to the Loser Company, a Canadian public company, for the years 1997 through 2000:

Year	Income (Loss) Before Taxes	Depreciation Expense	Capital Cost Allowance	Tax Rate
1997	($ 75,000)	$100,000	$100,000	40%
1998	(1,000,000)	100,000	-0-	40%
1999	250,000	100,000	-0-	50%
2000	1,800,000	100,000	250,000	50%

Other Information:

1. In 1996, the Loser Company had accounting income of $100,000, taxable income of $50,000, and paid taxes at a rate of 40 percent or $20,000 in total. The Loser Company had no accounting or taxable income or loss in 1994 and 1995. At the end of 1996, the Loser Company had taxable temporary differences of $700,000, all related to an excess of capital cost allowance taken over depreciation. This was reflected in a December 31, 1996 balance in the Future Income Tax Liability account of $280,000.

2. During both 1997 and 1998, annual dues of $15,000 were paid for membership in the

Kelly Lake Yacht Club. The Company discontinued its membership at the end of 1998 and no dues were paid in 1999 and 2000.

3. In 1999 and 2000, the Loser Company's income includes dividends from taxable Canadian companies in the amount of $35,000 per year, a total of $70,000 for the two years.

4. In 1999, the Loser Company incurs a gain of $20,000 from the sale of long term investments. For tax purposes the $20,000 qualifies as a capital gain.

5. There are no extraordinary items in any of the years under consideration.

6. There is no amendment of any previous year's capital cost allowance. It is expected that depreciation expense under generally accepted accounting principles will remain at $100,000 per year until at least the year 2008.

7. With respect to the benefits associated with unused losses, management indicates that they are "more likely than not" to be realized only to the extent that income would result from the reversal of temporary differences that are present in the year of the loss.

8. The tax rate increase for 1999 was not anticipated at the end of 1998.

Required: For each of the four years under consideration, prepare journal entries to record income taxes and a condensed Income Statement. Your solution should comply with all of the Recommendations of Section 3465 of the *CICA Handbook* and include any required note disclosure.

ASSIGNMENT PROBLEM SIXTEEN - 7

It is early January, 1999. Since its formation, the Changor Company has accounted for income taxes using the provisions of Section 3470 of the *CICA Handbook*. However, management knows that the Recommendations of this Section are out of line with accounting standards in the U. S. and most other countries. They see this as a problem in that Changor has foreign suppliers, foreign creditors, and foreign equity investors. They have recently been made aware of the new Section 3465 of the *CICA Handbook* and the fact that its Recommendations are largely consistent with U. S. standards applicable to accounting for income taxes. As a consequence, they intend to apply this new *Handbook* Section as of the year ending December 31, 1998. They have asked you to assist them with this transition.

For 1997 and previous years, the Company's tax rate was 40 percent. For 1998, the rate has increased to 50 percent. The legislation to implement this increase was passed during November, 1997.

To the present time, the Company's accounting records have been kept on the basis of Section 3470. On this basis, condensed comparative Balance Sheets for December 31, 1997 and 1998, along with a condensed Statement Of Income And Change In Retained Earnings for the year ending December 31, 1998 would be as follows:

Changor Company
Condensed Balance Sheets
As At December 31

	1998	1997
Current Deferred Income Taxes (Note 1)	$ 26,000	$ 16,000
Other Current Assets	342,000	309,000
Non Current Deferred Income Taxes (Note 2)	48,000	48,000
Other Non Current Assets	863,000	787,000
Total Assets	$1,279,000	$1,160,000

	1998	1997
Current Liabilities	$ 123,000	$ 113,000
Non Current Liabilities	247,000	226,000
Non Current Deferred Income Taxes (Note 3)	96,000	50,000
Common Stock	450,000	450,000
Retained Earnings	363,000	321,000
Total Equities	$1,279,000	$1,160,000

Note 1 The current Deferred Income Taxes reflects estimated warranty costs that have been expensed in the accounting records, but cannot be deducted for tax purposes until the costs are incurred. The amounts are $40,000 on December 31, 1997 and $52,000 on December 31, 1998.

Note 2 The non current Deferred Income Taxes of $48,000 reflect a write down of a long term investment for a non temporary decline in value. The accounting loss was $160,000. However, for tax purposes the net capital loss was calculated as $120,000 [(3/4)($160,000)].

Note 3 The non current Deferred Income Taxes of $50,000 on December 31, 1997 reflects an accumulated difference between Depreciation Expense and CCA of $200,000. However, the balance has been reduced in order to recognize the unrealized benefit of a loss carry forward of $75,000 that was accrued in the 1997 taxation year. While management was able to claim that it was more likely than not that this loss would be realized, they could not claim that it was virtually certain that realization would occur. This leaves a balance of $50,000 [(40%)($200,000 - $75,000)]. During 1998, the loss carry forward was applied against current taxes payable, resulting in $30,000 being restored to the balance. In addition, a further $16,000 was added to reflect the current year's excess of Depreciation Expense over CCA of $32,000. This leaves the 1998 balance of $96,000 ($50,000 + $30,000 + $16,000).

Changor Company
Condensed Statement Of Income And Change In Retained Earnings
Year Ending December 31, 1998

Revenues (Note 4)		$862,000
Expenses Other Than Taxes		(650,000)
Income Before Taxes		$212,000
Tax Expense:		
Current (Note 5)	($33,500)	
Deferred (Note 6)	(36,000)	(69,500)
Net Income		$142,500
Dividends Declared		(100,500)
Increase In Retained Earnings		$ 42,000

Note 4 The Changor Company's 1998 Revenues include $50,000 in dividends from taxable Canadian corporations.

Note 5 Current taxes payable can be calculated as follows:

Income Before Taxes	$212,000
Beginning Warranty Costs	(40,000)
Ending Warranty Costs	52,000
Loss Carry Forward	(75,000)
Excess Of Depreciation Expense Over CCA	(32,000)
Non Taxable Dividends Received	(50,000)
Taxable Income	$ 67,000
Rate	50%
Taxes Payable	$ 33,500

Note 6   Deferred taxes for the current year would be calculated as follows:

Beginning Warranty Costs	$ 40,000
Ending Warranty Costs	(52,000)
Excess Of Depreciation Expense Over CCA	32,000
	$20,000
Rate	50%
	$10,000
Loss At 40 Percent	30,000
Opening Warranty Cost Adjustment [(50% - 40%)($40,000)]	(4,000)
Total Deferred Taxes	$36,000

Required: Prepare condensed comparative Balance Sheets as at December 31, 1997 and 1998, along with a condensed Statement Of Income And Change In Retained Earnings for the year ending December 31, 1998, using the provisions of Section 3465. As per the Recommendation in that Section's transitional provision, the provisions should be applied retroactively, with all prior periods restated.

Chapter 17

Accounting For Income Taxes Part Two: Additional Issues

Introduction

17-1.   Chapter 16 provided comprehensive coverage of the basic issues associated with accounting for income taxes as described in Section 3465 of the *CICA Handbook*. The determination of taxable and deductible temporary differences, the recording of future income tax assets and future income tax liabilities required by the presence of such temporary differences, intrastatement allocation of taxes related to such items as discontinued operations and capital transactions, as well as the Income Statement and Balance Sheet disclosure to be generally given to income taxes, were dealt with in considerable detail in that Chapter.

17-2.   However, the coverage of Section 3465 is much broader than that of the now superseded Section 3470 and, as a consequence, there are a number of issues that have not been dealt with at this point. The most important of these is the income tax considerations related to business combination transactions. As described in Chapter 3 of this text, these transactions can be very complex, with relevant considerations involving marketing issues, human resources considerations, finance policy, accounting procedures, and tax planning strategies.

17-3.   The tax considerations which will arise in a business combination transaction will depend on the legal form of the combination. You may recall from Chapter 3 that some business combinations are legally structured as an acquisition of assets. If no rollover provision is used, the acquired assets will have an initial tax basis equal to their initial carrying value and no unique accounting for tax problems occur. However, if a rollover provision is used, temporary differences will be present at the time the assets are acquired.

17-4.   If the form of the business combination is such that shares are acquired, the situation becomes more complex. As noted in Chapter 3, this legal form of business combination gives rise to the need to prepare consolidated financial statements. As there is no statutory provision for filing a consolidated tax return, the individual legal entities that are party to the business combination transaction will continue to file separate tax returns. This means that there will be ongoing temporary differences between the information presented in the consolidated financial statements, and the information presented in the corporate tax returns.

17-5.   The now superseded Section 3470 did not provide specific guidance for dealing with the tax considerations that may arise in business combination transactions. As a consequence, it appears that a wide variety of practices were used in this area. One of the most important features of Section 3465 is that it will correct this situation. This new Section provides detailed Recommendations for accounting for taxes in the context of business combinations in general and consolidated financial statements in particular. This should result in improved reporting practices in this important area.

17-6.   While the tax problems associated with business combinations and consolidated financial statements are the major subject matter of this Chapter, there are other issues that require attention. They are as follows:

- Dealing with temporary differences on assets acquired other than in a business combination.

- Dealing with temporary differences resulting from the translation of the financial statements of integrated foreign operations.

- Procedures to be used for refundable taxes.

- Procedures related to certain issues pertaining to financial instruments.

- Problems related to alternative minimum taxes and capital taxes.

- Additional transitional problems related to business combination transactions.

17-7.   Before proceeding to these issues, we would note that much of the material in this Chapter will not be fully comprehensible unless you have an understanding of the material in Chapters 1 through 7 of this text on business combinations and consolidated financial statements. A good understanding of corporate taxation is also required.

Temporary Differences On Assets Acquired Other Than In A Business Combination

Background

17-8.   In the great majority of situations, when an asset is acquired it will have an initial tax basis that is equal to its initial carrying value. For accounting purposes the asset will be recorded at its cost and, at that point in time, its adjusted cost base or capital cost for tax purposes will be this same amount. The most common exceptions to this general rule are assets acquired in certain types of business combination transactions that are accounted for by the purchase method. For accounting purposes, these assets are recorded at their fair value which is, in effect, their cost to the acquiree. However, if a tax rollover provision is used or, if the business combination involves an acquisition of shares, different values can be used for tax purposes. The procedures required in such situations will be dealt with in the next Section of this Chapter.

17-9.   In addition, there are situations, other than those involving business combination transactions, in which a newly acquired asset will have an initial carrying value that is different than its initial tax basis. These situations may involve cases where the tax basis of the asset is greater than its cost, as well as cases where the tax basis is less than cost. The following Recommendation deals with both of these possibilities:

> **Paragraph 3465.43**   *When an asset is acquired other than in a business combination and the tax basis of that asset is less than its cost, the cost of future income taxes recognized at the time of acquisition should be added to the cost of the asset. When an asset is acquired other than in a business combination and the tax basis of that asset is greater than its cost, the benefit related to future income taxes recognized at the time of acquisition should be deducted from the cost of the asset.* (January, 2000)

Cost Greater Than Tax Basis

17-10.   As an example of the application of Paragraph 3465.43 to a situation where cost exceeds the tax basis of an acquired asset, consider the following:

Example   A corporation acquires a depreciable asset outside of a business combination for cash of $20,000 plus $30,000 in no par value common shares. Because it has been acquired under the provisions of ITA Section 85, its elected tax basis is the UCC of $20,000. The asset had an original cost of $90,000. The corporation is subject to a tax rate of 40 percent.

17-11.   The economic concept which underlies Paragraph 3465.43 is that, because the amount paid for the asset in the example is not fully deductible to the purchaser, the $50,000 paid for the asset is less than the corporation would have paid for the same asset if the cost was fully deductible. Given this, the recorded value for the asset will be increased to reflect the future income tax liability that exists when the asset is acquired.

17-12.   At first glance, one is inclined to say that the future income tax liability is equal to $12,000, the corporation's 40 percent tax rate multiplied by the $30,000 difference between the cost of $50,000 and the tax basis of $20,000. This, however, does not work. Adding this amount to the carrying value of the asset results in an amount of $62,000. If the asset were sold for $62,000, the tax liability would be $16,800. This amount is 40 percent of the $42,000 ($62,000 - $20,000) recapture of CCA.

17-13.   What has to be established here is a new carrying value for the asset, such that when the corporation's tax rate is multiplied by the difference between this new carrying value and the $20,000 tax basis of the asset, the product is equal to the difference between the new carrying value and the $50,000 acquisition cost. If we let X equal this new carrying value, the correct amount can be determined as follows:

$$X = \$50,000 + [(40\%)(X - \$20,000)]$$
$$X = \$70,000$$

17-14.   Using this value, the entry to record the acquisition of the asset would be as follows:

Asset	$70,000	
Future Income Tax Liability		$20,000
Cash		20,000
No Par Value Common Stock		30,000

17-15.   The logic of this approach is illustrated by the fact that, if the asset were sold for $70,000, there would be a tax liability of $20,000 [(40%)($70,000 - $20,000)]. In other words, instead of showing the asset at its tax reduced value of $50,000, it will be shown at its full $70,000 value, accompanied by the future income tax liability that would have to be paid if this value was realized.

Cost Less Than Tax Basis

17-16.   A simple example will also be used to illustrate the application of Paragraph 3465.43 to a situation where the cost of a newly acquired asset is less than its tax basis:

Example   A corporation acquires an asset in an arm's length transaction for $100,000 in cash. As an inducement to make this investment in a particular industry, it gains the right to deduct 125 percent of its cost for tax purposes. The corporation's tax rate is 45 percent.

17-17.   The economic interpretation here is that the corporation paid a higher than normal amount for this asset because of its associated tax benefits. While we are dealing with a future income tax asset, as opposed to a future income tax liability in the previous case, the basic idea is unchanged. We need to establish a new carrying value for the asset, such that when the corporation's tax rate is multiplied by the difference between this new carrying value and the $125,000 tax basis of the asset, the product is equal to the difference between the new carrying value and the $100,000 in cash paid. If we let X equal this new carrying value, the correct amount can be determined as follows:

X = $100,000 + [(45%)(X - $125,000)]
X = $79,545

17-18.   The entry to record this value would be as follows:

Asset	$79,545	
Future Income Tax Asset	20,455	
Cash		$100,000

17-19.   The logic of this approach is illustrated by the fact that, if the asset were sold for $79,545, there would be a tax deduction of $20,455 [(45%)($79,545 - $125,000)].

Business Combinations

Temporary Differences At Time Of Combination
Pooling Of Interests Method
17-20.   Under the provisions of Section 1580 of the *CICA Handbook*, business combinations are accounted for by the purchase method if an acquirer can be identified or, in those unusual cases where an acquirer cannot be identified, by the pooling of interests method.

17-21.   When the pooling of interests method is used, assets and liabilities retain their old carrying values in the financial reports issued by the combined companies. If the business combination transaction is effected by one company acquiring the shares of the other, or by a new company acquiring the shares of both combining companies, the tax basis of the combined companies' assets and liabilities will be equal to the old values that are being used in the consolidated financial statements prepared for the combined companies. In this situation, no temporary differences will be created at the time of combination and no special accounting for tax problems arise.

17-22.   Given the nature of the Recommendations in Section 1580, pooling of interests situations are fairly rare in Canada. Further, when they do occur, their legal structure is normally based on share issuance, rather than exchanges of assets. This being the case, it is unusual for a business combination accounted for by the pooling of interests method to have special accounting for tax problems. The exception to this is when one of the parties to a pooling of interests transaction has an unrecognized loss carry forward benefit. While we will give some attention to this problem in a later Section of this Chapter, we will not provide general coverage of income tax aspects of pooling of interests transactions.

Purchase Method
17-23.   When purchase accounting is used for a business combination transaction, Section 1580 requires that the identifiable assets and liabilities acquired be recorded at their fair values at the time of acquisition, and that any excess of the purchase price over the acquirer's share of these fair values be recorded as goodwill. This process may or may not create temporary differences at the time of the business combination transaction. With respect to this issue, there appear to be three different possibilities:

Acquisition Of Assets - No Rollover   In this situation, the acquiring enterprise pays cash or issues shares in order to acquire the assets and liabilities of the acquiree and does not apply a rollover provision. For both tax and accounting purposes, the cost of the acquisition will be allocated to the fair values of the identifiable asset and liabilities acquired, and to goodwill. These values will then be the carrying values for accounting purposes and the tax basis for income tax purposes. There will be no temporary differences arising at the time of the business combination transaction.

Acquisition Of Assets - Rollover Used   In this situation, the acquiring enterprise pays cash or issues shares in order to acquire the assets and liabilities of the acquiree and makes use of a rollover provision on the transfer of the assets (e.g., ITA Section 85 or 85.1). For accounting purposes, the carrying values will be the fair values of the various assets and liabilities acquired. However, in order to minimize or eliminate taxes for the acquiree, it is likely that some or all of the old tax values will be elected under the rollover provision. This means that, for the acquirer, these old values will be the tax basis of these assets and liabilities acquired. In this situation, temporary differences will arise at the time of the business combination transaction.

Acquisition Of Shares   If the business combination is carried out through an acquisition of shares, the acquiree will continue to exist as a separate legal entity and the tax basis of its assets and liabilities will remain unchanged (this would be the case even if push down accounting were applied). However, in the consolidated financial statements that will be prepared for the combined company, the purchase method of accounting will require that these assets and liabilities be recorded at their fair values. Here again, temporary differences will occur as a result of the business combination transaction.

17-24.   In this Section, we will present examples which illustrate these three possibilities. The appropriate procedures will be considered both at the time of the business combination transaction (acquisition date) and in periods subsequent to acquisition. However, before proceeding to these examples, we will give more detailed consideration to the treatment that is given to the temporary differences that occur at the time of a business combination transaction. In addition, we will have to consider the fact that fair value increases on capital assets may result in capital gains, only three-quarters of which will be taxable.

Treatment Of Temporary Differences

17-25.   You should also note that, in conjunction with the introduction of Section 3465, Section 1580, "Business Combinations", was revised. While the term temporary differences was not used, the older version of Section 1580 recognized that the tax basis of the acquiree's assets was often different from the fair values that were to be recorded under purchase accounting. More specifically, the following statement was made:

Paragraph 1580.47 (Old Version)   The value to the acquirer of an asset which is not fully claimable for tax purposes will be less than the value of an identical asset which is fully claimable for tax purposes. Similarly, a liability, such as a warranty provision, on which tax relief is available only when it is discharged, will be assigned a lower value than a liability on which such tax relief is not available.

17-26.   The suggestion here was that fair values should be recorded net of their tax implications. For example if an asset had a replacement cost of $150,000 but was being transferred with a tax basis of $80,000, this old approach would have the asset recorded at some value less than the full $150,000 replacement cost. Unfortunately, little guidance was provided on how to implement this approach and, it would appear that there was no consistent treatment of this issue in practice.

17-27.   If this approach had been retained, the approach to valuing assets and liabilities that was Recommended under Paragraph 3465.43 would have been appropriate (see Paragraphs 17-8 through 17-19). However, Paragraph 3465.43 specifically excludes assets acquired in a business combination transaction from its coverage. The reason for this exclusion is that the Section 1580 approach to determining fair values has been revised as follows:

Paragraph 1580.47 (As Revised)   The values placed by an acquirer on the assets and liabilities of an acquired company are determined based on their fair values, without reference to their values for tax purposes, or tax bases. "Income Taxes", Section 3465, requires that the tax effects of differences between the assigned values of the identifiable assets and liabilities acquired and their tax bases be recorded as future income tax assets and liabilities and included in the allocation of the cost of the purchase.

17-28.   Under this approach, if an asset had a replacement cost of $150,000, this amount would be recorded as its fair value without regard to its tax basis. If, as was the case in our Paragraph 17-26 example, the tax basis was $80,000, there would be a taxable temporary difference of $70,000 and a Future Income Tax Liability would have to be accrued at the appropriate tax rate.

17-29.   Given this revision of Section 1580, temporary differences arising on a business combination transaction will normally be given the same treatment as other temporary differences. There is, however, an exception for goodwill. This is noted in the following general *CICA Handbook* Recommendation on taxable temporary differences:

Paragraph 3465.22   *At each balance sheet date, except as provided in paragraphs 3465.33, 3465.35 and 3465.37, a future income tax liability should be recognized for all taxable temporary differences other than those arising from any portion of goodwill which is not deductible for tax purposes.* (January, 2000)

17-30.   The *Handbook* continues, justifying the exclusion of goodwill as follows:

Paragraph 3465.23   Goodwill is the excess of the cost of an acquisition over the acquirer's interest in the fair value of the identifiable assets and liabilities acquired. In some cases (e.g., in a share purchase transaction) taxation authorities do not allow the amortization of goodwill as a deductible expense in determining taxable income. Any difference between the carrying amount of goodwill and its tax basis is a taxable temporary difference that would usually result in a future income tax liability. This Section does not permit the recognition of such a future income tax liability because goodwill itself is a residual and the recognition of the future income tax liability would merely increase the carrying amount of that residual.

17-31.   Summing up these rules, the combination of the revisions in Section 1580 and the new Recommendations in Section 3465 will result in temporary differences which arise at the time of a business combination generally being treated like other temporary differences. To the extent they are taxable, they will result in Future Income Tax Liabilities. To the extent they are deductible, they will result in Future Income Tax Assets. The exception to this is temporary differences between the carrying value and tax basis of goodwill. No asset or liability will be recorded to reflect these differences. All of these procedures will be illustrated in the examples which follow.

Temporary Differences Involving Capital Gains

17-32.   The problem here is that if a taxable temporary difference on a capital asset is realized, it may result in a capital gain, only three-quarters of which is taxable. Outside the context of situations involving rollovers or business combinations, such situations would not be common. For non depreciable capital assets the carrying value and the tax basis will normally be equal. For depreciable capital assets, it is very unlikely that the tax basis of the asset (UCC) would be more than its cost. As a consequence, we did not discuss temporary differences involving capital gains in Chapter 16.

17-33.   This situation changes when we deal with certain business combination transactions in that the fair values assigned in purchase accounting may exceed the cost of the asset for tax purposes. Consider a tract of land with a capital cost of $100,000 and a current fair value of $150,000. If it is acquired through a business combination transaction involving an acquisition of shares, the tax basis of the asset will remain at the same capital cost of $100,000. In contrast, the fair value of $150,000 will be recorded in the consolidated financial statements. If the $150,000 carrying value is realized, the result will be a capital gain of $50,000.

17-34.   In similar fashion, this asset might be transferred to a corporation in a transaction other than a business combination. If the transfer was made under the provisions of ITA 85(1), the elected value would likely be the capital cost of $100,000. Depending on the circumstances, the transferee corporation may record the land at its fair value of $150,000.

17-35.   As only three-quarters of the $50,000 capital gain is taxable, it raises the question of how to calculate the appropriate amount of the Future Income Tax Liability that is related to this temporary difference. You will recall that the tax basis of an asset is described in Section 3465 as "the amount that could be deducted in the determination of taxable income if the asset were recovered for its carrying amount". While we would normally think of the tax basis of the land in the example as being $100,000, it does not fit this definition. As defined for the purposes of Section 3465, the tax basis would be $112,500, reflecting the fact that, in the determination of taxable income, the taxpayer could deduct the cost of $100,000 plus the non taxable $12,500 one-quarter of the capital gain. This means that the temporary difference here would be $37,500, with the Future Income Tax Liability being the $37,500 taxable three-quarters of the capital gain multiplied by the relevant tax rate.

17-36.   An alternative approach to this situation would be to view the temporary difference as $50,000 and calculate the Future Income Tax Liability on the basis of an "effective tax rate" equal to three-quarters of the normal tax rate. The two approaches will, of course give the same value. Assuming a normal tax rate of 40 percent, the Future Income Tax Liability in the example will be $15,000, whether we calculate it as 40 percent of $37,500 [(3/4)($150,000 - $100,000)] or, alternatively, 30 percent [(40%)(3/4)] of $50,000 ($150,000 - $100,000).

17-37.   Legally, the former approach is preferable. In Canada, there is no special tax rate on capital gains. We simply apply the regular rate to less than the full amount of the capital gain. However, many people will be uncomfortable with the idea that Land which costs $100,000 has a "tax basis" of $112,500. While this approach is consistent with Section 3465's definition of tax basis, it is inconsistent with the definition of "tax value" in ITA 248. Given this, we will use the alternative "effective tax rate" approach.

Procedures At Time Of Acquisition

Basic Example

17-38.   As previously noted, when the purchase method is used to account for a business combination transaction, temporary differences may arise, resulting in a need to record a Future Income Tax Asset or Future Income Tax Liability. We will use one example to illustrate the procedures associated with the following three situations:

   Case 1: An acquisition of assets with no rollover provision being used;

   Case 2: An acquisition of assets with the use of a rollover provision; and

   Case 3: An acquisition of shares with consolidated financial statements being prepared.

17-39.   The information that will be used in all three of these cases is as follows:

Example   On December 31, 1998, the Balance Sheets of Monson Inc. and Little Ltd., including the fair values for the balances of Little Ltd., are as follows:

	Monson Inc. Carrying Values	Little Ltd. Carrying Values	Fair Values
Cash	$ 500,000	$ 250,000	$ 250,000
Accounts Receivable	1,600,000	650,000	650,000
Inventories	2,300,000	1,200,000	1,200,000
Land	800,000	450,000	500,000
Plant And Equipment (Net)	4,400,000	2,400,000	2,600,000
Total Assets	$9,600,000	$4,950,000	$5,200,000
Current Liabilities	$ 700,000	$ 340,000	$ 340,000
Long Term Liabilities	1,200,000	910,000	910,000
Future Income Tax Liability	400,000	160,000	N/A
Common Stock - No Par	4,300,000	2,500,000	N/A
Retained Earnings	3,000,000	1,040,000	N/A
Total Equities	$9,600,000	$4,950,000	

Both companies are taxed in the same jurisdictions and are subject to a rate of 40 percent on all of their income. The Future Income Tax Liability of both companies reflect an excess of the carrying value of Plant And Equipment over its UCC balance. The balances are recorded at the current tax rate of 40 percent.

It is the policy of Monson Inc. to amortize Goodwill resulting from business combination transactions over a period of five years on a straight line basis.

Little's Plant And Equipment has an original cost of $3,000,000 and is being depreciated over 10 years at a rate of $300,000 per year. The UCC on December 31, 1998 is $2,000,000. This balance is subject to a declining balance rate of 20 percent.

In all of the cases which follow, Monson Inc. can be identified as the acquirer and, as a consequence, the business combination will be accounted for by the purchase method.

Case One - Acquisition Of Assets - No Rollover Provision

17-40.   In this first Case we will assume that, on December 31, 1998, Monson Inc. issues Common Stock - No Par with a fair market value of $4,100,000, in return for all of the assets and liabilities of Little Ltd. Note that in this case, as no rollover provision is being used, all of the assets and liabilities that have been transferred to Monson Inc. will have a tax basis equal to their carrying value. Given this, the analysis of the investment is as follows:

Investment Cost	$4,100,000
Fair Values Of Net Identifiable Assets	
($5,200,000 - $340,000 - $910,000)	(3,950,000)
Goodwill	$ 150,000

17-41.   Note that the tax basis of the goodwill will also be $150,000. For tax purposes, three-quarters of this amount will be added to Monson's Cumulative Eligible Capital (CEC) balance. However, because the other one-quarter of this amount can be realized without tax consequences, the tax basis of Cumulative Eligible Capital is $150,000 (the $112,500 balance in CEC, plus the $37,500 portion of the capital gain that would not be taxed on the realization of the $150,000 fair value).

17-42. Given this analysis, the Balance Sheet of Monson Inc. subsequent to the business combination transaction would be as follows:

Monson Inc. Balance Sheet
As At December 31, 1998

Cash ($500,000 + $250,000)	$ 750,000
Accounts Receivable ($1,600,000 + $650,000)	2,250,000
Inventories ($2,300,000 + $1,200,000)	3,500,000
Land ($800,000 + $500,000)	1,300,000
Plant And Equipment (Net) ($4,400,000 + $2,600,000)	7,000,000
Goodwill	150,000
Total Assets	**$14,950,000**
Current Liabilities ($700,000 + $340,000)	$ 1,040,000
Long Term Liabilities ($1,200,000 + $910,000)	2,110,000
Future Income Tax Liability (Monson's Only)	400,000
Common Stock - No Par ($4,300,000 + $4,100,000)	8,400,000
Retained Earnings (Monson's Only)	3,000,000
Total Equities	**$14,950,000**

Case Two - Acquisition Of Assets - Rollover Used

17-43. In the previous Case we assumed that Monson Inc. was prepared to pay $4,100,000 for the assets and liabilities of Little Ltd. when no rollover provision is used. This price was based on the fair values of the identifiable assets and liabilities of Little Ltd., and the belief that this acquiree had above normal earning power that was worth an additional payment of $150,000 for Goodwill. It was also based on the assumption that all of these items would have a tax basis equal to their carrying value.

17-44. In this Case we will assume that Section 85(1) of the *Income Tax Act* is used to transfer the assets of Little Ltd. with fair values in excess of their tax values (Land, Plant And Equipment, and Goodwill). Assuming that minimum tax values will be elected under ITA 85(1), Monson Inc. will have lower future tax deductions from these assets. As a consequence, Monson Inc. would pay a lower price as the assets are clearly less valuable due to their lower tax values. If we ignore the time value of money, the reduction in value of Little Ltd. would be based on the Future Income Tax Liability associated with these lost tax deductions. This amount can be calculated as follows:

	Fair Value From No Rollover Case	Election: Minimum Tax Value	Temporary Differences	
Land	$ 500,000	$ 450,000	$ 50,000	
Plant And Equipment	2,600,000	2,000,000		$600,000
Goodwill*	150,000	Nil	150,000	
			$200,000	$600,000
Effective Tax Rate			30%	40%
Future Income Tax Liability			$ 60,000	$240,000

*While the prohibition against recognizing a Future Income Tax Liability on temporary differences related to Goodwill removes it from the Future Income Tax Liability that is reported, the effective tax rate on these temporary differences is 30 percent. This reflects the fact that only three-quarters of Cumulative Eligible Capital amounts is recorded on the acquisition or disposition of Goodwill.

17-45. The proceeding calculation would suggest that, with the use of the rollover provision, Little Ltd. is worth $300,000 less to Monson Inc. than in the previous example. Based on this, we will assume that, on December 31, 1998, Monson Inc. issues Common Stock - No Par with a fair market value of $3,800,000 in return for the assets and liabilities of Little Ltd. transferred under the provisions of Section 85(1).

17-46. While the preceding calculations reflect the economics of the described transaction, Paragraph 3465.22 introduces a significant complication by prohibiting the recognition of a Future Income Tax Liability based on temporary differences related to Goodwill (see our Paragraph 17-29). Given this, the Future Income Tax Liability to be recorded will be $255,000 ($15,000 on Land and $240,000 on Plant And Equipment). It follows from this that the amount of Goodwill to be recorded in the Balance Sheet of the combined company would be as follows:

Investment Cost	$3,800,000
Fair Values Of Net Identifiable Assets	
($5,200,000 - $340,000 - $910,000)	(3,950,000)
Excess (Deficiency) Of Cost Over Fair Values	($ 150,000)
Future Income Tax Liability (As Above)	255,000
Goodwill	$ 105,000

17-47. What this Case makes clear is that, under the Recommendations of Section 3465, Goodwill is recorded net of its associated Future Income Tax Liability. The $105,000 to be recorded in the Balance Sheet is the original $150,000, less $45,000 in taxes at the effective tax rate on Cumulative Eligible Capital of 30 percent.

17-48. Based on the preceding calculations, the required Balance Sheet for Monson Inc. as at December 31, 1998 would be prepared as follows:

Monson Inc. Balance Sheet
As At December 31, 1998

Cash ($500,000 + $250,000)	$ 750,000
Accounts Receivable ($1,600,000 + $650,000)	2,250,000
Inventories ($2,300,000 + $1,200,000)	3,500,000
Land ($800,000 + $500,000)	1,300,000
Plant And Equipment (Net) ($4,400,000 + $2,600,000)	7,000,000
Goodwill	105,000
Total Assets	$14,905,000
Current Liabilities ($700,000 + $340,000)	$ 1,040,000
Long Term Liabilities ($1,200,000 + $910,000)	2,110,000
Future Income Tax Liability ($400,000 + $255,000)	655,000
Common Stock - No Par ($4,300,000 + $3,800,000)	8,100,000
Retained Earnings (Monson's Only)	3,000,000
Total Equities	$14,905,000

Case Three - Acquisition Of Shares

17-49. In this Case we will assume that Monson Inc. acquires all of the shares of Little Ltd. Use of this legal form means that Little Ltd. will continue to operate as a separate legal entity. This, in turn, means that the tax basis of its assets will be unchanged. In effect, the tax values for Little Ltd.'s assets in this case will be the same as in the previous case where the assets were acquired using an ITA 85(1) rollover.

17-50. As we used Little's underlying tax values as our elected values in Case Two, the tax values here will be the same. As a consequence, we will use the same $3,800,000 purchase price. Monson Inc. will issue Common Stock - No Par shares with a fair market value of $3,800,000 in return for all of the outstanding shares of Little Ltd. We would note, however, that in actual practice, the price might be lower. There are factors which provide incentives to the vendor of a corporation to sell shares rather than assets (e.g., the lifetime capital gains deduction on shares of a qualified small business corporation). These factors could lead to a lower price for Little Ltd.

17-51.   As the temporary differences in this Case Three are the same as in Case Two, the same amounts for the Goodwill and Future Income Tax Liability will be recorded. Given this, the required Balance Sheet is as follows:

Monson Inc.
Consolidated Balance Sheet
As At December 31, 1998

Cash ($500,000 + $250,000)	$ 750,000
Accounts Receivable ($1,600,000 + $650,000)	2,250,000
Inventories ($2,300,000 + $1,200,000)	3,500,000
Investment In Little Ltd. ($3,800,000 - $3,800,000)	Nil
Land ($800,000 + $500,000)	1,300,000
Plant And Equipment (Net) ($4,400,000 + $2,600,000)	7,000,000
Goodwill	105,000
Total Assets	$14,905,000
Current Liabilities ($700,000 + $340,000)	$ 1,040,000
Long Term Liabilities ($1,200,000 + $910,000)	2,110,000
Future Income Tax Liability ($400,000 + $255,000)	655,000
Common Stock - No Par ($4,300,000 + $3,800,000)	8,100,000
Retained Earnings (Monson's Only)	3,000,000
Total Equities	$14,905,000

17-52.   This Balance Sheet is identical to the one which was prepared in the previous case. The only difference is that we have indicated that Monson Inc. had a $3,800,000 Investment In Little Ltd. that had to be eliminated in the consolidation procedures. This fact would not, of course, be disclosed in the actual financial statements.

17-53.   We would also note that the $255,000 addition to the Future Income Tax Liability includes the $160,000 that is included in Little's single entity Balance Sheet. Our calculation of this amount included all temporary differences, including those that apply to Little Ltd. as a separate legal entity.

Procedures Subsequent To Acquisition

Dealing With The Equity Pickup

17-54.   In this Section we will extend Case Three of the Monson Inc./Little Ltd. example to illustrate the appropriate accounting for tax procedures in periods subsequent to acquisition. However, before proceeding to this issue we have to deal with the treatment of something that is commonly referred to as the equity pickup. When full consolidation procedures, proportionate consolidation procedures, or the equity method of accounting are applied to a long term investment, the financial statements of the investor will reflect its share of the retained earnings of the investee since the acquisition of the investment. This investor's share of the unremitted earnings of the investee is commonly referred to as the equity pickup.

17-55.   This equity pickup is not recognized in current tax legislation and, as a consequence, the tax basis of such investments remains their cost. This means that, whenever an investor company recognizes an equity pickup in their financial statements, there will be a temporary difference between carrying values and tax basis values.

17-56. While this type of temporary difference has some of the same characteristics as other temporary differences, it also has some different properties which have led the Accounting Standards Board to give equity pickup timing differences the special attention that is contained in the following Recommendation:

> **Paragraph 3465.37** *At each balance sheet date, a future income tax liability or future income tax asset should be recognized for all temporary differences arising from investments in subsidiaries and interests in joint ventures, except with respect to the difference between the carrying amount of the investment and the tax basis of the investment when it is apparent that this difference will not reverse in the foreseeable future. Any future income tax asset should be recognized only to the extent that it is more likely than not that the benefit will be realized.* (January, 2000)

17-57. Section 3465 goes on to describe such differences as follows:

> **Paragraph 3465.38** Temporary differences may arise from investments in subsidiaries and interests in joint ventures in a number of different circumstances, for example:
>
> (a) differences between the carrying amounts (in the consolidated financial statements) of individual assets and liabilities of subsidiaries and joint ventures and their tax basis ("inside basis differences"); or
>
> (b) differences between the carrying amount of an investment in a subsidiary or an interest in a joint venture and its tax basis ("outside basis differences") because of items such as:
>
>> (i) the existence of undistributed income of subsidiaries and joint ventures; or
>>
>> (ii) changes in foreign exchange rates when a parent and its subsidiary are based in different countries.

17-58. The meaning of this material is not completely clear to us. In particular, we have not encountered the terms "inside basis" and "outside basis" in any other source. Further, Section 3465 does not provide any definition of these terms. Accordingly, what follows is our interpretation of these terms.

17-59. It would appear to us that the differences referred to in Paragraph 3465.38(a) are the fair value changes and goodwill that exist at the time of a subsidiary's acquisition. As other Recommendations make it clear that future income tax assets and liabilities should be recognized for these types of temporary differences, we would assume that these items are not covered by the Paragraph 3465.37 Recommendation.

17-60. The differences referred to in Paragraph 3465.38(b)(i) are what we have referred to as the equity pickup. As we have noted, this type of situation results in a temporary difference between the accounting basis of the investment and the corresponding tax basis.

17-61. The concern here is that the amount of this difference will be determined by the amount of dividends paid by the investee and, in the case of both subsidiaries and joint ventures, the investor company is in a position to influence this policy. Further, the investor in the subsidiary or joint venture often views this interest in undistributed profits as an additional permanent investment in the investee.

17-62. Given an investor's ability to control the reversal of such temporary differences, as well as the fact that there may be no intention to implement such a reversal, a future income tax liability will not be recognized unless it is apparent that all or part of the related temporary difference will reverse in the foreseeable future.

17-63. Temporary differences like those just described for subsidiaries and joint ventures also exist for investments subject to significant influence and accounted for by the equity method. Section 3465 indicates that a future income tax liability should be recorded in this case since the investor is not normally able to control the timing of the reversal of temporary differences. We are not in complete agreement with this conclusion in that the degree of influence here may be equal to or greater than the degree of influence that is present with an investment in a joint venture. This would suggest similar treatment for these two types of investees.

17-64. A further problems arises if we do record future income tax liabilities on temporary differences resulting from equity pickups on significantly influenced companies. Such differences could be realized either through the sale of the investment or through dividend distributions by the investee. In the former case, the result would be a capital gain, only three quarters of which would be taxable. If dividends are distributed, taxation will vary depending on the status of the recipient (e.g., dividends from taxable Canadian corporations paid to a public corporation would not be taxed). These alternatives create complications with respect to the amount of the Future Income Tax Liability to be recorded.

17-65. There is an additional reference in Paragraph 3465.38(b)(ii) to differences resulting from changes in foreign exchange rates when a parent and its subsidiary are based in different countries. It would appear that this is a reference to the special shareholders' equity balance that is used to accumulate the exchange gains and losses of self sustaining foreign operations. In this case, the Paragraph 3465.37 Recommendation would prohibit the recognition of a future income tax asset or liability related to a temporary difference on this Balance Sheet item, except where there is an intent to liquidate the self sustaining foreign operation.

Basic Example - Subsequent To Acquisition

17-66. In order to illustrate income tax procedures in the years subsequent to a business combination transaction, we will extend the Monson Inc./Little Ltd. example that was presented in Paragraph 17-39 assuming shares were acquired. The single entity Statements Of Income And Retained Earnings for the year ending December 31, 1999, along with the single entity Balance Sheets as at December 31, 1999, for these two companies are as follows:

Statements Of Income And Retained Earnings
Year Ending December 31, 1999

	Monson Inc.	Little Ltd.
Revenues	$1,460,000	$ 872,000
Expenses Other Than Taxes	(1,060,000)	(662,000)
Pre Tax Income	$ 400,000	$ 210,000
Income Tax Expense (Note One)		
Current	(110,000)	(44,000)
Future	(50,000)	(40,000)
Net Income	$ 240,000	$ 126,000
Retained Earnings - January 1, 1999	3,000,000	1,040,000
Dividends	(75,000)	Nil
Retained Earnings - December 31, 1999	$3,165,000	$1,166,000

Note One All of the Income Tax Expense of both companies have been accrued at a rate of 40 percent. The Future component of this expense results from an increase in taxable temporary differences on Plant And Equipment. For Little Ltd., these differences increased from $400,000 ($2,400,000 - $2,000,000) at the beginning of the year, to $500,000 ($2,100,000 - $1,600,000) at the end of the year.

Balance Sheets
As At December 31, 1999

	Monson Inc.	Little Ltd.
Cash	$ 610,000	$ 280,000
Accounts Receivable	1,840,000	830,000
Inventories	2,265,000	1,516,000
Investment In Little Ltd.	3,800,000	N/A
Land	820,000	450,000
Plant And Equipment (Net)	4,500,000	2,100,000
Total Assets	**$13,835,000**	**$5,176,000**
Current Liabilities	$ 770,000	$ 420,000
Long Term Liabilities	1,350,000	890,000
Future Income Tax Liability	450,000	200,000
Common Stock - No Par*	8,100,000	2,500,000
Retained Earnings	3,165,000	1,166,000
Total Equities	**$13,835,000**	**$5,176,000**

*As we are looking at an extension of Case Three, Monson's Common Stock - No Par includes the $3,800,000 in shares that were issued to acquire the Little Ltd. shares. When added to the original balance of $4,300,000, we have the total of $8,100,000.

Case Three Extended - Acquisition Of Shares

17-67.   The required consolidated Statement Of Income And Retained Earnings would be prepared as follows:

Monson Inc. And Subsidiary
Consolidated Statement Of Income And Retained Earnings
Year Ending December 31, 1999

Revenues ($1,460,000 + $872,000)		$2,332,000
Expenses Other Than Taxes (Note One)		(1,763,000)
Pre Tax Income		$ 569,000
Income Tax Expense (Note Two)		
Current ($110,000 + $44,000)	($ 154,000)	
Future (Note Three)	(82,000)	(236,000)
Net Income (Note Four)		$ 333,000
Consolidated Retained Earnings - January 1, 1999 (Monson's Only)		3,000,000
Dividends		(75,000)
Consolidated Retained Earnings - December 31, 1999		$3,258,000

Note One   The consolidated Expenses Other Than Taxes would be calculated as follows:

Monson's Single Entity Expenses	$1,060,000
Little's Single Entity Expenses	662,000
Fair Value Depreciation On Plant And Equipment ($200,000 ÷ 10)	20,000
Goodwill Amortization Expense ($105,000 ÷ 5)	21,000
Total Expenses Other Than Taxes	$1,763,000

Note Two The statutory rate of 40 percent applied to the $569,000 of Income Before Taxes would give an Income Tax Expense of $227,600. The reported Income Tax Expense of $236,000 exceeds this amount by $8,400. This difference reflects the fact that no reduction in Future Income Tax Expense is recognized for the $21,000 in Goodwill amortization.

Note Three The consolidated Future Tax Expense would be calculated as follows:

Monson's Single Entity Expense	$50,000
Little's Single Entity Expense	40,000
Reduction In Temporary Differences Resulting From Fair Value Depreciation [(40%)($200,000 ÷10)]	(8,000)
Total Consolidated Future Income Tax Expense	$82,000

Note Four The consolidated Net Income Figure can be verified as follows:

Monson' Net Income	$240,000
Equity Pickup [(100%)($126,000)]	126,000
Fair Value Depreciation On Plant	(20,000)
Future Income Tax Expense Reduction - Fair Value Depreciation	8,000
Goodwill Amortization	(21,000)
Consolidated Net Income	$333,000

17-68. The required consolidated Balance Sheet would be prepared as follows:

Monson Inc. And Subsidiary
Consolidated Balance Sheet
As At December 31, 1999

Cash ($610,000 + $280,000)	$ 890,000
Accounts Receivable ($1,840,000 + $830,000)	2,670,000
Inventories ($2,265,000 + $1,516,000)	3,781,000
Investment In Little Ltd. ($3,800,000 - $3,800,000)	Nil
Land ($820,000 + $500,000)	1,320,000
Plant And Equipment (Net) (Note Five)	6,780,000
Goodwill ($105,000 - $21,000)	84,000
Total Assets	$15,525,000
Current Liabilities ($770,000 + $420,000)	$ 1,190,000
Long Term Liabilities ($1,350,000 + $890,000)	2,240,000
Future Income Tax Liability (Note Six)	737,000
Common Stock - No Par (No Change)	8,100,000
Retained Earnings (From Statement)	3,258,000
Total Equities	$15,525,000

Note Five The consolidated Plant And Equipment (Net) would be calculated as follows:

Monson's Plant And Equipment	$4,500,000
Little's Plant And Equipment	2,100,000
Fair Value Increase	200,000
Amortization Of Fair Value Increase	(20,000)
Total Consolidated Plant And Equipment	$6,780,000

Note Six The consolidated Future Income Tax Liability would be calculated as follows:

Monson's Future Income Tax Liability	$450,000
Little's Future Income Tax Liability	200,000
Liability On Land [(40%)(3/4)($50,000)]	15,000
Liability On Plant And Equipment Fair Value Change [(40%)($200,000 - $20,000)]	72,000
Total Future Income Tax Liability	$737,000

This amount could also be calculated by adding the $82,000 change for the year (see Income Statement) to the opening consolidated balance of $655,000.

Unrealized Intercompany Profits

17-69. While this is not illustrated in the preceding example, the preparation of consolidated financial statements normally involves the elimination of unrealized intercompany profits. As described in Chapter 6, these are profits on transfers between companies within a consolidated group that have not been realized through a subsequent transfer to an entity outside the consolidated group. From a purely accounting point of view, we gave this subject comprehensive coverage in Chapter 6. However, as tax returns are not filed on the basis of consolidated information, there are tax implications associated with the elimination of unrealized intercompany profits.

17-70. In order to discuss these tax implications, consider the following simple example:

Example A parent company sells merchandise with a cost of $45,000 to a 100 percent owned subsidiary for $60,000. At the end of the period, the merchandise is still in the inventories of the subsidiary. Both companies are subject to a tax rate of 40 percent.

17-71. From a tax point of view, the parent company has $15,000 of income as a result of this transaction, and the subsidiary has acquired merchandise with a tax basis of $60,000.

17-72. The problem here is that, in the preparation of consolidated financial statements, unrealized intercompany profits must be eliminated, leaving the carrying value of the asset at the original $45,000. This means that there is a deductible temporary difference between the carrying value of the merchandise and its tax basis of $60,000, a situation which would normally result in the recording of a future income tax asset of $6,000 [(40%)($60,000 - $45,000)]. In dealing with this situation, Section 3465 makes the following Recommendation:

Paragraph 3465.35 *When an asset is transferred between enterprises within a consolidated group, a future income tax liability or asset should not be recognized in the consolidated financial statements for a temporary difference arising between the tax basis of the asset in the buyer's tax jurisdiction and its cost as reported in the consolidated financial statements. Any taxes paid or recovered by the transferor as a result of the transfer should be recorded as an asset or liability in the consolidated financial statements until the gain or loss is recognized by the consolidated entity.* (January, 2000)

17-73. This approach is supported as follows:

Paragraph 3465.36 Although the difference between the buyer's tax basis and the cost of transferred assets as reported in the consolidated financial statements technically meets the definition of a temporary difference, the substance of accounting for it as such would be to recognize income taxes related to inter company gains or losses that are not recognized under "Consolidated Financial

Statements", Section 1600. Similar principles would apply to investments subject to significant influence and interests in joint ventures.

17-74.   We find these statements to be somewhat confusing as can be illustrated by extending our simple example. On the books of the purchasing company, the merchandise would be recorded at $60,000, an amount that would be fully deductible to that company. The entries on the books of the selling company would be as follows:

Cash or Accounts Receivable	$60,000	
Sales		$60,000
Cost Of Goods Sold	$45,000	
Inventories		$45,000
Income Tax Expense [(40%)($60,000 - $45,000)]	$6,000	
Taxes Payable Or Cash		$6,000

17-75.   The normal elimination entries for the sale and profit would be as follows:

Sales	$60,000	
Cost Of Goods Sold		$60,000
Cost Of Goods Sold	$15,000	
Inventories		$15,000

17-76.   In conflict with the statements made in Paragraph 3465.35 and 3465.36, if we do not recognize a Future Income Tax Asset, we will be leaving a $6,000 Income Tax Expense on the selling companies, for which there is no corresponding amount of taxable income. In our opinion it is essential that an additional entry be made as follows:

Future Income Tax Asset	$6,000	
Tax Expense		$6,000

17-77.   In the following period, when the merchandise is sold and the profit realized, the $6,000 Future Income Tax Asset would be charged to Tax Expense. While this is in conflict with the Paragraph 3465.35 statement that "a future income tax liability or asset should not be recognized in the consolidated financial statements for a temporary difference arising between the tax basis of the asset in the buyer's tax jurisdiction and its cost as reported in the consolidated financial statements", it would appear to us to be the only reasonable solution to this problem. Further, it is supported by the Paragraph 3465.35 statement that "Any taxes paid or recovered by the transferor as a result of the transfer should be recorded as an asset or liability in the consolidated financial statements until the gain or loss is recognized by the consolidated entity". In short, it would appear to us that Paragraph 3465.35 contains contradictory advice and, in our view, the second position taken in this Recommendation is the correct one.

17-78.   Unrealized intercompany profits are also eliminated in the application of the equity method for significantly influenced investments, and in the application of proportionate consolidation to joint venture investments. The same principles would be applicable to any taxes related to these eliminations.

Loss Carry Overs
Purchase Method Business Combinations

17-79.   In a business combination accounted for by the purchase method, the acquiree may have unused tax loss carry forwards. Depending on the legal form of the business combination, as well as the applicability of the acquisition of control rules, some or all of these losses may be available to the combined company. When this is the case, the following Recommendation is applicable:

Paragraph 3465.46   *When, at the time of a business combination accounted for as a purchase, the acquirer considers it more likely than not that it will realize a fu-*

ture income tax asset of its own that was previously unrecognized, it should in-clude a future income tax asset as an identifiable asset when allocating the cost of the acquisition. (January, 2000)

17-80.   A simple example will serve to illustrate the application of this provision:

Example   On December 31, 1998, Bondor Ltd. pays $1,200,000 in cash to ac-quire 100 percent of the outstanding shares of Bondee Inc. Bondee Inc. can be identified as the acquiree and, as a consequence, purchase method accounting is appropriate. Both Companies have a December 31 year end and are subject to a tax rate of 35 percent.

At the time of the business combination, Bondee Inc. has net identifiable assets with a carrying value and tax basis of $600,000. The fair value of these assets is $850,000. In addition, the Company has an unused non capital loss carry forward of $200,000. This loss carry forward has not been recognized on Bondee Inc.'s books.

17-81.   If Bondor Ltd. is able to claim that it is more likely than not that the benefit of the $200,000 loss carry forward will be realized, the $1,200,000 purchase price will be allo-cated as follows:

Investment Cost	$1,200,000
Fair Value Of Identifiable Assets	(850,000)
Excess Of Cost Over Fair Values	$ 350,000
Future Income Tax Asset [(35%)($200,000)]	(70,000)
Future Income Tax Liability [(35%)($850,000 - $600,000)]	87,500
Goodwill (Residual)	$ 367,500

17-82.   As specified in Section 3465, no Future Income Tax Liability has been recog-nized for the temporary difference associated with the goodwill.

17-83.   In contrast to the preceding analysis, if Bondor Ltd. was not able to claim that it is more likely than not that the benefit of the $200,000 loss carry forward will be realized, the allocation would be altered as follows:

Investment Cost	$1,200,000
Fair Value Of Identifiable Assets	(850,000)
Excess Of Cost Over Fair Values	$ 350,000
Future Income Tax Liability [(35%)($850,000 - $600,000)]	87,500
Goodwill (Residual)	$ 437,500

17-84.   As can be seen in the preceding allocation schedule, if the loss carry forward benefit is not recognized at the time of acquisition, it effectively becomes part of the goodwill balance. To some degree, this explains the basis for the following Recommenda-tion:

Paragraph 3465.48   *When a future income tax asset acquired in a business com-bination accounted for as a purchase that was not recognized as an identifiable as-set by the acquirer at the date of the acquisition is subsequently recognized by the acquirer, the benefit should be applied:*

(a) first to reduce to zero any unamortized goodwill related to the acquisition; then

(b) to reduce to zero any unamortized intangible properties (see "Capital Assets", Section 3060) related to the acquisition; and then

(c) to reduce income tax expense. (January, 2000)

17-85.   Continuing the simple example that we have presented, assume that the allocation of the purchase price was as presented in Paragraph 17-83. If, in a subsequent accounting period, the management of Bondor Ltd. concluded that Bondee Inc.'s loss carry forward benefit was more likely than not to be realized, a future income tax asset of $70,000 would be recorded, along with a corresponding reduction in the amount of goodwill to be disclosed.

17-86.   Similar problems with the recognition of acquired loss carry forward benefits arise in a number of other situations. These are covered by the following additional Recommendations:

> **Paragraph 3465.51**   *The principles in paragraphs 3465.46 and 3465.48 should be applied:*
>
> (a) *when accounting for an investment subject to significant influence or an interest in a joint venture; and*
>
> (b) *when recognizing future income tax assets in periods subsequent to the application of push down accounting (see "Comprehensive Revaluation Of Assets And Liabilities", Section 1625). (January, 2000)*

> **Paragraph 3465.52**   *When a future income tax asset that was not recognized at the date of a comprehensive revaluation as a result of a financial reorganization (see "Comprehensive Revaluation Of Assets And Liabilities", Section 1625) is subsequently recognized, the benefit should be applied:*
>
> (a) *first to reduce to zero any unamortized intangible properties (see "Capital Assets", Section 3060) that were recorded at the date of the comprehensive revaluation; and then*
>
> (b) *in a manner consistent with the revaluation adjustment recorded at the date of the comprehensive revaluation. (January, 2000)*

Pooling Of Interests Business Combinations

17-87.   In a business combination accounted for by the pooling of interests method, it is possible that one or both of the combining companies will have unused loss carry forwards. In this situation, the following Recommendation is applicable:

> **Paragraph 3465.53**   *When, at the time of a business combination accounted for as a pooling of interests, it is considered more likely than not that the enterprise will realize a future income tax asset of one of the parties to the combination that was previously unrecognized, a future income tax asset should be recognized in the financial statements of the combined enterprise. The related benefit should be recognized:*
>
> (a) *as a capital transaction, to the extent that the change related to a change in the tax basis of assets and liabilities that occurred as a result of the combination; and*
>
> (b) *any additional amount, as part of the restatement of the financial statements of the combined companies for periods prior to the date of the business combination. (January, 2000)*

17-88.   An example will serve to illustrate the application of this provision:

Example   As at December 31, 1998, the net identifiable assets and shareholders' equity of Barton Ltd. and Fink Inc. are as follows:

	Barton Ltd	Fink Inc.
Net Identifiable Assets	$950,000	$1,050,000
Contributed Capital	$500,000	$ 800,000
Retained Earnings	450,000	250,000
Total Shareholders' Equity	$950,000	$1,050,000

On this date, Fink Inc. has a non capital loss carry forward of $300,000. Both Companies are subject to a tax rate of 40 percent, and the $120,000 potential benefit of Fink's unused loss carry forward has not been recognized in that Company's financial statements. On this date, the two companies are combined in a transaction that qualifies for pooling of interests accounting. The legal form of the combination involves Fink Inc. issuing shares to the shareholders of Barton Ltd., thereby acquiring 100 percent of the Barton Ltd. shares. The benefits related to carrying out this business combination are such that it is now more likely than not that Fink Inc. will be able to realize the benefit of its unused loss carry forward.

17-89.   Given the legal form of the combination, there is no change in the tax basis of the assets or liabilities of either company. As a result, Fink's statements would be restated to include the benefit of the loss carry forward. On this basis, the condensed Balance Sheet of the combined company would be as follows:

Combined Company Balance Sheet
As At December 31, 1998

Net Identifiable Assets ($950,000 + $1,050,000 + $120,000)	$2,120,000
Contributed Capital ($500,000 + $800,000)	$1,300,000
Retained Earnings ($450,000 + $250,000 + $120,000)	820,000
Total Shareholders' Equity	$2,120,000

17-90.   If Fink's loss carry forward benefit had not been recognized at the time of the business combination transaction, the following Recommendation would be applicable:

Paragraph 3465.54   *When an unrecognized future income tax asset that existed at the time of a pooling of interests is subsequently recognized, the benefit should be recognized in income.* (January, 2000)

17-91.   This would mean that the net identifiable assets recorded at the time of the business combination transaction would be limited to $2,000,000 ($950,000 + $1,050,000). In the period when the $120,000 loss carry forward benefit is recognized, it would be set up as a Future Income Tax Asset, with the accompanying credit being included in the Accounting Income of that period.

Other Income Tax Issues

Integrated Foreign Operations

17-92.   In Chapter 16, we noted that Section 3465 generally requires the recognition of future income tax liabilities for taxable temporary differences, and future income tax assets for deductible temporary differences. In this Chapter we have discussed exceptions to this general rule for temporary differences related to Goodwill, and for temporary differences related to the equity pickup in the application of consolidation procedures. A further exception occurs with respect to integrated foreign operations.

17-93. As described in Section 1650 of the *CICA Handbook*, "Foreign Currency Translation", integrated foreign operations are foreign operations which are financially or operationally interdependent with the reporting enterprise such that the exposure to exchange rate changes is similar to the exposure which would exist had the transactions and activities of the foreign operation been undertaken by the reporting enterprise. As they essentially operate in Canadian dollars, the Canadian dollar is considered to be the appropriate currency of measurement. This view is implemented by translating the foreign currency financial statements using the temporal method of translation.

17-94. Under the temporal method, most non monetary assets are translated at historical rates of exchange. Consider, for example, a Canadian company with a German subsidiary classified as an integrated foreign operation. If that subsidiary acquired Land at a cost of DM1,000,000 at a point in time when DM1 = $.80, the Land would be recorded in the consolidated financial statements at $800,000. If, at a later point in time, the rate for the Deutsche Mark changed to DM1 = $.85, the Land would continue to be disclosed in the consolidated financial statements at its historic cost of $800,000. The problem is that its tax basis in Germany is still DM1,000,000 and, at current exchange rates, the cost of DM1,000,000 is $850,000. In other words, there is a deductible temporary difference between the $800,000 carrying value of the asset, and its $850,000 tax basis.

17-95. The situation described in the preceding paragraph would normally require recognition of a future income tax asset based on the deductible temporary difference. However, in this situation, the following Recommendation is applicable:

> **Paragraph 3465.33** *A future income tax asset or liability should not be recognized for a temporary difference arising from the difference between the historical exchange rate and the current exchange rate translations of the cost of non-monetary assets or liabilities of integrated foreign operations.* (January, 2000)

17-96. Section 3465 justifies this position as follows:

> **Paragraph 3465.34** ... Although that difference technically meets the definition of a temporary difference, the substance of accounting for it as such would be to recognize future income taxes on exchange gains and losses that are not recognized under Section 1650. In order to resolve that conflict and to reduce complexity by eliminating cross-currency (Canadian dollar cost versus foreign tax basis) computations of future income taxes, recognition of future income tax assets and future income tax liabilities for those differences is prohibited.

Refundable Taxes

General Application

17-97. Section 3465 provides the following definition of refundable taxes:

> **Paragraph 3465.09(b)** **Refundable taxes** are taxes that are based on certain types of income and that are refundable when certain amounts are paid to shareholders.

17-98. Without going into great detail, a certain portion of the Part I tax that must be paid on investment income earned by Canadian controlled private corporations is designated as refundable. In addition, a refundable Part IV tax is assessed on certain types of intercorporate dividends received by private companies. These taxes are refundable on the basis of $1 for each $3 of dividends distributed by the corporation paying the dividends.

17-99. With respect to the accrual of such taxes, the following Recommendation is made:

> **Paragraph 3465.73** *Refundable taxes should be accrued with respect to all related elements of income recognized in the period, whether the taxes with respect to such amounts are payable currently or in the future.* (January, 2000)

17-100.   With respect to the treatment of taxes paid but not, as yet, refunded, the basic accounting issue is whether they should be treated as a Future Income Tax Asset, an increase in the Income Tax Expense, or as a reduction in shareholders' equity. General guidance on this issue is in the form of the following two non italicized paragraphs:

> **Paragraph 3465.75**   Any taxes that will be refundable on payment of an amount related to an item classified as equity would not be treated as an asset since they do not represent a potential economic benefit - the benefit could only be realized by a decrease in net assets.

> **Paragraph 3465.76**   Any taxes that would be refundable on payment of amounts related to an item classified as a liability represent an advance payment in respect of an expense and would therefore be recorded as an asset.

17-101.   These two paragraphs suggest that refundable taxes related to equity items be treated as a capital transaction while, in contrast, refundable taxes related to liabilities be treated as an asset.

Financial Instruments Recommendations

17-102.   The Recommendation on refundable taxes found in the now superseded Section 3470 was less equivocal. It simply stated that refundable taxes represented advance distributions to shareholders and should be charged to Retained Earnings.

17-103.   Since that Recommendation was made, the world has become a more complex place. More specifically, Section 3860, "Financial Instruments - Disclosure And Presentation", was introduced into the *CICA Handbook* in 1995. This Section had the effect of changing the traditional classifications of certain items on the equity side of the Balance Sheet as follows:

- A portion of newly issued convertible bonds must now be treated as part of shareholders' equity. In the past, the entire issue price was allocated to liabilities.

- Certain types of preferred shares, those with contractual obligations for the issuers to make cash payments to the holders, must now be classified as liabilities.

17-104.   While these changes have been incorporated into the *CICA Handbook*, they have not affected Revenue Canada's position on these items. From a tax point of view, convertible bonds do not have an equity component and all preferred shares are equity instruments. This means that there may be refundable taxes on items that are accounted for as liabilities, as well as no refundable taxes related to items that are accounted for as equity. In the context of this somewhat confusing situation, Section 3465 puts forward the following Recommendations:

> **Paragraph 3465.71**   *When a payment related to a component of an instrument classified as a liability under "Financial Instruments - Disclosure And Presentation", Section 3860, will give rise to a refund of income taxes previously paid, the refundable amount should be recognized as a future income tax asset.* (January, 2000)

> **Paragraph 3465.72**   *Refundable taxes that are in the nature of advance distributions related to a component of an instrument classified as equity under "Financial Instruments - Disclosure And Presentation", Section 3860, should be charged to retained earnings when it is more likely than not that such taxes will be recovered in the foreseeable future. The recovery of such refundable taxes should be credited to retained earnings. The charge and the recovery should be disclosed separately. When it is not more likely than not that the taxes will be recovered in the foreseeable future, the taxes should be charged to income.* (January, 2000)

17-105.   The treatment of refundable taxes under these two Recommendations can be summarized as follows:

Refundable Taxes As An Asset This would be appropriate when a payment related to an item classified as a liability will give rise to a refund.

Refundable Taxes As A Shareholders' Equity Item This would be appropriate when the taxes paid are in the nature of an advance distribution to holders of an item classified as equity, and it is more likely than not that the taxes will be recovered in the foreseeable future. The taxes will be charged to Retained Earnings when paid, and credited to Retained Earnings when refunded.

Refundable Taxes As An Expense This would be appropriate when the taxes paid are in the nature of an advance distribution to holders of an item classified as equity, and it cannot be claimed that it is more likely than not that the taxes will be recovered in the foreseeable future.

Mutual Fund Corporations

17-106. Mutual fund corporations differ from other corporations in a variety of ways. For one thing, they are generally required to distribute a major part of their earnings in order to retain some of the tax advantages associated with this form of organization.

17-107. In addition, shares in mutual fund corporations are redeemable at the holder's option. The redemptions take place at a net asset value which is determined on a daily basis. To maintain equity between various investors leaving at different points in time, it is necessary to include in this net asset value any refundable taxes that are available on the shares. Given this, it is not surprising that Section 3465 requires that refundable taxes paid by mutual fund corporations be treated as assets:

Paragraph 3465.79 *Refundable taxes on mutual fund corporations should be recorded as an asset.* (January, 2000)

Convertible Debt

17-108. As noted in the preceding section, Section 3860 of the *CICA Handbook* requires that the proceeds from issuing convertible bonds be split between a debt component and an equity component. As this split is not recognized by Revenue Canada, there will be a temporary difference between the carrying value of the liability and its tax basis. However, the settlement of such liabilities may not have tax consequences for the issuer (e.g., if it is converted). As a consequence, Section 3465 indicates that where the enterprise is able to settle the instrument without the incidence of taxes, the tax basis of the liability component is considered to be the same as its carrying amount and there is no temporary difference.

Alternative Minimum Tax (Capital Taxes)

17-109. Some taxes are levied without regard to the amount of income earned by the enterprise. The most common types of such taxes are provincial capital taxes and the federal large corporations tax. Such taxes sometimes involve some form of carry over provision. For example, the Canadian surtax paid can be applied against the federal large corporations tax, with any excess carried over to prior and future years to be applied against the large corporations tax paid in those years. When this is the case, the following Recommendation is applicable:

Paragraph 3465.81 *Any amounts of income tax payable currently that may reduce income taxes of a future period should be recorded as a future income tax asset if it is more likely than not that income taxes will be sufficient to recover the amounts payable currently. Any amounts not more likely than not to be recovered should be included in current income tax expense.* (January, 2000)

Other Disclosure Recommendations

17-110.   For the most part, we have tried to present disclosure requirements as part of the discussion of particular income tax issues. However, a number of disclosure Recommendations do not relate directly to the issues that we have discussed. As a consequence, they are presented in this separate Section.

17-111.   The first two of these Recommendations cover situations where the enterprise is not subject to income taxes. These Recommendations are as follows:

> **Paragraph 3465.98**   *An enterprise that is not subject to income taxes because its income is taxed directly to its owners should disclose that fact.* (January, 2000)

> **Paragraph 3465.99**   *A public enterprise, life insurance enterprise, deposit taking institution or co-operative business enterprise that is not subject to income taxes because its income is taxed directly to its owners should disclose the net difference between the tax bases and the reported amounts of the enterprise's assets and liabilities.* (January, 2000)

17-112.   There is no statutory provision under Canadian income tax law that provides for the filing of a consolidated tax return. It appears, however, that administration rules allow some consolidated groups to file such returns. When this is the case, the following Recommendation applies:

> **Paragraph 3465.101**   *If an enterprise is a member of a group that files a consolidated income tax return, the enterprise should disclose in its separately issued financial statements:*

> *(a) the aggregate amount of current and future income tax expense for the period and the amount of any tax-related balances due to or from affiliates as of the balance sheet date.*

> *(b) the principal provisions of the method by which the consolidated amount of current and future income tax expense is allocated to members of the group and the nature and effect of any changes in that method (and in determining related balances to or from affiliates) during the periods for which the disclosures in (a) above are presented.* (January, 2000)

Transitional Rules For Business Combinations

Business Combinations - Section 3465 Guidance

17-113.   The general rule in Paragraph 3465.106 makes reference to business combinations which took place prior to the implementation of Section 3465 for the first time. Further guidance on this issue is included as follows:

> **Paragraph 3465.109**   *A business combination may have taken place prior to the beginning of the first period for which financial statements have been restated. If the values assigned to assets and liabilities arising from those business combinations took into account the tax effect of differences between the fair values and the tax base of those items, the remaining balances of such items as of the beginning of the first period restated would be adjusted to remove the effects of such differences. A future income tax liability or asset would be recognized for the differences between the adjusted balances and the tax basis in accordance with the Recommendations of this Section. The remaining carrying amount of goodwill and intangible properties would be reduced by the amount of future income tax assets recognized at the date of adoption of the recommendations of this Section. Any additional difference between the future income tax liability or asset recognized and the deferred income taxes previously recorded would be included in the adjustment to opening retained earnings of the first period restated.*

17-114.   When adjustments such as those referred to in Paragraph 3465.109 are not practicable, the Section offers additional guidance:

> **Paragraph 3465.110**   If, for a particular business combination, determination of the adjustment for any or all of the assets and liabilities referred to in paragraph 3465.109 is impracticable, none of the remaining balances of any assets and liabilities acquired in that combination would be adjusted. A future income tax liability or asset would be recognized for the differences between the remaining balances and the tax base in accordance with the Recommendations of this Section. The remaining carrying amount of goodwill and intangible properties would be reduced by the amount of future income tax assets recognized at the date of adoption of the recommendations of this Section. Any additional difference between the future income tax liability or asset recognized and the deferred income taxes previously recorded would be included in the adjustment to opening retained earnings of the first period restated.

Business Combination Transitional Example

Basic Data

17-115.   A simple example will serve to illustrate the transitional rules as they relate to business combination transactions that take place prior to the implementation of Section 3465:

> **Example**   An enterprise completes a business combination transaction on January 1, 1997. The transaction is accounted for by the purchase method and, on the date of the combination, the identifiable assets of the acquiree have a fair value, without regard to their tax basis, of $800,000.
>
> The tax basis of the assets is $350,000. The fair value of the assets, taking into consideration their tax basis, was $680,000. (This is the value that was used prior to the 1997 amendment of Section 1580.)
>
> Other Information:
>
> - All of the common shares of the acquiree were purchased.
>
> - The purchase price of the acquiree was $1,200,000.
>
> - The acquiring company will depreciate the identifiable assets acquired over five years and any goodwill recorded in the combination over 10 years.
>
> - At the date of acquisition, the acquiree had an unrecognized loss carry forward of $300,000. As management did not believe that it was more likely than not to realize the benefit associated with this loss carry forward, it is not recognized at the time of the business combination.
>
> - The tax rate for both companies in all years under consideration is 40 percent.
>
> - Both companies have a December 31 year end. During 1998, the acquiree did not use any of the loss carry forward and did not claim any CCA.
>
> - On the date of acquisition, the acquired company did not have any deferred income taxes on its Balance Sheet.
>
> On January 1, 1998, the enterprise decides to adopt the recommendations of Section 3465 for the first time. At this time, it is decided that the benefit of the acquiree's loss carry forward is more likely than not to be realized. The allocation of the purchase price as at January 1, 1997, and the carrying values for these amounts as at January 1, 1998, prior to the implementation of Section 3465, are as follows:

	January 1, 1997	January 1, 1998*
Identifiable Assets	$ 680,000	$ 544,000
Goodwill	520,000	468,000
Total	$1,200,000	$1,012,000

*These amounts have been reduced by one year's amortization.

Case One - Retroactive Application With Restatement

17-116.   In this case we will assume that the enterprise decides to implement Section 3465 by applying its provisions retroactively, with restatement of all prior years. Under this approach, the restated values as at January 1, 1997 and January 1, 1998 would be as follows:

	January 1, 1997	January 1, 1998
Identifiable Assets	$ 800,000	$ 640,000
Goodwill	580,000	522,000
Future Income Tax Liability*	(180,000)	(116,000)
Total	$1,200,000	$1,046,000

*The January 1, 1997 liability is $180,000 [(40%)($800,000 - $350,000). The January 1, 1998 liability is $116,000 [(40%)($640,000 - $350,000)]. The $640,000 is $800,000, less one year's amortization at 20 percent. The $350,000 is the same tax basis that was used on January 1, 1997 as no CCA has been taken.

17-117.   The preceding analysis does not take into consideration the fact that management has decided that it is more likely than not that the loss carry forward benefit will be realized. This will require recording a future income tax asset with a value of $120,000 [(40%)($300,000)]. Under the Recommendation contained in Paragraph 3465.48, this recognition must first be applied to reduce any unamortized goodwill related to the acquisition. Applying this Recommendation results in the following revised amounts for the January 1, 1998 assets and liabilities acquired in the business combination transaction:

Identifiable Assets	$ 640,000
Goodwill ($522,000 - $120,000)	402,000
Future Income Tax Asset (Net) ($116,000 - $120,000)	4,000
Total	$1,046,000

Case Two - Retroactive Application Without Restatement

17-118.   In this case we will assume that the enterprise decides to implement Section 3465 by applying its provisions retroactively, but without restatement of any prior years. Under this approach, we do not return to the purchase price allocation that would have taken place on January 1, 1997 if Section 3465 had been in effect. However, in order to implement Section 3465, we must adjust the net of tax values that are being used for the identifiable assets. To do this, we use the values for these assets that would have resulted if their pre tax fair values had been recorded on January 1, 1997. We do not, as part of this process, go back and revalue the amount of goodwill that was acquired in the business combination transaction.

17-119.   If we had recorded the $800,000 pre tax fair value on January 1, 1997, it would now be amortized to $640,000 ($800,000, less one year's amortization at 20 percent). With the value of the Identifiable Assets written up from $544,000 to $640,000, the Future Income Tax Liability will be $116,000 [(40%)($640,000 - $350,000)]. The entry to record these adjustments would be as follows:

Identifiable Assets ($640,000 - $544,000)	$ 96,000	
Retained Earnings	20,000	
Future Income Tax Liability		$116,000

17-120.   As we will retain the Goodwill figure that is on the books ($468,000), the balances remaining from the business combination transaction are as follows:

Identifiable Assets [$800,000 - (20%)($800,000)]	$ 640,000
Goodwill	468,000
Future Income Tax Liability	(116,000)
Total	**$ 992,000**

17-121.   Note that the net total is $20,000 ($1,012,000 - $992,000) less than the net total in Case One. This reflects the $20,000 debit that was made to Retained Earnings because prior years were not adjusted.

17-122.   With the application of the loss carry forward benefit to the goodwill balance, the final figures would be as follows:

Identifiable Assets	$ 640,000
Goodwill ($468,000 - $120,000)	348,000
Future Income Tax Asset (Net) ($116,000 - $120,000)	4,000
Total	**$ 992,000**

Case Three - Impracticable To Determine The Required Adjustments

17-123.   Paragraph 3465.110 considers the possibility that it will be impracticable to determine the amounts required to make a full retroactive application. Under this approach the carrying value of the identifiable assets will remain at $544,000 and the goodwill will remain at $468,000. However, a future income tax liability will be recognized in the amount of $77,600 [(40%)($544,000 - $350,000)]. This amount will reduce the total asset balance and will be charged to Retained Earnings. The resulting asset and liability figures, before recognition of the loss carry forward benefit, would be as follows:

Identifiable Assets	$544,000
Goodwill	468,000
Future Income Tax Liability	(77,600)
Total	**$934,400**

17-124.   With the application of the loss carry forward benefit to the goodwill balance, the final figures would be as follows:

Identifiable Assets	$544,000
Goodwill ($468,000 - $120,000)	348,000
Future Income Tax Asset (Net) ($77,600 - $120,000)	42,400
Total	**$934,400**

Assignment Problems

(The solutions to these problem are only available in
the solutions manual that has been provided to your instructor.)

ASSIGNMENT PROBLEM SEVENTEEN - 1

The following two independent cases involve the acquisition of an asset in a transaction other than a business combination. In both cases, the initial tax basis of the asset is different from its cost.

Case A A corporation acquires a new building at a cash cost of $341,000. As a special tax incentive, it will be allowed to deduct CCA on 150 percent of its cost. The corporation is subject to a tax rate of 48 percent.

Case B An individual transfers a depreciable asset with a capital cost of $450,000 and a fair market value of $267,000 to a corporation, using the provisions of Section 85(1) of the *Income Tax Act*. It is the last asset in its CCA Class and the balance in the class is $132,000. The value elected for the transfer is the Class UCC of $132,000. In return for the asset, the corporation issues a note with a fair market value of $132,000 and common shares with a fair market value of $135,000. The corporation is subject to a tax rate of 51 percent.

Required: In both of the preceding cases, provide the journal entry to record the acquisition of the asset on the books of the acquiring corporation. Your entries should comply with all of the Recommendations of Section 3465 of the *CICA Handbook*.

ASSIGNMENT PROBLEM SEVENTEEN - 2

On December 31, 1998, the Pentogram Company purchased 70 percent of the outstanding voting shares of the Square Company for $875,000 in cash. The Balance Sheets of the Pentogram Company and the Square Company before the business combination transaction on December 31, 1998 were as follows:

	Pentogram	Square
Cash	$1,200,000	$ 50,000
Accounts Receivable	400,000	250,000
Inventories	2,000,000	500,000
Plant And Equipment	4,000,000	1,400,000
Accumulated Depreciation	(1,000,000)	(300,000)
Total Assets	$6,600,000	$1,900,000
Current Liabilities	$ 200,000	$ 150,000
Long Term Liabilities	1,000,000	350,000
No Par Common Stock	2,000,000	1,000,000
Retained Earnings	3,400,000	400,000
Total Equities	$6,600,000	$1,900,000

All of the Square Company's identifiable assets and liabilities have carrying values that are equal to their fair values except for Plant and Equipment which has a fair value of $800,000, Inventories which have a fair value of $600,000 and Long Term Liabilities which have a fair value of $400,000.

The tax basis of all of the assets and liabilities of both companies are equal to their carrying values. Both the Pentogram Company and the Square Company are taxed at a rate of 38 percent on all of their income. The taxes on the two companies are levied in the same jurisdiction.

Required: Prepare a consolidated Balance Sheet for the Pentogram Company and its subsidiary, the Square Company as at December 31, 1998, subsequent to the business combination. Your solution should comply with all of the requirements of the *CICA Handbook*, including Section 3465, "Income Taxes".

ASSIGNMENT PROBLEM SEVENTEEN - 3

This problem is extended in Assignment Problem 17-4.

On December 31, 1998, the Shark Company pays cash to acquire 70 percent of the outstanding voting shares of the Peril Company. On that date the Balance Sheets of the two Companies are as follows:

	Shark	Peril
Cash	$ 590,000	$ 200,000
Accounts Receivable	2,000,000	300,000
Inventories	2,500,000	500,000
Investment In Peril (At Cost)	1,050,000	-0-
Plant And Equipment (Net)	4,000,000	1,000,000
Total Assets	$10,140,000	$2,000,000
Liabilities	$ 2,000,000	$ 400,000
Common Stock (No Par)	4,000,000	400,000
Retained Earnings	4,140,000	1,200,000
Total Equities	$10,140,000	$2,000,000

On the acquisition date, the fair values of the Peril Company's assets and liabilities are as follows:

Cash	$ 200,000
Accounts Receivable	250,000
Inventories	550,000
Plant And Equipment (Net)	700,000
Liabilities	(500,000)
Net Fair Values	$1,200,000

The tax basis of all of the assets and liabilities of both companies are equal to their carrying values. Both the Shark Company and the Peril Company are taxed at a rate of 46 percent on all of their income. The taxes on the two companies are levied in the same jurisdiction.

Required: Prepare a consolidated Balance Sheet for the Shark Company and its subsidiary the Peril Company, as at December 31, 1998. Your answer should comply with all of the Recommendations of the *CICA Handbook*, including Section 3465, "Income Taxes".

ASSIGNMENT PROBLEM SEVENTEEN - 4

This problem is an extension of Assignment Problems 17-4.

On December 31, 1998, the Shark Company pays cash to acquire 70 percent of the outstanding voting shares of the Peril Company at a cost of $1,050,000 in cash. On that date the Peril Company had Common Stock (No Par) outstanding of $400,000 and Retained Earnings of $1,200,000.

On the acquisition date, all of Peril's identifiable assets and liabilities had fair values that were equal to their carrying values except for the following:

	Carrying Value	Fair Value
Accounts Receivable	$ 300,000	$ 250,000
Inventories	500,000	550,000
Plant And Equipment (Net)	1,000,000	700,000
Liabilities	(400,000)	(500,000)

At this time, the Plant And Equipment has a remaining useful life of 8 years. It is Shark's policy to amortize goodwill arising on business combination transactions over a period of 10 years. The Liabilities mature on December 31, 2003.

On December 31, 1998, the tax basis of all of the assets and liabilities of both companies are equal to their carrying values.

Both the Shark Company and the Peril Company are taxed at a rate of 46 percent on all of their income. The taxes on the two companies are levied in the same jurisdiction. All of the taxable temporary differences in the single entities' books which arise during 1999 are related to an excess of the carrying values of Plant And Equipment over the corresponding UCC value.

The single entity Statements Of Income And Retained Earnings for the year ending December 31, 1999, and the single entity Balance Sheets as at December 31, 1999, for the Shark Company and its subsidiary the Peril Company are as follows:

Shark And Peril Companies
Statement Of Income And Retained Earnings
Year Ending December 31, 1999

	Shark	Peril
Revenues	$4,300,000	$1,411,500
Expenses Other Than Taxes	(3,700,000)	(1,149,000)
Income Before Taxes	$ 600,000	$ 262,500
Tax Expense:		
Current	(207,000)	(86,250)
Future	(69,000)	(34,500)
Net Income	$ 324,000	$ 141,750
Retained Earnings At January 1, 1999	4,140,000	1,200,000
Dividends	(102,000)	Nil
Retained Earnings At December 31, 1999	$4,362,000	$1,341,750

Shark And Peril Companies
Balance Sheets
As At December 31, 1999

	Shark	Peril
Cash	$ 301,000	$ 209,750
Accounts Receivable	2,140,000	327,500
Inventories	2,970,000	514,000
Investment In Peril (At Cost)	1,050,000	-0-
Plant And Equipment (Net)	4,150,000	1,125,000
Total Assets	$10,611,000	$2,176,250

	Shark	Peril
Liabilities	$ 2,180,000	$ 400,000
Future Income Tax Liability	69,000	34,500
Common Stock (No Par)	4,000,000	400,000
Retained Earnings	4,362,000	1,341,750
Total Equities	$10,611,000	$2,176,250

Required: Prepare a consolidated Balance Sheet for the Shark Company and its subsidiary the Peril Company, as at December 31, 1999, as well as a consolidated Statement Of Income And Retained Earnings for the year ending December 31, 1999. Your answer should comply with all of the Recommendations of the *CICA Handbook*, including Section 3465, "Income Taxes".

Appendix

Solutions To
Self Study Problems

Solution to Self-Study Problem Two - 1

Part A   As we are assuming here that a 25 percent investment does not give the Miser Company significant influence over the Mercy Company, the use of the cost method would be appropriate. The required journal entries under this method would be as follows:

1995 Journal Entries

Investment In Mercy	$4,000,000	
Cash		$4,000,000

Cash	$ 75,000	
Investment Income		$ 75,000

(To record the investment transaction and Miser's 25 percent share of Mercy's dividends)

1996 Journal Entry

Cash	$ 100,000	
Investment In Mercy		$ 100,000

(To record Miser's 25 percent share of the dividends which Mercy has paid out of earnings retained prior to Miser's investment)

1997 Journal Entry

Cash	$ 125,000	
Investment In Mercy		$ 125,000

(To record Miser's 25 percent share of the dividends which Mercy has paid out of earnings retained prior to Miser's investment)

1998 Journal Entry

Cash	$ 250,000	
Investment Income		$ 250,000

Or

Cash	$ 250,000	
Investment In Mercy	225,000	
Investment Income		$ 475,000

(To record Miser's 25 percent share of Mercy's dividends which have been paid out of earnings retained subsequent to acquisition)

With respect to the entry for 1998, the *CICA Handbook* is not clear as to the appropriate treatment. The Investment In Mercy was written down in both 1996 and 1997 to reflect the fact that dividends were being paid out of Retained Earnings that were present at the time of the Miser Company's acquisition of the Mercy Company shares. By the end of 1998, earnings have been sufficient to more than replace the Retained Earnings balance that was present on July 1, 1995. The first of the preceding entries treats this situation prospectively and is probably more consistent with other *CICA Handbook* recommendations. The second entry reflects a retroactive treatment of this situation and has the advantage of maintaining the integrity of the cost method definitions.

Part B Given the assumption that the Miser Company has significant influence over the Mercy Company, the use of the equity method would be required. The entries under this method would be as follows:

1995 Journal Entries

Investment In Mercy	$4,000,000	
Cash		$4,000,000

Cash	$ 75,000	
Investment Income		$ 75,000

(To record the investment transaction and Miser's 25 percent share of Mercy's income which also equals dividends paid)

1996 Journal Entry

Cash	$ 100,000	
Investment Loss	500,000	
Investment In Mercy		$ 600,000

(To record Miser's 25 percent share of Mercy's loss and dividends)

1997 Journal Entry

Cash	$ 125,000	
Investment In Mercy	250,000	
Investment Income		$ 375,000

(To record Miser's 25 percent share of Mercy's income and dividends)

1998 Journal Entry

Cash	$ 250,000	
Investment In Mercy	500,000	
Extraordinary Loss	200,000	
Investment Income		$ 950,000

(To record Miser's 25 percent share of Mercy's ordinary income, extraordinary loss and dividends)

Solution to Self-Study Problem Two - 2

Part A - Income Statement Under Equity Method - If the Buy Company used the equity method to account for its investment in Sell Company, its Income Statement for the year ending December 31, 1998 would be as follows:

Sales	$5,000,000
Cost of Goods Sold	$3,000,000
Other Expenses	800,000
Investment Loss - Ordinary ([25%][$200,000])	50,000
Total Expenses and Losses	$3,850,000
Income Before Extraordinary Items	$1,150,000
Extraordinary Investment Income (Net of Taxes of $100,000)	150,000
Net Income	$1,300,000

Part A - Statement Of Retained Earnings Under Equity Method - The Buy Company's Statement of Retained Earnings for the year ending December 31, 1998, if its Investment in Sell was accounted for by the equity method would be as follows:

Opening Balance - As Previously Stated	$15,000,000
Prior Period Error (Net of Taxes of $5,000)	(12,500)
Opening Balance - As Restated	$14,987,500
Net Income	1,300,000
Balance Available	$16,287,500
Dividends	500,000
Closing Balance	$15,787,500

Part B - Income Statement Under Cost Method - The Buy Company's Income Statement for the year ending December 31, 1998, if its Investment in Sell was accounted for by the cost method, would be as follows:

Sales	$5,000,000
Investment Income ([25%][$150,000])	37,500
Total Revenues	$5,037,500
Cost of Goods Sold	$3,000,000
Other Expenses	800,000
Total Expenses	$3,800,000
Net Income	$1,237,500

Part B - Statement Of Retained Earnings Under Cost Method - If the Buy Company had used the cost method to account for its Investment in Sell since its acquisition, the January 1, 1998 Retained Earnings balance of the Buy Company would not have been the $15,000,000 stated in the problem. The difference arises from the fact that the equity method includes in that $15,000,000, Buy Company's share of the Sell Company's Net Income between January 1, 1995 and December 31, 1997, while the cost method would have included instead the Buy Company's share of the dividends declared by Sell Company. This means that the January 1, 1998 Retained Earnings of the Buy Company would have been equal to $14,750,000 ($15,000,000 - [25%][$3,000,000] + [25%][$2,000,000]), if its Investment in Sell had been carried using the cost method since its acquisition. The Statement of Retained Earnings under this assumption would be as follows:

Opening Balance	$14,750,000
Net Income	1,237,500
Balance Available	$15,987,500
Dividends	500,000
Closing Balance	$15,487,500

Part C - Investment Account Balance Under Equity Method - The December 31, 1998 balance in the Investment in Sell account would be $1,800,000 if the equity method of accounting was used. This amount can be calculated as follows:

Investment Cost	$1,500,000
Equity Pickup to December 31, 1997	
([25%][$3,000,000 - $2,000,000])	250,000
Ordinary Investment Loss	(50,000)
Dividends Received	(37,500)
Extraordinary Investment Income	150,000
Prior Period Error	(12,500)
Balance in Investment in Sell Account	$1,800,000

An alternate calculation, using end of period figures, is as follows:

Investment Cost	$1,500,000
Equity Pickup to December 31, 1998	
([25%][$3,400,000 - $2,150,000])	312,500
Prior Period Error	(12,500)
Balance in Investment in Sell Account	$1,800,000

Solution to Self-Study Problem Two - 3

Case One - Part A The potential gain on the plant is $2,800,000 ($5,000,000 - $2,200,000). However, with CL's ownership interest at 60 percent, only 40 percent of this gain, or $1,120,000 ([40%][$2,800,000]) can be recognized.

With respect to the amount to be included in income at the time of transfer, this will be determined by the amount of unencumbered cash that CL received as consideration for the plant. Of the $3,500,000 received, $1,000,000 was from VI's capital contribution, with the remaining $2,500,000 coming from the bank loan proceeds. CL's 60 percent share of this financing must be removed from the proceeds of the sale, leaving an amount of $2,000,000 ($3,500,000 - [60%][$2,500,000]). Given this, the gain that is included in income at the time of transfer is calculated as follows:

Proceeds From Sale ($3,500,000 - [60%][$2,500,000])	$2,000,000
Cost Of Asset Considered To Be Sold	
([$2,000,000 ÷ $5,000,000][$2,200,000])	(880,000)
Gain To Be Recognized On Transfer	$1,120,000

In this Case, the gain that can be recognized is equal to the gain that can be taken into income at the time of transfer. This reflects the fact that the unencumbered cash received was equal to 40 percent of the asset's fair value, the same percentage as the ownership interest of the non affiliated venturer VI.

Case One - Part B The carrying value of CL's initial investment in the joint venture would be calculated as follows:

Carrying Value Of The Plant	$2,200,000
Total Gain Recognized	1,120,000
Value Of Capital Contribution	$3,320,000
Equity Returned	(3,500,000)
Initial Investment	($ 180,000)

The journal entry to record this initial investment would be as follows:

Cash	$3,500,000	
Plant		$2,200,000
Gain		1,120,000
Investment In SL		180,000

The credit balance in the Investment In SL would be shown in CL's single entity statements as a liability. This conclusion is reinforced by the following calculation:

Net Investment Contribution ($5,000,000 - $3,500,000)	$1,500,000
Share Of Borrowings ([60%][$2,800,000])	(1,680,000)
Net Obligation	($ 180,000)

Case Two - Part A The maximum gain that can be recognized in this case is equal to $750,000. This is based on the interest of the other non affiliated venturer, VI's 60 percent interest multiplied by the potential gain of $1,250,000 ($2,650,000 - $1,400,000).

The amount of this total recognized gain that can be taken into income at the time of transfer is calculated as follows:

Sale Proceeds	$650,000
Cost Of Asset Considered To Be Sold	
([$650,000 ÷ $2,650,000][$1,400,000])	(343,396)
Gain To Be Recognized On Transfer	$306,604

Case Two - Part B Given this amount of gain to be recognized in income, the initial Investment In SL would be calculated as follows:

Carrying Value Of The Plant	$1,400,000
Total Gain Recognized	750,000
Value Of Capital Contribution	$2,150,000
Equity Returned	(650,000)
Initial Investment	$1,500,000

The journal entry to record this initial Investment In SL would be as follows:

Cash	$ 650,000	
Investment In SL	1,500,000	
Plant		$1,400,000
Gain - Current Income		306,604
Gain - Deferred ($750,000 - $306,604)		443,396

Solution to Self-Study Problem Three - 1

Case A If we assume that the Graber Company can be identified as the acquiring Company, purchase accounting would be appropriate. The Balance Sheet which would result from the application of purchase accounting would be as follows:

Balance Sheet

Cash ($50,000 + $70,000 - $10,000)	$ 110,000
Accounts Receivable ($250,000 + $330,000)	580,000
Inventories ($400,000 + $300,000)	700,000
Plant and Equipment (Net) ($1,200,000 + $800,000)	2,000,000
Land ($800,000 + $300,000)	1,100,000
Goodwill (See note which follows)	260,000
Total Assets	$4,750,000

Current Liabilities ($75,000 + $50,000)	$ 125,000
Long Term Liabilities ($800,000 + $450,000)	1,250,000
Future Income Tax Liabilities (Graber's Only)	200,000
Common Stock - Par $20	1,600,000
Contributed Surplus ($400,000 + $600,000)	1,000,000
Retained Earnings (Graber's Only)	575,000
Total Equities	$4,750,000

Notes As Graber acquired the assets of Grabee, their accounting value and their tax base will be the same. Therefore, no future income tax asset or liability of Grabee's is included in the combined Balance Sheet. The $260,000 Goodwill consists of the $150,000 that was initially on the books of the Graber Company plus an additional $110,000 resulting from the business combination transaction which is calculated as follows:

Investment Cost	$1,410,000
Book Value	(1,200,000)
Differential	$ 210,000
Fair Value Increase On Plant	(200,000)
Fair Value Decrease On Land	100,000
Fair Value Increase On Long Term Liabilities	50,000
Fair Value Decrease On Future Income Tax Liabilities	(100,000)
Fair Value Decrease On Grabee's Goodwill	50,000
Goodwill	$ 110,000

Net Income And Earnings Per Share Under the purchase method, the Net Income of the combined company for the year ending December 31, 1998 is equal to the Graber Company's Net Income of $125,000. The earnings per share for the year amount to $3.13 per share ($125,000 ÷ 40,000).

Case B If we assume that neither Company can be identified as the acquirer, pooling of interests accounting would be appropriate. This method requires the elimination of the intercompany profits that are unrealized at the combination date, even though the sales transactions took place prior to the business combination. The Balance Sheet which would result from the application of pooling of interests accounting would be as follows:

Balance Sheet

Cash ($50,000 + $70,000 - $10,000)	$ 110,000
Accounts Receivable ($250,000 + $330,000)	580,000
Inventories ($400,000 + $300,000 - $50,000)	650,000
Plant and Equipment (Net) ($1,200,000 + $600,000)	1,800,000
Land ($800,000 + $400,000 - $20,000)	1,180,000
Goodwill ($150,000 + $50,000)	200,000
Total Assets	$4,520,000

Current Liabilities ($75,000 + $50,000)	$ 125,000
Long-Term Liabilities ($800,000 + $400,000)	1,200,000
Future Income Tax Liabilities ($200,000 + $100,000)	300,000
Common Stock - Par $20	1,600,000
Contributed Surplus ($400,000 + $100,000)	500,000
Retained Earnings ($575,000 + $300,000 - $10,000	
- $50,000 - $20,000)	795,000
Total Equities	$4,520,000

Note The preceding solution is completely consistent with the concepts that are involved in pooling of interests accounting. However, the shareholders' equity presentation would be in conflict with the requirements of the Canada Business Corporations Act and the carry forward of Grabee's Future Income Tax Liabilities would not be appropriate given that the assets are being transferred to a new entity.

Net Income And Earnings Per Share Under the pooling of interests method, the Net Income of the combined company for the year ending December 31, 1998 is $255,000 ($125,000 -$20,000 + $200,000 - $50,000). The Earnings Per Share for the year would be $3.19 per share ($255,000 ÷ 80,000).

Solution to Self-Study Problem Three - 2

Case A As the shareholders of the Ero Company remain the majority shareholder group in the combined company, this Company will be deemed the acquirer and purchase accounting will be required. The resulting solution would be prepared as follows:

Investment Analysis

Investment Cost	$4,000,000
Book Value	(4,200,000)
Differential	($ 200,000)
Fair Value Decrease on Non-monetary Assets	600,000
Goodwill	$ 400,000

Depreciation and Amortization The depreciation decrease resulting from the fair value change on Tick's Non-monetary Assets would be $150,000 per year ($600,000 ÷ 4). Goodwill amortization would be $20,000 per year ($400,000/20).

Balance Sheet

Monetary Assets ($200,000 + $1,000,000)	$1,200,000
Non Monetary Assets ($3,800,000 + $3,400,000)	7,200,000
Goodwill (As per the investment analysis)	400,000
Total Assets	$8,800,000
Monetary Liabilities ($100,000 + $800,000)	$ 900,000
Common Stock - Par $10 ($2,000,000 + $1,000,000)	3,000,000
Contributed Surplus ($500,000 + $3,000,000)	3,500,000
Retained Earnings (Ero's Balance)	1,400,000
Total Equities	$8,800,000

Net Income and Earnings Per Share   For the year ending December 31, 1998, the Net Income would be $400,000 and the Basic Earnings Per Share would be $2.00 per share.   For the year ending December 31, 1999, the Net Income would be $1,630,000 ($700,000 + $800,000 + $150,000 - $20,000) and the Basic Earnings Per Share would be $5.43 per share.

Case B   In this Case, both shareholder groups hold an equal number of shares in the combined company. As a reflection of this fact, the pooling of interests method should be used to account for this business combination. This means that no investment analysis is required and that no fair value changes or goodwill will be recorded. As a consequence, no adjustment need be made to depreciation expense or any goodwill amortization recorded. The solution would be prepared as follows:

Balance Sheet

Monetary Assets ($200,000 + $1,000,000)	$1,200,000
Non Monetary Assets ($3,800,000 + $4,000,000)	7,800,000
Total Assets	$9,000,000
Monetary Liabilities ($100,000 + $800,000)	$ 900,000
Common Stock - Par $10 ($2,000,000 + $2,000,000)	4,000,000
Contributed Surplus ($500,000 + $1,000,000)	1,500,000
Retained Earnings ($1,400,000 + $1,200,000)	2,600,000
Total Equities	$9,000,000

Net Income and Earnings Per Share   The Net Income for the year ending December 31, 1998 would be $1,000,000 and the Basic Earnings Per Share would be $2.50 per share. For the year ending December 31, 1999, the Net Income would be $1,500,000 and the Basic Earnings Per Share would be $3.75 per share.

Case C   Since the shareholders of the Tick Company received a majority of the shares in the newly formed Erotick Company, this Company would be deemed the acquirer and purchase accounting would be required. The solution is as follows:

Investment Analysis

Investment Cost	$4,800,000
Book Value	(3,900,000)
Differential	$ 900,000
Fair Value Increase on Non-monetary Assets	(400,000)
Goodwill	$ 500,000

Depreciation and Amortization The increased depreciation due to the fair value change on Ero's Non-monetary Assets would be $100,000 per year ($400,000 ÷ 4). Goodwill amortization would be $25,000 per year ($500,000 ÷ 20).

Balance Sheet

Monetary Assets ($200,000 + $1,000,000)	$1,200,000
Non Monetary Assets ($4,200,000 + $4,000,000)	8,200,000
Goodwill (As per investment analysis)	500,000
Total Assets	$9,900,000
Monetary Liabilities ($100,000 + $800,000)	$ 900,000
Common Stock - No Par ($3,000,000 + $4,800,000)	7,800,000
Retained Earnings (Tick's Balance)	1,200,000
Total Equities	$9,900,000

Net Income And Earnings Per Share Since the date of formation of the Erotick Company is December 31, 1998, there is no income earned by the Company for the year ending December 31, 1998 and no Earnings Per Share. For the year ending December 31, 1999 the Net Income is $1,375,000 ($700,000 + $800,000 - $100,000 - $25,000) and the Basic Earnings Per Share is $4.58 per share.

Case D As both shareholder groups receive an equal number of shares in the newly formed Erotique Company, the pooling of interests method is appropriate for dealing with this business combination. Given this choice, no investment analysis is required and no fair value changes or goodwill need be recorded. Further, no adjustments to depreciation or amortization expense will be needed. The resulting solution would be as follows:

Balance Sheet

Monetary Assets ($200,000 + $1,000,000)	$1,200,000
Non Monetary Assets ($3,800,000 + $4,000,000)	7,800,000
Total Assets	$9,000,000
Monetary Liabilities ($100,000 + $800,000)	$ 900,000
Common Stock - No Par	5,500,000
Retained Earnings ($1,400,000 + $1,200,000)	2,600,000
Total Equities	$9,000,000

Net Income and Earnings Per Share As the Erotique Company is formed on December 31, 1998, there is no income for the year ending December 31, 1998 or Earnings Per Share. For the year ending December 31, 1999, the Net Income is $1,500,000 and the Earnings Per Share are $15.00 per share.

Solution to Self-Study Problem Four - 1

Investment Analysis - The analysis of Shark's investment in the Peril Company is as follows:

	70 Percent	100 Percent
Investment Cost	$ 910,000	$1,300,000
Book Value	(1,120,000)	(1,600,000)
Differential	($ 210,000)	($ 300,000)
Fair Value Changes:		
Accounts Receivable	35,000	50,000
Inventories	(35,000)	(50,000)
Plant And Equipment (Net)	210,000	300,000
Liabilities	70,000	100,000
Goodwill	$ 70,000	$ 100,000

Consolidated Balance Sheet - Based on the preceding analysis, the required December 31, 1998 Balance Sheet is as follows:

Cash	$ 790,000
Accounts Receivable	2,265,000
Inventories	3,035,000
Plant And Equipment (Net)	4,790,000
Goodwill	70,000
Total Assets	$10,950,000
Liabilities	$ 2,470,000
Non Controlling Interest	480,000
Common Stock (No Par)	4,000,000
Retained Earnings	4,000,000
Total Equities	$10,950,000

Solution to Self-Study Problem Four - 2

Investment Analysis The analysis of Potvin Company's investment in the Shroder Company is as follows:

	60 Percent	100 Percent
Investment Cost	$1,200,000	$2,000,000
Book Value	(600,000)	(1,000,000)
Differential	$ 600,000	$1,000,000
Fair Value Changes:		
Inventories	(30,000)	(50,000)
Plant And Equipment (Net)	150,000	250,000
Long-Term Liabilities	60,000	100,000
Copyright	(120,000)	(200,000)
Goodwill	$ 660,000	$1,100,000

Consolidated Balance Sheet Based on the preceding analysis, the required December 31, 1998 Balance Sheet is as follows:

Cash	$ 400,000
Accounts Receivable	2,190,000
Inventories	3,430,000
Plant And Equipment	6,650,000
Accumulated Depreciation	(2,000,000)
Copyright	120,000
Goodwill	660,000
Total Assets	**$11,450,000**
Accounts Payable	$ 1,690,000
Long Term Liabilities	2,360,000
Non Controlling Interest	400,000
Common Stock (No Par)	3,000,000
Retained Earnings	4,000,000
Total Equities	**$11,450,000**

Solution to Self-Study Problem Four - 3

Investment Analysis   The analysis of the Pentogram Company's investment in the Square Company is as follows:

	70 Percent	100 Percent
Cost	$875,000	$1,250,000
Book Value	(980,000)	(1,400,000)
Differential	($105,000)	($ 150,000)
Fair Value Changes:		
Plant And Equipment	210,000	300,000
Inventories	(70,000)	(100,000)
Long Term Liabilities	35,000	50,000
Goodwill	$ 70,000	$ 100,000

Consolidated Balance Sheet   The required Consolidated Balance Sheet as at December 31, 1998, is as follows:

Cash ($1,200,000 + $50,000 - $875,000)	$ 375,000
Accounts Receivable ($400,000 + $250,000)	650,000
Inventories ($2,000,000 + $500,000 + $70,000)	2,570,000
Plant And Equipment ($4,000,000 + $1,100,000 -$210,000)	4,890,000
Accumulated Depreciation (Pentogram's Only)	(1,000,000)
Goodwill	70,000
Total Assets	**$7,555,000**
Current Liabilities ($200,000 + $150,000)	$ 350,000
Long Term Liabilities ($1,000,000 + $350,000 + $35,000)	1,385,000
Non Controlling Interest [(30%)($1,400,000)]	420,000
No Par Common Stock (Pentogram's Only)	2,000,000
Retained Earnings (Pentogram's Only)	3,400,000
Total Equities	**$7,555,000**

Solution to Self-Study Problem Five - 1

Investment Analysis The analysis of the Pastel Company's Investment In Shade as at the acquisition date is as follows:

	90 Percent	100 Percent
Purchase Price	$5,175,000	$5,750,000
Book Value	(5,400,000)	(6,000,000)
Differential	($ 225,000)	($ 250,000)
Fair Value Decrease On Equipment	900,000	1,000,000
Fair Value Increase On Land	(90,000)	(100,000)
Fair Value Decrease On Receivables	45,000	50,000
Fair Value Decrease On Liabilities	(180,000)	(200,000)
Goodwill	$ 450,000	$ 500,000

Step A - Investment Elimination The journal entry that would be required to eliminate the Pastel Company's Investment In Shade would be as follows:

Common Stock - No Par	$2,000,000	
Retained Earnings	4,000,000	
Land	90,000	
Long Term Liabilities	180,000	
Goodwill	450,000	
Investment In Shade		$5,175,000
Equipment (Net)		900,000
Accounts Receivable		45,000
Non Controlling Interest		600,000

Step B - Depreciation Of The Fair Value Change On Equipment The entry to record the reduction in Depreciation Expense related to the fair value change on the equipment would be as follows:

Equipment (Net)	$450,000	
Depreciation Expense		$ 90,000
Retained Earnings		360,000

(Annual Adjustment = $900,000/10 = $90,000)

Step B - Fair Value Change On Land No adjustment is required.

Step B - Realization Of The Fair Value Change On Accounts Receivable The entry to record the realization of the fair value change on Accounts Receivable is as follows:

Accounts Receivable	$45,000	
Retained Earnings		$45,000

Step B - Amortization Of The Fair Value Change On The Liabilities The entry to record the increase in Other Expenses (interest expense) related to the fair value change on liabilities is as follows:

Other Expenses	$ 36,000	
Retained Earnings	144,000	
Long Term Liabilities		$180,000

(Annual Adjustment = $180,000/5 = $36,000)

Step B - Goodwill Amortization The entry to record the amortization of the Goodwill recorded in this business combination is as follows:

Other Expenses	$15,000	
Retained Earnings	60,000	
Goodwill		$75,000

(Annual Adjustment = $450,000/30 = $15,000)

Step B - Intercompany Management Fees   Two entries are required here. The first is to eliminate the $100,000 in intercompany revenue and expense while the second is required to eliminate the intercompany asset and liability. The entries are as follows:

Other Revenues	$100,000	
Other Expenses		$100,000

Current Liabilities	$100,000	
Current Receivables		$100,000

Step B - Intercompany Merchandise Sales   Two entries are also required here. The first will eliminate the total intercompany merchandise sales of $650,000 ($500,000 downstream + $150,000 upstream) while the second will eliminate the intercompany asset and liability of $225,000 ($75,000 downstream + $150,000 upstream). The entries are as follows:

Sales	$650,000	
Cost Of Goods Sold		$650,000

Current Liabilities	$225,000	
Current Receivables		$225,000

Step B - Intercompany Dividends   Two entries are also required here. The first will eliminate the intercompany Dividends Declared against the Other Revenues and Non Controlling Interest while the second will be required to eliminate the unpaid balance from the consolidated assets and liabilities. The entries are as follows:

Other Revenues	$90,000	
Non Controlling Interest (Balance Sheet)	10,000	
Dividends Declared		$100,000

Dividends Payable	$90,000	
Current Receivables		$ 90,000

Step C - Distribution Of Retained Earnings   The analysis of the opening balance of the Shade Company's Retained Earnings is as follows:

Retained Earnings - Opening Balance	$5,500,000
Balance At Acquisition	(4,000,000)
Balance Since Acquisition	$1,500,000
Non Controlling Interest Percentage	10%
Non Controlling Interest	$ 150,000

Balance Available To The Controlling Interest (90 Percent)	$1,350,000
Fair Value Depreciation On Equipment	360,000
Fair Value Realization On Accounts Receivable	45,000
Long Term Liabilities Amortization	(144,000)
Goodwill Amortization	(60 000)
To Consolidated Retained Earnings	$1,551,000

Based on the preceding analysis, the journal entry required to distribute the opening Retained Earnings balance of the Shade Company is as follows:

Retained Earnings - Shade	$1,701,000	
Consolidated Retained Earnings		$1,551,000
Non Controlling Interest		150,000

Part A - Consolidated Income Statement   The consolidated Income Statement for the Pastel Company and its subsidiary, the Shade Company, is as follows:

Sales ($8,000,000 + $2,000,000 - $650,000)	$ 9,350,000
Gain on Sale of Land	500,000
Other Revenues ($800,000 + $100,000 - $100,000 -$90,000)	710,000
Total Revenues	$10,560,000
Cost Of Goods Sold ($3,800,000 + $800,000 -$650,000)	$ 3,950,000
Depreciation Expense ($1,400,000 + $300,000 -$90,000)	1,610,000
Other Expenses ($2,000,000 + $400,000 + $36,000	
+ $15,000 - $100,000)	2,351,000
Non Controlling Interest (.10)($600,000)	60,000
Total Expenses	$ 7,971,000
Consolidated Net Income	$ 2,589,000

Part B - Consolidated Statement Of Retained Earnings   The opening balance of consolidated Retained Earnings consists of the Pastel Company's opening balance in the amount of $18,100,000 plus the allocation that was established in Step C in the amount of $1,551,000. Beginning with this total of $19,651,000, the consolidated Statement Of Retained Earnings for the Pastel Company and its subsidiary, the Shade Company, is as follows:

Opening Consolidated Retained Earnings	$19,651,000
Net Income (From Part A)	2,589,000
Balance Available	$22,240,000
Less Dividends Declared (Pastel's Only)	200,000
Closing Consolidated Retained Earnings	$22,040,000

Verification Of The Closing Balance   The closing balance in the consolidated Retained Earnings can be verified as follows:

Pastel's Closing Retained Earnings	$20,000,000
Equity Pickup ([.90][$6,000,000 - $4,000,000])	1,800,000
Fair Value Depreciation On Equipment	450,000
Fair Value Realization On Accounts Receivable	45,000
Fair Value Amortization On Long Term Liabilities	(180,000)
Goodwill Amortization	(75,000)
Closing Consolidated Retained Earnings	$22,040,000

Part C - Consolidated Balance Sheet   The consolidated Balance Sheet for the Pastel Company and its subsidiary, the Shade Company, is as follows:

Cash And Current Receivables ($2,625,000 + $800,000	
- $45,000 + $45,000 - $100,000 - $225,000 -$90,000)	$ 3,010,000
Inventories ($8,000,000 + $2,000,000)	10,000,000
Equipment (Net)($24,000,000 + $4,000,000	
- $900,000 + $450,000)	27,550,000
Buildings (Net)($10,000,000 + $2,000,000)	12,000,000
Investment In Shade ($5,175,000 - $5,175,000)	-0-
Land ($2,000,000 + $1,200,000 + $90,000)	3,290,000
Goodwill ($450,000 - $75,000)	375,000
Total Assets	$56,225,000
Dividends Payable ($100,000 - $90,000)	$ 10,000
Current Liabilities ($1,800,000 + $900,000	
- $100,000 - $225,000)	2,375,000
Long Term Liabilities ($10,000,000 + $1,000,000	
- $180,000 + $180,000)	11,000,000
Non Controlling Interest (.10)($8,000,000)	800,000
Common Stock - No Par (Pastel's Only)	20,000,000
Retained Earnings (See Part B)	22,040,000
Total Equities	$56,225,000

Note that, as you would expect in the absence of unrealized intercompany profits, the Non Controlling Interest is simply ten percent of the book value of the Shade Company's net assets.

Solution to Self-Study Problem Five - 2

Investment Analysis   The analysis of the Prude Company's Investment in Sybarite as at the acquisition date is as follows:

	60 Percent	100 Percent
Investment Cost	$750,000	$1,250,000
Book Value at Acquisition	(780,000)	(1,300,000)
Differential	($ 30,000)	($ 50,000)
Fair Value Decrease on Receivables	30,000	50,000
Fair Value Decrease on Inventories	270,000	450,000
Fair Value Increase on Plant	(210,000)	(350,000)
Fair Value Increase on Liabilities	60,000	100,000
Goodwill	$120,000	$ 200,000

Step A - Investment Elimination   The journal entry that would be required to eliminate the Prude Company's Investment in Sybarite would be as follows:

Common Stock - No Par	$1,000,000	
Retained Earnings	300,000	
Accumulated Depreciation	300,000	
Goodwill	120,000	
Plant and Equipment		$ 90,000
Investment in Sybarite		750,000
Non Controlling Interest		520,000
Current Receivables		30,000
Inventories		270,000
Long Term Liabilities		60,000

While there is a net increase in Plant and Equipment of $210,000, it is accomplished by removing all of the Accumulated Depreciation of Sybarite on the acquisition date. This reflects the fact that, from the point of view of the newly combined company, these assets are newly acquired and it would not be appropriate for Accumulated Depreciation to be recorded.

Step B - Realization Of The Fair Value Change On Accounts Receivable   The entry to record the realization of the fair value change on Accounts Receivable is as follows:

Current Receivables	$30,000	
Retained Earnings		$30,000

Step B - Fair Value Change On Inventories   The entry to record the fair value change on the Inventories is as follows:

Inventories	$270,000	
Retained Earnings		$270,000

Step B - Depreciation Of The Fair Value Change On The Plant   The entry to record the increased Accumulated Depreciation related to the fair value change on the Plant would be as follows:

Retained Earnings	$105,000	
Accumulated Depreciation		$105,000

(Annual Adjustment = $210,000/14 = $15,000/year)

Step B - Amortization Of The Fair Value Change On The Liabilities   The entry to record the amortization of the fair value change on the Long Term Liabilities is as follows (this adjustment is required even though the long term liabilities have matured):

Long Term Liabilities	$60,000	
Retained Earnings		$60,000

(Annual Adjustment = $60,000/5 = $12,000/year)

Step B - Goodwill Amortization   The entry to record the amortization of the Goodwill recorded in this business combination is as follows:

Retained Earnings	$42,000	
Goodwill		$42,000

(Annual Amount = $120,000/20 = $6,000/year)

Step B - Intercompany Merchandise Sales   Since no Income Statement is required, no entry is necessary to eliminate the intercompany sales of $50,000. An entry is required to eliminate the intercompany asset and liability arising from the outstanding merchandise payable of $50,000 and the accrued interest of $5,000 which is also outstanding. This entry is as follows:

Current Liabilities	$55,000	
Current Receivables		$55,000

Step C - Distribution Of Retained Earnings   The analysis of the closing balance of the Sybarite Company's Retained Earnings is as follows:

Sybarite's Balance At December 31, 1998	$1,400,000
Balance At Acquisition	(300,000)
Balance Since Acquisition	$1,100,000
Non Controlling Percentage	40%
Non Controlling Interest	$ 440,000

Balance Available to the Majority	$ 660,000
Fair Value Realization on Current Receivables	30,000
Fair Value Realization on Inventories	270,000
Fair Value Depreciation on Plant (7 years @ $15,000)	(105,000)
Long Term Liabilities Amortization (5 years @ $12,000)	60,000
Goodwill Amortization (7 years @ $6,000)	(42,000)
To Consolidated Retained Earnings	$ 873,000

Based on the preceding analysis, the journal entry required to distribute the closing Retained Earnings balance of the Sybarite Company is as follows:

Retained Earnings - Sybarite	$1,313,000	
Non Controlling Interest		$440,000
Consolidated Retained Earnings		873,000

This results in a December 31, 1998 balance in consolidated Retained Earnings of $3,373,000 ($2,500,000 + $873,000).

Non Controlling Interest   Using the steps in the general procedures, the Non Controlling Interest would be calculated as follows:

Step A Allocation at Acquisition	$520,000
Step C Allocation Since Acquisition	440,000
Non Controlling Interest, December 31, 1998	$960,000

This same balance can be calculated more directly by noting that on December 31, 1998, the Sybarite Company has No Par Common Stock of $1,000,000 and Retained Earnings of $1,400,000. If we multiply this total net worth of $2,400,000 by the non controlling ownership percentage of 40 percent, we arrive at the same $960,000.

Consolidated Balance Sheet   Given the preceding calculations, the consolidated Balance Sheet as at December 31, 1998 for the Prude Company and its subsidiary, the Sybarite Company, would be as follows:

Prude Company And Subsidiary
Consolidated Balance Sheet
As At December 31, 1998

Cash ($50,000 + $300,000)	$ 350,000
Current Receivables ($300,000 + $400,000	
- $30,000 + $30,000 - $55,000)	645,000
Inventories ($700,000 + $1,750,000 - $270,000 + $270,000)	2,450,000
Investment in Sybarite ($750,000 - $750,000)	-0-
Plant and Equipment ($9,000,000 + $1,000,000 -$90,000)	9,910,000
Accumulated Depreciation ($3,000,000 + $650,000	
- $300,000 + $105,000)	(3,455,000)
Goodwill ($120,000 - $42,000)	78,000
Total Assets	$9,978,000

Current Liabilities ($300,000 + $100,000 - $55,000)	$ 345,000
Long Term Liabilities ($1,000,000 + $300,000	
+ $60,000 - $60,000)	1,300,000
Non Controlling Interest	960,000
No Par Common Stock (Prude's Only)	4,000,000
Retained Earnings	3,373,000
Total Equities	$9,978,000

Solution to Self-Study Problem Five - 3

Investment Analysis For First Purchase   The investment analysis for the first purchase would be as follows:

	30 Percent	100 Percent
Cost	$3,000,000	$10,000,000
Book Value	(2,100,000)	(7,000,000)
Differential	$ 900,000	$ 3,000,000
Fair Value Increase on Plant	(600,000)	(2,000,000)
Goodwill	$ 300,000	$ 1,000,000

Write Off Of Fair Value Change And Goodwill   The depreciation of the fair value change on the Plant and Equipment would increase expenses by $60,000 per year ($600,000/10). Goodwill amortization would be $15,000 per year ($300,000/20).

Investment Analysis For Second Purchase   The investment analysis for the second purchase would be as follows:

	30 Percent	100 Percent
Cost	$3,600,000	$12,000,000
Book Value	(2,400,000)	(8,000,000)
Differential	$1,200,000	$ 4,000,000
Fair Value Increase on Plant	(900,000)	(3,000,000)
Goodwill	$ 300,000	$ 1,000,000

Write Off Of Fair Value Change And Goodwill   The depreciation of the fair value change on the Plant and Equipment would increase expenses by $100,000 per year ($900,000/9). Goodwill amortization would be $15,000 per year ($300,000/20).

Plant And Equipment   The consolidated value for Net Plant and Equipment is independently calculated in the schedule which follows:

Port's Book Value	$10,000,000
Ship's Book Value	4,000,000
Fair Value Change from First Purchase	600,000
Less Two Years Depreciation @ $60,000/year	(120,000)
Fair Value Change for Second Purchase	900,000
Less One Year of Depreciation	(100,000)
Consolidated Net Plant and Equipment	$15,280,000

Goodwill   The amortized balance of consolidated Goodwill can be calculated as follows:

Goodwill Arising From First Purchase	$300,000
Less Two Years Amortization @ $15,000/year	(30,000)
Goodwill Arising From Second Purchase	300,000
Less One Year of Amortization	(15,000)
Consolidated Goodwill	$555,000

Consolidated Retained Earnings   The December 31, 1998 balance for this account would be as follows:

Port's Balance	$10,000,000
Equity Pickup from First Purchase	
(30%)($4,500,000 - $3,000,000)	450,000
Equity Pickup from Second Purchase	
(30%)($4,500,000 - $4,000,000)	150,000
Goodwill Amortization ($30,000 + $15,000)	(45,000)
Fair Value Depreciation ($120,000 + $100,000)	(220,000)
Consolidated Retained Earnings	**$10,335,000**

Consolidated Balance Sheet   Given the preceding computations, the consolidated Balance Sheet would be prepared as follows:

Port Company And Subsidiary
Consolidated Balance Sheet
As At December 31, 1998

Net Monetary Assets	$ 7,900,000
Plant and Equipment (Net)	15,280,000
Goodwill	555,000
Total Assets	**$23,735,000**
Non Controlling Interest (40%)($8,500,000)	$ 3,400,000
Common Stock - No Par	10,000,000
Retained Earnings	10,335,000
Total Equities	**$23,735,000**

Solution to Self-Study Problem Five - 4

Investment Analysis   The analysis of the Puberty Company's Investment in Senile Company as at the acquisition date is as follows:

	80 Percent	100 Percent
Purchase Price	$4,000,000	$5,000,000
Book Value	(2,400,000)	(3,000,000)
Differential	$1,600,000	$2,000,000
Fair Value Increase on Building	(3,200,000)	(4,000,000)
Fair Value Increase on Liabilities	1,600,000	2,000,000
Senile's Goodwill	800,000	1,000,000
Consolidated Goodwill	**$ 800,000**	**$1,000,000**

Step A - Investment Elimination   The journal entry that would be required to eliminate the Puberty Company's Investment In Senile would be as follows:

Common Stock - Par Value	$ 400,000	
Contributed Surplus	600,000	
Retained Earnings	2,000,000	
Plant and Equipment (Net)	3,200,000	
Consolidated Goodwill	800,000	
Investment In Senile		$4,000,000
Long Term Liabilities		1,600,000
Senile's Goodwill		800,000
Non Controlling Interest		600,000

Step B - Fair Value Change On Building   The entry to record the increase in Depreciation Expense related to the fair value change on the building would be as follows:

Retained Earnings	$ 768,000	
Other Expenses	128,000	
Plant and Equipment (Net)		$ 896,000

(Annual Adjustment = $3,200,000/25 = $128,000/Year)

Step B - Fair Value Change On Liabilities   The entry to record the decrease in Other Expenses (interest expense) related to the fair value change on liabilities is as follows:

Long Term Liabilities	$ 700,000	
Retained Earnings		$ 600,000
Other Expenses		100,000

(Annual Adjustment = $1,600,000/16 = $100,000/Year)

Step B - Senile's Goodwill   The entry to record the realization of the fair value change on Senile's Goodwill, which was fully amortized by December 31, 1996, is as follows:

Goodwill (On Senile's Books)	$ 800,000	
Retained Earnings		$ 800,000

Step B - Consolidated Goodwill Amortization   The entry to record the amortization of the Goodwill recorded in this business combination is as follows:

Retained Earnings	$ 120,000	
Other Expenses	20,000	
Consolidated Goodwill		$ 140,000

(Annual Adjustment = $800,000/40 = $20,000/Year)

Step B - Intercompany Merchandise Sales   The entry to eliminate intercompany merchandise sales is as follows:

Sales	$1,000,000	
Cost of Goods Sold		$1,000,000

Step B - Intercompany Note And Interest   Three entries are required here. The first is to eliminate the intercompany note payable and receivable, the second is required to eliminate the related interest expense and revenue and the third is to eliminate the interest payable and receivable at the year end. The entries are as follows:

Notes Payable	$500,000	
Long Term Receivables		$500,000

Other Revenues	$ 30,000	
Other Expenses		$ 30,000

($500,000)(12%)(1/2 year)

Current Liabilities	$ 15,000	
Cash and Current Receivables		$ 15,000

($500,000)(12%)(1/4 year)

Step B - Intercompany Dividends   The entry to eliminate the intercompany dividends declared is as follows:

Other Revenues	$ 240,000	
Non Controlling Interest	60,000	
Dividends Declared		$ 300,000

Step B - Intercompany Management Fees   Two entries are required. The first entry is to eliminate the intercompany revenue and expense while the second is required to eliminate the intercompany asset and liability. The entries are as follows:

Other Revenues	$100,000	
Other Expenses		$100,000
Current Liabilities	$100,000	
Cash and Current Receivables		$100,000

Step C - Distribution Of Retained Earnings   The analysis of the opening balance of the Senile Company's Retained Earnings is as follows:

Retained Earnings - Opening Balance	$3,200,000
Balance At Acquisition	(2,000,000)
Balance Since Acquisition	$1,200,000
Non Controlling Percent	20%
Non Controlling Interest	($ 240,000)
Balance Available to the Controlling Interest (80 Percent)	$ 960,000
Fair Value Depreciation on Plant	(768,000)
Long Term Liabilities Amortization	600,000
Senile's Goodwill	800,000
Consolidated Goodwill Amortization	(120,000)
To Consolidated Retained Earnings	$1,472,000

Based on the preceding analysis, the journal entry required to distribute the opening Retained Earnings balance of the Senile Company is as follows:

Retained Earnings - Senile	$1,712,000	
Consolidated Retained Earnings		$1,472,000
Non Controlling Interest		240,000

Part A - Consolidated Income Statement   The consolidated Income Statement for the Puberty Company and its subsidiary, the Senile Company is as follows:

Sales ($9,000,000 + $2,500,000 - $1,000,000)	$10,500,000
Other Revenues ($1,000,000 + $300,000 - $30,000 - $240,000 - $100,000)	930,000
Total Revenues	$11,430,000
Cost of Goods Sold ($5,000,000 + $1,500,000 -$1,000,000)	$ 5,500,000
Other Expenses ($3,000,000 + $800,000 + $128,000 - $100,000 + $20,000 - $30,000 - $100,000)	3,718,000
Total Expenses	$ 9,218,000
Combined Income	$ 2,212,000
Non Controlling Interest (20%)($500,000)	100,000
Consolidated Net Income	$ 2,112,000

Part B - Consolidated Statement Of Retained Earnings The opening balance of consolidated Retained Earnings consists of the Puberty Company's opening balance of $8,000,000 plus the allocation of $1,472,000 that was established in Step C. Beginning with this total of $9,472,000, the consolidated Statement of Retained Earnings for the Puberty Company and its subsidiary, the Senile Company is as follows:

Opening Consolidated Retained Earnings	$ 9,472,000
Consolidated Net Income (From Part A)	2,112,000
Balance Available	$11,584,000
Dividends (Puberty's Only)	400,000
Closing Consolidated Retained Earnings	$11,184,000

The closing balance of consolidated Retained Earnings can be verified as follows:

Puberty's Closing Retained Earnings	$ 9,600,000
Equity Pickup ([80%][$3,400,000 - $2,000,000])	1,120,000
Fair Value Depreciation On Plant	(896,000)
Fair Value Amortization On Long Term Liabilities	700,000
Senile's Goodwill Amortization	800,000
Consolidated Goodwill Amortization	(140,000)
Closing Consolidated Retained Earnings	$11,184,000

Part C - Consolidated Balance Sheet The consolidated Balance Sheet for the Puberty Company and its subsidiary, the Senile Company is as follows:

Cash and Current Receivables ($1,100,000 + $400,000 - $15,000 - $100,000)	$ 1,385,000
Long Term Receivables ($1,000,000 + $200,000 -$500,000)	700,000
Inventories ($4,000,000 + $1,300,000)	5,300,000
Plant and Equipment (Net) ($6,000,000 + $6,000,000 + $3,200,000 - $896,000)	14,304,000
Investment in Senile ($4,000,000 - $4,000,000)	-0-
Goodwill ($800,000 - $140,000)	660,000
Total Assets	$22,349,000

Current Liabilities ($300,000 + $400,000 -$15,000 - $100,000)	$ 585,000
Notes Payable ($200,000 + $600,000 - $500,000)	300,000
Long Term Liabilities ($2,000,000 + $2,500,000 + $1,600,000 - $700,000)	5,400,000
Non Controlling Interest (20%)($4,400,000)	880,000
Common Stock - Par Value (Puberty's Only)	3,000,000
Contributed Surplus (Puberty's Only)	1,000,000
Retained Earnings	11,184,000
Total Equities	$22,349,000

Solution to Self-Study Problem Six - 1

Investment Analysis The analysis of the Pastel Company's Investment In Shade as at the acquisition date is as follows:

	90 Percent	100 Percent
Purchase Price	$5,175,000	$5,750,000
Book Value	(5,400,000)	(6,000,000)
Differential	($ 225,000)	($ 250,000)
Fair Value Decrease On Equipment	900,000	1,000,000
Fair Value Increase On Land	(90,000)	(100,000)
Fair Value Decrease On Receivables	45,000	50,000
Fair Value Decrease On Liabilities	(180,000)	(200,000)
Goodwill	$ 450,000	$ 500,000

Step A - Investment Elimination The journal entry that would be required to eliminate the Pastel Company's Investment In Shade would be as follows:

Common Stock - No Par	$2,000,000	
Retained Earnings	4,000,000	
Land	90,000	
Long Term Liabilities	180,000	
Goodwill	450,000	
Investment In Shade		$5,175,000
Equipment (Net)		900,000
Accounts Receivable		45,000
Non Controlling Interest		600,000

Step B - Depreciation Of The Fair Value Change On Equipment The entry to record the reduction in Depreciation Expense related to the fair value change on the equipment would be as follows:

Equipment (Net)	$450,000	
Depreciation Expense		$ 90,000
Retained Earnings		360,000

(Annual Adjustment = $900,000/10 = $90,000)

Step B - Fair Value Change On Land No adjustment is required.

Step B - Realization Of The Fair Value Change On Accounts Receivable The entry to record the realization of the fair value change on Accounts Receivable is as follows:

Accounts Receivable	$45,000	
Retained Earnings		$45,000

Step B - Amortization Of The Fair Value Change On The Liabilities The entry to record the increase in Other Expenses (interest expense) related to the fair value change on liabilities is as follows:

Other Expenses	$ 36,000	
Retained Earnings	144,000	
Long Term Liabilities		$180,000

(Annual Adjustment = $180,000/5 = $36,000)

Step B - Goodwill Amortization   The entry to record the amortization of the Goodwill recorded in this business combination is as follows:

Other Expenses	$15,000	
Retained Earnings	60,000	
Goodwill		$75,000

(Annual Adjustment = $450,000/30 = $15,000)

Step B - Intercompany Management Fees   Two entries are required here. The first is to eliminate the $100,000 in intercompany revenue and expense while the second is required to eliminate the intercompany asset and liability. The entries are as follows:

Other Revenues	$100,000	
Other Expenses		$100,000
Current Liabilities	$100,000	
Current Receivables		$100,000

Step B - Intercompany Merchandise Sales   Two entries are also required here. The first will eliminate the total intercompany merchandise sales of $650,000 ($500,000 downstream + $150,000 upstream) while the second will eliminate the intercompany asset and liability of $225,000 ($75,000 downstream + $150,000 upstream). The entries are as follows:

Sales	$650,000	
Cost Of Goods Sold		$650,000
Current Liabilities	$225,000	
Current Receivables		$225,000

Step B - Unrealized Intercompany Inventory Profits   Two entries are required to eliminate the unrealized intercompany profits in both the opening inventories and the closing inventories. The unrealized opening inventory profits equal $240,000 ([60%][$300,000] + $60,000) while the unrealized inventory profits in the closing inventories equal $165,000 ([60%][$125,000] + $90,000). The entries are as follows:

Retained Earnings	$240,000	
Cost of Goods Sold		$240,000
Cost of Goods Sold	$165,000	
Inventories		$165,000

Step B - Realization Of Equipment Sale Loss   The piece of equipment was sold at a loss of $30,000 ($120,000 - $150,000) on January 1, 1995. This upstream loss will be realized through an increase of Depreciation Expense of $2,000 per year ($30,000/15). The entry to record this adjustment is as follows:

Depreciation Expense	$ 2,000	
Equipment (Net)	22,000	
Retained Earnings		$24,000

Step B - Elimination Of Gain On Land And Building Sale   The total gain of $500,000 must be eliminated against the Building and Land accounts by the amounts that they have been increased over their carrying values on Pastel's books. The entry to record this adjustment is as follows:

Gain on Sale of Land	$500,000	
Building (Net)		$300,000
Land		200,000

Step B - Intercompany Dividends   Two entries are required here. The first will elimi-nate the intercompany Dividends Declared against the Other Revenues and Non Control-ling Interest while the second will be required to eliminate the unpaid balance from the consolidated assets and liabilities. The entries are as follows:

Other Revenues	$90,000	
Non Controlling Interest (Balance Sheet)	10,000	
Dividends Declared		$100,000

Dividends Payable	$90,000	
Current Receivables		$ 90,000

Step C - Distribution Of Retained Earnings   The analysis of the opening balance of the Shade Company's Retained Earnings is as follows:

Retained Earnings - Opening Balance	$5,500,000
Balance At Acquisition	(4,000,000)
Balance Since Acquisition	$1,500,000
Unrealized Upstream Opening (Profits) Losses:	
Inventories	(180,000)
Sale of Equipment	24,000
Realized Profits Since Acquisition	$1,344,000
Non Controlling Interest Percentage	10%
Non Controlling Interest	$ 134,400

Balance Available To The Controlling Interest (90 Percent)	$1,209,600
Fair Value Depreciation On Equipment	360,000
Fair Value Realization On Accounts Receivable	45,000
Long Term Liabilities Amortization	(144,000)
Goodwill Amortization	(60,000)
To Consolidated Retained Earnings	$1,410,600

Based on the preceding analysis, the journal entry required to distribute the opening Re-tained Earnings balance of the Shade Company is as follows:

Retained Earnings - Shade	$1,545,000	
Consolidated Retained Earnings		$1,410,600
Non Controlling Interest		134,400

Part A - Consolidated Income Statement   The consolidated Income Statement for the Pastel Company and its subsidiary, the Shade Company, is as follows:

Sales ($8,000,000 + $2,000,000 - $650,000)	$ 9,350,000
Gain on Sale of Land ($500,000 - $500,000)	- 0 -
Other Revenues ($800,000 + $100,000	
- $100,000 - $90,000)	710,000
Total Revenues	$10,060,000
Cost Of Goods Sold ($3,800,000 + $800,000	
- $650,000 - $240,000 + $165,000)	$ 3,875,000
Depreciation Expense ($1,400,000 + $300,000	
- $90,000 + $2,000)	1,612,000
Other Expenses ($2,000,000 + $400,000 + $36,000	
+ $15,000 - $100,000)	2,351,000
Non Controlling Interest ([10%][$600,000 + $180,000	
- $75,000 - $2,000])	70,300
Total Expenses	$ 7,908,300
Consolidated Net Income	$ 2,151,700

Part B - Consolidated Statement Of Retained Earnings   The opening balance of consolidated Retained Earnings consists of the Pastel Company's opening balance in the amount of $18,100,000 plus the $1,410,600 allocation that was established in Step C less the downstream unrealized opening inventory profits of $60,000. Beginning with this total of $19,450,600, the consolidated Statement Of Retained Earnings for the Pastel Company and its subsidiary, the Shade Company, is as follows:

Opening Consolidated Retained Earnings	$19,450,600
Net Income (From Step A)	2,151,700
Balance Available	$21,602,300
Less Dividends Declared (Pastel's Only)	200,000
Closing Consolidated Retained Earnings	$21,402,300

Verification Of The Closing Balance   The closing balance in the consolidated Retained Earnings can be verified as follows:

Pastel's Closing Retained Earnings	$20,000,000
Equity Pickup ([90%][$6,000,000 - $4,000,000	
- $75,000 + $22,000])	1,752,300
Fair Value Depreciation On Equipment	450,000
Fair Value Realization On Accounts Receivable	45,000
Fair Value Amortization On Long Term Liabilities	(180,000)
Goodwill Amortization	(75,000)
Downstream Unrealized Closing Intercompany Profits:	
On Inventories	(90,000)
On Building and Land Sale	(500,000)
Closing Consolidated Retained Earnings	$21,402,300

Part C - Consolidated Balance Sheet   The consolidated Balance Sheet for the Pastel Company and its subsidiary, the Shade Company, is as follows:

Cash And Current Receivables ($2,625,000 + $800,000
   - $45,000 + $45,000 - $100,000 - $225,000 -$90,000) $ 3,010,000
Inventories ($8,000,000 + $2,000,000 - $165,000)   9,835,000
Equipment (Net)($24,000,000 + $4,000,000
   - $900,000 + $450,000 + $22,000)   27,572,000
Buildings (Net)($10,000,000 + $2,000,000 - $300,000)   11,700,000
Investment In Shade ($5,175,000 - $5,175,000)   -0-
Land ($2,000,000 + $1,200,000 + $90,000 - $200,000)   3,090,000
Goodwill ($450,000 - $75,000)   375,000

Total Assets $55,582,000

Dividends Payable ($100,000 - $90,000) $ 10,000
Current Liabilities ($1,800,000 + $900,000
   - $100,000 - $225,000)   2,375,000
Long Term Liabilities ($10,000,000 + $1,000,000
   - $180,000 + $180,000)   11,000,000
Non Controlling Interest ([10%][$8,000,000
   - $75,000 + $22,000])   794,700
Common Stock (Pastel's Only)   20,000,000
Retained Earnings (See Part B)   21,402,300

Total Equities $55,582,000

Solution to Self-Study Problem Six - 2

Step A - Investment Analysis   The analysis of the Investment in Stone is as follows:

	80 Percent	100 Percent
Cost	$7,800,000	$9,750,000
Book Value	(5,600,000)	(7,000,000)
Differential	$2,200,000	$2,750,000
Inventories	(800,000)	(1,000,000)
Land	400,000	500,000
Plant And Equipment	(1,600,000)	(2,000,000)
Loss Carry Forward	(400,000)	(500,000)
Long Term Liabilities	1,200,000	1,500,000
Goodwill	$1,000,000	$1,250,000

Step A - Elimination Entry   The Step A journal entry that would be required to eliminate the investment would be as follows:

Common Stock - No Par	$3,000,000	
Retained Earnings	3,000,000	
Reserve For Contingencies	1,000,000	
Inventories	800,000	
Loss Carry Forward Benefit	400,000	
Goodwill	1,000,000	
Plant and Equipment	1,600,000	
Accumulated Depreciation	3,000,000	
Plant And Equipment		$3,000,000
Land		400,000
Long Term Liabilities		1,200,000
Investment In Stone		7,800,000
Non Controlling Interest (20% Of $7,000,000)		1,400,000

The debit to Accumulated Depreciation and the credit to Plant and Equipment for $3 million is necessary since the accumulated depreciation of the acquired company cannot be brought forward to the consolidated books.

Step B - Adjustment   The entry to adjust the fair value increase on the acquisition date inventories is as follows:

Retained Earnings	$800,000	
Inventories		$800,000

Step B - Adjustment   The entry to adjust the Plant And Equipment for the depreciation on the fair value change is as follows:

Retained Earnings	$320,000	
Other Expenses	80,000	
Accumulated Depreciation		$400,000

(Annual Adjustment - $1,600,000/20 = $80,000)

Step B - Adjustment   The entry to adjust for the realization of the fair value change on the Loss Carry Forward Benefit is as follows:

Retained Earnings	$400,000	
Loss Carry Forward Benefit		$400,000

Step B - Adjustment   The entry to adjust the interest for the fair value change on the Long Term Liabilities is as follows:

Long Term Liabilities	$600,000	
Other Expenses ($1,200,000/10)		$120,000
Retained Earnings		480,000

Step B - Adjustment   The entry to record Goodwill amortization since the acquisition date is as follows:

Retained Earnings	$100,000	
Other Expenses ($1,000,000/40)	25,000	
Goodwill		$125,000

Step B - Elimination   The entry to eliminate the intercompany dividend payment is as follows:

Total Revenues	$800,000	
Non Controlling Interest (Balance Sheet)	200,000	
Dividends Declared		$1,000,000

Step B - Elimination   The entry to eliminate the unrealized profit on the intercompany sale of the patent is as follows:

Retained Earnings	$800,000	
Other Expenses ($1,000,000/10)		$100,000
Patents		700,000

Step B - Elimination   The entry to eliminate the unrealized profit on the intercompany sale of land is as follows:

Total Revenues	$500,000	
Land		$500,000

Step B - Elimination   The entry to eliminate intercompany sales of merchandise is as follows:

Total Revenues	$2,000,000	
Cost Of Goods Sold		$2,000,000

Step B - Elimination   The entry to eliminate unrealized intercompany profits in the closing inventories is as follows:

Cost Of Goods Sold (30%)($500,000)	$150,000	
Inventories		$150,000

Step B - Elimination   The entry to eliminate the unrealized intercompany profits in the opening inventories is as follows:

Retained Earnings (30%)($800,000)	$240,000	
Cost Of Goods Sold		$240,000

Step C - Distribution Schedule   The allocation of the balance in the Retained Earnings account of the Stone Company would be as follows:

Opening Balance		$6,700,000
Step A Elimination		(4,000,000)
Balance Since Acquisition		$2,700,000
Upstream Unrealized Profits:		
On Patent Sale	($800,000)	
Opening Inventories	(240,000)	(1,040,000)
Realized Profits Since Acquisition		$1,660,000
Non Controlling Percent		20%
Non Controlling Interest		$ 332,000
Available To Controlling Interest		$1,328,000
Inventory Realization		(800,000)
Plant And Equipment Depreciation		(320,000)
Loss Carry Forward Realization		(400,000)
Long Term Liability Amortization		480,000
Goodwill Amortization		(100,000)
To Consolidated Retained Earnings		$ 188,000

Step C - Distribution Entry   The entry to distribute the Stone Company's Retained Earnings as per the allocation in the preceding schedule is as follows:

Retained Earnings	$520,000	
Consolidated Retained Earnings		$188,000
Non Controlling Interest		332,000

The opening consolidated Retained Earnings is $11,188,000, the total of Plate's opening Retained Earnings of $11,000,000 and the preceding $188,000 allocation to consolidated Retained Earnings.

Part A - Income Statement   The required consolidated Income Statement would be prepared as follows:

The Plate Company And Subsidiary
Consolidated Income Statement
For The Year Ending December 31, 1998

Total Revenues ($16,500,000 + $7,000,000 - $800,000 - $500,000 - $2,000,000)	$20,200,000
Cost Of Goods Sold ($6,400,000 + $3,400,000 - $2,000,000 + $150,000 - $240,000)	$ 7,710,000
Other Expenses ($3,800,000 + $1,600,000 + $80,000 - $120,000 + $25,000 - $100,000)	5,285,000
Non Controlling Interest - [(.20)($2,000,000 + $100,000 - $150,000 + $240,000)]	438,000
Total Expenses	$13,433,000
Consolidated Net Income	$ 6,767,000

Part B - Statement Of Retained Earnings   The required consolidated Statement Of Retained Earnings would be prepared as follows:

The Plate Company And Subsidiary
Consolidated Statement Of Retained Earnings
For The Year Ending December 31, 1998

Opening Balance	$11,188,000
Consolidated Net Income	6,767,000
Balance Available	$17,955,000
Dividends Declared (Plate Company's Only)	2,000,000
Closing Balance	$15,955,000

Part C - Balance Sheet   The required consolidated Balance Sheet would be prepared as follows:

The Plate Company And Subsidiary
Consolidated Balance Sheet
As At December 31, 1998

Cash ($3,000,000 + $700,000)	$ 3,700,000
Accounts Receivable ($7,500,000 + $2,100,000)	9,600,000
Inventories ($14,300,000 + $5,600,000 + $800,000 - $800,000 - $150,000)	19,750,000
Land ($9,000,000 + $2,500,000 - $400,000 - $500,000)	10,600,000
Plant And Equipment ($26,400,000 + $12,000,000 - $1,400,000)	37,000,000
Accumulated Depreciation ($10,600,000 + $6,500,000 - $3,000,000 + $400,000)	(14,500,000)
Patents ($1,400,000 - $700,000)	700,000
Goodwill ($1,000,000 - $125,000)	875,000
Total Assets	$67,725,000

Current Liabilities ($8,500,000 + $1,200,000)	$ 9,700,000
Long Term Liabilities ($15,000,000	
+ $4,500,000 + $1,200,000 - $600,000)	20,100,000
Non Controlling Interest [(.20)($10,700,000	
- $700,000 - $150,000)]	1,970,000
Common Stock (Plate Company's Only)	20,000,000
Retained Earnings (See Part B Solution)	15,955,000
Total Equities	$67,725,000

Solution to Self-Study Problem Six - 3

Step A - Investment Analysis The analysis of the Prime Company's investment in the Sublime Company would be as follows:

	60 Percent	100 Percent
Investment Cost	$3,000,000	$5,000,000
Book Value	(3,000,000)	(5,000,000)
Differential	$ -0-	$ -0-
Accounts Receivable	60,000	100,000
Plant And Equipment (Net)	240,000	400,000
Goodwill	$ 300,000	$ 500,000

Step A - Investment Elimination Entry The entry to eliminate the Investment In Sublime would be as follows:

No Par Common Stock	$3,000,000	
Retained Earnings	2,000,000	
Goodwill	300,000	
Investment In Sublime		$3,000,000
Non Controlling Interest		2,000,000
Current Receivables		60,000
Plant And Equipment (Net)		240,000

Step B - Adjustment The entry to adjust the fair value change on the Accounts Receivable is as follows:

Current Receivables	$60,000	
Retained Earnings		$60,000

Step B - Adjustment The entry to adjust the fair value change on Plant And Equipment would be as follows:

Plant And Equipment (Net)	$160,000	
Retained Earnings		$160,000

(Annual Adjustment = $240,000/3 = $80,000 Per Year)

Step B - Adjustment The entry to amortize consolidated Goodwill is as follows:

Retained Earnings	$20,000	
Goodwill		$20,000

(Annual Adjustment = $300,000/30 = $10,000 Per Year)

Step B - Elimination   No elimination is required in the preparation of an end of the year Balance Sheet for the upstream profits that were unrealized at the beginning of the year. Sublime's cost for the merchandise that remains in Prime's Inventories is $160,000 ($200,000/1.25) resulting in an unrealized profit of $40,000. The entry to eliminate the unrealized profits of Sublime that are in the ending inventories of Prime is as follows:

Retained Earnings	$40,000	
Inventories		$40,000

Step B - Elimination   The entries to eliminate the unrealized loss on the intercompany sale of Plant And Equipment and the related asset/liability balance are as follows:

Plant And Equipment (Net)	$45,000	
Retained Earnings		$45,000

(Annual Adjustment = $50,000/5 = $10,000 Per Year. The remaining life on December 31, 1998 is 4.5 years)

Current Liabilities (80%)($150,000)	$120,000	
Current Receivables		$120,000

Step B - Elimination   The entries to eliminate the intercompany profit on the sale of Land and the related asset/liability balance are as follows:

Retained Earnings	$1,000,000	
Land		$1,000,000

Current Liabilities	$ 400,000	
Current Receivables		$ 400,000

Long Term Liabilities	$1,200,000	
Long Term Receivables		$1,200,000

Step C - Distribution Schedule   The schedule for the allocation of the balance in the Retained Earnings account of Sublime is as follows:

Sublime's Closing Balance		$5,000,000
Balance At Acquisition		(2,000,000)
Balance Since Acquisition		$3,000,000
Upstream Unrealized Profits:		
Closing Inventories	($40,000)	
Loss On Equipment	45,000	5,000
Adjusted Balance Since Acquisition		$3,005,000
Non Controlling Interest Percent		40%
Non Controlling Interest Since Acquisition		$1,202,000
Available To Controlling Interest		$1,803,000
Accounts Receivable		60,000
Plant And Equipment		160,000
Goodwill		(20,000)
To Consolidated Retained Earnings		$2,003,000

Step C - Distribution Entry   The entry to allocate the remaining balance of Sublime's Retained Earnings would be as follows:

Retained Earnings $3,205,000
    Non Controlling Interest $1,202,000
    Consolidated Retained Earnings   2,003,000

The December 31, 1998 consolidated Retained Earnings would be made up of Prime's $12,000,000, the above allocation of $2,003,000, less the downstream unrealized profit on land of $1,000,000. This gives a total of $13,003,000.

Non Controlling Interest   The Non Controlling Interest shown on the consolidated Balance Sheet consists of the Non Controlling Interest at acquisition of $2,000,000 from the Step A elimination entry and the Non Controlling Interest since acquisition of $1,202,000 that was calculated in the Step C Retained Earnings distribution schedule.

Solution   The required consolidated Balance Sheet is as follows:

The Prime Company And Subsidiary
Consolidated Balance Sheet
As At December 31, 1998

Cash And Current Receivables ($1,600,000 + $1,000,000 - $60,000 + $60,000 - $120,000 - $400,000)	$ 2,080,000
Inventories ($2,400,000 + $1,500,000 - $40,000)	3,860,000
Investment In Sublime ($3,000,000 - $3,000,000)	-0-
Long Term Receivables ($1,500,000 - $1,200,000)	300,000
Plant And Equipment ($14,000,000 + $8,500,000 - $240,000 + $160,000 + $45,000)	22,465,000
Land ($5,000,000 + $2,000,000 - $1,000,000)	6,000,000
Goodwill ($300,000 - $20,000)	280,000
Total Assets	**$34,985,000**

Current Liabilities ($4,500,000 + $2,000,000 - $120,000 - $400,000)	$ 5,980,000
Long Term Liabilities ($5,000,000 + $3,000,000 - $1,200,000)	6,800,000
Non Controlling Interest ($2,000,000 + $1,202,000)	3,202,000
No Par Common Stock (Prime's Only)	6,000,000
Retained Earnings (See Step C)	13,003,000
Total Equities	**$34,985,000**

Solution to Self-Study Problem Six - 4

Investment Analysis For First Purchase   The investment analysis for the first purchase would be as follows:

	20 Percent	100 Percent
Purchase Price	$600,000	$3,000,000
Book Value	(00,000)	(2,500,000)
Differential	$100,000	$ 500,000
Fair Value Decrease on Inventories	40,000	200,000
Fair Value Increase on Plant	(80,000)	(400,000)
Goodwill	$ 60,000	$ 300,000

Investment Analysis For Second Purchase   The investment analysis for the second purchase would be as follows:

	55 Percent	100 Percent
Purchase Price	$1,705,000	$3,100,000
Book Value	(1,540,000)	(2,800,000)
Differential	$ 165,000	$ 300,000
Fair Value Increase on Land	(27,500)	(50,000)
Fair Value Increase on Plant	(110,000)	(200,000)
Fair Value Increase on Liabilities	55,000	100,000
Goodwill	$ 82,500	$ 150,000

While the fact that a subsidiary acquisition occurs in more than one step does not change the general principles involved in the preparation of consolidated financial statements, it does make their application more complex. This is largely related to two factors. First, there will be an allocation of fair values and a goodwill calculation for each step in the acquisition. This will subsequently be reflected in the need to amortize and depreciate all of the various balances arising in the two or more steps required by the acquisition. In addition, the Step A Elimination Entry necessary for each acquisition ignores the fact that there is more than one acquisition. As a result, the combination of the two elimination entries has meaningless results for some accounts, such as Ginko's Common Stock and Retained Earnings and the Non Controlling Interest.

The second complicating factor relates to the calculation of consolidated Retained Earnings. Because the acquisition takes place over a period of time, there is no single figure that can be designated as Retained Earnings since acquisition. This results in the need to calculate the parent's share of post acquisition Retained Earnings for each step in the purchase.

Step B - Adjustment   The entry to adjust the fair value decrease on the inventories at the first acquisition date is as follows:

Inventories	$40,000	
Retained Earnings		$40,000

Step B - Adjustment   The entry to adjust the Plant And Equipment for the depreciation on the fair value changes at both acquisition dates is as follows:

Retained Earnings (7 years)	$56,000	
Retained Earnings (4 years)	62,856	
Other Expenses	23,714	
Plant and Equipment (Net)		$142,570

(Annual Adjustment - First Purchase = $80,000/10 = $8,000)
(Annual Adjustment - Second Purchase = $110,000/7 = $15,714)

Step B - Fair Value Change On Land   No adjustment is required.

Step B - Adjustment   The entry to adjust the interest for the fair value change on the Long Term Liabilities is as follows:

Long Term Liabilities	$13,750	
Other Expenses		$ 2,750
Retained Earnings (4 years)		11,000

(Annual Adjustment = $55,000/20 = $2,750)

Step B - Adjustment   The entry to record the Goodwill amortization is as follows:

Retained Earnings (7 years)	$21,000	
Retained Earnings (4 years)	16,500	
Other Expenses	7,125	
Goodwill		$44,625

(Annual Adjustment - First Purchase = $60,000/20 = $3,000)
(Annual Adjustment - Second Purchase = $82,500/20 = $4,125)

Step B - Elimination The entry to eliminate the unrealized loss on the intercompany sale of the machine is as follows:

Plant and Equipment (Net)	$25,000	
Other Expenses and Losses	25,000	
Retained Earnings		$50,000

(Annual Adjustment = $100,000/4 = $25,000)

Step B - Elimination The entry to eliminate the unrealized upstream loss and receivable and payable resulting from the intercompany sale of land is as follows:

Land	$43,000	
Other Expenses and Losses		$43,000
Current Liabilities	$37,500	
Current Receivables		$37,500

Step B - Elimination The entry to eliminate the intercompany dividend payment is as follows:

Other Revenues	$75,000	
Non Controlling Interest (Balance Sheet)	25,000	
Dividends Declared		$100,000

Step B - Elimination The entry to eliminate intercompany sales of merchandise is as follows:

Sales of Merchandise (Downstream)	$550,000	
Sales of Merchandise (Upstream)	190,000	
Cost Of Goods Sold		$740,000

Step B - Elimination The entry to eliminate unrealized intercompany profits in the closing inventories and the receivable and payable resulting from the merchandise purchases is as follows:

Cost Of Goods Sold (Downstream)	$110,000	
Cost Of Goods Sold (Upstream)	27,000	
Inventories		$137,000
Current Liabilities	$175,000	
Current Receivables		$175,000

Step B - Elimination The entry to eliminate the unrealized intercompany profits in the opening inventories is as follows:

Retained Earnings (Downstream)	$75,000	
Retained Earnings (Upstream)	12,000	
Cost Of Goods Sold		$87,000

Step C - Distribution Schedule The allocation of the opening balance in the Retained Earnings account of the Ginko Company would be as follows:

Balance at December 31, 1993		$1,800,000
Balance at December 31, 1990		1,500,000
Retained Earnings Realized Before Second Purchase		$ 300,000
Percentage Ownership		20%
To Consolidated Retained Earnings		$ 60,000

Balance at January 1, 1998		$2,200,000
Balance at Second Purchase		(1,800,000)
Balance Since Second Acquisition		$ 400,000
Upstream Unrealized (Profits) Losses:		
On Machine Sale	$ 50,000	
Opening Inventories	(12,000)	38,000
Realized Profits Since Acquisition		$ 438,000
Non Controlling Interest Percent		25%
Non Controlling Interest		$ 109,500

Available To Controlling Interest		$ 328,500
Inventory Realization		40,000
Plant And Equipment Depreciation:		
First Purchase (7 years @ $8,000)		(56,000)
Second Purchase (4 years @ $15,714)		(62,856)
Long Term Liability Amortization (4 years @ $2,750)		11,000
Goodwill Amortization:		
First Purchase (7 years @ $3,000)		(21,000)
Second Purchase (4 years @ $4,125)		(16,500)
To Consolidated Retained Earnings		$ 223,144

Step C - Distribution Entry The entry to distribute the Ginko Company's Retained Earnings based on the allocation in the preceding schedule is as follows:

Retained Earnings	$392,644	
Consolidated Retained Earnings		$ 60,000
Consolidated Retained Earnings		223,144
Non Controlling Interest		109,500

The required consolidated Income Statement would be prepared as follows:

The Rosebud Company And Subsidiary
Consolidated Income Statement
For The Year Ending December 31, 1998

Sales Of Merchandise ($5,000,000 + $2,000,000 - $550,000 - $190,000)	$6,260,000
Other Revenues ($200,000 + $100,000 - $75,000)	225,000
Total Revenues	$6,485,000
Cost Of Goods Sold ($2,500,000 + $800,000 - $550,000 - $190,000 + $137,000 - $87,000)	$2,610,000
Other Expenses and Losses ($1,000,000 + $900,000+ $8,000 + $15,714 - $2,750 + $3,000 + $4,125 + $25,000 - $43,000)	1,910,089
Non Controlling Interest (25%)($400,000 - $25,000 + $12,000 - $27,000)	90,000
Total Expenses	$4,610,089
Consolidated Net Income	$1,874,911

The required consolidated Statement Of Retained Earnings would be prepared as follows:

The Rosebud Company And Subsidiary
Consolidated Statement Of Retained Earnings
For The Year Ending December 31, 1998

Opening Balance	$2,708,144
Consolidated Net Income	1,874,911
Balance Available	$4,583,055
Dividends Declared (Rosebud Company's Only)	600,000
Closing Balance	$3,983,055

The Opening Consolidated Retained Earnings balance consists of the opening balance for the Rosebud Company of $2,500,000 plus the $60,000 and the $223,144 from the Ginko Company less the opening downstream unrealized inventory profits of $75,000.

The required consolidated Balance Sheet would be prepared as follows:

The Rosebud Company And Subsidiary
Consolidated Balance Sheet
As At December 31, 1998

Cash and Current Receivables ($500,000 + $600,000 - $37,500 - $175,000)	$ 887,500
Inventories ($600,000 + $1,200,000 - $40,000 + $40,000 - $137,000)	1,663,000
Investment in Ginko ($2,305,000 - $600,000 -$1,705,000)	-0-
Land ($795,000 + $500,000 + $27,500 + $43,000)	1,365,500
Plant And Equipment ($2,900,000 + $2,200,000 + $80,000 + $110,000 + $25,000 - $142,570)	5,172,430
Goodwill ($60,000 + $82,500 - $44,625)	97,875
Total Assets	$9,186,305
Current Liabilities ($500,000 + $400,000 - $37,500 - $175,000)	$ 687,500
Long Term Liabilities ($1,000,000 + $600,000 + $55,000 - $13,750)	1,641,250
Non Controlling Interest (See Following)	874,500
Common Stock - No Par	2,000,000
Retained Earnings (See Statement)	3,983,055
Total Equities	$9,186,305

Non Controlling Interest   The Non Controlling Interest can be calculated as follows:

Book Value of Ginko - December 31, 1998	$3,500,000
Unrealized Upstream Loss on Machine	25,000
Unrealized Upstream Profits in Closing Inventories	(27,000)
Total	$3,498,000
Non Controlling Interest Percent	25%
Non Controlling Interest	$ 874,500

An alternate calculation is as follows:

Non Controlling Interest - December 31, 1993	
(25%)($2,800,000)	$700,000
Non Controlling Interest Subsequent to Second Acquisition	109,500
Non Controlling Interest in Consolidated Net Income	90,000
Non Controlling Interest in Ginko's Dividends Declared	(25,000)
Non Controlling Interest	$874,500

Solution to Self-Study Problem Six - 5

Step A - Investment Analysis   The analysis of the Pork Company's investment in Salt is as follows:

	80 Percent	100 Percent
Investment Cost	$1,000,000	$1,250,000
Book Value	(800,000)	(1,000,000)
Differential	$ 200,000	$ 250,000
Bonds Payable	(80,000)	(100,000)
Goodwill	$ 120,000	$ 150,000

Step B - Bonds Payable Adjustment   The amortization of the fair value change on the Bonds Payable will be charged to income at the rate of $8,000 per year ($80,000/10).

Step B - Goodwill Amortization   The amortization of the Goodwill will be charged to income at the rate of $4,000 per year ($120,000/30).

Step B - Realization Of The Gain On Building Sale   The total unrealized gain on the intercompany sale of the building was $375,000 ($4,500,000 - $4,125,000). This will be realized as a reduction in Other Expenses at the rate of $25,000 per year ($375,000/15).

Part A   The consolidated Income Statement is as follows:

The Pork Company And Subsidiary
Consolidated Income Statement
For The Year Ending December 31, 1998

Sales ($600,000 + $400,000)	$1,000,000
Cost Of Goods Sold ($250,000 + $300,000)	$ 550,000
Other Expenses ($300,000 + $150,000 + $8,000 - $25,000)	433,000
Goodwill Amortization	4,000
Non Controlling Interest (.20)(- $50,000 + $25,000)	(5,000)
Total Expenses	$ 982,000
Income Before Extraordinary Items	$ 18,000
Extraordinary Gain (Pork's)	100,000
Extraordinary Loss (.80)($200,000)	(160,000)
Consolidated Net Income (Loss)	($ 42,000)

Part B   If we assume that the Pork Company uses the equity method to account for its investment in Salt, there are two alternate ways to adjust for the effects of the realization of the intercompany gain in its Income Statement. Paragraph 3050.15 of the *CICA Handbook* describes these alternatives as follows:

The elimination of an unrealized intercompany gain or loss has the same effect on net income whether the consolidation or equity method is used. However, in consolidated financial statements, the elimination of a gain or a loss may affect sales and cost of sales otherwise to be reported. In the application of the equity method, the gain or loss is eliminated by adjustment of investment income from the investee or by separate provision in the investor's financial statements, as is appropriate in the circumstances.

The solution which follows is based on an adjustment of Investment Income rather than disclosure through a separate provision. The Income Statement of the Pork Company would be as follows:

Pork Company
Income Statement
For The Year Ending December 31, 1998

Sales	$600,000
Cost Of Goods Sold	$250,000
Other Expenses	300,000
Investment Loss - Ordinary (Note One)	32,000
Total Expenses	$582,000
Income Before Extraordinary Items	$ 18,000
Extraordinary Gain	100,000
Investment Loss - Extraordinary (.80)($200,000)	(160,000)
Net Income (Loss)	($ 42,000)

Note One The Ordinary Investment Loss would be calculated as follows:

Salt's Ordinary Income (Loss)	($50,000)
Realization Of Intercompany Gain	25,000
Adjusted Loss	($25,000)
Pork's Ownership Percent	80%
Pork's Share Of The Loss	($20,000)
Bonds Payable Amortization	(8,000)
Goodwill Amortization	(4,000)
Ordinary Investment Loss	($32,000)

Pork's Net Loss of $42,000 when the equity method is used is equal to the previously calculated consolidated Net Loss. This result is a reflection of a requirement stated in Paragraph 3050.08 of the *CICA Handbook* as follows:

> *Investment income as calculated by the equity method should be that amount necessary to increase or decrease the investor's income to that which would have been recognized if the results of the investee's operations had been consolidated with those of the investor.*

Solution to Self-Study Problem Six - 6

Investment Analysis The problem implies that there are no fair value changes in Plantee's identifiable assets and liabilities since the entire excess of the purchase price over 75 percent of the carrying values of the net assets is to be allocated to goodwill.

Goodwill Amortization The amortization of Goodwill arising from this business combination will be charged to income at the rate of $5,000 per year ($100,000/20).

Intercompany Merchandise Sales The intercompany merchandise sales must be eliminated from the consolidated Income Statement, but will have no effect on the Income Statement of Plantor if it does not consolidate its Investment in Plantee. The intercompany merchandise sales total $150,000 ($100,000 downstream + $50,000 upstream). Adjustments must be made in both cases for the unrealized inventory profits of $16,000 ([40%][$15,000] downstream + [50%][$20,000] upstream)

Realization Of The Loss On Equipment The total unrealized loss on the upstream intercompany sale of the equipment was $35,000 ($100,000 - $135,000). This will be realized as an increase in Other Expenses at the rate of $7,000 per year ($35,000/5).

Part A - Consolidated Income Statement The consolidated Income Statement of the Plantor Company and its subsidiary, the Plantee Company is as follows:

Plantor Company And Subsidiary
Consolidated Income Statement
For The Year Ending December 31, 1998

Sales ($500,000 + $200,000 - $150,000)	$550,000
Cost of Goods Sold ($300,000 + $100,000	
- $150,000 + $16,000)	$266,000
Other Expenses ($140,000 + $76,000 + $7,000)	223,000
Goodwill Amortization	5,000
Total Expenses	$494,000
Combined Income	$ 56,000
Non Controlling Interest ([25%][$24,000 - $10,000 - $7,000])	1,750
Consolidated Income Before Extraordinary Items	$ 54,250
Extraordinary Gain ([75%][$6,000])	4,500
Consolidated Net Income	$ 58,750

Part B - Plantor's Income Statement Without Consolidation If we assume that the Plantor Company uses the equity method to account for its investment in Plantee, there are two alternate ways to adjust for the effects of unrealized intercompany profits in its Income Statement. Paragraph 3050.15 of the *CICA Handbook* describes these alternatives as follows:

> The elimination of an unrealized intercompany gain or loss has the same effect on net income whether the consolidation or equity method is used. However, in consolidated financial statements, the elimination of a gain or a loss may affect sales and cost of sales otherwise to be reported. In the application of the equity method, the gain or loss is eliminated by adjustment of investment income from the investee or by separate provision in the investor's financial statements, as is appropriate in the circumstances.

The solution which follows is based on an adjustment of Investment Income rather than disclosure through a separate provision.

Plantor Company
Income Statement
For The Year Ending December 31, 1998

Sales	$500,000
Cost of Goods Sold	$300,000
Other Expenses	140,000
Investment Loss - Ordinary ([75%][$24,000 - $10,000 - $7,000] - $6,000 - $5,000)	5,750
Total Expenses and Losses	$445,750
Income Before Extraordinary Items	$ 54,250
Investment Income - Extraordinary (.75)($6,000)	4,500
Net Income	$ 58,750

If the alternative form of disclosure had been used, one possibility would be to have Investment Income of $250 and the $6,000 downstream unrealized profit disclosed as a separate deduction from the Plantor Company's income.

Note that the equity method Net Income of Plantor of $58,750 is equal to the consolidated Net Income calculated in Part A. This result is a reflection of a requirement stated in Paragraph 3050.08 of the *CICA Handbook* as follows:

> *Investment income as calculated by the equity method should be that amount necessary to increase or decrease the investor's income to that which would have been recognized if the results of the investee's operations had been consolidated with those of the investor.*

Solution to Self-Study Problem Six - 7

Part A - Investment Analysis   The fair value of the net assets of Numa Inc. is $1,000,000 ($100,000 + $900,000). As both investor Companies have paid a purchase price equal to their proportionate share of Numa Inc.'s fair value, there is no goodwill arising from this acquisition. In addition, since the difference between the fair value and carrying value of the non current assets arises from Land, there is no amortization of this fair value increase.

Part A - Proportionate Consolidation Balance Sheet   Under the Recommendations of Section 3055 of the *CICA Handbook*, Sentinel Resources Ltd. would have to use proportionate consolidation to account for its investment in Numa. Given this requirement, on April 1, 1997, the consolidated Balance Sheet of Sentinel Resources and its investee Numa Inc., is as follows:

Net Current Assets ($1,050,000 + [45%][$100,000])	$1,095,000
Investment in Numa ($450,000 - $450,000)	-0-
Other Non Current Assets ($5,300,000 + [45%][$900,000])	5,705,000
Total Assets	$6,800,000
Common Stock - No Par (Sentinel's Only)	$4,000,000
Retained Earnings (Sentinel's Only)	2,800,000
Total Equities	$6,800,000

Part B - Proportionate Consolidation Income Statement   Under the Recommendations of Section 3055, intercompany gains and losses can only be recognized to the extent of the interests of the other non affiliated venturers. Given this general provision, Sentinel would have to remove its $36,000 ([45%][$175,000 - $95,000]) percent share of the $80,000 loss resulting from Numa's sale of Equipment to Sentinel. With respect to the remaining $44,000 or 55 percent of the loss, it would be removed from the consolidated Income Statement as a result of applying proportionate consolidation procedures (these procedures remove the interests of other non affiliated venturers from all of the joint venture's accounts). Taken together, these procedures remove 100 percent of the upstream loss from the proportionate consolidation Income Statement. Note, however, only 45 percent of the loss would be removed from the equipment balance in the proportionate consolidation Balance Sheet. This difference reflects the fact that the equipment is on the books of the venturer and would not be reduced by proportionate consolidation procedures.

Given this analysis, the proportionate consolidation Income Statement of Sentinel Resources and its investee Numa Inc., is as follows:

Revenues ($7,800,000 + [45%][$660,000])	$8,097,000
Expenses and Losses ($6,400,000 + [45%][$480,000 - $80,000])	6,580,000
Consolidated Net Income	$1,517,000

When the intercompany transaction results in a loss, Section 3055 indicates that this may serve as evidence of a reduction in the net realizable value of the asset. In these circumstances, the venturer should recognize the full amount of the loss. If this approach is taken here, the Expenses And Losses would be $6,616,000 ($6,400,000 + [45%][$480,000]) and consolidated Net Income would be $1,481,000 ($8,097,000 - $6,616,000).

Part C - Proportionate Consolidation Income Statement   In this case we have an upstream profit of $76,000 ($390,000 - $314,000). The Recommendations of Section 3055 will require that Molar's 55 percent share of this intercompany transaction be removed from consolidated revenues and expenses. In addition, proportionate consolidation procedures will require the removal of the remaining 45 percent that reflects the interest of the other non affiliated venturers. The resulting proportionate consolidation Income Statement would be as follows:

Revenues ($9,600,000 + [55%][$660,000 - $390,000])	$9,748,500
Expenses And Losses ($8,500,000 + [55%][$480,000 - $314,000])	8,591,300
Consolidated Net Income	$1,157,200

Note again that, in upstream transactions such as this, only 55 percent of the gain would be removed from the inventory balance on the books of Molar.

Solution to Self-Study Problem Seven - 1

Investment Analysis - Cost Method   While in this problem the Pip Company uses the equity method to carry its Investment in Squeak account, it will be useful to analyze the initial cost of the investment and the subsequent write offs of fair value changes and goodwill.

	75 Percent	100 Percent
Investment Cost	$4,875,000	$6,500,000
Book Value at Acquisition	(4,500,000)	(6,000,000)
Differential	$ 375,000	$ 500,000
Fair Value Increase on Government Bonds	(60,000)	(80,000)
Fair Value Increase on Liabilities	150,000	200,000
Fair Value Decrease on Equipment	375,000	500,000
Goodwill	$ 840,000	$1,120,000

Write Off Of Fair Value Changes And Goodwill   The fair value change on the long term Government Bonds would have no effect on income. Amortization of the fair value change on the Long Term Liabilities would reduce expenses by an amount of $15,000 per year ($150,000/10) while depreciation of the fair value change on the Plant and Equipment would reduce expenses by $75,000 per year ($375,000/5). Goodwill amortization would be $28,000 per year ($840,000/30).

Step A - Investment Analysis   The analysis of the Pip Company's Investment in Squeak as at December 31, 1998, accounted for by the equity method is as follows:

Investment At Equity	$6,398,000
Book Value on January 1, 1998 (75%)($7,300,000)	(5,475,000)
Differential	$ 923,000
Fair Value Increase on Government Bonds	(60,000)
Unamortized Fair Value Increase on Liabilities	105,000
Undepreciated Fair Value Decrease on Equipment	150,000
Investment Income	(512,000)
Squeak's Dividends Declared (75%)($200,000)	150,000
Goodwill, January 1, 1998	$ 756,000

Step A - Investment Elimination   The journal entry that would be required to eliminate the Pip Company's Investment in Squeak would be as follows:

Common Stock - No Par	$5,000,000	
Retained Earnings January 1, 1998	2,300,000	
Long Term Government Bonds	60,000	
Investment Income (Exclusive of		
Intercompany Dividends)	362,000	
Goodwill	756,000	
Investment In Squeak		$6,398,000
Non Controlling Interest January 1, 1998		1,825,000
Long Term Liabilities		105,000
Plant and Equipment (Net)		150,000

Step B - Amortization Of Fair Value Change On Long Term Liabilities   The entry to record the decrease in Other Expenses (interest expense) related to the fair value change on the Liabilities is as follows:

Long Term Liabilities	$15,000	
Other Expenses		$15,000

Step B - Depreciation Of The Fair Value Change On Equipment   The entry to record the reduction in Other Expenses (depreciation expense) related to the fair value change on the equipment is as follows:

| Plant and Equipment (Net) | $75,000 | |
| Other Expenses | | $75,000 |

Step B - Goodwill Amortization   The entry to record the amortization of the Goodwill recorded in this business combination is as follows:

| Other Expenses | $28,000 | |
| Goodwill | | $28,000 |

Step B - Intercompany Dividends   The entry to eliminate the intercompany dividends declared by Squeak is as follows:

Investment Income	$150,000	
Non Controlling Interest	50,000	
Dividends Declared		$200,000

Step B - Intercompany Merchandise Sales   Two entries are required here. The first will eliminate the total intercompany sales of $500,000 ($400,000 downstream + $100,000 upstream) while the second will eliminate the intercompany asset and liability of $250,000 ($200,000 downstream and $50,000 upstream). The entries are as follows:

| Sales | $500,000 | |
| Cost of Goods Sold | | $500,000 |

| Current Liabilities | $250,000 | |
| Cash and Current Receivables | | $250,000 |

Step C - Distribution Of Retained Earnings   As in this problem, the investment is carried by the equity method, there is no January 1, 1998 balance in the Retained Earnings of Squeak that requires distribution at this point. That is, the entire balance in this account was eliminated in the Step A Investment Elimination Entry.

Part A - Verification Of Investment In Squeak   The $6,398,000 in the Investment in Squeak account can be verified as follows:

Investment Cost	$4,875,000
Equity Pickup ([75%][$2,700,000 - $1,000,000])	1,275,000
Liabilities Amortization (4 years @ $15,000)	60,000
Plant Depreciation (4 years @ $75,000)	300,000
Goodwill Amortization (4 years @ $28,000)	(112,000)
Investment in Squeak, December 31, 1998	$6,398,000

Part A - Verification Of Pip's Investment Income   The $512,000 of Investment Income on the books of Pip arising from the accounting of its Investment in Squeak by the equity method can be verified as follows:

Pip's Share of Squeak's Income ([75%][$600,000])	$450,000
Amortization of Fair Value Increase on Liabilities	15,000
Depreciation of Fair Value Decrease On Plant	75,000
Goodwill Amortization	(28,000)
Investment Income for 1998	$512,000

Part B - Pip's Retained Earnings Under The Cost Method   If the Pip Company had carried its Investment In Squeak using the cost method, its Retained Earnings balance would have been $9,350,000 as shown in the following schedule:

Pip's Opening Retained Earnings Using Equity Method	$10,511,000
Equity Pickup Included ([75%][$2,300,000 -$1,000,000])	(975,000)
Liability Amortization Added (3 years @ $15,000)	(45,000)
Plant Depreciation Added (3 years @ $75,000)	(225,000)
Goodwill Amortization Deducted (3 years @ $28,000)	84,000
Retained Earnings, Using Cost Method - January 1, 1998	$ 9,350,000

Part C - Consolidated Income Statement　Using the Step B adjustments, the required consolidated Income Statement of the Pip Company and its subsidiary, the Squeak Company is as follows:

Sales ($14,000,000 + $3,030,000 - $500,000)	$16,530,000
Investment Income ($512,000 + $20,000 - 　$362,000 - $150,000)	20,000
Total Revenues	$16,550,000
Cost of Goods Sold ($7,000,000 + $1,850,000 - $500,000)	$ 8,350,000
Other Expenses ($1,062,000 + $600,000 - $15,000 　- $75,000 + $28,000)	1,600,000
Total Expenses	$ 9,950,000
Combined Income	$ 6,600,000
Non Controlling Interest [(25%)($600,000)]	150,000
Consolidated Net Income	$ 6,450,000

The consolidated Net Income is equal to the income of the Pip Company since the Investment in Squeak is being carried by the equity method.

Part C - Consolidated Statement Of Retained Earnings　The required consolidated Statement of Retained Earnings of the Pip Company and its subsidiary, the Squeak Company is as follows:

Opening Balance (Pip's Book Value)	$10,511,000
Consolidated Net Income for 1998	6,450,000
Balance Available	$16,961,000
Less Dividends Declared (Pip's Only)	400,000
Closing Consolidated Retained Earnings	$16,561,000

Part C - Consolidated Balance Sheet　The required consolidated Balance Sheet for the Pip Company and its subsidiary, the Squeak Company, is as follows:

Cash and Current Receivables ($740,000 + $400,000 　- $250,000)	$ 890,000
Inventories ($3,400,000 + $2,100,000)	5,500,000
Long Term Government Bonds ($150,000 + $60,000)	210,000
Investment in Squeak ($6,398,000 - $6,398,000)	-0-
Plant and Equipment (Net) ($13,500,000 + $6,400,000 　- $150,000 + $75,000)	19,825,000
Goodwill ($756,000 - $28,000)	728,000
Total Assets	$27,153,000

Current Liabilities ($977,000 + $350,000 - $250,000)	$ 1,077,000
Long Term Liabilities ($1,500,000 + $1,000,000	
+ $105,000 - $15,000)	2,590,000
Non Controlling Interest ([25%][$7,700,000])	1,925,000
No Par Common Stock (Pip's Only)	5,000,000
Retained Earnings	16,561,000
Total Equities	$27,153,000

Solution to Self-Study Problem Seven - 2

Part A - Solution   The calculations for the write off of the fair value changes and goodwill were presented in the investment at cost version of this problem. The investment analysis and relevant journal entries are repeated here for your convenience.

	60 Percent	100 Percent
Investment Cost	$3,000,000	$5,000,000
Book Value	(3,000,000)	(5,000,000)
Differential	$ -0-	$ -0-
Accounts Receivable	60,000	100,000
Plant And Equipment (Net)	240,000	400,000
Goodwill	$ 300,000	$ 500,000

Current Receivables	$ 60,000	
Retained Earnings		$ 60,000
Plant And Equipment (Net)	$160,000	
Retained Earnings		$160,000
(Annual Adjustment = $240,000/3 = $80,000 Per Year)		
Retained Earnings	$ 20,000	
Goodwill		$ 20,000
(Annual Adjustment = $300,000/30 = $10,000 Per Year)		

The balance in the Investment In Sublime Company account can be verified as follows:

Investment Cost		$3,000,000
Equity Pickup:		
Earnings Since Acquisition	$4,000,000	
Closing Upstream Inventory Profits	(30,000)	
Unrealized Loss on Machine Sale	25,000	
Realized Earnings Since Acquisition	$3,995,000	
Controlling Interest	60%	2,397,000
Accounts Receivable Realization		60,000
Plant And Equipment Depreciation		
(Totally Depreciated)		240,000
Goodwill Amortization (4 Years @ $10,000)		(40,000)
Land Profit		-0-
Downstream Closing Inventory Profits		
($420,000 - $300,000)		(120,000)
Downstream Equipment Sale ($60,000 - $20,000)		(40,000)
Investment At Equity		$5,497,000

Step A - Investment Analysis   The analysis of Prime's investment in Sublime would be as follows:

Investment At Equity	$5,497,000
Book Value At December 31, 1998 [(.60)($3,000,000	
+ $6,000,000)]	(5,400,000)
Differential	$ 97,000
Upstream Adjustments:	
Profits in Closing Inventories [(.60)($30,000)]	18,000
Loss on Machine Sale [(.60)($25,000)]	(15,000)
Downstream Adjustments:	
Closing Inventories	120,000
Profit On Equipment Sale	40,000
Goodwill	$ 260,000

At this point all of the initial fair value changes have been taken into income and would no longer be reflected in the balance that is found in the Investment In Sublime account.

Step A - Investment Elimination Entry   The entry required to eliminate the Prime Company's investment in Sublime would be as follows:

No Par Common Stock	$3,000,000	
Retained Earnings	6,000,000	
Plant And Equipment (Net)	25,000	
Goodwill	260,000	
Investment In Sublime		$5,497,000
Inventories ($30,000 + $120,000)		150,000
Plant And Equipment (Net)		40,000
Non Controlling Interest		3,598,000

The Non Controlling Interest credit is 40 percent of the $9,000,000 book value of Sublime, adjusted downward by $30,000 for unrealized profits in the closing inventories of Prime and upward for the $25,000 remaining unrealized loss on the machine.

Step B - Elimination   The entry to eliminate the intercompany asset/liability balance from sales is as follows:

Current Liabilities	$420,000	
Current Receivables		$420,000

Step B - Elimination   Since the land has been sold outside the consolidated entity, the downstream profit on the land sale has been realized and there is no need for any adjustment of the intercompany profit. The entries to eliminate the remaining current and long term liabilities resulting from the intercompany sale of land are as follows:

Current Liabilities	$400,000	
Current Receivables		$400,000
Long Term Liabilities	$400,000	
Long Term Receivables		$400,000

Step B - Elimination   The entry to eliminate the intercompany Dividends Payable is as follows:

Dividends Payable	$180,000	
Current Receivables		$180,000

Part B - Solution   The required consolidated Balance Sheet would be prepared as follows:

The Prime Company And Subsidiary
Consolidated Balance Sheet
As At December 31, 2000

Cash And Current Receivables ($2,003,000 + $1,000,000 - $420,000 - $400,000 - $180,000)	$ 2,003,000
Inventories ($3,200,000 + $2,000,000 - $150,000)	5,050,000
Investment In Sublime ($5,497,000 - $5,497,000)	-0-
Long Term Receivables ($800,000 + $1,500,000 - $400,000)	1,900,000
Plant And Equipment - Net ($17,000,000 + $8,000,000 + $25,000 - $40,000)	24,985,000
Land	5,000,000
Goodwill	260,000
Total Assets	$39,198,000
Current Liabilities ($2,503,000 + $1,200,000 - $420,000 - $400,000)	$ 2,883,000
Dividends Payable ($300,000 - $180,000)	120,000
Long Term Liabilities ($8,500,000 + $2,000,000 - $400,000)	10,100,000
Non Controlling Interest (Step A Elimination)	3,598,000
Par Common Stock (Prime's Only)	6,000,000
Retained Earnings	16,497,000
Total Equities	$39,198,000

Note that the consolidated Retained Earnings is simply that of the Prime Company. This will always be the case when the equity method is applied.

Solution to Self-Study Problem Seven - 3

Step A Investment Analysis   The analysis of the January 1, 1997 investment in Smelt Company would be as follows:

	80 Percent	100 Percent
Investment Cost	$800,000	$1,000,000
Book Value	(520,000)	(650,000)
Differential	$280,000	$ 350,000
Fair Value Change On Land	(40,000)	(50,000)
Fair Value Change On Equipment	(140,000)	(175,000)
Goodwill	$100,000	$ 125,000

In the presentation of the information in this problem the book value at acquisition was not provided. It was derived above by noting that $280,000 of the purchase price represented an excess of cost over book value and, therefore, 80 percent of book value must be equal to $520,000. This gives the total book value of $650,000. Smelt's Retained Earnings balance at January 1, 1998 is $340,000. Since the increase in Retained Earnings in 1997 consisted of Net Income of $120,000 less dividends of $20,000, Retained Earnings at January 1, 1997 equalled $240,000 and Smelt's Common Stock equalled $410,000.

Step A Elimination Entry   The entry to eliminate Pelt's investment in Smelt is as follows:

Common Stock	$410,000	
Retained Earnings	240,000	
Land	40,000	
Equipment	140,000	
Goodwill	100,000	
Investment In Smelt		$800,000
Non Controlling Interest		130,000

Step B Adjustment   The entry to record the depreciation on the fair value change for Equipment is as follows:

Depreciation Expense	$20,000	
Retained Earnings	20,000	
Equipment (Net)		$40,000

(Annual Adjustment = $140,000/7 = $20,000)

Step B Adjustment   No adjustment would be required with respect to the fair value change on the Land.

Step B Adjustment   The entry to record the amortization of Goodwill is as follows:

Goodwill Amortization Expense	$4,000	
Retained Earnings	4,000	
Goodwill		$8,000

(Annual Adjustment = $100,000/25 = $4,000)

Step B Elimination   The entry to eliminate the intercompany management fees is as follows:

| Miscellaneous Revenues | $21,000 | |
| Operating Expenses | | $21,000 |

Step B Elimination   The entry to eliminate intercompany sales cannot be made as this problem does not provide the 1998 information on the amount of such sales. However, since only a computation of consolidated Net Income is required, this entry is not needed.

Step B Elimination   The entry to eliminate the intercompany profits in the closing inventories is as follows:

| Cost Of Goods Sold | $32,000 | |
| Inventories | | $32,000 |

($24,000 Upstream + $8,000 Downstream)

Step B Elimination   The entry to eliminate the intercompany profits in the opening inventories is as follows:

| Retained Earnings | $30,000 | |
| Cost Of Goods Sold | | $30,000 |

($20,000 Upstream + $10,000 Downstream)

Intercompany Bond Sale   The required information for dealing with the intercompany bond holdings can be calculated as follows:

Liability - January 1, 1998 [(.60)($420,000)]	$252,000
Asset	224,000
Total Gain	$ 28,000

This total gain will be amortized over five years at a rate of $5,600 per year.

Smelt's Carrying Value	$252,000
Par Value	240,000
Smelt's Share Of Gain	$ 12,000

Smelt's share of the gain will be amortized over five years at a rate of $2,400 per year.

Par Value	$240,000
Pelt's Carrying Value	224,000
Pelt's Share Of Gain	$ 16,000

Pelt's share of the gain will be amortized over five years at a rate of $3,200 per year.

Step B Elimination   The entry required to eliminate all aspects of the intercompany bond holding at December 31, 1998 is as follows:

Bonds Payable - Par (60%)($400,000)	$240,000	
Bonds Payable - Premium (60%)($16,000)	9,600	
Interest Revenue	17,600	
Bond Investment ($224,000 + $3,200)		$227,200
Interest Expense		12,000
Net Income - Pelt		16,000
Net Income - Smelt		12,000

The difference between the Interest Revenue of $17,600 ([$240,000][6%] + $3,200) and the Interest Expense of $12,000 ([60%][$400,000][6%] - $2,400) is equal to the annual realization of the total gain for the consolidated entity.

Step C Distribution Schedule   The schedule to allocate the balance in the Smelt Company's Retained Earnings account is as follows:

Smelt's Balance At January 1, 1998	$340,000
Balance At Acquisition	(240,000)
Balance Since Acquisition	$100,000
Upstream Profits In Opening Inventories	(20,000)
Realized Profits Since Acquisition	$ 80,000
Non Controlling Interest Percent	20%
Non Controlling Interest	$ 16,000
Available To The Controlling Interest	$ 64,000
Equipment Depreciation	(20,000)
Goodwill Amortization	(4,000)
To Consolidated Retained Earnings	$ 40,000

Step C Distribution Entry   The entry to distribute the Retained Earnings of Smelt is as follows:

Retained Earnings	$56,000	
Non Controlling Interest		$16,000
Consolidated Retained Earnings		40,000

Part A Solution The required computation of consolidated Net Income is as follows:

Pelt's Net Income		$160,000
Intercompany Dividends		(16,000)
Equity Pickup:		
Smelt's Net Loss	($60,000)	
Unrealized Opening Inventory Profits	20,000	
Unrealized Closing Inventory Profits	(24,000)	
Gain On Bonds (Smelt's)	12,000	
Amortization Of Smelt's Bond Gain	(2,400)	(54,400)
Downstream Unrealized Profits:		
On Opening Inventories		10,000
On Closing Inventories		(8,000)
Gain On Bonds (Pelt's)		16,000
Amortization Of Gain On Bonds (Pelt's)		(3,200)
Depreciation On Fair Value Change		(20,000)
Goodwill Amortization		(4,000)
Income Before The Non Controlling Interest		$ 80,400
(Negative) Non Controlling Interest [(.20)($54,400)]		10,880
Consolidated Net Income		$ 91,280

Part B Solution The closing balance in consolidated Retained Earnings is $2,481,280. This can be calculated by taking the opening balance in consolidated Retained Earnings of $2,430,000 ($2,400,000 - $10,000 + $40,000), adding consolidated Net Income of $91,280, and subtracting Pelt's Dividends of $40,000. This required balance can also be calculated directly as per the following schedule:

Pelt's December 31, 1998 Balance		$2,520,000
Equity Pickup:		
Retained Earnings Since Acquisition	$20,000	
Unrealized Closing Inventory Profits	(24,000)	
Gain On Bonds (Smelt's Share)	12,000	
Amortization Of Gain On Bonds	(2,400)	
Realized Earnings	$ 5,600	
Controlling Interest Share	80%	4,480
Equipment Depreciation (2 Years At $20,000)		(40,000)
Closing Downstream Unrealized Inventory Profits		(8,000)
Goodwill Amortization (2 Years At $4,000)		(8,000)
Gain On Bonds (Pelt's Share)		16,000
Amortization Of Gain On Bonds (Pelt's)		(3,200)
Consolidated Retained Earnings - December 31, 1998		$2,481,280

The preceding solution has used all of the usual steps in the consolidation procedures developed in our material. However, this is an excellent example of the type of problem where the use of these procedures is an inefficient way of arriving at a solution. Clearly, the direct calculation of the information required would be much less time consuming.

Solution to Self-Study Problem Seven - 4

Step A Investment Analysis   The analysis of the Above Company's investment in the Center Company is as follows:

	70 Percent	100 Percent
Investment Cost	$4,000,000	$5,714,286
Book Value	(3,500,000)	(5,000,000)
Differential	$ 500,000	$ 714,286
Plant And Equipment	(210,000)	(300,000)
Goodwill	$ 290,000	$ 414,286

Based on this analysis, we would record at acquisition an additional $210,000 in consolidated Plant And Equipment and $290,000 in consolidated Goodwill. This would result in increased Depreciation Expense on Plant And Equipment of $10,500 per year ($210,000/20) and Goodwill Amortization Expense of $29,000 per year ($290,000/10).

Step A Investment Analysis   The analysis of the Center Company's investment in the Below Company is as follows:

	60 Percent	100 Percent
Investment Cost	$2,000,000	$3,333,333
Book Value	(1,800,000)	(3,000,000)
Differential	$ 200,000	$ 333,333
Plant And Equipment	300,000	500,000
Goodwill	$ 500,000	$ 833,333

Based on this analysis, we would record at acquisition a reduction of $300,000 in consolidated Plant And Equipment and an additional $500,000 in consolidated Goodwill. This would result in decreased Depreciation Expense on Plant And Equipment of $15,000 per year ($300,000/20) and Goodwill Amortization Expense of $50,000 per year ($500,000/10).

Step B Eliminations   In calculating income and asset balances, it will be necessary to remove $20,000 in unrealized upstream profits from the inventories of the Center Company and $30,000 in unrealized upstream profits from the inventories of the Above Company.

Goodwill   The consolidated Goodwill balance would be calculated as follows:

Goodwill On Above's Investment In Center	$290,000
Two Year's Amortization at $29,000 per year	(58,000)
Goodwill On Center's Investment In Below	500,000
One Year's Amortization	(50,000)
Consolidated Goodwill	$682,000

Nonmonetary Assets   The consolidated Nonmonetary Assets balance is calculated as follows:

Above's Balance		$3,500,000
Center's Balance		2,500,000
Below's Balance		2,500,000
Fair Value Change -		
Above's Investment In Center	$210,000	
Amortization (2 years at $10,500)	(21,000)	189,000
Fair Value Change -		
Center's Investment In Below	($300,000)	
One Year's Amortization	15,000	(285,000)
Unrealized Profits In Closing Inventories		(50,000)
Consolidated Nonmonetary Assets		$8,354,000

Non Controlling Interest   The Non Controlling Interest would be calculated as follows:

Below Non Controlling Shareholders' Interest In Below [(.40)($3,200,000 - $20,000)]	$1,272,000
Center Non Controlling Shareholders' Interest In Center [(.30)($5,400,000 - $30,000)]	1,611,000
Center Non Controlling Shareholders' Interest In Below Since Acquisition [(.30)(.60)($1,200,000 - $1,000,000 - $20,000)]	32,400
Total Non Controlling Interest	$2,915,400

Retained Earnings   The ending consolidated Retained Earnings balance can be calculated as follows:

Above's Balance	$3,000,000
Equity Pickup In Center (.70)($2,400,000 - $2,000,000 - $30,000)	259,000
Equity Pickup In Below (.70)(.60)($1,200,000 - $1,000,000 - $20,000)	75,600
Fair Value Depreciation:	
Above in Center	(21,000)
Center in Below	15,000
Goodwill Amortization ($58,000 + $50,000)	(108,000)
Consolidated Retained Earnings	$3,220,600

Balance Sheet   Based on the preceding calculations, the required consolidated Balance Sheet for the Above Company and subsidiaries can be prepared as follows:

Above Company And Subsidiaries
Consolidated Balance Sheet
As At December 31, 1998

Net Monetary Assets ($1,500,000 + $900,000 + $700,000)	$ 3,100,000
Nonmonetary Assets	8,354,000
Goodwill	682,000
Total Assets	$12,136,000
Common Stock (Above's Only)	$ 6,000,000
Non Controlling Interest	2,915,400
Retained Earnings	3,220,600
Total Equities	$12,136,000

Consolidated Net Income The consolidated Net Income for the year is calculated as follows:

Above's Net Income	$400,000
Equity In Center [(.70)($250,000 - $30,000)]	154,000
Equity In Below [(.70)(.60)($200,000 - $20,000)]	75,600
Fair Value Depreciation ($10,500 - $15,000)	4,500
Goodwill Amortization ($29,000 + $50,000)	(79,000)
Consolidated Net Income	$555,100

Solution to Self-Study Problem Seven - 5

Investment Analysis The analysis of the Push Company's investment in Shove as at December 31, 1997 is as follows:

	80 Percent	100 Percent
Investment Cost	$3,400,000	$4,250,000
Book Value	(3,200,000)	(4,000,000)
Goodwill	$ 200,000	$ 250,000

The $200,000 Goodwill to be recognized would be amortized over the required 10 years at the rate of $20,000 per year.

While the cost of Shove's investment in Push also implies the presence of Goodwill, it would not be recognized as Shove is not the acquiring company in this business combination.

December 31, 1997 Balance Sheet The Balance Sheet that would be required on this acquisition date would be as follows:

Push Company And Subsidiary
Consolidated Balance Sheet
As At December 31, 1997

Identifiable Assets ($10,000,000 - $3,400,000 + $4,000,000 - $1,100,000)	$9,500,000
Goodwill (As Previously Calculated)	200,000
Total Assets	$9,700,000
Non Controlling Interest (20 Percent Of $4,000,000)	$ 800,000
Common Stock (Push's Only)	5,000,000
Retained Earnings (Push's Only)	5,000,000
Shares In Push Company Held By Subsidiary Company	(1,100,000)
Total Equities	$9,700,000

Income Statement For 1998 The required consolidated Income Statement would be as follows:

Push Company And Subsidiary
Consolidated Income Statement
For The Year Ending December 31, 1998

Revenues ($2,000,000 + $800,000 - $400,000)	$2,400,000
Expenses ($1,500,000 + $600,000 - $400,000 + $85,000)	$1,785,000
Goodwill Amortization	20,000
Non Controlling Interest (Note One)	50,109
Total Expenses	$1,855,109
Consolidated Net Income	$ 544,891

Note One   In order to arrive at the non controlling interest figure, it will be necessary to solve the following two equations simultaneously:

Push Income = [($500,000 - $75,000 - $20,000)] + [(.80)(Shove Income)]

Shove Income = [($200,000 - $10,000)] + [(.10)(Push Income)]

Solving these equations gives a value for Push of $605,434 and for Shove of $250,543. The Non Controlling Interest in consolidated Net Income is then 20 percent of $250,543. This result can be verified by noting that 90 percent of $605,434 is $544,891, the consolidated Net Income disclosed in the preceding statement.

December 31, 1998 Balance Sheet   The Balance Sheet that would be required on this date would be as follows:

Push Company And Subsidiary
Consolidated Balance Sheet
As At December 31, 1998

Identifiable Assets ($7,100,000 + $3,100,000 -$85,000)	$10,115,000
Goodwill ($200,000 - $20,000)	180,000
Total Assets	$10,295,000
Non Controlling Interest ($800,000 + $50,109)	$ 850,109
Common Stock (Push's Only)	5,000,000
Retained Earnings ($5,000,000 + $544,891)	5,544,891
Shares In Push Company Held By Subsidiary Company	(1,100,000)
Total Equities	$10,295,000

Solution to Self-Study Problem Seven - 6

Case A Solution   The cost of the Preferred Stock investment exceeds the investor's share of the book value of the shares by $25,000 [$175,000 - (.50)($300,000)]. This amount would be charged to Retained Earnings as reflected in the following elimination entry:

Preferred Stock - Par $100	$300,000	
Retained Earnings - Pointer	25,000	
Investment In Setter Preferred Shares		$175,000
Non Controlling Interest [(.50)($300,000)]		150,000

An excess of cost over the investor's share of book value is also involved in the Common Stock investment. This excess would be $16,000 [$610,000 - (.90)($660,000)] and, in the absence of fair value changes on the Setter Company's net identifiable assets, the entire amount would be allocated to Goodwill as per the following elimination entry:

Common Stock - Par $50	$450,000	
Contributed Surplus	90,000	
Retained Earnings - Setter	120,000	
Goodwill	16,000	
Investment In Setter Common Shares		$610,000
Non Controlling Interest [(.10)($660,000)]		66,000

Based on these elimination entries, the consolidated Balance Sheet would be prepared as follows:

The Pointer Company And Subsidiary
Consolidated Balance Sheet
As At December 31, 1998

Net Identifiable Assets ($1,400,000 - $175,000	
- $610,000 + $960,000)	$1,575,000
Goodwill	16,000
Total Assets	**$1,591,000**

Non Controlling Interest ($150,000 + $66,000)	$ 216,000
Common Stock - Par $50 (Pointer's Only)	900,000
Contributed Surplus (Pointer's Only)	230,000
Retained Earnings ($270,000 - $25,000)	245,000
Total Equities	**$1,591,000**

Case B Solution   With the two years of preferred dividend arrearages, the relevant book value of the Setter Company's Preferred Stock is $354,000 [$300,000 + (2)($27,000)]. In paying $140,000 for 40 percent of this total, the Pointer Company's purchase is at a cost $1,600 less than its share of book value [$140,000 - (.40)($354,000)]. This would be allocated to Contributed Surplus as per the following entry:

Preferred Stock - Par $100	$300,000	
Retained Earnings - Setter	54,000	
Contributed Surplus - Pointer		$ 1,600
Investment In Setter Preferred Shares		140,000
Non Controlling Interest [(.60)($354,000)]		212,400

In the case of the investment in Setter Company's common stock, there is an excess of cost over the investor's share of book value of $65,200 [$550,000 - (.80)($660,000 - $54,000)]. The adjustment to the book value of the common stock is, of course, for the two years of preferred dividend arrearages. In the absence of fair value changes on the Setter Company's net identifiable assets, the entire amount of $65,200 would be allocated to Goodwill as per the following elimination entry:

Common Stock - Par $50	$450,000	
Contributed Surplus	90,000	
Retained Earnings - Setter ($120,000 - $54,000)	66,000	
Goodwill	65,200	
Investment In Setter Common Shares		$550,000
Non Controlling Interest		
[(.20)($660,000 - $54,000)]		121,200

Based on these elimination entries, the consolidated Balance Sheet would be prepared as follows:

The Pointer Company And Subsidiary
Consolidated Balance Sheet
As At December 31, 1998

Net Identifiable Assets ($1,400,000	
- $140,000 - $550,000 + $960,000)	$1,670,000
Goodwill	65,200
Total Assets	$1,735,200
Non Controlling Interest ($212,400 + $121,200)	$ 333,600
Common Stock - Par $50 (Pointer's Only)	900,000
Contributed Surplus ($230,000 + $1,600)	231,600
Retained Earnings (Pointer's Only)	270,000
Total Equities	$1,735,200

Case C Solution   This Case is complicated by the fact that the preferred shareholders of the Setter Company have the right to participate in the accumulated Retained Earnings of the Company. The participation ratios are based on the par values of the two classes of shares and would be calculated as follows:

Preferred Stock = [$300,000/($300,000 + $450,000)] = 40 Percent
Common Stock = [$450,000/($300,000 + $450,000)] = 60 Percent

Based on these ratios the relevant book values of the two classes of shares would be calculated as follows:

Preferred Stock = [$300,000 + (.40)($120,000)] = $348,000
Common Stock = [$450,000 + $90,000 + (.60)($120,000)] = $612,000

This means that the cost of the Pointer Company's investment in Setter preferred stock would involve an excess over their proportionate share of book value of $16,200. This would be charged to Retained Earnings as reflected in the following elimination entry:

Preferred Stock - Par $100	$300,000	
Retained Earnings - Pointer	16,200	
Retained Earnings - Setter [(.40)($120,000)]	48,000	
Investment In Setter Preferred Shares		$225,000
Non Controlling Interest [(.40)($348,000)]		139,200

For the investment in the Setter Company's common stock, there is an excess of cost over the investor's share of book value of $49,200 [$600,000 - (.90)($612,000)]. In the absence of fair value changes on the Setter Company's net identifiable assets, this entire amount would be allocated to Goodwill as per the following elimination entry:

Common Stock - Par $50	$450,000	
Contributed Surplus	90,000	
Retained Earnings - Setter [(.60)($120,000)]	72,000	
Goodwill	49,200	
Investment In Setter Common Shares		$600,000
Non Controlling Interest [(.10)($612,000)]		61,200

Based on these elimination entries, the consolidated Balance Sheet would be prepared as follows:

Pointer Company And Subsidiary
Consolidated Balance Sheet
As At December 31, 1998

Net Identifiable Assets ($1,400,000 - $225,000	
- $600,000 + $960,000)	$1,535,000
Goodwill	49,200
Total Assets	$1,584,200
Non Controlling Interest ($139,200 + $61,200)	$ 200,400
Common Stock (Pointer's Only)	900,000
Contributed Surplus (Pointer's Only)	230,000
Retained Earnings ($270,000 - $16,200)	253,800
Total Equities	$1,584,200

Solution to Self-Study Problem Seven - 7

Investment Analysis   The analysis of the Pick Company's investment in Shovel would be as follows:

	80 Percent	100 Percent
Investment Cost	$1,900,000	$2,375,000
Book Value	(1,600,000)	(2,000,000)
Differential	$ 300,000	$ 375,000
Fair Value Change On Equipment	(200,000)	(250,000)
Goodwill	$ 100,000	$ 125,000

The increase in the Depreciation Expense due to the fair value change on Equipment would be $20,000 per year ($200,000/10) while the Goodwill would be amortized at $10,000 per year ($100,000/10).

Case One Solution   The required consolidated Income Statement for this Case would be as follows:

The Pick Company And Subsidiary
Consolidated Income Statement
For The Year Ending December 31, 1998

Total Revenues ($4,000,000 + $1,000,000)	$5,000,000
Total Expenses ($3,200,000 + $700,000 + $20,000 + $10,000)	(3,930,000)
Non Controlling Interest [(.20)($300,000)]	(60,000)
Consolidated Net Income	$1,010,000

The consolidated Balance Sheet for Case One would be as follows:

The Pick Company And Subsidiary
Consolidated Balance Sheet
As At December 31, 1998

Identifiable Assets ($5,900,000 + $2,300,000 +	
$200,000 - $20,000	$8,380,000
Goodwill ($100,000 - $10,000)	90,000
Total Assets	**$8,470,000**
Non Controlling Interest [(.20)($2,300,000)]	$ 460,000
No Par Common Stock (Pick's Only)	4,000,000
Retained Earnings ($3,000,000 + $1,010,000)	4,010,000
Total Equities	**$8,470,000**

Case Two   In this second Case, the Pick Company purchases an additional 10 percent of the outstanding shares of Shovel on December 31, 1998 for a total consideration of $280,000 in cash. Ten percent of the Shovel Company's book value at this time is $230,000, leaving a differential of $50,000. Of this amount, $30,000 will be allocated to the fair value change on Equipment (10 Percent Of $300,000) while the remaining $20,000 will become part of the Goodwill balance.

The required consolidated Income Statement for this Case would be as follows:

The Pick Company And Subsidiary
Consolidated Income Statement
For The Year Ending December 31, 1998

Total Revenues ($4,000,000 + $1,000,000)	$5,000,000
Total Expenses ($3,200,000 + $700,000 + $20,000 + $10,000)	(3,930,000)
Non Controlling Interest [(.20)($300,000)]	(60,000)
Consolidated Net Income	**$1,010,000**

Note that this Income Statement is identical to that in Case One, reflecting the fact that while the Non Controlling Interest at year end had been reduced to 10 percent, the Non Controlling Interest in the subsidiary income during the year remained at 20 percent.

The consolidated Balance Sheet for Case Two would be as follows:

The Pick Company And Subsidiary
Consolidated Balance Sheet
As At December 31, 1998

Identifiable Assets ($5,900,000 - $280,000	
+ $2,300,000 + $200,000 - $20,000 + $30,000)	$8,130,000
Goodwill ($100,000 - $10,000 + $20,000)	110,000
Total Assets	**$8,240,000**
Non Controlling Interest [(.10)($2,300,000)]	$ 230,000
No Par Common Stock (Pick's Only)	4,000,000
Retained Earnings ($3,000,000 + $1,010,000)	4,010,000
Total Equities	**$8,240,000**

Case Three   In this Case, the Pick Company sells 20,000 of the shares of Shovel for cash of $600,000. The first step in dealing with this situation is to determine the Pick Company's equity in Shovel at the time it disposed of 25 percent (20,000/80,000 Shares) of its holding. This equity can be calculated as follows:

Investment Cost	$1,900,000
Equity Pickup [(.80)($300,000)]	240,000
Fair Value Depreciation	(20,000)
Goodwill Amortization	(10,000)
December 31, 1998 Equity In Shovel	$2,110,000
Percent Sold	25%
Equity Sold	$ 527,500

Since this equity of $527,500 was sold for $600,000, the gain to be recognized is $72,500. This gain would be reflected in the required Case Three consolidated Income Statement which follows:

The Pick Company And Subsidiary
Consolidated Income Statement
For The Year Ending December 31, 1998

Total Revenues ($4,000,000 + $1,000,000 + $72,500)	$5,072,500
Total Expenses ($3,200,000 + $700,000 + $20,000 + $10,000)	(3,930,000)
Non Controlling Interest [(.20)($300,000)]	(60,000)
Consolidated Net Income	$1,082,500

The Balance Sheet for this Case Three would be as follows:

The Pick Company And Subsidiary
Consolidated Balance Sheet
As At December 31, 1998

Identifiable Assets ($5,900,000 + $2,300,000 + $200,000 - $20,000 + $600,000 - $45,000)	$8,935,000
Goodwill ($100,000 - $10,000 - $22,500)	67,500
Total Assets	$9,002,500
Non Controlling Interest [(.40)($2,300,000)]	$ 920,000
No Par Common Stock (Pick's Only)	4,000,000
Retained Earnings ($3,000,000 + $1,082,500)	4,082,500
Total Equities	$9,002,500

Two items in the preceding Balance Sheet require further explanation, both relating to the sale of 25 percent of Pick's proportionate interest in Shovel. With respect to Identifiable Assets, the $45,000 represents 25 percent of the net fair value change on Equipment of $180,000 ($200,000 - $20,000). In a similar manner, the $22,500 deduction in the calculation of Goodwill reflects the disposal of 25 percent of the net Goodwill of $90,000 ($100,000 - $10,000).

Case Four   In this Case, the issue of new shares by Shovel reduces Pick's percentage holding to 64 percent (80,000/125,000), a reduction of 16 percentage points. In effect this is like selling 20 percent (.16/.80) of Pick's investment in Shovel. The resulting gain can be calculated as follows:

Proceeds (.64)($750,000)	$480,000
Equity [(.20)($2,110,000)]*	422,000
Gain	$ 58,000

*Pick's December 31, 1998 Equity In Shovel - See Case Three Solution

The required consolidated Income Statement for this Case is as follows:

The Pick Company And Subsidiary
Consolidated Income Statement
For The Year Ending December 31, 1998

Total Revenues ($4,000,000 + $1,000,000 + $58,000)	$5,058,000
Total Expenses ($3,200,000 + $700,000 + $20,000 + $10,000)	(3,930,000)
Non Controlling Interest [(.20)($300,000)]	(60,000)
Consolidated Net Income	$1,068,000

The consolidated Balance Sheet for Case Four would be as follows:

The Pick Company And Subsidiary
Consolidated Balance Sheet
As At December 31, 1998

Identifiable Assets ($5,900,000 + $2,300,000 + $200,000 - $20,000 + $750,000 - $36,000)	$9,094,000
Goodwill ($100,000 - $10,000 - $18,000)	72,000
Total Assets	$9,166,000

Non Controlling Interest [(.36)($2,300,000 + $750,000)]	$1,098,000
Common Stock (Pick's Only)	4,000,000
Retained Earnings ($3,000,000 + $1,068,000)	4,068,000
Total Equities	$9,166,000

In the preceding Balance Sheet, as in Case Three, two items require explanation, both related to the sale of 20 percent of Pick's equity interest in Shovel. The $36,000 deduction from the identifiable assets is 20 percent of the net fair value change of $180,000, while the $18,000 deduction from Goodwill is 20 percent of the net Goodwill of $90,000.

Solution to Self-Study Problem Seven - 8

Investment Analysis   The analysis of Patco's investment in Stand is as follows:

	80 Percent	100 Percent
Investment Cost	$720,000	$900,000
Book Value	(600,000)	(750,000)
Differential	$120,000	$150,000
Fair Value Change On Fixed Assets	(96,000)	(120,000)
Fair Value Change On Goodwill	48,000	60,000
Goodwill	$ 72,000	$ 90,000

The fair value change on fixed assets would be depreciated over four years at a rate of $24,000 per year. Note, however, that only one-half year's depreciation or $12,000 would be taken for 1998. The fair value change on Stand's existing Goodwill will be amortized at ten percent for the half year, the same rate that Stand appears to be using on its books ($6,000/$60,000 for July 1 to December 31). The new Goodwill will be amortized at 12.5 percent for the half year, the rate that is being used by Patco for its existing Goodwill ([1/2][$175,000/$700,000]). This gives values of $4,800 and $9,000, respectively.

Part A(1)   The consolidated Goodwill would be calculated as follows:

Patco's December 31, 1998 Balance	$525,000
Stand's Goodwill	54,000
Fair Value Reduction On Stand's Goodwill	(48,000)
Amortization Of The Fair Value Reduction	4,800
New Goodwill	72,000
Amortization Of New Goodwill	(9,000)
Goodwill	$598,800

Part A(2)   The Non Controlling Interest would be calculated as follows:

Stand's December 31, 1998 Book Value	$819,000
Inventory Profits ($85,000 - [$85,000/125%])	(17,000)
Loss On Equipment ($112,000 - $98,000)	14,000
Loss Realization For One-Fourth Year ($14,000/40)	(350)
Adjusted Book Value	$815,650
Non Controlling Percent	20%
Non Controlling Interest	$163,130

Part A(3)   The consolidated Retained Earnings would be as follows:

Patco's Balance	$ 975,000
Equity In Stand's Earnings Since	
Acquisition - [(.80)($69,000 + $14,000 - $350 - $17,000)]	52,520
Amortization - Fair Value Change On Goodwill	4,800
Amortization - Consolidated Goodwill	(9,000)
Depreciation - Fair Value Change On Fixed Assets	(12,000)
Retained Earnings	$1,011,320

This figure can be verified by taking the opening consolidated Retained Earnings which is Patco's January 1 balance plus the consolidated Net Income from Part B which equals $1,011,320 ($675,000 + $336,320).

Part B   The calculation of consolidated Net Income for the year ending December 31, 1998 would be as follows:

Patco's Net Income	$300,000
Equity In Stand's Net Income [(.80)($69,000	
+ $14,000 - $350 - $17,000)]	52,520
Amortization - Fair Value Change On Goodwill	4,800
Amortization - Consolidated Goodwill	(9,000)
Depreciation - Fair Value Change On Fixed Assets	(12,000)
Consolidated Net Income	$336,320

Part C   Cash From Operations can be calculated as follows:

Consolidated Net Income	$ 336,320
Depreciation ($525,000 + $120,000 + $12,000)	657,000
Amortization Of Goodwill ($175,000 + $6,000 - $4,800 + $9,000)	185,200
Non Controlling Interest [(.20)($69,000 + $14,000 - $350 - $17,000)]	13,130
Funds from Operations	$1,191,650
Decrease in Noncash Current Assets From Operations	
($1,000,000 + $140,000 - [$663,000 + $84,000 -$17,000])	410,000
Increase in Current Liabilities ($450,000 + $60,000	
- [$450,000 + $75,000])	15,000
Cash From Operations	$1,616,650

The cash used in acquiring the subsidiary can be calculated and disclosed as follows:

Total Cash Paid	$720,000
Cash Acquired	(10,000)
Net Cash Applied	$710,000

The acquisitions of Fixed Assets can be calculated as follows:

December 31 Balance ($1,680,000		
+ $1,050,000 + $14,000 - $350)		$2,743,650
January 1 Balance (Patco Only)	$1,500,000	
Depreciation Expense ($525,000 + $120,000)	645,000	
December 31 Balance Before Acquisitions		(855,000)
Total Acquisitions		$1,888,650
Stand's Fixed Assets At Acquisition		(900,000)
Other Acquisitions		$ 988,650

The consolidated Statement Of Changes In Financial Position would be prepared as follows:

Patco Company And Subsidiary
Consolidated Statement Of Changes In Financial Position (Cash Basis)
Year Ending December 31, 1998

Operating Activities		
Cash From Operations		$1,616,650
Financing Activities		
Issuance Of Mortgage		75,000
Investing Activities		
Investment In Subsidiary	($710,000)	
Purchase Of Fixed Assets	(988,650)	(1,698,650)
Decrease in Cash		($ 7,000)

This agrees with the decrease in cash for the year of $7,000 ($12,000 + $6,000 - $25,000).

The intercompany sale of the equipment for $98,000 is not disclosed in the consolidated Statement of Changes in Financial Position. The unrealized loss was eliminated in the consolidated Net Income calculation. Since the sale was not arms length, neither the proceeds nor the purchase of the machine affect consolidated cash.

Solution to Self-Study Problem Eight - 1

Account	Temporal	Current Rate
Cash	$125,000	$ 125,000
Long Term Receivables	375,000	375,000
Inventories	500,000	500,000
Plant And Equipment	500,000	1,250,000
Accounts Payable	(175,000)	(175,000)
Long Term Liabilities	(300,000)	(300,000)
Accumulated Depreciation on Plant and Equipment	(250,000)	(625,000)
Net Asset Balance	$775,000	$1,150,000

Solution to Self-Study Problem Eight - 2

Part A - December 31 Journal Entries   The journal entries that would be required to account for the loan on December 31 of the years 1995 through 1999 would be as follows:

December 31, 1995

Cash (D5,000,000 @ $1.80)	$9,000,000	
Long-Term Liability		$9,000,000

December 31, 1996

Deferred Exchange Loss	$1,125,000	
Exchange Loss	375,000	
Long-Term Liability		$1,500,000

D5,000,000 times the increase of $.30, one quarter of the balance is taken into income while the other three quarters is deferred.

December 31, 1997

Exchange Loss	$208,333	
Long-Term Liability	500,000	
Deferred Exchange Loss		$708,333

At the new exchange rate of $2.00, the Long-Term Liability has a translated value of $10,000,000 in comparison to an old value of $9,375,000 ($10,500,000, less the deferral of $1,125,000). This gives a loss of $625,000 of which one third, or $208,333 should be charged to income in the current period and two thirds, or $416,667, should be deferred. To reduce the balance in the deferred exchange loss account from $1,125,000 to this required balance of $416,667, necessitates the above credit of $708,333. The debit to the Long Term Liability reduces it from $10,500,000 to $10,000,000.

December 31, 1998

Exchange Loss	$208,333	
Deferred Exchange Loss		$208,333
(One-half the remaining Deferred Exchange Loss)		

December 31, 1999

Long-Term Liability	$1,500,000	
Deferred Exchange Loss		$ 208,333
Exchange Gain		1,291,667

At the new exchange rate of $1.70, the translated value of the D5,000,000 Long Term Liability is $8,500,000. At the beginning of 1999, this Long-Term Liability was being carried at a value of $9,791,667 ($10,000,000, less the balance in the deferral of $208,333). This difference explains the Exchange Gain of $1,291,667 that is shown in the preceding entry. The Deferred Exchange Loss account must, of course, be reduced to zero and this is accomplished with the credit in the amount of $208,333. The $1,500,000 debit to the long-term liability reduces it from $10,000,000 to the required balance of $8,500,000 and when this amount is paid, the entry will be as follows:

Long-Term Liability	$8,500,000	
Cash		$8,500,000

Note the May, 1996 CICA Re-Exposure Draft, "Foreign Currency Translation", would require the immediate recognition of exchange gains and losses on long term debt unless the debt meets the criteria for hedge accounting.

Part B - Income Effects Schedule   The schedule of income effects associated with the long term debt is as follows:

Year	Gain (Loss)
1996	($ 375,000)
1997	(208,333)
1998	(208,333)
1999	1,291,667
Total Gain	$ 500,000

Note that this total gain is equal to D5,000,000 ($1.80 -$1.70).

Solution to Self-Study Problem Eight - 3

Part A   In this Case the forward exchange contract would be classified as the hedge of a commitment to purchase goods. Given this classification, the journal entries would be as follows:

December 1, 1998

No Entry Required

December 31, 1998

It would be possible to set up the forward exchange contract as an asset and credit a deferred gain for a total of $40,000 [(SF2,000,000)($.98 - $.96)]. However, it is clear that any gain that is recorded will never be taken into income and that the forward contract has no value beyond its ability to establish the price to be paid for the inventories that will be acquired on March 31. As a result, we would not make any entry at this point.

March 31, 1999

Inventories	$2,000,000	
Cash		$2,000,000

Part B In this Case the forward exchange contract would be classified as the hedge of a monetary liability position. Given this classification, the journal entries would be as follows:

December 1, 1998

Inventories	$1,920,000	
Accounts Payable		$1,920,000
(SF2,000,000 @ $.96)		

December 31, 1998

Forward Exchange Contract	$40,000	
Accounts Payable		$40,000
[(SF2,000,000)($.98 - $.96)]		

Hedge Expense	$20,000	
Premium Liability		$20,000
[(.25)(SF2,000,000)($1.00 - $.96)]		

March 31, 1999

Forward Exchange Contract	$ 100,000	
Accounts Payable		$ 100,000
[(SF2,000,000)($1.03 - $.98)]		

Hedge Expense	$ 60,000	
Premium Liability		$ 60,000
[(.75)(SF2,000,000)($1.00 - $.96)]		

Accounts Payable	$2,060,000	
Premium Liability	80,000	
Forward Exchange Contract		$ 140,000
Cash		2,000,000

Part C In this Case the forward contract is not serving as a hedge but, rather, is being used for purely speculative purposes. Given this, the required journal entries would be as follows:

December 1, 1998

No Entry Required

December 31, 1998

Forward Exchange Contract	$100,000	
Exchange Gain		$100,000
[(SF2,000,000)($1.05 - $1.00)]		

March 31, 1999

Cash [(SF2,000,000)($1.03 - $1.00)]	$60,000	
Exchange Loss [(SF2,000,000)($1.03 - $1.05)]	40,000	
Forward Exchange Contract		$100,000

Solution to Self-Study Problem Eight - 4

November 1, 1997   The journal entry required on this date would be as follows:

Accounts Receivable (DM5,000,000 @ $.70)	$3,500,000	
Sales		$3,500,000

No entries would be required to record the forward exchange contracts.

December 31, 1997   The following journal entries would be required on this date for the receivable and its related hedge contract:

Accounts Receivable (DM5,000,000)($.73 - $.70)	$150,000	
Forward Exchange Contract		$150,000
Hedge Expense (DM5,000,000)($.70 - $.69)(2/3)	$ 33,333	
Premium Liability		$ 33,333

December 31, 1997   With respect to the contract which was entered in order to hedge the purchase commitment, it would be possible to make an entry setting up the forward exchange contract as an asset and crediting a deferred gain for $600,000 [(DM20,000,000)($.73 - $.70)]. However, it is clear that any gain that is recorded will never be taken into income and that the forward contract has no value beyond its ability to establish the price to be paid for the equipment that will be acquired on March 1, 1998. As a result, we would make no entry at this point.

December 31, 1997   With respect to the speculative contract, the following entry would be required:

Exchange Loss (DM10,000,000)($.81 - $.80)	$100,000	
Forward Exchange Contract		$100,000

February 1, 1998   The following journal entries would be required for the receivable and its related hedge contract:

Accounts Receivable (DM5,000,000)($.74 - $.73)	$50,000	
Forward Exchange Contract		$50,000
Hedge Expense (DM5,000,000)($.70 - $.69)(1/3)	$16,667	
Premium Liability		$16,667
Cash	$3,450,000	
Forward Exchange Contract	200,000	
Premium Liability	50,000	
Accounts Receivable		$3,700,000

March 1, 1998   The following journal entry would be required to record the use of the contract to implement the purchase commitment.

Equipment (DM20,000,000)($.75)	$15,000,000	
Cash		$15,000,000

June 1, 1998   The following journal entry would be required to record the fulfillment of the speculative contract:

Exchange Loss (DM10,000,000)($.82 - $.81)	$100,000	
Forward Exchange Contract	100,000	
Cash (DM10,000,000)($.82 - $.80)		$200,000

Solution to Self-Study Problem Nine - 1

Part A - Integrated Foreign Operation

Loss On Long-term Debt

	DM	Rate	Dollars
Closing	9,000,000	.85	$7,650,000
Opening	9,000,000	.75	(6,750,000)
Current Year's Loss			$ 900,000
Deferred Portion (4/5)			(720,000)
Income Portion - 1998			$ 180,000

Note the May, 1996 CICA Re-Exposure Draft, "Foreign Currency Translation", would require the immediate recognition of exchange gains and losses on long term debt unless the debt meets the criteria for hedge accounting.

Income Statement
For The Year Ended December 31, 1998

	DM	Rate	Dollars
Revenue	1,000,000	.80	$ 800,000
Expenses:			
Interest Expense	990,000	.80	$ 792,000
Other Expenses	10,000	.80	8,000
Exchange Loss	- 0 -	see above	180,000
Total Expenses	1,000,000		$ 980,000
Income (Loss)	- 0 -		($ 180,000)

Balance Sheet
As At December 31, 1998

	DM	Rate	Dollars
Cash	- 0 -		$ -0-
Land	12,000,000	.75	9,000,000
Deferred Exchange Loss	- 0 -	see above	720,000
Total Assets	12,000,000		$9,720,000
Bond	9,000,000	.85	$7,650,000
Common Stock	3,000,000	.75	2,250,000
Retained Earnings (Deficit)	- 0 -		(180,000)
Total Equities	12,000,000		$9,720,000

Part A - Self-Sustaining Foreign Operation

Deferred Exchange Gain On Net Assets

	DM	Rate	Dollars
Net Assets, Opening	3,000,000	.75	$2,250,000
Net Assets, Closing	3,000,000	.85	2,550,000
Deferred Exchange Gain			$ 300,000

Income Statement
For The Year Ended December 31, 1998

	DM	Rate	Dollars
Revenue	1,000,000	.80	$800,000
Expenses:			
Interest Expense	990,000	.80	$792,000
Other Expenses	10,000	.80	8,000
Total Expenses	1,000,000		$800,000
Income	- 0 -		$ - 0 -

Balance Sheet
As At December 31, 1998

	DM	Rate	Dollars
Cash	- 0 -		$ - 0 -
Land	12,000,000	.85	10,200,000
Total Assets	12,000,000		$10,200,000
Bond	9,000,000	.85	$ 7,650,000
Common Stock	3,000,000	.75	2,250,000
Deferred Exchange Gain	- 0 -	see above	300,000
Total Equities	12,000,000		$10,200,000

Part B   Economic exposure is the impact of changes in the relative values of the currencies on the earnings ability of the foreign subsidiary. The foreign debt is hedged by the foreign nonmonetary land investment if DM proceeds from the sale of the land in five years are adequate to pay off the DM debt. Therefore, reflecting an exchange loss on the bond (temporal method) does not reflect economic exposure.

The current rate method better reflects economic exposure. Investco Ltd. is exposed to the extent of this net asset investment (DM 3,000,000 at historic values) and in fact enjoyed favorable unrealized exchange gains on this investment during 1998, a year when the Canadian dollar was depreciating relative to the German mark.

Part C   According to the criteria of Section 1650, the German subsidiary is a self-sustaining foreign operation because:

1. There is no interrelationship between the day-to-day activities of the German subsidiary and the Canadian parent

2. The activities of the German subsidiary are financed by DM debt and DM rental inflows.

3. The DM debt will be repaid out of DM proceeds from the sale of the land in five years.

In effect, there is no exposure of the Canadian parent to short-term fluctuations in the DM exchange rate and it would be inappropriate to include unrealized foreign exchange gains or losses in the Canadian parent's income for each of the five years. Therefore, the current rate method would be required.

Part D If the bond is translated at the current exchange rate and a portion of the loss is expensed, then the company will recognize a loss on the bond without recognizing any change in the value of the land. In effect, the foreign currency debt is hedged by a non-monetary item (land); accordingly, any loss on the bond is deferred entirely until the maturity date in four years, in accordance with Section 1650.54 of the *CICA Handbook*. If DM proceeds from the sale of land are sufficient to repay the DM debt (which they are expected to be), then there is no exposure to DM exchange rate fluctuations. In other words, Canadian dollars are not expected to be required to repay the DM debt when it comes due. According to Section 1650.48, deferral is acceptable if the land is identified as a hedge and there is reasonable assurance that the land will be effective as a hedge.

Solution to Self-Study Problem Nine - 2

Part A The temporal method of translation should be adopted because Cellular is dependent on its parent and therefore is not a self-sustaining entity. Factors that lead to this conclusion are:

1. All management have been appointed by Sentex.
2. Top management of Cellular are paid directly by Sentex.
3. Seventy-five percent of Cellular's sales are to Sentex.
4. The majority of the profits will be distributed to the parent after the two-year freeze on profit distributions.
5. 80% of initial financing was provided by Sentex.

Part B The translation gain and loss would be calculated as follows:

Translation Loss on Net Current Assets

	Cuzos	Rate	Dollars
Opening Net Current Monetary Assets	30,000	2.00	60,000
Sales	600,000	1.82	1,092,000
Purchases Of Raw Materials And Labour	(370,000)	1.82	(673,400)
Selling And Admininistrative Expenses	(70,000)	1.82	(127,400)
Interest	(20,000)	1.82	(36,400)
Income Taxes	(4,500)	1.82	(8,190)
Land Held For Future Development	(10,000)	1.65	(16,500)
Calculated Closing Net Current Monetary Assets			290,110
Actual Closing Net Current Monetary Assets	155,500	1.65	256,575
Translation Loss On Net Current Monetary Assets			33,535

Translation Gain on Long-Term Debt

	Cuzos	Rate	Dollars
Long-term Debt, Beginning Of The Year	180,000	2.00	360,000
Long-term Debt, End Of The Year	180,000	1.65	297,000
Gain			63,000
Deferred To Future Years ([6/7] [63,000])			54,000
Gain To Be Reported In Current Year ([1/7] [63,000])			9,000
Translation Loss On Net Current Monetary Assets			33,535
Net Translation Loss			24,535

Note the May, 1996 CICA Re-Exposure Draft, "Foreign Currency Translation", would require the immediate recognition of exchange gains and losses on long term debt unless the debt meets the criteria for hedge accounting.

Part C The translated Income Statement and Balance Sheet of Cellular Company Inc., would be as follows:

Cellular Company Inc.
Income Statement For the year ending December 31, 1998

	Cuzos	Rate	Dollars
Sales	600,000	1.82	1,092,000
Depreciation Included In Cost Of Sales	(98,000)	2.00	(196,000)
Raw Materials And Labour Included			
In Cost Of Sales ($400,000 -$98,000)	(302,000)	1.82	(549,640)
Selling And Administrative Expenses	(70,000)	1.82	(127,400)
Interest Expense	(20,000)	1.82	(36,400)
Income Taxes	(4,500)	1.82	(8,190)
Net Income Before Foreign Exchange Loss	105,500		174,370
Foreign Exchange Loss	N/A		24,535
Closing Retained Earnings	105,500		149,835

Cellular Company Inc.
Balance Sheet As At December 31, 1998

	Cuzos	Rate	Dollars
Cash	25,000	1.65	41,250
Note Receivable	100,000	1.65	165,000
Accounts Receivable	65,000	1.65	107,250
Inventory	22,000	2.00	44,000
	68,000	1.82	123,760
Fixed Assets - Net	230,000	2.00	460,000
Land For Future Development	10,000	1.65	16,500
Total Assets	520,000		957,760
Accounts Payable	30,000	1.65	49,500
Taxes Payable	4,500	1.65	7,425
Long-term Debt	180,000	1.65	297,000
Deferred Exchange Gain	-0-		54,000
Common Stock	200,000	2.00	400,000
Retained Earnings (see Income Statement)	105,500		149,835
Total Equities	520,000		957,760

Solution to Self-Study Problem Nine - 3

Part A - Balance Sheets   Using the translation procedures required for integrated foreign operations, the Brazal Company's Balance Sheets are as follows:

Brazal Company (Integrated Foreign Operation)
Balance Sheet As At December 31, 1997

Cash And Current Receivables (NC6,500,000 @ $.040)	$ 260,000
Long-Term Receivable (NC5,000,000 @ $.040)	200,000
Inventories (NC9,500,000 @ $.045)	427,500
Plant And Equipment (NC17,000,000 @ $.100)	1,700,000
Accumulated Depreciation (NC4,000,000 @ $.100)	(400,000)
Land (NC3,000,000 @ $.060)	180,000
Deferred Exchange Loss (See Note One)	80,000
Total Assets	**$2,447,500**
Current Liabilities (NC5,000,000 @ $.040)	$ 200,000
Long Term Liabilities	-0-
No Par Common Stock (NC18,000,000 @ $.100)	1,800,000
Retained Earnings (Balancing Figure)	447,500
Total Equities	**$2,447,500**

Brazal Company (Integrated Foreign Operation)
Balance Sheet As At December 31, 1998

Cash And Current Receivables (NC11,000,000 @ $.030)	$ 330,000
Long-Term Receivable (NC5,000,000 @ $.030)	150,000
Inventories (NC8,000,000 @ $.032)	256,000
Plant And Equipment (NC13,000,000 @ $.100 + NC10,000,000 @ $.038)	1,680,000
Accumulated Depreciation (NC4,250,000 @ $.100 + NC750,000 @ $.038)	(453,500)
Land (NC3,000,000 @ $.060 + NC3,000,000 @ $.035)	285,000
Deferred Exchange Loss (See Note Two)	7,500
Total Assets	**$2,255,000**
Current Liabilities (NC3,000,000 @ $.030)	$ 90,000
Long-Term Liabilities (NC10,000,000 @ $.030)	300,000
No Par Common Stock (NC18,000,000 @ $.100 + NC2,000,000 @ $.038)	1,876,000
Retained Earnings (Deficit) ($447,500 - $458,500)	11,000
Total Equities	**$2,255,000**

Note One   The Deferred Exchange Loss relates to the presence of the Long-Term Receivable. The amount can be calculated as follows:

January 1, 1997 Balance (NC5,000,000 @ $.060)	$300,000
December 31, 1997 Balance (NC5,000,000 @ $.040)	(200,000)
Total Loss during 1997	**$100,000**
Amount Charged to 1997 Income (1/5)	(20,000)
Deferred Exchange Loss	**$ 80,000**

Note Two   For 1998, the Deferred Exchange Loss reflects the presence of both the Long-Term Receivable and the Long-Term Liabilities. The deferred gain on the Long-Term Liabilities is calculated as follows:

December 31, 1998 Balance (NC10,000,000 @ $.030)	$300,000
January 1, 1998 Balance (NC10,000,000 @ $.040)	(400,000)
Total Gain During 1998	($100,000)
Amount Added to 1998 Income (1/10)	10,000
Deferred Exchange Gain	($ 90,000)

The deferred exchange loss on the Long-Term Receivable is as follows:

January 1, 1998 Net Balance (NC5,000,000 @ $.040 plus January 1, 1998 Deferred Exchange Loss)	$280,000
December 31, 1998 Balance (NC5,000,000 @ $.030)	(150,000)
Exchange Loss For Year	$130,000
Charged to 1998 Income (1/4)	(32,500)
Deferred Exchange Loss	$ 97,500

Combining the deferred gain of $90,000 with the deferred loss of $97,500, gives the net Deferred Exchange Loss of $7,500. Note the May, 1996 CICA Re-Exposure Draft, "Foreign Currency Translation", would require the immediate recognition of exchange gains and losses on long term debt unless the debt meets the criteria for hedge accounting.

Part A - Statement Of Income And Change In Retained Earnings   Using the translation procedures required for integrated foreign operations, the Brazal Company's Statement of Income and Change in Retained Earnings would be as follows:

Brazal Company (Integrated Foreign Operation)
Statement of Income and Change in Retained Earnings
Year Ending December 31, 1998

Sales (NC50,000,000 @ $.035)	$1,750,000
Interest Revenue (NC1,000,000 @ $.035)	35,000
Total Revenues	$1,785,000
Opening Inventories (NC9,500,000 @ $.045)	$ 427,500
Purchases (NC28,500,000 @ $.035)	997,500
Closing Inventories (NC8,000,000 @ $.032)	(256,000)
Taxes (NC10,000,000 @ $.035)	350,000
Depreciation Expense (NC1,250,000 @ $.100 + NC750,000 @ $.038)	153,500
Other Expenses (NC5,000,000 @ $.035)	175,000
Exchange Loss (See Note Three)	104,000
Total Expenses	$1,951,500
Income (Loss) Before Extraordinary Items	($ 166,500)
Extraordinary Loss (See Note Four)	(260,000)
Net Income (Loss)	($ 426,500)
Dividends (NC1,000,000 @ $.032)	(32,000)
Increase (Decrease) in Retained Earnings	($ 458,500)

Note Three The current portion of the exchange loss is as follows:

Opening Current Net Monetary Assets (NC1,500,000 @ $.040)	$	60,000
Sales (NC50,000,000 @ $.035)		1,750,000
Interest Revenue (NC1,000,000 @ $.035)		35,000
Proceeds From Equipment		
Expropriation (NC1,000,000 @ $.040)		40,000
Sale Of Common Stock (NC2,000,000 @ $.038)		76,000
Purchases (NC28,500,000 @ $.035)	(	997,500)
Taxes (NC10,000,000 @ $.035)	(	350,000)
Other Expenses (NC5,000,000 @ $.035)	(	175,000)
Land Purchase (NC3,000,000 @ $.035)	(	105,000)
Dividends (NC1,000,000 @ $.032)	(	32,000)
Liabilities Issued (NC10,000,000 @ $.040)		400,000
Equipment Purchased (NC10,000,000 @ $.038)	(	380,000)
Computed Closing Current Net Monetary Assets	$	321,500
Actual Closing Current Net Monetary Assets	(	240,000)
Current Exchange Loss	$	81,500

In addition to the preceding loss on current monetary items, there is also a net loss of $22,500 on noncurrent monetary items. This is made up of a loss of $32,500 on the Long Term Receivable and a gain of $10,000 on the Long Term Liabilities. The total exchange loss to be recognized in 1998, including current and noncurrent portions, is $104,000 ($81,500 + $32,500 - $10,000).

Note Four The amount of the translated Extraordinary Loss would be calculated as follows:

Proceeds From Expropriation (NC1,000,000 @ $.040)	$ 40,000
Net Book Value (NC3,000,000 @ $.100)	(300,000)
Extraordinary Loss	($260,000)

Part B - Balance Sheets Using the translation procedures required for self sustaining foreign operations, the Brazal Company's Balance Sheets are as follows:

Brazal Company (Self Sustaining Foreign Operation)
Balance Sheet As At December 31, 1997

Cash And Current Receivables (NC6,500,000 @ $.040)	$	260,000
Long-Term Receivable (NC5,000,000 @ $.040)		200,000
Inventories (NC9,500,000 @ $.040)		380,000
Plant And Equipment (NC17,000,000 @ $.040)		680,000
Accumulated Depreciation (NC4,000,000 @ $.040)	(	160,000)
Land (NC3,000,000 @ $.040)		120,000
Total Assets		$1,480,000

Current Liabilities (NC5,000,000 @ $.040)	$	200,000
No Par Common Stock (NC18,000,000 @ $.100)		1,800,000
Retained Earnings (From Part A Solution)		447,500
Cumulative Translation Adjustment (Note Five)	(	967,500)
Total Equities		$1,480,000

Note Five   The calculation for determining the balance in this account at the end of the year preceding the first application of the requirements for a self sustaining foreign operation is as follows:

Net Assets As Per Current Rate Method On December 31, 1997 (NC32,000,000 @ $.040)	$1,280,000
Net Assets As Per Temporal Method On December 31, 1997 (See Part A Solution)	(2,247,500)
Beginning Cumulative Translation Adjustment	($ 967,500)

Brazal Company (Self Sustaining Foreign Operation)
Balance Sheet
As At December 31, 1998

Cash And Current Receivables (NC11,000,000 @ $.030)	$ 330,000
Long Term Receivable (NC5,000,000 @ $.030)	150,000
Inventories (NC8,000,000 @ $.030)	240,000
Plant And Equipment (NC13,000,000 @ $.030 + NC10,000,000 @ $.030)	690,000
Accumulated Depreciation (NC4,250,000 @ $.030 + NC750,000 @ $.030)	(150,000)
Land (NC3,000,000 @ $.030 + NC3,000,000 @ $.030)	180,000
Total Assets	$1,440,000
Current Liabilities (NC3,000,000 @ $.030)	$ 90,000
Long Term Liabilities (NC10,000,000 @ $.030)	300,000
No Par Common Stock (NC18,000,000 @ $.100 + NC2,000,000 @ $.038)	1,876,000
Retained Earnings (Note Six)	475,500
Cumulative Translation Adjustment (Note Seven)	(1,301,500)
Total Equities	$1,440,000

Note Six   The Retained Earnings balance in the Brazal Company's December 31, 1998 Balance Sheet can be calculated as follows:

Balance - December 31, 1997 (From The Part A Balance Sheet)	$447,500
Increase in Retained Earnings for 1998	28,000
Balance - December 31, 1998	$475,500

Note Seven   On December 31, 1997, the balance in the Cumulative Translation Adjustment account was a debit of $967,500. The closing balance on December 31, 1998 is a debit of $1,301,500 and this represents an increase of $334,000. This increase is calculated as follows:

Opening Net Assets (NC32,000,000 @ $.040) $1,280,000
Sales (NC50,000,000 @ $.035)   1,750,000
Interest Revenue (NC1,000,000 @ $.035)   35,000
Proceeds From The Sale Of Common Stock
   (NC2,000,000 @ $.038)   76,000
Cost Of Goods Sold (NC30,000,000 @ $.035)   (1,050,000)
Taxes (NC10,000,000 @ $.035)   (350,000)
Depreciation Expense (NC2,000,000 @ $.035)   (70,000)
Other Expenses (NC5,000,000 @ $.035)   (175,000)
Extraordinary Loss (See Income Statement)   (80,000)
Dividends (NC1,000,000 @ $.032)   (32,000)

Computed Closing Net Assets $1,384,000
Actual Closing Net Assets (NC35,000,000 @ $.030)   1,050,000

Change In Cumulative Translation Adjustment $ 334,000

Part B - Statement Of Income And Change In Retained Earnings   Using the translation procedures required for self sustaining foreign operations, the Brazal Company's Statement of Income and Change in Retained Earnings would be as follows:

Brazal Company (Self Sustaining Foreign Operation)
Statement of Income and Change in Retained Earnings
Year Ending December 31, 1998

Sales (NC50,000,000 @ $.035) $1,750,000
Interest Revenue (NC1,000,000 @ $.035)   35,000

Total Revenues $1,785,000

Cost Of Goods Sold (NC30,000,000 @ $.035) $1,050,000
Taxes (NC10,000,000 @ $.035)   350,000
Depreciation Expense (NC2,000,000 @ $.035)   70,000
Other Expenses (NC5,000,000 @ $.035)   175,000

Total Expenses $1,645,000

Income Before Extraordinary Items $ 140,000
Extraordinary Loss (See Note Eight)   (80,000)

Net Income (Loss) $ 60,000
Dividends (NC1,000,000 @ $.032)   (32,000)

Increase (Decrease) in Retained Earnings $ 28,000

Note Eight   The amount of the translated Extraordinary Loss is calculated as follows:

Proceeds (NC1,000,000 @ $.040) $ 40,000
Net Book Value (NC3,000,000 @ $.040)   (120,000)

Extraordinary Loss   ($ 80,000)

Solution to Self-Study Problem Ten - 1

Part A   The capital balances of the two partners on February 28 of the current year are as follows:

	George Brown	Terry Green
Assets Contributed	$50,000	$ 170,000
Liabilities Assumed	-0-	30,000
Net Capital Balances	$50,000	$ 140,000

Part B   The total capital balance would be $190,000 ($50,000 + $140,000) and, if the agreement called for this amount to be split equally, George Brown and Terry Green would each be allocated $95,000 ($190,000/2).

Part C   Given the large difference in tangible assets contributed by the two partners, it would appear that George Brown is bringing goodwill into the Partnership. The amount would be calculated as follows:

Identifiable Assets From Green	$140,000
Identifiable Assets From Brown	(50,000)
Implied Goodwill	$ 90,000

George Brown and Terry Green would each be allocated $140,000 in capital.

Solution to Self-Study Problem Ten - 2

The development of a distribution schedule must take into account the amount of loss that can be absorbed by each partner's capital account. If we assume that in liquidation Portly's loan will be added to his capital account, the loss bearing capability of each partner can be calculated as follows:

    Portly = $160,000/.10 = $1,600,000
    Brawn = $320,000/.40 = $ 800,000
    Large = $480,000/.50 = $ 960,000

Portly's loss bearing capability exceeds that of Large by $640,000 and, as a consequence, he would receive the first $64,000 to be distributed to the partners (10 percent of $640,000). This would leave the partners with the following loss bearing capabilities:

    Portly = $ 96,000/.10 = $960,000
    Brawn = $320,000/.40 = $800,000
    Large = $480,000/.50 = $960,000

In order to reduce the loss bearing capabilities of Portly and Large they would receive the next $96,000 with $16,000 going to Portly (10 percent of $160,000) and $80,000 going to Large (50 percent of $160,000). At this point each partner would have a loss sharing capability of $800,000. Alternatively, it can be seen that the partners' remaining capital balances ($80,000, $320,000 and $400,000) are in the same ratio as their profit sharing ratios. Subsequent distributions would be made on the basis of their profit and loss sharing ratios.

The schedule of distributions would be as follows:

	Creditors	Portly	Brawn	Large
First $72,000	$72,000			
Next $64,000		$64,000		
Next $96,000		$16,000		$80,000
Any Balance		10%	40%	50%

Solution to Self-Study Problem Ten - 3

Part A   The entry to record the transfer of interest of Tom Jones to his sister Shirley would be as follows:

Tom Jones, Capital	$26,000	
Shirley Jones, Capital		$26,000

As the transfer took place directly between the two individuals, no further explanation of this entry is required.

Part B   Under the new entity approach, assets would be revalued on the basis of the price paid by Shirley. The fact that she paid $40,000 for a 20 percent interest in the Partnership would indicate that the equity interest will be worth $200,000 ($40,000/.20) after her admission. This means that the present ownership interests would have a current value of $160,000 ($200,000 - $40,000) and that the total assets would be valued at $205,000 ($160,000, plus the Liabilities of $45,000). As the fair value given for the Partnership's Identifiable Assets is only $189,000, Goodwill in the amount of $16,000 appears to be present. The entries to record the fair value change on the Identifiable Assets and to admit Shirley to the Partnership are as follows:

Identifiable Assets ($189,000 - $164,000)	$25,000	
Goodwill	16,000	
Tom Jones, Capital (20%)		$ 8,200
Dick Jones, Capital (30%)		12,300
Harry Jones, Capital (50%)		20,500
Cash	$40,000	
Shirley Jones, Capital		$40,000

Part C   As the Partnership assets will not be revalued in this Case, the excess of the retirement price over the book value of Dick Jones' equity interest must be allocated to the other partners on the basis of their profit and loss sharing ratios. The required entry would be as follows:

Dick Jones, Capital	$41,000	
Tom Jones, Capital ([2/7][$13,000])	3,714	
Harry Jones, Capital ([5/7][$13,000])	9,286	
Cash		$54,000

Part D   If the assets were sold for $189,000, the transaction would result in a gain of $25,000 ($189,000 -$164,000). This would be allocated to the three partners on the basis of their profit sharing ratios. This means the sale of the assets would be recorded as follows:

Cash	$189,000	
Tom Jones, Capital (20%)		$ 5,000
Dick Jones, Capital (30%)		7,500
Harry Jones, Capital (50%)		12,500
Identifiable Assets		164,000

Given the preceding entry, the entry to record the distribution of the final cash balance to the partners would be as follows:

Liabilities	$ 45,000	
Tom Jones, Capital ($26,000 + $5,000)	31,000	
Dick Jones, Capital ($41,000 + $7,500)	48,500	
Harry Jones, Capital ($52,000 + $12,500)	64,500	
Cash		$189,000

Solution to Self-Study Problem Ten - 4

Case 1   The price paid by Breem for a one-third interest implies a total value for the partnership of $1,620,000 [(3)($540,000)] and a value for the partnership prior to this admission of $1,080,000 ($1,620,000 - $540,000). Given the book value for the Partners' capital of $1,000,000, this would imply Goodwill of $80,000. The entries to record this Goodwill and the admission of Breem would be as follows:

Goodwill	$ 80,000	
Jones, Capital (30 Percent)		$ 24,000
Smith, Capital (45 Percent)		36,000
Doe, Capital (25 Percent)		20,000

Cash	$540,000	
Breem, Capital		$540,000

Case 2   Doe is giving up his interest in the Partnership for an amount that is $20,000 less than its book value. If assets are not to be revalued, this deficiency will have to be viewed as a bonus to the other Partners. The entry which reflects this interpretation of the retirement of Doe is as follows:

Doe, Capital	$191,000	
Jones, Capital [(30/75)($20,000)]		$ 8,000
Smith, Capital [(45/75)($20,000)]		12,000
Cash		171,000

Case 3   On December 31 of the current year, the total capital of the Partners is $1,000,000 and, if we assume that the $100,000 is the only payment that will be received by the Partners, the loss would be $900,000. Based on this assumption, the distribution to the Partners can be calculated as follows:

	Jones	Smith	Doe
Capital Before Installment	$327,000	$482,000	$191,000
Share Of Liquidation Loss	(270,000)	(405,000)	(225,000)
Adjusted Capital	$ 57,000	$ 77,000	($ 34,000)
Distribution Of Doe's			
Capital Deficiency	(13,600)	(20,400)	34,000
Cash Distribution	$ 43,400	$ 56,600	$ -0-

Based on the preceding analysis, the journal entry to reflect the distribution of the first $100,000 would be as follows:

Jones, Capital	$ 43,400	
Smith, Capital	56,600	
Cash		$100,000

Index

F